NELSON'S
ILLUSTRATED ENCYCLOPEDIA
OF
BIBLE FACTS

J. I. Packer
Merrill C. Tenney
William White, Jr.

THOMAS NELSON PUBLISHERS
Nashville • Atlanta • London • Vancouver

MAJOR CONTRIBUTORS: Raymond J. Calvert, E. Clark Copeland, Leonard J. Coppes, Willem van Gemeren, Louis Goldberg, Victor P. Hamilton, Horace D. Hummel, Harold L. Phillips, Glenn E. Schaefer, Robert Tuten, Howard Vos, William White, Jr.

Published in Nashville, Tennessee, by Thomas Nelson, Inc.

The section entitled "Paul and His Journeys" was adapted and abridged from *A Man of Tarsus: Life and Work of Paul,* by Harold Phillips, copyright © 1955 by Gospel Trumpet Company, by permission of Harold Phillips.

Other acknowledgments appear at the end of the text.

Unless otherwise indicated, all Scripture quotations are from The Open Bible edition of the King James Version, copyright © 1975 by Thomas Nelson Inc., Publishers. All rights reserved.

Verses marked "NASB" are taken from the New American Standard Bible, copyright © 1960, 1962, 1963, 1968, 1971, 1972, 1973, 1975 by the Lockman Foundation.

Verses marked "RSV" are taken from the Holy Bible: Revised Standard Version, second edition, copyright © 1946, 1951, 1972 by the Division of Christian Education of the NCCCUSA.

Verses marked "NIV" are taken from the Holy Bible: New International Version, copyright © 1978 by the New York International Bible Society.

Library of Congress Cataloging-in-Publication Data

Nelson's illustrated encyclopedia of Bible facts / edited by
    James I. Packer, Merrill C. Tenney, William White, Jr.
      p.   cm.
    Rev. ed. of: The Bible almanac. c 1980.
    Includes bibliographical references and index.
    ISBN 0-8407-1974-4
    1. Bible—History of contemporary events.   2. Sociology,
Biblical.   3. Bible—Antiquities.   4. Jews—Civilization —To 70
A.D.   5. Palestine—Civilization.   I. Packer, J. I. (James Innell)
    II. Tenney, Merrill Chapin, 1904–   . III. White, William,
1934–   . IV. Thomas Nelson Publishers.   V. Bible
almanac.   VI. Title:
    Illustrated encyclopedia of Bible facts.
    BS635.2.B48   1995
    220.3—dc20   94-44337
                                               CIP

7 8 9 10—01 00 99 98 97

CONTENTS

CONTENTS

PUBLISHER'S PREFACE

Nelson's Illustrated Encyclopedia of Bible Facts is a key to unlocking the wonder and mysteries of the Bible and learning about its people and cultures. Forty-five major sections cover a wide variety of important biblical subjects, such as law, forms of trade and transportation, political systems, family life, eating habits, clothing, and plants.

Over 6,000 significant topics of interest are illustrated with more than 300 black and white and full color photos, and are supplemented by an extensive collection of maps, tables, and diagrams. The outlines and introductions for each book of the Bible will enrich personal study or lesson preparation, and its comprehensive easy-to-use subject index makes fact-finding simple.

Written and edited by dedicated biblical scholars, *Nelson's Illustrated Encyclopedia of Bible Facts* will provide reliable, fascinating answers to your questions about the drama of Bible times and people. It will soon become one of the most useful Bible reference books in your library.

Nelson's Illustrated Encyclopedia of Bible Facts is written for both the experienced and the beginning student to make Bible study and teaching more rewarding. The publisher sends it forth trusting that it will provide a gateway of understanding to the full riches of the Word of God.

EDITOR'S PREFACE

Works of reference—dictionaries, timetables, handbooks, gazetteers, and the like—are not usually thought of as inspirational reading. Nor should they be. Their job is not to inspire, but to inform. They are repositories of classified facts where from time to time you look up what you need to know. Their value depends on the importance of the information they provide. The facts given in the phone book, for instance, are vital; we should be lost without them. But anyone who hopes to have his heart warmed by reading all the names, addresses, and numbers straight through from A to Z would probably be disappointed.

Holy Scripture, by contrast, is thought of as supremely inspiring; and rightly so. It is magnificent literature, displaying with unrivalled vividness some of the most lively, colorful, and uninhibited people who ever lived. It is the written Word of God, "quick and powerful, and sharper than any two-edged sword, piercing even to the dividing asunder of soul and spirit, and of the joints and marrow, and is a discerner of the thoughts and intents of the heart" (Heb. 4:12). It shows us God and ourselves, and sets us in communion with Him. Bible readers worldwide in each generation testify that Jesus Christ has walked out of its pages into their lives. It is the mystery and marvel of the Bible, indeed the miracle of it, that nobody ever gets beyond it. The witness of the ages is that it (or should I say, God in and through it) always proves to have more to say than has yet been heard, and no life problem ever arises on which it does not in one way or another throw decisive light. That this book from an out-of-the-way corner of the ancient Middle East should have such universal and inexhaustible power reflects its inspiration, the fact that in a unique way it comes from God and is a unique instrument in His hands. It inspires in the secular sense of imparting vision and strength and a sense of God's aliveness and nearness. It is inspired in the biblical sense of originating from God as His own written instruction, taking the form of human witness to His work in world history and individual lives.

The truth of redemption entitles each Christian to say, with Paul, that Christ "loved me, and gave himself for me" (Gal. 2:20). Even so the truth of inspiration entitles each Bible reader to say, "God loved me, and had this book written for me." One statement is as true as the other.

Where then does *Nelson's Illustrated Encyclopedia of Bible Facts* fit in? An earlier version of this work was titled *The Bible Almanac* and almanacs (tables of dates, times, and circumstances) certainly belong among non-inspirational works of reference. So what can this volume offer to ordinary Christians who rightly want help and hope from Scripture? Will not its mass of information about the remote past make them feel as did the schoolgirl who wrote of her biology text, "This book told me more about worms than ever I wanted to know"? Why spend good money on such a book as this? What use will it be? The answer to these questions is as follows.

As God's climactic revelation took the form of an historical human life—the life of Jesus Christ, God's incarnate Son—so His entire revelation, first to last, took an historical form. What Scripture gives us is an interpreted record of that historical revelation. And though the truths that God taught are timeless in the sense of being universally true, they are not timeless in the sense of being fully understandable out of their historical context. We only catch their meaning properly by viewing them in the situations in which God spelled them out and enforced them. This necessitates having the kind of information that *Nelson's Illustrated Encyclopedia of Bible Facts* contains. Without that information we shall constantly be missing the point. We shall miss the fascination of being able to visualize Bible scenes. Through not knowing things that Bible writers took for granted, we shall find Bible history (the most poignant and dramatic history in the world) and Bible doctrine (the most electrifying communication ever) to be remote, mystifying, and boring. What a tragedy that would be!

History is the backbone of the Bible. Prophets' and apostles' sermons, with psalmists' praises, must be slotted into their place in the history, or the organism of Holy Scripture will not work in our minds as it should to bring us knowledge of God. Spine trouble limits what a person's other limbs can do, and uncertainty about Bible history—by limiting our insight into the rest of Scripture—limits what God's Word as a whole can do for us. Without some historical study a vast amount of the meaning of Scripture gets lost. Not that a man who has no historical aids to Bible study cannot understand the Word at all; on the contrary, its saving message is spelled out so

EDITOR'S PREFACE

often and so clearly that only the spiritually blind can miss it. But with historical aids one will understand Scripture much more fully than one could otherwise. This is where *Nelson's Illustrated Encyclopedia of Bible Facts* will help.

Nelson's Illustrated Encyclopedia of Bible Facts treats biblical statements of fact as trustworthy. It offers interpretations of them that, to the best of our linguistic and historical knowledge, seem natural. The world of technical biblical studies today is a jungle of skeptical speculations. But the approach of *Nelson's Illustrated Encyclopedia of Bible Facts* reflects the teaching of Scripture on prophets, apostles, our Lord Jesus Christ, and the whole Christian church till very recently. It is the approach that responsible scholarship and sober common sense demand when dealing with serious authors (and the Bible writers were certainly that). Moreover, this approach has stood up successfully to more than a century of critical challenge, and it seems to have come out of the academic furnace all the stronger in consequence. The adherence of *Nelson's Illustrated Encyclopedia of Bible Facts* to this approach seems therefore to need no apology, nor to require defense.

James I. Packer

BIBLE HISTORY

Think for a moment about this remarkable volume that we call "The Bible." Three major religions—Christianity, Judaism, and Islam—claim the Bible or portions of the Bible as a holy book, and Christianity claims the Bible as its *only* Holy Book. Christians believe the Bible is God's Word for every age, including our own. That is why we study it and try to understand it better in every new generation. To gain more than a casual understanding of the Bible, we must get a clear picture of the history recorded in it. We can divide this history into the Old Testament and New Testament periods.

I. OLD TESTAMENT HISTORY
A. From Creation to Abraham
B. From Abraham to Moses
C. From Moses to Saul
D. The United Monarchy
E. The Divided Monarchy
F. From the Exile to the Return

II. INTERTESTAMENTAL HISTORY

III. NEW TESTAMENT HISTORY
A. The Life of Christ
B. The Ministry of the Apostles
1. In Jerusalem
2. From Jerusalem into All Judea
3. From Antioch to Rome

I. Old Testament History. It is convenient to study Old Testament history in four sec-

THE CREATION STORY. *At first, archaeologists believed this cylinder seal from Mesopotamia showed a man and woman sitting under a tree, with a serpent (left) whispering in the woman's ear. The scene would naturally suggest the Creation story. However, many scholars now believe both figures are male deities.*

tions: (1) from Creation to Abraham, (2) from Abraham to Moses, (3) from Moses to Saul, and (4) from Saul to Christ.

"There is *one* central theme which . . . runs through all the stories of the Old Testament," William Hendriksen says. "That theme is the coming Christ."[1] Keep this in mind as we look at each section of the Old Testament.

A. From Creation to Abraham. God revealed to Moses how He created all things, and Moses described Creation in the Book of Genesis, the first book of the Bible. According to Genesis, God made the world and all that is in it within the space of six days, and He declared it all "to be very good." On the seventh day, He rested from His creating. Christian scholars disagree about how long these "days" might have been or even if they were periods of time at all.

But we must lay our understanding of the meaning of "day" on what the Bible itself has to say. Whatever other questions it leaves open, the biblical account makes it impossible for us to accept the modern theory that human life evolved over millions of years.

Christians also differ on the *date* of Creation. The Bible's lists of generations might skip names, as other genealogies sometimes do, so many scholars feel that we cannot safely add up the ages of the people listed to get the number of years in Old Testament history. The number thus reached could be far too small. There are other difficulties, too, in figuring the date of Creation—difficulties too complex to discuss here (*See* "Bible Chronology").

After God created man (Adam), He placed him in a garden called Eden. There, God decreed the first man and woman (Eve) to worship Him and rule the earth. (This is sometimes called our "cultural mandate.") God commanded the man and woman not to eat any fruit from the tree of knowledge of good and evil. If they did, they would know what it meant to participate in evil, and the happy life of Eden would be taken away from them!

We might think Adam and Eve would have

---

[1]William Hendriksen, *Survey of the Bible* (Grand Rapids: Baker Book House, 1977), p. 79.

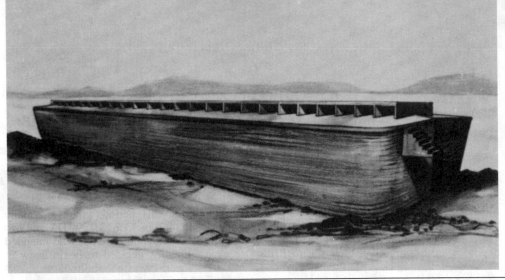

NOAH'S ARK. *This is an artist's conception of how the ark looked just after it was built. The sketch is based on information from George Hagopian, who claimed he saw the ark on Mount Ararat in 1908.*

had no trouble obeying this commandment. But someone else entered the picture: Satan, who leads the evil spirits who conspire to defeat God. Satan became a serpent; his lies seduced Eve into eating the forbidden fruit, and Adam joined her. They both sinned against God. Instead of living in harmony with God, they began a life of sin and misery and they fell from God's favor.

God promised Adam and Eve that He would send a Redeemer (also called a Savior, or a Messiah), who would destroy Satan and restore them to a right relationship with Him (Gen. 3:15). The Bible tells how God accomplished this plan of salvation. Of course, since the Bible focuses on that one aspect of world history, we can't expect it to tell us everything that happened in ancient times. It records only what we need in order to understand the history of redemption.

Several important things happened between the time of Adam and the time of Abraham, "father of all who believe" (Rom. 4:11,

NASB). For example, there was the first murder. Adam and Eve had many sons and daughters (Gen. 5:4), but the Bible names only two because they are important to the history of redemption. Eve thought that her firstborn, Cain, was the one who would destroy Satan and deliver them from the curse of sin and death (Gen. 4:1). But Cain jealously killed his brother Abel. God punished Cain by driving him out of the community of people who served God. (We know Adam and Eve continued to worship God because their sons offered burnt sacrifices to Him [Gen. 4:3–5], and the New Testament calls Abel a man of true faith [Heb 11:4]. Yet God saved Cain from the full penalty of his crime; He marked Cain so that other people would know God did not want him killed. We are not certain what God's mark was, but it must have been clearly visible to other people.

Then God gave Adam and Eve a third son, Seth, who replaced Abel. The Redeemer of the world would come from Seth's family.

ZIGGURAT OF UR. *This temple at Ur was used in the pagan worship that Abraham left behind when he traveled to the Promised Land. The word* ziggurat *is an English rendering of the Assyrian* ziqquratu *("height, pinnacle").*

But what about Cain's family? The Bible shows that Cain's son, Lamech, inherited his father's evil ways (Gen. 4:19–24). Lamech boasted that he did not need God's protection, for he could use his sword (Gen. 4:23–24). He rejected God's holy standards of marriage and took more than one wife. In fact, he set such a low value on human life that he killed a man for striking him.

Evil spread to all mankind (Gen. 6:1–4). The Bible says human giants or "mighty men" lived during this time, but their spiritual life certainly didn't stack up to their physical stature!

God sent a great Flood to punish sinful mankind, and this was the most important event of the ancient period. However, God preserved the lives of Noah and his family in an ark (a large wooden ship), so that He could eventually keep His promise to redeem mankind. Many Christians are now convinced that the Flood covered the entire world. According to 2 Peter 3:6, ". . . The world that then was, being overflowed with water, perished." Gleason L. Archer shows in detail that the ark was large enough to hold all the varieties of animals that exist today.[2] If that is so, it certainly could have held all the varieties of life in Noah's day. Notice that God sent the clean animals to the ark seven by seven (Gen. 7:2), and unclean animals two by two (Gen. 7:15).

After the Flood, God set the death penalty for murder and appointed human agents as executioners (Gen. 9:1–7). He also put a rainbow in the sky to remind His people that He would never destroy all mankind by water (Gen. 8:13–17).

Yet right after the Flood, Noah's son Canaan (or "Ham") sinned against God (Gen. 9:20–29). God cursed Canaan because of his disrespect for his father, Noah (v. 25).

Then God spoke through Noah to describe the course of subsequent history. He said a descendant of Shem would bring salvation into the world, and the descendants of Japheth would share in that salvation. Japheth's family moved north and became progenitors of the Gentiles of New Testament times (Gen. 10:2).

One more thing happened before Abraham appeared on the scene. Proud city-dwellers tried to get to heaven by building a tower in Babel (Gen. 11). God condemned their arro-

gant ways by breaking them up into different language groups, then scattering them to live in different areas (Gen. 10:4; cf. 9:1). This, it seems, is how the large language families of the world began.

So what does all this tell us? Clearly, it shows that evil continued to increase from the time of the Flood to Abraham. We know that people during this period worshiped many gods (Josh. 24:2; cf. Gen. 31:29–31), and immorality was rampant. So God, who intended to save humanity, decided to begin anew in one family . . . "through whom all the families would be blessed."

B. From Abraham to Moses. God chose Abraham's family to bring this salvation to the rest of mankind. Abraham lived in the city of Ur (capital of the ancient kingdom of Sumer). Sometime around 2000 B.C., God called Abraham to leave his father's home and go to a

HARAN. *The mound at the left in the background is believed to be the site of Haran, where Abraham stopped on his way to Canaan. The cone-shaped buildings are native Syrian homes.*

[2] Gleason L. Archer, *A Survey of Old Testament Introduction* (Chicago: Moody Press, 1964), p. 199 ff.

new land. The Bible traces Abraham's steps from Ur to Haran (north of Palestine), through the land of Palestine, into Egypt, and back into Palestine. God promised to give Abraham a son, whose children would become a great nation. God also promised to make Abraham's descendants a blessing to all nations (Gen. 12:2–3; 17:1–6). At first, Abraham believed what God said; but later he doubted that God would do as He promised, and tried to force God's hand by his own action. Thus, when God didn't give him a son as soon as he expected, Abraham took his wife's servant girl Hagar and had a son by her. Though the ancient world accepted this means of securing an heir, it violated God's law for marriage (Gen. 2:24), and Abraham suffered sorely for his sin. His firstborn son Ishmael turned against Isaac, the promised son who was born 13 years later. So Ishmael had to leave Abraham's household.

But Abraham came to trust God more completely as the years went by. Finally, God told him to offer Isaac as a burnt sacrifice to prove his love for God (Gen. 22). By this time, Abraham knew that God expected him to obey, and so, trusting God, he laid his son on the altar (cf. Heb. 11:17–19). At the last minute, God ordered him not to kill Isaac and gave him a ram for the sacrifice.

MIDIAN. *In this rugged wilderness, Moses joined the family of Jethro and found refuge from the Egyptians for 40 years. Midian lies east of the Gulf of Aqaba, the northeastern arm of the Red Sea.*

Another time, Abraham asked God to spare the sinful cities where his nephew Lot lived. But Lot failed to redeem his community (cf. 2 Pet. 2:8); God could not find even ten righteous men there. So God destroyed the cities as He had planned. Again, God was training Abraham and his family to obey Him.

Then the Bible turns our eyes to the life of Jacob, Isaac's second son. Jacob lived around 1850 B.C. God chose Jacob to inherit the promises He had given to Isaac. He named Ja-

MAKING BRICKS. *Murals from the tomb of Rekhmire, the vizier of Pharaoh Thutmose III, show how bricks were made in Egypt at the time of the Exodus (1446 B.C.) At the top left, two men are shown drawing water from a pool to make the mud. Beside them, two men work the clay. Slaves press the clay into wooden molds to form the bricks, which are left to dry in the sun. Notice that the slave kneeling in the middle of the upper panel has lighter skin than the other slaves; this indicates that he was of Semitic origin, perhaps a Hebrew. The bottom panel shows how the bricks were laid with mortar.*

cob's family as the one that would bring the Redeemer to the world.

But what an unlikely choice! Jacob grew up a self-seeking and deceitful fellow. He tricked his brother Esau and lied to his father so he could steal Esau's birthright. Then he fled to his uncle Laban's home to escape his brother's wrath. God confronted him as he ran away, and yet Jacob held his ground.

So God began a long, slow job of teaching Jacob how to trust Him. He gave Jacob a good wife and great possessions. His uncle tricked him into marrying Leah, a girl he did not want, so Jacob pressed on to marry her sister Rachel as well. Jacob grew rich, but his greed led to

family trouble and he had to leave Laban's land. He returned to his father's home in Palestine. There he found that God had prepared the way for him, and his brother was no longer angry.

But Jacob's troubles were not over. Years later, ten of Jacob's sons got jealous of their youngest brother, Joseph, because Jacob obviously preferred him. Joseph had dreamed they would bow down to him someday, along with their parents. The ten brothers resented this. They trapped Joseph, sold him into slavery, and told their father that he was dead.

Slave traders carried Joseph to Egypt, where he became one of the pharaoh's servants. God used Joseph to interpret the pharaoh's dreams, and the young man rose to become second in command under the pharaoh.

Then a famine in Palestine drove Joseph's family to Egypt in search of food. His older brothers came first. When they bowed before Joseph, he immediately recognized them; but he did not tell them who he was. Eventually, Joseph forced them to bring his younger brother Benjamin to Egypt, too. Then he revealed his identity and forgave them for selling him into slavery. Joseph invited them to bring his entire family. The pharaoh received them warmly and allowed them to settle in a rich part of Egypt.

C. From Moses to Saul. Now the Bible moves its spotlight to Moses (*ca.* 1526–1406 B.C.), who holds a vital place in the history of redemption. Jacob's descendants had so many children that the pharaohs feared they would take charge of the country. So a new pharaoh put them into slavery and ordered all of the Israelites' boy babies to be killed. Moses' mother put him in a little basket and set him afloat in the river, near the place where the pharaoh's daughter bathed. When the princess found the baby, she took him to the palace to raise as her adopted son. Moses' mother became his nursemaid and she probably took care of him well beyond the time he was weaned (Exod. 2:7–10).

As a young man, Moses began to feel burdened for his people; he wanted to bring them out of slavery (Exod. 2:11; Acts 7:24–25). When Moses was about 40 years old, he saw an Egyptian beating an Israelite; he flew into a rage and killed the Egyptian. Afraid the pharaoh would execute him, Moses fled into the Midian Desert (Exod. 2:14–15). There he married into the family of Jethro (also called

MOUNT SINAI. *Tradition says that this craggy peak in the wilderness of Sinai is Mount Sinai, where Moses received the stone tablets of Law from God. The Arabs call the peak Jebel Musa, which means "Mount Moses."*

"Reuel"), a pagan priest. Moses agreed to tend Jethro's flock (Exod. 2:16–21).

After about forty years, God spoke to Moses from a bush that burned but was not consumed. He ordered Moses to go back to Egypt and lead the Israelites into Palestine, the land He had promised to Abraham. Moses didn't believe he could do this, and he made excuses for not going. But God answered every one of them, and gave him power to work miracles that would induce the Israelites to follow him. God revealed His holy name *YHWH* (sometimes translated "Jehovah") to Moses. Moses tried to beg off by saying, "I am slow of speech. . . ," perhaps because he had a speech impediment. So God sent Moses' brother Aaron along with him, to translate what Moses had to say (Exod. 7:1).

Moses and Aaron persuaded the people of Israel to follow them, but the pharaoh refused to let them leave Egypt. Then God sent ten devastating plagues on Egypt to change the pharaoh's heart (Exod. 7:17—12:36). The last plague killed the firstborn son in every home whose doors were not marked with blood. Because the people of Israel obeyed God's instructions, the death angel passed over Israel's firstborn. (God commanded the Israelites to celebrate this event with a yearly festival that is actually named "the Passover.") The death plague made the pharaoh give in; he agreed to let the Israelites go back to their native land. But as soon as they left, the pharaoh changed his mind. He sent his army to bring the Israelites back.

God led His people to the Red Sea, where He parted the waters and led them through on dry ground. Several scholars, such as Leon Wood, estimate that it happened around 1446 B.C.[3]

Moses led the people from the Red Sea to Mount Sinai. On the way, God miraculously gave them bread and quail to eat. At Mount Sinai, God revealed through Moses the laws and social plans that would mold the Israelites into a holy nation (*See* "Laws and Statutes"). These included the Ten Commandments.

From Sinai, God led the Israelites to Kadesh, where they sent spies into Palestine. The spies reported that the land was rich and fertile, yet full of giants. Most of the spies believed that the giants would destroy them if they tried to take the land. Only two—Caleb and Joshua—believed it was worth the fight. The Israelites accepted the skeptical advice of the majority and turned away from Palestine. God condemned them to wander in the wilderness for 40 years because they hadn't trusted Him.

At the end of their wandering, they camped on the plains of Moab. Here Moses spoke to them for the last time, and his words were recorded in the Book of Deuteronomy. Moses turned his leadership over to Joshua. Then he gave the Israelites his final instructions and ended with a hymn of praise to God. Notice that Moses could not enter the Promised Land because he had rebelled against God at Meribah (Num. 20:12). But after Moses gave his farewell to the Israelites, God led him to the top of Mount Nebo to see the land they would enter. There he died.

Joshua had proven himself a capable leader of Israel's army in the battle of Amalek (Exod. 17:8–16). Now God used Joshua to lead the people of Israel in conquering and settling the Promised Land. He had been one of the spies who had first looked at the Promised Land. Because they trusted God to give them the land, Joshua and Caleb were the only adults of their generation that God allowed to enter it. All the others had died in the wilderness.

So Moses ordained Joshua to replace him, and he announced that God would give Palestine into Joshua's hands. After Moses died, God spoke to Joshua, encouraging him to stay true to his calling (Josh. 1:1–9).

Immediately, Joshua led Israel into the Promised Land. God rewarded Joshua's faith by helping Israel to take possession of it. First, God divided the overflowing Jordan River so they could cross over on dry land (Josh. 3:14–17). Then the angel of the Lord led the Israelites in their miraculous defeat of Jericho, the first city conquered in the Promised Land. When the people blew their trumpets as God had ordered, the walls of the city fell down (Josh. 6). Under Joshua, Israel proceeded to conquer the entire country (Josh. 21:23–45). They suffered defeat only at Ai, when one of their men disobeyed God's battle orders (Josh. 7). Having learned their lesson, the Israelites decided to follow God's orders and try again, and this time they defeated Ai. In all, they conquered 31 kings in the new territory. Joshua divided the land among the Israelite tribes according to God's directions. Just before he died, Joshua urged his people to keep trusting God and obeying His commands.

---

[3] Leon Wood, *A Survey of Israel's History* (Grand Rapids: Zondervan, 1970), p. 88 ff. Cf. Archer, p. 212 ff. *See also* "Bible Chronology."

BIBLE HISTORY

Moses

The most crucial figure of Old Testament history was Moses, who led the people of Israel out of bondage. Some commentators believe that his name is a combination of the late Egyptian words for "water" (*ma*) and "take" (*shi*). Thus it may be a reminder of how the pharaoh's daughter took the infant Moses from a basket on the Nile (Exod.2).

Moses had an older brother named Aaron and a sister named Miriam. He was born just after the Egyptian pharaoh ordered his soldiers to kill all new Israelite boy babies to control the population of the slaves. Moses' mother made a basket of bulrushes, placed him in it, and floated it on the Nile River under the watchful eye of his sister. When the pharaoh's daughter found the baby, she adopted him into the royal family.

When Moses was a young man, he killed an Egyptian slave driver in a fit of rage (Exod. 2:11 ff.). He escaped into the rugged land of Midian, where he married a priest's daughter named Zipporah. Together they had two sons—Gershom and Eliezer (Exod. 2:22; 18:4).

After Moses had lived in Midian for about 40 years, the Lord appeared to him in a burning bush on the side of Mt. Sinai or Horeb (Exod. 3). He instructed Moses to lead his people out of Egypt to the Promised Land of Canaan. Moses protested that he would not be able to convince the pharaoh to let the Israelites leave, so the Lord allowed him to take Aaron as his spokesman.

Moses went back to Egypt and conveyed God's message to "let my people go." When the pharaoh demanded a sign of divine power to confirm Moses' message, Moses was pitted against the pharaoh's court magicians. (According to Jewish tradition, they were named Jannes and Jambres.) Though the pharaoh saw Moses and Aaron perform miracles more spectacular than those of his own magicians, he refused to let the people of Israel leave his land. So God sent a series of ten plagues, culminating in the death of all the firstborn sons of Egypt—including the pharaoh's own son—to convince the ruler who finally decided to honor Moses' request. Even so, the pharaoh changed his mind while the Israelites were leaving. He tried to stop them at the shores of the Red Sea, but God parted the waters so that the Israelites could escape.

Moses led his people to Mt. Sinai, where he met with God and received a system of law to govern them in the Promised Land. God summarized this Law in the Ten Commandments, which He engraved on tablets of stone that Moses brought back to the Israelite camp. Moses found that his people had turned to pagan worship, and he angrily dashed the tablets to the ground, symbolizing the people's breaking of the covenant. After the people repented of their sin, Moses returned to the mountain and received the Ten Commandments once again.

For 40 years the Israelites wandered in the wilderness between Sinai and Canaan. During this time, Moses and Aaron were their civil and religious rulers. God prevented Moses from entering the Promised Land because he had disobeyed the Lord at Meribah, where he struck a stone with his rod to receive water. Yet God allowed Moses to view the Promised Land from the top of Mt. Nebo. Then Moses died.

In the 120 years of his life, Moses had led his people in their journey from bondage to freedom. He had recorded their past history by writing what are now the first five books of the Old Testament, and he had received the Law that would govern them for centuries to come.

But they didn't. After Joshua died, "every man did what was right in his own eyes" (Judg. 21:25). The great leaders of this period acted much like Moses and Joshua; they were military heroes and chief judges in the courts of Israel, and we call them the "judges." The most noteworthy were: Othniel, Deborah (the only woman judge), Gideon, Jephthah, Samson, Eli, and Samuel. (Ruth also lived during this period.)

As you read the colorful stories of these ancient heroes, spend some extra time on the life of Samuel. He was one of the most important figures of this era.

Samuel's mother had prayed for a son, so she praised God to see him born (1 Sam. 2:1–10). Samuel's parents gave him to the chief priest Eli so that he could be trained to serve the Lord. While Samuel was still a child, he helped Eli care for the Tent of Meeting.

ARK OF THE COVENANT. *This bas relief from the synagogue of Capernaum shows the ark of the covenant. The ark was kept in the holy of holies of the temple in Jerusalem. It disappeared when Nebuchadnezzar's armies razed the city in 586 B.C.*

(*See* "Laws and Statutes.") There he heard God calling him to become the new leader of Israel, as a prophet and judge.

Before Samuel's time, the Israelites called a prophet a "seer" (1 Sam. 9:9; cf. Deut. 13:1–15; 18:15–22). But Samuel, like other later prophets, was not just a forecaster of the future. He spoke God's messages to the nation about the lives they lived, often rebuking the people for their wicked ways. He stands as the first of Israel's great prophets, and the last of the judges. At God's direction, he anointed Saul to be the first human king over Israel (1 Sam. 8:19–22; cf. Deut. 14:14–20), though he later regretted it.

D. The United Monarchy. In his early years, Saul appeared as a man of humility and self-control. Over the years, however, his character changed. He became a man of self-will, disobedience to God, jealousy, hatred, and superstition. His anger turned against David, a young warrior who had killed the giant Goliath, and who served as his court musician. He often tried to murder David, being jealous of David's popularity (1 Sam. 18:5–9; 19:8–10).

But God had secretly chosen David to be the next king, and He promised the kingship to David's family forever (1 Sam. 16:1–13; 2 Sam. 7:12–16). Yet Saul continued to be king for many years.

After Saul's death, King David brought the ark of the covenant to Jerusalem (cf. Deut. 12:1–14; 2 Sam. 6:1–11). The ark was a wooden box that held the stone tablets on which God wrote for Moses the Ten Commandments; the Israelites had carried it with them through their years of wandering in the wilderness, and they prized it as a holy object. David brought it to his capital city so that Jerusalem would become the spiritual center of the nation, as well as its political center.

David had the kind of qualities they were looking for—military skill, political savvy, and a keen sense of religious duty. He had made the nation stronger and more secure than it had ever been.

But David was only a man, with weaknesses like everyone else. He toyed with the idea of starting a harem such as other kings had, and he arranged the murder of an officer in his army so he could marry the man's wife whom he had already seduced. He took a census of the men of Israel because he no longer trusted God for military victory; he only trusted the strength of his army. God punished David and Israel with him for his sin. David was the head of the nation; so when he sinned against God, all of his people suffered the punishment.

David's son Solomon was Israel's next king. Despite Solomon's legendary wisdom, he did not always live wisely. He did carry out David's political plan, strengthening his hold on the territories conquered by his father. He was a shrewd businessman, and he made some trade agreements that brought great wealth to Israel (1 Kings 10:14–15). God also used Solomon to build the great temple in Jerusalem (cf. Deut. 12:1–14). But Solomon's lavish style of living increased the burden of taxes upon the common people. He inherited his father's desire for women, and he concluded trade agreements with foreign kings which involved "political marriages" and thus he put together a harem of brides from many foreign lands (1 Kings 11:1–8). These pagan wives enticed him to worship pagan gods, and he soon set up their rites and ceremonies in Jerusalem.

E. The Divided Monarchy. After Solomon, the fortunes of Israel went downhill. The nation rebelled against God and His laws. God might have destroyed Israel; but He did not do so for He still planned to use the House of David to introduce the Redeemer who would save the world from sin. He had promised to raise this Redeemer from Abraham's family, and He intended to keep His promise.

BIBLE HISTORY

THE KINGS OF ISRAEL

Name	Length of Reign (Years)	Reference
Jeroboam I	22	1 Kings 11:26—14:20
Nadab	2	1 Kings 15:25–28
Baasha	24	1 Kings 15:27—16:7
Elah	2	1 Kings 16:6–14
Zimri	(7 days)	1 Kings 16:9–20
Omri	12	1 Kings 16:15–28
Ahab	21	1 Kings 16:28—22:40
Ahaziah	1	1 Kings 22:40—2 Kings 1:18
Jehoram (Joram)	11	2 Kings 3:1—9:25
Jehu	28	2 Kings 9:1—10:36
Jehoahaz	16	2 Kings 13:1–9
Jehoash (Joash)	16	2 Kings 13:10—14:16
Jeroboam II	40	2 Kings 14:23–29
Zechariah	$1/2$	2 Kings 14:29—15:12
Shallum	(1 month)	2 Kings 15:10–15
Menahem	10	2 Kings 15:14–22
Pekahiah	2	2 Kings 15:22–26
Pekah	20	2 Kings 15:27–31
Hoshea	9	2 Kings 15:30—17:6

THE KINGS OF JUDAH

Name	Length of Reign (Years)	Reference
Rehoboam	17	1 Kings 11:42—14:31
Abijam	3	1 Kings 14:31—15:8
Asa	41	1 Kings 15:8–24
Jehoshaphat	25	1 Kings 22:41–50
Jehoram	8	2 Kings 8:16–24
Ahaziah	1	2 Kings 8:24—9:29
Athaliah	6	2 Kings 11:1–20
Joash	40	2 Kings 11:1—12:21
Amaziah	29	2 Kings 14:1–20
Azariah (Uzziah)	52	2 Kings 15:1–7
Jotham	18	2 Kings 15:32–38
Ahaz	19	2 Kings 16:1–20
Hezekiah	29	2 Kings 18:1—20:21
Manasseh	55	2 Kings 21:1–18
Amon	2	2 Kings 21:19–26
Josiah	31	2 Kings 22:1—23:30
Jehoahaz	$1/4$	2 Kings 23:31–33
Jehoiakim	11	2 Kings 23:34—24:5
Jehoiachin	$1/4$	2 Kings 24:6–16
Zedekiah	11	2 Kings 24:17—25:30

Figure 1

BIBLE HISTORY

The Divided Monarchy

Biblical Events	Secular Events
The Division of the Kingdom (931) **Asa's Reformation in Judah (910)**	**Pharaoh Shishak I Invades Palestine (927)**
900 B.C. Omri Makes Samaria His Capital (879) Ahab and Jezebel Lead Israel to Idolatry (*ca.* 870) Elijah and Elisha (*ca.* 850) Jehu Pays Tribute to Shalmaneser III (841)	Assyria Begins Its Rise to Power (*ca.* 900) The Battle of Qarqar (853) Tyre Pays Tribute to Shalmaneser III (841)
800 B.C. Moabite Bands Invade Israel (795) Uzziah Is Struck Leprous (*ca.* 750) Beginning of Isaiah's Ministry (*ca.* 739) The Fall of Israel (723)	Assyria Destroys Damascus (732) Tyre Falls to Assyria (723) Sennacherib Invades Judah (701)
700 B.C. Manasseh Carried to Babylon (*ca.* 648) Jeremiah Begins His Ministry (*ca.* 627) Josiah's Reformation (621) Daniel and His Friends Carried to Babylon (605)	Esarhaddon of Assyria Captures Sidon (677) Egypt Overthrows Its Ethiopian Rulers (663) Nabopolassar Overthrows the Assyrians (625) The Fall of Nineveh (612) Nebuchadnezzar Defeats Egypt at Carchemish (605)
600 B.C. The Fall of Jerusalem (597) The Fall of Judah and The Exile (586)	Nebuchadnezzar Invades Egypt (568)

Figure 2

MOUNT CARMEL. *Beyond the Bay of Haifa lies historic Mount Carmel, where Elijah defeated the prophets of Baal (1 Kings 18).*

When Solomon died, Israel stumbled into a bloody civil war as Solomon's sons and generals fought for the throne. Rehoboam had his father's blessing to be the new king; but his rival Jeroboam wielded more influence among the military chiefs of the land. In the end, Rehoboam took the southern half of the country and called it Judah. Jeroboam set up his own government in the northern half and retained the name of Israel. Each claimed to be the king God had chosen.

Look at the two charts covering this period, and you'll see the main leaders in Israel and Judah, including the major prophets. The first chart (Fig. 1) shows who ruled Israel and Judah in each generation. The other chart (Fig. 2) shows what else was happening during the time of the divided monarchy. None of Israel's kings served God, and Judah wasn't much better; only Kings Asa, Jehoshaphat, Joash (Jehoash), Amaziah, Azariah, Jotham, Hezekiah, and Josiah were faithful to God's Word. Finally, God allowed the pagan empires of Assyria and Babylonia to destroy both kingdoms and carry the people away into exile.

Two important leaders emerged in the time of the divided monarchy. The first was the prophet Elijah. He stands out as a uniquely rugged character in the Bible story. We don't know where he came from; he just suddenly appeared before the wicked King Ahab and

BIBLE HISTORY

declared that God would bring a long drought because the people were so wicked. Elijah fled to the wilderness and stopped by the brook Cherith, where God miraculously provided food for him. When the stream dried up, God sent Elijah to help the widow of Zarephath, who was suffering under the drought. She was nearly out of food when Elijah came to her door, but she fed him anyway. Because she did, the prophet decided to stay at her house and miracles followed; her supplies never ran out while he was there, and when her son died, Elijah raised him from the dead.

Then the prophet returned to King Ahab and told him to summon all the prophets of the pagan god Baal whom Jezebel, Ahab's wife, worshiped, to meet him on Mount Carmel. There Elijah challenged the prophets to a contest to prove which god was stronger. Elijah asked God to send fire from heaven to light a water-logged sacrifice, and He did. Elijah killed all the false prophets (cf. Deut. 13:5). Then he asked God to end the drought, and God sent a cloudburst of rain. Elijah was so happy that he raced to the gates of Jezreel, outrunning the king and his chariots.

But Jezebel's threats against his life kept Elijah discouraged and frightened, and he asked God to let him die. Instead, God sent angels to minister to Elijah, and ordered him to recruit two future kings and his own successor. Elijah obeyed, appointing a farmer named Elisha to be the new prophet.

Elijah confronted Ahab again, condemning him and Jezebel for murdering their neighbor Naboth to get his vineyard. The king sent two companies of soldiers to capture the prophet, but Elijah called fire down from heaven to destroy them. Once more he declared the doom of the king.

Soon after that, Elijah and Elisha went for a walk, discussing the problems their nation faced. When they came to the Jordan River, Elijah divided the water by striking it with his mantle (a cape). They calmly walked across to the other side, as if they'd done it every day! As they stood on the river bank talking, a chariot of fire swooped down from the sky. It picked up Elijah and carried him away in a whirlwind, while his mantle fell on Elisha.

The second great personality of the divided monarchy was Elisha. He was like his teacher in many ways. Both men parted the waters of the Jordan, brought rain in times of drought, increased a widow's supply of food, raised a boy from the dead, performed miracles for Gentiles, pronounced doom upon kings, and destroyed their enemies with supernatural power. But there were also differences between them. Just before Elijah was taken into heaven, he prayed that God would give Elisha a double portion of his spirit. No doubt this had something to do with the differences between the two men. While Elijah fell under times of depression, Elisha had an attitude of triumph and confidence. He never seemed to complain or lose courage. The Scriptures show that he performed more miracles than any other prophet of the Old Testament (e.g., 2 Kings 4:38—5:19).

Isaiah, Jeremiah, Amos, Hosea, Micah, Ezekiel, and other prophets warned Israel and Judah that God would punish their wickedness. Isaiah and Ezekiel also had words of consolation for them after they went into exile. God used these men as His holy spokesmen in this crucial epoch of His people's history (*See* "Outline of the Books of the Bible").

F. From the Exile to the Return. The Jewish people were taken into exile more than once. So when we discuss the "Exile," we should be careful to say *which* exile we mean. The Assyrians twice conquered the Northern

ANTIOCHUS III. *This Seleucid king took Palestine from the Egyptians in 198 B.C. But the Romans subdued Antiochus in 190 B.C. and seized much of the territory he had conquered.*

BETHLEHEM. *This small city 10 km. (6 mi.) south of Jerusalem was the birthplace of David and Jesus. The Old Testament prophet Micah had predicted that the Messiah would be born in this city (Micah 5:2).*

Kingdom (Israel); the Southern Kingdom (Judah) was conquered once by Assyria and three times by the Babylonians. Each time, the conquerors carried off many captives. Most often when we talk about "the Exile," we mean the 70-year Babylonian captivity of Judah.

Religiously speaking, the Babylonian Captivity had three successive phases: one of unrealistic hopefulness (cf. Jer. 29; Ezek. 17:11–24); one of truer and humbler hopefulness, when God used Ezekiel to comfort the people (Ezek. 36—38); one of revived hopefulness in the time of Daniel. The Jews returned from the Exile in two stages: One group was led by Sheshbazzar and Zerubbabel (Ezra 1:8—2:70). The second was led by Ezra and Nehemiah (Ezra 8:1–14). Just as Isaiah had predicted (Isa. 44:28; 45:1), God raised up a kind-hearted pagan king—Cyrus of Persia—who let the Jews return to Palestine. The people who had taken their place tried to ruin their plans; but the Jews rebuilt the temple in Jerusalem and resettled in their land. The prophets Zechariah and Haggai encouraged the people in their work. But toward the end of this period, Malachi condemned them for slipping back into their sinful ways.

II. Intertestamental History. It is not always clear what happened in the 400 years between the writing of Malachi and the time Jesus was born. We call this the "Intertestamental Period" because it is the time between the writing of the Old and New Testaments.

We know the restored nation of Israel had serious political upsets during this time. After Alexander the Great conquered the Persian Empire, Greek princes and generals wrestled for the right to govern the Near East. The Se-leucid king Antiochus III took Palestine away from Egypt in 198 B.C. and tried to make it a base for building a new empire in the East. But Antiochus III was no match for the Roman legions. They defeated his army in 190 B.C. and made him a puppet ruler in the Roman chain of command.

The Maccabee family (the offspring of the high priest Mattathias) began a civil war against the Seleucid governors and captured Jerusalem in 164 B.C. But they weren't able to

SYNAGOGUE AT CAPERNAUM. *This is one of the best-preserved examples of synagogue architecture in Palestine. The style of the columns proves that the Jewish architects copied Greek models when they rebuilt the synagogue in the second or third century A.D.*

push the Seleucids completely out of their affairs until 134 B.C. In that year, John Hyrcanus I of the Maccabee family set up his own dynasty, known as the Hasmoneans. They ruled until 37 B.C., when Rome established the Herodian family as the new puppet government in Palestine.

The books entitled First and Second Maccabees describe the Maccabean revolt and the chaos of Palestine up to the time of the Hasmoneans. Roman Catholics include these books and other writings from the Intertestamental Period in their Bible, but Protestants do not, although translations of them are often included in Protestant versions of the Bible.

III. New Testament History. Old Testament history paints a colorful picture of God's dealings with man; but it doesn't give us the whole story of God's plan to redeem men from sin. The New Testament brings us to the climax of God's redemptive work, because it introduces us to the Messiah, Jesus Christ, and to the beginning of His church.

A. The Life of Christ. The writings of Matthew, Mark, Luke, and John tell us about Jesus' ministry. These writers were either eyewitnesses of Jesus' life or they wrote down what eyewitnesses told them, but they do not provide a full biography of Jesus. Everything they recorded actually happened, but they concentrate on Jesus' ministry and leave gaps elsewhere in the story of His life.

Imagine someone writing a letter to a friend to introduce him to an important person. Would the writer be able to describe *everything* about that person's life? Of course not. He could only write about what he knew—and he probably would not try to tell all of that, either. The writer would concentrate on what he thinks his friend wants and needs to know.

The men who wrote the Gospels did the same thing. They aimed to explain the *person* and *work* of Jesus by recording what He did and said. And each writer presents a slightly different view of Jesus and what He did. (*See* "Outline of the Books of the Bible.") The Gospel writers did not try to relate all the events of Jesus' boyhood, because that was not their reason for writing. They did not try to give us a daily diary of Jesus' life, either. They stuck to what matters for salvation and discipleship.

In this section we will take our cue from the Gospel writers. We will simply sketch the major events of Jesus' life and summarize how He brought the history of redemption to its climax. For more information about His life, see "Jesus Christ."

Many people know about the birth and infancy of Jesus Christ. Every Christmas we hear the well-known carols about the Virgin Mary (the mother of Jesus), her trip to Bethlehem on the back of a donkey, and the birth of the baby Jesus Christ—true man and true God, who came to earth to save God's people. We hear the familiar story of how Jesus was born in Bethlehem, of the manger where He lay, and of the angels who announced His birth to the shepherds. We know the angels declared Jesus to be the long-promised Davidic king.

The wise men who brought gifts to the Christ child are mystery figures. We don't know which country (or countries) they came from, only that they were "from the East"

THE STREET CALLED STRAIGHT. *A small arch is all that remains of the old city gate that stood in Damascus in Paul's day. The arch leads to "the street called Straight," where Paul stayed just after his conversion (Acts 9:11).*

BIBLE HISTORY

(Matt. 2:1). They may well have come from the great eastern empires of Mesopotamia, Babylonia, or Persia. They studied the stars and realized that a new king was being born among the Jews, and so they came to the Jewish capital of Jerusalem to pay their respects. How surprised they were to learn that King Herod had no new children! Then they followed a clear prophecy from Micah 5:2 that led them to Bethlehem, where they found the baby Jesus.

The Bible does not say there were *three* wise men, but artists have usually painted three to show the three gifts that they brought—gold, frankincense, and myrrh (Matt. 2:11). Apparently the *magi* came to see Jesus several months after He was born, and some scholars think Jesus may have been as much as two years old when they came.

After Jesus was born, His parents dedicated Him at the Temple in Jerusalem (Luke 2:22–28). They began training Him to live "in favor with God and man" (Luke 2:52).

King Herod wanted to be certain that the people did not rally around the infant king to start a rebellion, so he ordered his soldiers to kill all the boy babies in Bethlehem (Matt. 2:16). Jesus' family fled into Egypt to escape the evil decree. After Herod died, they returned to Palestine and settled in the town of Nazareth.

The Bible says nothing else about Jesus until He was 12 or 13 years old. Then, to assume His proper role in the Jewish congregation, He had to make a special visit to Jerusalem and offer a sacrifice at the Temple. While He was there, Jesus talked with religious leaders about the Jewish faith. He showed an extraordinary understanding of the true God, and His answers amazed them. Later, His parents started home and discovered that Jesus was missing. They found Him at the Temple, still talking with the Jewish experts.

Again, the Bible falls silent until it introduces us to the events that began Jesus' ministry when He was about 30 years old. First we see John the Baptist coming out of the wilderness and preaching in cities along the Jordan River, urging the people to prepare for their Messiah (Luke 3:3–9). John had been born

EPHESUS. *Paul visited the seaport of Ephesus on his second and third missionary journeys. A major landmark of the city was this theater, which the Romans built to seat about 25,000 people. In this arena the silversmith named Demetrius led a riot against the Christian evangelists (Acts 19:24–29).*

BIBLE HISTORY

into a godly family, and he grew up to love and serve God faithfully. God spoke through John, and crowds of people clamored to hear his preaching. He told them to return to God and begin obeying Him. When he saw Jesus he cried that this man was the ". . . Lamb of God which taketh away the sin of the world" (John 1:29). John baptized Jesus; and as Jesus came up from the water, God sent the Holy Spirit in the form of a dove that settled upon Jesus.

The Holy Spirit led Jesus into the wilderness, where He went without food for 40 days. While He was in this weakened condition, the Devil came and tried to tempt Him in various ways. Jesus refused and sent the Devil away. Then angels came to feed Jesus and comfort Him.

At first, Jesus was a popular man. In the area around the Sea of Galilee, He attended a wedding feast and changed water into wine to serve the guests. This is the first of His miracles that the Bible mentions. It demonstrated that He truly was God, just as His later miracles did. From Galilee, He went to Jerusalem and drove a group of religious hucksters out of the temple. For the first time, publicly He asserted His authority over the religious life of His people. This turned many of the other religious leaders against Him.

One of those leaders, Nicodemus, saw that Jesus was teaching the truth about God. He came to Jesus one night and asked how He could get into the kingdom of God, which is the realm of redemption and salvation. Jesus told Nicodemus that he must "be born again" (John 3:3); in other words, he had to become a new person. From this conversation between Jesus and Nicodemus, we learn that a Christian is a person who has been "born again."

When John the Baptist began preaching and drawing great crowds in Judea, Jesus went back to the district of Galilee. There He performed many miracles and was surrounded by large crowds. Unfortunately, the crowds were more interested in the miracles than Jesus' teachings.

Yet Jesus kept on teaching. He entered private homes, sat at public feasts, and worshiped with other Jews at their synagogues. He denounced the religious leaders of His day because their faith was a sham. He didn't reject their formal religion; on the contrary, Jesus respected the temple and temple worship (cf. Matt. 5:17–18). But the Pharisees and other leaders failed to see that He was the

Messiah, and they didn't care about being saved from sin. Furthermore, they were not satisfied with what God had revealed to them in the Old Testament, but kept adding to it and revising it. They believed their worked-over version of the Scriptures gave them the only true religion. Jesus called them back to God's original words. He was very careful about the way He quoted Scripture, and He prodded his followers to understand it better. He taught that even a basic knowledge of Scripture should show a person God's will for salvation through faith in Himself.

Near Galilee, Jesus performed His most amazing miracle yet. He took seven loaves of bread and two fish, blessed them, and broke them into enough pieces to feed 4,000 people! But this did not draw more people to faith in Jesus; in fact, they turned away because they couldn't figure out why and how He wanted them to "eat" His body and "drink" His blood (John 6:52–66).

The twelve disciples stayed true to Jesus, and He began to focus His efforts on training

CORINTH. *The ruins of the temple of Apollo give mute testimony to the pagan worship of Corinth, where Paul directed two of his earliest epistles. Located on the narrow isthmus of Achaia, Corinth had two harbors—one on the Aegean and one on the Adriatic Sea. Thus it was an important crossroads of the ancient world.*

BIBLE HISTORY

HITTITE ART. *Excavations in Turkey have uncovered many relics of the Hittite civilizations, including this bas relief of a lion hunt from the Hittites' capital city of Hattushash. A century ago, critics complained that the Bible described civilizations that were not confirmed by secular evidence, citing the Hittite nation as a prime example (cf. Deut. 7:1; Ezek. 16:3). But the digs at Hattushash since 1906 prove that the Hittites did exist, and were a powerful nation.*

them. He increasingly taught them about His coming death and resurrection, explaining that they also could expect to suffer death if they kept on following Him.

This brings us to the end of Jesus Christ's life on earth. Judas Iscariot, one of Jesus' twelve disciples, betrayed Him to the hostile leaders of Jerusalem, and they nailed Him to a wooden cross to die among common criminals. But He rose from the grave and appeared to many of His followers, just as He had promised, and gave final instructions to His closest disciples. As they watched Him ascend into heaven, an angel appeared and said they would see Him return in the same way. In other words, He would come back visibly and in His physical body.

B. The Ministry of the Apostles. Bible history ends in the Book of Acts, which describes the ministry of the early church. In Acts we see how the message concerning Jesus—the message of redemption—spread from Jerusalem to Rome, the center of the Western world. The Book of Acts shows the expansion of the church (a) in Jerusalem,

(b) from Jerusalem into Judea, Samaria, and the surrounding area, and (c) from Antioch to Rome.

1. In Jerusalem. The early experiences of Jesus' disciples in Jerusalem reveal a great deal about the early church. The Book of Acts shows how earnestly these Christians spread the news about Jesus.

The book opens on a hillside near Jerusalem, where Jesus was about to ascend into heaven. He told His disciples: ". . . after that the Holy Ghost is come upon you: and ye shall be witnesses unto me both in Jerusalem, and in all Judea, and in Samaria, and unto the uttermost part of the earth" (Acts 1:8). That was Jesus' plan to evangelize the world.

A few days later the disciples replaced Judas, who had killed himself after he betrayed Jesus. They chose Matthias to round out the group of twelve.

Then the risen Christ gave the church His Holy Spirit, who enabled the Christians to fulfill their worldwide task (Acts 1:8).

Peter spoke for the church on the Day of Pentecost; he unfolded the importance of

Christ as the Lord of salvation (Acts 2:14–40). The Holy Spirit empowered the church to perform signs and wonders that confirmed the truthfulness of this message (Acts 2:43). Especially significant was the apostles' cure of a beggar at the door to the temple (Acts 3:1–10), which brought the apostles into conflict with the Jewish authorities.

The church maintained a close fellowship among its members. They shared meals in their homes; they also worshiped together and shared their wealth (Acts 2:44–46; 5:32–34). One couple named Ananias and Sapphira tried to deceive the church; having sold their property, they claimed to be giving *all* of the proceeds to the Lord, but they gave only a portion. God struck them dead for lying (Acts 5:1–11).

As the church continued to grow, government authorities began to persecute Christians openly. When Peter and some of the apostles were imprisoned, an angel released them, but they were called back before the authorities who ordered them to stop preaching about Jesus (Acts 5:17–29). But the Christians refused to stop preaching, even though the Jewish religious leaders beat them and threw them into prison several times.

The church grew so rapidly that the apostles needed help in some of the practical matters of church administration, notably their ministry to widows. They ordained seven deacons for this task. One of the seven, Stephen, began to preach in the streets. Eventually the religious authorities stoned him to death (Acts 7:54–60).

2. From Jerusalem into All Judea. The second stage of the church's growth opened with a violent persecution of the church in Jerusalem. Almost all the believers fled from the city (Acts 8:1). Wherever the Christians went they witnessed, and the Holy Spirit used their testimony to win other people to Christ (Acts 8:3 ff.). For example, another of the apostles' seven helpers named Philip talked to an Ethiopian diplomat, who became a Christian and took the good news to his homeland (Acts 8:26–39).

At this point the Bible describes the conversion of Saul of Tarsus. Before his conversion Saul persecuted the church. He obtained letters from the Jewish leaders in Jerusalem, authorizing him to proceed to Damascus to make sure that the Christians there were imprisoned and put to death. On his way, Christ struck him down and challenged him. Saul surrendered and thus began a new life in which he was to use his Roman name, Paul, in place of his Jewish name, Saul. God led him blind to Damascus, where God sent a Christian man named Ananias to him. Through Ananias, Paul's sight was restored and he was filled with the Holy Spirit. Paul began to preach about Jesus in the Jewish synagogue, and the Jewish leaders drove him out of Damascus. Some time later (cf. Gal. 1:17—2:2) he went to Jerusalem, where he established a working relationship with the apostles.

We should also notice the ministry of Peter, which was especially marked with miracles. In Lydda he healed a man named Aeneas (Acts 9:32–35). In Joppa, God used him to raise Tabitha from the dead (Acts 9:36–42). Finally, God gave him a vision that summoned him to Caesarea, where he introduced the gospel to the Gentiles (Acts 10:9–48).

Peter was the foremost leader of the apostles and his ministry rallied the enthusiasm of the early church. An *apostle* was a person whom Christ had chosen for special training in ministry (cf. Gal. 1:12). The apostles laid the foundation of the church by preaching the

CHRISTIAN SYMBOLS. *The early Christians used the cross and other basic symbols to identify themselves. This mosaic floor from the Jewish Christian synagogue at Nazareth shows the cross (representing Christ) within the sun (representing the heavens).*

gospel of Christ (cf. Eph. 2:20; 1 Cor. 3:10–11; Jude 3:20. *See also* "The Apostles"). God used Peter to open the door of salvation to the Gentiles.

At this point the record of Bible history turns briefly to the expansion of the gospel among the Gentiles in Antioch (Acts 11:19–30). Then we read of James' martyrdom in Jerusalem, and how Peter was miraculously delivered from prison (Acts 12:1–19).

3. From Antioch to Rome. The rest of the Book of Acts describes the expansion of the church through the ministry of the Apostle Paul. Barnabas brought Paul to Antioch (Acts 11:19–26). There the Holy Spirit called Barnabas and Paul to be missionaries, and the church ordained them for this task (Acts 13:1–3).

The map entitled "Paul's First Missionary Journey" traces the route of their first church-planting campaign. (*See also* "Paul and His Journeys.") Generally, Paul and Barnabas would begin by preaching in a local Jewish synagogue. Thus the early church consisted primarily of converts from among Jews and "God-fearers" (Gentiles who worshiped with the Jews). This first journey saw a dramatic confrontation with evil when God used Paul to defeat the sorcerer Elymas (Acts 13:6–12). Young John Mark accompanied Paul and Barnabas, but he decided to turn back at Perga; this must have been very disappointing to Paul (cf. Acts 15:38).

Read the sermon Paul delivered in the synagogue at Antioch of Pisidia (Acts 13:16–41). In it he gives a brief summary of the history of redemption, emphasizing its fulfillment in Jesus Christ. Paul declared that believing in Christ is the only way to be free from sin and death (vv. 38–39).

At Lystra, hostile Jews stirred up crowds so that Paul was stoned and left for dead (Acts 14:8–19). The journey ended with Paul and Barnabas returning to Antioch, where they reported all that God had done through them and how the faith had spread to the Gentiles (Acts 14:26–29).

Later a serious disagreement arose in the church. Some Christians argued that the gentile converts had to follow the Old Testament laws, particularly the law of circumcision. Finally, the issue went before an assembly of church leaders from Antioch and Jerusalem. God directed this council (which met in Jerusalem) to declare that Gentiles did not have to keep the Law to be saved. But they instructed the new converts that they should abstain from eating things sacrificed to idols, blood, and strangled animals (Acts 15:1–29), so as not to offend the Jewish converts. The council sent a letter to Antioch, where the church read it and accepted it as God's will.

Paul soon decided to return to all the churches he and Barnabas had established on the first missionary journey. And so the second missionary journey began (Acts 15:40–41). Especially note the vision God

CATACOMBS. *The Romans often buried their dead in underground tombs or catacombs, such as this one in Rome. Christians suffered sporadic persecution at the hands of the Romans until A.D. 313; during these times of oppression, they sometimes held their worship services in the catacombs.*

BIBLE HISTORY

gave Paul in Troas, which summoned them to Macedonia (Acts 16:9–10). In Macedonia, they led "God-fearers" (Gentiles who believed in God) and Jews into the faith.

One day the missionaries encountered a demon-possessed slave girl. Her owners profited from her ability to tell fortunes. Paul cast the demons out of the girl and she lost her powers, so her owners arrested the missionaries (Acts 16:19–24). While in prison, Paul and his friends converted the jailer. They were released in the morning and went to Thessalonica, where many people were converted under their ministry. Next they went to Berea, where they also had great success (Acts 17:10–12). In Athens, Paul preached a remarkable sermon to the Greek philosophers on Mars Hill.

The next stop was Corinth, where Paul and his friends stayed a year and a half. From there they journeyed back to Antioch via Jerusalem (Acts 18:18–22). All this time, Paul and his companions continued to preach in the synagogues, and faced opposition from some Jews who rejected the gospel (Acts 18:12–17).

The third missionary journey covered many of the same cities Paul had visited on the second journey. He also made a quick visit to the churches in Galatia and Phrygia (Acts 18:23).

In Ephesus he baptized 12 of John the Baptist's disciples who had accepted Christ and they received the Holy Spirit (Acts 19:1–6). He preached in the Ephesian school of Tyrannus for nearly two years (Acts 19:9–10).

From Ephesus he went to Macedonia and finally back to Philippi. After a brief stay in Philippi he journeyed to Troas, where a young man named Eutychus fell asleep while listening to one of Paul's sermons and plummeted from a third-story window to his death. God worked through Paul to bring Eutychus back to life (Acts 20:7–12). From there, the missionaries went by way of Miletus to Caesarea where the prophet Agabus predicted that danger awaited Paul in Jerusalem.

In Jerusalem, Paul met trouble and imprisonment. The Bible records a speech he made there in defense of his Christian faith (Acts 22:1–21). Eventually the religious authorities succeeded in sending him to Rome for trial. On the way to Rome, the ship carrying him wrecked on the island of Malta ("Melita"). There a poisonous snake bit Paul, but he was not harmed (Acts 28:3–6). Paul then cured the sick father of Publius, the political leader of the island (Acts 28:7–8). After three months on Malta, Paul and his guards sailed for Rome.

The Book of Acts ends with Paul's activities in Rome. We read that he preached to the leading Jews there (Acts 28:17–20). He lived for two years in a rented house, continuing to preach to the people who visited him (Acts 28:30–31). For a more detailed description of Paul's life, see "Paul and His Journeys."

This closes the Bible's history of redemption. The gospel had been effectively planted in Gentile soil, and most of the New Testament Epistles had been written. The church was in the process of separating itself from the Jewish synagogue and becoming a distinct organization. (*See* "The Early Church.")

BIBLE CHRONOLOGY
Finding the Dates of Bible Events

Scripture tells how God revealed Himself at specific points in time. To help grasp the relation of these divine revelations to other historical events, we need to know the dates of the biblical events themselves.

The word *chronology* comes from the classical Greek word *chronos,* which signifies time viewed as a flowing stream—a stream that cannot be stopped, but can be measured. *Chronology* is simply the dating of historical events within the "stream" of time. The Bible devotes quite a lot of space to matters of chronology.

For instance, the prophets dated their writings to show the background of their message. Their chronological notes help us understand why God said what He said, and why He did what He did at each particular time.

Jewish people followed their calendar with great care. Ancient Israel had a lunar calendar that pegged religious festivals to certain seasons of the year. The Israelites harvested barley in the spring during Abib, the first month of the religious year (Exod. 23:15). After the Exile, they called this month Nisan. They celebrated the Feast of Weeks during the month of Sivan, which began the summer harvest of wheat (Exod. 34:22). Their Feast of the Ingathering (or Feast of Booths) coincided with their general harvest in the autumn month of Ethanim, later called Tishri (Exod. 34:22). Generally their months were 30 days long. But since each month was counted from a new-moon day, the calendar sometimes called for a 29-day month. The lunar calendar was 11 days shorter than the solar year and yet had to match the seasons, so the Israelites sometimes had to add a thirteenth month to the year. This gave them some leap-year days. Their pattern of inserting leap-year days repeated itself in a 19-year cycle.

I. ESTABLISHING ABSOLUTE DATES
  A. Assyrian Lists
  B. Two Systems of Figuring Dates
  C. Two Systems of Elapsed Time

II. RULERS OF THE DIVIDED KINGDOM

III. THE FIRST THREE KINGS OF ISRAEL

IV. MOSES AND THE PATRIARCHS
  A. The Date of the Exodus
    1. The Early Date
    2. The Late Date
  B. The Life of Moses
    1. Early Life
    2. Confrontation with the Pharaoh
    3. Life in the Desert
  C. The Patriarchs and the Move to Egypt
    1. Israel's Stay in Egypt
    2. Joseph
    3. Jacob
    4. Isaac
    5. Abraham

V. DATING PRIOR TO ABRAHAM
  A. From the Flood to Abraham
    1. Abraham's Father, Terah
    2. Nahor
    3. Serug
    4. Reu
    5. Peleg
    6. Eber
    7. Salah
    8. Cainan
    9. Arphaxad
    10. Shem
  B. From Creation to the Flood
    1. Adam to Enoch
    2. Methuselah to Noah

VI. DATING FOR ISRAEL AND JUDAH FROM 841 B.C.

VII. DATING FOR JUDAH FROM 696 B.C. to 587/86 B.C.

VIII. EXILIC AND POSTEXILIC DATING

IX. THE LIFE OF JESUS
  A. Birth
  B. Beginning of Ministry
  C. Length of Ministry

I. Establishing Absolute Dates. The Bible doesn't give its chronology according to the calendar in use today. To establish absolute dates, we need to figure out the Bible's system for recording the dates of the kings and then lay it alongside the dates for rulers of Assyria and Babylon. The Assyrians based their history on the data of astronomy, and so we can

BIBLE CHRONOLOGY

JEHU OFFERS TRIBUTE. *Shalmaneser III of Assyria recorded his military victories on a large black lime-stone obelisk near his palace at Calah. This panel from the obelisk shows King Jehu of Israel (wearing a pointed hat) bowing down to Shalmaneser. On either side of Shalmaneser are servants with parasol, fan, and scepter. The Bible does not mention Jehu's tribute.*

check the Assyrian dates against the movement of the stars, which our present knowledge enables us to plot accurately. Then we can use that information to pinpoint the dates of Old Testament events.

A. Assyrian Lists. The Assyrians' *eponym* lists give the dates of the Assyrian kings. An *eponym* is a person for whom a period of time has been named; for example, Queen Elizabeth I of England was the eponym of the Elizabethan Age. So the Assyrian lists put a number of important officials in sequence and name each year after a particular leader. Clay tablets from Nineveh and other Assyrian cities list the names of these leaders, along with the consecutive years of Assyrian history. These lists give us a history from 892 to 648 B.C. During that time, several Assyrian leaders made contact with the Hebrew kings.

The tablets mention Bur-Sagale, governor of Guzana. The Assyrian record says that an eclipse of the sun occurred in the month of Simanu during Bur-Sagale's term of office. Astronomers tell us that the eclipse occurred on June 15, 763 B.C. Therefore, Bur-Sagale governed in 763 B.C., and we can use this date to establish the dates of other Assyrian leaders.

A tablet about the Assyrian leader Daian-Assur says that he governed during the sixth year of Shalmaneser III. In that same year, the Assyrians fought an important battle at Qarqar

against a group of kings from the Mediterranean seacoast, and the tablet lists King Ahab of Israel among them. Other information in the Assyrian lists sets the date of this battle—and of Ahab's death—at 853 B.C.

Still another eponym list says that a certain "King Ia-a-u" began paying tribute to Shalmaneser III in the eighteenth year of Shalmaneser's reign. Most likely this was King Jehu of Israel. The Assyrian list shows that the date was 841 B.C.

By comparing Assyrian and Hebrew records in this fashion, we can learn a great deal about the chronology of the kings of Israel and Judah.

B. Two Systems of Figuring Dates. How did the chroniclers of the Bible date the reigns of the kings? After the death of King Solomon and the division of the kingdom, it seems that chroniclers in the Southern Kingdom of Judah counted the official reign of their kings from the Hebrew month of Ethanim, or Tishri (September-October)—the beginning of the civil year. In the Northern Kingdom of Israel, scribes used the month of Abib, or Nisan (March-April)—the beginning of the religious year.

Compare 2 Kings 22:3–13 and 23:21–23 for proof of this. These texts tell how King Josiah's men discovered a book of the Law in the temple, and how Josiah restored the Passover observance on the traditional four-

BIBLE CHRONOLOGY

ASSYRIAN CALENDAR. *This cuneiform tablet from Assyria ties the political events of the nation to movements of the planets and stars. Such calendars help modern scientists to figure the exact dates of key events in Assyrian history, which in turn allow us to calculate the dates of biblical events.*

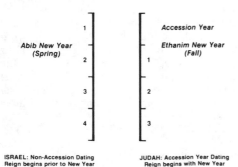

NON-ACCESSION AND ACCESSION-YEAR DATING

c Thomas Nelson, Inc.

Abib New Year
(Spring)

1

2

3

4

Accession Year

Ethanim New Year
(Fall)

1

2

3

ISRAEL: Non-Accession Dating
Reign begins prior to New Year

JUDAH: Accession Year Dating
Reign begins with New Year

Figure 3

OBELISK OF SHALMANESER. *King "Ia-a-u" offering tribute to Shalmaneser III appears as the second panel on this side of the obelisk describing the triumphs of Shalmaneser.*

teenth day of Abib. The Bible says all of this happened in the eighteenth year of Josiah's reign. If the writer of 2 Kings began counting the years of Josiah's reign with the month of Abib, he would be saying that the priests cleansed the temple for the Passover in a maximum of 14 days—from between the first and the fourteenth of Abib. This is not very likely. Therefore he may have figured that the eighteenth year of Josiah's reign began the previous fall, in the month of Ethanim.

No Scripture passage indicates when the reigns of Israel's kings began. However, Edwin R. Thiele has shown that if we assume Judah began her year with the month of Ethanim and Israel began her year with Abib, "the perplexing discrepancies disappear and a harmonious chronological pattern results."[1]

C. Two Systems of Elapsed Time. But knowing about these two different ways of counting years doesn't solve all the problems. Ancient historians were not consistent when they talked about a king's "first year" on the throne because each king decided for himself how his history books would handle this. A king might call the year in which his reign commenced his "first" year; scholars refer to this as *non-accession year* dating. On the other hand, he might call the first year after he took the throne his "first" year; scholars label that *accession year* dating. To accurately establish absolute dates, the method a king was using to designate the years of his reign must be established.

Suppose the kings of Israel used non-accession year dating, while the kings of Judah used accession year dating. Figure 3 shows how these systems would give different dates for the reign of a king. If this really happened, Israel's records would always give one year more for the reign of a king than Judah's records would. As each king of Israel came to the throne, the total span of the kings' reigns would seem to increase by one year. To correlate the royal chronologies of the two nations, we would therefore need to subtract one year from the reign of each king who sat upon the throne in the North.

Have we reason to think Israel's custom was to use the nonaccession year system of dating? Yes, we have. We have already learned from the Assyrian list that King Jehu probably paid tribute to Shalmaneser III in 841 B.C., 12 years after King Ahab fought in the battle of Qarqar. The records of Israel (from which the relevant dates in Kings and Chronicles are presumably taken) say that Ahab was succeeded by

TOMB OF THE KINGS, JERUSALEM. *All the kings of Judah, from David to Hezekiah, were buried in the capital city of Jerusalem. Many were placed in these royal tombs near the pool of Shelah. Josephus noted that the royal tombs were very lavishly furnished, but John Hyrcanus (son of Simon Maccabeus) robbed them of much of their treasure.*

Ahaziah, who ruled for two years (1 Kings 22:51). Then Joram (Jehoram) was king for 12 years (2 Kings 3:1), making a total of 14 years for these two kings. After Joram, Jehu came to the throne and began paying tribute to Shalmaneser III. It is possible to match the 12 years in Assyrian chronology with the period of 14 years in Israel's chronology only if Israel followed the nonaccession year dating scheme. That means we should take one year from the reign of each of Israel's kings. Thus, Ahaziah actually reigned for only one year and Joram for 11 years. That means Ahaziah and Joram actually reigned for a total of 12 years, and this corresponds with the Assyrian chronology for Jehu. The evidence fits together only if Israel followed the nonaccession year dating.

On the other hand, the scribes of Judah undoubtedly used the accession year dating scheme for their kings. They may have changed this system occasionally when the Northern Kingdom had a close influence on Judah. For instance, the two nations became more friendly when princess Athaliah of Israel married Jehoram, the son of Judah's King Jehoshaphat. The Bible says Jehoram "walked in the way of the kings of Israel, as did the house of Ahab" (2 Kings 8:18; 2 Chron. 21:6). Under Jehoram's reign, as we shall see, Judah adopted the nonaccession method for dating her kings, and used it for a number of years.

[1] Edwin R. Thiele, *The Mysterious Numbers of the Hebrew Kings* (Grand Rapids: William B. Eerdmans Publishing Company, 1965), p. 30.

BIBLE CHRONOLOGY

DATING SOLOMON'S REIGN
©Thomas Nelson, Inc.

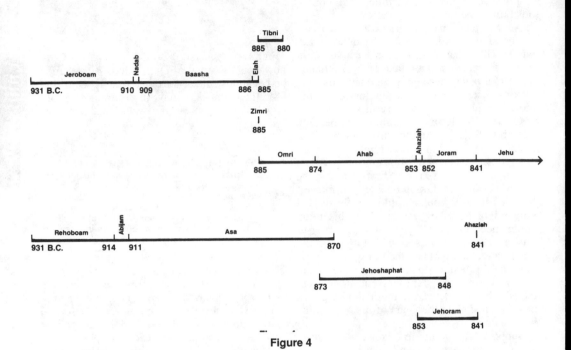

Figure 4

When studying the dates of the kings, we also need to allow for overlappings of kings' reigns. This happened when a son reigned as co-regent with his father. The same years were then reckoned to both reigns. There are several instances of this, as will appear.

II. Rulers of the Divided Kingdom. We are now ready to work back to the pivotal date of King Solomon's death, when the kingdom split. Figure 4 uses the biblical dates for rulers of the divided kingdom, keeping in mind the methods of dating we have already discussed.

Since we're assuming that Israel followed a nonaccession dating scheme, we need to deduct one year from the reign of each king of Israel as we work our way back from the Assyrian dates of 841 B.C. (the beginning of Jehu's reign) and 853 B.C. (the death of Ahab). Use Figure 2 to compare the dating of Israel's and Judah's kings. For clarity, the name of each king of Israel is shown in boldface type while the name of each king of Judah is shown in large and small capital letters.

Joram—2 Kings 3:1; "12 years" (11 years). Joram began his rule in the eighteenth year of Jehoshaphat (see page 26); since he reigned for 11 years before Jehu, his first year of sole reign was 852 B.C. (841 B.C. plus 11 years).

AHAZIAH—2 Kings 8:25; one year. Ahaziah began his rule in the eleventh year of Joram's reign (2 Kings 9:29). (The reason why 2 Kings 8:25 states that he began in the twelfth year of Joram is that Judah had adopted Israel's nonaccession dating scheme at this time.) Both Joram of Israel and Ahaziah of Judah died in 841 B.C. (2 Kings 9:24, 27); so Ahaziah probably reigned for only a few months, even though Israel's records say he reigned for "one year." (Remember that Israel's nonaccession dating method would have called the first months of Ahaziah's reign his "first year.")

JEHORAM—2 Kings 8:17; "eight years" (seven years). Jehoram evidently adopted Israel's nonaccession dating scheme, so one year should be deducted from his reign. Apparently Jehoram reigned with his father for five years before his official reign began. We know this because, when 2 Kings 8:16 says Jehoram began ruling Judah, it also mentions Jehoshaphat as king of Judah. Compare this text with 2 Kings 3:1 and 2 Kings 1:17, which say that Joram ("Jehoram") of Israel became king in the eighteenth year of Jehoshaphat's sole reign and in the second year of Jehoram of Judah. (We have already learned that this year was 852 B.C.) This indicates that Jehoram ruled with his father Jehoshaphat for five years before his official reign began in Joram's fifth year (fourth year according to non-accession dating), or 848 B.C. (852 B.C. minus four years).

Ahab—1 Kings 16:29; "22 years" (21 years). Ahab died in 853, so he must have begun his reign in 874 (853 B.C. plus 21 years).

JEHOSHAPHAT—1 Kings 22:41–42; 25 years. Settling the dates of Jehoshaphat is difficult because his reign overlapped with those of both his father and his son. He began his rule in the fourth year of Ahab, whose reign began in 874 B.C. Ahab's fourth year (the year Jehoshaphat took the throne of Judah) was 870 B.C. Since Jehoshaphat joined Ahab in the battle with the Syrians in 853 B.C., he would naturally have put his son Jehoram on the throne as co-regent at that time, in case he did not come back. We've already noted that Jehoram began his *sole* reign in the fifth year of Joram (the fourth year in the accession dating system). So if we take 852 B.C. (the first year of Joram's reign) and subtract four years, we find that Jehoram became sole ruler of Judah in 848 B.C., and we assume that was the year Jehoshaphat died. We know that Jehoshaphat reigned for 25 years (1 Kings 22:42), so we can infer that his reign began in 873 B.C. (848 B.C. plus 25 years). As we saw, his sole reign formally began in 870 B.C. He reigned with his father Asa for about three years, because Asa suffered from a disabling disease in his feet that had come on in his thirty-ninth year as king (2 Chron. 16:12).

Ahaziah—1 Kings 22:51; "two years" (one year). Ahaziah began his rule in the seventeenth year of Jehoshaphat's sole reign, 853 B.C. (870 B.C. minus 17 years).

ASA—1 Kings 15:10; 41 years. Since we know Jehoshaphat took the throne in 870 B.C., that must have been the year Asa died. And he must have begun his reign in 911 B.C. (870 B.C. plus 41 years).

Omri—1 Kings 16:15–16, 23; "12 years" (11 years). Since we know that Ahab began his reign in 874 B.C., Omri must have died that year. That means Omri began his reign in 885 B.C. (874 B.C. plus 11 years).

Zimri—1 Kings 16:15; seven days. Zimri killed Elah, son of Baasha. In turn, Omri deposed Zimri (1 Kings 16:17–18).

Elah—1 Kings 16:8; "two years" (one year). Elah was killed in Zimri's coup of 885, so he began his rule in 886.

Tibni—1 Kings 16:21–24. We are not told how long this rival of Omri ruled. We assume he began his rule at the same time as Omri in 885; they simply reigned in different parts of Israel. We know that Omri ruled in Tirzah for six years (actually five), until 880. Then he moved to Samaria and established his rule there, which suggests that Tibni was dead.

Baasha—1 Kings 15:33; "24 years" (23 years). Since Elah took the throne in 886, we know Baasha died that year. So he began his reign in 909 B.C. (886 B.C. plus 23 years).

Nadab—1 Kings 15:25–31; "two years" (one year). Baasha seized control of Israel by murdering Nadab, so Nadab must have reigned from 910 to 909 B.C.

Jeroboam—1 Kings 14:20; "22 years" (21 years). Jeroboam's reign began in 931 (910 B.C. plus 21 years).

ABIJAM—1 Kings 15:2; three years. Since Abijam began his reign three years before his successor Asa, this would have been in 914 B.C. (911 B.C. plus three years).

REHOBOAM—1 Kings 14:21; 17 years. Rehoboam started his rule in 931 B.C., 17 years before Abijam (914 B.C. plus 17 years). He began to reign over Judah in the same year as his rival Jeroboam took Israel, when the kingdom divided. This also would have been the year Solomon died.

III. The First Three Kings of Israel. Having established the date of Solomon's death (931 B.C.), we can proceed backward in Israel's history even further, using the chronology of the Bible to establish specific dates. (*See* Fig. 5.)

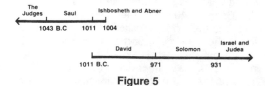

Figure 5

BIBLE CHRONOLOGY

DAVID. *David is portrayed here as a boy with his sling. Based on the dates of the Assyrian King list, it appears that he became king in 1011 B.C.*

RAMESES II (1304–1238 B.C.). *Some scholars believe that the Exodus occurred during the reign of this pharaoh. Rameses' royal records show that he used slave laborers to build his grain-storage cities, but other evidence indicates that the Israelites left Egypt before Rameses' reign.*

Jeroboam I and Rehoboam divided the kingdom in 931 B.C. and Solomon died that year. The Bible says that Solomon reigned over all Israel for 40 years (1 Kings 11:42). And so in Figure 5 the start of Solomon's reign is set in 971 B.C. That would have been the year of David's death.

David was king for 40 years, which places the start of his rule in 1011 B.C. However, David ruled only Judah while Saul's son Ish-bosheth had the other tribes' allegiance. First Kings 2:11 and 2 Samuel 2:11 say that David was king in Hebron for seven years and six months. When Ish-bosheth's enemies assassinated him, the tribal leaders of Israel met in Hebron and gave their allegiance to David (2 Sam. 5:3). Thus David's sole rule began in the year of 1004 B.C., and it lasted for 33 years.

Saul, who died in 1011 B.C., also had a long reign; we are told it lasted 40 years (Acts 13:21). (Something has dropped out of the Hebrew text in 1 Samuel 13:1. "Two years" could not be the complete number.) However, this figure of 40 may include both the reign of Saul and his son Ish-bosheth. If so, this would leave about 33 years for the sole reign of Saul, which means that he would have begun his rule in 1043 B.C. rather than 1057 B.C.

IV. Moses and the Patriarchs. There are two pivotal points in the chronology of the Old Testament. The first is the date the foundations of the first temple were laid. First Kings 6:1 says that Solomon began building the temple in the fourth year of his reign, in the second month (Ziv), 480 years after the Israelites came out of Egypt. We know that Solomon began his reign in 971 B.C., and so his first year on Israel's dating scheme would have begun in the fall of 970 B.C. The fourth year would be 967/66 B.C., reckoned on a fall-to-fall basis. Since Ziv was the second month on the religious calendar, we conclude that Solomon began the temple in the spring of 966 B.C. On this basis, Israel's Exodus from Egypt would have begun in 1446 B.C., and Canaan would have been conquered around 1406 B.C.

The other pivotal date in the Old Testament

BIBLE CHRONOLOGY

AMENHOTEP III (1410–1377 B.C.). *Clay tablets from Amarna show that the princes of Canaan appealed to Pharaoh Amenhotep III for help in fighting invaders known as the* Habiru. *The Israelites fleeing from Egypt may have been part of this wave of invaders.*

is that of Jacob's move to Egypt, which was 430 years before the Exodus (Exod. 12:40–41). This brings us to 1876 B.C. (1446 B.C. plus 430 years).

With these numbers as a start, we can fill in dates for events in the period from the time of Abraham until Israel's first king, Saul.

A. The Date of the Exodus. Many Bible students still question the date of the Exodus. They have developed two dating schemes for the Exodus—an early date that takes 1 Kings 6:1 as a precise note of time, and an alternate suggestion that we call "the late date." Here are the arguments for both sides:

1. The Early Date. This argument insists that the ancients knew how to construct a calendar and keep accurate records of time, and that they stated the length of epochs with chronological exactness. So it accepts the 480 years of 1 Kings 6:1 and the statement of Jephthah, a judge who declared that Israel had occupied the land of Canaan for about 300 years (Judg. 11:26). Since we have already calculated that Israel's Exodus began in 1446 B.C., we can deduct 40 years for their wilderness wanderings to place them entering Canaan in 1406 B.C. If we subtract the 300 years mentioned in this verse, we see that Jephthah would have lived in 1106 B.C. This provides ample time for the period of the

Judges, who ruled various sections of Israel prior to Saul's monarchy.

Bible students who support the early date of the Exodus on these grounds also point to the Amarna tablets, dated at about 1400 B.C. These tablets, discovered in Egypt, contain international correspondence during Egypt's eighteenth dynasty under Pharaoh Amenhotep III (1410–1377 B.C.). They contain numerous requests from the Canaanite city-states begging the Egyptians to help them drive out the *Habiru,* or nomadic invaders; but there is little evidence that this group included the Israelites. If we accept the early date of the Exodus (1446 B.C.), then allow 40 years for the Israelites' sojourn in the wilderness, they would have invaded Canaan in 1406 B.C. and would have been the *Habiru.*

2. The Late Date. Students who hold this view believe Moses led the Israelites out of bondage during Egypt's nineteenth dynasty, which began in 1318 B.C. The chief line of evidence for the late date is the appearance of new cultural forms in Palestine, specifically the destruction of Jericho by outside invaders at about this date. Scholars who advocate this date point out that the pharaoh of the time was Rameses II (*ca.* 1304–1238 B.C.), and they believe Hebrew slaves built the Egyptian store cities of Pithom and Rameses during his reign (Exod. 1:11; 12:37; Num. 33:3). Rameses II mentions using slave labor of the *Apiru*—per-

FOREIGN CAPTIVES. *The pharaohs used foreign slaves to erect their massive temples and tombs. This relief from the tomb of Rameses III shows (from left to right) Libyan, Hittite, Philistine, and Semitic captives being led to the pharaoh's compound.*

BIBLE CHRONOLOGY

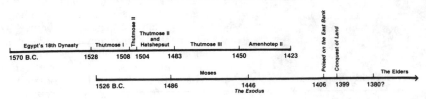

Figure 6

haps the Egyptian word for "Hebrew"—to build his grain cities. Other scholars believe an earlier pharaoh first built these cities, but in that case Rameses II certainly rebuilt and named one of them for himself. Archaeological evidence seems to indicate this. If we assume that the Hebrews built these cities for Rameses II, they would have left Egypt some years later, about 1275 B.C., and conquered Canaan after 1235—a date that these scholars believe is confirmed by archaeological evidence that Canaanite cities were destroyed.

But we should note that the pharaohs of Rameses' time used the very names employed by the Hyksos kings of Egypt (1730–1570 B.C.; *see* "Egyptians"). Rameses worshiped the same gods that the Hyksos kings worshiped. So the Hebrew slaves could have worked on these cities under the Hyksos. In fact, the Hyksos would have had good reason to oppress the Israelites, since they were also of Semitic origin and considered the Israelites bitter rivals.[2] In that case, Exodus 1:13 ff. may describe events under the eighteenth dynasty, which drove out the Hyksos.

We run into many difficulties if we suppose the Exodus took place in the thirteenth century. If the Exodus is dated at about 1275 B.C., and the conquest after 1235 B.C., and if Saul came to the throne in about 1043 B.C., only about 230 years would have elapsed from the Exodus until Saul, and only 190 from the conquest to Saul.

B. The Life of Moses. Figure 6 shows Egypt's eighteenth dynasty and the events of Israel from the birth of Moses until the time of Saul's reign. We have divided Moses' life into three parts:

1. Early Life. Since Moses was 120 years old when the Israelites were ready to enter Canaan in 1406 B.C. (Deut. 34:7), he must

have been born in 1526 B.C. near the beginning of Egypt's eighteenth dynasty. Until he reached 40 years of age, he lived in the royal palace as the adopted son of Hatshepsut, the daughter of Thutmose I. In 1486 B.C. (1526 B.C. minus 40 years) he fled into the wilderness (cf. Acts 7:23).

2. Confrontation with the Pharaoh. Moses spent 40 years in the wilderness, caring for the flocks of his father-in-law, Jethro. Then God called Moses to lead Israel from Egypt to be a free people, in 1446 B.C. (cf. Acts 7:30).

3. Life in the Desert. Until 1406 B.C., Moses led the Israelites on a wayward course to the Promised Land.

God chose Joshua to lead Israel in the conquest of Canaan, which took six years—to about 1400 B.C. (Josh. 14:7, 10). We know this because Caleb was 40 years old when he spied on Canaan in the second year of the Exodus, 1444 B.C., and he was 85 years old when the Israelites divided the territory of Canaan in 1400 B.C. (1445 B.C. minus 45 years).

Joshua lived to be 110 years of age (Josh. 24:29), but we do not know exactly when he died. The elders ruled Israel for a time after Joshua's leadership (Josh. 24:31). We can assume a period of 15 to 20 years from the end of the conquest (1400 B.C.) until the elders who served with Joshua died (about 1380 B.C.).

The Book of Judges covers a period of about 337 years, from 1380 to 1043 B.C. The judges' terms of service and the periods of oppression total about 410 consecutive years. Since Paul says the judges ruled "about the space of 450 years" (Acts 13:20), many of the judges' careers may have overlapped. In Figure 7, we attempt to reconstruct this period. However, these are approximate figures because we do not know exactly when Joshua and his elders died, nor how long certain tribes of Israel rebelled against God. But Jephthah's statement in Judges 11:26 that the Israelites

---

[2] *See* Gleason Archer, *A Survey of Old Testament Introduction* (Chicago: Moody Press, 1964).

BIBLE CHRONOLOGY

The Judges

Description	Reference	Date
Assume 5 years of apostasy		1380–1375 B.C.
Oppression, 8 years	Judg. 3:8	1375–1367 B.C.
Deliverance by Othniel; 40 years' rest	Judg. 3:11	1367–1327 B.C.
Assume 5 years of apostasy		1327–1322 B.C.
Oppression by Moab, 18 years	Judg. 3:14	1322–1304 B.C.
Deliverance by Ehud; 80 years' rest	Judg. 3:31	1304–1224 B.C.
Deliverance by Deborah; 40 years' rest	Judg. 5:31	1224–1184 B.C.
Oppression by Midian, 7 years	Judg. 6:1	1164–1177 B.C.
Deliverance by Gideon; 40 years' rest	Judg. 8:28	1177–1137 B.C.
Abimelech's reign, 3 years	Judg. 9:22	1137–1134 B.C.
Tola and Jair, 45 years	Judg. 10:2–3	1134–1089 B.C.
Jephthah, 6 years	Judg. 12:7	1089–1083 B.C.
Ibson, Elon, and Abdon, 25 years	Judg. 12:9, 11, 14	1083–1058 B.C.

Figure 7

conquered Canaan about 300 years before his time gives a reference point. If he is speaking in 1106 B.C. (1406 B.C. minus 300 years), it is very close to the date of 1089 B.C. that we have estimated for the raids by the Ammonites.

However, we will use the 1106 B.C. date for Jephthah to reconstruct the dates of the later judges. This new chart brings us down to the days of Samuel, the battles of Israel and the Philistines in the West and Southwest, and Saul's appointment as king in 1043 B.C.

C. The Patriarchs and the Move to Egypt. Having accepted the Exodus date of 1446 B.C., we can work our way back into the history of the patriarchs. Figure 8 shows the layout of this chronology.

1. Israel's Stay in Egypt. We have already seen that the Israelites lived in Egypt about 400 years (Gen. 15:13). Exodus 12:40 tells us that Jacob's family arrived in Egypt 430 years before the Exodus, or about 1876 B.C. (cf. Gal. 3:17). This means that Jacob's family entered Egypt at a time when Egypt was not a particularly strong nation.

Some scholars insist that the family of Ja-

cob must have entered Egypt after the time of the Hyksos, because the Israelites would have found easier access to Egypt after their time. However, the Hyksos did not leave Egypt until 1570 B.C. That would push the Exodus down to 1270 B.C., the "late date," which we saw to be doubtful on other grounds.

The Scriptures say Jacob was 130 years old when he entered Egypt (Gen. 47:9, 28). Joseph was 39 years old (age 30 plus seven years plus two years, Gen. 41:46–47; 45:6). With the date of 1876 B.C. for Jacob's move to Egypt, we can plot out the dates of these men.

2. Joseph. Joseph's birth date would be 1915 B.C. (1876 B.C. plus 39 years). According to Genesis 50:26, he would have died in 1805 B.C. (1915 B.C. minus 110 years).

3. Jacob. Jacob was 130 years old when he entered Egypt and lived there 17 years. So he was 147 years old when he died in 1859 B.C. (1876 B.C. minus 17 years). Working the other way, we find that he was born in 2006 B.C. (1876 B.C. plus 130 years).

4. Isaac. Jacob's father, Isaac, was 60 years old when Jacob was born (Gen. 25:26), and so Isaac himself was born in 2066 B.C. (2006 B.C.

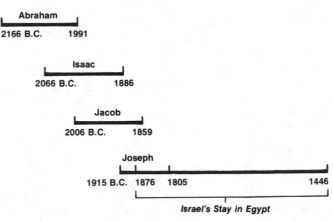

ISRAEL'S PATRIARCHS
©Thomas Nelson, Inc.

Abraham
2166 B.C.   1991

Isaac
2066 B.C.   1886

Jacob
2006 B.C.   1859

Joseph
1915 B.C. 1876   1805   1446

Israel's Stay in Egypt

Figure 8

plus 60 years). He lived to the age of 180, which means that he died in 1886 B.C., about 10 years before Jacob took his family into Egypt.

5. Abraham. The Bible says Abraham was 100 years old when Isaac was born (Gen. 21:5), and so Abraham himself was born in 2166 B.C. in Ur of the Chaldees. He entered Canaan at age 75 (Gen. 12:4) in 2091 B.C.. He died at 175 years of age in 1991 B.C. (Gen. 25:7).

V. Dating Prior to Abraham. Our study of the chronology prior to Abraham is divided into two sections: (1) from the Flood until Abraham and (2) from the Creation to the Flood. Needless to say, this span of time poses the greatest problems because we can no longer compare biblical dates with historical records of the nations surrounding Israel. The ancient histories of these other nations are very sketchy and poorly understood. Even different versions of the Old Testament disagree sharply about the events of history before the patriarchs. We will generally follow the Masoretic (Hebrew) text, but we will compare its account with the other ancient versions at specific points.

A. From the Flood to Abraham. Abraham's family list (Gen. 11:10–26) provides the information we need for this period. Figure 9 charts the lives of Abraham's ancestors. First, notice that Abraham has a birth date of 2166 B.C. and a death date of 1991 B.C. These

figures are based on the calculations we have already done.

1. Abraham's Father, Terah. Abraham's father, Terah, had worshiped idols for several years (Josh. 24:2) when he moved his family from Ur to Haran. Terah lived there until he died at the age of 205 (Gen. 11:32).

God called Abraham to go to Canaan at the age of 75 (Gen. 12:4). It appears that this was immediately after Terah's death. This would fix Terah's death at 2091 B.C. (2166 B.C. plus 75 years), making him 130 years old when Abraham was born (age 205 minus 75 years).

UR OF CHALDEES. *Ruins on the western bank of the Euphrates River mark the site of Abraham's hometown in Mesopotamia. Clay tablets found here identify the ancient city as "Uri."*

BIBLE CHRONOLOGY

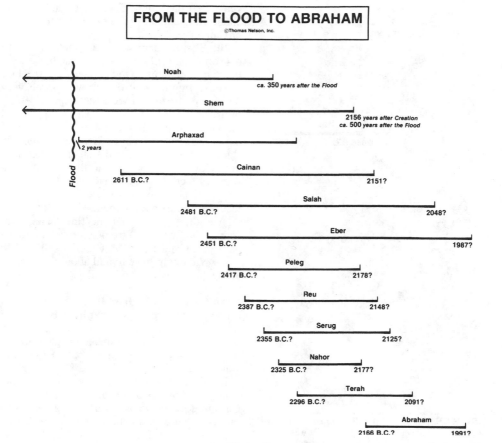

FROM THE FLOOD TO ABRAHAM

©Thomas Nelson, Inc.

Noah
ca. 350 years after the Flood

Shem
2156 years after Creation
ca. 500 years after the Flood

Arphaxad
2 years

Cainan
2611 B.C.?   2151?

Salah
2481 B.C.?   2048?

Eber
2451 B.C.?   1987?

Peleg
2417 B.C.?   2178?

Reu
2387 B.C.?   2148?

Serug
2355 B.C.?   2125?

Nahor
2325 B.C.?   2177?

Terah
2296 B.C.?   2091?

Abraham
2166 B.C.?   1991?

Figure 9

Thus we find that Terah was born in 2296 B.C. (2166 B.C. plus 130 years or 2091 B.C. plus 205 years).

2. Nahor. Terah was born when his father, Nahor, was 29 years of age (Gen. 11:24). Nahor lived for 119 more years (Gen. 11:25), so he must have been born in 2325 B.C. (2296 B.C. minus 119 years).

3. Serug. Nahor's father, Serug, was 30 years old when Nahor was born, and he lived 200 years afterward (Gen. 11:22–23). Therefore, Serug's birth date was 2355 B.C. (2325 B.C. plus 30 years) and he died in 2125 B.C. (2325 B.C. minus 200 years).

4. Reu. Serug's father, Reu, was 32 years old when Serug was born, and he lived 207 years afterward (Gen. 11:20–21). So the date of birth for Reu was 2387 B.C. (2355 B.C. plus 32 years), and he died in 2148 B.C. (2355 B.C. minus 207 years).

5. Peleg. Reu's father, Peleg, was 30 years old at the birth of Reu, and he lived 209 years afterward. So Peleg's birth date was 2417 B.C. (2387 B.C. plus 30 years) and his date of death was 2178 B.C. (2387 B.C. minus 209 years).

6. Eber. Eber was 34 years old when he became the father of Peleg, and he lived 430 years after Peleg's birth (Gen. 11:16–17). So we calculate that Eber was born in 2451 B.C. (2417 B.C. plus 34 years) and died in 1987 B.C. (2417 B.C. minus 430 years). This means that Eber lived beyond the time Abraham entered the land of Canaan. If the evidence from the tablets excavated at Ebla is correct, the term *Hebrew* may be derived from this man's name.

7. Salah. Eber's father, Salah, was 30 years old when Eber was born; he lived for 403 years more (Gen. 11:14–15). So Salah's birth date was 2481 B.C. (2451 B.C. plus 30 years)

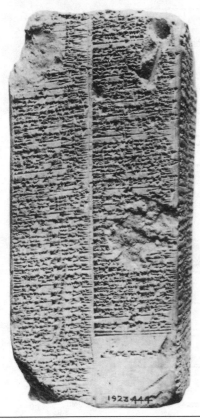

SUMERIAN KING LIST. *An historian in ancient Sumer recorded the reigns of the Sumerian kings on this prism sometime between 2000–2250 B.C. The list mentions a great flood that destroyed the world, just as the Book of Genesis does.*

years after the Flood (Gen. 11:10) and he lived about 400 years after the birth of either Salah or Cainan.

10. Shem. Shem was 100 years old when his son Arphaxad was born, and he had a total lifespan of about 600 years (Gen. 11:10–11).

These figures confront us with some very distinct problems. In view of the great length of life ascribed to the earlier patriarchs, should the years always be understood as full calendar years? Why does the Septuagint include Cainan in the list, while the Hebrew text does not? Could there be gaps in the genealogical lists? In fact, it appears that the lists of Genesis 5 and 11 are not complete records, but selections of outstanding men.

In addition, note that the time span from Cainan (in 2611 B.C.) to the entrance of Abraham into Canaan (in 2091 B.C.) is about 520 years. We might have to add about 60 years to allow for whether Arphaxad is the father of Cainan or Salah.

And what about Eber? If we take the Masoretic text at face value, Eber lived beyond the time Abraham entered Canaan. Was this really so? Not necessarily. If there are gaps in the list, Eber may have died long before Abraham was in Canaan.

Here's another problem: The 520-year span from Cainan to Abraham's entrance into Canaan does not square with the figures given by other versions of the Old Testament. The Septuagint says 1,232 years elapsed from the Flood to Abraham's journey into Canaan, while the Samaritan Pentateuch says it was 942 years. We have no way of testing either of these figures. But ever since the discovery of the Qumran scrolls, the Masoretic text has been viewed as probably authentic. Still, the Masoretic text disagrees with the records of early Egyptian and Mesopotamian history. Accounts of Egyptian and Mesopotamian history for these regions begin at about 3000 B.C. The Flood must have occurred prior to that time, and at an earlier time than what we see in Figure 9.

The best conclusion is that the list in Genesis 11 is not strictly genealogical so much as *epochal*. In other words, it gives the names of certain outstanding individuals in the correct genealogical line, but not always in a father-to-son sequence. Thus the length of time covered is longer than it might appear.

The Bible offers us several other examples of epochal lists, as in Matthew 1:8, where Jehoram appears to be the father of Uzziah. Ac-

and the date of his death was 2048 B.C. (2451 B.C. minus 403 years).

8. Cainan. The Hebrew text of Scripture does not mention Cainan's life, but there is a statement about him in the Septuagint version of Genesis 10:24 and 11:12–13, as well as 1 Chronicles 1:18. Luke 3:36 also mentions him. The Septuagint indicates that Cainan was 130 years old at the birth of Salah and lived 330 years beyond Salah's birth. This would mean that Cainan was born in 2611 B.C. (2481 B.C. plus 130 years) and died in 2151 B.C. (2481 B.C. minus 330 years).

9. Arphaxad. The Hebrew text says Arphaxad was the father of Salah, but the Septuagint states that Arphaxad was the father of Cainan. In view of these conflicting statements, we will not try to date Arphaxad's birth or death. We do know that he was born two

BIBLE CHRONOLOGY

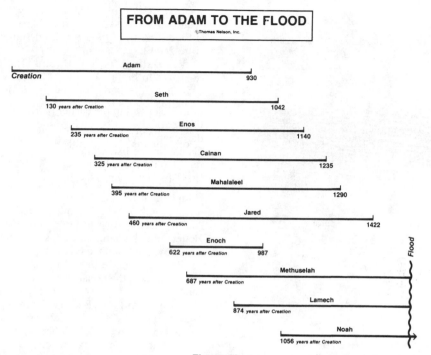

Figure 10

tually, Jehoram was the great-great-grand-father of Uzziah. Matthew could not have expected this omission to go unnoticed by his readers, nor did he seem to expect them to find fault with it. However strange it is to us, this method of epochal genealogy was well understood in the ancient world.

B. From Creation to the Flood. Since we cannot establish a specific date for the Flood, we will have trouble proceeding backward to the date of Adam and Eve. All we can do is trace the family line of Adam to the time of the Flood, using the chronologies found in Genesis 5 and 7:11. Refer to Figure 10 as we explore this pre-Flood history.

1. Adam to Enoch. Adam was 130 years old when Seth was born (Gen. 5:3). We can ignore the family of Cain, since Genesis gives us no specific dates for his descendants. And the Bible mentions no descendants of Abel when he was murdered. So the genealogy must begin with Seth. Adam lived for 800 years after Seth's birth (Gen. 5:4).

Seth was 105 years old when he became the father of Enos. He lived 807 years after Enos was born (Gen. 5:6–7).

Enos was 90 years old when his son Cainan was born, and he lived 815 years after that

(Gen. 5:9–10). Cainan was 70 years old when Mahalaleel was born, and he lived 840 years more (Gen. 5:12–13).

Mahalaleel was 65 years old when his son Jared was born, and he continued to live for 830 years (Gen. 5:15–16). Jared was 162 years old when he fathered Enoch, and he lived beyond Enoch's birth for 800 years (Gen. 5:18–19).

Enoch was 65 years old when Methuselah was born, and then he lived for 300 years. Enoch "walked with God" and God took him up into heaven (Gen. 5:21–24).

2. Methuselah to Noah. Methuselah was 187 years old when his son Lamech was born, and the Bible tells us that he lived beyond Lamech for 782 years (Gen. 5:25–26). The length of Methuselah's age would put his death in the year of the Flood, according to the Bible's account. Does this mean that Methuselah died during the Flood? Perhaps. The Bible doesn't say.

Lamech was 182 years old at the birth of Noah and lived another 595 years (Gen. 5:28–31).

Noah was 500 years old when his three sons were born (Gen. 5:32). Noah built a ship to carry himself and his family, along with cer-

BIBLE CHRONOLOGY

SENNACHERIB PRISM. *King Sennacherib of Assyria instructed his scribes to record his victories on this massive clay prism. The prism tells of Sennacherib's siege against Jerusalem in 701 B.C., during the reign of Hezekiah. The narrative says, "Hezekiah himself I shut up like a caged bird in Jerusalem, his royal city. I erected fortifications against him and blocked the exits from the gate of his city . . ."*

tain animals, through the Flood that God sent to destroy the wicked life of the earth in Noah's six hundredth year (Gen. 7:6). Noah lived 350 years after the Flood, dying at the age of 950 years (Gen. 9:28–29).

If we add up the ages of each of these men (from Adam to Noah), we get a total of 1,656 years from the time of Adam to the Flood. But other versions of the Old Testament give us different figures. The Septuagint puts 2,242 years between Adam and the Flood, the Samaritan version 1,307 years. These differences, all else apart, would make it impossible to fix a definite date for Adam. According to this chronology, Noah was born 1,056 years after Creation (1,656 years minus 600 years).

We have no reliable secular records from this period. The Sumerian king lists show six to eight kings ruling for about 30,000 years before the Flood! Obviously these are legends. We can't give an exact answer to the question of how long man had lived on the earth, but we would not favor the suggestion of millions of years. We only venture to say that many generations passed between Adam and the Flood, and the Flood occurred sometime before 2611 B.C. (Cainan's birth).

VI. Dating for Israel and Judah from 841 B.C. In Figure 4 we established two dates: 853 B.C. (the battle of Qarqar) and 841 B.C. (Shalmaneser's tribute from King "Ia-a-u," or Jehu). We have worked our way back in Israel's history from these dates. Now let us work forward to the fall of Israel and Judah. This is more difficult than one might suppose. Figure 11 lays out the history of these two kingdoms, with the bottom half referring to kings of Judah and the top half to the kings of Israel. In this text the name of each king of Judah will be shown in large and small capital letters and the name of each king of Israel will be shown in boldface type.

Once again, we need to remember that Israel followed the nonaccession dating scheme, and so one year must be subtracted from the reign of each king. Because Israel influenced Judah from the time of Jehoram, Judah followed a nonaccession scheme at that time also. But both nations switched to an accession scheme during this period.

Jehu—2 Kings 10:36; "28 years" (27 years). This king killed his predecessor in Israel, Joram, and also the king of Judah, Ahaziah. Since we're assuming that Jehu be-

BABYLON. *These brick walls are the last remnants of the great city of Babylon. Nebuchadnezzar erected many lavish buildings in the capital city and adorned it with its world-famous hanging gardens.*

BIBLE CHRONOLOGY

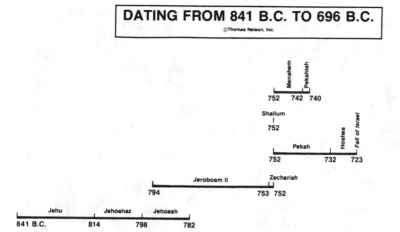

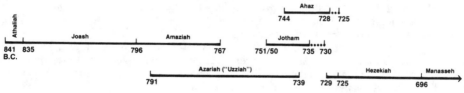

Figure 11

gan his reign in 841, his reign would have ended in 814 B.C. (841 B.C. minus 27 years).

ATHALIAH—2 Kings 11:4, 21; "seven years" (six years). This was the wife of Jehoram and daughter of Jezebel of Israel. When she saw that Jehu had killed her son, Ahaziah, she executed all the royal offspring so she could take the throne. (However, some loyal followers of Ahaziah spirited the king's son, Joash, away into hiding.) Athaliah came to the throne in 841 B.C. and ruled for seven nonaccession years or six actual years. Her reign was completed in 835 B.C. (841 B.C. minus six years).

JOASH ("Jehoash")—2 Kings 12:1; "40 years" (39 years). Joash began his reign as the boy king in 835 B.C. and reigned for 40 nonaccession years, or 39 actual years. This means he was assassinated in 796 B.C. (835 B.C. minus 39 years).

Jehoahaz—2 Kings 13:1; "17 years" (16 years). Jehoahaz began his reign upon the death of Jehu in 814 B.C., and he ruled for 17 nonaccession years or 16 actual years, until 798 B.C. (814 B.C. minus 16 years).

Jehoash—2 Kings 13:10; 16 years. It appears that Israel now adopted an accession

dating until the end of the kingdom. Jehoash began his reign in 798 B.C. and ruled until 782 B.C. (798 B.C. minus 16 years).

AMAZIAH—2 Kings 14:1-2; 29 years. By this time, Judah had evidently returned to the accession system of dating. Amaziah took the throne from Joash in 796 B.C. and reigned for 29 years, until 767 B.C. The Bible also says that Amaziah lived 15 years after the death of Jehoash of Israel—782 B.C. minus 15 years, or 767 B.C. (2 Kings 14:17).

Jeroboam II—2 Kings 13:10; 2 Kings 14:23; 41 years. While Jeroboam's total reign was 41 years, he seems to have reigned with Jehoash for a time. He officially became king in the fifteenth year of Amaziah, 781 B.C. (796 B.C. minus 15 years). Azariah ("Uzziah") followed his father Amaziah on the throne of Judah 14 years later (29 years minus 15 years), yet he became king in the twenty-seventh year of Jeroboam's reign (2 Kings 15:1-2), 794 B.C. (767 B.C. plus 27 years). So there must have been a 13-year overlap between Jeroboam and his father, Jehoash. This means that Jeroboam's joint reign with Jehoash began in 794 B.C., and his sole reign began in 781 B.C. (Apparently his official rule began with the new year, since the calendar says Jehoash died in 782 B.C.). He ruled until 753 B.C. (794 B.C. minus 41 years). Perhaps Jehoash set up joint rule with Jeroboam to protect the throne of Israel while he fought Amaziah of Judah (2 Kings 14:8–11).

Zechariah—2 Kings 15:8; six months. Zechariah's rule spanned 753–752 B.C., and then he was assassinated.

AZARIAH ("Uzziah")—2 Kings 15:1–2, 8; 52 years. We know that Zechariah became the king of Judah in the thirty-eighth year of Uzziah, so Uzziah became king in 791 B.C. (753 B.C. plus 38 years). But the Bible also says that Uzziah became king in the twenty-seventh year of Jeroboam II, in 767 B.C. Therefore, Uzziah must have had a dual reign of 24 years with Amaziah, and his sole reign began in 767 B.C., when Amaziah died. Since Uzziah's total reign began in 791 B.C., he ruled until 739 B.C. (791 B.C. minus 53 years). Uzziah's joint reign with Amaziah probably began on account of the battle between Amaziah and Jehoash of Israel, in which Amaziah was captured and taken to Israel (2 Kings 14:8–11). He remained there until Jehoash died. Then Amaziah returned to Judah, where he lived for 15 years beyond the death of Jehoash.

Shallum—2 Kings 15:13; one month. Shallum ruled in the thirty-ninth year of Uzziah, so he ruled and died in 752 B.C. (791 B.C. minus 39 years).

STONE WEIGHT. *A Babylonian merchant used this one-mina weight during the time of King Nebuchadnezzar. The cuneiform inscription describes other weights and measures then in use.*

Menahem—2 Kings 15:17; ten years. He also began his reign in the thirty-ninth year of Uzziah, 752 B.C., and ruled for ten years, until 742 B.C.

Pekahiah—2 Kings 15:23; two years. Becoming king in 742, he reigned until 740 B.C. (Second Kings 15:23 tells us Pekahiah began his reign in the fiftieth year of Uzziah, or 741 B.C. Evidently this is another case where the new king took the throne at the beginning of the new year.)

Pekah—2 Kings 15:27; 20 years. This appears to be a real problem. Second Kings 15:27 tells us that Pekah became king in the fifty-second year of Uzziah, which would be in 739 B.C. (791 B.C. minus 52 years). If we take that at face value, we would begin Pekah's reign in 739 and terminate it in 719 B.C. Then we would need to add the nine-year reign of Hoshea, placing the end of Hoshea's reign in 710 B.C. But this does not correspond with Assyrian records of the fall of Israel.

It is often suggested that the reigns of Jotham and Ahaz paralleled the reign of Pekah, which began in 752 B.C. In other words, Pekah began ruling Israel simultaneously with Menahem. On this assumption, Pekah would have ruled from 752 to 732 B.C. The reference to the fifty-second year of Uzziah's reign indicates the year Pekah became the sole ruler in the North, and the statement about his reign lasting 20 years refers to the total reign of Pekah, beginning in 752 B.C.

PERSIAN SUBJECTS. *This relief from a wall in Persepolis shows a man from Bactria (now southern Russia) bringing tribute to his Persian conquerors. The Persians extended their empire across much of the Near East.*

BIBLE CHRONOLOGY

JOTHAM—2 Kings 15:32–33; 16 years. Jotham began his reign in the second year of Pekah—751 or 750 B.C. (depending on the month when Pekah began his reign). We have seen already that Uzziah reigned until 739 B.C., so Jotham and Uzziah must have reigned together for several years. Indeed, the Bible says that Uzziah became leprous at the end of his life (2 Chron. 26:21); this would have made a co-regency necessary, since lepers had to be isolated. Second Kings 16:1 says that Ahaz succeeded Jotham in the seventeenth year of Pekah, or 735 B.C. (752 B.C. minus 17 years). So Jotham must have reigned from 750 to 735 B.C. While the Bible says Jotham reigned 16 years, it also indicates that he lived to what would have been the twentieth year of his reign, 730 B.C. Hoshea of Israel plotted Pekah's assassination in Jotham's twentieth year (2 Kings 15:30). So we show the end of Jotham's life at about 730 B.C. on Figure 11. Scripture says that the Ammonites paid tribute to Jotham until the third year of his official reign (2 Chron. 27:5). That would be about 736 B.C. (739 B.C. minus three years).

Hoshea—2 Kings 17:1; nine years. Beginning his rule at the death of Pekah in 732 B.C., Hoshea saw his reign end in 723 B.C. when the Assyrians carried off the Northern Kingdom. Here again, the official records of Assyria help to confirm the chronology of the Bible. They tell us that Shalmaneser V died in 722 B.C., just after capturing an important city in Palestine (cf. 2 Kings 17:3–6). Shalmaneser's successor, Sargon II, boasted of capturing Israel in the year he came to the throne of Assyria; apparently the government of Assyria changed hands during this conquest.

AHAZ—2 Kings 16:1–2; 16 years. Second Kings 17:1 says King Hoshea of Israel came to the throne in the twelfth year of Ahaz, so Ahaz's rule began in 744 B.C. (732 B.C. plus 12 years) and ended in 728 B.C. (744 B.C. minus 16 years). This means that Ahaz overlapped the reign of his father, Jotham, by nine years.

HEZEKIAH—2 Kings 18:1–2, 13; 29 years. Second Kings 18:1 says that Hezekiah came to power in Hoshea's third year, or 729 B.C. (732 B.C. minus three years).

Second Kings 18:13 says that Sennacherib attacked Jerusalem in the fourteenth year of Hezekiah's reign, which would be 715 B.C.; but Assyrian records show that this attack came in 701 B.C. Perhaps a scribe copied 2 Kings 18:13 incorrectly, and should have written 24 instead of 14. (It's easy to confuse these numbers in the Hebrew script.) In that case, Hezekiah's sole "reign" began in 725 B.C. (701 B.C. plus 24 years) and ended in 696 B.C. (725 B.C. minus 29 years).

Let us suppose that Hezekiah set up a rival government against his father, Ahaz. Let us also suppose that Ahaz left his throne but lived for a few more years, exerting a powerful influence in the country. If this was the case, we can understand why 2 Kings 18:1 says Hezekiah became king in 729 B.C., when 2 Kings 18:13 suggests that he became king in 725 B.C.—both would be right because of the way Ahaz's abdication muddied the political waters in Judah.

Of course, this still leaves unanswered questions. Why would the same book date a king's reign two different ways? How could Uzziah, Jotham, and Ahaz rule Judah at the same time (744—739 B.C.)? What power struggles were going on in Judah? Frankly, we don't know. But it is better to live with some of these questions and continue to investigate, than to reject one section of Scripture in favor of another. That course cannot be right.

VII. Dating for Judah from 696 B.C. to 587/86 B.C. By this time, the Northern Kingdom of Israel had ceased to exist, and so we can no longer compare dates for the kings of Israel and Judah. We will begin at 696 B.C. (the end of Hezekiah's reign) and lay out the reigns of the remaining kings of Judah. Figure 12 does this.

MANASSEH—2 Kings 21:1; 55 years. Manasseh began his reign in 696 B.C. and reigned for 55 years, until 641 B.C.

AMON—2 Kings 21:19; two years. Amon began his reign in 641 and ruled until 639 B.C.

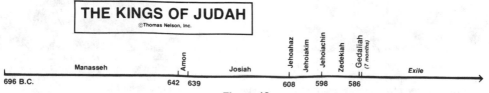

THE KINGS OF JUDAH
©Thomas Nelson, Inc.

| | | Manasseh | | Amon | | Josiah | | Jehoahaz | Jehoiakim | Jehoiachin | Zedekiah | Gedaliah (7 months) | Exile | |
| 696 B.C. | | | | 642 | 639 | | | | 608 | | 598 | 586 | | |

Figure 12

BIBLE CHRONOLOGY

JOSIAH—2 Kings 22:1; 31 years. Josiah began his reign in 639 B.C. and ruled until 608 B.C., when he lost his life on the battlefield trying to stop Pharaoh Necho and the Egyptians on their way to join the Assyrians in their battle against the Babylonians (2 Kings 23:29).

JEHOAHAZ—2 Kings 23:31; three months. The people chose the first son of Josiah, Jehoahaz, to be their new king. But Pharaoh Necho did not want him and placed another son of Josiah on the throne, Jehoiakim.

JEHOIAKIM—2 Kings 23:36; 11 years. During this king's reign Nebuchadnezzar came to Jerusalem for the first time and brought Judah under the domination of Babylon. Jehoiakim was confirmed as king in the year 605 B.C. We can fix this year without any doubt, because two eclipses established 605 B.C. as the date when Nebuchadnezzar began his reign. One of these eclipses took place in the fifth year of Nabopolassar, father of Nebuchadnezzar. We also know that Nebuchadnezzar came to the throne in his father's twenty-first year. The other eclipse took place on July 4, 568, when Nebuchadnezzar had ruled for 37 years. This

places Nebuchadnezzar's accession to the throne in 605 B.C. Also, Daniel was taken to Babylon and the 70-year Judean exile began in 605 B.C. (cf. Jer. 25:9–12; Dan. 9:2). Jehoiakim began his rule in 608 B.C. and reigned for 11 years, until 597 B.C. (608 B.C. minus 11 years), when he died.

JEHOIACHIN—2 Kings 24:8; three months. Jehoiachin became king after Jehoiakim, but Nebuchadnezzar attacked Judah a second time and deported Jehoiachin to Babylon. Nebuchadnezzar then placed another son of Josiah, Zedekiah, on the throne.

ZEDEKIAH—2 Kings 24:18; 11 years. This was the last king of Judah's first commonwealth. He ruled from 597 until 586 B.C., when Nebuchadnezzar came a third time, destroying the temple and ending the Judean kingdom.

GEDALIAH—2 Kings 25:22–26; seven months. Gedaliah became governor in the nineteenth year of Nebuchadnezzar, which confirms Gedaliah came to power in 586 B.C. (2 Kings 25:22). Apparently Nebuchadnezzar had to quell another rebellion in Judah, since

HEROD'S TEMPLE. *Dr. Conrad Shick has constructed this scale model of the temple in Jerusalem as it might have looked after Herod's massive restoration program (19 B.C.–A.D. 63). The model reflects information from early Jewish writers and archaeological finds in the temple area.*

some of the people did not accept the fact that the first commonwealth had come to an end. This happened in the twenty-third year of Nebuchadnezzar, or 582 B.C. (cf. Jer. 52:30).

VIII. Exilic and Post-Exilic Dating. The Bible provides some dates for the period of the Exile. Jehoiachin was released in the thirty-seventh year of his exile (2 Kings 25:27). This would place it at about 560 B.C. (597 B.C. minus 37 years). Ezekiel also gives us specific dates for the events of his ministry, from the time of Jehoiachin's captivity (Ezek. 1:1–2; 29:17). Ezekiel heard that Jerusalem had fallen in the twelfth year of his exile, which would place it at about 586 B.C. (Ezek. 33:21).

Babylon fell to Cyrus and the Persians in 539 B.C., and Cyrus immediately decreed that all refugees could return to their homelands (2 Chron. 36:22; Ezra 1:1). Again we see God working in history to accomplish His purpose for His people Israel. The Jewish people took about a year to return to their homeland and settle down to begin the second common-wealth. The Persian calendar system was different from the Jewish calendar, but we can calculate that the Jews began to lay the foundations for the second temple in 536 B.C. It is interesting to note that the Exile indeed ended 70 years after the Babylonians seized Judah in 606 B.C., as God had foretold (Jer. 25:11). The building of the temple came to a halt not too long after the start of construction. It began again in the second year of Darius I, in 520 B.C., under the preaching ministry of Haggai and Zechariah (Ezra 4:24; 5:1–2; Haggai 1:1–15; 2:1–9). It was completed in the sixth year of Darius (Ezra 6:15), which would be about 516 B.C. This is another way to mark the 70-year interval of Exile—from the destruction of the first temple in 586 B.C. to the completion of the second temple in 516 B.C.

Esther lived in the days of Ahasuerus or Xerxes (486–464 B.C.); and she is dated at about 483 and 479 B.C. (Esther 1:3; 2:16).

The closing historical events of the Old Testament occurred within the reign of Artaxerxes I (464–423 B.C.). Ezra took a contingent of Jews to Jerusalem in the seventh year of Artaxerxes (Ezra 7:7–9), about 458 B.C. To help Ezra and the Jewish community, Nehemiah arranged for an appointment as governor of the land. He was permitted to return in the twentieth year of Artaxerxes (Neh. 1:1), which would be about 444 B.C. There appears to be an interval between this first journey to Jerusalem (Neh. 2:1–11) and a second journey in the thirty-second year of Artaxerxes (Neh. 13:6), which would have been about 432 B.C.

Daniel predicts that the Messiah will redeem His people after 70 sets of seven years ("weeks"), beginning with Nehemiah's return to Jerusalem in 444 B.C. (Dan. 9:24). The Messiah is to be "cut off" at the end of 69 sets of sevens (Dan. 9:25–26), or 483 years starting with the proclamation of Artaxerxes in 444 B.C. This turns out to be the very week Jesus was crucified, taking into account all the necessary calculations.[3]

IX. The Life of Jesus. The New Testament gives us some important chronological indications. But it does not speak in terms of our calendar, and so we must compare it with other historical sources to find dates for the events of Jesus' life.

A. Birth. Herod the Great was king in Judea when Jesus was born (Matt. 2:1). Josephus writes in his *Antiquities* that there was an eclipse of the moon just before the death of Herod (Bk. XVII, Chap. xiii, Sect. 2). This might refer to any of three eclipses in 5 and 4 B.C.; the most likely choice is March 12, 4 B.C. Furthermore, this Jewish historian states that the king died just before Passover (Bk. XVII, Chap. vi, Sect. 4) and Passover occurred on April 11 in 4 B.C. So we must conclude that Herod died in the early part of April that year.

Wise men from the East came to worship God's Messiah. But when they did not report back to him, Herod ordered his soldiers to kill all babies in Bethlehem, two years and under (Matt. 2:16). This suggests that Jesus was born in 6 or 5 B.C. and He was between one and two

POST-EXILIC EVENTS
©Thomas Nelson, Inc.

The Fall of Babylon | Start of Second Temple | Temple Building Resumed | Temple Completed | Esther | Return of Ezra | Nehemiah and the Walls

539/38 536 520 516   458   444
B.C.

Figure 13

[3] *See* Robert Anderson, *The Coming Prince* (Grand Rapids, Mich.: Kregel Publications, 1975) and Alva J. McClain, *Daniel's Prophecy of the Seventy Weeks* (Grand Rapids, Mich.: Zondervan, 1940).

years old when Herod died. He was probably born in 5 B.C., and was taken to Egypt sometime in 4 B.C.

We don't know the exact month and day when Jesus was born. The date of December 25 is not very likely. The church in Rome chose that day to celebrate His birth in the second or third century in order to obscure a thoroughly pagan holiday that was traditionally celebrated on that day. Earlier the Eastern Orthodox church chose to honor Christ's birth on January 6, Epiphany. But why set the date in the winter? The shepherds would have been least likely to tend their flocks on the hillsides at that time. More likely, Jesus was born in the fall or spring.

Many scholars think the star of Bethlehem (Matt. 2:2) was some astronomical event. They say that perhaps it was a time when the planets Saturn and Jupiter appeared to cross paths in the sky; that happened in 7 or 6 B.C. Others note that Chinese records tell of a very bright star or comet in 5 and 4 B.C. But there are great problems with either theory. The Scriptures say that the star guided the wise men on their journey and even marked out the house, so that they would not be mistaken (Matt. 2:9–10). While the star did spark the interest of these wise men, it does not help us determine when Jesus was born.

B. Beginning of Ministry. The New Testament tells us much concerning Jesus' service in public; but again we must correlate these statements with outside sources to find the dates.

John the Baptist crossed the careers of several historical figures in Judea and the Roman Empire (Luke 3:1). For our purposes, the most important was Tiberius Caesar, who, Luke tells us, had been in office four years at the be-

GOLDEN GATE. *Located in the eastern wall of the temple area, this fifth-century A.D. structure is thought to have been built on the place where Christ made His triumphal entry into Jerusalem (cf. Matt. 21:8–11). The Turkish governor of Jerusalem blocked the gate in 1530.*

ginning of John's ministry. Josephus indicates that Tiberius became emperor at the death of Augustus in A.D. 14 (*Antiquities* Bk. XVIII, Chap. ii, Sect. 2). His fifteenth year would therefore have been A.D. 28 or 29, depending on whether he used an accession or a non-accession scheme of dating. John and Jesus began their ministry at about the same time. Let us assume that Jesus had a ministry of three and a half years and was about 30 years of age, as Luke 3:23 says, when He began to serve. At once a problem emerges: Josephus' date for Tiberius requires us to place the death of Jesus in about A.D. 31 or 32, and to move His birth date to 3 or 2 B.C., which as we saw is too late.

However, the problem is not insuperable. We know that Tiberius ruled with Augustus Caesar for two or three years before Augustus died. This means he began his official duties in about A.D. 11 or 12, and on this reckoning the fifteenth year of his rulership came in A.D. 26 or 27. The date of A.D. 26 is probably the best choice for the beginning of John's and Jesus' ministry, because it squares with the 5–6 B.C. birth date of Jesus.

The Bible says that Jesus was about 30 years of age when He began His ministry, right after His baptism (Luke 3:1–2, 21–23). But what did "*about* 30 years" signify? The priests began their service at 30 years of age, but Jesus was not a Levitical priest and was not bound to this rule. On the other hand, it was a respectable age. From a Jewish point of view, a man of 30 was not too young to be in a position of spiritual authority, yet not too old

to carry on a vigorous ministry. We should accept that Jesus began his ministry very near the age of 30.

Herod's reconstruction of the temple confirms our date for the beginning of Jesus' ministry. Roman history shows that Herod became king of Judea in 37 B.C. Josephus says that the Jews began to refurbish the second temple in the eighteenth year of Herod's reign, or in 19 B.C. (37 B.C. minus 18). When Jesus was in Jerusalem for the Passover, people told Him that the reconstruction was in its forty-sixth year (John 2:13, 20). This would place Jesus' first visit in A.D. 27. We assume that Jesus had already begun His ministry when He visited Jerusalem; so He would have begun His work sometime in the fall of A.D. 26.

C. Length of Ministry. Many regular events of Jewish life appear in Jesus' ministry. The most prominent of these was the feast of the Passover. The Gospel of John mentions three Passovers during Jesus' ministry (John 2:13; 6:4; 12:1). A. T. Robertson's *Harmony of the Gospels* shows that John 5:1 also refers to a Passover feast. Since Jesus began His ministry before the first of the four Passovers, the length of His ministry was three-and-one-half years, beginning sometime in the fall of A.D. 26 and concluding in the spring Passover season of A.D. 30.

Can we be more precise about the date of Jesus' death? Perhaps. The Jewish calendar shows that the Passover came on April 7, A.D. 30. Tradition says that Jesus was crucified on Friday; that would put the Passover on Thursday evening—Nisan 14 on the Jewish calen-

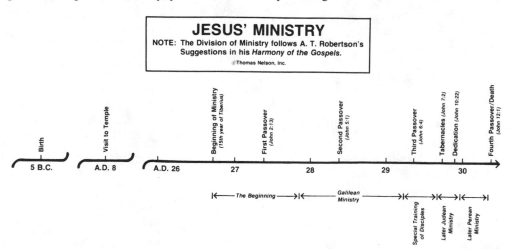

JESUS' MINISTRY
NOTE: The Division of Ministry follows A. T. Robertson's Suggestions in his *Harmony of the Gospels.*
©Thomas Nelson, Inc.

Birth — 5 B.C.
Visit to Temple — A.D. 8
A.D. 26
Beginning of Ministry (15th year of Tiberius) — 27
First Passover (John 2:13)
Second Passover (John 5:1) — 28
29
Third Passover (John 6:4)
Tabernacles (John 7:2)
Dedication (John 10:22) — 30
Fourth Passover/Death (John 12:1)

The Beginning — Galilean Ministry

Special Training of Disciples — Later Judean Ministry — Later Perean Ministry

Figure 14

dar. Some scholars, however, think that the crucifixion took place on Thursday, or even Wednesday.

And there is another problem: Did Jesus really eat a Passover meal, or just some *kind* of significant meal? It is inconceivable that Jesus would have sent His disciples to prepare the Passover (Luke 22:8, 13), without expecting them to offer the proper sacrifice in the temple and set an actual Passover table. Any other feast at that time of the year would have been unthinkable.

And how did the Jewish people calculate the new moon, which sets the date of the Passover meal? (They celebrated Passover 14 days after the new moon of the first month of Nisan.) If they reckoned the day of the new moon by a calculation of astronomy, they would have celebrated Passover on April 7, A.D. 30. But if they used a visual observation of the moon to determine the date of Passover, they could have made some error. But A. T. Robertson argues for the traditional date of Passover—April 7, A.D. 30—because it allows us to harmonize the narratives of the Synoptics (Matthew, Mark, and Luke) with the Gospel of John. Figure 14 shows how these dates plot the various phases of Jesus' ministry.

TEXT AND TRANSLATIONS

How authentic is our Bible? Do we really possess the Word of God? Or have distortions of God's truth crept in?

These questions concern the *text* of the Bible, which our ancestors have relayed to us from the original writers. In the following discussion of the *text* of the Bible, we shall try to see how God inspired the first writing of the Scriptures; how the scribes of past centuries preserved God's truth when they copied the original manuscripts; and what standards we can use to test the reliability of the ancient manuscripts that have survived, since some of them disagree. We shall also look into the different *translations* of the Bible, since few of us read it in its original Hebrew, Aramaic, and Greek. Can we trust the English translations we have? Do they give us an accurate rendering of the Bible text? What standards can we use to evaluate the various translations?

God's servants wrote the books of the Old Testament many generations before the New Testament was written. These were the holy books of the Jewish people; so we have received them through channels that were quite different from the route the New Testament text has followed. The text of the Old Testament has withstood the rigors of time for centuries more than the New Testament. And its writers wrote it in Hebrew and Aramaic, while virtually all of the New Testament was written in Greek. Because of these differences, we will discuss the text of the Old and New Testaments separately.

I. THE OLD TESTAMENT TEXT
A. How the Old Testament Was "Inspired"
B. How We Received the Old Testament

II. THE NEW TESTAMENT TEXT
A. New Testament Inspiration
B. How We Received the New Testament Text

III. ENGLISH TRANSLATIONS OF THE BIBLE
A. Psalters and Other Early Translations
B. The King James Version
C. Revisions of the King James Version
1. English Revised Version
2. American Standard Version
3. New King James Version

D. New Translations
1. Revised Standard Version
2. New English Bible
E. Recent Revisions and Paraphrases
1. New American Standard Bible
2. New American Bible
3. New International Version
4. Goodspeed's Paraphrase
5. J. B. Phillips' Paraphrase
6. Today's English Version (Good News Bible)
7. Living Bible

IV. STANDARDS FOR EVALUATION

I. The Old Testament Text. Of the Old Testament, Jesus said that "one jot or one tittle shall in no wise pass from the law, till all be fulfilled" (Matt. 5:18). Thus He taught that God had inspired the entire text of the Old Testament, even to the smallest details.

The early church considered the inspiration of the Old Testament to be a vital and basic part of its teaching. The New Testament books were still being written during the first century; so when New Testament writers referred to "Scripture," they generally meant the books that we now know as the Old Testament.[1] Peter wrote that "no prophecy of the scripture is of any private interpretation. For the prophecy came not in old time by the will of man: but holy men of God spake as they were moved by the Holy Ghost" (2 Pet. 1:20–21). Paul told Timothy, "All scripture is given by inspiration of God . . ." (2 Tim. 3:16a). And since God inspired these writings, they are "profitable for doctrine, for reproof, for correction, for instruction in righteousness" (2 Tim. 3:16b).

These statements arouse our curiosity about the way God worked in the writing of the Old Testament, and we need to understand this process before we study how the text was handed down to us. So we must consider the matter of inspiration before we proceed further.

A. How the Old Testament Was "Inspired." Traditionally, the church has taught

---

[1] Note, however, that Paul specifically referred to the books of Moses as the "old testament" or "old covenant" (2 Cor. 3:14–15). Also note that in 1 Timothy 5:18 he appears to be quoting Luke 10:7 as "scripture."

TEXT AND TRANSLATIONS

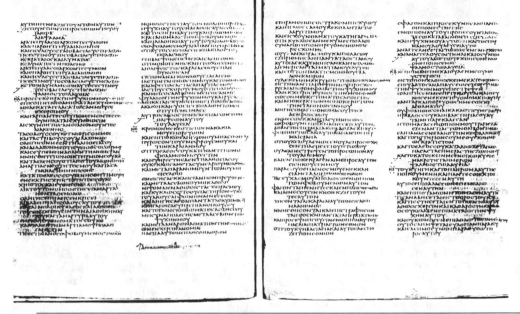

CODEX SINAITICUS. *Count Constantine von Tischendorf discovered this Greek manuscript of the entire Bible at the Monastery of St. Catherine on Mt. Sinai in 1859. It was written in large Greek letters (uncials) on vellum sheets measuring 38 x 33 cm. (15 x 13 in.). Count von Tischendorf considered the manuscript to be so valuable that he called it* Aleph *(the first letter in the Hebrew alphabet). It was copied in the fourth century A.D., making it the earliest complete copy of the New Testament in existence. Many other manuscripts were written earlier, but are not complete copies.*

the *plenary inspiration* of the Bible. Simply stated, this is the doctrine that (1) God gave and guaranteed all that the Bible writers had to say on all of the subjects they discussed, and (2) He determined for them by inward prompting (plus providential conditioning and control) the manner in which they should express His truth. In this way, Scripture was written exactly as He planned, and thus is as truly His Word as it is man's witness. Both of these teachings come from Scripture itself.

The Old Testament writers remind us again and again that they are communicating God's Word. The prophets introduce their statements with "thus saith the Lord," "the word of the Lord that came unto me," or something similar. René Pache found 3,808 of these declarations in the Old Testament; as he rightly concluded, they emphasize that Scripture "conveys the express word of God."[2]

Here are some passages that illustrate the point: ". . . The Lord said unto Moses, Write

thou these words: for after the tenor of these words I have made a covenant with thee and with Israel" (Exod. 34:27). "All this, said David, the Lord made me understand in writing by his hand upon me . . ." (1 Chron. 28:19). ". . . This word came unto Jeremiah from the Lord, saying, Take thee a roll of a book, and write therein all the words that I have spoken unto thee . . ." (Jer. 36:1–2; cf. vv. 21–32). Each writer explains that he is recording what God has revealed to him, expressing it in the same terms in which he received it from God.

However, God did not dictate the manuscript of the Old Testament to these writers, as if they were secretaries. He revealed His truth to them and showed them how they should present it; but in so doing He led them to express His Word in terms of their own outlook, interests, literary habits, and peculiarities of style.[3] As Benjamin B. Warfield put it, ". . .

---

[2] René Pache, *The Inspiration and Authority of Scripture* (Chicago: Moody Press, 1969), pp. 65, 81.

[3] See James I. Packer, *"Fundamentalism" and the Word of God* (London: InterVarsity Press, 1958), pp. 78ff.

TEXT AND TRANSLATIONS

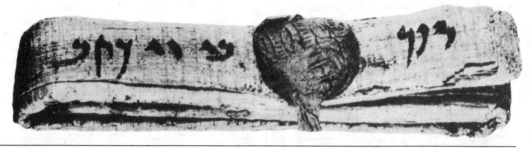

ELEPHANTINE PAPYRUS. *During the Exile, Jews who fled to Egypt established a colony on Elephantine Island in the Nile River near Aswan. Here archaeologists have found many Aramaic manuscripts written on papyrus, which show the Aramaic script that was commonly used during this period (5th century B.C.). This papyrus letter from Elephantine is clasped by the wax seal placed upon it over 2,500 years ago. The Aramaic characters read: "Letter concerning a house, written by . . . ."*

Every word of the Scriptures, without exception, is the word of God; but, alongside of that . . . every word is the word of man."[4] This is why the writer of Hebrews says that God "at sundry times and in divers manners spake in time past unto the fathers by the prophets" (Heb. 1:1). Instead of binding the Old Testament writers to produce one scripted account of His message, all in the same style, God spoke "in divers manners" according to the circumstances and abilities of each writer. Hence the marvelous variety of material from the prophets, poets, historians, wise men, and visionaries through whom God spoke.

The Old Testament writers tell us the methods whereby God inspired some phases of their work. At times He revealed His message to men through visions consisting of sights and sounds (e.g., Isa. 6:1 ff.); at other times He spoke directly through them (2 Sam. 23:2). We do not know exactly how He inspired every part of every Old Testament book, and that really does not matter. What is important is that we know the Scriptures are His Word, in both their substance and structure. This is what we mean when we say the Scriptures are the product of *plenary inspiration.*

Of course, we can say this about the original manuscripts only, and we no longer have them. (The technical term for the original manuscripts is *autographs.*) How can we be sure that the manuscript copies we have are still the Word of God?

To answer this question, we need to explore the way our ancestors copied the original

manuscripts of the Old Testament and passed the copies along to us. Scholars call this process *textual transmission.*

B. How We Received the Old Testament. When the Old Testament writers finished their scrolls, there were no copying machines or printing presses to duplicate their writing for the public. They depended on *scribes*—men who patiently copied the Scriptures by hand when extra copies were needed and when the original scrolls became too worn to use any longer. The scribes attempted to make exact copies of the original scrolls, and the scribes who followed them attempted to make exact copies of the copies. Even so, they did not always avoid mechanical slips in copying at some points. Anyone who has ever done any copying will sympathize!

By the time Jesus was born, the most recent Old Testament book (Malachi) had been copied and recopied over a span of more than four hundred years; the books that Moses wrote had been copied this way for more than *fourteen* hundred years. Yet during that time the scribes guarded the Old Testament text very well. It has been computed that, on the average, they mistakenly copied one out of every 1,580 letters; and they usually corrected these errors when they made new copies.[5]

The Hebrew language slowly changed, as languages do, across the centuries after the Old Testament writers. The language of Moses would seem very strange to a modern Israeli, just as the language of Chaucer or even Shakespeare is a long way from our own present-day speech. (*See* "Languages and

---

[4] Benjamin B. Warfield, *The Inspiration and Authority of the Bible,* ed. by Samuel G. Craig (Nutley, N.J.: Presbyterian and Reformed, 1948), p. 421.

[5] Pache, *The Inspiration and Authority of Scripture,* p. 190.

TEXT AND TRANSLATIONS

Writing.") Along the way, the meanings of some Hebrew words and some rules of grammar were lost. This gives Bible translators real headaches when they try to decipher some sections of the Old Testament manuscripts. Yet it's remarkable how much they can understand overall. Charles Hodge, professor of theology at Princeton Seminary a century ago, once said that the remaining problems of translation and interpretation affect the Bible no more than a tiny streak of sandstone would detract from the marble beauty of the Parthenon.[6] And that is even truer today.

Long before the time of the great writing prophets (seventh and eighth centuries B.C.), Hebrew scribes were copying and recopying the Scriptures. But Jeremiah is the first to mention the scribes as a professional group: "How do ye say, We are wise, and the law of the Lord is with us? Lo, certainly in vain made he it; the pen of the scribes (*sopherim*) is in vain" (Jer. 8:8). The word *sopherim* literally means "the counters"; the early scribes earned this title because they counted every letter of every book of Scripture to make sure they didn't leave out anything. To make doubly sure, they checked the letter that appeared in

the middle of each book and in the middle of each major section of the book. They took great care to preserve the original wording of the text, even though the changing Hebrew language made it seem archaic.

An important change in the Hebrew language occurred around 500 B.C., when the *sopherim* began using a square Aramaic script that they learned during their Exile in Babylon. (Aramaic had been introduced to Babylon in the Persian royal letters.) From the time of King David, the *sopherim* had used a rounded Paleo-Hebrew (early Hebrew) script to copy the Old Testament manuscripts, because they could write it on parchment, unlike the wedge-shaped script of the Canaanites. But by 500 B.C., Aramaic had become the common language of commerce and education in the Near East, so the Hebrews adopted its writing system. Papyrus manuscripts from a Jewish colony on Elephantine Island (in the Nile Delta) prove that the old cursive script was no longer used in 250 B.C. The Dead Sea Scrolls cover this period of transition; some of them are written in the rounded Paleo-Hebrew script, but most are in the square Aramaic.

Note that Hebrew scribes did not begin using the Aramaic *language;* they simply borrowed its script and used it to express their own Hebrew words. They could do this because both Hebrew and Aramaic were *Semitic*

---

[6] Charles Hodge, *Systematic Theology, Vol. 1* (Grand Rapids, Mich.: William B. Eerdmans Company, 1965), p. 169.

Scribal Customs

After the Jews returned from Exile, they formed communities of scribes to preserve and circulate the Scriptures that had become so precious to them. These scribes (later called the *Masoretes*) tried to explain the variations in different manuscripts. They eventually developed a system of vowel pointing that preserved the pronunciation of the Hebrew words.

Before he began his work each day, the scribe would test his reed pen by dipping it in ink and writing the name *Amalek,* then crossing it out (*cf.* Deut. 25:19). Then he would say, "I am writing the Torah in the name of its sanctity and the name of God in its sanctity." The scribe would read a sentence in the manuscript he was copying, repeat it aloud, and then write it. Each time he came to the name of God, he would say, "I am writing the name of God for the holiness of His name." If he made an error in writing God's name, he had to destroy the entire sheet of papyrus or vellum that he was using.

Although the scribes were careful to preserve the

text, they sometimes made changes to soften embarrassing statements. For example, they often changed *Jehovah* (*Yahweh*) to "the name" or "heaven," as in Leviticus 24:11: "And the Israelitish woman's son blasphemed the name." In some cases, they changed the name of the pagan god *Baal* to *Bosheth* ("shame"). In this way, they changed several proper names (e.g., Ish-bosheth for Ish-baal). They also shortened some names to remove or obscure references to pagan deities; for example, they shortened Baal-meon to Beon (*cf.* Num. 32:3, 38).

After the scribe finished copying a particular book, he would count all of the words and letters it contained. Then he checked this tally against the count for the manuscript that he was copying. He counted the number of times a particular word occurred in the book, and he noted the middle word and the middle letter in the book, comparing all of these with his original. By making these careful checks, he hoped to avoid any scribal errors.

TEXT AND TRANSLATIONS

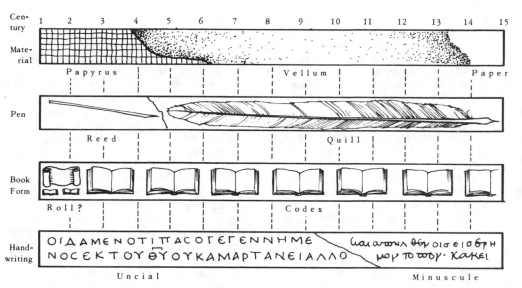

Figure 15

languages,[7] and their scripts stood for the same alphabet, which in turn signified many of the same sounds in both languages.

(We see a modern example of this in English and French. Since they were both shaped by the same classical language, Latin, their alphabets and some of their sounds are the same.) When Hebrew scribes had borrowed the Aramaic script, they also started borrowing Aramaic words and phrases to express traditional Hebrew ideas (just as we commonly use the French words *coiffure* and *lingerie*). Gradually they came to insert Aramaic words into the text to take the place of older Hebrew words that they no longer used. And sometimes they added editorial notes in Aramaic to clarify what the text said; Jeremiah 10:11 is such a note.

Paleo-Hebrew had no vowels, and early scribes probably used dots to separate their words, as the Phoenicians did. They did not put spaces between words, as we do. In the tenth century B.C., the Arameans (who lived in what is now Syria) had begun putting special letters at the end of each word to indicate final long vowels. Two centuries later, Moabites of Canaan began doing the same, and they passed the idea on to the Hebrew scribes. After the Exile, Hebrew scribes began to associate four of the Hebrew consonants with vowel sounds (*Aleph* = ā, *heth* = a, *vav* = o, *ayin* = i). Language experts call these letters the *matres lectionis* (Latin, "mothers of reading"). But the Hebrew scribes did not develop a system for showing the vowel sounds until after A.D. 500. (*See* "Languages and Writing.")

So a person who read an Old Testament manuscript in the time of Jesus found a continuous string of letters, and had only these three simple devices (dots between words, final long vowels, and the *matres lectionis*) to guide him in identifying, breaking up and pronouncing the words. He had to supply a good deal, in fact, from memory. For example, let us say we were going to write Isaiah 61:1 (in English!) the way it would have appeared in the scroll that Jesus read in the synagogue at Nazareth (Luke 4:18): "The Spirit of the Lord is upon me, because he has anointed me. . . ." If we use the letters from our English translation but write it in the old Hebrew style, it would look something like this:

TH.SPRT.F.TH.LRD.S.PN.ME.

That's not easy to read, is it? Actually, we have made it a bit easier by printing it from left to right, in normal English fashion. But Hebrew and other Semitic languages ran from right to left; so to get a better picture of what the verse looked like, try this:

.ƎM.Иꟼ.Ƨ.ᗡЯ⅃.HT.ꟻ.TЯꟼƧ.HT

---

[7] We call them *Semitic* languages because they were spoken by nations that descended from Noah's son, Shem (Gen. 10:21–31).

TEXT AND TRANSLATIONS

By the time the Hebrew scribes began to insert vowel markings into the text, they had lost the meanings of a few words (mostly very ancient or rare ones) in the Old Testament. They were able to determine the meaning of most of these words in the light of the surrounding material. We call these later scribes *Masoretes,* and the manuscripts they produced the *Masoretic Text.* These terms come from the Hebrew word *Masorah* ("tradition"), because the Masoretic scribes tried to preserve the traditional meaning of the Scriptures. A small Jewish sect in Babylon known as the Qaraites developed an effective system of vowel marks around A.D. 500, which led the Masoretes to deal more seriously themselves with this problem.

A Masoretic family named ben Asher produced a better system of vowel markings in the ninth and tenth centuries. Soon afterward, Aaron ben Moshe ben Asher issued a complete text of the Old Testament with the vowel

marks. Because the ben Asher system represented the vowels with dots and short dashes, above and below the line of letters, scholars refer to it as *vowel pointing.* The ben Naphtali family of Masoretes developed a different pointing system and a slightly different Old Testament text at this same time. But late in the twelfth century A.D., the noted Jewish philosopher Moses Maimonides declared the ben Asher text to be the *textus receptus* (Latin, "received text").

However, the ben Asher text comes to us in several different forms. Our earliest manuscript of the ben Asher text is the Cairo Codex of the Prophets (otherwise known as Codex C), which was made in A.D. 950. Moshe ben Asher supplied the vowel markings for this manuscript and presented it to the Qaraite community in Jerusalem. The Crusaders seized it in 1099, but eventually it was returned to the Qaraite community in Cairo. The Leningrad Codex B3 of the Major

Some Extant N.T. Manuscripts

Manuscript	Synoptics	John	Acts	Epistles	Revelation	Date
Rylands (p 52)		John 18:31–33, 37–38				*ca.* A.D. 115–125
Bodmer II (p 66)		√				*ca.* A.D. 150–175
Bodmer XIV–XV (p 75)	Luke 3–24	Portions 1–15				*ca.* A.D. 175–200
Chester Beatty (p 45–47)	Portions	Portions	Portions	Portions	Portions	2nd and 3rd Centuries A.D.
Vaticanus (B)	√	√	√	Portions		4th Century A.D.
Sinaiticus (Aleph)	√	√	√	√	√	4th Century A.D.
Alexandrinus (A)	Most of Matt. missing 1:1–25:6	Portions missing 6–8	√	All except 2 Cor. 4–12	√	5th Century A.D.
Ephraemi (C)	Fragmentary	Fragmentary	Fragmentary	Fragmentary	Fragmentary	5th Century A.D.
Washingtonensis (W)	√	√				4-5th Century A.D.
Bezae (D)	√	√	√			5th Century A.D.
Papyrus 2 (p 2)		John 12:12–15				6th Century A.D.

Figure 16

and Minor Prophets (also known as Codex P) was written in A.D. 916. The Aleppo manuscript of the ben Asher text (Codex A) was probably written before A.D. 940. However, one-fourth of that manuscript was lost during a raid on the Aleppo monastery in 1948. Finally, the Leningrad Codex B19 A (or Codex L) of the Old Testament was finished in A.D. 1008. These manuscripts provide the basic information we have about the ben Asher text.

In 1524, Jacob ben Hayyim published a printed text of the Hebrew Old Testament, using manuscripts that had been copied from the ben Asher manuscripts we have mentioned above. Because this was the first printed edition of the Hebrew Old Testament it became a standard for printed Bibles. Gerhard Kittel's *Biblia Hebraica,* perhaps the best-known Hebrew Old Testament of the twentieth century, listed the variations of the ben Hayyim text in its footnotes and did not include them in the text.

However, the Old Testament has come down to us in other languages besides Hebrew. Around 300 B.C., Greek versions began to appear. A community of Greek-speaking Jewish scholars in Alexandria compiled a Greek version of the Old Testament called the Septuagint.[8] For the Pentateuch, the Septuagint translators used a Hebrew manuscript very like the ben Hayyim text that we have today. But they seem to have used a much different manuscript for the other books, because the Septuagint often departs from the ben Hayyim text.

After A.D. 200, Jewish scholars began compiling Aramaic paraphrases of the Old Testament. We call these Aramaic versions *targums.* The targums were made from Hebrew manuscripts written in the time of Jesus or later.

II. The New Testament Text. The writers of the New Testament completed their work within about sixty years of Jesus' crucifixion. Being written in an age when literature flourished, and being copied constantly from the start, the New Testament text has survived the centuries well. J.H. Greenlee estimates that we have altogether 15,000 complete manuscripts

and quotations of the New Testament in our hands today.[9]

A. New Testament Inspiration. God moved the writers of the New Testament faithfully to record His Word as He did the Old Testament writers. Paul and the Gospel writers often showed themselves conscious of what the Holy Spirit was doing through them. We will review some of these texts briefly, because they give us valuable insights into the way God inspired His written Word.

Luke opens his Gospel by saying that "many" had attempted to write an account of Jesus' life and ministry, but that he himself is doing so because God has given him "perfect understanding of all things from the very first" (Luke 1:3). Likewise, we are assured that we can trust John's Gospel because he was an eyewitness of the events he records (John 21:24). God gave the Gospel writers firsthand exposure to the events of Jesus' ministry and a "perfect understanding" of those events; this uniquely qualified them for their writing task.

Similarly, when writing to the churches on practical matters of morals and ethics (1 Cor. 4:14; 5:9; 2 Cor. 9:1), Paul knew that he was expressing what the Holy Spirit directed him to write. Of his detailed directions about the conduct of worship in the Corinthian church, he said, "If any man think himself to be a prophet, or spiritual, let him acknowledge that the things that I write unto you are the commandments of the Lord" (1 Cor. 14:37). He was an apostle, one whom God enabled to declare His revealed wisdom "not in the words which man's wisdom teacheth, but which the Holy Ghost teacheth" (1 Cor. 2:13). What Paul laid down, therefore, was to be received as divine instruction. As Peter said, Paul had written "according to the wisdom given to him" (2 Pet. 3:15).

Again, the apostle John explained that he did not write to the churches to reveal any new instructions from God (1 John 2:7–8). Nor did he write because his readers were ignorant of the truth that Christ had already revealed (1 John 2:21). Rather, he wrote because his readers already knew the truth and his letters would encourage them to obey the truth (1 John 1:4; 2:21b). This shows that the Holy

---

[8] It got this name from the Latin word for *seventy,* because tradition says that seventy scholars translated the text of the Hebrew Bible into Greek. It is usually referred to by the symbol LXX, which is 70 in Roman numerals.

[9] J. Harold Greenlee, "Text and Translations of the New Testament," *The Zondervan Pictorial Encyclopedia of the Bible, Vol. 5,* ed. by Merrill C. Tenney (Grand Rapids, Mich.: Zondervan Publishing House, 1975), p. 697.

TEXT AND TRANSLATIONS

ISLE OF PATMOS. *The apostle John received his vision of God's judgment on this small, rocky island off the southwestern coast of Asia Minor. Tradition says that the Roman emperor Domitian (A.D. 81–96) banished John to Patmos because he refused to honor the state religion of Rome. The Book of Revelation confirms that the vision was received on Patmos (Rev. 1:9), and seems to indicate he wrote the book here (Rev. 1:11, 19; 10:4).*

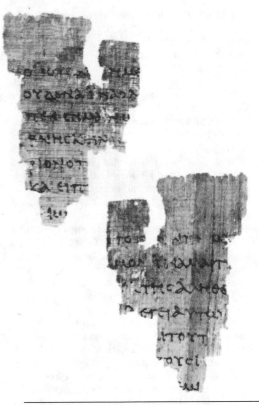

PAPYRUS 52. *This piece of papyrus manuscript from Egypt is the oldest confirmed fragment of the New Testament. (What appear to be two fragments here are actually two different sides of the same fragment.) Housed in the John Rylands Library in Manchester, England, it is commonly called the Rylands Fragment or Papyrus 52. It contains several lines from John 18 and was copied between A.D. 115–125. This indicates that the Gospel of John itself was written much earlier—most likely during the first century.*

Spirit inspired the New Testament writers to work in perfect harmony with the truth that had already been revealed. They knew it was that truth, stemming from Christ Himself, that they were expressing and enforcing.

B. How We Received the New Testament Text. We have many fragments of the New Testament text that were written in the second century A.D. Some of these are on *ostraka* (scraps of pottery that early writers used as a cheap form of stationery) and *talismans* (pendants, bracelets, and other objects that early Christians wore to ward off evil spirits). But these objects contain only very short quotations from the New Testament, so they give us little information about the original text.

More important are the papyrus manuscripts of the New Testament. Written on an early form of paper made from matted papyrus reeds, these manuscripts date from the second to the fourth centuries after Christ.

The earliest known fragment of a New Testament papyrus manuscript dates from about A.D. 115 or 125. It is commonly called the Rylands Fragment because it is housed in the John Rylands Library of Manchester, England. A mere 6 cm x 9 cm (2½ in. x 3¼ in.),

the fragment contains a portion of John 18:32–33, 37–38. Archaeologists recovered the Rylands Fragment from the ruins of a Greek town in ancient Egypt. Despite its early date, the fragment is too small to provide much information about the text of the Gospel of John in the second century.

The next oldest papyrus manuscript is one of those called the Chester Beatty Papyri, because most of it is owned by the Chester Beatty Museum of Dublin. This manuscript consists of 76 leaves of papyrus (46 at Dublin, 30 at the University of Michigan). Each leaf measures about 16½ x 28 cm (6½ in. x 11 in.) and contains about 25 lines of writing. Hand-

TEXT AND TRANSLATIONS

DESIDERIUS ERASMUS (1466–1536). *Though he was admitted to the Catholic priesthood and took the vows of a monk, Erasmus joined Martin Luther and other reformers in demanding that the Scriptures be published for lay readers. In 1516 he published a Greek text of the New Testament. He was unable to find a complete manuscript or manuscripts which he considered good, so he had to rely heavily upon two late and inferior manuscripts, as well as the Latin Vulgate. His text became known as the* textus receptus *and was used by the leaders of the Reformation as the basis of their common-language versions of the New Testament.*

scholars have traditionally supposed. The fragments date from A.D. 50, and it is very likely that they are copies of a manuscript written years before that. Therefore, most Bible scholars are doubtful about O'Callaghan's identification of the fragments.[10]

The earliest copies of the New Testament were written entirely in capital letters with no space between words and on vellum (parchment) or papyrus. Scholars call the manuscripts *uncials,* and nearly 275 have been found. Scribes used the uncial style of writing on vellum and papyrus until about the ninth century, when they began copying the manuscripts in a small, cursive Greek script. These later manuscripts are called *minuscules.* We have over 2,700 New Testament manuscripts written in minuscule style.

Scholars consider Codex Vaticanus (or "Vaticanus B") to be one of the most important uncial manuscripts. Written shortly after A.D. 300, this manuscript originally contained all of the Septuagint and all the New Testament. Part of the Letter to the Hebrews, the Pastoral Letters, and the Book of Revelation have been lost. Some portions of the Old Testament section of this manuscript also have been lost, but what remains is a useful source of information about the text of the Old Testament. It is housed in the Vatican Library.

Another valuable uncial manuscript is called Codex Sinaiticus, because Constantine von Tischendorf (1815–1874) found it in a monastery at the foot of traditional Mount Sinai in 1859. Written shortly after Codex Vaticanus, it is the earliest complete manuscript of the New Testament.

We should also note Codex Alexandrinus, an uncial manuscript that dates from just after A.D. 400. It originally contained the entire Bible in Greek, along with the apocryphal books of 1 and 2 Clement and the Psalms of Solomon. The Greek Orthodox patriarch of Constantinople gave this manuscript to the British ambassador in 1624, as a gift to England's King James I. It is now housed in the British Museum.

Another interesting uncial manuscript is the Codex Ephraemi Rescriptus, so called because it contains some of the writings of Ephraem Syrus. This manuscript was written about the same time as the Codex Alexandri-

writing experts believe that this manuscript was written in the second century. It contains most of Paul's letters.

Another important manuscript is called the Bodmer Papyrus (or Bodmer II). Also written in about A.D. 150–175, this manuscript contains chapters 1–14 of John and fragments of the last seven chapters. It is housed in the private library of Martin Bodmer in Cologny, Switzerland.

Jose O'Callaghan of Barcelona, a professor of the Pontifical Institute in Rome, believes that some papyrus fragments from Cave 7 of Qumran contain a portion of Mark's Gospel; if this is true, these fragments are the earliest New Testament finds to date. It would mean that the Gospel was written much earlier than

---

[10] David Estrada and William White, Jr., *The First New Testament* (Nashville: Thomas Nelson, Inc., 1978), pp. 13–27.

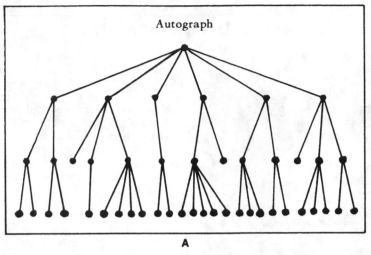

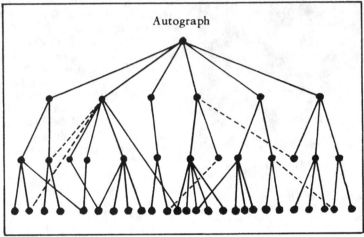

Figure 17

TEXTUAL TRANSMISSION. *Scribes usually made several copies of a manuscript, and sometimes they made errors while copying. The question is, Which copies give us the most genuine reading of the original? Scholars use textual criticism to try to recover the wording of the original manuscripts ("autographs") of the Scriptures.*

Figure A shows the copying process in its simplest form. For the sake of discussion, suppose that the scribes made six copies of the original manuscript. Notice that each of these copies was copied in turn and the new copies were copied yet again. It would seem that each new generation would introduce more errors into the text. For example, if two of the first six copies contain significant errors, these errors would be carried forward ("transmitted") to the copies made from them. We would logically assume that errors also crept into some of the copies made from the four other manuscripts. Thus it would seem that the last copies—those at the bottom of the diagram—would contain many different errors, and so they would disagree with one another. But scholars have found that more than 80 percent of the existing New Testament manuscripts are in agreement. The basic assumption of Westcott and Hort's theory of textual transmission is that this majority of manuscripts were all derived from a single manuscript exemplar somewhere in history and can be reduced to a single manuscript in their procedure. They use the agreement of Alexandrian and Western manuscripts as a "two-against-one" weighting system to totally discredit this majority of manuscripts.

Figure B shows what some scholars think is a better explanation of the copying process. As scribes made copies of the Scripture manuscripts, they consulted the manuscripts that were most readily available (indicated by the solid line), as well as older manuscripts and copies that had been passed down through different traditions (indicated by the dotted lines). At the first stage of copying, only a few copies would be in error; so scribes of the next generation would follow the reading of the majority, correcting their own manuscripts to make them agree. Thus, according to this theory, the reading given by the greatest number of copies ("the majority text") would be the most reliable version of the autograph.

TEXT AND TRANSLATIONS

Early Versions and Their Sources

Version and Date	Latin Vulgate	Greek and Hebrew Mss.	Luther's German Bible	Tyndale's Version	Coverdale's Version	Matthew's Bible	Great Bible	Geneva Bible	Bishop's Bible
Wycliffe (1380)	✓								
Tyndale (1525–1530)	✓	✓							
Coverdale (1535)	✓		✓	✓					
Matthew's Bible (1537)		✓		✓					
Great Bible (1540)				✓	✓				
Geneva Bible (1560)				✓			✓		
Bishop's Bible (1568)							✓		
Rheims (1582)	✓	✓							
Douay (1610)	✓	✓							
King James Version (1611)	✓	✓		✓	✓			✓	✓

Figure 18

nus, and it also contained the entire Greek Bible. Thrifty scribes produced it by erasing the parchment of the earlier manuscript of the Scriptures and jotting the new manuscript of Ephraem's sermons at a right angle to the old one. Scholars call this type of manuscript a *palimpsest* (Greek, *palimpsēstos*—"scraped again"). This makes the text very difficult to read, but in most places researchers can discern portions of the earlier manuscript as well as the newer one.

Most minuscule manuscripts contain the same type of cursive Greek script. In the nineteenth century, Bible scholars rejected hundreds of these manuscripts as being the poorest examples of the New Testament text. However, the minuscules have been reconsidered in recent years in an effort to produce what is now called a "majority text."

We gain some evidence of the New Testament text from early *lectionaries* (books containing Scripture lessons to be read on holy days). Also, the early church fathers often quoted New Testament Scriptures in their writings. But as M. M. Parvis notes, ". . . The Fathers did not always quote accurately. They harmonized their texts, and they misquoted just as often as does the modern writer. . . . They often paraphrased."[11] But these quotations still serve as an important witness to the original text.

When there came to be many Latin-speaking Christians, the Bible was translated into Latin so that the Christians of that area could understand it. It is believed that this was done around A.D. 200, although no Latin manuscripts survive from that time. Christian scribes copied this "Old Latin" version many times, and eventually their copies picked up some striking differences.

Pope Damasus I commissioned the scholar Jerome (A.D. 340–420) to produce a standard text of the Latin Bible, and Jerome completed this project around A.D. 400. His version

[11] M. M. Parvis, "Text, NT," *Interpreter's Dictionary of the Bible,* Vol. 4, ed. by George A. Buttrick (Nashville: Abingdon Press, 1962), p. 599.

(called the "Vulgate" because it used the "common language" of early medieval times) was based on the Old Latin versions. But Jerome used a good Latin text and compared it with some Old Greek manuscripts that were available.

Pope Leo X was the greatest scholar and manuscript collector among the Renaissance popes. He suggested a scholarly edition of the Bible to be edited by Cardinal Ximines of Spain. In 1517, a printer in Alcala, Spain, completed this printed Bible with the Vulgate and the Greek arranged in parallel columns. It became known as the *Complutensian Polyglot* (Latin, *Complutum*—"Alcala"; Greek, *Polyglot*—"set forth in many languages"). The editors of this edition said they used "very ancient and correct" Greek manuscripts that Pope Leo X provided for their work. But we cannot be sure which manuscripts these were, nor whether they have survived to the present day. They were probably burned in one of the papal wars of Renaissance Italy. The pope did not give permission to release this book until 1522, and by that time another printer named Joannes Froben had issued a printed Greek New Testament.

Froben, a printer in Basel, Switzerland, had persuaded the noted biblical scholar Erasmus of Rotterdam to come to that city to prepare this edition. Using manuscripts from the library of Basel University, Erasmus and Froben produced their Greek text in March 1516. Erasmus' text became the *textus receptus* (Latin, "received text") of the New Testament. It served as a basic guide for the translators of the King James Version.

Two hundred years later, scholars began to replace Erasmus' text with printed texts based on earlier Greek manuscripts, which they assumed to be better than the *textus receptus*. In 1831, Charles Lachmann published such a text. Scholars call Lachmann's work the first *critical text* of the New Testament. It was called a critical text because he set aside the *textus receptus* and constructed a text from what he thought were the most ancient witnesses. *Critical* comes from a Greek word meaning "judge."

Later, Constantine von Tischendorf zealously collected ancient manuscripts and issued several editions of the Greek text, with notations of variant readings in the margins. Also, from 1856 to 1879, Samuel Prideaux Tregelles tried to develop an "improved" text, seeking the best reading at each point where selected manuscripts diverged. Tregelles sought to evaluate the Greek manuscripts by the age of the various readings, not the age of the manuscripts themselves.

Two of the great names in the history of textual studies were Brooke Foss Westcott (1825–1901) and Fenton John Anthony Hort (1828–1892). They also classified the Greek texts according to the age of the various readings, and they concluded that there were four basic text types: Syrian, Western, Alexandrian, and "Neutral." In 1881, after 30 years' work, they published their own Greek text of the New Testament, entitled *The New Testament in the Original Greek*. It soon replaced Erasmus' text as the *textus receptus* of the New Testament. But, it began to appear that some classic translations, such as the King James Version, had been made from Erasmus' *textus receptus*.

Textual study has made some notable advances since the days of Westcott and Hort. Now scholars agree that "the early textual history of the Greek New Testament was more complicated than [Westcott and Hort] supposed. These two Anglican scholars assumed that the earliest text would be the purest, with the least difficulties and the simplest readings; but this does not now appear to be the case. Also, Westcott and Hort knew nothing at all about papyri or their readings. Therefore, they were unsuccessful in tracing the text back beyond the second century by the aid of text types."[12] Nevertheless, scholars still basically follow the Westcott and Hort principles and conclusions. But many scholars now believe that the "internal evidence" (content) should carry more weight than the text types in determining which readings are the most reliable.

The Christian can approach his Greek New Testament today with great confidence. Not one word in a thousand is seriously uncertain, and no established doctrine is called in question by any of the continuing doubts about the correct reading in this or that text.

III. English Translations of the Bible. Entire books have been written on the history of English translations of the Bible, but here we will review the translations very briefly. We will also attempt to evaluate the usefulness of each.

---

[12] J. Harold Greenlee, *Introduction to New Testament Textual Criticism* (Grand Rapids, Mich.: William B. Eerdmans Publishing Company, 1964), p. 79.

TEXT AND TRANSLATIONS

WILLIAM TYNDALE (1484–1536). *Though a member of a Catholic order, William Tyndale stirred considerable opposition to the repressive church policies of his day. He decided to translate the Scriptures into English, going to Germany to begin the work in 1524. Catholic authorities tried to stop Tyndale's research, so he had to labor in secret. He published part of the New Testament in 1525 and the rest at Worms in 1526. In 1530 he issued his translation of the Pentateuch. With the permission of King Henry VIII, English religious authorities sent agents to arrest Tyndale; he was strangled and his body burned at the stake. His last words were, "Lord, open the King of England's eyes."*

A. Psalters and Other Early Translations.

Bishop Aldhelm of Sherborne (d. A.D. 709) translated the Psalms into Anglo-Saxon, an early form of the English language. Very early, English bards put the Psalms into regular poetic form, which made them easy to remember. And so the Psalms became the most popular portion of Scripture in the English tongue. Peasants sang them in the fields and parents taught them to their children. We have manuscripts of the Psalms in Anglo-Saxon dialects dating back to the tenth century.

A tenth-century priest named Aldred wrote an English translation of the Gospels between the lines of a Latin text he was copying. This manuscript is our earliest evidence of an English translation of the New Testament. Around A.D. 1000, Alfric of Bath produced an English translation of the Gospels.

John Wycliffe published the first complete Bible in English in 1382. Wycliffe used primarily the Latin Vulgate, and his translation was weak in some respects. But the common people of England gladly received the book, and Wycliffe organized a group of ministers known as the Lollards (because they used the "lollardy," or common, speech) to travel throughout the country, preaching from his translation. The official Roman Catholic Church condemned Wycliffe's work and burned many of the handwritten copies. Nevertheless, about one hundred and fifty copies of Wycliffe's Version have survived, but only one is complete.

Another Englishman, William Tyndale, began printing the next important English translation of the New Testament at Cologne, Germany, in 1525. Because Tyndale was a close friend of Martin Luther, Roman authorities attempted to halt the project. Yet Tyndale succeeded in finishing the book and smuggled his printed New Testaments into England. In 1535, after he had completed translations of the Pentateuch and Jonah, British agents captured him in Belgium, strangled him, and burned him at the stake.

Also in 1535, an Englishman named Miles Coverdale published an English translation of the whole Bible in the city of Zurich. This edition had the support of King Henry VIII, because Coverdale translated many passages in a way that supported Anglican Catholic doctrine and undermined the use of the Latin Vulgate.

Coverdale then began work on another English Bible that would incorporate the best of Tyndale and other English translators, as well as new insights from the Greek and Hebrew manuscripts. He prepared huge 23 cm x 38 cm (9 in. x 15 in.) pages for this volume, earning it the name of the "Great Bible." He completed it in 1539, and the British government ordered the clergy to display the book prominently in churches throughout the land. This stirred popular interest in the Scriptures.

In 1553, Mary Tudor came to the throne of England and enforced strict Catholic policies upon the people. She banned the use of all English Bibles, in favor of the Latin versions. Coverdale and many other Bible translators fled to the city of Geneva, Switzerland, where John Calvin had established a Protestant stronghold. William Whittingham of Geneva organized several of these scholars to begin work on a new English Bible, which they published in 1560. It was the first Bible to divide the Scriptures into verses. (This was the work

KING JAMES VERSION (FIRST EDITION). *Robert Barker, the official printer of King James I, completed this first edition of the King James Version early in 1611. Its pages measure 22.5 x 35.7 cm. (8.9 x 14.5 in.) with double columns of type. Notice the sparse marginal notes. Scholars call this a "He" Bible because it renders Ruth 3:15 as ". . . He went into the city" instead of ". . . She went into the city." Different copies of the KJV published between 1611 and 1614 contain either* he *or* she, *which indicates that two presses were producing the Bible. Later editions accepted* she *as the proper wording.*

of Robert Estienne, a Parisian printer of Greek New Testaments.) Booksellers called this book the Geneva Bible or the "Breeches Bible," because of the peculiar way it translated Genesis 3:7: "They sewed fig leaves together and made themselves breeches."

Whittingham and his colleagues dedicated this translation to Queen Elizabeth I, who had

THREE VERSIONS COMPARED

	Coverdale (1535)	Geneva Bible (1560)	King James Version (1611)
Job 14:1	Man that is born of a . woman hath but a short time to live and is full of diverse miseries	Man that is born of a woman is for short continuance and full of trouble.	Man that is born of a woman is of few days, and full of trouble.
Psalm 46:1	In our trouble and adversity, we have found that God is our refuge, our strength and help.	God is our hope and strength and help in troubles, ready to be found.	God is our refuge and strength, a very present help in trouble.

Figure 19

taken the throne of England in 1558. The people of England used the Geneva Bible very widely for the next two generations.

B. The King James Version. In 1604, James VI of Scotland became King James I of England and began a program of peacemaking between the hostile religious factions of Great Britain. That same year he convened a meeting of religious leaders at Hampton Court. Dr. John Reynolds, the Puritan spokesman, proposed that a new English translation of the Bible be issued in honor of the new king. The King James Version was to become an important watershed in the history of English Bible translations.

King James appointed 54 scholars to the task of making a new translation. For the Old Testament, they relied primarily upon ben Hayyim's edition of the ben Asher text; for the New Testament, they relied upon the Greek text of Erasmus and a bilingual Greek-and-Latin text of the sixth century, found by Theodore Beza. The translators followed chapter divisions made by Archbishop Stephen Langton in 1551 and the verse divisions of Robert Estienne.

Because King James had authorized this project, the new Bible became known as the "Authorized Version." It was first published in 1611 and revised in 1615, 1629, 1638, and 1762.

We should especially note an edition of the KJV published by Bishop William Lloyd in 1701, because it was the first Bible to contain marginal notes dating biblical events in relation to the birth of Christ (B.C. and A.D.). Lloyd's edition also contained the chronology laid out by Archbishop James Ussher (1581–1656), which dated the Creation at 4004 B.C. This chronology was first used in an Oxford edition of the KJV published in 1679.[13] Many subsequent editions of the KJV have reprinted this chronology.

The 1762 revision is what most people now know as the King James Version. Current biblical knowledge invites both revision of the KJV, and new translations based on a re-edited majority text.

C. Revisions of the King James Version. Among the many attempts to revise the KJV, we should note the English Revised Version (ERV or RV) and the American Standard Ver-

sion (ASV). Both of these attempted to maintain the dignity of language that had become a hallmark of the KJV, while drawing upon the new insights provided by recent manuscript discoveries and improved knowledge of Hebrew words and grammar. They also sought to exclude obsolete words and usages left over from the Tudor speech of the King James Version.

1. English Revised Version. Bishop Harold Browne and Bishop C. J. Ellicott—both respected Anglican leaders—headed two committees that attempted to revise the KJV in the 1870s; an American committee joined them in 1872. These groups produced a Revised Version of the New Testament in 1881, which the public greeted enthusiastically in Great Britain and the United States. The committees issued the Revised Version of the entire Bible in 1885. By that time, the Revised Version had a reputation of being oriented toward British spelling and figures of speech, so the ERV lost popular support in the United States.

2. American Standard Version. Some members of the American committee for the ERV banded together to produce their own revision of the King James. Headed by J. Henry Thayer, this new committee substituted American expressions for British and reverted to the King James rendering of many words. The committee also made parallel passages read the same when the Greek text was identical; the KJV had not been consistent in doing this. The ASV committee aimed at a word-for-word translation of the Greek and Hebrew wherever possible, and in some cases this made the ASV rather awkward to read. The complete ASV Bible was published in 1901.

3. New King James Version. In 1979, Thomas Nelson Publishers issued a new edition of the KJV New Testament. This edition was based on the 1894 edition of the *Textus Receptus*. While it preserved the integrity of the text, it eliminated many archaic expressions that made the old KJV difficult to read.

The publisher assembled 119 scholars to work on this new publication. Dr. Arthur Farstad coordinated the work on the New Testament section. "We chose to follow the same theory of manuscript selection as was employed by the 1611 translators," Dr. Farstad said.

In 1982, Thomas Nelson published the complete NKJV Bible, which quickly gained wide acceptance.

---

[13] A. S. Herbert, *Historical Catalogue of Printed Editions of the English Bible* (London: British and Foreign Bible Society, 1968), pp. 217, 233–234.

TEXT AND TRANSLATIONS

D. New Translations. Besides revising the KJV, modern scholars have produced several totally new translations of the Bible.

1. Revised Standard Version. In 1929, the International Council of Religious Education (an agency of the World Council of Churches) began work on a revision of the ASV. After several false starts, the committee resolved on an entirely new translation, based in the New Testament on the latest scholarly Greek texts. The committee finally settled for an *eclectic* or reading-by-reading type of text that differed at many points from Westcott and Hort. The New Testament section of this Revised Standard Version was published in 1946, and the Old Testament in 1952.

The RSV met a mixed response. Many major denominations welcomed it as a more readable translation and a more reliable rendering of the ancient texts. It was one of the most consistent translations ever made into English. However, it brought on itself a storm of criticism for two features: (1) It altered the wording of many classic passages. (2) It chose new readings for a number of passages with far-reaching theological implications.

2. New English Bible. In October 1946, representatives of the major Protestant churches in Great Britain met at Westminster Abbey to commission a new translation that would be better suited to British readers. The New Testament portion of this New English Bible was released in 1961, exactly 350 years after the publication of the KJV. The complete NEB was released in 1970, listing C. H. Dodd as director of the project.

Donald Ebor, at that time Archbishop of York, Chairman of the Joint Committee for the NEB, stated that the NEB translators were "free to employ a contemporary idiom rather than reproduce the traditional 'biblical' English."[14] Nevertheless, the NEB reflects many British characteristics that have made it less desirable in the United States.

The NEB translators used Kittel's *Biblia Hebraica* (with a number of speculative and perhaps needless amendments) and an eclectic New Testament text by R.V.G. Tasker, published in 1964. They produced an entirely new translation, without trying to imitate the KJV or other earlier versions.

E. Recent Revisions and Paraphrases. We cannot discuss all of the revised editions and paraphrases of the Bible published in recent years. But we should note how several of these recent editions have attempted to present the biblical text.

1. New American Standard Bible. In the New American Standard Bible, evangelical scholars have attempted to update and clarify the ASV. The NASB's New Testament translators mainly used Nestle's improved text, based on Westcott and Hort; but they also referred to some of the papyrus manuscripts and recent studies of the New Testament text. Generally, the Old Testament committee used Kittel's Hebrew text; they noted in the margin any alternative translations from other manuscripts and versions, particularly the Septuagint.

The NASB translators made it their policy to *transliterate* (write in English letters) most of the Hebrew and Greek names. They capitalized personal pronouns that referred to deity and used "Thou" and "Thee" whenever a biblical speaker addressed God. When a literal translation would confuse the reader, the NASB gave the *meaning* of the text and put the literal reading in the margin. The marginal notes seem to follow the highly regarded Hebrew text of the Jewish Publication Society, known to scholars as the JPS. The complete NASB appeared in 1971, and was well received by Christian readers from different backgrounds.

2. New American Bible. A committee of prominent Roman Catholic scholars was gathered in 1944 and worked for many years to produce a new translation. They first established an Old and New Testament text of their own and then produced an English translation of it. The text chosen for translation varies slightly in character with each section of the Bible. But a textual guide and a complete introduction have been published to inform the reader what judgments were made. The entire NAB was published in 1970 and a complete concordance of it in 1978. At some points, the NAB contains readings based upon the tradition of Catholic biblical interpretation, which differs widely from the Protestant tradition. But the version is vigorous in style and reflects weighty scholarship.

3. New International Version. This version attempts to give the meaning of the Bible text more effectively than the ASV or the other contemporary versions. It was begun in 1965 by a number of scholars representing a

---

[14] Donald Ebor, "Preface to the New English Bible," *The New English Bible: Oxford Study Edition* (New York: Oxford University Press, 1976), p. ix.

TEXT AND TRANSLATIONS

group of evangelical denominations. The group worked for a decade under the direction of the New York Bible Society. The translation had two basic characteristics: (1) It was to be an ecumenical effort, which would first establish a critical text. The most recent edition of Kittel's *Biblia Hebraica* was used for the Old Testament, but major differences in the Septuagint were noted. The Greek text of the New Testament was adopted from a number of sources. (2) A principle of translation popularized in the 1960s, known as *dynamic equivalence,* was used in translating a number of passages. This principle calls for using a word or phrase that makes the impact that the original had on its first readers, rather than using a simple grammatical or lexical equivalent (which in our changed culture might not convey any meaning at all).

The New Testament of the NIV was published in 1973 and the Old Testament in 1978. The NIV's English style is quite contemporary and similar to that of the RSV.

The NIV has many helpful features. It seeks to communicate the meaning of the original text in modern English. On the whole, it reads smoothly and is easy for the average reader to understand. The NIV places quotation marks around direct quotes and brackets around words that the translators have supplied to aid the English reader.

4. Goodspeed's Paraphrase. In 1923, Edgar J. Goodspeed (1871–1962) issued his English-language version of the New Testament, entitled *An American Translation.* Goodspeed was trying to translate the Greek text of Westcott and Hort into the "simple, straightforward English of the daily expression." To avoid confusing the reader with the structure of Greek sentences, he had to paraphrase much of the text. This book enjoyed good success in the United States, and in 1931 it was combined with a similar translation of the Old Testament by J. M. Powis Smith and others.

5. J. B. Phillips' Paraphrase. J. B. Phillips' *New Testament in Modern English* appeared in 1957, bringing together a series of paraphrased New Testament books that Phillips began in 1947 with his *Letters to Young Churches.* Phillips rendered the text very freely, often departing entirely from the Greek manuscripts. His paraphrase attracted considerable attention because of its vivid (and sometimes earthy) language. But serious Bible students do not use it as their basic ver-

sion because it takes such liberties with the New Testament text.

6. Today's English Version (Good News Bible). This rendering (New Testament—1966; Old Testament—1976) was sponsored by the American Bible Society. The main TEV writer, Robert G. Bratcher (1920–   ), used a new critical text of the Greek New Testament that the Bible Society prepared for this project. Bratcher saw his work as one of translation rather than paraphrase, but he used the dynamic equivalence method more liberally than the earlier translations did. This placed the TEV in a class apart. It departs radically from the precise lexical meaning of the Hebrew and Greek at many points.

7. Living Bible. Kenneth Taylor (1917–   ), an editor at a Chicago publishing house, began writing this version, an avowed paraphrase, in an effort to make the Bible more understandable to his children. His colleagues found it very helpful, and Taylor founded his own publishing company—Tyndale House—in order to produce a paraphrase of the entire Bible. He published the New Testament section in 1956 and the Old Testament in 1972.

The Living Bible is marked by great clarity and simplicity, and thousands of readers find that they can understand the LB more easily than the KJV or other translations. But Bible scholars and religious leaders have criticized the LB for its free handling of many passages.

IV. Standards for Evaluation. The modern Christian finds himself in a situation that is both bewildering and exciting, because he has so many English translations and paraphrases available. John H. Skilton (1906–   ) lists 107 English translations that have appeared from 1881 to 1973 (*See* pp. 80–84.) More have been prepared.

Often, however, Christian readers are not sure how to weigh the different translations and paraphrases against each other. Here we will suggest some simple guidelines for evaluating the various English-language editions.

In general, there are three things to check in a Bible translation: (1) its attitude toward the original text, (2) its way of rendering that text, and (3) whether or not it communicates clearly to the modern reader.

People who have no knowledge of Greek or Hebrew can pass judgment only on the last point—whether the translation communicates clearly to them. But they can learn a great deal

English Versions

English readers have had access to many versions of the Bible in the past four centuries. This list gives the date, title, and translator of over 200 English versions of Scripture. It is based upon more extensive lists by John H. Skilton and A. S. Herbert.* Where the translator's name is unknown, or where a group of translators contributed to a particular work, the version is identified by the publisher's name (shown in parentheses):

1526 (The New Testament: untitled) WILLIAM TYNDALE	**1549** The first tome or volume of the Paraphrase of Erasmus vpon The newe Testament (Edward Whitchurch)	**1731** The New Testament . . . Translated out of the Latin Vulgat by John Wiclif. . . about 1378. JOHN LEWIS
1530 The Psalter of David in Englishe GEORGE JOYE	**1557** The Nevve Testament of ovr Lord Jesus Christ WILLIAM WHITINGHAM	**1741** A new version of St. Matthew's Gospel DANIEL SCOTT
(The Pentateuch: untitled) WILLIAM TYNDALE	**1560** The Bible and Holy Scriptvres conteyned in the Olde and Newe Testament (The Geneva Bible) WILLIAM WHITTINGHAM	**1745** Mr. Whiston's Primitive New Testament WILLIAM WHISTON
1531(?) The Prophete Jonas WILLIAM TYNDALE		**1761** Divers parts of the holy Scriptures MR. MORTIMER
1534 Jeremy the Prophete, Translated into Englisshe GEORGE JOYE	**1562** The Whole Booke of Psalmes THOMAS STARNHOLD and I. HOPKINS	**1764** All the books of The Old and New Testament ANTHONY PURVER
The New Testament GEORGE JOYE	**1568** The holie Bible. (The Bishops' Bible) MATTHEW PARKER	The New Testament RICHARD WYNNE
1535 Biblia: The Byble MILES COVERDALE		**1765** The Psalms of David CHRISTOPHER SMART
1536 The Newe Testament yet once agayne corrected WILLIAM TYNDALE	**1582** The Nevv Testament of Iesvs Christ (Rheims New Testament) GREGORY MARTIN	The New Testament PHILIP DODDRIDGE
1537(?) (The New Testament) MILES COVERDALE	**1592** Apocalypsis THOMAS BARBAR	**1768** A Liberal Translation of the New Testament EDWARD HARWOOD
1537 The Byble (Richard Grafton and Edward Whitchurch)	**1610** The Holie Bible (Douay Old Testament) GREGORY MARTIN	**1770** The New Testament or New Covenant JOHN WORSLEY
1539 The Most Sacred Bible (Taverner's Bible) RICHARD TAVERNER	**1611** The Holy Bible (The King James Version) (ROBERT BARKER)	**1771** The Book of Job THOMAS SCOTT
The Byble in Englyshe (The Great Bible) (Richard Grafton and Edward Whitchurch)	**1612** The Book of Psalmes HENRY AINSWORTH	**1773** The Pentateuch of Moses and the Historical Books of the Old Testament JULIUS BATE
The newe Testament of oure Sauyour Jesu Christ MILES COVERDALE	**1657** The Dutch Annotations upon the whole Bible THEODORE HAAK	**1779** Isaiah ROBERT LOWTH
The Nevv Testament in Englysshe RICHARD TAVERNER	**1700** The Psalmes of David C. CARYLL	Essay towards a literal English version of the New Testament, in the Epistle of the Apostle Paul directed to the Ephesians. JOHN CALLANDER
The new Testament in Englyshe (Richard Grafton and Edward Whitchurch)	**1726** A new version of all the Books of the New Testament (J. Batly and S. Chandler)	**1782** The Gospel of St. Matthew GILBERT WAKEFIELD
1540 The Byble in Englyshe MILES COVERDALE	**1727** The books of Job, Psalms, proverbs, Ecclseastes, and the Song of Solomon (J. Walthoe)	**1784** Jeremiah and Lamentations BENJAMIN BLAYNEY
1548(?) Certayne Psalmes chose out of the Psalter THOMAS STARNHOLD		

* John Skilton, *The New Testament Student at Work* (Nutley, N.J.: Presbyterian and Reformed, 1975). A. S. Herbert, *Historical Catalogue of Printed Editions of the English Bible, 1525–1961* (London: British and Foreign Bible Society, 1968).

TEXT AND TRANSLATIONS

1787 The First (-Fifth) Book of
Moses
DAVID LEVI

The Apostle Paul's First
and Second Epistles to the
Thessalonians
JAMES MACKNIGHT

1789 A new English Translation
of the Pentateuch
ISAAC DELGADO

The Four gospels
GEORGE CAMPBELL

1790 The Book of Psalms
STEPHEN STREET

1791 The New Testament
GILBERT WAKEFIELD

1795 The New Testament
THOMAS HAWEIS

1796 Jonah
GEORGE BENJOIN

An Attempt toward revising
our English translation of
the Greek Scriptures
WILLIAM NEWCOME

1797 The Holy Bible
ALEXANDER GEDDES

1799 A Revised Translation and
Interpretation of the Sacred
Scriptures
DAVID MACRAE

1805 The Book of Job
JOSEPH STOCK

1807 The Gothic Gospel of Saint
Matthew
SAMUEL HENSHALL

1808 The Holy Bible
CHARLES THOMSON

1810 The Book of Job
ELIZABETH SMITH

1811 Canticles: or Song of
Solomon
JOHN FRY

1812 The Book of Job
JOHN MASON GOOD

The New Testament
W. WILLIAMS

1816 The English Version of the
Polyglott Bible
(Samuel Bagster)

1819 Lyra Davidis (Psalms)
JOHN FRY

1822 The Epistles of Paul the
Apostle
THOMAS BELSHAM

1825 The Book of Job
GEORGE HUNT

The Psalms
J. PARKHURST

1827 An Amended Version of the
Book of Job
GEORGE R. NOYES

Liber Ecclesiasticus, the
Book of the Church
LUKE HOWARD

1828 The Gospel of God's
Anointed
ALEXANDER GREAVES

1831 The Book of Psalms
GEORGE R. NOYES

1833 A literal translation from the
Hebrew of the twelve Minor
Prophets
A. PICK

A New and Corrected Ver-
sion of the New Testament
RODOLPHUS
DICKINSON

1834 The Gospel according to
Matthew
WILLIAM J. AISLABIE

1835 The Book of the Law from
the Holy Bible
[The Pentateuch]
JOSEPH ABLETT

1837 A New Translation of the
Hebrew Prophets
GEORGE R. NOYES

The Gospel of John
WILLIAM J. AISLABIE

1843 The Gospel according to
Saint Matthew, and part of
the first chapter of the Gospel according to Saint Mark
SIR JOHN CHEKE

Horae aramaicae: compris-
ing concise notices of the
Aramean dialects in gen-
eral and of the versions of
the Holy Scripture extant in
them: with a translation of
Matthew
J. W. ETHERIDGE

1846 The book of Psalms
JOHN JEBB

A New Translation of the
Proverbs, Ecclesiastes and
the Canticles
GEORGE R. NOYES

The Four Gospels from the
Peschito
J. W. ETHERIDGE

1848 The New Testament
JONATHAN MORGAN

St. Paul's Epistle to the
Romans
HERMAN HEINFETTER

1849 The Apostolic Acts and
Epistles
J. W. ETHERIDGE

1850 The Bible Revised
FRANCIS BARHAM

1851 The New Testament
JAMES MURDOCK

The Epistle of Paul to the
Romans
JOSEPH TURNBULL

The Epistles of Paul the
Apostle to the Hebrews
HERMAN HEINFETTER

1854 The Epistles of Paul the
Apostle
JOSEPH TURNBULL

1855 The Book of Genesis
HENRY E. J. HOWARD

A Translation of the
Gospels
ANDREWS NORTON

1857 The Books of Exodus and
Leviticus
HENRY E. J. HOWARD

1858 The New Testament
LEICESTER A. SAWYER

1859 A Revised Translation of
the New Testament
W. G. COOKESLEY

1860 The Psalms
LORD CONGLETON

1861 Jewish School and Family
Bible
A. BENISCH

1861(?) The New Testament . . .
As Revised and Corrected
by the Spirits
LEONARD THORN

1862 The New Testament
H. HIGHTON

1863 The Holy Bible
ROBERT YOUNG

The Psalms
W. KAY

The Book of Daniel
JOHN BELLAMY

1864 The Book of Job
J. M. RODWELL

The Emphatic Diaglott
BENJAMIN WILSON

1867 The Minor Prophets
JOHN BELLAMY

1869 The Book of Job in metre
WILLIAM MEIKLE

The Book of Psalms
CHARLES CARTER

1870 The New Testament
JOHN BOWES

1871	The Book of Job FRANCIS BARHAM	**1900**	St. Paul's Epistle to the Romans W. G. RUTHERFORD	**1923**	The New Testament. An American Translation EDGAR J. GOOD- SPEED
	The Book of Psalms FRANCIS BARHAM AND EDWARD HARE	**1901**	The Holy Bible: American Standard Version (Thomas Nelson and Sons)		The Riverside New Testa- ment WILLIAM G. BALLAN- TINE
	St. John's Epistles FRANCIS BARHAM		The Five Books of Moses FERRAR FENTON	**1924**	The Old Testament JAMES MOFFATT
1871(?)	The Gospels, Acts, Epis- tles, and Book of Revela- tion JOHN DARBY		The Historical New Testa- ment JAMES MOFFATT		Centenary Translation of the New Testament HELEN B. MONT- GOMERY
1876	The Holy Bible JULIA E. SMITH	**1902(?)**	The Bible in Modern En- glish FERRAR FENTON	**1925**	Hebrews F. H. WALES
1877	The New Testament JOHN RICHTER	**1903**	The Book of Psalms KAUFMAN KOHLER	**1927**	The Old Testament J.M. POWIS SMITH, T.J. MEEK,
	Revised English Bible (Eyre and Spottiswoode)		The New Testament in Modern Speech RICHARD WEYMOUTH		ALEXANDER R. GORDON, LEROY WATERMAN
1881	The New Testament: En- glish Revised Version (Kambridgel University Press)		The Revelation HENRY FORSTER		St. Matthew's Gospel (T. and T. Clark)
1882(?)	St. Paul's Epistle to the Romans FERRAR FENTON	**1904**	The New Testament ADOLPHUS S. WORRELL	**1928**	The Psalms Complete WILLIAM W. MARTIN
1884	The Psalter . . . and cer- tain Canticles RICHARD ROLLE	**1906**	St. John's Gospel, Epis- tles, and Revelation HENRY FORSTER		The Christian's Bible: New Testament GEORGE LeFEVRE
	The Book of Psalms T. K. CHEYNE	**1908**	Thessalonians and Corinthians W. G. RUTHERFORD	**1933**	The Four Gospels accord- ing to the Eastern Version GEORGE M. LAMSA
	St. Paul's Epistles in Mod- ern English FERRAR FENTON	**1912**	The Book of Ruth R.H.J. STEUART		The Four Gospels CHARLES C. TORREY
1885	The Old Testament Scrip- tures HELEN SPURRELL	**1913**	The New Testament JAMES MOFFATT	**1936**	The Song of Songs W.O.E. OESTERLEY
	The Holy Bible: Revised Version (Oxford University Press)	**1914**	The Poem of Job EDWARD G. KING	**1937**	The Psalms and the Canti- cles of the Divine Office GEORGE O'NEILL
1894	A Translation of the Four Gospels from the Syriac of the Sinaitic Palimpsest AGNES S. LEWIS	**1916**	The Wisdom of Ben-Sira (Ecclesiasticus) W.O.E. OESTERLEY		The New Testament JOHANNES GREBER
1897	The New Dispensation: The New Testament ROBERT WEEKES	**1917**	The Holy Scriptures ac- cording to the Masoretic text (The Jewish Publication Society of America)		The New Testament CHARLES B. WILLIAMS
1898	The Book of Job FERRAR FENTON				St. Paul from the Trenches GERALD CORNISH
	The Twentieth Century New Testament (W. and J. Mackay and Co.)	**1918**	The New Testament (The Shorter Bible) CHARLES FOSTER KENT	**1938**	Job GEORGE O'NEILL
					The New Testament EDGAR L. CLEMENTSON
	The Four Gospels SEYMOUR SPENCER	**1920(?)**	Amos THEODORE H. ROBIN- SON	**1939**	Ecclesiasticus A. D. POWER
1899	The Old and New Testa- ments (J. Clarke and Co.)	**1921**	The Old Testament (The Shorter Bible) CHARLES FOSTER KENT	**1944**	The New Testament RONALD A. KNOX
			Mark's Account of Jesus T. W. PYM	**1945**	The Berkeley Version of the New Testament GERRIT VERKUYL

TEXT AND TRANSLATIONS

1946	The Psalms . . . Also the Canticles of the Roman Breviary (Benziger Bros.)

1946 The Psalms . . . Also the Canticles of the Roman Breviary
(Benziger Bros.)

The New Testament (Revised Standard Version)
(Thomas Nelson and sons)

1947 The Psalms
RONALD A. KNOX

The New Testament
GEORGE SWANN

Letters to Young Churches: Epistles of the New Testament
J. B. PHILLIPS

1949 The Old Testament
RONALD A. KNOX

1950 The New Testament of Our Messiah and Saviour Yahshua
A. B. TRAINA

New World Translation: New Testament
(Watchtower Bible and Tract Society, Inc.)

1951 The New Testament
(Brotherhood Authentic Bible Society)

1952 The Four Gospels
E.V. RIEU

The Holy Bible: Revised Standard Version
(Thomas Nelson and Sons)

1954 The New Testament
JAMES A. KLEIST and JOSEPH LILLY

The Amplified Bible: Gospel of John
THE LOCKMAN FOUNDATION

1955 The Authentic New Testament
HUGH J. SCHONFIELD

1956 The Inspired Letters in Clearest English
FRANK C. LAUBACH

1957 The Holy Bible from Ancient Eastern Manuscripts
GEORGE M. LAMSA

1958 The New Testament in Modern English
J. B. PHILLIPS

The Amplified Bible: New Testament
THE LOCKMAN FOUNDATION

1959 The Holy Bible: The Berkeley Version in Modern English
(Zondervan Publishing Co.)

1960 The Holy Bible (New American Standard)
(Thomas Nelson and Sons)

The New World Translation: Old Testament
(Watchtower Bible and Tract Society, Inc.)

1961 The New English Bible: New Testament
(Oxford University Press and Cambridge University Press)

1962 The Children's Version of the Holy Bible
J. P. GREEN

Modern King James Version of the Holy Bible
(McGraw-Hill)

Living Letters: The Paraphrased Epistles
KENNETH TAYLOR

The Amplified Bible: Old Testament Part II
THE LOCKMAN FOUNDATION

The New Jewish Version
JEWISH PUBLICATION SOCIETY

1963 The New Testament in the Language of Today
WILLIAM BECK

New American Standard Bible: New Testament
THE LOCKMAN FOUNDATION

1964 The Amplified Bible: Old Testament Part I
THE LOCKMAN FOUNDATION

1966 Good News for Modern Man: The New Testament
(American Bible Society)

The Living Scriptures: A New Translation in the King James Tradition
(American Bible Society)

The Jerusalem Bible

1968 The Cotton Patch Version of Paul's Epistles
CLARENCE JORDAN

The New Testament of Our Master and Saviour
(Missionary Dispensary Bible Research)

1969 The New Testament: A New Translation
WILLIAM BARCLAY

Modern Language New Testament
(Zondervan Publishing Co.)

The Cotton Patch Version of Luke and Acts
CLARENCE JORDAN

1970 New American Bible
(St. Anthony Guild Press)

New English Bible
(Oxford University Press and Cambridge University Press)

The Cotton Patch Version of Matthew and John
CLARENCE JORDAN

1971 Letters From Paul
BOYCE BLACKWELDER

New American Standard Bible
THE LOCKMAN FOUNDATION

King James II Version of the Bible
(Associated Publishers and Authors)

The Living Bible
(Tyndale House)

1972 The New Testament in Modern English, Revised Edition
J. B. PHILLIPS

1973 The New International Version: New Testament
(Zondervan Bible Publishers)

The Translator's New Testament
(The British and Foreign Bible Society)

The Cotton Patch Version of Hebrews and the General Epistles
CLARENCE JORDAN

The Poetic Bible
VEO GRAY

1976 Good News Bible
(American Bible Society)

1977 The Holy Bible in the Language of Today
WILLIAM BECK

1978 The New International Version
(Zondervan Bible Publishers)

1979	The New King James Version: New Testament (Thomas Nelson Publishers)	1989	New Revised Standard Bible (Thomas Nelson Publishers and others)		(American Bible Society and Thomas Nelson Publishers)
1982	The Holy Bible, New King James Version (Thomas Nelson Publishers)		Revised English Bible (Oxford University Press and Cambridge University Press)	1995	Contemporary English Version (American Bible Society and Thomas Nelson Publishers)
1986	The New Jerusalem Bible ( )	1991	Contemporary English Version, New Testament	1996	New Living Bible (Tyndale Publishers)

about the way each version has handled the work of translation by seeing what it does with certain key passages. For example, we shall get some idea of the translators' theological viewpoint by checking these references:

Deity of Christ—John 1:1; Romans 9:5; Titus 2:13

Atonement—Romans 3:25; Hebrews 2:17; 1 John 2:2; 4:10

Justification—Romans 3:25; 5:1

Repentance—Matthew 3:2

Baptism—Matthew 28:19

Eternal Punishment—Matthew 25:46

Church Government—Acts 14:23; 20:17, 28; James 5:14

Inspiration of Scripture—2 Timothy 3:16

A more thorough New Testament checklist of key passages is provided by the proof texts to the Westminster Confession of Faith. [15]

Some of the most difficult Old Testament sections are Genesis 1:1–10; 49; Job 9–11; and Ezekiel 1–10. By comparing how various translations render these sections, a reader will soon discern the theological flavor of each.

Of course, if one does not know Hebrew or Greek, he must depend upon the opinions of reputable Bible scholars concerning the reliability of the translation. He will get a clue to the integrity of a particular version by reading its preface and noting which Hebrew and Greek manuscripts the translators used. Beyond this, he will be wise to note what is said in reviews by trusted Bible scholars.

---

[15] John H. Skilton, *The New Testament Student at Work* (Nutley, N.J.: Presbyterian and Reformed, 1975), p. 227.

ARCHAEOLOGY

The English word *archaeology* comes from two Greek words, *archaios,* meaning "ancient," and *logos,* meaning "word," "matter," "account," or "discourse." *Archaeology* literally means "account (or discourse) of ancient matters," and people occasionally use the word to refer to ancient history in general. Usually, however, the word *archaeology* is applied to the *sources* of history that were unknown until excavations brought them to light.

Archaeologists are students of the past who dig up ancient sites and study what they find in relation to each site. In the Near East archaeologists depend on these historical objects for their knowledge much more than they do when they excavate cities in Italy or Greece because very little literature survives from the ancient Near East. If the archaeologist finds written texts, he turns them over to a specialist in the language or culture, who translates them and compares them with other bits of literature from that time.

I. Biblical Archaeology. Scholars disagree about whether we can speak of "*biblical* archaeology." Some say that archaeology is archaeology—that is, its methods and goals are essentially the same everywhere, whether the Bible is involved or not. They also have valid concerns about the unscientific (occasionally even fraudulent) claims that have been perpetrated in the name of "biblical" archaeology. They believe we should use another term, such as "*Palestinian* archaeology," or speak of "archaeology and the Bible."

Perhaps the term *biblical archaeology* has fallen into disfavor because scientists today are simply not very interested in biblical matters. Scholars with a professional interest in the Bible are not as actively engaged in archaeological work as they once were. Today, professional archaeologists study a broad spectrum of cultural and anthropological interests that may not be immediately relevant for the student of the Bible. The long-standing alliance between biblical studies and archaeology is not as firm as it once was.

The major funding and staffing of archaeological projects in Bible lands has never come from church organizations or institutions. It has come from universities, museums, or other private sources. This trend will probably become even stronger in the future because of inflation, the increasing specialization in archaeology, and archaeology's growing skepticism toward traditional Christianity. Nevertheless, churches and their institutions should seek to be involved to the maximum practical extent.

Does archaeology "prove the Bible true"? Not exactly. It is true that archaeology has enhanced our confidence in the broad outlines of

ARCHAEOLOGY

YIGAEL YADIN. *Archaeologist Yadin, one of the most renowned of the Israeli archaeologists, painstakingly studies an ancient letter from the Judean wilderness. This letter dates from A.D. 135 and was written during the second Jewish revolt.*

the biblical report. Archaeological finds have supported many, many specific statements in the text. Archaeology has often been useful in refuting the attacks of skeptics. But much of the Bible has to do with relatively private, personal matters that archaeology cannot verify. And the farther back we go into history, the less evidence we have.

A. Its Limitations. The "truth" of the Bible is not only a matter of facts, but of their interpretation. Even if we could demonstrate the factuality of the entire Bible, that would not prove its redemptive significance. Because the Christian faith is based on historical events, Christians welcome any evidence that archaeology can provide—but they do not anchor their faith to it. No lack of evidence nor

critical skepticism can disprove God's Word. It is better to emphasize how archaeology helps us *understand* the Bible than to insist that it proves the Bible true. In fact, it cannot do so much, nor is there need that it should.

B. Its Value. Archaeology can provide background information thousands of years after the Bible was written. Although archaeology deals primarily with concrete, material objects, it can help us comprehend the spiritual message of the biblical writers—especially their illustrations and figures of speech. There must be a "dialogue" between the biblical text and archaeological finds, because each can help us understand and interpret the other. The Bible helps us understand the archaeologists' new discoveries, while archaeology

ARCHAEOLOGY

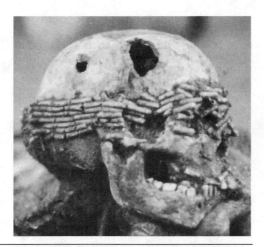

SKULL WITH BEADS. *Objects buried with the dead, such as this beaded headdress, help archaeologists determine the age of the skeletal remains. They also reveal something of the artistic values and skills of the people who made them.*

helps us "read between the lines" of the inspired record.

For example, the historical records of ancient Babylon do not mention Belshazzar, even though the Bible says he succeeded Nebuchadnezzar as king (Dan. 4–5). For a time, some Bible scholars doubted the Bible at this point. But in 1853 archaeologists found an inscription in Ur, which showed that Belshazzar reigned with his father, Nabonidus.

C. Its Reliability. How objective or truly scientific is the archaeological method, and to what extent can its results be trusted? Fortunately, we are past the day when we think that even the "hard" or physical sciences (physics, chemistry, and so on) are absolutely objective. We know that the scientists' attitudes and notions of truth will affect the way they interpret the facts. On the other hand, the degree of personal opinion in the "soft" or social sciences (history, sociology, psychology) is not so great that we should refuse to call them "scientific." Archaeology occupies a middle ground between the "hard" and the "soft" sciences. Archaeologists are more objective when unearthing the facts than when interpreting them. But their human preoccupations will affect the methods they use in making the "dig," too. They cannot help destroying their evidence as they dig down through the layers of earth, so they can never test their "experiment" by repeating it. This makes archaeology unique among the sciences. Moreover, it makes archaeological reporting a most demanding and pitfall-ridden task.

Yet archaeology does overlap with other scientific disciplines, such as history, geography, and cultural anthropology (the study of man's ways of thinking and living). Specialists in biology, anthropology, or geology often join excavation teams in order to analyze seeds, bones, pollen, soil, and the like. The study of comparative religion or the "history of religions" often plays a prominent part in interpreting the finds, because so many finds are cult-related. Geology deals with natural layers or strata of earth, in contrast to the man-made layers that claim the archaeologists' attention; yet archaeologists often consult geologists to learn more about the nature of the sites they are excavating.

D. Its Geography. Which geographical areas attract the interest in biblical archaeology? For the New Testament period, that area largely coincides with the Roman Empire. For Old Testament times the area is somewhat smaller, and the center shifts eastward to in-

GRAVE POTTERY. *Buried for centuries under layers of gravel and dirt, this pottery was found in a grave at Tell el-Far'ah (ancient Tirzah). The articles are shown as they were excavated. Archaeologists must carefully catalog their finds and begin the tedious job of reassembling the shattered objects.*

clude the Mesopotamian valley and Persia (modern Iran).

It is simplest, however, to begin at the hub—Palestine or Israel (Canaan)—and fan out from there. The great empires in the Nile and Mesopotamian valleys are almost as interesting as Palestine itself. The culture of Phoenicia (modern Lebanon) had much in common with that of Canaan to the south. Syria to the east is also of prime concern—its history often intertwined with that of Israel and it was always the major corridor for invaders of Palestine. Still farther north, Asia Minor was the homeland of the Hittites and other important peoples.

II. The Rise of Modern Archaeology. The history of modern Near Eastern archaeology begins at about the same time as did other modern sciences, during the eighteenth century. Before that, there had always been collectors of antiquities (usually museums or rich individuals). The resulting "excavations" were little more than treasure hunts that destroyed most information of value to the scientific archaeologist. Unfortunately, some people still have these attitudes, and every Near Eastern country must wage a difficult battle against diggers who are trying to meet the black-market demand for artifacts.

STRATIFICATION LEVELS AT JERICHO. *This cutaway view of the dig at Jericho shows the area's various levels of stratification. Archaeologists assume that the levels are in chronological order. Therefore they think that pottery and implements found at lower levels are older than those closer to the surface, and they can study these artifacts in the context of their ages.*

Biblical archaeology probably began with the discovery of the Rosetta Stone (named after a nearby village in the Nile Delta) when Napoleon invaded Egypt in August 1799. Written in three columns (Greek, Egyptian hieroglyphics, and a later Egyptian script), the stone was soon deciphered by Jean François Champollion. More relics of the past remained visible above ground in Egypt than anywhere else in the ancient Near East, and Napoleon's discovery of these ancient writings spurred further exploration of that country.

A similar breakthrough was made in Mesopotamia in 1811, when Claude J. Rich found dozens of baked clay tablets at Babylon with *cuneiform* ("wedge-shaped") writing. In 1835, Sir Henry Creswicke Rawlinson deciphered an inscription in three languages (old Persian, Elamite, and Akkadian), which Darius the Great had made on a cliff near Behistun in western Persia. A decade later, Sir Austen Henry Layard and other pioneer archaeologists opened mounds containing the remains of great Assyrian cities such as Nineveh, Ashur, and Calah. In these mounds they discovered more cuneiform tablets. Since they had already learned how to read cuneiform, the tablets allowed them to review the entire history, culture, and religion of ancient Assyria and Babylon. They found many parallels to the history of the Bible.

A. Petrie's Contribution. But scientific archaeology was nearly another half-century in coming to Palestine. In 1890, Sir W. M. Flinders Petrie turned his attention to the mound of Tell-el-Hesi (now considered to be the biblical city of Eglon, although Petrie thought it was Lachish). Petrie was not the first to dig in Palestine, but he was the first to recognize the real significance of *stratigraphy*—the study of the various layers of occupation in a mound, and of the pottery belonging to each *stratum* (Latin, "layer"). But even Petrie's first step was a faltering one. Petrie's method of *sequence dating* simply made "stratigraphical" divisions every foot down into the dig, instead of following the irregular lines of occupation itself.

It is not possible to mention all of the scientists who built upon Petrie's achievements. However, the next major step was taken by W. F. Albright at Tell Beit Mirsim, west of Hebron, in a series of "digs" from 1926 to 1932. (Albright identified the site with biblical Debir or Kirjath-sepher, but this has been seri-

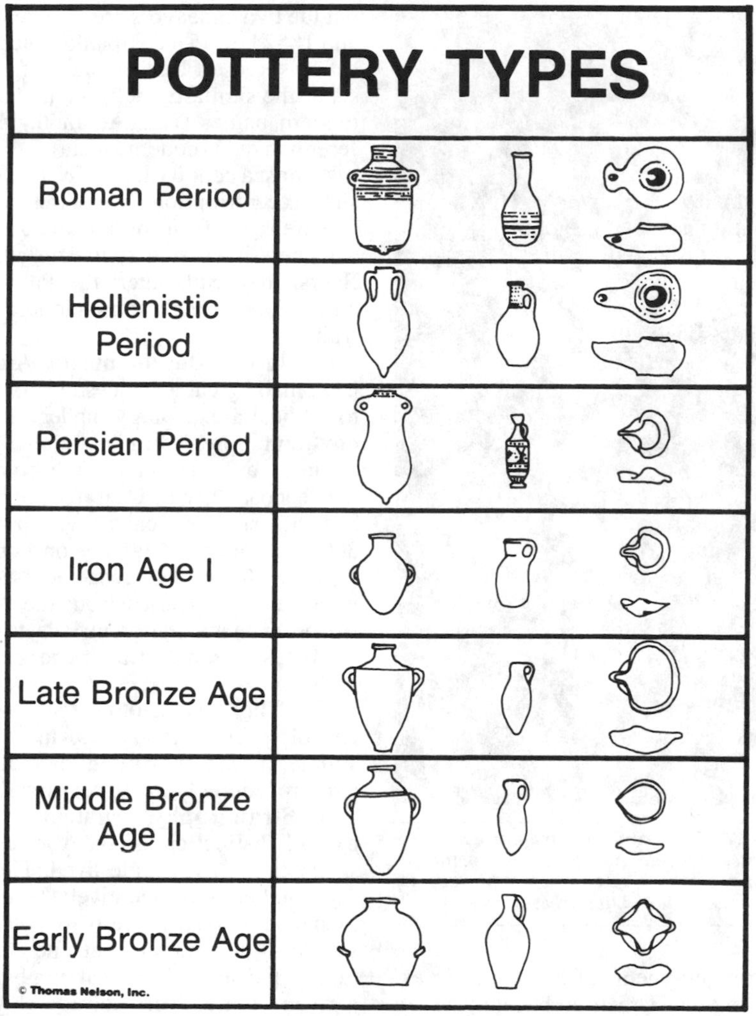

ARCHAEOLOGY

Figure 20

This chart shows several pottery types characteristic of Palestine in Bible times. They are arranged from the most recent (top) to the oldest (bottom), as they would be found in the progressively deeper layers of a tell.

Dr. W. M. Flinders Petrie developed a method for finding the approximate date of artifacts in a tell by observing the depth and physical context of each layer (stratum) of dirt. By using this method, called stratigraphy, archaeologists have learned which type of pottery was common to each period of the ancient past.

The left row shows the development of large two-handled water pots. Women used such pots to carry drinking water from the town well; these pots could also be used to store water, wine, or other liquids. The middle row shows the development of simple clay pitchers, used for household meals. The row on the right shows the evolving design of oil lamps; each section of this row gives a top view and a side view of the lamp.

Notice that the earlier designs (e.g., those of the Bronze Age) tended to be quite simple and functional. Later designs, which show the influence of Persian and Greek art, were more delicate and often had ornamental painting.

ously challenged.) By his meticulous methods, Albright established once and for all the correct sequence of Palestinian pottery. Albright and his successors (especially G. E. Wright) recommended and practiced the most painstaking procedures. Other improvements in excavation technique were made by G. A. Reisner and Clarence S. Fisher at Samaria (1931–1935), and by Kathleen Kenyon at Jericho and elsewhere beginning in 1952. Specialists still debate the best procedures. Different methods must be used simply because of

ARCHAEOLOGY

GLASS VASE. *This small Roman vase is typical of the glassware used in Palestine during the New Testament era. This particular object dates from the time of Herod the Great (37–4 B.C.).*

the varying requirements of the sites. For example, present-day Israeli archaeology is often forced to forgo more desirable procedures in order to beat the bulldozers of new construction.

As noted earlier, modern archaeologists tend to have a much broader concept of their task than is signaled by the term *biblical archaeology.* They want to explore the entire spectrum of human experience in connection with a site's history. This approach is not necessarily at loggerheads with the concept of biblically oriented archaeology. But unfortunately, conflict often results.

B. Robinson and Glueck. Our sketch of the history of Palestinian archaeology would be incomplete without including the name of Edward Robinson. His contributions were more in the area of geography or surface exploration than in archaeological excavation,

but the two endeavors are inseparable. In 1838 and 1852 he and a companion succeeded in locating scores of biblical sites, often on the basis of the similarity between their biblical and modern names (e.g., Anathoth, the home of Jeremiah, and modern Anata).

Almost a century later, Nelson Glueck made similar contributions by his treks over the barren areas of Transjordan, the Jordan Valley, and the Negev (the semi-arid region around Beersheba). Still later, the Palestine Exploration Fund brought those pioneering labors to fruition.

C. Recent Developments. Archaeologists have made great advances in two areas related to biblical archaeology: underwater archaeology and "prehistoric" studies. Underwater methods affect biblical archaeology only at the seacoast city of Caesarea Maritima. "Prehistoric" studies, dealing with periods before 3000 B.C., depend largely on comparing the styles of flint tools. Archaeologists have made important discoveries from the "prehistoric" period at many points in Palestine, and they are focusing more of their energies in that direction.

III. The Archaeologist's Methods. Archaeological methods are, in essence, very simple. In fact, they might be reduced to only two procedures—*stratigraphy* and *typology.*

A. Stratigraphy. Stratigraphy makes a careful distinction of the various levels (or *strata*) at which people lived. These are simply numbered consecutively (usually by Roman numerals) from top to bottom, the top *stratum*—the most recent one—being "Stratum I" and so on. The total number of strata at a given site may vary considerably, as well as the depth of the individual strata. A *tell* (mound of debris of an ancient city) may well reach 15 to 22 m. (50 to 75 ft.) above virgin soil, and in Mesopotamia they frequently exceed that height. Occasionally a mound has been occupied almost continuously for thousands of years; and if it is still occupied, excavation will be very difficult or impossible. At other times, there will be long gaps in the occupational history of the site. One can know this only after thorough excavation, although a study of the *sherds* (broken pieces of pottery) that have washed down the slopes of the mound will give the archaeologist a good advance picture of the civilizations to be uncovered within the tell. Sometimes the various strata will be distinguished by thick layers of ash or other destruction debris; at other times

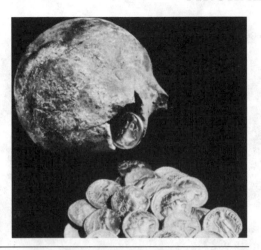

JUG AND COINS FROM SHECHEM. *This small pottery jug filled with 35 silver coins probably was the private bank of some resident of Shechem, a town of Ephraim, in the second century B.C. Because they are easily dated, coins can help archaeologists determine the age of the sites in which they are found.*

wick, the lamp eventually developed a lip on one side to hold the wick, then four lips at right angles to one another. Finally the top was covered over to leave only a spout for the wick. By Byzantine and Christian times, the covered top was crowned with a variety of artistic symbols. Tools, weapons, and architectural styles changed through the centuries, as did the design of pagan idols.

On those rare occasions when writing is found in Palestine, we have another important test for historical dates, and paleography (the study of the history of writing) has become quite a precise science.

Coins did not appear in Palestine until the very end of the Old Testament period (c. 300 B.C.). Since the people sometimes hoarded coins or kept them as heirlooms, this evidence may mislead the archaeologist. The same is true of imported objects, where a time lag of 25 to 50 years will often have to be taken into consideration.

C. Other Techniques for Dating. Pottery typology is the most basic way of dating archaeological sites. All the other methods are supplementary. In recent years, scientists have developed new procedures for dating ancient objects. But none of these threatens to replace the analysis of pottery types. Specialists are able to date pottery to within at least half a century; the margin of error is considerably greater with other procedures, and it generally grows larger the farther back in time we go. Only in a few "dark ages," for which we have no pottery clues, have the newer techniques proved to be worth the time and expense.

Of the newer procedures, the best established and most important is that of *radiocarbon* dating. Carbon isotope 14 is a form of carbon with a half-life of about 5,600 years. It "decays" to form carbon-12, the most common form of carbon. By measuring the proportion of carbon-14 to carbon-12 in an object, scientists can determine the age of the object. Although carbon-14 is supposed to disintegrate at a constant rate, some scientists still question its accuracy and reliability. It can be found only in organic substances (wood, cloth, and so on), which are rare in Palestinian excavations. A sizeable piece of the sample is destroyed in the process of testing, which makes archaeologists reluctant to use this method. Nevertheless, it has been useful, especially in quieting the skepticism of people who are not yet convinced of the archaeologists' ability to date pottery.

only by differences in soil color or compactness. If a mound lay uninhabited for a long time, erosion and robbing of the site may completely disrupt a stratum. Later inhabitants often dig trenches, cisterns, and pits deep into earlier strata, adding to the modern excavator's problems.

B. Pottery Typology. Identifying the strata enables the scientist to determine a relative sequence of layers, not absolute dates. For dates, he must use pottery *typology* (i.e., the study of different forms of pottery). Over the course of time, archaeologists have developed a very detailed knowledge of the characteristic pottery of each period. By relating each stratum to the pottery fragments in it, the archaeologist is usually able to date the stratum within a relatively narrow period of time.

When they were introduced, the scientific community was reluctant to adopt the methods of stratigraphy and typology. At Troy, Heinrich Schliemann concluded in the nineteenth century that tells or mounds concealed the layers of more than one ancient city. This earned him the ridicule of learned circles all over Europe until he proved his point. There was similar initial rejection of pottery typology.

Typologies of other ancient objects are also useful. For example, the development of the lamp helps the archaeologist in identifying broader periods. From a simple saucer with a

TELL OF BETH-SHEAN. *This is an overview of the tell, or mound, of Beth-shean in the valley of Jezreel. Such mounds are centuries-old accumulations of rubble created when new cities are continually built over old cities on the same site.*

Some other techniques are more promising for biblical archaeology. *Thermoluminescence* measures electronic emissions from reheated pottery to determine when it was first fired. *Spectographic analysis* bombards a piece of pottery with electrons in order to measure the chemical spectrum of the minerals within it. Somewhat similarly, in *neutron activation* ceramic material is placed in a nuclear reactor and the chemical composition of the clay is determined from the radioactivity it can give off. The latter two methods are more helpful in determining the source of the clay from which the pottery was manufactured than its date; but often the two investigations go together. (The naked eye of a skilled pottery expert can often detect much about the original source of clay without these scientific helps.)

Scientific techniques may also help in the search for sites. So many ancient tells remain untouched by modern excavation that there has been little demand for these helps. But in the lesser populated areas of Transjordan and the Negev, infrared aerial photography has been able to isolate ancient cities by picking out differences in vegetation. An object gives off heat in the form of infrared rays; the hotter the object is, the more infrared rays it gives off. Thus infrared photographs reveal differences in the temperature of the plants that grow over ancient walls and floors. In Italy,

archaeologists used the *proton magnetometer* (comparable to the Geiger counter) to locate the city of Sybaris.

D. Supervising the Work. In addition to stratigraphy and typology, careful recording and publication of the data is a third major principle of scientific archaeology. Unlike other sciences, archaeology cannot repeat its "experiments" to verify them. So the concern for careful records lies at the heart of a successful "dig."

Initially, archaeologists will plot a site on a "grid system," paralleling the latitude and longitude of the area. They usually divide the mound into "fields." Within each field, they measure certain "areas" and stake them off for excavation. The fields may be of varying sizes depending on the situation, but customarily the areas are 6 m. (19 ft.) square. Archaeologists will further subdivide each area into four squares, leaving dividers ("balks") a meter wide between each quadrant. These balks provide catwalks for observation and inspection while the work is in progress and make points of reference if questions arise later on. Not even an entire quadrant is dug uniformly; the workers will sink "probe trenches" at right angles to other trenches, in an effort to anticipate what they may uncover as they proceed.

Each area has an area supervisor, who in turn is supervised by the director of the exca-

ARCHAEOLOGY

vation. The area supervisor has two tasks: (1) to supervise and direct the actual digging in his area, and (2) to carefully record everything as it appears.

The laborers are basically of three types: (1) *pickmen,* who carefully break up the compacted soil (a very skilled procedure, to be distinguished from ordinary ditch-digging); (2) *hoemen,* who work over the newly loosened soil, watching for anything of significance; and (3) *basketmen,* who carry off the dirt after inspection. Sometimes the basketmen also use sieves, as well as trowels and brushes for scraping and cleaning.

The area supervisor keeps careful notes in a field notebook, a diary of everything that his workers do. He assigns an arbitrary location number to each subdivision of his area, both vertically and horizontally. The workers collect all pottery in special baskets and tag them to indicate the date, area, and location. Then the pottery is washed and "read" by experts, who save and register pieces of special interest. They photograph or sketch anything of special interest before they take it apart. At the end of each day (or before a new phase of the excavation continues), the area supervisor must make scale drawings of both the vertical walls and the floor of his area. At the end of

PORTRAIT HEAD. *A resident of Jericho during the Neolithic Period covered this skull with plaster to give it the lifelike appearance of a human face. Archaeologists believe these skulls belonged to beloved ancestors of Jericho residents or were trophies of their enemies.*

the season, he must write a detailed report of all that happened in his area. The director of the entire excavation pulls all of these reports together into his own preliminary report and then into a detailed publication. However, many a project director has failed to follow through on these final steps, depriving the scholarly world of the fruit of his labors.

IV. Periods of Ancient History. Archaeologists arrange the earliest historical and cultural evidence according to a three-period system, consisting of the Stone, Bronze, and Iron Ages (each with various subdivisions). We inherited this scheme from the early nineteenth century, and it is now antiquated. But it has become so much a part of archaeology that it seems impossible to change it. Archaeologists have attempted to substitute something more satisfactory, but these new systems have had only limited success and often they have introduced more confusion. The most successful of these new proposals have used sociological or political labels, while the traditional scheme is based on the most vital metal of those periods. After the Iron Age (that is, beginning with the Persian Period) political or cultural names

ISRAELI ARCHAEOLOGISTS. *As a team of Israeli archaeologists and students explored several Judean desert caves in 1961, they unearthed a cache of Canaanite artifacts at a site they named the "Cave of Treasure." The cave contained 429 copper artifacts wrapped in a straw mat, which included crown and wands of various designs dating from c. 3000 B.C.*

ARCHAEOLOGY

have always been standard for the archaeological periods.

The dates are approximate, of course, because cultural changes always come gradually. In later periods, where we usually know the history more precisely, some exact dates can be given.

When assigning dates to archaeological finds, the biggest problems occur in the earlier periods. Not until the patriarchal period (generally the Middle Bronze Age, c. 2000 B.C.) do we begin to reach firm ground. And not until a millennium later (at the time of David and Solomon) do we find it easier to determine the dates of Bible events. (*See* "Chronology.") The extremely early dates that some scientists offer for the Paleolithic or Old Stone Age are based more on theories of evolution and geology than archaeology. Such dates clash with the Bible—not only on the surface, but on the level of underlying concepts.

However, it is not easy to say precisely where to draw the line. It is difficult to interpret the chronologies of the Bible itself, and so conservative interpreters sometimes reach different conclusions.

Many believe that the Bible portrays a relatively young earth, in contrast to the millions of years assumed in modern thought. The accompanying table (Fig. 21) suggests 10,000 B.C. as the earliest date we can entertain. Certainly, no precise archaeological evidence *requires* us to go back farther than that.

A. The Stone Age. The earliest archaeological time period—the Stone Age—is divided into the Paleolithic Period, the Mesolithic Period, and several Neolithic Periods.

1. The Paleolithic Period. The Paleolithic or "Old Stone Age" may be described as an age of hunting and food-gathering. People lived in caves or temporary shelters. They made implements of flint or chipped stone, and subsisted from what they could gather from nature itself.

2. The Mesolithic Period. The Mesolithic or "Middle Stone Age" was a transitional stage to a food-producing economy, in which real settlements first appeared; it was a revolution that matured in the Neolithic era. We can say there was an evolution of the arts of civilization during this period, but not an evolution of man or his native capacities.

3. The Neolithic Periods. The invention of pottery around 5000 B.C. ushered in a new era of antiquity, the Neolithic or "New Stone Age."

The most spectacular Palestinian site illustrating these developments is Jericho. In the eighth millennium B.C., Mesolithic hunters built a sanctuary near a spring at Jericho. Gradually they developed their homes from nomadic shelters into mud-brick houses, and began irrigation farming. Four Neolithic Periods are distinguished at Jericho after this: two pre-pottery, and two in which pottery was known. While the first period apparently began in peace, this was certainly not the case with the other three. In fact, the first Neolithic period was characterized by the construction of massive defensive walls—the earliest known in the history of man. After the wall was destroyed, an entirely new culture moved in at Jericho. Pottery was still unknown, but a high degree of artistic ability was evident otherwise. The people of Jericho molded mud around human skulls to make realistic portraits with shells inset for eyes, probably for some kind of ancestor worship.

The next wave of invaders into Palestine was culturally retarded in many respects. But there was one major exception: they knew how to make pottery. After one more wave of settlers, Jericho went into temporary eclipse around 4000 B.C. During the Chalcolithic Period the city of Ghassul on the other side of the Jordan River assumed the power Jericho had known.

B. The Chalcolithic Period. The Chalcolithic (Copper-Stone) Period, covering most of the fourth millennium B.C., saw a transition to a significant use of copper. (Chalcolithic people did not use bronze, an alloy that was not yet known.)

Until this period, Palestine had kept pace with the two great river cultures of Egypt and Mesopotamia. Beginning around 4000 B.C., however, those two legs of the Fertile Crescent began to forge ahead, and Palestine began to assume the geopolitical role it played throughout most of the biblical period. It became a cultural and political backwater, but a strategic bridge for trade and communication for much of the ancient Near East. The two great rivers helped the other regions become more dominant by unifying the vast territory and opening it up to commerce. By the end of this era, these regions had developed patterns they would follow for thousands of years.

1. Ghassulian Culture. In Palestine, as we noted, Jericho appears to have been replaced by Ghassul (we know only this modern Arabic name), to the east of Jericho. The absence of

ARCHAEOLOGY

fortifications indicates that it was a peaceful period. Ghassul was most famous for its sophisticated art, particularly for its multicolored frescoes containing geometric motifs, stars, masks, and other images (probably having religious or mythological significance).

Ghassul flourished during the latter half of the fourth millennium. Since it was the first known Palestinian culture of the period, the era has been given its name, "Ghassulian." Increasingly, however, archaeologists are finding that other cultures were also strong during this period. They are also finding that other Chalcolithic cultures had customs that resembled the practices of Ghassul. For example, archaeologists have documented the Ghassulian custom of burying the dead in *ossuaries* (ceramic receptacles for bones) in many other areas, particularly the coastal cities near modern Tel Aviv. These ossuaries were usually shaped like animals or houses, in imitation of those used in daily life. After the body was cre-

mated, mourners buried the ossuary in a stone cist together with provisions for the afterlife.

Two sites near Beersheba (Tel Abu Matar and Bir es-Safadi) illustrate the use of copper during the Chalcolithic Period. Some of the dwellings at both of these sites were underground, entered by shafts from the surface and connected by tunnels. Copper working was found in the many pits, ovens, and fireplaces in the area, indicating the dominance of copper in the two villages' economy. The ore had to come from mines in the southern Negev, a considerable distance away, which indicates that the villages had a sophisticated social and economic organization.

Probably the most spectacular Chalcolithic site in Palestine is near En-Gedi, the oasis on the western shores of the Dead Sea. High above the spring (where the Israelite city was later excavated) was a walled complex. Inside its largest structure was an open-air temple with an altar. We know nothing of the rites of the shrine, but archaeologists commonly assume that the large collection of copper objects (mace heads, scepters, processional standards) discovered in a cave nearby were used in this temple. Presumably they were hidden in the cave when the temple was threatened, and no one was able to return and save them.

2. Megalithic Culture. The Megalithic remains of Palestine straddle the Chalcolithic and Early Bronze Periods. The term *Megalithic* simply means "large-stoned," referring to the boulders that people employed in these early constructions. In Europe such structures seem to be characteristic of the Neolithic Period, but in the Near East they appear later. However, any pottery or other remains that were originally buried with them have long since disappeared, and only quite recently have their dates been established more firmly.

The Palestinian "megaliths" are usually very simple: one or more horizontal blocks were laid over a few vertical ones averaging a meter (39 in.) or less in height, with a low entrance on one side. These may have been monuments to the dead, designed as imitations of everyday dwellings. More technically, this type of structure is called a *dolmen* (meaning literally, "stone table"). Originally, they were probably covered with small stones and earth, which has been washed away. Occasionally one or two circles of small stones surrounded them. Nearly always they are clustered in "fields" or groups, mostly in northwestern Jordan on the slopes above the east bank of the

BASALT BOWLS. *These basalt bowls, a pestle, and grindstones were discovered at the site of Ghassul, to the east of Jericho. The city flourished during the Chalcolithic Period and was famous for its sophisticated art and advanced culture.*

ARCHAEOLOGIST AT WORK. *Archaeological finds are remarkably fragile, requiring great care and patience for their preservation. Here Dr. Gustav Jeeninga unearths an ancient skeleton at Caesarea Maritima. This entails the painstaking removal of centuries-old deposits, which must be cleaned away without disrupting the site where the remains are found.*

Jordan River, or in upper Galilee, especially around Chorazin.

C. The Bronze Age. Archaeologists have found many artifacts from the Bronze Age— so many that they have been able to discern several distinct cultural periods within the Bronze Age.

1. Early Bronze Age. With the Early Bronze Age and the third millennium B.C., we leave "prehistory" and enter the "historical" period—if we define *history* as the presence of written records. The cultures of the two great river valleys (Nile and Tigris-Euphrates) gained many advantages over Palestine, especially as they developed the art of writing in the latter half of the fourth millennium. The Mesopotamians (proto-Sumerians?) pioneered writing, but Egypt was quick to recognize the benefits of it.

The evolution of writing can be traced in considerable detail, from its origins in business dockets through pictographs (picture-writing) into more abstract symbols. (*See* "Languages and Writing.") Mesopotamia developed *cuneiform* writing—that is, using a stylus to impress wedges into soft clay tablets, which were then baked. Originally the non-Semitic Sumerians devised cuneiform for themselves, but it was soon adopted by their Semitic successors, and even by various Indo-European language groups (that is, the family

of languages scattered from India to Western Europe). It became a virtually universal script until the Aramaic alphabet replaced it under the Persian Empire.

The roots of the modern alphabet are in Egypt. In one sense, the Egyptians did not develop writing beyond the earlier pictographic stage, resulting in the familiar Egyptian *hieroglyphs* (literally "sacred carvings"). Although the Egyptian symbols represented syllables (just like the Mesopotamian ones) they also contained an early alphabetic significance; each symbol stood for a letter instead of a syllable.[1]

Even though the Canaanites could not match the cultures of the great river valleys, the Early Bronze Period was a period of great urbanization here, too. In fact, virtually all of the great Canaanite cities were founded in this period. In Palestine, these cities remained independent, and never coalesced into larger empires. We find essentially the same city-state political system over 1,000 years later at the time of Joshua's invasion. The empire of King David was probably the first to supersede it completely.

Despite tradition, it is not accurate to call this period the Early Bronze Age in Palestine. "Bronze" implies an alloy of copper and tin, which was not widely used until at least a thousand years later. If a metal term were satisfactory at all, "copper" would be much better. Alternative names for the period have never caught on widely. However, two types of suggestions have some merit.

Kathleen Kenyon wanted to call this the Urban Period, because the people tended to build great cities. However, Israeli scholars prefer to call it the Canaanite Period (followed by the Israelite Period and the Persian Period); these labels identify the political power of each period.

The problem of terminology is even more acute for the third millennium B.C. The ques-

---

[1] But the Egyptians never allowed a genuine alphabet to develop; this step was taken in about 1500 B.C. by political prisoners at the turquoise mines at Serabit el-Khadem in central Sinai. From their proto-Sinaitic inscriptions, the idea of an alphabet spread northward to Canaan, where we find evidence of experiments with alphabets shortly afterwards. One of the most famous of these is the writing of Ugarit (Ras Shamra). The scribes of Ugarit used cuneiform symbols alphabetically to express their own Semitic dialect, which closely resembled Hebrew. Other experiments undoubtedly led into the Hebrew alphabet, although we cannot trace its beginnings.

ARCHAEOLOGY

tion is, which terminology will best indicate the continuity as well as the contrast between the periods?

a. Mysterious Invaders. No one denies the abrupt contrast between the Chalcolithic and the Early Bronze Periods. Several tells from this era indicate that the cities that stood on these sites were destroyed between the Chalcolithic and Early Bronze periods. The only evidence about the nature of the people who destroyed these cities is their new burial customs. They practiced communal burials in single chambers, pushing the bones of previous generations against the wall as the newly deceased were "gathered to their fathers."

It seems obvious that the invaders brought a new way of life. They were not nomads who gradually settled down (as we noted many times in Neolithic Jericho). This seems evident from their tendency to prefer the plains instead of the hill country, and brick instead of stone (even in the hill country where stone was so abundant). This pattern of sparse occupation of the hill country continued through the subsequent Middle Bronze Age until well into the Israelite settlement.

Who were these invaders? Without written records we cannot be sure. By calling them "Canaanites," the Israeli archaeologists are suggesting that they were related to the people who lived in Canaan at the time of the Israelite invasion. That may well be true, but not everyone agrees. And how much of these invaders' cultural influence remained after the Amorite and Hurrian invasions of the Middle Bronze eras? The geographical names of the land are quite uniformly Semitic, which indicates that the Semitic languages were certainly dominant from hoary antiquity. But what was that date? And what was the origin or identity of the people who first introduced it? Some of these invaders lived along the Mediterranean coast in the fourth millennium B.C., and archaeologists usually assume that the invasion moved southward along the coast. Perhaps this was the beginning of a pattern that prevailed throughout much of the biblical period—namely, that the term *Canaanite* referred to a southern extension or subdivision of a general Phoenician culture all along the coast. At any rate, many aspects of the Canaanite culture took shape at this time.

Among these aspects was the Canaanite pattern of city planning. Most structures within the Canaanite city walls were public buildings; for the most part, the masses lived in hovels outside the walls, perhaps working or trading within the gates and fleeing to their security in times of war. Among the most prominent of the Canaanite public buildings were temples or related structures, which proves that the Canaanites had highly developed rituals and priesthoods from antiquity. Many clues from this period indicate Palestine's trade relations with Egypt and Mesopotamia. We do not know whether Egypt's cultural influence at this early date was accompanied by some measure of political control. During this period the Canaanites began forests from the Palestinian hills. Also, lamps appeared in this period.

b. Biblical Sites. Archaeologists have found several Early Bronze sites with biblical significance. These sites include Ai, Arad, Jericho, Megiddo, and Tirzah. John Garstang identified the double walls of Jericho (which were destroyed toward the end of the Early Bronze Age) with those miraculously overwhelmed by Joshua. In later excavations, Kathleen Kenyon found only scant remains of the Late Bronze city.

The site of Ai et-Tell lay vacant throughout the Middle and Late Bronze periods after the Early Bronze metropolis was destroyed. Apparently the Ai of Joshua 7–8 was located elsewhere in the vicinity, but archaeologists do not agree where it was. We are interested in the Early Bronze site of Ai because its sanctuary was divided into three parts, much like Solomon's temple about 1,500 years later. An altar was found in Ai's holy of holies and many animal bones throughout. Archaeologists unearthed a simpler temple with only two chambers (no outer court) at Tirzah, later one of the capitals of the Northern Kingdom. At Megiddo they uncovered no temple, but they did find an open-air shrine with walls enclosing an altar—apparently the type of idolatrous installation that the Bible calls a *bamah* or "high place" (*cf.* Num. 22:41; 33:52). The altar was round, about 70 feet in diameter and five feet high, ascended by seven steps. The Bible prohibited altar steps because the priests became guilty of "indecent exposure" when they climbed them (Exod. 20:26).

Archaeologists also uncovered temples at the Bronze Age city of Arad (near, but not identical to the Iron Age city of Arad that is frequently mentioned in the Bible). The main significance of the settlement was the well-planned nature of the city.

We should mention two other Early Bronze

sites that the Bible does not name (probably because they were uninhabited throughout that period). Beth-Yerah (Arabic name: *Khirbet el-Kerak*), on the southwestern shores of the Sea of Galilee, was another major urban center. It lent its name to some typical pottery of the period, characterized by a beautiful red burnish. Another site near the southeastern corner of the Dead Sea (known only by its Arabic name, *Bab edh-Dhra*) has an odd reputation. It was also a major city, but its major "industry" was burial. There archaeologists found a vast number of burials of various types, in various cemeteries and charnel houses. It must have been a favorite burial ground for a wide area. Because of the present arid and desolate nature of the area, it may have served the "Cities of the Plain" (Sodom and Gomorrah, and others) near the Dead Sea before they were destroyed.

c. Ebla (Tell Mardikh). One very important Early Bronze site outside of Canaan is the recently discovered city of Ebla in northern Syria. Also known by its modern name of Tell Mardikh, this site has already revolutionized our knowledge of the period. During the third quarter of the third millennium B.C., Ebla was the capital of a large empire. For a time it even eclipsed the empire of Akkad in Mesopotamia. Thus, Syria cannot have been quite the backwater that it was assumed to be in this period. We are not sure of its political ties with Canaan, to the south, but there certainly were trade contacts.

Ebla's business records mention a large number of Canaanite sites for the first time, among them Jerusalem—and even Sodom and Gomorrah, whose existence some scholars had previously doubted. Ebla's records also mention some personal names similar to biblical ones. One of Ebla's major kings was Eber, the same name as that of one of the "Hebrew" ancestors (Gen. 10:25; 11:14; the names are very similar in the Hebrew language).

Although Ebla's religion was polytheistic, one of its deities may have been named the same as the "Jehovah" of the Old Testament. If so, the Ebla tablets provide interesting evidence for the antiquity of the personal name of the true God.

2. Middle Bronze I. Toward the end of the third millennium (beginning around 2300 B.C.) the flourishing urban culture of the Early Bronze Period began to crumble in the face of nomadic invaders, who brought upon Palestine one of the most violent devastations of its

history. Not a single Early Bronze city escaped total destruction, and all lay unoccupied for at least a couple of centuries. Transjordan did not get back on its feet for nearly a thousand years (just in time to resist the Israelites!). Some sites were never resettled. In Palestine, a "dark age" ensued (although new discoveries are filling out the picture). In many respects, the invaders were culturally "backward." They lived mostly in caves or in camps atop city ruins. But plainly they brought some highly developed traditions of their own. Their pottery differed from that of Early Bronze inhabitants in shape as well as decoration; often it was poorly fired and brittle.

But the invaders distinguished themselves by their prolific tomb building. Archaeologists have found their large burial grounds, especially near Jericho and Hebron. In contrast to the multiple burials of the preceding Early Bronze Period and the rest of the Middle Bronge era, these nomads generally made only one burial per tomb. Usually the tomb was of a "shaft" type—i.e., with a vertical shaft sunk to the horizontal entrance to the tomb. Most of the bones were disorganized, indicating that mourners carried their dead back to the tribal burial grounds when the seasonal migration was over (*cf.* Jacob and Joseph, Gen. 50). Near Jericho archaeologists discovered an unwalled open-air shrine that the migrants dedicated by child sacrifice (*cf.* Psa. 106:37–38, which tells how the Israelites adopted this practice).

Who were these new invaders? We have no written records, of course. But most scholars think that they were at least a part of that general group labeled *Amorite*. The term originally means "Westerner," and the Mesopotamians applied it to invaders who entered their country from the West. Other members of this group may have invaded Egypt at about the same time (Egypt's so-called First Intermediate Period).

The Bible uses the term *Amorite* in a slightly more general and popular sense, referring to the pre-Israelite native population of the land. This makes it essentially synonymous with *Canaanite*. By the time of the Israelite invasion, the two terms had become interchangeable. But what was the original relationship between the two groups? Archaeologists who believe that the Amorites lived in Palestine during Middle Bronze I assume that the "Canaanites" were the invaders of Middle

ARCHAEOLOGY

DIAGRAM OF A TELL. *Before excavating a tell, archaeologists make a limited excavation to determine whether the site will justify the very expensive process of excavation. This photograph shows an experimental trench on Tell Judeideh in northern Syria. Each stair marks a different archaeological level.*

Bronze II A, who moved down along the Mediterranean coast from Phoenicia. But the literature of the Near East does not mention Canaan until much later. Then it is referred to as a geographical location, from which the adjective *Canaanite* appears to be derived. So most modern archaeologists believe that "Canaanites" was simply a later name for the Amorites. Unfortunately, scholars do not agree on this point. It is an urgent question for the Bible believer, however, because it would help to identify the date of the patriarchs.

For a long time Albright, Glueck, and many other archaeologists suspected that the patriarchs were somehow connected with the Amorites. After all, the Amorites settled the semi-arid region of the Negev where the patriarchs wandered. However, the patriarchs also settled in various cities (Shechem, Bethel, and Hebron), and there were no such urban centers in Palestine during Middle Bronze I. In addi-

tion, the patriarchs practiced multiple burials (Gen. 23:7–20), in contrast to the Middle Bronze I custom of individual burials. So we are reluctant to identify the patriarchs with the "Amorites"; it just doesn't seem to fit with events in Palestine, nor with the events in neighboring countries. Current archaeologists do not even attempt to identify the Middle Bronze I invaders, and they date the patriarchs sometime after 1900 B.C.

Some evidence from outside of Palestine indicates that the patriarchs lived in desert areas close to the urban centers of this era. The Mesopotamian cities of Mari and Nuzi resemble the culture of the patriarchs in many ways. Mari dates back to the eighteenth century B.C., and Nuzi to the sixteenth century B.C. This suggests that the patriarchs lived in Middle Bronze II A, instead of Middle Bronze I (the time of the new invaders).

Some information from Ebla suggests that

ARCHAEOLOGY

the patriarchs may have lived well before 2000 B.C. However, some of the secular records from outside Palestine do *not* confirm that they lived in this period.

3. Middle Bronze II. We have noted that another wave of northern invaders entered Palestine during Middle Bronze II A (*ca.* 1900 B.C.). Colin McEvedy observes that "presumably this was another facet of the Amorite migration."[2]

The Middle Bronze II B period was ushered in by still another invasion from the north. These invaders pushed down through Palestine into Egypt, beginning that country's Second Intermediate Period. In Egypt the new invaders came to be known as the *Hyksos* ("foreign invaders"). They centered their activities around the cities of Tanis and Avaris in the northeastern part of Egypt, which was nearer to their homeland. The Bible refers to Avaris as *Zoan,* and Numbers 13:22 dates its founding after the time of Abraham. Because the Hyksos may have been relatives or descendants of the Amorites, they probably would have felt the Israelites were rivals to the throne. Many scholars believe the Hyksos ruled Egypt during the years the Israelites lived in bondage.

Multiple burials again became common in the Hyksos period. In fact, tombs were reopened many times. Hyksos cavalrymen were sometimes buried with their horses and weapons, along with pottery, jewelry, and other articles of daily living. Near Jericho, Dr. Kenyon discovered several well-preserved Middle Bronze II tombs of this type.[3]

The Hyksos period probably lasted from 1750 to 1550 B.C. The later half of that period (after 1650 B.C.) is usually called Middle Bronze II C. An "Indo-Aryan" tribe (a group of non-Semitic people originally from the plateau of Iran) rose to power in the Near East at this time. They were probably the Hurrians (or as the Bible calls them, "Horites"). About a century later, they established the empire of Mitanni, which for a time was equal in power to Egypt. The Hurrians intermarried with the Amorites. This probably explains why the Hurrian city of Nuzi shows close similarities with the culture of the patriarchs.

Archaeologists have found that the Indo-Aryans exerted a strong influence upon Palestine. Apparently they introduced many new weapons and tools. They brought horse-drawn chariots, the composite bow, and new types of city fortifications. They outfitted nearly every major city from central Syria to the Nile Delta with a defensive wall called a *glacis.* The glacis contained alternating layers of pounded earth, clay, and gravel, covered with plaster. It sloped down from the rock city walls to a dry moat below. Perhaps it was designed to frustrate cavalrymen and battering rams. The Indo-Aryan cities also had huge cyclopean walls—a row of boulders leaning against a massive earthen fill. The people often built rectangular enclosures next to the walled city, surrounded by high ramparts. These enclosures may have been used for army camps or horse parks; but soon private homes were built inside them, and they became suburbs of the walled citadels. Hazor in the Holy Land provides a superb example of this.

Middle Bronze II (probably the time the patriarchs entered Canaan) was one of Palestine's most prosperous periods. Archaeologists have unearthed many massive fortress-temples that were built during this period. However, we have very few documents from this time, and so we know little about its politics or secular history. The Bible says little about the secular world.

SIFTING DIRT. *To archaeologists, every fragment of history is precious. These scientists at an excavation of Caesarea Maritima (A.D. 100–500) sift dirt through a screen box to search for small relics.*

[2] Colin McEvedy, *The Penguin Atlas of Ancient History* (Middlesex: Penguin Books, 1967), p. 28.

[3] Howard M. Jamieson, "Jericho," *The Zondervan Pictorial Encyclopedia of the Bible* (Grand Rapids: Zondervan, 1975), pp. 451–452.

4. Late Bronze Age. The Late Bronze Period began about 1550 B.C. The Egyptians regained their throne and drove the Hyksos from their country about this time. Moses was born during this troubled time. By 1500 B.C., most Hyksos cities in Palestine had been destroyed.

In 1468 B.C., Thutmose III defeated the Hyksos in a famous battle at the Megiddo Pass. The Pharaoh left many accounts of this battle in his inscriptions. Egyptian troops pressed north, eventually reaching the Euphrates. However, Egypt's full political control did not extend quite that far.

a. Palestine: The Amarna Age. Canaan did not prosper during this period, on the eve of the Israelite conquest. It appears that the Egyptian pharaohs gave poor leadership to their puppet governments in Palestine; their time was consumed by military adventures to the north. So the land of Canaan gradually fell into a disconnected group of petty, quarrelling city-states. These quarrelsome tendencies peaked in the fourteenth century, the so-called Amarna Age. That title comes from our modern name for the ruins of the capital of Egypt's heretic king, Amenhotep IV or Akhnaton. He spurned Egypt's traditional capitals and priesthoods to found his own capital on the middle Nile. Moreover, Akhnaton disliked politics and the business of administering the Egyptian empire, such as it was, in Palestine.

Out of this situation came the so-called Amarna letters, which the petty princes of Palestine sent to the pharaoh. Apparently he simply discarded them where they awaited modern archaeologists. Although written in Akkadian cuneiform (the language of international diplomacy at that time), the Amarna letters are heavily influenced by the local Canaanite dialect. They give us much information on the local language shortly before the Israelite invasion. The rulers of these city-states professed their loyalty to the pharaoh, but it is obvious that many of them were simply trying to promote their own careers at the expense of their neighbors.

Of special interest are the many letters that appeal to the pharaoh for aid against the incursions of the *Habiru.* One prince wrote, "The *Habiru* are plundering all the lands of the king. If no troops come in this very year, then all the lands of the king are lost."[4] Linguistically, this word is very similar to "Hebrew," but they have nothing to do with one another. The term *Habiru* could be found all over western Asia from the end of the third millennium until the end of the second. The term was not basically ethnic or political, but sociological. It signified landless people of almost any sort, usually semi-nomads who sold their services to city-dwellers in times of peace, but who threatened their stability when the cities became weak. The leaders of the Canaanite city-states may well have reckoned the Israelites among the *Habiru,* but the term referred to many other groups of people as well. Note that the Israelites did not refer to themselves as "Hebrews" until much later; instead, they called themselves "children (sons) of Israel."

Some scholars believe that the "Israelite invasion" was actually an internal rebellion of oppressed serfs against the landed aristocracy in the cities, abetted by newcomers from across the Jordan. While the Canaanite peasants may have indeed rebelled against the land owners, the Bible clearly shows that these serfs had only a secondary role in the invasion, if they were involved in it at all.

b. Egypt: The Nineteenth Dynasty. After Akhnaton's neglect brought Egypt to the brink of collapse, the nineteenth or Rameside dynasty brought a brief revival of Egypt's power in the thirteenth century, or Late Bronze II. But it turned out to be Egypt's last gasp. The gargantuan statues and temples of the Rameses, especially Rameses II, could not conceal the fact. Although Egypt continued to meddle in Canaanite affairs throughout biblical history, never again was she able to become much more than a "broken reed of a staff, which will pierce the hand of any man who leans on it" (Isa. 36:6, RSV). Powerful nations were contending for the Near East, and Egypt was scarcely able to survive.

A major barbarian force moved down from the Balkan and Black Sea regions, engulfing and obliterating every civilization in its path: the Mycenaeans in southern Greece, the Hittites in Asia Minor, and Canaanite settlers along the Mediterranean coast to the gates of Egypt. In a last-ditch stand at Medinet Habu, Rameses III stopped the barbarian horde, but the effort drained the last of Egypt's resources. The Egyptian inscriptions call these would-be invaders the "Sea Peoples," but there is little doubt that these are the people that the Bible calls "Philistines." Ironically, this area was ultimately named after them—*Palestine.* After

---

[4] George Steindorff and Keith C. Seele, *When Egypt Ruled the East,* rev. ed. by Keith C. Seele (Chicago: University of Chicago Press, 1957), p. 221.

DURA-EUROPAS. *The ruins of this forgotten city in the Syrian Desert were discovered in 1921 by the British Army, which was digging trenches at the site. Seven years later, archaeologists began to excavate the city. It was founded in about 300 B.C.*

their defeat, the "Sea Peoples" agreed to become a buffer state against further invasion of Egypt. That may still have been their status when they collided with the Israelites, streaming in from the southeast.

Archaeological evidence suggests that the Israelites arrived before the Philistines, were pushed back by the Philistine invaders, and then conquered the Philistines under Joshua. The biblical accounts that say Joshua swept all the way to the Mediterranean coast (Josh. 10:40–41) are not simple boasting. They are supported by the first mention of Israel in extrabiblical history by Pharaoh Merneptah (*ca.* 1224–1211 B.C.), who led a raid into Canaan *before* Rameses III's confrontation with the Philistines. Upon his return, Merneptah boasted that "Israel is laid waste, his seed is not." His report characterizes Israel only as a people, not as a nation. That certainly would have been their status shortly after entering Canaan under Joshua.

Archaeological evidence does not support the biblical account of the conquest as firmly as we might wish. At best, of course, archaeology can only "prove" the destruction of certain cities at a certain time; it cannot tell us why the cities were destroyed, or by whom. However, the lack of evidence does not entitle

us to contradict the Bible; that would be an argument from silence.

There are many good explanations for the scarcity of evidence from cities of this period. For example, the severe erosion of the Jericho site during the centuries it lay unoccupied accounts for our lack of Late Bronze evidence there. A similar explanation may apply to Gibeon; but it may also be that the city was located at a different place in Joshua's time. (It was not all that unusual for Near Eastern people to relocate their cities when they were destroyed by war or natural disaster.) The lack of destruction evidence at Shechem agrees with the Bible account that no destruction was necessary there—probably because an "advanced guard" of Israelites was already in control (*cf.* Gen. 34). And the Bible's report of destruction is beautifully corroborated by finds at Hazor, Lachish, and Debir (*cf.* Josh. 10:11, 30–31, 38–39).

D. The Iron Age. We are not surprised that the remains of Iron Age I are of relatively poor quality. The Israelites were not experienced in the arts of civilization, and they really did not establish their culture in Canaan until the days of David and Solomon. As the Book of Judges shows, a protracted and troubled period of consolidation followed Joshua's initial lightning victories. Recent excavations at Ashdod have illustrated, by way of contrast, the high level of Philistine culture at the same time. Often the relics from the Philistine cities show clear evidence of the people's Aegean backgrounds. A high-water mark of Philistine imperialism came with their capture of the ark of the covenant and the destruction of Shiloh (1 Sam. 4:1–10). Archaeological research at Shiloh has now confirmed this defeat. Saul's citadel at Gibeah, just north of Jerusalem, is another excellent example of the crude architecture of Iron Age I. It is just the rustic fortress one might have expected. As W. H. Morton says, "The unpretentiousness of its structure and the simplicity of its furnishings . . . are suggested by the smallness of its rooms and the common quality of its artifacts."[5]

With the rise of David's empire, we have more secular histories to confirm the Bible record, and so we depend much less upon archaeology than we did for information about earlier periods. The records of the great empires of the period, especially those of Assyria, often parallel and give more detail to the biblical testimony.

Only recently have archaeologists found some remains of the Jebusite city of Jerusalem (Ophel), which David and Joab captured. The nearly vertical shaft to the water supply was discovered early, as well as Hezekiah's later replacement, bringing water from the Gihon spring to the pool of Siloam within the walls. A new round of excavations just beginning may uncover even more of the early history of this pivotal spot.

Because the Israelis are creating many new buildings, archaeologists have uncovered more of Solomon's efforts in the past decade. Among them are his massive fortifications throughout the land, including standard-size gateways at many sites (e.g., Gezer, Megiddo, and Hazor).

Israeli archaeologists have just begun to publish their newest discoveries at Solomon's temple. We know of many parallels to its floor plan and some details of its structure.

Early archaeological literature touted the importance of "Solomon's stables" at Megiddo; but now scholars debate whether they are really either stables or Solomon's.

They almost certainly must be redated to the time of Ahab.

Shortly after the time of Solomon, someone prepared the document that we know as the famous "Gezer calendar." Apparently, it was only a schoolboy's exercise for memorizing the agricultural activity for each month of the year; but until recently it was our oldest known specimen of Hebrew writing.[6]

We can trace archaeologically Baasha's first attempts to construct a capital at Tirzah (1 Kings 15:33) and Omri's founding of Samaria (1 Kings 16:24). Among the many magnificent finds at Samaria, two stand out: the ivory plaques and the *ostraca*. The former were apparently inlays in the "ivory house" of Ahab (1 Kings 22:39) and other kings very similar to those popular in Phoenicia and Assyria at the time. The *ostraca* (inscribed potsherds) probably came from the reign of Jeroboam II. They contain commonplace records of taxes or contributions to the throne but they are important for the work of linguistic scholars.

Beginning about the time of Omri and Ahab, the Assyrians increased their pressure on Israel and Judah. The archaeological record of that conflict is too plentiful to detail here. The famous Lachish *ostraca* (discovered in the guardhouse of one of that city's gates) are nearly contemporary with the fall of Jerusalem to Babylon in 587 B.C. Recent excavations at Jerusalem have uncovered some of the walls toppled by the Babylonians, and even some of the arrowheads that the attackers fired.

We know as little about some periods after the Exile (such as the Persian Period) as we do about the patriarchal age. Archaeological finds for these periods are correspondingly meager. But archaeologists have found Nehemiah's rebuilt walls around Jerusalem, as well as inscriptions naming his three enemies—Sanballat, Tobiah, and Geshem (*cf.* Neh. 6:1).

E. The Hellenistic Period. Archaeology gives us no direct information concerning Alexander the Great's invasion of Palestine (330 B.C.) and the beginning of the Hellenistic Period. However, we have ample written records from this period, especially from Greek and Roman sources. This lessens our

4

ARCHAEOLOGY

---

[5] W. H. Morton, "Gibeah," *Interpreter's Dictionary of the Bible,* Vol. 2 (Nashville: Abingdon Press, 1962), p. 391.

[6] Now the Gezer calendar has been upstaged by an inscription found at Izbet Sarta (probably the biblical Ebenezer) near Aphek. This newly-found inscription is at least a century older.

ARCHAEOLOGY

dependence on archaeology. The most important archaeological material from the time of the Maccabean struggles is the renowned Qumran scrolls, found in caves along the northern shore of the Dead Sea in 1947. These scrolls had been stored in huge clay jars by members of a hermit Jewish sect, probably the Essenes. However, the scrolls' importance for the Old Testament is largely limited to the area of textual criticism. For the New Testament scholar, they help to illuminate the religious and political ferment of the times.

F. The Roman Period. Generally, biblical archaeology deals far less with the New Testament than with the Old. There are good reasons for this. The wealth of literary information about the New Testament period makes us much less dependent on archaeological sources. Also the history of the New Testament is largely that of a small, private group that affected external history only occasionally. Christianity left no architecture of its own until after it became a state religion in the fourth century.

Many excavations have been made at the traditional sites of New Testament events. Much of this work has been done by the Franciscans, who traditionally have had custody of Palestinian "holy places." However, they generally discover only the remains of the churches or shrines erected at these spots shortly after the early fourth century. Many of these shrines were probably erected at the behest of Helena, mother of the Emperor Constantine. The archaeologist can rarely prove (or disprove!) the authenticity of these sites or discover evidence to clearly associate them with New Testament times.

However, there are some notable exceptions in which the evidence clearly does reach back to New Testament times. The most important of these have been sites in or around Jerusalem itself, where modern habitation generally makes excavation very difficult. Archaeologists made several probes in connection with the renovation of the Church of the Holy Sepulchre, covering the traditional site of Calvary and Joseph's tomb. (There are competing claims for these sites, especially "Gordon's Calvary" and the "Garden Tomb" outside the present walled city. But these sites are discounted by virtually all scientific scholarship.)

Other significant finds have emerged in the course of Israeli excavations around the Temple Mount. It has long been known that the so-called "Wailing Wall" represents part of the western wall that Herod's builders erected in connection with rebuilding the temple.

At the back of St. Anne's Church on the northern edge of the Temple Mount grounds, archaeologists have found the probable site of Jesus' cure of the paralytic (John 5:1–9). Underneath a fifth-century basilica on the site, the researchers found remains of various pools and baths. Jesus' miracle apparently took place at a small pool near the entrance to a cave at the site.

Many details of the surrounding city are unclear, however. For example, it has been demonstrated that "Robinson's Arch," jutting out from the western wall of the temple, was *not* the beginning of a bridge across the Tyropean Valley, as previously thought. Rather it was the last link in a grandiose stair system that led up from the main street to the temple precincts themselves. South of the Temple Mount archaeologists have uncovered a magnificent plaza and broad steps leading up to the "Hulda Gates," the main entrance to the temple courtyards at the time of Christ. (They

OIL LAMP AND FLASK. *This oil lamp and oil flask were used in Jerusalem during the first century A.D. A householder poured olive oil from the flask into the center hole of the lamp to fuel the wick, which was lighted where it protruded from the spout.*

ARCHAEOLOGY

proved that Josephus' descriptions of this and of other nearby structures were phenomenally accurate.)

Across the valley on the western hill of Jerusalem, archaeologists have found luxurious residences of the Herodian period. They have also established that this area had already been inhabited and enclosed in a wall when Solomon's Temple was built. This section of town was probably the "Second Quarter" mentioned in 2 Kings 22:14 and Zephaniah 1:10.

Other Herodian sites have been cleared recently. Probably the most famous is Herod's resort at Masada, overlooking the southern end of the Dead Sea. After Titus' destruction of Jerusalem (A.D. 70), Masada became a refuge for fanatical zealots fleeing from the Roman armies. The Romans finally captured the site after a long siege, only to find nearly all the defenders dead in a suicide pact.

The "Herodium," which dominates the skyline a few miles southeast of Bethlehem, has also been cleared recently. It may be called Herod's "mausoleum," although it is debated whether he was actually buried in this luxurious structure at the top of the hill or somewhere on its lower slopes. Finally, we should mention the "digs" at the site of New Testament Jericho (about a mile west of the Old Testament site, at the foot of the mountains). It was one of Herod's most luxurious retreats, replete with palaces, baths, pools, sunken gardens, and the like. Undoubtedly it was the scene of some of his most infamous debaucheries.

Nearby is Qumran, excavated by the Dominican scholar, Roland de Vaux. Most of our knowledge of the important site is based on the famous scrolls found there. (*See* "Text and Translations.") However, de Vaux's excavation illuminated the community's life. For example, he found elaborate devices for catching and storing the sparse rainfall. De Vaux also uncovered the "scriptorium," where the famous scrolls had originally been copied.

On the Mediterranean seacoast to the west, at Caesarea Maritima, continuing excavations have exposed much of the layout of that great Roman and Byzantine city. In many respects, Caesarea was quite typical of urban construction in those days. The relics of Caesarea illustrate how Jews, Christians, and pagans lived and worked side by side in such metropolitan centers.

The relatively well-preserved synagogue of

CRUSADER FORTRESS. *European-style castles built during the Crusades surprise many visitors to the Middle East as their soaring Gothic architecture contrasts sharply with the low-built cities native to the area. The well-preserved "Krak des Chevaliers," shown here, was a fortress of the Knights Hospitallers commanding the road from Hama to Tripoli.*

Capernaum can hardly be the very one in which Jesus taught (Mark 1:21). The existing synagogue was built in the third or fourth century. But it may well be the successor of the synagogue Jesus knew, and perhaps it is of very similar design. Archaeologists think they may have discovered Peter's house at the same site (Matt. 8:14 ff.). Graffiti on the plastered walls of this second-century house clearly link it with Peter. Later it was replaced by a succession of octagonal churches.

Atop Mount Gerizim, excavations have uncovered the foundations of the Samaritan temple that competed with the temple of Jerusalem in New Testament times. Visitors can now see traces of a massive staircase down the mountainside to the city below. Near the bottom of this staircase is the traditional

ARCHAEOLOGY

site of "Jacob's Well" (*cf.* John 4:1–42), which may well be genuine.

The search for the scenes of the Gospel narratives has been going on for centuries. A few traditions report very early sites. Justin Martyr was told the location of a cave in Bethlehem where Jesus was born. (This would have been before A.D. 130.) The supposed location of Golgotha at the end of the Via Dolorosa was first mentioned by A.D. 135 and was officially recognized by the Emperor Constantine after A.D. 325. Both sites (that of Jesus' birth and death) have been continually venerated to modern times. The excavations in and around Jerusalem are beginning to provide a much better idea of how that city looked in the days of the New Testament.

The Archaeological Periods of Palestine

Period	Dates	Bible Events
I. Stone Age		
A. Paleolithic (Old Stone)	10,000–8000 B.C.	See Genesis 1–11
B. Mesolithic (Middle Stone)	8000–5500 B.C.	
C. Neolithic (New Stone)	5500–4000 B.C.	
II. Chalcolithic Period		
A. Megalithic	4000–3200 B.C.	See Genesis 1–11
B. Ghassulian	3500–3200 B.C.	
III. Bronze Age		
A. Early Bronze	3200–2200 B.C.	
B. Middle Bronze I	2200–1950 B.C.	Abraham born (2166 B.C.)
C. Middle Bronze II A	1950–1750 B.C.	Jacob enters Egypt (1876 B.C.)
D. Middle Bronze II B	1750–1550 B.C.	
E. Late Bronze	1550–1200 B.C.	The Exodus (1446 B.C.)
IV. Iron Age		
A. Iron Age I	1200–970 B.C.	David becomes king (1004 B.C.)
B. Iron Age II	970–580 B.C.	Israel's fall (586 B.C.)
C. Iron Age III	580–330 B.C.	The Jews return (539 B.C.)
V. The Hellenistic Period	330–63 B.C.	
VI. The Roman Period	63 B.C.–A.D. 330	Christ crucified (A.D. 30)

Figure 21

PAGAN RELIGIONS AND CULTURES

The Israelites of Old Testament times came into contact with Canaanites, Egyptians, Babylonians, and other people who worshiped false gods. God warned His people not to imitate their pagan neighbors, yet the Israelites disobeyed Him. They slipped into paganism again and again.

What did these pagan nations worship? And how did it pull the Israelites away from the true God?

By studying these pagan cultures we learn how man attempted to answer the ultimate questions of life before he found the light of God's truth. Also, we come to understand the world in which Israel lived—a world from which she was called to be radically different, both ethically and ideologically.

Before beginning such a study, we should note some cautions. First, we need to remember that we stand at least two millennia from the pagan cultures we are about to describe. The evidence (texts, buildings, artifacts) is often very sketchy. So we need to be cautious in drawing conclusions.

Secondly, we should realize that we live in a pluralistic society in which every person is free to believe or disbelieve as he chooses; but ancient peoples felt that some sort of religion was necessary. An agnostic or "free thinker" would have had a hard time living among the Egyptians, the Hittites, or even the Greeks and Romans. Religion was everywhere. It was the heart of ancient society. A person worshiped the deities of his town, city, or civilization. If he moved to a new home or traveled through a foreign land, he was duty-bound to show respect to the deities there.

I. COMMON FEATURES OF PAGAN RELIGIONS
  A. Many Gods
  B. Worship of Images
  C. Self-Salvation
  D. Sacrifice

II. OFFICIAL RELIGION VS. POPULAR RELIGION
  A. Categories of Gods
  B. Abstract Philosophy
  C. Akhnaton's Belief

III. PAGAN RELIGION IN LITERATURE
  A. Egyptian Creation Stories
  B. Babylon's Creation Story
  C. Pagan Flood Myths
  D. Divination Texts
  E. Ritual Literature

IV. HOLY DAYS

V. VIEWS OF THE AFTERLIFE

I. Common Features of Pagan Religions. Certain features were common to most of these pagan religions. They all partook of the same world view, which was centered on the locality and its prestige. The differences between Sumerian and Assyro-Babylonian religions or between Greek and Roman religions were marginal.

KNEELING WORSHIPER. *This ancient statue from a Sumerian temple depicts a man kneeling in worship. The Sumerians often made images of themselves, placing them in the temples to show their constant devotion to the gods. This statue was dedicated to the god Amurru.*

PAGAN RELIGIONS AND CULTURES

PAGAN GODS. *This illustration from a vase depicts the Greek gods watching over Darius I of Persia (in the bottom row, with scepter in right hand and sword in left), who attempted to conquer Greece in the fifth century B.C. Zeus, the central figure among the gods in the top row, is shown with the scepter and thunderbolt that symbolize his status as ruler of the gods.*

A. Many Gods. Most of these religions were *polytheistic,* which means that they acknowledged many gods and demons. Once admitted to the *pantheon* (a culture's collection of deities), a god could not be eliminated from it. He or she had gained "divine tenure."

Each polytheistic culture inherited religious ideas from its predecessors or acquired them in war. For example, what Nanna was to the Sumerians (the moon god), Sin was to the Babylonians. What Inanna was to the Sumerians (the fertility goddess and queen of heaven), Ishtar was to the Babylonians. The Romans simply took over the Greek gods and gave them Roman names. Thus the Roman god Jupiter was equal to Zeus as sky god; Minerva equaled Athena as goddess of wisdom; Neptune equaled Poseidon as god of the sea; and so forth. In other words, the idea of the god was the same; just the cultural wrapping was different. So one ancient culture could absorb the religion of another without changing stride or breaking step. Each culture not only claimed gods of a previous civilization; it laid claim to their myths and made them its own, with only minor changes.

The chief gods were often associated with some phenomenon in nature. Thus, Utu/Shamash is both the sun and the sun god;

Enki/Ea is both the sea and the sea god; Nanna/Sin is both the moon and the moon god. The pagan cultures made no distinction between an element of nature and any force behind that element. Ancient man struggled against forces in nature that he couldn't control, forces that could be either beneficent or malevolent. Enough rain guaranteed a bumper crop at harvest, but too much rain would destroy that crop. Life was quite unpredictable, especially since the gods were thought to be capricious and whimsical, capable of either good or evil. Human beings and gods participated in the same kind of life; the gods had the same sort of problems and frustrations that human beings had. This concept is called *monism.* Thus when Psalm 19:1 says, "The heavens declare the glory of God, and the firmament showeth his handiwork," it mocks the beliefs of the Egyptians and Babylonians. These pagan people could not imagine that the universe fulfilled an all-embracing divine plan.

The Egyptians also associated their gods with phenomena of nature: Shu (air), Re/Horus (sun), Khonsu (moon), Nut (sky), and so on. The same tendency appears in the Hittite worship of Wurusemu (sun goddess), Taru (storm), Telipinu (vegetation), and several mountain gods. Among the Canaanites, El was the high god in heaven, Baal was the storm god, Yam was the sea god, and Shemesh and Yareah were the sun and moon gods respectively. Because of this bewildering array of nature deities the pagan could never speak of a "*uni*verse." He did not conceive of one central force that holds all together, and by which all things exist. The pagan believed he lived in a "*multi*verse."

B. Worship of Images. Another common trait of pagan religion was religious *iconography* (the making of images or totems to worship). All of these religions worshiped idols. Israel alone was officially *aniconic* (i.e., it had no images, no pictorial representations of God). Images of Jehovah, such as Aaron's and Jeroboam's bull-calves (Exod. 32; 1 Kings 12:26 ff.) were forbidden in the second commandment.

But aniconic religion was not always the whole story. The Israelites worshiped pagan idols while they lived under Egypt's bondage (Josh. 24:14); and even though God banished their idols (Exod. 20:1–5), the Moabites lured them into idolatry again (Num. 25:1–2). Idolatry was the downfall of Israel's leaders in different periods of her history, and God finally allowed the nation to be defeated "because of their sacrifices" to pagan idols (Hos. 12:19).

Most pagan religions pictured their gods *anthropomorphically* (i.e., as human beings). In fact, only an expert can look at a picture of Babylonian gods and mortals and tell which is which. Egyptian artists usually represented their gods as men or women with animal heads. Horus was a falcon-headed man, Sekhmet was a lioness-headed woman, Anubis was a jackal, Hathor a cow, and so forth. Hittite gods can be recognized by the drawing of a weapon they place on their shoulder, or by some other distinctive object such as a helmet with a pair of horns. The Greek gods also are pictured as humans, but without the harsh characteristics of the Semite deities.

C. Self-Salvation. What is the significance of portraying the gods like human beings? The opening chapters of Genesis say that God made man in His image (Gen. 1:27), but the pagans attempted to make gods in their own image. That is to say, the pagan gods were merely amplified human beings. The myths of the ancient world assumed that the gods had the same needs as humans, the same foibles and the same imperfections. If there was a difference between the pagan gods and men, it was only a difference of degree. The gods were humans made "bigger than life." Often they were the projections of the city or township.

D. Sacrifice. Most pagan religions sacrificed animals to soothe their temperamental

EGYPTIAN GODS. *This papyrus from the tenth century* B.C. *depicts the Egyptian universe. The sky goddess Nut, arched as the heavens, is supported by the upstretched arms of the air god Shu. At Shu's feet, the earth god Geb stretches his left arm along the ground. Other gods look on from the sides.*

PAGAN RELIGIONS AND CULTURES

gods; some even sacrificed human beings. Because the heathen worshipers believed their gods had human desires, they also offered food and drink offerings to them (*cf.* Isa. 57:5–6; Jer. 7:18).

The Canaanites believed sacrifices had magical powers that brought the worshiper into sympathy and rhythm with the physical world. However, the gods were capricious, so worshipers sometimes offered sacrifices to secure a victory over their enemies (*cf.* 2 Kings 3:26–27). Perhaps this is why the decadent kings of Israel and Judah indulged in pagan sacrifice (*cf.* 1 Kings 21:25–26; 2 Kings 16:23). They wanted magical aid in fighting their enemies, the Babylonians and Assyrians—preferably the aid of the same gods that had made their enemies victorious.

II. Official Religion vs. Popular Religion. Ancient polytheistic religions operated at two levels: the official religion of the archaic religious state and popular religion, which was little more than superstition.

A. Categories of Gods. Each ancient religious system had a chief god who was more powerful than the rest. For the Egyptians, this might be Re, Horus, or Osiris; for the Sumerians and Akkadians, it might be Enlil, Enki/Ea, or Marduk; for the Canaanites, it would be El; and for the Greeks, Zeus. In most instances, the pagans built temples and recited liturgies in honor of these high gods. Usually the king presided over this worship, acting as the god's representative in a ritual meal, marriage, or combat. This was the official religion.

"The temple was the home of the god, and the priests were his domestic staff. . . . Every day it was the duty of the staff of the temple to attend to the god's 'bodily needs' according to a fixed routine. . . .

"But the god was not merely the householder of the temple, he was also the lord and master of his people, and as such entitled to offerings and tributes of many kinds. . . ."[1]

The gods of the official state religion were too far removed from the local man to be of any practical value.

Ancient Egypt was divided into districts called *nomes*. In the early days of Egypt there were 22 of these in Upper Egypt (the southern part) and 20 in the northern delta area. Each *nome* had a key or capital city and a local god who was worshiped in that territory: Ptah in

AMUN-RE. *Egypt's sun god, Amun-Re, was considered the king of the gods. Egyptians believed he traveled across the sky in his boat by day, then continued his journey at night into the underworld, using a second boat. Egyptian mythology also pictured him as a falcon soaring through the skies or as a young hero in a constant struggle with the powers of darkness. In his right hand, Amun-Re carries the ankh, a religious symbol of life.*

Memphis, Amun-Re in Thebes, Thoth in Hermopolis, and so on. In Mesopotamia too, each city was sacred to one god or goddess: Nanna/Sin in Ur (Abraham's birthplace), Utu/Shamash in Larsa, Enlil in Nippur, and Marduk in Babylon. The Canaanites worshiped "the Baal" (the local fertility deity) but the people of each community had their own *baal,* as we can tell by place names like Baalzephon, Baal-peor, and Baal-hermon (all mentioned in the Old Testament—e.g., Exod. 14:2; Num. 25:5; Judg. 3:3). In the ancient Near East, official religion was oriented to the state, while popular religion was oriented to the geographical locale. Ancient man saw no inconsistency between believing in gods "up there" and another god "right here"—all competing for his attention and servitude. This was a partial recognition of the ultimate problem of immanence and transcendence.

B. Abstract Philosophy. The ancients be-

---

[1] O. R. Gurney, *The Hittites* (Baltimore: Penguin Books, 1952), pp. 149–150 (see also 2d ed., 1990).

PAGAN RELIGIONS AND CULTURES

gan to move away from pure superstition and deified various abstract ideals under the names of ancient gods.

In Mesopotamia, "Justice" and "Righteousness" appear as minor deities in the retinue of Utu/Shamash, the sun god; they were called Nig-gina and Nig-sisa, respectively. Their "boss" was Shamash, the Mesopotamian god of law. Ancient thinkers conceived of these abstract ideas as gods, rather than dealing with the ideas themselves.

The Egyptians did this more than anyone else. Some of the major Egyptian gods fell into this category. For example, Atum expresses the concept of universality. The name *Amon* means "hidden"—the Egyptians thought he was a formless, unseen being who might be anywhere, and anyone could worship him. For that reason, they later grafted the idea of Amon on to Re, and the god became Amun-Re, "the king of eternity and guardian of the dead."[2] The most massive temples of Egyptian history were built in honor of Amun-Re at Karnak. The goddess Maat was another Egyptian idea-become-god. She was supposed to personify truth and justice, and was the cosmic force of harmony and stability.

The Canaanites represented truth and justice with the gods Sedeq and Mishor, who were supposed to serve under the god Shemesh. But even though pagan thinkers could deal with these ideas more easily this way, few of the gods lived up to their ideals, according to legend. Canaanite religion continued the ancient desire for sexual harmony with nature, and it encouraged particularly obscene rituals.

C. Akhnaton's Belief. The pagan religions of Mesopotamia never broke out of their polytheistic mold. One scholar of ancient religions, W. W. Hallo, speaks of the Mesopotamians' "unsurmountable antipathy to an exclusive monotheism."[3] The same can be said for other people of antiquity: Hittites, Persians, Canaanites, Greeks, and Romans.

There is perhaps one exception. Typically Egypt was polytheistic; but during her eighteenth dynasty she produced the famous pharaoh Amenhotep IV (1387–1366 B.C.). He outlawed the worship of all gods except Aton (the "sun disk"), and then changed his own name to Akhnaton. Prior to Akhnaton, the Egyptian deities had often been merged or coalesced into a single god-concept (usually Re); this, however, is not monotheism. But the Egyptians called the god Aton "the sole god, like whom there is no other." This had far-reaching political effects and could not have been accomplished without the support of the army and the priests. But Akhnaton's religion fell far short of saying anything like, "Hear, O Israel, the LORD our God is one" (Deut. 6:4). Akhnaton's "reform" was short-lived, however, and his successors purged Egypt of this "heresy." The old political priesthood returned to power and supported their own pharaoh.

In the ancient world, only Israel was fully monotheistic. But let us be sure we understand what this means. Monotheism is not simply a matter of arithmetic. Perhaps the most succinct statement is that of W. F. Albright, who says that monotheism is "the belief in the existence of only one God, who is the Creator of the world and the giver of all life, . . . [Who is] so far superior to all created beings . . . that He remains absolutely unique." This made Israel radically different from her pagan neighbors.

AKHNATON. *A king of Egypt in the fourteenth century B.C., Akhnaton believed exclusively in Aton, the sun god. For this reason, his polytheistic countrymen considered him a heretic. This relief shows him with Queen Nefertiti and their three daughters. The sun god is depicted by the shining orb at the upper center of the picture.*

---

[2] George Steindorff and Keith C. Seele, *When Egypt Ruled the East,* rev. ed. by Keith C. Seele (Chicago: University of Chicago Press, 1957), p. 77.

[3] W. W. Hallo and W. K. Simpson, *The Ancient Near East: A History* (New York: Harcourt Brace Jovanovich, 1971).

PAGAN RELIGIONS AND CULTURES

III. Pagan Religion in Literature. When we turn to the literature of the ancient world we get the clearest picture of pagan religions. Almost all ancient literature reflects the religion of its culture: hymns, prayers, royal inscriptions, incantations, historical texts, and epics. The beliefs of a people are seen most clearly when they address themselves to questions such as: Who am I? Where did I come from? What is this world? How does one explain pleasure and pain? We find their answers to most of these questions in ancient creation stories (technically called *cosmogonies*), and hardly any group of people is without some tradition at this point.

A. Egyptian Creation Stories. Egypt had at least five different stories that explained the origin of the world, the gods, and man. Two of these five will be enough to illustrate what the Egyptians believed.

The city of Heliopolis hands down the story that Amun-Re came forth from the watery mass (Nun) by his own power. He then reproduced from himself the first divine couple, Shu and Tefnut (air and moisture, male and female). This couple mated and produced another generation of gods, Geb (earth) and his wife Nut (sky). And so the process of life started.

In another story (this one from the city of Hermopolis), creation began with four couples of gods. These four couples created an egg from which the sun (Re) was born. Re then created the world.

Egyptians told these creation stories to try to prove that their city was the place of creation. Memphis, Thebes, Heliopolis, and Hermopolis claimed to be the territory where it all started.

B. Babylon's Creation Story. The most complete creation account from Babylon is usually called the *Enuma Elish*. These are the first two words of the narrative, and they translate into English as "When on high. . . ."

In the beginning there were two gods, Apsu and Tiamat, who represented the fresh waters (male) and the marine waters (female). They cohabited and produced a second generation of divine beings. Soon Apsu was suffering from insomnia because the young deities were making so much noise; he just could not get to sleep. He wanted to kill the noisy upstarts, despite the protests of his spouse, Tiamat. But before he managed to do

that, Ea, the god of wisdom and magic, put Apsu to sleep under a magic spell and killed him.

Not to be outdone, wife Tiamat plotted revenge on her husband's killer and those who aided the killing. Her first move was to take a second husband, whose name was Kingu. Then she raised an army for her retaliation plans.

At this point the gods appealed to the god Marduk to save them. He happily accepted the challenge, on the condition that if he was victorious over Tiamat, they would make him chief of all gods.

The confrontation between Tiamat and Marduk ended in a blazing victory for Marduk. He captured Tiamat's followers and made them his slaves. Then he cut the corpse of Tiamat in half, creating heaven from one half of it and the earth from the other half. He ordered the earlier supporters of Tiamat to take care of the world.

Shortly thereafter, Marduk conceived another plan. He had Kingu killed and arranged for Ea to make man out of his blood. In the words of the story, man's lot is to be "burdened with the toil of the gods." To demonstrate their gratitude to Marduk, the gods then helped him to build the great city of Babylon and its imposing temple. The story ends by describing the gods' great feast in Marduk's honor and by listing Marduk's fifty names, each of which is supposed to indicate some power or accomplishment that characterizes him.

Note some of the emphases of this story. It says that in the beginning there were two gods, Apsu and Tiamat, male and female. This is markedly different from the creation account of Genesis 1–2, which states that in the beginning there was one God, not two. Why is it important to know that God had no spouse or consort, and was alone? Because it shows that God finds fulfillment in himself, and needs no resources outside himself. The opening chapters of Genesis refer to nothing else that finds fulfillment in itself. All of God's creatures find fulfillment in something or someone outside themselves.

The pagan Babylonian had no problem believing that there were two gods in the beginning. As far as he was concerned, there could be no future with only one god. How could there be creation or procreation if there was only one god? When the pagan talked about his gods, he talked only in human categories.

PAGAN RELIGIONS AND CULTURES

He could not imagine a god who was any different.

It seems strange that the Babylonian god Apsu complains that he wants to sleep. But when the Psalmist said that our God "shall neither slumber nor sleep" (Psa. 121:4), he was stating something that was not obvious in his day. It underscores the fact that Israel's be-

Emperor Worship

The Romans found many different languages, religions, and cultures among the people they conquered. The Roman Empire gradually absorbed these foreign beliefs, including the worship of political leaders.

The eastern provinces had customs of worshiping their living rulers. Egyptians thought that the pharaohs had descended from the sun god, while the Greeks worshiped their great warriors who had died. Alexander the Great established for himself a cult of worshipers in Alexandria. The Seleucids of Syria and the Ptolemies of Egypt followed this tradition, calling themselves gods living on earth. When the power of Rome began to replace these monarchs, the worship of *Roma* (a deification of the Roman state) began to supplant their cults. The conquered people began to worship great individual Romans—Sulla, Mark Antony, and Julius Caesar.

At first, the Romans disdained this ruler worship. However, they did revere the spirits of their dead ancestors (the *lares*) and the divine spirit of the family head (the *paterfamilias*).

Augustus Caesar combined the ideas of ruler worship and ancestor worship in the imperial cult. In the provinces, his Roman subjects worshiped Roma and Augustus together as a sign of their loyalty to the emperor.

Throughout the empire, Roman subjects incorporated emperor worship into the local religion. In the provinces, leading citizens became priests in the imperial cult to cement their ties with Rome. However, Augustus exempted the Jews from the imperial cult.

The Roman emperor Caligula (A.D. 37–41) proclaimed himself a god; he built two temples for himself—one at public expense, one at personal expense. Dressed as Jupiter, he uttered oracles. Turning the temple of Castor and Pollux into the vestibule of his palace, he appeared between the statues of the gods to receive adoration. He was accused of following the Ptolemaic custom of marrying his sister. In A.D. 40, possibly provoked by the fact that some Jews had destroyed an altar erected to him, Caligula ordered a statue of Jupiter with his own features to be placed in the temple in Jerusalem. The Jews responded by saying that "if he would place the image among them, he must first sacrifice the whole Jewish nation" (Flavius Josephus, *Wars,* Vol. 2, Bk. 10, Sec. 4). The Syrian governor Petronius succeeded in having the order rescinded.

Claudius, Caligula's successor, restored the religious exemption to the Jews and shunned attempts to worship him. "For I do not wish to seem vulgar to my contemporaries," he said, "and I hold that temples and the like have by ages been attributed to the gods alone."

The most famous account of the policy of the Romans toward the Christians is found in the correspondence between Pliny the Younger (A.D. 62–113) and the emperor Trajan (reign A.D. 98–117). Pliny was sent to Bithynia (modern Turkey) to investigate charges of misgovernment. The Bithynians denounced their Christian neighbors, but Pliny was not sure how to handle them. He told the emperor:

". . . The method I have observed towards those who have been denounced as Christians is this: I interrogated them whether they were Christians; if they confessed it I repeated the question twice again, adding the threat of capital punishment; if they still persevered, I ordered them to be executed. . . . Those who denied they were or had ever been, Christians, who repeated after me an invocation to the gods, and offered adoration, with wine and frankincense, to your image . . . and who finally cursed Christ—none of which acts, it is said, those who are really Christians can be forced into performing—these I thought it proper to discharge . . . For the matter seemed to me well worth referring to you—especially considering the numbers endangered. Persons of all ranks and ages and both sexes are and will be involved in the persecution. For this contagious superstition is not confined to the cities only, but has spread through the villages and rural districts; it seems possible, however, to check and cure it" (Epistle X, 96).

Trajan's reply sums up this policy: "The method you have pursued, my dear Pliny, in sifting the cases of those denounced to you as Christians is extremely proper . . . No search should be made for these people; when they are denounced and found guilty they must be punished; with the restriction, however, that when the party denies himself to be a Christian, and shall give proof that he is not (that is, by adoring our gods) he shall be pardoned on the ground of repentance" (Epistle X, 97).

Emperor worship continued as the official pagan religion of the empire until Christianity was recognized under the Emperor Constantine (reign A.D. 305–337).

PAGAN RELIGIONS AND CULTURES

ENUMA ELISH. *These cuneiform tablets contain the Enuma Elish, the Babylonian creation epic. Although the story bears similarities to the biblical story of creation, there are striking differences. The Babylonians perceived their gods in human terms and believed that there must be two gods, a male and a female, for creation to take place. This is in sharp contrast to the monotheistic view of Creation in the Bible.*

lief in God was radically unique among the people of the ancient world.

Apsu was ready to kill because his children kept him awake. He had no clear-cut moral motive. The god is angry—not because man has filled the earth with violence or corruption, but because it is so noisy he cannot sleep! It seems strange that a god like Apsu could act out of such selfish motives. But the pagan mind reasoned that if mortal man conducts himself this way, why not the gods, too?

The real purpose of the *Enuma Elish* is not to tell about the creation of the world. The story is intended to answer the question: How did the god Marduk become chief god of the mighty city, Babylon? More than likely, the Babylonians read this particular composition at their New Year's festival, in the hopes of guaranteeing a good year ahead. Marduk represented the forces of order and Tiamat the forces of chaos. This line of thinking concludes that, if a person says the right words at the right time, his chances of success will increase. It sees celebration or invocation of the gods as a kind of magic charm.

Pagan myths view the creation of man as an afterthought. They say that man was created to be a servant of the gods, to do their "dirty work." The Babylonians believed that man

was evil because Marduk had created him from the blood of the rebellious god, Kingu. Certainly this account has none of the majesty that we find surrounding the creation of man in Genesis.

The Bible says God created man in His own image, distinct from all else that God had made (Gen. 1:26f.). And the Bible alone, of all ancient literature, has a separate account of the creation of woman (Gen. 2:21–25).

C. Pagan Flood Myths. In the Bible, the creation story is soon followed by the Flood, God's response to man's repeated iniquities (Gen. 6–9). In both Egypt and Canaan we find narratives about angry gods who unleashed their fury on mankind, sometimes accompanied by a great flood.

In Egyptian mythology the goddess Sekhmet intended to wipe out the human race. She was thwarted only when others flooded the world with beer, which had been dyed blood-red. Bloodthirsty as she was, Sekhmet drank all she could and was put to sleep by the beer.

Canaanite literature tells a similar story about the goddess Anath (wife of Baal), who went on a rampage against man. No gory detail is omitted from the story as she wades into battle with a club and bow: "Under Anath

PAGAN RELIGIONS AND CULTURES

(flew) heads like vultures/Over her (flew) hands like locusts . . . She plunges knee-deep in the blood of heroes/Neck-high in the gore of troops . . . Anath swells her liver with laughter/Her heart is filled with joy/For in the hand of Anath is victory."[4]

The literature of Mesopotamia includes a crucial text that describes a flood as divine punishment. This particular text is called the Gilgamesh Epic. The main character is himself a combination of history and legend. He was in fact the fifth king of the Uruk dynasty (around 2600 B.C.), and appears in legend as a Samson-like individual. Two things stand out in the traditions about Gilgamesh. First, the story says he was one-third human and two-thirds divine. Second, he supposedly was of mixed human and divine parentage; his mother was the goddess Ninsun and his father was Lugal-banda, an earlier king of Uruk.

The Gilgamesh Epic tells how Gilgamesh brutalized his subjects. To tone him down, the people of Uruk persuaded the goddess Aruru to create a man named Enkidu. Enkidu eventually met Gilgamesh and the two became the best of friends. Subsequently, they waged war against all types of monsters, such as the evil dragon Humbaba. Gilgamesh is handsome—so handsome that the goddess Ishtar proposes marriage. Gilgamesh rejects her proposal because she is a promiscuous wife and lover. Fuming, Ishtar obtains permission from her father, Anu, to destroy Gilgamesh with the Bull of Heaven. Ferocious fighting follows, and again Gilgamesh and Enkidu are victorious.

But then Enkidu becomes ill and dies. Brooding over the death of his companion, Gilgamesh determines to find a man called Utnapishtim, the only mortal who had ever become immortal by surviving the flood, because Gilgamesh wants to learn how to do the same. After much hair-raising adventure through the underworld, Gilgamesh finally meets Utnapishtim.

Utnapishtim tells Gilgamesh how the gods secretly decided to send a flood on the earth, principally through the storm god Enlil. One of their own, Ea, divulged the plan to Utnapishtim and urged him to build a boat to save himself, his family, some precious metals, and various species of animals. Utnapish-tim took all of these aboard, along with several skilled crewmen. The rains fell for seven days and nights, after which Utnapishtim's boat landed on a mountain. Utnapishtim sent out various birds to determine whether or not the waters had receded. When he finally left the ship he made a sacrifice to the gods, who "gathered like flies" around it. Enraged that two humans had escaped his catastrophic blow, Enlil at first threatened but then conferred divinity upon Utnapishtim and his wife—not as a reward, but as an alternative to destroying humanity.

But all this means nothing for Gilgamesh. Utnapishtim's rescue was an exception, not a precedent. As a consolation, Utnapishtim offers Gilgamesh the Plant of Life; but even this is stolen by a serpent. Frustration upon frustration! Drearily Gilgamesh trudges home to Uruk. He knows he must die, but at least he will be remembered for his building accomplishments—his immortality being in the work of his own hands. This is one of the great poetic epics of the Akkadian language.

Woven into this myth is a Mesopotamian flood story, with fascinating parallels to Scripture. But in no way does the Mesopotamian myth cast doubt on the authenticity of Genesis.

There are many ideological differences between the two flood stories. The Gilgamesh Epic gives no clear-cut reason for Enlil to send the flood. Certainly he was not moved by the moral degeneracy of mankind. How could he be? These pagan gods were not paragons of virtue nor did they champion it. One modern scholar, C. H. Gordon, says, "The modern student must not make the mistake of thinking that the ancient Easterner had any difficulty in reconciling the notion of divinity with carryings-on that included chicanery, bribery, indecent exposure for a laugh, and homosexual buffoonery."[5]

Also, note that the Gilgamesh Epic emphasizes Utnapishtim's use of human skill in saving himself from the flood. That's why there were navigators on board; it is a match of human wits and divine wits. There is nothing like this in the Genesis account; there were neither navigational equipment nor professional sailors on board. If Noah, his wife, and

---

[4] J. B. Pritchard, ed., *Ancient Near Eastern Texts Relating to the Old Testament* (Princeton, N.J.: Princeton University Press, 1969).

[5] C. H. Gordon, "Ancient Near Eastern Religions," *Encyclopedia Britannica,* 15th ed., Vol. 12 (Chicago: Encyclopedia Britannica Educational Corporation, 1974).

PAGAN RELIGIONS AND CULTURES

MODEL OF SHEEP'S LIVER. *This clay model of a sheep's liver, found in Babylonia, dates from about 1700 B.C. Divided into over 50 sections inscribed with omens and magical texts, it was used for a guide for diviners.*

family were to be saved, it would happen by God's grace, not human expertise or ingenuity.

Third, the Gilgamesh story is basically without educational and long-range moral value. Scripture explains the significance of the Flood for subsequent generations by the words of a covenant from God: "And I will establish my covenant with you; . . . neither shall there any more be a flood to destroy the earth" (Gen. 9:11).

Fourthly, the Bible shows that God saved Noah to preserve the human race. The myth of Utnapishtim does not reflect any such divine plan. He was saved by accident, because one of the gods tattled to him about Enlil's intentions.

D. Divination Texts. Texts dealing with divination represent the second largest single category of the cuneiform literature of Mesopotamia (after economic texts). At its most elementary level, *divination* is an attempt to decipher the will of the gods through the use of magical techniques. The pagans believed they could use human skill and ingenuity to acquire from the gods knowledge about certain situations. In the words of Yehezkel Kaufmann, a diviner is "a scientist who can dispense with divine revelation."[6]

Divination usually followed either the inductive or intuitive method. In the former, the diviner observes events and then draws conclusions from them. The most common method was to observe the inner parts of slaughtered sheep or goats. Diviners usually studied the liver (a technique called *hepatoscopy*). A typical divination formula might run something like this: "If the liver has the shape X, then the outcome of the battle/sickness/journey will be as follows. . . ."

This particular system was fine for the king and the wealthy, but for average citizens a variety of cheaper techniques was needed. There were at least a half dozen of these, such as *lecanomancy* (letting drops of oil fall into a cup of water and observing the patterns that appear) or *libanomancy* (watching the various shapes from the smoke of incense).

In the intuitive type of divination, the diviner is less active; he is more of an observer and interpreter. The best-known type of intuitive divination was dream interpretation (*oneiromancy*). This method produced a body of dream interpretation literature that said, "If you dream such and such, it means. . . ." Other means of divination were the texts known as *menologies* and *hemerologies*. The first type listed the months of the year and told which months were favorable for certain kinds of tasks. The latter listed activities that a person should engage in or avoid for each day of the month. From all of this, astrology was born.

The Old Testament forbids all techniques of divination (*cf.* Deut. 18:10; Lev. 20:6; Ezek. 13:6–8). The Bible calls divination an "abomination"; for that reason, there were no professional diviners in Israel. The confidence that divination put in human wisdom was an insult to God, for it reflected unwillingness to trust His revelation of truth.

E. Ritual Literature. The vast majority of the texts that tell of pagan temples, offerings, sacrifices, and clergy are describing the religion of the king. They are not usually applicable to the commoner's religion. Leo Oppenheim has said correctly, "The common man . . . remains unknown, the most important unknown element in Mesopotamian religion."[7] The same could certainly be said for

---

[6] Yehezkel Kaufmann, *The Religion of Israel* (Chicago: University of Chicago Press, 1960), p. 21.

[7] A. Leo Oppenheim, *Ancient Mesopotamia: Portrait of a Dead Civilization,* 2nd ed. (Chicago: University of Chicago Press, 1976).

PAGAN RELIGIONS AND CULTURES

INCENSE STAND. *This incense stand found in the Megiddo dates from 1100 B.C. Priests used it in religious ceremonies, where the bowl served as a vessel for burning incense.*

Egypt. It was unthinkable that "the man on the street" could receive revelations from the gods. This was a prerogative of the king.

The chasm between Christian Scripture and pagan religions is enormous here. In the Old Testament, God speaks not only to leaders like Moses and David, but also to harlots, outcasts, sinners, and others. For example, note that the first person of whom Scripture says, "He was filled with God's Spirit," was a man named Bezaleel (Exod. 31:3), the foreman in charge of building the tabernacle.

Whether in Egypt or in Mesopotamia, pagans believed that their gods lived in the temples they built for them. As such, they considered the temple to be sacrosanct. Hymns to temples are quite common in pagan literature.

In this respect, Solomon's prayer of dedication at the Jerusalem temple reveals a clear anti-pagan emphasis. Consider this verse: "But will God indeed dwell on the earth? Behold, heaven and the highest heaven cannot contain thee; how much less this house which I have built!" (1 Kings 8:27, RSV).

The pagan king administered the temple and performed the priestly services for his gods. He was thought to be the mediator between man and the gods. He reigned for gods (as in Mesopotamia) or as god (as in Egypt).

Incidentally, here we meet one of the most distinctive characteristics of biblical faith. The pagan religions never produced spokesmen who ventured to contradict the king, as the biblical prophets did. The pagans had no concept of "prophetic immunity." Only in Israel could a king be reproached by a prophet with the words, "Thou art the man!" (2 Sam. 12:7). After all, if the king is sovereign, divine, and the head clergyman, who can tell him that he is out of line? This is why Jezebel, being of Phoenician background, could not understand why her Israelite husband cowered before the prophet Elijah (*cf.* 1 Kings 16:31; 21:6, 20–27).

IV. Holy Days. The Israelites celebrated a number of religious festivals during the year. (*See* "Jewish Rituals.") Their pagan neighbors had holy days of their own, and these observances give us further insight into their spiritual outlook.

The Babylonians observed moon festivals on fixed days of the month: the first, seventh, fifteenth, and twenty-eighth. In addition, they had special "seventh" days—the seventh, fourteenth, twenty-first, and twenty-eighth of each month. They took special precautions to avoid bad luck on these "seventh" days. And they did not work at all on the fifteenth day of the month, because they believed there was no chance for good fortune on that day; this day of rest was called *shappatu*. On the *shappatu*, the Babylonians tried to pacify the gods and appease their anger with a day of penitence and prayer.

In pagan religions a sacrifice was a meal for the god, the source of his nutrition. "Like flies" the gods converged on the sacrifice of Utnapishtim after he got off his boat. It is hard to believe that anyone really believed the idol ate a morsel when no one was looking. Probably the dishes were brought to the king for consumption after being presented to the image. The food, having an aura of the holy, was supposed to sanctify the consumer—in this case, the king. When very large amounts of food were presented for sacrifice, as in Egypt or Persia, the food would go to temple personnel. The apocryphal story of Bel and the Dragon describes this practice.

In addition to the lucky and unlucky days we discussed earlier, the greatest festival in Babylon was the *akitu* (i.e., the New Year

PYRAMIDS. *Built as the tombs of kings, the pyramids of Egypt have themselves achieved a kind of immortality among the peoples of the world, who marvel at their magnificence. In fact, they were constructed to insure the immortality of the royalty, whose bodies they contained.*

Feast). The Babylonians celebrated *akitu* in March and April, when nature began to revive. They spent the first four days making prayers to Marduk, the chief god of Babylon. In the evening of the fourth day they recited the creation story (the *Enuma Elish*). By recounting the original victory of order (Marduk) over chaos (Tiamat), the Babylonians hoped that the same victory would be evident in the new year. The Babylonians believed that the spoken word had power. And so on the fifth day, the king appeared before Marduk's statue and declared his innocence from faults and his fulfillment of his obligations. We are not sure what the people did for the next few days, but on the ninth and tenth days they held a banquet. On the eleventh day soothsayers divined the destinies of the following year.

V. Views of the Afterlife. Two radically different concepts of the afterlife appeared in

the pagan Near East. In Mesopotamia, very few people believed there was life after death. The Gilgamesh Epic had this to say: "Gilgamesh, whither runnest thou? Life, which thou seekest, thou wilt not find. When the gods created mankind, they allotted to mankind Death, but Life they withheld in their hands."[8]

At the other end of the spectrum were the Egyptians. Their religion was saturated with a belief in the afterlife. The Egyptians believed the dead go to a territory ruled by Osiris, where a person must give an account of his good and bad deeds. Behind this was the Osiris legend, which tells how the benevolent ruler Osiris was killed by his wicked brother Seth, who cut his body into pieces. His wife,

---

[8] *The Tree of Life* (New York: Viking Press, 1942), p. 263.

PAGAN RELIGIONS AND CULTURES

Isis, searched for his dismembered body and restored it to life. Eventually Osiris descended into the underworld as the judge of the dead. His son, Horus, avenged his father's death by killing Seth. Subsequently the myth of Osiris' death and resurrection stimulated the Egyptians' hope for immortality. For Osiris, life won out over death; good won over evil. So the Egyptian reasoned the same could happen to him.

At this point, however, we meet another basic contrast between Egyptian religion and biblical faith. The Old Testament affirms that, at least for the righteous, life continues after physical death (*cf.* Psa. 49:15; Prov. 14:32; Isa. 57:2). So in the biblical faith there is an afterlife for everyone who is faithful to God, whether that person is king or slave. The Egyptian religion was obsessed with the afterlife; but this afterlife was only for the pharaoh and his high-ranking officials. The Bible teaches that no man has a special claim on the presence of God, and no man is exempt from God's moral law. In essence, the difference boils down to a religion for the king (pagan) versus a faith for all believers (biblical).

ALTAR. *This domestic altar illustrates the meaning of the biblical phrase, "four horns of the altar"—as when Adonijah clung to the horns of the altar, for fear of Solomon (1 Kings 1:50–51). This tenth-century limestone altar from Megiddo served an undetermined function in religious ceremonies.*

THE EGYPTIANS

Many barriers seemed to separate Egypt from the Promised Land. It was on a different continent, separated from Palestine by the rocky Sinai Peninsula and the marshes and lakes between the Mediterranean and the Red Sea. Egypt was rich in crops, livestock, and precious metals, while Palestine could offer few goods in exchange. The culture of Egypt was radically different from that of the Canaanites and Israelites, and its people came from a different race. Yet some unexpected turns of history brought the Egyptians and the Israelites together, and the Old Testament refers to Egypt more than 550 times. For centuries, Egypt ruled the coastland of Palestine; its culture and religion was dominant from Gaza to Suez.

I. THE EGYPTIAN PEOPLE AND THEIR LANGUAGE

II. GEOGRAPHY AND AGRICULTURE

III. RELIGION AND HISTORY
  A. Early Dynastic Period and Old Kingdom
  B. First Intermediate Period
  C. The Middle Kingdom
  D. Second Intermediate Period
  E. The New Kingdom
  F. Third Intermediate Period
  G. The Late Period
  H. The Ptolemaic Period

I. The Egyptian People and Their Language. We do not know the exact racial origin of the Egyptian people, but their statues and temple paintings give us a detailed picture of them during biblical times, and the embalmed bodies of Egyptian kings give us further evidence of how they looked.

Most Egyptians were fairly short, brown-skinned, with the stiff brown hair that was typical of people on the southern Mediterranean coasts. Nubians from the Upper Nile in the south did not move down the river and mingle with the Egyptians until around 1500 B.C.

By contrast, the Israelites originally came from the settled city life of southern Mesopotamia. So Abraham and his descendants were probably about the same height as the Egyptians, but they had a light olive-colored complexion and dark brown or black hair.

Egyptians referred to the people of other lands according to their geographical location: "the Libyans," "the Nubians," and so on. But they simply called themselves "the people."[1]

Their language came from a Hamito-Semitic background. In other words, it carried some traits of languages from Northern Africa ("Hamitic," supposedly from Ham's family—Gen. 10:6–20) and from southern Asia Minor ("Semitic," supposedly from Shem's family—Gen. 10:21–31). Although the basic structure of the Egyptian language (such as the construction of verb forms) resembled the Semitic languages such as Hebrew, it was much more like the Hamitic languages of Egypt's African neighbors along the Mediterranean coast.

Captain Bouchard of Napoleon Bonaparte's army discovered the Rosetta Stone in the western Nile Delta in 1799. It bore one inscription in three languages—Greek and two forms of Egyptian—honoring Ptolemy V Epiphanes, a Hellenistic ruler of Egypt who lived 200 years before Christ. An English

---

[1] J. A. Wilson, "Egypt," *Interpreter's Dictionary of the Bible,* Vol. 2 (Nashville: Abingdon Press, 1962), p. 42.

THE BOOK OF THE DEAD. *This papyrus manuscript contains the Book of the Dead, a vast collection of Egyptian incantations to aid the journey of the soul through the netherworld. In this illustration, two gods carry the dead man's soul on a silver boat across a mystical sea. The three figures at left are glorified ancestors of the deceased, awaiting his arrival.*

physicist named Thomas Young and a French linguist named Jean François Champollion used the Greek portion of the stone to decipher the two Egyptian scripts.

Champollion and Young found that one of the Egyptian texts on the Rosetta Stone was written in the *demotic* script (from the Greek *demotikos,* "pertaining to the people"); this was a simple form of writing that Egyptians began using around 500 B.C. The other text was written in the classic Egyptian script called *hieroglyphics* (from the Greek *hieroglyphikos,* "sacred carvings"). Champollion and Young deciphered both of the Egyptian texts by 1822, and their work opened the way for further study of ancient Egyptian literature.[2]

II. Geography and Agriculture. Egypt's territory covered the northeast shoulder of Africa, bordered by the Sahara Desert to the west, the tropical forests of Nubia to the south, the Red Sea to the east, and the Mediterranean to the north. The Nile River was like the bloodstream of ancient Egypt. The waters of

the Nile brought life to the parched plains that the Egyptian people cultivated in Bible times.

The Nile flooded each year in mid-July, providing water for the irrigation systems

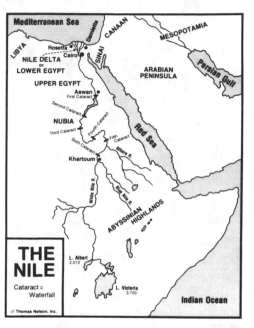

6

THE EGYPTIANS

---

[2] The Egyptians also used a simplified form of hieroglyphics called the *hieratic* script (from the Greek *hieratikos,* "pertaining to the priest's office").

EGYPTIAN WALL PAINTING. *This wall painting from the fourth dynasty (ca. 2700 B.C.) depicts the Egyptians as a brown-skinned people with stiff, dark hair.*

THE EGYPTIANS

THE NILE. *"Egypt is the gift of the Nile," said Hecataeus of Miletos. The river which gave Egypt life brought both blessing and curse. So strong was its influence that the Egyptians deified it as the god Hapi, and in many ways the river was the center for Egyptian culture. Deserts surround the Nile Valley, but the fertile river lowlands are green and bountiful. Cooperation among the area's people in constructing and operating dams and irrigation systems unified the country politically. Efforts to predict the river's cycles led to Egyptian discoveries in astronomy, which in turn led to the creation of a calendar. As Egyptian scribes recorded annual changes of the river, they developed the Egyptian system of writing.*

the Nile each signalled disaster, for farmers in the first case, for whole settlements in the second. The river was both a blessing and a curse to the Egyptian farmers (*fellahin*).

The Nile River watered a green valley that varied from one to twenty miles in width. Egyptians called the rich soil of this valley "Black Land," and the surrounding desert the "Red Land."

Every June, the rains of central Africa and the melting snows of Abyssinia raised the river waters more than fifteen feet over their banks. The flood reached Syene (modern Aswan) in the middle of June, and the river remained at flood stage for more than a week. Normally, the *fellahin* were glad to see the Nile cover their land with its sluggish waters, for they knew it would leave behind a deep layer of silt that would give them an abundant harvest that fall. If the Nile did not rise as much as usual, they would have a "lean year" (cf. Gen. 41:30 ff.). But if the river rose too much, it destroyed everything in its path. So the peasants and herdsmen were at the mercy of the river.

At the city of Heliopolis, the Nile River split into the Rosetta and Damietta Branches, then broke into the many arteries of the Nile Delta. The small branches of the river crisscrossed the Delta, irrigating the land even dur-

built to benefit from this inundation. But while the timing of the flooding was predictable, its extent was not. Too small or too large a rise in

WOODEN MODEL OF BOAT. *Dating from the eleventh dynasty of Egypt (ca. 2000 B.C.), this model boat is equipped with a rudder, mast, sail, and cabin. Within the cabin sit models of an Egyptian ruler, his son, and a singer to entertain them.*

THE EGYPTIANS

ing the dry winter months. For this reason, the Delta became the "bread basket" of Egypt.

The Nile was Egypt's most important trade route. Because the prevailing winds blew south, boats could sail upstream on the Nile. The waters were smooth for about six hundred miles from the Mediterranean coast to Syene. There caravans from the Upper Nile unloaded their cargo for shipment to the outside world. (Egyptians called the land upstream [south] from Syene "Upper Egypt," while the land downstream [north] was "Lower Egypt." Just above Syene was the first of several *cataracts*—rapids and waterfalls that blocked navigation. So the port city naturally became an important landmark for the Egyptians.)

". . . From prehistoric times on, the Egyptians were a river-faring people, and by [3000 B.C.] they had taken their boats out into the open sea. . . . On the Red Sea the Egyptian vessel was dominant in the trade southward to the land of incense, myrrh, gums, and ivory . . ."[3]

As Egypt expanded her trade and became a prosperous nation, she had to develop better agricultural methods. Food crops and textile fibers were the mainstays of her economy, so the farmers had to devise more efficient methods for irrigating their fields, making the most of their narrow strip of soil along the Nile. They built dikes to protect their crops from the river in years of severe flood; they drained the marshes of the Delta region; they installed crude wooden irrigation devices to lift water from the river; and they abandoned the hand-held hoe in favor of ox-drawn wooden plows.

Compared to the lush river valley of the Nile, the eastern coastal region was bleak and hostile. "Along the coast there appear to have always been a number of lagoons, separated from the sea by low bars of sand, and used as salt-pans. In Greek and Roman times the largest of these was known as the Serbonian [Sirbonian] Bog or Marsh. It had a very evil repute. The dry sand blowing across gave it the appearance of solid ground, which was sufficient to bear those who ventured on it, only until they were beyond flight or rescue, and it swallowed up more than one unfortunate army."[4]

The Delta and coastal regions had high tem-

peratures and high humidity in the summer and heavy rain in the winter. A hot, scorching wind known as the *Khamsin* blew across the Delta between March and May, leaving the people fatigued and irritable. The *Sobaa* wind generated blinding dust storms that could bury a merchant caravan in minutes.

This variable climate brought many diseases to the Egyptian people. In fact, Moses warned the Israelites that if they were not faithful to God, He would afflict them with "the diseases of Egypt" (Deut. 7:15; 28:60). Men of Napoleon's army suffered from boils and fever when they camped in Lower Egypt; even modern visitors find it difficult to adapt to the climate there.

Yet the climate of Egypt benefitted her people in other ways. The warm Mediterranean breezes gave Egypt a year-round growing season, which the *fellahin* exploited to the limits

PALETTE OF NARMER. *This palette (an inscribed plaque of slate) from 3000 B.C. is the first great historical record. It depicts the conquest of Lower Egypt by King Narmer, who wears the white crown of Upper Egypt and strikes a kneeling prisoner with a mace. Narmer claimed Lower Egypt but was unable to subdue it. His successor, Menes, was the first Egyptian leader since prehistoric times to conquer the delta lands and reunite them with Upper Egypt. (Some scholars believe Narmer and Menes are identical.)*

---

[3] J. A. Wilson, "Egypt," p. 42.

[4] George Adam Smith, *The Historical Geography of the Holy Land* (New York: A. C. Armstrong and Son, 1906), p. 157.

THE SPHINX. *This massive figure with the body of a lion and the head of King Khaf-Re represents the god Horus guarding the city of the dead at Giza. Built during the Old Kingdom period of Egypt (2800–2250 B.C.), the Sphinx has come to symbolize the mystery of the past.*

of their technical abilities. At the same time, the dryness of arid wastelands along the edge of the Nile Valley preserved the pharaohs' embalmed bodies (*mummies*) and other relics. And the desolate lands surrounding Egypt made natural borders that were fairly easy to defend.

III. Religion and History. When the Egyptian priest Manetho (*ca.* 305–285 B.C.) wrote a history of Egypt in Greek, he divided the history of the kings into 30 (later expanded to 31) periods known as "dynasties." The dynasties were then grouped into kingdoms: the Old Kingdom (*ca.* 2800–2250 B.C.; dynasties 3–6), the Middle Kingdom (*ca.* 2000 B.C.–1786 B.C.; dynasties 11–12), and the New Kingdom (1575–1085 B.C.; dynasties 18–20). Manetho labeled the time of the last pharaohs the Late Period (*ca.* 663 B.C.–332 B.C.; dynasties 26–31). The first two dynasties belonged to the Early Dynastic Period (3100–2800 B.C.). Between the Old and the Middle Kingdom and between the Middle and the New Kingdom were tumultuous times, known respectively as the First and the Second Intermediate Period. The period between the New Kingdom and the Late Period was known as the Third Intermediate Period (1085 B.C.–661 B.C.).

The conquest of Alexander the Great introduced a new period in Egypt's history, known as the Ptolemaic Period (332–30 B.C.). With the victory over Cleopatra VII, Augustus incorporated Egypt into a Roman province (30 B.C.–A.D. 395).

The development of Egyptian religion is reviewed in the section entitled "Pagan Religions and Cultures," but here we should note the allegiance of different pharaohs to differ-

ent Egyptian gods. A pharaoh's religious beliefs often revealed something of his personal character and political ambitions.

A. Early Dynastic Period and Old Kingdom. Before Menes united Egypt (*ca.* 3200 B.C.), the land was divided into two kingdoms that roughly corresponded to Upper and Lower Egypt. Seth, the patron god of the city Ombos, had become the god of Lower Egypt while Horus, the patron god of the city Behdet, had become the god of Upper Egypt. When Menes of Thinis united the two Egypts (*ca.* 3200 B.C.), he made the sky god, Horus, the national god and claimed that he was the incarnation of Horus. Most pharaohs of the Old Kingdom (2800–2250 B.C.) did the same, and the Egyptians built up a large collection of myths about Horus. The Old Kingdom is also remembered for its famous pyramids.

B. First Intermediate Period. The First Intermediate Period followed the Old Kingdom. This time of social upheaval saw the total collapse of the central government. Local princes and barons gained power during the sixth dynasty; at last they became completely independent. Rulers of Thebes restored order to the troubled nation during the eleventh dynasty, but they were not able to reunite Egypt. During this time Abraham came to Egypt for relief from the famine in Palestine (Gen. 12:12–20). The "pharaoh" that Abraham tried to deceive may have been a king of Thebes, but most likely he was a ruler of the region of Upper Egypt.

C. The Middle Kingdom. The Middle Kingdom began around 2000 B.C. when Amenemhet I of Thebes forced the princes of the land to give their grudging allegiance to him. Amenemhet made Amun, the god of

THE EGYPTIANS

Thebes, the national god of his new Middle Kingdom. By setting up Amun as the spiritual symbol of his new dynasty, Amenemhet tested the political allegiance of his subjects. Loyal Egyptians worshiped Amun in obedience to their new pharaoh, much as in later days the patriots of a country would rally around its flag. For more than 200 years (2000–1780 B.C.) the Amenemhet and Senwosret pharaohs used Thebes as their central seat of power and worshiped Amun as the "king of the gods."

Joseph was brought to Egypt as a slave around 1876 B.C. (cf. Gen. 37:5–28). Several years later he became the *vizier* (an officer second only to the pharaoh) in a united, powerful Egypt (cf. Gen. 41:38–46). During this Middle Kingdom period Egypt was awakening to the world. It traded commercial goods with Crete, Palestine, Syria, and other lands. Art and literature blossomed and peaceful conditions generally prevailed. When Jacob and his family migrated to Egypt, they no doubt felt secure from attack and persecution.

D. Second Intermediate Period. Shortly before 1700 B.C., the Hyksos ("foreign rulers") seized control of Egypt and made Heliopolis their new capital. They adopted the local god of Heliopolis, Re, as the national god of their new kingdom. Re was another sun

GOLD COFFIN OF TUTANKHAMEN. *Tutankhamen, who ruled Egypt for nine years between 1366 and 1357 B.C., is sometimes known as "The Boy King." He was 18 years old when he died under mysterious circumstances. A minor pharaoh, his principal accomplishment was to restore the worship of Amun to Thebes. His modern-day fame lies in the fact that his was the only Egyptian tomb that archaeologists have discovered intact. This miniature gold coffin in the likeness of the king was one of four containing the embalmed internal organs. The lid is inlaid with semi-precious stones and colored glass, and the figure bears a crook and flail, symbols of authority. He wears a headdress featuring the vulture and the serpent, national divinities of Upper Egypt and Lower Egypt, respectively.*

QUEEN NEFERTITI. *This famous bust of Akhnaton's queen shows the high quality of Egyptian artwork, which at this period (fourteenth century B.C.) has become less formalized and more realistic in its approach.*

god; artists portrayed him as a falcon-man with a solar disk over his head. The Hyksos used Re to emphasize that Heliopolis dominated all of Egypt. Actually, the Hyksos controlled only Lower Egypt, while the kings of the Upper Nile Valley stood firm in their own local domains. The Egypt of the Hyksos was not as well organized as under the Old

Kingdom and Middle Kingdom. But its literature and culture far surpassed anything in Palestine at that time, which was also in political and economic chaos.

Some scholars believe the Exodus took place during the time of the Hyksos; while others maintain that it occurred after the Hyksos were expelled from Egypt. Unfortunately, Scripture and archaeological evidence do not obviously enforce one another at this point. The most probable date of the Exodus (1446 B.C.) is discussed under "Bible Chronology." A Hyksos ruler was probably the "pharaoh who did not know Joseph" (Exod. 1:8). The Semitic Hyksos probably felt a rivalry with

THE GREAT HYPOSTYLE HALL, KAR-NAK. *One of the greatest monuments of antiquity, the Hypostyle Hall is the largest of many massive structures at Karnak, the city of temples at Thebes. Its interior space of 6,000 square yards is enough to contain the entire Cathedral of Notre Dame in Paris. Begun by the pharaoh Seti, it was dedicated to the sun god Amun-Re. The structure was completed by the pharaoh Rameses II. Its 134 sandstone columns are covered with hieroglyphs. The 12 largest columns line the central avenue and are 69 feet tall and 33 feet in circumference; 100 men could stand atop each.*

the Hebrews and wanted to suppress them as much as possible. Even after the Hyksos were overthrown, the rulers of Egypt oppressed the Hebrews.

After about a century, King Kamose of Thebes broke the power of the Hyksos in Egypt and united the nation under the city of Thebes once again. Kamose, his younger brother Ahmose, and their successors reformed the religion of Egypt once again. These alterations in religion were a political tactic. The priests who controlled the various shrines and towns fought to gain political power over the pharaoh. They revived the worship of Amun, combined it with the religion of Re, and named the new national god Amun-Re. This prepared the way for a new epoch in Egyptian politics, called the New Kingdom (1575–1085 B.C.). Ahmose married his sister, Princess Ahmose-Nofretari, and claimed that she was the wife of Amun. This gave both of them spiritual prestige.

E. The New Kingdom. The New Kingdom formally began when Ahmose's son, Amenhotep I, succeeded him in 1546 B.C. Notice that Amenhotep named himself after his father's god, Amun-Re; he also called himself the "Son of Re."

Gradually the Egyptians came to think of their pharaohs as gods in the flesh, and they worshiped them as such. For example, the official Egyptian history showed that when Thutmose II died (*ca.* 1504 B.C.), he "went forth to heaven and mingled with the gods."[5]

Other pharaohs of the New Kingdom followed the custom of naming themselves after Amun-Re (e.g., Amenophis, Tutankhamen). When Hatshepsut assumed the power of the pharaoh after the death of Thutmose II (she was the only woman to ever do so), she called herself "Daughter of Re." She described herself as "altogether divine" and said that all the gods of Egypt promised to protect her.

Her son, Thutmose III, also held this idea of divine protection for the pharaoh. When his general, Djehuti, won a great victory at Joppa, he sent a dispatch to Thutmose III that said: "Rejoice! Your god Amun has delivered to you the enemy of Joppa, all his people, and all his city. Send people to lead them off as captives, in order that you may fill the house of

[5] George Steindorff and Keith C. Seele, *When Egypt Ruled the East* (Chicago: University of Chicago Press, 1957), p. 40.

your father Amun-Re, king of the gods, with male and female slaves . . ."[6]

The succeeding pharaohs of the New Kingdom, especially Amenhotep III (1412–1375 B.C.), constructed great tombs for themselves that extolled the powers of Amun-Re. He was their claim to immortality.

Amenhotep IV shunned the worship of Amun-Re in favor of the sun god, Aton. He renamed himself Akhnaton and founded a new capital city at Amarna, where he tried to establish Aton as the new universal god of Egypt. But when he died in 1366 B.C., his successor Tutankhamen moved the capital back to Thebes and restored Amun-Re as the leading god of the empire. Tutankhamen's tomb contained many symbols of Osiris, the god of the dead; and other evidence indicates that the worship of Osiris was becoming more prominent at this time.

The elderly king Rameses I began the nineteenth dynasty with his short one-half year reign (1319–1318 B.C.). This dynasty revived the glory of ancient Egypt for a brief time, following the political disorder that Akhnaton had caused. Rameses' son, Seti I, began new wars of conquest that pushed into Palestine, driving out the Hittites.

The pharaohs of this new dynasty established their capital at Karnak in the Nile Delta. Though they still gave homage to Amun-Re, they raised the worship of Osiris to a new level of royal favor. They dedicated the city of Abydos in honor of Osiris and glorified the god of the dead in their majestic tombs at Abu Simbel and the temples of Medinet Habu. The Rameses pharaohs also elevated the worship of Re-Harakhti, in whom they combined the qualities of Horus (the sky god) and Re (the sun god). But they still considered Amun-Re to be the chief god of their religious system.

Rameses II chose his son, Merneptah, to succeed him in 1232 B.C. Merneptah and the remaining kings of the nineteenth dynasty gradually lost the power that the Rameses kings had acquired; but Merneptah launched ruthless raids against Palestine. Archaeologists have translated an inscription from a stone column called the Israel Stele, on which Merneptah describes his victories in that area: "Carried off is Ashkelon; seized upon is Gezer; Yanoam is made as that which does not

exist; Israel is laid waste, his seed is not. . . ."[7]

This would have been during the time of the judges; so Merneptah's description confirms the disorganized situation in Israel, where "there arose another generation . . . which knew not the Lord nor yet the works which he had done for Israel" (Judg. 2:10). However, Merneptah's troubles at home did not allow him to stay in Palestine, and so he left the scat-

---

[7] J. B. Pritchard, *Ancient Near Eastern Texts Relating to the Old Testament* (Princeton, N.J.: Princeton University Press, 1969), p. 231.

THE MERNEPTAH STELE. *Merneptah ruled Egypt in the latter half of the thirteenth century B.C. He fought to defend the Egyptian Empire against the invasion of Mediterranean peoples into the Delta. The Merneptah Stele commemorates the king's Palestinian campaign, in which he claims to have destroyed Israel. This is the first historical monument on which the name of Israel is inscribed.*

---

[6] Steindorff and Seele, *When Egypt Ruled the East*, pp. 57–58.

tered tribes of Israel at the mercy of the Philistines.

Pharaoh Sethnakht reunited the Egyptian city-states in about 1200 B.C. His son, Rameses III (1198–1167 B.C.), fought off invasions by the "Peoples of the Sea"—Philistines who landed on the Mediterranean shores of Egypt. His artists chiseled great relief carvings in the Temple of Medinet Habu that describe these victories. But Rameses III died at the hand of an assassin, and his successors slowly lost their grip on the government. Ironically, the priests of Amun gained more prestige during the same periods.

F. Third Intermediate Period. Around 1100 B.C., a Nubian general named Panehsi appointed one of his lieutenants named Hrihor as the high priest of Amun at Karnak. Hrihor soon became commander-in-chief of the army itself and took the throne from Rameses XI (1085 B.C.). This began a new pattern in Egyptian government: Each pharaoh appointed one of his sons to become the high priest of Amun as the boy's first step to the throne. The royal family claimed to be the high religious family from this point on, using the influence of Amun to assert their authority.

At this time, David and Solomon were building Israel to the height of its power. When David's commander-in-chief, Joab, drove young Prince Hadad of Edom out of his native land, Hadad's servants took him to Egypt (1 Kings 11:14–19). One of the pharaohs took him in, and Hadad married the pharaoh's sister-in-law. Hadad then returned to harass King Solomon (1 Kings 11:21–25). So Egypt figured in the political affairs of Israel throughout this period (cf. 1 Kings 3:1; 9:16).

But the Egyptian empire gradually disintegrated, and princes of Nubia carved out the southern territory with their capital at Napata. These Nubian kings also claimed to have the special favor of Amun. "The state was to be considered as a model theocracy and its king the true guardian of unadulterated Egyptian character and culture."[8] Egypt's troubles were much like Israel's during this time; both had a divided kingdom. (*See* "Chronology.")

Kings of Libya (to the west) toppled the weak pharaohs of Thebes in the tenth century B.C. They hired soldiers from the region of the Nile Delta to keep the peace in Lower Egypt.

One of these Libyan kings, Sheshonk I, sacked the temple of Jerusalem in the fifth year of King Rehoboam (1 Kings 14:25–26; note that the Bible calls him "Shishak"). Sheshonk and the other Libyan kings adopted the traditional worship of Amun-Re. But even

---

[8] Steindorff and Seele, *When Egypt Ruled the East,* pp. 270–271.

The Valley of the Kings

For a thousand years, the pharaohs of Egypt were buried in the desolate area known as the Valley of the Kings. Located along the Nile near the city of Thebes, it became the resting place of 30 or more kings, among them Egypt's greatest.

The Egyptian culture took great care in preparing the dead, to insure their security in the afterlife. It was believed that one must place in his tomb everything needed to make the afterlife happy. So the kings filled their tombs with great wealth and then marked the site of the tomb with a huge stone monument (*pyramid*).

Many workers were used to build the elaborate tombs, and they knew that within them lay treasures of all descriptions. In order to protect these treasures, the king of the reigning dynasty hired guards to patrol the valley. In spite of these precautions, grave robbers began to plunder the tombs, stripping them clean. Thus, many of the kings were moved to secret burial sites to protect and preserve their bodies and coffins.

King Thutmose, greatly disturbed by this looting, decided to keep secret the location of his tomb. He hired a trusted friend, Ineni, to oversee its construction. It is believed that Ineni hired prisoners to do the actual work and then slaughtered them when it was completed, in order to guard the royal secret. Even this plan failed, for thieves continued to plunder the riches that lay within the tombs. When King Thutmose's tomb was discovered in 1899, little remained in it but the massive stone sarcophagus.

No area has ever been surrounded with such mystery as the Valley of the Kings. The riches that lay there evoked wickedness in the hearts of men who sought to strip it bare. As late as the 1800s, men continued to seek its wealth. However, the valley was eventually saved by the efforts of archaeologists who unearthed the greatest find to date, the tomb of King Tutankhamen.

THE EGYPTIANS

with this symbol of national power, they failed to realize their dream of reviving the Egyptian empire.

The Nubian (Ethiopian) princes moved down the Nile and defeated the Libyan kings around 700 B.C. For the next 50 years, they attempted to reunite Egypt. One of these new kings (the Bible calls him "Zerah") attacked Judah with an enormous army. Undoubtedly, he was trying to secure his eastern border, as so many pharaohs had done before him. But Asa soundly defeated him: ". . . Ethiopians were overthrown, that they could not recover themselves" (2 Chron. 14:13).

The Assyrians attacked Judah soon afterwards. King Hoshea of Judah appealed to a new Ethiopian king for help, but the Ethiopians could do nothing. ". . . Therefore the king of Assyria shut him [Hoshea] up, and bound him in prison" (2 Kings 17:4). The Assyrians captured Judah, then marched into Egypt and overthrew the Ethiopian monarchy in 670 B.C.

G. The Late Period. But the Assyrians could not maintain their hold on Egypt, and seven years later Prince Psamtik of Sais drove them back to the Sinai Peninsula. Psamtik reunited Upper and Lower Egypt and established the twenty-sixth dynasty, reviving Egyptian culture until 663 B.C. (when the Persians conquered Egypt). Psamtik reestablished

CLEOPATRA VII. *A Macedonian by birth, Cleopatra was an ambitious, intelligent, and cultured queen. She was unique in Egypt's line of Ptolemaic rulers because she took the Egyptian religion seriously and spoke the language of the people. When her dreams of empire were lost with Antony's fleet at Actium, she committed suicide by allowing herself to be bitten by an asp, the symbol of Amun-Re.*

the worship of Amun-Re as the national god of Egypt. But his priests were not able to exert the controlling and unifying influence that royal priests once had over the Egyptian people.

Egyptian religion now degenerated into a variety of animal cults. The kings of the twenty-sixth dynasty built temples in honor of certain sacred animals, such as the crocodile and the cat. "So extreme was the zeal of this epoch that it became the custom to embalm each one of the sacred animals at death and bury it ceremoniously in special cemeteries dedicated to the purpose."[9]

Nekau ("Necho") succeeded his father Psamtik I as pharaoh in 610 B.C. He recognized the growing menace of Babylon and marched through Canaan in order to help the Assyrians fight this common enemy. King Josiah tried to stop him at Megiddo, but Nekau defeated him and continued on his march (2 Kings 23:29–30). Nebuchadnezzar destroyed the Egyptian army at Carchemish

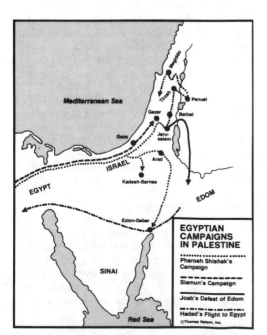

Mediterranean Sea

Megiddo

Tirzah

Penuel

Gezer

Bethel

Gaza

Jeru-
salem

Arad

ISRAEL

Kadesh-Barnea

EGYPT

EDOM

Ezion-Geber

SINAI

Red Sea

EGYPTIAN CAMPAIGNS IN PALESTINE

•••••••••••••••••
Pharoah Shishak's Campaign

▬ ▬ ▬ ▬ ▬ ▬
Siamun's Campaign

▬ ▬ ▬ ▬ ▬ ▬
Joab's Defeat of Edom

▬ ▬ ▬ ▬ ▬ ▬
Hadad's Flight to Egypt

©Thomas Nelson, Inc.

---

[9] Steindorff and Seele, *When Egypt Ruled the East,* pp. 139–140.

THE EGYPTIANS

on the Euphrates River in 605 B.C. But Nekau escaped, captured the new king of Judah, and made Judah a buffer state between Babylon and Egypt (2 Chron. 36:4). When Nebuchadnezzar attacked Judah in 601 B.C., Egypt was able to stop him temporarily. Pharaoh Apries encouraged King Jehoiakin to resist the Babylonian intruders. But Nebuchadnezzar succeeded in capturing Jerusalem in 586 B.C. and carried its people into exile. Nebuchadnezzar installed Gedaliah as governor of the new Judean province; but Gedaliah's subjects murdered him within a few months (2 Kings 25:25). Afraid that the Babylonians would slaughter them in revenge, the remaining Jews of Jerusalem fled to Egypt. Among them was the prophet Jeremiah (Jer. 43:5–7).

King Cyrus of Persia conquered the Babylonian Empire in 539 B.C.; his successor, Cambyses, took Egypt in 525 B.C. The Persians placed puppet kings on the throne of Egypt for the next century, and each of them gave lip service to the god Amun-Re. But the real power behind the throne was the army of Persia, not the traditional mystique of the Egyptian gods.

H. The Ptolemaic Period. Alexander the Great conquered Egypt in 332 B.C. He died nine years later and the Ptolemy family took charge of Egypt and Palestine. The Ptolemies placed members of their own family on the throne at Thebes, and they tried to recapture the grandeur of Egypt's golden age. For example, Ptolemy Euergetes II made Amenhotep I a god in 140 B.C.; by revering this pharaoh who established Egypt's New Kingdom, Euergetes hoped to pass himself off as a true Egyptian. But the native people of Egypt only gave him token loyalty. He had to depend on the Roman armies to protect him from the attacks of the Seleucid Empire north of Palestine.

The Roman general Pompey captured Jerusalem in 63 B.C. and broke the back of the Seleucid threat; but Egypt was tottering on the brink of collapse. At last Cleopatra emerged from the Ptolemy family to try to save the nation by political chicanery and bribes. She courted the favor of both Augustus Caesar and Mark Antony; but when Caesar's fleet defeated hers at Actium in 30 B.C., Cleopatra committed suicide in despair. From that time, Egypt came under the shield of imperial Rome.

During their brief time on the throne, the Hellenistic rulers planted Greek cities on the coast of Egypt and brought Greek settlers into the country. Thus they added foreign elements to the Egyptian way of life, especially to Egyptian religion.

The Egyptians were more receptive to the process of Hellenization than the Jews were. (*See* "The Greeks and Hellenism.") Priests gave Egyptian gods the names of their Greek counterparts: Horus became Apollo; Thoth became Hermes; Amun became Zeus; Ptah became Hephaistos; Hathor became Aphrodite; and so on. Egyptians worshiped the Ptolemaic rulers and their wives, much like they had worshiped the pharaohs.

Jews who settled in Egypt during the Babylonian exile developed thriving Jewish communities there. Aramaic papyri show that there was a prominent Jewish colony at Aswan, on the island of Elephantine. This group did not live in close conformity with the Law of Moses, and they finally abolished animal sacrifice. The community was destroyed soon after 404 B.C.

Other Jewish communities fared better, and under the Ptolemies they received legal status. The Letter of Aristeas claims that Ptolemy I carried off over 100,000 Jews from Palestine and used them as mercenaries in the Egyptian armed forces. These Jews continued to worship God, but they were able to adjust to the Graeco-Roman way of life.

Ancient tax receipts show that there were Jewish tax collectors in Egypt. Jews also served in other government offices. In a letter that Claudius wrote to the Alexandrines, he asked that Jewish candidates not be allowed to run for the office of *gymisiarch,* who was in charge of the athletic games that were offensive to strict Jews (cf. 1 Macc. 1:14–15).

The ancient historian Philo says that 1,000,000 Jews lived in Egypt. They knew little Hebrew or Aramaic. For this reason, the Hebrew Bible was translated into Greek, the *Septuagint* version. The Jews of Alexandria were the first to use the Septuagint; later it was read in synagogues throughout the Roman Empire.

Philo of Alexandria was a Jewish philosopher who adopted the Greek ideas of Stoicism and Platonism. He dressed Jewish beliefs in the categories of Greek philosophic thought.

From Alexandria came the allegorical interpretation of Scripture. This Egyptian city became an important center of Jewish scholarship in the intertestamental period. (*See* "Jews in New Testament Times.")

When Mary and Joseph hid the infant Jesus

THE EGYPTIANS

there in about 4 B.C. (Matt. 2:13–15), several Jewish communities remained in the Nile Delta area where they had settled in Jere- miah's time. We assume that Mary and Joseph found refuge in one of these villages.

Periods of Egyptian History

Period	Dates	Bible Events
I. Early Dynastic Period (Dynasties 1–2)	3100–2800 B.C.	
II. The Old Kingdom (Dynasties 3–6)	2800–2250 B.C.	
III. First Intermediate Period (Dynasties 7–9)	2250–2000 B.C.	Abraham comes to Egypt
IV. The Middle Kingdom (Dynasties 9–12)	2000–1786 B.C.	Joseph and Jacob come to Egypt
V. Second Intermediate Period (Dynasties 13–17)	1786–1575 B.C.	Hyksos Period (c. 1667–1559 B.C.)
VI. The New Kingdom (Dynasties 18–20)	1575–1085 B.C.	The Exodus (1446 B.C.)
VII. Third Intermediate Period` (Dynasties 21–25)	1085–663 B.C.	Sheshonk I ("Shishak") sacks the temple (927 B.C.)
VIII. The Late Period (Dynasties 26–31)	663–332 B.C.	The Exile (586 B.C.); refugees flee to Egypt
IX. The Ptolemaic Period	332–30 B.C.	
X. The Roman Era	30 B.C.–A.D. 395	Mary and Joseph escape to Egypt (4 B.C.)

6

THE EGYPTIANS

THE BABYLONIANS AND ASSYRIANS

The Babylonians and Assyrians lived in the region known as *Mesopotamia* (Greek, "between the two rivers"). The ancient historian Herodotus gave this name to the broad plains between the Tigris and Euphrates Rivers, bounded on the north by the Zagros Mountains and on the south by the Persian Gulf. The Bible mentions several cities of Mesopotamia and some of the significant leaders of the Babylonians and Assyrians. Indeed, these two cultures brought the eventual downfall of Israel and Judah. Yet the people of Mesopotamia were affecting the lives of the Israelites many centuries before that final encounter.

I. THE SUMERIANS
A. "Ur of the Chaldees"
B. Larsa
C. Erech

II. THE AKKADIANS
A. Agade (Akkad)
B. Sargon of Agade

III. THE EARLY BABYLONIANS
A. Hammurabi (ca. 1792–1750 B.C.)
B. Babylonian Literature

IV. THE EARLY ASSYRIANS
A. Shalmaneser I (ca. 1300 B.C.)
B. Assyrian Literature

V. THE GOLDEN AGE (1211–539 B.C.)
A. Nebuchadnezzar I (ca. 1135 B.C.)
B. Tiglath-Pileser I (ca. 1100 B.C.)
C. Ashurnasirpal III (885–860 B.C.)
D. Shalmaneser III (860–824 B.C.)
E. Tiglath-Pileser III (745–727 B.C.)
F. The Destruction of Israel (721 B.C.)
G. The Destruction of Judah (586 B.C.)
H. The Glory of Nebuchadnezzar II (605–562 B.C.)

VI. YEARS OF DECLINE

VII. ART AND ARCHITECTURE

VIII. RELIGION

IX. LITERATURE OF THE GOLDEN AGE

X. OTHER ARCHAEOLOGICAL EVIDENCE

SUMERIAN DAIRY. *This bas relief from a Sumerian temple shows dairying activities in about 2500 B.C. At top right a man is milking a cow. To the left of the stable a man churns butter, while farther to the left three men are preparing and stirring clarified butter, which is still the principal product of rural Iraq.*

THE BABYLONIANS AND ASSYRIANS

UR. *This is all that remains of the city in which Abraham lived before migrating into Palestine. The mound in the rear was the ziggurat, or temple tower. The ruins of the city lie in the foreground.*

I. The Sumerians. The earliest known inhabitants of Mesopotamia lived in the southern part of what is now Iraq. These people are simply called "proto-Euphrateans," for lack of a better term. The first identifiable people of this group were known as *Sumerians.* Their culture greatly influenced all of the ancient Near East, including the Israelites. The word "Shinar," which occurs several times in the Old Testament, refers to the area that includes the Sumerian homeland.[1] The Sumerians were not Semites, nor were they Indo-Europeans. They spoke a language unlike any other, either ancient or modern.

The Sumerians began building small towns along the banks of the Tigris and Euphrates sometime after 7000 B.C. The relics of these early communities show that the people were primitive farmers.

The Sumerians developed a township system of government, in which the temple of the local deity was the center of economic, cultural, and religious life. So integrated were the religious and civil functions that these ancient societies are called the "archaic religious states." This term describes the antiquity and the religious character of their organization.

The town was ruled by a council led by a

mayor or *ensi.* The *ensi* also acted as the high priest of the town, ministering at a temple that stood at the center of the community. The temple was the town's center for worship, education, and government. At the temples of E-Anna in Uruk archaeologists have found evidence of writing dating from about 3000 B.C. (*See* "Languages and Writing.")

Each Sumerian city developed its own style of pottery. Archaeologists have found beautiful examples of their pottery art at Hassuna, Samarra, Halaf, Ubaid, and Uruk (Warka). The Sumerians also developed great skill as jewelry makers.

A. "Ur of the Chaldees." One of the foremost cities of Sumer was Ur. This city-state came to the chief position among the towns of Sumer several times in its history. The Bible refers to it as "Ur of the Chaldees" (Gen. 11:28). This city was the home of Terah and Abram (Abraham), ancestors of the Hebrew nation (Gen. 11:28–31).

Located on the banks of Euphrates River, Ur was an important trading post dedicated to the god Sin and the goddess Nin-gal. Clay tablets from Ur explain that it was located in the district of the Kaldu people, which is why

GUDEA. *This is one of a series of statues representing Gudea, the governor or king of Lagash, one of the major Sumerian cities. The serenity and dignity of this portrait sculpture make it a remarkable work of art.*

---

[1] Walter Bodine, "The Sumerians," in Alfred Hoerth, Gerald Mathingly, and Edwin Yamauchi, eds., *Peoples of the Old Testament World* (Grand Rapids: Baker, 1994), 19.

THE BABYLONIANS AND ASSYRIANS

the biblical writers called it "Ur of the Chaldees."

B. Larsa. Northeast of Ur stood the city of Larsa. The Bible probably refers to this site when it mentions the "king of Ellasar" who attacked Sodom and Gomorrah and the other "cities of the plain" (Gen. 14:1–2). The people of Larsa worshiped the sun god Shamash.

C. Erech. Just over 24 km. (15 mi.) west of Larsa stood the town of Erech. Many scholars believe this was the home of the "Archevites" who later petitioned King Artaxerxes to stop the restoration of Jerusalem (Ezra 4:9).

Erech was the center for the worship of the goddesses Ishtar and Nana, two of the best-known pagan deities. (*See* "Pagan Religions and Cultures.") Unlike the other Sumerian towns, Erech was the home of Semitic people. In its ruins archaeologists have found bricks bearing the names of Semitic kings.

II. The Akkadians. In the central region of Mesopotamia lived the Akkadians, who had a more advanced civilization than their neighbors to the south. The Akkadians developed one of the first systems of writing. (*See* "Languages and Writing.") They were ingenious builders and military strategists. Like the Sumerians, the Akkadians built each of their cities around a temple that honored a local deity.

A. Agade (Akkad). The central region took its name from the town of Agade, which many English-speaking scholars call Akkad. Some believe that the Bible calls this city Sepharvaim (cf. 2 Kings 17:24).

B. Sargon of Agade. The Akkadian cities were eventually dominated by Elam, a strong city-state to the southeast. In about 2300 B.C., King Sargon of Agade rebelled against the Elamites and united the Akkadians under his rule. He called himself "King of the Four Zones," referring to the major cities of the region—Kish, Cutha, Agade-Sippar, and Babylon-Borsippa.

Sargon established an efficient system of roads and postal service to unite his domain. He began an imperial library that eventually collected thousands of clay tablets.

Sargon's dynasty lasted for only three generations. Akkad then came under the influence of Ur, the great commercial center of Sumerians. A few Akkadian cities, such as Langash (ruled by a priest named Gudea) resisted this trend. But the Sumerian city-states of Ur and Larsa dominated Mesopotamia for over 200 years. The region gradually drifted back to the control of Elam.

III. The Early Babylonians. Semitic invaders from Canaan and the Arabian Desert wrested Mesopotamia from Elamite control in about 2000 B.C. The ruler of Babylon, a man named Hammurabi, emerged as the new ruler of the land "between the two rivers."

A. Hammurabi (1792–1750 B.C.) Hammurabi united the cities of Mesopotamia much as Sargon had done before him. He set up a royal postal system, a new network of roads, and an effective chain of command for his government officials. Hammurabi organized the laws of Mesopotamia into a simplified written form. These laws were carved upon a massive stone column found at Susa. Modern scholars have acclaimed Hammurabi's Code of Law as "a monument of wisdom and equity."[2]

B. Babylonian Literature. The cuneiform tablets and stone monuments of Babylon pro-

BABYLON. *This painting by Maurice Bardin shows the city of Babylon in its glory during the reign of Nebuchadnezzar (605–562 B.C.). The city proper was surrounded by double-walled fortifications and connected to the newer area across the Euphrates River by a pontoon bridge. To the left behind the wall is a ziggurat; to the right, the temple of Marduk.*

[2] Lewis Spence, *Myths and Legends of Babylonia and Assyria* (London: George G. Harrap and Company, 1916), p. 21.

THE BABYLONIANS AND ASSYRIANS

vide considerable information about life in the Babylonian Empire not long after the time of Abraham. This literary evidence runs the gamut from very personal letters to huge public inscriptions boasting of the king's power and prestige.

The best-known document from this period is Hammurabi's Code of Law. Hammurabi used this great declaration to assert that the gods sanctioned his rule. He wrote: "I, Hammurabi, the perfect king among perfect kings, was neither careless nor inactive in regard to the citizens of Sumer and Akkad, whom Enlil bestowed upon me and whose shepherding

Marduk committed unto me. Safe places I continually sought out for them, I overcame serious difficulties, I caused light to shine for them. With the awesome weapons that Zababa and Ishtar entrusted to me, with the wisdom Ea allotted to me, with the ability Marduk gave me, I uprooted enemies above and below, I extinguished holocausts, I made sweet the expanse of the fatherland with irrigation. . . . I am the preeminent king of kings, my words are precious, my ability has no equal. According to the command of the sun god, the great judge of heaven and earth, may my law be displayed in the fatherland."

Nineveh

The powerful city of Nineveh (built by Nimrod, the great-grandson of Noah) presents us with mystery piled on mystery. Even so, as scholars assemble the puzzle, the accuracy of the Bible becomes more apparent.

Nineveh was undoubtedly one of the oldest large cities in the world. The record of its beginnings go back to Genesis 10:11–12: "From that land he went into Assyria, and built Nineveh, Rehoboth-Ir, Calah, and Resen between Nineveh and Calah; that is the great city" (RSV).

The Khoser River flowed eastward from the Tigris through Nineveh. These two rivers, plus a canal that was constructed to carry water from the Tigris to the edge of the city's western wall, provided water for moats, fountains, irrigation, and drinking purposes.

From 1100 B.C., Nineveh was a royal residence. During the reign of Sargon II (722–705 B.C.), it served as the capital of Assyria. Sennacherib (705–681 B.C.) especially loved Nineveh and made it the chief city of his empire: "So Sennacherib king of Assyria departed, and went and returned, and dwelt at Nineveh" (2 Kings 19:36).

Sennacherib made many improvements at Nineveh. He had massive walls constructed and built the oldest aqueduct in history there. It was part of a canal that brought water from the mountains 56 km. (35 mi.) away.

All of these improvements cost money; but the conqueror Sennacherib had no problem raising money, a great deal of which came from tribute.

No one knows the precise age of Nineveh, but the city is mentioned in Babylonian records that extend back to the twenty-first century B.C. Nineveh was also mentioned in the records of Hammurabi, who lived between 1792 and 1750 B.C. We do, however, fix a more precise date for the city's destruction.

The prophet Nahum wrote lyrically about Nin-

eveh's destruction: "Woe is the bloody city! It is full of lies and robbery. . . . The noise of a whip, and the noise of the rattling of the wheels, and the prancing horses, and of the jumping chariots" (3:1–2).

Nineveh was destroyed in August 612 B.C. It fell after a two-month siege carried out by an alliance among Medes, Babylonians, and Scythians. The attackers destroyed Nineveh by releasing the Khoser River into the city, where it dissolved the buildings' sun-dried brick. This was a remarkable fulfillment of Nahum's prophecy: "The gates of the river shall be opened, and the palace shall be dissolved" (Nahum 2:6). Nineveh was lost for well over 2,000 years.

Two centuries after Nineveh's destruction, the Greek soldier and historian Xenophon passed near it on his famous trip to the Black Sea. Although he mentioned seeing the remains of the quay as he marched along on the dry riverbed, he assumed it was a wall belonging to ancient Larsa.

Writing about the city of Mosul in the twelfth century A.D., Benjamin of Tudela wrote: "This city, situated on the Tigris, is connected with ancient Nineveh by a bridge. . . . Nineveh lies now in utter ruins, but numerous villages and small towns occupy its former space." Others also wrote about the place that was Nineveh, but Henry Layard was the first archaeologist to identify the site; he made the discovery on December 22, 1853.

The most famous biblical person connected with the drama of ancient Nineveh was Jonah. Controversy has swirled about this man during the last two centuries, as some scholars have questioned the three days that he spent in the "great fish." But the story of Jonah and Nineveh was in wide circulation during the ministry of Jesus, and Jesus referred to Jonah several times (e.g., Matt. 12:39–41; 16:4).

THE BABYLONIANS AND ASSYRIANS

This passage illustrates the governmental ideals of one of the great conquerors of history. On this great stone stele, Hammurabi lists 282 laws to regulate everyday life in the empire. (*See* "Laws and Statutes.")

Archaeologists have found many clay tablets that describe the worship of various Babylonian gods. Statues and carvings of these gods are not very impressive. In fact, it seems that the Babylonians paid more homage to the king than to the god he represented. The gods were patriotic symbols of the various Babylonian cities. Thus Babylonian travelers were careful to honor the gods of cities that they visited, lest they offend the native citizens.

Religion colored every aspect of Babylonian life. The ruins of Babylonian cities contained inscriptions of prayers for every conceivable occasion. Some of these prayers are addressed to no god in particular and run something like this: "May the god who is unknown be favorable to me."

Other religious texts from Babylon confess the sins of the worshiper and call upon the gods for forgiveness. Scholars call one of these tablets "The Lament of the Righteous Sufferer."

Unfortunately, few of the documents from ancient Babylon describe the political events of that day. We must reconstruct the history from casual clues on royal monuments and letters. So Babylonian literature is of little help in establishing the dates of biblical events; for this we must depend on the records of the third great culture of Mesopotamia—the Assyrians.

IV. The Early Assyrians. In the northeastern reaches of Mesopotamia lived the Assyrians, a warlike people who used the Zagros Mountains as their stronghold. These Semitic tribes settled in the area before Sargon of Agade united the lower Mesopotamian region. They were proud and independent.

Because they were proud of their heritage, the Assyrians kept careful records of their royal lineage. These Assyrian king lists help us to establish the dates of many Old Testament events. (*See* "Chronology.")

The king lists show that the Assyrians began flexing their muscles in the Near East shortly after Hammurabi's dynasty ended. An eastern nation known as the Kassites seized control of Babylon around 1750 B.C. and began a series of wars with Assyria that lasted until 1211 B.C. These wars covered the time of

MESOPOTAMIA

Israel's bondage in Egypt, the Exodus, the conquest of Canaan, and the early years of the judges. At the same time Egypt was vying for control of the Near East. All three nations—Assyria, Babylon and Egypt—marched their armies across Palestine in their pursuit of world supremacy.

A. Shalmaneser I (ca. 1300 B.C.). The first great Assyrian conqueror was Shalmaneser I, who built the capital city of Calah. Shalmaneser expanded the Assyrian territory beyond the Euphrates River and his son, Tiglath-Ninib, captured the enemy city of Babylon. With the aid of the Hittites, Tiglath-Ninib's son incited a civil war that divided the Assyrian nation.

Subsequent Assyrian leaders were able to unite their nation in the face of rather formidable foes. By the time Assyria entered the Old Testament record, it had earned a reputation for military prowess.

B. Assyrian Literature. Most of the Assyrian literature that modern archaeologists have found comes from its later history. It records Assyria's incessant wars with Babylon and other rival nations. Most of the Assyrian king lists were written after 1200 B.C., using older records that have not survived.

V. The Golden Age (1211–539 B.C.). The last Kassite king of Babylon drove the Assyrians out of his territory by 1211 B.C. This established an uneasy balance of power between the Babylonians and Assyrians, allowing both nations to rise to their zenith.

A. Nebuchadnezzar I (ca. 1135 B.C.). The people of Babylon ousted the Kassite kings in

THE BABYLONIANS AND ASSYRIANS

1207 B.C. and placed a new family of native kings on the throne. The sixth king in this line was Nebuchadnezzar I, who began his reign around 1135 B.C. Nebuchadnezzar suffered several defeats at the hands of the Assyrians, but he was able to expand the realm of Babylon. He was also successful in pushing back the Elamites on his eastern border. His son and grandson made successful raids upon Assyrian territory.

B. Tiglath-Pileser I (ca. 1100 B.C.). The Assyrian king Tiglath-Pileser I conquered many surrounding nations during his reign. He plunged deep into the heart of Babylonian territory and captured the city of Babylon for a short time. Tiglath-Pileser's court scribes erected an eight-sided stone monument to record his victories, and he rebuilt the old capital city of Asshur. Saul took the throne of Israel at about this time.

For the next two centuries, Babylon and Assyria fell on hard times. Civil war, conspiracy, and siege combined to weaken them and

WINGED BULL. *This winged, man-headed bull guarded the palace of the king of Assyria during the ninth century B.C. A fine example of Assyrian art, the figure with its long plaited beard and hair tells us something of the appearance of the people of that day.*

thwart their desire for conquest. As these two giants struggled with their problems, the nation of Israel enjoyed its own "golden age" under the reigns of David and Solomon.

Tiglath-Pileser II (*ca.* 950 B.C.) began a new line of kings in Assyria. These kings renewed Assyria's efforts to build an empire that would blanket the known world.

C. Ashurnasirpal II (883–859 B.C.). The next king of Assyria, Ashurnasirpal II, led his armies against the Arameans of the north and then marched west to the Mediterranean coast. Ashurnasirpal forced conquered cities to pay heavy tribute to his royal treasury and he often sent captured kings to the prisons of his capital city (Nineveh) to guarantee that his subjects would remain loyal. He conducted these military campaigns during the reigns of Ahaziah and Athaliah of Judah. He also rebuilt the old Assyrian capital of Calah.

D. Shalmaneser III (858–824 B.C.). The next Assyrian king, Shalmaneser II, continued the conquests of his father. He turned his eyes south to the divided kingdoms of Israel and Judah. King Ahab of Israel and Ben-hadad of Damascus joined forces to resist these invaders (1 Kings 20:13–34). Ahab's successor, King Jehu, submitted to the Assyrians. A black obelisk-shaped monument of Shalmaneser shows Jehu bowing down to the Assyrian king. Shalmaneser boasted that he was "trampling down the country like a wild bull."[3]

The Assyrian Empire suffered serious setbacks under Shalmaneser's descendants. His son Shamshi Adad V (823–811 B.C.) defeated an alliance of Babylonians, Elamites, and other eastern peoples. The next king tried to unite Babylon and Assyria by bringing Babylonian religious symbols into Nineveh. But the strategy failed. His Babylonian subjects rebelled and a series of famines and military defeats pointed to Assyria's gradual decline.

E. Tiglath-Pileser III (745–727 B.C.). Tiglath-Pileser III revived Assyria's hope of becoming a world empire. He regained the Babylonian territory, recaptured the Aramean cities, and returned Assyria's army to the battlefield of Palestine. Tiglath-Pileser's royal documents say that foreign cities were "desolated like an overwhelming flood" by his

[3] George W. Gilmore, "Assyria," *The New Schaff-Herzog Encyclopedia of Religious Knowledge*, Vol. 1, ed. by Lefferts A. Loetscher (Grand Rapids, Mich.: Baker Book House, 1977), p. 330.

THE BABYLONIANS AND ASSYRIANS

sudden advance.[4] Tiglath-Pileser captured Israel and Damascus in 732 B.C., setting Hoshea on the throne of Israel as a puppet ruler (2 Kings 15—16).

F. The Destruction of Israel. King Hoshea foolishly decided to rebel against Tiglath-Pileser's successor, Shalmaneser V. He made an alliance with the pharaoh of Egypt and stopped paying tribute to the Assyrian capital. Shalmaneser attacked and captured Hoshea, then laid siege to the city of Samaria. Shalmaneser died just before the city surrendered in 721 B.C. (2 Kings 17).

This was Israel's final gasp. The new Assyrian king, Sargon (722–705 B.C.), deported the people of Israel to the hinterlands of the expanding Assyrian Empire. These tribes would never return to the Promised Land.

G. The Destruction of Judah. Shalmaneser and his successors, Sargon (722–705 B.C.) and Sennacherib (705–681 B.C.), had to quell several revolts in the defeated nation of Israel (2 Kings 17:24—18:12). Sennacherib captured the fortified cities of Judah and demanded the surrender of Jerusalem (2 Kings 18), but he had to withdraw his forces to fight Merodach-baladan, the rebel king of Babylon.

Having lived under Assyrian rule since 1100 B.C., the Babylonians took this opportunity to declare their independence from the expanding Assyrian Empire. Sennacherib defeated Merodach-baladan, but a more powerful king named Nabopolassar came to the throne of Babylon. He was able to unite the city-states of the old Babylonian Empire and restore much of the former glory of Babylon. Nabopolassar and his son Nebuchadnezzar II led their armies against the Egyptian pharaoh Necho, who was trying to gain control of the weakening Assyrian Empire. Their armies met at Carchemish, where the Babylonians defeated the Egyptians in one of the great battles of the ancient world (604 B.C.).

The Egyptian pharaohs provoked rebellion among the kings of Judah to distract their Babylonian foes. When Jehoiakim of Judah refused to pay tribute to Nebuchadnezzar II, the Babylonian king captured Jerusalem and deported part of its population in 597 B.C. (2 Kings 24:8–17). Jehoiakim's successor Zedekiah also followed the bad advice of the Egyptians, and Nebuchadnezzar attacked

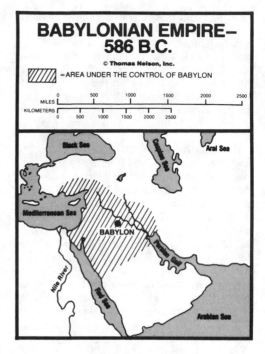

BABYLONIAN EMPIRE– 586 B.C.

© Thomas Nelson, Inc.

////// = AREA UNDER THE CONTROL OF BABYLON

Jerusalem again. This time he destroyed the city's defenses and took most of the population into captivity (2 Kings 25). Thus the divided kingdom of Israel and Judah met its final end in 586 B.C.

H. The Glory of Nebuchadnezzar II. Nebuchadnezzar invaded Egypt and the coastal cities of Palestine to secure the borders of his new empire. For more than 20 years after the fall of Jerusalem, Nebuchadnezzar reigned over the mighty Babylonian Empire. His architects raised the capital city of Babylon to the height of its splendor, adorning it with the famed hanging gardens.

"There was a conscious effort on the part of the leaders to return to the old forms and customs. It has been said that this period might properly be called the Renaissance of Old Babylonia."[5]

VI. Years of Decline. The Babylonians began to lose their grasp of Mesopotamia as the Persian Empire grew stronger. Nineveh, capital of already weakened Assyria, fell to a group of Scythian tribes known as the Umman-Manda in 606 B.C. These tribes used the resources of Nineveh to build an empire of their own.

---

[4] Dorothy Ruth Miller, *A Handbook of Ancient History in Bible Light* (New York: Fleming H. Revell Company, 1937), p. 102.

[5] Miller, *A Handbook of Ancient History in Bible Light*, p. 117.

THE BABYLONIANS AND ASSYRIANS

ISHTAR GATE. *A procession moves along Marduk's Way and enters Nebuchadnezzar's palace through the massive Ishtar Gate in this painting by Maurice Bardin. The famous hanging gardens are pictured in the upper right-hand corner, and the city's ziggurat appears behind them.*

control of all Mesopotamia. (*See* "The Persians.")

VII. Art and Architecture. We have learned much about the life of the Babylonians and Assyrians from relief carvings found in the ruins of Nimrud and Nineveh (magnificent capitals in the prime of Assyria). For example, one carving depicts a savage lion "hunt" in which lions are released into an arena and slaughtered by a king in his chariot, shooting arrows while protected by his spearmen!

From an early period, Babylonian and Assyrian altars showed scenes of war. Their wall paintings and cylinder seals portrayed scenes of animal and plant life. Only a few sculptures have survived from the Assyrian culture, the best-known being the statue of Ashurnasirpal II now in the British Museum.

Assyrian architecture emphasized the ziggurat and is probably represented best by the palace built by Sargon II in what is now known as Khorsabad.

The palace had a triple entrance leading into a large court measuring 90 m. (300 ft.) on each side. The walls were carved with reliefs of the king and his courtiers and were plastered in sections with vari-colored designs. To one side of the court were offices and service quarters, and to the other were six temples and a ziggurat. Behind the court were the living quarters of the king. Beyond these were rooms of state including a brightly painted throne room.

Much Assyrian art focuses on battle scenes showing dead and dying soldiers or on hunting scenes depicting wounded and dying animals. Babylonian art reflects the Sumerian influence. They used brick panels (some enameled and in relief) on walls and gates. They also built ziggurats, a Sumerian contribution. Babylon itself was the site of the ziggurat known in the Bible as the "Tower of Babel" (Gen. 11:1–9). All that remains are the ground plan and traces of three large stairways leading to its summit. A geometrical description found on a cuneiform tablet (dated about 229 B.C.) describes the tower as having two stories plus a tower of five stages, crowned by a sacred shrine at the top. However, the Greek historian Herodotus said the Tower of Babylon was built in eight stages surrounded by a ramp and having a sanctuary.

The Babylonian palaces often were decorated with paintings. During the dynasty of Hammurabi, the painted themes were mainly

To the south in Babylonia, Nebuchadnezzar's successors made corruption and assassination a way of life. They broke off diplomatic relations with the Medes—the tribal chieftains of Nineveh and enemies of the Scythians—thinking that these renegades had no use in their political schemes.

Nabonidus took the throne of Babylon in 555 B.C. and attempted to revive popular interest in the ancient religions of the empire, neglecting the status of his armed forces. He did not anticipate the sudden rise of Cyrus the Great, who absorbed the Medes and pushed north to subdue other tribes of Asia Minor. Finally Cyrus sent his armies against Babylon. The stodgy government of Nabonidus and his son Belshazzar proved to be an easy prey. Babylon fell to the Persians, giving Cyrus

THE BABYLONIANS AND ASSYRIANS

mythological motifs, war scenes, and religious rites.

Babylonian sculpture is represented by cult statues of deities and rulers. One of the most important discoveries is a head in black granite, which might be that of King Hammurabi. The rendering is almost impressionistic.

VIII. Religion. Assyrian religious practices were almost identical with those of Babylonia, except that their national god was called Ashur while Babylonia's national god was called Marduk.

The Babylonians modified the Sumerian religion. Besides Marduk, their important gods were Ea (god of wisdom, spells, and incantations), Sin (moon god), Shamash (sun god and god of justice), Ishtar (goddess of love and war), Adad (god of wind, storm, and flood), and Marduk's son, Nabu (scribe and herald of the gods).

Babylonian temple services were held in open courts where there were sacrifices, burning of incense, and festivals.

IX. Literature of the Golden Age. The inscribed clay tablets unearthed by archaeologists have contributed greatly to our knowledge of Assyria, Babylonia, and the ancient Middle East.

Most of the inscriptions are administrative, economic, and legal documents. Many are dated in relation to significant historical events. They bear the distinctive *cuneiform* (wedge-shaped) writing.

Archaeologists have found more than 5,000 tablets inscribed with myths, epic tales, hymns, lamentations, and proverbs. Except for the proverbs and some essays, all the Babylonian and Assyrian literary works are written in poetic form.

The literary influence of Babylonia and Assyria upon the Old Testament is seen in the fact that hundreds of words and phrases used in the Hebrew Bible are directly paralleled in the cuneiform tablets. Three primary texts found in cuneiform are very similar to Old Testament themes. These are the creation, the flood, and the lament of the righteous sufferer (cf. the Book of Job). For a further description of the cuneiform stories of the creation and flood, see "Pagan Religions and Cultures."

X. Other Archaeological Evidence. Sifting through other archaeological clues, we find that Assyrian culture closely resembled Babylonian culture—except that the Assyrians tended to be more barbaric. For example, the Assyrians buried their dead with knees drawn up to chins. They buried them under houses instead of in cemeteries.

The favorite pursuits of Assyrian kings were war and hunting, which is reflected in their art and writings. Archaeological finds indicate that the Assyrians were generally a merciless and savage people.

In 1616, Italian traveler Pietro della Valle (1586–1652) recognized the ruins of Babylon. And between 1784 and 1818, several "digs" took place at this site. But the most important was done here after 1899, by the Deutsche Orient Gesellschaft under the direction of German archaeologist Robert Koldewey (1855–1925). He traced the outermost wall of Babylon over about 31 sq. km. (12 sq. mi.) and excavated the Processional Street, the Ishtar Gate, and the foundations of two palaces of King Nebuchadnezzar II.

What do the archaeological discoveries tell us about Babylonia? First, that the people were essentially urban, although their economy was based on agriculture. Babylonia consisted of 12 or more cities surrounded by villages and hamlets. The people served under an absolute monarch.

Second, these finds tell us there were three social levels of citizens: *awelin,* the free man of upper class; *wardu* or slave; and *mushkenu,* free man of lower class. Parents could sell their children into slavery if they desired.

LYRE. *This reconstructed Lyre from Ur (twenty-fifth century B.C.) consists of a sound box attached to two uprights, which are decorated with mosaic inlay and the gold head of a bull. Attached to the uprights is a crossbar, half of which consists of silver tubing. A Mesopotamian craftsman probably fixed the strings at the bottom of the sound box*

THE BABYLONIANS AND ASSYRIANS

However, it seems that most slaves were acquired as prisoners of war and were treated humanely (considering the era).

The family was the basic unit of society, with marriages arranged by parents. Women had a few legal rights but were subordinate to men. Children had no rights.

Third, we find that the population of Babylon was perhaps half a million at its height. Babylonian streets were winding, unpaved, and meandering. But after Nebuchadnezzar's rebuilding, many were straight and paved. The average house was a one-story mud brick structure with several rooms grouped around an open court.

The well-to-do Babylonian usually had a two-story house that was plastered and white-washed. The ground floor had a reception room, kitchen, lavatory, servants quarters and sometimes a private chapel. Furniture consisted of low tables, high-backed chairs, and beds with wooden frames. Utensils were made of clay, stone, copper, and bronze. Reeds were utilized for baskets and mats. Like the Assyrians, the Babylonians buried their dead (in many cases) underneath the house. Pots, tools, weapons, and other items were buried with them.

Babylonians had considerable engineering "know-how" that they used in maintaining canals and reservoirs. They prepared maps, mastered early mathematics, and developed timetables for planting and harvesting.

UGARIT AND THE CANAANITES

The Canaanites lived in the land of Palestine before the Hebrews arrived. Until 1928, our knowledge of the Canaanites was limited to three sources.

One source was the archaeological work at cities in Palestine such as Jericho, Megiddo, and Bethel. These cities yielded pre-Israelite building remains, pottery, house utensils, weapons, and similar items—but no inscriptions. Scholars certainly value these other items, but written evidence is usually the most important tool in reconstructing the past. In the long run the historical value of inscriptions outweighs physical evidence. Here we have in mind such things as myths, legends, royal

chronicles, legal texts, and business records.

The second source of our information on Canaan was the literature of contemporary people who lived outside Canaan. A good example of this is the Tell el-Amarna Letters, sent by Canaanite princes in Palestine to the pharaoh in Egypt. These letters were written mainly to Amenhotep III and his son Akhnaton in the 1400s or early 1300s B.C. (*See* "Egyptians.") As we shall see, Canaan was an extension of Egyptian power for much of the Canaanites' history.

A late Egyptian story (11th century B.C.) gives us another view of Canaan. This story concerns the journey of Wenamon, an official

---

UGARIT. *This aerial view shows part of the excavation at Ugarit (Ras Shamra), located in present-day Syria near the Mediterranean coast. The Canaanites worshiped the god Baal, and the Old Testament prophets frequently condemned them for their religious practices. Written records at Ugarit have enabled scholars to understand the beliefs and rituals so abhorred by the prophets. Clay tablets found at the site have also provided keys to the meanings of Old Testament Hebrew words not previously understood.*

UGARIT AND THE CANAANITES

MINET-EL-BEIDA. *This harbor town was capable of handling great quantities of merchandise for the nearby city of Ugarit. At the site, archaeologists have found over 1,000 vessels filled with perfumed oil for export to Palestine and Egypt, indicating that the manufacture of cosmetics was one of Ugarit's primary industries.*

Scripture is amazingly accurate and objective, and does not exaggerate the truth when it tells us of the Canaanites. An archaeological discovery in northern Syria in 1928 confirms the Bible's portrayal of the Canaanites. This discovery provided a vast new store of information about Canaanite civilization.

In the spring of 1928, a Syrian peasant farmer working in his fields heard a blade of his tilling machine strike what he assumed was a hidden rock. Looking closer, he saw that his blade had sliced off the top of an unusually large hole in the ground; it looked like an ancient tomb. This accidental discovery began an exciting excavation of a Canaanite city, which yielded fascinating historical objects and the remains of several significant monuments.

As French archaeologists dug deeper into the city, they found vast amounts of ancient texts on clay tablets. Could it be that they had stumbled upon Canaanite literature, written by Canaanites in their native language? The answer was yes.

of the Temple of Amun at Karnak, to Byblos in Phoenicia to get lumber for the sacred boat of his god. The story suggests that Egypt's control over Canaan had slipped severely from the time of the Tell el-Amarna Letters, for the Canaanites treated Wenamon disrespectfully and were slow to meet his request.

Various Akkadian texts from the east and Hittite texts from the north also give us interesting facts about Canaanite customs. For example, Hittite laws are very specific and seem to deal with every possible civil offense. Akkadian texts describe elaborate temple rituals and sacrifices. These documents suggest that the cultures of that area were quite sophisticated.

Our third source of facts on Canaan and its people was the Old Testament. Scripture tells us the Hebrews pushed the Canaanites out of their land and in some cases eliminated entire cities (Josh. 11:10—12:24). Even a quick reading of Scripture shows us that the Canaanites never ranked highly with Old Testament writers. The Old Testament writers spare no effort in painting the Canaanites as evil and immoral people, and their religion as strange and obnoxious (Judg. 2:2; 10:6–7). The account of such an unsparing attack convinces some modern scholars that the Old Testament is unduly biased against the Canaanites. But

8

UGARIT AND THE CANAANITES

I. The City of Ugarit. The ancient name of this site was Ugarit. Although the name of

UGARIT AND THE CANAANITES

Ugarit was mentioned in documents such as the Tell el-Amarna Letters, biblical scholars did not know Ugarit's exact location. The discovery of 1928 solved the problem. The modern Arabic name for this territory in Syria is Ras Shamra, meaning "fennel head." (*Fennel* is a fragrant flower whose seeds are used for making aromatic ointments; much of it is grown in this area.)

A. Description of the Area. What survives of Ugarit today is a large mound of earth about 20 m. (65 ft.) high, over 900 m. (1,000 yds.) at its widest point, and almost 640 m. (700 yds.) at its greatest length. It is located about 0.8 km. (0.5 mi.) from the Mediterranean coast, in line with the easternmost tip of the island of Cyprus. Scientists began excavating the area in 1929 and have continued to the present, except for the years during World War II.

B. Ugaritic Texts. Scholars soon deciphered the Canaanite texts from Ugarit and translated them into several modern languages. This was due largely to the efforts of Hans Bauer, a German, and the Frenchmen Charles Virolleaud and Edouard Dhorme.

We might say the Ugaritic texts were "cosmopolitan," since the writings were found in seven different languages: Egyptian, Cypro-Minoan Linear B, Hittite, Hurrian, Sumerian, Akkadian, and Ugaritic. So the Ugaritic tablets contained *hieroglyphic* (Egyptian),
cuneiform (Hittite), and *linear* (the remaining five) forms of writing. (*See* "Languages and Writings.")

Researchers found that most of the texts were in the Akkadian syllabic script, which they knew from the cities of Mesopotamia. Akkadian was used for most of the business, law, administrative, and international documents at Ugarit. But archaeologists found that a unique Ugaritic alphabetic script was used for recording the great myths, epics, and legends of the city.

The traditional cuneiform script uses hundreds of different symbols; but on many tablets of Ugarit only 30 separate symbols appeared, suggesting that they used a system like an alphabet. The words were often separated by a divider symbol, something archaeologists had not seen on other cuneiform tablets. Most of the words were built from three basic consonants, the same pattern followed by Semitic languages such as Hebrew, Aramaic, and Phoenician. Also, a few of the Ugaritic texts were written from right to left, while cuneiform is nearly always written from left to right. These peculiarities convinced the researchers that Ugarit's tablets introduced them to an alphabet that had been unknown, yet related to the Phoenician system of writing.

Here is the Canaanite alphabet:

a	y	p
b	k	s
g	s	q
h	l	r
d	m	t
h	d	g
w	n	t
z	z	i
h	s	u
t	c	s

The following sequence of letters of our English alphabet survived from this old alphabet: ab-d-h-klmn-pqr-t.

C. Other Archaeological Data. Archaeologists noticed five separate levels in the mound of Ugarit, and they found signs of human occupation at each level. Level Five (at ground level) contained evidence of a small fortified town at Ugarit as far back as a major flood. No pottery was discovered at this level. Level Four and part of Three date back to the Chalcolithic Period. (*See* "Archaeology.") Diggers did find pottery here. Level Three dates to the Early Bronze Age, about 1,000 years before Abraham. Here the excavators found signs of skillful work with metals. The

WEAPONS AND TOOLS. *Archaeologists examine a hoard of 74 copper and bronze artifacts hidden under the house of Ugarit's high priest. The weapons and tools, never used, may have been an offering made by a bronze smith to the high priest.*

UGARIT AND THE CANAANITES

top layers, Levels One and Two, bring us into the golden age of Ugarit, 1550–1200 B.C. This takes us from the Old Testament patriarchal period into the time of the judges. Ugarit was destroyed at the end of this period, apparently the victim of earthquake and invaders that the scribes of Ugarit called "Sea Peoples." (*See* "Archaeology.") There are only traces of occasional settlement at Ugarit after 1200 B.C.

Diggers unearthed two temples at Ugarit dedicated to the god Baal and his father Dagon. These temples are similar in structure to the one Solomon built. Both of the Ugaritic temples have rooms that might have been used somewhat like the holy place and the holy of holies in Solomon's temple.

Archaeologists unearthed several other buildings at Ugarit; some of these contained the libraries that give us most of our Ugaritic literature. The diggers found what must have been a plush royal palace, with 67 rooms and halls. It measured 119 m. by 82 m. (130 yd. by 90 yd.). The researchers discovered that many people of Ugarit placed burial vaults directly beneath their homes. Channels carried water from ground level into the tombs. Some archaeologists believe these channels were used to make pagan offerings to the dead.

Scientists also found storage jars over one meter (39 in.) high, and several beautiful golden bowls that were surely the work of professional goldsmiths. One bowl featured the engraved picture of a hunter on a chariot aiming his arrows at gazelles and bulls.

Archaeological researchers found 74 weapons and tools under the floor of a single Ugaritic house. Inscriptions on five of these items show that the collection belonged to a high priest (*rb khn,* as the letters would be written in their English counterparts). Apparently, ancient worshipers gave the priest these tools and weapons as offerings or gifts for their blessings and rituals.

Archaeologists also discovered several religious statues and cult objects at Ugarit. Among them were a few small golden amulets in the shape of nude women, surely relating to Ugarit's fertility cult. On the lid of an ivory box, the excavators found a carved picture of a bare-breasted goddess, holding several ears of grain in each hand. A goat on each side stood on hind legs, trying to nibble on the grain. Another ivory slab has a picture of a goddess nursing two children. This is a familiar feature in Near Eastern religious literature and art. Mortals and minor gods were supposed to re-

GOLDEN BOWL. *This artifact from Ras Shamra shows wild goats in the inner circle. In the outer circle a hunter stands in a two-wheeled chariot with drawn bow, pursuing a gazelle that leaps gracefully away. Running ahead are three wild bulls and one of the hunter's dogs. Hunting from the chariot was popular sport for the wealthy Canaanites. The hunter tied the reins to the chariot pole and then wrapped the ends around his waist to give greater stability and to leave his hands free for shooting.*

ceive power and prestige by suckling at the breasts of a goddess.

The researchers found a few small bronze statues of the god Baal, showing his left hand lowered and right hand raised, as if he were ready to strike a blow or lead a war cry. A larger slab of stone featured a picture of Baal wearing helmet and skirt and waving a club or mace in his right hand. He holds a spear in his left hand.

II. Canaanite Government. Unlike Egypt, Mesopotamia, or Asia Minor, early Canaan had no single ruler whose power extended over the entire country. The Canaanites never produced a famous pharaoh or king. The cities were each governed by a petty ruler. The association of rulers held power over all Canaan.

A. City-State Concept. Canaan was composed of several city-states, self-ruling and to some degree, self-sufficient. A king, more properly called a lord, ruled in each city-state. In the Middle Bronze Age (2000–1500 B.C.) and the Late Bronze Age (1500–1100 B.C.), each of these territories was usually under the actual control of the Egyptians or the neo-Hittites. Note that Joshua 12 lists 31 kings with whom the Israelites battled in the conquest of Canaan.

B. Ugarit's Kings. It is hard for historians to establish exactly when, and by whom, the dynasty of petty kings started in Ugarit's history. Kings of the Late Bronze Age employed a seal that bears the inscription, "Yaqarum son of Niqmad King of Ugarit." This seal probably dates back to the nineteenth century B.C.

Biblical scholars don't know who provided community leadership in Ugarit over the next few centuries. But we are able to trace the rulers of Ugarit from the fourteenth century B.C. to the destruction of Ugarit in the eleventh century B.C. These late Ugaritic rulers, in order of succession, are:

1. Ammishtamru I
2. Niqmad II
3. Ar Khalba
4. Niqmepa
5. Ammishtamru II
6. Ibiranu
7. Niqmad III
8. Hammurapi' (no relation to Hammurabi, p. 131)

At least the first two in this list were faithful vassals of Egypt and wrote regularly to that country. We find evidence of this in the Amarna letters.

Niqmad II (or Niqmaddu, as it may be spelled) lived at the same time as a famous Egyptian pharaoh, Akhnaton, also known as Amenhotep IV (*ca.* 1360 B.C.). The names of Akhnaton and his equally famous wife, Nefertiti, appear on alabaster vases found at Ugarit. Coaxed by the promise of more land, Ugarit's Niqmad II shifted his loyalty from the Egyptian pharaoh to a Hittite king, Shuppiluliuma. Niqmepa enjoyed one of the longest reigns of all the Ugaritic rulers, (*ca.* 1336–1265 B.C.) He sided with the Hittites against the Egyptians and the Pharaoh Rameses II at the famous battle of Kadesh in 1285 B.C. The fight ended in a stalemate and the rival nations formed a peace treaty. Ugarit benefited from this pact.

The fifth king on our list, Ammishtamru II, was Niqmepa's son. Ammistamru should be remembered for a written record of his marriage and divorce from his wife, who was an adulteress. The Hittites forced Ammistamru II and his son, Ibiranu, to provide money and troops to defend them against a new menace on the horizon, the Assyrians. These easterners were led by Shalmaneser I and Tukulti-Ninurta I.

The reigns of the final Ugaritic kings, Niqmad III and Hammurapi', were brief and without significance. During their time a western enemy, the "Sea Peoples," appeared to have become a more dangerous threat than the Assyrians while some natural disasters such as earthquakes may have weakened the city-states. The "Sea Peoples" attacked, burned, decimated, and buried the city of Ugarit in about 1200 B.C. So it remained until it was rediscovered in A.D. 1928 by the Syrian farmer.

III. Land of Canaan. Though Ugarit is never mentioned in the Bible, it is part of the land of Canaan. Let us look at the wider area of Canaan as it is described in the Old Testament.

A. The Meaning of *Canaan*. Scholars still debate the meaning of *canaan,* as they do the boundaries of the territory indicated by this term. In the nineteenth century, scholars thought *canaan* was linked with the Semitic verb *knc,* which in Arabic means "to bow, be low," and in Hebrew, "to be subdued, humble oneself." So they interpreted *Canaan* to mean something like "lowland." Language experts have now abandoned this approach, but we should not overlook the words of Genesis 9:25, "Cursed be Canaan, a servant of servants shall he be unto his brethren." It is hard to miss the idea of inferiority here. Here *Canaan* may indeed be tied with the Hebrew root *knc,* "to be low."

Most scholars today feel *canaan* is related to the cuneiform word *kinahhu,* which comes to us from the Hurrians of Mesopotamia. This word means "reddish purple," and it refers to the murex snail found on the shores of the Mediterranean, which secretes a purple dye. The dye was one of the chief products of Canaan; hence it was called "the land of the purple dye." Phoenicians used the dye in the clothing industry. In fact, the Canaanite word for *Phoenician—phoinike—*is very close to the word *phoinix,* meaning "reddish purple."

B. Canaanite Boundaries. It is one problem to define *canaan.* It is just as difficult to determine the country's boundaries.

1. Biblical Evidence. We find the first clear biblical statement on this matter in Genesis 10:19: ". . . And the border of the Canaanites was from Sidon, as thou comest to Gerar, unto Gaza; as thou goest, unto Sodom and Gomorrah, and Admah, and Zeboim, even unto Lasha (in the Dead Sea area?)." On the basis of this verse, we may define Canaan as a long, thin area parallel to the southeast shore of the Mediterranean, covering areas populated by southern Phoenicians (Sidonians) and

UGARIT AND THE CANAANITES

FUNERAL VAULTS. *This photograph shows the burial vaults located under many of the dwellings in Ugarit. The dead were laid on the vault floors, possibly wrapped in mats, surrounded by food, water, and other articles to use in the afterlife.*

Philistines. No eastern boundary is designated, but we think it was the Jordan River. For a more detailed discussion of the boundaries of the Promised Land, *see* "Geography."

2. Akkadian References. God's promise of land to Abraham takes on more significance when compared to an Akkadian text found at Ugarit. The text is a letter from the Hittite king Hattusilis III (thirteenth century B.C.) to his vassal, Niqmepa, king of Ugarit. Niqmepa had complained to the Hittite king that traveling merchants from Ur were making life difficult for residents of Ugarit. Some scholars believe Abraham was a traveling merchant with far-flung commercial interests. His 318 troops (Gen. 14:14) may have been bodyguards for the traveling merchants.

To relieve the situation at Ugarit, the Hittite king placed several restrictions on the merchants. One was that they could visit Ugarit only at harvest. The merchants were also prohibited from buying land or personal real estate in Ugarit with profits from their business. If Abraham was a merchant forbidden to buy

real estate, then the promise offering him "all this land" takes on a new meaning. Man says: You can't have this land. God says: I am giving it to you.

C. God's Word and Canaan. Beginning with Abraham, and through following generations, God promised Canaan to individuals (a patriarch), then groups (the Israelites under Moses and Joshua). But the land of Canaan had to be conquered; it was not delivered on a silver platter to the Israelites.

God's word to His people was: "And the city [Jericho] shall be accursed, even it, and all that are therein, the Lord . . . And they utterly destroyed all that was in the city, both man and woman, young and old, and ox, and sheep, and ass, with the edge of the sword" (Josh. 6:17a, 21).

IV. Conquest of Canaan. It is easy to say, as some scholars do, that Canaan was not conquered as the Bible describes, but was instead penetrated slowly by the Israelites. Some people feel the description of these "holy wars" or "wars of extermination" springs from the imagination of later writers who distorted the historical events. It is equally convenient to view the events as historical, but chalk them up as an early stage in the development of the conscience of the old Israelites. But perhaps the conquest of Canaan can be better understood in light of these facts:

A. Mercy Grant. The land of Canaan was given to the Israelites on the basis of God's mercy, not their merit. We find no suggestion that the Israelites considered themselves a superior people. Their God was superior—the *only* God.

B. God's Orders. Canaan was attacked by the Israelites because God gave the order. Israel did not take the first step on its own. This was not a fulfillment of any long-held dream of expansion on Israel's part. In fact, Scripture makes no reference to Israel's having a standing army until David's time.

C. War as a Way of Life. The wars against Canaan never became models for later action by the Israelites. God's will for His people in the world was spelled out first in Genesis 12:3: "And in thee shall all families of the earth be blessed."

D. Booty. Taking booty from the defeated enemy was a common practice in that day and has remained so throughout history. But God's Word prohibited the Israelites from taking personal booty from the conquered people. Everything was to be devoted to the Lord.

UGARIT AND THE CANAANITES

Silver, gold, and vessels of bronze and iron were to be placed in the Lord's treasury, not private coffers (Josh. 6:18–19).

E. No Dual Standard. The Israelites are not exempt from God's Word. There was no dual standard here. An Israelite named Achan gave in to the temptation to sneak a bit of Canaanite spoil for himself. As a result, he and his family were devoted to destruction (Josh. 7, especially vv. 24–26). When the Israelites sinned as a nation, they were punished—i.e., defeated by their enemies—just as other nations were.

F. Enslavement. When the Israelites entered Canaan, they could have followed three courses of action regarding the Canaanite people. They could kill them, expel them, or make them slaves. Except in actual battle situations, the Israelites appear to have chosen the last option most often, for the Canaanites continued to live in Palestine long after Joshua's death. This is seen in the story about Solomon's father-in-law, the Egyptian pharaoh, who marched against the city of Gezer in Canaan, wrested it from the Canaanites, and gave it to his daughter as a wedding present (1 Kings 9:16). Judges 3 states that Canaan was a nation left by God to test the Israelites (Judg. 3:1–3).

G. Immorality. The Bible firmly states that the Canaanites' religion and lifestyle were immoral. The Canaanites destroyed themselves by their sinful living. This is what God means when He tells Abraham, "but in the fourth generation they [Abraham's descendants] shall come hither again: for the iniquity of the Amorites [Canaanites] is not yet full" (Gen. 15:16). God will not give the land to His people too soon. He will wait until evil has run its full course.

The Lord said to His people through Moses, "Thou shalt not bow down to their gods, nor serve them, nor do after their works. . . . Thou shalt make no covenant with them, nor with their gods. They shall not dwell in thy land, lest they make thee sin against Me: for if thou serve their gods, it will surely be a snare unto thee" (Exod. 23:24a, 32–33).

V. Ugaritic Literature. Does the literature found at Ugarit confirm what the Old Testament says about the Canaanites?

Let us look at the texts from Ugarit written in the unique alphabetic cuneiform script discussed above. These texts may be divided into two groups. The first is *legends* or *epics,* in which the main characters are human. The

second category is *myths,* in which the action of the gods is the main feature. Let us first look at the myths.

A. Myths. Most of the Ugaritic myths revolve around Baal and the other gods associated with him. Baal was the god of sky and rain. His two major opponents were Yamm (god of the sea) and Mot (god of death).

1. The Baal Cycle. We call the longest of the Canaanite myths the Baal Cycle. Scholars do not agree on the sequence of this story's episodes, which are found on about one dozen clay tablets. But we can accept this general version:

Baal and Yamm are engaged in a fierce war. It is not merely a wrestling match in the sky to be observed by amused spectators. The outcome is deadly serious for believers in Baal. If Baal triumphs, the land will be fertile that year, and farmers and residents can breathe a bit easier. But if Mot wins, disaster will follow—death and sterility will rule. It may mean the year of the locust plague, or one of drought.

We learn from one of the first tablets in this series that Yamm sends two messengers to El, head of the gods, to ask that he give Baal to the messengers: "Give up, O gods, him whom you harbor. . . . Give up Baal . . . Dagon's son, so that I may inherit his gold." El yields and hands over Baal. Angered, Baal lashes out in revenge, but is restrained by the goddesses Anath and Ashtoreth. For the moment, Yamm is victor over Baal.

But we see that another text puts the shoe on the other foot. In this episode, Baal defeats Yamm. Baal's weapons are two magic clubs furnished by Kothar-wa-Khasis, god of craftsmanship and inventor of tools, weapons, and musical instruments.

A long text of the Baal Cycle introduces us to the goddess Anath, Baal's consort. Baal had three daughters as well: Talliya, goddess of dew; Padriya, goddess of the clouds; and Arsiya, goddess of the earth.

Anath is both goddess of war (She fights for her husband's causes.) and goddess of love and sensuality, a common combination of attributes in ancient goddesses. Her slaughterhouse tactics against Baal's opponents are described in detail: "Anath swells her liver with laughter/Her heart is filled with joy/For in Anath's hand is victory/For knee-deep she plunges in the blood of soldiers/Neck-high in the gore of troops/Until she is sated." This slaughter results in fertility for the land:

UGARIT AND THE CANAANITES

EL. *Many scholars believe the seated deity shown on this stone relief was El, the leader of the Ugaritic gods. His left hand is upraised in a gesture of benediction as he accepts an offering from a worshiper.*

by a bull) has carnal relations with a young cow before going to the underworld in order to provide an heir. Apparently the Canaanites saw nothing wrong in allowing their gods to practice bestiality.

These texts allow us to understand the cosmic battles in Ugaritic myths between the god-forces of barrenness and productivity, sterility and fertility—Yamm and Baal, Mot and Baal. The Old Testament has many passages that read much like these showdowns in the sky. One example is: "Awake, awake, put on strength, O arm of the Lord . . . Art thou not it that hath cut Rahab, and wounded the dragon? Art thou not it which hath dried the sea, the waters of the great deep . . . ?" (Isa. 51:9–10). Or Psalm 74:13–14: "Thou didst divide the sea by thy strength: thou brakest the heads of the dragons in the waters. Thou brakest the heads of leviathan in pieces, and gavest him to be meat to the people inhabiting the

"She draws water and washes/With dew of heaven/Fat of earth." Similar blessings are contained in Isaac's words to Jacob (or Esau, as Isaac thought), in Genesis 27:28: "God give thee of the dew of heaven, and the fatness of the earth." This blessing is found again in Isaac's word to Esau (Gen. 27:39).

The next story tells us how Baal attempts to lure Anath into convincing El to give him a palace. No favor or request from Baal seems too much for Anath to honor. She tells Baal that all he need do is ask, and she will deliver. She reminds him of her past achievements: "Have I not crushed Yamm, El's darling?/Nor annihilated the great god River?/Have I not muzzled the dragon/Nor crushed the crooked serpent/Mighty monster of seven heads?/I have crushed Mot, darling of the earth gods. . . ." As the narrative ends, Anath appears before El and demands that he honor Baal's request for a palace. She threatens El with violence if he does not fulfill the request. El is so frightened by his daughter that he hides from her in his own house!

Another text describes a different meeting between Baal and Yamm, with Yamm the victor. But in this version Baal (often symbolized

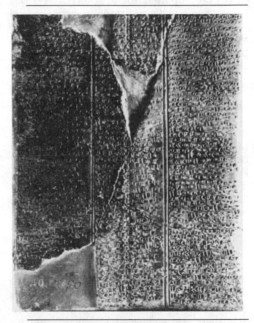

THE LEGEND OF KERET. *This epic, written on four tablets in cuneiform alphabetic script, tells of the prosperous King Keret of Ugarit. The story says that Keret was distressed by the death of his wife and her failure to bear any heirs to the throne. The god El told him to demand the hand of the beautiful daughter of the king of Udum. Keret made the appropriate vows, besieged the capital of Udum, and won the king's daughter. In time, he had sons and daughters of his own. Keret fell ill, but El intervened to restore his health.*

wilderness." We find similar declarations in the New Testament, in connection with the great red dragon with seven heads and 10 horns, defeated by Michael and his angels (Rev. 12:3–17).

How shall we interpret verses such as these? Did the poets of Israel borrow the myth of the cosmic battle from her Canaanite neighbors? Probably not. Literary material such as this was common currency throughout the ancient Near East.

Biblical writers deliberately made references to familiar myths. It seems impossible to avoid this conclusion. What would allusions to a dragon or leviathan mean to Isaiah's audience, unless the people were already familiar with stories about the creatures? But the Israelite authors did not simply copy Canaanite thoughts in their writing. If they had, we would expect to find Canaanite creation myths in the Pentateuch and the opening chapters of Genesis, and we do not. Instead, the mythical beasts crop up in Scripture at a relatively late date, when Israel was firm in its belief in God who is One, without rival. Isaiah and the Psalmist are not affirming Canaanite myths as truths, but borrowing their contents to use as poetic imagery for celebrating God's sovereignty.

2. Fertility Myths. Two more myths from Ugarit will round out our discussion of this branch of literature. One myth concerns the marriage of Yarih, the moon god, to Nikkal, moon goddess from Mesopotamia. Nikkal bears a child to Yarih. Yarih's words to Nikkal show that fertility of the womb and fertility of the land are linked: "I shall make her fields into vineyards/The field of her love into orchards."

The second myth is often called "The Birth of the Good and Gracious God." It opens with a banquet at which wine flows freely. The text is divided into sections, the tenth being the last and most crucial. El is about to create two women who will become either his wives or daughters, depending on his ability to impregnate them. He creates these females and seduces them, and they both become pregnant. One bears a child called Dawn (Shahar), and the other a child called Dusk (Shalim). Later, El makes love to these same women and they produce seven sons between them. These sons are "the good and gracious gods." They are destined to be gods of fertility, and are first suckled at the breasts of "the Lady" (Asherah, wife of El?). El sends them to the wilderness

for over seven years, until things take a turn for the better. It has been suggested this text was connected with a ritual intended to end a string of bad years and start a productive cycle for Ugarit.

Fertility religions such as Ugarit's place great emphasis on reproduction in the land, in crops, and in the womb. This emphasis helps explain their stress on sexual unions.

The Bible and the Canaanite texts at Ugarit use the words *qadesh* and *qedesha,* which mean "holy one"—the first masculine, the second feminine. At Ugarit these "holy ones" were homosexual priests and priestesses who acted as prostitutes.

We find strong Hebrew reaction against this "cultic prostitution" in passages such as Leviticus 19:29, "Do not prostitute thy daughter, to cause her to be a whore," and Deuteronomy 23:17, "There shall be no whore (*qedesha*) of the daughters of Israel, nor a sodomite (*qadesh*) of the sons of Israel." One of Josiah's reforms was "to break down the houses of the sodomites" (2 Kings 23:7).

B. Legends. We should examine two important Canaanite legends about ancient kings. One story is the Legend of Keret, named for its major character, the son of El. Keret is king of Hubur. His wife is taken from him and his family killed. Much of this story contains the advice from El to Keret on where to find a new wife. Keret is told to go to Udum (Edom?), where King Paebel has a beautiful daughter, Hurriya. Keret's quest is successful. The couple is happily united and starts a new family, which grows to seven boys and a girl. Later Keret becomes fatally ill.

Here El, leader of the gods, steps in again. He uses magic to restore Keret's health: "I myself will perform the magic/I shall indeed stay the hand of the disease/Exorcising the demon . . . ." We find it interesting that in using magic, the god appeals to an outside power.

One of Keret's sons, Yassib, soon rebels against his father for his bland leadership. Keret says, "May Horon (god of the plague and the nether world) break, O my son/May Horon break your head/Ashtoreth, name of Baal, your pate. . . ." So we see this story begin and end with a troubled father.

The second legend deals with a king called Aqhat, son of Danel (sometimes "Daniel," but *not* the Daniel of Scripture) and his wife Donatiya. Kothar-wa-Khasis (the god of crafts) makes a beautiful bow for Aqhat, which draws

UGARIT AND THE CANAANITES

the attention of Anath, goddess of war. Anath desires the bow for her arsenal, but Aqhat rejects her offers for it.

Anath has Aqhat killed by one of her cohorts, Yatpan, who assumes the form of an eagle.

Father Danel retrieves Aqhat's remains from the stomach of the eagle and buries his son. Aqhat's sister, Pigat, goes to Yatpan to revenge her brother's death. Meanwhile, Danel enters a seven-year period of mourning for

CORBELLED VAULT. *A passage or stairway probably led to this stone vault under the main floor of a Canaanite house. The people of Ugarit believed the dead could not rest if they were deprived of water, and so they devised elaborate systems to provide it. Often water was poured into a pipe above ground and flowed into a gutter, which led into a pit next to the burial chamber. A window cut into the wall supposedly allowed the dead access to the water. Archaeologists call this type of chamber a corbelled vault, because the tightly-fitted stone masonry forms a stone gable or corbel.*

CITY GATE. *Past this entrance lay Ugarit, one of the oldest cities in the world and one of the largest city-states of the Phoenicians. At the king's palace of Ugarit, excavators discovered the foreign office archives, which contained letters to the Egyptians and the Hittites and bills of shipping to Tyre, Sidon, Ashdod, Crete, and other ancient sites. The people of Ugarit built a massive trading empire.*

Aqhat. The text ends here, but many scholars feel there is probably more to the legend.

Why was this legend written? Nobody is certain. The story probably hints at the sacred office of the king as holder of fertility, because the text says that after Aqhat's death "Baal failed for seven years . . . without dew, without showers." Danel is called several times *mt rp'e,* "the healer," or "dispenser of fertility."

Aqhat's father, Danel, is especially interesting to us in this legend. The prophet Ezekiel dampened his people's false hopes of deliverance (14:12–23) by saying that an individual will be saved only if he is righteous. To stress the point, Ezekiel says: "Though these three men, Noah, Daniel, and Job, were in [the land], they should deliver but their own souls by their righteousness" (vv. 14, 16, 18, 20). Three verses insert, "they shall deliver neither sons nor daughters."

Scholars have no problems identifying Noah and Job in the Bible. But who is Daniel? Is it the same Daniel of whom Ezekiel speaks in 28:3: "Thou [the prince of Tyre] art wiser than Daniel; there is no secret that they can hide from thee"? Many writers have suggested that the Daniel whom Ezekiel mentions is not his contemporary, the prophet Daniel, but the Danel of Canaanite legend. In the Book of Daniel, Daniel is spelled in Hebrew *dny'l.* But in all of Ezekiel's passages, Daniel is spelled *dn'l,* exactly as the name Danel is spelled in the Aqhat story.

If the Hebrews knew of the Canaanite leviathan and mentioned it in their religious literature, could they not have done the same with Danel?

VI. Conclusion. We know that the Hebrews lived next to the Canaanites and were familiar with their lifestyle, world view, religion, and literature. Many times the Hebrews adopted the Canaanite religion. Think of the bull image built by Jeroboam at Bethel and Dan (1 Kings 12:28–29); in Ugaritic texts, El is often called "the Bull." Or recall the frequent references to such Canaanite objects as the Asherah or Asherim (Exod. 34:12; Deut. 7:5; 12:3; 16:21; Judg. 6:25; 1 Kings 14:15; and others).

Much of the prophets' stern warning was a reaction against the Canaanites. At times the Hebrews freely borrowed from the Canaanites.

From which areas of Canaanite life did they borrow? Certainly from their architecture and their literary techniques. Our knowledge of the workings of Hebrew poetry (especially Psalms and Proverbs) is due in great part to valuable poetic texts found at Ugarit. (*See* "Poetry.") The Hebrews even referred to their language as "the language of Canaan" (Isa. 19:18).

But these borrowings were rarely religious. To be faithful to its God, Israel had to stand apart from its pagan neighbors. It dared not tamper with what God called loathsome and unacceptable to Him. Yahweh and His spokesmen challenged Israel to live above the surrounding cultures, to be separate from them, and to be a witness and a challenge to them.

THE PERSIANS

Persians ruled Palestine during the last century of Old Testament history. The Bible speaks of that period in the narratives of Esther, Daniel, Ezra, Nehemiah, and two verses at the end of 2 Chronicles. For the Jews this was a period of restoration and reconstruction. For the Persians it was a period of imperial expansion.

The Jews had been exiled to Babylonia for nearly 60 years when the Persians conquered that land in 539 B.C. Two years later Cyrus II, the Persian king, granted the exiles permission to return to their homeland. He then pressed on toward the conquest of Egypt, a feat accomplished by his son in 525 B.C.

Palestine was swept into the great empires of Babylon, Persia, Greece, and Rome over a period of 550 years. However, only the Persians are remembered for their contributions to the Jewish people. The other empires are regarded in the Bible as evil and hostile to the Jews.

I. EARLY HISTORY

II. THE RISE OF CYRUS THE GREAT (550–529 B.C.)
  A. The Reign of Nabonidus
  B. Daniel and the Writing on the Wall
  C. The Identity of "Darius"
  D. Cyrus' Decree
  E. The Jewish Response
  F. Daniel under the Persians
  G. Cyrus' Death

III. CAMBYSES II (529–522 B.C.)

IV. DARIUS I (522–486 B.C.)
  A. Strengthening the Empire
  B. Darius and Palestine
  C. Darius and the Greeks

V. XERXES I (486–465 B.C.)

VI. ARTAXERXES I (465–424 B.C.)

VII. PERSIA'S DECLINE
  A. Political Maneuvers
  B. Growing Jewish Power
  C. Final Phase

VIII. PERSIAN CULTURE
  A. Art and Architecture
  B. Language
  C. Religion

I. Early History. The Persians knew what it meant to be exiled. They had been forced to migrate for over a thousand years. Their ancestors had originally lived near the steppes of southern Russia. They were pressured by other migrating peoples about 2000–1800 B.C. to move into the plains of Central Asia. They took with them their Aryan names, traditions, and language. This Indo-Iranian language has some closeness to Greek and Latin. When these Aryans reached their new homeland in the vast region between India and Mesopotamia, it appears they introduced the horse and chariot. Pottery from that period has been discovered showing pictures of horses. Iron and copper reins have also been uncovered.

Of the tribes which settled in northern Iran only the Medes and Persians are of significance to this study, since they had the most influence on Bible people and times. Their emergence as a formidable political power took nearly a thousand years.

By about 700 B.C. Media and Persia were established, although they were subject to Assyria. Assyria had by that time conquered the northern kingdom of Israel. The Persians freed themselves from Assyrian dominance in 681 B.C., when Achaemenes was their king. However, the Assyrian cuneiform became the basis for the Persian system of writing. His two sons quarreled among themselves when they inherited the throne, and they divided the kingdom into two parts. Very soon, however, one of those kingdoms, called Parsa, was absorbed by Media. The other kingdom, centered in a region called Anshan, provided the basis for the eventual Persian Empire and the first dynasty, the Achaemenid dynasty, that lasted until 330 B.C.

At the beginning of the seventh century B.C., when Judah was subject to Nebuchadnezzar of Babylon, the Medes were still a semi-nomadic people. Their ruler was Phraortes (675–653 B.C.), who resided at Ecbatana (near modern Hamadan), a city that later became one of the capitals of the Persian Empire. In a battle against Assyria in 653 B.C. Phraortes was killed.

Cyaxares, his son, reorganized the army and

THE PERSIANS

GOLDEN ARMLET. *The Persians were fine craftsmen. In this golden armband, the two carefully detailed creatures represent griffins, mythological beasts that were part eagle and part lion. Persian artists often pictured griffins with rams' horns.*

Cambyses I, Persian king of Anshan. The son born out of this marriage was Cyrus II, known as Cyrus the Great. Under Cyrus II the Persian power had to be reckoned with. When he was crowned king of Anshan in 559 B.C., the Persians still paid tribute to Media. By about 550 B.C. Cyrus had defeated his grandfather, Astyages, king of the Medes, and taken his capital, Ecbatana. Cyrus then gave himself the title of "king of the Medes" and made Ecbatana his headquarters. By permitting the Median officials to remain in office, he won their allegiance to him.

All of the Median Empire fell to Cyrus. He marched westward and claimed Armenia, Cappadocia, Cilicia, Lydia, Greek city-states in Asia Minor, and Greek islands. Eastward, his conquests included all of Iran. There were still two powerful rivals, however: Babylon and Egypt. Before a march against Egypt

introduced better weapons for his warriors. He extended his control over the Persian kingdom, which paid tribute to him. When he was about to defeat the Assyrians, however, the Medes were forced to withdraw to protect their eastern regions from Scythian invaders. Twenty-eight years later Cyaxares attacked Assyria again and took the city of Asshur in 614 B.C. He joined forces with Nabopolassar of Babylon, who had defeated Assyria in battle on an earlier occasion (626 B.C.), to capture Assyria's capital, Nineveh, in 612 B.C.

Babylonia continued westward conquests. She defeated the alliance of the Assyrians and Egyptians at Carchemish in 605 B.C. and took over the Assyrian Empire. The Babylonians would control affairs in the Near East for the next 60 years.

Babylonia and Media marched on parallel routes westward in order to subdue the nations under them. Cyaxares took his forces on campaigns into northern Mesopotamia, capturing Armenia and Cappadocia as far as the kingdom of Lydia to the west and Parthia to the east. The Babylonians campaigned in Syria, Phoenicia, and Palestine. However, while these two kingdoms rivaled each other for power, Persia began its rise toward dominance of the Near East.

II. The Rise of Cyrus the Great (550–529 B.C.). Cyaxares' granddaughter was married to

A MEDE. *This relief portrait of a Mede, from the Apadana at Persepolis, shows a figure with tightly-curled hair clasping the fringe of his garment. The hand of a second figure touches him in a gesture of comradeship. Media was located in northwestern Iran, west of the Caspian Sea and south of the Zagros Mountains. The Medes were steppe-dwellers who overthrew Babylon. Their customs and laws gradually affected those of their conquerors, the Persians (Dan. 6:8, 15).*

THE PERSIANS

could be made, Babylon had to come under Persian rule.

In conquering Babylonia, Cyrus entered the arena of biblical history. To understand the impact Cyrus had upon the ancient world, we should review the last days of Babylonia, his arch rival.

A. The Reign of Nabonidus. Nabonidus, the last ruler of the Babylonian Empire (555–539 B.C.), believed that an alliance with Cyrus II of Anshan might destroy his rival, Media. He relied on the alliance for protection and made no efforts to strengthen his own country. Instead of building his military forces, Nabonidus spent his time with literature, religion, and a study of Babylon's past. The work of Nabonidus has proved invaluable in establishing dates. He brought in the cult of the moon-god, Sin, the patron deity of Haran, from which his family originally came. Before long he was driven from Babylon by priests who did not like his religious reforms. He lived in exile in Teima in northern Arabia for 10 years, beginning in 552 B.C. Nabonidus left his son Belshazzar as regent in Babylon during this time. When Nabonidus returned to Babylon in 543 B.C., the kingdom was weakened and divided. The priests were still dissatisfied, for they felt themselves robbed of their former glory since Sin had replaced Marduk as the god of Babylon.

B. Daniel and the Writing on the Wall. The Old Testament records that Daniel served under Belshazzar, who ruled Babylon in the absence of his father, Nabonidus. The book bearing Daniel's name tells that Belshazzar provided a banquet for a thousand nobles. Among the excesses at the party were drunkenness and the defiling of vessels captured from the Jerusalem temple. When the handwriting on the wall appeared, neither the king nor his sages could read the strange inscription. Finally, Daniel was called. He first rebuked the king for his pride. The same pride which brought Nebuchadnezzar down for a short time, would bring Belshazzar down, according to the meaning Daniel gave to the inscription: "MENE, MENE, TEKEL, UPHARSIN" (Dan. 5:25). Daniel interpreted these Aramaic words (literally, "number, number, weight, divisions") to mean that "God hath numbered thy kingdom, and finished it. . . . Thou art weighed in the balances and art found wanting. . . . Thy kingdom is divided and given to the Medes and Persians" (Dan. 5:26–28).

Even after hearing this dire message, Belshazzar did not repent. Instead, he made Daniel the third in rank in the kingdom, as if to overrule God's decision by including this man of God in his government. The Bible solemnly observes: "In that night was Belshazzar the king of the Chaldeans slain. And

NABONIDUS CYLINDER. *This clay cylinder from Babylon recorded events during the reign of Nabonidus, last king of the Babylonian Empire. Nabonidus and his son Belshazzar were conquered by Cyrus, the first king of the Persian Empire. The Persians eventually reigned over the lands between Ethiopia and India, as described in Esther 1:1.*

PERSEPOLIS. *Darius the Great (r. 522–486 B.C.) moved his capital from Pasargadae to Persepolis, where he and his successors raised a magnificent group of buildings. In one monumental structure, called the "Hall of 100 Columns," sleek pillars rose sharply to end in the sculptured heads of unicorns or bulls. The stairway shown here led to the reception hall of the king. There were harems, a treasury, palaces, and temples in the complex as well.*

Darius the Median took the kingdom, being about three-score and two years old" (Dan. 5:30–31).

C. The Identity of "Darius." Critics have been quick to argue that the Bible is mistaken in the reference to Darius in Daniel 5:31. Secular records bear out that Cyrus II took Babylon in 539 B.C., and they do not know of a Darius who conquered and ruled Babylon. Some critics feel the book was not written by Daniel or even during his lifetime but by a second-century B.C. writer who wanted to encourage the Jews to be faithful to God in resisting Antiochus IV, who had attempted to Hellenize Palestine. (*See* "Jews in New Testament Times.") Such a writer might be more interested in telling an inspiring story than in carefully recording facts. Other scholars suggest possible identifications of Darius.

Some have speculated that Darius was really Gobryas (or Gubaru), one of Nebuchadnezzar's generals. He had become Babylonian governor of the province of Elam, a province at the edge of Persia. When he saw the rise of

Persian power, he deserted to Cyrus and joined him in undermining the power of Babylon. Gobryas and Cyrus easily took Babylon since the priesthood of the god Marduk was waiting to aid the Persians. Belshazzar, left by Nabonidus to defend the city, was unable to defend his capital because of his drunkenness. Cyrus followed Gobryas into Babylon without a battle. There he received a hero's welcome and was immediately crowned "king of Babylon."

Documents of that period reveal why Cyrus was so popular as the conqueror of Babylon. He restored Marduk as the deity of the state, along with the priestly order. He also maintained strict discipline among his occupation forces so that plundering and rape were avoided.

D. Cyrus' Decree. Cyrus committed himself to a policy of restoration. Unlike the Assyrians and Babylonians, who uprooted and exiled conquered people from their countries, Cyrus believed that it was in his best interest to permit the people to return to their native

THE PERSIANS

SHUSHAN (SUSA). *This ancient city in southwestern Persia became a capital city of the Persian Empire. Here Darius I built his palace, which was restored by Artaxerxes I and Artaxerxes II. Many of the events in the Book of Esther occurred in this palace.*

countries and to rebuild their temples. His was a policy of religious polytheism.

The new policy was welcomed by the Jewish communities. Jews had been in exile from Israel since 723 B.C. and from Judah since 586 B.C. They viewed the growing power of Persia as a God-sent sign of the end of their captivity. They comforted themselves with prophetic messages of Babylon's downfall such as Jeremiah 25; 50; 51. Isaiah assured them that Cyrus was anointed by God for a special mission even though he did not know God (Isa. 45:1, 4).

Ezra 1 records the decree of Cyrus to restore captured people to their homelands as the Jews received and understood it. In addition to releasing them, the decree granted the Jews permission to rebuild the temple and to set up organized worship of the God of Israel. Ezra has the decree instructing the neighbors of the Jews to send them off with a personal travel gift as well as a free-will offering for the reconstruction of the temple. Cyrus even returned those valuable articles which had been taken out of Solomon's temple by Nebuchadnezzar in 586 B.C. The items included 30 gold platters, 1000 silver platters, 29 vessels of various kinds, 30 golden bowls, 410 bowls of sil-

ver, and 1000 "other vessels" (Ezra 1:9–10). Cyrus also contributed to the reconstruction from the royal treasury. This contribution was later verified during the reign of Darius when a memorandum in Aramaic was found in the fortress in Ecbatana. That memorandum is recorded in Ezra 6:3–4.

E. The Jewish Response. The Jews responded with enthusiasm to Cyrus' offer. The year the order was issued (538 B.C.), many Jews prepared to return home. We should remember their decision to return was not an easy one. Those who had followed Jeremiah's advice (Jer. 29:5 ff.) had become rooted in Babylonia. They had bought homes, planted orchards, and established businesses in exile. Babylonian business tablets reveal to us Jewish names, indicating the Jews' good standing in Babylonia at that time. These ancient "Zionists" had to give up all they had built in exile to return to a poor homeland. Those starting the long and dangerous journey from Babylon to Palestine needed trust in God, a pioneering spirit, and a strong will to rebuild their land.

Sheshbazzar, "the prince of Judah," was the first governor of Judah. Sheshbazzar, whose name in Babylonian (*Shamash-apalusur*)

THE PERSIANS

means "Shamash has guarded the sonship," was responsible for temple treasures during the trek to Jerusalem (Ezra 1:11; 5:14). He was possibly the son of Jehoiachin, Shenazzar (1 Chron. 3:18).

Historians do not agree on Sheshbazzar's identity. Some argue that the Sheshbazzar named in Ezra 1:11 is identical with Zerubbabel of the family of David, who led the first return (Ezra 2:2). Zerubbabel was a leader next to Jeshua. But we are not told that Sheshbazzar was an active leader, while Ezra lays special emphasis on Zerubbabel's role as Davidic leader in the reconstruction period. In the Jewish response to Darius, Sheshbazzar is mentioned as the governor who saw the foundations of the temple laid. Sheshbazzar may have died soon after his return to Jerusalem, and perhaps his middle-aged relative, Zerubbabel, took over the governorship. The prophet Haggai refers to Zerubbabel as "governor" (Hag. 1:1, 14).

Soon after the Jews' arrival in Jerusalem, Sheshbazzar instructed his people to follow Cyrus' order to rebuild the temple. Zerubbabel of David's family and Jeshua the high priest led the people in thanksgiving and laid the foundation of the temple. The priests and Levites led the people in praise. "Because he is good, for his mercy endureth for ever toward Israel" (Ezra 3:11). Only those who had seen the glory of Solomon's temple could compare it with the humble structure being built before their eyes. Those who remembered cried, while younger Jews shouted for joy at witnessing this new beginning. They knew this fulfilled God's promises to the prophets based on His covenant with Abraham (Ezra 3:12–13).

The Jews in Palestine sought to obey Mosaic Law. They sacrificed burnt offerings morning and evening (Ezra 3:2; cf. Deut. 12:5–6); celebrated the Feast of Booths (Num. 29:12); and observed the fixed festivals (Num. 29:39). They willingly gave what they could afford for building the temple—a total of 61,000 gold drams, 5,000 pounds of silver, and 100 priestly garments (Ezra 2:69).

TOMB OF CYRUS. *Isaiah prophesied the coming of Cyrus, first king of the Persian Empire, to deliver the Jews from their Babylonian Exile (Isa. 44:28; 45:1). A powerful ruler, Cyrus united the Medes and the Persians to conquer Babylon, Assyria, and Lydia. He then permitted the exiles within these conquered lands to return to their homes. It was Cyrus who ordered the rebuilding of the temple at Jerusalem. He died in 530 B.C. and was entombed at Pasargadae, Persia in this vault built in limestone blocks tied together by iron clamps.*

F. Daniel under the Persians. Daniel's life in exile had covered the rise and fall of Babylonia. He had witnessed the beginning of the Exile (*ca.* 606 B.C.), the fall of Babylon (539 B.C.), and the first waves of Jewish people returning to Palestine (*ca.* 538 B.C.). God had used Daniel to proclaim Babylon's fall into Persian hands (Dan. 5). Daniel then served the Persians for a few years after the fall of Babylon.

It seems most likely that the "Darius" of Daniel 6 should be identified with the Persian ruler named Gubaru. Gubaru became governor of the largest Persian province, "Babylonia and across the River." His domain included Babylonia, Assyria, Syria, Phoenicia, and Palestine. He appointed 120 governors and three commissioners (Dan. 6:1) to protect his province. Gubaru made Daniel a commissioner. Daniel's two colleagues and the governors wanted Daniel dismissed, even though his work and judgment were beyond criticism. They attacked his personal life. A pious Jew, Daniel regularly prayed to God, facing Jerusalem (6:10). His enemies convinced Gubaru to order that no one should pray to any god or person, save the king (6:12). As the governors expected, Daniel defied this order. He was tried and found guilty, and cast into a lions' den, from which God rescued him by a miracle (6:22).

During Gubaru's first year of rule, Daniel meditated on Jeremiah's prophecy of the 70 years of exile (Jer. 25:11–12; 29:10). Daniel confessed the sins for which the Jews were exiled, and prayed that the Lord might again deal graciously with His people and restore them to Jerusalem. Suddenly the archangel Gabriel revealed to Daniel that after 70 weeks (an unknown period of time) the people and Jerusalem would be restored, and atonement for their sins would be made. Gabriel said everlasting righteousness would be accomplished on their behalf (Dan. 9:24).

Daniel's last prophetic vision appeared in the third year of Cyrus, king of Persia (Dan. 10:1). By this time Daniel was too old to join the Jews returning to Palestine. God revealed His glory to Daniel as Daniel sat on the bank of the river Tigris (10:4 ff.). God's messenger told Daniel of the future of the Persian Empire. Daniel's vision foretold that three kings after Cyrus would rule Persia (Cambyses, Pseudo-Smerdis, and Darius), before a fourth (Xerxes) would spend his life fighting the Greeks (11:2). One hundred years later the

DARIUS AND XERXES. *This relief from Persepolis shows King Darius I on the throne and crown prince Xerxes behind him. A very powerful Persian king, Darius compiled a code of laws, quelled revolutions within the empire, and established Susa as its new capital. The Jews prospered under the reign of Darius I. The Book of Esther refers to his son, Xerxes, by the name "Ahasuerus."*

Persian Empire was taken by Alexander the Great (*ca.* 323 B.C.). For the next century and a half, two divisions of Alexander's empire would fight on the soil of Palestine—the Ptolemaic kingdom of Egypt ("king of the south") and the Seleucid kingdom of Syria ("king of the north"). Indeed, Palestine would be captured by the Seleucids around 200 B.C. (Dan. 11:17 ff.), and ruled by them until the coming of Antiochus Epiphanes. Antiochus was to battle the Ptolemies of Egypt until the Romans' "ships of Kittim" demanded his withdrawal (11:30). Enraged, Antiochus would go to Jerusalem and "set up the abomination of desolation" (11:31).

The kingdom of God triumphed over the enemy forces in Daniel's vision. God's guidance of history assured Daniel and the Jews that God would accomplish everything according to His purpose. The Jews' future was not bright; they were destined to be ruled by Persians, Greeks, and Romans, and would endure great suffering (Dan. 11:40–45; 12:1). But ultimately the Jews would be raised and "shine brightly like the brightness of the expanse of heaven" (12:3). God made a special promise to Daniel: "You will enter your rest and rise again for your allotted portion at the end of the age" (12:13).

G. Cyrus' Death. Cyrus reached his goal of building an empire even greater than Babylon. He organized his empire into 20 satrapies (provinces). A satrap (governor) ruled each province, and was responsible to the king. Each satrap was checked by officers who also answered directly to the great king. The officers were the king's "eyes" in each province. Any attempt to go against the king's interests was reported to Cyrus at his great palace at Pasargadae, near the eastern shore of the Persian Gulf. Cyrus created a large park there with his palace, shrines, and other structures.

Cyrus continued to fight in the East until he died in 530 B.C. He was buried at Pasargadae in a tomb 10.7 m. (35 ft.) high. (The tomb chamber is only 3.2 × 2.2 m. [10.5 × 7.5 ft.].) Guards stood near the tomb to protect the body of the dead king Cyrus. The corpse was placed inside the tomb in a limestone sarcophagus, which was placed on a funeral couch. The beloved Cyrus was buried with swords, earrings, fine clothing, and tapestries.

III. Cambyses II (529–522 B.C.). Cyrus' son, Cambyses, took over the kingdom after his father's death. Like his father, he was a capable man and a good general. Cambyses had represented Cyrus at the new year's festival (called "the Akita Festival") in Babylon ever since Cyrus became king of Babylon. Cambyses had also stood in the capital as the king's official successor when Cyrus was on a military trip, in case harm came to the king. After his coronation, Cambyses looked westward to expand his empire.

Egypt had escaped foreign rule until this time. Pharaoh Amasis, who was disliked by his people, ruled Egypt with the aid of hired Greek soldiers. Cambyses took Memphis in 525 B.C., when neither Amasis nor his son, Psamtik II, could resist the Persian troops. This marked the start of Persian rule over Egypt.

Egyptians hated foreign rule. The false rumor that Cambyses had killed the sacred Apis bull was an outrage easily believed by simple people. The priests of certain temples were angry because they no longer received free supplies from the state. They were required instead to work the soil and raise fowl for sacrifice. These changes were all the Egyptians needed to reject the Persian rule. Archaeological evidence suggests that Cambyses respected Egypt's religion. But the Egyptian revolt forced him to pull the reins tighter. On his return from Egypt, Cambyses was told that Smerdis had seized rule of Persia. Cambyses knew it could not have been Smerdis, his half-brother (also known as Barfiya), because his aides had already killed Smerdis to prevent an uprising of this sort. Gaumate, a Median who claimed to be Smerdis (Pseudo-Smerdis), had really led the revolt. Cambyses did not live to

deal with Gaumate. He died near Mount Carmel in 522 B.C., possibly by suicide.

IV. Darius I (522–486 B.C.). Darius was a distant relative of Cambyses. He bore Cambyses' spear in his battle with Egypt, and kept up with new political developments. Darius plotted against Gaumate, who backed the religious interests of the Medians and Magian priests. Darius and his forces killed Gaumate in a fortress in Media.

A. Strengthening the Empire. Darius first acted to unite the empire. It was crumbling on all sides because of separate patriotisms in the satrapies. Leaders of the provinces tried to grab power in Media, Elam, Babylon, Egypt, and even in Persia. Darius stemmed each revolt by sending loyal generals to subdue rebel forces. In two years Darius was recognized as great king over most of the empire. He established Susa as the new capital of the kingdom, and built a palace there (521 B.C.). Next he created a code of law to be obeyed throughout his empire (*ca.* 520 B.C.). This law code resembles the Code of Hammurabi (*ca.* 1775 B.C.). Darius also appointed Persians to sit with native leaders as judges, and imposed taxes to be enforced by new officers.

B. Darius and Palestine. In the first difficult years of his reign, Darius had to deal with the temple in Jerusalem. Builders had laid the foundation of the temple, but no further work had been done (Ezra 4:5). The Jews concentrated on building homes and reestablishing their lives in the desolate land. Knowing the rumors of Cambyses' opposition to Egypt's

DARIUS I ON LION HUNT. *This impression of a cylinder seal, dating from about 500 B.C., shows Darius I on a lion hunt. The cuneiform inscription gives his name and title, "The Great King," in three languages—Old Persian, Elamite, and Babylonian. Obviously, the Persian kings were proud of their position. Darius' son, Xerxes, followed his father's model when he declared, "I am Xerxes, the great king, king of kings, king of lands containing many men, king in this great earth far and wide. . . ."*

TOMBS OF THE KINGS. *These tombs of three Persian kings are cut into the rock at Naqsh-i-Rustan in Iran. They are the tombs of Kings Darius I (522–486 B.C.), Artaxerxes I (465–424 B.C.), and Darius II (423–404 B.C.). While Darius I enlarged and strengthened the empire through better organization, Artaxerxes I ruled an empire weakened by internal rebellion. He stopped work on the temple at Jerusalem, but later reconsidered and allowed the work to resume. Darius II (mentioned in Nehemiah 12:22 as "Darius the Persian") chose not to intervene when Egyptians under his rule persecuted Jewish inhabitants of Elephantine Island.*

religious practices, the Jews in Palestine may not have felt eager to request Cambyses' aid in rebuilding the temple.

But Darius wanted to win the Jews' loyalty to his throne, and he was more tolerant of the Jews than earlier Persian rulers had been. God sent two prophets to stir the hearts of Jews in Palestine: Haggai and Zechariah. Both of these men stressed the importance of finishing the temple. Haggai shamed the people by pointing out the poor progress they had made on the temple since their arrival in Jerusalem. The Jews had been in Palestine for over 15 years, but only the foundations of the temple were in place. The Jews were continually frustrated by drought (Hag. 1:10–11), blasting winds, hail, and mildew (2:17). Still, they found time to build fine houses for themselves. Haggai twice challenged them with these words: "Consider your ways!" He warned that God would withhold His blessing until the temple was rebuilt (Hag. 2:18–19).

Zechariah prophesied between 520 and 518 B.C., a longer time than Haggai. Zechariah's gloomy picture of the disillusioned Jews agrees with that of Haggai (Zech. 1:17; 8:10). God reassured the people through Zechariah of the future glory of Jerusalem.

The Jews and their leaders were stunned by the prophetic words. Their new eagerness to obey God led them back to work. Zerubbabel and Jeshua (Joshua) began rebuilding three weeks after the first prophetic oracle (late 520 B.C.). Their loyalty to the Lord was noted by Haggai: "Then Zerubbabel the son of Shealtiel, and Joshua the son of Jehozadak,

the high priest, with all the remnant of the people, obeyed the voice of the Lord their God and the words of Haggai the prophet, as the Lord had sent him. And the people showed reverence for the Lord" (Hag. 1:12, NASB). God sent Haggai words of further encouragement: "I am with you" (Hag. 1:13), and "take courage, Zerubbabel, take courage also, Joshua . . . , and all you people of the land take courage . . . and work; for I am with you" (Hag. 2:4, NASB).

But opposition soon came. Tatnai, the newly appointed Persian governor, tried to halt the renewed efforts to rebuild the temple. The Jews claimed they were carrying out Cyrus' orders. They asked Tatnai to check royal records for Cyrus' memorandum telling the Jews to go to Jerusalem and restore their temple (Ezra 5:10–16). The order was found at Ecbatana, Cyrus' home in his first years of rule. The order was written in Aramaic, and its instructions are recorded in Ezra 6:3–5.

Now it was clear to the Jews that God was with them! Darius told Tatnai not to interfere with the work on the temple (6:6–7). Further, Darius ordered that the royal provincial treasury pay for the building expenses, as well as for the necessary sacrifices—young bulls, rams, and lambs for a burnt offering to the God of heaven, and wheat, salt, wine, and anointing oil; "according to the appointment of the priests, which are at Jerusalem, let it be given to them day by day without fail" (6:9). It seems that Darius continued Cyrus' custom of allowing nations in the empire to worship their native gods, that "they may . . . pray for

THE PERSIANS

the life of the king, and of his sons" (Ezra 6:10). Anyone who disobeyed this order was warned of severe penalties: destruction of his house and execution (6:1).

Darius established good relations with his Jewish subjects. As his forces marched through Palestine on their way to fight in Egypt, the Jews assured Darius that they would not trouble his men. During the winter of 519–518 B.C., Darius managed to regain control of Egypt, by the same quiet manner he had used with the Jews. He respected the religious traditions of Egypt and encouraged the digging of a canal from a branch of the Nile to the Gulf of Suez. (The project had been started by the Pharaoh "Necho" 70 years earlier and abandoned.) Before Darius left their land, Egyptians accepted him as their ruler and gave him the title of Egyptian king.

C. Darius and the Greeks. Darius reestablished the Persian Empire from Egypt to India, as far east as the Indus River. He did not bring the Scythians in southern Russia under his rule, though he gained a foothold across the Bosporus by taking Thrace (513 B.C.).

At his death in 486 B.C., Darius I controlled a larger and stronger empire than he had inherited. Darius improved the government of the empire, placed strict military control on the semi-independent governors, introduced coinage, standardized weights and measures, and took an interest in the welfare of his subjects. But his new taxes were to cause the empire's downfall.

Darius was buried in a royal tomb at Persepolis. After his burial, his son Xerxes was made king.

V. Xerxes I (486–465 B.C.). Some scholars think Xerxes I is the famous "Ahasuerus" of the Book of Esther. He faced the same problems as his father, Darius. His empire was crumbling, largely because of new taxes. But Xerxes did not have Darius' interest in holding the loyalty of his subjects. He made grave errors of judgment in his military actions. He angered the priests of Egypt by taking their temple treasures. He burned Athens, and lost any support he might have claimed in Greek cities. He destroyed Babylon's temples and ordered that Marduk's golden statue be melted down. The Jews had prospered under the peaceful reign of Darius and had completed

---

The Book of Esther: A Glimpse of Persia

The Book of Esther records events that occurred during the reign of Ahasuerus (Xerxes) in the fifth century B.C., at Shushan (Susa), a capital city of the Persian Empire. Since Esther's story centers around intrigues at the royal court, it gives much detail about the customs and life at this time.

Persian feasts were famous for their magnificence. Esther 1 gives a glimpse of the opulence of these feasts. It describes the common Persian manner of eating by reclining on couches or beds (v. 6), and it states that all drinking utensils were made of gold, no two being alike (v. 7). The Greek historian Xenophon said the Persians prided themselves on their number of drinking vessels. When the Greeks destroyed the Persian Empire, a part of their spoil consisted of golden drinking horns and cups.

Esther shows the inner workings of the royal Persian court, as well as special laws relating to the king. Esther 1:14 mentions the seven princes of Persia and Media who "saw the king's face." These were chief nobles who were intimate advisors of the king (cf. Ezra 7:14).

Only a person summoned by the king could visit him without penalty. This gave dignity to the monarch and protected him from assassination. Esther feared going to Ahasuerus without being called because the punishment for such a visit was death (Esther 4:11). Also, no one was allowed to visit the king in mourning clothes, such as sackcloth (Esther 4:2). Yet Esther did so.

Bowing in reverence to nobles was a common custom (Esther 3:2). Everyone bowed in the presence of the king; to refuse to bow was an insult.

Herodotus mentions that the king kept records of royal benefactors. These records are probably referred to in Esther 2:23 and 6:1–3. One of the greatest favors the king could bestow upon a loyal subject was to dress him in clothing the king himself had worn (Esther 6:8).

The Book of Esther tells of other interesting Persian customs outside the royal court. The Persian Empire boasted a highly organized postal system. Letters sent by couriers were forwarded with amazing speed (Esther 3:13). Swift horses or other animals were used to make the dispatch travel even faster (Esther 8:10). As in other areas of the ancient Near East, letters were "signed" by the imprint of one's seal of a signet ring on the document.

By faithfully reflecting the manners and customs of Persia during the days of the empire, the Book of Esther serves as a reliable historical record of the period.

their temple. But when the Jews wanted to rebuild the walls of Jerusalem, their enemies falsely accused them of rebellion. The Jews were not permitted to complete the walls.

In his third year of rule, Xerxes organized a royal party for all of the princes, governors, and high army personnel in the empire's 127 satrapies from India to Nubia (Esther 1:1–3). All of the events of the Book of Esther occurred under Xerxes' reign.

VI. Artaxerxes I (465–424 B.C.). Xerxes was murdered in his bedroom in 465 B.C. His younger son, Artaxerxes (Longimanus) took over a weakened Persian Empire. Artaxerxes tried to keep the empire together with many battles in Bactria, Egypt, and Greece. He accepted the peace formula known as the treaty of Callias (449 B.C.), which postponed a full-fledged war with Greece.

We can appreciate the activities of Ezra and Nehemiah against this background of international rebellion and plotting. The Jews again attempted to rebuild the walls of Jerusalem. The nobles of Samaria this time saw the building as a sign of rebellion. They told Artaxerxes that a strong Jerusalem would be a danger to the security of the empire. They told the king he should check the records to see for himself that Jerusalem was a "rebellious and evil city" (Ezra 4:12, RSV), and that the king's treasury was in danger: "If this city be builded, and the walls set up again, then will they not pay toll, tribute, and custom, and so thou shalt endamage the revenue of the king" (Ezra 4:13). They also advised that in that case the king "will have no possession in the province beyond the River" (4:16, NASB). The search of records in the royal library confirmed the nobles' point. ". . . It is found that this city [Jerusalem] of old time hath made insurrection against kings, and that rebellion and sedition have been made therein" (4:19). Artaxerxes ordered work on the walls stopped until a later order changed the situation (4:21).

Despite his feelings against a walled Jerusalem, Artaxerxes viewed the Jews favorably. He gladly provided funds for Ezra's mission (*ca.* 458 B.C.). The loyalty of Jews in Judea strengthened his position in Syria, and in Egypt. He reinforced Cyrus' order in a special order of his own that permitted Jews in the Persian Empire to return to Palestine. We know from Scripture that Artaxerxes gave gold, silver, and lavish utensils to the temple (cf. Ezra 8:26–27), and promised to pay for all the temple needs from the royal treasury (7:16–20). The king impressed the Jewish leaders with his gifts, promises, and encouragement to do "whatever is commanded by the God of heaven . . . for why should there be wrath against the realm of the king and his sons?" (7:23). Artaxerxes also exempted priests, Levites, and temple workers from paying taxes (7:24).

Artaxerxes supported Ezra's wish to teach the people of Judea the Law of God. Ezra was well qualified by his own study and careful observance of the Law. "Ezra had prepared his heart to seek the Law of the Lord, and to do it, and to teach in Israel statutes and judgments" (Ezra 7:10). Artaxerxes ordered Ezra to teach the people of the Law, and to make them accountable for their actions before courts and judges (7:25). The sword of the Persian government backed up the God-centered Jewish system of law: "Whosoever will not do the law of thy God, and the law of the king, let judgment be executed speedily upon him, whether it be unto death, or to banishment, or to confiscation of goods or to imprisonment" (7:26).

Fifteen hundred Jews, including Levites who were responsible for the temple treasures (Ezra 8:24 ff.), joined Ezra in his mission early in 458 B.C. This group experienced God's presence during their long and dangerous journey. Ezra records: "He delivered us from the hand of the enemy, and of such as lay in wait by the way" (8:31). They arrived late the same year.

By this time over 50,000 exiles had returned to Judea. According to Nehemiah 7, most lived in towns located in and around Jerusalem. The region from Jericho to Bethel was the northern limit, from Bethel to Zanoah the western, from Zanoah to En-Gedi the southern, and from Beth-Zur to Jericho the eastern. The big problem Ezra faced on arriving in Palestine was intermarriage. He knew the history of his people well enough to recall that in the past intermarriage had caused idolatry and corruption. Ezra pleaded with his people to stay pure as the people of God living by the Law of Moses, lest they return to exile. In prayer (Ezra 9:6–15), Ezra shows us his deep hope that the present generation would not repeat the mistakes of the past. Ezra was aware God might leave no remnant in another act of judgment.

Those who had intermarried confessed their sins and were willing to divorce their "foreign" wives (10:3, 11, NASB). The Jews set

GOLDEN DRINKING HORN. *Many Persians made a hobby of collecting drinking vessels, like this beautifully crafted horn made of gold. Note that it features the head and forebody of a griffin at its base. This horn is probably similar to vessels carried by Nehemiah, governor of Judea, when he was cupbearer to the king of Persia (Neh. 2:11).*

In 445 B.C., Nehemiah's mission accomplished what the Jews had hoped for. Nehemiah, a Jew, was a cup-bearer to King Artaxerxes at Susa. Nehemiah had heard that his fellow Jews were not allowed to rebuild the walls of their city. He realized how dangerous the situation was for the Jews. The changeable times, the dislike of the Samaritan leaders for the Jews of Judea, and the nearly successful extinction of the Jewish people by Haman were good reasons for Nehemiah's distress. After prayer (Neh. 1:5–11), and with deep concern for his brothers in Judea, Nehemiah spoke with Artaxerxes. The king gave Nehemiah permission to rebuild the walls of Jerusalem (2:5, 7–8). Escorted by the royal cavalry, Nehemiah arrived in Jerusalem in 445 B.C.

Nehemiah was soon opposed by Sanballat, Tobiah, and Geshem (Neh. 2:10, 19; 4:1–2). But Nehemiah checked the work to be done on the walls and made sure that construction was started immediately, before the Jews' opponents could gather forces. During these tense days workers used one hand to build and the other to hold a weapon for defense (4:17). The wall was finished after only 52 days of work. The Israelites had worked very hard during the day and guarded the walls at night. When the walls were done, Levites and singers came from all around Jerusalem to dedicate the structure with song. Nehemiah arranged two choirs to walk in opposite directions around the walls, singing praises to God as they drew nearer each other. Amid the singing and sacrifice at the temple, the people were so happy that their enemies could hear the joyous sounds from a great distance (Neh. 12:43).

Nehemiah remained governor of Judea for 12 years. He wanted to restore Jerusalem to its former glory. Until now few people had risked living in Jerusalem, exposed to invaders and surprise attacks (Neh. 7:4). With their wall rebuilt, the Jews agreed that at least 10 percent of their people would move from their homes and villages to live in Jerusalem (11:1). In this way Jerusalem quickly became a thriving city in which all the citizens of the province had an interest—many had friends or relatives there now. Nehemiah was also successful in gaining social reforms in his province: He abolished lending money at unfairly high rates (Neh. 5:7), and restored lost property (5:11).

Sometime during Nehemiah's governorship, Ezra returned to Jerusalem. Ezra read the

up a divorce court, and by the winter of 458 B.C. they had settled the matter of intermarriage. A list of the divorces was added to the end of the Book of Ezra (chap. 10).

We know little about Ezra's whereabouts after this episode until we find him some years after in Jerusalem with Nehemiah (Neh. 8). Perhaps Ezra fulfilled his mission of teaching the Law throughout Judah, or had been away reporting the success of his mission to the Jews of Babylonia or to the court of Artaxerxes.

Persian troops moved through Palestine four years later (454 B.C.) on their way to Egypt. The mood was tense in the satrapy of "beyond the River," to which Judea belonged. The satrap of this province revolted against Artaxerxes. Fortunately for Judea, Artaxerxes quickly stemmed this rebellion.

Law to the assembly of people (Neh. 8:2) and helped the Jews understand how they should live according to the Law. This instruction continued during the Feast of Booths (8:18). A solemn assembly at Jerusalem (9:38; 10:29) made its own agreement to uphold the Law. This group also faced specific problems of its community: intermarriage (10:30); Sabbath observance (10:31); contribution of one-third of a shekel for the temple service (10:32–33); and support of priests and Levites with first fruits and tithes (10:34–39).

Nehemiah returned to Artaxerxes in 433 B.C. He was privileged to return to Jerusalem later (Neh. 13:6), when he used his royal authority to expel Tobiah (13:7). Nehemiah also required the citizens of Jerusalem to support the Levites and singers (13:10 ff.), to enforce the Sabbath observance (13:15 ff.), and to forbid intermarriage (13:23 ff.).

VII. Persia's Decline. Like other great powers of the ancient world, Persia eventually passed its peak of influence and began a long period of decay. Military defeat, political intrigue, and economic blunders contributed to the empire's failure.

A. Political Maneuvers. The death of Artaxerxes in 424 B.C. opened a new era of secret plotting in the royal courts of Persia. Xerxes II was killed while intoxicated. His assassin, a son of Artaxerxes' concubine, was killed by Ochus, son of another concubine. Ochus, who already had support from the Babylonian army, found Susa's army unsympathetic to its new ruler, Darius II. Darius was forced to deal with Ochus and other pretenders to the throne by having them cruelly executed. He maintained Persian interests in Greece with Sparta's help. When tension arose between the Jews in the Elephantine region of Egypt and the local Egyptians, Darius and the Persians did not intervene.

B. Growing Jewish Power. The Jews enjoyed good relations with the Persians during the years of Persia's decline. They served as hired soldiers in Persian forces. Jews stationed at Syene (modern Aswan) at the southern border enjoyed relative independence. On the island of Elephantine opposite Syene in the Nile River, one Persian fortress was manned entirely by Jews. They even built a temple on the island, where they sacrificed animals to God. The sacrifice of rams offended the native Egyptians, especially the priests of Khnum, who regarded the sacrificial ram as a sacred animal. The priests destroyed the Jews' temple

APADANA AT PERSEPOLIS. *The Apadana, or audience hall, of the capital city was covered in beautifully-sculpted relief work depicting soldiers, courtiers, and tribute-bearing foreigners. This view shows Susian and Persian guards standing at attention along the eastern stairway of the Apadana. It represents the very best sculpture produced during the time of the Persian Empire.*

when the Jewish governor left to report to Susa in 410 B.C. Jews of the Nile asked Jerusalem for advice on rebuilding their temple. They said the temple had stood since before Cambyses' conquest of Egypt. After repeated requests for aid, Jewish leaders in Jerusalem told the colony in Egypt to rebuild their temple and to continue offering meal and incense. But because the local Egyptians strongly disliked them, the Jews never rebuilt their temple at Elephantine.

C. Final Phase. The last 70 years of the Persian Empire were filled with plotting and murders. The last Persian king, Darius III, was a capable ruler who faced the impossible task of uniting a splintering empire while trying to withstand the onslaught of the great general of Macedonia, Alexander the Great. Alexander reached Persepolis in 330 B.C. after defeating Darius at Gaugamela. In 330 B.C., Alexander looted and burned Darius' palace.

The Persians' rule had brought relative peace and prosperity to Jews in Palestine. The Jews' temple and Torah had flourished, and much of the Oriental culture of Persia had been adopted by the Jews. Jewish life in Palestine under the Greeks would change for the worse.

VIII. Persian Culture. The Persians left an indelible mark upon the life of the Jews. Various aspects of Persian culture changed the

TRILINGUAL TABLETS. *These inscriptions were found at Ganj Name near the modern Iranian city of Hamadan (ancient Ecbatana). The inscription at the left was ordered by Darius and the one on the right was ordered by his son Xerxes. Three languages appear on each tablet (from left to right): Old Persian, Akkadian, and Elamite. Each inscription describes the triumphs of the Persian kings.*

life of Jewish people in New Testament times and beyond.

A. Art and Architecture. Persian art reflected the life of the court. Persian rulers cut fine royal reliefs into rocks to celebrate their victories over enemies. In the Behistun relief, Darius is shown defeating the rebels (521 B.C.). These victory reliefs show foreign subjects offering tribute to Darius.

Persian rulers also prided themselves on their beautiful palaces. Cyrus followed the style of the Median palace of Ecbatana in building his capital, Pasargadae.

King Darius chose Persepolis as the setting for his palace in 520 B.C. Building and magnifying Persepolis began with Darius' successor, and lasted to the fall of Persepolis under Darius III in 330 B.C.

Even after eight years of warfare, Xerxes found time to develop the buildings of Persepolis. Achaeminid art reached its peak during the last 13 years of Xerxes' reign.

The royal tombs also show us the Persians'

desire for lavishness. The tomb of Cyrus II was simple compared to the rock-hewn tombs of Darius I, Artaxerxes I, and Darius II near Persepolis.

The whole Persian Empire contributed materials and artisans to imperial projects. Natural, three-dimensional figures; a fondness for animal themes; and the refined art of miniatures are contributions of the Persians. We find many of these characteristics in synagogues and other Jewish buildings of the postexilic period in Palestine, such as the synagogue at Capernaum.

B. Language. Persian is a branch of the Indo-Iranian language group. It has similarities to Latin and Greek. (The Persian word for god is *daiva,* related to Latin *deus* and English *divine.*) The ancient Persians knew and used the Elamite, Babylonian, and Old Persian languages. The Behistun Rock records the Achaeminid dynasty up to Darius I in these three languages.

Old Persian was written in *cuneiform,* or

THE PERSIANS

wedge-shaped figures. People used the language only for official court documents and inscriptions. Official correspondence was aided by the use of Aramaic, a language that was used from Persia to Egypt. The Aramaic script became the model for a new Hebrew script that was used to record the Old Testament. (*See* "Languages and Writing.") The Jews borrowed many Aramaic words. In Hebrew, for example, the word *dat* ("decree") comes from the Persian *data*.

Aramaic words found their way into other languages as well. Our English word *paradise* comes from the Persian word for garden palace, *pairi-daeza*.

C. Religion. The chief god of the Persian system of religion was Ahura-Mazda, "the wise Lord." The official priests were called the Magians. The king believed Ahura-Mazda granted him the right to rule; he was the "image" of the god, in a very real sense.

The Persians believed in nature gods such as Air, Water, Heaven, Earth, Sun, and Moon. They did not worship these gods in temples. Instead, they sacrificed animals in open fields, to the accompaniment of chanting from a Magian priest. The Persians also burned sacrifices to their gods.

In the middle of the sixth century B.C., Zarathustra began to reshape Persian religious thought into what later became known as Zoroastrianism.

The conflict of good and evil was basic to Zarathustra's teachings. Zoroastrianism recognized Ahura-Mazda as its only god, but Ahura-Mazda was in eternal conflict with the evil spirit Angra Mainyu. Zarathustra opposed sacrifices and offerings of drink. He started the worship of Ahura by perpetual fire. The Persians built fire temples for this purpose.

This popular religion challenged the Jews to state their faith in clear terms. Jewish rabbis founded academies to preserve the truth of God's Word and to combat the intriguing doctrines of the Zoroastrians.

In the New Testament we read how "the magi" came to worship the baby Jesus in Bethlehem (Matt. 2:2). They may have been representatives of the priestly caste of the Zoroastrian religion.

Persia profoundly altered the course of Israelite history. The apocalyptic ideals of Persian philosophy are strongly represented in the apocryphal books of the intertestamental period. So pervasive was the influence of Persia that it is difficult to isolate Israelite art and architecture from the Persian influences. The Aramaic language (a late Persian dialect of Assyrian) became the standard language of Jewish politics and religion after the intertestamental period.

THE GREEKS AND HELLENISM

Ancient Greeks called their land Hellas and they called themselves Hellenes. The most influential of the Greek city-states was Athens, which provided the major inspiration for the achievements of the Greek Empire that was briefly to stretch across territories nearly as large as the United States of America.

When we speak of "*Hellenic* culture," we mean the Greek cultural achievements that reached their highest point in Athens in the fifth century B.C. "Hellenic culture" signifies the arts, commerce, and thought of the Greek mainland as it was influenced by Athens. "*Hellenistic* culture" is the subsequent development of Greek culture among other eastern Mediterranean peoples who reflected the culture begun in Athens. This Greek way of life was carried as far as India by the armies of Alexander the Great. It remained long enough in Egypt, Palestine, Asia Minor, and Persia to influence their religion, government, language and art.

I. Early Greek History. War and political intrigue checkered the early history of Greece. The Greeks' ability to overcome these problems indicated their strong character and hopeful vision of the future.

A. Roots of Greek Culture. The Greek islands and the Greek mainland were inhabited by people called the Aegeans by about 3000 B.C. The Minoans inhabited the island of Crete. The people we call Greeks did not begin arriving until about 1900 B.C. They seem to have come from the Balkan region now called Bulgaria.

These migrating peoples had gradually moved into Europe from the regions east of the Caspian Sea. As they gradually settled in northern and western Europe respectively, their language developed into what are now known as German and the Romance languages (for example, French, Italian, and Spanish as regional descendants of the Latin language of the Romans). Other groups had

BLACK-FIGURE POTTERY. *Warriors battle on the side of this* amphora *(two-handled jar) dating from about 540 B.C. Decorated in black on light-colored background, the jar is a fine example of the black-figure pottery developed in Athens and very popular until it was supplanted in 525 B.C. by red-figure pottery. At this point in the evolution of Greek art, the two warring figures are still stylized. But black-figure pottery was beginning to take on some form of realism, associated with the best Greek art.*

THE GREEKS AND HELLENISM

GOLDEN MASK. *Heinrich Schliemann discovered this golden death mask in a Greek tomb in Mycenae, Greece in 1876. He thought it was a mask of the face of Agamemnon, a hero in the Trojan War. But the carefully crafted golden artifact actually dates from between the sixteenth and nineteenth centuries B.C., long before the Trojan War.*

moved further east across the Himalayas into India, where their language was preserved in Sanskrit. These wanderers with their *Indo-European* language provided a common ancestry for scores of civilizations, as revealed by similarities between words in the languages of widely separated countries.

The first group of this great family arrived in the Greek peninsula about 1900 B.C. and were called Achaeans. Some settled in the Plains of Thessaly. Others moved to the southernmost part of the land called the Peloponnesus. By 1200 B.C. King Agamemnon of Mycenae, a powerful city-state in the northeast section of the Peloponnesus, emerged as the foremost leader of these settlements. Agamemnon led an attack force to Troy on the Asian shore of the Aegean Sea. His destruction of Troy opened the door for more Achaeans to migrate to Asia Minor, where they set up cities of Greek-speaking peoples.

The Achaeans' migration to Asia Minor was probably prompted by invasions of more tribes from the Balkans. The Dorians moved into Greece over a period of three centuries (1500–1200 B.C.). They too spoke a form of Greek, but they were hostile to the settled peoples of the Greek peninsula. They burned Mycenae and other cities, including Cnossus in Crete (the center of the Minoan civilization). Thus they destroyed the culture and commerce that had steadily developed over about 2,000 years.

However, the Ionians moved to the eastern side of the Aegean and preserved their heritage. They spread north and south along the

rim of Asia Minor in a region eventually called Ionia. Homer, the great Greek poet, produced his literary masterpieces there sometime between 900 and 700 B.C.

The next people to invade and settle Greece were the Aeolians, who occupied west central Greece, the northern Peloponnese, and the islands offshore. The exact time at which these invaders appeared in Greece is uncertain.

While Greece was being invaded from the Balkans over a period of about eight centuries (1900–1100 B.C.), the Israelites were developing into a nation. This period spans the time of the patriarchs Isaac and Jacob, Israel's stay in Egypt and the Exodus (1446 B.C.), the conquest of Canaan (1399 B.C.), and a large portion of the period of the judges, which ended in 1043 B.C. when Saul was made king.

B. Age of the Kings. The next stage in early Greek history can be called the age of the kings (*ca.* 1000–750 B.C.). The waves of new people that surged into Greece often settled in towns and villages with the original inhabitants. Hundreds of valleys and plains provided convenient settlement centers. These city-states were ruled by kings.

The region called Attica included Athens, a city that eventually absorbed the many self-governing townships around it. Legend says that King Theseus united Attica under Athenian rule, forcing everyone to pay taxes and be enrolled as a citizen of Athens.

Athens became a prominent city-state by about 700 B.C. Others also developed—including Megara, Corinth, Argos, and Sparta to the east and south, and Thebes to the north. The Greek word for city (*polis*) referred to the entire political state ruled by a city.

The city-states constantly quarreled among themselves, sometimes one-on-one and sometimes in groups called *leagues.* In addition to warring, they carried on extensive trading and exploration throughout the Mediterranean and even as far as the British Isles.

During the age of the kings, the Greeks began to develop distinctive patterns of art and commerce. They learned commercial skills from the Phoenicians, who dominated Mediterranean trade at that time. They also borrowed the Phoenician alphabet and added vowels to it. The Greek literature of this period is best preserved in the epic poems known as the *Iliad* and the *Odyssey,* which are usually attributed to Homer.

This period in Greece's history roughly par-

THE ACROPOLIS, ATHENS. *In Greek antiquity,* acropolis *was the name of any fortress overlooking a populated area. An acropolis was built on a hill as a place of refuge and defense, with the growing city at its base. The acropolis at Athens was the most famous of these sites. Most of its temples and public buildings were erected during the fifth century B.C., Athens' period of greatness.*

allels the monarchy of Israel, which began when Saul became Israel's first king in 1043 B.C. and ended when the Assyrians defeated Israel in 722 B.C.

C. The Rise of Democracy. The rule of Greek kings was slowly usurped by nobles, who enjoyed great wealth and power at the expense of the peasants.

The nobles vanished from the scene by about 600 B.C. and merchants became the most important leaders in the Greek city-states. A system of metal coinage had been adopted in the early 600's, so that wealth was now accumulated in lands, slaves, and money. All of these gains were no help to the poverty-stricken peasants, so the city-states passed laws to limit the power of wealthy tyrants. By 500 B.C., democracy had a strong foothold in Greece.

Greek democracy gave citizens a voice in their own affairs—an innovation in ancient government. There was no sense of citizenship among the Egyptians or Mesopotamians, not even among the Old Testament Jews. When a Hebrew prophet denounced social wrongs, he appealed to the justice of Jehovah rather than the rights of man. The Greeks were the first to develop a system of government that guaranteed civil liberties and focused upon civic obligations.

During this period, Greek culture produced lyric poetry, architecture, sculpture, and religious thought that would continue to affect the world for centuries to come. Pindar, Tyrtaeus, and Sappho were well-known poets of this period. Greek architects abandoned the flat Egyptian style of construction to design buildings with soaring columns, sloping roofs, and carved friezes. Greek sculptors carved their works in marble that would last through the ages.

Greek gods were no longer thought of as acting unjustly or capriciously. Greek philosophers raised the cry for social justice. They began teaching that the deeds of men would be judged after death in the court of Minos and Rhadamanthus.

While Greece was making these great cultural strides, the Jews were facing a bleak future. The people of Judah were exiled by their Babylonian enemies in 586 B.C. Persia conquered Babylon in 539 B.C., and although Cyrus the Great allowed the Jews to return home, there could be no real resurgence of Jewish nationalism until the time of the Seleucids, who inherited part of the domain of Alexander the Great. (*See* "Jews in New Testament Times.")

D. The Brief Unification of Greece. The city-states were so jealous of each other and so fiercely independent that they could unite only for brief periods to fight a common enemy. This eventually led to their own downfall.

Cyrus the Great conquered Asia Minor and made Persia the strongest military power in the world. A Persian army attempted to invade Greece in 490 B.C., but Athenians defeated them at Marathon. A second Persian invasion by land and sea in 480 B.C. plunged all the way to Athens, which was partially destroyed. It was during this invasion that the Spartan king Leonidas made his heroic stand at the pass of Thermopylae. The Athenians formed a league of city-states and drove out the Persians in 479 B.C., having inflicted a crushing defeat on the Persian navy at Salamis.

E. The Peloponnesian Wars. Because Athens had led this military victory, Athens became the dominant force of the Greek world. Sparta resented this power and pulled Corinth and Megara into a league to squelch Athens. The series of battles between Athens and Sparta came in two phases (459–446 B.C.

THE GREEKS AND HELLENISM

Greek War Tactics

Greece's domination of the ancient world and the spread of the Greek language throughout the Mediterranean area are two of the most startling facts of history. Modern Greece is only slightly larger than the state of New York, it is filled with mountains, and its soil is rather unproductive. Ancient Greece knew little political unity. So what was the secret of Greek military success? Here are a few possible answers:

Ancient Greeks were raised to be soldiers. In Sparta, children belonged to the state. Defective boys were thrown out on the hills to die; strong ones were educated by the state, and most education was physical. Boys were taught to run, wrestle, endure pain without flinching, live on reduced rations, obey commands—and to rule. They were also taught mathematics, philosophy, music, and the love of reading.

These qualities can be seen in some famous Greek battles. Feeling it was time to conquer Greece, Darius I of Persia assembled a huge army and 600 ships. Drunk with success (he had just destroyed Miletus), Darius was confident that he could subdue Greece within days.

The Persians landed on the east side of Attica at a place near Marathon. News of the oncoming battle alarmed Greece. Slaves and freemen were enlisted at Athens and forced to march across the mountains to Marathon. By the time the Greeks assembled, there were only 20,000 of them. (The armies of Sparta were delayed and did not arrive in time). The Persians, on the other hand, had 100,000 hardened veterans.

The Persians filled the air with arrows; but they had little effect, for the Greeks were well-armored. Under the leadership of Miltiades, the Greeks attacked as a team. Teamwork was something the Persians did not understand; they fought as individuals.

The battle was a disaster for Darius. According to Greek records, 6,400 Persians lost their lives while only 192 Greeks fell. At the end of the battle, the delayed Spartans arrived and praised the victors. Darius failed to conquer Greece, but his son Xerxes had the same dream; he collected troops and war materials, and by 481 B.C. he was ready. According to Herodotus, this army had 2,641,000 fighting men in addition to slaves, engineers, and others.

As the huge army marched westward toward Greece, it passed through Thrace and by Philippi and Macedonia. Many Greeks on the way surrendered, either because of terror or bribes. These Greeks allowed their armies to become a part of the Persian army.

Rising to the occasion, Themistocles, commander of the Athenian contingent, requested his sailors to paint huge signs on the rocks that the Persian fleet could see as they passed by. These signs implored the Greeks in the fleet to either desert or refuse to fight against their native land. Themistocles knew that even if the Greek sailors did not desert, Xerxes would be worried about using them.

The rival fleets finally clashed and fought until darkness stopped them. Many Greeks turned traitor and showed the Persians secret passes over their mountains. Undaunted, King Leonidas of Sparta gathered 300 Spartans to guard the pass at Thermopylae. Knowing that this was extremely dangerous, he only chose men who had sons, so that their family names would not be extinguished. Including other garrisons, his army consisted of only 6,000 men.

When the fighting got tough, most of the Greeks escaped. But Leonidas and all but two of his Spartans died fighting. The Persians lost 20,000, the Greeks 300. (One of the two Spartan survivors fell later in a battle at Plataea; the other survivor hanged himself to avoid shame.)

The following year, an army of 110,000 Greeks attacked the Persians. Though outnumbered, they killed 260,000 Persians.

One hundred and twenty-three years after the defeat of Xerxes, King Philip of Macedonia had a son named Alexander. Alexander became the greatest Greek general of all times. Inspired by Homer's *Iliad,* he early determined that he would conquer the world. Macedonian training and Alexander's phalanx were vital factors in Greek victories.

There were 9,000 men in a phalanx, divided into squares with 16 men on each side. Each man was protected with armor and a four-m. (13-ft.) spear. Standing about 1 m. (3 ft.) apart, shields in position, they formed a human tank.

In addition to the phalanx and cavalry, Alexander had war machines designed by Diades, a Greek engineer. These bow-like machines could shoot huge arrows or hurl 22-kg. (50 lb.) stones more than 180 m. (200 yds.). Alexander's army also carried huge towers with which they could scale enemy walls.

Alexander was a master of propaganda. He loved to terrify foes by scattering enormous bridle bits where they could easily be seen. This gave the impression that he possessed supersized horses!

So the Greeks used shrewd psychology as well as mechanical genius to conquer their foes. They overcame enormous odds to establish themselves as masters of the Mediterranean world.

ALEXANDER THE GREAT. *This youthful king of Macedonia (ca. 356–323 B.C.) changed the world militarily and culturally. He destroyed the Persian Empire and swept through Syria, Palestine, and Egypt, marching as far as India's Indus River before his tired troops mutinied, forcing him to turn back. Alexander spread the Hellenistic culture and established Greek as the dominant language throughout the known world.*

and 431–404 B.C.), called the Peloponnesian Wars.

This period has also been called the "golden age of Athens." Under Pericles, Athens surpassed its former glory. The buildings of the Acropolis, including the famed Parthenon, belong to this period. The greatest Greek writers lived in the Periclean era—Aeschylus, Sophocles, Euripides, and Aristophanes. The debates of Socrates began the Greek philosophical tradition that Plato and Aristotle were to adorn in the next century. The Athenian fleet ruled the Aegean Sea, and with that superiority came wealth and power.

Yet Sparta defeated Athens in 404 B.C., and the victorious Spartans used ruthless methods to dominate the Hellenic mainland. Corinth, Athens, Argos, and Boeotia formed a league to resist Sparta. But the Corinthian War (as it was called) ended when Sparta made an alliance with Persia. With this extra support, Sparta forced Athens and its allies to recognize Spartan authority over the Hellenic mainland. They agreed upon the Peace of Antalcidas or King's Peace of 386 B.C. This treaty yielded Hellenic cities in Asia Minor to Persian rule, allowed the Aegean islands to remain independent, and placed

Sparta in absolute military control of the mainland.

Spartan power did not last long. In 378 B.C., the people of Thebes—a city-state 48 km. (30 mi.) north of Athens—recaptured their citadel. They were led in their battle by a man named Epaminondas, who developed a new military tactic that revolutionized Hellenic warfare. Until this time, battles had been fought in parallel lines, with opposing armies meeting each other head-on in wave after wave of fighting men. Epaminondas created the "oblique order" of battle. He divided his army into two units: one for defense, the other for offense. The offensive wing was strengthened with additional men. While the defensive wing advanced slowly toward the enemy, the offensive wing advanced on the left to break through a given point. The Thebans surprised the Spartan armies with this tactic, crushing Spartan units at Leuctra around 371 B.C. This victory gave Thebes control over Greece.

While Thebes was fighting Sparta, units were mobilizing 160 km. (100 mi.) north of Athens and Thebes in an area called Thessaly. The leader of this growing threat was Jason of Pherae, who turned Thessaly into a powerful armed camp. But he was assassinated before he could move against Thebes.

In 362 B.C., Epaminondas of Thebes gained

HORSEMAN. *This bronze statuette of a horseman dates from about 575 to 560 B.C. Found at Dodone, it has a static quality that gradually disappeared as Greek art neared its perfection in the following century.*

THE GREEKS AND HELLENISM

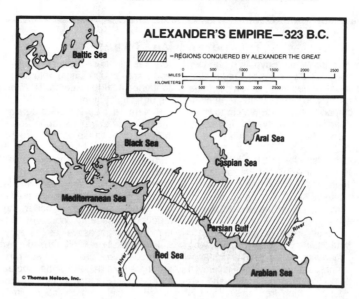

ALEXANDER'S EMPIRE— 323 B.C.

= REGIONS CONQUERED BY ALEXANDER THE GREAT

another victory over the Spartans at Mantinea. However, Epaminondas died in the battle. Thebes could not control Greece without him. Nor was Athens capable of assuming leadership, having been weakened by the Peloponnesian Wars. And Thessaly had lost Jason of Pherae. In short, not one of the city-states was strong enough to unify Greece, and the stage was set for the rise of Alexander the Great of Macedon. This came during the Intertestamental Period, when the Jews under Nehemiah rebuilt the walls of Jerusalem, with Persia's permission.

II. The Rise of the Macedonians. In 359 B.C. a young man named Philip II became the new king of Macedonia. Before he ascended to the throne, Philip had been captured in a battle with Thebes. While a prisoner, he learned war tactics from Epaminondas and planned his own variation of the oblique order of battle—a variation now known as the *phalanx.*

Philip created a powerful new Macedonian army. His cavalry consisted of about 2,000 horsemen in eight squadrons. He established the king's bodyguard of both cavalry and foot soldiers and six infantry battalions of 1,536 men each. Philip also invented an impressive array of siege engines for storming city walls.

His soldiers were heavily armed. In addition to small shields, helmets, and breastplates, the front line infantry who led the wedge-shaped phalanx carried four-m. (13-ft.) spears. The cavalry and other infantrymen carried larger shields, plus short thrusting swords and spears.

To free himself for conquest, Philip made a peace agreement with Athens in 358 B.C. He then quickly conquered the Macedonian city-states of Amphipolis and Pydna. By 352 B.C. he penetrated south into the Greek peninsula and took Thermopylae, a mere 112 km. (70 mi.) from Athens. In 348 B.C. he made a new alliance with Athens and ended what has been called the "Sacred Wars." During the next 10 years Macedonia established its control over much of the Hellenic peninsula. Macedonia— a nation that the Hellenes had considered to be barbaric—was soon to spread Greek culture across many lands.

The golden age of Greek culture was over by the time Macedonia rose to power. One of the last great political figures was Isocrates (436–338 B.C.). Isocrates was a great orator, and his public speaking swayed political thought in Athens. His passion was the defeat of Persia. Isocrates saw the eastern power as a menace to Hellenic society. He felt the Persians were vile and disgusting, and he spent his life arousing hatred and hostility toward them. His most notable follower was none other than Philip II of Macedon.

A. The Advance of the Hellenistic Empire. It did not take long for the Hellenic city-states to mobilize against the Macedonians. The Athenians and Thebans unified to face them, and in 338 B.C. the two forces engaged in battle. The Macedonians soundly defeated

The Alexandrian Library

Alexander the Great reached Egypt in November 332 B.C. On January 20, 331 B.C., Alexander himself drew in the sands an outline for a new city to be the center of his navy and Greek culture—Alexandria. It would incorporate the old Egyptian town of Ratotis and Neopolis (new city) in its walls. Dinocrates, the architect of Rhodes, was left in charge of the building project.

Alexandria became the site of three wonders of the ancient world: the lighthouse of Pharos (an island connected to the mainland with a causeway); the Soma, which housed Alexander's golden coffin; and the most famous library in the ancient world, the Alexandrian Library.

The idea for a library in Alexandria seems to have originated with Ptolemy I Soter (d. 283), who began collecting manuscripts for it. The actual library building was probably erected by Ptolemy II Philadelphus (285–246 B.C.). Most of Alexandria's archeological evidence dating from this period is lost, although scholars accompanying Napoleon Bonaparte recorded in 1799 that the city's ruins (which had served for centuries as a quarry for new building) still constituted a considerably large complex. Modern Alexandria was built on the same site and obliterated most of the ruins, including the library.

The library was a part of the *Mouseion* ("House of the Muses," or house of arts and sciences), which was patterned on Aristotle's Lyceum in Athens. The Mouseion was a complex of buildings connected by long colonnades. In these colonnades were study rooms, lecture halls, and administrative offices where scholars could teach and do research. Among the scholars who used the library were the mathematicians Euclid and Apollonios of Perga, the geographer Eratosthenis (who first said the world was round), the astronomer Aristarchos of Samos, and the medical researchers Ersistratos and Eudemos.

The library building had two parts: "the library within the palace" (the *Brucheion*) and the smaller "library outside the palace" (the *Serepheum*). By 250 B.C., the Brucheion contained 400,000 "mixed volumes" (longer scrolls containing more than one work) and 90,000 single volumes; the Serepheum contained 42,800 volumes. The Serepheum served the ordinary students and citizens.

Ptolemy II also issued orders that his soldiers should seize any books found on ships unloading in Alexandria. These books were then copied and a copy was returned to the owners. Books received in this manner were labelled "from the ships." The ancient writer Galen recounted how Ptolemy III Euergetes tricked the Athenians into lending him their official copies of the tragedies—the copies which the actors used in their performances—and then forfeited the security deposit of 15 talents when he kept the original as well as the copy he had made.

The books were first housed in warehouses until they could be processed. Library workers took great care in labelling the copies, to show the source of each manuscript. The books might be labelled by the geographical origin, by the name of the corrector or editor of the copy, or by the name of the owner. Callimachus, who may have been one of the chief librarians, is said to have compiled a document called the *Pinakes* for library users. The *Pinakes* was subtitled, "Tables of Those Who Were Outstanding in Every Phase of Culture, and Their Writings."

The decline of the Mouseion and library seems to have begun about 100 B.C., amid wars and civil unrest. It seems that the Brucheion was accidently burned by Julius Caesar in the Alexandria War in 48 B.C. Although much irreplaceable material was lost when the Brucheion was destroyed, Mark Antony compensated for the loss by giving Cleopatra 200,000 manuscripts from the library at Pergamum. From this time, the Serepheum took the place of the Brucheion as the royal library.

The library declined further after the beginning of the Christian Era. It was burned again by the Roman emperor Aurelian in A.D. 273 as he reconquered Egypt. Whatever was left of the library was finally destroyed by the Moslem conqueror Omar in A.D. 645.

---

the Hellenic units at Chaeronea and took control of Greece. At this battle a young Macedonian cavalry officer appeared for the first time on the battlefield. He was Philip's son, Alexander.

Philip called a meeting at Corinth of representatives from all the Greek city-states, except Sparta. Delegates to this League of Corinth sat on a council, the *Synhedrion* (cf. Jewish *Sanhedrin*). Representation was based on the population of the districts in the city-states. Philip was elected as the *hegemon* (ruler) of the Hellenic League. For the first time since the Persian Wars, the Hellenic cities were unified under one powerful ruler.

Interestingly, though, the conquered Greeks still considered the Macedonians to be foreigners, largely because the Macedonians did not speak one of the Hellenic dialects. However, the Macedonians soon absorbed the

THE GREEKS AND HELLENISM

Hellenic culture and dialects. Attic Greek—the language spoken in Athens—was adopted as the official language of state under Philip. Thus for the first time on the Hellenic peninsula all the people began to speak a common language. It was called *koine* (meaning "common") Greek. As Alexander marched, this *koine* language went with him, influencing the surrounding communities which he conquered.

B. Alexander the Great. Alexander was born around 356 B.C. His mother was of royal lineage, as was his father, Philip II. When Alexander was 14, he studied under the Athenian philosopher, Aristotle. Perhaps no culture has ever produced a greater mind than Aristotle's. So searching and profound was Aristotle's work that in the twelfth and thirteenth centuries A.D. much of the Christian church regarded his teachings as being divinely inspired. No subject was untouched by his contemplation. Philosophy, botany, geography, zoology, astronomy, and art were all subjects of deep concern for him. Aristotle was the student of Plato and the teacher of Alexander the Great. Either role would have earned him an important place in history.

Most likely Aristotle instructed Alexander by reading and discussing Homer and the Greek tragedies. Aristotle also trained Alexander in politics. Through Aristotle, Alexander acquired his deep love for Hellenic culture, which drove him to the Far East in order to spread the Hellenic "spirit." Tradition says that Alexander even carried a copy of the *Iliad* throughout his Persian and Oriental campaigns.

One of Alexander's most cherished possessions was the horse he had trained as a youth; it was named Bucephalus. This was his mount in all of his major battles and conquests. The horse died in India, and Alexander built the city of Bucephala on the Hydaspes River in memory of his horse.

In 336 B.C., when Alexander was 20 years old, his father Philip was assassinated under mysterious circumstances and Alexander was made the new Macedonian king. His rivals spread rumors of Alexander's own death and he spent much of the following year in quelling revolts that these rumors inspired. He destroyed Thebes in the process. This gave him undisputed control over the Hellenic peninsula.

1. The March toward Persia. In spring of 334 B.C. Alexander led his army of 40,000

GREEK RELIEF. *This relief from the Parthenon dates from the fifth century, the time of Pericles, when Greek artists had completely mastered both form and material. Flowing drapery, following the shape of the human form, revealed the sculptors' special attention to detail.*

men across the Dardanelles into Asia Minor and first engaged the Persians at the Granicus River. The Persian advance guard, lightly armed and unaccustomed to Macedonian tactics, was overwhelmed. Alexander had planned only to free the Greek cities then under Persian control, but the resounding victory spurred him to strike at the heart of the empire itself.

This was no madcap venture. Darius III, the Persian king, was a poor leader and his provincial officials were unreliable. The unwieldy empire was ready to fall in pieces.

The victory at the Granicus River quickly opened the towns of Sardis, Ephesus, and Miletus to Alexander's conquest. Miletus was the traditional birthplace of Hellenic philosophy; Sardis and Ephesus would play significant roles in the New Testament church (cf. Rev. 1:11; 3:1, 4).

In 333 B.C., Alexander moved on Gordium, the capital of Phrygia. The goal of this offensive was the Cilician Gates, a narrow mountain pass to Syria and Palestine. Moving through the pass, Alexander advanced onto a plain near the village of Sollioi. The leader of Darius' Greek mercenaries advised the Persian king to keep his forces on the open plain. But Darius established a defensive position on the Pniaurus River. Here would be the first encounter between the Macedonians and the Persian royal units. The phalanxes of the Macedonians again proved too powerful for the Persian army. Darius swiftly retreated, relinquishing Asia Minor to the Macedonian conqueror.

During 332 B.C., Alexander swept through Syria, Palestine, and Egypt. He captured the Phoenician naval base of Tyre, once thought to be invulnerable to attack from land. (The city was on an island, but Alexander built a causeway to it. Some consider this his greatest victory.) Egypt hailed him as the deliverer who freed them from their Persian overlords.

While wintering in the Nile valley, he chose the site for a new commercial center to take the place of Tyre. Alexandria, as the new city was called, occupied a highly favorable position for linking the trade of the Mediterranean with India and the Far East.

As a result of Alexander's conquests, the center of Western civilization was shifting—culturally and economically. Alexandria replaced the cities of Greece as the focus of Greek intellectual and artistic life.

In 331 B.C., Alexander resumed his eastward march and this was perhaps the most significant period in his career. He crossed the Syrian desert to confront the Persians in one final epic battle. This battle has been given two names, Arbela or Gaugamela. On the open plains, Darius III faced Alexander with the remainder of his armies and a line of battle elephants. Alexander's troops were at first startled by the appearance of the beasts—but not startled enough for this to be of help to Darius III. The Persian king was killed by his own troops as he attempted to flee from the battle. The tactics of phalanx and cavalry again carried the day, and the Macedonians achieved a signal victory. After the battle Alexander was crowned king of Asia. Thus the crusade for Hellenic vengeance was accomplished. The Persian Empire was soundly defeated.[1]

---

[1] In later years, however, remnants of the Persian kingdoms would plague the eastern Roman Empire. The Parthians freed themselves from Greek control about 235 B.C. and wrested Persia from Seleucid control about 155 B.C. In about A.D. 225, a Persian named Ardashir overthrew the Parthians and set up the Sassanid kingdoms. These kingdoms became the cultural context for the rise of the Islamic religion.

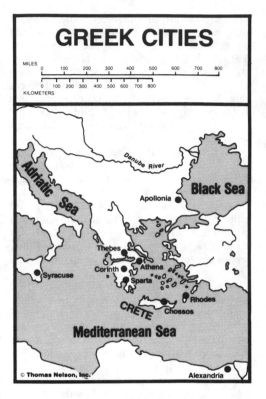

GREEK CITIES

2. Alexander and the Orient. After Alexander defeated Darius III at the Battle of Arbela, he immediately captured the old Persian seats of power in Susa, Babylon, and Ecbatana. He took enough booty in the capture of Susa to finance all of his later expeditions.

Thus the first chapter of the great Hellenistic conquest opened a second chapter.

While in Ecbatana, Alexander decided to explore the Orient. The Persians had long claimed the territories of western India as a part of their empire. Indeed, they had brought their battle elephants from the region of India. However, Alexander's new plan for conquest and exploration was the first known instance of a European's venturing into the mysterious East.

In 330 B.C. Alexander began the march north and east from the capital cities near the Persian Gulf. By 329 B.C. his forces had crossed the Hindu Kush mountains, threading their way through Afghanistan and overrunning the provinces of Bactria and Sogdiana. It took two years to pacify the area. While there, Alexander married Roxane, a princess of noted beauty.

On this eastward move, Alexander under-

THE GREEKS AND HELLENISM

went some rather deep personal changes. He began to adopt Persian and Oriental costumes for his dress. He also introduced the Oriental custom of *proskynesis* (Greek, "worship"). In other words, he required his troops to make a display of worship by lying on the ground before him in the Oriental fashion. This rankled the Macedonian units. Though they respected their king, they still regarded him as a mortal being, not a god. Because he opposed this policy, Callisthenes—the historian for Alexander's campaigns and a nephew of Aristotle—was arrested, tried, and executed under Alexander's orders. Perhaps this marks the lowest ebb in Alexander's career.

In the latter part of 327 B.C. Alexander began to move his units south, again crossing the Hindu Kush mountains. As Alexander approached the Indus River, people of the village Taxila met his army with a massive assault of battle elephants. The Macedonians won the battle, but were exhausted and frightened at the prospect of fighting more elephant armies on the other side of the Indus. Alexander's beloved horse, Bucephalus, died during the conflict. The army mutinied and refused to go any farther east. Alexander had no choice but to lead them back across the terrible desert of Gedrosia in present-day Pakistan and Iran.

Alexander returned to Ecbatana, then to his capital city of Babylon, where he began prepa-

rations for the conquest of Arabia and the organizing of his empire. Weakened by heavy drinking, he was unable to survive a bout with malaria. He died in 323 B.C. at the age of 33. His body was placed in a beautiful tomb in Alexandria.

3. The Jews under Alexander. According to tradition, Alexander treated the Jews favorably, and they fought in his army. Both the historian Josephus and the Jewish Talmud mention this as they describe Alexander's attack on Tyre. Alexander ordered the Jews to help him with troops and supplies, but the high priest Simon the Just refused because he was loyal to Persia. However, after both Tyre and Gaya fell to Alexander, Simon had a dream that told him to go out with the people and meet the victor. When he did this, Alexander bowed before the divine name on the priest's headdress, because he too had had a dream in which he had seen the headdress. Alexander then worshiped in the temple and granted the Jews a certain amount of self-rule in his territories.

Palestine was included in the province of Coele-Syria, whose governor Andromachus lived at Samaria. Jealous over the privileges that Alexander granted the Jews, the Samaritans revolted and burned the governor to death in his house. In retaliation, Alexander expelled the population of Samaria and settled Macedonians in the city. They rebuilt the old Semite city into an outpost of Greek civilization with a theater and enormous public buildings.

Deuterocanonical references to Alexander are found in 1 Maccabees 1:1–8; 6:2. Daniel 7 and 11:3–4 also refer to Alexander the Great, and some scholars feel that Zechariah 9:1–8 refers to Alexander's conquest of Palestine.

4. Alexander's Legacy. Alexander's campaigns profoundly influenced subsequent history. His personal achievements were largely military, but he laid the foundations for the cultural development of Western civilization. Alexander's marriage of the Oriental culture of the East and the Hellenic culture of the West can be seen in the fourth- and third-century B.C. statuary of Gautama Buddha, which bear striking Hellenic characteristics, especially in the faces.

Through his conquests, Alexander managed to spread the language of *koine* Greek among the people of many lands and cultures. The *koine* Greek would come to dominate this portion of the Mediterranean and Oriental regions until the period of the Byzantine Empire (A.D.

PTOLEMY I. *A general of Alexander the Great, Ptolemy received Egypt as his share of the Greek Empire after Alexander's death. His descendants ruled Egypt from 323 to 30 B.C., infusing the land of pharaohs with Hellenistic culture and running the state on a business basis, with profits payable to the crown. The Ptolemies also controlled Palestine until the Seleucids of Syria wrested it away.*

395). This common language facilitated the spread of the gospel of Christ during Paul's time. In fact, the earliest New Testament manuscripts were written in this *koine* dialect.

Alexander built several "Alexander" cities along his route of conquest. These cities radiated Greek language, arts, and government. They had a profound impact on their surrounding regions.

5. The Aftermath of Alexander's Death. However, all was not well in the Hellenistic empire. When Alexander died, he left no successor. His son by Roxane was not born until after his death, so his field marshals scrambled to claim the lands they had conquered. These generals and their successors, primarily the Ptolemies of Egypt and the Seleucids of Syria, warred among themselves until the Roman conquests began in 197 B.C. These struggles had a profound effect upon the Jews.

Antiochus III of the Seleucid Empire died *ca.* 187 B.C. He was succeeded by his son Antiochus IV (Epiphanes) in 175 B.C. Under his leadership, the Seleucid Empire carried out a thorough Hellenistic reconstruction of its subject lands. Particularly affected by this new campaign were the Jews.

III. Hellenism in Palestine. When Antiochus IV inherited the Seleucid part of the Greek Empire in 175 B.C. he had a burning passion to unite all of his territory by spreading Hellenism throughout. Known as one of the cruelest tyrants of all time, he used harsh methods that stirred opposition, particularly in Jerusalem. The city's dwellers were caught between rival and faithless priests who contended for leadership of the city. Antiochus smashed the civil strife, massacred thousands of the people, and robbed the temple of its treasures. The governor that Antiochus left in charge of Jerusalem was also cruel. The people chafed under his control.

IV. Influence on Bible History. Not a great deal of the history from the period following the sixth century B.C. may be found in the books included in the Protestant Bible canon. Much of the Jewish literature from this period has been classified as *apocryphal* ("hidden," books rejected by the Reformers but viewed as having canonical authority by Catholics) and *pseudepigraphical* ("false names," that is, written by someone other than those to whom the works are attributed) writings. Yet some of these writings provide us with a view of this history through the eyes of Jews influenced by Hellenistic culture.

THE PARTHENON. *Considered the peak of Greek architecture, the Parthenon was built by Pericles between 446 and 438 B.C. and dedicated to the goddess Athena Parthenos (the virgin) of Athens. The architects Ictinus and Callicrates designed the building. Sitting majestically astride the Acropolis, it has long been considered one of the most beautiful buildings in the world. It remained in good condition for centuries and was used as both a church and a mosque in medieval times. However, while the Venetians were besieging the Turks in 1687, an explosion of a powder stockpile destroyed the interior of the building.*

The Jews did not easily give themselves to the ways of their conquerors, such as the Persians and Greeks. Though some nations adopted the customs of their victors, the Jews tried to withstand this temptation.

Not all Jews returned to Judea. Many scattered throughout the Persian Empire, seeking official positions and establishing new communities. This scattering of the Jewish race and culture has been referred to by the Greek word *Diaspora* ("Dispersion").

A rather large Jewish community established itself in Alexandria, Egypt, under the Ptolemies. The Ptolemies made certain that their Alexandria was a center of Hellenistic culture equal to Athens. Artwork and literature abounded in this metropolitan city. The architecture of Alexandria was famous—from the towering Pharos lighthouse at the entrance of the eastern harbor to the city's museum and great library. The Ptolemies collected a large quantity of existing literature. The dry desert air of Egypt helped to preserve this great body of ancient literature.

An outstanding literary accomplishment under the Ptolemies was the translation of the Hebrew Scriptures into the *koine* Greek dialect. This translation was called the *Septuagint*. (*See* "Text and Translations.") The translation project is said to have been sponsored by Ptolemy II Philadelphus around the third century B.C. According to tradition, 72 Jewish scholars (six from each tribe) were summoned for the project and the work was finished in 72 days; the Jewish scholars were then sent away with many gifts. This story may be nothing more than a legend; but the translation indeed came out of the Alexandrian determination to preserve the great writings of the time in Greek.

The Septuagint provided a bridge between the thoughts and vocabulary of the Old and New Testaments. The language of the New Testament is not the *koine* of the everyday Greek, but the *koine* of the Jew living in Greek surroundings. Learned men throughout the Mediterranean became acquainted with the Septuagint. By the New Testament era, it was the most widely used edition of the Old Testament.

Alexandrian Jews adopted *koine* Greek as their language. In their attempt to persuade their Gentile neighbors that the God of the Jews was the one true God, they used *koine* diction, Hellenistic literary patterns, and Gentile thought-forms. All of these are reflected in the Septuagint and many other Jewish writings, such as Philo's *Against Flaccus* and the *Embassy to Caligula*. Hellenism also influenced the writing of 2 and 3 Maccabees and the New Testament. Philo Judaeus was the leading Jewish philosophical thinker of the time. He said the God of Israel was the God of the philosophers, and he equated the teachings of Hebrew Scriptures with the ideologies and ethics of Greek philosophy, Platonism in particular.

Alexandria also played an important role in early Christendom. A Christian school there was headed by such famous church fathers as Clement and Origen; it flourished from the second to the late fourth century A.D. The school taught that Scripture had three meanings: the literal, the moral, and the spiritual. The most vital of these was the spiritual meaning, and the school's use of allegory for biblical interpretation surpassed the complexity of similar methods used by earlier Hellenistic Jews.

Antiochus IV returned to Jerusalem in 168 B.C. and destroyed the city, killing most of the men and selling the women and children into slavery. Only a few men escaped into the hills under the leadership of a priest named Mattathias Hasmon.

From this base his son Judas Maccabeus

staged a revolt. The books of 1 and 2 Maccabees give a detailed description of this struggle, in which the Judeans formed an alliance with Rome. This backlash brought the eventual collapse of the Hellenistic kingdoms under the growing power of Rome.

By 165 B.C. the Greek rulers had been driven from Palestine. Judea proper was ruled by the high priest, the leading figure in the Jewish religion and society. The new Judean state was dominated by the officials of the religious cult.

Around 143 B.C. Simon, a descendant of the Maccabees, was named both high priest and ethnarch. (*Ethnarch* was a position very much like that of a medieval vassal king. He was the royal ruler of a given district; however, his rule was authorized by one who ruled the larger region of which his district was a member.) Simon and the Maccabeans resisted attempts to make Judea a Hellenistic state. But their efforts were only partially successful. Judea soon found itself under the rule of the wealthy Sadducee sect, a high priestly group who tended toward Hellenizing influences. (For a thorough discussion of the Pharisees and Sadducees, *see* "Jews in New Testament Times.")

The subtle Hellenizing influence entered many areas of Palestinian life. Architecture was one of those areas. The Jerusalem temple built by Herod the Great was one of the best examples of Hellenism in local architecture. The temple was built like other eastern Hellenistic temples; it stood within a network of courts surrounded by porticoes with freestanding Corinthian colonnades.

The city of Caesarea, which became the official capital of Palestine under the procurators, had buildings that were characteristic of a Hellenistic city: a theater, an amphitheater, a colonnaded street, a hippodrome (an arena for racing), and a temple.

It is hard to identify original Jewish art, for it was so strongly influenced by Hellenism. Also, we must remember that the Law of Moses forbade the making of any graven images (Exod. 20:4). This inhibited the Jews from developing any notable works of pictorial art.

V. Influence on the New Testament. The New Testament refers to some Christians as "Hellenists" (Acts 6:1; 9:29; RSV). We do not know exactly what this meant. (Some scholars believe that these people were Jews of the *Diaspora* who had adopted a Hellenistic

THE GREEKS AND HELLENISM

THE AREOPAGUS. *Sixteen steps lead to the top of rocky Mars Hill in Athens, called the Areopagus. This rocky bluff served as a meeting place of the city court and council of elders. Here Paul preached his famous sermon to the Athenians (Acts 17:21–34). A stronghold of the Athenian aristocracy during the sixth and fifth centuries B.C., the council of the Areopagus gradually lost power in subsequent years.*

man" who could come into fellowship with God (Eph. 2:15). He spoke of Christ "being in the form of God," yet taking "the form of a servant" (Phil. 2:6–7) or being "the image (i.e., the visible expression) of the invisible God" (Col. 1:15). These statements struck fire in the minds of Greek readers who were well-acquainted with Plato's teachings about visible forms and invisible ideals.

At times, Paul interpreted Old Testament events in an allegorical way, as Hellenistic Jewish writers commonly did. The best example is his interpretation of the story of Sarah and Hagar. He explained that their experience was an allegory of people who still lived

lifestyle.) At any rate, other Christians snubbed these Hellenists in distributing aid to widows (Acts 6:1 ff.); and the tension between the Hellenists and other Christians threatened to divide the early church. The apostles overcame this problem by appointing seven deacons, including the Hellenistic leader Stephen, to supervise the distribution of goods.

Some commentators believe that Hellenistic Christians did much of the early missionary work in Gentile lands (cf. Acts 8:1–3; 11:19–30). This would have been a logical development, but Scripture does not give us concrete proof that it happened this way.

We find a number of Hellenistic influences in Paul's letters. It seems that Paul absorbed a considerable amount of Greek wisdom during his years in Tarsus, for he was able to express the gospel in terms that the Greek mind could readily understand.

Throughout his letters, Paul tried to articulate the "deep things of God" (1 Cor. 2:10). He frequently used Greek philosophical concepts to do this. For example, he described how Christ united Gentiles and Jews in "one new

THE LAOCOON. *This sculpture graphically depicts the agony of Laocoon, a Trojan priest of Apollo, and his two sons. The three men are trapped in the coils of twin sea-serpents. The statuary group dates from about 50 B.C., and is characteristic of Hellenistic art at this time.*

THE GREEKS AND HELLENISM

under the old covenant while others lived under the new covenant of Christ (Gal. 4:21–31). As we have seen, Hellenistic thinkers at Alexandria later developed this method of interpretation to its height.

Yet Greek philosophy did not provide the *substance* of Paul's teachings. Paul differed sharply with the Greek thinkers; in fact, he was sometimes hostile toward them. He told the Colossians, "Beware lest any man spoil you through philosophy and vain deceit, after the tradition of men, after the rudiments of the world, and not after Christ" (Col. 2:8).

The classical scholar William M. Ramsay noted that "the influence of Greek thought on Paul, though real, is all purely external. Hellenism never touches the life and essence of Paulinism . . . but it does strongly affect the expression of Paul's teaching. . . ."[2]

VI. A Roman World; A Greek Culture. After Judea fell to the Romans in 63 B.C., Egypt was the only remnant of the Hellenistic kingdoms. Egypt lasted as a sovereign state until 31 B.C., when the Roman generals Octavian (Augustus) and Mark Antony fought the Battle of Actium. Mark Antony had married the Ptolemaic queen Cleopatra; thus his defeat

---

[2] William M. Ramsay, *The Teaching of Paul in Terms of the Present Day* (London: Hodder and Stoughton, 1913), pp. 161–162.

brought Egypt under the effective control of Rome.

The Roman forces brought military and governmental unity to the fractured Hellenistic Empire. Rome became the center of government. The formal naming of Augustus as Roman emperor in 27 B.C. signaled the end of the Hellenistic period and the beginning of the Roman imperial period.

Greece was no longer a political power; but its culture and spirit formed the foundations of imperial Roman culture. As the Roman writer Horace observed, "Captive Greece captivated her conqueror." Hellenistic art, literature, and government thrived throughout most of the Roman period. Even *koine* Greek remained the official language of business in the Near East, and New Testament literature was written in this dialect.

Two Greek schools of philosophy flowered during the Roman period. Each offered a path to personal happiness, but their paths went in opposite directions. The Stoics felt that the body should be controlled, denied, even ignored in order to free the mind. Epicureans taught that the body must be satisfied if the mind was to know happiness. Thus the philosophers of Alexandria perpetuated the spirit and culture of fifth-century Athens. In so doing, they perpetuated the spirit of ancient Greece.

THE ROMANS

The people of Rome developed the last great civilization of the ancient world in the West. They based their culture in the land now known as Italy, but expanded to cover North Africa, much of Western Europe and much of Western Asia. They were to have a significant impact upon Palestine in the Intertestamental and New Testament eras.

I. Early History (3000–1000 B.C.). Around 3000 B.C., tribes from different areas of Europe and Asia formed small towns and farming communities in mountain pockets of the Italian peninsula. The rough shape of the Apennine Mountains allowed many of these small tribes to exist separately. Some of them had migrated to Italy from areas north of the Black and Caspian seas. Historians call these people *Indo-Europeans*—that is, they came from Europe, southwest Asia, and India. These Indo-Europeans also influenced the Greek culture of the time.

Among them were the Etruscans, who came from the area of Asia Minor that is occupied by modern Turkey. By about 800 B.C. (when Jehoahaz was on the throne of Israel and Joash on the throne of Judah), the Etruscans had formed the first city-state in Italy. We know very little about the Etruscans, except that they made tools and weapons with copper, bronze, and iron. They gained control of the

city now called Rome about the sixth century B.C. during the time of the Exile of the Jews.

While the Etruscan culture was developing on the western side of the Apennines, Phoenicians had begun to move across the Mediterranean Sea. Their homeland was on the seacoast of northern Syria. The Phoenicians built a great city-state at Carthage on the northern coast of Africa, across from Sicily. Historians call this the *Punic* civilization (from the Latin word *Punicus,* "of Carthage").

About this same time Greece controlled colonies in Sicily, Sardinia, and southern Italy. The Greek territory in Italy was called *Magna Graecia,* or "Greater Greece."

II. The Rise of the Roman Republic (750–133 B.C.). While the Greeks and Phoenicians tried to resist the Persians, they lost their grip on the Mediterranean lands. The city of Rome arose in this political setting.

Rome's birth is clouded in legend. One legend said the Trojan warrior Aeneas founded Rome after the fall of Troy in the 1100's B.C. Another legend maintained that two of his

TRIBES ENTERING ITALY—1500 B.C.

© Thomas Nelson, Inc.

| MILES | 0 | 500 | 1000 | 1500 | 2000 | 2500 |
| KILOMETERS | 0 | 500 | 1000 | 1500 | 2000 | 2500 |

THE ROMANS

ETRUSCAN SOLDIERS. *This tomb painting depicts two Etruscan soldiers—an archer and a spearman—accompanied by the goddess of victory, Nike. The Etruscans, who controlled Rome during the sixth century B.C., may have come from what is now Turkey. Great builders and engineers, they cleared the forests, drained marshes, and built fortified cities. The Etruscan kings were driven out of Rome by the unified Latin tribes, who established the Roman Republic in 510 B.C.*

empire: As it absorbed other peoples, either peacefully or by war, it granted them citizenship and treated them as allies. Rome even absorbed some major Greek colonies, such as Naples, in this manner. Rome controlled all of central Italy by 400 B.C., and began to use its citizen-soldiers against the Greeks of the south. (This was about the time Ezra brought the Law to Jerusalem.) The Romans learned how to read and write from the Greeks, and how to appreciate the finer points of culture and society.

A. Early Warfare. While the Greeks and Phoenicians fought the Persian Empire, they drew their troops away from the Western Mediterranean. Rome grew stronger in the absence of foreign power, basing its strength on the citizen-soldier. The Roman army trained its men to act according to standard rules. Every commander, archer, and foot soldier knew exactly what was expected of him. Roman warfare required many dams, defense walls, and weapons; often these preparations took more time and effort than the actual battle. A universal draft provided a constant supply of fresh troops for the Romans. This well-drilled army was also used to build excellent roads and *aqueducts*—bridge-walls used to transport water from the mountains to Roman cities. These projects allowed the Romans to move from one area to another faster than ever before.

During this early period of Rome's growing

descendants, Romulus and Remus, founded Rome in 753 B.C. This would have been while Azariah (Uzziah) ruled Judah and Zachariah and Shallum ruled Israel.

Archaeologists tell us that Rome was much like other tribal centers of its time, though it was older. According to tradition, Etruscan kings ruled Rome until unified Latin tribes drove out Tarquinius Superbus, the last king, in 510 B.C. (This would have been about the time of the completion of the second temple in Jerusalem.) This rebellion established the Roman republic. Under this republic, there were two classes of citizens—*patricians* and *plebeians*. *Patricians* were persons of nobility or higher social rank; *plebeians* were people of lower class. The republic assigned two judges to decide civil cases for the patricians, while the plebeians elected tribunes to serve as their officials. Rome suffered from the intense class struggle between patricians and plebeians.

Rome absorbed small Latin kingdoms that surrounded it, but continued fighting with Etruscans in the north and Greek cities in the south. In time, Rome formed a policy that was to be carried through the building of its

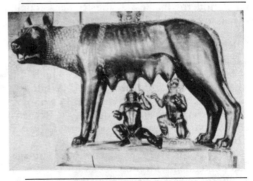

ROMULUS AND REMUS. *According to legend, Rome was founded by Romulus, a son of the god Mars and a woman named Rhea Silvia. Rhea had taken vows of virginity. As punishment for her violation of the vows, her twin infants Romulus and Remus were abandoned on the banks of the flooding Tiber River. There a she-wolf found and nursed them. On reaching manhood in 753 B.C., Romulus traced the outline of Rome with a plow and became its first king.*

THE ROMANS

HANNIBAL (247–183 B.C.). *This famous general led his troops against the Romans during the Second Punic war, a major conflict between Rome and Carthage, located in present-day Tunisia. Hannibal is best remembered for crossing the Alps with elephants, which he planned to use in fighting the Roman troops. Although he posed a threat to Rome for a time, he was defeated in 201 B.C.*

power, the Romans engaged in constant warfare. The Gauls invaded Italy in 390 B.C. and occupied Rome for seven months. They left only after receiving a large ransom from the Romans. Then in 340 B.C. (the Intertestamental Period for the Jews), the Romans fought off an invasion by the Latin League, their former allies who had become jealous of Rome's power. Rome also had to conquer the Samnites, a tribe in the central Apennines, in 290 B.C.

Then Rome was ready to challenge the wealthy cities of *Magna Graecia.* While the successors of Alexander the Great fought over the division of his vast conquests, the Romans conquered the Greeks of southern Italy. By 270 B.C., Romans controlled all of Italy.

B. Foreign Wars. The people of Carthage had contended with the Greeks for control of Sicily for over a century. Now the Greek ruler of Syracuse invited Rome to join him in the fight for control. For the next 64 years (264–201 B.C.), Rome fought a series of long wars with Carthage known as the Punic Wars. The Romans finally defeated the famous Carthaginian general Hannibal in 202 B.C. After adding Spain to its conquests, Rome turned to the east.

The Greek (Hellenistic) kings of Syria (the Seleucids) and of Egypt (the Ptolemies) fought over Palestine from 323 B.C. (when Alexander died) until 301, when the Ptolemies established control. Then in 198 B.C. the Seleucids wrested control from the Ptolemies. While the Ptolemies had not forced the Jews to accept Hellenistic religious ways, the Seleucids did. While this was going on in Palestine, Rome sought to conquer Greece.

Antiochus IV of Syria (175–163 B.C.) launched a program to exterminate Judaism in 167, making such religious observances as circumcision and Sabbath keeping and the possession of a copy of the Law punishable by death. The temple was dedicated to Zeus, and it was desecrated with a sacrifice of a swine on the altar. A Jewish priest named Mattathias, of the house of Hasmon, took to the hills with his five sons and began a revolt. Mattathias's third son was Judas Maccabeus, who led a series of raids against Antiochus (1 Macc. 3:1–9, 42–60; 4:1–61). By 160 B.C., the leaders of the house of Hasmon, called Hasmoneans, were accepted as rulers of Judea.

III. The Romans Enter Judea (63 B.C.). Much of what we know of the Roman conquest of Judea comes from the *History of the Jewish Wars,* by the Jewish statesman and soldier Flavius Josephus.

While the leaders of the Hasmon family had gained a measure of self-rule, they held office by permission of the Seleucids. The Book of the Maccabees tells of the Jews' rejoicing over Hasmonean victories—but they were small, unimportant victories. The Jews were not a real threat to the Seleucids; the Greek rulers had more to fear from the Parthians, people from the area now called Iran. The Parthians inherited much of Persia after that empire fell to Alexander the Great. They raided and threatened the Seleucids in the north and east, and later fought many wars with the Romans.

A. Hasmonean Rule. During the rule of the Hasmon family, devout Jews had strong disagreements with those who accepted Greek ways. The Hasmoneans combined the offices of king and high priest in one family. To maintain this double role, they had to balance carefully the various sects of Judaism. (*See* "Jews in New Testament Times.") The Hasmoneans appealed to the Roman Senate in 161 B.C. for defense against the Seleucids and Ptolemies (1 Macc. 8). Rome promised to aid the Hasmonean family and their people in the event they were attacked.

THE ROMANS

THE SENATE HOUSE. *Built in the Roman Forum at the time of Diocletian (ca. A.D. 300), this building housed the Roman Senate. During the imperial period, the Senate fell under the domination of the emperors and lost most of its powers.*

11

THE ROMANS

ideas of late Greek culture. Hyrcanus's eldest son, Aristobulus, succeeded his father in 104 B.C. Aristobulus died within a year; but before he did, he pushed Judea's borders into Galilee, which had been known as "Galilee of the Gentiles." Aristobulus's widow, Salome Alexandra, married Aristobulus's younger brother, Alexander Janneus. Janneus then became king and high priest. He further extended the borders of Judea and severely persecuted the Pharisees, causing a civil war that lasted six years. When he died, his widow Salome ruled in his place for the next seven years. Salome supported the Pharisees and separated the offices of ruler and high priest. She died in 69 B.C.

B. Julius Caesar. Until this time, the Romans had been primarily concerned with the two Greek-influenced kingdoms of the Seleucids and Ptolemies. Historians tell us that major changes now occurred. In defeating Carthage, Rome became master of all the former Semitic colonies—Carthage, Spain, Sicily, Sardinia, Corsica, and the Balearic Islands. Rome also adopted two major Punic traditions: the building of enormous plantations worked by slaves, and the use of cruel measures such as crucifixion to keep the slaves under control. The spread of plantations forced many private Roman farmers from their land and into the city of Rome. The old republican government could not rule the widespread colonies Rome was taking on; a stronger executive rule was needed.

The first person to grab this absolute power was the general named Julius Caesar. He showed the advantages of befriending the tribal peoples on Rome's borders, and he made popular appeals to quiet the mobs in Rome. Julius Caesar was the model of today's popular politician. He was a brilliant, able leader who proved his strength by extending Rome's border north to the Rhine and west to Britain.

Rome's chief ruler in the east was the general named Pompey. He cleared the Mediterranean of pirates and defeated Mithridates IV, the king of Pontus in Asia Minor. Pompey captured the coast of Syria/Palestine, and in 63 B.C. he stormed Jerusalem. Pompey captured Jerusalem's ruler, Aristobulus II, and ended the independent rule of the Hasmon family. Aristobulus II was pulled through the streets of Rome behind Pompey's chariot. Pompey released many of the Hasmonean territories from Jewish control and divided the kingdom of Judea into five districts:

The true Hasmonean line of kings began with Simon, who established independence of the Jewish state in 142 B.C. His successor, John Hyrcanus (135–104) brought his kingdom to the height of its power. Hyrcanus captured the area of Galilee and the southern area known as Edom (or Idumea). He made Antipater the governor of Galilee and forced all of the surrounding people to become Jews. He also conquered territory east of the Jordan.

Hyrcanus' successors were not as capable of ruling the enlarged Judea. They were influenced more by Greece than by their Hebrew background, and they took on the ways and

Roman Citizenship

During the New Testament era, Rome ruled the Mediterranean world. Its dominion stretched north to the borders of barbaric Gaul (France) and Germany, and encircled the Mediterranean Sea. Egypt was in its grip, as well as the cities of northern Africa.

Yet wherever Romans went, they brought good roads and public works, government officials, soldiers, and sometimes entire colonies of Roman citizens. Despite talk of Roman brutality, Rome was not a vengeful conqueror. Its aim was to make good Romans out of its new subjects, so that the Roman Empire would be truly Roman. This was quite a challenge, because the conquered people burned with hatred toward Rome.

The Roman Senate decided to allow an area as much self-rule as prudence permitted. In Judea, this meant that the native king (Herod the Great) was allowed to rule the Jews. When he died, the kingdom was divided among his three remaining sons: Philip, Archelaus, and Herod Antipas. Jewish nationalists did not accept this, and they finally appealed to Augustus Caesar to abolish the kingship in Judea. This he did in A.D. 6. Though Palestine was still thick with Roman soldiers and tax collectors, Jews were allowed to manage their own internal disputes.

Rome also consolidated the empire by granting Roman citizenship to certain non-Romans. "Never before or since," says historian Will Durant, "has citizenship been so jealously guarded or so highly prized."[*] A man holding Roman citizenship had ties to the ruling elite, though he might be an otherwise unimportant person. Under Rome's tolerant laws, a person could hold dual citizenship. Thus Paul the apostle could enjoy the civic rights of both Tarsus and Rome.

The benefits of Roman citizenship were clear.

Roman citizenship was valued not only for the right to vote, but for the protection it afforded. A Roman citizen could not be bound or imprisoned without a trial. He could not be scourged—the common means of wringing a confession from a prisoner. If he felt he was not receiving justice under local rule, he could appeal to Rome.

No wonder Roman authorities in Philippi quaked when they realized that Paul and Silas were not just a pair of rabble-rousing Jews! These men insisted they were Roman citizens, a matter which could be confirmed by a simple check of the census rolls. Emperor Claudius executed men who falsely claimed Roman citizenship; so it was not an assertion to be made lightly. No, the Philippians had unwittingly bound, beaten, and imprisoned Roman citizens. But Paul and Silas were willing to settle for an apology. Paul suggested that, since the magistrates had publicly thrown him in jail they could now publicly free him. Gladly the magistrates complied—and begged the wronged missionaries to leave town (Acts 16:12–40).

Later, in Jerusalem, Paul again made use of his "Roman connections." He was taken into protective custody when the howls of his Jewish enemies attracted the Roman militia. When Paul surmised that he was about to be scourged—probably for disturbing the peace—he mentioned his Roman citizenship. Not only did this save him a beating, but it assured him safe passage out of Jerusalem.

The Book of Acts concludes by stating that Paul lived two years in Rome under house arrest. He was permitted to preach and make converts. It is said that Emperor Nero crucified Peter, as common criminals were routinely executed, but Paul was beheaded. This was considered a more honorable and merciful death—the final prerogative of Paul's Roman birthright.

[*] Will Durant, *The Story of Civilization: Caesar and Christ.* (New York: Simon & Schuster, 1944), p. 25.

Jerusalem, Gadara, Amathus, Jericho, and Sepphoris.

IV. The First Triumvirate. In 59 B.C., Caesar, Pompey, and Crassus (a rich real estate speculator) joined forces to form a triple leadership called the First Triumvirate. The rulers of Rome's states and colonies suspected that one man would soon emerge as the complete ruler. Antipater, ruler of Idumea, played one ruler against the other to seek favor. In 54 B.C., Crassus invaded Jerusalem and stole the temple treasure while war broke out between Pompey and Caesar. Antipater sided with Pompey until Pompey was defeated, then switched his loyalty to Caesar. Caesar abol-

ished the five districts and named Antipater procurator of all Judea in 47 B.C. Antipater was killed in 43 B.C., shortly after Caesar's own death.

Caesar's friend, Antony, defeated Caesar's enemies in northern Greece. He then named Antipater's sons, Herod and Phasael, as *tetrarchs* ("rulers of fourths") of Galilee (cf. Matt. 14:1; Luke 3:1, 19). When the Parthians invaded Syria/Palestine in 40 B.C. to aid a Hasmonean attempt to regain power, Herod fled to his fortress at Masada on the western shore of the Dead Sea. His older brother, Phasael, was captured and committed suicide.

Herod traveled to Rome, where the Roman

THE ROMANS

JULIUS CAESAR (100–44 B.C.). *A brilliant soldier and statesman, Caesar extended Rome's border north to the Rhine River and west to Britain. Between 49 and 45 B.C., he eliminated his political rivals to become sole ruler of Rome. His appetite for power led to his assassination in 44 B.C.*

Senate named him king of Judea. Antony and his troops finally overpowered the Parthians and their Seleucid allies, and Antony settled in Jerusalem in 37 B.C.

The strain of imperial expansion was so great that Rome took in no new territories for at least 50 years after Caesar's birth. Rome ruled most of Greece, Syria, Judea, and North Africa. Only one Greek-influenced nation remained intact. This was Egypt, ruled by Queen Cleopatra.

V. The Second Triumvirate. Cleopatra became Julius Caesar's friend after he defeated Pompey. When Caesar was murdered, Cleopatra tried to pick the winner in the struggle for power that followed. The major contenders were Antony, Lepidus (who had served under Julius Caesar), and Caesar's nephew and adopted son, Octavian. These three kept a temporary peace by forming another triple dictatorship, the Second Triumvirate.

Antony met Cleopatra in 41 B.C. in Cilicia, a region in southern Asia Minor. Cleopatra was neither a ravishing beauty (as modern stories would have us believe) nor an Egyptian. She

was Macedonian, and a crafty politician who sought to preserve her kingdom at all costs. Cleopatra married Antony and plotted with him to rule the Roman Empire.

When civil war broke out between Antony and Octavian, Cleopatra convinced Antony to send Herod to fight the Arabians (Nabateans), instead of supporting Antony. She hoped that each nation would weaken the other; Egypt could then absorb both. This move saved Herod's kingdom, for Octavian crushed the forces of Antony and Cleopatra at the Battle of Actium in 31 B.C. and ordered their deaths.

VI. The Jews under Rome. In early 30 B.C., Herod met with Octavian and bargained to keep his life and throne. Through the years, Herod had rid himself of any possible claimants to the throne. He had "playfully" drowned his young brother-in-law Aristobulus, executed his uncle Joseph as an adulterer, and framed Hyrcanus II for plotting with the Nabateans. Herod was subject to deep moods of depression, when he would order the murders of friends and family. For example, he or-

POMPEY (106–48 B.C.). *This Roman general captured Jerusalem and made Syria a Roman province. An early ally of Julius Caesar, he became a rival for control of the Roman state. He was defeated by Caesar in battle in 48 B.C. and fled to Egypt, where he was assassinated.*

11

THE ROMANS

THE COLOSSEUM. *Between A.D. 72 and 80, the Emperors Vespasian and Titus built the Colosseum, a massive structure with rising tiers of seats circling an open space. Gladiatorial battles—fights between animals, and between men and animals—were favorite sports of the Roman spectators. A vast network of underground tunnels provided spaces for the caged animals and human participants, who fought to the death in the arena. The Roman engineers even devised a method to flood the arena for mock sea battles.*

dered the execution of his favorite wife, Mariamne, then brooded over her death.

Herod broke many of the Jewish laws. He introduced Greek-style games and races to his kingdom and ordered many large building projects. Among these were Greek temples, forts, and a palace. His greatest project was a new temple in Jerusalem, which he began in 20 B.C. (Matt. 4:5; 24; Mark 11:27; 13:1; Luke 19:45; 20:1; John 2:14).

In 27 B.C., Octavian took the title *Augustus* and founded the Roman Empire. Augustus Caesar brought peace to the Roman Empire through strict control of his army and land; he created the image of Rome's golden age. (Jesus was born during the rule of Augustus, who died in A.D. 14.)

In 22 B.C., Herod sent his children to Rome to be educated and pay respect to Augustus. Augustus visited Syria in 20 B.C. and gave Herod even more land. Fearing revolt, Herod banned large public gatherings during the visit.

Herod had to deal with the power of Greek-influenced officials in Asia, as well as the power of Augustus in Rome. Herod's other problem was the discontent of Jewish sects and parties. He remembered how the Maccabees had driven Greek sympathizers from their temple in Jerusalem in 165 B.C. He determined to prevent this kind of revolution.

Judaism was the only religion to survive the strong influence of Greek ways. Through the translation of the Old Testament into Greek, Judaism actually increased its influence during the Hellenistic Age. But Judaism's popularity attracted Herod's envy. Though he was not of Jewish birth, he spent large sums of money on the new temple in hopes of winning the Jews' loyalty.

But plots and counterplots marked the last years of Herod's reign. In all, Herod married 10 wives, and his many sons fought for his throne. Time and again, Herod promoted a son, discovered a plot, and then killed the son. As he neared his seventieth year, Herod became obsessed with destroying all but his chosen heir. Shortly before his death, he heard the disturbing news that a long-awaited king of Israel had been born in Bethlehem. Herod ordered his soldiers to kill all newborn infants of the Jews, much as he had murdered rivals in his own family (cf. Matt. 2).

Herod lived in Jericho, and he ordered that a number of the Jewish leaders there be killed when he died, so that it would be a time of national grief. Herod had his son, Antipater, killed in early 4 B.C. Five days later Herod himself died. Another of Herod's sons, Archelaus, was left to inherit the throne. Archelaus tried to win over the people through kindness and patience. But rebellion mounted—not so much against Archelaus as

THE ROMANS

Pax Romana

Historians have given the title *Pax Romana* ("the Roman peace") to the period from 30 B.C. to about A.D. 180, when Rome flourished in a time of imperial greatness. During this period, the Roman Empire brought peace, prosperity, and good government to an area that ranged from Britain to the Euphrates, and from the North Sea to the Sahara.

The Pax Romana began with the rule of Octavian, who became emperor of Rome after defeating the last of his opponents for that title in the Battle of Actium in 31 B.C. After a century of civil strife, Rome was at last united under one ruler. Octavian, given the title *Augustus* by a respectful Roman Senate, concentrated on his empire's internal problems and laid the foundation for two centuries of strong rule and peace.

The Pax Romana brought a great increase in Rome's trade and prosperity. The imperial navy swept the Mediterranean of pirates who imperiled shipping between Rome, the provinces in Asia Minor, and the African coast. The great Roman roads were built primarily as military routes to the provinces. But they also allowed grain to be brought to the city of Rome, and wine and olive oil to be brought to outer provinces. Tolls and many other artificial barriers to trade were removed. A stable coinage and improved methods of banking and credit encouraged economic expansion. Manufacturing sprang up in Roman provinces, and soon pottery from Gaul, textiles from Flanders, and glass from Germany could be found in Rome.

A key to the maintenance of peace was Augustus's willingness to allow provinces local self-government, coupled with his quick use of military force to stifle rebellion or terrorism. Augustus allowed conquered nations to keep their language, customs, and religion, as long as the people stayed on peaceful terms with Rome.

Agriculture remained the basic economic activity in the Roman Empire under the Pax Romana, but this period also saw the rapid increase of cities and the creation of a cosmopolitan world-state, where races and cultures intermingled. At its height the Roman Empire had over 100 million people, including Italians, Greeks, Egyptians, Germans, Celts, and others. By the time of Hadrian (reign A.D. 117–138), the empire covered an area of over 1 1/4 million square miles.

Augustus funneled the wealth of his provinces to Rome through taxes. He rebuilt Rome from a city of bricks to a city of marble. The state also supported many artisans, who belonged to *collegia,* or guilds. Recreation and sports came to play an increasingly large role in the public lives of Roman citizens.

The Pax Romana had come to an end by the time of Rome's real money crisis in the third century A.D., when political anarchy and monetary inflation caused the collapse of its economy.

against the dead Herod. At Passover a new revolt broke out while Archelaus was on his way to Rome to be confirmed. Roman soldiers looted Herod's temple, and when Archelaus returned many Jews and Samaritans were killed. Rome banished Archelaus from the tetrarchy of Judea and replaced him with a procurator named Coponius in A.D. 6.

Archelaus's younger brother Antipas was tetrarch of Galilee and Perea from 4 B.C. to A.D. 39. He had John the Baptist beheaded and is often mentioned in the Gospels.

Antipas feared that Jesus was John the Baptist resurrected (Matt. 14:1–2; Mark 6:14–16; Luke 9:7–9). Pharisees warned Jesus to flee the region because Antipas was plotting against Him (Luke 13:31–33). Antipas scornfully tried Jesus during Passion Week, then turned the whole matter over to Pontius Pilate (Luke 23:6–12).

VII. Augustus Organizes the Empire. While the family of Herod ruled in Judea, Augustus organized his empire. The Rome he inherited from Julius Caesar was a political hotbed of rival classes and contenders for power. Augustus had seen Caesar's rise to power and the awful way in which Caesar's rule was ended. So Augustus gradually transformed the structure of Roman government to assure his control.

First he introduced a system called the *principate,* which seemed to follow the old republican order and the power of the Senate. It really brought the republic under the personal control of Augustus. The principate provided the basic structure of the Roman Empire for almost 200 years.

Under the empire, Augustus ruled only a few provinces directly. One of these was Judea. Romans saw Syria/Palestine as a small but troublesome part of their empire.

Augustus brought the *Pax Romana* ("Roman peace") to all provinces within the borders of the empire. There were no major wars within the Roman Empire in the time of Jesus, only minor skirmishes along the borders. But

11

THE ROMANS

THE ROMANS

PRAETORIAN GUARD. *This relief shows the Praetorians, who served the Roman emperor as personal bodyguards. The unit was instituted by Augustus, who made them his crack troops stationed in Rome. The Praetorian guard was part of the massive army that expanded the Roman Empire and then policed its boundaries.*

lowest-ranking active group was the *contubernium* of eight soldiers, who shared a leather tent that enclosed about 9 sq. m. (30 sq. ft.) in the field. A half *contubernium* (four men) was assigned for very small work details and patrols. Ten *contubernia* comprised one *century*. While *century* strictly meant 100, a *century* usually consisted of only 70 or 80 men. Six *centuries* made a *cohort,* and 10 *cohorts* made a *legion*. The average Roman legion contained about 6,000 men with their pack animals, cavalry horses, and servants.

Legions were stationed in the two main Roman cities in Palestine: Sebaste (Samaria) and Caesarea, Herod's main seaport (Acts 10:1). This put the legions in much closer contact with Rome. We know that a large number of Roman troops marched up to Jerusalem for the feasts to keep order among the Jewish sects and pilgrims. Jewish authorities had few troops, possibly no more than 500, under their

the emperor still relied on his army to keep the peace.

We learn from tomb inscriptions and other writings that troops were drafted from all over the empire and required to become Roman citizens. The legions included Britons, Spaniards, Slavs, Germans, Greeks, Italians, and even Jews. Unfortunate soldiers were assigned to lonely outposts on distant frontiers. We find an example of this in Acts 10:1, which describes the "Italian Cohort" in Palestine. By the time Augustus reached complete power, unrest and civil war had swelled the army to about 25 legions and 25 auxiliary forces. Since Rome itself was safe from attack during the early period of the empire, native Italians usually avoided military service.

The people of conquered colonies saw volunteer service as a path to Roman citizenship and other benefits. The government granted immediate citizenship to army volunteers and paid them a pension on retirement. The military groups made up of non-Romans were called *auxiliaries;* they were about equal in number to the regular army.

The army was organized as follows: The

CAESAR AUGUSTUS (63 B.C.–A.D. 14). *Grand nephew and adopted son of Julius Caesar, Octavian took the honorary title Augustus (i.e., "the exalted") when he became sole ruler of Rome after defeating Mark Antony at Actium. (Augustus became the official title for later emperors of Rome.) The reign of Augustus Caesar was a period of peace and prosperity for the empire.*

THE ROMANS

AQUEDUCT. *This aerial view of the Roman-built Pont du Gard in Provence, France shows the aqueduct (water-way) on the upper level and a roadway on the lower level. The Romans constructed aqueducts to bring running water into their cities from hilly areas outside. The ruins bear testimony to the monumental engineering feats of Rome.*

command. They also had a semi-military temple guard (probably referred to in Matt. 26:47; John 18:31).

Roman forces in Palestine were still directly under Roman control. A Roman military tribune acted as chief of police and his men were responsible for keeping civil order. These men were stationed in the fortress of Antonia (which guarded Herod's temple) and in Herod's palace (which occupied a prominent spot just south of the modern Jaffa Gate of Jerusalem).

Julius Caesar and Augustus gave Jews a great amount of religious freedom, as the very events of Holy Week attest. (Those events took place during the Jewish observance of Passover.) But relations between Romans and Jews of Judea continued to crumble throughout the first century. Romans still appointed the head of the *Sanhedrin,* the chief Jewish political assembly, and they still chose the Jewish high priest. The Sanhedrin was the

MASADA. *This aerial view shows the excavated remains of Masada, on the western shore of the Dead Sea. Rebel Jews who camped here killed their women and children and then one another, rather than face capture by Roman troops in A.D. 73.*

THE ROMANS

religious court of Judaism, and the high priest was the head of the Jewish religious structure (Matt. 26:57–68; Luke 22:66–71; Acts 22:30). To most Roman officials, Jewish religion was too complex to bother with.

The Romans were very practical and they brought many Greek innovations to the marketplace. The Romans surpassed previous cultures in their financial and political success. They developed a thorough code of laws and an elaborate structure of officials to enforce those laws. Rome made two basic demands of its people: that they pay taxes and accept the rule of Rome (John 18:19; Rom. 13:1–7). Any rebellion or revolt was met with terrible violence. We see proof of this in the writings of Josephus, as well as in the New Testament (Luke 13:1). But Judea with its vast wastelands had no natural boundaries on three sides, so it was a difficult area for the Romans to police.

The Roman government exercised the power of capital punishment over its colonies, and many Jews were killed as political trouble-makers (cf. Luke 23:18–19). The main

TIBERIUS. *Augustus's stepson and successor, Tiberius ruled Rome from A.D. 14 to 37. He was an experienced soldier and administrator, as well as a capable ruler, although he did not have the cooperation of the Senate. In A.D. 31, he discovered his friend Sejanus plotting to overthrow him. Embittered, Tiberius became a suspicious tyrant. During his last six years of rule, the empire suffered a reign of terror. Informers were everywhere and treason trials increased. Christ was crucified during Tiberius' reign.*

conflict between Jews and Romans arose over Roman taxes. The Jews had paid taxes to Rome since 63 B.C. But when Judea was added as a Roman province, Jews were also expected to pay provincial taxes. The Romans thought it wise to choose the lowest persons in the tax-collecting system from among the natives of the country. The taxpayers' hatred would be turned against these "traitors," and not against the Romans themselves. (*See* section on Matthew in "The Apostles.")

The people of Judea had to pay three major taxes. The first was the tax on land, the *tributum soli.* The second was the *vectiqalia,* a general tax of the empire that included tax on imported goods at ports. Matthew probably collected this tax from returning fishermen at Capernaum, a town on the northwest shore of the Sea of Galilee. Last was the head tax, *tributum capitis,* the "tribute" we read of in the Gospels. Augustus started this tax and Quirinius, governor of Syria, attempted to carry it out. He ordered all natives of Judea to return to the town of their family to be counted for the new tax. Thus Mary and Joseph traveled to Bethlehem (Luke 2:1–3) at the time Jesus was born.

The tax issue continued to be a sore spot with the Jews and many small groups attempted revolt. During Jesus' ministry, taxes were still a serious matter (Matt. 17:24–27; Mark 12:13–17; Luke 20:21–26).

Quirinius' last act as governor was to install a new high priest, Annas (Luke 3:2; John 18:13, 24). Annas took office in A.D. 7 and was forced to resign after Augustus' death in A.D. 14.

Augustus's stepson, Tiberius (A.D. 14–37), became emperor after Augustus's death. He appointed Gratus as new governor of Judea. Gratus chose a number of high priests before selecting Caiaphas in about A.D. 18. Caiaphas held office until A.D. 36. During this time, he found Jesus guilty of blasphemy and sent him to Pilate for sentencing (Matt. 26:3, 57; Luke 18:13–14, 24, 28).

Pontius Pilate had replaced Valerius Gratus as governor in A.D. 26. He had gotten off to a bad start by ordering the legion of soldiers in the fortress of Antonia to carry a bust of the emperor Tiberius as its emblem. The Jews considered this emblem to be an idol; they rebelled when the soldiers paraded it through the streets during the Day of Atonement.

The trial of Jesus in about A.D. 32 was another in a long series of skirmishes between

THE ROMANS

Pilate and the Jews. Pilate feared that if he were lenient with Jesus, the Jews would stage another uprising, so he had Jesus crucified (Matt. 27:11–26; Mark 15:1–15; Luke 23:1–25; John 18:28–19:16). Pilate was removed from office in A.D. 36, when he reacted too strongly to a meeting of Samaritans on Mount Gerizim. Pilate's journey to Rome for punishment was stopped when Tiberius died in A.D. 37.

Tiberius and his successors—Caligula, Claudius, and Nero—were known as the Julio-Claudian emperors. Caligula (A.D. 37–41) was a madman who once installed a horse as an official in his government. Being convinced of his own divinity, he ordered a statue of himself to be placed in the Jerusalem temple. He was assassinated before this command could be executed.

At the beginning of his reign (A.D. 41–54), Claudius (cf. Acts 11:28; 18:2) tried to suppress the anti-Jewish activities that Caligula had begun. But later he turned against the Jews. Suetonius says Claudius "expelled from Rome the Jews, who were constantly rioting under the leadership of Chrestus."

The immoral behavior of Nero (A.D. 54–68) is well known. He ordered his wife and mother killed, and persecuted Christians dur-

ing his rule. Nero's rumored resurrection may be symbolically mentioned in Revelation 13:3.

Vespasian took the imperial throne in A.D. 69. He had served as commander of the Syrian frontier army when the final fight between Romans and Jews began to surface in A.D. 66. In the summer of that year, Jewish terrorists slaughtered the Roman troops at Masada and prepared for a strong defense. The leader of the temple in Jerusalem stopped the daily offerings for the emperor's well-being. Vespasian was given the task of subduing the Jewish revolt. By the summer of A.D. 68, Jerusalem was near defeat and Vespasian was made emperor. He allowed his son Titus to make the final assault. In A.D. 70, Jerusalem was destroyed. Herod's temple was burned and its sacred furniture carried off to Rome. The remaining Jewish guerillas were defeated during the next two years. By A.D. 73, all traces of Jewish revolt were suppressed and the Jewish population of Judea largely exterminated. The remaining Jewish population was almost completely killed off during the Bar Kochba revolt of the second century, and there were very few Jews remaining in Palestine until the Zionist effort to bring them back from abroad late in the nineteenth century.

VIII. Rome's Contributions. The Romans were not very original in their abstract think-

ARCH OF TITUS. *Emperor Titus of Rome (rule A.D. 79–81) built this imposing monument to commemorate his victories. Among the scenes depicted on the arch is the Romans' looting of the temple at Jerusalem (A.D. 70). Titus was the commander of the Roman army at that time.*

MARK ANTONY. *A friend of Julius Caesar, Antony fought Octavian (later, Augustus) in a power struggle after Caesar's death. In 31 B.C., the two met in a sea battle near the Greek port city of Actium. Defeated, Antony fled to Egypt, where he committed suicide.*

THE ROMANS

ing, but they were quick to adopt good ideas from people they conquered. The remains of Roman roads, walls, bridges, amphitheaters, and basilicas still impress tourists today.

The Romans held law and order above all other things. They treated conquered people with justice and tact. Many aspects of Roman law survive in modern governments around the world.

The Latin language flowered in the first century B.C., giving us classic poetry and prose. Pliny the Elder and other Latin writers recorded excellent histories of the empire. For centuries, Latin influenced the languages and literature in Europe, and about 40 percent of the English language comes from Latin. English words such as *citizen, census, senate,* and *fiscal* survive from Roman days.

The Romans had little use for a complex religion; they invoked gods only to help their family or state. Their chief gods were Jupiter, who controlled the universe; Mars, god of war; Juno, patron goddess of women; and Minerva, goddess of war, wisdom, and skill.

The Romans found a way to build concrete domes that allowed them to enclose large areas. Their engineers produced aqueducts, bridges, colosseums, roads, stadiums, and other important structures. Many of the Romans' contributions still affect Western life today. The Roman world order was the greatest single influence upon the life of the Jews in the New Testament era.

THE GEOGRAPHY OF PALESTINE

Palestine is the heartland of three major religions of the world. Judaism, Christianity, and Islam each trace their beginnings to this small tract of land. Here God revealed Himself to the patriarchs and prophets, to Jesus and His apostles.

Studying the geography of Palestine is not a recent pursuit. Early church fathers such as Jerome felt it was important for an understanding of the Bible.

Many Christians no longer depend on maps and globes to show them the face of Palestine. They can see the ancient sites with their own eyes. Place names leap to life as they walk the ground where biblical cities once stood. Scripture takes on new reality when they step into the Holy Land.

Palestine is a magnificent country rich in history, a land of contrasts. Modern and ancient ways of life go on side by side. Barren deserts clash with the lush foliage of oases.

I. THE GREAT RIFT VALLEY
  A. The Surrounding Land
  B. Earthquakes

II. THE FERTILE CRESCENT
  A. Palestine: A Strategic Location
  B. The Canaanites

III. THE PROMISED LAND
  A. Abraham's Journey
  B. Land of the Patriarchs
  C. Extent of the Promised Land
  D. Efforts to Expand
  E. Fertility of the Land
    1. Soil
    2. Precipitation
    3. Winds

IV. THE JORDAN VALLEY
  A. The Upper Jordan
    1. Mount Hermon
    2. Sources of the Jordan
    3. Hula Lake
  B. The Jordan Valley Proper
    1. A Natural Boundary
    2. The Beth-Shean Valley
  C. The Lower Jordan

V. GALILEE
  A. Upper Galilee
  B. Lower Galilee
  C. The Sea of Galilee

VI. SAMARIA

VII. JUDAH
  A. Bethel Hills
  B. Jerusalem Hills
  C. Hebron Hills
  D. The Coastal Plains
  E. The Philistine Coast
  F. The Shephelah
  G. The Sharon and Carmel Coast
  H. The Plain of Asher

VIII. THE DEAD SEA

IX. THE TRANSJORDAN
  A. Bashan
  B. Gilead
  C. Perea
  D. Ammon
  E. Moab
  F. Edom

I. The Great Rift Valley. What can compare with the beauty of the Jordan River Valley? Barren slopes of the Judean wilderness loom over the curves of the Jordan River. But since the 1967 cease-fire, this river has marked the boundary between the modern states of Israel and Jordan. Unfortunately, it is now dangerous even to approach the Jordan.

Impressive though it is, the Jordan Valley is only a small part of the Great Rift Valley, which stretches from Syria to Africa. South of the Jordan Valley and the Arabah wilderness, the Red Sea covers over 2,200 km. (1,400 mi.) of the Great Rift Valley's floor. The Red Sea extends to the Indian Ocean; its waters lap against East Africa on one side and the Arabian Peninsula on the other. In Central Africa, the Great Rift Valley cradles the Rudolf, Albert, Victoria, Tanganyika, and Nyasa Lakes.

Thousands of years ago, immense pressures beneath the earth's surface created the Great Rift Valley. As the earth cracked in the upheaval, parts of the earth's crust were pushed up. Thus mountains follow the valley for its full length on both sides.

A. The Surrounding Land. In northern Palestine, the Lebanon and Hermon mountain ranges flank the valley. During certain months of the year these mountains cool the moisture-filled clouds causing heavy rainfall, and in

THE GEOGRAPHY OF PALESTINE

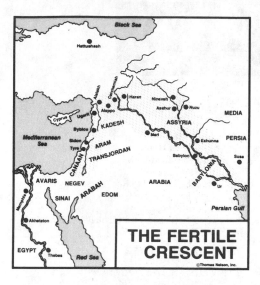

THE FERTILE CRESCENT
©Thomas Nelson, Inc.

The Jordan meanders southward from the Sea of Galilee through the valley, finally bringing its waters into the Dead Sea. Here the water is trapped; it cannot escape except by evaporation because at the south end of the Sea the ground rises.

The higher ground becomes the Arabah wilderness, which reaches from the Dead Sea south to the Gulf of Eilat on the Red Sea. On the east are the sharp mountains of Edom; to the west are the Negev Desert and the Mediterranean Sea.

Biblical authors introduce us to the geographical divisions of Palestine. Moses told the people of Israel, "Turn you, and take your journey, and go to the mount of the Amorites, and unto all the places nigh thereunto, in the plain, in the hills, and in the vale, and in the south, and by the sea side, to the land of the Canaanites, and unto Lebanon, unto the great river, the river Euphrates" (Deut. 1:7). Later we are told that "Joshua smote all the country of the hills, and of the south, and of the vale, and of the springs, and all their kings" (Josh. 10:40).

winter they collect snow. Springs and runoff waters create streams that flow into the Sea of Galilee to the south and are eventually channeled out into the Jordan River.

PALESTINE. *This aerial photograph taken in 1930 shows the western edge of the Jordan Valley in the foreground. The houses and roads of modern Jericho lie in the center of the picture, and a white arrow indicates the dark oval mound of the Tell es-Sultan (biblical Jericho). To the left, behind the mountains, lies the desert of Judah. In the distance is the Mediterranean Sea. Although the picture was probably retouched (due to technical imperfections of aerial photography when it was taken), it gives a striking impression of the Palestinean highlands.*

JERICHO. *The oldest city in Palestine, Jericho was attacked and conquered by Joshua during the Israelites' conquest of Canaan. The city lies 16 km. (10 mi.) northwest of where the Jordan River enters the Dead Sea, and about 27 km. (17 mi.) northeast of Jerusalem. The mountains of Judea rise abruptly from the plains just west of the city.*

B. Earthquakes. The subterranean forces that formed the Great Rift Valley are still at work. Even today the land rests uneasily, at the mercy of tremors caused by shifts of the great blocks of land that form the earth's crust. Through the centuries tremors and quakes have shaken the valley.

The Bible mentions some of these earthquakes. Such a forceful quake shook Palestine during King Uzziah's reign that the prophet Amos dated a message by it: ". . . two years before the earthquake" (Amos 1:1). Zechariah referred back to it 270 years later: ". . . ye shall flee, like as ye fled from before the earthquake in the days of Uzziah king of Judah: . . ." (Zech. 14:5).

Another earthquake took place half a millennium later. It occurred at the moment Jesus died on the cross: ". . . and the earth did quake, and the rocks rent; And the graves were opened; . . ." (Matt. 27:51–52).

Poets and prophets saw earthquakes as instruments of God's judgment: "Thou shalt be visited of the Lord of Hosts with thunder, and with earthquake, and great noise, with storm and tempest, and the flame of devouring fire" (Isa. 29:6). And "Then the earth shook and trembled; the foundations also of the hills moved and were shaken, because he was wroth" (Psa. 18:7).

Genesis 19:24–28 chronicles the destruction of Sodom and Gomorrah by "brimstone and fire." Some believe this was a divinely-ordered earthquake that released a cloud of natural gas, which exploded. Located in the southern part of the Jordan Valley, the ruins of

these cities were gradually covered with the water of the Dead Sea, to remove any trace of the wickedness practiced in them.

Ancient sources mention other earthquakes. Archaeologists have unearthed the results of their devastation in Jericho, Qumran, Hazor, and elsewhere.

II. The Fertile Crescent. God promised the land of Canaan to Abraham and his descendants. It is a fertile country, bounded by deserts to the east and south and shaken by an occasional earthquake.

Canaan is the southern tip of the area known as the Fertile Crescent. Unlike the terrain around it, this narrow semicircle of land in the Near East receives enough moisture to grow crops. The green horseshoe starts at the Persian Gulf on the eastern end and extends to the southern part of Canaan on the western end. It is bordered by the Mediterranean on the west, mountains to the north, and desert regions to the south and east. From this well-favored strip of land rose the great nations of the Old Testament.

A. Palestine: A Strategic Location. God chose a prominent place for His people to prove themselves to be a "holy nation." The land of Canaan was strategically located between the great civilizations of the Near East. Egypt lay to the southwest, Phoenicia and Aram (Syria) to the north, and Assyria and Babylonia to the east. Unlike Egypt, Canaan could not isolate herself from her neighbors.

In fact, the inhabitants of Canaan were *forced* to get involved in world politics. In times of war they were never safe. Canaan was the land-bridge over which Egypt passed on her way to the north. Assyrians, Babylonians, and Greeks also trampled Canaan when they headed south in their conquest of the Near East.

Yet there were advantages to being crisscrossed by surrounding cultures. Canaan was enriched by the art and literature of other nations, as well as by their building techniques and scientific accomplishments. In the teeming center of the ancient Near East, God called His people in Canaan to be a challenge to the nations.

". . . a goodly heritage of the most beauteous hosts of nations" (Jer. 3:19)—so did the prophet Jeremiah describe Palestine, the Promised Land. It is a pleasant land, this southwestern branch of the Fertile Crescent. In contrast to the sea, mountains, and deserts that enclose it, Palestine offers fertile soil,

THE GEOGRAPHY OF PALESTINE

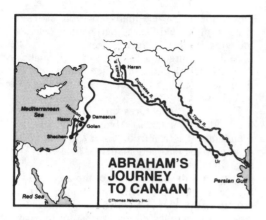

ABRAHAM'S JOURNEY TO CANAAN

III. The Promised Land. Even in twentieth-century ears, those words create excitement. From the very first book of the Bible, God's promise of the land to Abraham emerges as a theme again and again.

A. Abraham's Journey. Genesis 11:31—12:10 describes the incredible journey that Abraham made in search of the land of promise. From the Persian Gulf he traveled the full length of the Fertile Crescent, even going as far as Egypt.

In 1866, archaeologists positively identified a site in southern Iraq as Ur, the place of Abraham's birth (Gen. 11:28). The city was located on the Euphrates River, and in ancient times it was an important commercial center. (*See* "Ugarit and the Canaanites.") It prospered for thousands of years, up to the fourth century B.C. Excavations at Ur have unearthed a ziggurat (a three-staged step tower) dedicated to the moon god, Nanna.

Abraham's father, Terah, led the family's migration from Ur. Abraham, his brother Nahor, and his nephew Lot took their families, servants, and possessions on the long trek. They journeyed over 1,100 km. (700 miles) to Haran, another thriving city on one of the trade routes from Assyria to the Mediter-

water, and a pleasant climate. These favorable conditions enticed early man to settle there. Indeed, whole civilizations rose and fell on the soil of Palestine before Israel claimed it as her own.

B. The Canaanites. By the time Abraham came into the land, Canaan had long been inhabited. The first settlers dwelled in caves in the Mount Carmel region. They lived by hunting wild game and collecting wild grains, vegetables, and fruits. Gradually they moved to small villages and planted fields of wheat, barley, and legumes. Herds and flocks further expanded their diet. As the villagers produced more than they could use, they began trading. The small communities then developed road systems for traders to move from village to village with their wares of produce, textiles, pottery, and jewelry. (*See* "Trade.")

Jericho is a good example of such developments. This well-watered region is a gorgeous oasis in the desert north of the Dead Sea and several miles west of the Jordan River. Archaeologists have found few signs of the early stages of the city's growth. They surmise that the people lived in flimsy tents and huts. At first the people of Jericho were semi-nomadic, moving from place to place in search of food. But with the development of the flint, sickle, and primitive plow, they could support themselves off a smaller parcel of land. They built houses and the population increased, and gradually the village became a city. To protect against destruction by jealous neighbors or passing enemies, they erected a wall around the settlement. When Abraham arrived in Canaan, Jericho had already passed through several cycles of building, destruction, and rebuilding. (For more information about the Canaanites, *see* "Ugarit and the Canaanites.")

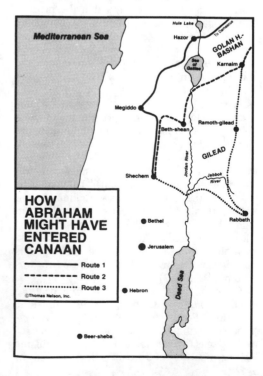

HOW ABRAHAM MIGHT HAVE ENTERED CANAAN
——— Route 1
- - - - Route 2
······· Route 3

THE GEOGRAPHY OF PALESTINE

WAR PANEL FROM UR. *This mosaic panel from the twenty-fifth century* B.C., *discovered at Ur, depicts the triumph of a king over his enemies. In the upper lefthand corner, four asses pull an enemy's four-wheeled chariot, preceded by a groom and soldiers bearing axes and spears. The larger center figure is probably the king, receiving prisoners who are escorted by soldiers (right).*

ranean Sea. Haran was located at the Balikh River, a northern tributary of the Euphrates. The people here also worshiped the moon god.

Abraham was 75 when God told him: "Get thee out of thy country, and from thy kindred, and from thy father's house, unto a land that I will show thee" (Gen. 12:1). He left Haran, taking his wife Sarai and nephew Lot, and their possessions. They took a road leading through Syria to Damascus.

After that point, it is interesting to speculate on the routes Abraham might have taken to Canaan. From Damascus one road led past the Hermon Mountain range and over the Golan Heights to the Hula Valley. The Hula Lake was a swampy reservoir of water from the melting snow of Mount Hermon, runoff rain water, and springs at the foot of the mountain ranges. South of the lake, the water ran through a narrow canal to the Sea of Galilee. Caravans crossed the narrow canal at a ford. From there the road passed by Hazor and the Sea of Galilee to Megiddo, then through the valley of Dothan to Shechem.

Or Abraham's caravan may have used the Bashan Road, which leads through the Golan Heights (Bashan). At the eastern edge of the Yarmuk gorge, the road turns westward and gradually descends to the Jordan Valley. There the Sea of Galilee, the Jordan River, and the

Yarmuk come together. Once in the Jordan Valley, a traveler can quickly go to Beth-Shean and from there to Shechem through the valleys of Jezreel and Dothan. This route was not traveled as frequently as the Hula Valley road. The trail from the Golan Heights to the Jordan Valley descended sharply, and part of the way it followed secondary roads less fit for large caravans or troops.

A third route that Abraham may have taken was probably used by Jacob when he deserted Laban in Haran. It led directly south, passing by the cities of Karnaim and Ashtaroth, and between Irbid and Ramoth-Gilead. Ten miles before Rabbath-bene-ammon (the present city of Amman, capital of Jordan), it veered slightly north and due west toward the Jordan Valley. The road descended to the gorge of the Jabbok River, crossed it at the ford of Mahanaim, then turned southward to Adam, where it could cross the Jordan River. From there to Shechem, the road leading out of the valley followed a rather steep incline by the Wadi Far'a for nearly 32 km. (20 mi.).

We know Abraham came through Shechem. It was a major intersection, controlling traffic going every direction. Archaeologists believe that Shechem was not a fortified city until the time of Jacob (*ca.* 1900 B.C.). But it was strategically located at a pass between Mount Ebal on the north and Mount Gerizim on the

12

THE GEOGRAPHY OF PALESTINE

THE GEOGRAPHY OF PALESTINE

south. The road from Wadi Far'a came into the Tirzah-Shechem road, which south of Shechem was called "the plain of Meonenim" (Judg. 9:37), or "the direction of the Diviners' Oak" (in the RSV). At Shechem a road turned off toward the Mediterranean, connecting Shechem with the major highway of Palestine, the Via Maris (Latin, "Way of the Sea").

At Shechem, the Lord promised to give the land to Abraham's descendants (Gen. 12:7). As a memorial of the promise, Abraham built an altar on the plain of Moreh (Gen. 12:6). God did not give Abraham exact boundaries, but He later assured the patriarch that the land on all four sides would be granted to his descendants (cf. Gen. 13:14–15).

God's covenant with Abraham stated the promise even more clearly: "Unto thy seed have I given this land, from the river of Egypt unto the great river, the river Euphrates" (Gen. 15:18). The promise was confirmed to Isaac (Gen. 26:3) and to Jacob (Gen. 28:13). God Himself established the relationship between the *people* and the *land*.

B. Land of the Patriarchs. God revealed to the patriarchs the lines of Israel's conquest. Biblical history continued to revolve around the cities, regions, and shrines where the patriarchs lived and worshiped. God commanded Abraham, "Arise, walk through the land in the length of it and in the breadth of it; for I will give it unto thee" (Gen. 13:17). Until they could gain control of Canaan, the patriarchs obeyed that command and took the land in faith for their descendants.

The patriarchal family was forced to leave Shechem after Jacob's sons Simeon and Levi rashly killed all the males of the city. Jacob rebuked them: "Ye have troubled me to make me to stink among the inhabitants of the land, . . . and I being few in number, they shall gather themselves together against me, and slay me; and I shall be destroyed, I and my house" (Gen. 34:30). God sent them to Bethel, where Jacob built another altar. To prepare for that holy experience, Jacob's household buried all their foreign gods by an oak tree and purified themselves. They took the Way of the Diviners' Oak to Bethel, where God had revealed Himself in Jacob's dream of the ladder 20 years earlier (Gen. 28). Again at Bethel, God reassured Jacob that his descendants would occupy the land (Gen. 35:12).

Bethel and Shechem were not the only places where the patriarchs lived and built altars. Their footsteps led to Hebron and as far

THE DEAD SEA. *The lowest body of water in the world, the Dead Sea is about 390 m. (1,300 ft.) below sea level. Its depth is estimated at another 91 m. (1,300 ft.). Located in southern Palestine, the Dead Sea is 80 km. (50 mi.) long and not more than 18 km. (11 mi.) at its widest point. The sea has no outlet. It is so filled with salts and other minerals that fish brought down by the Jordan River are killed within a few moments. The Dead Sea is referred to as the "Salt Sea" in the Old Testament (cf. Gen. 14:3).*

south as Beersheba in the Negev Desert. They canvassed the area that Joshua would later conquer.

Indeed, the patriarchs laid the groundwork for both good and ill for their descendants in the land of Canaan. Abraham's and Isaac's involvement with the king of Gerar in the Philistine plain (Gen. 20:1–18; 26:17–22) foreshadowed future conflicts, when the Philistines would press hard against the Israelites in the hill country. But many sacred sites of the Israelites in this period became important cities. Jerusalem, where the priest-king Melchizedek blessed Abraham, became the royal residence of King David and the very center of the Jewish religion after Solomon built the temple there.

Jacob's son Joseph brought the Israelites into Egypt. They entered Egypt as the *people* (clan) of Israel (Jacob); but there God forged them into a *nation*. The Egyptians felt threatened by the "population explosion" of the Israelites. To thwart their growing power, the Egyptians forced them to serve as slaves in the land of Goshen. Yet at the appointed time, God promised them: "And I will bring you in unto the land, . . . I did swear to give . . . to Abraham, to Isaac, and to Jacob; and I will give it you for an heritage: I am the Lord" (Exod. 6:8). God sent Moses to lead the people ". . . up out of the affliction of Egypt

THE GEOGRAPHY OF PALESTINE

unto . . . a land flowing with milk and honey" (Exod. 3:17).

God planned that His people would enter the Promised Land and become a nation unlike the surrounding nations. They would show their faith in God by grateful obedience. Keeping God's commandments would ensure their success: "Hear therefore, O Israel, and observe to do it; that it may be well with thee, and that ye may increase mightily . . ." (Deut. 6:3).

God chose the Israelites to be His witnesses in the Promised Land. They could demonstrate the faith of the patriarchs, who had successfully dealt with the nations around them. God's chosen people would grace the chosen land. This was God's third promise to Abraham, that through him and his descendants the nations would be blessed (Gen. 12:3).

Israel's possibilities within the Promised Land—its very future—depended on two things: its responsible use of the land and its faithful obedience to the terms of the Covenant. God looked for the day when Israel's observance of His laws would cause the nations to declare: ". . . Surely this great nation is a wise and understanding people" (Deut. 4:6).

C. Extent of the Promised Land. We don't know the exact boundaries of the Promised Land. God revealed to Abraham that he and his descendants would receive the land of Canaan, but He originally promised them a much larger area than that. When Lot's and

---

Hula Basin Project

Hula Lake no longer exists. Where gentle waters once shimmered in the shadow of Mount Hermon, farmers now cultivate an "agricultural paradise." In draining this lake and its papyrus marshes, the modern Israelis reclaimed about 45,000 acres of rich peat soil, enough farming land to support 100,000 people.

For the tiny nation of Israel, both water and land are in short supply. After the State of Israel was established, waves of immigrants landed upon the shores of the Promised Land. Though Israel welcomed the newcomers, it agonized over the lack of space available for settlement. Clearly the government had to make the best possible use of the land it had.

The new nation immediately adopted a far-reaching policy of land and water use. Officials began a comprehensive inventory of the land. All waters—surface, subterranean, even sewage—were declared public property and put under governmental control. At Israel's request, the Food and Agricultural Organization of the United Nations sent a team to help develop a soil and water conservation program, and to determine the best use of all available resources.

The Hula Basin Project was Israel's first major reclamation program. Waters converged in Hula Lake to form the nation's water lifeline, the Jordan River. In Roman times and earlier, the Hula Basin was fertile and populated. But by the twentieth century, it consisted primarily of 90 sq. km. (44 sq. mi.) of swamps. The area was a public menace. Its humid marshlands bred malaria and black-water fever; they also made a fine hiding place for enemy infiltrators. Worst of all, the water there was being wasted. Wildlife inhabited the area, but the water was of no use to the people of Israel.

Reclaiming the marshes of Hula Lake was not a new idea. During the Ottoman Empire (A.D. 1300–1500), Syrians got permission from their Turkish overlords for a similar project, but never followed through. In 1869, a Scottish adventurer named John MacGregor explored the area via canoe. He suggested that someone should cut a hole at the bottom end of the lake and drain it. Three generations later (1951–1957), Israel did.

Workmen began by blasting a hole in the basalt rock that dammed the southern end of the lake. This widened and deepened the mouth of the lake, and lowered the water level. With a temporary partition holding back the water, giant dredges dug channels through the swamps. When the partition was removed, the water flowed through 46 km. (29 mi.) of drainage canals.

Israel's gains are many. The peat deposits of the former lake bed have been called the finest soil in Israel. Grapes, sugar cane, cotton, vegetables, grains, and fruits are grown on the valley floor. The first yield was three times as great as anticipated. Processing and canning plants were built in the region to take care of the surplus.

A 750-acre plot was preserved for a wildlife refuge. In this natural aviary, more than 450 species of birds have been sighted. Pelicans soon discovered that fish were still available, lake or no lake. This posed a serious problem for certain Israeli entrepreneurs, who built ponds in the Hula district to raise fish commercially.

Water still flows into Hula Basin from the slopes and springs of Mount Hermon. But that water now serves Israel. Some stays in the valley to irrigate local crops; conservationists say that enough water is saved to irrigate 17,000 to 25,000 acres.

12

THE GEOGRAPHY OF PALESTINE

Abraham's shepherds quarreled over the land, Abraham wisely offered to give his nephew Lot first choice of the territory. Lot decided to settle in the well-watered Jordan Valley in the east. God then told Abraham: ". . . Lift up now thine eyes, and look from the place where thou art northward, and southward, and eastward, and westward: For all the land which thou seest, to thee will I give it, and to thy seed for ever" (Gen. 13:14–15). The boundary lines were not settled, though Abraham's territory obviously ended where Lot's flocks grazed.

God made the "land of promise" a part of His covenant with Abraham. Abraham ". . . believed the Lord; and he counted it to him for righteousness" (Gen. 15:6). In return, God solemnly promised to give to his descendants the land ". . . from the river of Egypt unto the great river, the river Euphrates" (Gen. 15:18).

Several hundred years later, when Moses reminded the Israelites of that promise, he described the boundaries of the Promised Land: the Arabah, the mountainous regions, the Shephelah, and the Negev and the coastal plains by the Mediterranean Sea, from the southern border of Canaan through Lebanon up to the Euphrates (Deut. 1:7).

By this time the Israelites already lived in the Transjordan. God allowed the tribes of Reuben and Gad, as well as part of the tribe of Manasseh, to settle in the newly-occupied land of the Amorites east of the Jordan (Num. 21:21—35:32). This territory extended the borders of the Promised Land even farther. But Moses still did not set a definite eastern boundary.

God ordered Joshua to take all the territory specified by Moses: "From the wilderness and this Lebanon even unto the great river, the river Euphrates, all the land of the Hittites, and unto the Great Sea toward the going down of the sun, shall be your coast" (Josh. 1:4). However, during the conquest of Canaan the people of Israel failed to take the total area promised them, partly because they were unfaithful to God. God punished the Israelites by holding them back from complete victory. ". . . I sware in my wrath that they should not enter into my rest" (Psa. 95:11). Each tribe lacked part of its inheritance.

D. Efforts to Expand. During the period of the judges, Israel tried unsuccessfully to enlarge its tribal territories. Even Saul, the first king, was not powerful enough to drive out or subdue the other nations.

Yet God allowed Saul's successor, King David, to control the land of promise except for "the land of the Hittites" (cf. Josh. 1:4). David was a man "after God's heart." Because he honored God in his military pursuits, God granted him victory over the Ammonites, Moabites, and Edomites in the east, over the Philistines in the west, and over the marauding nomadic bands in the south. In fact, his conquests reached almost to the Euphrates River, as far north as Hammath (2 Sam. 8).

Solomon inherited the kingdom at its peak. "For he had dominion over all the region on this side the river, from Tiphsah even to Azzah, over all the kings on this side the river: and he had peace on all sides round about him" (1 Kings 4:24). But from the latter part of Solomon's reign, the nation of Israel went steadily downhill. First the kingdom was divided into two nations: Israel and Judah. Wars wracked both of these kingdoms until their enemies forced them out of the land.

E. Fertility of the Land. A tourist to Palestine from the fertile plains of America might wonder if Moses was in his right mind when he described the Promised Land as ". . . a good land, a land of brooks of water, of fountains and depths that spring out of the valleys and hills; A land of wheat, and barley, and vines, and fig trees, and pomegranates; a land of olive oil, and honey; a land wherein thou shalt eat bread without scarceness, thou shalt not lack any thing in it; . . ." (Deut. 8:7–9). But Moses addressed those words to a people who had just spent 40 years in the desert! The earliest American pioneers, crossing the desert into the coastal plain areas of California, might have found similar soil conditions and geographical contrasts. The Promised Land held boundless possibilities in contrast to the harsh, dry regions of the Sinai, Negev, and Arabah.

However, the Promised Land was no Garden of Eden. The Israelites may have envisioned endless valleys of crops and hillsides adorned with grasses, herbs, and flowers; but that is not what they found. Thorns and thistles cover the rocky land. During summer months a dull reddish-brown color on the slopes indicates parched vegetation. Nevertheless, the land is highly fertile compared to the surrounding deserts.

The Promised Land offered good opportunities for making a living with its water and tillable soil. But the Israelites discovered that it was not easy to take advantage of those opportunities. They had to tame the land. The Is-

THE GEOGRAPHY OF PALESTINE

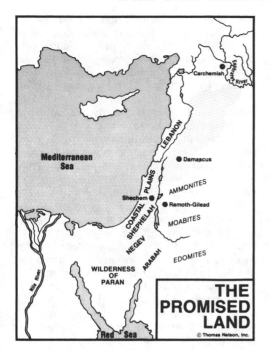

gather but little in; for the locust shall consume it. Thou shalt plant vineyards, and dress them, but shalt neither drink of the wine, nor gather the grapes; for the worms shall eat them" (Deut. 28:38–39). If the Israelites did not heed the Lord, they would lose the very land God promised to them: ". . . Ye shall be plucked from off the land whither thou goest to possess it" (Deut. 28:63b). Sadly, that very thing happened.

1. Soil. When Israel first occupied the land, they lived in the hill country near the central mountain range of Canaan. The Israelite farmers had to learn how to eke out an existence from the hills, which were largely composed of limestone rock. Though limestone weathers into soil very slowly, it is very fertile.

Rains easily wash the rich hillside soil down streams to low-lying valleys. To prevent erosion, farmers planted fruit trees and vines or built terraces.

Terraces abounded in the hill country. Sometimes a layer of rock resisted weathering and formed a natural wall. This held in place the reddish soil that the farmer could plant with wheat, barley, legumes and vegetables, in addition to fruit trees and vines. When there was no natural wall, the farmer had to clear the area of ever-present stones and use them to build a wall at the lower side of the hill.

Vineyards also abounded in Palestine, and biblical authors often mentioned them symbolically, as Isaiah did: ". . . My well-beloved hath a vineyard in a very fruitful hill: and he fenced it, and gathered out the stones thereof, and planted it with the choicest vines . . ." (Isa. 5:1–2). In this passage, God is the owner of the vineyard Israel. The work of preparing the vineyard represents God's love and care for Israel, who nonetheless failed to produce the harvest of righteousness He desired.

Israelite farmers cultivated fruit trees, vines, and grains in the low-lying hills, the Shephelah, and the coastal plains. The soft chalk of the Shephelah weathered easily and mixed with organic materials. Farmers could till this soil at a deeper level, and it was less subject to rain runoff.

2. Precipitation. Have you ever wondered what the Bible means by "former rains" and "latter rains"? Farmers in Palestine counted on the "former rains" of fall, which permitted seeds to germinate and seedlings to develop into strong plants. Equally essential were the "latter rains" of February and March, which

raelite farmer had to deal with rocks, thorns, thistles. He feared the sun, which scorched young seedlings that were not rooted deeply enough to draw water from a depth. He learned dependence on the Lord, ". . . for he maketh his sun to rise on the evil and on the good, and sendeth rain on the just and on the unjust" (Matt. 5:45).

Jesus nicely illustrated the farmer's plight with His parable of the sower. The sower spread the seed all over the field, but only the seed which fell on "good soil" produced a crop. The remaining seed fell on rocks and among thistles and soon died (Matt. 13:3–8).

What the Israelites could accomplish with the soil of Palestine depended entirely on their relationship with the Lord. He promised to bless them materially for their obedience: "The Lord shall open unto thee his good treasure, the heaven to give the rain unto thy land in his season, and to bless all the work of thine hand: . . ." (Deut. 28:12). Disobedience, however, would bring material judgment: "But . . . if thou wilt not hearken unto the voice of the Lord thy God, . . . thy heaven that is over thy head shall be brass, and the earth that is under thee shall be iron. The Lord shall make the rain of thy land powder and dust" (Deut. 28:15a, 23–24). "Thou shalt carry much seed out into the field, and shalt

WADI FAR'A. *Wadi is the Arabic word for a dry ravine that fills with water in the rainy season. There are numerous wadis throughout Israel. The Wadi Far'a, shown here, lies near the Judean city of Anathoth, the home of the prophet Jeremiah.*

enabled plants to mature in the following months. October to April is considered the winter season and is cold and rainy.

In Palestine, summer's warm air makes rain unlikely. Rain is also rare in May and September. Weather varies in the transition months between spring and summer (April to mid-June) and between summer and fall (September and October). The onset of cold weather may trigger heavy showers and endanger ripening crops: "As snow in summer and as rain in harvest, so honor is not seemly for a fool" (Prov. 26:1).

To the prophets, the rain signaled God's continued blessing and favor upon his children: "Be glad then, ye children of Zion, and rejoice in the Lord your God: for he hath given you the former rain moderately, and he will cause to come down for you the rain, the former rain, and the latter rain in the first month" (Joel 2:23).

Hosea likened God's presence to the refreshing spring rain: ". . . he shall come unto us as the rain, as the latter and former rain unto the earth" (Hos. 6:3b).

Lack of rain spelled failure for the farmer. As we have seen, God made His gift of rain depend on His people's continued faithfulness (cf. Deut. 11:13–14).

Israel's unfaithfulness brought many sea-

sons of drought. Naomi and her family left Bethlehem for the fields of Moab because of drought (Ruth 1:1). Elijah prayed that no rain or dew would fall for three years so that the people of Israel, seeing God's judgment on them, might return to Him (1 Kings 17:1; cf. Amos 4:7). Of course, drought often led to famine, a condition frequently mentioned in the Bible (e.g., Luke 15:14).

The rainfall in Palestine varies widely from place to place. At one extreme, the southern Negev receives 5 cm. (2 in.) per year, while Mount Hermon may be drenched with 152 cm. (60 in.) of precipitation.

Palestine's rainfall is directly related to the latitude and height of the land. The mountainous regions receive the most—from 61 to 91 cm. (24 to 36 in.) in northern Galilee and from 51 to 71 cm. (20 to 28 in.) in Samaria and Judah. South of the line between Gaza and Engedi a mere 31 cm. (12 in.) of rain falls; south of Beersheba, only 20 cm. (8 in.). The rain also decreases from west to east. Perhaps 20″ falls on the coast at Tel Aviv, or at Jerusalem, but only 10 to 20 cm. (4 to 8 in.) falls a few miles to the east at Jericho and the Jordan River.

An estimated 60 to 70 percent of the precipitation is lost through evaporation because of the land's high temperatures and low humidity. Only 10 to 25 percent is absorbed for agricultural purposes.

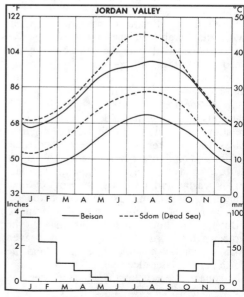

Figure 23. Annual Temperature and Rainfall

THE GEOGRAPHY OF PALESTINE

So the dew that falls approximately 250 nights of the year is very essential. Some vegetation depends entirely on the dew's moisture. We understand why Elijah included dew in his prophecy to Ahab: ". . . there shall not be dew nor rain these years, but according to my word" (1 Kings 17:1b). It is an exhilarating experience to wake up in the Negev desert on a summer morning and see a thick fog! A visitor to this region can appreciate why the Psalmist said: "Behold, how good and pleasant it is for brethren to dwell together in unity! It is like the dew of Hermon, and as the dew that descended upon mountains of Zion" (Psa. 133:1, 3). Yet the dew evaporates quickly, and it became proverbial to compare Israel's faithlessness to dew (cf. Hos. 6:4).

Palestine also gets snow. The majestic snow of Mount Hermon can be seen from a great distance until midsummer. Jeremiah referred to the snowy mountains when he flailed Israel's faithless ways: "Does the snow of Lebanon leave the crags of Sirion? Do the mountain waters run dry, the cold flowing streams? But my people have forgotten me . . ." (Jer. 18:14–15a, RSV).

The hill country of Judah averages two days of snow, which melts rapidly when the daytime temperature rises. However, a blizzard hit Palestine in 1950, bringing 69 cm. (27 in.) of snow to Jerusalem and 53 cm. (21 in.) to Acre!

3. Winds. Wind is both a boon and a bane to Palestine. Her hot climate is eased by cool Mediterranean winds during the day. Chill evenings provide a welcome change from the day's heat in desert and hill country. The moisture-laden sea winds combine with cool air at night to give Palestine her vital dew.

A southeasterly wind marks the change of seasons in Palestine, from spring to summer and from summer to fall. Jeremiah 4:11 mentions "a hot wind from the bare heights in the desert." This dry wind loaded with dust makes the people very uncomfortable.

The Bible's "east wind" may be what the Arabs call a *khamsin*. The *khamsin* leaves people irritable and they feel like doing nothing, because of the oppressive heat. "When the sun did arise, God prepared a vehement east wind: and the sun beat upon the head of Jonah, that he fainted, and wished in himself to die, and said, 'It is better for me to die than to live' " (Jon. 4:8).

The land of Israel may be divided into six regions. The Jordan Valley runs down the center of Palestine:

The *Upper Jordan* extends from the Lebanon Mountains to the Sea of Galilee. The area that is usually called the *Jordan Valley* lies between the Sea of Galilee and the Dead Sea.

Galilee is the northernmost area of Palestine between the Jordan River and the Mediterranean coast. *Samaria* spreads between these natural boundaries in central Palestine, while *Judah* does so in the extreme south.

Transjordan is all the land east of the Jordan River, east and south of the Dead Sea. Its eastern border is the Syrian Desert.

Now that we have taken a bird's-eye view of the land of Palestine, let's look more closely at its distinctive parts.

IV. The Jordan Valley. The Jordan River courses through the center of Palestine. It has also been the center of Israel's social and economic life, both in ancient times and today.

A. The Upper Jordan. God first gave the coastal plains to the tribe of Dan for their

SNOW IN JERUSALEM. *A little snow may fall once or twice during Jerusalem's rainy season, but it usually melts quickly. A very heavy snowfall occurs about once in 15 years. The Israelis welcome the wet weather, despite the discomfort it brings, because rain and snow will improve the next season's harvest.*

12

THE GEOGRAPHY OF PALESTINE

inheritance. However, as the Philistines grew in power the Danites couldn't hold the land, and they moved to the Upper Jordan Valley, far from the political centers of Jerusalem and Samaria (Judg. 18). They never fully used the 26 sq. km. (11 sq. mi.) of the valley, as it held many streams, swamps, and small lakes. Mountains hedge the valley on three sides: the Naphtali Range to the west, the Hermon Range to the north, and the Golan Heights (Bashan) to the east.

The encircling mountains, drawing abundant rain and snow, give this region the highest precipitation in Israel, 7 to 15 cm. (3 to 6 in.) annually. Runoff water and melting snow flow underground into springs to provide a year-round supply of fresh water.

1. Mount Hermon. The Danites settled in the fruitful valley at the foot of majestic Mount Hermon. They built their towns and planted their crops by the icy waters that flowed to the Sea of Galilee and the Dead Sea via the Jordan River.

Over 2,700 m. (9,000 ft.) high, Mount Hermon juts against the horizon to the northeast. Snow covers its highest peaks until midsummer. The mountain can be seen from a remarkable distance. One visitor told of distinguishing the white snowcap of Mount Hermon above the Golan Heights from the western side of the Jordan Valley—a distance of 97 km. (60 mi.)!

The imposing heights, abundant water, and luxurious vegetation struck awe in the hearts of those who settled in the shadows of the Hermon range. Even before the Israelites came, Canaanites linked the region with their fertility god, Baal. Part of the range is called Baal-hermon (Judg. 3:3; 1 Chron. 5:23), and there is a city of Baal-gad (Josh. 13:5).

Idolatrous Israelites viewed Mount Hermon as a fertility symbol, as the pagan Canaanites did. But the Israelites credited fertility and might to the Creator, not to His creation. To them, the power and magnificence of God dwarfed even the mighty peaks of the north—Lebanon, Tabor, and Hermon: "The voice of the Lord breaketh the cedars; yea, the Lord breaketh the cedars of Lebanon. He maketh them to skip like a calf; and Lebanon and Sirion [Hermon] like a young wild ox" (Psa. 29:5–6). In their eyes the mountains themselves worshiped Yahweh: "Tabor and Hermon shall rejoice in thy name" (Psa. 89:12).

The many names of Mount Hermon attest its importance. Before the Israelites conquered them, the Amorites called it Shenir (Deut. 3:9) or Mount Senir (Deut. 3:9; Ezek. 27:5). To the people of Sidon it was Mount Sirion (Deut. 3:9), and the Hebrew of Deuteronomy 4:48 refers to it as Mount Sion, though the Syriac version has Sirian.

When war threatened Israel's northern border, the Hermon range absorbed the first shock of invading forces. With the Lebanon mountains to the west, it provided a natural barrier to the Aramaean kingdom of the north. But in times of peace the great Mount Hermon

MOUNT HERMON. *Over 2,700 m. (9,000 ft.) high, Mount Hermon rises above the floor of the Upper Jordan Valley, marking the northern boundary between the Israelites and the Amorites. Snowcapped for most of the year, the mountain is visible from a remarkable distance.*

THE JORDAN RIVER. *The Hebrew name of the Jordan River literally means "the descender." Beginning 70 m. (230 ft.) above sea level, it drops to 213 m. (700 ft.) below sea level 16 km. (10 mi.) south of the Sea of Galilee. By the time it reaches the northern end of the Dead Sea, the river has plunged to 393 m. (1,290 ft.) below sea level. The distance of about 120 km. (75 mi.) from its source to the Dead Sea is more than doubled by the river's meandering. No other river figures more prominently in the Bible.*

still helped the people of Canaan. She quietly gave birth to springs around her base, as melting snows seeped through the porous rocks that make up her foundation.

2. Sources of the Jordan. The Jordan River begins in the Hula Valley of northern Palestine. Actually, four rivers—the Senir, Dan, Ayyon, and Hermon—flowed into Hula Lake and their waters emerged at the southern tip of the lake as the Jordan River.

Springs in the northern recesses of Lebanon created the Senir River. These springs are situated 52 km. (32 mi.) northeast of Metulla, Israel's northernmost settlement, and are fed by runoff water from the western slope of Mount Hermon.

A larger river, the Dan, comes from the ancient springs of Dan. Here the water flows into a crystal pool of ice-cold water and drops quickly into rapids. Smaller springs in the area ooze out of the ground and trickle from the rocks to water the dense foliage of mosses, bushes, and trees.

The tribe of Dan scouted this land and decided it was an ideal spot to settle. So they wiped out the peaceful inhabitants of Laish, rebuilt the town, and renamed it Dan. Instead of going to worship at Shiloh, about 128 km. (80 mi.) away, they set up their own shrine with stolen idols (Judg. 18).

The Ayyon River (which in biblical times drained the Ayyon Valley in Lebanon) contains Palestine's most impressive waterfall, the Tannur. At Abel Beth-maacah, a mile south of the waterfall, King David's men besieged that "worthless fellow" Sheba who drew away Israel's allegiance with his cry: "We have no portion in David" (2 Sam. 20:1).

The fourth river feeding into the Jordan River, the Hermon, spills from beneath a high rock wall at what was once the village of Banias. The Banias springs were originally named *Paneas* after Pan, Greek god of forests and meadows. *Banias* reflects the Roman term for *bath*. There are waterfalls about a mile southwest of this place also.

Herod the Great built a temple at Banias and dedicated the site to Caesar Augustus. Later the tetrarch Philip made his home there and renamed it Caesarea Philippi, after himself.

At Caesarea Philippi, a profusion of rocks was scattered along the river bank. Idols were nestled in the niches of a high rock wall dedicated to Pan. In the Master's powerful way He welded the setting to His response: "Blessed art thou, Simon Barjona! . . . Thou art Peter, and upon this rock I will build my church, and the gates of hell shall not prevail against it" (Matt. 16:17–18).

What a contrast! Peter voiced his faith in Christ amid rampant paganism and Rome's worldly might. Yet on the rock of Peter's confession all other rocks—the power of Rome included—would crumble.

THE GEOGRAPHY OF PALESTINE

Since they were traveling in the region of Caesarea Philippi, Jesus might have led Peter and James to one of Mount Hermon's ridges to witness His transfiguration. (Some believe the "high mountain" of Matthew 17:1 was Mount Tabor, but the preceding passage places the group near Mount Hermon.)

3. Hula Lake. Hula Lake nestles close to the Lebanon and Hermon ranges in the Upper Jordan Valley. In Bible times, river waters drained into the shallow water of the Hula swamps, and then into the lake. The swamps north of the lake were filled with semi-tropical plants. Alligators, hippopotamuses, and water buffalo made their homes there. Since drainage was poor, settlers often contracted malaria, and at certain seasons the area flooded. With so many hazards, the land was not fully used.

A layer of basalt blocked the southern end of Hula Lake. Volcanic activity in the Golan Heights had dumped lava on the mountains north of Galilee. These areas were equally hostile to settlers.

In Old Testament times, river water cut a canal 16 km. (10 mi.) through the basalt. The canal drops 750 feet in that stretch and deepens as it goes. Consequently, travelers could cross the Jordan at only one point of the canal, just below the lake. Travelers who were willing to wait until the water was low could ford the river there. Caravans loaded with wares from Egypt and Israel regularly crossed the Jordan at that ford on their way north to Damascus or Mesopotamia.

In our time, the Bridge of the Daughters of Jacob spans the ancient ford. Modern Israeli tanks and trucks loaded with ammunition rumble over it to reach the Golan Heights.

Twentieth-century Israelis have made other changes in the region as well. From 1951 to 1958 they drained Hula Lake and reclaimed over 78,000 sq. km. (20,000 acres) of highly fertile land from the lake bed and swamps.

JABBOK RIVER. *The Jabbok flows westward into the Jordan River about 32 km. (20 mi.) north of the Dead Sea. Over 96 km. (60 mi.) long, it is known as the Wadi Zerqa today. The river marked a boundary line between Ammon and the tribes of Reuben and Gad (Deut. 3:16). It was also the river that Jacob forded when he wrestled with the angel (Gen. 32).*

THE GEOGRAPHY OF PALESTINE

They also straightened and deepened the canal to the Sea of Galilee.

B. The Jordan Valley Proper. The Jordan River Valley stretches out in the middle of Palestine for 105 km. (65 mi.). Elevation drops gradually as the Jordan leaves the Sea of Galilee at an altitude of 195 m. (650 ft.) below sea level and enters the Dead Sea at 387 m. (1,290 ft.) below sea level. Since the river depth varies and the water is full of sandbars, sailors do not try to navigate between the two seas.

About 8 km. (5 mi.) south of the Sea of Galilee, the Jordan doubles in size as the Yarmuk River adds roughly 459,000 cu. m. (16.2 million cu. ft.) of water to its flow every minute. Other rivers such as the Jabbok swell the Jordan by an additional 94,500 cu. m. (3.3 million cu. ft.) per minute.

The watercourse of the Jordan is ever-changing. The entire Jordan Valley was once under water. This left debris of loose soil and gravel, especially to the south in a land now called the *qattara* or "badlands." Little rivers feed soil as well as water into the Jordan, and its own currents eat away the riverbed. Earthquakes and tremors have dumped dirt into the river also, sometimes blocking the Jordan's flow and forcing it to seek a new course.

Desolate mountain ranges flank the river. To the west, Samaria and Bethel reach 450 m. (1,500 ft.) in Lower Galilee. East of the Jordan, the humps of the Gilead rise to 600 m. (2,000 ft.).

At one point the valley is only 3 km. (2 mi.) wide. It spreads out to 11 km. (7 mi.) near Beth-shean and the Jezreel Valley, and by Jericho it widens to a span of 22.5 km. (14 mi.). A narrow pass in the hill country of Samaria separates the Jordan Valley into the Beth-shean and Lower Jordan valleys.

1. A Natural Boundary. The Jordan River served Canaan as a natural boundary, holding back eastern invaders.

From the Book of Genesis onward, the Scriptures speak of the Jordan River as a boundary or border. Several Scripture texts refer to crossing the Jordan: Genesis 32:10; Deuteronomy 3:20, 25; 27:4; Joshua 1:1; Numbers 34:10–12.

As the tribes of Israel moved north from the Sinai, they approached the Jordan Valley from the east. At the time, plundering tribes from the desert controlled that land, and the Jordan was a frontier. Three tribes wanted to stay and graze their cattle there, but Moses urged them to go along across the Jordan to help in the conquest of Canaan. They did so, with the provision that after the conquest they could return to the eastern shore to settle. The tribes of Reuben and Gad and half the tribe of Manasseh eventually received their inheritance east of the river, as they had requested. Still, the prospect of being separated from the other tribes troubled them: "In time to come your children might speak unto our children, saying, What have ye to do with the Lord God of Israel? For the Lord hath made the Jordan a border between us and you, ye children of Reuben and children of Gad; ye have no part in the Lord. So shall your children make our children cease from fearing the Lord" (Josh. 22:24–25).

Many gospel songs have been written about going over the Jordan, and with good reason. It was not an easy river to cross. The Israelites could ford the Jordan only at traditional spots, and even those places were useless when the Jordan flooded its banks.

The Israelites knew the value of the fords and wrested them from their enemies as soon as possible. Ehud's forces ". . . took the fords of Jordan toward Moab, and suffered not a man to pass over" (Judg. 3:28). Gideon recruited men for his army with the cry, "Come down against the Midianites and take before them the waters . . ." (Judg. 7:24).

For the most part, the Jordan Valley was sparsely settled, partly because of the heat and dryness. More people settled in the Beth-shean Valley to the north, where it was at least possible to irrigate crops.

2. The Beth-shean Valley. Tributaries on both sides of the Jordan flood their banks in winter and spring. Though the climate in the Beth-shean Valley resembles a desert, the plentiful amount of water and high temperatures produce dense subtropical brush. The Israelis eventually dug canals to control the flooding and used the Jordan's waters to irrigate crops in the valley.

A modern city of 15,000 people, Beth-shean lies at the foot of Mount Gilboa 24 km. (15.5 mi.) south of the Sea of Galilee where the Valley of Jezreel meets the Jordan Valley.

C. The Lower Jordan. The Lower Jordan Valley contains three distinct levels. They appear on both sides of the river, and are known as the *zor,* the *qattara,* and the *ghor.*

Closest to the river is the *zor,* a narrow strip of land one or two miles wide, which the Bible

THE GEOGRAPHY OF PALESTINE

calls the "thickets of the Jordan" or the wilderness. Thanks to seasonal floods, the zor was a veritable jungle of dense brush, shrubs, and tamarisk trees. Wild beasts hid in its shelter. Jeremiah speaks of ". . . a lion from the swelling of the Jordan . . ." (Jer. 49:19). The sons of the prophets were cutting down trees in the Jordan thickets when Elisha made an iron axe head float on the river (2 Kings 6:1–7).

John the Baptist prepared the way for the Messiah in the zor near Jericho: "John did baptize in the wilderness, and preach the baptism of repentance for the remission of sins" (Mark 1:4). He also baptized Jesus in the Jordan (1:9).

Away from the river, beyond the zor, are the *qattara* badlands. This territory is covered by ancient deposits of sediment from the lake that once filled the Jordan Valley. Seasonal streams carve deep crevices in the qattara. No one grew crops there because the soil was salty. Modern Israeli scientists are reclaiming the soil by washing it with river water.

The *ghor* is a steep but fertile terrace between the qattara and the mountains. Farmers irrigate and cultivate these fields.

V. Galilee. Jesus proclaimed the Good News in the lowlands of Galilee. The prophet Isaiah had predicted that He would minister in "The land of Zebulun, and the land of Naphtali, by the way of the sea, beyond Jordan, Galilee of the Gentiles" (Matt. 4:15).

Volcanoes and earthquakes shaped the landscape of Galilee. The area holds isolated mountains, high plateaus, valleys and gorges, rocky ridges and steep cliffs. Galilee divides naturally into two parts, with obvious differences in altitude, climate, and vegetation.

A. Upper Galilee. Upper Galilee lies south and west of the Hula Valley. It extends eastward from the Mediterranean Sea to the town of Safed, and south to the Beth-haccerem Valley. In this fertile valley live olive trees that are hundreds of years old.

At one time Upper Galilee was probably a single block of mountain, but massive natural forces split it into many pieces. Some parts were thrust up, others sank down, and all were eroded by water.

The tribe of Naphtali settled the mountainous area to the east. From the Naphtali Range (about 600 m. or 2,000 ft. above sea level), the traveler gets a splendid view of the Hula Valley. The scattered peaks of Mount Meiron, Mount Shammai (or Mount Hillel), and Mount Ha-ari, rising between 1,000 and 1,200 m. (3,400 to 3,900 ft.), tower above the relatively high mountain ranges of Upper Galilee.

Few people settled in Upper Galilee. The rugged mountains and sharp cliffs mostly offered protection for fugitives and refugees. King Solomon gave 20 cities in the northwestern territory to King Hiram of Tyre. But the biblical timber baron didn't appreciate the gift: "And Hiram came out from Tyre to see the cities which Solomon had given him; they did not please him. And he said, What cities are these which thou hast given me, my brother? And he called them the land of Cabul to this day" (1 Kings 9:12–13). Roughly translated, *Cabul* meant "obscurity." Hiram's discourteous remark immediately strained relations with his new subjects in the cities of Galilee.

On Upper Galilee's eastern border stands the modern city of Safed, 540 m. (1,800 ft.) above sea level. Safed is visible from the northern shore of the Sea of Galilee. The twinkling night lights of such a town might have prompted Jesus' remark: "A city set on a hill cannot be hid" (Matt. 5:14).

B. Lower Galilee. Lower Galilee is literally lower than Upper Galilee, being a plateau about 350 feet above sea level. In Lower Galilee we find Jesus' hometown (Matt. 2:23). Nazareth perches atop a steeply tilted hunk of earth. It seems impossible to enter Nazareth from the south, but a tenacious road curves and twists up the narrow ridge into the city. The attempt made on Jesus' life at Nazareth no doubt occurred on the cliffs to the south: "And they rose up and put him out of the city, and led him to the brow of the hill on which their city was built, that they might throw him down headlong. But passing through the midst of them he went away" (Luke 4:29–30, RSV).

Looking away from Nazareth one sees Mount Tabor, a cone-shaped volcanic mountain almost 600 m. (2,000 ft.) high. In the days of the judges, Deborah sent Barak and his troops to Mount Tabor to attack the Canaanites (Jer. 4:6). Jeremiah evoked the name to pronounce doom on Egypt: "Surely Tabor is among the mountains, and as Carmel by the sea, so shall he come" (Jer. 46:18).

Mount Tabor's beautiful foliage contrasts with the rather barren grassy hills at its base. Some say that Mount Tabor was the site of Jesus' transfiguration. It is difficult to climb.

Another volcanic crater, the Horns of Hittin, can be seen from many parts of Galilee. In

MOUNT TABOR. *Rising from the Plain of Jezreel to almost 600 m. (1,000 ft.), Mount Tabor is located on the tribal boundary between Zebulun and Issachar. There is a magnificent view from the summit, where an idolatrous shrine was set up during Hosea's day (ca. 730 B.C.).*

A.D. 1187 a decisive battle took place there between the Crusaders and the Arab leader Saladin.

Earthquakes produced two other mountains in Galilee that are really escarpments: long cliff-like ridges. Mount Arbel rises only to 180 m. (600 ft.), yet from it one can see the arena of Jesus' ministry: the valley of Gennosar, the Mount of the Beatitudes, Capernaum, and the blue waters of the Sea of Galilee, and the Golan Heights beyond. Wadi Arbel served as a junction between the road of Galilee (from Hazor and Damascus) and Horns of Hittin.

The second escarpment overlooks the Jordan Valley, Golan Heights, and the Sea of Galilee. Though Ramat Kokav is the highest mountain in Lower Galilee, the Scriptures do not mention it. But the Crusaders built a fortress on its summit. They named the stronghold *Belvoir* (good lookout point), because of the excellent view which includes even the snow-capped peaks of Mount Hermon.

C. The Sea of Galilee. Many people think of this as a large body of water. Actually, the Sea of Galilee is a lake below sea level, and not a very large one. Roughly pear-shaped, the water is only 10 km. (6 mi.) wide and 24 km. (15 mi.) from north to south. It is 39 to 47 m. (120 to 155 ft.) deep, and its surface is 206 m. (650 ft.) below sea level. Its circumference is about 51 km. (32 mi.). It is listed as the Lake (or Sea) of Chinnereth on Old Testament maps. Later it was called Lake Gennesaret (Luke 5:1), the Sea of Tiberias (John 6:1), or most frequently, the Sea of Galilee.

The territories of Naphtali, Zebulun, and Issachar bordered Lake Chinnereth in Old Testament times. They constituted the region of Galilee, a subdivision of the Northern Kingdom. Under Rome's rule, the provinces of Galilee, Judah, and Samaria were part of Herod's kingdom. Herod the Great supposedly rid Galilee of robbers and repopulated the north with Jews. Once known as "Galilee of the nations" (Isa. 9:1; RSV "Gentiles"), it became a vigorously Jewish region. Still, the people of Judea despised the Jews of Galilee. However, Jesus conducted most of his ministry in the vicinity of the Sea of Galilee.

Steep hills skirt most of the shoreline. Streams by Bethsaida, Gennesaret, and Sennabris created fertile valleys that the Israelites cultivated. They often built villages on hills and mountaintops. The Arbel cliffs above Magdala offer a panoramic view of the northern region of the lake. The map helps us visualize some familiar New Testament events.

"As he walked by the Sea of Galilee, he saw two brothers, Simon who is called Peter and Andrew his brother, casting a net into the sea; for they were fishers" (Matt. 4:18).

About 3.5 km. (2 mi.) west of Capernaum stands the Hill of the Beatitudes, where Jesus may have delivered the Sermon on the Mount (Matt. 5). On one of these hills He fed the 5,000 with a few loaves and fishes.

When Nazareth rejected Jesus (Luke 4:29–31), he made Capernaum the center of his ministry. Jesus taught in their synagogue, performed many miracles, and then set out on a preaching mission. After the Resurrection, Jesus returned to the shores of Galilee.

VI. Samaria. North of the Dead Sea and west of the Jordan is the hill country of Samaria. A harsh, mountainous land full of fissures and valleys, its boundaries run from the Jordan Valley on the east to the Plain of Sharon on the west. The valleys of Jezreel and Esdraelon border it on the north. The southern boundaries tended to shift, since there is no sharp division between the hill country of Samaria and that of Judah.

If you were to stand on Mount Nebo and

THE GEOGRAPHY OF PALESTINE

SEA OF GALILEE. *Located in the northern part of the Jordan Valley, the Sea of Galilee is really a lake 24 km. (15 mi.) long and 10 km. (6 mi.) wide. This body of water is called the "Sea of Chinnereth" in Numbers 34:11 and the "Lake of Gennesaret" in Luke 5:1. Christ's ministry often took Him to the towns on its shores. This photograph shows the southern portion of the lake, where the Jordan River leaves it; the mountains of Syria are in the background.*

look westward across the Jordan, Samaria might appear to be an impenetrable mountain mass. From the floor of the Jordan Valley, 240 m. (800 ft.) below sea level, the Samarian hills climb steeply to 600 m. (2,000 ft.) above sea level within 11 km. (7 mi.). The coastal side drops more gradually, taking 40 km. (25 mi.) to descend to sea level. Understandably the west offers easier ways into the hill country of Samaria than the passes of the east.

Mountain passes made Samaria's hills accessible and connected the country with other towns and peoples. Several important routes passed through Samaria. One road passes Beth-shean north of Mount Gilboa to Megiddo, connecting Samaria to the Via Maris, Canaan's major north-south highway. Just west of Mount Gilboa one branch heads south, passing through the Valley of Dothan. Northeast of Shechem is the pass of Wadi Far'a by which a traveler can reach the Jordan Valley. The Wadi Far'a descends gradually 300 m. in 16 km. (or 1,000 ft. in 10 miles), compared to the steep cliffs (750 m. or 2,500 ft.) through which it passes.

The Via Maris ran parallel to the main watershed of the Samarian hill country in the Plain of Sharon. From early times, settlers of the hill country maintained connections with the coastal highway for trade and cultural purposes.

Many place names of Samaria are familiar to Bible readers. At Shechem both Abraham and Jacob built altars (Gen. 12:6–8; 33:18). There the Israelites buried Joseph's bones (Josh. 24:32) and renewed the covenant God had made with Moses.

Remember when the lad Joseph went to look for his brothers? He found them in the Valley of Dothan (Gen. 37:17). Several judges were active in the region: Deborah, Gideon, Tola, and Abdon. The first prophet, Samuel, grew up at the Tabernacle of Shiloh. Later he made his birthplace, Ramah, his headquarters and traveled a circuit that included the towns of Bethel, Gilgal, and Mizpah (1 Sam. 1:1—2:11; 7:15–17).

The northern kingdom of Israel made Samaria its capital, and many battles were fought in its open valleys. Such characters as Ahab, Elijah, Jehu, and Elisha appeared in this hilly country to play important parts in the history of Israel.

At the northern tip of Samaria is Mount Gilboa, a significant place in Israel's military history. Here the Lord once instructed Gideon

SAMARIA. *The ancient capital of the northern kingdom of Israel, Samaria was ideally situated amid fertile hills at the junction of important roads. A natural acropolis made this a strategic military site. This view shows the gentle contours of the surrounding countryside, so different from the harsh landscapes of Judea.*

to reduce his forces from 32,000 to 300 men so that it would be obvious that God was responsible for their victory against the Midianites and Amalekites. The "people of the East" had crossed the Jordan and camped in the valley of Jezreel, by the hill of Moreh. Gideon's forces camped near the spring of Harod, at the foot of Mount Gilboa. Gideon obeyed the Lord, and his tiny army routed the enemy (Judg. 7:1–25).

In a later battle, Saul did not fare as well. "Now the Philistines fought against Israel; and the men of Israel fled from before the Philistines, and fell down slain in Mount Gilboa" (1 Sam. 31:1). Saul's sons were killed in the battle, and Saul committed suicide. The Philistines hung the bodies of Saul and the royal sons on the wall of Beth-shean in the Harod Valley (31:10). On hearing of their ignoble deaths, David lamented: "Ye mountains of Gilboa, let there be no dew, neither let there be rain, upon you. . . . for there the shield of the mighty is vilely cast away, the shield of Saul, as though he had not been anointed with oil" (2 Sam. 1:21).

Jesus also visited Samaria. In fact, it was at Jacob's well near Shechem that He met the "woman of Samaria" (John 4:5–7).

Samaria was one of three specific places named in the Great Commission Jesus gave just before His ascension: ". . . Ye shall be witnesses unto me in Jerusalem, and in all Judea, and in Samaria and unto the uttermost part of the earth" (Acts 1:8). When the early church was scattered by the persecution in Jerusalem, Philip took the gospel to Samaria, where it was well received (Acts 8:1–6, 14).

VII. Judah. No one can say for certain where the land of Samaria ended and Judah began. Some say the road from Ajalon to Jericho, passing between Bethel and Gibeon, marks the boundary. Others think Samaria ended with the road from Beth-shemesh to Jerusalem. Between the two were the Bethel hills, the shifting border of the northern kingdom of Israel.

Judah encompasses a spine of mountains and the barren desert sands of the wilderness.

JUDEAN WILDERNESS. *The Judean Wilderness mentioned in Judges 11:6 is probably identical with the wilderness of Judah, a desert to the west of the Dead Sea and to the east of the Judean hill country. Sharp outcroppings of bare rocks pierce the desolate and barren stretches of rolling sands. Hot, dusty winds shift the dunes about. Rain seldom falls here.*

THE GEOGRAPHY OF PALESTINE

The hill country of Judah runs parallel to the plateau of Moab which lies on the other side of the Dead Sea. It goes roughly in a northeast-southwest direction from Bethel to Hebron, with the mountains tapering off in the south, at Beersheba. The mountains are even higher than those of Samaria, rising to 990 m. (3,300 ft.).

A. Bethel Hills. The Bible says little of the Bethel hills, though the tribes of Benjamin and Ephraim settled in this region. Manasseh to the north and Judah to the south are mentioned more frequently in the Scriptures. Yet the Bethel hills contained fertile valleys, such as the plateau between Gibeon and Michmash. Since rainfall was heavy, the region was soon cultivated.

B. Jerusalem Hills. South of the Bethel hills, in line with the northern tip of the Dead Sea, are the Jerusalem hills and the city of Jerusalem. The city lies 600 m. (about 2,000 ft.) above sea level, and the hills that surround it are lower than those of Bethel or Hebron. "As the mountains are round about Jerusalem," said the Psalmist, "so the Lord is

round about his people . . ." (Psa. 125:2a). Even from 13 km. (8 mi.) away, Jerusalem can be seen from the encircling mountains.

Ravines cut Jerusalem off from all directions but the north, for several valleys converge at this location.

When Jesus came to Jerusalem, the palaces of Herod and the high priest Caiaphas were within the walled city. From their windows they could look down upon the Valley of Hinnom, to the west. King Ahaz had "burned his sons as an offering in the valley of the sons of Hinnom, and practiced soothsaying and augury and sorcery, and dealt with mediums and with wizards. He did much evil in the sight of the Lord, provoking him to anger" (2 Chron. 33:6, RSV). Jesus used the name of the region (*Ge-hinnom,* in Greek *Gehenna*) for hell, the ultimate place of God's judgment. Judas, it seems, committed suicide in this valley, where it curves from south to east.

By the Pool of Siloam the Hinnom and Kidron Valleys come together. The Kidron River runs between the Mount of Olives and the Hill of Jerusalem, also known as Mount

JERUSALEM. *The recently discovered Ebla Tablets contain the earliest known reference to Jerusalem, indicating that the city existed in the early second millennium B.C. Some scholars think this is the city called "Salem" in Genesis 14. This aerial photograph shows the large open space surrounding the dome-topped Mosque of Omar built on what is thought to be the site of the Holy of Holies in Solomon's Temple.*

THE GEOGRAPHY OF PALESTINE

Moriah. The events of history mingle in Jerusalem, for it was on Mount Moriah that Abraham prepared to sacrifice Isaac (Gen. 22:2), and where the Lord appeared to David (2 Chron. 3:1). From the confluence of the Hinnom and Kidron Rivers, rainwater flows through the Judean wilderness to the Dead Sea.

C. Hebron Hills. If we continue our journey south, we approach the Hebron range. At over 900 m. (3,000 ft.), it is the highest range in Judah. On Hebron's slopes Abraham and Isaac tended their flocks. Near Hebron, Abraham purchased the Cave of Machpelah to bury Sarah, and the patriarchs were also interred there. After Saul's death, David ruled Judah from Hebron for about seven years before he captured Jerusalem.

D. The Coastal Plains. Alongside the mountain ranges of Judah and Samaria lies the coast of the beautiful Mediterranean Sea. It is a remarkably smooth coastline. Sea currents straightened much of the shoreline by depositing sand picked up from the Nile delta. Northward, the sand deposits decrease until, by the Ladder of Tyre, the coast is rocky.

Between sand deposits and rocks, it seemed impossible to develop a harbor for international shipping until late in Israel's history. The Phoenicians used the natural harbors at Sidon and Tyre. But on Palestine's stretch of the Mediterranean, only small vessels could dock at Joppa. Solomon's main harbor was Ezion-Geber, on the Red Sea's Gulf of Eilat. Other kings of Judah unsuccessfully contested the Edomites for control of that region.

During the rule of Herod the Great, the Romans developed two more ports, Ptolemais (Acre) and Caesarea. The Apostle Paul docked at Caesarea at the close of his second missionary journey, then visited both Ptolemais and Caesarea after his third journey. Later, Festus sent Paul from Caesarea to Rome as a prisoner (Acts 27:2).

The Palestinian coast has extensive deposits of *kurkar,* a type of sandstone. Kurkar disintegrates slowly and hardens when it meets water, so it tends to prevent erosion of the shoreline. Little islands of kurkar and a sandstone ridge follow the coastline by Samaria. Until modern times, the Sharon Plain was swampy because that ridge held back water draining from the Samarian hills. Thus the water flooded the plain, where rivers slowly carried it to the sea.

E. The Philistine Coast. The Philistines controlled the coast from the Yarkon River (near Joppa) to Gaza. Dune belts skirt the shore, especially to the south. The dunes are approximately 6 km. (4 mi.) wide by Gaza, and south of the Philistine Coast the sand extends even farther inland. A fertile plain about 16 km. (10 mi.) wide lies east of the dunes. Sediment and sand create a rich soil, and many types of crops are grown there.

In this region the Philistines lived and worshiped.

Five major cities controlled Philistia and its trade routes. To go from Phoenicia to Egypt, or through Israel's Shephelah into the Judean hills, traders had to pass through Philistia. Gaza, Ashdod, and Ashkelon were near the coast and served as small harbors. Gath and Ekron were further inland, on a road running parallel to the Via Maris. Goliath, the Philistine giant, came from Gath.

F. The Shephelah. The Shephelah, a strip of land 13 by 64 km. (8 by 40 mi.) between Philistia's coastal plain and the Judean hills, was a much-disputed territory. Its low-lying hills are mostly of chalk, which easily erodes to form passes and caves. The most important pass into the hills is the Valley of Ajalon, where Joshua said, "Sun, stand thou still upon Gibeon; and thou, Moon, in the valley of Ajalon" (Josh. 10:12).

Judah could have been quite isolated, except for the Philistines on the west. International roads crossed through Samaria, but the coastal plains insulated Judah's hills from the

12

THE GEOGRAPHY OF PALESTINE

PHILISTINE COAST. *This section of Palestine's Mediterranean coast is located near the ruins of the Philistine city Ashkelon. There are few natural seaports along this coast, which explains why ancient Israel never became a seafaring nation.*

THE GEOGRAPHY OF PALESTINE

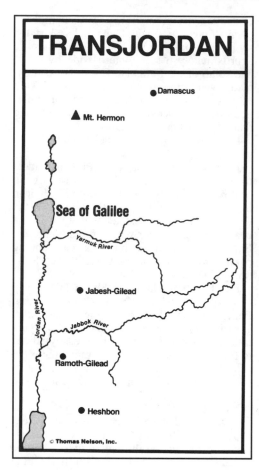

TRANSJORDAN

● Damascus

▲ Mt. Hermon

Sea of Galilee

Yarmuk River

Jordan River

● Jabesh-Gilead

Jabbok River

● Ramoth-Gilead

● Heshbon

© Thomas Nelson, Inc.

fense centers, then leads northward into the Valley of Elah. The other originates farther north at Ashdod, passes by Gath, and reaches the Valley of Elah after a journey of 32 km. (20 mi.). Merging in the valley, the roads continue northward via Beth-Horon and Gibeon to Michmash, an ancient outpost of the Philistines (1 Sam. 13:5). Saul's son Jonathan boldly routed the Philistine forces at the pass of Michmash, forcing them to retreat to the Valley of Ajalon (1 Sam. 14:1–31).

One of the most famous biblical dramas was staged in the Valley of Elah: "Now the Philistines gathered together their armies to battle, and they were gathered together at Shochoh, which belongeth to Judah, and pitched between Shochoh and Azekah, in Ephesdammim. And Saul and the men of Israel were gathered together, and pitched by the Valley of Elah, and set the battle in array against the Philistines. And the Philistines stood on a mountain on the one side, and Israel stood on a mountain on the other side: and there was a valley between them. And there went out a champion out of the camp of the Philistines, named Goliath . . ." (1 Sam. 17:1–4).

The newly anointed king, David, heard the challenge as he brought supplies to his brothers. Over the protests of his brothers and despite King Saul's reservations, David met Goliath. His only assurance was: "The Lord that delivered me out of the paw of the lion, and

Via Maris ("Road to the Sea") thoroughfare. Judah could easily check traffic on the road from Shechem to Jerusalem, and in times of war with Israel she simply closed the northern border. The Judean Desert to the east and the Negev Desert on the south helped isolate the southern kingdom.

But that vulnerable western front remained. The kings of Judah poured much effort and expense into strengthening the fortified cities of the Shephelah. It was Solomon's idea to flank Jerusalem with defense cities, such as Gezer and Beth-Horon (1 Kings 9:15–17). Rehoboam, Abijah, Asa, and Jehoshaphat also reinforced Judah's western frontier (2 Chron. 11:5–12, 23; 13:7; 14:6 f.; 17:1 ff.).

A modern traveler can still take one of the two roads that led from the domain of the five Philistine kings into the heart of Saul's kingdom in the Shephelah. One road passes through Lachish, one of Judah's military de-

WADI MUGHARA, MOUNT CARMEL.
The caves at this site contain evidence of human occupation during the Paleolithic period (before 800 B.C.). Mount Carmel is the name given to the main ridge of the Carmel range about 28 km. (12 mi.) inland from the Mediterranean Sea. Mount Carmel marked the border of Asher (Josh. 19:26).

THE ARABAH. *Derived from a Hebrew word meaning "steppe" or "desert," Arabah is the name given to the southern extension of the Jordan Valley. This depression extends more than 160 km. (100 mi.) from the Dead Sea to the Gulf of Aqaba.*

out of the paw of the bear, he will deliver me out of the hand of this Philistine" (17:37).

The first stone he slung felled the giant, and the Israelites chased the astonished Philistines all the way back to the coastal plains.

G. The Sharon and Carmel Coast. The Philistine territory ended at the Yarkon River, where the Plain of Sharon begins. Largest of the coastal plains, the Sharon reaches to the Crocodile River in the north.

Though it seemed to be too swampy and

QUMRAN CAVE. *The harsh landscape of the Judean Wilderness is evident in this photograph of caves at Qumran just northwest of the Dead Sea and about 13 km. (8 mi.) south of Jericho. In these caves, archaeologists found the Dead Sea Scrolls, one of the greatest discoveries of biblical archaeology in this century.*

shrub-filled to be much good for human settlement, the Sharon Valley was quite fertile, according to the Old Testament. The region was best suited for pasturage (Isa. 65:10), and in it the "rose of Sharon" grew wild (Song of Sol. 2:1). Isaiah spoke of the "majesty of Carmel and Sharon" (Isa. 35:2). Perhaps the Israelites regarded the extensive swamps of the Sharon much as we today value America's wilderness regions.

A few cities dotted the Plain: Shocho (1 Kings 4:10), Gilgal (Josh. 10:7), Aphek, Gathrimmon, Lod, and Ono (1 Chron. 8:12). A small harbor at Dor provided international contacts for the Canaanites.

H. The Plain of Asher. According to the prophetess Deborah, the tribe of Asher "continued on the seashore, and abode in his breeches" (Judg. 5:17b). This small plain hugs the coast above the Plain of Sharon. For the most part, the Asher Valley is about five miles wide, though it widens south of the port of Accho (modern Acre). At the north end, the mountains of Galilee almost touch the sea, leaving a narrow passage to Phoenicia known as the Ladder of Tyre.

Because of its strategic location between Phoenicia and Egypt, the plain was important to commerce. In times of peace, the tribe of Asher enjoyed cultural prosperity, but during wars it suffered devastation.

VIII. The Dead Sea. The lowest body of water in the world is the Dead Sea, an oblong lake three-fourths as long as the Jordan Valley north of it. Eighty km. (50 mi.) in length, it does not measure more than 18 km. (11 mi.) at

THE GEOGRAPHY OF PALESTINE

the widest; across from the Lisan Peninsula it narrows to 3 km. (2 mi.) or less.

The water surface of the Dead Sea is about 390 m. (1,300 ft.) below sea level. Its depth has been estimated at another 1,300 feet.

Tourists enjoy floating on the incredibly buoyant water of the Dead Sea. Because the sea has no outlet and evaporation is high, the concentration of minerals is as much as 30 percent. The water abounds with salt, bromide, magnesium chloride, potassium chloride, and sulfur. Modern Israelis mine the chemical salts of the rich waters for potash, bromine, and other industrial chemicals.

Long ago the Dead Sea was part of a huge inland lake that covered the Jordan Rift from the Hula Valley southward. A salt rock at Mount Sedom (at the southwest corner of the Dead Sea) and the *qattara* of the Jordan Valley are signs that eroding soil made the ancient lake more salty.

The level of the Dead Sea is dropping. In recent times both Israel and Jordan have diverted huge quantities of water from the Sea of Galilee and the Yarmuk River, so less water flows into it. At one time it was convenient to cross the Dead Sea by the Lisan Peninsula, where the water was about three feet deep. The water level has since dropped so much that only a narrow canal separates the western shore from the widening Lisan.

The third hottest temperature on world record (72°C. or 129°F.) was taken in this area on June 21, 1942. You would think no one would want to live where temperatures are so high, precipitation perhaps 5 cm. (2 in.) per year, and the scenery so bleak. Yet people have settled in the Dead Sea region from ancient times.

When Abraham and Lot went their separate ways, this region appeared fertile and desirable to Lot. Unfortunately for Lot, he moved into bad company. "But the men of Sodom were wicked and sinners before the Lord exceedingly" (Gen. 13:13). The tragic fate of Sodom and her sister city Gomorrah has been recalled by preachers from the Old Testament prophets down to the present day.

Archaeologists speculate that Sodom and Gomorrah were located in the southern portion of the Dead Sea. When the Lord reduced them to rubble because of their wickedness (Gen. 19), an earthquake probably dropped the land on which they stood and the waters of the Dead Sea inundated the debris.

In the midst of the Judean wasteland bordering the Dead Sea, the oases of En-gedi and Ein-Faschka provide food and springs of fresh water. Remains of an ancient temple show there was a settlement there as early as 4000 B.C. David and his men hid from Saul at En-gedi (1 Sam. 24:1). The Song of Solomon speaks of "a cluster of camphire blossoms in the vineyards of En-gedi" (Song of Sol. 1:14).

Near Ein-Faschka is the site of Qumran, where the Dead Sea scrolls were found in 1947. During Jesus' time, this Essene community believed that they were the righteous remnant, sole heirs to God's covenant. They interpreted literally Isaiah's words: "The voice of him that crieth in the wilderness, Prepare ye the way of the Lord, make straight in the desert a highway for our God" (Isa. 40:3). Separating themselves for this purpose, they awaited the Lord's coming in the desert. The sweet waters at Ein-Faschka permitted vegetation to grow, supplying the community's physical needs.

The fortress of Masada overlooks the Dead Sea from the rocky Judean wilderness farther south. There the last Jewish forces of the Great Revolt took their own lives in A.D. 73, rather than submit to Rome's rule.

The Dead Sea region is aptly named. Even fish struggle against being carried into the sea, for its high mineral content brings immediate death. Yet the oases are a vivid reminder of

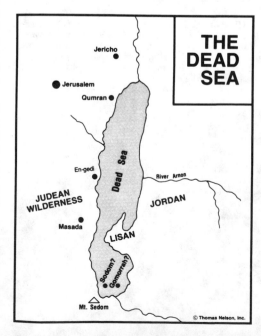

THE GEOGRAPHY OF PALESTINE

how beautiful the region could be if the lake contained sweet water.

The prophet Ezekiel envisioned the restoration of the Dead Sea valley. In his vision, water poured forth from the temple altar and flowed into the Kidron through the Judean wilderness to the Dead Sea (Ezek. 47:8–12). Revelation 22:1–5 tells of a strikingly similar vision.

IX. The Transjordan. The term *Transjordan* means "on the other side of the Jordan," and in its widest sense this area includes all the land east of the Jordan River to the vast Syrian Desert. The area takes in the land east of the Upper Jordan Valley as well as that east and southeast of the Dead Sea—and everything in between. Today it includes the nations of Lebanon and Israel, and the Gaza Strip.

From a high vantage point in Palestine, the mountains of Transjordan seem to jump from the valley floor. Higher than Palestine's mountains (though no less bleak), their western rim gently runs down to the plateau of the desert.

Canyon-like riverbeds, running east and west, marked the divisions of tribal territory in Transjordan.

Bashan is the northern area between the Hermon and Yarmuk Rivers; Gilead lies between the Yarmuk and Jabbok. Next comes the land of the Ammonites (partly shared with the Moabites), whose southern border was the Arnon River. Moab extended from the Arnon to the Zered River. Finally, Edom stretched from the Zered to the Red Sea's Gulf of Eilat and the modern port of Aqaba.

A. Bashan. Bashan is the biblical name for an area that includes one of the modern world's political "hot spots," the Golan Heights, from which Syria shelled Ein Gev, precipitating Israel's Six-Day War in June 1967. This highly-coveted district follows the eastern side of the Upper Jordan Valley for about 64 km. (40 mi.), almost to Damascus.

In New Testament times, Herod the Great made Bashan's wheatlands the granary of the Near East. Even in the Old Testament era, the rich soil of this well-watered tract produced grain aplenty. Animal husbandry flourished, and the huge bulls and well-fed cows of Bashan were known far and wide. Exiled in the land of the Chaldeans, the prophet Ezekiel spoke of the "fatlings of Bashan" (Ezek. 39:18). Amos railed against the noblewomen of Samaria, calling them "cows of Bashan, who are in the mountain of Samaria, who op-

VOLCANIC POOLS. *Just northeast of Capernaum, in the valleys that lace the Golan Heights, the volcanic pool of Berekhat Ha Meshushim reminds visitors of Palestine's geological origins. This natural swimming pool is surrounded by pentagonal lava formations. A cool mountain stream brings fresh water to the pool, which is a striking contrast to the barren hills around it.*

press the poor, who crush the needy, who say to their husbands, 'Bring, that we may drink!' " (Amos 4:1, RSV). The Psalmist compared his enemies to the powerful beasts: "Many bulls have encompassed me: strong bulls of Bashan have beset me round" (Psa. 22:12).

Mighty oaks grew in Bashan. Isaiah mentioned "all the cedars of Lebanon . . . all the oaks of Bashan" (Isa. 2:13). Though Lebanon's cedars were more highly prized than Bashan's oaks, the Israelites used the timber and even exported it. According to Ezekiel, the oaks of Bashan were used to make oars for Phoenician ships (Ezek. 27:6).

Ten cities in southern Bashan and northern Gilead organized to form the *Decapolis* mentioned in Matthew 4:25, as well as Mark 5:20 and 7:31. Each city was a strategic point in the political division of the region. Hippos, for instance, controlled the road to Damascus, for which Paul was heading to persecute early Christians when he was converted (Acts 9:3). Today that road overlooks the modern kibbutz of Ein Gev near the Sea of Galilee.

For the most part, Bashan is unlike the rest of Transjordan. It is a high country, with mountains rising ever higher to the east. In the north, dense foliage pushes back the desert, compared to a narrow strip of cultivated land south of the Yarmuk River. Most of the Bashan gets rain or snow.

The Lower Golan (i.e., southern Bashan) starts at the eastern shore of Galilee, below sea level. Not far from the lake, barren hills rise steeply to a plateau about 400 m. (1,600 ft.) above the Sea of Galilee. In recent years, Syrian gunners trained their weapons on Israeli forces from that shelf. The Lower Golan held a prosperous Jewish community in New Testament times.

The Upper Golan is breathtaking, with exalted cone-shaped peaks and craters of extinct volcanoes. Erosion of the basalt soil has made a good grazing land. Less rain—3 to 3.5 cm. (12 to 14 inches)—falls on the plateau to the southeast, which was called Argob in the Old Testament. Moses reminded the Israelites that he led them to Bashan: "So the Lord our God delivered into our hands Og also, the king of Bashan, and all his people: . . . And we took all his cities at that time, there was not a city which we took not from them, threescore cities, all the region of Argob, the kingdom of Og in Bashan" (Deut. 3:3-4; cf. Deut. 3:13; 1 Kings 4:13; Num. 21:33).

Still farther east is the Hauran, which Ezekiel included as part of the northeastern boundary of Israel (Ezek. 47:16, 18). The Hauran is jagged terrain, once having been the center of volcanic activity. Jebel Druz, the mountain of the Arabic-speaking Druze sect, pierces the sky at 1,500 m. (5,000 ft.). This rugged country made an ideal hideout for robber bands, and later was a refuge for the persecuted Druze. Yet the area has enough moisture and good soil to grow crops.

Herod the Great took control of Bashan as early as 20 B.C., and left it to his son, Herod Philip, as an inheritance. Philip built up Caesarea Philippi as his capital, naming it in honor of the Caesar as well as himself. The province was given to Agrippa I in A.D. 37.

B. Gilead. The mountains of Gilead are an eastern counterpart to the hill country of Samaria, and the landscape, vegetation, and climate are somewhat similar. However, the eastern mountains rise higher: 1,000 to 1,200 m. (3,281 to 3,937 ft.) as compared wit Mount Hebron's 990 m. (3,300 ft.). They also receive more rainfall, 75 cm. (30 in.) per year, instead of the 50 cm. (20 in.) per annum of Palestine.

A person who visits Gilead after being in Palestine is usually surprised at the many springs, villages, and shrub-covered hillsides.

GOLAN HEIGHTS. *A scene of modern conflicts between the Israelis and Arabs, the Golan Heights is a tableland east-northeast of the Sea of Galilee. In Old Testament times it was part of the inheritance of Manasseh.*

The visitor might also be surprised to learn that the famous "balm of Gilead" was not just a spiritual cure for the sin-sick soul. The ancient people used to export the "balm of Gilead"—probably tiny balls of sap from slashed evergreen trees—used for medicinal purposes. Joseph was sold to a caravan from Gilead, on its way to Egypt with "camels bearing spicery and balm and myrrh" (Gen. 37:25).

Gilead is an oval dome roughly split in two by the Jabbok River. The half-tribe of Manasseh settled northern Gilead, which was covered with thick brushwood and oaks. The

HILLS OF GILEAD. *Gilead was the hilly wooded country north of Heshbon and the Dead Sea. The hills flatten out into plains about 29 km. (18 mi.) south of Yarmuk and their northern extension forms the territory of Bashan. In its widest application the term Gilead can include all of Israel Transjordan.*

more mountainous southern Gilead was allocated to Reuben. The high amount of precipitation, plus heavy dew in summer, produced lush growth. Year-round tributaries of the Yarmuk and Jordan rivers drained the excess water.

Several judges of Israel were natives of Gilead. Jair ruled Israel for 22 years from Camon, his home in northern Gilead. The judge Jephthah was the son of Gilead, but his mother was a harlot, so his step-brothers refused him a share of the inheritance. He fled to the land of Tob, where he formed a band of raiders. Later his brothers recalled his prowess as a warrior, and promised him the leadership of Gilead if he would lead their army against the Ammonites. Jephthah's forces attacked and defeated the Ammonites (Judg. 11:32).

For the most part, the Ammonites left the Israelites alone until the days of Saul. As Saul was about to assume the reign of Israel, an unsavory character named Nahash besieged the city of Jabesh-gilead. The inhabitants offered to serve him under a treaty, but he would agree only if they allowed him to gouge out their eyes! And Saul gathered the forces of Judah and Samaria to go to their rescue (1 Sam. 11:1–11). The people of Jabesh-gilead never forgot this act of kindness: "And when the inhabitants of Jabesh-gilead heard of that which the Philistines had done to Saul; All the valiant men arose, and went all night, and took the body of Saul and the bodies of his sons from the wall of Beth-shean, and came to Jabesh and burnt them there. And they took their bones, and buried them under a tree at Jabesh, and fasted seven days" (1 Sam. 31:11–13).

Elijah the prophet also came from Gilead (1 Kings 17:1), bringing God's word to Israel's King Ahab. During a three-year famine, he stayed by the brook Cherith in Gilead, where the water refreshed him and ravens brought food (1 Kings 17:3 ff.). When his earthly ministry was finished, Elijah again crossed the Jordan into Gilead, where God's chariots snatched him up in a whirlwind (2 Kings 2:8 ff.).

C. Perea. Looking at a map of the New Testament era, we would see the names *Perea* and *Decapolis* on the area of Gilead. Decapolis was roughly equivalent to northern Gilead. Multitudes followed Jesus from this region, which extended to both sides of the Jordan River (Matt. 4:25).

"Beyond the Jordan" referred to Perea, a

PETRA'S ARCHITECTURE. *The rose-red city of Petra is one of the most unusual sites in the territory of Edom. This Nabataean town was carved from sheer sandstone rock cliffs around 300 B.C. The photograph shows a detail from the Petran structure which local Arabs call El Deir Monastery.*

province bordering the Jordan River on the southeast. This was the territory of Herod Antipas, who had John the Baptist beheaded (Mark 6:14–29).

It was customary for Jews to avoid Samaria, so on His way to Jerusalem, Jesus generally crossed the Jordan to Perea. Opposite Jericho He crossed back over by fording the Jordan or taking a ferry, then continued His journey through the Judean wilderness to Jerusalem.

D. Ammon. Ammon is a vast grassland between the desert on the east and the green mountains of Gilead on the west. The mountains level off into a plateau, and since Ammon has no high mountains, there is little rainfall. But at Rabbah, "the city of waters" (2 Sam. 12:27), springs gush forth to make the beginnings of the Jabbok River. The well-watered areas of Ammon could be cultivated, but it was best suited for pasture. Ezekiel once prophesied that Rabbah would become "a stable for camels, and the Ammonites a couching place for flocks . . ." (Ezek. 25:5).

E. Moab. Moab was another high pastureland. The 3,000-foot plateau bordering the Dead Sea between the Arnon and Zered rivers was partially planted in wheat and barley. Moab's King Mesha was a sheep breeder who paid a large tribute to King Ahab of Israel. After years of this, he rebelled against Ahab's successor, Jehoram (2 Kings 3:4–5).

The cities just north of the Arnon River—Dibon (modern Dhiban) and Aroer—were Moab's outposts. But the Moabites wanted the northern tableland of Heshbon and Medeba.

THE GEOGRAPHY OF PALESTINE

Moses told of a time when Sihon, king of Heshbon, had pushed the Moabites back to the Arnon: "For there is a fire gone out of Heshbon, a flame from the city of Sihon: It hath consumed Ar of Moab, and the lords of the high places of Arnon. Woe to thee, Moab!" (Num. 21:28–29).

Eventually God gave Sihon's power into Israel's hand. When King Balak of Moab saw what had become of Sihon's Amorites, he panicked at the sight of the Israelites encamped below him in the plains of Moab. He sent for the diviner Balaam to come and curse the Israelites on his behalf, saying, "I know that he whom you bless is blessed, and he whom thou cursest is cursed" (Num. 22:6). But God told Balaam, "Thou shalt not curse the people: for they are blessed" (Num. 22:12). Though Balak was furious with Balaam for not doing as he asked, the invasion he feared did not come. Instead the Israelites settled down at Shittim and got into trouble by being overly friendly with the Moabites (num. 25:1–2).

In the days of the judges, a famine in Judah caused Elimelech and Naomi and their sons to sojourn in Moab (Ruth 1:1). The sons married Moabite women. After their husbands died, Naomi and her daughter-in-law, Ruth, returned to Bethlehem, Naomi's former home. Ruth then married Boaz and became the great-grandmother of King David.

Both the Ammonites and the Moabites coveted the fertile Jordan Valley. When the Israelites conquered the kingdoms of Sihon and Og, the Ammonites and Moabites retreated to the safety of their borders. But each time one nation weakened, another would try to expand. Thus Israel, Ammon, and Moab were a constant threat to each other.

The Ammonites and Moabites pressed hard on the Israelites during the period of the judges. Eglon of Moab penetrated beyond the Jordan as far as Jericho (Judg. 3:12–14). Later, when Israel sinned, the Lord "sold them into . . . the hand of the Ammonites" (Judg. 10:7), who oppressed both the Israelites in Gilead and those west of the Jordan—in Judah, Benjamin, and Ephraim.

King David turned the tables on the Ammonites, forcing them to work for him (2 Sam. 12:29–31). The Ammonites escaped the conquering Babylonians in 586 B.C., and they gloated as Judah was exiled to Babylonia (Ezek. 25:6). Time did not lessen the ancient animosity. When the Jews returned from exile and started to rebuild the walls of Jerusalem,

MOAB AND EDOM. *The land of Moab lay on the north (right) and the land of Edom to the south (left) of the Wadi Zered, which flows westward into the Dead Sea. The Edomites (descendants of Esau) inhabited a mountainous territory extending from the Zered to the Gulf of Aqaba. The descendants of Moab (a son of Lot) settled on the plateau east of the Dead Sea, between Wadi Zered and the Arnon River.*

Ammonites showed up to taunt the workmen (Neh. 4:1–9). The Tobiad family ruled the Ammonites from the fifth to the second century B.C., and they never did learn to like the Jews.

F. Edom. Edom was another name for Esau, son of Isaac and brother of Jacob (Gen. 25:30; cf. 32:3). Originally Esau went to live in the hills of Seir, southeast of the Dead Sea. The area came to be known by his name, and the people were called Edomites.

Edom also means "red," and speaks of the reddish color of the sandstone mountains in south Edom. Here we find Petra, the fabled "red-rose city." In the time of Christ, the Nabateans built the impenetrable fortress of Sela there, carving it from sandstone rocks. Visitors can see how these ancient people used the natural rocks of Edom for their protection. A narrow passage of steep rocks leads into Petra, and many of the caves they hollowed out and ornately decorated are well-preserved to this day.

The stark and imposing mountains of Edom are a radical change from the northern edge of Edom territory, the valley of Zered, as well as from the northern stretch of the King's Highway crossing the tableland of Moab. In Bible times, the northern cities of Tophel and Bozrah had more abundant vegetation. Their wood was sent south to make charcoal for the

THE GEOGRAPHY OF PALESTINE

copper smelters at Punon. Even today the village of Tofileh (Tophel) harvests fine olive groves.

The peaks of south Edom exceed 1,500 m. (5,000 ft.)—a composite of sandstone, basalt, and crystalline rocks. The 45 to 50 cm. (16 to 20 in.) of yearly precipitation sometimes includes snow. The resulting vegetation encouraged people to settle there in biblical times.

Edom and Judah contended fiercely for control of a very important highway junction near the port of Ezion-geber. Here the King's Highway from the northeast met the road to Egypt across the Sinai, and a third highway took caravans farther south, to Tema. Edom's economy hinged on access to this junction, but it was also valuable to Israel. Therefore the Israelites fought numerous battles attempting to subjugate Edom, Ammon, and Moab.

David did manage to conquer Edom (2 Sam. 8:13–14). Solomon extracted tribute from the Edomites, and they did not endanger his shipping ventures at Ezion-geber. But soon after Solomon's death they rebelled and shipping became unsafe. Later, King Jehoshaphat of Judah tried to send ships to Ophir for gold, but the ships were wrecked at Ezion-geber (1 Kings 22:48).

In further strife between the two peoples, the Edomites got the upper hand over Judah's King Jehoram (2 Kings 8:24) and King Ahaz (2 Kings 16:5–18). God may have permitted these nations to threaten Israel in order to force His people to depend on Him. With God's help, Israel would prosper and limit the conquests of her eastern neighbors.

12

THE GEOGRAPHY OF PALESTINE

THE MINERALS AND GEMS OF PALESTINE

Bible writers tell us the Israelites found a wide variety of minerals and precious stones in the Promised Land. They used these resources for building, jewelry, and fine crafts. In fact, these minerals became vital to Israel's export business. (*See* "Trade.")

I. CONSTRUCTION MATERIALS
    A. Hewn Stone
    B. Bricks
    C. Mortar and Plaster

II. METALS
    A. Gold
    B. Silver
    C. Iron
    D. Lead
    E. Tin
    F. Copper

III. GEMS AND PRECIOUS STONES
    A. "Adamant"
    B. Agate
    C. Alabaster
    D. Amber
    E. Amethyst
    F. Beryl
    G. Carbuncle
    H. Chrysolite
    I. Chrysoprasus
    J. Coral
    K. Crystal
    L. Diamond
    M. Emerald
    N. Jacinth
    O. Jasper
    P. Ligure
    Q. Onyx
    R. Pearl
    S. Ruby
    T. Sapphire
    U. "Sardine"
    V. Sardonyx
    W. Topaz

IV. OTHER MINERALS
    A. Brimstone
    B. Flint
    C. Nitre
    D. Salt

I. Construction Materials. Building projects consumed the largest quantity of Israel's mineral resources, but we have no evidence that the Hebrews ran short of mineral supplies. They used the most easily available minerals for building.

A. Hewn Stone. Most Israelites lived in houses built of hewn stone. (*See* "Architecture and Furniture.") The prophet Amos tells us that even the wealthy preferred "houses of hewn stone" (Amos 5:11), and Solomon used stone for the temple in Jerusalem (1 Kings 5:17; 7:12). Many kinds of building stone were available in Palestine, but it seems that marble and cheaper grades of limestone were most popular. Even in New Testament times, stone was the most common building material in the Holy Land, and Peter referred to Christians as "lively stones" in the structure that Christ built (1 Pet. 2:4–5).

The patriarchs gathered field stones to erect monuments and altars of worship (Gen. 35:14; Josh. 4:4–7). These landmarks lasted for many generations (cf. Gen. 35:20; Josh. 4:9).

True marble is a fine grade of limestone that will take a high polish. When the Bible refers to "marble," it most often means common limestone, which was more plentiful in Palestine. But in some cases it probably means true marble, as in God's plan for the temple (1 Chron. 29:2). Builders used different colors of marble to make mosaics and terrazzo floors, as in the palace of the Persian King at Shushan (Esther 1:6).

B. Bricks. Baked clay bricks were the Israelites' second favorite building material. The Bible first mentions brick in the construction of the Tower of Babel. There the builders said to one another, "Go to, let us make brick, and burn them thoroughly" (Gen. 11:3). So we think the builders baked their bricks in kilns, as the ancient Babylonians did. Archaeologists have found Babylonian bricks that were quite large, sometimes 30 cm. (about one foot) square, and flat. This shape could support the weight of large buildings better than today's rectangular bricks. Researchers think some of the early Israelite bricks may have followed this Babylonian pattern.

THE MINERALS AND GEMS OF PALESTINE

BRICK MAKING. *The Israelites probably made bricks much the same way as the worker shown here. A wooden frame is still used to form the wet clay into a brick, which is then dried in the sun. Scholars believe that some Israelites dried their bricks in kilns.*

Clay was plentiful in Palestine, and the Hebrews used it for various jobs besides brickmaking; for example, they fashioned it into pottery and lamps. But the Hebrews molded clay bricks by the thousands, usually baking them in the sun. These bricks did not last as long as hewn stone. To make clay bricks more durable, kings and wealthy householders hardened them in charcoal-fired kilns (cf. Nah. 3:14). The Book of Exodus tells us how the Egyptians forced their Hebrew slaves to make bricks for the pharaoh (Exod. 5:6–7). No doubt the Hebrews taught this skill to their descendants, who entered the Promised Land.

C. Mortar and Plaster. The Hebrews often used "pitch" as mortar for their stone work. Pitch was asphalt, which the Hebrews dug from tar pits around the Dead Sea. The Bible also calls soft asphalt "slime" (Gen. 14:10). "Pitch" or "slime" exposed to the air for several days hardened to form a tight, resilient bond between the stones of Hebrew buildings. The Israelites also used pitch to seal their boats and fuel their torches (cf. Gen. 6:14; Exod. 2:3). The Egyptians used it to coat the linen wrappings of embalmed corpses, in order to keep out moisture.

The Israelites burned limestone, shells, and other materials to make lime for brick mortar. Isaiah said the wicked would be "as the burnings of lime" (Isa. 33:12), and Amos tells us that the Moabites "burned the bones of the king of Edom into lime" (Amos 2:1). So we are sure the ancients understood how to make lime. They mixed lime with clay and other materials to make a simple form of mortar. When they mixed these ingredients poorly, their "untempered mortar" crumbled very quickly (cf. Ezek. 13:10–11).

Sand was not as plentiful for the ancients as we might suppose. Most of Palestine was covered with coarse gravel and dust; sand was found only along riverbanks and the seacoast—but the Philistines controlled most of the coast. Yet the Israelites dredged sand from the Kishon River near Accho and other sites to make mortar, glass, and other products.

II. Metals. The Bible names only six metals as known to the Israelites: gold, silver, iron, lead, tin, and copper (also called "steel"). Although archaeologists have uncovered a wide variety of metal objects in Palestine, we have little evidence of mining operations there. Palestinians probably found metal ore along riverbeds and exposed areas of rock, or dug shallow trenches where metal-bearing minerals lay near the surface. The Israelites traded precious metals for farm products and other goods.

A. Gold. Gold was the heaviest metal known to the Israelites, and the easiest to shape into intricate artistic designs. The Egyptians had large quantities of gold. Classical historian Walafrid Strabo (A.D. 808–849) noted that the Nabateans, who inhabited Moab and Edom, mined gold along the Sinai peninsula. The Bible says the Israelites bought gold from Ophir and Parvaim (which may have

THE MINERALS AND GEMS OF PALESTINE

been in India—1 Chron. 29:4; 2 Chron. 3:6), as well as from Sheba and Raamah, which were probably on the southern coast of Arabia (Ezek. 27:22).

Despite being scarce, gold was widely used in building Solomon's temple (1 Kings 7:48–50), in decorating the homes of the kings (1 Kings 10:17–22), and in making jewelry. Gold displayed its owner's prestige or royal power (Dan. 5:29; James 2:2).

Gold ore usually has impurities of other metals, which lend their characteristic color (e.g., copper impurities make yellow gold). Metalworkers in biblical times did not know how to remove these impurities, so they tested gold by rubbing it across a black stone called a *touchstone* and observing the color of its mark. Zechariah suggests this when he describes how God will test His people (Zech. 13:9).

B. Silver. The Israelites imported silver from several countries, but most of it came from "Tarshish"—possibly the town of Tartessus in southern Spain (1 Kings 10:22; 2 Chron. 9:21). Amazing as it seems, the Bible says King Solomon imported so much silver for the temple project that he "made silver to be in Jerusalem as stones" (1 Kings 10:27),

GOLD HELMET. *Hammered from a single piece of metal, this gold helmet (twenty-fifth century B.C.) was found in a tomb in Ur. Fragments of cloth and wool stuffing suggest that the helmet was fitted with a quilted cap for comfort. The inner cap was probably held in place by laces threaded through the small holes around the rim of the helmet.*

and he refused to make any of his drinking cups of silver because "it was nothing accounted of" (1 Kings 10:21)!

Because silver does not combine easily with other metals, it is easy to recognize in its natural state. Even the patriarchs prized it as a valuable commodity, and Genesis says that "Abram was very rich in cattle, in silver, and in gold" (Gen. 13:2). The Israelites used silver to decorate the tabernacle and the temple (Exod. 26:19; 1 Chron. 28:14–17), to make trumpets (Num. 10:2), and to make idols in their decadent days (Isa. 40:19).

Merchants carried silver pieces as a common medium of trade; as a matter of fact, the Old Testament often uses the Hebrew word for silver (*keseph*) to mean "money." Even in Abraham's day, the value of property was determined in silver (Gen. 23:15–16). However, Israel did not make silver coins until after the Exile; early traders simply used standard bits of silver. (*See* "Trade.")

C. Iron. This was the most plentiful of the heavy metals the Hebrews learned to use. Genesis 4:22 says that Tubal-cain was the "instructor of every artificer in brass and iron," so iron was being used even before the age of the patriarchs. The Hebrew word for iron was *barzel.*

Scripture emphasizes the abundance of iron ore in Palestine, where the "stones are iron" (Deut. 8:9). Jeremiah suggests that the "northern iron"—perhaps from the mountains of Lebanon—was stronger than the iron from other regions of the Near East (Jer. 15:12).

We know the Israelites had iron tools when they entered Canaan, for God instructed them not to use iron instruments to build the altar of the tabernacle (Deut. 27:5). They made iron axe heads (2 Kings 6:5–6), spear tips (1 Sam. 17:7), harrows (2 Sam. 12:31), and other tools and weapons. Iron technology gave the Israelites' enemies an advantage in war. The Israelites complained to Joshua that "all the Canaanites that dwell in the land of the valley have chariots of iron" (Josh. 17:16). The Israelites rapidly mastered skills with iron, but did not learn how to make steel. When the KJV mentions "steel," it means bronze, an alloy of copper and tin (e.g., Psa. 18:34).

D. Lead. This heavy white metal was familiar to the people of Old Testament days. They used it to purify silver in crude furnaces (Jer. 6:29) and to strengthen alloys of other metals (Ezek. 22:20). When Job wished that his works "were graven with an iron pen and

THE MINERALS AND GEMS OF PALESTINE

Minerals in the Dead Sea

The sparkling blue waters of the Dead Sea contain a high concentration of minerals. Rivers and streams flowing over the land near the Dead Sea dissolve salts from the soil and deposit them into the sea. The fresh water evaporates, leaving the chemicals in the sea and making it the saltiest body of water on earth. The Dead Sea concentration of mineral salts is nine times saltier than that of the oceans.

The minerals in the Dead Sea include the chlorides of sodium (salt), magnesium, potassium, calcium, and magnesium bromide. The presence of bituminous material in the sea has been known since ancient times. These lumps of bitumen, found floating on the surface, provide evidence of petroleum springs in the sea bed.

Ancient Hebrews enjoyed an unlimited supply of salt. They formed brine pits called "salt-pans" along the Dead Sea's flat coastal area. The sun evaporated the water in the pits, leaving behind an abundant supply of mineral salts.

Salt was the chief economic product of the ancient world, and the Hebrews used it in a variety of ways: for flavoring foods, preserving fish, curing meat, and pickling olives and vegetables. Salt was an ingredient in the sacred anointing oil and ritual sacrifices. Infants were rubbed in salt to insure good health before swaddling (Ezek. 16:4). Salt was believed to have been an antidote for tooth decay and was considered a treatment for toothache. The modern Jewish custom of laying meat in salt, to drain it of blood, was no doubt observed in Bible times. The use of salt in every sacrifice symbolized God's perpetual covenant with Israel (Num. 18:19).

Today only five percent of the world's salt is used for seasoning. Many other chemicals are derived from salt, such as lye and chlorine. Lye is used to make soap, paper, rayon, and to purify petroleum, while chlorine is used to whiten paper, and to purify water.

Modern Israelis extract large amounts of mineral resources from the Dead Sea. A network of dikes form shallow pools over 100 sq. km. (40 sq. mi.) of the sea. As the temperature in the area sometimes rises to 125° F, the water evaporates, leaving chemical salts that are manufactured into potash for fertilizer and magnesium bromide for drugs, ethyl gasoline, and many other products. Jordan extracts only a small percentage of the minerals in the Dead Sea, and exports 70 percent of its output to other Arab countries.

lead in the rock for ever" (Job 19:24), he referred to the practice of pouring molten lead into inscriptions in rock, to make them more easily readable. The Egyptians believed this metal had mystical powers, so they sometimes buried an embalmed corpse with a plate of lead on its chest.

E. Tin. Archaeologists have discovered many objects made of bronze scattered across the Near Eastern world. However, only small amounts of tin ore, used to make this alloy, were available in the Near East. The best supplies of tin ore were in Britain, Spain, and India. Ezekiel 27:12 tells us the Israelites got their tin from Tarshish; Tarshish may in turn have gotten its tin from Britain.

The Hebrews used tin in Moses' time (Num. 31:22). They called it *bedhit*. The prophets knew of the process of smelting tin with other metals to make strong alloys (Ezek. 22:20).

F. Copper. Ezra tells us that this versatile metal was "precious as gold" when the Israelites returned from the Exile (Ezra 8:27). Copper was used to make brass and bronze and was known in the biblical world as early as the time of Tubal-cain (Gen. 4:22).

The Hebrew word for copper was *nechosheth*. The King James Version sometimes translates this word as "brass" when copper is clearly meant, as when God promised to lead His people into Canaan, "out of whose hills thou mayest dig brass" (Deut. 8:9).

Although the Israelites had a good supply of copper ore, they did not master the skills of refining it and shaping it. Thus, Solomon had to depend on Phoenician craftsmen to make copper furnishings for the temple (1 Kings 7:14 ff.).

III. Gems and Precious Stones. The Israelites valued precious stones much as we do today. The Bible often links precious stones with the architecture of the temple (2 Chron. 3:6; 9:10), and John saw the heavenly Jerusalem "garnished" with them (Rev. 21:19).

Jewelers of Bible times used vague terms to describe their stones, and this causes some confusion. They might call any hard stone an "adamant," and any clear stone "crystal." They might switch the names of stones with similar colors. Or they might use names we no longer understand. So when we study the gems of the Bible, we must admit some mystery still shrouds the subject.

For example, Exodus 28:15–22 describes

THE MINERALS AND GEMS OF PALESTINE

the breastplate worn by the high priest, which had four rows of precious stones. Each stone bore the name of one of the tribes of Israel, "like the engravings of a signet" (v. 21). Because the Israelites did not know how to engrave the hardest gems, it is doubtful whether the breastplate really held a diamond, sapphire, emerald, and topaz. We feel it is more likely these terms refer to softer stones, such as chalcedony, lapis lazuli, garnet, and chrysolite.

The Bible mentions over 20 gems and precious stones, which we will discuss in alphabetical order:

A. "Adamant." As we have already noted, this word refers to any number of hard gems. It comes from the negative form of the Greek word *damazō,* which means "to subdue" or "to crush"; so adamant signifies something that cannot be broken. The Hebrew word behind this is *shamir,* which literally means "a thorn." It is the same word Israelites used to denote a diamond.

Ezekiel said, "As an adamant harder than flint have I made thy forehead . . ." (Ezek. 3:9). Zechariah said that his rebellious people "made their hearts [as hard] as an adamant stone" (Zech. 7:12). Clearly the adamant stood for toughness and hardness, even though we do not know what specific gem(s) it identifies.

B. Agate. The King James Version uses this word to translate two Hebrew words— *cadcod* and *shebo.* The first word occurs in Isaiah 54:12 and Ezekiel 27:16, and it literally means "ruddy" or "reddish." German scholar Wilhelm Gesenius (1786–1842) believed it actually refers to the ruby, and most Bible interpreters follow this idea. The second word (*shebo*) occurs in Exodus 28:19 and 39:12, and it probably refers to the true agate.

This stone is a form of chalcedony, with stripes or layers in various shades of black, brown, or blue. It can be polished to a high gloss, making it a favorite decorative material of architects in biblical times. The second

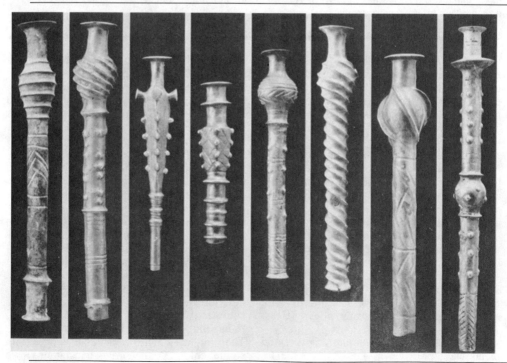

COPPER WANDS. *About 80 copper wands were found in the "Cave of the Treasure" in 1961 at Nahal Mishmar in Palestine. These objects date from the end of the fourth millennium B.C. Copper ore was plentiful in Israel, although the Israelites did not learn to refine it until after the reign of Solomon. The word brass in the King James Version probably refers to copper, instead of the alloy developed at a later time.*

THE MINERALS AND GEMS OF PALESTINE

BREASTPLATE OF HIGH PRIEST. *This is a replica of the high priest's breastplate (cf. Exod. 28:15–21), which was set with stones representing the 12 tribes of Israel. The name of a tribe was engraved on each stone.*

stone of the third row in the high priest's breastplate was an agate (Exod. 28:19).

C. Alabaster. This white mineral is easy to carve and polish, so Israelites used it to make beautiful jars and vases. Two varieties of alabaster are found in the Near East: one is a pure form of gypsum; the other a reddish marble. The first kind crumbles too easily to be used for carving. The second kind has colorful markings and is partially transparent, so it appeals to the eye.

Archaeologists have recovered alabaster jars from Greek, Kanan, Egyptian, and Assyrian ruins. Ancient traders often sealed costly perfume in an alabaster jar, allowing the scent to escape only gradually through the jar's porous shell over many years. Greek poet Theocritus (third century B.C.) reports that the merchants of Palestine used alabaster jars in the same way. This explains why Jesus' disciples rebuked the woman who broke an alabaster vessel of perfume and poured the perfume upon Jesus' head (Mark 14:3). The disciples felt the precious scent could have been sold for money to give to the poor. Shortly after Jesus' time, the Romans and Greeks called any thin-necked vial an *alabastron,* or "alabaster," because that was the familiar shape of alabaster perfume jars. Some Bible commentators believe that when the

woman opened the jar over Jesus' head, she broke the neck of such a vial.

D. Amber. This is the fossilized resin of trees. Deep yellow or orange in color, amber could be polished to a high luster. Our English versions use this word to translate the Hebrew *hashmal,* which probably was some kind of metal. The Septuagint and the Latin Vulgate take *hashmal* to mean electrum, the shiny alloy of silver and gold. So when the Bible mentions "the color of amber" (Ezek. 1:4, 27; 8:2), it may mean a bright silvery hue, rather than the orange or yellow color we associate with amber.

E. Amethyst. Westerners know amethyst as a rare variety of quartz, a six-sided purple crystal that is hard enough to scratch glass. But the people of the Near East are better acquainted with amethyst as a deep purple or violet form of corundum. The Hebrew word for it is *achlamah,* which may come from the stone's mythical ability to cause dreams (Hebrew, *halam*—"dream"). An amethyst was the third stone in the third row of the high priest's breastplate (Exod. 28:19), and John saw that the twelfth layer of the wall of New Jerusalem was amethyst (Rev. 21:20).

F. Beryl. The Hebrew word for this stone was *tarshish,* perhaps because this gem was imported from the city of Tarshish. We know the beryl of biblical times as *aquamarine;* it is a yellow, green, or bluish crystal (depending on the chemical impurities in the gem). A beryl was the tenth stone in the fourth row of the high priest's breastplate (Exod. 28:20). The wheels of Ezekiel's vision and the man of Daniel's vision were the color of beryl (Ezek. 1:16; Dan. 10:6). Solomon and the King of Tyre wore jewelry of beryl (Song of Sol. 5:14; Ezek. 28:13), and other wealthy people prized this stone for its brilliance and vivid color.

G. Carbuncle. The King James Version uses this word to translate two Hebrew words: *ekdāch,* which literally means "fiery glow," and *bārkath,* which means "flashing" or "sparking." Exodus 28:17 and 39:10 use carbuncle to name a jewel in the first row of the high priest's breastplate, but it may refer to any sparkling gem. The first word designates the deep red color we find in the true carbuncle. This word occurs in Isaiah 54:12, where the prophet describes the "gates of carbuncles" of New Jerusalem.

H. Chrysolite. John says that the seventh foundation of New Jerusalem was made of

THE MINERALS AND GEMS OF PALESTINE

chrysolite—a golden yellow stone we feel may have been the same as the "beryl" of the Old Testament (Rev. 21:20). This stone was a yellow topaz or sardonyx.

I. Chrysoprasus. This grass-green gem formed the ninth foundation of New Jerusalem in John's vision (Rev. 21:20). Mineral experts believe it was the same basic crystal as the chrysolite, but with nickel impurities that gave its greenish cast. The Septuagint stated that the Garden of Eden had gold, bdellium, and "chrysoprase" (Gen. 2:12); but later versions translate that word (*shoham*) as "onyx stone" or "beryl."

J. Coral. The merchants of Tyre sold coral to the wealthy people of Syria (Ezek. 27:16), who polished it for use in fine jewelry and inlaid work on buildings. Coral is the brilliant reddish or orange skeleton of sea animals, which forms reefs in the Mediterranean and other warm seas. It can be cut and polished like inorganic stone. The Old Testament uses two words for coral: *râmôth,* which refers to coral in a general sense (Ezek. 27:16), and *peninim,* which refers to red coral (Job 28:18).

K. Crystal. Rock crystal is a completely transparent form of quartz. The Hebrew word for crystal (*gerach*) also means "frost" or "ice." The ancients thought crystal was only ice congealed by intense cold. They valued it highly for its great beauty. Crystal's clarity is suggested in Revelation 4:6; 21:11; 22:1. Ezekiel describes the heavenly firmament as "the terrible crystal" (1:22). This mineral's beauty has given rise to such expressions as "clear as crystal."

L. Diamond. Diamond is pure crystallized charcoal or carbon. It is named as the third precious stone in the second row of the high priest's breastplate (Exod. 28:18; 39:11). But many scholars feel that this stone in the breastplate should have been translated as onyx, and that diamond was intended by the word translated *jasper* (e.g., Exod. 28:20).

In biblical times all diamonds were brought from India. The ancients supposed diamonds were indestructible in fire—but we now know this is not true. Jeremiah tells us the diamond was used as an instrument for engraving on hard materials (Jer. 17:1).

M. Emerald. This crystal stone owes its chief value to its deep green color. The emerald is named as the first stone in the second row on the high priest's breastplate (Exod. 28:18; 39:11). Many biblical scholars feel, however, that this stone should have been

translated as "carbuncle." In any case, the ancients got emeralds from Cyprus, Egypt, and the mountains of Ethiopia. The emerald is mentioned in the description of the rainbow around God's throne (Rev. 4:3), and it makes up the fourth foundation of the walls of the heavenly Jerusalem (Rev. 21:19).

N. Jacinth. Biblical scholars have not had an easy time identifying this stone, which is mentioned in Revelation 21:20. Some historians consider it the same as amethyst; others link it with ligure (Exod. 28:19). Jacinth may have been a puce-red stone which came in brown and yellow varieties.

O. Jasper. Jasper is an opaque, impure variety of quartz that is mentioned in both the Old and New Testaments. Jasper comes in red, yellow, and some duller colors. When the colors are in stripes or bands, jasper is called striped quartz. As with a number of other precious stones mentioned in the Bible, scholars dispute whether modern jasper is meant in Scripture. But scholars agree that the Hebrew and Greek names (*yashpeh* and *iaspis*) have the same origin as our word *jasper.* Jasper was the third stone in the fourth row of Aaron's breastplate (Exod. 28:20). Revelation mentions jasper several times: He that sat upon the throne was "like a jasper and a sardine stone" (Rev. 4:3). (*See* "Sardine" below.) The light of the New Jerusalem appeared "like a jasper stone" (Rev. 21:11). And the first of the New Jerusalem's 12 foundations was jasper (Rev. 21:19).

P. Ligure. Modern scholars know of no stone with this name. Students of the Bible have very little idea what is meant by this stone, which was the first of the third row of precious stones on the breastplate of the high priest (Exod. 28:19; 39:12).

The Hebrew and Greek words for ligure (*leshem* and *ligurion*) suggest "to attract." Because amber has a magnetic attractive quality, some scholars think it is ligure. But this could not be so, because true amber is not a precious stone and is not hard enough for an engraver to work with. Therefore, it could not have been part of the high priest's breastplate.

Q. Onyx. Onyx is a type of agate stone with two or more colors in parallel bands or layers. The Hebrew word for onyx is *shoham.* The ancients found onyx in the land of Havilah (Gen. 2:12). Today onyx is a semiprecious stone. But in biblical times it was obviously of high value, since it is mentioned among pre-

THE MINERALS AND GEMS OF PALESTINE

cious stones and metals (Job 28:16; Ezek. 28:13). Onyx adorned the high priest's breastplate and the two shoulders of his outer vestment (Exod. 28:9–12, 20).

R. Pearl. A pearl is a smooth, hard white or bluish-gray growth formed inside the shell of some oysters and other mollusks. Usually roundish, the most valuable pearls are produced by the oyster species. In ancient times, pearls were used in the East as personal ornaments, as they are today (1 Tim. 2:9; Rev. 17:4; 18:12–16).

From the way pearls are mentioned in the New Testament, we know they were held among the most precious substances. Compared with gems, pearls were considered in biblical times even more valuable than today (Matt. 7:6; 13:45–46; Rev. 21:21).

S. Ruby. The ruby is a clear, deep red variety of corundum, a mineral second only to diamond in hardness. The price and value of wisdom has been likened to that of rubies (Job 28:18; Prov. 3:15; 8:11), and the value of a virtuous woman (Prov. 31:10).

T. Sapphire. This is a hard, clear deep blue type of corundum stone. The sapphire was one of the stones in the high priest's breastplate and in the foundation of the apocalyptic city (Exod. 28:18; Rev. 21:19).

The sapphire is often mentioned in the Old Testament. Sapphire is next to the diamond in luster, beauty, and hardness. Bible scholars generally agree, however, that the usual sapphire of biblical times is the same as our *lapis lazuli,* an opaque, dark blue mineral.

U. "Sardine." We find the word *sardine* only in Revelation 4:3, where we are told that the Deity was like "a jasper and a sardine stone" to look upon. Most scholars feel it is the same stone referred to in the Old Testament under the Hebrew name of *ōdhem,* and the Septuagint as *sardion,* and the *sardius* of the Authorized Version.

Sardius is mentioned among the precious stones on the breastplate of the high priest (Exod. 28:17; 39:10) and is mentioned in connection with diamonds in Ezekiel 28:13. Sardine is a gem of blood-red or flesh color and may have a high polish. It got its name from Sardis, the capital city of ancient Lydia (modern Turkey), where it was first found. Sardine has long been a favorite of engravers, because it is very hard, yet easy to work with, and beautiful in color. Sardine comes under a variety of quartz called sarde.

V. Sardonyx. This stone is mentioned only

ALABASTER JAR. *Fashioned as a container for oil, this Egyptian vessel from the tomb of Tutankhamen (fourteenth century B.C.) consists of an inner shell and an outer shell carved with open-work designs and inscriptions. The Israelites frequently made jars and vases from alabaster, since it was easy to carve and polish. Alabaster jars were often used for costly perfumes, because its porous texture allowed the scent to escape slowly into a room.*

in Revelation 21:20, where it is said to be the foundation of a wall. Sardonyx is a variety of chalcedony, a grayish or milky quartz. In this gem, a white opaque layer rests upon a clear red layer. Thus sardonyx combines the qualities of sarde and onyx—thus, its name.

W. Topaz. Scholars agree that topaz is the same as modern chrysolite, a soft and clear or translucent gem, usually pale green in color. A true topaz is usually clear with a yellowish tint, but may be brown, blue, green, or even colorless. The topaz was the second stone on the first row of the high priest's breastplate (Exod. 9:10; 28:17). The "topaz of Ethiopia" (Job 28:19) was known for its beauty and value.

THE MINERALS AND GEMS OF PALESTINE

IV. Other Minerals. The Bible also tells us of other minerals the Hebrews knew. We shall discuss them as a group because of their various uses.

A. Brimstone. The Hebrews used this term to describe any substance that caught fire easily, especially sulphur. We find brimstone mentioned in seven passages of the Old Testament (Gen. 19:24; Deut. 29:23; Job 18:15; Psa. 11:6; Isa. 30:33; 34:9; Ezek. 38:22).

Brimstone is also used as a symbol of God's fiery wrath and the future suffering of the wicked (Rev. 14:10; 19:20; 20:10; 21:8).

B. Flint. Flint is a very hard kind of quartz stone that produces sparks when struck against iron. It is usually brown, black, or gray. The Hebrews, like other ancient peoples, used flint to start fires for cooking and sacrifices. Flint was well-known and plentiful in Palestine and nearby districts (Psa. 114:8).

Bible writers also considered flint a symbol of things firm and constant (Isa. 50:7; Ezek. 3:9).

C. Nitre. This is an earthly alkaline salt that resembles soap. Indeed, the Hebrews often used it as soap. Nitre separated from the bottom of the Natron Lakes in Egypt and rose to the top, where it was condensed by the heat of the sun into a dry, hard substance like soap. Nitre is found in many other parts of the East.

Nitre is our translation of the Hebrew word *nether.* Vinegar has no effect on common nitre, but vinegar does affect *natron,* or soda. Probably the English translation of the substance referred to in Proverbs 25:20 and Jeremiah 2:22 should have been *natron* instead of *nitre.*

D. Salt. Salt held a place of great importance in the primitive and simple society of the ancient Israelites. Job tells us that salt was used from the oldest times to flavor food (Job 6:6). Ancient man sacrificed to God food he found pleasant, so salt was included among these offerings (Ezek. 43:24). By biblical times, salt had become linked with health, hospitality, purity, and durability. Ezekiel tells us that in ancient times the Israelites rubbed newborn children with salt (Ezek. 16:4).

Later religious rites emphasized the cleansing property of salt. Salt came to stand for the most sacred and binding of obligations. God said of His covenant with the Israelites, "It is a covenant of salt for ever" (Num. 18:19). Second Chronicles relates that "the Lord God of Israel gave the kingdom over Israel to David for ever, even to him and to his sons by a covenant of salt" (2 Chron. 13:5). Jesus told His disciples they were "the salt of the earth" (Matt. 5:13). Paul linked salt with wisdom: "Let your speech be always with grace, seasoned with salt" (Col. 4:6).

Plants and crops cannot grow in land that has too much salt. The Bible also deals with this aspect of the mineral. When Abimelech took the city of Shechem, we are told he sowed the land with salt, so that it would always remain barren and unfruitful (Judg. 9:45).

Salt was plentiful in Palestine. The famous Jebel Usdum is actually a mountain of rock salt, about 11 km. (7 mi.) long. This ridge extends along the south and southwest corners of the Dead Sea. Jews used rock salt from this ridge. They also got salt by evaporating the waters of the Mediterranean and Dead seas.

Bible critic Edward A. Robinson believes the large plain east of Jebel Usdum is the "valley of salt" where David's army defeated the Edomites (2 Sam. 8:13; 1 Chron. 18:12; 2 Chron. 25:11).

THE ANIMALS AND INSECTS OF PALESTINE

"And God made the beast of the earth after his kind, and cattle after their kind, and every thing that creepeth upon the earth after his kind: and God saw that it was good" (Gen. 1:25).

From the creation account in Genesis to the symbolic beasts of Revelation, the Bible abounds with animals of every description. God paraded the animals before the first man, so Adam could name them (Gen. 2:19–20). When Adam and Eve discovered their nakedness, God clothed them with animal skins. Throughout history animals have been an integral part of mankind's existence. They provided food as well as clothing, carried his burdens, drew his plow. They even spilled their blood for his sins.

The biblical writers were not naturalists, but many had keen eyes. The prophet Habakkuk watched the sure-footed deer nimbly pick their way across the treacherous rocks of the Judean hills. Then he exulted, "The Lord God is my strength and he will make my feet like hinds' feet, and he will make me to walk upon mine high places" (Hab. 3:19). Others taught lessons by comparing the natures of beast and man.

About 80 mammals are named in Scripture. And that is not a complete list of the animals which live in the little land of Palestine. Sometimes we read and wonder. Are there really such things as unicorns, satyrs, dragons? What on earth is—or was—Behemoth? Leviathan? Did lions and bears really prowl the Holy Land? What of such strange-sounding beasts as the chamois or pygarg? The Bible mentions everyday animals too—cattle and horses, sheep and goats. Did puppies and kittens amuse little children in biblical days?

I. IDENTIFYING THE ANIMALS

II. MAMMALS
A. Domestic Animals
1. Asses
2. Camels
3. Cats
4. Cattle
5. Dogs
6. Goats
7. Horses
8. Mules
9. Sheep
10. Swine
B. Wild Animals
1. Wild Asses
2. Badgers
3. Bears
4. Boars
5. Coneys
6. Deer
7. Foxes
8. Wild Goats
9. Hares, Ferrets, Weasels
10. Hyenas
11. Jackals
12. Leopards
13. Lions
14. Mice
15. Moles
16. Pygarg, Chamois
17. Wolves
C. Mammals in Modern Israel

III. BIRDS AND FISH
A. Birds
1. Bitterns
2. Cormorants
3. Cranes
4. Cuckoos (Cuckows)
5. Doves or Turtledoves
6. Eagles
7. Gier Eagles
8. Hawks
9. Herons
10. Kites
11. Lapwings
12. Nighthawks
13. Ospreys (Oprays)
14. Ossifrages
15. Ostriches
16. Owls
17. Partridges
18. Peacocks
19. Pelicans
20. Pigeons
21. Quail
22. Ravens
23. Sparrows
24. Storks
25. Swallows
26. Swans
27. Vultures

THE ANIMALS AND INSECTS OF PALESTINE

I. Identifying the Animals. Not all of these questions have answers. Some of the animal knowledge has been lost or distorted in transmission. Thus various translations of the Bible differ considerably in animal identification. Take a verse like Exodus 25:5 or Isaiah 34:14 and trace it through several Bible translations. For example, in the Exodus passage badgers' skins in the KJV become goatskins in the RSV. This is only one of the changes you will find.

We must remember that the King James Version was written in the 1600s. At that time most people believed that unicorns and satyrs and dragons, for instance, were real. Now we know that they were imaginary beasts that came into our language through Greek and Roman myths. Such fanciful beasts are rarely mentioned in modern translations. "Unicorn" is generally replaced by "wild ox," as in Job

39:9 (RSV): "Is the wild ox willing to serve you?" One of the earliest translations, the Vulgate, called it a rhinoceros. Though the Hebrew term (*reem*) appears several times, only Psalm 92:10 indicates an animal with a single horn.

Satyrs are still found in the Revised Standard Version of 1952. But the Hebrew term is translated "devils" in other verses, and "he-goats" in other versions. The mythical satyr is half-man, half-goat. That image fits easily into Isaiah's prophecy of desolation: "But wild beasts of the desert shall lie there; and their houses shall be full of doleful creatures; and owls shall dwell there, and satyrs shall dance there" (Is. 13:21; cf. 34:14).

You can find a real dragon in the encyclopedia, but it is only an overgrown lizard that neither flies nor spouts flames. You will also find the word "dragon" in most modern Bibles. However, it is used only in a symbolic sense. Where a literal animal was intended, as in Jeremiah 9:11, the RSV substituted "a lair of jackals" for "a den of dragons." *Serpents* in the RSV replaces *dragons* in Deuteronomy 32:33: "Their wine is the poison of dragons

ANIMALS ON POTTERY. *Cattle and various birds decorate these pieces of pottery from the sixteenth century B.C., found at Tell Ajjul in Palestine.*

THE ANIMALS AND INSECTS OF PALESTINE

(serpents, RSV), and the cruel venom of asps."

Satyrs and unicorns lend color to the King James Version. For a precise rendering of the Hebrew terms for animals, however, we need to consult additional translations and study aids. Even that cannot insure total accuracy. Thousands of years have passed since some of these animals walked the earth. During that period both languages and the distribution of animals have undergone changes. Some species are even extinct.

Yet we are intrigued by the mysterious creatures of the Bible. Even today scholars disagree on the meaning of *behemoth* and *leviathan* (Job 40:15–24; 41). Some think these words referred not to real animals, but to mythological beasts, larger than life—as we speak of "monsters." Others think the behemoth was an elephant or a hippopotamus, and that leviathan was a crocodile. On the other hand, the New English Bible translates *behemoth* as "crocodile" and *leviathan* as "whale"! We can see how they reach such divergent conclusions. The verses in Job, though strikingly detailed, could apply to more than one animal. "He moveth his tail like a cedar" (Job 40:17), for instance, could be said of either an elephant or a crocodile. "He drinketh up a river" (Job 40:23) sounds very much like an elephant. But a hippo's home is the river, and he may appear to consume it as he submerges. Elephants and hippos were not unknown to the ancient Hebrews, and crocodiles once sunned themselves on the banks of the Jordan River.

Three continents converge at the Holy Land: Europe, Asia, and Africa. Animals from these areas have made their way into Palestine. Mountain sheep may have come from the island of Cyprus, gazelles from Africa, bears from Syria.

At times the Israelites lived in exile—as in Egypt or Persia. They became acquainted with the wildlife of those countries as well as the animals of their homeland.

As far back as King Solomon, exotic animals were imported. "Once in three years," according to 1 Kings 10:22, "came the navy of Tarshish, bringing gold, and silver, ivory, and apes, and peacocks." Such neighboring countries as Assyria had public zoos and even bred lions for the royal hunt.[1]

II. Mammals. The Hebrews found a prolific variety of mammals in the Promised Land itself. They domesticated many of these animals for agricultural power and other uses.

A. Domestic Animals. For the most part, the animals we read of in the Bible are the common animals, although not considered to be pets. Keeping animals solely as pets was a luxury the Israelites could not afford. The common animals of the Bible were what we would think of as farm animals—sheep and goats, cattle, beasts of burden.

1. Asses. The lowly ass—our donkey—was the conventional beast of burden. The Hebrew term *hamor* ("red animal") referred to the domestic ass. Able to subsist on very coarse food, this hardy creature also had multiple uses. The female (she-ass) was often ridden, and could be milked. Like the ox, the ass helped plow the fields and trample in the seed.

If you wanted to ride instead of walk, the ass was your most probable conveyance. Persons of rank, such as governors, could afford white asses (Judg. 5:10). The ass was a symbol of humility and patient service. Jesus entered Jerusalem as Zechariah foretold: "Lo, your king comes to you; triumphant and victorious is he, humble and riding on an ass, on a colt the foal of an ass" (Zech. 9:9, RSV).

2. Camels. To the Hebrews, camels (*gamal*) were predominantly a beast of burden. Camels are bad-tempered, a bit dense, and complain when they have to carry a load. But God must have created the camel expressly for desert nomads. This animal is superbly engineered to cope with a hot, harsh environment. Long legs keep the camel's belly comfortably away from the blazing sands. (A rider careens along about 2 m. [6.5 ft.] off the ground.) The camel conserves water admirably. Its thick wool coat provides natural insulation; it maintains an even body temperature and hardly perspires at all. Though a thirsty camel may gulp 105 l. (25 gal.) of water within ten minutes, he can go for long periods without food and even longer without water. The dromedary camel familiar to Bible writers had but one hump—his reserve fuel tank. It is not a hollow cistern of water, as some believe, but a mass of muscle and fat. After an arduous journey, the once-firm hump may be floppy and soft and have to be built up again.

Arabs prized the camel much as Israelites valued the goat. It supplied transportation, milk and meat, and clothing from its soft hair;

---

[1] A. H. Brodrick, *Animals in Archaeology* (New York: Praeger Publishers, 1972), p. 49.

THE ANIMALS AND INSECTS OF PALESTINE

CAMELS. *The Hebrews used camels as beasts of burden. Bad-tempered though they are, camels are well-adapted to desert life. Their thick coats provide insulation against the extreme heat, and they can go for long periods without food and even longer without water. These camels are about to be sold at a camel market in Beersheba.*

even the dung chips were burned for fuel. Jews did not eat camel as the Arabs did, because camels were considered unclean (cf. Deut. 14:7). But rich men like Abraham and Job counted camels among their possessions (Gen. 22:16; Job 1:3; 42:12). Jeremiah's comment, "Thou art a swift dromedary traversing her ways" (Jer. 2:23), indicates that a dromedary camel was their equivalent of our racehorse. The dromedary could cover 13 to 16 km. (8 to 10 mi.) per hour.

The two-humped Bactrian camel of central Asia is probably the type of camel referred to in Isaiah 21:7.

3. Cats. Though there's no shortage of cats in modern Israel, they were practically unknown in ancient Mesopotamia. But they were worshiped in ancient Egypt, so cats may have entered the Palestinian scene at any time. The Bible does not mention them.

4. Cattle. The soft lowing of cattle was as familiar in Bible times as the baas of sheep and goats. Cows, calves, heifers, and bulls are mentioned, but the *ox* appears more frequently. *Oxen* are the adult cattle used as draft animals. With sheep and goats to supply meat and milk, Israelite farmers depended on oxen as modern farmers rely on tractors. Broken to service at three years, oxen pulled plows,

threshed grain, and drew carts. The full-grown animals were regarded as too valuable for slaughter, either for food or sacrifice.

One had to be wealthy, as Abraham was, to keep many cattle (Gen. 12:16; 21:27). Being larger animals, they needed more and better pasture than goats or sheep. Some areas of Palestine were better for grazing herds—Bashan in the north and Gilead east of the Jordan. When pasture was scant, or an animal was to be eaten, cattle were penned and given fodder. The "stalled ox" of Proverbs 15:17 had been fattened up for the table.

In the Bible, "cattle" had the broader meaning of "livestock." Thus cattle included sheep and goats as well as asses, mules, horses, and even camels. This may explain why the tribes of Gad and Reuben proposed to "build sheepfolds . . . for our cattle" (Num. 32:16).

5. Dogs. Dogs had value as service animals and were domesticated quite early in history. Job spoke of "the dogs of my flock" (30:1). Some were trained as watchdogs. Greyhounds, described in Proverbs 30:30–31 as "comely in going," were used by kings for hunting. Many dogs were half-wild scavengers. They roamed the streets in search of food and would even consume human flesh. Queen Jezebel, you may recall, was thrown into the streets and her corpse was eaten by dogs (2 Kin. 9:35–37).

"Dog" was a term of derision. In this symbolic sense it appears several times in Hebrew and Greek texts. "Dog" (Greek, *kuon*) stood for a false teacher (Phil. 3:2) or a sinner (Rev. 22:15). *Keleb*, the most common Hebrew term for dog, symbolized a persecutor of God's people (Ps. 22:16). Jesus spoke of casting food for the "children"—i.e., the Jews—to the non-Jews who were "dogs" (Greek, *kunarion*; Matt. 15:26). In later history, Muslims showed their contempt for Christians by calling them "dogs."

6. Goats. Goats, sometimes called "the poor man's cow," were also domesticated early. They did not need good pasture; they liked to eat bark and tender twigs. Goats were terribly hard on vegetation; they ate everything within reach, including fledgling trees and shrubs. Their excessive numbers and indiscriminate grazing have been blamed for some of the barren hills of present-day Israel.[2]

But to the Israelites in Bible times, goats had great value. They supplied milk and milk products. The meat tasted like venison; the young kids were especially tender. Goat hair was not shorn, but combed from the animals and woven into coarse cloth. (Curtains of the tabernacle were made of goats' hair—Ex. 26:7.) Goatskin made good leather and water bottles. Even the horns of rams were used for drinking vessels and musical instruments. A man with a large flock of goats was indeed well off. By careful breeding of his flocks, Jacob became a rich man (Gen. 30).

Goats had their drawbacks—they stank, and they were lively, strong-willed creatures, unlike their docile cousins the sheep. In Jesus' parable, when the sheep and goats were separated, the goats wound up on the left, a position of disfavor (Matt. 25:32–33).

7. Horses. Horses were also latecomers to Israel and never did attain a position of great importance. They were used by the Egyptians and Assyrians for warfare, but Israel's king was told not to "multiply horses to himself, nor cause the people to return to Egypt, to the end that he should multiply horses" (Deut. 17:16). Isaiah warned, "Woe to them that go down to Egypt for help; and stay on horses, and trust in chariots" (Is. 31:1). Nevertheless, King Solomon "had a thousand and four hun-

LION AND DOG FIGHTING. *This relief was found in the fourteenth-century* B.C. *stratum at the tell of Beth-shean in Palestine. Above, a dog and a lion rise up on their hind legs to fight; below, the dog bites the rump of the standing lion.*

dred chariots, and twelve thousand horsemen, whom he bestowed in the cities for chariots, and with the king at Jerusalem" (1 Kin. 10:26). He imported them from Egypt at a cost of 600 silver shekels per chariot and 150 shekels per horse (1 Kin. 10:29). Even in the New Testament book of Revelation, horses are linked with war (Rev. 6:1–8).

As time passed, horses took their place as riding animals, along with the ass, mule, and camel. They even served in a primitive "pony express": "he . . . sent letters by posts on horseback" (Esth. 8:10). But Psalm 32:9 expressed a disparaging view: "Be ye not as the horse, or as the mule, which have no understanding."

8. Mules. Mules (Hebrew, *pered*) were the hybrid offspring of a male ass and a female horse. They were stronger and more enduring

---

[2] Walter Ferguson, *Living Animals of the Bible* (New York: Charles Scribner's Sons, n.d.), p. 37.

THE ANIMALS AND INSECTS OF PALESTINE

RELIEF FROM KHORSABAD. *This relief from the eighth century B.C. was discovered at the palace of Sargon, king of Assyria, at Khorsabad. The Persians used horses to maintain an efficient postal system. King Solomon had thousands of horses for warfare.*

than asses and more sure-footed and longer-lived than horses. Yet the Israelites were prohibited from mating ass and horse (Lev. 19:19). Mules were probably not used in Israel until the time of King David, and then were likely imported from Egypt. David's son Absalom was astride a mule when his head caught in the boughs of an oak, leaving him at the mercy of his enemies (2 Sam. 18:9).

9. Sheep. Sheep are mentioned about 750 times in Scripture, and are undoubtedly the most familiar biblical animal symbol.

Often flocks were mixed, goats and sheep grazing amicably together. Sheep were well-suited for a nomadic life, but they were very dependent on their shepherd. He led them to pasture, found water to quench their thirst, protected them from wild beasts. A good shepherd cared deeply for his sheep. He not only knew how many were in his flock, but could call them by name. The sheep in turn knew their shepherd's voice. Jesus illustrated God's tender concern for His children by comparing Himself to a good shepherd, willing even to lay down his life for his sheep (John 10:1–15).

"Keeper of sheep" was the first profession

named in the Bible (Gen. 4:2). Throughout Israel's history shepherding continued to be a very respectable calling, although shepherds as a class were distrusted in Jesus' day as being a wild lot. The beloved King David was once a shepherd boy. And unpretentious shepherds were the first to be told of the Messiah's arrival.

Sheep have not changed since Bible times. The broad-tailed sheep was, and still is, prevalent in Israel. Some sheep had such fat tails that they pulled little wagons on which to rest them! The ewes were milked. Since sheep were considered to be clean (Deut. 14:6), mutton was an everyday meat.

The sheep's precious wool (often dark-colored) provided warm garments. Once a year the sheep were herded into an enclosure for shearing. Like the "husking bees" of the American farm heritage, sheep-shearing made a good excuse to socialize. Absalom killed his brother Amnon during the hubbub of one sheep-shearing (2 Sam. 13:23–29).

10. Swine. *See* "Boars."

B. Wild Animals. It is difficult to identify many of the wild animals mentioned in the Bible. Biblical writers may have referred to several species with one general term. In this section, we will attempt to distinguish between them by noting the various types of wild animals found in Palestine today.

1. Wild Asses. The wild ass of Syria (Hebrew, *peres*) is mentioned several times (Job 24:5; Ps. 104:11; Is. 32:14). They were occasionally found in northern Palestine. Daniel 5:21 may refer to the larger species, which was common in Arabia.

2. Badgers. Although badger skins are mentioned several times in the KJV, that is a disputable translation of the Hebrew. Exodus 26:19 states that craftsmen working on the tabernacle made "a covering for the tent of rams' skins dyed red, and a covering of badgers' skins." One naturalist makes a good case for retaining that interpretation.[3] The honey badger, he notes, ranges from Africa to India, and has a thick loose skin. Such a hide would be durable, suitable for weatherproofing the tabernacle. Since badgers are small animals, quite a quantity of their pelts would be needed. This would raise their value and explain their place among such listed treasures as gold and jewels.

---

[3] Peter Farb, *Land, Wildlife, and Peoples of the Bible* (New York: Harper and Row, 1967), pp. 85–86.

THE ANIMALS AND INSECTS OF PALESTINE

However, later translators did away with badgers entirely. The New English Bible reads "porpoise hides" where badger skins were named in regard to the tabernacle. The RSV uses *goatskins*. *Leather* is substituted in Ezekiel 16:10: "I clothed you also with embroidered cloth and shod you with leather" (RSV). According to some authorities, the Hebrew term (*tachash*) translated *badger* designates not an animal but a color (black or blue). It may have referred to the tough skin of a marine animal, such as the dugong or even the whale, which can be found in the Red Sea. There is evidence that "porpoise hides" were highly prized by the other nations of antiquity.

3. Bears. Now found mostly in the mountains of Lebanon, the Syrian bear once roamed the entire area. This light-colored bear liked to prey on sheep and goats. A "bear robbed of her whelps" was a popular expression to indicate a state of uncontrollable rage. There are not many references to bears in Scripture, though they cropped up as symbols in visions given to Isaiah, Daniel, and John (Is. 11:7; Dan. 7:5; Rev. 13:2).

4. Boars. The Israelites contended with wild boars from the Hula Valley all the way down to the desert near the Dead Sea. Boars were so damaging to crops that farmers sometimes had to set a watch for them. They were vicious when crossed by man and seemed to delight in trampling and destroying his carefully tended vineyards. The psalmist compared the cruel ravishing of Israel by her enemies to a vine at the edge of a woods: "The boar out of the wood doth waste it" (Ps. 80:13).

Domestic swine were raised too, though pigs were abhorred throughout the Middle East, not only by the Jews. Yet someone, even in Bible days, kept pigs, for Christ cast demons into a herd of swine (Matt. 8:28–34). He mentioned them more than once in His teaching, always as a symbol of degradation, as in the story of the prodigal son (Luke 15:15). They were strictly forbidden as food. "Many will be slain by the Lord," Isaiah predicted direly, "those who eat the flesh of pigs and rats and all vile vermin." (66:17, RSV).

5. Coneys. The coney of the Bible is really a rock hyrax, which looks somewhat like a rabbit-sized guinea pig. Proverbs 30:26 states, "The conies are but a feeble folk, yet make they their houses in the rocks." Hyraxes easily scramble about seemingly inaccessible ter-

rain. Their feet have a built-in suction that gives them incredible clinging power on even the steepest rock surfaces.

6. Deer. After the Flood, wild animals became part of the food supply. God told Noah, "Every moving thing that liveth shall be meat for you" (Gen. 9:3).

Two types of deer are mentioned in the Bible, the fallow deer and the roe deer. (Males and females are not called bucks and does, but harts and hinds.) The true fallow deer (Hebrew, *yahmur*) are beautiful creatures, similar to North American deer. Deuteronomy 14:5 and 1 Kings 14:23 refer to this type.

The roe deer or roebuck was noted for its swiftness. In Song of Solomon 2:8–9, the young lover comes "leaping upon the mountains, skipping upon the hills" like a roe or a young hart.

Gazelle has replaced "roe deer" in many translations. These two animals closely resemble each other. The gazelle is buff-colored and fine-featured, with large liquid eyes and distinctive horns. In numerous biblical comparisons they exemplify beauty, affection, and agility (Song 2:17; 8:14).

Deer hunting is an ancient sport. Esau was "a cunning hunter" (Gen. 25:27–28); the venison he brought home endeared him to his father Isaac. King Solomon's menu included "harts, and roebucks, and fallow deer" (1 Kin. 4:23).

7. Foxes. Foxes were not dangerous, but they were destructive. The fox is a member of the dog family, with a sharp pointed nose and bushy tail. They are cunning hunters, eating small animals and birds and having a fondness for certain fruit. Song of Solomon 2:15 tells of "the little foxes, that spoil the vines." But they helped keep down the mouse population.

Foxes live alone or in pairs, but do not go in packs as jackals do. This explains a later version of Judges 15:4, which tells that Samson caught 300 jackals (KJV, "foxes") and sent them into the fields with firebrands tied between their tails. They live in holes or rocky caves, often secondhand burrows abandoned by other animals. Jesus pointed out that even foxes had holes, but He had no dwelling of His own (Matt. 8:20). He also tartly called King Herod a fox (Luke 13:32).

Two species of fox are now found in Palestine: the tawny fox and the Egyptian fox.

8. Wild Goats. There were goats everywhere in Palestine, both tame and wild. En-Gedi (Spring of the Kid), an oasis near the

THE ANIMALS AND INSECTS OF PALESTINE

Dead Sea, still teems with wild goats, particularly a breed now known as the Nubian ibex. "The high hills are a refuge for the wild goats," according to Psalm 104:18.

9. Hares, Ferrets, Weasels. This trio was mentioned only as forbidden for food (see Lev. 11:6, 29–30). Hares, which are plentiful in Palestine, appear to chew a cud because of a peculiar movement of their mouths. Thus they were considered unclean. But they are not true ruminants. The common hare of Palestine looks like a jumbo rabbit; but unlike baby rabbits, hares are born with a coat of hair and are able to see.

Ferrets are rat-catchers related to weasels. Later translators substituted a wall lizard, *gecko,* in the Levitical list.

Weasels (Hebrew, *haled*) exist in almost every part of the world. They are small furry animals with long slender bodies and short legs, adept at squeezing through small openings. They dine on small rodents, and, like skunks, can spray attackers with a foul odor. The weasel is found throughout Palestine.

10. Hyenas. The hyena is not mentioned in the KJV. But hyenas do live in Palestine and may be among the "wild beasts" of such passages as Jeremiah 7:33: "And carcases of this people shall be meat for the fowls of the heaven, and for the beasts of the earth." A hyena resembles a wolf, but is a dirty gray color with dark stripes. Hyenas are scavengers, despised by man. They will even dig up and devour human corpses. They have such strong jaws that they can easily crack the bones of an ox. Though savage, they are rather cowardly when confronted by man.

11. Jackals. Jackals are not specified in the KJV either. But they were probably meant in certain scriptures which mention dragons, such as Micah 1:8, and were probably the animal meant in some passages reading *foxes.* The RSV reads: "For this will I lament and wail; I will go stripped and naked; I will make lamentations like the jackals." Until recent times the chorus of jackals was a familiar night noise in Palestine. They tended to travel in packs and inhabit deserted places. Isaiah refers to "the haunt of jackals" (34:13, RSV).

12. Leopards. Flocks, herds, and humans had to beware of leopards. "A leopard shall watch over their cities: every one that goeth out thence shall be torn in pieces" (Jer. 5:6). The leopard is intelligent and wary; it is a better fighter than a lion, and more savage. Leopards lived in the mountains of Carmel and Lebanon, as well as in the woody "jungle" near the Jordan.

The cheetah is a smaller version of the big spotted cat and is probably the beast meant in Habakkuk 1:8: "Their horses also are swifter than the leopards." Jeremiah doubted the likelihood of Israel's repentance, asking sardonically, "Can the Ethiopian change his skin, or the leopard his spots?" (Jer. 13:23).

13. Lions. Fierce predators also stalked the hills and the thickets of Palestine. Lions, found in almost half the books of the Bible, were a very real danger. The biblical lion was smaller than the African lion and had a short curly mane, but was no less feared. Even thinking about "the roaring of the lion, and the voice of the fierce lion, and the teeth of the young lions" (Job 4:10–11) could send shivers down one's spine.

Though some brave souls killed lions in individual combat (Judg. 14:5–6), Ezekiel 19:1–9 tells of capturing lions in a pit with nets. Lion hunting was a favorite sport of Near Eastern kings. Darius of Persia was not eccentric in keeping a den of lions (cf. Dan. 6:16–23). Early Christians were thrown to the lions when Rome raged against the fledgling church.

SHEEP. *Sheep provided milk, meat, and wool for the Israelites. This common sheep was found in the Judean desert and is about to be auctioned at a sheep market in Jerusalem.*

THE ANIMALS AND INSECTS OF PALESTINE

Kings may have hunted lions for sport, but shepherds and common men killed them in self-protection. Lions had lairs in the thickets bordering the Jordan River. When rising flood waters forced them out, they made irascible neighbors. Jeremiah anticipated the rising judgment of God: "He shall come up like a lion from the swelling of Jordan" (Jer. 49:19).

Mentioned more than any other wild beast in the Bible, the lion symbolized royalty, courage, and power. It was the symbol of the tribes of Judah, Dan, and Gad. In Revelation 5:5, Jesus is referred to as "the Lion of the tribe of Judah."

14. Mice. Some wild animals were pests. Mice were a common scourge, especially in grain-growing areas. Twenty-three species of mice consider the Promised Land their land too. They could be as destructive as locusts, destroying grain as it sprouted in the fields. When the Philistines captured the ark of the covenant, they were afflicted with *buboes* (the characteristic lesion of the lice-borne plague) and mice. In restitution they had to make golden images of both the tumors and of the "mice that mar the land" (1 Sam. 6:5). The Israelites were not supposed to eat mice, but apparently some did so (Is. 66:17).

15. Moles. When *moles* appear in the Bible record, probably the mole-rat is meant, since there are no true moles in Israel. Like our gophers, mole-rats are the bane of farmers. They live underground and burrow tunnels that wreak havoc with gardens. Despite their silky, silvery fur, the mole-rats are rather ugly little beasts. No eyes, ears, or tail can be seen—just a pig-like snout and beaver-like teeth. Isaiah foresaw a day when men would cast away their idols "to the moles and to the bats" (Is. 2:20).

16. Pygarg, Chamois. Since these animals appear only in Moses' list of clean animals (Deut. 14:5), translators didn't have much to go on. "Pygarg" is replaced by "ibex" in later versions, suggesting a type of bearded wild goat.

KJV translators were acquainted with the chamois, a goatlike antelope found in Europe's colder climate. But *zemer,* the original Hebrew term, probably refers to some kind of wild mountain sheep.

17. Wolves. Wolves were fierce, cruel enemies. Light-colored and resembling large dogs, wolves in Palestine traveled singly or in groups of three or four. They were a variety of the European wolf and are still found in Pales-tine. They were a particular threat to sheep. The tranquility of the Messiah's reign will indeed be miraculous when "the wolf also shall dwell with the lamb," as Isaiah 11:6 foretold.

The patriarch Jacob, foreseeing the warlike character of one son, predicted "Benjamin shall ravin as a wolf" (Gen. 49:27). Jesus used the wolf to warn of treachery: "Beware of false prophets, which come to you in sheep's clothing, but inwardly they are ravening wolves" (Matt. 7:15).

C. Mammals in Modern Israel. The passing years have reshaped the face of Palestine. Areas once wooded are now barren hills. Swamps where hippos wallowed have been drained and reclaimed for cropland. In the modern state of Israel, space is precious. Wild places are dwindling.

Gone are the bears and lions, the formidable crocodiles, even the wild asses. The fallow deer has not been seen in Israel in this century. Modernization has left little need for beasts of burden. But camels, mules, asses, and horses are still in evidence.

Sheep and goats still dot the landscape. The beef and dairy industries are thriving. Many common animals still live there: foxes, coneys, hares, mole-rats, and of course mice.

Two species very nearly disappeared from the area entirely, the Nubian ibex (wild goat) and the gazelle. However, the State of Israel instituted strict protective measures and they have been preserved. In fact, gazelles are now agricultural pests.

The wild boar is the largest game animal left in Israel. Wolves, hyenas, and leopards are protected; jackals are rare.

The people of Israel, along with thoughtful people the world over, are awakening to their serious responsibility for the animals God placed in their dominion. Modern Israelis are planting trees where forests once flourished, and they are attempting to reintroduce wildlife that had vanished. At the National Biblical Zoo in Jerusalem it is possible to see many types of animals mentioned in the Bible.

III. Birds and Fish. The first chapter of Genesis tells us that God said, "Let the waters bring forth abundantly the moving creature that hath life, and fowl that may fly above the earth in the open firmament of heaven" (Gen. 1:20). On the fifth day of creation, God "created great whales, and every living creature that moveth, which the waters brought forth abundantly, after their kind, and every winged fowl after his kind" (Gen. 1:21). These crea-

THE ANIMALS AND INSECTS OF PALESTINE

tures received God's command to "be fruitful, and multiply . . ." (Gen. 1:22).

A. Birds. Birds were common in Palestine and the people of biblical times used them for many different purposes. (For example, they used the pigeon and dove for sacrifice when a lamb was unavailable.)

Bible writers often used bird symbols to describe man's spiritual condition. For example, the church is compared to a "turtledove" (Ps. 74:19), as being gentle and vulnerable. Again, the writers of Scripture were fascinated by the magnificence of the eagle and its ability to soar in the sky. For this reason, they used the symbol of the eagle to challenge man to rise above his circumstances and follow God (cf. Prov. 23:5).

The Jewish law code forbade anyone to kill a mother bird, though a hunter could take her young (Deut. 22:6–7). The hunters usually caught their prey with a snare.

God's Law divided birds into clean and unclean categories, like the other animals. The distinction was made on the basis of a bird's diet. Unclean birds were those that ate flesh, while clean birds were those that ate grain or seeds (Lev. 11:13–21).

Scripture mentions some species of birds that are unfamiliar to us. Some of these are native to the Near East, others are common to many parts of the world (though they are designated in the Bible by less familiar names).

1. Bitterns. The bittern (Hebrew, *kippod*) is a solitary bird whose booming cry echoes mysteriously through the stillness of marshes. Prophets such as Zephaniah felt that the bittern epitomized utter solitude and desolation. The bittern is mentioned three times in Scripture (Is. 14:23; 34:11; Zeph. 2:14). Isaiah 14:23 probably refers to a long-necked, long-legged wading bird similar to the heron. The other two passages refer to the "short-eared owl."

2. Cormorants. This bird (Hebrew, *kaath* or *shalak*) is linked with the bittern by two biblical writers—Isaiah and Zephaniah—who evidently see them as similar. However, the cormorant is essentially a seabird that lives by catching fish. Perhaps the similarity between the two lies in their solitary and lonely life.

An unclean bird by Levitical law, the cormorant is mentioned four times in the Bible (Lev. 11:17; Deut. 14:17; Is. 34:11; Zeph. 2:14). The *shalak* is probably the common cormorant or the pygmy cormorant, which breeds at the area formerly occupied by Hula Lake. The Hebrew *kacta* is probably more properly rendered *pelican*. (See below.)

3. Cranes. The crane (Hebrew, *agur*) is one of the largest birds in the Holy Land, with

DEER. *This ancient Hittite relief shows a hunter pursuing a deer. The Hebrews admired the deer for its grace and speed. It was a clean animal according to the Scriptures (Deut. 14:5), and could be used for food.*

THE ANIMALS AND INSECTS OF PALESTINE

an extended wingspan of 2.1 m. (7 ft.) and a standing height of approximately 1.2 m. (4 ft.). The crane has a loud, trumpeting voice that resounds as it takes flight. It is a wading bird that feeds on frogs, fish worms, and insects; therefore the Jews considered it to be unclean. This bird is mentioned twice in Scripture (Is. 38:14, Jer. 8:7).

4. Cuckoos (Cuckows). Many scholars feel the Hebrew word *shahaph* has been improperly translated as *cuckoo* or *cuckow*. The Bible writers were probably describing some form of sea gull or the common tern. It is unlikely that the two species of cuckoos that do visit Palestine in the summer—the common cuckoo and the great spotted cuckoo—are meant, for they are not flesh-eating birds. The cuckow was considered an unclean bird, so it is mentioned only twice in Scripture (Lev. 11:16; Deut. 14:15).

5. Doves or Turtledoves. Doves were listed as clean birds, and therefore could be eaten and sacrificed. They lived in the craggy holes of rocks and were known for their passive dispositions, never retaliating or resisting their enemies. For this reason, the dove became known as the symbol of peace. Jesus exhorted His followers to be "harmless as doves" (Matt. 10:16), emphasizing the peaceable characteristics that are pleasing to Him. The dove is also a symbol of the Holy Spirit (Luke 3:22).

Four species of doves are found in Palestine: the ringdove or wood pigeon, the stock dove, the rock dove, and the ash-rumped dove.

The Hebrew *yonah* and Greek *peristera* are both rendered as *dove*. This bird is mentioned many times in Scripture (e.g., Gen. 8:8–12; Psa. 55:6; Isa. 38:14; Matt. 3:16; Mark 1:10).

The turtledove (Hebrew, *tor*) is a special type of pigeon. The most abundant in Palestine is the common turtledove. Also found there are the collared turtledove and the palm turtledove. Like the dove, this bird is gentle and harmless; hence in appearance it was an emblem of a defenseless and innocent people (Psa. 74:19). The Israelites often used turtledoves as burnt offerings (Lev. 1:14).

6. Eagles. Bible scholars disagree about which species of eagle is meant by the Hebrew word *resher*. Some think it might be the griffon or great vulture, a bird that is very common in Palestine and adjacent countries. Others believe it may be the golden eagle, which is common in Syria, or the imperial eagle. In any case, the eagle was a bird of high honor in the Bible and was often used as a prophetic symbol.

The eagle displays great tenderness toward its young, but has destructive power as well. It is noted for its ability to fly quickly to high altitudes (Prov. 23:5; Is. 40:31; Obad. 4). It builds its nest high on cliffs and rocks away from danger. It has long been believed that an eagle renews its strength after molting and takes on the appearance of a young bird (cf. Psa. 103:5).

Small living creatures are the natural food of the eagle; but mainly the bird is a scavenger, feeding on dead carcasses. Though an unclean bird by Levitical law (Lev. 11:13), the eagle is mentioned often in the Bible. Prophets saw the symbol of the eagle in their visions of God (Ezek. 1:10; 10:14; Rev. 4:7).

7. Gier eagles. This unclean bird (Hebrew, *rahamah*) was the Egyptian vulture. It displays many of the same characteristics as the eagle, and is mentioned twice in the Scriptures (Lev. 11:18; Deut. 14:17).

8. Hawks. Even though God's law designated hawks as unclean, Greeks and Egyptians considered them to be sacred. The Egyptian sun god Re was represented with the head of the hawk.

The hawk (Hebrew, *nea*) is a general name for more than one species of predatory birds known for their fierceness—such as the sparrow hawk and the kestrel. In Scripture, the hawk is mentioned three times (Lev. 11:16; Deut. 14:15; Job 39:26).

9. Herons. Considered unclean because it eats fish, the heron (Hebrew, *anaphah*) is a waterfowl. The buff-backed heron is the most common and is often called the white ibis. With it are found the common heron and the purple heron.

10. Kites. This bird (Hebrew, *ayyak*) is said to have extremely keen eyesight. It is an unclean bird of the falcon family and breeds in northern Palestine. In winter, the kite travels extensively.

Various kinds of kites are common to Palestine: the black kite, the yellow-billed kite, and the red kite. The kite is mentioned twice in Scripture (Lev. 11:14; Deut. 14:13).

11. Lapwings. Sometimes called a "hoopoe," the lapwing is a small, double-crested bird of many colors. It is commonly found in Palestine and the warmer parts of the Old World. A lapwing (Hebrew, *dukiphath*) builds its nest in holes along pathways, where travelers pack the earth firmly and prevent in-

THE ANIMALS AND INSECTS OF PALESTINE

vasion by jackals. The lapwing is mentioned twice in Scripture (Lev. 11:19; Deut. 14:18).

12. Nighthawks. Because of its dietary habits, this bird was considered unclean by Levitical law. Some biblical scholars believe the bird (Hebrew, *talmas*) was a barn owl. Others believe it was indeed the familiar nighthawk that abounds in the Near East. While rare in North America, this species thrives in the woodlands of Asia Minor, darting about with the swiftness of a swallow. It is mentioned twice in the Scriptures (Lev. 11:16, Deut. 14:15).

13. Ospreys (Oprays). This bird (Hebrew, *ozniyyah*) feeds on fish and can be found in the vicinity of seas, lakes, rivers, and pools. The Levitical law declared it unclean. Different species of the osprey are found in Europe, Asia, Africa, North America, and Australia. However, the Hebrew word may also refer to the short-toed eagle, the most abundant member of the eagle family in Palestine. It is mentioned twice in Scripture (Lev. 11:13; Deut. 14:12).

14. Ossifrages. Declared an unclean animal by Levitical law, this bird (Hebrew, *peres*)

HARE. *Plentiful in Palestine, hares look like large rabbits; but unlike rabbits, they are born with a coat of hair and are able to see at birth. They were considered unclean and forbidden as food to the Israelites (Lev. 11:6).*

is the bearded vulture or eagle. It was one of the most formidable birds of its tribe; in fact, the name *ossifrage* literally means "bone-breaker." The bird is thus named for its habit of dropping dead animals from great heights onto rocks to crack their bones, in order to eat the bone marrow. The ossifrage lacks the strength of many eagles, so it can't carry off living prey. But its throat muscles give it an enormous swallowing ability. It is mentioned twice in Scripture (Lev. 11:13; Deut. 14:12).

15. Ostriches. The ostrich (Hebrew, *yaen* or *yaanah*) was considered unclean because of its fleshy diet. Ostriches lay eggs in conspicuous places and quickly abandon their eggs or young when danger approaches. An ostrich can easily outrun a horse, though because of its tremendous weight—33 to 36 kg. (70 to 80 lb.)—it cannot fly. Scripture explicitly mentions the ostrich twice (Lam. 4:3; Job 39:13), and other verses may allude to the bird (Isa. 13:21; Mic. 1:8).

16. Owls. Even though it was an unclean bird, the owl is referred to as being "beautiful." It is sometimes referred to as the "mourning owl," because it habitually visits cemeteries.

The owl prefers solitary and desolate surroundings. Combined with its doleful hooting in search of food at night, these characteristics give the owl a dismal reputation. It is common in Egypt and Syria.

The King James Version translates several Hebrew words as "owl"; they may actually refer to different kinds of fowl.

Bath hayyaanah (Lev. 11:16) is probably the ostrich.

Kos (Lev. 11:17; Deut. 14:16; Ps. 102:6) is probably the little owl found throughout Palestine, considered a good-luck omen by Arabs.

Yenshuph or *yanshoph* is the "great owl" (Lev 11:17; Deut. 14:16), which lives in wastelands (Is. 34:11). This is probably the Egyptian eagle owl.

Tinshe-meth. See "Swan."

Lilith may have been the screech owl. But some scholars think *lilith* does not refer to an owl (cf. Isa. 34:14).

Kippoz (Isa. 34:15) may be the scops owl, common around ruins in the Near East.

17. Partridges. This bird (Hebrew, *kore*) is very common in Palestine, making its home in mountainous cliffs. The partridge lays its eggs on the sand and rocks, thus exposing them to breakage. Partridge eggs were greatly prized

THE ANIMALS AND INSECTS OF PALESTINE

by the ancient Syrians, who gathered them in large numbers. Because of its unwillingness to take flight, the bird was chased on foot until it became exhausted; then the pursuer hit it with a stick or rock. The partridge is mentioned in Jeremiah 17:11.

Two species of partridge are found in Palestine—the desert of Hey's sand partridge and the chukar partridge. The former is the only species at En-Gedi, where David compared himself to a hunted partridge (1 Sam. 26:20).

18. Peacocks. It seems from 1 Kings 10:22 and 2 Chronicles 9:21 that King Solomon brought the peacock by ships from abroad. The magnificent bird (Hebrew, *tukkiyyim*) is known by its long tail that trails gracefully behind it. But scholars disagree as to whether the peacock is really the bird that the Scripture writers intended to portray.

In Job 39:13, the "peacock" referred to (Hebrew, *renanim*) is said to have "goodly wings," but there is no mention of the striking tail feathers. It has generally been thought that this text refers to the Indian peacock.

Others feel that the Hebrew word *tukkiyyim* refers to a kind of monkey. The Egyptian word *t.kyw* means monkey; this is very similar to *tukkiyyim* without the vowels.

19. Pelicans. The pelican makes its home among the reeds and rushes of lakes and rivers in Western Asia. Toward the end of each day, the pelicans gather in flocks and soar in circles before landing on an island or open plain.

When pelicans roost, they form a circle, keeping their heads forward to ward off enemies. The female of the species has a large pouch that can hold up to 11.4 liters (3 gal.) of water and enough food to feed six men. She feeds herself and her young from this pouch. This bird also gorges itself on fish, then flies into the wilderness to sit in some lonely, isolated spot for days, its bill resting on its breast. For this reason, the pelican is used to describe melancholy (Ps. 102:6).

There are two species of pelicans in the Near East—the white pelican and the Dalmatian pelican. Jewish law declared the pelican unclean (Lev. 11:8; Deut. 14:17).

20. Pigeons. This bird was acceptable as an Israelite sacrifice if a person were unable to bring a lamb. In Scripture, the pigeon may be any member of a widely distributed sub-family of birds (*columbinae*). The term *dove* is loosely applied to many of the smaller species found in this sub-family. (See "Dove.") The term "young pigeon" is usually used when referring to its cultic or sacrificial use. The pigeon is almost always mentioned with the turtledove; doves are actually pigeons.

21. Quail. The Lord used quail (Hebrew, *selaw*) to supply food to the Israelites in the wilderness. God caused a mighty wind to bring enough quail to feed them for more than a month (Ex. 16:13). The Israelites spread the quail around the camp to dry in the sun and air (Num. 11:32).

ASHURNASIRPAL HUNTING LIONS. *Lions once roamed in the hills and thickets of Palestine, posing a real danger to the population. Smaller than their African counterparts, they were no less feared. Kings made a sport of lion hunting. In this relief (ca. ninth century B.C.), King Ashurnasirpal of Assyria is shown aiming at a lion. His driver stands with him in the chariot while two footmen prod the injured beast into the king's range.*

THE ANIMALS AND INSECTS OF PALESTINE

Quail are considered a small game bird of great delicacy. They fly in large flocks across the Mediterranean, sometimes in such numbers as to cover small islands. The quail is weak of wing and often flies with the wind. When it does land, it is often exhausted and easily caught by hand, which is how the Israelites caught them. The quail of Scripture was the European, not American, quail.

22. Ravens. Eight or more species of ravens are found in Palestine. The raven (Hebrew, *oreb;* Greek, *korax*) resembles the crow in size, shape, and color; but its black feathers are more iridescent. Ravens live in pairs and are devoted parents, while crows are so solitary that they drive their young from the nest as soon as they can fend for themselves.

The raven of the Scriptures is undoubtedly the common raven, which is found in all parts of Palestine.

The raven was an unclean bird by the Hebrew law. The world has commonly portrayed the bird as an omen of evil, but the Bible makes no such connection. In fact, the raven seemed to be favored by God, since it was used to bring meat and bread to the prophet Elijah (1 Kin. 17:4, 6). Also, Christ used the raven in His illustration of God's providence (Luke 12:24). Scripture refers to the raven 11 times (e.g., Gen. 8:7; Job 38:41; Ps. 147:9; Prov. 30:17; Is. 34:11).

23. Sparrows. The Hebrew word *sippor*—rendered *sparrow* in Psalms 84:3 and 102:7—more properly refers to the whole family of small birds that do not feed exclusively on grain. The very poor used sparrows as offerings (Matt. 10:29; Luke 12:6). The sparrow was considered a domestic bird.

24. Storks. An unclean bird by Levitical law (Lev. 11:19; Deut 14:18), the stork is much like the crane but larger. It feeds on insects, snails, and frogs. The common stork stands about 1.2 m. (4 ft.) high with a wing span 2.1 m. (7 ft.). The white stork has black only on the tips of its wings. The black stork, also found in Palestine, has a black neck and back. Because of its long legs, the stork can find its food in the water as well as on the land. The bird builds its nest in high places, usually trees or lofty ruins (Ps. 104:17).

In most places where the stork lives, it is protected by man. Ancient people believed that the offspring could recognize its parents throughout its life. The Hebrew word for stork, *hasidah,* meant "affectionate." Storks have powerful wings, and they regularly migrate to Africa. The bird has no vocal organs; the only sound it makes is created by rapidly snapping its long bill, making a sound similar to castanets. The stork is also mentioned in Jeremiah 8:7 and Zechariah 5:9.

25. Swallows. Swallows (Hebrew, *deroi, sus* or *sis,* and *egur*) inhabit the Holy Land in abundance, making their nests atop high places. These migratory birds are known for their swiftness (Prov. 26:2). Some believe that the swift (*cypselus apus*) is meant by these Hebrew words.

26. Swans. The swan (Hebrew, *tinshemeth*) was an unclean bird of great strength, but which rarely attacked any living thing. It is mentioned only twice in Scripture (Lev. 11:18; Deut. 14:16). Some scholars believe that the word actually denotes the white owl. The Old Testament also used *tinshemeth* to refer to a reptile classed with the lizard.

27. Vultures. Different translations apply the Hebrew words for kite, gier eagle, and ossifrage to the vulture. This large bird is a scavenger of flesh, and was therefore considered unclean by Levitical law (Lev. 11:14; Deut. 14:13). Vultures have poor eyesight (Job 28:7) and rely on their sense of smell to locate food. Vultures are also mentioned in Isaiah 34:15.

B. Fish. The subject of fish and fishing weaves its way through much of the Bible. At least seven of the apostles—Peter, Thomas, Nathaniel (probably Bartholomew), John, James the elder, and "two other of His disciples"—made fishing their livelihood upon the Sea of Galilee, or Gennesaret (Matt. 4:18; Luke 5:6–9; John 21:3). We learn in John 21:1–6 that these apostles returned to fishing after Jesus' resurrection. Like many other fishermen of their day, the disciples fished with nets and hooks. They may have also fished with a baited hook on the end of a line. Peter probably fished with pole and hook when Jesus told him to cast a hook and catch a fish for the tribute tax (Matt. 17:27).

The fish quickly became Christianity's chief symbol. Early Christians who gathered for secret meetings in the catacombs of Rome used the sign of a fish to signal fellow Christians that a meeting was near. They probably chose the Greek word for fish (*ichthus*) as a code for the name of Christ: *Iesous Christos Theou Huios Soter* (Jesus Christ, God's Son, Savior). The first letters of these Greek words combine to make the word *ichthus* in Greek.

THE ANIMALS AND INSECTS OF PALESTINE

HORUS. *Egyptians believed the predatory hawk represented the god Horus. This statue of Horus, which dates from the seventh century B.C., wears the crown of Upper and Lower Egypt.*

1. Species of Fish. The ancient Hebrews caught and ate fish from the many lakes and rivers of Palestine and Syria. Unfortunately, the Bible names no particular kinds of fish that the Hebrews favored. So we must assume they went after the same types of fish that are popular in the Near East today.

a. Freshwater Fish. Fish are plentiful today in the Jordan River and its tributaries, as well as in the other tributaries to the Dead Sea. Even small ponds and fountains in this area have plenty of fish. The pond called Mezereib, near Jordan, and the fountains of Capernaum and Elisha, near Jericho, are well supplied with water life.

The barbel, the bigger species of carp, has grown to such size in the Euphrates River that it is called the "camel fish." The Hebrews probably saw many fish of the "black fish" family. Many scholars believe that the Hebrews generally refused to eat the black fish; but it was held in high esteem by the Romans. Black fish are caught today with a large hook fixed to a pole; this method may be suggested in Matthew 17:27. The catfish may reach large sizes. Josephus recorded that these were present in the Nile.

Carp are still plentiful throughout Syria, where they originated before passing into Europe. The carp was the sacred fish at Urfah, and is found in many other fishponds throughout the Jordan area.

The mormyrus swims upriver, like the bass, and is considered one of the tastiest fish produced in freshwaters. We also find perch, loach, bream, and the common eel in Palestine. Trout are plentiful in its mountain streams, and a species of salmon is among the

14

What Swallowed Jonah?

As long as there are little children, Bible storybooks, and Sunday schools, the story of Jonah will be told. Some of those storybooks will tell about Jonah and the whale, and some will tell about Jonah and the great fish. Which is right?

The answer seems simple enough if one checks only the Book of Jonah. Virtually every English translation says that Jonah was swallowed by a "great fish" (Jon. 1:17). Other verses (2:1, 10) refer only to "the fish."

Yet when Jesus refers to the story of Jonah in Matthew 12:40, He says, "For as Jonah was three days and three nights in the whale's belly; so shall the Son of man be three days and three nights in the heart of the earth." Thus the confusion.

Jonah began his voyage at the seaport of Joppa, which is on the Mediterranean Sea. Very few whales are found in the Mediterranean. But the sperm whale, which is sometimes found here, can swallow a person whole.

A 30-m. (100-ft.) whale captured off Cape Cod in 1933 had a mouth nearly 4 m. (12 ft.) wide. This was easily large enough to have engulfed a man. Interestingly, an enlargement of the whale's nasal sinus provided a storage compartment of air.

A newspaper article in the *Cleveland* (Ohio) *Plain Dealer* reported that Dr. Ransome Harvey found a little dog in the head of a whale after it had fallen from a ship six days earlier. Dr. Harry Rimmer, President of the Research Science Bureau of Los Angeles, has documented reports from the 1920s which tell of a sailor being rescued from the stomach of a shark 48 hours after he had been swallowed.

What swallowed Jonah? We can't be certain. But whatever it was, it caused him to repent of his stubbornness and carry God's message to Nineveh.

THE ANIMALS AND INSECTS OF PALESTINE

edible fish of the Nile and the large rivers of Syria.

b. Saltwater Fish. Fish of many different species are still found along Syria's seacoast—barracuda, great sea bream, mackerel, flying fish, gudgeon, mullet, herrings, shad, and sharks and one species of sea mammal.

We are told that "God created great whales" (Gen. 1:21). By the term *whale,* the ancients no doubt meant sea monsters in general. The root of the Hebrew word for whale (*tan*) clearly suggests a creature of great length—without necessarily meaning that the creature was a sea animal. In fact, *tan* is often translated *dragon* or *leviathan,* but *dragon* is incorrect. From other Semitic languages such as Ugaritic we know that both *tanin* and *leviathan* refer to whales.

Neither the Old nor the New Testament clearly states that a whale swallowed Jonah, although the KJV improperly uses this term in Matthew 12:40. Scripture tells us simply that Jonah was swallowed by a "great fish" (Jon. 1:17).

But whales were not unknown in the Mediterranean. Sightings of whales have been recorded in this area occasionally throughout history. The whales most likely to be encountered would be the humpback whale and the fin whale.

Toothed whales were probably more common in early times than at present. In fact, the bones of a great toothed whale were on exhibit in pre-Roman times at a pagan temple at Joppa (now called Jaffa), the very place from which Jonah set sail. At the time, legend said these were the bones of a dragon monster slain by Perseus. The bones remained at Joppa until conquering Romans carried them triumphantly home to their capital.

2. Methods of Fishing. We can see people in the act of fishing in Egyptian and Assyrian sculptures and paintings. These show us that the ancients used methods of fishing very similar to those used by fishermen today. They employed the line and hook, rod and hook, rod and line, and net.

a. Nets. The ancient Hebrews used nets for fishing and hunting. Scripture mentions several kinds of nets for different purposes. The Hebrew word *cherem* denoted a net used for either fishing or hunting (Ezek. 26:5, 14; 47:10; Hab. 1:15, 17). The word *mikmōreth* denoted the net of a fisherman (Isa. 19:8; cf. Hab. 1:15–16, where "drag" is a rendering of the same word).

The New Testament mentions the use of nets for fishing only. We believe the ancient Hebrews used woven nets much like the nets of Egypt, which are mentioned more than once in Scripture (cf. Isa. 19:8).

b. Hooks and Rods. The Egyptians mastered the art of catching fish by hook in ancient times. Job 41:1–7 suggests that very large fish were probably caught with hooks or spears. The apostles who fished upon the Sea of Galilee probably used hooks and rods, as well as nets (Matt. 17:27).

c. Spears. Fishermen used spears in very early times to capture the crocodile and the larger species of fish (Job 41:2). Some fishermen in Arab countries still practice spearfishing.

3. Fish in Ancient Trade. Laws concerning fish as food (Lev. 11:9–12; Deut. 14:9–10) suggest that the methods of catching fish were known even in the time of the Exodus. Fishermen may have used the net even in Egypt's early period (Job 18:8; 19:6). They preserved fish in pools, from which the prey was easily taken (Song 7:4; Is. 19:10).

Mosaic law declared that fish having scales and fins were proper for food, while those without scales were unclean (Lev. 11:9–10). This ruled out eels, sharks, and some other saltwater creatures. The Jews in the wilderness fondly remembered the fish that they ate in Egypt (Num. 11:5), but we do not know which kinds of fish they recalled. Fish was a favorite food in the Promised Land so we assume that the Israelites found a ready supply in the lakes and rivers from Palestine and Syria, as well as in the sea.

Freshwater fish, especially the black fish, were salted like sea fish. The historian Strabo (808–849) tells us that the fish wharf of Taricheaea on the Sea of Galilee got its name from this practice.

The Jews enjoyed eating and trading sea fish quite as much as fresh fish. Sidon got its name from being a popular place where fish trade was carried on. We learn from Nehemiah 13:16 that the Phoenicians of Tyre frequented Jerusalem as fish dealers.

A gate on Jerusalem's northeast border was named the Fish Gate (2 Chr. 33:14; Neh. 3:3; 12:39; Zeph. 1:10). This gate is elsewhere called "the first gate" (Zech. 14:10). Some Bible scholars believe that fish from the Sea of Galilee were brought in through this gate.

IV. Reptiles and Insects. It seems as though most of the animals mentioned in the

THE ANIMALS AND INSECTS OF PALESTINE

OSTRICH. *Ostriches once inhabited the semi-desert areas of Israel. Considered unclean and "cruel" by the early Israelites (Lam. 4:3), the ostrich lays its eggs in conspicuous places and quickly deserts them when danger approaches. The birds are too heavy to fly, but can easily outrun a horse.*

Bible are big, colorful ones that do spectacular things. But notice how many history-making events in the Bible turn on the actions of small reptiles and insects.

Sin and temptation were first introduced by the actions of a snake (cf. Gen. 3). Three of the terrible plagues that God sent upon the Egyptians were plagues of insects—lice, flies, and locusts (Ex. 8:16–32; 10:1–20). Aaron proved that God was with him by turning his rod into a snake (Ex. 7:8–12). John the Baptist lived on locusts and wild honey made by bees (Mark 1:6). In fact, the Promised Land was described as a land "that floweth with milk and honey" (Lev. 20:24).

A *reptile* is an animal, always cold-blooded, that zoologists classify between birds and amphibians in its complexity of physical structure. The reptiles of the Bible are much like the ones we know: snakes, lizards, turtles, crocodiles, and so on.

Likewise, insects of biblical times were very much like the ones we know. Flies, grasshoppers, beetles, and mosquitoes are commonly known insects. Many different insects are mentioned in the Bible.

A. Why They Flourished. Several factors combined to give reptiles and insects a notable influence upon the lives of the Hebrew people.

1. Climate. The climate of the Holy Land varied greatly for such a small nation. High mountains, dry deserts, hot river valleys and barren, stony ground gave opportunity for a wide variety of insects and reptiles to make their homes in the land. In the desert, lizards abounded and the sand fleas made life miserable for the wandering Hebrew people. Flies also swarmed in hot, jungle-like lowlands and in the desert in summer.

2. Inadequate Control. Man had little control over nature in Bible times; there were no insecticides and no insight into the diseases that some insects carried. The semi-nomadic life of the early Hebrews brought them into contact with a wide variety of reptiles and insects, and their lack of knowledge about these creatures often brought hardships.

3. Food Value. Unlike our Western culture today, many Near Eastern societies used reptiles and insects for food. Reptiles were considered unclean among the Israelites, but neighboring people did eat snakes, lizards, and turtles. Even the Hebrews were permitted to eat locusts, grasshoppers, and perhaps beetles (Lev. 12:22).

In taking a look at the reptiles and insects of the Bible, we need to remember the Bible is an ancient Semitic book, so many of the terms it uses are inexact by our standards. (For example, we really don't know what organism is meant in many places where the word *lice* is used.) Even so, the Bible gives us some inter-

THE ANIMALS AND INSECTS OF PALESTINE

FISH. *Fish from the Sea of Galilee are as important to the diet of the modern Israelis as they were to their ancestors. In 1965, the Sea of Galilee yielded 304 tons of this particular species, the Tilapia.*

esting glimpses of the reptiles and insects that were familiar to the Israelites and early Christians of Palestine. (These species are still there today.)

B. Reptiles. Reptiles were the earliest living things; in fact, they were created on the same day as man (cf. Gen. 1:24–25, where "creeping thing" is usually interpreted to mean reptiles and insects).

1. Chameleons. *Chameleon* is the KJV's rendering of two Hebrew words, *tinshemeth* and *koah*. The chameleon is listed as an unclean animal (Lev. 11:30).

2. Lizards. Called *leta'ah* in Hebrew, lizards were regarded as unclean (Lev. 11:30).

In Bible lands, green lizards were plentiful in cultivated land and in woods. Much of the present land of Israel was covered with thick forests in Bible times; agriculture has stripped much of this wooded land.

Wall lizards of the same *Lacertidue* family also abounded in farm areas, crawling over any stony surface available. The warm weather associated with the growing season brought out many varieties of lizards.

The yellowish lizards of the dry desert lands hid under rocks and burrowed in the ground, but didn't climb well. The sandy deserts often produced lizards up to 61 cm. (2 ft.) in length.

Southern Judea had "land monitors" that were from 1 to 1.5 m. (4 to 5 ft.) in length and lived as far south as the Sinai. They had long snouts with sharp, pointed teeth and long tails. Leviticus 11:30 refers to this type of lizard. "Water monitors" lived in the streams, rivers

and lakes of the area. They were even larger and could be quickly identified in the water by the high ridge on their backs.

3. Snakes (Serpents). The word *serpent* is used in the Bible as freely as we now use the word *snake*. In Genesis 49:17, *adder* (Hebrew, *shephiphon*) probably refers to the horned sand snake of Arabia and Egypt. This poisonous snake often coils and waits—perhaps in a sandy imprint of a camel's hoof—until a small animal comes along. Then it strikes, bites, poisons its victim, and kills for food. Most mature animals can smell the adder and are terribly afraid of it.

The Hebrew word *pethen* in Psalms 58:4 and 91:13 probably refers to the Egyptian cobra, *Naja háje*. Some feel that another Hebrew word for adder (*aksub*, as in Ps. 140:3; Prov. 23:32) might mean the horn viper, the puff adder, or the common adder. The Septuagint translators believed this word in Psalm 5:9 referred to the asp; so did Paul when he quoted this verse in Romans 3:13.

The "asp" (Hebrew, *pethen*) is also thought to refer to the Egyptian cobra (see above), for it was said to live in holes in the ground. The asp was small and very poisonous (Deut. 32:33), for it was most dangerous to allow an infant child to play at the hole of such a snake (Isa. 11:8).

The Egyptian cobra has a hood that flares when it is about to strike. Its diet consists of frogs and mice. It has been called "the spitter," due to its habit of spitting just before it bites. Queen Cleopatra of Egypt is said to have committed suicide by putting an asp to her breast.

The King James Version of the Bible uses the word *cockatrice* for a very poisonous snake (Is. 11:8; 14:29; Jer. 8:17), although we cannot identify exactly what snake is meant by the Hebrew phrase behind it. Some think it is the yellow viper, some the cerastes, and others think the KJV uses the term to apply to any venomous serpent. The Hebrew terms *siph'oni* and *seph'a* are rendered *cockatrice* in some passages but *adder* in others.

Viper is the KJV's rendering of the Hebrew word *'eph'eh*. The Old Testament use of this word is unclear and could mean any of several snakes (cf. Job 20:16; Is. 30:6).

The most familiar New Testament reference to a viper is in Acts 28:1–6, which tells how Paul was bitten by one. But the New Testament word (*echidna*) can also be used for any poisonous snake. The passage in Acts 28 probably refers to the common viper, which is of-

THE ANIMALS AND INSECTS OF PALESTINE

ten found on the Mediterranean coast. Vipers were different from other snakes in that they gave live birth to their young, instead of laying eggs.

The "brass serpent" of Numbers 21 indicates a classical respect for snakes; they are still highly regarded in some places today. At God's command, Moses erected a brass snake on a pole so that people who had been bitten by live snakes could look at it and be healed. The New Testament's direct symbolism of the "brass serpent" (cf. John 3:14–15) refers to Jesus' death on the cross. The serpent has become an important symbol in other instances too.

4. Other Reptiles. One whole section of reptile study in the Bible could concern itself with what appears to have been a giant land/water animal. It has been variously translated as *dragon, whale,* and *satyr* in the Old Testament; the only New Testament reference to this creature (Rev. 12:3–17 ff.) is translated simply as *dragon.*

Most likely these animals were crocodiles (cf. Ps. 74:13; Is. 34:14; Jer. 51:34). Whales are also a possibility, but the Bible writers were more familiar with whales and probably would have identified them as such. Most New Testament scholars agree that the use of *dragon* in the Book of Revelation is a symbolic reference to Satan and not to an actual dragon.

Again, the *leviathan* (Hebrew, *livyathan*) in Job 41 probably refers to the Nile crocodile. In two other places similar reference is made (Ps. 74:14; Is. 27:1). However, in Psalm 104:26 *livyathan* probably means a whale.

There were indeed many crocodiles in Bible lands in former centuries. However, man's taming of the land has crowded out the mighty crocodile; the last one was killed in the Jordan River in the mid-1800s, and there have not been any since.

V. Insects. For every star you can see in the sky on a clear night, scientists have estimated that there are 100 kinds of insects—a total of over 800,000 kinds. There are billions of insects of each kind. Throughout history, insects have covered the earth in great numbers.

Some insects are mentioned in the Bible as they affected events and people. Others are mentioned to illustrate a spiritual truth. Locusts and other locust-like insects are the most often mentioned, but others are frequently more important.

Of one thing we may be sure: In the Med-

FISHING BOATS. *Fishermen cast their nets while moored at the Sea of Galilee, north of Tiberias. Snow-topped Mount Hermon rises majestically above the northern shores of the lake, which has provided food for the region from antiquity.*

iterranean area with its heat, humidity, and poor health conditions, insects were a sad fact of everyday life for the Israelites.

A. Ants. Two sections of the Book of Proverbs mention ants in order to point out the hardworking nature of these tiny insects. Proverbs 6:6–8 and 30:25 point out that ants work without supervision and plan ahead for times when food will be scarce.

Ants are any of the myriad insects belonging to the *Formicidae* family. There are 104 types of ants in the Eastern Hemisphere and only two are "harvesting ants," as described in Proverbs. These ants nested near grain fields, threshing floors, or granaries. Since the harvester ants also collected their grain from the sown seed, they often prevented germination entirely.

The people in Bible lands accepted and even admired the ants for their hard work. Historical records outside the Bible document the presence of ants from earliest times.

14

THE ANIMALS AND INSECTS OF PALESTINE

THE ANIMALS AND INSECTS OF PALESTINE

B. Bees and Hornets. Bees and wasps (called "hornet wasps" in the Hebrew, from a word that refers to their stinging power) are "social insects" that cooperate to do their work. The honeybee seems to be the only variety in the Bible, for each time that Scripture describes the bee, it also mentions the fact that it produces honey.

Samson found a swarm of bees in a lion carcass (Judg. 14:8), and wild bees placed honey in other odd locations (Deut. 32:13; Ps. 81:16).

The Septuagint rendering of Proverbs 6:8 tells us, "Go to the bee, and learn how diligent she is, and how earnestly she is engaged in her work, whose labors kings and private men use for health, and she is desired and respected by all. Though weak in body she is advanced by honouring wisdom." Obviously the ancient writers admired the bee's industrious traits.

Honey was the most highly prized sweet treat of the Bible (1 Kin. 14:3; Song 5:1; Ezek. 27:17). This was another reason for this insect's good reputation.

While the bee produced something that man desired, the hornet or wasp was a pest. The Hebrew word for hornet is *sir' ah*. This insect is of the same genus as the wasp, but it is larger and more vicious. The hornet's troubles for man are described in Exodus 23:28, Deuteronomy 7:20, and Joshua 24:12. These small, stinging flyers could do much harm; ancient secular accounts tell of whole cities that had to flee from swarms of wasps or hornets.

As the Bible records, God used these tiny fighters to teach His people much-needed lessons. Read, for example, Deuteronomy 7:20–23.

C. Beetles, Crickets. Biblical references to "beetles" or "crickets" (Lev. 11:22) seem to be a poor translation of the Hebrew word *hargāl*. The Hebrew word most likely refers to one of the three related families of insects—locusts, grasshoppers, or crickets. However, there can be little doubt that many varieties of true beetles did live in the Bible lands, among them the house cricket and the field cricket. Some experts feel that Exodus 8:21 refers to a true beetle, since the Egyptians worshiped the beetle as a god of fertility and immortality.

COBRA OR ASP. *The desert cobra is a glossy black snake found in Israel and throughout the Middle East. It does not rear up or have a hood like the Egyptian or Indian Cobra. Some think Ecclesiastes 10:11 refers to this snake.*

THE ANIMALS AND INSECTS OF PALESTINE

LOCUSTS. *Great clouds of locusts still periodically devour crops and forests, especially in the Middle East. The picture at left shows a fig tree in full leaf. The second picture, taken 15 minutes later, shows how a swarm of locusts has stripped the tree bare of all greenery.*

D. Caterpillars. The caterpillar (also the *cankerworm* of Joel 1:4; Nah. 3:15–16, and the *palmerworm* of Joel 1:4) was a wormlike crawler that may simply have been an earlier developmental stage of the locust.

The caterpillar (Hebrew, *hasil*) devoured foodstuffs, according to the Bible (1 Kin. 8:37). Thus God sometimes used the caterpillar as a punishment (Ps. 78:46; 105:34).

The cankerworm (Hebrew, *yelek*) may also have been the locust in one of its molting stages. In this stage, the insect is even more to be dreaded than as a mature creature.

The palmerworm (Hebrew, *gayam*—the word means "pilgrim worm") mentioned in Joel 1:4 is known for its wide-ranging habits. One translation calls it a "creeping locust," as though it were the same insect as the locust, without wings. Its destructiveness is well described in Amos 4:9.

E. Fleas. Fleas (Hebrew, *par'osh*) live on the blood of animals and make their homes on and under the skin of animals. The flea's ability to leap is astounding; it can jump 200 times its own body length.

Fleas were well-known pests in Bible times, but the insect is mentioned only twice in Scripture (1 Sam. 24:14; 26:20). The area around Tiberias was known for having many terrible fleas. A popular saying was that the king of the fleas had his court in Tiberias.

F. Flies. Flies have been pests to man since the beginning of time. But in our English Bibles, the word *fly* refers to any one of a variety of bothersome insects. The plague of flies (Hebrew, *arab*) in Exodus 8:21 ff. probably refers to a mixture of tiny insects. It could

mean that flies, mosquitoes, and many other kinds of bugs plagued the Egyptians. (*See* "Beetles, Crickets.")

The phrase "diverse sorts of flies" in Psalm 78:45 continues that idea. Yet some translations of the Bible take this phrase to mean "dog fly" or "gadfly."

We who live in more temperate climates cannot comprehend the abundance of flies in the Bible lands. Cattle were literally bothered to death by them. Larger flies so troubled humans with their bites that deaths were credited to them. The heat, the lack of sanitation, and the people's inability to fight the flies only added to their numbers.

Farming has always been difficult in the Holy Land, and the pests such as flies only made the task harder. One tribe—the Ekronites—worshiped a god they called *Baalzebub* ("the lord of flies"), because they believed he controlled the flies (2 Kin. 1:2). The Hebrew word *zebub* meant one of the order *Diptera*, especially the domestic fly.

In Ecclesiastes 10:1, the writer likens a little folly to the trouble caused by a few flies (again the Hebrew, *zebub*). The flies laid eggs under the skin of some animals, which brought painful ulcers.

G. Gnats. These tiny pests were in the same family as the mosquito and are an extremely troublesome insect. They grow and reproduce in wet climates and move about mainly at night. The only time the gnat is mentioned in the Bible is in reference to its small size (Matt. 23:24).

H. Lice. Lice (or ticks) are mentioned as the third plague on Egypt in Exodus 8:16. Lice

14

THE ANIMALS AND INSECTS OF PALESTINE

THE ANIMALS AND INSECTS OF PALESTINE

are parasite pests that live on the skin of animals and humans. Perhaps the sand fly is meant in Exodus 8:16, since "dust" is mentioned in this passage. Both sand flies and lice are common in the Nile Valley. Two Hebrew words (*kinnam* or *kinnim*) are translated both as *lice* and *gnats*.

I. Locusts. Great clouds of locusts have been mentioned in the earliest records of man. They are still seen today, especially in the Near East. The KJV uses seven different names to refer to the same insect that one Hebrew word (*'arbeh*) records—the locust, bald locust, beetle, cankerworm, caterpillar, grasshopper, and palmerworm.

1. True Locusts. English Bibles often use the word *locust* as the rendering of the Hebrew *'arbeh*. This word probably refers to the migratory locust or similar insects. Migratory locusts are about 5 to 8 cm. (2 to 3 in.) long and move throughout their lives, searching for food. They travel in large swarms and cause a great deal of destruction by their eating habits. These locusts should not be confused with the 17-year locust, which North Americans commonly call the "locust."

Migratory locusts eat vegetation of any kind. The huge swarms can strip fields, trees, grasslands, and any other plant life in their path. Their wings carry them upward, where they travel much like gliders; locusts have been known to sail for 160 km. (100 mi.) or more before coming down.

They land at night in trees or in grasses. When the morning sun comes up, they take off again to find food.

When locusts come to a river, they try to fly over. If wind currents do not carry them across, they simply fall into the river by the thousands, forming a bridge for the other locusts. Thus, even in dying they cause trouble; downstream the millions of dead locusts become a breeding ground for disease.

Read of the destruction of crops by locusts in Joel 1:1–12. The Romans called them the "burners of the land," because of the destruction they caused.

Farmers have tried many ways of fighting

Could the Ark Hold the Animals?

Children as well as adults find their imaginations stirred by the Old Testament's account of Noah's building an enormous ark and gathering the animals, and of the great Flood that covered the earth.

Many have often wondered whether such an ark could really have held so many animals. Encyclopedias tell us that there are about 500,000 species of animals on earth, yet Noah brought the animals into the ark by pairs and sometimes groups of seven. Imagine the space required to contain them and their food supply for a year!

The Bible tells us the ark was 300 cubits long, 50 cubits wide, and 30 cubits high. The cubit was a common unit of measurement in ancient times, but the length of a cubit was determined differently by each nation. Some considered a cubit to be the distance from the elbow to the middle finger; others thought it to be the distance of the entire arm; while still others measured it as the length of a newborn baby. A cubit could vary in length from about 45 to 58 cm. (18 to 22 1/2 in.). Using the cubit's lower standard of 45 cm., we find that the ark measured 22 1/2 by 135 m. (75 by 450 ft.) with a height of 13 1/2 m. (45 ft.). That would make the ark considerably larger than a football field and about three stories high. The ark was divided into three floors, providing a total of 3,037 sq. m. (101,250 sq. ft.) of living area. All this space was usable, since the ark did not require engines to propel it through the water.

Even with such a tremendous capacity, could the ark have housed the animals described in the Bible? To answer that question, we must determine what Genesis means by the term *kind* (Gen. 3:7). Some scholars feel that *kind* approximates our modern classification of "family," which would put the maximum number of animals on the ark at about 700. But other scholars feel that *kind* refers to species instead of animal "families." There are approximately 1,072,300 animal species (a figure provided by the American taxonomist Ernst Mayer), and many did not need to be aboard. Fish, sponges, many insects, and amphibians would have survived the flood waters. But even if we assume that as many as 50,000 animals were on the ark, there was sufficient room to accommodate them.

Could the ark have supported a full cargo of animals? Biblical scholars are divided on this point, and they disagree about the type of wood used to construct the ark. Some believe the "gopher wood" mentioned in the biblical account was cypress. But this is doubtful because cypress wood shrinks and withers and is easily attacked by insects. Others believe the wood used was the highly prized teak of India. Teak was available close to where the ark was built.

oncoming locusts; the most popular method through the centuries has been to start fires, in hopes that the smoke would steer them away. Even this is not entirely successful.

Mosaic Law allowed the Hebrews to eat locusts (Lev. 11:22; Matt. 3:4). However, some think that John the Baptist's food was not the locust, but the fruit of the carob tree—"husks" much like the prodigal son ate (Mark 1:6; Luke 15:16). The most popular way to prepare locusts for eating was to dry them, put them in a sack, and simply make them available for visitors to "dig in" and eat as snacks.

Other Bible references to locusts speak of God's judgment and punishment by plagues of locusts (Ex. 10:4–15; Deut. 28:38–42; 1 Kin. 8:37; Joel 2:1–11). In Joel 2:25, the invading armies are compared to a swarm of locusts.

2. Grasshoppers. Our English Bibles mention the *grasshopper* in Judges 6:5, Job 39:20, Ecclesiastes 12:5, and Jeremiah 46:23. The destructiveness of grasshoppers is described in Amos 7:1. The Bible also uses the grasshopper as an example of something that has little importance or value (Num. 13:33; Is. 40:22).

In biblical parlance, the main difference between locusts and grasshoppers lies in the insect's ability to fly. The locusts take wing and go great distances, while the grasshopper "hops" on the ground.

Grasshopper is the English rendering of four Hebrew words: *'arbeh* (as is *locust*), *hagab, gob,* and *gobay.* The second word (found in Lev. 11:22; Num. 13:33; Eccles. 12:5; Is. 40:22) is probably referring to the English grasshopper.

J. Moths. In the Bible, this word refers to the ordinary genus clothes moth, of which there were several species in Israel. Both the worm stage and the full-grown moth were a threat to clothing in Bible times.

Jesus referred to the moth as a constant threat to man's savings for the future (Matt. 6:19–20). This statement refers to material goods, since there was no paper money in biblical times. (*See* "Money and Economics.") The ancients had no mothballs, so it was risky business for them to store clothing and other fragile goods for the future.

Moths are mentioned elsewhere (Job 13:28; Ps. 39:11; Is. 50:9; Hos. 5:12; James 5:12). Job 4:19 uses the moth as a symbol of vulnerability.

K. Spiders. The Bible symbolically emphasizes the weakness of the spider's web. These tiny insects were known from the beginning of time, and the climate and life-style of Bible times must have made them very common. Indeed, over 600 varieties of spiders have been identified in Palestine.

Job 8:14 and Isaiah 59:5 mention the spider's web as both marvelous and easy to destroy. In the same way, Scripture says that man has false hope if he trusts in his own strength. In these verses, *spider* is a rendering of the Hebrew word *akkabish.*

L. Worms. The insect called *worm* (generally translating the Hebrew *toleah* or *tolath*) might have been any number of other creatures. Perhaps it was the common earthworm or the maggot so familiar in Bible times as the consumer of dead flesh.

When the Bible speaks of man as a worm, it probably means the common earthworm. But other varieties are meant when Exodus 16:24 says there were no "worms" in the manna; and when Deuteronomy 28:39 speaks of "worms" in the vines. Still other worms preyed on human flesh (Job 7:5; Is. 14:11). Luke writes that Herod Agrippa had a terrible affliction of worms (Acts 12:23).

Isaiah 66:24 and Mark 9:44 tell how fires were kept burning in the Hinnom Valley near Jerusalem, because the filth and rotting flesh dumped there bred many worms.

The "horseleech" mentioned in Proverbs 30:15 was a well-known Palestinian worm that lived in stagnant waters. It fastened itself to the nose or mouth of animals that drank from the water. Once in the animal, it multiplied quickly and lived on the animal's blood, finally killings its host. The Hebrew for *horseleech* was *alukah.*

VI. Clean and Unclean Animals. Even before the Flood, animals fell into these two divisions. Noah was told to take into the ark seven pairs of clean beasts and two pairs of unclean beasts (Gen. 7:2). At that time animals were not eaten, so the clean/unclean designation was probably for sacrifices. When Noah and his family left the ark, God told them, "Every moving thing that liveth shall be meat for you; even as the green herb have I given you all things" (Gen. 9:3).

Later Moses included dietary restrictions in the Law he handed down to the Israelites. Only certain creatures would be acceptable as food, that is, clean. The Lord told Moses, "Whatsoever parteth the hoof, and is cloven-footed, and cheweth the cud, among the

THE ANIMALS AND INSECTS OF PALESTINE

beasts, that shall ye eat" (Lev. 11:3). Basically the clean animals were ruminants, grazing animals that swallow their food quickly and bring it up later in small quantities to chew as a cud. Cattle, sheep and goats, and such wild game as deer and antelope fit this requirement. Yet ruminants without a cloven hoof—the camel for one—were unclean (Lev. 11:4–8). For a more detailed discussion of clean and unclean foods, *see* "Laws and Statutes."

VII. Animals in Worship. Though animal sacrifice seems repulsive to modern readers, it was the acceptable method of worship in ancient times. The Israelites at least refrained from human sacrifice, which was all too common among their peers. The first sacrifice the Bible tells of was Abel's. Adam and Eve's second son "brought of the firstlings of his flock and of the fat thereof. And the Lord had respect unto Abel and to his offering" (Gen. 4:4). His brother's offering of "the fruit of the ground" was not accepted.

In a sense, the sacrifice of animals for man's propitiation was a measure of God's mercy. For some crimes no animal substitution was permitted; the sinner's life must be forfeited. When it was possible, the Israelites redeemed their own lives by offering an animal.

Only three kinds of animals were offered in sacrifice, in addition to birds. These were cattle (oxen), sheep, and goats. The kind of animal to be sacrificed depended not on the seriousness of the sin, but on the social standing of the sinner. Thus a priest who sinned had to offer a bullock, a ruler required a male kid, and the common people could get by with only a female kid or a lamb (Lev. 4). Pigeons or turtledoves were an acceptable substitute for people who could not afford even that much. Whatever the animal, it was to be perfect, worthy of sacrifice. (An exception is found in Lev. 22:23.) For more information about the use of animals in worship, *see* "Worship Rituals."

PLANTS AND HERBS

From the beginning of Bible history, the land of Palestine has supplied a sufficient amount of food for the people and their cattle. The people of Bible lands found a use for nearly every plant, from the forests on Mount Lebanon to the scrubby shrubs of the desert.

The three main crops of Palestine were "wine that maketh glad the heart of man, and oil to make his face to shine, and bread [grain] which strengtheneth man's heart" (Ps. 104:15).

I. GRAINS
A. Barley
B. Corn
C. Millet
D. Rye
E. Wheat

II. VEGETABLES
A. Beans
B. Cucumbers
C. Gourds
D. Leeks
E. Lentils
F. Mandrakes
G. Onions

III. HERBS AND SPICES
A. Aloes
B. Anise
C. Balm or Balsam
D. Baytree or Laurel
E. Bdellium
  1. An Aromatic Substance
  2. A Mineral
F. Bitter Herbs
G. Calamus
H. Camphire
I. Cassia
J. Cinnamon
K. Coriander
L. Cummin
M. Fitches
N. Frankincense
O. Gall
  1. A Poisonous Herb
  2. A Secretion of the Liver
P. Garlic
Q. Hyssop
R. Mallow
S. Mint
T. Mustard
U. Myrrh
V. Myrtle
W. Rue
X. Saffron
Y. Spikenard
Z. Stacte

IV. FRUITS
A. Almonds
B. Apples
C. Figs
D. Grapes
E. Husks
F. Mulberries
G. Pistachio Nuts
H. Pomegranates
I. Sycamine
J. Sycamore Fruit

V. WOOD
A. Almug; Algum
B. Ash
C. Box Tree
D. Cedar
E. Chestnut
F. Cypress
G. Ebony
H. Fir
I. Gopher Wood
J. Oak
K. Pine
  1. An Evergreen
  2. A Deciduous Tree
L. Shittah or Acacia
M. Teil
N. Thyine

VI. ADDITIONAL PLANTS
A. Bulrushes
B. Cockles
C. Cotton
D. Flax
E. Grass
F. Hay
G. Juniper Bush
H. Lily
I. Nettles
J. Olives
K. Palms
L. Papyrus
M. Reeds
N. Roses
O. Soapwort
P. Straw
Q. Tares
R. Thorns and Thistles
S. Willows
T. Wormwood

PLANTS AND HERBS

I. Grains. Grain has always been one of the main ingredients in man's diet. Various grains have been grown where climate and soil conditions allow. Especially rich were the areas of the Tigris and Euphrates Rivers in the east, the Nile River in Egypt, and the Jordan Valley of Palestine.

Grain was used in many different ways in Bible times: for export, for food, and for sacrificial offerings (Gen. 4:3; Lev. 2:1). Also, Jesus used grain as an object for teaching, as in His parable of the sower (Mark 4:3) and His teaching about the Sabbath (Matt. 12:1).

Grain ("corn") and wine are used in the Old Testament as symbols of plenty and prosperity. In Deuteronomy 11:14, grain is mentioned as a gift of God; in Deuteronomy 18:4, it is described as an offering of obedience; and in Deuteronomy 28:51, the loss of grain is foretold as a warning of Israel's destruction.

When threshing season began, the grains were tossed into the air to remove the chaff. Isaiah suggests that the chaff was later burned (Is. 5:24). For a more complete description of this process, *see* "Agriculture."

A. Barley. The Hebrew word for barley is *seorah,* meaning "a hairy or bristling thing." It was so called because of the rough and prickly beard covering the ears. Barley belongs to the genus *Hordeum,* which was cultivated in Palestine (Ruth 1:22), in Egypt (Ex. 9:31), and in adjacent regions.

Barley was used in ceremonial offering (Num. 5:15), baked into cakes (Judg. 7:13), and fed to horses and camels (1 Kin. 4:28). Jesus used barley loaves to feed the five thousand (John 6:9). For food, it was held in low esteem and was believed to be a symbol of poverty. According to Adam Clarke, barley had scarcely one-third the value of wheat in ancient trade.[1]

B. Corn. When Americans or Britons think of corn and cornfields, they visualize long rows of tall, green stalks, tasseling for the harvest. This is not what the Bible means by "corn." In fact, the plant we now call "corn" was introduced to us by the American Indians, who called it "maize."

When the KJV speaks of "corn" in Mark 4:28 and Matthew 12:1, the Bible actually means "grain." The RSV correctly uses this term instead of "corn."

C. Millet. The Hebrew word for millet is

[1] *Adam Clarke's Commentary,* Vol. 1 (New York: Abingdon Press, n.d.), p. 557.

STALKS OF WHEAT. *Wheat was cultivated throughout Palestine, Egypt, and Mesopotamia from the earliest times. An important part of the diet of the Israelites (Ruth 2:23), wheat became a symbol of God's goodness and provision (Psa. 81:16).*

dohan. This term might refer to at least two kinds of grain. One is the cultivated grass known as *Panicum miliaceum,* the other is *Sorghum vulgare.* Both of these grains were cultivated in Palestine, Egypt, and other parts of the ancient world. God instructed Ezekiel to use "millet" for bread (Ezek. 4:9), and it was probably a staple item in the Israelite diet.

D. Rye. The Hebrew word for rye, mentioned in Exodus 9:32, is *kussemeth,* meaning "hairy or bearded grain." The same Hebrew noun is used in Ezekiel 4:9, where the KJV has *fitches.* The RSV translates it as *spelt.*

It is generally believed that this grain had less food value than wheat and was mixed with other grains to make bread (Ezek. 4:9). The Hebrew word may also refer to another inferior grain, emmer, which grows in the area today. Spelt is no longer grown there.

E. Wheat. The Hebrew word for wheat is *hittah.* The kind grown in biblical Egypt (Gen. 41:5–7) is believed to have been the variety with many heads on one stalk. This may also have been the kind of wheat grown in Palestine; but some scholars believe that another species was the "wheat" of Palestine.

Whatever the species, wheat had been cultivated from earliest times in Palestine, Egypt,

PLANTS AND HERBS

and Mesopotamia. In Egypt it was grown in abundance and was exported during early Christian times (Acts 27:38).

II. Vegetables. Everywhere the Hebrew people traveled, they included vegetables in their diet. Vegetables were boiled, eaten raw, or mixed with other foods. (*See* "Food and Eating Habits.") Some of the vegetables we have today have been known from ancient times.

A. Beans. The "beans" mentioned in the Bible were not found on a bushy plant like the beans of North America or Great Britain, although they were of the same family. The plant grew 91 cm. (3 ft.) high, with white peashaped blooms. The beans are large, coarse seeds. Sometimes the Israelites mixed these beans with other grain for bread (2 Sam. 17:28; Ezek. 4:9). Generally, these beans were eaten by the poorer classes of people.

B. Cucumbers. The Hebrew word for cucumber, *kishshu'ah,* could refer to either of two species of cucumbers grown in Egypt and Palestine today.

As Moses led the people through the desert, they still longed for the cucumbers of Egypt (Num. 11:5). They planted cucumber gardens in Palestine (Is. 1:8); in this text, the "lodge in a garden of cucumbers" refers to a shelter used by watchmen to guard the crops.

C. Gourds. The gourd that shaded Jonah (Jon. 4:6–10) may have been either the castor-oil plant or the pumpkin. Either of these could be considered a member of the gourd family.

Most scholars believe that the Hebrew word for gourd (*kikayon*) refers to the castor-oil plant. (This word is similar to the Egyptian word for the castor-oil plant, *kiki*.) The castor-oil plant grows rapidly up to 4.6 m. (15 ft.), with purplish-red stems, broad leaves, and fiery red fruit. Any slight injury causes it to wilt. Grown in southern Asia and Egypt, it is sometimes referred to as the "Christ Palm."

The wild gourd (Hebrew, *pakkuoth*) mentioned in 2 Kings 4:39 was gathered in Gilgal near Jericho and was very poisonous. It was a wild vine of the gourd family that flourished

DATES. *An important food for the Middle East, dates are eaten fresh or dried; they are also used in making wine. The date palm grows 18 to 24 m. (60 to 80 ft.) tall and lives for over 200 years. It reaches its fruit-bearing peak between its thirtieth and eightieth years.*

PLANTS AND HERBS

during extreme droughts. The fruit was gourd-like, eight or more centimeters (three or more inches) in diameter. Images of the same fruit (called *knops* in 1 Kings 6:18; 7:24) were carved in the cedar beams of Solomon's temple.

Some botanists believe that the plant *Ecballium elaterium* was the "wild gourd" of 2 Kings 4:39. Although the fruit of this plant was similar to the wild gourd, the plant grew upright with no tendrils, and could hardly have been the vine referred to.

D. Leeks. The Hebrew word *hasir* (spelled *chatzir* in Num. 11:5) usually meant grass. But Numbers 11:5 probably refers to the leek, which grew extensively in Egypt. When the children of Israel grew tired of eating manna, they remembered the foods of Egypt that they considered to be delicacies, such as the leek.

E. Lentils. This plant is from the pea family. The Hebrew word for lentils is *adhashim.* It has five or six pairs of oblong leaves on each stem and white, violet-striped flowers. These legumes are harvested and boiled to produce the red pottage mentioned in Genesis 25:30.

Lentils are grown in all parts of Palestine (cf. 2 Sam. 23:11). They were combined with other ingredients to make bread (Ezek. 4:9).

The *pulse* mentioned in Daniel 1:12, 16 and in 2 Samuel 17:23 is believed to have been the lentil plant.

F. Mandrakes. Mentioned in only two passages in the Bible (Gen. 30:14–16; Song 7:13), mandrakes were thought to aid fertility. The Hebrew word for this plant was *dudaim.*

We do not know whether the mandrakes of the Bible were the same as the plant known as mandrakes in Palestine today. This plant has a large, forked root with broad, wavy leaves sprouting from the base. The small purple flowers produce yellow fruit. Song of Solomon 7:13 notes the mandrakes' strong fragrance.

G. Onions. The only mention of the onion in the Bible is Numbers 11:5. The Hebrew word is *basal.* Grown in Egypt and other parts of the East, these onions are very large and of exceptional flavor.

III. Herbs and Spices. This large group of plants were in abundant supply in Bible times. They were found growing on mountains, hillsides, along riverbanks, and in valleys. Herbs grew wild in fields and were sometimes cultivated in gardens. The existence of some herbs is well documented by the Bible, while others are rarely mentioned.

Sometimes the Bible refers to herbs by name (e.g., mustard, Mark 4:31–32). At other times, it alludes to them in general terms (Rom. 14:2).

The Latin word for herb is *herba,* meaning "grass," "green stalks," or "blades." Some herbs grow as annuals and die soon after maturing. These usually multiply by reseeding themselves. Others are perennials, which multiply from the root; after a short period of winter dormancy, they sprout again when the spring rains begin. Psalm 37:2 and Matthew 6:30 mention herbs as symbols of a brief life.

A *spice* is a vegetable substance possessing a sharp taste and aromatic qualities. The Bible sometimes uses the Hebrew word for spices in general (*bosem*), which literally refers to the rich fragance of spices (Ex. 25:6; 1 Kin. 10:10). At other times, specific spices are mentioned, as in Exodus 30:23, Song of Solomon 4:14, and Ezekiel 27:19.

Spices were grown in Arabia, India, Persia, Syria, Palestine, and Egypt. There was an extensive commerce in spices between these countries (Gen. 37:25). For further information, *see* "Trade." The people of the ancient world possessed an incredible knowledge of how to use spices and herbs. When royal emissaries sent gifts to rulers of other countries, spices and herbs were usually included in their cargo.

These plants were used for many purposes, including medicines, food, flavorings, cosmetics, dyes, disinfectants, and perfumes. Often every part of the plant was used: leaves, branches, bark, blossoms, berries, and roots. Many of these herbs and spices are still in use today.

A. Aloes. The King James Version often uses this word in reference to a large tree, known in Hebrew as *ahalim.* Resin and perfume were made from the *ahalim.*

But the *ahalim* is not the true aloe of the lily family; instead, the Bible species had long, lance-shaped leaves. The fragrant substance extracted from the wood of this plant was used to embalm the dead (John 19:39) and for perfume (Ps. 45:8; Prov. 7:17; Song 4:14).

The "Lignaloes" to which Israel is compared (Num. 24:6) was probably the true aloe plant (genus *Aloe*). Botanists believe this plant originated in India.

B. Anise. The term *anise* mentioned in

PLANTS AND HERBS

Matthew 23:23 is derived from the Greek word *anethon*. It refers either to the dill or to the true anise. Both plants are similar and of the same plant family. Both grow about 91 cm. (3 ft.) high with clusters of yellow flowers. The seeds, leaves, and stem are used for medicine and cooking, and were a part of the ancient temple tithe. (Jesus denounced the Jews of His day for carefully obeying small laws, such as the spice tithe, and forgetting the more important ones.) Anise was cultivated in ancient Egypt and other Mediterranean countries, and still grows there today.

C. Balm or Balsam. The *balm* mentioned in Genesis 37:25 is an extremely fragrant resinous substance extracted from the balsam tree. This was highly esteemed among the ancients (Jer. 46:11).

We do not know whether the balsam tree native to Arabia is the same one mentioned in Jeremiah 8:22 as the "balm of Gilead." The Hebrew word has a variety of spellings— *tzari, sori,* and *tsori;* it literally refers to the fragrance of the plant.

The balsam was a bushy evergreen growing 3.7 to 4.3 m. (12 to 14 ft.) high. The pale yellow gum was used as incense (Exod. 35:28) and dissolved in water as an ointment. The oil obtained from the bark, leaves, and berries was used as medicine. This medicinal "balm" is referred to in Jeremiah 8:22, 51:8 as a symbol of spiritual healing.

D. Bay tree or Laurel. The meaning of the *bay tree* in Psalms 37:35 is obscure. The Hebrew word (*ezrah*) means "a green tree in its native soil." The Septuagint, Latin Vulgate,

A Bible Garden

The Bible refers often to gardens, fields, foods, feasts, and eating habits of people. Food was certainly an important aspect of life for the ancients. By cultivating a Bible garden, we can learn much about the eating habits and other customs of Bible times.

Many people find the experience of growing plants mentioned in the Scriptures an exciting way to learn about Bible lands. This project is well-suited to the home garden, a plot on the church campus, or a small garden space elsewhere.

A Bible garden would include many vegetables that can be grown in the temperate climate of North America, Great Britain, or Western Europe. For example, one could plant beans, lentils, cucumbers, leeks, onions, radishes, and garlic. In warmer climates, a Bible garden could also include melons, grapes, apricots, figs, and pomegranates.

One authority notes that biblical people crushed watermelon and mixed it with water to satisfy their thirst. They mixed juices of fruit with honey to make a tasty fruit punch and dried spring flower petals to brew fragrant teas.

A variety of herbs would also be in a Bible garden. Caraway, cumin, mint, mustard, parsley, sage, and thyme are but a few plants that were used for seasoning food.

Remember that the Israelites observed certain methods of planting that were quite different from our traditional gardening practices. So if you wish to make your Bible garden truly authentic, you may choose to follow these ancient methods.

For example, modern gardeners often plant two crops in the same furrow to take advantage of different growing seasons; but the Israelites could not

do this. Seed symbolized the Israelites themselves—the "seed" (descendants) of Abraham— and just as God forbade the Israelites to marry pagan peoples, He forbade them to mix their garden seed (Lev. 19:19; Deut. 22:9). This law constantly reminded the Israelites that they must remain a separate people. God's Law also prohibited planting trees near a place of worship (this assured that the Israelites would not revert to pagan tree worship—Deut. 16:21), so gardens near the temple had no fruit trees.

In the dry climate of Palestine, the Israelites customarily planted their crops beside streams (cf. Ps. 1:3; Is. 19:7), or dug irrigation ditches between the rows of plants (cf. Ezek. 17:7). Our gardens seldom require such special provisions for watering; but you may decide to lay out your Bible garden in this fashion to illustrate the methods that Israelite farmers used. It would also remind you of the symbolic importance of water in the Bible. Isaiah said that when God's people disobeyed Him, they would "be as an oak that fadeth, and as a garden that hath no water" (Is. 1:30). The writer of Proverbs said that God could direct a king's heart "as the rivers of water: he turneth it whithersoever he will" (Prov. 21:1)—a phrase that reminds us of the irrigation ditches which the Israelites used to channel water wherever they desired. The Bible often cites water as a spiritual symbol, and it was a very familiar commodity for the Hebrew gardener.

The ancients planned, planted, and tended their gardens with care. They enjoyed the fruits of their labor and celebrated the yield with great thanksgiving. We can do the same.

15

PLANTS AND HERBS

PLANTS AND HERBS

and RSV render it "cedar of Lebanon." But the NEB translates it to mean "a spreading tree in its native soil."

Henry B. Tristram, author of *Fauna and Flora of Palestine* (1884), theorized that this word refers to the sweet bay tree or laurel. This evergreen is found in northern and western Palestine. It branches from the base, becoming an upright tree with fragrant leaves fitting the psalmist's description of the "spreading bay tree."

E. Bdellium. This term has two possible meanings:

1. An Aromatic Substance. The Hebrew word (*bedolah*) may refer to a gum resin, similar to balm or myrrh. Genesis 2:12 states that bdellium is a product of the Havilah region in Persia. Numbers 11:7 says that bdellium is the color of manna. Some believe this substance came from a tree that produces a waxy, transparent substance that hardens and resembles pearls.

2. A Mineral. On the other hand, *bdellium* may refer to a mineral; but if so, we do not know which. (*See* "Minerals and Gems.")

F. Bitter Herbs. The people of Israel were commanded to eat the Passover lamb with "bitter herbs" (Ex. 12:8; Num. 9:11) to symbolize their Egyptian bondage. We do not know the kind of herbs or salad that is intended by this Hebrew word (*merorim*, "bitter"). According to the Mishna, these were lettuce, endive, coriander seeds, horehound, tansy, and horseradish. Modern Jews in Egypt and Arabia eat the Passover with lettuce and endive.

G. Calamus. This was a tall, reed-like grass with hollow stems. The Hebrew term for this plant (*Keneh bosem*) means "reed of fragrance." It is indeed a very sweet-smelling plant (Song 4:14).

The oil extracted from this grass was an ingredient in the anointing oil of Exodus 30:23. The calamus was grown throughout Palestine.

H. Camphire. The only mention of this plant in the Bible is in Song of Solomon 1:14; 4:13. Most scholars consider it to have been the henna. The Hebrew word for the plant is *kopher.*

This shrub grows approximately 3 m. (10 ft.) high. It flourished during Solomon's time at En-gedi and is still growing there today.

The leaves and young twigs were ground into powder and mixed with paste and hot water to produce a reddish-orange dye, which women used to paint their fingernails, toe-

nails, and the soles of their feet. (*See* "Clothing and Cosmetics.") Men also used this cosmetic to paint their beards. The "camphire" also grows in Egypt and other countries in the East today.

I. Cassia. The ingredients of the anointing oil referred to in Exodus 30:24 included the product of the cassia tree. The bark of this tree is similar to cinnamon and is valued for its aromatic qualities. The spice was available to the Israelites during the Exodus, having perhaps come to them from India by caravan. The Hebrew word for the cassia is *kiddah.* Ezekiel 27:19 implies that the people of Tyre purchased this spice in Dan on the northern border of Palestine.

In Psalm 45:8, the Hebrew word translated as *cassia* is *kesiah,* meaning "fragrant." It seems to be referring to another kind of plant.

J. Cinnamon. A native of Ceylon, cinnamon is a member of the laurel family. The tree grows about 9 m. (30 ft.) high with clusters of

FLOWERING ALMOND. *The almond tree blooms as early as January in the Holy Land. Ornamental architecture often copied the almond's beauty (Ex. 25:33–34), and Jacob sent almonds to Egypt as a gift (Gen. 43:11). The Israelites called it "the wakeful tree" (Jer. 1:11–12).*

PLANTS AND HERBS

MULBERRY. *The mulberry grows in southern Palestine, and it is still cultivated in Syria for its leaves, on which silkworms feed. Its berries furnished the ancients a tasty drink, which they sweetened with honey and flavored with spices.*

yellow and white flowers. Its very fragrant bark yields a golden yellow oil, which was used as one ingredient of the anointing oil (Ex. 30:23) and as perfume (Prov. 7:17).

The Hebrew word for this plant is *kinnamon*. It was one of the chief spices of the ancient Near East.

K. Coriander. The coriander plant belongs to the parsley family. It is an annual that grows 60 to 90 cm. (2 to 3 ft.) high, producing pink or white flowers. When dried, the coriander seeds are pleasant to taste and are used to flavor foods. The Hebrew word for coriander is *gad.*

This plant, known throughout Mediterranean countries from ancient times, was probably introduced to the Israelites in Egypt. When they saw manna in the wilderness, it reminded them of the white seeds of the coriander plant (Ex. 16:31; Num. 11:7).

L. Cummin. The plant is also a member of the parsley family. The Hebrew word for it is *kammon*. Cummin is a low-growing herb with heads of white flowers. When the seeds are dried, they are used for flavoring foods.

Isaiah 28:25, 27 says that, just as the farmer carefully plants his cummin, so God will deal wisely and justly with His people. Jesus used cummin to demonstrate the importance of keeping the whole law (Matt. 23:23).

M. Fitches. Many botanists believe this was the black poppy, commonly known in Palestine. It has fine, thin leaves resembling the fennel and is sometimes called the "fennel

flower." It grows 30 to 60 cm. (1 to 2 ft.) tall with yellow or blue flowers. Its black, aromatic seeds are used for seasoning, and in Bible times they were usually beaten out with a rod (Is. 28:25, 27).

For the reference to "fitches" in Ezekiel 4:9, see the section on "Rye."

N. Frankincense. Although many types of plants were used as incense, only one is mentioned in Scripture as *frankincense*. The Hebrew word for this plant is *lebonah*, which means "incense" or "freely burning." It is a large, pink-flowering tree, producing a white gum that hardens quickly and is very aromatic when burned. This was used in ceremonial offerings (Ex. 30:34; Lev. 2:1), as an article of luxury (Song 3:6), and as a gift for the Christ child (Matt. 2:11).

The "frankincense" tree did not grow in Palestine, but the product was brought there by caravan (Is. 60:6; Jer. 6:20).

O. Gall. There are two meanings of the word *gall* in the Bible:

1. A Poisonous Herb. When the Hebrew word *rosh* was translated as *gall,* it was probably designating the hemlock or the opium poppy. Hosea 10:4 says that gall grew wild in the field. (In this passage, the word *rosh* is rendered *hemlock* in the KJV.) Punishment was sometimes likened to gall water (Jer. 8:14; 9:15; 23:15).

2. A Secretion of the Liver. The *gall* mentioned in Job 16:13 and 20:25 represents the Hebrew word *mererah*. It refers to the gall produced by the liver. The "gall of bitterness" in Acts 8:23 probably refers to the same thing. It is a symbol of spiritual enmity to God.

P. Garlic. This plant is known for its strong taste and aroma. It has flat, pointed leaves, and its bulbous root grows in sections called *cloves.*

The Hebrews called the garlic plant *shum*. It is a member of the amaryllis family, closely related to the onion.

Garlic grew abundantly in Egypt and other countries of the Mediterranean. The Israelites cherished memories of eating garlic in Egypt (Num. 11:5), where it was used to flavor breads.

Q. Hyssop. Many different plants may have been the *hyssop* of the Bible. The Hebrew word for this herb is *ezob.*

The common hyssop is a sweet-smelling plant of the mint family. It is a bush growing 30 to 46 cm. (12 to 18 in.) high, with small pointed leaves and spikes of various colored

PLANTS AND HERBS

flowers. It was grown in Egypt and Palestine (Ex. 12:22), and was used in the ceremonial rituals of the Israelites (Lev. 14:4, 6; Num. 19:6, 18; Heb. 9:19). Psalm 51:7 refers to the hyssop as a symbol of inner cleansing. First Kings 4:33 shows that Solomon was aware of its vigorous growing habits.

Some think the Bible uses *hyssop* to refer to marjoram. Both plants have similar qualities, and both grow in Egypt and Palestine. The reference to hyssop in John 19:29 shows that hyssop was still commonly known in the New Testament era.

R. Mallow. This spice is mentioned in the Bible only once (Job 30:4). The Hebrew word for this plant is *malluah* ("salty"); it denotes a plant that has a salty taste or is raised in salty places. The mallow fits this description.

The mallow bush grows abundantly in salt marshes along the Mediterranean and on the shores of the Dead Sea.

It reaches about 3 m. (10 ft.) in height and has tiny purple flowers. Its leaves are eaten by the poor when food is desperately scarce.

S. Mint. The Greek word *heduosmon* is translated *mint* in the New Testament. There are two varieties of wild mint; both grow in Syria and Palestine.

POMEGRANATE. *The fruit of this tree provides a refreshing juice that is sometimes used as a base for wine. The pomegranate tree grows 3 to 4 m. (10 to 15 ft.) high and has bright red flowers. Its reddish-maroon fruit is the size of an orange and has many seeds.*

In ancient times, mint was used for medicine and seasoning foods. It may have been one of the "bitter herbs" that the Israelites ate with the Passover lamb. Mint was considered to be one of the least important herbs, even though it was used as a tithe at the temple.

T. Mustard. The black mustard grew wild in Palestine on the shores of Galilee. This herb reached 1.8 to 2.4 m. (6 to 8 ft.) in height and was covered with yellow flowers. The seeds were used to flavor meat and vegetables, and were a favorite food of the birds.

Jesus compared the kingdom of heaven to the mustard seed (Matt. 13:31–32; Mark 4:31–32; Luke 13:19). He also used it to teach the power of small faith (Matt. 17:20; Luke 17:6).

Some think the mustard of the Bible was the yellow mustard. But this is not likely, because it is a low-growing plant and not a true herb.

U. Myrrh. The King James Version uses the word *myrrh* with reference to different plants. One of these was a small tree with bushy branches and three-sectioned leaves, bearing a plum-like fruit, and producing a fragrant gum that had many uses. The Hebrew word for this plant was *mor*. It was used in anointing oil (Ex. 30:23), in perfume (Ps. 45:8; Prov. 7:17; Song 3:6), and in ceremonial cleansing (Esth. 2:12). The magi brought it to the baby Jesus (Matt. 2:11) It was offered to Jesus on the cross (Mark 15:23), and was used to prepare Jesus' body for burial (John 19:39).

The *myrrh* mentioned in Genesis 37:25 and 43:11 was probably the tree *Cistus creticus*. The Hebrew word for this plant is *lot*. This shrub produces pink flowers and is sometimes known as the "rock rose." It is very fragrant and valued for its perfume.

The tree that produces the myrrh used in modern times is not of the same genus or species as the myrrh of Bible times.

V. Myrtle. The myrtle tree (Hebrew, *hadas*) of the Bible was probably the common myrtle. Growing 4.6 to 6 m. (15 to 20 ft.) high, it has dark, shiny leaves and bears clusters of star-shaped flowers.

The myrtle tree was common to Galilee and northern Palestine and Syria. It also grew around Jerusalem, but was rarer there. Zechariah 1:9–11 mentions that it also grew in the Jordan Valley.

Its branches were used for booths in the Feast of Tabernacles (Neh. 8:15; cf. Lev. 23:40). It reminded the Israelites of God's

PLANTS AND HERBS

goodness (Is. 41:19), by contrast with the brier (Is. 55:13).

The myrtle was sacred to the ancient Greeks. They used it in their worship of Aphrodite, the goddess of love.

W. Rue. This important herb is mentioned in the Bible only once (Luke 11:42). The Greek word for it is *peganon.* It is a small shrub with clusters of yellow flowers that have a very strong odor. It is a native to the Mediterranean region, but was cultivated in Palestine as a garden herb. It was used as a disinfectant, medicine, and as the temple tithe.

X. Saffron. The saffron has been cultivated in southern Europe and Asia from very early times. The Hebrew word for it is *karkom.*

The plant, which grows from a bulb, blooms in the fall, with light lavender blossoms, veined red. Their stigmas are dried, pulverized, and pressed into cakes that are used for making yellow dyes, in medicine, and for flavoring. Saffron has a sweet smell but a bitter taste. It is mentioned as one of the common spices of the Old Testament (Song 4:14).

Y. Spikenard. This is one of the most precious spices of the Bible. The Hebrew for it is *nerd;* the Greeks called it *nardos.* It grew extensively in northern India, and has been found high in the Himalaya Mountains.

It grows small with many spikes on one root, bearing pink blossoms; thus it is sometimes called the "Indian spike." Perfumed oil is extracted from these spikes.

The New Testament tells how a woman anointed Jesus with this most costly liquid (Mark 14:3–4). According to Werner Keller, "The receptacles for these often expensive items (i.e., perfumes) have been found by archaeologists under the debris of walls, among the ruins of patrician houses, and in royal palaces."[2]

Z. Stacte. The Hebrew word for this spice is *nataph,* which means "a drop." It is generally believed that this word denotes the gum from the storax tree.

Grown in the region of Galilee, Asia Minor, and Syria, the storax tree reaches up to 6 m. (20 ft.) with dark green leaves. Its clustered white blossoms appear in March. When in bloom, it resembles the orange tree.

The resin of the storax is used as an expectorant. It is mentioned in the Bible only once,

as an ingredient for the anointing oil (Ex. 30:34).

IV. Fruits. The various fruits mentioned in the Bible show not only the fertility of Palestine but the Israelites' ingenuity in growing, harvesting, and preparing them for use. Fruits were eaten fresh, dried, pressed into cakes, and squeezed for juice. Some were used as medicine. According to God's Law, all fruit-bearing plants had to be three years old before their fruit could be harvested (Lev. 19:23). Farmers made provision for the poor and widows by leaving some fruit for them.

A. Almonds. The almond has been known since early Bible times (cf. Gen. 43:11). The Hebrews called it *shaked,* which means "hasten." This may refer to the fact that the pink blossoms of the almond tree are the first blooms to appear in the spring (Jer. 1:11–12).

Some visitors think that Palestine grows the best almonds in the East. They have been found in the northern regions of Mount Lebanon and Hebron, east of the Jordan, and in Egypt. Under favorable conditions, the tree grows to 6 m. (20 ft.) in height.

Note that when Aaron's rod budded, it brought forth almonds (Num. 17:8).

B. Apples. Different scholars identify the *apple* referred to in Joel 1:12 and the Song of Solomon 2:3, 5; 7:8; 8:5 with apple, quince, and apricot. The Hebrew word used in these passages is *tappuah.*

The ancient Romans prized the apple tree for its fruit. Scholars believe that the Romans introduced them into England. Although our apple tree grows in Palestine today, it is not certain that the Bible refers to it.

Henry B. Tristram and others think that the apple tree of the Bible was actually the apricot (*Prunus armeniaca*), which originated in southern Asia and grows abundantly in the Holy Land. It reaches approximately 9 m. (30 ft.) with very sweet, golden fruit. This tree could fit the description of the "apple" in Proverbs 25:11.

C. Figs. The fig tree was cultivated in Palestine and other Mediterranean countries (cf. Deut. 8:8). Although it is not tall, its large leaves and widely spreading branches provide excellent shade. Sitting under a fig tree was typical of peace and prosperity (1 Kin. 4:25; Mic. 4:4; Zech. 3:10). The Hebrew word for the fig tree was *teenah,* meaning "to spread out." The Greeks called this tree *syke* and the fruit *sykon.*

There were two crops of figs in ancient

---

[2] Werner Keller, *The Bible as History* (New York: William Morrow and Company, 1964), p. 215.

Palestine. The early harvest appeared in June and was called the *bikkore* (Hos. 9:10; Is. 28:4). The later crop ripened continually from August through March; it was called the *kermouse*.

The fig is small and pear-shaped and often forms before the leaves appear. In biblical times, figs were eaten fresh, dried, or pressed into cakes (1 Sam. 25:19; 30:12). Sometimes figs were used as a poultice (2 Kin. 20:7). Jesus used a fig tree to teach His disciples the need for spiritual fruitfulness (Matt. 24:32; Luke 13:6).

D. Grapes. The Holy Land has rightly been called "the land of the grapes." Climate and soil conditions in Palestine are well suited for growing grapes.

The Israelites found enormous clusters of grapes growing in Canaan (Num. 13:23). A single grape was reported to be as large as a plum. Since the grapes of Egypt were small, the Israelites naturally were impressed.

Grapes have been the principal agricultural product of Palestine since ancient times. Besides furnishing raisins and wine, the grapes provided juice that was boiled down to the consistency of molasses; the Hebrews called this *debash*, or "honey." This was probably the "honey" mentioned in Genesis 43:11 and Ezekiel 27:17.

E. Husks. This is thought to be the fruit of the carob tree. The carob is a tall-growing evergreen with clusters of pea-shaped flowers. The fruit appears in large, flat pods, 15 to 20 cm. (6 to 8 in.) long. The pods themselves are very sweet, with flat beans inside. Israelite farmers dried the pods and fed them to cattle; humans ate them only in extremity (cf. Luke 15:16).

Tradition says that carob pods were eaten by John the Baptist, and so the fruit is sometimes called "Saint John's bread."

The tree grows wild in Mediterranean countries today. It is related to the North American locust tree.

F. Mulberries. The Hebrew word *baka* ("weeping") is thought to have referred to the mulberry, which grew in southern Palestine. When David fought the Philistines in the Valley of Rephaim, the rustling of the mulberry leaves was his signal to attack (2 Sam. 5:24). Psalm 84:6 refers to the Valley of Baca, which literally meant "valley of mulberries."

New Testament references to the mulberry (Greek, *sykaminos*) denote the black mulberry. In Luke 17:6, most English Bibles

CEDARS OF LEBANON. *Ranging from 21 to 24 m. (70 to 80 ft.) tall, the cedar of Lebanon has long, spreading branches that occasionally grow over 30 m. (97 ft.) across. The ancient Assyrians, Babylonians, and Egyptians used its fine timber, noted for beauty and strength. It was also used in the temple at Jerusalem (1 Kin. 7:12). In ancient times, the mountains of Lebanon were covered with these magnificent trees; but after 40 centuries of logging, only a few isolated plantations remain today.*

translate this word as *sycamine*. The fruit of this tree resembles the blackberry; the leaves are rough and jagged. First Maccabees 6:34 suggests that the juice of these berries was used as a refreshing drink in Palestine.

G. Pistachio Nuts. When Jacob sent gifts to Joseph in Egypt, he included "nuts" (Gen. 43:11). The Hebrew word for this is *botnim*. Most scholars believe this was the pistachio nut. These grow in parts of Palestine, Syria, and southern Europe.

The pistachio tree grows 6 to 9 m. (20 to 30 ft.) high. The oval nuts hanging in clusters resemble the almond; but they are smaller than the almond and very sweet. The Israelites enjoyed eating these nuts just as they came from the tree; they also made them into a confection.

A few scholars believe the word *botnim*

PLANTS AND HERBS

SEED CONES. *The species of cedar that grows on the Lebanon mountains produces 20 cm. (5 in.) cones that take three years to mature. These cones will produce trees that repel insects and resist rot so well that they will live for hundreds of years.*

refers to the pine nut, walnut, acorn, or some other nut. But these interpretations are not generally accepted.

In describing the "garden of nuts," Song of Solomon 6:11 probably refers to the English walnut. The Hebrew word here is *egoz*. This tree is cultivated in the region of Galilee and along the slopes of Mount Lebanon and of Mount Hermon. Blossoms appear in February and the tree bears fruit in August.

H. Pomegranates. The Hebrew word for pomegranate is *rimmon*. Known in Palestine since earliest times (cf. Num. 13:23), the pomegranate grew wild in western Asia and northern Africa and was cultivated in Palestine.

This sweet-tasting fruit was used in many ways. Its juice was enjoyed as a cooling drink and as wine (Song 8:2). Symbols of the fruit were embroidered as decorations around the bottom of the high priest's robe (Ex. 28:33–34) and carved on the pillars of Solomon's Porch at the temple (1 Kin. 7:20).

The pomegranate tree grew 3 to 4 m. (10 to 15 ft.) high with bright red flowers. Its reddish-maroon fruit was the size of an orange and had many seeds. The rind contained a large amount of tannin, which today is used as an astringent and in tanning leather.

I. Sycamine. For information on this plant, see the section on "Mulberries."

J. Sycamore Fruit. The Hebrews called this tree *shikmāh*. It belongs to the fig family. The biblical sycamore grew in Egypt (Ps.

78:47), along the coast of Palestine, and in the Jordan Valley (1 Kin. 10:27). Its small yellow fruit is similar to the common fig; it is very sweet and grows in clusters close to the branches. The tree's heart-shaped leaves resemble the mulberry, and so the plant is sometimes called the "fig mulberry." The large spreading branches growing close to the ground provided Zacchaeus an opportunity to get a better view of Jesus (Luke 19:4). Amos gathered the fruit of this tree for a living (Amos 7:14).

V. Wood. From earliest times, man has depended on the earth to provide the resources for his survival. Wood was an important source of shelter, fuel, and decoration.

Wood was always available to the people of Israel, and they became skilled in woodcutting. In fact, they were called "hewers of wood" (cf. Deut. 29:11; 17:15–18). The Israelites used wood for four main purposes: fire, worship, shelter, and commerce.

A. Almug; Algum. These English words are just forms of the same Hebrew word. Solomon requested "algum" wood from Lebanon (2 Chr. 2:8) and "almug" was sent from Ophir (1 Kin. 10:11–12). We are not sure what kind of tree this was, but Bible scholars generally believe that it was sandalwood.

The almug tree was used for making the columns in Solomon's temple, and for musical instruments. As we have noted, Solomon imported this wood from great distances.

B. Ash. The Bible mentions this tree only once, in Isaiah 44:14. The true ash is not native to Palestine, so the Septuagint translators understood the Hebrew word (*oren*) to mean the fir tree. Jerome took it to mean the pine. The RSV translates it *fir,* and puts *ash* in the margin. Some scholars are of the opinion that the Syrian fir is the one mentioned. This tree grew on Mount Lebanon and was used to make idols.

C. Box Tree. The box tree was one of those mentioned as the "glory of Lebanon." It has small, glossy foliage and grows about 6 m. (20 ft.) high. The Hebrews called it *teashur.*

The hard, highly polished wood of the box tree was used in Solomon's temple (Is. 60:13). Boxwood has been used for musical instruments since Roman times.

D. Cedar. The most valuable and majestic trees described in the Bible are the "cedars of Lebanon." The Hebrew word for this tree was *erez.* It grows to a height of 21 to 24 m. (70 to 80 ft.), with long, spreading branches. The branches of one tree were 33.8 m. (111 ft.) across. The trunks of some cedars are 9 to 12 m. (30 to 40 ft.) in circumference. These huge trees continue to grow for hundreds of years. They were symbols of strength and durability, and noted for their toughness (cf. Ps. 92:12; Ezek. 31:3).

The cedar produces 20 cm. (5 in.) cones that take three years to mature. The wood is red and free of knots. Fragrant sap exudes from the trunk and cones (Psa. 104:16; Song of Sol. 4:11). The bitter wood repels insects and resists rot.

The cedar had many uses. Its wood was used for building David's and Solomon's houses (2 Sam. 7:2; 1 Kin. 7:12), making idols (Is. 44:14–15), and constructing ships (Ezek. 27:5).

Cedars grow on Mount Lebanon today; but less than a dozen of these trees stand in the actual groves mentioned by the Bible, near the Lebanon coast of the Mediterranean. All of them have trunks more than 3 m. (10 ft.) in diameter.

The Bible first mentions the cedar tree in Leviticus 14:4. However, some scholars believe this text refers to the juniper, since the Israelites were sojourning in the Sinai Peninsula and the juniper was common in that area. See the section on "Juniper."

E. Chestnut. Most scholars agree that the *chestnut* mentioned in the Bible is the Oriental plane. Jacob's speckled rod was made from the wood of this tree (Gen. 30:37).

Ezekiel mentions the plane tree along with others growing on Mount Lebanon (Ezek. 31:8). The Hebrew word used here is *armon,* meaning "naked" or "bare." This points to the way the bark continually breaks and peels off, exposing the light-colored trunk. The plane tree resembles North America's sycamore or buttonwood trees and will grow to enormous size if left undisturbed. It produces small, spiny balls that hang from the branches. Its leaves are heavily veined, and resemble the maple. It is native to southern Europe, western Asia, and Palestine.

F. Cypress. The Hebrew word *tirza* in Isaiah 44:14 probably refers to the cypress. It is very durable, making it suitable for building, carving, or any fine woodwork. The beautiful red wood of this tree is heavily aromatic. A native of Persia, the cypress was known throughout the Near East and is thought to have grown on Mount Lebanon. Cypress trees were planted in ancient cemeteries, and several mummy cases found in Egypt were made from cypress wood.

G. Ebony. The wood of this tree is mentioned only once in the Bible, when traders from Dedan in Arabia brought it to Tyre (Ezek. 27:15). The Hebrew word for ebony (*hobnim*) literally means "stonewood."

The ebony tree is now found in many Asian countries, as well as India and Ethiopia. It is sometimes 60 cm. (2 ft.) in diameter with a smooth bark; it has white flowers and small, edible fruit. Its bark is a whitish gray, but the heart of the wood is black, sometimes streaked with light brown, red, or yellow. Ethiopia is said to have the best ebony wood today.

Highly polished ebony wood was used in Bible times for making musical instruments and ornamental work. The North American persimmon tree belongs to the same genus as the ebony.

H. Fir. Our English Bibles render the Hebrew word *berosh* in a variety of ways to denote different trees of the pine family—especially the fir. The word probably referred only to the Aleppo or Sipcon pine, which is almost as large as the cedars found on Mount Lebanon. The Aleppo pine was common in Palestine (Hos. 14:8); it was an emblem of nobility (Is. 41:19–20).

The Aleppo pine has smooth bark, grows up to 8 m. (60 ft.), and produces cones 13 to 15 cm. (5 to 6 in.) long. It was used for making

PLANTS AND HERBS

musical instruments (2 Sam. 6:5), floors (1 Kin. 6:15), decks of ships (Ezek. 27:5), and houses (Song 1:17). Its wood was also used for Solomon's temple (1 Kin. 5:8, 10). Storks built their nests in this tree (Ps. 104:17).

I. Gopher Wood. "Gopher wood" is mentioned only once in the Bible (Gen. 6:14). Some scholars believe this is an alternate reading for the Hebrew term *kopher,* which probably means *pitch* or some other resinous material. The Septuagint translates it as *squared wood,* and in the Vulgate it is *planed wood.*

Since cypress trees were used extensively for shipbuilding and grew abundantly in the area, many believe that Noah used cypress wood for the ark. Others have suggested it was the cedar, pine, or fir tree.

J. Oak. English versions translate many different Hebrew words as *oak, terebinth,* or *elm.* They may also translate these words as *place* or *plain.* Some of the Hebrew words are *el, elah, elon,* and *allon.* They generally mean the terebinth or elm trees (Gen. 35:4, 8; Judg. 6:11; 2 Sam. 18:9). The Old Testament often uses *oak* to denote any strong tree or grove. There are 5 species of oak tree in modern Palestine:

Quercus pseudo-coccifera, which has small, prickly leaves like the holly. This was Abraham's "oak of Mamre" (Gen. 13:18; 14:13, RSV).

Quercus calliprinos grows large on Mount Tabor and east of the Jordan River. This is believed to have been the "oak of Bashan" (Is. 2:13; Zech. 11:2).

Quercus aegilops is a deciduous tree that grows in Samaria and Galilee. It does not seem to be mentioned in the Bible.

Quercus sesiliflora grows at high elevations in Lebanon. Such a tree was probably the "oak of Moreh" (Gen. 12:6, RSV).

Quercus coccifera is the type of tree that Rebekah's nurse, Deborah, was buried under. The Bible called that particular tree the "oak of Bethel" or the "oak of tears" (Gen. 35:8).

Though Mount Lebanon was famous for its great cedar trees, Palestine was the land of the oaks. The wood of oak trees was often also used for making idols.

K. Pine. The *pine* of the Old Testament represents the Hebrew word *tidhar.* Actually the word has two meanings.

1. An Evergreen. *Tidhar* may refer to an evergreen, such as cedar. This fits Isaiah's ref-

TEREBINTH. *The terebinth is a spreading tree, usually less than 8 m. (25 ft.) high, which grows in warm, dry, and hilly places in Palestine. It is often considered sacred. This particular tree is part of a small grove surrounding the ruins of a Roman temple at Yajuz in Gilead.*

erences to the "pine" that he says grew on Mount Lebanon and was used for Solomon's temple (Isa. 41:19; 60:13).

2. A Deciduous Tree. *Tidhar* may also refer to the "oil tree," as in Nehemiah 8:15. The RSV uses the term "wild olive" in this instance. See the section on "Olive."

L. Shittah or Acacia. The Hebrew word for the acacia tree was *shittah.* Thus the Old Testament often refers to acacia wood as "shittim wood."

Two species of the acacia are found in Palestine: the *Acacia nilotica* and the *Acacia seyal.* These are quite similar. They grow 4 to 8 m. (15 to 20 ft.) high, with large thorns and hard wood suitable for building. Both have yellow flowers and produce long pods with beans inside.

God instructed the Israelites to build a tabernacle of shittim wood. The tree was probably growing in the region of the Sinai Peninsula, so it was familiar to the Israelites at that time. The Hebrews used shittim wood for boards, altars, pillars, tables, staves, and bars for the tabernacle (Ex. 25:5, 10, 13; 26:15, 26; 27:1; 30:1). Acacia trees grew along the Jordan Valley from the Sea of Galilee to the Dead Sea (Is. 41:19).

M. Teil. The Hebrew word *elah* is often translated *oak, elm,* or *terebinth.* But in Isaiah 6:13, the King James Version translates it as "teil tree." This is another name for the linden

15

PLANTS AND HERBS

tree, also known as the basswood. This tree does not grow in modern Palestine.

Many scholars believe this passage refers to the terebinth, which grew throughout Palestine. It produced clusters of red berries and may have yielded a form of turpentine. In the Apocrypha, Ecclesiasticus 26:16 gives a poetic description of this tree. Gideon may have met the angel under the wide-spreading branches of a terebinth tree (Judg. 6:11–12).

N. Thyine. Mentioned only in Revelation 18:12, this small, low-growing, coniferous tree belongs to the cypress family. It is native to North Africa and may have been used in the construction of Solomon's temple. The thyine tree was highly valued by the Romans for cabinet making, and its aromatic wood was burned for incense.

VI. Additional Plants. Some plants mentioned in the Bible were used in a variety of ways. Since these plants served very useful purposes in Bible times, they deserve individual consideration.

A. Bulrushes. Two Hebrew words refer to this plant—*gome* and *agmon*. Sometimes our English versions simply call it the "rush" (cf. Is. 9:14; 35:7).

Scholars generally believed this plant was the papyrus. It grew abundantly in northern Egypt along the banks of the upper Nile. Although it still grows there today, overuse has made it scarce. It also grows in northern Galilee at the mouth of the Jordan.

Papyrus is a shallow-rooted plant that grows in mire (Job 8:11). It reaches about 3 m. (10 ft.) high on an unbranched stem, which is 5 to 8 cm. (2 to 3 in.) in diameter at the base. A large tufted head at the top of the stem droops when the plant is mature (Is. 58:5).

The Egyptians used this plant for making boats (Is. 18:2) and fishing rope (Job 41:2, RSV). They used its sap for sugars, medicine, and fuel. The pithy substance inside the stem was eaten. More important for us today is the fact that the Egyptians first manufactured paper from this plant. Many manuscripts on papyrus have helped us learn more about the text of the Bible. (*See* "Text and Translations.")

B. Cockles. No one is certain what the *cockle* really was. The Hebrew word *boshah* literally means "stinking like carrion."

The word probably refers to weeds in general, as Job 31:40 seems to imply. Perhaps it refers to weeds with a foul odor, as the Hebrew word suggests.

Some think it denotes the *Arum* genus of marsh plants that grow in Asia today. However, this explanation does not fit the Bible's references to cockles growing "instead of barley" in open fields (Job 31:40).

C. Cotton. The RSV renders the Hebrew word *karpas* as *cotton*. It literally means "to be white," so the KJV often translates it as *fine linen* (Gen. 41:42; 1 Chr. 4:21).

India first cultivated cotton, and subsequent growth of the crop probably spread to Persia (Esther 1:6) and Egypt. Cotton was an important commodity of trade in the ancient world. (*See* "Trade.")

D. Flax. Flax was cultivated in Egypt from ancient times (cf. Ex. 9:31). The Hebrew word for this plant was *pishtah*.

Flax grew in fertile soil. It reached about 90 cm. (36 in.) high, with delicate light blue flowers.

Flax was an important crop in Egypt and the rest of the ancient world. To harvest flax, farmers pulled it up by the roots and spread it to dry on housetops. (*See* "Architecture and Furniture.") It was customary for women to perform this task, and this chore was consid-

SHITTAH. *Also known as the acacia tree, two species of the shittah are found in Palestine, growing between 4 and 8 m. (15 to 20 ft.) high. The wood is commonly used in building. The tabernacle was primarily built of shittah (pl., shittim) wood (Ex. 25:10–11; 26:15).*

ered the mark of a virtuous woman (Prov. 31:13). Hebrew flax was grown in Canaan before the conquest under Joshua. Its woody stems furnished fiber for fine linen (Is. 19:9; Luke 23:53).

Today, linseed oil is extracted from flax seeds. We do not know whether this was done in Bible times.

E. Grass. Of all the plant kingdom, grass is probably the item most useful to man. Many kinds of grasses are listed in the Bible.

Sometimes the Bible uses *grass* to refer to cereal grains or to herbs in a general way (Is. 51:12). At other times, Scripture makes a distinction between "grasses" intended for man and those that were food for cattle (Psa. 104:14). Grass was used to symbolize man's brief life on earth (Ps. 90:5; 103:15–16). In teaching His disciples their worth to God, Jesus mentioned the custom of burning dry straw, herbs, and stubble in ovens (Matt. 6:30).

F. Hay. When the word *hay* is mentioned in English versions of the Bible, it does not mean dried grass stored for cattle. Hebrew farmers did not store food for their cattle in this way. Instead, *hay* refers either to green shoots of grass or mown grass (Prov. 27:25; Is. 15:6).

G. Juniper Bush. This should not be confused with the juniper tree. This shrub grows about 4 m. (12.1 ft.) high in the sandy soil of the Jordan Valley and along the Sinai Peninsula.

Its twiggy, almost leafless branches bear clusters of pinkish flowers. It is a member of the broom family. The Hebrew word for it is *rothem.*

Desert travelers used this bush for shade. For example, Elijah rested under a juniper bush in the wilderness of Judah as he tried to escape from Jezebel (1 Kin. 19:4). Sometimes, in dire situations, the bitter roots of the juniper were eaten (Job 30:4).

Bedouins used the root of the juniper for charcoal, and this may have been done during Old Testament times (Ps. 120:4).

H. Lily. Flowers grew abundantly in Palestine—on hills, in valleys, in gardens, beside water, and in open fields. Yet Scripture mentions the lily more often than any other type of flower.

No particular lily may have been meant by the Song of Solomon (2:1–2; 5:13; 6:2). The Hebrew word for this was *shushan.* Arabs use the word *susan* to refer to beautiful flowers in general.

ANEMONE. *The "lily" is the most frequently mentioned flower in Scriptures. Probably no particular species of flower is meant in most references; but in Christ's description of the lily (Matt. 6:28–29), the flower referred to may well be the anemone. This bright red species grows abundantly throughout Palestine.*

Because of its bright color, abundance, and beauty, the anemone could be the flower referred to in Matthew 6:28–29. Various other kinds of flowers grew in Palestine—such as gladiolus, anemone, lily, hyacinths, tulips, and irises. So it is doubtful whether Jesus had any specific flower in mind when He referred to the "lily" in His Sermon on the Mount.

I. Nettles. The plants that the Bible calls *nettles* were probably thorny weeds growing over neglected or uncultivated land (Prov. 24; Is. 34:13; Hos. 9:6; Zeph. 2:9). The Hebrew word behind this term is *kimmosh.* Although the term may not refer to a specific plant, it could possibly mean the "Roman nettle." This species is still growing in Palestine today.

J. Olives. The olive tree has been known since very early times (Gen. 8:11). It is generally believed to have come from North India and was flourishing in Canaan before the conquest under Joshua (Deut. 6:11). The olive tree is approximately the size of the American apple tree and produces beautiful clusters of white flowers (cf. Hos. 14:6). The olives are green when immature, then turn black as they ripen.

In autumn, the olives were harvested by beating the branches with a stick. Some were left on the tree for the poor (Deut. 24:20).

Olives were grown chiefly for their oil, which was used in cooking. The oil was also used for fueling lamps, grooming the hair and

PLANTS AND HERBS

skin, and for religious rites. Olive wood was used for Solomon's temple (1 Kin. 6:23, 31–33), and olive branches formed booths for feast days (Neh. 8:15).

An olive tree does not bear fruit until its fifteenth year, but it grows for hundreds of years. The "wild olives" mentioned by Paul in Romans 11:17–24 grew on a low bush.

K. Palms. The date palm grows from 18 to 24 m. (60 to 80 ft.) high and lives over 200 years. The Hebrew name for it was *tamar*. The Bible describes it as being "upright" (Jer. 10:5). Indeed, 2 m. (6 ft.) leaves branching from the top give this tree a very tall appearance. The date palm flourished throughout the Near East, especially around the Nile River and the Red Sea. Bethany was called the "house of dates" and Jericho "the city of palm trees."

The palm tree was useful in many ways, most of all because of its fruit. It bears the most fruit between its thirtieth and eightieth years. Dates are eaten fresh or dried, and some are made into wine.

Carvings of palm trees decorated Solomon's temple (1 Kin. 6:29, 32, 35). Palm branches were used to make booths for feast days (Neh. 8:15). The shoots that sprouted around the bottom of the trunk were used for ropes, sandals, and baskets.

In Psalm 92:12, the palm is a symbol of the righteous. Palm branches were spread before Jesus as he entered Jerusalem (John 12:13).

L. Papyrus. See the section on "Bulrushes."

M. Reeds. The *reed* of Egypt and Palestine resembled bamboo; it grew very thick in marshy areas (Job 40:21). Its 4-m. (12-ft.) stems are hollow and may have been used for musical instruments. The reed has a massive purple bloom at the top that bends in the slightest breeze (Matt. 11:7). Isaiah and Jeremiah refer to it as "cane" (Is. 43:24; Jer. 6:20).

OLIVE. *Approximately the size of an apple tree, the olive produces beautiful clusters of white flowers. The olive will not produce fruit until its fifteenth year, but will live for hundreds of years. In biblical times olives were grown primarily for their oil, which was used in cooking, fueling lamps, and grooming the hair and skin. The trees shown here are in a garden at Emmaus.*

PLANTS AND HERBS

The Hebrew word for it was *kaneh;* the Greeks called it *kalamos.*

The Bible used cane to symbolize the punishment of Israel (1 Kin. 14:15). It denoted weakness (2 Kin. 18:21; Ezek. 29:6). It also functioned as a unit of measure, because of its uniformly jointed stem (Ezek. 40:3, 5). The Roman soldiers used a reed to ridicule and abuse Jesus (Matt. 27:29–30).

N. Roses. The Hebrew word signifying the true rose (*rhodos*) is only mentioned in the deuterocanonical books of Ecclesiasticus (24:14; 39:13; 50:8) and The Wisdom of Solomon (2:8). However, the maid who recognized Peter at the gate was named *Rhoda*—literally meaning "a rose" (Acts 12:13–16).

It is doubtful whether the Hebrew word *habazeleth* actually means *rose* in Song of Solomon 2:1 and Isaiah 35:1. Some scholars suggest that the "rose of Sharon" was in fact the narcissus, which blooms in the spring on the Plain of Sharon. Others think this term refers to the meadow saffron, with its lilac-colored flowers. Still others think that the "rose of Sharon" was a form of the papyrus, which blooms on Sharon each autumn.

The wild rose is seen only in the extreme northern portions of Palestine, while the true rose is a native of Media and Persia. The true rose was later brought to the countries of the Mediterranean and grows today on the mountains of Palestine.

O. Soapwort. Before the manufacture of soap as we know it today, people in Palestine used a crude form of soap made from the ashes of the roots of the soapwort, mixed with olive oil.

The Hebrew words for these soap plants—*bor* and *borith*—literally meant "that which cleanses." For making soap, the Hebrews used several types of scrubby alkaline plants that grew in the area of the Dead Sea and the Mediterranean. They often used this soft soap for bathing (Job. 9:30; Jer. 2:22).

Generally, Hebrew women used the root of the soapwort for washing linens, because they believed it would not make them shrink. Men used the ashes of the glasswort and the saltwort to make potash for smelting metals (Is. 1:25; Mal. 3:2).

P. Straw. After Israelite farmers threshed their grain, they fed the remaining straw to cattle and work animals (Gen. 24:25, 32; Judg. 19:19; Is. 25:10). During their Egyptian bondage, the Israelites mixed straw with clay to make bricks; this was to prevent the bricks

from cracking. When the pharaoh took their straw away, they gathered stubble in the field and chopped it for straw (Ex. 5:7, 12, 16).

Straw was used as a symbol of weakness in Job 41:27.

Q. Tares. The Bible mentions "tares" only in Matthew 13:25–40. The Greek word for this plant is *zizanion.* The seeds are poisonous, producing dizziness and sometimes death if swallowed. The modern name for this plant is the "bearded darnel" (*lolium temulentum*). It is a grass very common in the Near East, and looks very similar to wheat until it begins to head. Darnels are usually left in the field to ripen until harvest, and then are separated when the wheat is winnowed. Since the grain of the "tares" is smaller and lighter than the wheat, it is blown away with the chaff. If any tares remain, they are passed through a sieve and separated from the wheat.

R. Thorns and Thistles. Many Hebrew words denote thorny plants, and are variously

PALM. *The palm tree flourishes throughout the Near East, and carvings of palms decorated King Solomon's temple (1 Kin. 6:29–35). Palm leaves called "branches" were used to make booths for feast days (Neh. 8:15). They were also woven into baskets, ropes, and sandals.*

PLANTS AND HERBS

translated as *bramble, brier, thorns,* or *thistles.* For example, the Hebrew word *choach* is usually translated *thistle.* Actually, it refers to many kinds of prickly plants (Judg. 8:7, 16).

Probably the most well-known of the thorns of Palestine is called the "crown of thorns." This is a small tree that grows 6 to 9 m. (20 to 30 ft.), whose thorny boughs Roman soldiers plaited for Jesus' head at the Crucifixion (Matt. 27:29).

The shrubby plant called "burnet" grows in Judea, Galilee, and around Mount Carmel. It was used for feed and for fueling the baker's oven (Eccl. 7:6).

Many of these prickly plants cover the land and choke the crops (Matt. 13:7). Modern Israeli farmers sometimes cut them before they go to seed.

Hosea alludes to the way the Israelites fortified their walls by placing thorny branches along the top (Hos. 2:6). The Old Testament often spoke of thorns as symbols of punishment (Num. 33:55; Judg. 2:3; Prov. 22:5).

S. Willows. The Septuagint, the Latin Vulgate, and most English versions have rendered the Hebrew word *aravah* as *willow.* Although several species of willow grew in Palestine, it is generally believed that this word refers to the Babylon willow, which flourished on the banks of the Euphrates (Ps. 137:2; Is. 44:4).

God instructed the Israelites to build booths for the Feast of Tabernacles out of willow branches (Lev. 23:40). After the captivity in Babylon, the willow became an emblem of sorrow (Ps. 137:1–2).

The true willow has long narrow leaves, hanging on drooping branches. The flowers are small furry catkins that appear before the leaves. The seed pods split open and release furry seeds to the wind. This beautiful tree is rarely seen today in the Holy Land.

T. Wormwood. This plant is distinguished for its bitter juice (Lam. 3:15). Several species grew in the arid regions of Palestine and northern Africa.

Scholars believe that wormwood (Hebrew, *laanah*) was either the absinthium, which yielded oil for medicinal purposes, or a low-growing shrub with small leaves and heads of yellow-greenish flowers.

The Bible refers to wormwood—along with gall and hemlock—to signify bitterness (Rev. 8:11). In Deuteronomy 29:18 it symbolizes the disobedient, and in Jeremiah 9:15; 23:15 it is used to denote punishment.

AGRICULTURE

Agriculture refers to the various operations connected with the cultivation of the soil. It includes the sowing and harvesting of vegetables, grains, and fruits or flowers, as well as the raising of animal herds. Hebrew agriculture developed with the growth of the Hebrew nation.

I. THE DEVELOPMENT OF FARMING

II. A HOLY PARTNERSHIP
A. Feasts and Festivals
B. Property Protection

III. CONDITIONS AFFECTING AGRICULTURE
A. Soil
B. Rainfall Patterns
C. Control of Water
D. Hot Winds
E. Insects

IV. CROP STORAGE

V. METHODS OF CULTIVATION
A. Grapes
B. Grains
C. Olives
D. Dates and Figs
E. Flax
F. Other Crops

VI. AGRICULTURAL TOOLS
A. Plows and Harrows
B. Sickles
C. Winnowing and Threshing Tools
D. Sieves
E. Mills and Presses

VII. AGRICULTURAL SYMBOLS

I. The Development of Farming. Tilling the soil became mankind's first occupation when God put Adam and Eve in the garden "to dress it and keep it" (Gen. 2:15). Adam's son Cain tilled the soil while his other son, Abel, tended sheep (Gen. 4:2). Noah kept the first vineyard (Gen. 9:20).

The patriarchs became skillful herdsmen, and Joseph described his brothers as shepherds. But by the time the Hebrews entered Canaan, they had mastered many other agricultural skills. They had seen the Egyptians using the waters of the Nile for irrigation and cultivating large fields of cotton. However,

Moses warned his companions that they would face very different agricultural problems in Canaan: "For the land, whither thou goest in to possess it, is not as the land of Egypt" (Deut. 11:10–11).

Mosaic Law encouraged agricultural development among the Hebrew landowners (Deut. 26:1–11). Farming became an honorable career as people of the soil earned a living by the sweat of their brows. When the Hebrews entered the Promised Land, each family received its own allotment of land. The Law did not permit a family to sell its land or to relinquish permanent rights to it; it was to remain the family inheritance (Deut. 19:14).

II. A Holy Partnership. The Hebrew farmer looked upon his land as a gift from God, and he believed that he was to be a faithful steward of it (Deut. 11:8–17). The farmer engaged in many activities that expressed this holy partnership with God.

A. Feasts and Festivals. The Hebrews' religious calendar revolved around the cultivation of crops, and the major fasts and feasts had an agricultural significance, for they marked the seasons of planting and harvesting. (*See* "Worship Rituals.") These events enhanced the worker's sense of personal worth and enriched his faith in God. The Hebrew farmer worked with God to produce the best crop possible. He usually began the farming season with fasting and concluded it with feasting and worship at the time of harvest (e.g., Deut. 16:13–17).

Each farmer paid one-fifth of his produce to God (Lev. 27:31), just as the Egyptians paid one-fifth of their produce to the pharaoh after Joseph bought all the land during Egypt's drought (Gen. 47:20–26).

Every seventh year was a sabbatical year when Israelite farmers did not plant any crops on their lands. It provided rest for the soil and emphasized the people's dependence upon God, since they depleted their reserves of food during the sabbatical year. (*See also* "Laws and Statutes.")

B. Property Protection. Israelite farmers enclosed their gardens and vineyards with hedges or walls (Is. 5:5). But it was not possible to build walls around large fields. To pre-

AGRICULTURE

TERRACING. *A series of retaining walls prevents soil erosion in hilly areas of Palestine. Stony ledges often provide natural terraces. Olive trees grow on these man-made terraces at Bethlehem.*

vent border disputes in the fields, the Law placed severe punishment upon anyone who removed the boundary stones used as landmarks (Deut. 27:17). The Romans later considered such stones to be minor deities under the god Terminus.

The Hebrew landowner seldom visited his fields during the growing season. Instead he hired watchmen to stay in crude lounges (also called "towers"—Mark 12:1), where they protected the crop from beasts, birds, and marauders.

III. Conditions Affecting Agriculture. The farmers of Israel found unique challenges in the water and soil of Palestine.

A. Soil. The country's irregular land surface offered a variety of soil, frequently fertile but shallow and rocky (Is. 5:2). The soil varied from dark, heavy loam to light, well-aerated sand. (*See also* "Geography.")

The coastal plains provided the most productive area, where even bananas and oranges flourished. The land of the plains supported almost every kind of cultivated fruit and vegetable.

The Lower Jordan Valley provided one of the most naturally fertile growing areas in the world. Its tropical climate produced abundant fruit.

The hill country of Judah offered excellent grazing pastures and natural terraces where the soil had built up behind rock walls. The higher elevations received snow during the winter, providing additional water. The plateau of Perea, east of the Jordan, contained soil from eroded lava beds that made it exceedingly fertile. Decayed limestone enriched the soil around Bashan, making it a vast natural wheat field.

Some areas produced two crops per year because they were so fertile (Amos 7:1). Today, after much soil erosion, the land of Palestine still yields rich crops where water is available.

The Israelite farmer found a variety of weather patterns in his native land. The extreme difference in the rain of the mountains and the drought of the desert, plus the contrast between freezing cold and tropical heat, allowed the farmer to grow many different crops. Modern visitors may find snow in Jerusalem while open markets only a few kilometers away sell strawberries.

Biblical Palestine was more heavily wooded than Palestine is today; it had more ground cover and orchards than now. Deuteronomy 8:7–8 accurately describes the land as the Hebrews found it. Since that time, overproduction of crops, wartime pillage, and

AGRICULTURE

other changes have stripped away much of this ground cover. The modern state of Israel is attempting to restore trees and grass that will hold the vital top soil.

B. Rainfall Patterns. The pattern of rainfall dictated the way a season would develop. Steady rainfall, coming at critical times, produced better crops than heavy, intermittent rainfall.

The farmer in Palestine had to contend with a five-month rainless summer (May to October); and if the following autumn rains were sporadic, the results could be disastrous (Amos 4:7). Three months without rain during autumn would destroy most crops. The Bible speaks of "early" and "latter" rains (Deut. 11:14). The "early" rains were the first autumn showers and the "latter" rains were the last spring showers. Between these were the rains of January. The "early" rains prepared the soil for the seed and the "latter" rains filled out the crops for harvest. The amount of rain received in different locations varied greatly. For example, in modern Palestine, Jericho receives 14 cm. (5.5 in.) of rainfall per year while areas in Upper Galilee have gotten 117 cm. (47 in.) per year.

However, the farmers of Israel could not rely solely upon the rainfall. When the dry season arrived they depended upon the dews and mist (Gen. 27:28; Deut. 33:28). A heavy dew comes in late August and September. Even today, dew in the hill country and coastal plains will roll off a tent like an early morning rain. This extra moisture provided daily sustenance through the long dry seasons. The absence of dew was considered a sign of God's disfavor (Hag. 1:10).

Winters were moderately cold but could be severe at night, especially in the highlands. Frost and snow lay upon the mountains until April or May. When the frost and snows of winter departed, harvest came quickly.

Jordan Valley wheat ripened in May. Grain crops on the coastal plains followed in late May, but harvest in higher elevations sometimes waited until late June. Too much moisture during the season would cause mildew and blight, which could destroy various crops (Deut. 28:22; Amos 4:9).

C. Control of Water. The Israelites tried to control their supply of water with wells and irrigation. Shepherds and herdsmen generally provided wells for their flocks, often at great expense (2 Chr. 26:10). A well became a natural center for many social gatherings (Gen. 24:11), a resting place for weary travelers (John 4:6), and the campsite for hungry armies. It was community property. To stop up a well was considered an act of hostility (Gen. 26:15). Tribes frequently clashed over the right to use a well.

A small stone usually covered the well opening. A low stone wall surrounded the well to protect it from blowing sand and to prevent people and animals from falling in.

The farmers of Palestine also depended upon cisterns. They dug these reservoirs underground and cemented them tightly to prevent the water from evaporating. Sometimes farmers carved a cistern out of solid rock, which held the moisture better than a clay-lined cistern. The Nabateans and Romans built dams and reservoirs under their respective governments in the first century B.C. These methods greatly increased the productivity of the land.

The Hebrews practiced irrigation on a much smaller scale than the Egyptians. They used artificial trenches to distribute the water. Irrigation water nourished the large city gardens

DRAWING WATER. *This painting from a tomb at Thebes shows an Egyptian gardener drawing water by means of a fulcrum-counterweight device. The painting dates from about thirteenth century B.C. The Hebrews depended on irrigation less than the Egyptians did.*

16

AGRICULTURE

SILOS. *Fossilized grains of wheat, barley, and lentils were found in these underground silos near Beer-sheba, dating back to 4000 B.C. The Hebrews stored grain in such pits, some as large as 8 m. (25 ft.) in diameter and nearly as deep. They also kept provisions in clay jars that were sunk into smaller pits in their homes.*

of Israel. These quadrangular plats were subdivided into smaller squares, bordered by walkways and stone-lined troughs that conveyed water to every plant and tree. Royal palaces were famed for their gardens, which were often used for festivities (Song 5:1). There were also public gardens, such as the Garden of Gethsemane.

Palestine's dependence upon the rain made it especially vulnerable to famine. When the rains failed, dry easterly and southerly winds parched the earth. The Bible mentions numerous famines, beginning with Abram's journey to Egypt because of famine (Gen. 12:10). Such droughts could last for several years.

Famine was one of the most fearful judgments that God brought upon the land (1 Kin. 8:35).

D. Hot Winds. *Siroccos* (hot winds from the eastern desert) worried the farmer from mid-September through October. Siroccos lasted from three days to a week, raising the temperature as much as 20° F. above average. Humidity dropped sharply when the siroccos blew. A prolonged sirocco could spell disaster for the farmer (Is. 27:8; Ezek. 17:10; Hos. 13:15; Luke 12:55).

E. Insects. Locusts or other insects could destroy a crop. For a complete description of insects and the problems they caused, *see* "The Animals and Insects of Palestine."

IV. Crop Storage. After the harvest, a farmer had to dispose of his produce or store it. He stored most of his crops for his own household, though his harvests often supplied exports (Ezek. 27:17).

Storage places for grain ranged from clay jars to pits in the ground, as large as 7.6 m. (25 ft.) in diameter and nearly as deep. The Hebrews used storage jars to keep their grains, oils, and wines, especially in their homes or shops.

Cisterns and silos stored larger amounts of produce. A circular opening of about 38 cm. (15 in.) made the top easy to seal. Some farmers built their bins under the women's apartments, the most secluded part of their home. (*See* "Architecture and Furniture.")

Jesus described a wealthy man who stored his crops in barns, sometimes called granaries (Luke 12:13–21). The kings of Israel and Judah often built store cities that were filled with such barns. Solomon built several store cities to supply his royal court (1 Kin. 9:19).

V. Methods of Cultivation. The farmers of Israel raised a great variety of crops and some required special methods of cultivation. (All of the crops mentioned below are discussed more fully in "Plants.")

A. Grapes. Grapes grew plentifully in Palestine and the Hebrews devoted as much time to their vineyards as they did to all other forms of agriculture. The planting, pruning, and cropping of grapevines was hard work that many people considered to be menial (2 Kin. 25:12). Yet the hill country of Judah offered grapevines a perfect climate. Walled vineyards and watchtowers came to symbolize the land of Judah.

To prepare a hillside for planting a vineyard, a farmer had to clear rocks from the

WINE-MAKING. *This painting from the fifteenth century B.C., found in a tomb at Thebes, shows the process of Egyptian wine-making. To the right, two men gather grapes from an arbor. To the left, five men tread out the grapes. The juice flows out of the vat to be stored in stopper jars.*

ground and build stone hedges to hold the soil. The vines were planted in rows 2.4 to 3.0 m. (8 to 10 ft.) apart. They trailed upon the ground or crept upon stone ridges in search of warm, dry exposure for their fruit, which was sometimes propped up on forked sticks. Trimmed down to permanent stock, the vines were fastened to a stake or trellis, trained upon upright frames, or hung on the side of a house or in a tree.

By forbidding farmers to gather grapes for the first three years (Lev. 19:23), Mosaic Law guaranteed that the vines would be well-tended in their formative years. The first pruning came in March. After clusters began to form again, the pruners cut off twigs having no fruit. Again the vine grew new clusters and again the barren branches were pruned.

Once or twice during the growing season, the soil around the vines was dug and cleared of weeds. The vinedressers removed stones and trained the vines upon their trellises.

Wine was squeezed in September, and the Hebrews celebrated this occasion with even more festivity than the harvest (Is. 16:9). It sometimes resulted in wicked mirth (Judg. 9:27).

B. Grains. Cereal grains were another vital crop of Palestine, and wheat gave the highest yield. We might say the Plain of Esdraelon (Jezreel) was the bread basket of Palestine. The area of Galilee produced the best wheat, but every available valley in the rough West Jordan hill country produced grain. The high Transjordan plateau was also an important grain producer.

Galileans planted fall wheat as the winter rains were beginning, harvesting it between May and June. Farmers in lowland areas like the Jordan Valley harvested their wheat in early May.

The Hebrews harvested abundant barley crops. Since it grew best in the drier climates, they grew much of it in the southeast near the Arabah. Because the climate was too warm to cultivate oats and rye, barley became the Israelites' primary animal feed.

Fitches, spelt, and emmer were inferior grains planted around the border of the fields. They were mixed with wheat or barley to make coarse breads.

C. Olives. The olive touched nearly every phase of Jewish life. Olive wood was used in carpentry and fuel; the olive fruit served as food; and olive oil found its way into a variety of medicines and ointments, as well as being fuel for light.

The cultivation of olive trees was routinely simple, requiring only occasional loosening of the soil. Olive trees flourished in the shallow, rocky soil of Palestine and required little water. However, the trees could not withstand severe cold, so they found southern Palestine more hospitable than the north.

Olives ripen slowly and the farmer picked them as time permitted. Olives could be eaten after being pickled, but they were valued most for their oil, which was used as a substitute for scarcer animal fats. Farmers extracted the oil in stone presses. They rolled a thick stone wheel over the olives on another flat, circular stone which was grooved to carry the oil to a basin (Mic. 6:15).

D. Dates and Figs. Dates flourished in Palestine, especially in the Jordan Valley north of the Dead Sea. Although the Bible never mentions dates as food, it frequently mentions palm trees, so it is logical to assume that the

16

AGRICULTURE

AGRICULTURE

PLOWING. *In this wooden model dating from about 2000 B.C., an Egyptian guides a two-handled plow drawn by a pair of oxen. This shows the crude methods of farming that Abraham would have seen when he visited Egypt (Gen. 12:10–20).*

fruit contributed to the diet of the Hebrews. Ancient writers such as Pliny, Strabo, and Josephus wrote of the syrup made from dates. The Mishna refers to date honey and the Talmud mentions date wine. Dates were pressed into cakes, as were figs.

Cultivated from very early times, figs grew on low trees with thick-spreading branches. The pear-shaped fruit of the green fig appeared before the leaves. When the leaves attained some size, their interiors filled with small white flowers. If the leaves came out and no fruit appeared among them, the tree would remain barren for the season (Matt. 21:19).

Figs could be gathered as early as June but the main crop ripened about August; this main crop was the green fig (Song 2:13). Figs came from the tree ready to eat, but could be dried and made into cakes.

E. Flax. The Hebrews made linen cloth and rope from flax (Judg. 15:14; Hos. 2:5, 9), which they harvested in March and April. Farmers used their hoes to chop off the stalks at the ground so that none of the valuable plant would be lost. After the flax was cut, it was laid out to dry in the sun (Josh. 2:6).

F. Other Crops. Lentils, coarse beans, and chick peas were also grown in Palestine. Cucumbers, onions, leeks, and garlic were other plants on the menu of the Israelites.

VI. Agricultural Tools. The Hebrew farmer had only primitive tools. This made his work even more difficult.

A. Plows and Harrows. The plow of biblical times was little more than a forked stick with a pointed end. Handles added control. In patriarchal times the farmers added a copper point to the plow; later, bronze improved on that. Later still, after the tenth century B.C., the iron plow penetrated the soil to a depth of about 12 cm. (5 in.).

Plows were pulled by oxen, camels, or asses, but never by more than a pair of animals. The plow demanded the farmer's constant attention to keep it in the ground; only a careless man would look away. Jesus used this as an example of one not fit to enter the kingdom of God (cf. Luke 9:62).

Once the early rains came ground could be broken. The farmer tilled the hard-to-reach places with a mattock, a broad-bladed pickax, or a hoe. Sometimes a farmer would plow his field twice, crisscrossing directions.

Harrowing broke up the clods after the plowing. Early harrows may have been no more than a wooden plank or log, weighted with stones. Sometimes the farmer rode on the harrow.

B. Sickles. Farmers mowed their fields with hand sickles (cf. Deut. 16:9). The ancient sickle resembled the sickles still used in the Near East; Egyptian monuments show how they looked. Until the early tenth century B.C., the cutting blade of the sickle was made of flint; after that time, it was made of iron.

Workers who reaped grain with a sickle would cut it near the ear, leaving the stubble to

AGRICULTURE

be pulled up and used for straw. The grain ears were then carried away in baskets. Sometimes the entire stalk was cut close to the ground and the stalks were bound into sheaves (Gen. 37:7). Then workers removed the sheaves by cart, stacked them, or stored them.

C. Winnowing and Threshing Tools. Grain was threshed and then winnowed by throwing it against the wind, which blew away the chaff. Farmers still use this method in much of the Near East.

Ancient threshing places were high, flat summits 15 to 30 m. (50 to 100 ft.) in diameter and open to the winds on every side. Each year farmers would level and roll the dirt to keep the threshing floor hard. Often a village had only one threshing floor and each farmer took his turn in a fixed order.

The sheaves were piled in a heap and the grain was beaten out by a machine or by the trampling of oxen's feet. The threshing machine was a square wooden frame holding two or more wooden rollers. On each roller were three or four iron rings, notched like sawteeth. Oxen pulled the machine, and the driver sat on a crosspiece fastened into the frame. As the rollers passed over the grain, it was crushed out on every side and the straw was shredded for fodder. The threshing machine was a symbol of violence and destruction (cf. Amos 1:3).

Another threshing tool was a wooden plank 90 cm. (3 ft.) wide and 2 to 3 m. (6 to 8 ft.) long. On the lower side were many holes 2.5 to 5 cm. (1 to 2 in.) in diameter, where the farmer fastened pieces of stone, flint, or iron that projected from the board as teeth, tearing the grain loose. Unmuzzled oxen pulled the board behind them across the threshing floor, with the driver standing on the plank.

The grain and chaff gradually formed a big heap at the center of the floor. During the days of threshing, the owner slept nearby to protect the grain from thieves (cf. Ruth 3:2–14).

Farmers winnowed their grain with a fan, which was a semi-oval frame about 90 cm. (3 ft.) in diameter with a surface of woven hair or

---

The Kibbutz

Kibbutz (key-boots) is an Israeli name for any settlement that is operated on a collective system. Most *kibbutzim* (pl.) in Israel today are agricultural.

The first kibbutz was founded in 1904 by Aaron David Gordon, an immigrant from Russia, on a malaria-infested marshland near the southwestern tip of the Sea of Galilee. Gordon and others had arrived in Palestine with a dream to "repossess a land," but had little resources.

Pooling what they had, the immigrants purchased the land from absentee Persian owners who referred to it as the "Death Spot" because of the great toll of life it had already taken. The group constructed simple dwellings, built a communal dining room, moved tons of rock by hand, and drained swamps. Almost anyone joining the commune was made part of the whole, with no one owning anything personally. Known today as Degania, the settlement is the showpiece of the kibbutz movement, with attractive and substantial homes and communal buildings, blooming orchards, citrus groves, and flower beds.

Not long after Gordon's arrival, hundreds of thousands of Jews migrated to Palestine, fleeing from the growing political unrest and persecutions of Europe. Most immigrants had little or no possessions with them. To survive they followed the example of Degania *kibbutzniks* (kibbutz dwellers) in setting up communal property.

It is not unusual to find a kibbutz in which (aside from small personal possessions) no one owns anything at all, not even clothes. Community wardrobes, community toys, community books, community tools—even cots are not personally owned. Although mostly modest (some have neither electricity nor running water) a few kibbutzim have prospered to the point of having their own schools, cultural events, small factories, and even swimming pools.

A kibbutz has an executive committee, whose major decisions are subject to the approval of all members. A work committee assigns jobs, and meals are eaten in a communal dining room. Children live in a "children's home," frequently the best building on the kibbutz.

In biblical times, a Jew owned a plot of ground and passed it on to succeeding elder sons. Although early Hebrews lived together for safety and water supply, the family tenaciously held to its individual property. Such ownership of property has been retained in *moshavim* (communities of individual owners), where each member lives in his own house and farms his own land. But members of *moshavim* buy or rent heavy equipment and sell produce. The *moshav* parallels the small village of biblical days.

16

AGRICULTURE

palm leaves. A worker would hold the fan by hand while others poured the mixture of grain and chaff upon it. Then the winnower tossed the grain to the winds so the chaff would be blown away and the heavier kernels would fall to the ground (Ps. 1:4). Winnowing was done in the evening, when sea breezes blew the strongest.

D. Sieves. The first winnowing process did not remove all the unwanted material, so a final step—sifting—was necessary. Amos 9:9 and Isaiah 30:28 describe two kinds of sieves: the *kebarah* in Amos and the *naphah* in Isaiah. We are not sure which type of sieve is meant in either passage. One type of sieve now used in the Near East has a fine mesh that retains the good grain and lets the dust pass through. Another kind, with coarse mesh, allows the desired grain to fall through and retains the larger husks and pods, either to be thrown out or to be rethreshed.

E. Mills and Presses. Corn and other grains were ground with mortar stones. One or two persons in a household ground grain daily for the family's meals.

Vinedressers cut grapes from the vine with sickles and carried them in baskets to a winepress. This was usually a large stone vat with a small channel that allowed the grape juice to pour out the side into a tub. The grapes were trodden by foot, then pressed by machine. Farmers stored the grape juice in skin bottles, pitchers, and barrels, where it fermented into wine. They also obtained olive oil with presses.

VII. Agricultural Symbols. The Bible abounds with agricultural symbolism. For example, we read that a blessed man is one whose life is watered by God's Spirit as an irrigation stream waters a fruit tree (Ps. 1). God's favor comes like the dew on the grass (Prov. 19:12). An evil man is sifted like chaff (Ps. 1:4). Men faint for God while living in life's dry, barren deserts (Ps. 63:1). And forsaking God is like living with a leaky cistern (Jer. 2:13).

Jesus often used agricultural symbols in His teaching. He described a sower scattering his seed (Mark 4:1–20) and laborers who an-

WINNOWING WHEAT. *In the Near East, sheaves of wheat are still beaten with sticks and trampled by animals to separate wheat grains from the straw. After threshing, the grain is thrown up into the air so that the chaff blows away, in a process known as winnowing. Afterwards the grain is passed through a sieve to remove dirt. It is then ready to be ground into flour.*

swered a call to work in a vineyard (Matt. 20:1–16). He compared false prophets to trees that bear bad fruit (Matt. 7:15–20) and warned that "every tree is known by his own fruit" (Luke 6:43–44). Jesus promised to give His followers "living water" from everlasting wells (John 4). He used seeds, vines, trees, fruit, and other agricultural metaphors to express the truths of God.

The early Christian writers also used the common knowledge of agriculture to convey their message. For example, Paul recalled the unmuzzled ox at the threshing floor when he asked churches to support their spiritual reapers (1 Cor. 9:10). John described the angel of judgment thrusting in his sickle, "for the harvest of the earth is ripe" (Rev. 14:15). Seldom was a preacher or writer better understood than when he used the simple things of nature to illustrate his message.

TOOLS AND IMPLEMENTS

The Old Testament often refers to tools by using the collective Hebrew words *keli* (which literally means "vessels" or "instruments") and *hereb* (which refers to a sword, knife, or any sharp cutting instrument). When a scripture uses one of these general terms, the context can help us determine which tools the writer might have been referring to. Each craft or trade had its own particular tools.

Tools appeared on the scene of history very early. The Bible tells us that "Cain was a tiller of the soil" (Gen. 4:2). He must have used some kind of tool to break the ground, though the exact tool is not mentioned. Archaeologists have found flint knives, scrapers, and hoes from the early Neolithic era (*ca.* 7000 B.C.) in Palestine. Flint was used for rough tools such as reaping hooks even after metal was plentiful (*ca.* 1000 B.C.). But as metal workers learned to use copper, bronze, and meteoric iron, they developed various metal tools.

Archaeologists have found that woodworkers used metal saws with teeth that pointed toward the handle. These same saws were used for cutting stone (1 Kin. 7:9; Is. 10:15). Some people were executed by being sawn in two (Heb. 11:37). Tradition has it that Isaiah might have been killed in this manner.

Perhaps the Israelites were not as skilled in the use of tools as some of their neighbors. This might explain why Solomon employed the craftsmen of Hiram to build the temple (1 Kin. 7:13), and why Bezaleel and Oholiab were summoned for the building of the tabernacle (Ex. 31:1–11).

I. GENERAL TOOLS
A. Hammer
B. Axe

II. BARBER'S TOOLS
A. Razor
B. Mirror

III. BUILDER'S TOOLS
A. Measuring Line
B. Plumb Line ("Plummet")

IV. CARPENTER'S TOOLS
A. Marking Tool
B. Compass or Divider
C. Adze
D. Awl (Aul)
E. Saw
F. Maul or Hammer
G. Nail
H. Chisel
I. Bow Drill

V. FARMER'S TOOLS
A. Yoke
B. Plow
C. Goad
D. Harrow
E. Mattock
F. Axe
G. Sickle
H. Threshing Machine
I. Fan
J. Sieve
K. File

VI. FISHERMAN'S TOOLS
A. Casting Net
B. Dragnet, or Drawnet
C. Spear
D. Hook
E. Anchor

VII. HOUSEHOLDER'S TOOLS
A. Oven
B. Mill
C. Needle
D. Knife
E. Press

VIII. MASON'S TOOLS

IX. POTTER'S TOOLS
A. Wheel
B. Paddle and Scraper
C. Furnace

X. METAL SMITH'S TOOLS
A. Anvil
B. Bellows
C. Furnace
D. Tongs

I. General Tools. Scripture refers to two tools that were used in a variety of trades—the axe and the hammer.

A. Hammer. The ancient hammer looked much like the hammers we use today. More than one Hebrew word was used to denote the hammer. The type of hammer used to drive the tent peg into Sisera's head (Judg. 5:26) was called the *halmuth*. But the Hebrew words

TOOLS AND IMPLEMENTS

EGYPTIAN RAZOR BLADE. *Some of the tools used by ancient barbers were similar to modern-day shaving and grooming devices. This Egyptian razor blade, dating from about the sixteenth century B.C., is made of bronze.*

makkubhah and *makkebheth* also referred to the hammer (Judg. 4:21; 1 Kin. 6:7; Is. 44:12; Jer. 10:4).

B. Axe. Seven different Hebrew words are translated as *axe* in the English versions. The most commonly used is *garzen,* from a Hebrew root word that means "to be cut" or "sever." This type of axe had a head of iron (Is. 10:34) fastened to a handle of wood by leather straps. The axe head sometimes slipped off the handle during use (Deut. 19:5; 2 Kin. 6:4–7).

Axe blades might be short or long. They were set in the wooden handle, parallel or at a right angle to the handle. Materials for the axe head varied from stone (in the earliest times) to bronze and iron. Modern scholars believe that the Israelites learned iron-working from the Philistines (cf. 1 Sam. 13:20).

II. Barber's Tools. The types of tools used by barbers in Bible times were much the same as those used today. Barber items such as the razor and mirror are certainly familiar to us (2 Sam. 14:26).

A. Razor. The practice of shaving a man's head after he completed a vow indicates that the Israelites had barbers (Num. 6:9; 8:7; Lev. 14:8; Is. 7:20; Ezek. 5:1). In some instances the whole body was shaved (Num. 8:7).

Scripture gives us no exact account of what the ancient Hebrew razor looked like, but similar cultures used sharp pieces of obsidian glass and thin flakes of flint. The subject is, however, mentioned by ancient secular writers and illustrated by works of art. The trade of barbering was common among the Egyptians and other nations of antiquity.

B. Mirror. Mirrors dating from the Bronze Age have been found in Palestine. These mirrors or "looking glasses" were made of highly polished metal. Hebrew women may have brought mirrors with them when they came out of Egypt. The mirrors used by the Egyptians were made of mixed metals, chiefly copper. These could be polished to a high luster, but were liable to rust and tarnish (Wisdom 7:26; Ecclus. 12:11). The Hebrew word *gillayon* may refer to mirrors (cf. Is. 3:23). Isaiah considered them to be extravagant finery.

By New Testament times, the Romans had learned to make mirrors of glass. These mirrors often had a cloudy or distorted image (cf. 1 Cor. 13:12).

III. Builder's Tools. The Hebrew word *bana* was used to refer to construction workers, both skilled and unskilled. The tools used by the master builder as he supervised the construction (1 Cor. 3:10) included the measuring line and the plumb line.

A. Measuring Line. Builders used this tool to survey a building site. Scripture indicates that there may have been more than one type of measuring line. A rope or cord might have been used for this purpose (2 Sam. 8:2; Zech. 2:1); but a string or thread might also have been used. In any case, the measuring line was knotted or marked at one-cubit intervals (cf. 1 Kin. 7:15, 23). The cubit (Hebrew, *amma*) was an ancient measure of length that equaled about 45 cm. (17.5 in.). Originally, a cubit was the distance from the tip of the middle finger to the elbow.

In the New Testament, distance was measured in Roman measures (usually translated by the Elizabethan English term *furlongs*), which were approximately 220 m. (660 ft.) long (Luke 24:13; John 6:19; 11:18; Rev. 14:20; 21:16). Sometimes builders took measurements with reeds of a standard length (cf. Rev. 11:1; 21:15).

The measuring line was used as a symbol of God's judgment (Is. 28:17; Jer. 31:39).

B. Plumb Line ("Plummet"). The He-

TOOLS AND IMPLEMENTS

brew word *misqelet* is translated as "plummet" in the King James Version of the Bible (2 Kin. 21:13). In modern builder's terms, it would be called a plumb line.

A plumb line was used to measure and check the vertical line of a structure. This tool was a small lead cone, fastened by cord to a cylindrical piece of wood that was the same diameter as the cone. The wood cylinder was placed against the wall at the top. If the wall was straight, the lead cone at the end of the plumb line should barely touch the wall.

The plumb line was a symbol of God's action in testing men's lives: "Judgment also will I lay to the line, and righteousness to the plummet" (Is. 28:17), or as the NIV puts it: "I will make justice the measuring line and righteousness the plumb line."

IV. Carpenter's Tools. The trade of the carpenter is often mentioned in the Scriptures (cf. Gen. 6:14; Ex. 37). It seems that the carpenter was usually a talented wood carver (1 Kin. 6:18, 29). Isaiah mentions the tools of the carpenter's trade: "The carpenter stretcheth out his rule; he marketh it out with a line; he fitteth it with planes, and he marketh it out with the compass, and maketh it after the figure of a man" (Is. 44:13).

A. Marking Tool. The "rule" mentioned in Isaiah 44:13 was a measuring line, used much the same as we would use a measuring tape or ruler today. After measuring the correct distance on a piece of wood, the carpenter marked it with a stylus or some kind of marking device.

B. Compass or Divider. Ancient carpenters used the compass to mark a circle or portions of a circle. No description of the compass is given in the Scriptures, but archaeologists have found the remains of these ancient tools at several sites in Egypt and Palestine.

C. Adze. In Bible times the adze was used to shape wood (Is. 44:13). The blade of this tool was curved and attached to the handle at a right angle.

Archaeologists have found the remains of a type of adze used by the Egyptians in about 2000 B.C. This Egyptian adze had a copper blade and was strapped to the wooden handle at a right angle. It is possible that the "planes" mentioned in Isaiah 44:13 were made in the same way.

D. Awl (Aul). Carpenters of Bible times used the awl to poke holes in wood or leather. The awl was a tool with a small, pointed blade that stuck straight out the end of the wooden handle. Egyptian monuments picture the awl.

Tools of the Pharaohs

The Egyptian pyramid is a marvel, even in our modern age. But the question of how it was so precisely constructed has puzzled explorers for centuries.

As the pharaohs' tombs have been excavated, archaeologists have discovered details of Egyptian technology and the tools used in constructing the pyramids. The people of the Nile had a skill for cutting, dressing, transporting, fitting, cementing, and polishing hard and heavy rock. In the pharaohs' tombs, archaeologists have found tools used in the final stages of stonework, along with beautiful flint blades and arrowheads.

Some pyramids were built with iron tools. Colonel Howard Vyse found such a tool in the Great Pyramid—the first clue that the Egyptians used iron. An iron dagger was found in the tomb of King Tutankhamen. In the tomb of a first-dynasty king, archaeologists found scores of knives and swords with wooden blades, along with hoes, axes, and chisels—all fashioned out of metal. The tomb even contained slabs of copper, apparently put there so that coppersmiths in the "next world" could make more tools for the pharaoh. It seems extraordinary that so much metal would be found in the tomb of a first-dynasty king, but there is no reason to suppose that this hoard was an exception at that time.

Though archaeologists have found some saws in ancient ruins, these are rare discoveries. Saws of ancient Egypt cut on the pulling stroke, not on the pushing stroke as saws do today. Axes, chisels, and saws were commonly used to start wedge-slots in pyramid construction.

Having learned to work with metal, Egyptians were able to develop carpentry skills. They designed wooden chisels, hammers, mallets, scrapers, and squares; several specimens of these tools have been found in the ancient tombs.

While the Egyptians were skilled in the use of tools, the Hebrews were not. The Bible refers to the use of tools only incidentally, in connection with arts and crafts. The tools of the Egyptians surpassed those of other neighboring cultures as well, and enabled Egypt to develop a sophisticated technology that still amazes men today.

17

TOOLS AND IMPLEMENTS

TOOLS AND IMPLEMENTS

SAW. *This copper saw could be fitted into a wooden handle. It is part of a cache of tools discovered at Kfar Monash in Israel.*

The Israelites also used this tool to pierce a hole in the ear of a servant, indicating that he would be a servant forever (cf. Ex. 21:6; Deut. 15:17).

E. Saw. As we have noted, the ancient Egyptians used saws with teeth pointing toward the handle (instead of away from the handle, like those of modern saws). In most cases, these Egyptian saws had bronze blades, attached to the handle by leather thongs. Some ancient saws in the British Museum have blades inserted *into* the handle, much as do our modern knives.

F. Maul or Hammer. The ancient carpenter's hammer was usually made of heavy stone, drilled with a hole for inserting a handle (cf. 1 Kin. 6:7; Is. 41:7). The "maul" mentioned in Proverbs 25:18 is thought to have been a heavy wooden hammer or mallet that the carpenter may also have used (Judg. 5:26).

G. Nail. Carpenters used nails to hold pieces of wood together (Jer. 10:4; Is. 41:7). Iron was used to make these pins or nails (1 Chr. 22:3). Golden or gilded nails were also used (2 Chr. 3:9).

H. Chisel. Archaeological discoveries show that these sharp tools were made of copper. Looking somewhat like a wide screwdriver, the chisel was a thin wedge of metal and had to be continually resharpened. Copper chisels were used by the Egyptians from about 2000 B.C., and it is very possible that the same tool was used by the Hebrews.

I. Bow Drill. Archaeological discoveries indicate that a type of drill was used in Bible times. The *bit,* or sharp point, was inserted in the tip of a wooden handle. The string of the bow (shaped like the type used to shoot arrows) was wrapped around the wooden handle of the bit. When the carpenter moved the bow forward and backward, it caused the bow drill to rotate, thus boring into the wood.

Scripture makes no specific mention of this tool. However, the Bible does mention boring a hole in the lid of a chest (2 Kin. 12:9).

V. Farmer's Tools. Though Cain was a tiller of the ground (Gen. 4:2), the Bible does not mention specific farming tools until after the Flood. The tools Cain used were probably made of wood and were very primitive.

A. Yoke. Israelite farmers seem to have been well acquainted with plowing, since the yoke is often mentioned in Scripture (e.g., Gen. 27:40).

Farmers placed the yoke on the necks of oxen that pulled the plow. It was made of wood and kept the oxen in their places as they pulled (Deut. 21:3). *Traces* (leather straps) were connected to the yoke and the plow, thus pulling the plow along.

A pair of oxen were called a "yoke" of oxen, as we see in 1 Kings 19:19.

STELE OF ESARHADDON. *This stele (stone monument) dating from the seventh century B.C. bears the image of a seed plow on its lower half. To the left is an object representing either a stylized hill or an ear of corn. To the right is a palm tree with two bunches of dates. Many scholars believe that the royal figure on the upper level was Esarhaddon, Sennacherib's successor (2 Kin. 19:36–37).*

B. Plow. Deuteronomy 22:10 is the first scripture reference to the plow. The Law admonished, "Thou shalt not plow with an ox and an ass together."

This farming tool was made of wood, though the use of iron was known from the time of Tubal-cain (Gen. 4:22) and the Israelites had iron tools when they entered Canaan (Deut. 27:5).

The primitive Hebrew plow was made of oak. The bent parts were formed by the natural curves in the wood and were held together with iron bands. To this, the farmer fastened a single upright shaft with a short crosspiece to serve as a handle. The single-handed plow was lightweight, allowing the farmer to leave one hand free to use the ox goad.

C. Goad. The Hebrew plowman used a *goad* for urging on the oxen. The goad was a pole 213 to 240 cm. (7 to 8 ft.) long, having a point at one end. The point was sometimes tipped with iron and sharpened (1 Sam. 13:21).

Shamgar used the goad as a very effective weapon: "And after him was Shamgar the son of Anath, which slew of the Philistines six hundred men with an ox goad" (Judg. 3:21).

D. Harrow. The harrow was a well-known farming implement (Job 39:10). Some scriptures translate this word as "to break the clods," which probably conveys the proper meaning (Is. 28:24; Hos. 10:11).

The Hebrew noun for "harrow" (*charitz*) represents an instrument with teeth (cf. 2 Sam. 12:31; 1 Chr. 20:3). It might have been pulled along by an ox (Job 39:10). It was actually a kind of sled with stone or metal blades mounted on the underside. (*See* "Agriculture.")

E. Mattock. Israelites used the mattock to break the ground, much as we would use a hoe (Is. 7:25). The Hebrew word for "mattock" (*ma'der*) literally meant "an instrument used to dig in the ground" (Is. 5:6).

The head of this tool was made of iron,

Potter's Wheel

The potter's wheel was one of mankind's earliest inventions and has changed surprisingly little in the last 6,000 years. A potter's wheel is not one wheel, but two.

Primitive potter's wheels were made of stone. A disc-shaped stone was placed on the ground; another disc-shaped stone was notched in the center to fit over a pointed pivot in the center of the lower stone. A nudge of the potter's toe set the lower wheel in motion, which rotated the upper wheel. The upper wheel was where the potter shaped his clay.

In Bible times, potter's wheels were also made of wood. The two wheels were joined by a shaft, so that the upper wheel was at hand level. The foot moved to the lower disc and the connecting axle caused the upper wheel to revolve. Modern potter's wheels follow the same basic design; some are electrically powered, yet many are turned by foot.

Before using the wheel, a potter must knead his clay to rid it of impurities and air. He "wedges" it—slicing it in half and slamming the halves back together to force out air bubbles. When he feels the clay is ready, the potter places a container of water at his workbench (to keep his fingers wet) and turns to his wheel.

The potter next throws the ball of clay down on the upper wheel. Then he sets the wheel in motion and surrounds the clay with his hands, forcing it true to the center of the wheel head. Now the potter must "master" the clay, making it responsive to his touch. He applies pressure at the base of the clay ball, causing it to rise up in sort of rounded cone. Then he presses on top of the clay with his thumbs or the palms of his hands. Repeating this three or four times increases the flexibility of the clay and increases its strength.

At this point the potter "opens up" the clay ball by pressing his thumbs into the center, gradually hollowing it out. Applying pressure with his fingers, he evens out the thickness of the cylinder walls. Finally he shapes the clay into a vase, a pitcher, or whatever he chooses.

As the terms *force, master,* and *throw* imply, clay is not always easy to work with. Often a partially formed object will disintegrate into a shapeless heap of clay—perhaps because a tiny stone was overlooked when the clay was worked. The potter must begin to knead the clay again. Or he may dislike the way a pot is forming and sweep it off the wheel in disgust.

Jeremiah 18 describes God as a potter having trouble at His wheel because His people refused to obey Him. This was a familiar image to people in biblical times, because they could see the potter's wheel in the marketplace of virtually every village and town.

TOOLS AND IMPLEMENTS

IRON PLOW. *Although the Israelites had iron tools when they entered Canaan (Deut. 27:5), they did not use the iron-tipped plow extensively until the tenth century B.C. This iron sheath was found at Tell Beit Mirsim in Palestine. The iron plow greatly increased the yield from the soil.*

which could be sharpened (1 Sam. 13:20–21) and used as a weapon.

F. Axe. As we have already noted, the axe was used in various ancient trades. Several Hebrew words are translated as *axe,* and mentioned in connection with the carpenter's work.

The Hebrew word *kardom* probably refers to the "sharpness" of the axe (cf. Judg. 9:48; 1 Sam. 13:20–21; Ps. 74:5). Another Hebrew word, *garzen,* refers to the "cutting power" of the axe (cf. Deut. 19:5; 20:19). A third word, *barzel,* refers to the fact that an axe was made of iron (cf. 2 Kin. 6:5).

The axe had a handle of wood. As with the mattock and the goad, it could double as a weapon of war (1 Sam. 13:20).

G. Sickle. Jews used the sickle to harvest grain ("corn") and other crops (cf. Deut. 16:2). This tool had a short wooden handle, turned toward the point. Ancient Egyptian monuments show the type of sickle that was used in Egypt. Clay and wooden sickles with flint blades have been frequently found in excavations.

Prehistoric Mesopotamian sickles were made of flint teeth set in wood. In the tenth century B.C., small curved blades replaced the earlier flint.

The reaper grasped the stalks of grain with one hand and cut them off with the sickle, held in the other hand (Is. 17:5). The sickle is often mentioned in relation to the harvest (cf. Joel 3:13; Mark 4:29). (*See also* "Agriculture.")

H. Threshing Machine. After the harvest, the grain was spread on the threshing floor— usually a hard-packed patch of ground located at the outskirts of the city. Farmers separated grain from the straw by having oxen trample on it, or by pulling a threshing instrument over it.

There were two types of threshing machines—one made of flat boards and one that ran on small wheels or rollers (cf. Is. 28:27–28). The wooden sled-type machine had stones or iron fragments fastened to the underside (Amos 1:3). (*See also* "Agriculture.")

I. Fan. After the threshing machine had done its job, the farmers used winnowing fans to throw the stalks and grain into the wind (Is. 30:24; Jer. 15:7). The breeze separated the grain from the chaff.

The fan is still used in some remote areas of the Middle East. It is a wooden, semi-oval frame, about one meter (one yard) wide, crossed with a texture of hair or palm leaves. (*See also* "Agriculture.")

Isaiah 30:24 mentions that a "shovel" was used in the same manner; but this tool is not described.

J. Sieve. Israelites used the sieve to separate grain from the grit and dirt after it was threshed and fanned (cf. Is. 30:28). (*See also* "Agriculture.")

The Old Testament prophets used the sieve as a symbol of God's judgment, which would "sift" the nations (Is. 30:28; Amos 9:9). Jesus also used this symbolism (Luke 22:31).

K. File. The *file* was used to sharpen other types of tools: "Yet they had a file for the mattocks, and for the coulters, and for the forks, and for the axes, and to sharpen the goads" (1 Sam. 13:21). This is the only scriptural reference to the file, and the exact nature of the tool is not described.

VI. Fisherman's Tools. Fish was one of the most abundant foods of Bible times, and we find that fishermen used special tools for catching fish.

A. Casting Net. When Jesus called Simon and Andrew to be His disciples, He found them "casting a net into the sea; for they were fishers" (Mark 1:16–17; Matt. 4:18). The cast-

TOOLS AND IMPLEMENTS

ing net (*amphiblēstron*) had a circular form about 4.5 m. (15 ft.) in diameter, with a fine mesh. A fisherman placed lead sinkers around the edge of the net to take the net to the bottom of the lake. He attached a long piece of line to the center of the net. The fisherman held this line by the left hand, gathered the net up in the right hand, and cast it out into the shallow water.

B. Dragnet, or Drawnet (*sagēnē*, Matt. 13:47). Fishermen used this type of net in deeper water (Luke 5:4). It was a long net—sometimes nearly 100 m. (328 ft.) long—and about 2.5 m. (8 ft.) wide. The fisherman attached corks to one side to keep it buoyed up, and lead sinkers to the other side to make it sink.

Sometimes the net was stretched between two boats and the boats were rowed in a circle, drawing the net together. The ropes attached to the bottom of the net were drawn in faster than those at the top, which trapped the fish in the net (John 21:16).

C. Spear. Hebrew fishermen used the spear, and possibly a type of harpoon, for fishing (Job 41:7). The spear head and the barbs of the harpoons were probably made of iron. Ancient inscriptions prove that such tools were used by the Egyptians.

D. Hook. Hooks were also used for fishing. Peter used a fishhook to catch a fish (Matt. 17:27). We know that Assyrian fishermen used the hook and line for fishing, as shown by inscriptions from 700 B.C.

E. Anchor. Ancient fishermen used the anchor much as it is used today. However, early anchors were simply large stones or crooked pieces of wood weighted with stones. These crude tools were not capable of holding a large vessel, and metal anchors with hooks were soon developed.

At first, the metal anchor had only one barb to catch the ground; then anchors with as many as four barbs were developed. Acts 27:29 is thought to refer to a four-barbed anchor: "They cast four anchors out of the stern, and wished for day."

In ancient times anchors were thrown from

FLINTS AND BONE TOOLS. *Discovered at Jericho, these flints and the bone tools date from the Neolithic period (5000–4000 B.C.). Other tools and weapons made of flint were found on the same excavation level. Most appear to have been knife blades, some having fine, serrated edges.*

either end of the ship (Acts 27:30). When ships were at anchor near the shore, they were placed with their stern to the beach and their bow in deep water, having the anchor cast from the bow.

The anchor has long been a symbol of hope, as we see in Hebrews 6:19. Early Christians used the anchor to signify the successful end of the voyage of life. Thus it is found as an emblem on their tombs.

VII. Householder's Tools. Hebrew women used special tools in preparing food for the family. Most of the food preparation was done in a courtyard near their houses. (*See* "Architecture and Furniture.")

A. Oven. Ovens were usually built in the courtyard. These early ovens were hollow at the top, about 60 cm. (24 in.) in diameter at the base and about 30 cm. (12 in.) high. They often were constructed by alternating layers of clay and potsherds (pieces of broken pottery; Job 2:8). The women could bake flat cakes by sticking them to the sides of the oven or placing them over a fire on heated stones (Lev. 2:4; 11:35; 26:26). Archaeologists have found the remains of such ovens in the ruins of Megiddo.

B. Mill. We first read of the grain mill in Exodus 11:5, which describes the custom of hiring women to turn it: "even unto the first-born of the maidservant that is behind the mill." The wandering Israelites ground *manna* in mills (Num. 11:8). The mill was such an important item of domestic use that no one was allowed to take it as collateral for a loan (Deut. 24:6).

In Abraham's time, grain was pounded or ground by spreading it on a flat stone and rubbing it with a round stone muller (Gen. 18:6). This type of grinding tool was found in the ruins of Jericho.

The rotary mill came into use in the Iron Age. It consisted of two circular stone slabs 50 cm. (20 in.) across. A pivot secured the upper slab (Hebrew, *rekeb*) to the stone beneath. Women poured grain through the pivot hole in the upper stone, and it was ground as the wheel turned. The flour was forced out between the two stones as more grain was added. Often two women would grind, sitting on either side of the mill. They would turn the mill with a wooden handle attached to the outer surface of the upper stone (cf. Matt. 24:41).

C. Needle. Hebrew women used needles to make clothing. (*See also* "Clothing and Cosmetics.") The first scriptural reference to

BRONZE IMPLEMENTS. *These implements found at Megiddo were made of bronze. The Israelites used the knife for eating and for slaughtering animals. These implements were originally attached to wooden handles.*

needlework is found in Exodus 26:36, which gives specifications for the temple hangings. Needlework was common in Bible times (cf. Ex. 27:16; 28:39; 36:37; 38:18; 39:29; Judg. 5:30; Ps. 45:14).

D. Knife. The Hebrews used a knife called *ma'akeleth* (literally, "eating instrument") for slaughtering animals for food or sacrifice (Gen. 22:6). Another Hebrew word, *hereb,* meant a knife made of flint (Josh. 5:2) or perhaps a knife for shaving (Ezek. 5:1). The flint knife survived well into the Bronze Age for everyday use.

E. Press. Presses were used to extract the juice of grapes, olives, and other fruit. A full winepress was a sign of propriety. (*See* "Agriculture.")

VIII. Mason's Tools. Stone masons used many of the same tools that were used by

TOOLS AND IMPLEMENTS

builders and carpenters of that day, such as the hammer, plumb line, marking tool, measuring line, saw, and chisel.

Masons used saws to cut stone for the temple (1 Kin. 7:9). Some Bible passages suggest that they may have used a level and square (cf. Ezek. 41:21), but clear Scripture references to such tools cannot be found. Stones from both Herod's temple and his fortress-palace at Masada show that the stones were cut and fitted before being erected. They often have numbers or mason's marks carved in them.

IX. Potter's Tools. Until about 3000 B.C., pottery was hand-molded. After this time, it was made on a potter's wheel. The potter's work is described in Jeremiah 18:3–4.

A. Wheel. Examples of the potter's wheel have been discovered in archaeological diggings at Jericho, Megiddo, Gezer, Laish, Hazor, and other Palestinian cities. These relics show that the potter sat at the edge of a pit in which the "wheel" stood (Jer. 18:3). The lower stone of the wheel rested in the pit, while the upper stone was on a pivot. A wooden collar encircled the upper stone, and the potter turned this collar with his feet.

B. Paddle and Scraper. From archaeological finds, we know that the potter used various types of paddles and scrapers of wood and stone. But there is no record of these tools in the Scriptures.

C. Furnace. Furnaces were used for baking pottery. The remains of such furnaces or kilns have been discovered at Megiddo.

X. Metalsmith's Tools. In Bible times, the smith was often referred to as "he who blows the coals" (Isa. 54:16). The metalsmith poured liquid metal from ladles or buckets into clay molds or beat it on an anvil with a forge hammer. The coppersmith and ironworker (*haras barzel*) were also known as "hammerers" (Is. 41:7; 44:12), because they flattened and smoothed metal by pounding.

A. Anvil. The Hebrew word for *anvil* is found only in Isaiah 41:7: "And he that smootheth with the hammer him that smote the anvil." The earliest anvils were made of bronze. But when Israelites mastered the smelting of iron, they formed it into anvils. The anvil was a metal surface on which the smith would place an object to hammer it into the desired shape. He might place this metal surface on a large block of wood to deaden the sound of the pounding.

B. Bellows. The smith used this instrument to force a draft of air through clay pipes to the furnace, producing enough heat to melt metal (Ezek. 22:20). Usually the bellows (Hebrew, *mappuach*) was made of sewn goat or sheepskin (Jer. 6:22). The skin formed an airtight bag that was fitted in a frame of wood. When the smith compressed this bag, the air was forced out under the pressure.

C. Furnace. The smith used a furnace that could be heated to very high temperatures (cf. Dan. 3:19). But the ancient smiths were never able to get their furnaces hot enough to pour melted iron, as they did copper. Iron came from the furnace as a spongy mass of iron, slag, and cinders. The smith hammered it out to remove the slag and air bubbles. Then it was put in the furnace until it was forged into wrought iron, and finally worked by the skilled blacksmith (1 Sam. 13:18–20). If he needed to sharpen the edges of instruments, such as axes or knives, he might use a whetstone or file (Eccl. 10:10).

Archaeologists have found the remains of smiths' furnaces at Beth-shemesh in Palestine (Josh. 15:10). There were two different types of furnaces, both made of clay bricks. One had holes in the sides where air could be forced in by a blowpipe. The second type was long and narrow, and open to the air.

D. Tongs. Often the smith used tongs to lift iron from the furnace or fire (Is. 44:12). These early tongs were made of bronze; but as iron became available, they were made of that metal.

The smith's tongs had much the same shape as tongs used today. In the archaeological diggings at Tell el-Amarna, Egypt, tongs from 1350 B.C. have been discovered. The grasping ends on the ancient tongs were shaped like human hands.

TRADE

People of the ancient Near East communicated mostly in person, and merchants of the day exchanged news and ideas along with their merchandise. For this reason, trade deeply affected society in Bible times; it opened the way for new discoveries about the world.

Traders took their caravans of camels and donkeys to the far reaches of the Near East, giving little thought to the time involved in the travel. Sometimes they spent a year or more in other countries, hawking their wares.

Sea captains often traded their services for part of the merchandise they carried. Sometimes there were no roads between cities of trade, so merchants had to take the high seas unless they simply cut across the desert.

Trade improved in peacetime. As nations formed alliances, their tradesmen shuttled to and fro, in spite of the dangers of traveling across foreign soil. Government leaders set up military posts; soldiers patrolled the roads; and courts took severe action against thieves on the road. Tradesmen in Bible times needed constant protection from the danger of robbers.

But war meant trouble for tradesmen. The inflation rate soared; kings banned trade with some nations; and the roads were filled with armies instead of trade caravans. After war, the victors often imposed limits on the trade of conquered nations. This restricted their wealth and so prevented further rebellion.

Canaan was in a key trade position. The countries to her north (Phoenicia and Aram) and to the south (Egypt) used the public roads that ran through Canaan. She could not be isolated from her neighbors, even if she had wanted to be. This strategic location could have been used by Israel in order to proclaim God in her trade and cultural relations (Deut. 4:6). Instead, Israel became more and more like her ungodly neighbors, and she lost her distinctive quality of life as God's covenant people. God then allowed other nations to scatter the Israelites.

I. BEGINNINGS OF TRADE
   A. Egypt
   B. Canaan

II. TRADE IN THE KINGDOM OF DAVID AND SOLOMON

III. TRADE IN THE DIVIDED KINGDOM

IV. OBJECTS OF TRADE
   A. Gold
   B. Silver
   C. Copper
   D. Tin
   E. Iron
   F. Ivory
   G. Glass
   H. Wood
   I. Bitumen
   J. Flax
   K. Cotton
   L. Wool

I. Beginnings of Trade. The land determines what a nation can produce for trade. Climate, soil, raw materials, and the location of trade routes encourage or limit economic development.

Humans need food, and this is the most basic item of trade. In the earliest times, people collected wild grains and legumes and killed animals for meat. Because they constantly needed to search for food, they ignored most other needs. When they began running out of wild grain, they made a tough decision: they settled down and took the risk of trying to grow their own crops, and then faced the problems of lack of rain, locusts, untimely planting, wild animals, and floods. If the farming attempts failed, starvation would follow. When people decided to settle down, therefore, they had to consider such things as availability of water, fertility of the soil, and the ability to defend themselves against hostile neighbors.

People produced fruits and vegetables, dairy products, and meat products. They made tools and utensils with local raw materials. The producer traded with the consumer.

But as men formed larger communities and villages, their needs increased, and some of the settlers became tradesmen. They traded materials from several producers in their own villages for goods produced by neighboring villages. As these tradesmen moved about, they shared information about needs and supplies between one village and another, and soon particular communities began to special-

TRADE

ize in certain kinds of work. One area produced wine, another dyed textiles, and so on. The merchant arranged trades between these communities.

Some areas started producing copper, bronze, iron, and other metals. Tradesmen had to go long distances to find these metals, and this is how distant trade began. Merchants took raw materials from the mines and delivered them to craftsmen, who made them into needed tools and finished products. Then the merchants took the tools to farmers, hunters, and others who needed them.

The desire for raw materials explains why the ancient nations needed good trade relations. It also explains why they engaged in war to control areas that produced these materials. Egypt, Mesopotamia, Anatolia, Syria, Phoenicia, and Canaan were connected by trade routes before 3000 B.C. In fact, archaeologists have found evidence of a network of Near Eastern trade routes that existed before 3000 B.C. Caravans moved from one end of the "Fertile Crescent" to the other—from the Persian Gulf to Asia Minor, Syria, Canaan, and Egypt.

Sea trade soon became common. (*See* "Transportation.") The Phoenicians built a great fleet and used colonies along the coast of the Mediterranean as trading posts. The cities of Tyre and Sidon became trading centers for many nations; they had good harbors and lay near the important land routes. Many ships stopped there to unload their goods.

Merchants depended on special privileges to do their work. When kings made treaties, they gave special status for some merchants; they were considered to be the official representatives of the nation. Because the kings protected them, they were called "royal merchants." Solomon imported horses through "royal merchants" (1 Kin. 10:28). The king of Byblos wrote: "Aren't there 20 ships in my harbor which are in *commercial relations* with Ne-su-Ba-neb-Ded? As to Sidon . . . aren't there 50 more ships there which are in *commercial relations* with Werket-El, and which are drawn up to his house?" (italics ours).[1]

_____

[1] James B. Pritchard, ed., *The Ancient Near East: An Anthology of Texts and Pictures* (Princeton, N.J.: Princeton University Press, 1958), p. 19.

SYRIANS BRINGING TRIBUTE. *Syrian tribute-bearers deliver to the pharaoh of Egypt an ointment horn, an elaborate quiver, costly jars and jugs, and a decorated drinking vessel in this wall painting from a tomb at Thebes (ca. fifteenth century B.C.). This scene features objects that were particularly valued at the time.*

18

TRADE

GOLDWORKING. *This relief in an Egyptian tomb at Sakkarah (ca. 2300 B.C.) shows scenes from the process of goldworking. In the upper left, gold is weighed on scales and a scribe records the weight. To the right, men blow through tubes to make the fire hot enough to melt the metal. In the lower section, craftsmen fashion gold objects on tables. The finished objects rest on a shelf in the center frame.*

The prosperity of a nation depended on its raw materials and its trade relations with other countries. This is why the various countries needed an extensive system of transportation. Early merchants exchanged one product for another, a transaction that we call a *barter.* Later they paid for goods with gold or silver. Nations agreed on a set value for these metals, and this value might change over the years.

Abraham paid 400 shekels of silver for the cave of Machpelah, for example, and Joseph's brothers sold him for 20 shekels of silver. By the sixth century B.C., merchants were using coins for payment. Most merchants used coins by the time of Jesus. Thus, Jesus could ask about the image that was on the face of a Roman coin (Luke 20:19–26).

A. Egypt. Egypt soon controlled the metal market in the Near East. The Egyptian pharaohs kept a tight rein on the mining of gold in their country. This metal was so scarce that it became precious, and among merchants it was the most prized form of payment. Egypt actually became a superpower because of her control of gold. For example, the king of Mitanni wrote:

My brother, pray send gold in
* very great quantities, such*
* as cannot be counted;*
my brother may send me that;
and my brother may send me more
* gold than my father got.*
In the land of my brother is not
* gold as the dust upon the ground?*
  —Trans. by Herman Kees
  Ancient Egypt, pp. 137–138

The gold used for the burial of Tutankhamen ("King Tut") shows Egypt's riches, even in a time of lessening wealth.

Egypt was also rich in silver; Egyptian jewelers added it to gold as an alloy. About 3000 B.C., silver was valued more than gold, but merchants gradually came to value gold more. Thus, by 1500 B.C., gold was worth twice as much as silver; by 1000 B.C., the ratio of gold to silver was $3\frac{1}{2}$ to 1.

But Egypt's gold couldn't do everything. Egypt needed wood, turquoise, and copper, and she had to trade to get them. The fancy lifestyle of her pharaohs strained Egypt's economy, and crop failure caused widespread famine.

TRADE

First, therefore, Egypt had to make special trade deals to import the needed goods. Her earliest efforts brought trade contracts with Cyprus, Anatolia, Mesopotamia, and other Near East nations.

Egypt's next step was to colonize Syria and Palestine to safeguard the trade routes that brought in her raw materials. These routes brought foodstuffs and other vital supplies. Ships from Phoenicia brought timber for doors, paneling, coffins, and other special uses of the Egyptian royal family—including wood for the chambers of the tombs. Copper came by sea from Cyprus and Asia Minor.

Then Egypt explored the vast desert regions east of Egypt, especially Sinai and the southern Negev, searching for copper and turquoise. Egypt had much to offer the world, such as linens and papyrus (which was her most important contribution to Western civilization, in the long run). Papyrus (from which we get the word *paper*) was a sturdy writing material made from flax pulp, woven together with beaten strips of papyrus reed. Some papyrus manuscripts have lasted 4,500 years.

B. Canaan. Canaan has always been a very fertile and fruitful land. In his tomb inscriptions, Pharaoh Weni tells of his military campaigns in Canaan. He took cities and destroyed vineyards and orchards (around 2500 B.C.—about the time of Abraham). Sinuhe (about 1950 B.C.) tells of living in the Yarmuk Valley where figs, grapes, honey, olives, fruit, and barley were plentiful. He writes:

*Bread was made for me as a daily
fare; wine as daily provision,
cooked meat and roast fowl, besides
the wild beast of the desert . . .
and milk in every (kind of) cooking.*[2]

Moses' description of the land agrees. He said it was a land "of wheat and barley, of vines and fig trees and pomegranates, and a land of olive trees and honey" (Deut. 8:8). The people of Palestine have cultivated these products from early times, and they still form the backbone of the diet in Israel. When Joshua led the invasion of Canaan, the Israelites kept right on farming the crops the Canaanites had raised. Note: "The Lord your God brings you into the land . . . to give you . . . vineyards and olive trees which you did not plant, and you shall eat and be satisfied" (Deut. 6:10–11,

NASB). Ever since, the farming pattern of the Holy Land has stayed about the same.

Schoolboys in ancient Israel learned their farm calendar as set out in a poem found at Gezer in 1908. Some schoolboy learning to write at about Solomon's time recorded this breakdown of the farmer's year:

*1. His two months are (olive) harvest,
2. His two months are planting (grain),
3. His two months are late planting,
4. His month is hoeing up of flax,
5. His month is harvest of barley,
6. His month is harvest and feasting,
7. His two months are vine-tending,
8. His month is summer fruit.*

In ancient Israel, September and October were a harvest time for olives, grain, and grapes. In November and December, farmers planted grains and vegetables. In January and February, they sowed grains and vegetables

GEZER CALENDAR. *The inscription on this soft piece of limestone was probably a school exercise, recorded by a young boy learning to write. The verse traces the calendar of a farmer's year. The stone was found at Gezer and probably dates from the ninth or tenth century* B.C.

18

TRADE

---

[2] Pritchard, *op cit.,* p. 17.

TRADE

WEIGHTS. *In the interest of fair trade, vendors weighed the metal used as currency against standard stone weights. These weights were discovered on the hill of Ophel in Jerusalem; they date from the late seventh or early sixth century B.C. One weight bears the value of two shekels, another of four shekels, and the largest is valued at 24 shekels.*

for a later crop. In March, April, and May they harvested flax, then barley, wheat, and vegetables. Israelite farmers celebrated the end of the harvest with a time of feasting and praise to God. The hot, dry summer months produced little, so the farmer used that time to care for his vines and orchards; some orchards gave him fruit in August.

Canaan was a favorite trading spot, since it lay exactly on the major trade routes between Egypt, Syria, Phoenicia, Babylon, and Assyria. Canaan supplied honey, olive oil, grain, wine, and spices. Also, the ancient world had a growing need for tar and oil, which Canaan produced in great quantities. Many nations traded for it. Egypt readily sent supplies of pottery, metals, frankincense, and ivory in exchange for oil-related products. Ezekiel writes, "Judah and the land of Israel, they were your traders; with the wheat of Minnith, cakes, honey, oil and balm they paid for your merchandise" (Ezek. 27:17, NASB). By the way, when the Bible mentions "oil," it usually means olive oil for cooking.

Local trade followed supply and demand —what was needed most would cost the most. The siege of Samaria shows this. War made food prices go up for Samaria. Traders couldn't get in the cities, and farmers couldn't get out to harvest their crops. Soon the people were eating everything—a donkey's head sold for 80 pieces of silver; a tiny amount of common weed sold for 5 pieces of silver. Starvation isn't pretty. The siege victims were even eating babies (2 Kin. 6:28).

When the siege lifted, prices came down as food became available. "Tomorrow about this time a measure of fine flour shall be sold for a shekel, and 2 measures of barley for a shekel, in the gate of Samaria" (2 Kin. 7:1, NASB).

In ancient times, merchants conducted most of their business at the city gate. The gate soon became important in matters of government as well. The elders of the city met at the gate to deal with community and legal matters (Amos 5:10). Strangers were either welcomed to the city or refused entry at the gate.

So merchants came to Jerusalem with their grain, wine, figs, grapes and other products to sell at the main gate. But problems arose when they tried to do this on the Sabbath. Nehemiah would not allow trade at the gate on the Sabbath; he stationed guards there to enforce the law (Neh. 13:15–21).

False weights and measures were another kind of problem in Old Testament trade. "You shall have just balances, just weights, a just ephah and a just hin" (Lev. 19:36). The lack of honesty in daily life—shown in the trade problems—tells us of much deeper problems with Israel. Prophets pointed to sharp practices in business to show the sad religious state of Israel: "Hear this, you who trample the needy . . . saying, 'When will the new moon be over, So that we may buy grain, And the sabbath that we may open the wheat market, to make the bushel smaller and the shekel bigger, And to cheat with dishonest scales" (Amos 8:4–5, NASB). Some merchants tried to ruin their fellow citizens with sharp business deals. If a farmer had a bad harvest, he might need to borrow money to buy food and plant the next crop. If the next crop was just as bad, ungodly lenders might then take all his

TRADE

property and sell his family into slavery. Israel's prophets condemned these wheeler-dealers for their lack of pity or any sense of fairness. They attacked shrewd merchants who took advantage of poor people, widows, and orphans. Isaiah says God searched the streets of Israel for right living and found sin instead: "Thus He looked for justice, but behold, bloodshed; For righteousness, but behold, a cry of distress. Woe to those who add house to house and join field to field, Until there is no more room, So that you have to live alone in the midst of the land" (Is. 5:7–8, NASB). Amos says these ungodly merchants were anxious "to buy the helpless for money and the needy for a pair of sandals" (8:6; 2:6–8).

Women engaged in business as well as men. The writer of Proverbs tells us that a "virtuous" woman had many skills. She could weave the materials she purchased in the market to make cloth (31:13, 19, 21–22) and she could sew clothes and belts (31:24). She profited from wise buying, hard work, and good trading (31:24). Often she used her profits to buy land (31:16). The writer of Proverbs says an ideal woman is hardworking, mentally sharp, and alert in her business dealings. She is not shy or housebound. She proudly bids and pays for the things she buys. She is "like merchant ships," bringing profit to the family (31:14).

Theocratic (direct divine) rule was supposed not only to help Israel rule itself, but to enable it to influence other nations as well. But each time Israel began associating with strong nations, it suffered. Its strength lay in its religious commitment, but this commitment wavered. If Israel had allowed God to rule completely, other nations would not have overrun it. But Israel kept ignoring Him.

Now we will review Israel's economic development, starting with the period of the United Kingdom.

II. Trade in the Kingdom of David and Solomon. King Saul united the 12 tribes of Israel into one strong nation. By the time David ruled (tenth century B.C.), Israel was an established power. By war and by treaty, David brought the neighboring nations to his side, and many of them paid great sums of money to keep peace with Israel. The Bible doesn't give a total of this money (2 Sam. 8:2, 6, 11–12), but it must have been very large.

For instance, David received from Zobah 700 horsemen, 20,000 foot soldiers, 1,000

chariots and horses (2 Sam. 8:4; 1 Chr. 18:4). From Syria he received shields of gold and bronze; from Hamath, articles of silver, gold, and bronze; from Ammon, a heavy gold crown (2 Sam. 12:30). Israel lived at peace and became richer under David's rule. The Bible tells us little about trade during this time, but we know Israel grew rich from the agreements she made with her neighbors. David probably traded with his friend Hiram of Tyre, and the nation must have profited by this friendship. Both Tyre and Phoenicia traded with Israel, "for the Sidonians and Tyrians brought large quantities of cedar to David" (1 Chr. 22:4).

Solomon continued to receive payments from weaker nations to keep peace, as his father David had (1 Kin. 4:21). Notice how well the king's table was spread with foreign items: "And Solomon's provision for one day was 30 kors of fine flour and 60 kors of meal, ten fat oxen, 20 pasture-fed oxen, 100 sheep besides deer, gazelles, roebucks and fattened fowl. For he had dominion over everything west of the River, from Tiphsah even to Gaza, over all the kings west of the River; and he

HEBREW OSTRAKON. *This potsherd (ca. eighth century B.C.), was found at Tell Qasile. It is inscribed, "Gold from Ophir to Beth-horon—30 shekels." Costly papyrus was not normally used for everyday writing in antiquity. Instead, potsherds (Greek, ostraka) were inscribed in ink or engraved with a stylus.*

18

TRADE

TRADE

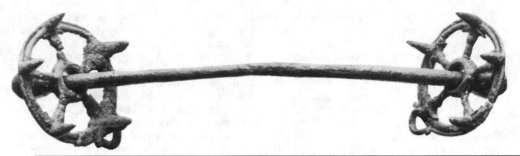

BRONZE HORSE'S BIT. *This bit comes from Palestine. Notice its circular cheek pieces, to which sharp spikes are fastened. It may date to the seventeenth century B.C.*

had peace on all sides around about him" (1 Kin. 4:22–24, NASB).

Governors taxed local products, and these taxes supplied the needs of the king's palace: "They brought tribute and served Solomon all the days of his life" (1 Kin. 4:21; 10:15). Surrounding kings paid their taxes in food, gold, silver, barley and even straw for the horses (cf. 1 Kin. 4:28).

More income for Israel's trasury came from merchants who wanted favors and would pay to get them. These traders would give gold or whatever was required to get special treatment from the king; Arab traders brought merchandise with them for this purpose (1 Kin. 10:15). Even the Queen of Sheba brought fine gifts when she visited Solomon, no doubt to get special treatment for her merchants (1 Kin. 10:2).

Solomon imported materials for the temple from neighboring lands (1 Kin. 9:15). From Tyre he got cedar, cypress, and gold (1 Kin. 5:8; 9:11, 14). In return, he gave Hiram of Tyre 20,000 kors of wheat and 20 kors of oil as an annual payment.

Solomon became an international dealer. His ships had Phoenician sailors on them; he used Ezion-Geber on the Gulf of Eilat as his own port (1 Kin. 9:26 ff.). The royal merchants brought him gold, almug trees, precious stones, ivory, silver, apes, peacocks, and horses (cf. 1 Kin. 9:28; 10:11–12, 14, 22, 26).

Solomon bought horses and chariots from Egypt and Que, paying 600 shekels of silver for a chariot and 150 shekels for each horse. In turn he sold these to Anatolia and Aram (1 Kin. 10:29).

III. Trade in the Divided Kingdom. When Israel split into two kingdoms, the wealth of the nation fell. Phoenicia became the strong commercial force in Palestine; her seaports and harbors on the Mediterranean helped greatly. Ezion-Geber never regained its place as a first-rate trading port, but the Arameans of the north quickly grew into a strong military power.

The Phoenicians took control of Near Eastern markets by developing sea routes to Egypt, Cyprus, Crete, Sicily, North Africa (Carthage), Italy, and Spain. Phoenician ships may have gone as far as Cornwall (England). From the Red Sea they traded with Africa, Arabia, and India.

The Phoenicians planted colonies of their own people in foreign lands, to control better the trade there. Trade was their strength; they never tried to gain power by making war. Phoenicians had a reputation for landing the best deal they could make. Other nations accepted this peaceful practice; they knew they had nothing to fear from the Phoenicians.

The northern kingdom of Israel tried to copy the Phoenicians. King Ahab sealed a friendship with Phoenicia when he married the daughter of Eth baal of Sidon (better known as Jezebel). He adopted Baal worship and copied Phoenician forms of art and building construction. When King Sargon II conquered Israel, he boasted that he received large tribute from Menahem, the last king. Archaeologists have found pieces of ivory from Israel in Sargon's palace at Nimrud; the ivory carvings copied Phoenician artwork. Similar carvings have been found in Samaria, showing the great influence that Phoenicia had on the northern kingdom.

Ezekiel tells us much about the Phoenicians' trading ways. He foretold that Babylon would take over the riches and power of Tyre, a Phoenician seaport. No longer could people say that Tyre "is perfect in beauty" (Ezek.

27:3), for she "will be no more" (27:36). Ezekiel lists commodities that the Phoenicians traded. They sought trading opportunities as they sailed the Mediterranean and Red Seas (1 Kin. 9:26–28; 2 Chr. 8:17–18). The Phoenicians were proud of their wealth, but Ezekiel predicted that they would crumble.

After the Phoenicians, the Arameans gained the upper hand in trading strength. They opened trading stalls in Samaria during Ahab's reign. As their armies conquered neighboring territory, they opened more markets and the Aramean kingdom grew stronger. Then Ahab overthrew King Ben-hadad of Aram, and the two men signed a treaty that allowed the northern kingdom to open trading posts in Damascus (cf. 1 Kin. 20:34).

Solomon's successors tried to use Ezion-Geber as a trade port. They did not succeed because they had no political clout with the surrounding nations. Ezion-Geber was Judah's southernmost city, about 200 miles below Jerusalem, and Judah could use it as a port only if she controlled the land of Edom. After Solomon's death, Edom grew strong and became a great trading power in its own right; the Edomites made good use of their key location at a crossing point in trade routes between Egypt and the Arabian Desert. But when Judah tried to use the port of Ezion-Geber, the Edomites forced them out.

Because King Jehoshaphat wanted to build up the trading power of the south, he made a trading agreement with Ahab in the north. His successor, Ahaziah, tried to build ships at Ezion-Geber and launch massive trading ventures for Jehoshaphat. But the ships never sailed; they were destroyed in the harbor (2 Chr. 20:37). That was the end of Judah's attempts at wide trade, even though King Uzziah of Judah brought Ezion-Geber back under Judah's control a hundred years later (2 Chr. 26:2). Uzziah had a great interest in Judah's business welfare. He strengthened vital cities, built additional military outposts, and expanded Judah's farming area. We believe he strengthened Judah's trading ties with other nations and may have planned a large fleet of merchant ships.

But Babylon defeated Judah, and her trading friends jeered at her misfortune (Ezek. 25:32). After the Exile, God improved the trading efforts of His people as Persia, Greece, Egypt, Syria, and Rome struggled for control of Palestine; but the big trading days were over. In Jesus' time the Jews were mainly farmers and shepherds. Their Roman masters encouraged this, so that Palestine became the Roman Empire's "bread basket."

IV. Objects of Trade. What items were traded in the Near East through these years? Ezekiel listed some of the items (Ezek. 27). He tells not only what was traded, but where it came from. He lists raw materials such as cloth goods, precious stones, animals, farming products, carpets, cords, and even clothing. Animals and farm products were discussed in the section on Canaan; but let us look at the other goods in trade:

A. Gold. In Egypt, the Pharaoh's government owned all of the gold. Egypt's eastern desert was rich in gold ore and the kings mined it for their own treasuries. They used gold for decorations in the palace and various temples. The Egyptians used every method they could to get the gold; washing sand and gravel, combing the beaches for nuggets tossed up by the sea, and mining the underground deposits with slave labor. They could mine silver along with the gold, since it was often found in the same places. The ancients called the alloy of gold and silver *electrum*.

Israel had no gold in her land. The Israelites could see tiny particles of gold in the quartzite and granite of the Eilat Mountains, but it was never worth mining. When Moses led the Israelites out of Egypt, the Egyptians gave them gifts of gold, just to get rid of these people who brought the plagues (Ex. 12:35). The Israelites used much of this gold to decorate the ark of the covenant and the tabernacle (Ex. 35:5). They wasted some of the same gold in making the golden calf (Ex. 32:3–4). As Joshua swept through Canaan, he collected a great deal of gold and other booty, but it was lost in later years when other conquerers defeated Israel.

David gathered gold by demanding taxes or tribute from nations he had defeated in battle, and from nations that were weak and "fearful of Israel's army" (2 Sam. 8:10; 12:30; 1 Chr. 18:10). David himself gave 100,000 talents of gold for the temple construction (1 Chr. 22:14), while the other leaders of Israel gave 5,000 talents and 10,000 darics of gold (1 Chr. 29:7, RSV).

As Israel flexed her military muscles, other nations paid tribute in gold and silver (1 Kin. 9:14; 10:14 ff.). For example, the Queen of Sheba gave lavish donations to the high-living court of Solomon: "And she gave the king one hundred and twenty talents of gold, and a very

18

TRADE

Barter in the Bible

Barter is the simple exchange of one item or service for another. In ancient times, a carpenter might build a house for a farmer, in return for some vegetables and grain; cattlemen might trade cattle for hay; and so on.

In Eastern countries today, a section of each city is still designated as the place where craftsmen, importers, farmers, and businessmen can meet to barter their goods and services. In times of national crisis, barter often takes the place of cash sales. People of the United States and other Western nations commonly used barter during the Great Depression of the 1930s.

The Bible mentions several interesting examples of barter. One involved trading cattle for bread during the famine described in Genesis 47:13–17; this example shows that barter was used when money was no longer worth anything. Another barter involved the Israelites' trading of wheat for cedar trees, in order to build Solomon's temple (1 Kin.

5:1–12); this shows that barter was used in prosperous times, when one people had something that another needed, and would trade for it. Yet another interesting barter was Hosea's exchange of grain and silver for a wife (Hos. 3:2); this incident shows that barter was one way that a groom could pay for a wife, whose absence from her father's household decreased the workforce in the home. (See "Marriage and Divorce.") This "dowry" concept is still used in some African nations.

Materials or services could be used for barter, as when Jacob bound himself to Laban as a servant to gain Laban's daughter for his bride (Gen. 29:15–30). When Joseph was sold into slavery, his services as a slave were exchanged for money or trade goods (Gen. 37:23–28). God ordained that the tribe of Levi should live by bartering their services as priests for food and meat, which were brought to the temple for sacrifice (Num. 18:25–32).

---

great amount of spices and precious stones. Never again did such abundance of spices come in as that which the queen of Sheba gave King Solomon" (1 Kin. 10:10, NASB).

Then Israel's state changed, and her neighbors demanded peace payment in gold and other precious metals, often in huge amounts (1 Kin. 14:26; 15:18 ff.; 23:33; 25:15).

The value of gold was great, yet the Israelites did not use it for money, but mainly for decorations. Since gold is a soft metal, craftsmen could shape it in a variety of ways for elaborate objects. The Bible mentions fancy cups and bowls, especially for royal use (Esth. 1:17); gold-leaf decorations on the tabernacle, the throne, and the walls of the palace; golden objects used in worship in the temple; and jewelry for women (Gen. 24:22; Num. 31:50).

B. Silver. People used silver for money in these early times. Traders recognized a set value for a given amount of silver. The Egyptians and early Sumerians got silver from northern Syria and parts of Egypt; as we have already noted, the Egyptian mines often produced a combination of gold and silver.

Silver became an important factor in trading in the ancient world. Conquered nations used it to pay tribute (1 Kin. 9:14). Worshipers brought it as a gift to the temple in Jerusalem (1 Chr. 29:4). The modern Hebrew word for

silver has extended its most common meaning to signify "money."

C. Copper. Copper and bronze are ancient products of Canaan. Looking back, we find that the Canaanites learned the art of *smelting* (heating ore to melt the metal and separate it from the rock) as early as 3500 B.C. The Arabah produced malachite, an ore that was high in copper content, and the people of that region mined it extensively. They built a copper-smelting factory at Tel Abu Matar, southwest of Beer-sheba, in about 3500 B.C. Arab craftsmen sent expeditions into the Sinai Desert to get their copper (about 3000 B.C.).

Archaeologists once thought King Solomon opened the mines at Timna and a smelting plant at Ezion-Geber. Nelson Glueck discovered these sites. But more recent researchers have found that the mines were Egyptian, and dated from about 1300 to 1150 B.C. We know this because the Timna mines were dedicated to an Egyptian goddess, Hathor. Diggers have unearthed a temple there with inscriptions in the Egyptian language.

Solomon used huge quantities of copper in building the temple at Jerusalem (1 Chr. 18:8), and explorers have tried to find where it all came from. They found evidence at Ezion-Geber of what they thought were Solomon's copper mines; it turned out to be a spot where caravans of traders stopped to rest. Most likely the copper came from the Arabah desert at

TRADE

Punon, a spot the Israelite caravans passed on their way across Jordan (Num. 33:42 ff.). Israeli archaeologists discovered large-scale copper mines at Timna in the Sinai that dated back to Egyptian times. These mines are now being exploited by modern mining techniques.

Egypt's business leaders combed the Sinai for copper; they used copper mines at Serabit-el-Khadem beside the Gulf of Suez and in the southern Negev near Ezion-Geber, on the Gulf of Eilat. But most of the Egyptian copper came from the island of Cyprus; in fact, our English word *copper* comes from the name of that island. Copper drew Cyprus into the trading plans of many nations—especially Greece, Asia Minor, and Syria. Between 2000 and 1000 B.C., Cyprus arose as a major trader in the Mediterranean world.

Researchers have found a letter from a ruler of Cyprus, agreeing to barter copper for famous Egyptian chariots and beds. It reads: "And have I not sent to thee through my messengers one hundred talents of copper? Furthermore, now, let thy messenger bring, for presents, one bedstead of ebony, inlaid with gold, and a chariot, with gold . . . and two horses."

So the discovery and use of copper pros-pered the trading world of the Near East. Copper had many more uses than silver or gold; its hardness made it ideal for many practical uses. And it was easier to find.

But many countries had no copper of their own. In Israel, for example, David needed more copper than the land could provide. So he accepted bronze (an alloy of copper and tin) as part of the tribute he demanded from Hadadezer of Aram (1 Chr. 18:8). David stored large quantities of copper for building the temple. Also, the king of Hamath sent bronze to David (1 Chr. 18:10). Armies used copper for helmets, swords, mace heads, and other weapons. Religious objects were made of copper—pans, wands, idols. Kitchen utensils were made of copper; women used it for mirrors and powder boxes; and most musical instruments were made of copper.

Archaeologists found that a spot called "the Cave of the Treasure," near the temple at Engedi, held a large store of copper objects. Priests from the temple stored 429 prized objects there, wrapped in straw mats (about 3000 B.C.). Of these, many were copper: 10 crowns, 80 wands and 240 mace heads.

D. Tin. People of the ancient world needed tin to make bronze. By combining copper and

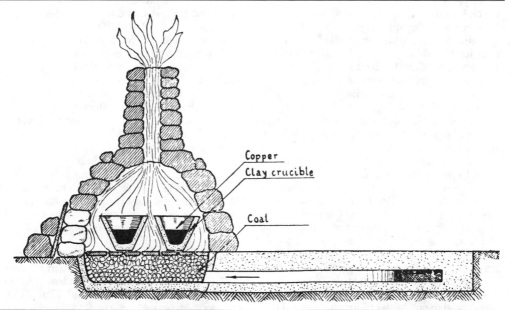

COPPER FURNACE. *This drawing reconstructs the copper-smelting furnace at Tell Qasile on Israel's central coast. Remains of two such furnaces, made of mud brick and stone tiles, were discovered here. Nearby, researchers found crucibles holding the remains of smelted copper.*

TRADE

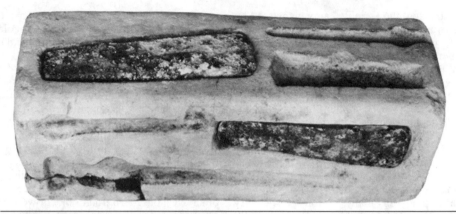

CASTING MOLD. *Two axes or chisels rest in a clay mold for casting metal implements. The mold was discovered at Shechem; it dates from about 1800 B.C.*

tin, they could produce a stronger, tougher metal. The Phoenicians sold tin, but we're not sure where they found it. Perhaps it came from Cornwall in England, which was rich in tin.

E. Iron. In early centuries, man learned how to take iron from iron ore. But the real surge towards an iron industry came when man discovered the ore could be heated to melt the iron away from the rock. This iron industry began in Asia Minor around 1400 B.C. In Egypt and parts of Asia, ironworkers built special iron furnaces that used very hot air blasts to melt the ore and produce liquid iron, that then could be cast into molds. Our Bible tells us that Moses and the Israelites knew of this process: "But the Lord has taken you out and brought you out of the iron furnace, from Egypt, to be a people for His own possession, as today" (Deut. 4:20, NASB). "And I will also break down your pride of power; I will also make your sky like iron and your earth like bronze" (Lev. 26:19, NASB).

The Israelites depended on the power of the Lord to defeat the Canaanites. We realize this even more when we look at the kinds of weapons they had. The Israelites were poorly equipped for war, for the Canaanites had "chariots of iron." In Judges we read: "Now the Lord was with Judah, and they took possession of the hill country; but they could not drive out the inhabitants of the valley because they had iron chariots" (Judg. 1:19, NASB).

Later, when Israel was weak, the Philistines threatened them. As the Philistines moved into the southwestern shore of Canaan (about 1200 B.C.), they brought the skills of casting iron tools and weapons—skills they had learned from the Hittites in Asia Minor. Soon the Israelites began to buy iron farming tools from the Philistines instead of developing their own iron industry. The Philistines tried to keep it that way: "Now no blacksmith could be found in all the land of Israel, for the Philistines said, 'Lest the Hebrews make swords and spears.' So all Israel went down to the Philistines, each to sharpen his plowshare, his mattock, his axe, and his hoe. And the charge was two-thirds of a shekel for the plowshares, the mattocks, the forks, and the axes, and to fix the hoes. So it came about on the day of the battle that neither sword nor spear was found in the hands of any of the people who were with Saul or Jonathan, but they were found with Saul and his son Jonathan" (1 Sam. 13:19–22, NASB).

David made sure his people got their fair share of the iron. As he extended the borders of Israel, more of this raw material became available.

David got as much iron as he needed for weapons and other military needs; and he got ready for building the temple by storing up great quantities of iron. The Bible says, "David prepared large quantities of iron to make the nails for the doors of the gates and for the clamps, and more bronze than could be weighed" (1 Chr. 22:3, NASB).

As David's armies won in battle, they brought back iron implements as part of their loot. The soldiers gave 100,000 talents of iron to help in building the temple (1 Chr. 29:7). Archaeologists realized how valuable iron was at that time when they discovered a stockpile of iron bars weighing a total of 330,000 pounds in the palace of Sargon II who lived at

Nineveh about 715 B.C. Surely King David forced the nations around him to give such iron bars to Israel as part of their peace tribute.

The Israelites never practiced iron smelting, as far as we know. Even though the Hermon Mountains in Carmel and the Arabah held plenty of iron ore, Israel depended on iron imports from Syria, Cyprus, and Asia Minor.

Iron was in great demand. It was harder and more plentiful than copper, so merchants all over the Near East traded with it. Armies used iron for daggers, shields, spearheads, and arrowheads. Farmers wanted iron for hoes, plowshares, picks, and sickles.

F. Ivory. Because ivory comes from the tusks of elephants, it was hard to get in the Near East. Rich families wanted it for jewelry and decorative furniture. Elephants once lived in Syria, but the search for ivory killed off all of them by 800 B.C. Most ivory used in the Near East came from the so-called Asiatic elephants.

Craftsmen around Beersheba made ivory figurines as early as 3500 B.C. Diggings in the Near East have turned up many ivory carvings, like those at Ugarit in Syria (dated about 1300 B.C.). At Megiddo archaeologists found 200 pieces of finely carved ivory below the palace of the governor; they dated from about 1150 B.C.

Solomon's merchant ships brought him ivory for his throne (1 Kin. 10:18–22). Ahab ordered his craftsmen to build an "ivory house," because he so admired the fine ivory work done by the Phoenicians (1 Kin. 22:39). Pieces of ivory were inlaid in the walls of this house, and it contained many hand-carved ivory figurines. These included figures of people, animals, flowers, plants, and mythological figures.

Ancient sculptures used ivory to make chairs, couches, beds, boxes and caskets. Soon the rich people of Samaria wanted these ivory creations. Because they'd gotten their riches by mistreating the people, Amos foretold that the rich Samaritan houses of ivory would be destroyed (3:15). The Assyrians made his forecast come true when they captured Samaria in 722 B.C. They looted the palaces of Samaria and took the ivory to Sargon II. Recent diggings show that the palace of Sargon II at Nimrud had ivory carvings much like the ones found in Samaria.

When Assyrians forced the southern kingdom to pay tribute, it included gifts of ivory. The Assyrian records say: "Hezekiah . . . did send me later to Nineveh . . . 30 talents of gold, 800 talents of silver, precious stones, antimony, large cuts of red stone, couches (inlaid) with ivory, nimedu chairs (inlaid) with ivory. . . ." (Pritchard, p. 201).

G. Glass. Because it was so rare, glass was a form of wealth; Job tells us "gold or glass cannot equal it (wisdom): nor can it be exchanged for articles of fine gold" (Job 28:17, NASB). Before craftsmen developed the art of glass blowing, they molded the glass around an inner core while the glass was in a sticky, plastic form. When the glass cooled and hardened, they took away the core and the glass object was ready for use. Artisans used this process widely in Egypt and Mesopotamia about 2500 B.C. Archaeologists have discovered a glass factory that operated at El-Amarna in Egypt about 1400 B.C.; it produced small glass bottles that were exported to Palestine. The Egyptians also sent these bottles to Haran, Cyprus, and the Aegean Islands. The Mesopotamians did not export their glass objects as far away as Palestine. The Phoenicians made glass vessels to resemble alabaster; the Egyptians were also good at making glass pots, bottles, and other vessels, and coloring them to look like the original containers.

The Phoenicians began making blown glass about 100 B.C. They could produce blown glass much more rapidly than molded glass, so this lowered the cost of glass objects and made them more common. Romans used these glass vessels nearly as much as pottery. You will remember that a woman anointed Jesus with ointment from a glass bottle (Matt. 26:7).

H. Wood. Wood is one of man's oldest working materials. People of the Near East developed many uses of wood, and the area still depends heavily on wood today. Carpenters and wood craftsmen made furniture, tools and idols (Deut. 4:28). They used it for paneling rooms, building homes, strengthening forts, and constructing ships. When woodsmen cleared hills near villages, the rains caused the bare soil to erode. This made much of the rocky, bare landscape of Israel today. Now the Near East has virtually no forests, though fine forests stood there in early centuries.

When the Israelites invaded Canaan, they took the hill country first and left the Canaanites in the valleys. On the hills, the Israelites steadily cut down all the trees for homes and for making farm tools. They also used the wood for fuel.

18

TRADE

Solomon wanted fine cedar lumber for the temple, and he had to get it from Phoenicia. For 25 years workmen cut timber and shipped it to Solomon, landing at the port of Joppa (2 Chron. 2:16). Solomon also ordered fir and almug trees for building his palace.

The area of Bashan had fine oak forests; Israelite craftsmen made oars and furniture from oak. The Phoenicians exported much of the oak wood from Bashan to distant ports of the Mediterranean, even as far as Egypt.

Egypt lacked wood, so the pharaohs sent merchant fleets out to countries like Lebanon to get wood for their fine palaces and temples.

I. Bitumen. The word *pitch* in the Bible refers to bitumen, a thick form of oil. Bitumen seeps to the surface of the earth from deep layers of rock. It is much like asphalt. We find large quantities of bitumen floating on the surface of the Asphalt Lake on the island of Trinidad, and near the Dead Sea. Genesis 14:20 says that the kings of Sodom and Gomorrah fell into bitumen pits by the Dead Sea, and Noah waterproofed the ark by coating it with bitumen (Gen. 6:14).

J. Flax. Egypt produced fine linens from the flax plants that grew so well along the Nile Valley. The Egyptians had a secret way of softening the flax fibers to make the linen more comfortable to wear; this made their products more popular. They placed the stalks of flax into water until it started to rot; then they dried the stalks and beat them to separate the fibers. Expert weavers spun the fibers into thread and wove it to make cloth.

The Egyptians used linen to wrap the embalmed bodies of the dead. They usually left the linen at its natural color, but they dyed some linen a red color to be used by the royal family. The Egyptians gave their word for linen (*sas*) to the Hebrew language.

The Israelites grew flax near Jericho and in the area of Galilee. They used dew water instead of running water to soften the stalks; this was easier, but it didn't give their linen the fine quality that Egyptian linen had. The Israelites learned the art of weaving from the Egyptians and the Bible often mentions how they used this skill. Sinai women made linens for the tabernacle (Exod. 35:25); priests and kings wore linen clothes (Exod. 28:39; 39:27–29; 1 Sam. 2:18; 2 Sam. 6:14; 1 Chron. 15:27–28). An angel who appeared to Daniel was dressed in linen (Dan. 10:5). Rich men like Mordecai wore linen (Esther 18:15); the rich man who spoke to Lazarus was dressed in fine linen (Luke 16:19). And remember that the body of Jesus was wrapped in linen for burial (Luke 25:53).

K. Cotton. Cotton was the poor man's cloth; it was more plentiful than linen and more widely used. Cotton came directly from the cotton plants of the field, and it needed far less processing to make it usable. Farmers raised the best quality cotton in the humid climate of Upper Egypt. Most often the Egyptians used cotton in its natural color, rather than dyed.

L. Wool. Wool comes from sheep, which were abundant and common in the ancient world. The people of the Near East raised sheep and goats from very early times, and they commonly wore clothing of wool. The weavers and dyers of the Near East developed cloth-making into a fine craft. Many villages became famous for their weaving and dyeing industries; for example, archaeologists have found a famous dyeing workshop at Tell Beit Mirsim.

TRANSPORTATION

The land in which Jesus walked and taught is small—just a narrow strip of land at the eastern end of the Mediterranean Sea. But the nations around Israel were often passing through it and needed its strategic location and they often fought over it. Egypt, Assyria, Babylon, Persia, Greece and Rome all wanted to control that special territory.

The world of the Near East is full of barriers—seas, rivers, deserts, and mountains. These barriers were vital to Israel's defense. For example, enemy armies were often stopped by mountains; they could go over them only if they found a natural pass. So Israel built fortified cities to guard these natural passes and the routes of travel. Settled people could live at the edge of a desert, but this was often dangerous. Nomads from the desert would invade these villages when food was scarce; they might invade them at other times simply to rob and steal. People could cross rivers by fords or by walking across shallow spots. They could sail the seas in ships. Thus, geographical barriers did not stop those who wished to cross them.

In the Near East no nation had everything it needed for daily life; each depended on others for some of its needs. Both raw materials and finished products had to be traded. (*See* "Trade.") Ships traveled between ports of trading nations.

I. ROAD SYSTEMS OUTSIDE PALESTINE
  A. Asia Minor
  B. Cyprus
  C. Syria (Aram)
  D. Phoenicia

II. ROAD SYSTEM IN PALESTINE

III. MESOPOTAMIA'S WATER AND ROAD SYSTEM

IV. SHIPPING

V. CARAVANS
  A. Camels
  B. Donkeys

I. Road Systems Outside Palestine. The nations surrounding Palestine used their roads for commerce and communication, as well as for military routes in times of war. Even before the Roman Empire brought its famous road system to the Near East, this area had developed effective routes for long-distance transportation.

A. Asia Minor. Asia Minor is a Central Plateau about 900 to 1500 m. (3,000 to 5,000 ft.) in altitude bordered by mountains on the south ranging up to 4,000 m. (13,000 ft.). Asia Minor has water on three of its sides: the Mediterranean Sea to the south, the Aegean Sea to the west, and the Black Sea to the north. Steep, rocky mountains rim the coast of the Black Sea, forming a natural barrier to roads linking the northern and southern territories of Asia Minor. The ancient Lydians settled in the fertile valleys of western Asia Minor along the Aegean Sea. In this area Croesus, the last king of Lydia (an ancient country of Asia Minor), was defeated in battle by the Persians. The Taurus Mountains in the south are a serious barrier to people wanting to come north from the Mediterranean Sea. But these travelers can follow gorges through the mountains. Paul used one of these passes—known as the Cilician Gates—on his second and third journeys through Derbe, Lystra, Iconium, and Antioch (Acts 15:41; 16:1; 18:23 ff.). The central plateau of Asia Minor is made up of rolling hills, basins, marshes, and volcanic cones. The mountains that hem it in limit the amount of rainfall. Its bare terrain is used by shepherds and their flocks.

The strength of Asia Minor in the ancient world lay in its mineral resources. Silver and copper were mined in Cappadocia, north of the Taurus Mountains. The Pontus region included the Hittite capital of Hattushash, which was a center for wood, silver, copper, and iron. Lead was mined near the Hellespont in northwest Asia Minor.

B. Cyprus. Cyprus was an island in the Mediterranean Sea, just 72 km. (45 mi.) south of Asia Minor and 96 km. (60 mi.) west of Syria. Its shape was much like a deerskin with its "tail" pointed toward Syria. It was 222 km. (138 mi.) long and 96 km. (60 mi.) wide at its widest point. The terrain resembled Asia Minor—mountains to the north (the Kyrenia Range) and the south, with the Mesaoria

TRANSPORTATION

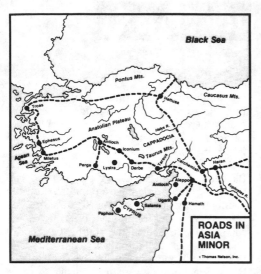

ROADS IN ASIA MINOR
© Thomas Nelson, Inc.

(2 Sam. 8:3 ff.; 10:6, 8), Aram-Damascus, Arpad, and Hamath. The Phoenicians controlled the coastal harbors (except for Ugarit) all the way to the Amanus Mountains; but Syria controlled the roads from Asia Minor to Mesopotamia, Palestine, Egypt, and the Syrian Desert. Syria's western border, comprised primarily by the Amanus mountain range, touched Phoenicia's coastal plains. The Orontes and the Khabur Rivers broke up this mountain range on their way to the Mediterranean. The valleys of these rivers were swamplands, where malaria posed a continual health problem.

The Anti-Lebanon Mountains formed the western border of Syria. These mountains rose up quickly out of the Beqa Valley; their layers of rock soaked up rainwater and drained it into a number of streams in the Syrian Desert. Damascus received its water from the southern slopes of the Anti-Lebanon Mountains, which made the city a desert oasis. As the capital of the Aramaean kingdom, Damascus was of great importance in the Near East.

Damascus lay at the crossing point of international trade routes: the desert route from Babylon by way of Mari and Damascus, the Beqa road from northern Mesopotamia to Asia Minor by way of Aleppo and Hamath, the inland route of the *Via Maris* from Egypt to Mesopotamia, and the King's Highway from Ezion-geber to Amman. All went by way of Damascus.

Trade caravans met at Damascus, and this became a key factor in the city's prosperity. Merchants of the area sold oil and wine to the passing caravans and bartered for their goods. The caravans exchanged news from all over the Near East as traders mingled in the streets of Damascus.

The Book of Acts tells how Saul, a follower of the Jewish rabbi Gamaliel, was traveling from Jerusalem to Damascus to rout out followers of Jesus who had been strengthening the church there. While he was on that road, Jesus spoke to Saul and convinced him to stop persecuting the Christians. Acts 9:17–22 tells of Saul in Damascus, where he became a firm believer in Christ. He left that city to spend three years in the desert before returning to Damascus and then to Jerusalem, where he met Peter (Gal. 1:16–18).

D. Phoenicia. The peoples of Canaan who lived along the coast were called *Phoenicians;* they earned their living in shipping and came to be great sailors. Their land was enclosed by

Plateau lying between. The plateau produced grain and the mountains yielded timber, copper, silver and possibly iron. Cyprus' wealth of natural products, its natural harbors (Salamis and Paphos), and its convenient position along Mediterranean trade routes made it a busy trading area in the earliest times. Acts 13:5 tells of Paul's arrival at Salamis by ship. He traveled by road from Salamis to Paphos, sharing the gospel of Christ as he went. At Paphos he rebuked a magician named Barjesus or Elymas. The governor heard Paul's preaching of the gospel, and believed in Jesus (Acts 13:12). Paul left Cyprus for Asia Minor, sailing from the port of Paphos (13:13).

C. Syria (Aram). The area along the eastern end of the Mediterranean Sea—from the Taurus Mountains in the north to the Sinai Desert in the south—encompassed several different kinds of geography and climate. The Egyptians named the region *Retenu,* "the land of the Asiatics." Its only unifying feature was the Rift Valley, running from the Amanus Mountains to the Gulf of Eilat.

The Orontes River drained the northern part of the Rift Valley, including part of the Beqa Valley. The Litani River drained between the Heman Mountains and Lebanon. The Jordan drained rainfall from the southern Beqa and the Hula Valley into the Dead Sea. The Aravah Valley ran southward from the Dead Sea to the Gulf of Eilat.

Modern Syria includes the area of ancient Phoenicia and Aramaea. The Aramaeans were seldom united. For example, we read about the rival Aramaean tribes of Aram-Zobah

TRANSPORTATION

the Mediterranean Sea on the west and two sets of mountains on the east: the Amanus and the Lebanon Mountains. Phoenicia expanded its influence by trade and by sending people to colonize other lands.

Water from the rains and snows in the highlands sank into the layers of rock in the mountains and came back out at lower levels as springs and rivers. This supply of water allowed the people of the coastal area to farm the slopes. Villages grew up on the mountainsides.

The Beqa Valley between the Lebanon Range and the Anti-Lebanon was up to 16 km. (10 mi.) wide and 161 km. (100 mi.) long. It had a deep, rich soil south of Baalbek, between the Orontes and Litani rivers. The Litani River ran for 112 km. (70 mi.) through the Beqa and turned for its last 32 km. (20 mi.) westward through gorges in the Lebanon Range to reach the Mediterranean. A road connected the seaports of Ugarit, Byblos, Sidon, and Tyre along the Mediterranean; but it never developed into a major highway because mountain spurs impeded traffic and travel was easier by sea. To make road travel worse, each of these cities charged a toll for use of the road near their city; such tolls would not be charged when traveling by sea. Sidon and Tyre were directly connected by road with Canaan; this road was called *Via Maris* or "Way of the Sea." These cities exercised a great influence on the more primitive cities of Canaan.

II. Road System in Palestine. The first roads of Palestine were sheep or cattle trails—dirt paths. Some roads followed *wadis,* dry river beds that carried water only during rainy seasons. Some roads were built through mountain passes. As trade grew, it became more important to get to and from neighboring countries by road. Nations bartered their own natural products, their ores or minerals. Many merchants had to pass through Palestine, because Palestine lay on the natural route from Egypt to the southwest, Asia Minor to the northwest, and Mesopotamia to the northeast. As caravans passed through, they shared information, art ideas, and the latest trade goods. So Palestine became a land-bridge for trade and ideas. Traders used the roads in peacetime and armies in wartime. No matter who was at war in the Near East, much of the fighting was done on Palestinian soil. So for its day, Palestine had a highly advanced set of roads.

The Via Maris (mentioned in Is. 35:8) was the way across Palestine from the Mediterranean. It cut through the Carmel Range at Megiddo. From there it went along the Mediterranean, across sand dunes and swamps southward, and through Sinai to Egypt. The Egyptian kings used this road as their armies marched northward in conquest. For example, Pharaoh Necho was marching along the *Via Maris* on his way to Carchemish on the Euphrates when he was halted at Megiddo by King Josiah of Judah. In their battle, Josiah was killed (2 Kin. 23–29) and Judah suffered a serious defeat.

At Megiddo the Via Maris split into two main branches: (1) the road to Tyre, Sidon, and Ugarit by the Mediterranean Sea and (2) the road by the Sea of Galilee to Hazor. At Hazor, the road again divided into: (1) a road to the north leading to Aleppo through the Beqa and (2) a road northeast to Damascus.

The *King's Highway* was the second major north-south road of Palestine. This was a mountainous road between Saudi Arabia and Damascus. It ran close to the desert in Transjordan and was rougher than the Via Maris. The King's Highway crossed lands that were controlled by Edomites, Moabites, Ammonites, and Israelites. In places it was not at all a "king's highway," for it followed *wadis* (Zered, Arnon, and Jabbok) that were too steep and rough for armies or caravans to travel.

Another road ran part of the way alongside the King's Highway. This road connected

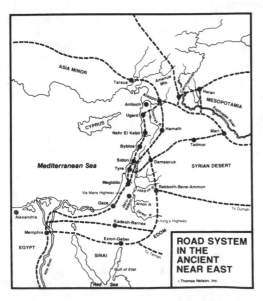

ROAD SYSTEM
IN THE
ANCIENT
NEAR EAST

© Thomas Nelson, Inc.

MODERN DAMASCUS. *Damascus, the capital city of Syria, lies northwest of the Ghuta Plain, a district famous for its orchards and gardens. Damascus is a natural communication center, linking the caravan route with the Mediterranean coast about 105 km. (65 mi.) to the west.*

Edom to Rabbath-bene-ammon across flat desert land. Although this road helped travelers escape the steep wadis, the lack of water along the way often caused problems.

Other caravan routes joined the King's Highway. From the east came the Dumah and Tema route; from the west a route from Egypt joined at Bozrah. The northern Transjordan enjoyed many contacts with Palestine; several roads ran down the mountains into the Jordan Valley. At shallow places—*fords*—travelers could cross the Jordan and then continue on the road to the cities of Beth-shean, Shechem, and Jericho.

Three roads crossed Canaan and Transjordan on the way to Egypt. All of these crossed the desert. The roads were developed in order to span the Arabah, Negev, and Sinai Deserts. From Edom in Transjordan, the way to Shur (Gen. 16:7) went down by way of Bozrah and Pinon from the high country into the Arabah. From there it went through the Wadi Zin (cf. Num. 27:14) and past Kadesh-barnea into the Sinai Peninsula. There a narrow strip of land between the sands and the hills gave access to Egypt. The southern route left Elath by the Gulf of Elath over the R-Tih Plateau to Egypt. The northern route connected Canaan with Egypt by the Via Maris; this was a popular route for most caravans and marching armies. This is most likely the route Joseph chose when he fled from Palestine

with Mary and the baby Jesus when King Herod gave orders for all baby boys to be killed (Matt. 2:14).

III. Mesopotamia's Water and Road System. Mesopotamia was the land that lay between the Tigris and the Euphrates Rivers. In the Bible it is called Padan-aram (Gen. 25:20; 28:2, 5) or "Aram of the two rivers." This second title is translated in the Greek as *Mesopotamia* (Gen. 24:10). Actually, it included the area from the mountains in the north to the Persian Gulf in the south. (*See* "The Babylonians and Assyrians.") An important civilization developed in this region between the rivers, just as the Nile River Valley in Egypt gave rise to another advanced civilization. Mesopotamia comprised much of the "Fertile Crescent," which stretched from the Persian Gulf to the Amanus Mountains, an arch of over 1,600 km. (1,000 mi.). The western area of the Fertile Crescent covered only about 800 km. (500 mi.).

The Tigris and Euphrates Rivers were fed by the melting snows of the mountains of Armenia (Ararat). These high mountains drained the melted snow into swamps at the head of the Persian Gulf. The larger of the two rivers, the Tigris, flowed over 1,800 km. (1,100 mi.) with a rapid current that caused a great deal of soil erosion. The Tigris was a very muddy river because of this eroding action. The Euphrates was a slow-moving river over most of

TRANSPORTATION

its 2,800-km. (1,700-mi.) course. The river was very steep, but also very wide, and the flow of water was more gradual. The two rivers came together in the marshy delta about 100 miles north of the Persian Gulf and flowed together into the Gulf. "The land between the two rivers" was rich when the extra water was drained off; but flooding was common in this area. Southern Mesopotamia's low rainfall made irrigation necessary for farming.

Farming was Mesopotamia's big business. People of the area had to trade for ore, timber, and metals. Their only local mineral resource was bitumen, used to waterproof boats and form a kind of cement for buildings. (*See* "Minerals and Gems.") Bitumen in this area came from the middle of the Euphrates, where it seeped out like thick oil (Gen. 6:14).

Mesopotamia was surrounded by mountains on the north and east and by desert on the west and south. Between the two rivers was a steppe—a flat, dry, almost desert-like area. It was about 400 km. (250 mi.) wide. The hills to the north provided streams that flowed downward to the Euphrates. These ran in grooves of rock that had been cut for thousands of years. On the banks of these rivers were the cities of Carchemish, Mari, Maran, and Asshur. When the water supply was good, the steppe provided grain, cattle, sheep, and orchards of fruit. The mountains to the north and east provided cheap lumber. The people of the area used the rivers for transportation.

The middle and lower parts of the rivers could be traveled easily. Small ships used canals. Ships on the Persian Gulf shuttled gold and timber between Babylonia and India.

Inland roads connected Mesopotamia with its neighbors to the north and west. Another road to the south followed the route of the Euphrates. Where the roads crossed, great trading cities grew up. At Mari the road split in three directions: (1) To the north it went to Haran, (2) to the northwest it went to Aleppo and Ugarit, and (3) to the southwest it crossed the desert to Tadmor and Damascus.

Another road ran parallel to the Tigris River to Nineveh. At Nineveh, other roads joined it from the northeast (the Caspian Sea) and from the west: One road ran to the northwest through the hill country to Asia Minor. Another ran southwest across the steppe between the rivers and connected Nineveh with Haran and Carchemish. At Carchemish on the Euphrates, this road split into two routes—one going north to Asia Minor and the other going

south to Aleppo. Only a few passes connected the Zagros Mountains in western Persia with Mesopotamia. The southern route to the east lay between Ur and Susa. It was often used as an army road, since the Elamites and Babylonians were often at war.

IV. Shipping. Forests and natural harbors encouraged shipbuilding in several countries of the ancient world. Phoenicia had both, whereas Egypt and Israel lacked the wood. The cedars of the Lebanon Mountains gave Phoenicia an abundant supply of sturdy wood.

Egypt had the great Nile River, which could be traveled by boat from the Mediterranean Sea to the first cataract at Aswan. Syria and Phoenicia had many bays that were developed into harbors (e.g., Ugarit, Byblos, Sidon, and Tyre). In contrast, Canaan's seashore was unfit for harbors. In spite of this, Canaanites (and later the Israelites) learned to build a seaport wherever a river flowed into the sea, such as at the Yarkon (Tell Qasile) and the Kishon. They also used small bays at Accho and Joppa. But shipping competition from the north and the Philistines to the southwest hurt Israel's sea development.

KING'S HIGHWAY. *The modern highway winding down into the Arnon Valley closely follows the route of the ancient King's Highway. The original road ran directly from the Gulf of Aqaba to Syria. Edomites and Ammonites closed the road to the Israelites when they tried to enter the Promised Land (Num. 20:17–18).*

TRANSPORTATION

The biblical writers were quite familiar with sea travel. Ezekiel calls sailors wise men (Ezek. 27:8). The psalmist praises God for the ships of the sea (Ps. 104:26). But the psalmist also knew of the dangers of the sea (Ps. 107:24).

Of course, the Book of Jonah includes much about sailing. The prophet came to the harbor of Joppa and booked passage to Tarshish. A storm broke (Jon. 1:4) and the sailors called on their god (1:5). God rescued them after they threw Jonah overboard and called on God for mercy (1:14).

Ezekiel describes a merchant ship like this: "They have made all thy ship boards of fir trees of Senir: they have taken cedars from Lebanon to make masts for thee. Of the oaks of Bashan they have made thine oars; the company of the Ashurites have made thy benches of ivory, brought out of the isles of Chittim. Fine linen with broidered work from Egypt was that which thou spreadest forth to be thy sail; blue and purple from the isles of Elishah was that which covered thee. The inhabitants of Zidon and Arvad were thy mariners: thy wise men, O Tyrus, that were in thee, were thy pilots. The ancients of Gebal and the wise men thereof were in thee thy calkers: all the ships of the sea with their mariners were in thee to occupy thy merchandise" (Ezek. 27:5–9).

Here Ezekiel uses the usual Hebrew word for ship (*'oniyah*). This word is also used in 1 Kings 9:26–27 and Isaiah 33:21. The phrase "navy of Tharshish" (1 Kin. 10:22) signifies a fleet of ships with trading goods from the city of Tarshish—a port often visited by Phoenicians (Ezek. 27:12) and the place to which Jonah tried to escape. The Old Testament also uses the words *sefinah* (Jon. 1:5) and *si* (Is. 33:21; Num. 24:24) to refer to ships. Barges or floats carried wood and other types of cargo (1 Kin. 5:9).

According to Ezekiel, the bottoms of boats were made of firwood and the masts were sometimes of cedar (27:5). Isaiah adds that the mast was placed in a socket and the ropes were tied to the top of the mast to hold it in place (Is. 33:23).

Observation posts at the top of the masts were common (Prov. 23:34). Sails were strung from the mast and a covering under the mast protected the sailors from the sun (Ezek. 27:7). They used both sails and oars to power the ships (27:8).

Egypt used ships as its main means of trans-

ROMAN ROAD. *This road between Antioch and Aleppo is 6 m. (20 ft.) wide and made of limestone blocks. Such roads crossed the entire Roman Empire, allowing rapid troop movement and facilitating trade.*

portation. Inside the country, the Nile made it unnecessary to build many roads. Even between villages small boats were used for travel. Ferryboats were common and smaller craft were seen everywhere.

The Egyptians made certain boats with bundles of papyrus reeds, tied with hemp or papyrus. Light and fast, these papyrus boats were used for personal transportation and not for trade.

The Egyptians had to import wood for shipbuilding; Nubia and Phoenicia sold most of this timber to Egypt. The Egyptians learned to build boats in pieces; they could be taken apart so that they could be carried over land and reassembled. This was especially helpful in wartime. In peacetime, the Egyptians used

How a Roman Road Was Built

The Romans were prodigious road builders. They spent five centuries completing a road system that extended to every corner of their empire and eventually covered a distance equal to 10 times the circumference of the earth at the equator. This included over 80,000 km. (50,000 mi.) of first-class highways and about 320,000 km. (200,000 mi.) of lesser roads.

Before the Romans built a road, they conducted a survey. They could calculate distances to inaccessible points, run levels with accuracy, measure angles, and lay out tunnels and dig them from both ends with a vertical shaft. Road surveyors considered the slope of the land and questions of defense. Where necessary (as in the regions of Cumae and Naples), they cut tunnels through mountains with a skill that aroused admiration for centuries. Because Romans tried to build straight roads—often over hills rather than around them—slopes frequently were steep; 10 percent grades were common.

When building an important road, Roman engineers dug a trench the full width of the road and 1.2 to 1.5 m. (4 to 5 ft.) deep. The roadbed was built up with successive layers of large and small stone and rammed gravel; sometimes there was a layer of concrete. Normally roads were surfaced with gravel, which might rest on a bed of mortar. Near cities, in places where traffic was heavy, or in the construction of an important road, engineers paved the surface with large, carefully fitted stones about 30 cm. (12 in.) thick and 45 cm. (18 in.) across.

The type of construction varied with expected traffic, terrain, and available materials. Mountain roads might be only 1.5 to 1.8 m. (5 to 6 ft.) wide, with wider places for passing. Main roads were 4.5 to 6 m. (15 to 20 ft.) wide. The Appian Way was about 5.5 m. (18 ft.) wide—wide enough for two wagons to pass abreast—and paved with basaltic lava.

Stone bridges were usually built where roads crossed streams. Such construction was possible because the Romans had concrete much like that in use today. To make lime mortar set under water and resist water action, the road engineers had to add silica to the mixture. The Romans had large quantities of volcanic sand (*pozzolana*), which had a mixture of silica in proper proportions.

Unfortunately, records do not tell us how long it took to build Roman roads or how large the road gangs were that built them. The Appian Way— "Queen of Roads" and forerunner of many other Roman roads on three continents—was begun in 312 B.C. as a road for use in the Samnite Wars. The 211 km. (132 mi.) to Capua must have been completed within about a decade. Ultimately, the Appian Way reached southward 576 km. (360 mi.) from Rome to Brundisium on the Adriatic Sea. The road system was gradually extended through the efforts of numerous Roman emperors. Augustus, Tiberius, Claudius, and Vespasian were among those who launched great road-building projects.

Some Roman roads have been used throughout the Middle Ages and into modern times. The Appian Way, on which Paul traveled to Rome (cf. Acts 28:13–15), is still an important artery of western Italy. It is a mute reminder of the glory of the time when all roads led to Rome.

---

these boats to open trade with the Red Sea. Ships could be built farther west and carried in pieces to the coast for assembly. History tells us that Queen Hatshepsut of Egypt sent five oceangoing ships to Punt on the African coast in this way. Temple drawings show this fleet brought back to Thebes a load of ivory, ebony, gold, eye paint, skins, and greyhound dogs.

Because water travel kept increasing in Egypt, the armies of Pharaoh Necho dug a canal from one of the branches of the Nile to the Red Sea (about 600 B.C.). In 279 B.C., Ptolemy Philadelphus reopened this same canal. The canal provided water travel for Egypt from Aswan to the Mediterranean, and from the Nile to the Red Sea.

Egypt learned how to use warships to protect its shores. A "relief drawing" at Medinet-Habu shows the Egyptian ships winning a sea battle against the Philistines and the "Peoples of the Sea." These invaders came from the Aegean Sea and attacked Egypt. The Peoples of the Sea were caught between the fire from Egyptian ships and archers shooting arrows from land. This may well be the earliest record of a naval battle.

Thus ships had two main uses: trade and defense. Pleasure travel was little known. If an extra space on a boat was available, a passenger might go along. Such people paid their fare (Jon. 1:3) and were given a place to sleep.

In Paul's day, people commonly traveled by ships. Paul used ships for his missionary journeys. On his way to Rome, his ship ran on a reef and broke into pieces (Acts 27:41). Since the island of Malta was nearby, everyone reached shore safely (27:44). From there the Romans took Paul on a ship to Rome (Acts

TRANSPORTATION

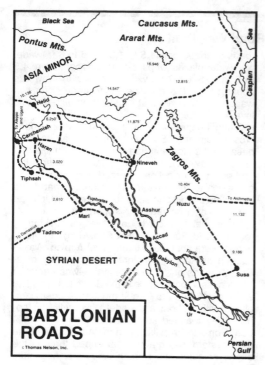

BABYLONIAN ROADS

© Thomas Nelson, Inc.

Hasan shows such a caravan entering Egypt (*ca.* 1890 B.C.). The 37 members of the caravan were all Semitic and included men, women, and children. They carried eye paint to Egypt, and the caravan was protected by armed warriors with bows, spears, and throwsticks. Desert regions and mountains were well-known hide outs for robbers, so bodyguards were a vital part of the caravan company.

The late William F. Albright, an archaeologist, argued that Abraham was himself a caravan leader. The Bible says he had 318 trained bodyguards (Gen. 14:14), and he migrated from Ur to Canaan. He moved around in Canaan, from Hebron to Beersheba, then to Gerar; he even traveled to Egypt during a famine. He most likely traded the products his herds produced for whatever needs he had along the road. But we have no real proof that he was a caravaneer.

Caravanserais grew up. These were roughly equivalent to our modern "truck stops," with all the needs of the traveling caravans in mind: food, water, bathing places, and supplies.

These caravanserais were usually found at points where roads crossed; some were near harbor cities and others at points where special help was needed, such as a water hole in the desert.

Inns were much like caravanserais but smaller, with less help for the traveler. An inn provided hospitality for the night. In the parable of the Good Samaritan, Jesus tells us about the travel from Jerusalem to Jericho (Luke 10:30–37): When a passing Samaritan stopped to help a traveler who had been attacked, he took him to an inn to recover.

A. Camels. By taming the camel, caravaneers shortened their travel routes, for the camel seemed able to go anywhere. Desert conditions that hurt man (dust, lack of water, too much sand, the heat, the rocks, and thorny grass) were natural conditions for the camel.

According to archaeological finds, the two-humped camel was being used as a pack animal in Turkestan in about 3500 B.C. Camels must have been domesticated much earlier than that. The camel also provided milk. Since its strong body could pull a plow or be ridden, it was called "the ship of the desert." Each camel could carry up to 230 kg. (500 lb.) for up to 160 km. (100 mi.) a day.

The patriarchs used camels in their travels. When Abraham sent his servant to get a bride

28:11), with stops at Syracuse (28:12) and Puteoli (28:13).

V. Caravans. We are not sure when caravan travel began; surely it must have been early. To make a profit, these strings of pack animals could move large amounts of goods over long distances. At first such long-distance caravans kept to main roads and missed cities along the way. But when man learned to tame the camel, he was able to travel across deserts to otherwise out-of-the-way places. Even today, caravans go to many places that planes and cars do not normally reach.

Each caravan had a leader who controlled the route of the journey. He would make business deals with others who wished to join the caravan for safety. Sometimes a family or tribe traveled the roads as a full-time work, buying and selling along the way. We see an example of this in the story of Joseph, who was sold as a slave to a caravan that passed by. He was purchased by Ishmaelite traders who came "from Gilead with their camels bearing spicery and balm and myrrh, going to carry it down to Egypt" (Gen. 37:25). The caravan people often traveled between Gilead and Egypt.

A picture in the tomb of an Egyptian at Beni

TRANSPORTATION

The Nile–Red Sea Canal

The idea of a canal linking the Mediterranean and Red seas is about 4,000 years old. The first canal was probably built by Pharaoh Sesostris I (reign 1980–1935 B.C.). Egypt's foreign commerce at that time was a royal monopoly. Middle Kingdom pharaohs believed in courting the favor of their neighbors. Sesostris I or another pharaoh of that era built a canal to increase commerce with his southern neighbors in Punt (possibly modern Somaliland).

During the time of the pharaohs, the Nile River divided into three great branches that passed through the delta and emptied into the Mediterranean Sea. The easternmost branch (which has silted up since the time of Christ) was the branch from which the Nile–Red Sea canal was built. The canal seems to have run from the Nile at Bubastis (modern Zagazig) through the land of Goshen to join Lake Timsah. There it turned south, passing through the Bitter Lake and another canal connecting it with the Red Sea. The earliest written record of the canal is the inscription of one of Hatshepsut's trading expeditions to the Punt. Remains of the canal's masonry work show that it was about 45 m. (150 ft.) wide and 5 m. (16 ft.) deep. The canal gradually fell into disuse.

About 600 B.C., Pharaoh Necho tried to reopen the Nile–Red Sea canal. Herodotus recorded the undertaking: "The length of this canal is equal to a four days' voyage, and is wide enough to admit two *triremes* (war galleys) abreast. . . . In the prosecution of this work under Necho, no less than 10,000 Egyptians perished. He at length desisted from his undertaking, being admonished by an oracle that all his labor would turn to the advantage of a barbarian."

Strabo (ca. 63 B.C.–A.D. 21) stated that Darius of Persia carried on the work, then stopped on the false opinion that the Red Sea was higher than the Nile and would flood Egypt. The Ptolemies made the canal navigable by means of locks.

During the Roman occupation of Egypt, Roman Emperor Trajan (reign A.D. 98–117) added a branch to the canal. This later fell into disuse, as the earlier canal had. A Muslim caliph ordered his men to fill in part of the canal as an act of war in A.D. 767, and it was never reopened.

The Suez Canal, opened in 1869, directly linked the Red Sea with the Mediterranean, without using the Nile.

---

for Isaac, the emissary went to Padan-aram with a caravan of 10 camels (Gen. 24:10). Jacob left Padan-aram with many camels; his wives and children sat on them (Gen. 31:17). Jacob sent a present of 30 milking camels and their colts to Esau (Gen. 32:15–16). The Ishmaelites who took Joseph to Egypt loaded their goods on camels (Gen. 37:25).

The roaming nomads who spent so much of their time in the desert commonly used the camel. The Amalekites, Hagarites, and Midianites especially were camel-raisers. The Israelite tribes took as many as 50,000 camels when they conquered the Hagarites (1 Chr. 5:21). Job owned 3,000 camels—a large herd for any one man to have. His troubles took them from him, but afterward he had twice as many.

The Jews who returned from the Exile brought with them 435 camels (Neh. 7:69). In the New Testament, the wise men most likely rode on camels to see Jesus (Matt. 2:1–12).

B. Donkeys. People who lived in the area we now call Saudi Arabia are credited with taming the donkey sometime around 4000 B.C. Early pictures show the donkey as a farm animal and a caravan worker (painting at Beni

Hasan, ca. 1890 B.C.). The donkey traveled well across the desert, for he was used to eating thin, thorny grasses that were hard to find.

MODEL OF MERCHANT SHIP. *This model depicts a merchant ship of the "Tarshish" type that Solomon used in his fleet about the thirteenth century B.C. (1 Kin. 10:22; 2 Chr. 9:21). Some scholars think "Tarshish" refers simply to a particularly well-constructed type of ship used for long voyages.*

TRANSPORTATION

BENI HASAN. *A group of Semitic nomads appears before an Egyptian official in this section of a wall painting from a tomb at Beni Hasan (ca. 1890 B.C.). The caravan carries merchandise for trade in Egypt. Notice that the men are armed against robbers, who made travel dangerous in the early days.*

CAMEL. *Caravans of pack animals moved large quantities of trade goods from place to place in the ancient East. The domestication of the camel allowed traders to go into previously inaccessible areas.*

Donkeys often ate coarse food that camels refused to eat.

The Bible mentions the donkey many times. Both rich and poor people owned and rode donkeys.

Ziba met David with donkeys and supplies when David was forced to leave Jerusalem (2 Sam. 16:1–2). Solomon equipped his mounted army with horses, so that the donkey came to be used for carrying heavy loads only. Donkeys were used less often as royal beasts of burden, and they were looked down upon. So in prophesying the coming Messiah, Zechariah said He would be riding on a donkey (Zech. 9:9)—a sign that He would be humble.

WARFARE AND WEAPONS

Early in the Book of Genesis we find warfare going on (the battle of the kings, chap. 14). The human pattern of war continues right to the end of the Book of Revelation, where the final battle between good and evil (Armageddon) is foretold.

As we survey the biblical material on warfare, we find that it falls into two categories: what the Bible says about war (teaching) and what actually happened (history).

I. HOW THE OLD TESTAMENT DEALS WITH WAR
    A. Promotion of Justice
    B. God's Protection
    C. God's Presence
    D. Ritual Cleanness
    E. Victory Expected
    F. Military Conscription
    G. Other Priorities
    H. Peace Offered
    I. Utter Destruction
    J. Trust in God
    K. Respect for Natural Resources
    L. Compensation for Troops

II. NEW TESTAMENT TEACHINGS
    A. The Principle of Love
    B. Sinful Man
    C. Unanswered Questions

III. THE CONDUCT OF WAR
    A. The Period of the Patriarchs
    B. The Period of the Egyptian Captivity through the Period of the Judges
    C. The Period of the United Monarchy
    D. The Period of the Divided Kingdom
    E. The Rise of Greece
    F. The Military Genius of Rome

I. How the Old Testament Deals with War. We can make some basic observations about the Old Testament's ideas of war and teachings concerning it. These ideas changed slightly in New Testament times.

A. Promotion of Justice. Properly conducted warfare was tied to defending and promoting justice and righteousness. Theologian John Murray builds a strong case for the just waging of war by comparing it to the power God gave to the civil magistrate (cf. Rom. 13:1–7; 1 Pet. 2:13–17).[1] This general princi-

ple was applied to national security, and Israel was organized into a fighting unit (Ex. 7:4; 12:51) to be led by God Himself into battle (Judg. 4:14; cf. Deut. 20:4). Whenever wars were fought under God's leadership, they were considered "holy" wars; they were for the purpose of establishing Israel in the Promised Land or protecting them from foreign invasions. In these "holy" wars, going into battle was preceded by sacrificing to God (1 Sam. 7:9; 13:9, 12) and consulting Him as the Leader of Israel's armies (Judg. 20:22, 28; 1 Sam. 14:37; 23:2, 4). So in the Old Testament God used war for just and righteous ends to promote and protect righteousness.

B. God's Protection. In a properly conducted "holy" war God promised His protection of the warriors (Deut. 20:1–4). Israel's enemies were God's enemies, and the people were called on to trust Him, rather than their own strength, for victory (Judg. 5:31; see Ex. 17:16). When they did this, God fought on their side, kept them from bodily harm, and sometimes used the forces of nature against the enemy (cf. Josh. 10:11; 24:7; and many other passages).

C. God's Presence. The ark of the covenant served as a symbol or sign of God's

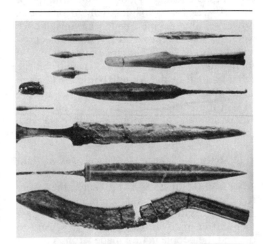

WEAPONS FROM PALESTINE. *These relics of war date from between the ninth and the early sixth centuries B.C. They include arrowheads, spearheads, daggers, and a sword.*

---

[1] John Murray, *Principles of Conduct* (Grand Rapids, Mich.: William B. Eerdmans Company, 1957), pp. 107–122, 178–180.

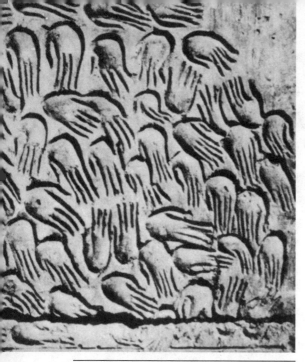

HEAP OF HANDS. *This limestone relief shows hands that were severed by the soldiers of Rameses III in their victory over the Libyans (ca. 1190 B.C.). This was common practice among the Egyptians, who used the hands to tally the number of enemy dead.*

presence with the Israelites during battle (Ex. 30:6; cf. 25:21–22). During the wanderings in the wilderness and in the conquest of the Promised Land the ark always went before the armies of Israel. This was to *symbolize* God's active presence with His people, not to suggest that His presence was localized in that object (see 1 Kin. 8:21), or that the bringing of the ark was like a magic spell. At one time, however, the people made the mistake of thinking that the ark as a physical object assured them of God's presence and guaranteed them victory (1 Sam. 4:1–11). David, on the other hand, took the ark into battle too (2 Sam. 11:11); but it appears that his trust was in God to win the battle, not in the ark as an object. His understanding of God's guidance was like that of Israel during the conquest of the Promised Land.

D. Ritual Cleanness. If God was to fight with and for His people, they were to be ritually clean (Deut. 23:9–14). Because they were to be completely separate from anything having to do with sin and pollution, God gave them strict instructions on what they were to do, and the people in turn made strong vows to the Lord (1 Sam. 21:4–5; 2 Sam. 11:11; cf. Ex. 19:15). The people and their cause were to be holy, for God would fight only in a war that was holy and just.

E. Victory Expected. The priests were to blow trumpets before battle to place their cause before God, to show that they expected victory, and to give God thanks for it (Num. 10:9–10). In the course of particular battles, trumpets often served as the means of sending instructions from the commanders to their troops (Josh. 6:5; Judg. 3:27; 7:16–17). The armies of Israel also plunged into battle using a war cry, sometimes consisting of a loud yell and sometimes of a loud petition to God. A similar cry was used in the worship of the Lord (see Lev. 23:24; Num. 29:1).

F. Military Conscription. In Israel's earlier history the army consisted of all men who were 20 years old or older (Num. 1:2–3, 18, 20, 45; 26:2–4). Some scholars have suggested that 50 was the upper limit for soldiers, just as it was for the priests (cf. Num. 4:3, 23). At other times there seems to have been a selective service system for particular battles in which only a limited number of men fought (see Num. 31:3–6).

G. Other Priorities. Certain social responsibilities had priority over warfare, and several categories of eligible men were exempted from a particular battle or war.

First, anyone who had recently built a home and had not dedicated it was excused (Deut. 20:5). Second, anyone who had planted a vineyard and not yet harvested it was not required to go to war (Deut. 20:6). Third, anyone who had just married and not yet consummated his marriage could stay at home (Deut. 20:7). In fact, the newly married were to be exempted for a year (Deut. 24:5). Fourth, any who were afraid or disheartened were to be excused, for they could demoralize the troops (Deut. 20:8). Fifth, Levites did not have to go to war (Num. 1:48–49), though a number of them voluntarily took up arms. Family and religious obligations had priority over going to war.

H. Peace Offered. Before distant cities were to be attacked, peace terms were to be offered them (Deut. 20:10–15). The terms of this peace included the subjection of the enemy to slavery or forced labor, which in effect made them vassals of Israel. Historical records from this period show that often these peace treaties were framed in a particular form, in which the vassal pledged his total obedience to the overlord while the latter promised protection to his vassal. To break this treaty was to rebel against the overlord and forfeit his mercy, protection, and any other blessings.

WARFARE AND WEAPONS

I. Utter Destruction. War was a grim and ugly affair. The instructions for the conquest of the Promised Land were that all the inhabitants that were found alive were to be destroyed lest they lead the people of God into their awful perversions (Deut. 20:16–18). Everything within Palestine proper was to be consecrated to God, and no treaty or covenant was to be made with these peoples (Deut. 2:34; 3:6; Josh. 11:14; and many other passages).

It is important to note that the ban on taking any kind of spoil in Canaan was more than a wartime regulation. It was part of the regular worship of God and included anything that was totally consecrated to Him (Lev. 27:21, 28–29; Num. 18:14). Since Palestine was the land God had claimed for Himself, He demanded that the entire land be consecrated to Him. In practice this meant that the land had to be thoroughly purified, for no unholy person or thing could stand in His presence and He was going to dwell in this land with His people. The Canaanites, who had been cursed in their distant ancestor (Gen. 9:25), had given themselves to dreadful sinfulness and practiced awful perversions of virtually every form as religious acts.

We should also note that every man is already under the sentence of death by God and lives only by His grace (Gen. 3:3), so there needs to be no further justification of God's curse on any man, including the Canaanites. Their abominations, however, went even beyond those of other sinful men. Furthermore, as the eternal Creator and sovereign Lord of the universe, God controls the lifespan of every person (Job 1:21; Ps. 31:15; 39:4–5; cf. Dan. 4:35). So whether death comes by natural means or through war, it is strictly in His hands.

Nations outside Palestine that refused Israel's offer of peace and bondage received death for every man; all the women, children, livestock, and everything else became booty for the Israelites (Deut. 20:12–14). Exceptions to these rules came either through specific divine directions (Num. 31:7; 2 Sam. 8:2) or through Israel's own disobedience (for example, 1 Sam. 30:17). Women prisoners could be taken as wives and thus made to serve the Lord. In this case, they would not later be subjected to slavery, which was to be their lot otherwise (Deut. 21:10–14).

J. Trust in God. The people of Israel were to trust in God and not in their own military strength. God originally planned for His people's government to be centralized in Him rather than in a human king, and that would have meant a minimum of taxation. Strong earthly rulers tend to require heavy taxation. Since cavalry and chariots as major military weapons of the time were extremely expensive to acquire and maintain, God forbade Israelite kings to have them (Deut. 17:16). They would have required a highly centralized government and very high taxes.

K. Respect for Natural Resources. God forbade the destruction of fruit trees to build siege machinery in attacking walled cities (Deut. 20:19–20). Even in times of warfare Israel was taught to respect the fruit of the ground, which was a source of life, and was reminded that war was against sinful men and not against nature.

L. Compensation for Troops. Adequate provision was made for paying the troops (Num. 31:21–31, 42; Deut. 20:14), binding their families to outfit and support them, and allowing them to take booty as their pay (1 Sam. 30:16; Ps. 119:162; Is. 9:3). The booty was to be divided among all the troops, including those who were "behind the lines" caring for the baggage or waiting at the rear for some other reason (Num. 31:26–47; Judg. 5:30; 1 Sam. 30:24–25).

A portion also had to be set aside for the Lord (Num. 31:28–30, 50–54; Josh. 6:24). In later Israelite history the king, as God's special representative, took the Lord's portion for the temple (2 Sam. 8:7–8, 11) and for the palace or the maintenance of government (2 Sam. 12:30; cf. 1 Sam. 21:9; 2 Kin. 14:14).

These are 12 general observations on the rules or principles of warfare in the Old Testament. The biblical record of the history of Israel shows repeated violations of them. Almost from the beginning of their history in the land, idolatry and superstition led the people away from the Lord. We see this in the idolatrous behavior of the judges Gideon and Micah (Judg. 8:22–28; 17:1–6). Later, the monarchy under Saul was founded on the same lack of trust in God. Solomon's large standing army and many chariots bear clear evidence of his attitude toward God's earlier instructions. Finally, during the divided monarchy, the kings of Israel and Judah paid little attention to the directives of God concerning warfare.

Interestingly, even though modern secular

WARFARE AND WEAPONS

man often harshly condemns what he thinks to be the barbarity of biblical war regulations, today's wars are conducted on a much more barbaric level, sparing neither land nor people. And this is just as true in wars between nations as it is in civil wars where various factions strive for the control of a particular country. We have developed weapons so destructive that they know no distinction between the military and civilians. The morality of warfare and those who fight in wars is lost in today's world because men basically disregard the issues of righteousness and justice. On the battlefield the end justifies the means, hate predominates, and no rules prevail.

II. New Testament Teachings. In the New Testament the emphasis is again on righteousness and justice. The issues are too complicated to discuss in detail; but Scripture suggests a Christian position on war.

It is clear that many practices of modern warfare must be denounced strongly. On the other hand, the same God is at the center of both Testaments; and in the Old Testament, God engaged in war Himself (Ex. 7:4; 12:41; 14:14; 15:1). He used war to punish His people (Deut. 28:49–57) and to judge the nations (for example, 1 Sam. 15:1–3).

A. The Principle of Love. We see that love undergirds both the Law of Moses and the teachings of Jesus. Both command the pious person to love God totally (compare Deut. 6:5 and Matt. 22:37) and his neighbor as himself (compare Lev. 19:18 and Matt. 22:39). Warfare for the cause of justice and righteousness—that is, waging war in defense of God or one's neighbor—is therefore an expression of love and is not contrary to the ethic of Jesus.

B. Sinful Man. According to the New Testament, man is still the same—a sinner who pursues evil ways (cf. James 4:1–4). John Murray has written, "War arises from failure to conform to the attitudes and principles inculcated by the Lord. If there were no sin there would be no war."[2] But sin is, in fact, universal.

Yet the world cries out for justice, and the Christian's ear should be open to this cry. "Love is not inconsistent with the infliction of punishment for wrong. Love is first of all love to God, and therefore love of justice."[3] The New Testament writers maintain that God has

brought government into being for the purpose of maintaining justice, and for those in power to be able to do that, He has given them the power and authority to wage war. Governments are to use this power—not vindictively, maliciously, or hatefully against other men—but as a means of protection and the carrying out of justice. It is interesting to note that many biblical passages that deal with the last times are full of references to warfare conducted by God or under His orders (cf. Is. 2:4 Matt. 24:6; and many others).

C. Unanswered Questions. The New Testament leaves many important questions unanswered. Thus, if governments have the right to wage warfare for a just cause, who determines whether a cause is just? Is it up to the individual Christian? Does this mean that every Christian (or a group of Christians) must have access to all information the government has with regard to the declaration of war? If this access is not given, may he (or they) refuse to participate?

Again, if a nation is justified in protecting its territory, what constitutes a nation and who determines what its territorial limits are? (Was the settling of America an act of aggression against a nation? If so, should the United States government return the whole territory to its original owners? Who can determine how this territory might be subdivided among them?)

Once more, how should a Christian conduct himself in the midst of war and battle? Should he give, for instance, aid to wounded enemies?

These questions need careful study, for the Bible does not give cut-and-dried answers to them.

III. The Conduct of War. Let us examine the historical record of war in the Old Testament and the weapons used throughout the four historical periods of Israel's existence.

A. The Period of the Patriarchs. This period was characterized by mass movements and wanderings of many peoples in the Near East. These movements brought different peoples into contact with one another, both peacefully and through warfare. They were quick to learn from these contacts, and the knowledge of the art of warfare grew accordingly.

During this period the light chariot first appeared, and its use spread from Asia Minor to Egypt. This period also saw the invention and use of the battering ram, metal breastplates, and metal helmets, and the development of

---

[2] Murray, *Principles of Conduct,* p. 179.
[3] Murray, *Principles of Conduct,* p. 179.

WARFARE AND WEAPONS

countermeasures against them. The response to the battering ram was the "casemated" wall (a term used for walls thickened with a space, sometimes a room, between the outer wall itself and the inner layer of stone). The composite bow or crossbow was used against the light chariot. These new weapons, including the piercing axe, helmets, and shields, greatly changed warfare during that time. They also enabled armies who used them (like the Hyksos) to conquer those who did not have them (like the Egyptians).

The Hebrew patriarchs fought only in the first half of this period (*ca.* 2166–1805 B.C.). The weapons used at this time differed somewhat between the Egyptians to the south of Palestine and the nations north of Palestine. Abraham and his allies probably used the latter kind.

Egyptian warriors of this period were protected by shields and wore no armor, as did their neighbors to the north. The axe in Egypt was designed primarily to be used against soldiers without armor, while other peoples used axes designed to penetrate armor. Semites introduced the eye-axe, or penetrating axe, into Egypt. But it was not generally accepted there. Some Semitic warriors carried a refined eye-axe (also called a duck-bill axe), with a handle that was often curved to increase leverage.

The sword of this period first appeared several centuries before and is called a sickle sword. It became prominent during the period of the Israelite conquest of Canaan. This was a curved cutting sword that was made from a single piece of metal and easily wielded in battle, even from a chariot. Soldiers also fought with many varieties of short straight swords or daggers, which were designed primarily for hand-to-hand combat.

Spears and javelins of this early period were attached to wooden stocks by a tang; the base was sometimes tipped with metal so the weapon could be stuck into the ground when not in use. The blunt edge could also be used as a club. These weapons were standard equipment in armies from this time on. Archaeological evidence associates these javelins, spears, and short narrow swords or daggers with the nomadic Semites who invaded Palestine from the north.

Long-range weapons of this period consisted of the bow and the sling. Soldiers mainly used the simple double-convex bow, while other types of simple bows are found in Egyptian tomb paintings and actually buried in the tombs. When not in use, bows were unstrung. The quiver for the arrows was a Semitic invention used rarely by the Egyptians, who preferred to carry their arrows in bundles that they piled at their feet while shooting. The bow was used as both an offensive and a

EGYPTIAN SOLDIERS. *These models of Nubian and Egyptian soldiers march in four columns of 10 each. The darker skinned Nubians carry bows and arrows while the Egyptians are armed with lances and shields. These models, found in an Egyptian tomb, date from about 2000 B.C.*

WARFARE AND WEAPONS

SICKLE SWORD. *The sickle sword was commonly used during the time of the Israelite conquest of Canaan. A curved cutting sword made of a single piece of metal, the weapon was easily wielded in battle. Its cutting edge was the outer edge of the bow, unlike the sickles used in agriculture.*

defensive weapon in all kinds of battles. Slingmen were used especially in siege warfare in support of archers.

This period also shows the existence of fortresses, such as Buhen in Egypt, which is similar to Palestinian fortifications of this period. Egypt also began using battering rams during this period.

The only battle in the Bible during this period fought by the Hebrew patriarchs was the surprise attack of Abraham on the four kings of the north (Gen. 14). We have no details of the battle tactics—apart from the surprise—or the weapons used, but the previous discussion gives us some idea of what Abraham and his soldiers might have used.

Archaeological evidence shows the development of new and improved weapons in the last half of the patriarchal period. Narrow-socketed axes have now been designed for even greater armor penetration, and socketed spears and javelins now begin to appear, since

the tang attachment often caused the staff to split. In the 1500s B.C. the composite bow, one that had greater range and penetration, made its appearance in Palestine. It was expensive to make and more easily affected by weather conditions, so it was not only unstrung when not in use but carried in a case. It must have been during this period that the heavier chariot became a major weapon, for there is little evidence that the Egyptians and Semites used it earlier as such.

B. The Period of the Egyptian Captivity through the Period of the Judges. This period was very important in the Near East, for it saw the rise of many warlike peoples, further migrations, and much conflict. Egypt was on the rise again; the Hittites emerged as a mighty military power; the Hebrews—now called Israelites—invaded Palestine; and the Sea People appeared on the coast of Palestine, introducing new weapons to the Near East. These included the long straight sword, smaller face shields, and better armor, including coats of mail or scaled armor. The composite bow became a major weapon in the hands of the major powers.

Because of the rise of new powers, weapons in this period went through considerable changes. The cutting sickle sword was improved by making the blade longer in comparison to the hilt. This one-edged sword perhaps explains the phrase "smite with the edge of the sword" (in Joshua and Judges), in which the victim was killed by the one edge of the sickle sword. The straight sword or dagger was refined because of the improvement in armor, which made the sickle sword obsolete. In addition to the dagger, a long straight sword made its appearance toward the end of the period, being brought into the Near East by the Sea People, among whom were the Philistines. It was originally Aegean in design.

The spear and the axe continued to be the basic weapons of the infantry. We find that Barak's forty thousand troops in Israel had neither sword nor spear (Judg. 5:8), and toward the end of the period the Philistines totally disarmed the Israelites (cf. 1 Sam. 13:19–22).

The chariots of the Assyrians, Canaanites, and Hittites had three riders—a driver, a man who carried the shield as defense, and the bowman or spearman. The spear was also the weapon of the driver and was carried in a special holder at the back of the chariot.

The difficult-to-make composite bow came

WARFARE AND WEAPONS

into fuller use at this time, in both its triangular and its recurved form. Arrows were usually made of reeds, and battle arrowheads were made of bronze and were spined to help them penetrate armor. Quivers holding 25 to 30 arrows came into general use in this period. (Quite a comment on Ps. 127:5 in terms of the number of children!)

Various types of shields were used during this period: the rectangular, slightly convex shield, the rectangular with a rounded top shield (Egyptian), the light round shield (introduced by and at first used exclusively by the Sea People), and the "figure eight" shield of the Hittites.

Armor became much more widely used by the major military powers, especially in conjunction with archery and chariot units. The disadvantages of armor were its excessive weight, which curtailed the ability of soldiers to move well, and the expense and difficulty of its manufacture. Soldiers also began to be equipped with helmets (another expensive piece of military equipment introduced by the Semites). The piercing axe was then improved further to combat the effectiveness of the helmet and armor.

Chariots became increasingly important weapons for the Egyptians, whose words for the horses and chariots were Canaanite because of their origin. This equipment also was expensive to build and maintain, but was highly effective in battle. Toward the end of this period cavalry units began appearing on the battlefields, though they were not as fully developed as they would become in later centuries.

Fortifications were used extensively in Palestine, as material for building strong and thick walls was readily available. Aramaean fortifications of this period seem to have been *casemated.* This kind of wall was strengthened regularly by supporting balconies and crenelated parapets or battlements. Yigael Yadin has described crenelated parapets as looking like a row of teeth with gaps between them. The "teeth" are called *merlons,* while the "gaps" are called *embrasures* or *crenels.* All this provided the defenders with excellent protection and effective angles to shoot at the enemy. The distance between the towers and battlements was never more than double the range of the defending archers. Smaller fortresses were called *migdolim,* the Hebrew term for "towers" (cf. Judg. 9:50–52; 2 Chr. 26:10; 27:4).

Battering rams were used to attack fortresses, but the Canaanites thickened the walls of their cities so that they were ineffective. Defenders would often begin their stand outside the wall, where they had greater mobility. They would then fall back into the city or be drawn up the walls by ropes if they were unsuccessful (cf. Josh. 2:15). From the tops of the walls the defenders would shoot arrows, throw spears and javelins, and drop stones and anything else that was movable on the attackers who might be climbing up scaling ladders, seeking to undermine the walls, attacking the walls and gates with battering rams, or trying to burn or hack through the city gates. The siege was complicated and costly in human life and money, so usually the attacking commander tried various means to capture the city without a siege. The attacking army would often build barriers, temporary walls, and bulwarks around its camp (cf. Deut. 20:19–20) to prevent sneak attacks by the defenders or from any allies that might come to their aid.

All these descriptions suggest that the Israelites faced tremendous opposition when they were on the threshold of entering the Promised Land (note the fortified cities of Deut. 1:28 and 3:5 and the iron chariots of Josh. 17:16–18). These former slaves were probably armed with Egyptian hand weapons (see Ex. 11:2) and any other arms captured from enemies during the 40 years of wandering. Moses, who had been trained in all the necessary arts in Egypt, including warfare,

COAT OF MAIL. *This fragment of a Hurrian coat of mail (made of bronze plates laced together with cord or thongs) was probably from an unfinished piece of armor. Discovered at Nuzi in Iraq, the armor dates from about 1400 B.C. The Hurrians lived in northern Mesopotamia; some scholars identify them as the Horites (cf. Gen. 36:20–29).*

WARFARE AND WEAPONS

must have trained the people accordingly. This does not mean that they had become a well-trained, professional army, for Israel had been taught to depend totally on God. He was to be the One who brought them victory and intervened when they obeyed Him. The biblical account records many battles during their wilderness years (cf. Exod. 17:8–16; Num. 21:3, 23–25, 32, 35), but we are not given any details except that they were won or lost according to God's intervention. The key to their victories was their dependence on the intervention of God.

We also know that every man except those exempted served in the army, which was organized according to units of 1,000, 100, 50, and 10 (cf. Num. 2). Every man in the army supplied his own weapons (see Num. 31:3; 32:20), applied or did not apply the ban according to God's directions (see Num. 11:2–11, 16–20), and divided the booty among all the people and the Lord. The army was mustered by various means, including the setting up of poles on hills, fire signals, and trumpets. Communication in battle was maintained by messengers on foot (Judg. 9:31; cf.

2 Sam. 11:19; 18:19) or on horseback (2 Kin. 9:17–18), by fire signals (Judg. 20:38; cf. Jer. 6:1), and by trumpets (Jer. 6:1).

The account of the conquest of the Promised Land tells us something of the battle tactics Israel used. They used a trick to draw the defenders of Ai out of their strongly fortified city (Josh. 8:3–22; cf. Judg. 20:29–41) and later confronted the chariots of the Canaanites and defeated them (Josh. 17:18). The overall strategy they used was to "divide and conquer." They invaded central Palestine, then turned south, and finally smashed the opposition in the north after a forced march by night. After the conquest they occupied the mountain regions, while the previous inhabitants still lived on the plains and coastal areas.

During the period of the judges each tribe pretty much went its own way and suffered for it, as various groups of peoples invaded the land. Some military cooperation did exist among the tribes (cf. Judg. 7:24), and once involved them all (Judg. 21:8–9). Most of their suffering and captivity came as a result of their disobeying the Mosaic Covenant of

Catapults

For about 2,000 years, catapults and other "engines of war" were feared as horrible weapons of destruction and death. As early as the eighth century B.C., the Bible mentions that Uzziah ". . . made in Jerusalem engines, invented by cunning men, to be on the towers and upon the bulwarks, to shoot arrows and great stones withal" (2 Chr. 26:15). The *catapult* was any type of war machine that could throw stones or arrows.

The simplest catapult (sometimes called *ballista*) was designed like a giant crossbow on a carriage. A more complex type had a rectangular wooden frame that housed a mechanical arm to hurl stones or arrows. Twisted rope, mule gut, or other animal sinew was wound around levers to create tension which, when released, propelled these objects through the air.

Some catapults could be carried in pieces by man or mule and assembled quickly on the battlefield. Alexander the Great was fond of these portable models. But most catapults were larger, sacrificing mobility for additional weight and force. The average range of a catapult was between 315 and 450 m. (350 and 500 yds.). It could throw a 2.5 m. (8 ft.) javelin or a 13-kg. (30 lb.) stone. In comparison, an enemy arrow could travel up to only

270 m. (300 yds.). The difference in range was significant.

During the siege of a city, a catapult could be kept out of the enemy archers' range. But large catapults were a disadvantage on the open battlefield, since they could not be easily moved if the enemy gained ground. A large catapult was helpless when it lost its advantage of range.

Some large catapults became almost legendary. The Roman catapult used at the siege of Carthage in 149–146 B.C. weighed several tons and threw to a distance of 360 m. (400 yds.). There are accounts of catapults with ranges up to 720 m. (860 yds.), but their accuracy was quite limited.

The inhabitants of a besieged city could never be sure what a catapult might hurl over their walls. While stones and arrows were the usual ammunition, flaming mixtures of sulphur and oil were sometimes used to set fire to the city. A catapult could also throw decaying animals or dead bodies into a city to cause disease among its population. Perhaps this was the earliest form of germ warfare.

Catapults and ballistas became obsolete with the development of more accurate and maneuverable cannons. But from 800 B.C. to A.D. 1500, they served as the most formidable weapons on the world scene.

WARFARE AND WEAPONS

BATTERING RAM. *Bowmen behind large shields of reeds support a four-wheeled battering ram in an attack against the walls of an enemy city. The bodies of three townsmen are impaled on stakes outside the city, and a citizen extends his hands in surrender from atop the wall. This Assyrian relief dates from the eighth century B.C.*

Sinai, with the result that God brought on them the punishments He had promised.

New tactics developed during this period as the tribes began to learn the art of warfare. Ehud assassinated Eglon with a short double-edged sword or dagger, which he had bound to his right side and smuggled past the bodyguards (Judg. 3:21). Barak lured the chariots of Sisera into the muddy flats of the Kishon River and destroyed him and his army (Judg. 5:21). Gideon used the unexpected tactic of a small raiding force that made much noise and surprised the Midianites at night with the added effect of lights in the hills (Judg. 7:16–22). Then, after the enemy was routed, Gideon summoned his reserve troops to the pursuit (vv. 23–25).

On one occasion the men of Succoth asked Gideon if he had the hands of two Midianite kings in his possession; they would not give his army food unless he had them (Judg. 8:6). This was a practice of the Egyptians and Assyrians, who amputated the hands of their enemies as proof of their victories and enemy casualties.

We are given many details of Abimelech's capture of the tower or fortress of Shechem (cf. Judg. 9). The battle had two stages. In the first, the open battle before the city, Abimelech divided his troops into three units and attacked at dawn—common tactics of the day.

In the second stage he attacked the fortress, breached the walls, and burned down the inner citadel.

Toward the end of this period we find that the tribe of Benjamin had trained 700 slingers, who were lefthanded and never missed (Judg. 20:16). We also discover that the recruited army of the other tribes numbered some 400,000 men, a large force indeed by any standards (Judg. 20:17). However, the large numbers quoted in the Old Testament have been questioned for centuries.

During the second half of this period we find the Egyptians and the Canaanites engaged in many battles. Egyptian tomb paintings show the chariots of the battling armies and the warfare against the Sea People. The Canaanites used three-man chariots, while the Egyptians used two men to man their chariots. Infantrymen carried two spears, a long straight sword, and a round shield; they fought in groups of four and marched in unison into battle. The Egyptians used mercenaries (often other Sea People) as their first striking force and as bodyguards in the palace to guard the pharaoh against any local intrigues.

Finally, we have one fascinating detail of how a city was breached in the account of the capture of Bethel. The Israelites spotted a man coming out of the city and forced him to tell them of the secret tunnel into the city. They came through it, surprised the inhabitants, and killed everyone in it except the man who had shown them the way in (Judg. 1:22–26). These secret entryways were used for launching attacks on the besiegers or as ways of escape should the city fall. The Israelites simply reversed the process.

C. The Period of the United Monarchy. In the early part of this period the Hittite kingdom all but vanished from the pages of history and the Egyptians were in decline. This helped the rise of a strong Israelite kingdom under Saul, David, and Solomon. Militarily the strength of Israel would not be broken till after the death of Solomon, when the pharaoh Shishak took and looted Jerusalem during the reign of Rehoboam (*ca.* 925 B.C.; cf. 1 Kin. 14:25–26).

During Saul's rule wars were fought pretty much as before. With the rise of the kingdom came the need for training, and the Bible mentions Saul's son Jonathan as an instructor in the use of the bow (2 Sam. 1:18); some scholars believe this passage to be a reference to instruction in warfare. This period saw the use of the bronze bow, which was probably a compound bow covered with bronze (cf. 2 Sam. 22:35; Ps. 18:34). One type of shield used by the Israelites was large and went with a man armed with a spear, while another was used with the bow to protect the archer.

Tactically the army was divided into three units and used the surprise attack of late night and early morning (cf. Judg. 7:16; 9:43; 1 Sam. 11:11; 14:36). With a king on the throne, a standing army was organized (apparently also into three units; 1 Sam. 13:2), fulfilling the request of the people for a king and an army. The Philistines against whom Saul fought had infantry (also organized into three units; 1 Sam. 13:17), chariots, and cavalry.

One of the interesting devices used by opposing Near Eastern armies was the tactic of the duel. Each army selected a champion, they fought one another, and the one who won represented victory for his army. The outcome of the duel determined the outcome of the war, and no additional battles were fought. So Goliath, the Philistine champion (who was perhaps 9 $^1/_2$ feet tall), challenged Israel to send out a man to fight him. The meaning of the Hebrew term translated "champion" (KJV) has the connotation of "dueler"; Goliath may have been a professional dueler (1 Sam. 17:4–10). His weapons consisted of the long sword in a scabbard (1 Sam. 17:51), a bronze

helmet, armor on his body and legs, and a spear (1 Sam. 17:5–7). His large shield was carried by his shield-bearer, a common practice of the time.

The potential duel was an ideal solution for Saul's army if they could but find someone to fight the giant Philistine. It would prevent many casualties for his outmanned force. When David finally volunteered for the duel, the Philistine made fun of him. The only weapon David had was a sling, and the Sea People did not use such a weapon; so Goliath saw no threat in it. Since he did not carry a bow, David's sling considerably outdistanced Goliath's close-combat weapons. And the tactical advantage—not to mention the help of the Lord—was with him.

A mass duel was fought later between David and the descendants of Saul. But because the duelists all killed one another, the armies subsequently fought and David was victorious (cf. 2 Sam. 2:12–17). Tomb pictures from Tel Halaf of the same period show duelists in action. There may have been certain rules for dueling, for we see the combatants grabbing one another by the hair and trying to finish each other off with daggers (cf. 2 Sam. 2:16).

Two additional sidelights on warfare of the time come in David's capture of Jerusalem for his capital (2 Sam. 5:6–8). After carefully studying the "tunnel" of Jerusalem ("gutter" in the KJV, v. 8), some archaeologists have concluded that it was too narrow for a man to get through.[4] They suggest that the Hebrew word, used only here and in Psalm 42:7, might be rendered *trident,* a three-pronged sea weapon. Thus the New English Bible translates the phrase: "Let him use his grappling-iron," probably also a three-pronged weapon. In the same passage (2 Sam. 5:6–8), there is mention of the "blind and the lame." Hittite records show that the killing of such unfortunates brought the curse of the gods down on the killers. The Jebusites may have posted these helpless people to defend the city, but David ignored the heathen curse and took it anyway.

The wars of David may be divided into two types—those close to home in which

---

[4] Other authorities believe that verse 8 may simply mean that David's men fought their way up to the spring of Gihon, located just outside the city wall, to cut off the Jebusites. They could have done this without crawling through the shaft.

WARFARE AND WEAPONS

GOLD DAGGER AND SHEATH. *The hilt of this beautifully made weapon from Ur (ca. twenty-fifth century B.C.) is a single piece of lapis lazuli, studded with gold and pierced by a hole edged with gold. The mark on the golden blade may identify the owner. The gold sheath is decorated with an openwork design of woven grass.*

Jerusalem served as the center of operations and wars away from the home base. The second type required a base of operations that had good communications with Jerusalem and the front lines. It had to be easily defended. It required a good supply of food, water, and facilities to manufacture and repair weaponry. And it must have a government loyal to David. Ma-

hanaim met all these qualifications, being a center for metal works and having a government especially loyal to David (cf. 2 Sam. 17:27–29).

David's first war with outside nations was against the Aramaean-Ammonite alliance (2 Sam. 10—12). There were three routes from Jerusalem to Rabbah, the capital of Ammon: (1) The first was the shortest and fastest route, but involved a 1,200-meter (1,300-yard) climb inside enemy territory that was exposed to the enemy and difficult to defend. (2) The second was a medium-long route that went through rough, broken territory inside the enemy country and was open to attack by the enemy. (3) The last was the longest route that led through Israelite territory and crossed the Jordan near Samaria, an Israelite stronghold. The army could then resupply at Succoth and be in a position to attack either to the north (Aram) or to the south (Ammon).

The incident in which General Joab was defeated by a surprise attack, being trapped between the Aramaeans and the Ammonites (cf. 1 Chr. 19:9–13), is best explained by assuming he had taken the shortest route (1). The Aramaean army had marched south and was encamped south of Rabbah at Medeba, where there was a good plain on which to use their chariots and where they would be able to strike Joab's forces from the rear. So Joab had the Ammonite army to his north, which he knew about, and the Aramaeans to the south, about whom he did not know till it was too late. He was able to avoid total disaster by counterattacking aggressively against these combined forces and turning the battle into a draw. The armies then returned to their respective home bases to fight again another time.

David learned from this incident and adjusted his strategy accordingly. He decided to fight against the Aramaeans first, to stop them from helping the Ammonites (2 Sam. 10:19), and then use the northern route (3) to attack Rabbah in Ammon. Yigael Yadin suggests that this long campaign was fought with the regular army as the main fighting force and the militia (conscripts) being held in reserve at Succoth. The ark was sent along on the campaign (cf. 2 Sam. 11:11), and finally Rabbah was taken (2 Sam. 12:26). As the Ammonite capital was about to fall, Joab called for David to join him and take the proper credit for winning the war. The king was to bring the militia with him to take the city (2 Sam. 12:28–29).

As under Saul, David's army consisted of

WARFARE AND WEAPONS

War Galleys

The mainstay of navies in the ancient Mediterranean world was the war galley. This was a long, slender boat powered by long oars arranged in rows. The galley usually had only one deck and the side of the ship rose only a little above the waterline.

Egyptians built galleys as early as 3000 B.C. At first the ships were used both as merchant vessels and warships. In later years, they were used exclusively for combat.

Around 700 B.C., the Phoenicians made several changes in the Egyptian galley design. One of their most important changes was the addition of a battering ram on the front of the boat. This device was a timber snout overlaid with bronze or iron, positioned just below the water. In battle, a ship with such a device would attempt to ram an enemy vessel; then the galley's crew attempted to board the enemy craft and overpower it.

Originally, each galley had a single bank (row) of oars. However, in the sixth century B.C., some armies developed galleys called *biremes;* these had two levels of oars. Within 100 years, the *trireme* (a vessel with three rows of oars on each side) was constructed; the *trireme* was the backbone of the Roman fleet during its time of conquest.

Early galleys required only one rower per oar. However, as the ships increased in size, more manpower was required. Some of the oars on the larger vessels were up to 15 m. (50 ft.) long, and six men were required to pull each one. At first being a rower was considered honorable; but this job was later done by slaves and captives of war, freeing combat soldiers to board the enemy craft.

Many galleys had a small square sail in addition to the oars. These sails could only be used for cruising when the wind was just right. In battle, the oars were used almost exclusively.

Although the Egyptians, Phoenicians, Greeks, and Romans relied on galleys, this type of craft was notoriously unseaworthy. It was not designed for prolonged use on the open sea; in rough weather, it sank rather easily. In fact, more vessels were lost in storms than in battles.

The galley continued in at least partial use until the eighteenth century A.D. Before its disappearance, it had been used by many countries in one form or another, having found a place in the navies of Southeast Asia as well as those of the Mediterranean area.

---

professional soldiers and the militia, or the drafted army. The first was divided into two groups—Israelites and Gentiles, the latter being mercenaries. The Israelite contingent was commanded by Joab and had grown out of the "mighty men" who had followed David before he was king. These were from among the original 400 friends of David, many of them having been dissidents under Saul (1 Sam. 22:1–2). These later grew to 600, with many of them distinguishing themselves in battle and perhaps in individual duels with the enemy (cf. 1 Sam. 23:13; 27:2; 1 Chr. 11—12). When David became king, these men became his royal strategists and advisors and were made the officers of the standing army, responsible for training and commanding the civilian militia. The top men were known as the *three,* with the next level being the *thirty.* The exact function of these two groups is not given in the Bible, but since they were the best warriors in the land, they occupied high positions in the army.

The professional army also included Gentile mercenaries, who were mostly Sea People (including some Philistines), commanded by Ittai the Gittite (2 Sam. 15:18–22). These men had probably been recruited at the time that David fled from Saul into Philistia and served as a mercenary to Achish, the king of Gath (1 Sam. 27).

As king, David hired Cherethites and Gittites as his personal bodyguard and placed Benaiah over them (2 Sam. 8:18). From among this group of Gentile mercenaries came the *runners,* the king's special escort corps. They first appeared under Saul (1 Sam. 22:17) and are mentioned during David's time (2 Sam. 15:1); they seem to have been a regular part of the king's retinue. David used this corps of foreigners to settle rebellion within his own family, as for example the war against Absalom (2 Sam. 15:17–21). This practice followed the example of the Egyptian pharaohs, who had provided themselves with men who were loyal only to the king.

The other part of the army was the militia, probably commanded by Amasa (cf. 2 Sam. 20:4–5). Since they were civilians and had home responsibilities, they were difficult to assemble quickly. But the militia was called out to join the army in its struggle against Absalom, and the whole was divided into three units, headed by Joab, his brother Abishai, and Ittai. Amasa had gone over to Absalom and was head of his army (2 Sam. 17:25). After the rebellion was crushed, Amasa returned to David's side and was appointed the commander of the militia (2 Sam. 19:13; 20:4–5), while Joab remained as the commander over the professional army. Later, in another time of crisis, Joab killed Amasa (2 Sam. 20:8–12) either because he doubted his loyalty to David or because of personal ambition. Subsequently Joab was restored to his former position as commander of the entire army (2 Sam. 20:23).

David organized the militia into twelve divisions of 24,000 men each, one division serving on active duty for one month each year. They were trained and readied for battle by the professionals (1 Chr. 27:1–15). Each tribe tended to specialize in the use of particular weapons (cf. 1 Chr. 12), and each of the twelve divisions may have consisted of specialized units from each of the twelve tribes. The central government assigned the number of units each tribe was to supply to the militia, while the local tribal authorities determined which men went on active duty (cf. 1 Chr. 27:16–22). The local authorities could also summon the tribal militia to meet local needs such as policing and emergency raids or withstanding invasions. As much as possible, the tribes supplied their own units.

David's census, for which he was judged by God, was probably a military one in which he sought the age and location of potential draftees for the militia (cf. 2 Sam. 24:2–9; 1 Chr. 21:6; 27:24). Other military censuses are recorded in Scripture (2 Chr. 17:14–18; 25:5; 26:11–13), but the motivation for this one was wrong. It is interesting to note that Joab, the professional soldier, was opposed to this plan of David's, reflecting perhaps the professional's disdain for the draftee.

Another change that came during David's reign was the use of chariots in Israel. In Saul's day the Canaanites fielded 30,000 chariots and 6,000 cavalry against him, but he as the judges before him had no such weapons (see 1 Sam. 13:5). The biblical record does not give us the details, but David began using chariots, probably those captured from the Canaanites (cf. 1 Chr. 18:3–4). When David hamstrung the Aramaean horses instead of capturing them, this may have indicated that he already had sufficient chariots. By this time the Aramaean chariots were manned by two soldiers, and perhaps so were David's.

Under Solomon, chariotry became a major unit in his army, involving many chariots, horses, and extensive housing for them (1 Kin. 4:26; 10:26; 2 Chr. 9:25). That he had so huge a force has been verified by Egyptian and Assyrian records of the time; he probably made good use of captured Canaanite chariotry. Having so large a force probably protected him from outside invasions and maintained peace in that part of the Near East. It is interesting to note that many years earlier Samuel had predicted that having a king would involve this expensive equipment, which would then have to be supported by much higher taxes (cf. 1 Sam. 8:11–18).

The extensive use of cavalry units would come at a much later time, but some were used in Israel. As neither saddles nor spurs were used by the troopers, they had less stability and less control over the animal than they needed. The horseman carried a small shield, which could easily be shifted to his back, freeing both his hands to handle other weapons. Apparently mules were also used by the cavalry, since they would be more agile in the hilly terrain (cf. 2 Sam. 18:9). It is interesting to note that in Palestine the mule at this time was the riding animal of the nobility (cf. 2 Sam. 13:29).

Solomon was especially active in building fortifications (1 Kin. 9:17–19; 2 Chr. 8:3–6). We know how Solomon built his fortifications, for archaeological discoveries at Megiddo, Hazor, and Gezer have given us a good picture of what they looked like (cf. 1 Kin. 9:15). Solomon simply copied the fortifications of the previous period by using casemated walls, whose outer shell he thickened, and also improved the gates.

D. The Period of the Divided Kingdom. The major military influences of this period were the great Mesopotamian powers of As-

WARFARE AND WEAPONS

CAVALRYMAN. *The Aramaean cavalryman astride his prancing horse on this basalt relief (ca. ninth century B.C.) is armed with a shield and a club or sword. His hair hangs in locks to his shoulders. He is beardless because clean-shaven soldiers could not be seized by the beard in combat.*

syria and Babylon. Warfare continued as before, with no particular changes being made offensively or defensively except in the improvement of existing weaponry. The Assyri-

ans improved their offensive weapons, so their enemies improved their defensive ones, particularly the architecture of their fortifications.

The period opened with warfare between the Northern and the Southern Kingdoms (Israel and Judah), as each tried to establish itself as an independent power. At this time, Aram was the major rival in the area and fought against both kingdoms. Assyria was on the rise and would soon be the major influence in Palestine. Although the Bible has little to say about him, Omri of Israel must have been a very capable military leader (885–874 B.C.). Assyrian records speak of his kingdom as the "Land of Omri" a century or so after his reign. Apparently his abilities in war and politics, which included his conquest of Damascus of Aram and his alliance with the Phoenicians, earned him the respect of Assyria. Omri and his son Ahab strengthened the fortifications of Samaria, the capital of the Northern Kingdom. Although the biblical accounts of warfare in this period are not too detailed, Assyrian monuments and inscriptions provide many detailed descriptions of their activities in the Near East including Palestine.

Assyria's major weapon was the chariot, though the Assyrians also used spearmen, bowmen, slingers, and cavalry well. For their soldiers' defense, they made good use of coats

ATTACK BY ASSYRIAN ARMY. *This drawing, made from a relief in Sennacherib's palace, depicts the Assyrian army's assault on the city of Lachish (ca. eighth century B.C.). The Assyrians attack with bows and arrows and battering rams, while the inhabitants of Lachish throw stones and shoot arrows at their enemies.*

WARFARE AND WEAPONS

TUNNEL OF SILOAM. *This tunnel dates from the reign of Hezekiah (eighth century B.C.), who diverted water from outside springs through the underground passage into Jerusalem's Pool of Siloam. The tunnel is over 500 m. (1,750 ft.) in length.*

only field 10 chariots, 50 horsemen, and 10,000 infantry (cf. 2 Kin. 13:7). Israel, and presumably Judah, became more and more dependent on the great powers and entered into an era of "power politics" to insure their survival as nations. This showed their continual lack of trust in the God of Israel in their looking for help in human strength and weaponry, and brought on them the condemnation of the prophets (cf. Is. 31:1, 3).

The biblical account of the wars between Ahab of Israel and Ben-hadad of Syria (860–841 B.C.) shows how God's people won some of their battles through superior tactics, such as maneuvering their enemy into an indefensible position (see 1 Kin. 20). Ben-hadad had besieged Samaria and demanded its surrender (vv. 2–3). The wording of the demand was interpreted to be figurative, so Ahab agreed to submit, expecting only the paying of the usual tribute (v. 4). The Aramaeans, however, wanted to loot Ahab's family, palace, and city, so after consulting with his elders the king of Israel agreed only to pay the tribute rather than surrender to the literal demands of the Aramaean (v. 9). An exchange of threats followed, and Ben-hadad, who had his army camped at Succoth, some miles to the east, set out with an advance force for the capital of Israel (v. 12). Since it took time for armies to march in those days, Ahab was able to muster his militia (v. 15) and lay a trap for the advancing Aramaeans. At noon they attacked the Aramaeans in a narrow valley near Tirzah and thoroughly routed them. They pursued the fleeing Syrians to their camp at Succoth and thoroughly defeated them, for Ben-hadad and his officers, certain of victory by the advance force, had become drunk and were not able to fight (vv. 16–21).

A prophet of God then came and warned Ahab that Ben-hadad would try again in the spring. That season was the favorite time for oriental kings to launch their invasion campaigns, for it allowed their armies to travel in dry weather and put them in enemy territory at harvest time when the farmer-militiamen would be busy in the fields and unprepared for battle. The time would also enable their armies to live off the foodstuffs of the land they were invading. Meanwhile Ben-hadad was told by his advisors that the "gods" of Ahab were mountain gods and that the Aramaean should therefore avoid the mountains and fight on the plains, where his chariots would prove to be superior. Ahab, however,

of mail and shields. They were excellent tacticians and were able to transport their troops and equipment over all kinds of terrain. Their tactics included fighting on all kinds of terrain, including amphibious operations.

Assyrian pictorial records show the development of the chariot in great detail. At first this offensive weapon was manned by two men, then by three men by the time of Sargon (722–705 B.C.), and finally by four men by the time of Ashurbanipal (669–633 B.C.). One Assyrian bas relief shows the capture of the city of Lachish by Sennacherib (704–681 B.C.). It shows a Judean battle chariot, which is like those of Assyria, having a yoke for four horses. The personal chariot of the king had a three-man crew, two soldiers and an armor-bearer, on whom the king's life might depend.

Israel, the Northern Kingdom, was still using chariots at the time of Ahab, for the records of Shalmaneser of Assyria (859–824 B.C.) record that Ahab sent 2,000 chariots and 10,000 infantry, perhaps his professional army, to help him at the Battle of Qarqar. After him Israel's chariot force diminished, till at the time of Jehoahaz (814–798 B.C.) he could

WARFARE AND WEAPONS

met the Aramaeans at a narrow pass leading to the plains and so defeated a larger and stronger force. Ben-hadad's troops fled to Aphek, which Ahab besieged and captured. Ben-hadad surrendered and begged for mercy. Contrary to God's instructions through the prophet, Ahab let him live and made an alliance with him rather than depending on his greater "ally"—God (vv. 31–34, 42).

Jehoshaphat of Judah (876–848 B.C.) used similar tactics against the Moabites, the Ammonites, and their allies. The enemy was ambushed in one of the Judean canyons and was so completely surrounded and exposed that they surrendered without battle (cf. 2 Chr. 20:16). The kings of Israel and Judah often used their knowledge of the geography of Palestine to fight against and win over their enemies (cf. 2 Kin. 6:8–12; 2 Chr. 13:13–14). A notable exception occurred toward the end of this period when Josiah went to battle against Pharaoh Necho (609–593 B.C.) and fought him on the plains near Megiddo instead of setting an ambush in the hill country. Josiah was killed in battle and Judah was defeated. This was a common tactic in ancient times, for to kill the king was to cut off the army's head (see the instructions of Ben-hadad in 1 Kin. 22:31).

After the decline of Aram came the rise of Assyria. That nation's superiority in open warfare drove the lesser nations of the Near East

to start building better fortifications to withstand Assyrian sieges. The cities of Judah and Israel apparently were successful in doing this, for Assyrians are often pictured as besieging them. The siege of Samaria, for example, took three years, and later God warned Judah against trusting in her fortresses (Jer. 5:17).

The Assyrians, to match their enemies' improved fortresses, developed the battering ram into a more effective weapon, but their enemies built new, thicker noncasemated walls to counter it. One type of Assyrian battering ram had six wheels, a wooden frame, and sides covered with wicker shields or other light material that would prevent spears or arrows from penetrating. These battering rams were approximately 4.5 to 6.5 m. (5 to 7 yds.) long with a 65-cm. (26-in.) base and a domed turret, possibly covered with metal, in which the ram was suspended by a rope and was used like a pendulum. Peepholes in the turret allowed the crew to guide the machine to the right part of the wall and fire arrows at the defenders. The turret was about four yards high and the front of the section housing the ram about a yard high. The head of the ram was like a large metal axe blade, which was driven against stone walls in an attempt to collapse them. The crews of some of the rams included "dowsers," who threw water on the firebrands the defenders threw on the weapon (see Sen-

SILOAM INSCRIPTION. *This six-line inscription is carved into the rock wall of the lower entrance of the Siloam tunnel, south of Jerusalem's temple area. Probably made by a workman, the inscription gives details on construction of the tunnel.*

WARFARE AND WEAPONS

nacherib's ram, 705–681 B.C.). Tiglath-Pileser III (745–727 B.C.), called "Pul" in the Bible (2 Kin. 15:19; 1 Chr. 5:26), developed a ram that moved on four wheels, had a lighter body than previous rams, and could be more easily dismantled, transported, and reassembled. Sennacherib improved even more on its lightness and ease of assembly. A century or so later, the pictures of Ashurbanipal's reign (669–633 B.C.) show no evidence of the use of rams. He used scaling ladders on enemy walls, because he apparently felt it was a waste of time to transport unwieldy rams around to the cities of the enemy.

The Assyrians also invented and used mobile towers, from which archers could cover the advance of the battering rams by shooting directly at the defenders on the walls. In order to get these weapons close to the walls, the attacking army would often build dirt ramps (cf. Ezek. 42:21–22) topped with rocks or logs to cover the sharp embankment at the lower walls to bring the rams and towers to the walls.

Often several rams would be concentrated on a single point of the wall while attempts to undermine or scale the wall were made at other points. Assyrian pictures of the period show enemy walls being attacked by battering rams, axes, swords, spears, fire, scaling ladders, and undermining at the same time. This forced the defenders to spread their men along the entire wall instead of concentrating at the place where the wall was being dangerously battered. The attackers were also protected by round and rectangular shields, the latter being of body length and curved at the top. They would protect the men doing the undermining. Supporting infantry was used to help those attacking the wall.

Another tactic employed by a besieging army was to try to cut off all food and water supplies to the enemy city (cf. 2 Kin. 6:26–29, where we read of a famine in Samaria when it was besieged by the Syrians). Kin. defending their cities tried to stock up and assure adequate food and water supplies if they were expecting a siege. Hezekiah's engineers dug a tunnel through almost 550 m. (600 yds.) of solid rock to give him a water supply (2 Ch. 32:30). The Siloam Inscription (Hebrew writing found on the walls of the tunnel) describes the work, which was begun at opposite ends and joined in the middle. Other fortress cities show evidence of wells, cisterns, complicated drainage systems, and un-

derground tunnels to provide water for the city. The Bible describes Rehoboam's efforts at building fortresses and how he provided supplies for them (2 Chr. 11:6–12). The kings of Israel and Judah studied the construction and defense of cities carefully. We are told that Uzziah (790–739 B.C.) invented "engines" that shot arrows and threw large stones at the besieging enemy (2 Chr. 26:15). Some scholars think these may have been catapults, but Assyrian pictures dating from this period and subsequent times show no evidence of them. Yigael Yadin suggests that these "engines" were special structures built on towers behind which the defenders could stand upright, still be protected, and be able to shoot at the enemy. However, the Lachish picture shows a screen of shields protecting standing defenders.

According to the Bible, Uzziah was the first king who equipped his entire army with helmets and breastplates (2 Chr. 26:14). Previously such equipment had been the possession only of kings and special fighters in Israel (cf. 1 Sam. 17:38; 1 Kin. 22:34), though other kings equipped all their troops with them.

Because of the difficulties and great expense of sieges, kings and commanders often tried threats and tricks to get a city to surrender. So it was that Jehoram was not willing to believe that the besieging Aramaeans had left (cf. 2 Kin. 7:10–12). Attackers also tried intimidation (cf. 1 Kin. 20:1–3) and direct threats. When Sennacherib besieged Hezekiah's Jerusalem, he verbally attacked Judah's army, the Egyptian allies, and God Himself (2 Kin. 18:19–23). Hezekiah's representatives in the negotiations asked the Assyrians to stop speaking Hebrew and use Aramaic so the defenders would not be panicked. The answer was that they were using Hebrew as a tactic to do exactly that—lower the morale of the defenders and cause them to revolt against Hezekiah. The soldiers stayed loyal and the siege was resisted. Sennacherib never took Jerusalem (as he did Lachish), but according to his records he "shut Hezekiah up like a bird in a cage."

Babylon finally managed to conquer Judah by taking all her fortresses and besieging and taking Jerusalem. Everything in the land was destroyed and the people taken into captivity, which was another military tactic to prevent the rebellion of captured peoples.

Later, in the restoration, only Jerusalem was

WARFARE AND WEAPONS

rebuilt (by Nehemiah). The land would not see war again till Maccabean times.

E. The Rise of Greece. During the fifth and fourth centuries B.C., the Greek city-states developed volunteer citizen armies to defeat mighty Persia. However, these city-states fell prey to a series of disastrous civil wars and a new power, Macedonia, arose. The Macedonian army copied the close-order battle tactic known as the *phalanx,* which had been developed by a general named Epaminondas.

Philip, king of Macedonia, willed his army and throne to his son, Alexander, under whom Greek military tactics and culture spread throughout the Asian world. Alexander's successors were the rulers of what were called the Hellenistic kingdoms.

F. The Military Genius of Rome. The Romans, who fought with the Greeks first in Italy and then in the Greek islands, copied and improved upon their enemy's well-organized military units. They built a truly citizen army and a powerful navy. It was the Romans' talent for building and organizing that brought down almost all their enemies.

One by one, small kingdoms of the eastern Mediterranean fell to Rome. The great visionary text of the Essene collection of the Dead Sea Scrolls, entitled *The War of the Sons of Light with the Sons of Darkness,* describes in detail the last great battle in which the Roman army destroyed the Jewish state in A.D. 70.

ISRAEL'S GOVERNMENT

When God created all things, He brought into being an orderly universe. With the creation of man and the multiplication of people throughout the earth, God ordained government for societies and nations.

When the people of Israel became a nation, government became a necessity. This chapter surveys the forms of Israel's government through the time of the divided monarchy.

I. THE THEOCRACY IN THE WILDERNESS
  A. Unique Nature
  B. Organization
  C. Administration
    1. Judicial Responsibilities
    2. Military Responsibilities

II. THE THEOCRACY IN CANAAN

III. THE UNITED MONARCHY
  A. Choosing a King
  B. The Reign of Saul
  C. The Reign of David
    1. Organization of the Militia
    2. Local Government
    3. Judicial System
    4. The King's Cabinet
    5. Minor Officials
  D. The Reign of Solomon
    1. The King's Cabinet
    2. The Queen Mother
    3. Centralized Government
    4. Policy toward the Canaanites
    5. The Central Province
  E. The Divided Kingdom
    1. Cabinet Officials
    2. Queen Mothers
    3. Minor Officials

IV. SUMMARY

I. The Theocracy in the Wilderness. After God rescued His people out of slavery in Egypt, He brought them to Mount Sinai, where He organized them into a nation. He constituted them "a kingdom of priests" (Exod. 19:6) with Himself as their ruler. (The term *theocracy* comes from two Greek words, *theos,* God, and *kratos,* rule, thus rule by God.) From that time on, Israel would always consider itself to be God's kingdom and God to be its ultimate king.

---

* God's personal name

Roland de Vaux has written, "Israel is Yahweh's* people and has no other maker but him. That is why from the beginning to the end of its history Israel remained a religious community."

A. Unique Nature. Because Israel's government was given directly by God, it had no true parallel with that of the city-states of the Canaanites, the great empires of later history, or the Greek republic.

Some scholars have tried to parallel Israel's government under Moses and the judges with that of the Greek city-states. From 6 to 12 Greek cities would bind themselves together around a central religious shrine, commit themselves to the same laws, consult together, and cooperate in matters that concerned them all. But the Greeks did not live under God's covenant as Israel did. God made a covenant with Abraham and with His people through Moses, in which He promised that He would be their God and they would be His special people. This made Israel's government distinctively different in character from that of other nations.

B. Organization. God organized His people into a 12-tribe structure, since He had given Jacob 12 sons (see Gen. 49). Other tribes in the Near East organized themselves into units of 12 (cf. Gen. 25:12–16; 36:10–14), but Israel's structure had been mandated by God.

C. Administration. At first, the governmental administration of Israel was very simple. Moses was the God-appointed leader to whom was delegated all authority over God's

SEAL OF SHEMA. *This jasper seal (ca. eighth century B.C.) discovered at Megiddo is inscribed, "Shema servant of Jeroboam." Seals were used to mark and verify documents and belongings.*

ISRAEL'S GOVERNMENT

people. But he soon discovered that there were too many people to rule, and he was busy all day long (Ex. 18:13). Jethro, his father-in-law, suggested that Moses appoint judges to rule over groups of thousands, hundreds, fifties, and tens (Ex. 18:25). With God's approval, Moses chose from among the heads of families. He gave them special instructions and commissioned them to judge the people's everyday problems (Deut. 1:12–18). However, Moses continued to decide the most difficult cases (Ex. 18:26).

The system of government, then, was one of a supreme judge and a court system. The courts settled both religious and civil matters, for in a theocracy no clear-cut line between religious and civil law could exist; all cases were ultimately brought before God (Ex. 18:19).

1. Judicial Responsibilities. The court system also included priests and Levites, who were primarily responsible for directly religious cases, such as murder (Deut. 21:1–9) and rituals for leprosy (Lev. 13—14). The judges also had administrative responsibili-

ties, including oversight of the courts' work (Deut. 19:12; 21; 22:15) and selecting men for warfare (Deut. 20:5–9). Both the judges and the priests were responsible to teach the law to the people (Deut. 17:9; 33:10).

2. Military Responsibilities. The judges had leadership roles; they were appointed as captains over thousands, hundreds, fifties, and tens. It is estimated that there were 78,000 captains in Israel.

II. The Theocracy in Canaan. When the people of Israel conquered the land of Canaan and settled in it, certain changes occurred in their government. They were no longer nomads in the desert; they were now living in cities. They had lost the unity they had while wandering in the wilderness. This transition did not change the structure of Israel's government, but it did change the duties of the judges and the manner of their selection.

The judges became responsible for the government of the towns in which they lived (cf. Num. 21:25, 32; Judg. 8:6, 14, 16). The elders of the tribes had exercised general governmental authority since the days of the Egyp-

Madame Pharaoh

Ancient governments seldom allowed women to attain positions of leadership. The few women who succeeded in claiming the throne did so by vio-

lence or by gradually assuming the powers of a weak male monarch. The first method was used by Athaliah, the only woman to rule Judah, who seized power by murdering her grandsons (2 Kings 11:1–3). The second method was used by Hatshepsut, who slowly assumed the role of pharaoh from her half-brothers.

Hatshepsut (reign 1486–1468 B.C.) was the only surviving child of Pharaoh Thutmose and Ahmose. Ahmose (her mother) was the only descendant of the old Theban princes who had fought and expelled their foreign rulers, the Hyksos. Many Egyptians believed that only the descendants of this line were entitled to rule. In fact, Thutmose had ruled by virtue of his marriage to Ahmose, since the country refused to submit to the rule of a woman.

To provide a pharaoh for the throne when her father died, Hatshepsut married Thutmose II, her step-brother by one of the Thutmose's lesser wives. (The Egyptians saw nothing wrong in brother-sister marriages. They felt this made the blood line purer.) But at the time of his coronation, Thutmose II was sickly. He was dominated by his wife, Hatshepsut, and her mother Ahmose. His reign lasted no more than three years.

Thutmose III, another half-brother of Hatshepsut, was then proclaimed pharaoh; but Hatshepsut acted as regent for the young pharaoh. An inscription tells us: "His sister, the Divine Consort, Hattian captivity (cf. Ex. 3:16–18; 19:7); so when they settled in Palestine, some of these elders were elected as judges in the cities (see Judg. 11:5, 11) and sat in the city gates. In other words, they judged civil cases at the city gates, where most civic business was transacted (Ruth 4:1–11).

In cities of refuge, the judges tried persons who were accused of murder (Deut. 19:12). They conducted inquests on people who had died (Deut. 21:2) and settled family and marriage problems (Deut. 21:18; 22:15; 25:7). Families generally settled their own problems according to the decision of the patriarch or family leader, but when there was still dissatisfaction the case would be taken to the judge at the city gates.

Bible scholars believe that Israel's court system included a battery of higher courts in addition to these city judges. Priests sat on the higher courts, to which more difficult cases were referred. However, we have no direct biblical evidence of these higher courts.

During Israel's first settlement of Canaan there was no central authority, king, or ruling body. Each tribe lived in its own area with a minimum of central administration. Since there were few officials, the people had few men to whom to give loyalty and obedience.

After a short period of time, the people of Israel turned from God and began to serve the gods of their Canaanite neighbors. God punished them by sending various nations to oppress them. During this time of oppression "every man did that which was right in his own eyes" (Judg. 17:6; 21:25). This form of anarchy was more than a breakdown in government; it was a breakdown of obedience to the Law of God given at Mount Sinai (Ex. 19—40).

However, God loved His people and periodically sent "judges" to deliver them from their oppressors. These men (and one woman) differed from the judges of the court system. They were primarily military leaders rather than judges of the people's disputes. (However, Deborah the prophetess was an exception—cf. Judg. 4:4–5.)

This office was not hereditary, but the Old Testament seems to suggest that the judges

shepsut, adjusted the affairs of the Two Lands [i.e., Upper and Lower Egypt] by reason of her designs; Egypt was made to labor with bowed head for her, the excellent seed of the god, who came forth from him."

Instead of surrendering her regency when Thutmose came of age, Hatshepsut assumed the titles of the pharaoh. At her temple in Deir el-Bahri, she expended great efforts to make her reign legitimate. Her architect, Senmut, sculptured on the walls a series of reliefs showing the birth of the queen. The god Amon is shown appearing to Ahmose, and he tells her as he leaves: "Hatshepsut shall be the name of this my daughter . . . She shall exercise the excellent kingship in this whole land." The artist followed court traditions so closely that he pictured Hatshepsut as a boy. The relief shows Hatshepsut's coronation by the gods and her parents' acknowledgment of her as queen. They represent Thutmose I as saying: "Ye shall proclaim her word, ye shall be united at her command. He who shall do her homage shall live, he who shall speak evil in blasphemy of her majesty shall die."

Hatshepsut's reign brought the greatest prosperity following the collapse of the Middle Kingdom. Extensive building and rebuilding of the temples was carried out under the direction of Senmut. Hatshepsut ordered huge obelisks from the Aswan quarries, had them inscribed to proclaim the queen, and topped them with gold, which reflected the sun so that they could be seen from both sides of the Nile.

Hatshepsut's relations with other nations were peaceful. She was most proud of an expedition to the land of Punt (perhaps modern Somaliland). Five vessels laden with jewelry, tools, and weapons, as well as a great statue of the queen, sailed down the Nile and through a canal connecting the Nile with the Red Sea. When the ships returned, they were loaded "very heavily with the marvels of the country of Punt; all goodly fragrant woods of god's land, heaps of myrrh-resin, of fresh myrrh-trees, with ebony and pure ivory, with the green gold of Emu, with incense, with baboons, monkeys, and dogs. . . . Never was the like of this brought for any king who has been since the beginning."

After Hatshepsut had been pharaoh for 17 years, young Thutmose III brought her reign to an abrupt end. Perhaps because he had waited so long in the background, Thutmose attempted to completely purge the records of her reign. Inscriptions in her temples were chiseled off. Obelisks were sheathed with masonry, covering Hatshepsut's name and the record of their erection. Her statues were hurled into the quarry. But Thutmose III did not succeed in obliterating Hatshepsut's fame.

ISRAEL'S GOVERNMENT

STATUE OF KING KHAF-RE. *Khaf-Re was a pharaoh of the fourth Egyptian dynasty, about 2700 B.C. The word of the pharaoh was absolute law. The god Horus, depicted as a falcon, extends his wings to cover the king's neck to signify his protection of the monarch. The Israelites did not believe their king was divine.*

tary leader who would keep them free of other nations' rule. The words "a king to judge" probably emphasize the *military* role that the judges played in the preceding centuries, rather than the judicial role of settling disputes among the people.

A. Choosing a King. The king was chosen by God (1 Sam. 9:15–16), as well as by the people (1 Sam. 11:15). But the people's demand for a king was seen as rejection of God's military leadership; they wanted deliverance from their enemies without obedience to God. Had their attitude toward God been different, God would have provided a king for His people in due course. This event had been planned for centuries before (see Deut. 17:14–20). God agreed to their request but predicted judgment against them. Ultimately the king would oppress the people through heavy taxation and by drafting people to work for him and serve in his army (see 1 Sam. 8:9–18).

B. The Reign of Saul. This prediction began coming true during the reign of Saul. Before he became king, he owned only the usual family property (1 Sam. 9:1–2; 21), but during his reign he distributed fields and vineyards to his officers (1 Sam. 22:7). He must have obtained this property through taxation. At his death he also left considerable property to his heirs (2 Sam. 9:9–10), property that he must have gained during his reign.

Government under King Saul continued to be quite simple, for he did not make any known changes from the previous ways. We know of no administrative or bureaucratic developments during his reign. His only administrators seemed to have been members of his immediate family. His son Jonathan and his cousin Abner served with him in the army and led the militia (1 Sam. 13:1–2, 16; 14:50–51). We also find that Saul established a permanent army in keeping with the desire of the people (1 Sam. 14:52).

C. The Reign of David. During the reign of David, many governmental changes occurred. David led the nation into an era of great military power. He subdued Israel's enemies and dominated over their lands. He had to consolidate the tribes and centralize the government in order to rule the conquered territories and run the government at home.

1. Organization of the Militia. The army was under the command of a general—Joab—and consisted of three sections. One was the original band of about 600 men under 30 com-

came from the ruling class of the people (the elders). Their military leadership lasted only as long as an enemy threatened the borders of Israel (Judg. 8:22–23).

III. The United Monarchy. Israel underwent a drastic change when theocracy gave way to monarchy (rule by a king). This period of history is usually divided into two parts, the United Kingdom (*ca.* 1043–930 B.C.) and the Divided Kingdoms (*ca.* 930–586 B.C.). Particularly in the first period, the governmental structure grew more complex.

Israel became a monarchy when Saul was enthroned. The Israelites had been oppressed by the Philistines for many years and wanted to have "a king to judge us like all the nations" (1 Sam. 8:5). They wanted a permanent mili-

ISRAEL'S GOVERNMENT

David's Cabinet

Title	2 Sam. 8:15–18	1 Chron. 18:14–17	2 Sam. 20:23–26
Recorder	Jehoshaphat, son of Ahilud	Jehoshaphat, son of Ahilud	Jehoshaphat, son of Ahilud
Scribe	Seraiah	Shavsha	Sheva
Priests	Zadok, son of Ahitub Ahimelech, son of Abiathar	Zadok, son of Ahitub Abimelech, son of Abiathar	Zadok and Abiathar
Chief Rulers	David's sons	David's sons	Ira the Jairite
"Over the Host" (Army)	Joab, son of Zeruiah	Joab, son of Zeruiah	Joab
"Over the Tribute" (Forced Labor)			Adoram
"Over the Cherethites and Pelethites"	Benaiah, son of Jehoiada	Benaiah, son of Jehoiada	Benaiah, son of Jehoiada

Figure 24

manders (cf. 2 Sam. 23:8–39; 1 Chr. 11:10–47); the other two were the drafted militia and the hired mercenaries. The militia was organized into 12 sections consisting of 24,000 men each. Each section served on active duty for one month a year, and its tribe was responsible to provide for its needs. Probably the elders of the tribes would be the ones who had to see that the support for the militia was raised (cf. 1 Chr. 27:6–22). It is possible that these men were also responsible for the judicial matters in their tribes.

2. Local Government. David either appointed governors over the people whom he conquered (2 Sam. 8:6, 14) or made their kings his vassals (2 Sam. 10:19). These governors and kings were then responsible to carry on the local government for King David. They had to raise the necessary taxes, tributes, levies, and gifts.

David also appointed men over various treasuries, storehouses, and agricultural enterprises (1 Chr. 26:25–31). The lists of his personal holdings show that the shepherd boy gained many possessions and properties during his reign.

3. Judicial System. As king, David made few changes in the previously existing struc-

ture of tribal government. He continued the judicial system established by Moses and allowed cities and tribes to manage their own affairs. The Bible tells us that David used the Levites as civil servants in the court system and the police force of that period (1 Chr. 26:29–32).

4. The King's Cabinet. The king surrounded himself with able men who formed a kind of "cabinet," roughly modeled on the form found in Egypt. These major officials are indicated in Figure 24. Two of the lists of his royal officers are from the early reign of David (2 Sam. 8:15–18; 1 Chr. 18:14–17) while the third is from the end of his reign (2 Sam. 20:23–26).

The office of royal *scribe* or secretary appears frequently throughout the history of the kingdom. (*See* Fig. 25.) This high official seems to have had special assignments from time to time, but his regular duties included writing the royal correspondence and keeping the royal records, the annals of the events during the king's reign (2 Sam. 8:17; 20:25; 1 Chr. 18:16).

The office of *recorder* seems to have been one of high rank from the reign of King David on. He was called *mazkir* in Hebrew ("one

ISRAEL'S GOVERNMENT

Royal Scribes

King	Scribe	Reference
United Monarchy		
David	Seraiah/Sheva /Shavsha	2 Sam. 8:17; 1 Chr. 14:17–18
Solomon	Elihoreph and Ahiah	1 Kin. 4:3
Judah		
Jehoash	(Unnamed)	2 Kin. 12:10
Uzziah	Jehiel	2 Chr. 26:11
Hezekiah	Shebna	2 Kin. 19:2
Josiah, Jehoiakim	Shaphan, Elishama	2 Kin. 22:3, 8–10; Jer. 36:10, 12
Zedekiah	Jonathan	Jer. 37:15, 20

Figure 25

BRONZE CROWN. *Discovered at Nahal Mishmar in Judea, this bronze crown (ca. 3000 B.C.) was a symbol of power and rank. It was worn by an unidentified Canaanite chieftain 1,000 years before the time of Abraham.*

who brings to mind"), and his official duty was to advise the king respecting important events. Jehoshaphat, the son of Ahilud, served as recorder for both David and Solomon (2 Sam. 8:16; 1 Kin. 4:3). The recorder represented Hezekiah in public business (2 Kin. 18:18, 37). During the reign of Josiah the recorder was placed in charge of repairs of the temple (2 Chr. 34:8).

David's cabinet also included several royal counselors or *advisors*. The king trusted these men, who were knowledgeable in many areas; he sought their advice in governing his kingdom. Among David's advisors was Hushai, who is termed the "friend" of the king (2 Sam. 15:37); evidently he was a close and respected advisor of David (2 Sam. 16:16; 1 Chr. 27:33). This position was held by only one person at a time. It appeared only under David and Solomon; there is no mention of it in later centuries. In addition to the court official with this title, David's sons were his chief advisors (2 Sam. 8:18; cf. 1 Chr. 18:17). But we do not know the functional relationship between the king's sons and his official advisor.

5. Minor Officials. The Bible mentions a

SCRIBES. *Royal scribes recorded the acts of the kings and kept tax records. This limestone relief (ca. 2300 B.C.) is from a tomb at Sakkarah in Egypt; it depicts scribes recording evidence as village leaders are questioned for nonpayment of taxes.*

number of minor officials in the king's court during David's reign. One of these was the *saris,* usually translated as "eunuch" (1 Chr. 28:1).

The pharaohs of Egypt had such men, who served as trustees of royal property (Gen. 37:36; 39:1). The neighboring Assyrians had a dignitary called a *sha-reshi,* "he who is at the head," a courtier that may have been a model for the *saris.* The *sha-reshi* was not necessarily a physical eunuch, although he may have been. Scripture indicates that the *saris* of Israel was a trustee much like the Egyptian eunuch or the Assyrian *sha-reshi* (cf. 2 Kin. 24:15; 1 Chr. 28:1).

Another official title was "the king's servant" or "the servant of the king." This seems to have been a general title that applied to the entire group of officials and royal household servants, from the royal guard to the highest office (1 Kin. 1:33; 11:26); in fact, to all those who "stood before" the king (1 Sam. 16:21)—that is, the courtiers in the royal palace (1 Kin. 12:6). Sometimes it may have been used as a special title, as in the case of David's uncle, Ahithophel (2 Sam. 15:12).

Finally, there was the *superintendent of forced labor.* This office first appears toward the end of David's reign (2 Sam. 20:24). At first, only non-Israelites were subjected to forced labor (Judg. 1:27–33). Under David foreign peoples were used extensively for this work, especially in the king's many building projects. The Hebrew word for forced labor or "tribute" is *mas,* and is of Canaanite origin. Perhaps David borrowed the institution from the Canaanites when the need arose.

D. The Reign of Solomon. Under Solomon the administrative structure of government increased greatly. His large standing army, his extremely lavish court, and his many building projects required a complex system of government.

David's son built his government on the foundation of existing structures. First, the elder/judge and the priestly/judge institution continued to be the main government of the cities. The elders continued to function as they had done under David and for centuries before. Wherever Solomon reorganized the government, he left intact the traditional tribal divisions and loyalties.

1. The King's Cabinet. When we compare Figure 24 with Figure 26 we find many similarities between the cabinets of David and Solomon. Solomon kept David's recorder and the office of royal scribe; in fact, Solomon had two secretaries. Some scholars suggest that he did this because of the increased record-keeping responsibilities during his reign.

The son of David's high priest was the high priest during Solomon's reign. Adoram, David's superintendent of forced labor, also kept his job under Solomon. (He is called Adoniram in 1 Kin. 4:6 and 5:14.) The need for forced labor increased during Solomon's reign because of the building of the temple, as well as the construction of palaces and fortifications. Solomon's policy was to fortify and hold the territory that David had conquered. He also had extensive personal properties that required maintenance and needed a large work squad. Solomon began using Israelites as well as non-Israelites in forced labor.

During Solomon's reign the superintendent of forced labor held an important office, for he supervised the work of thousands of people. Adoniram was responsible for 150,000 foreign men in the labor force with 3,600 Israelite supervisors over them. He also had 30,000 Israelites working for him, supervised by 300 officers. The entire structure of nearly 184,000 men must have been well organized and carefully policed, but we have no way of knowing exactly how that was done. We do not know whether the army or a special force was responsible to see that the work was done.

Solomon added three new officials to his cabinet: the king's friend, the chief of the prefects, and the official over the royal household. (*See* Fig. 26.)

The king's "friend" functioned much like the advisor of David's cabinet. Zabud held this post under Solomon (1 Kin. 4:5).

The chief of the prefects was the cabinet member responsible for all the internal affairs of the kingdom. Under him were the governors or prefects in charge of the 12 districts of the nation created by Solomon. These district governors were responsible for (1) collecting taxes, (2) collecting the temple tithe, (3) supplying the royal court with food for one month each year, (4) lodging soldiers and chariots in the district, (5) erecting public buildings in the district, and (6) constructing and maintaining roads in the district (see 1 Kin. 4:7, 21–28).

This office was similar to later administrative offices in the Babylonian Empire. Various nations of the Near East organized their government into 12 districts to provide for the court and army throughout the year (one district per month).

RECONSTRUCTION OF KHORSABAD. *This artist's reconstruction shows the palace of Sargon II (ca. eighth century B.C.) at Khorsabad. The size and sumptuousness of the structure attest to the wealth of the Assyrian kings. King Solomon also lived lavishly—but not to this degree.*

The third new official in King Solomon's structure was the officer over the royal household or *vizier* as he was known in other lands. Figure 27 shows that this office continued after Israel split into Northern and Southern Kingdoms.

This official probably was the manager of the king's palace, supervising the maintenance of the grounds, the upkeep of the royal palace, and the assigning of quarters to the court members. He was also responsible for maintaining all royal properties, including Solomon's extensive trade and mining operations.

Solomon's court was quite lavish when compared to David's. Many people were fed from the king's table. There were about 1,000 administrators and palace officials; Solomon's wives, concubines, and royal children; an unknown number of ambassadors; the entire military complex in the capital, and some of the Levites. The vizier was responsible for feeding all these people; this burden made a great demand on royal revenues. (It is interesting,

however, to note that Solomon's court was much smaller than that of ancient Ebla about 13 centuries before, which included 4,700 bureaucrats.)

The revenue of the palace greatly increased during Solomon's reign, and the vizier had to manage all of these finances. The support of the army and the Levites may have been managed by others. But the vizier was responsible for raising all the funds from the royal estates. Archaeological discoveries suggest that these revenues were used to support the palace courtiers, to supply military needs, and perhaps to provide for the Levites.

Solomon had inherited many estates from his father David, and probably added to these holdings throughout his reign. His lands came through gifts given him (2 Sam. 8:11; 1 Kin. 7:51; 15:15), purchases (2 Sam. 24:24; 1 Kin. 16:24), conquests and offerings (2 Kin. 12:10–11; 22:3–4), and by confiscating the properties of people who had fled the country (2 Kin. 8:1–6).

In Israel the king's lands were regarded as

ISRAEL'S GOVERNMENT

Solomon's Cabinet*

Title	Name
Recorder	Jehoshaphat, son of Ahilud
Scribes	Elihoreph and Ahiah, sons of Shisha
Priests	Zadok and Abiathar; Azaraiah, son of Zadok
"King's Friend"	Zabud, son of Nathan
"Over the Host" (Army)	Benaiah, son of Jehoiada
"Over the Tribute" (Forced Labor)	Adoniram, son of Abda
"Over the Officers"	Azariah, son of Nathan
"Over the Household"	Ahishar

* Based on 1 Kin. 4:1–6

Figure 26

Royal Viziers

King	Vizier	Reference
United Monarchy		
Solomon	Ahishar	1 Kin. 4:6
Israel		
Elah	Arza	1 Kin. 16:9
Ahab	Obadiah	1 Kin. 18:3
Jehoram	(Unnamed)	2 Kin. 10:5
Judah		
Uzziah	Jotham	2 Kin. 15:5
Hezekiah	Eliakim	2 Kin. 18:18, 37; 19:2

Figure 27

being God's lands, since He was the real King of the nation (cf. Lev. 25:23; Deut. 7:6). During Solomon's reign the royal estates, the royal fortresses, and the Levitical cities were closely tied together. The Levites were servants of the kingdom as much as they were servants of the priesthood. This may be why David and Solomon used Levites as civil servants. The kings naturally associated their estates and fortresses with the Levitical lands (Num. 35:1–8). Thus the Levitical lands were also under the vizier's supervision.

The vizier's office can be compared to the Egyptian office of vizier—though under Solomon this official had far less power than his Egyptian counterpart, who was more of a prime minister. He is named toward the bottom of the list of Solomon's court officials (cf. 1 Kin. 4:6), and there is no reference to his father.

2. The Queen Mother. Solomon was the first of Israel's kings to include a "queen mother" in his administration—Bath-sheba. She received great honor and sat at his right hand (1 Kings 2:19). Her power was not simply that of a mother over her son; because of her experience, she was considered an important advisor.

A similar office existed among the Hittites and among the people of Ugarit. But in these lands the queen mother often became more active in political affairs.

3. Centralized Government. Solomon's changes in the administrative cabinet served to centralize his government. He structured the district governments in a hierarchy of power, stemming from the power of the king.

Solomon introduced this system sometime during the second half of his reign. Two of the districts were governed by his sons-in-law, Ben-Abinadab and Ahimaaz (1 Kin. 4:11, 15). The empire was divided into the following districts:

(1) the house of Joseph
(2–5) former Canaanite territories
(6–7) conquered Transjordan territories
(8–10) the northern tribes
(11) Benjamin
(12) Gad (facing Benjamin on the other side of the Jordan).

These districts are listed in 1 Kings 4:1–19.

Solomon retained most of the old tribal boundaries, only making changes for economic or political reasons. Perhaps his division of districts reflected his suspicion of the northern tribes and was an effort to break up any potentially hostile situations. As a result, districts Three (Sharon and others) and Eleven (Benjamin) gained areas formerly belonging

ISRAEL'S GOVERNMENT

JUDEAN ROYAL SEALS. *These royal seals were stamped on jar handles in the eighth or seventh centuries B.C. to mark the property of the king. The jar on the top is stamped "Socoh," the one to the bottom reads "Ziph." Some scholars believe royal potteries were located at these cities, and the seal impressions may indicate that the size or volume of the jar was guaranteed by the government.*

to the house of Joseph, while district One (Joseph) kept the remaining territory. Ephraim and Manasseh had already claimed the Canaanite lands (cf. Judg. 1). So the Transjordan, which had been one administrative district under David, became two districts under Solomon. Solomon may also have made these divisions in order to distribute the tax burden more equally among the 12 tribes.

Solomon's new system eroded the administrative independence of the tribes. He now had a central government, with a local administrative staff appointed by the central government. Israel was no longer a kingdom; it had become an empire.

4. Policy toward the Canaanites. As for the areas where Canaanites still lived, Solomon's policy was to tie them directly to the palace, rather than allowing the Israelite tribes to have jurisdiction over them. Canaanite leaders were given new positions in Solomon's government. With few exceptions, these men were placed over former Canaanite districts (cf. Gen. 10:6–20). These Canaanite prefects or governors were responsible for the

collection of taxes and the payment of tribute. Probably Solomon kept the Canaanite districts that had existed during the reign of David (1 Kin. 5:1; 10:15).

5. The Central Province. The tribe of Judah does not appear as one of Solomon's 12 districts. Apparently this territory formed a central province, which itself was divided into 12 sections. The Septuagint mentions a "governor of the land" at the end of the list of Solomon's districts. In neighboring Assyria, the term "the land" referred to the central province in their civil administration. In the Assyrian form of government, the central province was not considered part of the overall administrative system of government; it was ruled directly from the palace. Perhaps Solomon's structure followed Assyria's.

E. The Divided Kingdom. The Bible does not tell us very much about the administrative structures of the two divided kingdoms, Israel and Judah. We suppose that the structures of Solomon's time were carried over into both kingdoms.

1. Cabinet Officials. We have some evidence that the kings of Israel and Judah continued to use the offices of recorder, scribe, vizier, and others. For example, under King Hezekiah the recorder Joah went to negotiate with officials of the invading Assyrian king, Sennacherib (2 Kin. 18:18, 27; Is. 36:3, 22). Another man named Joah was the recorder under King Josiah and was one of the three officials responsible for repairing the temple (2 Chr. 34:8).

When King Jehoash of Judah rebuilt the temple, he entrusted his scribe and high priest with the control of the money (2 Kin. 12:10–11). King Hezekiah sent his scribe Shebna with the elders of the priests and his vizier Eliakim to meet Sennacherib's envoy and later to confer with the prophet Isaiah (2 Kin. 19:2). Under King Josiah, Shaphan the scribe joined Joah the recorder and Maaseiah the governor of the city of Jerusalem in restoring the book of the Law to the temple (2 Chr. 34:8–21).

The office of vizier became more important with the passage of time. In Hezekiah's day, Shebna and his successor Eliakim had great power. Notice how Isaiah describes the office when he predicts that Eliakim will replace Shebna: "And I will clothe him with thy robe, and strengthen him with thy girdle, and I will commit thy government into his hand: and he shall be a father to the inhabitants of

ISRAEL'S GOVERNMENT

KING DARIUS. *This scene from a Grecian vase shows King Darius of Persia (reign 522–486 B.C.) with the symbols of his royal office—the crown, the scepter (in his right hand), and the mace (on his lap). A bodyguard or messenger is giving a report to the king.*

Scripture mentions "the governor of the city" of Samaria and Jerusalem (1 Kin. 22:26; 2 Kin. 23:8; 2 Chr. 18:25).

Early in Israel's history Abimelech appointed a governor over Shechem (Judg. 9:29–30). Much later Ahab ordered Amon, the governor of Samaria, to imprison the prophet Micaiah (1 Kin. 22:26). In Jehu's day, the governor of Samaria ("he that was over the city"), the vizier ("he that was over the house"), the elders, and the "bringers-up of the children" offered their support and loyalty to him (2 Kin. 10:5). Maaseiah administered Jerusalem under King Josiah (2 Chr. 34:8). In Jezebel's plotting to get Naboth's vineyard, she dealt with the elders and the nobles of the city (1 Kin. 21:8–11). We have no evidence of governors in the Northern Kingdom, except for the capital city of Samaria.

Eunuchs were more prominent in the divided monarchy than at previous times. Jeremiah lists them as men of rank with princes and priests (Jer. 34:19). Earlier, such men took Ahab's message to the prophet Micaiah, summoning him to appear before the king (1 Kin. 22:9). These "officers" or eunuchs restored the Shunammite's goods (2 Kin. 8:6). They were also among those who went into the Babylonian Captivity under Jehoiakim (2 Kin. 24:12; Jer. 29:2), having led the men of Israel in fighting against the Babylonians at the capture of Jerusalem (2 Kin. 25:19; Jer. 52:25).

2. Queen Mothers. We find mention of two queen mothers in the divided kingdom. Maakah misused her office and was deposed by King Asa (1 Kin. 15:13), and Athaliah later took control of the nation (2 Kin. 11:1–16).

3. Minor Officials. In light of the Scripture evidence that cabinet offices continued into this period, we may safely assume that priest administrators, military heads, administrators over local districts, and other minor officials continued in each kingdom.

A new minor official who appears in the divided monarchy is the "king's son." He appears to have been some kind of policeman and did not hold high rank in the governmental structure (cf. 1 Kin. 22:26–27; 2 Chr. 18:25). Perhaps the title indicates that a king's son originally held this office.

IV. Summary. The government of the nation of Israel began with a theocracy in the wilderness where Israel was a religious community ruled by God with a system of tribal

Jerusalem, and to the house of Judah. And the key of the house of David will I lay upon his shoulder; so shall he open, and none shall shut; and he shall shut, and none shall open" (Is. 22:21–22).

Adoram, the superintendent of forced labor, continued from David's and Solomon's reigns into the time of Rehoboam. In fact, Rehoboam arrogantly sent Adoram to the northern tribes to assert his rule over them; but they showed their contempt for the king of Judah by stoning Adoram (Hadoram) to death (1 Kin. 12:18; 2 Chr. 10:18). The office disappeared after the division of the two kingdoms. But in later days Asa forced some men to fortify Geba and Mizpah (1 Kin. 15:22) and Jeremiah denounced King Jehoiakim for forcing his people to build his palace (Jer. 22:13).

During the period of the divided kingdom the capital cities—Jerusalem and Samaria—were under a governor as well as the king. In other Near Eastern countries capital cities were administered by a governor. For example, the governor of the central administrative town of Ugarit had authority over the entire surrounding territory.

ISRAEL'S GOVERNMENT

courts. Moses was chief executive over a staff of judges who gave decisions in disputes and apparently served as leaders in battle.

The theocracy in Canaan remained simple, with its civil government centered in the cities where elder-judges settled disputes. Later God raised up another type of judge to deliver the Israelites from their oppressors.

The monarchy in Israel became centralized and more complex. The rule by Kings Saul, David, and Solomon eventually resulted in division of the nation.

Local administration in the divided kingdoms was adjusted from time to time by various reforms and changes of government. But the elders (or judges) still continued as the primary government officials responsible for the judicial processes and local civil needs. This best explains how the returning exiles were able to assume so quickly a form of government that was patterned after the pre-kingdom administrative structure.

MONEY AND ECONOMICS

The functions of money, finance, and economics may seem very difficult to understand. Actually, they are not. *Money* means anything of value that can be easily transported and exchanged. Coins, currency, and jewels are forms of money. *Finance* is the management of money. *Economics* is the study of what money does.

The Bible contains some interesting sidelights on the development of money. It even gives basic principles for its use and management.

I. DIVINE OWNERSHIP

II. MONEY
    A. Barter
    B. Pieces of Metal
    C. Coinage
        1. In the Old Testament
        2. In the New Testament
        3. In the Roman Era

III. FINANCE AND ECONOMICS
    A. The Tithe
    B. Property Rights
    C. Care of the Poor
    D. Solomon's Reign: An Era of High Finance
    E. The Divided Kingdom
    F. The New Testament Era
        1. The Economic Teachings of Jesus
        2. The Apostles' Principles

I. Divine Ownership. God owns everything! He owns the entire universe; everything that was, and is, and may become. "The earth is the LORD'S, and the fullness thereof; the world, and they that dwell therein" (Ps. 24:1). He rules over all: "Say among the heathen that the LORD reigneth: the world also shall be established that it shall not be moved: he shall judge the people righteously" (Ps. 96:10).

When God gave the Israelites the land of Canaan as an inheritance, He said: "The land shall not be sold forever: for the land is mine; for ye are strangers and sojourners with me" (cf. Ex. 15:17–18; Lev. 25:23). This made them *stewards* or caretakers of the land. Ever after, the people of Israel were expected to use their possessions as a scared trust. This understanding applied to their property, their money, and every-

thing else that they treasured. All belonged to God.

We see the Israelites speak of divine ownership from time to time throughout their history. But we should remember that it was always in the background of their thinking. Jesus spoke directly to this issue in many of His sermons.

II. Money. In the distant past, there were no paper money or coins. People *bartered*—in other words, they traded one thing of value for another. The precious metals gold, silver, and copper were often traded. Later, these metals were made into standard coins. The Bible does not tell us about the steps of this development. Rather, it shows that both systems of trade—barter and coinage—were in use about the same time.

A. Barter. Abram's wealth was counted in cattle, camels, other livestock, servants, silver, and gold (Gen. 13:2; 24:35). Cattle were a common form of money. They were a unit of trade especially well suited to Abram's way of life, for "not knowing whither he went," he followed the Lord's directions (Heb. 11:8). Pharaoh "entreated Abram well" because he believed that Abram's wife was actually his beautiful "sister." Pharaoh gave him sheep, oxen, donkeys, camels, and male and female servants (Gen. 12:14–16). Later, in an identical situation Abram (now called Abraham) again declared his wife Sarai (now called Sarah) to be his sister. Abimelech of Gerar, after learning the deception, returned Sarah to her husband and gave him sheep, oxen, and male and female slaves as an indemnity. In addition he gave Abraham "a thousand pieces of silver" (Gen. 17:5, 15; 20:14–16).

Jacob worked 14 years to pay the dowry for his two wives; he acquired a fortune in cattle, sheep, goats, camels, and donkeys by further labor (Gen. 29:30). King Mesha of Moab was a sheep breeder who paid tribute to Jehoram, the king of Israel—100,000 lambs and the wool of 100,000 rams annually (2 Kin. 3:4). Solomon traded 20,000 kors of crushed wheat, 20,000 kors of barley, 20,000 baths of wine, and 20,000 baths of oil annually for cedar, cypress, and algum timber from Lebanon (2 Chr. 2:10). The governors of Judah

MONEY AND ECONOMICS

TABLE OF MEASURES. *These ancient tables of measure are from Nippur, a city of Babylonia founded about 4000 B.C. The table at top lists measures of surface and length and weights; the table at bottom shows measures of capacity.*

before Nehemiah taxed the people in "bread and wine, beside forty shekels of silver" (Neh. 5:15).

B. Pieces of Metal. The word *money* appears in the King James Version of the Old Testament 112 times as the translation of the Hebrew word for silver. (The same word refers 287 times to objects made of silver.) Silver was a common unit of trade in ancient Israel. Merchants often exchanged small pieces of the metal to cinch a deal, as in the case of Jacob's dowry.

In the New Testament the Greek word for silver is translated 11 times as *money,* 9 times

as *pieces of silver,* and 3 times as a general indication of material wealth.

The value of the silver pieces was determined by weight. When Abraham bought the cave of Machpelah he "weighed to Ephron the silver, which he had named in the audience of the sons of Heth, four hundred shekels of silver, current money with the merchant" (Gen. 23:16). This transaction would have been made at the gate of the city, in the presence of witnesses. Jeremiah also weighed out the price of the land he bought from his relative and signed and sealed the deed (Jer. 32:9–10). David paid 50 shekels of silver to Araunah (Ornan) the Jebusite for his threshing floor, his oxen, and the instruments of threshing to make a sacrifice to the Lord (2 Sam. 24:24; cf. 1 Chr. 21:25). Likewise, the Queen of Sheba gave Solomon a gift of 120 talents of gold (1 Kin. 10:10).

Many kings required their subjects to pay an annual levy of silver or gold. For example, Solomon had an income of 666 talents of gold (1 Kin. 10:14–15). Hezekiah was forced to pay Sennacherib 300 talents of silver and 30 talents of gold (2 Kin. 18:14).

Jacob paid Hamor 100 *qesitah* of silver for a piece of land at Shechem (Gen. 33:19; Josh. 24:32). The Hebrew root for this word is unknown today; the Septuagint translates it "lamb." Perhaps this was the shape of the weight used in weighing out the silver; or perhaps the unit was a quantity of silver equal to the price of a lamb. Whatever it may have been, the name indicates that the biblical writers were thinking of the relative value of goods though the medium was silver.

C. Coinage. Archaeologists have found many ancient coins and coin inscriptions that show us how early coinage appeared. A gold talent and two gold half-talents were found in a twelfth-century grave at Salamis, Cyprus. Egyptian wall paintings depict Cretans and Syrians offering copper ingots in tribute to Pharaoh Thutmose III (1501–1447 B.C.). Many coins have been unearthed in the ruins of Israelite towns.

If we carefully examine Scripture, we can see the transition from barter to coinage. Joseph was sold for "twenty pieces of silver" to Ishmaelite traders (Gen. 37:28). This meant that the price was 20 shekels of silver by weight. The *shekel* was a weight unit in the payment of silver; the word was so common that it was often omitted. An example of this omission is when Scripture says that the sons

MONEY AND ECONOMICS

JEWISH COIN. *This silver coin from the fourth century* B.C. *shows a bearded male figure seated on a winged wheel, his right hand wrapped in his garment and his left holding a hawk. Hebrew characters on the coin can be read as either "Jehovah" or "Judea," depending on how the last letter is interpreted.*

of Jacob took "money" (silver) to buy grain in Egypt (Gen. 42:25, 27).

Standard coins gradually replaced these standard units of weight. The early Egyptians, Semites, and Hittites shaped gold and silver into bars, rings, and rounded nodules for convenience of exchange.

In the area of the Aegean Sea, a unit called a *talent* that had the value of an ox became the standard. These ox-talents were pellets or rings of gold weighing 8.5 grams (.29 oz.). A copper ingot of the same value weighed 25.5 kg. (60 lbs.).

The story of Joseph indicates that the patriarchs used silver pieces of a shekel weight. For this reason, Achan had no difficulty knowing the value of the gold and silver he stole from the spoil of Jericho (Josh. 7:21).

God decreed that "the shekel of the sanctuary" must be 20 gerahs (Num. 3:47). Since God was the true King, His priests and prophets were guardians of the money standards. "Ye shall do no unrighteousness in judgment, in meteyard, in weight or in measure," wrote Moses. "Just balances, just weights, a just ephah, and a just hin, shall ye have" (Lev. 19:35, 36a).

Honesty in weights and measures was even a part of Israel's law of holiness. The use of different weights (some true and some false) was absolutely forbidden in both the Law and the Prophets (cf. Deut. 25:13–16;

Prov. 11:1; 20:10; Hos. 12:7; Amos 8:5; Mic. 6:10–11).

The accompanying chart (*see* p. 331) shows approximate equivalents of the weights and measures used in Old Testament times. Ezekiel tells us the *bath* (liquid) and the *ephah* (dry) are equal in size (45:11–14).

For the return of his unfaithful wife, Hosea had to pay a homer and a lethech of barley (Hosea 3:2). Solomon bought lumber from Hiram for thousands of cors (kors) of grain and thousands of baths of oil and wine.

Religious fees also had to be paid; this amount was determined by the ritual service performed. For example, a man who had been cleansed of leprosy was required to pay two male lambs, a ewe, an ephah of fine flour, and a log of oil (Lev. 14:19). If a man dedicated himself to the Lord in a vow, the priest charged him according to his age. Males between 20 and 60 paid 50 shekels; those over 60 paid 15; those between 5 and 20 paid 20; and those between one month and 5 years paid the reduced rate of 5 shekels. Women between 20 and 60 were charged 30 shekels. Those above 60 were charged 10 shekels. Those from 5 to 20 had to raise 10 shekels; and those from one month to 5 were let off for 3 shekels (Lev. 27:2–9).

The very poor were charged according to what the priest thought they could pay. Such persons would be charged according to the value of their labor. Indeed, he might serve out his payment by working in the tabernacle under the priests (Lev. 27:2–9).

These passages illustrate why we cannot know when Israel changed from barter measurements to standard coinage. The earliest coins were named for the standard barter measures they represented. Often the Bible uses these terms without saying whether or not they refer to coins.

1. In the Old Testament. The first statement in the Old Testament that explicitly

EARLY COIN. *A fine example of one of the earliest coins, this electrum piece from Lydia dates back to the seventh century* B.C. *Electrum is an alloy of gold and silver.*

Thirty Pieces of Silver

One of the most infamous stories of the Bible is that of Judas Iscariot, the disciple who betrayed Christ for 30 pieces of silver. While it is difficult to determine exactly what 30 pieces of silver was worth, we know it was not a fortune.

The Roman *denarius,* was the most common coin used during Jesus' day. Struck from silver, this coin bore an imprint with the head of the emperor. Because of this, the Jewish people were not allowed to use coins as offerings in religious services; they converted their coins to pieces of silver. Money changers converted the *denarius* or *shekel* to silver for a fee of 12 percent.

The denarius would be worth about 44 cents in today's market, according to its silver weight and content. But one denarius equaled a day's wages of a common laborer at that time, so it had significant buying power. Even so, by this estimate we find that Judas betrayed Christ for a month's salary—hardly a fortune.

The Book of Zechariah prophesied that such an amount would be paid for the Messiah (Zech. 11:12). When Judas accepted 30 pieces of silver for the life of Christ, he fulfilled the prophecy (Matt. 26:15). The amount was also the typical price of a slave or servant during that time.

---

refers to coins is in regard to the 20 gold bowls worth 1,000 "drams" (darics), which Ezra carried to Jerusalem in 458 B.C. (Ezra 8:27). The *daric* was a Persian gold coin that derived its name from Darius I (522–486 B.C.). It weighed 8.4 grams (0.3 oz.), just a little over a shekel.

Archaeologists believe that the kings of Lydia were the first to coin money; they began doing this in the seventh or sixth century B.C. The Persians adopted coinage from the Lydians when they conquered Asia Minor. Thus the value of freewill offerings given for the rebuilding of the temple in 537 B.C. is said to have been 61,000 darics (Ezra 2:69). The recorded value of the gold contributed for the temple in David's time is also given in darics (1 Chron. 29:7); apparently a later historian inserted this information, giving the value of the contribution in terms of the currency used after the Exile.

Archaeologists have found some coins with the marking *YHD* (Judah), indicating that the Persian court authorized their production in that province. These coins are of Greek style, indicating that they were made by Persian governors; the Jews would have considered it idolatrous to mint coins stamped with the images of their rulers. The Bible does not mention these coins.

The Maccabean kings of Judea issued coins after 138 B.C., when the Seleucids granted them full sovereignty. The first Maccabean coins were silver; but since silver coinage was considered an exclusive privilege of the Roman emperor, later coins were made of copper. The first coin issued under this arrangement celebrated "Jerusalem the Holy." It bore

the emblem of a chalice on the face and a three-branched pomegranate on the reverse. These Jewish coins generally used symbols from nature or depicted articles used in the tabernacle and temple. Some of these copper coins were still in circulation in New Testament times.

2. In the New Testament. In New Testament times, the silver coin of Tyre and Sidon was called the "temple coin." It was widely known for its pure metal. But the Roman *denarius* quickly superseded all silver coins of the same value. A *denarius* was a soldier's daily wage and worth about 44 cents today. It was the wage mentioned in the parable of the laborers in the vineyard (Matt. 20:9–10, 13). This coin was also used to pay tribute to the emperor. Jesus recognized it as being Caesar's due (Matt. 22:19–21).

The Greek silver coin of the same value was the *drachma.* This was probably the coin in the parable of the lost coin (Luke 15:8).

As we have already noted, the Greek word for *silver* was frequently used for money. Jesus told His disciples to take no "money" (silver) with them when He sent them out two by two (Luke 9:3). Judas was paid 30 "pieces of silver" to betray Jesus (Matt. 26:15; 27:3, 5. These references cite Zechariah 11:12–13, which did not refer specifically to coins.)

One of the most famous givers in the New Testament was the poor widow (Mark 12:41–44). She dropped two *lepta,* which equaled the value of a *kodrantēs,* into the temple treasury. The *lepton* was first minted by the Maccabees while the *kodrantēs* was the tiniest Roman copper coin. The *kodrantēs* was about one-sixteenth of a soldier's daily pay.

MONEY AND ECONOMICS

SILVER DRACHMA. *Bearing the likeness of Alexander, this silver coin was found at the treasury of Persepolis. Coinage first appeared in Asia Minor in the seventh or sixth century B.C.*

Yet the widow's gift prompted Jesus' highest praise: "Verily I say unto you, That this poor widow hath cast more in, than all they which have cast into the treasury: For all they did cast in of their abundance; but she of her want did cast in all that she had, even all her living" (Mark 12:43b–44).

When the temple tax collector in Capernaum asked the disciples of Jesus if He paid the two-drachma tax, Jesus sent Peter to catch a fish, in whose mouth he found a coin. This coin was a *stater*—a four-drachma piece. It was sufficient to pay the tax for both of them.

Asked whether it was lawful to pay tribute to Caesar, Jesus said: "Show me the tribute money" (Matt. 22:19). The tax coin or *denarius* was shown to Him. It had the image of the emperor on its face.

3. In the Roman Era. Many other coins that are not mentioned in the New Testament still survive from the Roman era. Some of these bear witness to the history of the Jewish people. An example of this is a coin bearing the inscription of "Herod the King," or Herod the Great. This king's soldiers killed all the male babies in Bethlehem under two years of age, to make sure they eliminated the One who was "born King of the Jews" (Matt. 2:2–16).

Some coins bear the inscription *Herod Ethnarch,* referring to Archelaus, who succeeded his father without the title of king. When Archelaus was deposed and banished, Judea became a Roman province ruled by procurators appointed by Rome.

Herod Antipas built Tiberias, which became the capital of the Roman province of Galilee shortly before Jesus began His ministry. A coin bears his portrait and title on the face, and the inscription *Tiberias* on the reverse. Herod

Antipas also beheaded John the Baptist (Luke 9:7, 9) and participated in the trial of Jesus (23:8–12).

Herod Agrippa I minted a coin bearing his portrait with the inscription, "King Agrippa the Great, friend of Caesar." Agrippa persecuted the church; he beheaded James and imprisoned Peter. Luke recorded his agonizing death under the judgment of God. (Agrippa's officials minted another coin in Caesarea to mark the great prize fights, during which he suddenly fell ill.)

Some scholars have disputed Paul's reference to a Roman official called the *anthupatos* on the island of Cyprus (Acts 13:7). But a coin from Cyprus bears the head and superscription of Claudius Caesar on the face, and on the reverse the inscription, *Commenius Proculus anthupatos.* Paul visited Cyprus during the reign of Claudius.

Many other coins support the disputed accuracy of Luke. They confirm the existence of the *Asiarchs* or "chief (people) of Asia," who were listed among Paul's friends in Ephesus (Acts 19:31). Coins also confirm the fact that Philippi was a Roman colony and the chief city of Macedonia (Acts 16:12), and that Tarsus was "no mean city" (21:39).

III. Finance and Economics. The principles that control economics—the production, distribution, and consumption of the material means of satisfying human desires—are the same as those that direct finance, the management of an enterprise. The Bible provides useful guidance on all of these issues.

In God's first appearance to man, He let man know that the earth was good and delightful, and it was to be used to meet his

COIN OF VESPASIAN. *A mourning Jew and Jewess flank a palm tree (symbol of Judea) on the reverse of this coin bearing the likeness of Emperor Vespasian. Vespasian and his son Titus conquered Judea in A.D. 70, and the coin was struck in honor of their victory.*

needs (Gen. 1:29). But man's enjoyment of life should come from God, not from the things God had made! God Himself was to be the focus of man's desire and attention.

A. The Tithe. When he returned from destroying the Mesopotamian kings, Abraham gave Melchizedek the priest a tenth of the spoil (Gen. 14:20). This was his confession that God was his Lord, the Possessor of heaven and earth, and the Giver of victory (14:19).

Jacob recognized the same responsibility. He vowed to give God a tithe of all that he received if God would protect him in this journey and return him to his land. This humble confession of dependence on God stands against the proud boast, ". . . My power, and the might of mine hand hath gotten me this wealth" (Deut. 8:17; cf. Dan. 4:30). There was no middle road between these paths.

The giving of a tithe was man's acknowledgment that he is a steward of God's creation. The Old Testament clearly demonstrates that every spiritual relationship of man is expressed in some material way. Rites of worship gave the Israelites a way to confess the operation of their faith in every sphere—not the least of which was the economic sphere.

Israel came out of Egypt by faith in the promises of God. God then claimed the firstborn of Israel (Ex. 13:11–16) and commanded that they be redeemed by the payment of five shekels per male child (Num. 3:46–47). This token payment reminded the people of Israel that they belonged to the Lord; they were not their own (cf. 1 Cor. 6:19–20).

God brought the Israelites into the land promised their fathers (Ex. 6:8), where He would rule over them forever (15:17–18). God would drive out the inhabitants and give the land to them (Ex. 23:28–30). In return, they would acknowledge His bounty by offering to Him the firstborn of all clean animals and the first ripe grain and fruits, at the place He would choose (Deut. 12:11–12, 17–18). There they would bring annual tithes of the fruits of the ground and of the flock (Deut. 26:1–12).

When the Israelites offered their tithes, they confessed God's providence to their forefathers, His deliverance in their time of need, His redemption of them from oppression, and His gift of the land of Canaan (Deut. 26:5–9). They invited the Levites, the poor, the widows, and the orphans of their local community to join them at the central sanctuary as they made these offerings to the Lord. No man could appear at a feast empty-handed. The Law required each man to bring an offering proportionate to the way he had been blessed (Deut. 16:10, 17). (*See also* "Worship Rituals.")

Notice the economic dimension of Israel's worship. They offered the Lord a large part of their time; they presented the first fruits of their grain and livestock; they came to the feasts with offerings and tithes; they made freewill offerings of their lives and property; and they gave liberally for the building of the tabernacle and temple. When they returned with booty taken in battle, they set aside a portion for the Lord and Levites before dividing it among themselves (Num. 31:26–54). Their devotion to God cost them the best of all they had (cf. 2 Sam. 24:24). The tithe clearly expressed this costly devotion.

B. Property Rights. Every family received a tract of land as a perpetual inheritance. This land was a trust from the Lord. It enabled every family to produce enough for their own needs and share with their neighbors—especially the poor and strangers living among them. The land remained the Lord's (Lev. 25:23), although He gave each family the right to produce food and clothing from it. (*See* "Agriculture"; "Laws and Statutes.")

The Israelites were to exercise stewardship of the land. They were to use the land and its products unselfishly for those in need around them. Even the passer-by on the road was free to gather grain or fruit to satisfy his hunger (Deut. 23:24–25). They were to be gracious and bountiful to others, just as God had been bountiful to them.

C. Care of the Poor. The welfare of the individual was primarily the responsibility of the family. The closest male relative, known as the kinsman-redeemer, was the protector of the individual. He was to "avenge his blood" and redeem his kinsman from indebtedness (Num. 35:12, 19; Lev. 24—26).

The most notable example of the kinsman-redeemer was Boaz, who bought from Naomi all that had belonged to her husband and married her widowed daughter-in-law, Ruth. Thus Naomi was no longer obligated to Ruth and Boaz for her daily provision. Her property was eventually given to the child of Ruth, the heir of Naomi's son, Mahlon. (*See also* "Marriage and Divorce.")

Any crops that grew during the sabbatical year and the Year of Jubilee were set aside for the poor to gather. This made the poor respon-

MONEY AND ECONOMICS

TABLE OF WEIGHTS AND MEASURES**

| | Equivalents (approx.) | |
UNIT	Metric	English
*UNITS OF WEIGHT		
bekah, $^1/_2$ shekel	1.9 gram	.067 oz
shekel, 20 gerahs	3.8 gram	.134 oz
maneh, 50 shekels	.57 kg	$1^1/_4$ lbs
talent, 3000 shekels	34.02 kg	75 lbs
UNITS OF VOLUME (LIQUID)		
log	.32 liter	.67 pt
hin	6.5 liter	1.7 gal
bath, ephah, $^1/_{10}$ homer	37 liter	10 gal
cor (kor), homer, 10 baths	370 liter	100 gal
UNITS OF VOLUME (DRY)		
omer, $^1/_{10}$ ephah	4 liter	0.45 pk
ephah, $^1/_{10}$ homer	40 liter	1.1 bu
lethech, $^1/_2$ homer	200 liter	$5^1/_2$ bu
cor (kor), homer, 10 baths	400 liter	11 bu
cab (kab)	2.2 liter	2 qt

* Tables for gold and silver differed, as did the actual weights of light or normal shekels.
** Based on *Collier's Encyclopedia,* Vol. 23, ed. by William D. Halsey (New York: Crowell-Collier Publishing Company, 1965), p. 394.

Figure 28

sible to gather their own grain. Thus they preserved their personal dignity and self-respect.

The Law called upon the people in each community to take personal interest in the poor and give them individual encouragement. The third-year tithe was to be stored for the poor of the community, so that they "shall eat and be satisfied; that the LORD thy God may bless thee in all the work of thine hand which thou doest" (Deut. 14:29b; cf. 12:11–12; 26:1–19). Thus the Jewish congregation showed interest in the needy. This practice also helped to prevent division between the comfortable middle-class farmer and the gleaning poor.

The Law told individuals how to deal with neighbors in progressive stages of poverty (Lev. 25:35–43). If a poor man lost all sense of security, his neighbor was to treat him with hospitality, as if he were a stranger or sojourner (Lev. 25:23). If a poor man needed to borrow money, he was not expected to pay interest or return more goods than he borrowed. If the poor man became so indebted that he had to sell himself as a bond servant, he was to be treated as a hired servant. (*See* "Laws and

Statutes.") He remained a free man (cf. Deut. 15:18), and in the Year of Jubilee he would be freed. Further, the master was obligated to share with him grain, livestock, and wine (Deut. 15:14).

The Law calls the poor man "your brother" (Lev. 25:35, 39). He was a fellow Israelite; but more importantly, he was a brother in God's covenant. For this reason, an Israelite was not to begrudge the bond servant his freedom nor the goods he gave him.

The fourth commandment required a man to let his servants rest on the Sabbath, just as he refreshed himself. He was to pay his hired servants at the end of the day (Lev. 19:13).

The Lord promised that if Israel faithfully obeyed His commandments, there would be no poor in the land because He would bless them (Deut. 15:1–5). But notice the condition of the promise: "There shall be no poor among you; for the LORD shall greatly bless thee . . . Only if thou carefully hearken unto the voice of the LORD thy God" (Deut. 15:4–5). If God's people listened, they would be so prosperous that they would lend their wealth to many nations (15:6).

MONEY AND ECONOMICS

STONE SHEKEL WEIGHTS. *These Israelite stone weights were used to determine the value of gold and silver. The smaller stone equals the weight of one shekel; the larger equals four shekels. Archaeologists have discovered several stones of this type, most dating from the seventh century B.C.*

D. Solomon's Reign: An Era of High Finance. Solomon engaged in an extensive building program. This work demanded a complex organization of men, the gathering of imported building materials, and the accumulation of wealth.

At the beginning of his reign, Solomon loved the Lord and walked in His statutes (1 Kin. 3:3). In response to his request, God gave him great wisdom (1 Kin. 4:29–30). With this wisdom, Solomon organized his people, made international covenants for materials, collected wealth, and pursued his building programs. He gave his most careful attention to the building and dedication of the temple, for that was the central event of his life.

Solomon began by making a mutual trade agreement with Hiram (Huram), king of Tyre, to buy cypress, cedar, and algum lumber. He paid for it with wheat, barley, oil, and wine (1 Kin. 5:2–12; 2 Chr. 2:3–10). Solomon drafted 30,000 woodcutters from Israel and sent 10,000 of these men to Lebanon. They worked on a regular schedule: one month in Lebanon and two months at home.

Needing more workers, Solomon made slaves out of the Canaanites who remained in Israel. Of these, 70,000 worked in transportation, 80,000 were stone cutters, and 3,600 were overseers.

As Solomon's kingdom expanded, he demanded tribute from the kings of the territories he conquered (2 Chr. 9:13). Solomon also collected money from merchants who used Israel's trade routes (9:14).

Solomon's merchants bought chariots from Egypt and sold them to the kings of the Hittites and Syria (1 Kin. 10:28–29). They built a fleet of ships, manned them with Israelite sailors and the sailors of Hiram, and sent them to Ophir. These men returned with 420 talents of gold. From sources other than the Bible we learn that Solomon conducted a large mining and smelting enterprise in the Sinai Desert. As a result, silver became common in Jerusalem (1 Kin. 10:27; 2 Chr. 9:20, 27).

By the end of his life, Solomon had turned his heart away from the Lord. His extravagant living soon brought disaster to the realm. Indeed, 10 tribes broke away from Rehoboam to form the kingdom of Israel under Jeroboam (1 Kings 12:16–24).

The Bible says nothing about the care of the poor under Solomon's reign, nor about the sabbatical year or the Year of Jubilee.

In one generation, the agrarian economy of Israel had become a highly organized state machine. By concentrating the control of labor and the means of production in the hands of a government, Solomon sowed seeds of discontent among his people.

Solomon controlled kingdoms from the Euphrates to the Nile. He saw an end to the devastating wars of David's rule. But he achieved only a meager part of the promised reign of righteousness and peace (Ps. 72).

E. The Divided Kingdom. The economy of united Israel depended upon its agriculture and its control of the trade routes. But during the period of the divided kingdom, Syria became strong and took from Israel all the pasture lands east of the Jordan and the plain of Galilee and Jezreel. To Jehoahaz, Syria left but a little circle of land around Samaria. Indeed, Israel was reduced to poverty and near collapse (2 Kin. 13:3, 22; 14:26).

But by the time Jeroboam II ascended the throne, God had weakened Syria internally. The Syrian kings were worried by the rise of Assyria. This enabled Jeroboam to restore Israel's former borders (2 Kin. 14:25–26). By recovering its pasture and grain lands and regaining control of the trade routes, he made Israel prosperous once more.

MONEY AND ECONOMICS

But the new wealth was concentrated in the hands of a few rich people, who lived in luxury and oppressed the poor (Hos. 12:7–8; Amos 2:7–8; 4:1–7, 11; 8:4–6; Mic. 2:1–2). Prophets denounced the rulers and merchants for enriching themselves at the expense of the helpless poor. They predicted that the kingdom would crumble and fall before the powerful Assyrian armies.

By God's grace, the kingdom of Judah continued 150 years longer than the Northern Kingdom of Israel. But Judah's kings frequently broke their loyalty to the Lord by making treaties with pagan powers. They lost God's promised blessings, weakened their strategic position, and brought military destruction on themselves (cf. 2 Kin. 16:7–9; 2 Chr. 16:1–10; 2 Chr. 28:20). Prophets denounced these elders of Judah and princes of the house of David for their injustice and oppression of the poor (Is. 3:13–14; 10:1–4; Mic. 2:1–2; Jer. 22:1–5).

God had promised Moses that He would bless the land if Israel was obedient. But Israel was not obedient. The rulers no longer held the land in trust for the welfare of the people. Rather, they were using their power to enrich and glorify themselves. They perverted the entire economic system.

The prophets believed the divided kingdom was doomed. But they believed the Lord would raise up another David who would shepherd the flock in righteousness (Jer. 23:5–6; Ezek. 34:23–25). This new David would proclaim good news to the afflicted and liberty to the captives (Is. 11:4–5; 61:1–3). He would do what the Davidic kings had failed to do (Ps. 72), and would devote the unjust gains of the world to the Lord (Is. 60:1–12; Mic. 4:1–13).

F. The New Testament Era. The New Testament affirmed that God is the final authority over every part of our lives. Jesus and the apostles dealt with money, finance, and economics as areas of privilege and responsibility for the people of God.

1. The Economic Teachings of Jesus. Jesus proclaimed good news to the poor and liberty to the captives (Luke 4:16–19). He called people to demonstrate their single-hearted devotion to God in their economic pursuits (Matt. 6:19–21, 24). With profound simplicity, Jesus pointed out that God clothes the plants with beauty and gives the birds their food—and so will He care for the needs of His people. He insisted that His followers seek to live in righteousness, for then "all these things shall be added unto you" (Matt. 6:33).

When Jesus sent His disciples out to preach, He commanded them to take no money with them. He insisted that each man would be worthy of his support (Matt. 10:1–10). Thus He taught that the children of the Kingdom should support His servants with their material goods. Jesus demonstrated His own devotion to the will of God by refusing to lay up material wealth for Himself (cf. Luke 9:58). He was the King of kings, yet he lived like a pauper in His own world.

Jesus' life demonstrated that every spiritual condition has a material manifestation. For example, Jesus and His disciples had a common treasury; the responsibility for handling it was given to one of the group, Judas Iscariot. The unfaithfulness of Judas in this task (which they dubbed the "least") revealed his unworthiness to be entrusted with true riches (Luke 16:10–11; John 12:6).

Jesus made it clear that His true children distinguish themselves from hypocrites by the way they minister to their brothers who are in need (Matt. 25:31–46). He did not teach some new doctrine of material goods or try to establish a new economic system. He came to affirm the Law of Moses, not to destroy it. The difference lay in who He was: He was the Lord of glory who became a man and lived in perfect obedience to the Law of God.

2. The Apostles' Principles. The apostles reaffirmed that God created all things through Jesus Christ for Himself (Col. 1:16). All things have their origin, continuation, and goal in Him (Rom. 11:36). Believers exist for Him (1 Cor. 8:6); they were purchased to glorify Him with their bodies (6:20).

The apostles taught that, since Christ laid down His life for us, we ought to lay down our lives for the brethren (1 John 3:16). This means that if we have this world's goods and see a brother in need, we should love him in deed by sharing our goods with him (1 John 3:17–18).

The early church displayed its stewardship by placing its goods in the care of the apostles (and later the deacons) for distribution as people had need (Acts 2:44–45; 4:32–37; 6:1–7).

Paul asked the churches of Asia Minor and Greece to share their wealth with the needy church of Jerusalem. He wrote, "For I mean not that other men be eased, and ye burdened" (2 Cor. 8:13).

In other words, Paul made it clear that he

MONEY AND ECONOMICS

STEELYARDS. *These portable balances were designed to be suspended from a hook or from the user's hand. Note the movable weights shaped like the heads of Roman gods. These balances were unearthed at Pompeii; they were buried by an eruption of Mount Vesuvius in* A.D. *79.*

expected each congregation to give according to its ability. God gives abundance to one so that he may supply the want of another (2 Cor. 8:14). This is why Paul was so grateful for the gift he received from the Philippians. It demonstrated their liberality, it was the fruit of their love, and it was pleasing to God (Phil. 4:10–19).

James approved of Christians' engaging in business for profit; but he reminded them that their first concern should be the will of God. Anyone who failed to follow this course, he said, is boastful and arrogant (James 4:12–16). James also rebuked his fellow Christians for failing to pay their laborers adequately. He said that riches acquired through stinginess would rust, and the rust would witness against

them in the day of judgment (James 5:2–4). Paul spoke more positively. He instructed the rich to store for themselves a spiritual treasure by doing good works and sharing their material goods (1 Tim. 6:17–19).

John heard the heavenly choir singing: "Thou art worthy, O Lord, to receive glory and honor and power: for thou hast created all things and for thy pleasure they are and were created" (Rev. 4:11). At the end of John's Book of Revelation we see the kings of the earth bringing their glory to the new heaven and the new earth (Rev. 21:24, 26). Thus the fruits of man's toil would be remembered and celebrated in the presence of God to all eternity.

LANGUAGES AND WRITING

A century ago, many learned scholars doubted that the peoples and languages mentioned in the Bible had ever existed. However, as modern archaeology developed and more of the ancient inscriptions were deciphered, they opened a new view of the historical accuracy of the Bible.

I. KEYS TO DECIPHERMENT
    A. The Rosetta Stone
    B. The Behistun Rock
    C. The Tablets of Ugarit

II. SIGNIFICANT LANGUAGES
    A. Sumerian
    B. Akkadian
    C. Babylonian and Assyrian
    D. Eblaite and Amorite
    E. Ugaritic
    F. Hebrew
    G. Aramaic
    H. Syriac
    I. Greek
    J. Latin

I. Keys to Decipherment. This new understanding rests primarily on our ability to decipher three ancient sources—the Rosetta Stone, the Behistun Rock, and the clay tablets of Ugarit.

A. The Rosetta Stone. Napoleon Bonaparte invaded Egypt in 1798, sending teams of scholars and artists with his army. They surveyed the great ruins of ancient Egypt that were still above ground. While digging a trench near the city of Rosetta, some of Napoleon's soldiers turned up the famous trilingual inscription known as the Rosetta Stone. This marvelous find was written to celebrate the ascension of the Hellenistic ruler Ptolemy Epiphanes to the throne of Egypt on March 27, 196 B.C. The inscription had approximately the same text in three languages and three scripts. The first was hieroglyphic Egyptian, an ancient dialect; the second was demotic Egyptian, a much later dialect; and the third was *koine* Greek in the familiar Greek alphabet.

The stone was taken back to Europe. The Greek text could be read easily enough, but the hieroglyphics were puzzling. Most scholars just considered them to be some sort of se-

cret code or symbols not connected with speech. Many tried to break this code and failed. Then the young scholar Jean François Champollion compared segments of the three inscriptions. He began to recognize that the hieroglyphics were not merely pictographs or symbols, but phonetic characters. He was actually able to identify the names of the famous Egyptian rulers, Rameses and Thutmose. Within a half century, scholars could decipher and read most Middle Kingdom hieroglyphics.

B. The Behistun Rock. The wedge-shaped or *cuneiform* writing introduced by the Sumerians was at first more of a puzzle than the hieroglyphics. European travelers brought back the first cuneiform inscriptions from the

ROSETTA STONE. *The Egyptian priest of Memphis drew up this trilingual stele in honor of Ptolemy (203–181 B.C.). Named for the nearby Egyptian village of Rosetta, the stone was found in 1798 by an officer of Napoleon. The Rosetta Stone's message, written in Greek, Egyptian hieroglyphs ("holy writing"), and Egyptian demotic ("common writing"), provided scholars the key to deciphering the ancient Egyptian language.*

SCARAB OF QUEEN TIY. *This commemorative scarab (beetle-shaped seal) issued in 1422 B.C. records the construction of a pleasure lake for Queen Tiy by Amenhotep III. Some scholars believe that Amenhotep was the pharaoh of the Exodus.*

Middle East as early as the seventeenth century. No one realized it then, but several different languages of the ancient world were recorded in cuneiform.

One of the later languages to be written in cuneiform was Persian. Eighteenth-century scholars knew this language was still being used, although it was written in a different script. They consulted the sacred book of the Parsee religion, the *Avesta,* for clues to the meaning of certain Persian words and titles. Finally, a German high school teacher named Georg Friedrich Grotefend deciphered several Old Persian inscriptions of Darius and Xerxes. He published his findings in 1802.

In 1835 a British army officer named Henry Rawlinson, who was an advisor to the Persian government, discovered the large inscription of Darius on the high cliff of Behistun. Rawlinson studied this lengthy Old Persian inscription and soon discovered that it was closely akin to Sanskrit, the ancient literary language of India.

Like the Rosetta Stone, the Behistun in-

scription was written in three languages. The first segment was written in a script that had frequently turned up in excavations along the Tigris and Euphrates Rivers. A Frenchman named Paul Emile Botta had found similar records in the ruins of the Palace of Khorsabad, where the Assyrian King Sargon had reigned. An Englishman named Austen Henry Layard had uncovered many more from the remains of Nineveh.

The second segment of the Behistun inscription was written in Old Persian, while the third was in a late dialect of Elamite. But the first segment was the most crucial. It held the key to cuneiform.

Until the 1840s, scholars made slow progress in unravelling the cuneiform of the first segment. In 1845 a Swede named Isidor Löwenstern recognized that the language was Semitic and probably related to Hebrew, Arabic, and Syriac—all of which were well known. In 1850 the Irish scholar Edward Hincks announced that the signs represented syllables. Thus it appeared that both Egyptian hieroglyphics and Babylonian cuneiform were structurally the same. Both are syllabic systems in which there are at least three kinds of signs:

Simple ideographs, in which one sign stood for a word.

Syllable signs, in which one character could stand for a syllable or several different sounds making up a syllable.

Determinatives, in which a symbol indicated the class of things that the word represented—e.g., whether it was the name of a deity, the name of a country, an object made of wood, or the like.

Once these clues were discovered, the process of deciphering cuneiform went on very rapidly. In the century since Hincks' breakthrough, cuneiform has become a major source of our knowledge of the ancient world. It has added a great deal of background material for the study of biblical Hebrew, and it has given us the historical framework for understanding the rise and fall of the kingdoms of the Near East.

C. The Tablets of Ugarit. The last important advance in understanding ancient languages occurred in the twentieth century. For many years after World War I, a French archaeological team excavated the ruins of an ancient city near the Mediterranean in northern Lebanon. There they discovered a library of clay tablets from the ancient Canaanite cap-

LANGUAGES AND WRITING

ital of Ugarit. These texts were written in a very, very simple cuneiform that had only about 30 basic characters—unlike Sumerian or Babylonian, which had hundreds. In April of 1930, a German scholar named Hans Bauer suggested that the language was Semitic. Several French scholars deciphered the script, and thus recovered the West Semite language of Ugaritic from the dust of antiquity. Ugaritic studies proved to be an enormous boon to biblical scholarship. Hundreds of Hebrew words and dozens of phrases found in the Old Testament were also found in the tablets of Ugarit.

II. Significant Languages. Several ancient languages have a bearing on our interpretation of Scripture. These languages provided the basic framework within which the Bible writers did their work.

A. Sumerian. Scholars who examined the Akkadian, Babylonian, and Assyrian languages suspected that the cuneiform writing system had originally been devised for some other language. It suited these Semitic languages very poorly and it contained many picture-symbols that were based on a non-Semitic language. Henry Rawlinson proposed the term "Scythian" for the unknown tongue. Then archaeologists discovered tablets with this language at the ancient city of Sumer and Jules Oppert, a French scholar, suggested that the language be called "Sumerian."

The Sumerian language, like some modern Asian languages, was *tonal*—that is, similar sounding words were distinguished by the tone of voice in which they were said.

In the tablets, the Sumerians are found listing all the items of their experience in long inventories. Thus they carefully listed all the names of plants, animals, fish, and even grammatical constructions in long texts running to many tablets. They had even developed multilingual dictionaries, which listed terms in Sumerian with their equivalents in Akkadian, Hurrian, and even Hittite. In the last several years, archaeologists have found such lists at Ebla in North Syria. These tablets give equivalent words in Sumerian and Eblaite (a previously unknown West Semite language).

B. Akkadian. The oldest East Semitic language is called Akkadian. The first evidence of this language was found in the ruins of Agade (Akkad) in Mesopotamia. Akkadian texts from 2300 B.C. contain many Sumerian words and forms.

Akkadian was the official language of Sar-

gon of Agade, possibly the "Nimrod" of Genesis 10. It used very precise grammatical forms and the most complete phonetic system of all of the East Semitic dialects. The Akkadian language has helped Bible scholars understand the basic structure and historical changes in the other Semitic languages.

C. Babylonian and Assyrian. These were two dialects of Akkadian, written in a more simplified script. They are of vast historical importance, since the annals of many kings mentioned in the Old Testament were written in these languages. The philosophical, religious, and historical texts of these ancient cultures are also preserved. (*See* "The Babylonians and Assyrians.") For centuries scholars have debated the origins of the East Semite components of biblical speech. Many thought these were Aramaic. But there is now strong evidence that many of these foreign elements (as in the prophecy of Ezekiel) are Babylonian or Assyrian in origin.

D. Eblaite and Amorite. So far, researchers know little about either of these languages, which lie in a direct line behind biblical Hebrew. However, archaeologists have uncovered thousands of tablets that contain material in both languages. Many years will pass before all of it becomes available and can be accurately studied. Preliminary reports indicate that many of the place names of

HIEROGLYPHS. *The priests and scribes of ancient Egypt used this form of picture-writing to record their nation's historical and religious texts. Merchants used a more simple script called demotic.*

LANGUAGES AND WRITING

CUNEIFORM SCRIPT. *This section of the stele of Hammurabi shows the wedge-shaped cuneiform writing typically used in Babylon during the eighteenth century B.C. Cuneiform was inscribed in clay with a sharp pointed reed or carved in stone.*

Genesis appear on the texts. They are written in cuneiform.

E. Ugaritic. This is the West Semitic language of the Canaanites. It records in a shortened, nearly alphabetic script the legends and religious literature of the period 1800 to 1400 B.C. Many Ugaritic words—and some whole expressions—are identical with those in the

ADZE WITH UGARITIC ALPHABET. *Among the written languages discovered in the texts of Ugarit was a previously unknown Semitic language using an alphabetic cuneiform script. Because this language is related to biblical Hebrew, it helps to throw light on the meaning of ancient Hebrew words. This ceremonial adzehead, inscribed with the Ugaritic alphabet, belonged to a priest.*

earlier parts of the Hebrew Bible. (*See also* "Ugarit and the Canaanites.")

F. Hebrew. The Hebrew language was written in a consonantal script from right to left. It bore absolutely no resemblance to any European language. Yet it has been written at least since 1500 B.C., and a modified dialect of Hebrew is still spoken and written today.

Hebrew belonged to the Semitic group of languages. It was directly related to such ancient Semitic languages as Aramaic, Akkadian, and Ugaritic and to such modern ones as Arabic and Amharic. Hebrew shared all of the common characteristics of the Semitic group—especially the guttural quality of strong consonants, which we occasionally hear in modern German and Russian.

Most Hebrew nouns, verbs, adjectives, and adverbs consisted of three consonants—the "triliteral roots." Vowels were added before, between, and behind these consonants. To a large extent, the same root could be developed as several parts of speech.

Noun	Verb	Extended Meaning
davar "good word"	*divver* "speak about"	*devarynu* "our business"
harash "craftsman"	*harash* "plow"	*hersheth* "working of wood"

Figure 29

This process produced many words that had similar sounds. Thus the Hebrews would commonly write a sentence such as: "The smiter smote the smitten." While very poor form in English, this would be fine syntax and rhetoric in Hebrew. In fact, many common expressions of the Old Testament depended on the natural redundancy of the Hebrew roots for their effect. For example, *ra'oh ra'itiy,* which literally means, "Seeing I have seen." The corresponding English expression would be, "I have surely seen."

The Hebrews were able to develop more complex verbal forms with pronoun and voice alterations. Thus, for example, *meloshniy* ("intent on injuring with the tongue") came from *lashon* ("tongue").

The word order in the typical Hebrew sentence is very different from English. The Hebrew writer usually placed the verb first and followed it in order with pronoun and objects

LANGUAGES AND WRITING

The Behistun Inscription

Kings of the Ancient Near East often prepared monuments to commemorate their victories. From these monuments, scholars have learned a great deal about the ancient world. Biblical events and persons are frequently mentioned. One of these commemorative monuments, the Behistun inscription, enabled scholars to decipher ancient Akkadian (i.e., the eastern division of the Semitic languages).

The town of Bisitun or Behistun lay on the main caravan route between Baghdad and Tehran. King Darius I of Persia (522–486 B.C.) had a record of his exploits carved on the mountainside nearby, 108 m. (345 ft.) above a spring where travelers stopped and 31 m. (100 ft.) above the highest point to which a man could climb. To insure that his work would not be defaced, Darius instructed his workers to destroy the way to get to the inscription after their work was completed.

In 1835, a British officer named Sir Henry Rawlinson began the hazardous task of copying the inscription. To copy the top lines, he had to stand on the topmost step of a ladder, steadying his body with his left arm and holding his notebook with his left hand, while writing with his right hand.

To the top of the inscription is a winged disk (representing the god Ahura-Mazda) and 12 figures. The inscription shows Darius treading on his rival Gaumata. To Darius' left are two attendants and before the king are nine rebels, roped together.

The inscription itself is in three languages: Old Persian, Elamite, and Babylonian (a form of Akkadian). After they deciphered the Old Persian inscription, scholars worked on the hypothesis that the other two texts contained the same narrative. Edward Hincks, rector of a parish church in Ireland, and Henry Rawlinson published their interpretation of the cuneiform characters. This provided the key to the decipherment of other Akkadian inscriptions.

A copy of the Behistun inscription was also found at Babylon, and an Aramaic version was discovered among the Jews of Elephantine Island. Darius made sure his fame was spread from one end of his extensive empire to the other.

In part, the Behistun inscription reads: "I am Darius . . . By the grace of Ahura-Mazda I am ruler of 23 lands including Babylonia, Sparda (Sardis?), Arabia and Egypt. I put down the rebellions of Gaumata and (8) others . . ."

Due to the great height of the inscription from the road, one wonders how Darius expected travelers to read of his glory. However, his trilingual proclamation has benefited scholars in a marvelous way—a way the king never dreamed.

LANGUAGES AND WRITING

(direct or indirect), noun subject, and noun object. A literal rendering of a simple Hebrew sentence will demonstrate this: *waytsaw yosef eth-'avadayw eth-harofi'm lahanot eth-'aviyw.* This sentence literally reads, "And-commanded-he Joseph servants-his, physicians to-embalm father-his." Notice the enormous difference between this type of grammar and that of English and the other Indo-European languages.

The Hebrew language was written with some 22 consonantal signs and no vowels (except those added to the consonantal signs centuries later). Some words can no longer be construed with any certainty. An example is found in the narrative of Joseph. The Hebrew states: *Ketoneth passiym.* The first word is clearly *coat;* there is no difficulty with it. But the second word appears nowhere else in the Old Testament. Translators have had to guess at its meaning. It has been interpreted as a coat "of many colors," a coat "with long sleeves," a coat "with much embroidery," and even as a coat of "choice wool." The simple fact is that

A SCRIBE. *This statue dating from the fifth dynasty (ca. 2400 B.C.) shows an Egyptian scribe holding a partially open roll of papyrus. The scribe was a highly respected member of ancient society, recording the day-to-day details of the culture in which he lived.*

no one knows what the precise meaning is, and there is no way we can find out.

Over the centuries there were different dialects of Hebrew, and all of them affected the copying of the Old Testament manuscripts. For example, the Book of Genesis contains many Egyptian expressions as well as a few early Akkadianisms. Numbers, Joshua, Judges, and Ruth contain very early Canaanite words and expressions, as well as some of the oldest Hebrew in the Old Testament, such as the Song of Deborah in Judges 9. The former prophets (1 Samuel through 2 Kings) record some spoken Hebrew of the monarchy. The latter prophets (Isaiah through Malachi) have a vocabulary all their own, with both Aramaic and Babylonian influences. The books of the Persian Period (Ezra through Daniel) show a considerable Aramaic influence. In addition, some books have linguistic patterns completely out of the ordinary, such as Job and the Song of Solomon.

Very few sentences in the whole Old Testament can be translated word-for-word into English. There is just no way to bring over all the nuances of the Hebrew. Hebrew has no tense structure to the verb, so that the familiar past, present, and future tenses (e.g., "I went, I had gone—I go, I am going, I will go") simply do not exist in Hebrew. Thus the time aspects of Hebrew verbs are very unclear.

G. Aramaic. The origin of the Aramaic language has long been debated. Aramaic words and phrases frequently appear in the Old Testament, and it is the language of some whole passages (Dan. 2–7; Ezra 4–7; Jer. 10:11). Outside of the Bible, the oldest fragments of Aramaic are relatively late—from 820 B.C. and later. Of all known Semitic languages, Aramaic was certainly the most like Hebrew.

Among Jewish scholars, Aramaic has been held in higher esteem than Hebrew, simply because the primary works of Jewish tradition (the Talmud and its subsequent materials) were written in a dialect of Aramaic. No doubt the Persian Empire used Aramaic as its chief Semitic language, and it became the common language of the Jews after the Exile. From that time, they began translating the Old Testament into Aramaic. These Aramaic translations as we know them are called the *Targums.* It was generally thought that they had an influence on the Judaism of Greek and Roman times, and therefore on the early Christian church; but this now has been called in question by the

LANGUAGES AND WRITING

Dead Sea Scrolls, the majority of which were written not in Aramaic but in Hebrew.

The New Testament indicates that Aramaic was the language of Jesus and His disciples. We find a number of His Aramaic expressions transliterated into Greek. The most common is the phrase, "Amen, Amen" (translated by the archaic "Verily, Verily" in the King James Version). Others are: *Talithā qūmi* ("Maiden, arise!"—Mark 5:41); Ephphatha ("Be opened"—Mark 7:34); and the cry from the cross, *Eli, Eli, lemā sebaqtanī* ("My God, my God, why have you forsaken me?"—Matt. 27:46; Mark 15:34).

In the New Testament epistles there are several Aramaic words, such as *Abba* ("Father!"—Rom. 8:15; Gal. 4:6) and *Maranatha* ("Lord, come!"—1 Cor. 16:22). Some Bible scholars believe that we can gain a greater understanding of Jesus and the Gospels from the Aramaic and its later dialect, Syriac, but there is not much historical basis for this theory. The major contribution of Aramaic to Hebrew seems to be its script. By as early as 200 B.C., Hebrew was probably written in the square script introduced with Aramaic. (*See also* "Text and Translations.")

H. Syriac. Syriac was a late dialect of Aramaic, written in a number of flowing scripts. It was the language of a Bible version used in many eastern churches—a version known as the *Peshitta* (literally, "the simple" or "basic" version). This version was produced in the fourth century A.D.

Syriac was the principal literary language of a large Christian community that spread east from Edessa in the third to the thirteenth centuries A.D. It was very similar to Aramaic in grammar, structure, and vocabulary; but it also borrowed words from Arabic. In time Syriac was almost totally absorbed by Arabic. In a few passages the Syriac version of the Gospels preserves Aramaic statements that may be close to the actual speech of Jesus. But generally it is simply a translation of the Greek.

I. Greek. Greek has been written in one dialect or another for nearly 3,600 years, and undoubtedly it was spoken long before that. The first written Greek was the very ancient tongue of the Mycenaeans. They derived their written language from the Hittite hieroglyphs. But by 1000 B.C. the Greeks had adapted the simpler West Semite script to their language and added the all-important component of vowels, which none of the Semitic scripts had

developed. Thus the Greeks were the first to have a completely alphabetic system. It was easy to learn and it greatly enhanced the spread of Greek as a trade and commercial language. In fact, many cultures that could write their languages only with great difficulty adopted Greek for their written communication.

Greek was easy to read and became the vehicle for some of the greatest literary works of Western civilization. Among these were the poetry of Homer, the history of Herodotus, the medicine of Hippocrates, the mathematics of Archimedes, the drama of Sophocles and Aeschylus, and the philosophy of Plato and Aristotle.

Greeks used the classical dialect of Homer from 1050 to about 700 B.C. Two dialects—the Ionic (or East Greek) and the Attic (the dialect of Athens)—were used from the close of the Homeric period until the Roman era. These dialects combined in a simplified version of the language that was spread to all of the coun-

23

LANGUAGES AND WRITING

COPPER SCROLLS. *Discovered in the Dead Sea caves at Qumran near the Dead Sea, these copper scrolls describe a treasure—26 tons of gold and 65 tons of silver—hidden at 64 locations throughout Israel. Most scholars believe the treasure is a hoax or a myth, although others hold that the treasure was indeed taken from the temple and hidden before the Roman legions arrived in A.D. 70. It is very rare to find a Hebrew text on thinly beaten sheets of copper, such as these.*

tries conquered by Alexander the Great in the late fourth century B.C. The new dialect was called *koiné* (common) Greek. This was the language of the Greek Old Testament (the Septuagint) and the Greek New Testament.

Koiné Greek was similar to modern Indo-European languages, yet it had more elaborate word variations than any of them. The enormous Greek vocabulary and the full and precise system of grammar made it the premier language of philosophy. In this regard, it is closer to German or Russian than it is to English, French, or Spanish. The tonal system of Greek made it especially suitable for poetry. The work of poets such as Homer, Sappho, and Pindar is virtually impossible to reproduce in English. Even the *koiné* of the New Testament rises to levels of expression that defy translation. (*See* "The Poetry of the Bible.")

The details of Christian theology in the New Testament were greatly enhanced by the

GREEK WRITING. *Spoken for at least 3,600 years, the Greek language was the first to have a completely alphabetic system. The conquest of Alexander the Great spread a simple dialect of Greek called koine to the Mediterranean countries. This form of Greek was the language of the New Testament. This papyrus manuscript contains the end of the Epistle to the Romans and the beginning of the Epistle to the Hebrews, written in koine Greek.*

LANGUAGES AND WRITING

shades of meaning available in the Greek language. A good example of this is found in Galatians 6:2, 5. These verses seem to contradict one another, for verse 2 says, "Bear ye one another's burdens" while verse 5 says, ". . . Every man shall bear his own burden." But here our English versions have translated two different Greek words as *burden.* The word in verse 2 is *baros,* which Greek philosophers used to denote the burden of temptation. The word in verse 5 is *phortion,* which denoted the responsibility imposed by the Law (*cf.* Matt. 23:4; Luke 11:46). So in effect verse 2 means, "Support one another in carrying the weight of temptation," while verse 5 means, "Assume the duty that the Law places upon you." Hundreds of passages in the Greek New Testament can be given their full meaning only by referring to the Greek text.

After the writing of the Greek New Testament, the Greek language continued to change. At first, the language was under pressure from Latin. Later, Greece and its environs were conquered by the Turks, who further changed the language. Medieval or Byzantine Greek became the language of the Eastern Orthodox church, which preserved some of the old theological expressions. Modern Greek is very different from New Testament Greek. One who speaks modern Greek fluently will yet be hard put to make sense of the ancient text.

J. Latin. Latin was one of the many Indo-European languages of central Italy. As Rome became the queen city of the ancient world, the Latin language spread to influence generations of Europeans. By the year 50 B.C., Latin was spoken, written, and understood from the Atlantic coast of England to the shores of the Baltic Sea. It deeply influenced every European language, both medieval and modern. It has been estimated that as much as 80 percent of the vocabulary of educated English speech today is derived from Latin—in fact, thousands of classical Latin words came over directly into English, unchanged in form, spelling, or meaning.

While the see of Rome dominated Western Christianity, the pope required churches to use the Latin version of the Bible, the Vulgate, translated by Jerome. Thus Latin served as the common language of Western Christianity from A.D. 400 to nearly 1800. It was the international language used by the Reformers of the sixteenth century and their predecessors. Hus, Luther, Wycliffe, and Calvin all wrote and published in Latin. All the Reformers' Bible commentaries were written in Latin.

Jerome's Latin version of the Scriptures has had a tremendous influence on the church's thinking; it has influenced all of the great modern translations.

23

LANGUAGES AND WRITING

THE LITERATURE OF THE BIBLE

The Bible is not just one book—it is a library. It contains 66 books written over a span of many centuries. God inspired the writing of each book, but He allowed the personality of each writer to come through the Scriptures. So the books of the Bible are written in a variety of literary styles.

The Bible contains books of poetry, prophecy, history, letters, and apocalyptic literature. There are many styles of writing as well.

I. POETRY

II. PROPHETIC LITERATURE
A. The Message of Prophecy
    1. Messages of Faith
    2. Messages of Obedience
    3. Messages of Hope
    4. Messages on the Lordship of God
B. isaiah (741?—698 B.C.)
C. Jeremiah (626—571 B.C.)
D. Ezekiel (597—555? B.C.)
E. Daniel
F. Minor Prophets
    1. Hosea
    2. Joel
    3. Amos
    4. Obadiah
    5. Jonah
    6. Micah
    7. Nahum
    8. Habakkuk
    9. Zephaniah
    10. Haggai
    11. Zechariah
    12. Malachi

III. OLD TESTAMENT HISTORY
A. As History
B. As Literature

IV. NEW TESTAMENT HISTORY
A. The Gospels
    1. Jesus as a Literary Character
    2. Literary Features of the Gospels
      a. Matthew
      b. Mark
      c. Luke
      d. John
B. The Book of Acts

V. THE EPISTLES
A. Paul's Epistles
B. The Letter to the Hebrews
C. The Epistle of James
D. Peter's Epistles and Jude
E. John's Letters

VI. APOCALYPTIC LITERATURE
A. Daniel
B. Intertestamental Apocalyptic
C. Revelation

I. Poetry. Poetry is a very important form of biblical literature. The "poetical" books of the Bible—Psalms, Lamentations, and Song of Solomon—are all poetry. Poetry is found, however, in several other books of the Bible, especially in the books of wisdom and prophecy. Poems are even scattered through the books of history; the Bible scholar Theodore H. Robinson found nearly 50 poems in the first 12 books of the Bible. For a more thorough discussion of the Bible's poetic and wisdom literature, *see* "Poetry."

II. Prophetic Literature. The Old Testament contains much prophetic literature which the Jews classified as: (1) the former prophets—the books Joshua, Judges, First and Second Samuel, and First and Second Kings, and (2) the latter prophets—Isaiah, Jeremiah, Ezekiel, and the twelve minor prophets. The books called the "former prophets" were history written from a prophetic point of view or by professional prophets. The term "prophetic literature" in this article, however, means specifically the latter prophets plus the book of Daniel.

A. The Message of Prophecy. God commissioned each prophet to fulfill a particular role—to be "the servant of the Lord." The prophets conveyed God's message to men, and as "men of the Spirit" they had special abilities to carry out their tasks. As "interpreters," they explained God's acts to men; as "seers," they saw what was hidden from others; as "spokesmen," they voiced God's truth.

These writing prophets did not necessarily perform miracles, but they were excellent interpreters of history. Their writings reflect all

THE LITERATURE OF THE BIBLE

the conditions of their age (political, economic, religious, and social).

The contents of the Bible's prophetic literature falls into four categories:

1. Messages of Faith. The prophets encouraged God's people to trust in God alone and not to bow before human strength or military power (Isa. 30:12–14). They firmly believed that God is Almighty Ruler of the universe, the moral Governor of the world, and the covenant God of Israel. He controls all things for the good of those who love Him. Therefore, God's people should obey Him and not fear the empty threats of man.

2. Messages of Obedience. The prophets urged men to know, believe, and practice God's Word. They based their teachings upon the laws of Moses. Therefore, the prophets were keenly aware of the sinfulness and perversity of man. They preached that repentance

and returning obediently to God is necessary for salvation in this life and in the life to come. (e.g., 1 Sam. 15:22).

3. Messages of Hope. The prophets encouraged God's faithful people respecting the future. Moses had prophesied that God would cut off His people and send them into exile (Lev. 26; Deut. 28). The nation as a whole was again and again deteriorating. Yet the believers received encouragement from God. Exile was not the end for them because God would restore His faithful people and through them He would send the Messiah (e.g., Isa. 51:11; 54:10; Jer. 3:12).

4. Messages on the Lordship of God. The prophets taught the people that Jehovah was the Lord of all creation. They predicted future events, and as those events came to pass the people learned that these were true prophets and that Jehovah was the only true God (cf. Deut. 18:15–22).

B. Isaiah (741?—698 B.C.). Isaiah is one of the most noteworthy of the Old Testament prophets. As literature this book abounds in superb poetry. As theology it emphasizes the holiness of God and His hatred of Israel's sin.

A literary analysis of the book of Isaiah proves it to be a carefully structured collection of various prophetic utterances and historical narrative (i.e., an anthology) with the first half of the book paralleling the second half. The units are:

Ruin and Restoration: 1—5 and 34—35
Biographical Material: 6—8 and 36—40
Agents of Divine Blessing and Judgment: 9—12 and 41—45
Oracles against Foreign Powers: 13—23 and 46—48
Universal Redemption and the Deliverance of Israel: 24—27 and 49—55
Ethical Sermons: 28—31 and 56—59
The Restoration of the Nation: 32—33 and 60—66

The book contains many different literary genres including lyric poetry, encomium (praise of someone or something—e.g., Isa. 52:13—53:12), autobiography, historical narrative, and pastoral themes (e.g., Isa. 5:1—7). Isaiah is a master of high poetic art. His book contains an abundance of exalted poetry. For example, see Isaiah 34—35 for two vivid poems concerning the end times. Also note his parable in the form of a poem (Isa. 5:1—7) and a hymn of praise (Isa. 26).

C. Jeremiah (626—571 B.C.). Jeremiah

WRITING TABLE AND BENCH. *Scribes from Qumran sat at this table and copied the texts that we now know as the Dead Sea Scrolls. Tens of thousands of fragments, representing approximately 500 to 600 manuscripts, have been found in the Qumran Caves. About one quarter of these manuscripts are biblical books, including every Old Testament book except Esther.*

gave this book a thematic not a chronological arrangement. The first section (Jer. 1–25) labors to develop the theme of national sinfulness from the statement of the prophet's credentials to the final judgment. As a unit it forms a somewhat disjointed whole with varying kinds of literary forms interwoven: oracles of hope and doom and autobiographical, biographical, and conversational (dialogue) narrative. This is comparable with the literary style found, for example, in the Koran (the holy book of Islam). There too the material is not developed logically but is repeated and constantly interwoven both as to subject and form.[1] Thus he interweaves and repeats the theme of national sinfulness and coming judgment, often going back over material already presented, as a fugue does in music. The effect is powerful and moving (cf. Jer. 5; 17). Jeremiah's psalm style is especially evident in his second psalm of lamentation (Jer. 4:19–31).

The middle section (Jer. 26–45) on the whole proceeds chronologically although this is not consistent. In this section prose narrative predominates but poetic passages are also present. The third section (Jer. 46—51) is primarily prophetic poetry. The prophetic eye moves from Egypt to Elam-Babylon depicting in beautiful imagery the judgment of all Israel's enemies.

Jeremiah's style is excessively wordy, unlike the simplicity of Isaiah and Hosea. He often refers to other prophets but puts the material into a milder form. He also refers to the Pentateuch, especially Deuteronomy (cf. Jer. 3:1 and Deut. 24:4; Jer. 3:13 and Deut. 30:1; Jer. 4:4 and Deut. 10:6). He even refers back to himself (cf. Jer. 44:28 and 51:50). His discourses are like the frames of a moving picture; each presents the same characters but in slightly different positions. Indeed, the frames may be somewhat mixed up. Thus, the progression in the book is not straightforward and flowing. The transitions between the frames are abrupt and the repetitions frequent. He is sometimes charged with lack of originality, but this is a superficial judgment. The power of his imagination gives new depth and poignancy to the tradition out of which he speaks. His great poetical skill is seen especially in his vivid presentations of human loneliness and suffering. Jeremiah's poetry attains depths of pure emotion that reach every reader.

D. Ezekiel (597—555? B.C.). Ezekiel was a man with an overwhelming sense of God's majesty. His book is full of visions and symbols that can bewilder the modern mind. We are not accustomed to so pictorial a style.

Ezekiel's visions and ecstatic utterances usher in the whole class of powerfully symbolic exilic and postexilic writings that we call *apocalyptic* (hidden) literature (cf. "Apocalyptic Literature" below).

The literary structure of Ezekiel is tightly drawn. There are two major divisions, each with two subdivisions. The first division contains prophecies of judgment on Israel and the nations (1—32) and the second, prophecies of salvation for God's people (33—48). Most of the prophecies were first given to the exiles in Babylon. Much of the material within the first subdivision is arranged chronologically.

There are several unique aspects of Ezekiel's style. First, he uses symbol and allegory more than the other prophets. His figures are set forth in elaborate detail and are extremely bold (e.g., Ezek. 3:16–21; 13:8–16; 26; 29). Every discourse abounds in imagery that often includes strange comparisons and peculiar expressions. The language is obscure and sometimes difficult to follow. Once a subject is introduced, it is pursued to every detail and viewed from every angle. Ezekiel's vision of God's glory is a good example (Ezek. 1). Ezekiel employs parables, pictures, and proverbs. His symbolism is taken from the Jerusalem temple and various Old Testament precedents. The concept of Jesus as the Good Shepherd can be traced to Ezekiel 34:23. The vision of the new Jerusalem after God's judgment is found in Ezekiel 40—48.

Second, Ezekiel's style is marked by its sustained emphasis on the divine origin and contents of his message(s). He often uses the phrase "son of man" as the title by which God addresses him. Other phrases often repeated that reinforce this emphasis are: "the Lord God," "thus says the Lord," "the saying of the Lord," "You shall know that I am Jehovah."

Third, Ezekiel reveals his priestly descent and disposition, particularly in those visions that have to do with priestly functions (Ezek. 8; 44:9–31).

E. Daniel. Interestingly, Jewish scholars do not place this book among the prophetic books but among the writings because its author was a statesman not a prophet. However, since

---

[1] Edward J. Young, *Introduction to the Old Testament* (London: Tyndale Press, 1960), p. 234.

Daniel had the gift of prediction, the New Testament calls him a "prophet" (Matt. 24:15).

Daniel saw many symbols in his prophetic visions, and he often records them without attempting to interpret what they mean. This style of prophetic writing is called apocalyptic (from the Greek word *kalyptein,* "to cover"), because the true meaning lies behind the symbolic images of the vision. The only apocalyptic book that truly parallels the book of Daniel in its sustained use of symbolism is the New Testament book of Revelation.

The first section (chaps. 1—6) recounts the faithfulness of Daniel and his friends to their God during the Exile and ways in which God blessed and used them. It consists of good narrative prose with a few poetic passages interspersed (e.g., 2:20—23). We also find examples of dialogue (e.g., chap. 2), vision (4:14—17), and vision and interpretation (a monologue or speech by one person, 4:19—27). The skill of the author is seen in the way all of these elements are blended in his series of dramatic stories. These stories are exciting and easily remembered. Each one has a well-defined and carefully developed plot. The characters are presented interestingly and in many cases there is obvious character development, as with King Darius (Dan. 6). The stories have a strong two-level conflict—one between the hero and his adversaries and another between God and the forces of evil. Daniel, or whoever put his material together for him, was a gifted narrator.

The last section of the book (chaps. 7—12) records the prophetic visions of Daniel. For a discussion of the literary form and style of this section, see "Apocalyptic Literature" below.

F. Minor Prophets. The group of twelve shorter prophetic books are called "minor" only because of their length, not because they are less important. All of the books bear the names of the prophets who wrote them.

In our English translations of the Bible, these books are arranged according to the order in which tradition says they were written. The first of these prophecies was delivered around 850 B.C., and the last after the Exile. Most of them tell us their dates by the historical material they contain. Here are the books in order with their respective themes:

Hosea—Gomer's sin, punishment, and restoration; a symbol of Israel's sin, punishment, and restoration.

Joel—locust plague, penitence, God's promise.

Amos—woe and weal for Israel.

Obadiah—Jehovah will humble the pride of Elam who rejoiced in his brother's distress.

Jonah—mission to Nineveh; Jehovah's love contrasted to Jonah's anger.

Micah—Jehovah's controversy.

Nahum—Jehovah's vengeance and goodness revealed in Nineveh's overthrow.

Habakkuk—the righteous shall live by faith.

Zephaniah—Jehovah hides His people in the day of wrath.

Haggai—exhortation to rebuild Jehovah's house.

Zechariah—future glory of Zion and of its shepherd king.

24

THE LITERATURE OF THE BIBLE

JOEL. *One of the most lyrical prophets of the Old Testament, Joel predicted that God would judge Israel but save His faithful followers. This mosaic from the Cathedral of St. Mark in Venice shows the prophet with a Latin inscription of the prophecy: ". . . I will pour out my spirit upon all flesh; and your sons and your daughters shall prophesy . . ." (Joel 2:28).*

Malachi—Jehovah's love unrequited.

1. Hosea. The book of Hosea is unified by the development of the dual themes of God's love and wrath. There is an ever-present atmosphere of doom (e.g., Hos. 8:2–3; 9:1). Yet Hosea is uniquely a prophet of love. He shows that although Israel has rejected God's covenantal love and merits God's judgment (cf. Lev. 26; Deut. 28) and parental wrath (Deut. 21:18–21), yet God's elective love knows no conditions. He will restore them (Hos. 14:4). God is love.

The book presents two major literary problems. First, to what literary genre do chapters 1—3 belong? Is it allegory or biographical narrative? If allegory, then the marriage between Hosea and Gomer did not really occur, and the story is told to illustrate a truth. If biography, then the marriage really occurred. These first three chapters form a complete literary narrative with a beginning, middle, and end. The narrative is introduced and closed with prose sections. Most of it, however, consists of poetry.

The rest of the book (chaps. 4–14) exhibits no chronological sequence. These chapters repeat and develop the themes set forth by the first 3 chapters. (Compare chap. 2 with chap. 11.) They consist of three unequal sections. Each opens with a general condemnation of Israel (the Northern Kingdom). Then comes a condemnation of each layer of society, a description of the coming judgment, and finally a description of the ultimate redemption of the nation. Each section focuses increasingly on the fact that the only hope is God's mercy. Thus, the material is arranged somewhat thematically. The movement is not logical but progresses in broad strokes.

The poet often repeats themes for effect. The poetic texture of the book is typified with skillful use of parallelism, simile, and metaphor.[2] The skillful heaping up of poetic parallelism (e.g., Hos. 6:1) creates a strong emotional effect.

2. Joel. The book of Joel contains some of the foremost lyric poems in the Old Testament. Its basic literary form is a liturgy of lamentation. However, Joel also uses other forms, such as the address of admonition (Joel 1:2–3). The language is vividly descriptive,

STELE OF SETI I. *This stele of Seti I (fourteenth century B.C.), found at Beth-shean in Palestine, tells of the Egyptian king's success in overthrowing a coalition of Asiatic princes. At the top of the stele is the winged sun disk. Below, to the right, stands the hawk-headed Egyptian god Re-Harakhti. Seti I stands before him. Rulers ordered the erection of such commemorative steles to preserve the records of their achievements.*

compact, and very effective. Like the book of Amos, Joel uses pure classical Hebrew. It, too, uses much parallelism and rhythm of thought. God's judgment is depicted symbolically by a ravaging locust plague. Some understand this as a literal locust plague and others as a devastating army.

The book skillfully weaves together a variety of images, similes, hyperbole (literary exaggeration in order to make a point; Joel 2:30–31), paranomasia (plays on words and puns; Joel 1:12). The effect is a carefully developed proclamation in sophisticated poetry (except for the brief introduction).

The book uses the device of *anthological comparison*—In other words, it borrows earlier biblical language to express its ideas. For

---

[2] *Simile* is a literary technique that makes a symbolic comparison by saying that one thing is like another. *Metaphor* makes the comparison by saying that one thing is in fact something else.

THE LITERATURE OF THE BIBLE

example, Joel 2:6 comes from Nahum 2:10, while Joel 2:10 comes from Isaiah 13:13.

The first part of the book (Joel 1:1—2:27) is aligned with prophetic poetry in genre while the rest of the book (2:28—3:21) is nearly apocalyptic. Its imagery is more difficult to penetrate (cf. 2:30–31; 3:12 ff.) with frequent use of imagery from the heavenly bodies. The emphasis is on the coming day of judgment and after that, on the restoration. This book is not apocalyptic in the sense of Daniel, whose imagery is much more extensive and complex (e.g., Daniel's vision of the ram and goat—Dan. 8).

3. Amos. The book of Amos may be understood as an informal satire. It is not at all a subtle scorning, such as the book of Jonah. The satire is straightforward (e.g., Amos 4:4–5). The writer openly scorns the religious, social, and political practices of Israel, the Northern Kingdom (e.g., Amos 6:1–7). Again, there appears to be no carefully designed plot to the book. Like much satire it is disjointed structurally and evidences no change or development as it proceeds. It is a loosely arranged gathering of fragments from the prophet's ministry.

Elements of the following genres are included: "saying," narrative, predictive prophecy, vision, dialogue, dramatic monologue, lyric poetry, and pronouncement of woe.

The writer proves himself to be a master of ancient poetry. He uses clear, simple Hebrew—"some of the purest and most classical Hebrew in the entire Old Testament."[3] He also uses metaphor, simile, epithet (a striking use of titles), parallelism, rhetorical questions, sarcasm, conflict, and other devices.

4. Obadiah. The book of Obadiah is the shortest book in the Old Testament. It forms a compact literary unit whose theme is the destruction of Edom. Its poetic imagery and vocabulary are consistent throughout. Both sections (vv. 1–9 and 10–21) contain Hebrew words that occur only here in the Old Testament and words that occur elsewhere but only rarely. The entire poem is bold and lively.

5. Jonah. The book of Jonah may be understood as a satire designed to teach a lesson. It holds up for scorn the narrow-minded view that God is concerned only with the Jewish nation (Jonah 4:9–11). The writer skillfully hides his own identity and feelings, depicting

God as the One who scorns such strict nationalism. The two main characters are God, the merciful Judge, and Jonah, the bigot. The plot exhibits no character development since Jonah seems unmoved by the entire episode. Yet the book is a unified, carefully designed story. Therefore, Leland Ryken says Jonah is an example of an anti-plot.[4] The satirical tone of this work is light but effective. The writer employs narrative, dialogue, and lyric poetry. He uses the well-known literary motif of the death, burial, and resurrection of a hero with an unusual twist.

Most commentators until modern times have felt, and with reason, that this story is biographical—i.e., this is what actually happened to Jonah. The prayer (Jonah 2:2–9), expressed in very elaborate poetry, was no doubt composed in calmer circumstances than the belly of the large fish. Nonetheless, we need not doubt that it expresses what Jonah prayed in his heart in that traumatic situation.

6. Micah. The book of Micah is sometimes said to lack literary unity, but it displays a logical unity. Except for the superscription (introduction), it is written entirely in poetry. Each of its three divisions is structured similarly and in three stages: reproof, threat, and promise. The three major divisions are marked by different themes. The first division speaks of divine judgment, the second of Messianic salvation, and the third admonishes repentance if the readers are to enjoy this salvation.

Micah's poetic style is sometimes said to be rough. He moves abruptly from threats to promises (e.g., 2:1–11; 12), from one subject to another (e.g., 7:1–7), from one person to another (e.g., 1:8, 10; 6:16; 7:15–19), and so on. He is never clear and vivid in what he says. The book abounds in simile (e.g., 1:8–16; 2:12), paronomasia (esp. 1:10–16), and dialogue (6:3–5).

7. Nahum. The book of Nahum is a single poem consisting of 10 stanzas or *strophes* of nearly equal length. (The stanzas are 1:11–15; 2:1–5; 2:6–10; 2:11–13; 3:1–4; 3:5–7; 3:8–10; 3:11–13; 3:14–15; and 3:16–19.) These form three larger divisions, thematically treating expectation of the coming judgment of Nineveh, the judgment itself, and the guilt of the city. Thus, the poem has a single theme: Nineveh's destruction.

Nahum contains some of the most exalted

---

[3] George L. Robinson, *The Twelve Minor Prophets* (Grand Rapids: Baker Book House, 1926), p. 50.

[4] Leland Ryken, *The Literature of the Bible* (Grand Rapids: Zondervan, 1974), pp. 265–268.

poetry in the Old Testament. It displays a mastery of vivid description and Hebrew poetic style. Nahum's poetry is rich in simile (2:8; 3:15), metaphor (1:7), paronomasia (3:5 ff.), and rhetorical questions (2:11). Descriptive words are piled upon one another, creating rapidly moving pictures (e.g., 3:1 ff.).

8. Habakkuk. The book of Habakkuk forms a complete artistic unit. Except for the introduction, it is written entirely in poetry. The theme of the book is developed in three sections. The first section consists of a complaint set forth in a dialogue between the prophet and God (1:2—2:4). Then appear five woes (2:5–20), in which the personified nations oppressed by Nineveh sarcastically taunt their oppressor. The final section (chap. 3) is a psalm of praise (an *encomium*) to Jehovah. The theme of the book as a whole aligns it with the literary genre of *theodicy* (justifying God's righteousness in view of the presence of evil—cf. Job).

The style and concepts of this book are uniform throughout. Like all the prophets Habakkuk has mastered poetic parallelism (3:17). He also employs the rhetorical question (1:2–3), *hyperbole* (exaggeration for effect—1:8; 2:11), simile (1:9, 11; 2:5), *anthropomorphism* (attributing human characteristics to God—3:8, 15), and *personification* (attributing human personality to inanimate objects—e.g., 3:10). Much of the vivid imagery is drawn from the military and natural arenas.

9. Zephaniah. The book of Zephaniah is unified around the theme that a remnant of God's people will survive the day of judgment. Structurally the book is divided into three sections, which progress logically. The first (chap. 1) announces judgment on the surrounding nations. The second (chap. 2) describes the scope of the judgment. And the third (chap. 3) focuses on salvation for the remnant of Israel.

Other than the introduction and the brief passage of Zephaniah 2:1–11, the whole book is poetry. The poetic style is straightforward and forceful. Except in 2:8–11 and 3:16–20, Zephaniah uses the *qinâ* or dirge meter. This meter was frequently employed in Hebrew poetry to express mourning. (*See* "Poetry.")

Zephaniah's imagery draws heavily from other prophets, especially Isaiah. For example, Zephaniah 1:7 is a reference to Isaiah 13:6

OBELISK OF ASHURNASIRPAL II. *Two registers from a basalt obelisk depict the Assyrian king Ashurnasirpal II (883–859 B.C.) receiving tribute from his subjects. The fragmentary inscriptions repeat passages from other inscriptions of Ashurnasirpal.*

and 34:6. Nonetheless the author makes some unique poetic contributions. He frequently repeats words and phrases (1:10, 12)—a practice that makes his writing emphatic. He is fond of puns (e.g., 2:4), which unfortunately are often lost in translation. There are also striking *epigrams* (short, powerful phrases—e.g., 1:12, 17), anthropomorphisms (1:12; 2:13; 3:8, 17), similes (1:17; 2:2), personifications (2:2; 3:1 ff.), and metaphors (3:3). Poetic imagery appears rather infrequently in Zephaniah. He achieves his strong emotional effect primarily through the use of parallelism.

10. Haggai. The book of Haggai consists of four dated statements by the prophet. The unifying theme of the book is the rebuilding of the temple. Each section of the book appears to be a summary of a longer speech that Haggai delivered orally. These written oracles proceed in sequence to form a logically complete unit.

The book is written entirely in poetry. It introduces each oracle with the statement, "Thus says the Lord. . . ." Haggai often uses the rhetorical question (cf. 1:4, 9; 2:3, 12).

Haggai's style is compact, forceful, and at times stern. The sentences are short and sharp (1:5–7). The vocabulary of the book is limited, and the writer frequently repeats his statements.

11. Zechariah. The book of Zechariah may be divided into four sections, with the first three sections (1:1–6; 1:7—6:15; 7:1—8:23) forming a unity over against the last section (chaps. 9–14). All of the earlier sections are dated but the last is not. Furthermore, the imagery of the first section is quite different from that of the last. The first division deals with themes relating to the rebuilding of the temple and religious renewal following the hope of the return from the Exile (cf. Neh. 12:16), while the last section speaks of the final consummation of history.

Each section employs various literary genres. The first section is written entirely in prose and consists of a dialogue. The second is a series of visions containing dialogue and narrative. The third division is written in a question-and-answer format, containing a brief introductory dialogue and speeches by the Lord. The final section consists of both poetry and prose by which the Lord makes predictions about the future.

The overall unity of the book is sometimes questioned because of the difference in style, language, and form between the two major di-

visions. The unity, however, is evidenced in several ways. There are important and characteristic phrases and formulas recurring in both sections—e.g., "passed through" (7:14; 9:8); "saith the Lord" (1:4; 2:5; 8:11; 12:4), "the eyes of the Lord" or "mine eyes" (4:10; 9:8; 12:4), and "Lord of hosts" (1:6, 12; 2:9; 9:15; 10:3; 13:2). The similarity in language and ideas is illustrated by comparing 2:10 and 9:9:

" 'Sing for joy and be glad, O daughter of Zion; for behold I am coming and I will dwell in your midst,' declares the Lord" (2:10, NASB).

"Rejoice greatly, O daughter of Zion! Shout in triumph, O daughter of Jerusalem! Behold your king is coming to you; He is just and endowed with salvation, Humble, and mounted on a donkey, Even on a colt, the foal of a donkey" (9:9, NASB).

In both major sections, the writer is noteworthy for not borrowing words or phrases from other Semitic languages, as other prophets customarily did.

Zechariah makes frequent quotations from previous Old Testament prophets. There are echoes of the four beasts of Daniel 7:7 (1:18), the measuring rod of Jeremiah 31:39 and Ezekiel 40:3 (2:1), and many other prophetic images.

The author employs *anthropopathism* (attributing human emotions to God—1:2, 12; 8:2), vision and symbolism (1:8), metaphor (1:5; 7:14), personification (1:7), simile (7:1; 7:12), and *hyperbole* (exaggeration for effect—e.g., 7:14; 8:4).

Although generally similar in style to apocalyptic, the final chapters (9—14) do not have the intricate symbolism of apocalyptic elsewhere. Nor do they include several of the symbols prominent in other Old Testament apocalyptic passages (e.g., animals, numbers, and the Son of Man).

12. Malachi. The book of Malachi falls into two sections according to the themes treated (chaps. 1—2 and 3—4). The first section describes Israel's sin and apostasy while the second predicts the coming of the Messiah. Malachi consistently and logically pursues his argument. His book is ". . . the work obviously of a legal pleader and a moral reasoner who had a definite and detailed plan of argument."[5]

---
[5] Robinson, *The Twelve Minor Prophets,* p. 160.

THE LITERATURE OF THE BIBLE

This book is entirely in prose. Occasionally there are outbursts of poetic rhythm and parallelism (cf. 1:11; 3:1, 6, 10; 4:1). At points Malachi employs beautiful symbols (3:2; 4:1–3). Among the literary devices he uses are anthropopathism (1:2–3), hyperbole (2:13), and simile (3:2–3).

Malachi's favorite literary method is to pose and answer questions—a device unique to him among the prophets. It proceeds in a regular pattern of statement, question, and refutation. According to this pattern, the book has seven divisions (1:2–5; 1:6—2:9; 2:10–16; 2:17—3:6; 3:7–12; 3:13—4:3; 4:4–6). The transitions from theme to theme are abrupt. The effect of the book as a whole is vigorous and forceful.

III. Old Testament History. The historical literature of the Old Testament includes the books from Genesis to Esther, the prologue and epilogue of Job, Isaiah 36—39, a few chapters in Jeremiah, and Daniel 1—6.

A. As History. The Old Testament shows us ancient history from the divine perspective. It presents history as being *linear*—that is, as having a beginning, a center (Jesus Christ), and an end. The Bible explains that God is working to guide history according to His plan. It shows us that history is progressive with each stage building upon the preceding stage. God reveals more and more of His design for salvation as the stages of history unfold.

The historical literature of the Old Testament records and interprets the events of that particular era. As the authors wrote, God worked through them to insure a true interpretation and an accurate record of the facts. Sometimes He informed them of the facts or events which they could not otherwise know (e.g., Gen. 1—3 was no doubt directly revealed).

The Old Testament records a number of miracles, in which God's creative power becomes evident in shaping events. Miracles are scattered throughout the narrative but they especially appear in connection with Moses, Joshua, Samuel, Elijah and Elisha (e.g., 1 Kings 17:17–24). These miraculous events are not presented as ordinary happenings in the lives of these people. They represent the special activity of God. The Bible depicts God as being in control of all history; but He seldom introduced miracles into the course of events.

Unlike other histories written in the ancient world, the Bible does not indulge in hero worship. It shows the leading characters of history exactly as they were, even when this might raise serious questions. For instance, how could David (the author of so many beautiful psalms) commit murder, adultery, and polygamy (2 Sam. 11—12)? Yet Scripture frankly tells us that he did.

Old Testament history has many interesting traits. It describes events graphically, vividly, and concisely, but does not always follow a strict chronological order (e.g., Gen. 2; the book of Judges). Because the Bible focuses on matters of theological importance, it is silent at some points and goes into great detail at others. It records only what is important to its theological theme. In Samuel–Kings and Chronicles, the Old Testament confronts us with parallel accounts that are at some points difficult to harmonize. They contain repetitions, summarized speeches, and different theological perspectives—the same kinds of

GILGAMESH EPIC. *This portion of the Babylonian story of Gilgamesh tells of a flood with remarkable parallels to the Flood account found in Genesis. The kindly god Ea warns the character Utnapishtim that a flood is coming to destroy mankind. Utnapishtim builds a cube-shaped ark and takes silver, gold, and living creatures into it, along with his family. The storm lasts for six days and nights. Finally the ship comes to rest at Mount Nisir, and the gods grant immortality to Utnapishtim and his wife.*

THE LITERATURE OF THE BIBLE

AMPHITHEATER. *Theaters were built on slopes and hills in every major city of the ancient world. The original form of the amphitheater dates from the classical Greek period. Although the Romans made a number of modifications, they never abandoned the basic plan. This Greek theater at Epidaurus, on the coast of Argolis (the eastern side of the Greek peninsula), is one of the best preserved of the amphitheaters. It could accommodate over 16,000 spectators. The landscape forms a natural background behind the proscenium (stage).*

ture. Literary study views the books apart from their historical and cultural environment. It looks at literature as an art form rather than as a cultural form.

Literary criticism focuses on whatever unit it can isolate. There is no criterion by which these units are chosen, other than the student's judgment. This unit is then identified as a particular kind, or genre, of literature—such as heroic narrative (legend), chronicle, epic, lyric poetry, or wisdom.

Each kind of literature has its own ways of speaking. For example, when one says that an historical narrative is not a good story, he is evaluating it in terms of the way he thinks a story should go—its structure, plot, characters, imagery, and so on.

In the process of analyzing a given unit, the student may focus on the way the language is used. This is called *rhetorical* criticism. Rhetorical criticism has developed special criteria for analyzing such matters.

But many scholars prefer to look at the Bible from the perspective of pure literature. An example of this approach is set forth by Leland Ryken in his book, *The Literature of the Bible.* What follows is largely based upon his work.

The narrative literary genre reaches a peak of excellence in the Old Testament historical literature. Ryken advances Genesis 1—3 as a classic example of narrative; it forms a complete literary unit with a beginning, middle, and end. Genesis 1 exhibits *recurrence*—i.e., repetition in form, order, and design. This narrative also has unified progression, artistic balance, and an almost poetic vividness of imagery. All of these elements are typical of good quality narrative wherever it occurs. The biblical account deals with the origins of the earth; but unlike its counterparts in pagan literature, it is neither a *theogony* (a story of the origins of the gods) or a *cosmogony* (a story of the origin of the universe).

The middle section of the Creation narrative (Gen. 2:4–24) has an abundance of dialogue and emphasizes the relationship between God and man. Other ancient literature described places of paradise; in such narratives, paradise usually lies outside human experience. This biblical narrative credits God as the originator and ruler of the Garden of Eden, the place of mankind's trial.

Genesis 3 depicts man's fall to catastrophe. Ryken concludes, "There is a sense in which the story told in Genesis 1—3 fulfills the

problems that occur in the Gospels. The inner substance of Old Testament history is God's working out of salvation, with Christ as the fulfillment and goal. This message is plain in both Samuel–Kings and Chronicles, yet these two "histories" differ. The first shows us history through the eyes of the prophets, while the second describes history from a priestly point of view or merely presents a chronicle of events. These two histories supplement each other; they do not contradict each other, although their different interests led them to emphasize different features of what took place.

B. As Literature. There are many different ways to study Old Testament history as litera-

expectations of great narrative better than any other story in literature."[6]

The Old Testament contains several special kinds of narrative, such as heroic narrative (e.g., the story of Abraham) and epic (e.g., the Exodus). We find many different kinds of plot—tragedy, comedy, and so on. Unlike Greek history, the Old Testament seldom features the military exploits of its heroes. Nor does it fill in all the details of the events. But the reader receives enough information to understand what happened.

Old Testament narrative always focuses on God, who acts in history, and on His relationship with the human actors. There is always a double plot—the earthly and the spiritual—both of which move toward an ultimate goal. Both plots involve a conflict between good and evil, with the good being ultimately victorious. However, evil triumphs in some events, so that there is periodic tragedy (e.g., the stories of Samson, Saul, and Solomon).

Old Testament history exhibits a high artistic quality; yet the artistry of the narrative does not prevent a clear presentation of its theme.

The Pentateuch (Genesis through Deuteronomy) is a unique literary phenomenon. Other than the Pentateuch, there is no known historical writing from the period before 1000 B.C. There are pagan myths, stylized bragging material in royal inscriptions, records of business transactions and letters, but no sequential history of the world. The Old Testament is the only ancient document that gives us a factual account of history from the dawn of civilization.

IV. New Testament History. The New Testament writers lived at a time when the art of historical literature was beginning to flower. The historians of Greece and Rome have left us interesting accounts of their cultures.

But New Testament history is more than a cultural report. It is a record of God's interaction with mankind through the life of a man from Nazareth named Jesus.

A. The Gospels. The Gospels have no exact parallels in ancient literature. None of the usual literary categories fit them.

They are not heroic narratives. The heroic narrative is a single unified story—i.e., there is one plot. The structure of a gospel is more fragmented. Its elements may be rearranged or even omitted without damaging the movement of the narrative.

In this respect, the Gospels more closely parallel the structure of a chronicle, such as we saw in the histories of the Old Testament. Certainly the gospel genre parallels the *concept of history* found in these documents. Yet the Old Testament chronicles focus on the story of the nation (kingdom), whereas the Gospels focus on an individual or *protagonist* (main character).

The biographies of the Old Testament (e.g., that of Elijah) bear some similarities to the Gospels. But they lack the extended discourses and the parabolic devices so prominent in the Gospels. Also, the Old Testament biographies are intertwined into the overall structure of the "history of the kingdom." The Gospels cannot be called biography since they lack the detailed reconstruction of the life of the subject. Indeed, vast stretches of Jesus' life story are missing—elements that would be indispensable in a biography.

Certainly the Gospels are not tragedy. Although the main character faces much tragedy and ultimately dies, these accounts do not conform to the structure of tragedy. Jesus is not overcome by uncontrollable fate; He is in complete control of every moment and circumstance. He voluntarily goes to His death, and not as a defeated hero. His death is His victory. It is not the result of a tragic moral decision on His part, but it is the climactic step of His consciously chosen way to triumph and glorification. In tragic literature, the hero is admired because he accepts a defeat pressed upon him in spite of his undeserving character. How different from the plot set forth in the Gospels!

Certainly the Gospels are more than theological treatises. To be sure, each Gospel presents a slightly different portrait of Jesus. But the Gospels lack that systematic discussion of a given theme or themes, which typifies the theological treatise.

Neither are the Gospels essays, since the essay lacks the ever-present narrative thread so prominent in the Gospels. The Gospels bear some similarity to the classical history, except that their speeches do not follow the stylistic patterns of Greek rhetoric. Like the history of the book of Acts, the Gospels are religious history or religious biography. The distinctive literary quality of Jesus' discourses shows that

---

[6] Ryken, *The Literature of the Bible*, p. 41.

THE LITERATURE OF THE BIBLE

they originated with a single highly creative personality.[7]

1. Jesus as a Literary Character. As a literary character, Jesus is unique. In a heroic narrative, the main character is merely exemplary. What he does and what happens to him is held up as a pattern for all people. In the Gospels, however, Jesus is depicted as more than a human example. He is God incarnate who forgives sin, promises salvation to all who believe in Him, and performs miracles—literary themes foreign to heroic narrative.

In mythological narrative tales, the divine or semi-divine protagonist is a literary fiction—i.e., not an actual real-life character. Jesus is clearly a different kind of protagonist. He is an actual historical figure immersed in real life. Since this depiction was published very close to the time of His ministry, it would have been folly for the gospel writers to try to present fiction as fact, and there is no solid reason to think they did so. The Gospels show us Jesus as He was.

As a literary figure, Jesus is an anti-hero. He is neither a political king nor a military victor, but a suffering servant and a dying (but victorious) Messiah.

2. Literary Features of the Gospels. What then are the literary characteristics of a gospel? A gospel is a collection of stories that are unique in the great amount of action they set forth. Their purpose is to publish the facts and meaning of Jesus' life as well as to praise Him. There are many forms used in the gospel. First, there is narrative, extending in complexity from a simple, bare outline of events to an extended presentation of details surrounding events (e.g., Matt. 27). Dialogue appears with the same wide degree of complexity (e.g., Matt. 13:10–17). The gospel also frequently employs discourses or speeches (e.g., the Sermon on the Mount in Matthew 5 or the Olivet discourse in Matthew 24).

The final prominent device is the *parable*. A *parable* may be a story illustrating a single point, in which the details have no meaning (Matt. 13:33), or a story illustrating a major point and perhaps other minor points, in which the details are meaningful (e.g., Matt. 13:36–43).[8]

Miracle stories are also prominent in the Gospels. As literary devices, they demand to be taken at face value. The authors fully intend the reader to understand that Jesus performed miracles. To read them otherwise is to ignore the author's intent and is not responsible literary criticism.

All four Gospels depict Jesus as a literary genius. He is shown to be a master of all the devices of Old Testament poetry: parallelism (Matt. 13:13), metaphor (Matt. 15:14), simile (Matt. 13:47), paradox (Matt. 11:30), and hyperbole (Matt. 19:24). His teaching reflects the style and standpoint of both the prophets and the Old Testament wisdom literature. He stands authoritatively in the midst of His disciples, instructing them in the wise ways of living.

a. Matthew. Each of the Gospels is a unique literary production, although it is evident that the first three are related. Most scholars think that Matthew and Luke wrote with Mark open before them. Matthew is distinguished by its apologetic thrust. The writer wishes to convince his readers that Jesus is the Messiah promised in the Old Testament. Thus, he points out how He fulfilled specific Old Testament prophecies (cf. 1:23; 2:6, 15, 18, 23; 3:3; 4:15–16; 8:17; 12:18–21; 13:35; 21:5; 26:56). In every case except Matthew 2:6, he prefaces the Old Testament quote with a formula specifying that the Scripture is fulfilled. These quotes appear to be fresh translations of the Old Testament passages, while the other Old Testament citations in the Gospel are taken from the Septuagint (the Greek Old Testament). This Gospel has a pronounced Old Testament flavor: its emphasis on God's kingdom (Matt. 13), Christ the Messiah (texts given above), the new age (Matt. 24—25), and righteousness (Matt. 23) recall Old Testament prophecy and apocalyptic. Wisdom themes occur frequently both in the depiction of Christ's stance among His disciples and in the themes He uses. This is especially true of the contrast between the wise and the foolish (Matt. 25).

There are also many characteristics distinctive to this Gospel. It places a unique emphasis on the role of the Gentiles in the new Kingdom (e.g., Matt. 8:10–12; 10:18). It is the only Gospel that mentions the church (Matt. 16:18; 18:17). Matthew groups the sayings of Jesus together into five blocks of discourses, each ending with the formula, "When Jesus had finished. . . ." (Matt. 5:1—7:29; 10:5—11:1; 13:1–53; 18:1—19:1; 24:4—26:1).

---

[7] Ryken, *The Literature of the Bible,* pp. 291–314.

[8] Critics tend to call the first form *parable* and the second *allegory,* but the distinction is logical (or literary) and not in keeping with the New Testament use of the word *parable.* Here *parable* embraces the wider definition.

The book divides the ministry of Jesus into three large sections. First, there is the preparation for His public ministry closed by the phrase "from that time" (4:17). The second division focuses on the opening of His ministry. Then comes the closing phrase "from that time forth" (16:21), followed by emphasis on His private instruction of the Twelve and His death on the cross.

The book is consciously and artfully constructed as a literary work, with a blend of all the elements of the gospel literary genre.

b. Mark. The Gospel of Mark is distinguished by several aspects of its language. It uses more Latin words than any other Gospel. In some cases, it even explains a Greek word with a Latin word (Mark 12:42; 15:16). It also has a pronounced Aramaic flavor. The Greek of this book is rough, marked by broken sentence structure (e.g., 2:10; 11:32), the collo-quial intermingling of Greek tenses, parenthetical remarks (e.g., 3:30; 7:19), and slang expressions. Some scholars believe this indicates that Mark wrote down the material as Peter (who was Jewish and knew Aramaic better than Greek) spoke it for a Roman audience.

This Gospel moves more rapidly than the other Gospels. Yet Mark is not skimpy with details. In fact, when the three synoptic Gospels (Matthew, Mark, and Luke) all report an event, Mark usually gives more details than the others do. Rather, Mark wrote a book of action, focusing on the *deeds* of the main character (Jesus) rather than His words. These events pass before the reader in rapid succession, emphasized by Mark's use of the word *immediately* (more than 40 times).

Mark also depicts Jesus as a teacher and a real human being. The reader sees His compassion (e.g., 1:41; 6:34), His indignation

Hebrew vs. Egyptian Wisdom

The Hebrew sages who wrote the Old Testament books of Proverbs, Ecclesiastes, Job, and some of the Psalms may have been influenced by Egyptian sages who wrote similar literature. But Hebrew "wisdom literature" has a basic difference from the wisdom of other cultures.

Hebrew wisdom centered around Almighty God; it said that "the fear of the Lord is the beginning of wisdom" (Prov. 1:7). This wisdom would guide an individual in day-to-day living. The wisdom of God, as reflected through Old Testament wisdom literature provided the Jewish people with a basic common-sense morality that dictated individual conduct in many circumstances.

Egyptian wisdom also attempted to establish the rules of proper conduct for daily life. Wisdom for the Egyptian, however, centered on the individual. It was based on studying and recording wisdom of the sages, and on disciplining oneself to accept life with its many paradoxes. Being well-versed in the wisdom writings was an important part of Egyptian education; it opened doors to careers and privileges that were otherwise unobtainable.

The Egyptian scholars produced a sophisticated form of wisdom verse. One popular form is seen in the "Instructions" or accumulations of practical sayings. Many Bible scholars acknowledge that the "Instruction of Amen-em-opet" shows a strong similarity to the book of Proverbs. Amen-em-opet divides his "Instruction" into 30 parts, a structure that is similar to the 30 wise sayings of Proverbs 22:17 to 24:22. Both books show concern for the protection of the defenseless; they call for the

fair treatment of widows and orphans and emphasize the value of knowledge. Amen-em-opet advises: "Do not lean on the scales nor falsify the weights . . ." Proverbs 20:23 says, "The Lord hates people who use dishonest scales and weights." The Egyptian's philosophy on a life well lived was: "Better is poverty in the hand of the god than riches in a storehouse; better is bread, when the heart is happy, than riches with sorrow." It is similar to Proverbs 15:16–17: "Better to be poor and fear the Lord than to be rich and in trouble. Better to eat vegetables with people you love than to eat the finest meat where there is hate."

The injustices of life are reflected in "The Admonition of an Egyptian Sage," which observes: "In truth, the poor now possess riches and he who was not even able to make sandals for himself possesses treasures. . . . He who had not any servants is now become master of (many) slaves and he who was a nobleman has now to manage his own affairs." Ecclesiastes 9:11 and 10:7 declare a similar thought: "Wise men do not always earn a living, intelligent men do not always get rich, and capable men do not always rise to high positions . . . ," And "I have seen slaves on horseback while noblemen go on foot like slaves."

Study of these ancient documents has added to our understanding of the Old Testament, but there is still considerable debate over what relationship existed between Hebrew and Egyptian wisdom. Perhaps Hebrew wisdom influenced the development of the surrounding cultures, and what we see in Egypt is really a reflection of Hebrew work.

THE LITERATURE OF THE BIBLE

NAZARETH. *Jesus spent His boyhood years in this obscure village of the Galilee region. Nazareth was considered to be a crude, backward place; so many non-Christians scornfully called Jesus' followers "the sect of the Nazarenes"* (Acts 24:5).

(e.g., 3:5), and His distress and sorrow (e.g., 14:33–34). This Gospel focuses on the training of the Twelve, sometimes painting a poorer picture of them than is found in the other Gospels (e.g., 5:31; 9:10; 10:13–14). Structurally, about 40 percent of the book is given to Christ's passion (i.e., 10:32 ff.). Jesus is clearly pictured as the Son of God from the very beginning (1:1).

c. Luke. Only the Gospel of Luke seeks to bind the stories of Jesus to the secular world. The language of this Gospel is quite literary, somewhat comparable to that of classical Greek. The language of the birth and infancy passages is noticeably different from that of the prologue and rest of the book. These early narratives have a Semitic flavor. They also relate events otherwise not known.

This writer emphasizes the response of the crowds to Jesus. They were amazed at Him (e.g., 5:26; 7:16–17). Yet there is no mention of His compassion for the crowds. There is only mention of His compassion for individuals. Luke focuses especially on the poor, the rich and their wealth (e.g., 12:13–21; 13:11–17), and women. He portrays Jesus as the champion of society's outcasts. Luke also focuses on certain concepts: love, joy, praise, peace, and so on.

Luke usually tells us the time and place of the events narrated (e.g., Luke 2:1). He supplies more details about Christ's human life than do the other Gospels. He alone gives Jesus the title *Savior* (2:11). He emphasizes the mission of Christ, especially noticing His kingship and kingdom. He also traces the parallel between the prophetic pattern and Jesus' ministry.

d. John. The fourth Gospel is written in a very simple style. It uses common words, brief statements, picturesque language, and frequent repetition. The effect is simple but profound. The language is quite distinctive in its diction and its theological concepts (e.g., such key words as *witness, believe, life, love, abide* or *remain, truth* or *true, Jew, world, feast,* and *light*).

The structure of this Gospel is artistically balanced between an almost poetic prologue (John 1:1–18) and epilogue (chap. 21). Seven of Jesus' miracles are especially emphasized and called "signs" (2:1–12; 4:46–51; 5:1–16; 6:1–14, 15–21; 9:1–41; 11:17–46). However, other miracles are mentioned (2:33; 6:2; 20:30). John shows that Jesus used the miracles as opportunities to teach spiritual lessons (cf. John 9, esp. v. 41).

John highlights the "I am" sayings of Jesus

(e.g., 8:12). He places a unique emphasis on the Jewish feasts and festivals that Jesus attended. He demonstrates that Jesus was greater than the Law (cf. 1:17), the temple (cf. 2:19–21), the *shekinah* glory (cf. 1:14), and the entire ritualistic system (cf. 7:37–39). Here we see Jesus primarily addressing individuals rather than crowds. Some of the main characters associated with Jesus' life are pictured more fully here than elsewhere—e.g., John the Baptist and Judas Iscariot. There is special emphasis on the deity of Christ. John is unique in highlighting His preexistence and in calling Him the *logos* ("Word"). At the same time, John clearly sets forth Jesus' dependence on the Father and His full humanity (chap. 17).

B. The Book of Acts. Comparisons of the book of Acts with extra-biblical literature has produced interesting results. Students of classical Greek have concluded that Luke is a church historian in the tradition of Thucydides and Polybius. This is best seen in the speeches that are recorded in Acts. The Greek historians composed the speeches they reported, but gave careful attention to what the speaker really said. But in writing the book of Acts, Luke probably took shorthand notes of the speeches that he heard, and of others' memories of what they had heard. For example, Paul's address to the Ephesian elders gathered to him at Miletus (Acts 20:17–38) reflects distinctively Pauline concepts, while the speeches attributed to Peter (Acts 2:14–40; 3:12–26; 4:8–12; 10:34–43) reflect neither Pauline nor Lukan concepts, but do reflect the language and concepts of 1 Peter. All the speeches in Acts reflect the same general pattern, a pattern that probably follows the structure of early Christian preaching.

But we should not jump to the conclusion that Luke was a simple chronicler who merely recorded the events that occurred. The book's *rhetoric* (i.e., the way words are used), *diction* (the words that are used), structure, and theology are marked by his unique hand. Like all historians, Luke sets forth an interpretation of history.

The overall structure of the book is geared to show how the gospel spread from Jerusalem to "the uttermost parts of the world" (i.e., Rome, the capital of the empire) and how its center shifted from Judaic Christians to Gentile Christians. Many things not relevant to this theme are omitted. Especially noticeable in this regard is the way in which

the ministry of the apostles is recorded. The only one of the original 12 who is pictured to any degree is Peter, and he is soon eclipsed by the appearance of Paul.

On the other hand, there is clear evidence that this book is not only a theological creation. Luke's distinctive Greek style marks most of the book. It is among the most sophisticated Greek writing in the New Testament. This is especially true in Luke's "we" passages, where he reports as an eyewitness of the events recounted (cf. Acts 11:28; 16:10–17; 20:5—21:18; 27:1—28:16). Some of the other sections are couched in the same cultural style. Perhaps Luke composed them on the basis of interviews with other eyewitnesses.

Other sections are written in a rougher style marked by "Semiticisms" (i.e., reflections of Hebrew or Aramaic diction). These sections could reflect the use of Semitic written sources.[9]

Commentators disagree about the literary genre to which the book of Acts belongs. It certainly lacks the characteristics of the biography, heroic narrative, or epic. (There is no central political figure.) It has many similarities with the Old Testament presentations of the kingdom (Samuel–Kings and Chronicles). But these Old Testament chronicles report the history of the kingdom from different theological perspectives, which strongly influence the choice and framing of particular events. Therefore, they are not just neutral records of what happened in a given period. Like Acts, they contain summarized speeches. But the speeches of Acts are far more frequent and extended than the speeches of these Old Testament histories. Speeches play a most significant role in the structure of the book of Acts—e.g., Peter's sermon at Pentecost (Acts 2:14–39), Paul's speech on Mars Hill (Acts 17:16–31), and his address to the Ephesian elders (Acts 20:18–35).

Luke relates only the details that are relevant to his central thesis (unlike the Greek historians). The end result is high literature. The structure of the work as a whole and of the individual subdivisions presents an excellent balance of simplicity and clarity. Luke introduces each main character and describes his life only insofar as he contributes to the main theme. Minor themes are unobtrusively

---

[9] Donald Guthrie, *New Testament Introduction,* rev. ed. (Downers Grove, Ill.: InterVarsity Press, 1970).

introduced, treated, and set aside. Thus, Luke combines the individual units into a harmonious whole. In many cases, each unit forms a completed story with a beginning, middle, and end (e.g., Acts 1—2).

By analyzing Paul's speech on Mars Hill (Acts 17) from a literary perspective, Ryken further supports the thesis that Luke wrote as a historian.[10] He notes that the address follows the rules of Greek and Latin oratory. Verses 22–29 constitute the introduction (*exordium*) and are formulated according to the known rules of classical oratory. Verses 30–31 introduce the main thesis of Paul's address (*propositio*). But before he could proceed to a defense of this thesis, he was interrupted. Ryken observes that Paul's other speeches and epistles are quite similar in style.

V. The Epistles. Much of the New Testament consists of letters that we call *epistles*,[11] a well-known form of literature among the ancient Greeks. We will discuss the book of Hebrews with the epistles, even though it appears to be more of a theological treatise than an epistle.

A. Paul's Epistles. Paul's epistles (as the rest of the New Testament epistles) are unique literary productions. They differ from all letter styles found in extra-biblical literature.

The extra-biblical letters are structured as follows: (1) the author's name and title, (2) the recipient's name and title, (3) sometimes the secretary's or messenger's name, (4) a standardized greeting, (5) a discussion of the business in hand, and (6) closing greetings.

In many papyrus letters, the closing greeting is written in a hand different from the rest of the letter. This suggests that the author employed an *amanuensis* or secretary to write his letter. An amanuensis would listen to what the author wanted to say and would then compose the document in his own words. Then the author would read the amanuensis' work, making sure it said what he intended. A secretary might take down the author's words in shorthand, write them out, and submit the result to the author for the closing greetings (cf. Gal. 6:11–12; 2 Thess. 3:17).

Paul's letters follow this general structure. What makes them distinctive is the element of apostolic proclamation and exhortation, which gives them the force of written sermons. Paul expands the colorless, standardized greeting into a rich combination of "grace" and "peace"—characteristic Christian and Hebrew ideas. Then he replaces the next section (the thanksgiving for the recipient's health and happiness) with a *blessing* (i.e., thanksgiving for the blessings received from God).

The main part of Paul's letters opens with a well-known device taken from the rules of Greek and Roman public speaking. Seeking to establish a good relationship with his readers, Paul makes request, appeal, or injunction. Sometimes he uses a "formula of disclosure" (e.g., "I want you to know," and "I would not have you to be ignorant"). On other occasions, he congratulates his readers on the success of their work (cf. Phil. 1:3–6; 1 Thess. 1:2–10) and their healthy spiritual condition (1 Thess. 1:4–5; 2 Thess. 1:3–4).

Paul's letters may interweave practical and doctrinal concerns (e.g., 1 and 2 Cor., Phil., and 1 Thess.). At other times he separates these two concerns, placing the doctrinal before the practical (e.g., Rom., Gal., Eph.); in these cases, the doctrinal section constitutes the basis for the practical application.

Paul closes his epistles with notes of greetings, a doxology, and a benediction.

The tone of Paul's epistles is not intimate, like the typical letter genre. He does not write to a single reader (save in the case of Timothy, Titus, and Philemon), but to a more general audience. Conscious of his apostolic office, he regularly speaks as a public person rather than as a private individual. Whether the addressee is a church (e.g., 1 Cor.) or an individual (e.g., 1 Tim.), Paul does not relinquish his public stance. Nearly everything he says is ultimately a message to the church universal. His epistles are in effect thematic extensions of the Gospels—a trait that is reflected in their literary structure.

Paul proves himself to be a master of rhetoric and eloquent style. He loves to use long, suspended sentences that build to a powerful climax. He skillfully uses evocative words—vivid metaphors and similes, touching allusions to the life and person of Jesus—all the devices of effective literary communication. He is especially adept at *peroration* (attaining a strong climax—e.g., Eph. 6:10–17).

B. The Letter to the Hebrews. There is considerable debate concerning the literary genre to which Hebrews belongs. It is not really a letter, since it lacks the expected introduction. Yet the opening unit (Heb. 1:1–3)

---

[10] Ryken, *The Literature of the Bible*, pp. 327–331.

[11] From the Latin *epistola*, "letter."

SUPPER AT EMMAUS. *This is how the sixteenth-century Italian painter Caravaggio depicted Christ's supper with His disciples at Emmaus (cf. Luke 24:13–18). Modern artists tend to show Christ with a lean face and a long beard, following the pattern of Rembrandt and other "Old Masters." But earlier artists such as Caravaggio did not follow this model—which underscores the fact that the Gospels give us no detailed portrait of Jesus' physical features.*

serves as an excellent springboard to its argument. The book has several personal allusions (e.g., 2:1). Its argument, however, is much more cohesively developed than in an ordinary epistle, and its style is mostly that of a didactic treatise.

Some scholars conclude that Hebrews is an essay. But this literary category fails to include certain elements (e.g., personal allusions) present in Hebrews. Others see the book as a written sermon or a combination of several sermons. It seems truest to say that Hebrews is unique from a literary standpoint, with elements of the epistle, essay or theological treatise, and sermon all blended together.

The book of Hebrews presents a well-balanced argument. Like some Pauline epistles (e.g., Romans, Ephesians), it consists of an extended theological or doctrinal presentation (1:1—10:18), followed by a briefer section of practical exhortation (10:19—13:21). The doctrinal section itself, however, is punctuated by practical admonitions (e.g., 2:1–4; 3:7–19; 15:11–14), exhortations (4:11–13; 6:9–12), and warnings (6:1–8). These elements are masterfully interwoven. This epistle makes frequent reference to the Old Testament; indeed, it establishes every doctrinal point by expounding and applying Old Testament passages. The writer introduces Old Testament passages with formulae showing his respect for them as the utterances of God (e.g., Heb. 4:3; 10:15).

C. The Epistle of James. This letter was written by James the brother of Christ to the Jewish Christians scattered throughout the Roman Empire. James was not merely the physical brother of Jesus; he was a true believer. There is a striking parallel between the sayings of Jesus recorded in Matthew 5—7 and the Epistle of James; both of them use many images from nature. Some passages in this letter also remind us of the speech of James in Acts 15.

The epistle exhibits a strong Jewish background. This refutes the notion that James structured his letter after the Greek diatribe, common among the popular Greek moralists. The diatribe was not geared to speak to a particular historical situation.

The style of this book is authoritative, simple, and direct. It lacks the cohesiveness of Pauline presentation. So even though it is clearly didactic and pastoral in its purpose, it is quite different in structure and rhetoric from Paul's writings. It contains many epigrams, which demonstrate the influence of the Old Testament poetic style upon James' writing. The same poetic style was prominent in Jesus' teaching, and several passages in this book are obviously dependent upon that teaching. (For example, compare James 1:12 with Matt. 5:11–12.)

Some say that James is an example of New Testament wisdom literature. The writer appears as a wise teacher instructing his readers in the way of wise living. His short, rather disconnected maxims resemble the ancient proverbs of Solomon. This feature has led some scholars to suggest that James wrote in the manner in which he taught. They suggest that this epistle is written *catechetical* (instructional) material.

D. Peter's Epistles and Jude. The Apostle Peter wrote his first epistle from Rome. He addressed it to the predominantly Gentile churches of Asia Minor that were enduring severe persecutions at the hands of their unbelieving neighbors.

First Peter is in the form of an epistle. It has the expected opening and personal greetings at the beginning and a benediction at the end. The book presents the theme of Christian suffering in ever-increasing intensity. The doxology in 4:11 interrupts the flow of thought only momentarily.

The Chiasm

In several ways the *chiasm,* one of the writing styles of the Bible, resembles mountain climbing. Ascending to the summit, a mountaineer climbs past level upon level of rock in sequence, then reaches the peak. Descending the other side, he passes the same ledges in reverse order.

Using the same symmetrical approach, many Bible authors recorded each idea in sequence, built to a peak, then wrote again about each idea in inverted order. Their first concept was mirrored in their last, their second thought was next to last, the third idea was also third from the bottom, and so on—with a peak or platform in the center. This method of writing is called the *chiasm* (from the Greek word for "placing crossways"), and may be found in the poetry and prose of both the Old and New Testaments.

In poetry, the chiasmatic order of thoughts may be switched without changing meaning. The prophet Isaiah was familiar with this style:

(first idea)	For my thoughts
(second idea)	are not your thoughts,
(second idea)	Neither are your ways
(first idea)	my ways, says the Lord. (55:8, RSV)

God's methods open and close the verse, while man's wisdom forms a two-part central plateau. Similarly:

(first idea)	Ephraim shall not be jealous of Judah,
(second idea)	and Judah shall not harass
(second idea)	Ephraim. (Isa. 11:13b, RSV)
(first idea)	

Notice the symmetry of Ephraim-Judah-Judah-Ephraim.

We also find chiasms in biblical prose. Paul used this inverted style to describe God as the sovereign Creator and the all-powerful Sustainer of creation (recorded in Acts 17:24–25). The central plateau explains that God is beyond any need of human assistance:

(first idea)	God that made the world and all things therein,
(second idea)	seeing that he is Lord of heaven and earth,
(third idea)	dwelleth not in temples made with hands;
(third idea)	Neither is worshiped with men's hands, as though he needed any thing,
(second idea)	seeing he giveth to all life, and breath,
(first idea)	and all things.

A narrative could also be written as a chiasm. In the account of the Gadarene demoniac in Mark 5, the apostle clearly uses the chiasm to describe his story. The tale starts and concludes with the Lord physically entering and leaving the scene (vv. 1, 20). In the next and second to last episodes, Jesus actually faces the man who is later freed of his devils (vv. 2, 18). The description of the demoniac is third (vv. 3–5, 15), while the demons' request comes next (vv. 7, 10). The peak of the story is the moment when Christ asks the demons' name (v. 9). Mark methodically leads us up the mountain past each facet of demon control to the peak encounter with Jesus, then down the victorious side of the summit, free of Satan's power, all in carefully inverted sequence. In fact, he gives us a chiasm within a chiasm, for his first description of the demoniac is a chiasm in itself:

(first idea)	who had his dwelling among the tombs;
(second idea)	and no man could bind him,
(third idea)	no, not with chains: Because that he had been often bound with fetters and chains,
(third idea)	and the chains had been plucked asunder by him, and the fetters broken in pieces:
(second idea)	neither could any man tame him.
(first idea)	And always, night and day, he was . . . in the tombs . . . (Mark 5:3–5).

Mark uses this elaborate chiasm to dramatize the bondage of the man. The peak of the "mountain" describes how the demoniac was bound with fetters and chains, yet the bondage of demon possession was even more powerful. This is a vivid example of the chiasmic technique.

This document has been viewed in a variety of ways: as a written baptismal sermon with a general address attached to the end, as a double letter subsequently combined, and as a letter with an addition for a particular church. It probably was a general (or circular) epistle used as a vehicle to deliver an exhortation (cf. 5:12).

The style of this epistle is quite elegant, exhibiting similarities to classical Greek. On the

24

THE LITERATURE OF THE BIBLE

ANTIOCH. *The modern city of Antakya stands on the site of Antioch, where the early church launched Paul's first missionary campaign (Acts 13:1–3). This photo is taken from the ruins of the Seleucid fortress above Antioch, which was still standing in Paul's day.*

other hand, certain aspects of its style are somewhat rough. This may indicate two hands. The thought and substance are Peter's (the fisherman whose Greek may have been a little rugged), the composition was mostly if not wholly done by the Greek *amanuensis* Silvanus (1 Pet. 5:12).

A number of passages in 1 Peter are sometimes said to be *hymnic*—i.e., they may reflect ancient Christian hymns (1:3–12; 2:21–25; 3:18–22).

This epistle frequently quotes the Old Testament. It employs various figures of speech: simile (2:2), colorful epithets (2:25; 5:4), and metaphor (5:2).

The apostle wrote 2 Peter when he was facing certain death. He addressed the same readers, warning them against false teachers who were spreading dangerous doctrines, and urging his Christian friends to grow in the knowledge of the truth.

The Greek of 2 Peter is generally less elegant than that of 1 Peter. There is a difference in vocabulary. Probably this reflects use of a different amanuensis. Unlike 1 Peter, the second epistle does not refer frequently to the Old Testament. Second Peter 1:5–7 attains an in-teresting poetic quality by piling phrase upon phrase. The prose is highly descriptive at many points (cf. 2:12–13), employing powerful figures of speech (e.g., simile in 2:12; 3:10 and metaphor in 2:17).

Jude was a brother of James and Jesus. His letter picks up the theme of 2 Peter. Jude condemns the false doctrine that "whatever is done in the body is not chargeable to the soul." Christians who held this position believed that their acts did not affect their salvation, and so they committed many sinful acts.

This epistle presents two intriguing literary problems. First, it quotes from 1 Enoch 1:9 and the Assumption of Moses. These books were written before the time of the New Testament, but they were not accepted as inspired by the Jewish or Christian communities. Yet Jude used them to make his point. How much authority did he give them? All we can safely say is that he believed what he quoted was true.

Secondly, there is a strong similarity between Jude and 2 Peter. If they were not penned by the same writer, they were at least written with one another in mind.

Who borrowed from whom? We cannot be sure. The Greek language of Jude is strongly

Semitic. Perhaps this is due to his intimate knowledge of the Greek Old Testament (i.e., the Septuagint). His style is vivid, vigorous, and at times nearly poetic (vv. 12–13). It does not use the rugged broken sentence typical of Paul, the epigram (short powerful statements) of James, or the reasoned argumentation of Hebrews. His frequent use of a three-point argument and his carefully constructed doxology (vv. 24–25) point to an orderly mind. Only Jude and Paul end their letters with such an elaborate ascription of praise.

E. John's Letters. The New Testament contains three epistles from the Apostle John to the churches in Asia Minor, which have notable similarities to his Gospel and the book of Revelation. These letters contend against an error that later emerged as the heresy of Gnosticism.

First John is evidently a personal message from the writer. However, is does not have the introduction, writer's greeting, and thanksgiving typical of the epistle genre. Nor does it exhibit the influence of public speaking, typical of the sermon genre. Some scholars have related this epistle to the diatribe genre, but it speaks to a definite historical situation, which diatribes do not.

There is no unifying theme developed throughout the book. It presents a series of pastoral instructions on topics that appear not to be directly related. A close study reveals that the author is refuting a heresy similar to Gnosticism. (*Gnosticism* taught that the body and this world are evil and that salvation is gained by knowledge alone. In particular, the Gnostics argued that God could not have become incarnate. They maintained that a person could do as he wished in this world, as long as he thought the right thing.)

This epistle often repeats its leading ideas and terms (e.g., *light, truth,* and *love*). The sentence structure is simple and straightforward, involving much parallelism of idea (e.g., 3:6). The writer tends to present ideas in strong contrast to one another—i.e., in absolute blacks and whites. There appear to be for him no theological grey areas. Although these characteristics are similar to Old Testament prophetic writing, 1 John makes only one direct reference to the Old Testament (3:12).

Second and Third John are more personal than is 1 John. They also speak to specific (but differing) situations, and they include the opening and personal greetings typical of a letter. Their style is similar to that of 1 John, although it is closer to that of the Gospel of John. Each letter briefly addresses a specific subject and pursues that subject rather directly.

VI. Apocalyptic Literature. In the broadest sense, *apocalyptic* includes all religious literature that abounds in visions of God or revelations from God concerning the end of the present evil age. In this sense, apocalyptic includes certain sections of Joel, Amos, Zechariah, Daniel 7–12, Jesus' Olivet discourse (Matt. 24–25), 1 Thessalonians 4:13 ff., the book of Revelation, and certain extra-biblical literature.

A. Daniel. Daniel 7—12 is the prototype of apocalyptic literature. Apocalyptic writers take their major literary features and themes from Daniel.

First, Daniel presents a cosmic dualism—i.e., there are two mighty forces (God and evil) locked in a great struggle. Daniel sets forth abundant visions and revelations in highly symbolic language, which often alludes to ancient mythological figures and Old Testament prophetic symbolism. Daniel makes symbolical use of numbers, animals, and inanimate objects.

He condemns the evil of the present age even though the forces of evil apparently triumph. In the higher realm these evil forces are clearly losing the war. Daniel's strong emphasis on divine sovereignty shows that the outcome of the war is never in doubt. His pessimistic outlook on the present political situation is thematically balanced by this optimistic view of divine sovereignty and the outcome of world history. He knows that in the future age God will triumph and bless the faithful.

Another apocalyptic theme of Daniel is the resurrection of the righteous and judgment of the wicked (Dan. 12). Also prominent in Daniel's book is the figure of the "Son of Man," who appears as a supernatural preexistent being in the form of a man.

Because it abounds in mysterious figures or symbols, apocalyptic literature such as Daniel's is more difficult to interpret than other Old Testament literature.

B. Intertestamental Apocalyptic. Intertestamental apocalyptic differed from Old Testament apocalyptic in several tendencies. It was more deterministic and pessimistic. It urged upon its readers an ethical passivity—i.e., that the faithful should not struggle

24

THE LITERATURE OF THE BIBLE

against the forces of evil but let God deal with them. It also expanded the symbolism of Daniel. The Dead Sea Scrolls contain a wealth of apocalyptic material from this period.

C. Revelation. The book of Revelation (which has the unique literary form of letters plus visions of the future) borrows from Old Testament and intertestamental apocalyptic, as well as from Old Testament prophetic literature as a whole. For example, it highlights the Son of Man, the second coming of Christ, the ultimate glory of the kingdom of God (Rev. 21), and the resurrection of final judgment (Rev. 20:11–15). In intertestamental apocalyptic we also find a woman representing a people and a city (cf. Rev. 17:18), horns representing authority and eyes representing understanding (cf. Rev. 5:6), trumpets signifying a superhuman or divine voice (cf. Rev. 8:6—11:19), white robes symbolizing the glory of the coming age (cf. Rev. 6:11), crowns depicting dominion (cf. Rev. 6:21), the number seven standing for fullness or perfection (cf. Rev. 5:1; 8:6), the number 12 standing for the ultimate perfect people of God (cf. Rev. 7:5–8; 22:2), and the frequent appearance of angels (cf. Rev. 7:1; 10:1).

Apocalyptic writing of this sort was a kind of code, a way of communicating that unbelieving enemies would not understand. A person who wrote such literature could encourage his readers to stand against the pagan state and predict its downfall under divine judgment, without fear of official reprisal. Modern readers often miss this aspect of the apocalyptic genre, just as the ancient pagans did. It was designed to reveal its message to insiders in terms that an outsider could not understand.

An interesting stylistic trait of Revelation is its strong contrasts. These include contrasts in *conflict* (e.g., God struggles against Satan, the saints against the followers of the beast, the bride of Christ against the harlot Babylon), *imagery* (e.g., the Lamb and the dragon, the beautiful but deceptive [deadly] harlot, the Lamb that is a Lion), *actions* (e.g., the estab-

GOSPEL EVENTS. *These medieval drawings illustrate the text of Robert de Lisle's Psalter, which was prepared in England in the late thirteenth century. They show four key events from the Gospels: Jesus' resurrection (top left), the three Marys at Jesus' empty tomb (top right), the resurrected Christ speaking to Mary Magdalene (bottom left), and the Last Supper (bottom right).*

lishment of the new Jerusalem and the destruction of Babylon, Satan being allowed to harm his own human followers but not the followers of the Lamb), *location* (e.g., heaven and earth, land and sea) and *time* (i.e., time and eternity). These contrasts vividly convey the sense that vast forces of good and evil are in conflict in this world, and we cannot hope for stability until the day of Christ's triumph.

THE POETRY OF THE BIBLE

The Israelites used poetry and music from the earliest days of their history. Before that, Adam probably used a poem to praise God for his new mate (Gen. 2:23). Moses sang a song to God for delivering the Israelites from Egypt (Exod. 15). The Bible (Judg. 5:2–31; 14:14, 18) records many other poems from the time of the judges (1400—1000 B.C.). But most poetry recorded in the Bible comes from the time of King David (1012—972 B.C.) and afterward. By David's time, the poets and musicians of Israel had banded together to form their own guilds (1 Chron. 35:15), which stayed active until the time of the Exile. It is said that King Hezekiah (728—687? B.C.) sent a group of musicians as a part of his peace offering to Sennacherib.

Thus poets and musicians played an important part in the life of Israel. The New Testament does not contain any complete books of poetry as the Old Testament does, but it does contain a good deal of poetry all the same.

I. Types of Old Testament Poetry. The Hebrew language used several different words to refer to the various types of poetry that we find in the Old Testament. The *shîr* was a poem that was accompanied by musical instruments. The word literally means "song." The *mizmôr* was a song or hymn of worship; the *qînâ* a funeral eulogy or lament; a *tehillâ* a hymn of praise; and the *māshāl* a proverb or satire.

Each Hebrew poet expressed his own personal feelings in what he wrote, being inspired by the Holy Spirit. Most of the poetical books contained *lyric poetry* (poetry to be sung). Many biblical books contained *gnomic* (wisdom) poetry. *Prophetic poetry* usually described a vision from God, while *historical poetry* told about actual events of the past in epic fashion.

II. Nature of Old Testament Poetry. Any poet uses special techniques to express his message. Three techniques that most poets use to express their ideas are rhyme, meter, and parallelism.

Rhyme is concerned with the sounds of words. Most often rhyming poetry makes the same sound occur at the end of each line or every other line. Rhyme is common in English-language poems, but it was very rare in Hebrew poetry.

Meter is concerned with the measured beat of poetry. The poet uses the accents of his words to set up a rhythm in each line and a pattern of rhythms throughout the poem. Scholars disagree about whether Hebrew poetry really has a meter. If it does, it is a 3:3 meter—i.e., three beats for each line. Biblical poems seldom follow this pattern exactly, and so one cannot be sure whether Hebrew poetry actually had a system of meter in Old Testament times.

The third technique, *parallelism,* was the one Old Testament poets used most often. The Bible has three basic types of parallelism: *complete, incomplete,* and *"staircase."*

A. Complete Parallelism. When a poet used complete parallelism, he repeated the

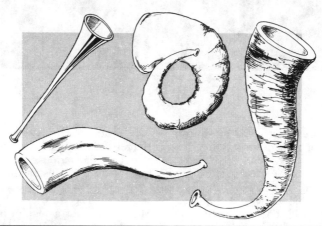

ANCIENT HORNS. *"Praise him with the sound of the trumpet," says Psalm 150:3. Music and singing were vital to early Hebrew life. The Psalms themselves were songs, frequently sung to the accompaniment of wind or stringed instruments. Horns and trumpets convened the congregation, announced festivals, sounded the attack, or proclaimed the ascension of the king.*

exact idea or the opposite idea of a line in the next line:

Israel doth-not-know
My-people doth-not-consider (Is. 1:3).

In this verse, *Israel* means the same thing as *My-people*. (The English words are joined by a hyphen to show the ideas contained in a single Hebrew word.) The word *doth-not-know* is parallel with *doth-not-consider*. The poet has used different words in each line to express the same idea.

Sometimes a Hebrew poet would express an idea in one line and the opposite in the next line; this type of complete parallelism is called *antithetic* parallelism:

A-wise son gladdens a-father
And-a-foolish man despises his-mother
(Prov. 15:20).

This kind of parallelism balanced the complete thought of each line. Yet another type of complete parallelism repeated the idea of a line in figurative or symbolic terms. Scholars call this *emblematic* parallelism:

As-coals are to-burning coals, and
wood-to-fire;
So-is-a-contentious man to-kindle strife
(Prov. 26:21).

The Hebrew poet might also reverse the idea of a line to make *introverted* or *chiastic* parallelism:

(1) *The-mouth of-a-righteous man*
(2) *Is a-well of-life*
  (1) *But-violence covereth*
  (2) *The-mouth of-the-wicked* (Prov. 10:11).

The poet contrasts the ideas in the first half of the first line (No. 1) to the last half of the second line. He contrasts the second half of the first line (No. 2) to the first half of the second line. In other words, he contrasts the ideas in reverse order. Also notice that this poem uses antithetic parallelism.

B. Incomplete Parallelism. If the Hebrew poet used incomplete parallelism, he would not repeat the *entire* idea of his first line in the second line of his poem:

(1) *Therefore-the ungodly*
(2) *Shall not stand*
(3) *In the judgment*
  (1) *Nor-sinners*
  (3) *In-the-congregation of-the-righteous*
(Psa. 1:5).

The three elements of the first line are numbered 1—3. Notice that the second line repeats elements 1 and 3, but not 2. The poet did not try to match the full idea of the first line in the second line, but he did set up a parallel pattern. In the Hebrew language, both lines of this verse have the same number of accented syllables. This is called *compensation*. Occasionally a Hebrew poet does not use parallel ideas at all, but he does use compensation.

THE POETRY OF THE BIBLE

THE TRUMPETER'S PLACE. *Taken from a niche of the northwest parapet of the temple at Jerusalem, this inscription reads "to the place of trumpeting . . . to herald. . . ." The stone indicates the site on which the priest blew the shofar (ram's horn) to signal the holy day.*

25

THE POETRY OF THE BIBLE

Of course, the Hebrew poet could make a very sophisticated poem by using incomplete parallelism *without* compensation. In the following verse, the poet uses his accented syllables to set up the pattern of 4:3::4:3. Of course, you can't see this in the English translation. But you *can* see that it is incomplete parallelism, because he does not try to parallel the full idea of each line:

I-saw the-earth and-lo waste and-void
And-the-heavens and-not their-light
    I-saw the-mountains and-lo they-were-
      trembling
    And-all the-hills moved-lightly
    (Jer. 4:23–24).

Most often this style was used for the *qînâ*, or "dirge pattern":

I-am-the-man that-hath-seen affliction
By-the-rod of-his-wrath (Lam. 3:1).

C. Climactic Parallelism. Perhaps one of the most interesting forms of parallelism was "staircase" or *climactic* parallelism:

(1) *For-lo thine-enemies,*
(2) *O Lord*
(1) *For-lo thine-enemies*
(3) *Shall-perish*
    (1) *All-workers of-iniquity*
    (3) *Shall be scattered* (Psa. 92:9).

Here the poet dropped the second element of his first line, which is marked as Number 2. He then carried the idea forward by adding a third element.

D. Other Devices. Hebrew poetry also used several other devices. The poet might begin each line of his poem with a different letter of the Hebrew alphabet to make what is called an *acrostic*. For instance, Psalm 119 is divided into 22 sets of 8 verses each, one set for each letter of the Hebrew alphabet. Each verse in each set begins with the same letter in Hebrew. The verses in the first set all begin with *aleph*, the first letter in the Hebrew alphabet. The verses in the second set all begin with *beth*, the second letter in the Hebrew alphabet, and so on.

Sometimes Hebrew poetry would repeat the sound of each word to make *alliteration*, like our English poem, "Peter Piper picked a peck of pickled peppers. . . ." Or the sound might be repeated at the end of each word, which is called *assonance* (like "potato–tomato"), but this was very rare in Hebrew.

Hebrew poetry used many figures of speech to help the reader visualize what the poet was talking about. The Hebrew poet often described God in human terms, with human emotions and body features—for instance, "It grieved him" (Gen. 6:6) and "His ears" (2 Sam. 22:7). Scholars call this technique *anthropomorphism*. A special kind of anthropomorphism, called *personification*, describes things as if they had the qualities of a person. For example, the Bible speaks of "the virgin Israel" (Amos 5:2).

Some poems exaggerated the facts to stress an idea. This is called *hyperbole*. Amos used it when he described an Amorite warrior as one "whose height was like the height of the cedars" (Amos 2:9). English-language poets compare a person with an object—a technique

THE POETRY OF THE BIBLE

that is called *simile*. Likewise, the Hebrew poets liked to use this technique as is seen in Hosea 14:8. Sometimes they would imply the comparison (a device called *metaphor*), as when the Psalmist said, "The Lord is my life" (Psa. 27:1).

At times the Bible poet said the opposite of what is intended, to give us a touch of grim and grotesque humor (Amos 4:4–5). Biblical poetry also used symbols to express much larger ideas. A famous example of this is the verse, "They shall beat their swords into plowshares" (Isa. 2:4). In this case, the sword stands for war and the plowshare stands for peaceful labor. This poetic use of symbols is called *metonymy*.

Although it only rarely used rhyme and meter (the two features most commonly associated with English poetry), Hebrew poetry was nevertheless rich and creative.

III. Literary Context. A great deal of poetry was composed in Egypt, Mesopotamia, and Canaan long before the appearance of the biblical books of poetry. The lyric poem, which comprises most of the poems in the Psalms, corresponds with the extensive lyric poetry of Egypt, Sumer, and Babylon.

The oldest ancient Near Eastern literature stems from the Sumerians (early occupants of the Mesopotamian Valley), whose literature contains many hymns or psalms of praise and prayers in poetic form. In Sumer the art of writing hymns was highly developed before 2000 B.C. Ancient Sumerian poets categorized their works according to subject and manner of performance (i.e., what instrument should be used). Such lyric poems may be as long as 400 lines. Egyptian poems were also of varying lengths and consisted of both prayer and praise. This literature includes love songs from as early as 1300 B.C. Interestingly, the lover in the Egyptian poems was called "brother" (cf. Song of Sol. 5:1–2; 8:1–3). We find extended lamentations among Sumerian and Egyptian literature from before 2000 B.C. Thus all three types of poetry have been found outside the Bible.

The artistic style of biblical poetry closely resembles Ugaritic (from 1700 to 1500 B.C.) and Babylonian poetry. There we see similar themes and imagery. In view of such material, the archaeologist William F. Albright concluded that the poetry of the Old Testament was written very early. In structure (i.e., in the use of parallelism) it was midway between Mesopotamian and Ugaritic poetry. The grammar, vocabulary, and imagery of the poetry throughout the Bible have remarkable parallels to Ugaritic poetry.[1] In spite of these similarities, biblical poetry is distinguished by its superior elegance, artistic expression, and moral and religious concepts.

IV. The Poetic Books. Six books of the Old Testament contain lyric and gnomic poetry. The *lyric* (song poem) books are Psalms, Lamentations, and the Song of Solomon. The *gnomic* (wisdom poem) books are Proverbs, Job, and Ecclesiastes.

A. Psalms. By far the largest book of Old Testament poetry is the Book of Psalms. Jewish scholars put this book in a section of the Bible that they call the "Writings."

The Book of Psalms stands apart from any other poetic literature of the ancient Near East, lifting praises to God and revealing God's will to His people. The poems of other Near Eastern people do not and could not do this.

The New Testament quotes the Psalms more often than any other section of the Old Testament except for the Book of Isaiah. The Psalms build upon the theological ideas of the Pentateuch, explaining and applying the laws of Moses. The Psalms also forge a strong link with the books of prophecy, in that they often warn the people of Israel concerning their disobedience to God's law. Some of the Psalms themselves contain prophecy (e.g., Psa. 2).

1. Classification. The Psalms are divided into five sections, or books. Psalms 1—41 form what is called the "Davidic Section," because King David wrote most of them. The Davidic psalms call God by the name *Jehovah* 272 times and by the name *Elohim* 15 times. The name *Elohim* refers to God as the Almighty Creator, the ruler of all the nations. The name *Jehovah*, on the other hand, refers to Him as the God of the covenant with Israel. It identifies God as the divine King of the Hebrew people.

Psalms 42—72 are called "Hezekiah's Collection" because they seem to have been compiled about the time of King Hezekiah (729—696 B.C.). However, many of them were written long before Hezekiah. Eighteen of them were written by King David. In this section the name *Elohim* appears 200 times and *Jehovah* appears 43 times. Some of these Psalms may have been written even before the time of David.

---

[1] *See* William F. Albright, *Yahweh and the Gods of Canaan* (New York: Doubleday and Company, 1968).

THE POETRY OF THE BIBLE

The third section includes Psalms 73—89. It is called "Josiah's Collection" because it was probably compiled during the time of King Josiah (638—608 B.C.).

Psalms 90—106 were designed to be used in the temple worship, and they only use the name *Jehovah*. Bible scholars believe these Psalms were collected between the time of King Josiah's reign and the fall of Israel.

The last section of the Book of Psalms (Psa. 107—150) was probably collected after the Jews returned to their homeland—after 536 B.C. Nearly all of these Psalms use the name *Jehovah* to refer to God, and 15 of them were written by King David. This section includes Psalms 107—150, and it has two different types of Psalms—the *Hallels* or "praises" (Psa. 113—118) and the "Songs of Degrees" (Psa. 120—134).

The theme of the Book of Psalms is "My God and Me," or "Our God and Us." It has been truly said that it is a "book of universal heart-appeal, covering the whole range of religious motions."[2] It is easy to see that the Book of Psalms is a very emotional book; but it also contains a great deal of religious teaching. It shows that every true believer in God should be marked by right feeling (experience) as well as right thinking (theology).

The Psalms lift up three important themes: (a) man's desire for rescue from sin and misery, (b) man's celebration of the deliverance God gives him, and (c) man's voicing of praise and gratitude toward God. Sometimes all three things will appear in a single Psalm (e.g., Psa. 51). But generally, the Book of Psalms leads us gradually through each of these themes. The first section focuses on misery, while the second and third sections stress the theme of deliverance. The fourth and fifth sections express praise and gratitude.

2. Authorship. Many different writers composed the majestic poems that we now find in the Book of Psalms. Often a Psalm tells who wrote it or to whom it was dedicated. Some Psalms mention a person's name at the beginning, but they do not really make it clear whether this person was the writer, the collector, or the person to whom the Psalm was dedicated. Seventy-three Psalms give the name of David; 10 or 11 name the sons of Korah; while 12 Psalms give the name of Asaph. Other Psalms carry the names of Moses, Solomon,

Heman, and Ethan. Fifty of the Psalms do not indicate who wrote them.

3. Subject Matter. The Psalms may be grouped according to their poetic style, the time in which they were written, and the persons who wrote them. But they may also be grouped according to subject.

Many of the Psalms are called *messianic* Psalms, because they refer to Christ. They foretell the coming of Jesus and His ministry; in fact, they make little sense unless read with Jesus in mind. Jesus said, "All things must be fulfilled, which were written in the . . . psalms concerning me" (Luke 24:44). Certainly these Psalms explain a great deal about the ministry of the Savior. Nine of the messianic Psalms are called *royal* Psalms because they exalt Jesus as the King of all nations (Psa. 2; 18; 20; 21; 45; 61; 72; 110; and 132). Ten messianic Psalms are called *prophetic* Psalms because they foretell the coming of Christ (Psa. 8, 16, 22, 40, 45, 68, 72, 97, 110, and 118). Six are called *passion* Psalms because they describe Jesus' suffering in death on the cross (Psa. 22; 35; 41; 64; 69; and 109).

There are nine *imprecatory* Psalms in which the writer asks God to destroy his enemies. These Psalms were written by King David. Some Bible critics wonder why these were included in the Bible. They think these Psalms arise from unworthy motives. However, we must realize that King David represented the entire nation of Israel, which was the kingdom of God. His enemies were really opposing God, and it was altogether fitting for David to summon God's help to preserve His kingdom.

Some Psalms celebrate the history of Israel. For example, Psalms 106 and 114 describe the days of Moses. Psalm 106:34–36 describes the time of the Judges. Psalms 3, 7, and others tell about the reign of King David. Psalm 72 paints a colorful picture of Israel under King Solomon. Psalms 74, 79 and others tell how the enemies of Israel carried God's people away into captivity during the Exile.

The Psalms also embody many different religious experiences. There are Psalms expressing repentance (Psa. 25), conversion (Psa. 40), consecration to God (Psa. 46), trust (Psa. 3), prayer (Psa. 55), praise (Psa. 96), and other uplifting experiences. There are also Psalms about affliction (Psa. 6), the hardships of old age (Psa. 71), vain pride (Psa. 39), and homesickness (Psa. 137).

Many Psalms describe the characteristics of God. For example, Psalms 18—20 describe

---

[2] E. J. Pace, *Sunday School Times*, July 21, 1941, p. 616.

God's wisdom, majesty, and power. Psalms 32, 85, and 136 tell about His mercy. Psalm 139 praises God's infinite knowledge, while Psalms 33, 89, and 104 laud His creative power.

4. Language. The language of the Psalms resembles the poetry of the ancient city of Ugarit. (*See* "Ugarit and the Canaanites.") The Psalms pick up some of the phrases and expressions that were popular during that time, but this does not mean that the Psalms were copied from the literature of Ugarit.

Psalm 104 is remarkably similar to the Egyptian "Hymn to Aton" in its use of poetic parallelism and in the thoughts of some verses. Although these similarities are too close to be incidental, a close comparison of the two poems shows that the biblical poem is clearly *monotheistic* (affirming the existence of one God) and quite different from the Egyptian poem in structure. Perhaps the Hebrew poet composed his hymn with the Egyptian piece before him. What the polytheistic poet ascribed to Aton, the monotheistic biblical poet attributed to Yahweh.

When the Israelites were carried away into exile in Babylon, their language began to change. By the time they returned from the Exile, their vocabulary and grammar were quite different from the ancient Hebrew period. Yet the Psalms preserved the old language. This is another proof that the Old Testament had been handed down faithfully. To understand the language of the Psalms, one must study the old Hebrew language and the expressions of the ancient Ugaritic poetry.

5. Literary Qualities. Above all, the Psalms are poems. Specifically, they are lyric poems—poems intended to be sung. They must be read as poems, with an understanding of all the characteristics of poetry, if they are to be properly understood. Their language is emotional, not logical. The use of symbols, imagery, and other poetic devices makes the language concentrated; i.e., a great deal is suggested and said with a few words. Like all lyric poetry, the Psalms display pattern or design, unity, theme (or centrality), balance, harmony, contrast, unified progression, recurrence, and variation.

All of the Psalms are immediately lyrical. Even if they are also *gnomic* (having to do with wisdom) or historical, they are above all lyrical. The poet expressed wisdom and historical reflection in emotional and spiritual terms. There are many kinds of lyric poems in

THANKSGIVING PSALMS. *This is a page from the Thanksgiving Psalms of the Dead Sea Scrolls. Quite similar in form to the Psalms of the Old Testament, these Intertestamental religious lyrics are written in the first person and express mourning for sin, a consciousness of weakness, and a conviction of God's goodness and mercy.*

the Psalter: lament or complaint (10, 35), acrostic (119, cf. above), and *encomium* (praising someone or something, 1, 15).

Three elements are necessary in analyzing a poem: (1) theme or topic, (2) structure, (3) poetic texture. Structurally, biblical poems may proceed from one thought to another (e.g., Psa. 13), they may contrast one thought with another (e.g., Psa. 1), or they may merely present a series of pictures without any apparent movement (e.g., Psa. 148). Most biblical psalms, however, have a three-part structure. They begin with a statement or theme; that theme is then developed or at least reacted to; then the theme is resolved or repeated.

Poetic texture concerns the minor elements, such as the figures of speech, the connotations or multiple meanings of words, imagery, tone (i.e., the use of vivid or colorful language), and allusion. The texture of the Psalms is amazingly uniform. This is due to the fact that this poetry arises against the background of a highly developed poetic art that had long existed in Mesopotamia, Ugarit, and Canaan. By the time the biblical Psalms were written, this art of composing poems was well-known in Israel. And so these Psalms tend to follow the same structural patterns and use similar poetic style. The actual grammar and specific motifs, however, change considerably from Psalm to Psalm. Hence, some scholars speak of Psalms with strong Ugaritic similarities (e.g., Psa. 29; 68; 72; 78) and strong Egyptian similarities (e.g., Psa. 104).

Although the Psalms are collected around certain themes, there is no overall unifying literary plot to the book.

B. Lamentations. Jewish scholars also put the Book of Lamentations in the section of the Old Testament literature that they call the "Writings." Jews read the book of Lamentations in the middle of July on the anniversary of the day when the temple was destroyed in 586 B.C. In our English versions of the Old Testament, Lamentations is found after the Book of Jeremiah because the translators believed Jeremiah also wrote the book of Lamentations. Some modern scholars doubt that Jeremiah wrote it, but recent studies of the Old Testament text suggest that he really was the writer.

Chapters 1, 2, and 4 are the writer's personal lament over the fall of Jerusalem; chapters 3 and 5 voice the nation's collective sorrow at the destruction of their holy city. Each chapter of this book takes up a different theme of sorrow: (1) the desolation and misery of Jerusalem, (2) the Lord's anger with His people, (3) reasons why the nations should be comforted, (4) the contrast between Israel's past and present, and (5) the nation's appeal for mercy from the Lord.

There are also several minor themes in the book. Lamentations 2:2–22 describes the horrors of the siege against Jerusalem. Lamentations 2:19 and 4:12–16 condemn the sins of the priests and the prophets. Lamentations 4:17 chides Egypt for failing to help Israel defend itself against the Babylonians. Lamentations 3:40–42 confesses the sin of the nation, while Lamentations 3:22–26 expresses Israel's hope in the Lord.

The Book of Lamentations is written in a very beautiful poetic style. Every chapter (except 5) uses the distinctive *qînâ* meter and is acrostic. The fifth chapter contains 22 lines; although it is not acrostic, it is alphabetical, having the same number of lines as the Hebrew alphabet has letters. In the first three chapters there are three lines of poetry for each letter of the acrostic, while the fourth chapter has two lines for each letter. Each of the five poems has a distinctive poetic character and a distinctive theme. There is no unifying structure to the book as a whole. Each poem is complete in itself. The style of the poems bears a striking similarity to those of the Book of Jeremiah. This is especially true with reference to certain images—e.g., the virgin daughter of Israel, the appeal to the righteous judge, and so on.[3]

Lamentations reflects a long tradition of ancient Near Eastern lament poetry. Even before 2000 B.C., the Sumerians lamented the destruction of Ur. Similar laments appear in Babylonian literature as well. This is especially significant since the poetic literature of Israel was primarily in the Mesopotamian tradition.

C. The Song of Solomon. Some older English versions of the Bible call this book *Canticles,* which means "song" or "chant" (from the Latin word *canticulum,* "chant"). Jews read this book at the Feast of the Passover in April because they feel it symbolically describes God's love for Israel.

Tradition says that Solomon wrote this book, but the Hebrew title may also mean "Song of Songs which refers to Solomon." Some Bible scholars, therefore, believe that the book was written later than Solomon and was dedicated to him.

Unlike all other books of the Old Testament except Esther, the Song of Solomon does not refer to God (unless one reads Song of Sol. 8:6 that way). Neither does the book mention sacrifices, the temple, priests, prophets, or religion in general. The New Testament does not quote the Song of Solomon. The book refers to many exotic plants and herbs found in northern Palestine in Old Testament times, and it uses many ancient Aramaic phrases that had disappeared from the language by the time of Jesus.

On the surface, the Song of Solomon describes passionate love. This causes many Bible scholars to disagree over the book's meaning. Most Christians follow the traditional belief that the book tells of God's love through allegory or *parable* (a symbolic story), but others believe that it is simply a collection of Hebrew love poems celebrating

[3] *See* E. J. Young, *An Introduction to the Old Testament* (London: Tyndale Press, 1960), p. 343.

25

THE POETRY OF THE BIBLE

Early Christian Hymns

It is impossible to determine what was the "first" Christian hymn. Christians adopted singing as an expression of thanksgiving or joy from the Jewish faith. Scripture tells us that Jesus sang a hymn with His disciples following the Last Supper (Mark 14:26); this most likely was Psalms 113–118, which were traditionally sung at the Passover celebration. The New Testament records other occasions when the apostles and other Christians sang. Paul and Silas, for example, prayed and sang hymns in the jail in Philippi (Acts 16:25).

What were these songs and hymns? It is impossible to say with certainty, but we find some fragments of these early songs throughout the New Testament. Ephesians 5:14 records part of what may have been a hymn of penitence: "Awake thou that sleepest, and arise from the dead, and Christ shall give thee light."

A hymn on the glory of martyrdom may have been the source of the saying in 2 Timothy 2:11–13: "For if we be dead with him, we shall also live with him . . ." Other examples are: Titus 3:4–7 on salvation; Revelation 22:17 on invitation; Philippians 2:6–11 on Christ as God's servant; and 1 Timothy 3:16 on Jesus' incarnation and triumph over death.

Besides serving as songs of praise, these songs were often intended to teach converts the basic truths of Christian faith and life.

Doxologies, or hymns praising God, were sung by early Christians and are recorded in fragments. For example, "Thou art worthy, O Lord, to receive glory and honor and power, for thou hast created all things, and for thy pleasure they are and were cre-

ated" (Rev. 4:11).

Luke records a number of spontaneous songs that were so joyful they were often repeated by early Christians. These *canticles* have found their way into songs sung today. They include the "Magnificat," Mary's song of praise on learning she would give birth to the Savior (1:46–55); the "Benedictus," Zachariah's joy in the arrival of the Messiah (1:68–79); the "Gloria in Excelsis," the angels' song of praise to God (2:14); and the "Nunc Dimittis," Simeon's joyous thanks that the Savior has at last come (2:29–32).

Other early Christian hymns were written after the time the New Testament was written. "A Hymn to the Savior" is credited to the second century A.D. teacher and writer Clement. A literal translation of the first line of this song, which was included at the end of Clement's three-volume work about Christ entitled "The Tutor," is: "Bridle of steeds untamed." However, an English translation reads, "Shepherd of tender youth." This hymn uses numerous metaphors to describe Christ: Fisher of Souls, Everlasting Word, Eternal Light, and so on. This hymn instructed pagan converts on the nature of Christ.

"The Candlelighting Hymn," or "A Hymn for the Lighting of Lamps," was written at about the same time, though the exact date and authorship are unknown. We do know that second-century Christians gathered at dawn and again at twilight to sing hymns, and this hymn would certainly have been appropriate. This song is still used in the Greek Orthodox church as the vesper hymn.

---

the mutual affection of bride and bridegroom. This uncertainty makes the Song of Solomon one of the most controversial books of the Old Testament. There is much debate regarding the literary genre of this book. Some say it is a drama. But unlike drama it exhibits no discernible chronology or sequence of events. If acted out it would consist of little more than one passionate love scene after another. This certainly is not the structure of ancient dramas. Therefore, it appears to be a collection of pastoral poems perhaps originally set to music (and, therefore, lyric poems).

The structure of the book is fragmented. Scholars cannot be sure what the structure is, due to the frequent and abrupt shifts in subject and speakers. (How can one analyze the structure and/or movement of thought if he cannot determine who the speaker is?)

The literary method in this book is similar to the stream of consciousness technique. It exposes the inner thoughts of the speaker, focusing on what he or she thinks rather than what is actually happening to them. Specifically, the poet uses the form both of poems (expressing his personal feelings) and of dialogue.

The poems in the book present traditional pastoral themes. There is the traditional invitation to love (Song of Sol. 2:10–15; 7:10–13), the *blazon* or praise of the beauty and virtue of the beloved (cf. 2:1–3; 4:1–15), a description of the delights of love (1:14, 16–17), and a complaint of unfulfilled love (8:1–4). The pastoral poem often is used to speak of human love.

V. Wisdom Books. The books of Job, Proverbs, and Ecclesiastes contain most of the

THE POETRY OF THE BIBLE

Old Testament's *gnomic* (wisdom) poetry. Other wisdom poetry is found in Psalms 1; 4; 10; 14; 18:20–26; 19; 37; 49; 73; 90; 112; and also in Habakkuk 3.

Gnomic poetry can be divided into three categories: (1) popular proverbs that express practical truths in short, colorful parallels to nature, (2) riddles or parables with a spiritual meaning, (3) lengthy discussions of the problems of life.

Many wisdom poems of the ancient Near East try to draw a parallel between the world of nature and the spiritual life of man. For example, the Egyptian proverbs of Amen-em-opet (*ca.* 1150—950 B.C.) seem to resemble Proverbs 22:17—23:23. However, we have no evidence that the Book of Proverbs copied its ideas from Egyptian proverbs or other ancient literature. Hebrew wisdom poems record *divine wisdom,* the revealed truth of God. During the period of the judges, Jewish leaders used riddles, proverbs, and fables to communicate God's truth (Judg. 14:14, 18; 8:21; 9:6–21).

In the most ancient times, kings kept wise men in their royal courts for advice. A special class of wise men served in the royal courts of Israel from the time of King Saul (*ca.* 1043 B.C.). These wise men advised the king in matters of administration (Jer. 18:18). Younger men studied under these counselors and began to write down their teachings (Prov. 1:6; 22:17). Later, these writings were collected to make the wisdom literature of the Old Testament.

There were also many sages who did not serve in the court. Their wisdom is sometimes known as "popular wisdom." Such sages apparently functioned throughout the Old Testament era, just as they did among other ancient Near Eastern peoples. We read of the wisdom of the city of Abel (2 Sam. 20:18). Jeremiah spoke of the wise men as sources of knowledge alongside the priests and prophets (18:18).

Hebrew wisdom poetry focused upon God as the Lord of wisdom (Job 12:13 ff.; cf. Isa. 1:2; Dan. 2:20–23). These poems praised God as the One who knows all things and who has infinite power to accomplish His holy will (Job 10:4; 26:6). The wisdom poems tell us that God created all the universe and that all life is under His control (cf. Isa. 28:23–29; 31:2). The wisdom writers explain that God truly knows what is good and evil; He rewards the righteous and punishes the wicked (cf. Psa. 1; 37; 43).

Job contains a good example of this teaching when he sighs that man can never understand the full extent of God's wisdom (Job 28:12–21). Job admits that man can understand only what God reveals to him (Job 28:23, 28).

The wisdom poetry of the Old Testament offers practical wisdom as well as religious wisdom. It attempts to apply God's truth to the many problems of everyday life. The Old Testament writers declare that anyone who does not know God does not have true wisdom and is doomed to failure (Isa. 5:21; Jer. 18:18–23).

It has already been suggested that Israel's wisdom movement was part of a movement found throughout the ancient Near East. The Old Testament itself refers to wise men outside Israel. Solomon's wisdom "excelled the wisdom of all the children of the east country, and all the wisdom of Egypt. For he was wiser than all men; than Ethan the Ezrahite, and Heman, and Chalcol, and Darda, the sons of Mahol" (1 Kings 4:30–31). Obadiah prophesied the destruction of the wisdom of Edom (Obad. 8) and Jeremiah spoke of the wisdom of Teman (Jer. 49:7). Job was an Edomite. Proverbs 30:1—31:19 is attributed to the sages of Massa in North Arabia.

There are records of wisdom both within and outside the ancient Near East. For example,

INSTRUCTION OF AMEN-EM-OPET. *Remarkably similar to the Book of Proverbs, the instruction of Amen-em-opet was written in the twelfth century B.C. or before.*

compare Proverbs 17:28 and its parallel in Sanskrit:

"Even a fool, when he holdeth his peace, is counted wise; and he that shutteth his lips is esteemed a man of understanding" (Prov. 17:28).

"Even a fool covered with fine clothes is fair in the assembly up to a point; yea a fool is fair so long as he utters no word."

Much of the similarity is due to the common observations of men.

The Egyptian sage Ipuwer (*ca.* 2200 B.C.) described the coming of a righteous pharaoh (king) "who will bring rest to men as a shepherd to his sheep." This is quite similar to Psalm 72 and other messianic Psalms. Such a similarity certainly suggests some kind of motif common to both ancient Egypt and Israel, but the exact relationship is difficult to determine.

The Book of Psalms contains other wisdom poems. Especially prominent is the struggle concerning the existence of evil. How could a good God have made such a godless world (e.g., Psa. 14; 19; 90)? How can a good God allow the wicked to prosper and the godly to suffer (e.g., Psa. 10; 37; 49; 73)?

Wisdom influences not only the prophetic and poetic movements but the apocalyptic movement as well. Daniel was known as a man "of illumination, insight, and wisdom like the wisdom of the gods" (NASB). He was said to possess "an extraordinary spirit, knowledge and insight, interpretation of dreams, explanation of enigmas, and solving of difficult problems" (Dan. 5:11–12, NASB). Daniel was told that those who are wise would understand, i.e., act wisely until the end. Revelation 13:18 describes wisdom as the ability to interpret visions.

Jesus is depicted as a sage, too. He stands in the midst of His disciples authoritatively instructing them in proper (wise) living (e.g., Matt. 11:28 ff.; cf. Ecclesiasticus 51:23–27; Prov. 8:4–21). He described Himself as being greater in wisdom than Solomon, and chided the Pharisees for not flocking to receive His instruction (Matt. 12:42; Luke 11:31).

A. Proverbs. The Book of Proverbs collects a variety of sayings, expressed in short poems that are easy to memorize. The motto of the book is "The fear of the Lord is the beginning of wisdom." Christians have found a great deal of help from Proverbs because it contains so much practical advice for daily living.

In general, the Book of Proverbs describes the source and value of wisdom. It reminds us that God gives all true knowledge and that we should use knowledge as a sacred trust from Him.

The Book of Proverbs is certainly in the tradition of wisdom literature. Chapters 1—24 are especially interesting, since they form a literary collection similar to the proverbs of the Egyptian sage Ptahhotep (*ca.* 2500—2400 B.C.). This Egyptian collection opens with a main title including the name and title of the author (cf. Prov. 1:1). This is followed by his discourse. Then comes a subtitle (cf. Prov. 10:1), followed by a series of maxims. Some have argued that Proverbs 8 must be a later product, since wisdom is treated as a human personality. Yet this occurs in Egyptian wisdom as early as the writings of Ptahhotep. Mesopotamian wisdom includes proverbs parallel to those in the Bible in style, theme, and poetic mechanisms.

Proverbs 1—9 is a section with a single poetic texture (i.e., it uses the same kinds of imagery and symbols throughout) and a single narrative viewpoint. However, the section employs a variety of poetic parallelism and literary genres—e.g., the lyric poem, dramatic monologue, *encomium* (praise of something), narrative, and dramatized scene. In short, it appears to be a discourse by a single sage. The entire passage is developed in a series of conflicts setting forth a kind of plot—i.e., pursue the good (wisdom) and avoid the foolish. The plot contrasts wisdom (depicted as a lady) and a harlot; a good and an evil man; life and death; wisdom and folly; wisdom and evil. The unifying topic is wisdom.

B. Job. The French novelist Victor Hugo once called the Book of Job "the greatest masterpiece of the human mind." We know very little about the man who wrote Job, but he probably lived before the time of Moses. The prologue of the book recounts how Job was a righteous man who suffered many calamities. The main section of the book traces the arguments and questions that Job raised about his sufferings. Job's friends offered many of the ideas that people have traditionally used to explain suffering. They said that God might have sent this crisis to punish Job's sin (chaps. 4—31), or to discipline him (chaps. 32—37).

We see Job growing through the agony of trying to understand why God allowed all of these distresses to fall upon him. At first he pleads for death (chaps. 3, 6), then for mercy

(7:12–21). God does not respond, and so Job wishes someone would resolve the quarrel between them (9:11–21; 10:8–17). Finally, he decides to face his problems with courage (13:13–28), and he asks God to bring him through his painful trials (16:18—17:3). Job declares that he trusts God to preserve his life in spite of all the pain and heartache he has experienced (19:25–27). He concludes that suffering is a mystery to man; only God knows the reason for it. When God finally speaks to Job, He gives him no hint as to why he has had to endure such distress.

Ancient Near Eastern literature attests several poems treating the same theme as Job—the theme of the righteous sufferer. Before 2000 B.C., Sumerians recited and read the poem now entitled "Man and His God." A lengthy treatise on this theme appeared amid the Babylonian literature; it was called *Ludlul bel Nemeqi,* or "I Will Praise the God of Wisdom."

Job is difficult to classify as to literary genre. It has been called wisdom, drama, and tragedy. Leland Ryken concludes that it is none of these, but a comic narrative that includes elements of all of the other three genres. By "comic," he means it parallels the structural pattern of the classical Greek comedies—i.e., the hero is plunged into tragedy and then is moved back into prosperity.[4] The Book of Job gives more attention to the tragic element than the Greek comedies do. It is much like the modern problem play, which poses a problem, offers several solutions, and leaves us to infer the final answer.

The structure of Job is very artfully designed. The prose introduction and prologue constitute the upward parts of a U-shaped plot. The middle poetic section (the discourse) moves ahead slowly, often folding back upon itself. To the reader unaccustomed to Oriental style, this part of the book might seem to lack coherence. Yet God's final vindication of Job is a clear and compelling conclusion. (*See also* "Outline of the Books of the Bible.")

C. Ecclesiastes. The ancient Jews read the Book of Ecclesiastes during the months of September and October. Tradition says King Solomon wrote it (Eccles. 1:1, 12).

Ecclesiastes argues that life has meaning only when a person serves God. If a person follows other goals, he will fall into utter hopelessness: "vanity of vanities" (Eccles. 1:2). Ecclesiastes says that a person can find happiness only when he pursues godliness, not when he pursues pleasure or comfort. The world was created to glorify God and only what a person does for God will endure. "Fear God, and keep his commandments: for this is the whole duty of man" (Eccles. 12:13).

The generally pessimistic outlook on "life under the sun" is paralleled in other ancient Near Eastern literature. Mesopotamian literature depicts such an outlook in the "Gilgamesh Epic" and the "Dialogue of Pessimism." However, Ecclesiastes does not conclude with pessimism, as do these other works. The writer declares that life is "vanity of vanities" only if it is lived apart from God. Though His ways are inscrutable, God gives meaning to life.

In its stance and literary technique, Ecclesiastes belongs to the genre of wisdom literature. The narrator speaks as a sage, advising his hearers on the path of wisdom. He attributes personality to impersonal objects and concepts. He uses brief narrative, portraiture, description, and commands to the reader—all well-known wisdom conventions. The key phrase, "life under the sun" or "under heaven," occurs 30 times. This provides a single theme throughout the book.

Ecclesiastes makes skillful use of the quest motif (a man seeking for the wise life) so frequently found in wisdom literature as a whole. There is no apparent narrative unity in this book; the unity is logical and stylistic. Its imagery embraces nearly every activity and situation of human living.

VI. New Testament Poetry. No book of the New Testament is written entirely in poetry, yet the New Testament abounds in poetry. There are also many prose passages that have a highly poetic character.

Paul quoted from various classical poets. When preaching to the Greek intellectuals on Mars Hill (Acts 17:22–31) he quoted from as many as three poets: Epimenides of Crete (Acts. 17:28, "For in him we live and move and exist," NASB), Aratus of Cilicia and/or the Stoic philosopher Cleanthes (Acts 17:28, "For we also are his offspring," NASB). In Titus 1:12 he again quoted Epimenides ("The Cretans are always liars, evil beasts, lazy gluttons," NASB), and in 1 Corinthians he used the words of Menander ("Evil company corrupts good morals," NASB).

There are many clearly poetic fragments in

---

[4] Leland Ryken, *The Literature of the Bible* (Grand Rapids, Mich.: Zondervan, 1974), pp. 109–118.

THE POETRY OF THE BIBLE

GREEK MUSICIAN. *The young Greek man in this marble frieze plays the lyre, a very popular stringed instrument (mid-fifth century B.C.). David may have played a similar instrument for King Saul (1 Sam. 16).*

Paul's writings. Some scholars suggest that these were originally parts of early Christian hymns. These fragments employ various kinds of parallelism, or at least very exalted rhythmical language that could have been set to music (e.g., 1 Tim. 3:16; 2 Tim. 2:11–13; Eph. 5:14; and Phil. 2:5–11).

Other poetical passages in the New Testament are directly patterned after Old Testament quotations. There are over 200 direct Old Testament quotations and probably 2000 literary asides. Luke 1 and 2 contain eight such passages (1:14–17, 32–33, 35, 46–55, 68–79; 2:14, 29–32, 33–35). Some of these passages are well-known among Christians because of their use in formal public worship.

Luke 1:46–55 is known as the *Magnificat* ("My soul doth magnify the Lord"), because of its opening words in the Latin translation. This outpouring of Mary's heart revealed that she was steeped in the Old Testament. She alludes to the song of Hannah (1 Sam. 2:7) and several Psalms (e.g., Psa. 31; 113; 126). The opening line is virtually identical with the Greek translation of Psalm 31:8. The poem

consists of three or four stanzas that repeat well-known praises from the prophetic perspective, celebrating God's grace, omnipotence, holiness, justice, and faithfulness.

Luke 1:67–79 is known as the *Benedictus,* from the Latin translation of its opening word, "blessed." This poem is also full of direct references to Old Testament poetry, such as Malachi 3:1; 7:20; Jeremiah 11:5; and Psalms 41; 72; 106; 107; 111; 132; 105. The resemblances are quite striking. This poem has two stanzas, with the first verse having three lines (68–69, 70–72, 73–75) and the second, two lines (76–77, 78–79).

Luke 2:14 is known by the Latin version of the words with which it opens, *Gloria in Excelsis* ("Glory in the highest"). This poem has two parts. Each part has three members in the poetic sequence a:b:c::b:a:c. Although it is consistent with Old Testament teachings, this poem has no Old Testament parallel as do the previous two poems.

Luke 2:29–32 also is known by the first words of its Latin translation—i.e., *Nunc Dimittis* ("Now, let depart . . ."). This poem has two stanzas (29–30, 31–32). The first stanza states what the coming of the Messiah means to the speaker and the second what that coming means to the world. It is an extremely moving and beautiful poem.

The Gospels and Epistles contain many passages that use well-known poetical devices or appear in smooth-flowing, highly intense language. All of these characteristics were exemplified in the Sermon on the Mount, in which Jesus appeared as an Old Testament wisdom teacher. He attacked the prevailing religious abuses, holding them up for ridicule (i.e., He used *satire*). The opening section of His sermon (the Beatitudes) employed the parallelism so well-known from Old Testament poetry. The entire mood of His presentation ran counter to what is ordinarily found in classical literature. "It is obvious that Jesus is setting up ideals that differ from those espoused in literature."[5]

---

[5] Ryken, *The Literature of the Bible*, p. 294.

Several of the verses in the Book of James recall the cadence and literary qualities of the Sermon on the Mount. The other epistles contain several *encomiums* (poetic songs of praise), such as the praise of the incarnate Christ (1 Cor. 1:15–20), the praise of love (1 Cor. 13), and the praise of faith (Heb. 11). Other exalted passages include Romans 8:35–38; 1 Corinthians 15:51–57; and Jude 24–25.

The Book of Revelation contains many psalms or hymns and poems (cf. 4:8, 11; 5:9, 12–13; 7:15–17; 11:17–19). These poems employ various kinds of parallelism that remind us of Old Testament prophetic poetry. Yet they differ from the Old Testament, because they ascribe to Jesus Christ the titles, names, and perfections of God. In addition, Revelation is marked by strong symbolism, repetition, parallelism of structure, and so on. All of its visionary material is couched in a rhapsodic, poetic type of prose.

LAWS AND STATUTES

God told Moses how the people of Israel should live, and Moses recorded these commands in the first five books (the *Pentateuch*) of the Old Testament. These laws teach us a great deal about Old Testament society; but they also suggest how our own society should work. God still expects His people to honor Him in their dealings with one another. The laws of the Old Testament teach us to lift up God and respect the rights of our neighbors. As interpreted by Jesus and His apostles, they form the foundation of modern Christian ethics.

I. UNIQUENESS OF BIBLICAL LAW
   A. The Form of the Law
   B. The Origin of the Law
   C. The Concept of Law
   D. Underlying Principles
      1. All Crimes Ultimately Crimes against God
      2. Total Submission to God
      3. National Responsibility
      4. Individual Responsibility
      5. Respect for Human Life
      6. Equitable Penalties
      7. Personal Punishment
      8. Universal Justice
   E. A Case Comparison

II. BODIES OF OLD TESTAMENT LAW
   A. The Book of the Covenant
   B. The Holiness Code
   C. The Deuteronomic Code

III. FUNCTIONAL DEVELOPMENT OF LAW
   A. Ceremonial Law
      1. Ark of the Covenant
      2. Central Sanctuary
   B. Dietary Law
   C. Quarantine Law
   D. Laws of Dedication
   E. Laws of Religious Symbolism
   F. Civil Law
      1. Political Leaders
      2. Israel's Army
      3. The Court System
   G. Criminal Law
      1. Crimes against Religion
      2. Crimes against Society
      3. Crimes against Morality
      4. Crimes against the Person
      5. Crimes against Property
   H. Laws of Benevolence
   I. Personal and Family Rights
   J. Obligations to God

IV. INTERTESTAMENTAL LAW

V. JESUS AND THE LAW
   A. Dialogue with the Pharisees
   B. Jesus' Attitude

VI. PAUL AND THE LAW
   A. Paul's World
   B. The Jerusalem Council
   C. Paul's Theme of Faith *vs.* Law
   D. Paul and Jesus

I. Uniqueness of Biblical Law. Since the legal system of the Bible helped to shape that of the West today, it does not seem strange to us. But we can discern the uniqueness of biblical law when we compare it with other ancient systems of law. Archaeologists have found collections of Near Eastern laws in the ruins of Ur-Nammu, Eshnunna, Sumer, Mari, Ugarit, and other cities.

King Hammurabi of Babylon produced a famous system of law around 1700 B.C. The Hittites of Asia Minor adopted similar ideas when they created their own well-known legal system. The Sumerians, the Babylonians, the Assyrians, and other peoples of Mesopotamia greatly influenced the laws of the world around them. S. M. Paul says that nearly every legal system of the ancient Near East "bore the imprint of Mesopotamia."

The various law-codes of Mesopotamia followed the same general pattern: instead of giving universal guidelines, they stated what had been traditionally decided in a series of actual court cases. In other words, Mesopotamian law was *case law.* (Scholars often call it *casuistic* law—a term that comes from the Latin word *casus,* meaning "case.") The people of the Near East believed their king could apply eternal truth to every new problem. After all, hadn't the gods chosen him to rule them? So when he made a judgment, he bound all of his people to it, and they did not demur. However, later kings just quoted tradition and did little to codify or modify law in terms of life situations.

Mesopotamian laws told people how to

handle their money and property, how to collect damages, how to get a divorce, and so on, but did not teach moral or religious lessons.

A code of Mesopotamian law usually opened by telling how gods gave the king power to rule the land. Then the book listed the rulings on a series of legal cases, arranged by topic. It closed with curses for anyone who disobeyed the king's laws and blessings for those who kept them. (There are sections of the Pentateuch that list God's rulings according to this pattern.)

Mesopotamian legal codes begin each rule by saying, "Thus you shall do . . ." Often a biblical commandment begins with the words, "Thus saith the Lord . . ." But notice the difference: In the Bible, God gives the command; in Mesopotamian law, the king does.

The content of biblical law often resembles other laws of the Near East. But in many more ways, biblical law is different. Biblical law codes are unique in their form, their origin, their concept of law, and their underlying principles.

A. The Form of the Law. As we have noted, most law systems of the Near East consisted of case laws; they laid out the age-old traditional decisions in various legal cases. They were cold, hard, and capricious. But the laws of the Bible point back to a personal lawgiver: God.

The Bible says that God gave His Law with a purpose of love. Though the laws of the Bible are firm, they point to a God who cares about human beings personally and therefore directs how they should live so as to please Him and enjoy His favor. Bible scholars call this the *apodictic* form of law, because it demonstrates how God governs His people. (*Apodictic* comes from the Greek word *apodeiktikos,* which means "demonstrative.") In Mesopotamia it was the king's *word* that was binding; his decree in a specific case was the law. When his word was written, everyone had to obey it—even the king himself (cf. Esth. 8:8; Dan. 6:12). But the Law of God was different. God's statements did not control Israel; God did. He was free to act on His own initiative and He chose to act according to His own righteous character, and obedience to His Law was a direct expression of love and loyalty to God Himself. This is why biblical law contains so much moral and religious material: it tells about God and His relationship with His people.

Most of God's commandments were meant

to last for centuries, but occasionally He gave short-term instructions. When the Israelites entered Canaan, for example, He told them to destroy the pagan shrines (Deut. 12:2), to set

CODE OF HAMMURABI. *An early king of Babylon (eighteenth century B.C.), Hammurabi set up one of the earliest known legal codes. He improved upon earlier codes and had the laws recorded on a stone stele, set up in the temple of Marduk at Babylon where the people could see it. Discovered at Susa, the Code of Hammurabi is the longest and the most complete legal document ever found in the Near East. It contains over 280 laws.*

BABYLONIAN CONTRACT. *This contract from the seventeenth century B.C. records the division of an inheritance among several heirs. It bears 25 impressions made by seven different seals that belonged to the contracting parties and witnesses.*

up a civil court system (Deut. 16:8), and to establish cities of refuge (Deut. 19:1–13). These short-term commands revealed God's love under the temporary conditions of conquest.

The Bible may express God's Law in the form of general statements of policy or as rulings for specific cases (cf. Ex. 21:16; Deut. 24:7). Sometimes both forms (general and specific, apodictic law and case law) appear side-by-side in the same text. The Bible doesn't use one legal form as the Mesopotamian law systems do. Because God spoke to His people in many different situations, His commands appeared in various forms.

B. The Origin of the Law. Rulers of the Near East were not trying to express universal wisdom through their laws. They were trying to maintain their personal political and economic power and their image as lawgivers. If a previous king had already done this they just borrowed the ideas for their own legal system. A king was supposed to hand down laws that were clear, just, and true, no matter where he got them.

In contrast, the Bible teaches that God's people received their laws from God Himself, not from their neighbors. Even laws whose content corresponded to those of other Near Eastern codes are presented as God-given. The Bible says to obey its laws because they are God's commands. Such a statement is called a *motive clause,* because it blesses those who obey God's Law and curses those who disobey it, or both (e.g., Lev. 26). The opening chapters of Deuteronomy (1—4) review Israel's history with a motivating purpose, to re-

mind God's people that they ought to obey His laws. The Israelites agreed with their neighbors that the Law was eternal and binding, but for a different reason—not because the king said so, but because God said so.

C. The Concept of Law. Laws usually deal with a nation's social order; they tell how citizens should act toward one another. But the laws of the Bible also tell how God's people should act toward Him. Indeed, they are primarily religious laws.

God introduces His Law by saying that He chose Israel to be a nation with its own land, not just a clan or a large family (see Gen. 12:2). God's Law then told the people of Israel how to live in harmony with Him. This was the message of the Ten Commandments or *Decalogue* ("ten words," Ex. 20), and the thrust of the civil laws in the legal section of Exodus (chs. 21—23) as well as of the rules of worship (Ex. 24–31). Man served God and His Law; man did not make the Law.

Hittite law assumed that a god was the *suzerain* (conquering ruler) of the nation. But in the Bible, the relationship between God and Israel is a more personal one. Israel is God's "treasured possession" (cf. Ex. 19:3–6).

Biblical law was public law, and this was another important difference from the pagan laws of the Near East. In many nations of the ancient Near East, the king carried the laws in his head, as they were his personal possession. He did not publish them until he was ready to give up his throne. Thus a person could be arrested for breaking a law he had never known. The laws were kept secret, even when a person was put on trial for breaking them. (There are few instances in which anyone cited the royal codes in a court case.)

But in Israel, the leaders of government read God's Law to the people at regular times of the year (cf. Deut. 31:10–13). Thus every citizen could learn the laws he had to obey. Other peoples of the Near East obeyed laws because they were enforced by the royal establishment; disobedience meant punishment. But God's people were to obey His Law because they loved Him (cf. Deut. 6:5, 20–25).

In Israel, the claim of the Law rested on the known character of the Lawgiver. Even though the judges and priests interpreted the Law, they did not make the Law (Deut. 17:8–13). So when people abided by the Law, they showed their love for God, rather than for His interpreters.

D. Underlying Principles. The principles

that stood behind the laws of the Bible are in marked contrast to those behind other Near Eastern laws. We have noted that the laws of the Bible were based upon the revealed character and purpose of God Himself. Rather than being the political whim of a human king or the mere traditions of the state, the Bible's laws point toward a transcendent goal—God's redemption of mankind. They show God's protection of each individual's integrity. They reflect the fact that God made man a steward of the earth (Deut. 21:22–23).

We see another fundamental difference in the social distinctions embodied in ancient Near Eastern codes. The Code of Hammurabi, for example, preserves three separate social classes and codifies the degradation of the lower class. It is a system designed to protect the position of the few people at the top of society. Biblical law sees all men as the creatures of God, equal to one another. Other important themes emerge as we study biblical Law.

1. All Crimes Ultimately Crimes against God. God built Israelite society on His own rules; so when a person offended society, he thereby offended God (1 Sam. 12:9–10). In

BUST OF HAMMURABI. *This diorite head discovered at Susa dates from the eighteenth century B.C. Many researchers believe it represents Hammurabi, who welded the small states of Babylonia into a single powerful kingdom. In addition to his well-known legislative abilities, Hammurabi was a military genius and a man of literary talent.*

26

LAWS AND STATUTES

fact, some social offenses were so serious that only God could pardon them.

2. Total Submission to God. God's laws showed that He cares about every aspect of a person's life. It was not enough to give Him formal worship or moral behavior. Since each person's whole being came from God, God expected all His people to serve Him with their whole being (Amos 5:21–24).

God enforced His Law when His human agents would not (Ex. 22:21–24; Deut. 10:18; Ps. 67:4). He undertook to punish His people when they did not apply His Law fairly. He was present as Judge at every court trial, no matter what verdict the human judge rendered (cf. Deut. 19:17).

3. National Responsibility. As we have seen, God's Law wasn't the private property of the upper class; each person knew the Law and the penalty for breaking it. Often the whole community punished the lawbreaker, because all of the people had to uphold the Law (Ex. 21:22–23).

BROTHERLY PACT. *This stele from Ras-Shamra (ca. fourteenth century B.C.) shows two men standing on opposite sides of a table with their hands extended to touch. This act probably marked the formalizing of a pact between the two parties. Genesis 31:44–53 tells how Laban and Jacob made a similar covenant.*

LAWS AND STATUTES

Judges represented God, but they also represented the law-abiding community. Executioners meted out punishment on behalf of the total community. Thus a murder case required evidence from two or three witnesses, and the verdict was announced publicly at the city gate. Sometimes the witnesses executed a murderer (Deut. 13:6–10; 17:7). Sometimes the victim's next of kin did it (Deut. 19:11–12), and sometimes the whole community took part (Num. 15:32–36; Deut. 13:6–10).

4. Individual Responsibility. The Bible stresses that each person's duty to God was more important than the duty to go along with his community. If his community was wrong, God still held him responsible for his own actions (cf. Ex. 32).

5. Respect for Human Life. Since man was created in God's image, God's Law protected human life. If someone injured a person of lower social status, he was not excused by the mere payment of a fine. The only equivalent of human life was human life itself. God said that every murderer should be executed (Gen. 9:6).

6. Equitable Penalties. Other laws of the Near East allowed a victim to inflict more injury than he had received. They also allowed some criminals to pay back less than they had stolen or less than the injury they had caused. God ruled that the courts could only require "eye for eye, tooth for tooth" (Ex. 21:24), which made the law more equitable. This is often called "the law of the claw" (Latin, *lex talionis*).

7. Personal Punishment. Outside Israel, rich people could buy their way out of punishment; but God declared that every lawbreaker must suffer for his own crime. If a judge was too easy on the lawbreaker, he became guilty of the crime too. No one could pay a ransom for the criminal (Num. 35:31)—except that when an animal committed an offense, its owner could buy it back (Ex. 21:29–30). Only the system of religious sacrifice allowed a person to offer a substitute for his punishment.

8. Universal Justice. God's Law protected the rights of the poor, the widow, the orphan, and the alien. God ruled that no Israelite could be enslaved forever (Ex. 21:2), and He guarded slaves from abuse (Ex. 21:20–21, 26–27), including foreigners who were enslaved (Lev. 25:44). He forbade heavy penalties for debt, and He told His people to share their goods with the needy.

E. A Case Comparison. Let's look at one specific example of how biblical law compares with other laws of the ancient Near East. We will compare what the different laws said about a "goring ox" (Fig. 30.) Notice that the law of the Bible:

—Placed greater value on human life than on animal life.

—Valued the life of a woman as much as the life of a man.

Laws Concerning a Goring Ox

Code of Eshnunna (Old Babylonian—*ca.* 2000 B.C.)	Code of Hammurabi (Babylonian—*ca.* 1700 B.C.)	The Pentateuch (Hebrew—*ca.* 1440 B.C.)
54—If an ox is known to gore habitually and the authorities have brought the fact to the knowledge of its owner, but he does not have his ox dehorned, it gores a man and causes [his] death, then the owner of the ox shall pay two-thirds of a mina of silver.	251—If a man's ox was a gorer and his city council made it known to him that it was a gorer, but he did not pad its horns [or] tie up his ox, and that ox gored a member of the aristocracy, he shall give one-half mina of silver.	Exodus 21:29 (RSV)—But if the ox has been accustomed to gore in the past, and its owner has been warned but has not kept it in, and it kills a man or a woman, the ox shall be stoned, and its owner also shall be put to death.
55—If it gores a slave and causes [his] death, he shall pay 15 shekels of silver.	252—If it was a man's slave, he shall give one-third mina of silver.	Exodus 21:32 (RSV)—if the ox gores a slave, male or female, the owner shall give to their master thirty shekels of silver, and the ox shall be stoned.

Figure 30

LAWS AND STATUTES

—Valued the life of a child as much as the life of an adult.

—Found the ox guilty of murder.

—Upheld the rule of "a life for a life."

—Condemned a careless owner to die along with his ox.

—Applied the *lex talionis* with mercy, putting the blame on the guilty party alone.

—Set a higher value on human life. (It may be worth all that a man has.)

—Recognized that a slave was still a human being.

—Restored a slave's services to his master. (It requires the ox's owner to pay him 30 shekels, the purchase price of a slave.)

—Put no price on a normal citizen. (Because he was God's servant, he was beyond price.)

—Allowed the community to decide the price of justice, instead of setting a stated fine for every case.

II. Bodies of Old Testament Law. It's interesting to compare the various collections of Old Testament laws: the Book of the Covenant (Ex. 20:22—23:33), the Deuteronomic Code (Deut. 12—26), and the Holiness Code (Lev. 17—27).

A. The Book of the Covenant. Technically, the "Book of the Covenant" was everything that Moses read to the Israelites at the foot of Mount Sinai (cf. Ex. 24:3–7), including the Ten Commandments (Ex. 20:2–17). Later Jewish leaders called the book of Deuteronomy the "Book of the Covenant" (2 Kin. 21:2; 23:2; Chr. 34:30). Deuteronomy is generally thought to be "the book of the law" discovered during the restoration of the temple under King Josiah of Judah (2 Kin. 22:8).

The Israelites accepted the entire Law as part of their covenant with God. They believed that the Decalogue stated the basic rules of the Law, while the other Old Testament laws applied these principles and clarified them. This is why both the Ten Commandments with the detailed Sinai Legislation and equally the entire book of Deuteronomy, in which the Sinai legislation is

SINAI. *The mountain slope on the left is Jebel Musa, the traditional Mount Sinai. Moses climbed the rugged face of Sinai to receive from God the set of laws now known as the Ten Commandments. These laws became the core of all biblical law.*

reapplied and amplified, may be called the "Book of the Covenant."

B. The Holiness Code. God unfolded His laws over a span of many generations. The Ten Commandments were expanded and explained in Exodus 20:22—23:33. In turn, the laws of Leviticus and Deuteronomy expanded and explained the laws of Exodus. Leviticus explained the first four commandments of the Decalogue—those that had to do with the worship of God—while most of Deuteronomy dealt with the rest of the Decalogue.

The collection of laws found in Leviticus 17—26 is called the Holiness Code; its primary concern was to keep Israel—God's chosen people—holy and pure. The purpose of the Holiness Code was clearly expressed in Leviticus 20:26: "And ye shall be holy unto me: for I the Lord am holy, and have severed you from other people, that ye should be mine."

C. The Deuteronomic Code. Bible scholars disagree about how much of the Book of Deuteronomy makes up the Deuteronomic Code. (Some believe that Deuteronomy 1—11 continues the discussion of worship from the Book of Leviticus; others include this section in the Holiness Code, because it differs from the rest of the book of Deuteronomy.)

But the Decalogue (Deut. 5) laid the foundation for the book of Deuteronomy. The laws that governed human relationships would have made no sense without the laws governing man's relationship with God. So it is more logical to see the Book of Deuteronomy as a complete work, and to call the entire book the "Deuteronomic Code." It covers the wide range of ethical and ritual concerns that Moses raised with the Israelites just before they entered the Promised Land.

Notice that the book of Exodus divides its case laws from its general legal policies (Ex. 21:1—22:17; 22:18—23:33). The fact that Deuteronomy blends these two forms of law together confirms that it was probably written later. Also notice that the laws of Deuteronomy were designed for a more settled way of life; for instance, the book adds laws of inheritance (Deut. 21:15–17) and interest on loans (Deut. 23:20) to the Exodus laws. These new laws reflected a life that would be less nomadic. When Deuteronomy was written, the Israelites were no longer destined to wander in the wilderness; they were ready to conquer Canaan and settle down. We find more of these domestic laws in the book of Numbers, such as the laws of a woman's inheritance (Num. 27:1–11; 36:1–12).

III. Functional Development of Law. The law of Israel developed over several hundred years as God gave each generation the instructions it needed for its way of life. When the laws of the Bible are grouped by topic, we get a picture of how they unfolded through the centuries.

A. Ceremonial Law. The ancient Israelites centered all of their activities on the worship of Jehovah. Each person was expected to worship God individually, just as the whole nation was to worship Him together. Jesus recalled this when He said He could sum up all the commands of the Old Testament in one commandment—to love God (Matt. 22:37; cf. Deut. 6:5; Lev. 19:18).

In great detail, the Bible described the ceremonies of worship that were so important to the life of God's people. These scriptures show that even though a person cannot please God on his own, God makes that person able to worship Him acceptably.

1. Ark of the Covenant. The Bible's ceremonial law mentioned several sacred objects that the Israelites kept at the center of their camp as they wandered in the wilderness. The most important of these was the ark of the covenant.

The ark of the covenant was a wooden box about 122 x 76 x 76 cm. (4 x 2 1/2 x 2 1/2 ft.), or 2 1/2 x 1 1/2 cubits. It was made of acacia (*"shittim,"* KJV) wood and covered with gold, inside and out. The Israelites believed this box was God's throne, and so they called its solid gold lid the "mercy seat." Two golden cherubim (angelic statues) stood on opposite ends of the box, facing the mercy seat (Ex. 25:10–22). Inside the box the Israelites kept the stone tablets on which God gave them the Ten Commandments, a pot of manna, and Aaron's rod—all reminders of God's love for them.

The Israelites carried this ark at the head of their procession across the Jordan River (Josh. 3—4). Arabian tribes carried similar arks into battle as a magic charm to gain their gods' favor. But the ark of the covenant was a symbol of the covenant between God and men, not a magic charm.

2. Central Sanctuary. God promised Israel that some day they would be at "rest" in a land of their own (cf. Heb. 4). When that day came, they were supposed to build a central

LAWS AND STATUTES

The Mezuzah

When the angel of death passed over Egypt, killing all first-born males, Jewish families were protected by the blood of the paschal lamb on the doorposts of their homes (Ex. 12:23). Today many Jews attach a *mezuzah* to their doorposts as a reminder of God's presence and the Jewish people's redemption from Egypt.

The *mezuzah* (Hebrew, "doorpost") is a small case containing a parchment on which the following prayer is written: "Hear, O Israel, the Lord our God, the Lord is One. And thou shalt love the Lord thy God with all thy heart, and with all thy soul, and with all thy might. And these words which I command thee this day shall be upon thy heart. Thou shalt teach them diligently unto thy children, and shalt speak of them when thou sittest in thy house, when thou walkest by the way, when thou liest down and when thou riseth up. And thou shalt bind them for a sign upon thy hand and they shall be for frontlets between thine eyes. And thou shalt write them upon the doorposts of thy house and upon thy gates" (Deut. 6:4–9).

The parchment continues with Deuteronomy 11:13–21, which emphasizes obedience to the commandments and the rewards of a righteous life.

Even today each mezuzah parchment is carefully written by qualified scribes, using the same strict procedures they use in writing the laws. It is then tightly rolled and placed in its case so that the word *shaddai* ("Almighty") appears through a small hole near the top. A special prayer is read when the mezuzah is attached near the top of the right-hand doorpost. Though the popularity of the mezuzah has diminished in recent years, many Jews still kiss the mezuzah by touching their lips with their fingers and raising the fingers to a mezuzah when entering or leaving the home. At the same time, they recite Psalm 121:8. "The Lord shall preserve thy going out and thy coming in from this time forth, and even forevermore."

The mezuzah is a Jewish family's daily reminder of their responsibility to God and their community. It is a sign to the community that this home is one where the laws of God reign supreme. Within this sanctuary, away from worldly influences, the Jewish family studies the Scripture, observes religious holidays, and instructs their children in the faith of their fathers.

An ancient Hebrew scholar explained the purpose of the mezuzah by comparing it to the guards of an earthly king. In the same way that a king has guards at the gate to assure him of his security, the people of Israel are safe within their homes because the Word of God is at the door to guard them.

---

sanctuary where they could worship Him. (*See* "Jews in New Testament Times.")

God chose all of the Israelites to be His priests (Ex. 19:6), but most of them had to earn a living. Therefore He ordered that the tribe of Levi should represent the whole nation in the sanctuary (Ex. 28:43—29:9). The Levites had to follow special rules to keep themselves pure for this kind of service. God chose the Levitical family of Aaron to be His priests, and they had to follow stricter rules (Lev. 10:8–11). From them, God chose one man to be the high priest and gave him even more special rules.

Why God would lay out such complex rules for worship puzzles many modern readers of the Bible. But the crucial idea behind the ceremonial laws was *holiness,* that is, separation, closeness, and conformity to God. Obedience to the laws assured that God's people would be different from all others. The worship of God was most important in their lives, so they devoted much time and care to it. (*See* "Worship Rituals.")

B. Dietary Law. God gave the Israelites a special diet to emphasize that they were His special people (Deut. 12:15). He did not allow them to eat meat that was improperly butchered (Lev. 7:22–27) or any of the first-fruits from a plant (Ex. 23:19; 34:26). He gave them many other rules about their diet. Here are some examples:

—They could not eat any blood, because life was in the blood (Deut. 12:23) and it was a covering (atonement) for sin (Lev. 17:11).

—They could not eat any animal fat, because it should be offered to God (Lev. 7:23, 31).

—They could not eat animals killed by wild beasts or animals that died of natural causes (Lev. 7:22–27).

—They could not eat scavenger animals,

such as vultures (Deut. 14:11–20), or organs that remove impurities from an animal's body (Ex. 29:13, 22).

—They could eat water animals with scales or fins, but not others, such as the otter (Deut. 14:9–10).

—They could eat any plant-eating animals which both chewed their cud and had a parted hoof (such as cows), but no others (Deut. 14:6–8).

—They could not eat any crawling or flying insects, except those of the locust and beetle families (Lev. 11:22–23).

—They could eat any fruits after the fourth harvest (Lev. 19:23), as well as any vegetables and grains (Gen. 1:29–30) or eggs (Deut. 22:6–7).

—They could not eat or drink anything that had been left open in a room with a dead or dying person (Num. 19:11–22).

—They could not eat a goat's kid boiled in its mother's milk because this was a pagan ritual of the Canaanites (Ex. 23:19).

Some basic concepts of biblical law emerge from this list. First, God's people were to give Him what was rightfully His (the blood and fat). Second, they were to avoid contact with sources of defilement, such as the dead. Third, they were to avoid anything pagan or idolatrous. Fourth, all of the dietary laws came from God; He alone decided what His people should eat.

C. Quarantine Law. God laid down strict rules about death, illness, childbirth, and a woman's monthly menstrual period. The Israelites learned that these things could make them unclean and unfit for acceptable worship (cf. Lev. 12; 14:1–32; 15).

The Israelites knew that God was a God of the living, so they accepted that they must keep death away from their worship. If they touched a corpse, they could not go to a worship service until they had cleansed themselves (Lev. 22:3–7).

God blessed marriage and the raising of a family (Deut. 28:11), but His laws on childbirth reminded the Israelites that they were born in sin. (A woman who bore a child had to cleanse herself by rituals; so did the midwife and anyone else who attended the birth—Lev. 12.) These laws also reminded the Israelites that sex was not a part of their worship. This set them farther apart from other ancient cultures, for whom fertility rites and temple prostitutes formed an important part of worship.

D. Laws of Dedication. God taught the Is-

raelites that the firstborn of every family, animal, and plant belonged to Him. They gave the firstborn to God as a symbol of giving all life back to Him. Because God counted Israel His firstborn among mankind, He called the nation to dedicate itself to serving Him (Ex. 4:22–23).

God claimed the Israelites as His people when they lived in Egypt. Answering His call, they followed Moses into the wilderness and entered into a *covenant* (a treaty or agreement) with God at Mount Sinai. They agreed to let the tribe of Levi represent the firstborn of the nation in its worship ceremony (Num. 3:40–41; 8:18). The other Israelites paid a fee to excuse their own firstborn children from this duty (Lev. 27:1–8). Once a year they sacrificed the firstborn of all flocks, herds, and fields to the Lord (Deut. 14:22–27). After the Israelites settled in Canaan, God told them to give these firstfruits to the Levites (Lev. 23:10, 17). This demonstrated that the land and all its fruits belonged to God.

The Israelites probably gave three tithes. They called the first "the Lord's tithe." It was one-tenth of their money and produce, and they gave it to the Levites, who weren't allowed to own any land (Num. 18:21–24). From what they received, the Levites gave a tithe to the priests (Num. 18:26).

The Israelites gave a second tithe three times a year when they went to the central sanctuary (Deut. 12:6–7, 17–18). They gave the third tithe once every three years; they left it at the city gate to be distributed among the Levites, strangers, orphans, and widows (Deut. 14:27–29). These tithes amounted to about 13 percent of a man's total income.[1] The tithe system allowed all of the Israelites to offer their possessions to God. It spread the responsibility for maintaining worship among the rich and the poor, the willing and the unwilling. God ordered the Israelites not to plant their land in the seventh year (Ex. 23:10–11), and He did not require a tithe in that year. Thus God expected men to recognize His Lordship, but He demanded only a relatively small portion of their property for Himself.

In addition to these tithes, every adult male of the wilderness generation paid a poll tax to raise funds for constructing the tabernacle

---

[1] R. J. Rushdoony, *Institutes of Political Law* (Nutley, N.J.: Craig Press, 1973), p. 53.

(Ex. 38:24–31). All Israelite men over the age of 20 paid this tax.

E. Laws of Religious Symbolism. God commanded the Israelites to wear certain symbols to show their dedication to Him. For example, Jewish men wore *phylacteries*—tiny containers that held key Bible texts. The Old Testament often mentions the phylacteries, but gives no specific command from God concerning them (Ex. 13:9; Deut. 6:8; 11:18). An Israelite would tie the phylactery to his forehead, his left hand, or the doorpost of his house.

God told the Israelites to wear blue fringes on their garments (Deut. 22:12; Num. 15:37–41). These fringes showed a person's commitment to God's royal law. Jesus wore them (Matt. 9:20), but He condemned Jews who made their fringes large to boast of their dedication to God (Matt. 23:5).

F. Civil Law. The people of Israel knew themselves called to worship God with their entire lives. This meant that their obedience extended to the realm of civil laws as well as of religious laws. They consulted God when they selected their leaders, and they looked to God to guide their government. They believed that God had set up the powers of civil government for their own good.

1. Political Leaders. God would not allow anyone who had a physical handicap to serve in a position of leadership. He banned from office any male who was sexually maimed, anyone who was born out of wedlock, and anyone who was a Moabite or Ammonite (mixed races). The law prevented these people from entering the "congregation of the Lord," the chief political body of the nation (Deut. 23:1–3).

These laws offend our modern sense of democracy, but we must remember that ancient Israel was not a democracy. It was a *theocracy* (a government ruled by God), and God stressed that His people should be pure. He wanted Israelites to be spiritually clean and perfect; He symbolized this by allowing only those who were physically and racially perfect to come into His presence.

God gave Israel specific instructions for choosing a king (Deut. 17:14–20). Some modern scholars believe that these laws date from after the time of Moses, but there is no proof of that. What is said is that God required a king who would submit to the laws of the covenant, and this is fully in keeping with the teachings of the rest of the Pentateuch.

Anticipating the Israelites' desire for a king, God laid down the laws of Deuteronomy to make sure that the king would not lead the people away to paganism. But the Israelites did not need these laws until many generations after Moses (cf. 1 Sam. 8:5).

2. Israel's Army. God allowed Israel to raise an army for defense (Num. 2:14), but He did not want His people to become a war-like nation, greedy for land and power. He would not let them have war horses (Deut. 17:16), nor would He let them keep anything they captured in war. But they could protect the borders of the Promised Land from any invaders, and they could crush rebel armies within their country. The generals of Israel could draft soldiers from the men over 20 years of age (cf. Num. 1:21–43), except for the Levites (Num. 1:48–49). God promised to help the army of Israel if the soldiers obeyed His laws (Deut. 23:9–14). Israel must try to make peace with its enemies before going into battle, but often Israel had to destroy its enemies (Deut. 2:34; 3:6). Sometimes God allowed the troops to spare young virgins and marry them. But if a soldier decided to do this, he could not treat the woman as a slave or captive (Deut. 21:10–14). Even in war, God told the Israelites to respect the life He had created. He ordered them to protect all innocent forms of life, including the fruit trees (Deut. 20:19–20).

3. The Court System. Israel had a dual system of courts. The nation elected judges to hear civil law suits, while the Levites judged religious matters (cf. Deut. 17:8–13; 2 Chr. 19:8, 11). Each court system had several layers of lesser courts (cf. Deut. 1:15–16). The judges heard cases of all kinds and taught the laws to the people (Deut. 17:11; 2 Chr. 17:7–9).

The law required witnesses to tell the truth or suffer the same penalty as the accused one (Ex. 23:1–3). Two or three witnesses had to give consonant testimony in order to convict a person of a serious crime. A person could not be convicted on the basis of only one witness's testimony (Deut. 17:6). Anyone who refused to accept the verdict of the court could be put to death (Deut. 17:12–13).

The courts had room for mercy, though. If someone committed murder by accident, he could go to a city of refuge—i.e., a city where he could live without being punished (Deut. 19:1–14). But the fugitive could enter the city only if he convinced the city's judges that the killing was indeed an accident. The Bible set up these cities of refuge to protect the lives of innocent people. (Anyone who fled to a city of refuge could go free when the high priest died.) The judges controlled these cities, which were an important feature of Israel's civil law.

G. Criminal Law. The criminal laws of Israel can be divided into several categories. Of course, all crimes were serious because they were sins against God. But some crimes were more destructive, and they carried a heavier penalty.

1. Crimes against Religion. Some crimes offended God directly, dishonoring Him by evil speech and rebellious action. A person might reject God and the life He offers; he might worship a pagan God, betray the people of God, or abuse the holy rituals of worship. If so, he would be put to death. In some cases, his own relatives would execute him (Deut. 13:6–9). When such a case came to trial, the judges investigated it very carefully. They cross-examined the witnesses and checked the evidence several times. If a witness gave false testimony on a matter of such importance, he was put to death.

The Bible listed several crimes of this type. Among them were child sacrifice (a form of murder), sorcery, and violation of the Sabbath. (The Sabbath law was strict because the Sabbath symbolized God's promise of eternal rest.)

2. Crimes against Society. Anyone who tried to bribe a judge or give false testimony was found guilty of a crime against society (Ex. 23:1–7; Deut. 19:16–21); for he was trying to injure the person on trial and undercut God's system of justice. This kind of crime was both a civil and religious offense.

God's Law did not allow judges to torture witnesses or to take bribes. They were required to treat all defendants with equity (Deut. 16:18–19). As the Law respected a witness so it required much of him. It forced him to pay the price of death for lying (Deut. 19:16–21). The Law also gave death to a son who cursed or struck his parents (Ex. 21:15, 17), because he was attacking the family, the foundation of his society. By the same token, it protected the son from evil parents because it did not permit child abuse.

The criminal law of the Old Testament affirms that God controls life. He creates life, and only He can decide to cut it off. The death penalty protected law-abiding citizens from

SAMARITAN SCROLL OF THE LAW. *Inhabitants of northern Israel, the Samaritans rejected all Old Testament Scripture except the Pentateuch. The Samaritans intermarried with foreign tribes after the restoration to Israel in the fifth century B.C., which created the ancient antipathy between the Samaritans and the Jews.*

any evil person who might want to seize power in their community.

It protected the family and the individual, too. A rebellious son who struck his parents was to be executed in the public marketplace as a lesson to other children (Ex. 21:18–21). God expected His people to raise their children so that they would respect the Law. But in the end, each child was responsible for what he did.

3. Crimes against Morality. The laws of the Bible form a unique moral system. While other laws of the Near East tried to show what a king thought was good and right, the Bible shows how to honor God; this theme runs through all of its laws and is the root of all its morality.

The Bible outlaws adultery, unnatural sex acts (such as homosexuality), prostitution, and other forms of perverted sex. God knew that

LAWS AND STATUTES

these things could destroy Israel, just as they had destroyed other nations. They were crimes against morality—in other words, crimes challenging the God-given order for human society.

God's Law ruled out greed, lying, strange marriages, and anything else that would upset society. God expected His people to live morally upright lives.

4. Crimes against the Person. These crimes included murder, abortion, rape, and kidnapping. Each carried the death penalty. Let us take a close look at the law concerning rape, because it sheds light on the Bible's understanding of woman.

If a woman was attacked and did not cry out for help, her attacker was not guilty of rape. But if she sought help without being able to get it and if she was married or betrothed, her attacker was put to death. If an unmarried woman was raped, the attacker had to pay a dowry price (50 shekels of silver)—in fact, he often had to pay a double dowry to make her a more desirable bride. The woman might decide to marry her attacker, or her father might decide the two should get married. In that case, the attacker paid 50 shekels to her father and married the girl; and the law never allowed him to divorce her (Deut. 22:23–30). This protected the right of the woman. (*See* "Family Relationships"; "Women and Womanhood.")

The Bible outlawed kidnapping to stop the slave trade. This especially protected the foreigners (Ex. 22:21–24), the blind and deaf (Lev. 19:14, 33–34), the hired servants (Deut. 24:14), and other helpless people (Deut. 27:19).

If a woman attacked a man's genital organs, even to defend her husband, the law would cut off her hand (Deut. 25:11–12). This was the only case in which the Bible would allow the court to mutilate a guilty person. The Old Testament taught that God set man over woman, and every woman must respect this order of things.

If a man claimed that his wife had not been a virgin and her family could prove otherwise, the husband had to pay her father a massive fine—100 shekels of silver. He would be beaten, he would lose his right to divorce his wife, and he would have to support her for the rest of his life. In court, a judge would assume that the woman was innocent until proven guilty, and it took two witnesses to prove her guilt. If she was indeed guilty, she was put to death. But no man would dare to accuse his wife of adultery unless he was very sure of it, because a lie would bring bankruptcy and would make him his wife's servant forever (Deut. 22:13–19).

Another law that sheds light on the Bible's understanding of woman is found in Exodus 21:22–25. If two men were fighting and one of them struck a pregnant woman and she miscarried, the person who struck her was fined an amount determined by her husband and administered by the judges. However, if the miscarriage caused further complications and she died, the Law provided for the death penalty. In this way unborn children and their mothers were valued and protected.

The law allowed no one to harm another person or his property. Notice the damages the offender had to pay in the matter of a goring ox (Ex. 21:28). God prized the rights of every person, and His Law protected them. A goring ox had to be locked up (Ex. 21:29), any open pit had to be covered (Ex. 21:33), and homeowners had to put railings around their roofs so that no one would fall off (Deut. 22:8).

5. Crimes against Property. God granted His people the right to own property, and He gave them special laws to protect that right. However, it is clear that the Bible placed a higher value on human life than on property. While murder carried the death penalty, theft carried only a fine. If someone stole an ox and couldn't return it, he had to pay its owner five times the normal value. If he stole a sheep, he had to pay four times the normal value. (Oxen were worth more because they were beasts of burden.) If the thief was able to return the beast he had stolen, he still had to pay the owner twice its value. If the thief couldn't afford to pay, he was sold into slavery to pay the debt (Ex. 22:1–5). And if the farmer discovered the thief at night and killed him, the judge would let the farmer go free.

God gave laws concerning "white-collar crime" too. If a person blackmailed a friend or refused to pay back a loan, a judge would order him to pay back what he had taken plus one-fifth more and to give a guilt offering to God (Lev. 6:1–7). If a merchant used false weights and measures, the courts would make him pay back the people he had cheated (Lev. 19:35–36; Deut. 25:13–16). The law required a person to return stray animals to their rightful owners; if he didn't know who the owner was, he was supposed to care for the animal until the owner claimed it (Ex. 23:4–5; Deut. 22:1–4).

A person who destroyed God's property received the full condemnation of the law. For example, God had ordered the leaders of Israel to place landmarks at the boundaries of each family's property. The Bible cursed anyone who moved these landmarks (Deut. 19:14; 27:17) because they belonged to God. The Bible also gave stern warnings to anyone who tampered with God's sanctuary (cf. Lev. 10:1–2).

H. Laws of Benevolence. Many biblical laws called for humane treatment of the poor and helpless, as well as kindness toward animals.

The law said that every animal was useful, and the Israelites were to feed each animal according to the work it did (Deut. 25:4). God did not allow his people to beat their animals cruelly. In fact, they had to let their animals rest on the Sabbath (Ex. 20:8–11; 23:72).

One law said that when an Israelite found a beast carrying a load that was too heavy for it—even if the animal belonged to his neighbor—he should take part of the burden himself (Deut. 22:1–4.) The Israelites were supposed to leave gleanings in the field for wild animals to eat (Lev. 24:4–7). Also, an Israelite could not take a mother bird and her eggs on the same day, nor a cow and its calf, nor a ewe sheep and its lamb (Lev. 22:28; Deut. 22:6–7). God's Law respected the source of life and demanded humane treatment of all animals.

Scripture directed God's people to care for the widow, orphan, and foreigner (Ex. 22:22–24). These people did not receive handouts, however; they were supposed to be able to earn their own living (Deut. 24:19–22). The Israelites respected and cared for their elders (Lev. 19:32). They could criticize a neighbor they did not like, but they were not allowed to hold a grudge against him (Lev. 19:17–18). They could not inflict excessive punishment on a criminal (Deut. 25:1–3). In every way, God expected His people to love their neighbors.

If an Israelite loaned someone a coat or some other necessary item, it had to be returned at nightfall. An Israelite could not enter someone's house to collect a bad debt (Deut. 24:10–13). God honored the right of the creditor, but He also guarded the right of the debtor.

The Law allowed travelers to enter a field and gather food to eat, but they could not carry off an extra supply (Deut. 23:24–25). A man had to pay wages to his hired hands every day, since they needed the money to buy their food (Deut. 24:14–15). He had to lend them money without interest in an emergency (Lev. 25:35–37). If a person could not make a living on his own, he could sign a contract to become another man's servant. His master had to treat him kindly, though (Lev. 25:39–43). A freeborn person could not be kidnapped and sold as a slave (Ex. 21:16; Deut. 24:7). And an Israelite had to protect a runaway slave from another country, making sure that his owner didn't harm him (Deut. 23:15–16). Each person could expect fair treatment under the legal system of Israel.

I. Personal and Family Rights. A survey of the laws of the Bible shows that they guard the rights of each individual and his family. The Law required children to respect and obey their parents and parents were supposed to raise their children to serve and obey God (Deut. 6:7). The Bible set strict limits on marriage to make sure that family life would be a decent and wholesome thing. (*See* "Marriage and Divorce.")

Each slave kept his dignity as a human being. No Israelite could be forced into slavery. Even if he signed a contract to become another man's servant, God's Law cancelled the contract at the end of seven years (Ex. 21:2–6). A slave became a member of his owner's family. He enjoyed the rights of any other family member (except the right of inheritance, of course). If the slave was a foreigner, his owner could circumcise him and invite him to worship with other Jews (Ex. 12:44; Deut. 12:18; 16:10–11).

If an owner punished a slave so harshly that he died, the Law branded him a murderer (Ex. 21:20). But if the slave did not die, the Law did nothing; God judged that the owner suffered enough by having a disabled slave (Ex. 21:21). If the owner inflicted a permanent injury—for example, if the slave lost an eye or tooth—the slave could go free (Ex. 21:36–27).

Even though the Bible allowed slavery, its regulations reminded the Israelites that every person was created in the image of God—including the slave.

We've already noticed that the Bible preserved each person's right to his own property. He could claim any property that had been lost or stolen and anyone who borrowed his property had to return it in good condition. If the

LAWS AND STATUTES

KUDURRU STONE. Kudurru *is an Akkadian (early Mesopotamian) term that refers to an oval or pillar-shaped boundary marker, set up to show that certain property was a royal grant. Each stone was usually engraved with the images of deities to protect the property, curses against those who would remove the stone, and blessings on those who honored it.*

price. If a man built a house inside a walled city, he could sell it. If he did not buy it back within a year, it would not return to him in the jubilee (Lev. 25:29–31). But if a Levite sold his house, it would in any case be restored to him at that time (Lev. 25:32–34).

Because God owned the land, He dictated the rules of inheritance. God said that a firstborn son could receive a double portion of the property and other special benefits (Deut. 21:15–17; 25:6). A wicked son might receive nothing. And if there was no son, a daughter could inherit the property (Num. 27:7–8). In that case, she had to marry a member of her own tribe to keep the property within the family (Num. 36:1–12). Anyone who inherited a piece of property had to use it to care for his relatives because he (or she) became the head of the family.

J. Obligations to God. The Law of God did not simply describe the rights of each person; it also described his responsibilities to God. Each person owed his life to Yahweh, and so the community expected him to serve God and remain loyal to His people.

This is why biblical law contains so many religious commands. For example, God told His people to tear down heathen shrines and stop pagan worship practices (Deut. 7:5). He commanded them to observe the laws of the Sabbath and to regard His sanctuary with proper reverence (Lev. 19:30).

26

LAWS AND STATUTES

borrower lost the property or if it was stolen from him, he still had to repay the owner. In fact, if the borrower schemed to "lose" the property in his care, he had to repay the owner *twofold* (Ex. 22:7–15). When he borrowed another man's property, he held a sacred trust.

The Bible explained that God still owned all the land of the Israelites, even though it had been divided among the families of Israel (Lev. 25:23). Each seventh year the land was to enjoy a sabbath, during which no crops would be gathered; but any passer-by might take what he needed (Lev. 25:1–7). The ancient landmarks showed the boundary of each family's portion. If they rented or sold the land to someone else, the property came back to the family in the jubilee at the end of 50 years (Lev. 25:8–24). Even before the end of 50 years, the Law allowed a member of the family to buy the property back at its original

CODE OF LIPIT-ISHTAR. *King of the small city kingdom of Isin in Sumer (nineteenth century B.C.), Lipit-Ishtar formulated a code of law to restore order to his kingdom. He probably derived most of his laws from existing Sumerian practices. The code contained 38 regulations dealing with matters such as the treatment of slaves, inheritance, and marriage.*

LAWS AND STATUTES

God bound His people to follow His Law and no other. He commanded the leaders of Israel to record His Law, and He commanded the people of Israel to study and remember it (Deut. 4:2; Num. 15:37–41; Lev. 18:4–5). God's Law demanded their reverence, obedience, and service. And as long as Israel obeyed God's commands, they lived in harmony with Him.

IV. Intertestamental Law. The Jewish notion of law changed somewhat between the writing of the Old and New Testaments. God had given His Word to the children of Israel through historic events—especially those involving Moses during the Exodus—and the later prophets and priests had interpreted that Law for their own day. Their interpretation usually included a hope for national independence and superiority (Is. 60:1–3; Jer. 31:3 f.; Joel 3:18f.)—a hope that rested on the Jews' obedience to God's covenant. After centuries of failing to actualize this hope, the Jews saw this theme disappear from their prophecy. In fact, the role of prophecy itself diminished during the intertestamental period.

For the Jews, making the Law meaningful for their own day became less important than making it meaningful for that future day when God would come to reward them. Thus they began to stress the Law's ceremonial prescriptions. Almsgiving, festivals, ritual prayers, and temple rites grew to be very important in the Jewish community. (*See* "Worship Rituals.")

Disaster was looming on the horizon. The temple of Jerusalem would be destroyed in A.D. 70 at the end of a bitter war between the Jews and the armies of Rome. This would affect the religious outlook of Jews and Christians alike—especially their hope for an immediate new age of the Messiah. The Jews would not be able to hold their festivals in the shambles of Jerusalem, for the Roman army would completely end the possibility of temple worship. Early communities of Christians, realizing that Jesus' return was delayed, would develop a new organization. (*See* "The Early Church.") But the traditional Jews would already have an organization to deal with the problems caused by the destruction of the temple. They would experience a shift in the balance of power between the religious parties, with the Pharisees emerging as the strongest Jewish faction.

The aristocratic Sadducees were closely connected with the temple, so their influence was to be destroyed when Jerusalem fell. The militant Zealots would lead the nation to the disastrous defeat, which would turn most Jews against them. The reclusive Essenes had always been a minority sect and would gain nothing from the war. But the Pharisees' concern for the Law assured them of a dominant place in Jewish life after the Roman conquest. They had developed many oral interpretations of the Law for their own day, and after the fall of Jerusalem they would establish a new center for studying the Law at Jamnia. There they would preserve and systematize the written Law and their oral interpretations of it. This would be the beginning of modern Judaism, commonly called *rabbinic* Judaism.

The Jewish War came a generation after Jesus. But this preview of the war and its aftermath helps to set the stage for Jesus' dialogue with the Pharisees. The Gospels (especially Matthew) often picture Jesus in conflict with the Pharisees' interpretation of the Law. This conflict foreshadowed the rift between the early Christians and Jews.

V. Jesus and the Law. Jesus' attitude toward the Law is a topic of much debate. Some scholars believe that He merely interpreted Mosaic Law like the Pharisees, without changing it. Others believe that Jesus penetrated past the letter of the Law to reveal its great moral and spiritual principles. In more recent years, commentators have noted that some of Jesus' statements seem to be in direct conflict with the Mosaic Law. These commentators have made several attempts to resolve these conflicts. At least three of their interpretations have gained some popularity:

The first may be called *the fulfillment view.* Most readers are familiar with Jesus' statement, "Think not that I have come to abolish the law and the prophets; I have come not to abolish them but to fulfil them" (Matt. 5:17, RSV). There are apparent conflicts between Jesus' teachings and Mosaic Law (e.g., His teachings on divorce); but the fulfillment view tries to show that, if we look beyond appearances, we can harmonize Jesus' actions with the Old Testament in every case.

The second interpretation may be called *the sovereignty view.* Commentators who take this approach hold that, when there is a disagreement between Jesus and Pharisaic law, Jesus' word is authoritative. They base this view upon Jesus' statements such as, "You have heard that it was said, 'You shall love your neighbor, and hate your enemy.' *But I say to*

LAWS AND STATUTES

you. . ." (Matt. 5:43–44a, NASB, italics added). Exponents of the sovereignty view would point out that the Old Testament nowhere says, "You shall hate your enemy"; this was a teaching of the Pharisees.

The third interpretation might be called *the inscrutability view.* Commentators who favor this approach believe that we cannot determine Jesus' attitude toward the Law. Even if we could determine His attitude, they doubt if it could be expressed in a clean, neat formula.

A. Dialogue with the Pharisees. But let us attempt to see what we can of the relationship between Jesus' teachings and Moses' Law, according to the biblical witness. We will rely heavily on the Gospel of Matthew, since Matthew and his audience were deeply concerned with Jewish matters.[2]

We find that Jesus said various things concerning the Law. For example, in controversies such as that about eating on the Sabbath (Matt. 12:1–8), Jesus made it clear that He superseded the Law. He said, "I tell you, something greater than the temple is here" (v. 6, RSV). The Pharisees were not looking for anything greater than the temple, where God's Law was preserved. They were amazed to hear anyone claim that something was greater than the repository of God's Word. Christ not only refused to submit to their interpretation of the Law, but He declared that He was greater than it: "For the Son of Man is Lord of the Sabbath" (Mark 2:28).

In other instances, though, Jesus preserved the Law. For example, in Matthew 23:2ff., Jesus admonished the crowd to do all that the scribes and Pharisees told them, for they had "seated themselves in the chair of Moses." Then, however, He attacked the Pharisees' hypocrisy! Does this mean that Jesus changes His position in the course of the sermon? Or is He making a distinction between the Pharisees' relaying Moses' Law faithfully and embroidering it falsely? Scholars disagree.

Second, Jesus emphasized that love is the proper motive for obeying God's Law. Pharisees would agree that love is important, but they had never said that everything else should be measured against it. The Pharisees had defined and redefined Mosaic Law so that it could be practiced as a complete code of righteousness. But for Jesus, righteousness did not depend upon following mechanically a prescribed pattern of action. His own love for other people often led Him to speak and act in ways that were unexpected and unconventional, as when He spoke harshly to the hostile Pharisees (Matt. 23:17; cf. Mark 3:5). This behavior did not fit any conventional idea of loving conduct; but Jesus' calculated attempt to bring the Pharisees to their spiritual senses was the most loving gesture He could make to them.

Does Jesus bring a new and greater Law? Or does He merely challenge the Pharisaic interpretations and hypocrisy? We see the dialogue between Jesus and the Pharisees in many circumstances, and more than one witness writes about it. But some common themes stand out:

—Jesus does not separate Himself from Mosaic Law (Matt. 5:17; Luke 9:31).

—Unlike the Pharisees, Jesus emphasizes God's love—though He does warn of God's judgment (Matt. 7:21).

—Jesus' behavior fits no mold of this world. He does not attempt to compete as a rabbi among rabbis, nor does He try to fill the traditional role of the Messiah. His relationship to the Law is truly unique (cf. Matt. 7:28–29).

B. Jesus' Attitude. Jesus both affirms and criticizes the Jewish law. He does not teach that fulfillment of the Mosaic Law means that one automatically enters into the saving relationship between God and His people that He calls God's "Kingdom." Rather, He says that people enter that Kingdom through faith in Christ Himself, and that it produces a completely regenerated life. Jesus teaches that we should obey God because He is our heavenly Father and we love Him; we do not obey in order to be made right with Him.

VI. Paul and the Law. Paul affirms and criticizes the Law. He declares that God is finished with it, but also that He has established it. Many of Paul's teachings on this subject are very strongly stated: "For Christ is the end of the law for righteousness to every one that believeth" (Rom. 10:4). "Do we then make void the law through faith? God forbid: yea, we establish the law" (Rom 3:31). "For I through the law am dead to the law, that I might live unto God" (Gal. 2:19).

How may we integrate these divergent emphases?

A. Paul's World. To make sense of this

---

[2] Luke plays down Pharisaic debates, while Mark never uses the Greek word *nomos* (law). John's portrayal of Jesus is so unique that it would be confusing to discuss it here.

tension in Paul's teachings, we need to understand the times in which he lived. When Paul wrote, Jerusalem was still intact. The Sadducees and Zealots were powers to be reckoned with, but there was no unified Jewish opposition to Christianity. Paul was part of a fledgling religious community that took its place alongside the other Jewish sects.

When the church began to spread into Gentile territory, a serious question arose: Should Gentiles who are unfamiliar with the Law be required to learn and practice it when they become Christians?

B. The Jerusalem Council. Acts 15 and Galatians 2 (by common interpretation) tell how the church convened an apostolic council to decide this issue. The congregation at Jerusalem was headed by James, brother of Jesus and the successor of Peter, whose leadership had been ended by Herod Agrippa (Acts 12:17; 15:13; 21:18; Gal. 1:19). James believed that the Jewish Christians should obey Jewish Law, but that Gentile Christians could be permitted a certain amount of freedom from it. A dissenting faction existed, though (Acts 15:5; Gal. 2:4). The dissenters believed that all Christians should obey the Jewish Law; they are therefore called the "Judaizers."

The real conflict came between James's faction and Paul's followers, who may have been more liberal than James (note Gal. 2:4 f.). Paul was summoned to Jerusalem to validate his preaching (Gal. 2:1–3), particularly on the relation of the Law to the gospel of Christ. The outcome was a brotherly agreement between Paul, James, and Peter. In principle, they agreed that the Gentile congregations were free from most of the Law, and they recognized that faith in Christ was sufficient to save the Gentiles. Peter said that the Holy Spirit "made no distinction between us and them, but cleansed their hearts by faith. Now therefore why do you make trial of God by putting a yoke [the Law] upon the neck of the disciples which neither our fathers nor we have been able to bear? But we believe that we shall be saved through the grace of the Lord Jesus, just as they will" (Acts 15:8–11, RSV).

This principle confirmed Jesus' teaching that law is not to be obeyed as a fetish, or as a system of salvation, since faith in Christ saves people. This principle came to dominate the early church, and it served as a springboard for Paul's rather sophisticated theology of Law and gospel.

Unlike Jesus, who wrote nothing that we know of, Paul wrote weighty doctrinal and pastoral letters. Although some of them circulated among several churches (cf. Col. 4:16), Paul often wrote with the local problems of a particular congregation in his mind.

For this reason, he seems to have different opinions on the Law in different letters. At Corinth, for example, Paul's opponents were Hellenistic; they had little use for law or morality. Paul took a very conservative stand in responding to them. In Galatia, on the other hand, he had to face the Judaizers. So Paul emphasized liberty from Law when writing this letter. While there was a definite theological development from the writing of 1 Thessalonians to Romans, Colossians and Ephesians, we should not ignore Paul's specific local themes. It is instructive to compare Paul's let-

MARASHU DOCUMENTS. *A family of Jewish businessmen living in the Mesopotamian city of Nippur in the fifth century B.C. left behind a collection of over 700 tablets recording their commercial and real estate transactions. These clay documents include business contracts, land leases, loan contracts, and receipts. Nippur was a rich city, and some Jews who specialized in banking became quite wealthy there.*

LAWS AND STATUTES

ters to a congregation where the general disposition is to practice the letter of the Law (e.g., Galatia) and his letters to a congregation where the feeling is opposite (e.g., Corinth).

After Paul left the Jerusalem Council, he ministered primarily to Hellenistic Jewish communities. Their people had some notion of Jewish law mixed with Gentile ideas. In most congregations, Jewish Christians worshiped beside Gentile Christians. One group was expected to obey the Law; the other was released from most of it. It is no wonder that the issue of Law required so much of Paul's attention.

C. Paul's Theme of Faith vs. Law. Probably the most dominant theme in all of Paul's writings is that the Law is subordinate to faith in Christ: "A man is not justified by the works of the law, but through faith in Jesus Christ" (Gal. 2:16; cf. Phil. 3; Rom. 1—4). Paul taught that no law brings justification in and of itself. The new covenant is based on the work of the Holy Spirit in the heart, and not on "letters in stone" (an obvious reference to Mosaic Law). Paul knew that God's Law can be made the basis of a legalistic, self-justifying habit of mind; and when it is thus abused we are doomed "under the Law." This legal condemnation is the opposite of being "under grace"—the grace, that is, of Christ's redeeming death (Rom. 6:14). Paul does not attack the righteous content of the Law, but the lethal manner in which it operates.

In what way has the Law been superseded by faith in Christ? Paul declares that all of us, Jews and Gentiles, have been under the judgment of the Law (Rom. 5:12–19), but Christ freed us from this judgment through the cross (Gal. 2:21; Rom. 7:4; 8:1ff.). All of Paul's preaching centers on Christ crucified (1 Cor. 1:17ff.). If we are to understand his attitude toward the Law, we must therefore see it in light of Jesus' Crucifixion.

Paul understood that Jesus died to open for us a way of salvation (Gal. 2:21). That is, Christ died so that we might cease from trying to right ourselves with God by obeying the Law. Jesus substituted Himself for us, taking our judgment upon Himself so that we would not have to bear it (2 Cor. 5:19–21; Gal. 3:13; Col. 2:14).

D. Paul and Jesus. Paul and Jesus affirmed the value of Jewish Law, but they directed early Christians beyond the Law. Jesus was somewhat more amiable toward the Law, perhaps because His circumstances allowed Him to speak more objectively. But neither Paul nor Jesus taught that the Jewish Law was evil in itself; they simply pointed out that it cannot justify sinners before God.

The early Christians did not understand the Law and gospel as opposites; nor did they simplify their way of relating Law and gospel to a formula. It is difficult to describe the early Christians' attitude toward Law in a few pages. But perhaps this brief study reflects the vital importance of the issue in New Testament times.

26

LAWS AND STATUTES

WORSHIP RITUALS

The people of Israel worshiped the living God in many ways and at many different places throughout the year. It is important to see what impact their worship rituals had upon their daily lives.

First, we need to understand how the people of the Bible felt about the God they worshiped. Moses told the people of Israel, "Thou art a holy people unto the Lord thy God: the Lord thy God hath chosen thee to be a special people unto himself above all people that are upon the face of the earth" (Deut. 7:6). God chose them not because of anything they did or were, but because *He loved them* (Deut. 7:7). God showed this love in many ways. He was faithful to His covenant (v. 9); He destroyed their enemies (v. 10); He blessed them with good harvests (v. 13); and He took away their diseases (v. 15).

In response to God's actions, the Israelites were a thankful people. The Psalmist said, "It is a good thing to give thanks unto the Lord, and to sing praises unto thy name, O Most High: to show forth thy loving-kindness in the morning, and thy faithfulness every night. . . ." (Ps. 92:1–2).

They stood in awe of God. As one sage observed, "The fear [awe] of the Lord is the beginning of knowledge" (Prov. 1:7). These responses were expressed in their worship. Of course, the Israelites responded to God with a whole range of thought and emotion; but these two—thankfulness and awe—seem to typify their relationship with Him.

We also need to understand how God and Israel interacted. For example, it was easy to see God in the lives of the patriarchs. He enabled Sarah to bear children at an old age (Gen. 18:9–10). He tested Abraham and spared Isaac from death (Gen. 22). He spoke with the people and they with Him (Gen. 13:14–17; 15:2). But the Israelites were never allowed to see God; Moses had to hide his face from God's presence "for he was afraid to look upon God" (Ex. 3:6).

We will see how the Israelites expressed their thankfulness and awe to the heavenly Father, how they engaged in worship.

I. BEFORE THE TIME OF MOSES

II. IN THE TIME OF MOSES
A. The Worship Site
B. The Priesthood
C. The Sacrificial System
1. Burnt Offerings
2. Cereal Offerings
3. Peace Offerings
4. Sin Offerings
5. Trespass Offerings
D. The Ritual Year
1. The Sabbath
2. Passover and the Feast of Unleavened Bread
3. The Feast of Weeks (Pentecost)
4. The Feast of Tabernacles (Booths)
5. The Day of Atonement

III. FROM THE MONARCHY TO EXILE
A. The Temple
B. The Priests, Prophets, and Kings
C. Feasts

IV. THE EXILE AND THE INTER-TESTAMENTAL PERIOD

V. THE NEW TESTAMENT ERA

I. Before the Time of Moses. The first clear mention of a worship act is found in Genesis 4:2–7: "And Abel was a keeper of sheep, but Cain was a tiller of the ground. And in process of time it came to pass that Cain brought of the fruit of the ground, an offering unto the Lord. And Abel, he also brought of the flock and of the fat thereof." The children of Adam and Eve recognized that God had given them "every herb" and "every beast" (Gen. 1:29–30), so they brought simple offerings to Him. We do not know precisely where and how the offerings were made. But we are told that they brought two types of offering, and that Cain's was rejected while Abel's was accepted.

This brief account tells us two very important things about worship: First, God acknowledges worship. We do not know whether He had spoken to the brothers at this particular site prior to this day. But on this day God spoke (v. 6) and acted (vv. 4–5) as they were worshiping. God made this time holy for them. Second, God is the focal point of worship. Scripture makes no mention of any altar

WORSHIP RITUALS

STONE ALTAR. *Found outside the gate leading into Beersheba, this stone altar is typical of those used in the Near East for offering sacrifices. The Israelites were supposed to offer sacrifice only at Jerusalem, but many disobeyed this law.*

or any words spoken by these men. We do not know what prayers they might have offered. But we *are* told what God did; His action was the vital part of worship.

Scripture does not tell us why Cain and Abel made offerings to God, simply that they did so "in process of time." We can suppose that they wanted to give thanks for what God had given them. They knew God had blessed them and would continue to bless them. So they were motivated not only by past events, but by their future hopes. Their sacrifices were made with dual intent: thankfulness for what God had given them and trust that He would continue to give. It is important to remember both aspects of worship and not downplay one or the other.

We cannot be sure why Abel's offering was accepted and Cain's rejected. We haven't been told of any rules regarding sacrifices at this time. The clue may appear in verse 7: "If thou doest well, shalt thou not be accepted?" In other words, Cain's faulty character may have rendered his sacrifice meaningless.

This is the first recorded instance of animal sacrifice. As time passed, the people learned

that God honored and accepted their sacrificial offerings.

The patriarchs erected altars and made sacrifices wherever they settled (cf. Gen. 8:20; 12:7–8). They erected stone monuments as well. Jacob took the stone that he used as a pillow and "set it up for a pillar, and poured oil upon the top of it" (Gen. 28:18–22). He called it *Bethel,* or "God's house."

The patriarchs also designated sacred trees (e.g., Gen. 12:6; 35:4; Deut. 11:30; Josh. 24:26) and sacred wells (Gen. 16:14). These objects reminded them of what God had done at particular times in their lives.

The patriarchs built simple earthen and stone altars ("cairn altars") for the slaughter of animal offerings. In fact, the Hebrew word usually translated as *altar* (*mizbeach*) literally means "a place of slaughter."

There seems to have been no formal priesthood in the time of the patriarchs, yet we read of a striking encounter between Abraham and Melchizedek, a mysterious "priest of the most high God." Some scholars speculate that Melchizedek was a Canaanite king from Salem. Abraham met him after rescuing some of his captive kinsmen (Gen. 14:17–20). Because God had enabled Abraham to bring about the rescue, he responded with worshipful gratitude. Rather than building an altar or offering an animal sacrifice, Abraham offered a "tenth of everything" as sacrifice and received God's blessing through the mediator, Melchizedek. This mysterious figure is the first priest mentioned in the Bible.

Were there other priests at this time? If so, why are they not named? Perhaps the patriarchs usually acted as their own priests. They were the only ones reported to offer sacrifice to God. But if they functioned for others as clergy, that is not clearly stated.

There was spontaneity in the worship of the patriarchs. At first they left their altars uncovered and exposed to the weather; this surely affected the time of the ceremonies, since burning was a vital part of them. Also, God acted and spoke when He chose, and the patriarchs could not know in advance when God would call them to worship. Since only a handful of people worshiped at one time, there was no need for a scheduled worship time.

II. In the Time of Moses. Moses inaugurated a new period in Israel's worship practices—a period that extended far beyond the lifetime of Moses. It began as Moses led the people of Israel out from Egypt (1446 B.C.),

WORSHIP RITUALS

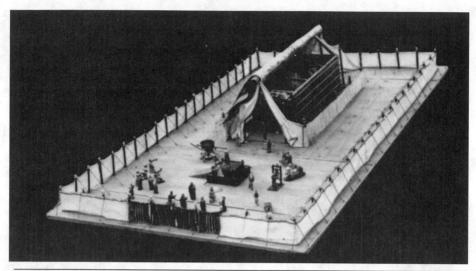

MODEL OF TABERNACLE. *This model constructed by Dr. Conrad Schick shows the tabernacle, a movable tent sanctuary made according to instructions that God gave to Moses on Mount Sinai. One special compartment of the tabernacle, called the "holy of holies," was revered as the place where God dwelled. Only the high priest could enter this place, and he did so only one day of the year—on the Day of Atonement.*

but Moses' direct influence on worship practice extended throughout Jewish history. For practical reasons, in this section let us focus on Moses' influence until the time of the judges (which ended in 1043 B.C. with the naming of Saul as Israel's first king). During the time of the judges, God's people still worshiped in tents or tabernacles. But when David was king, plans were made for construction of a temple; our next section deals with that.

A. The Worship Site. We have already mentioned that God sanctioned the use of earthen and stone altars (Ex. 20:24–26). In the days of Moses, God also sanctioned a new kind of worship site. When the great lawgiver climbed to the top of Mount Sinai, he received much more than the Ten Commandments. Among other things, he received a plan for an enclosed worship site, with an altar housed in a cloth tent. It is difficult to construct a picture of this new site. Many artists have drawn their impressions, based upon the Bible's descriptions; but there is no complete agreement on the plan of the tabernacle.

Yet we know that this worship site was distinctly different from the altars erected under the open sky. For one thing, it was much more elaborate. A description of the altar itself is found in Exodus 27:1–3: "Thou shalt make an altar of shittim wood, five cubits long, and five cubits broad; the altar shall be foursquare:

and the height thereof shall be three cubits. And thou shalt make the horns of it upon the four corners thereof: his horns shall be of the same: and thou shalt overlay it with brass. And thou shalt make his pans to receive his ashes, and his shovels, and his basins, and his flesh-hooks, and his firepans: all the vessels thereof thou shalt make of brass."

Not only were the materials different from the first altars, but the tools required to make it and the accompanying utensils were different (cf. Ex. 20:25). There is good evidence that Israel used both kinds of altars—those outdoors and the one in the tabernacle—during this time. Eventually, a more permanent, central altar was erected in the tabernacle.

Scripture also describes the tent that now covered the altar: "And Moses took the tabernacle, and pitched it without the camp, afar off from the camp, and called it the tabernacle of the congregation. And it came to pass, that everyone which sought the Lord went out unto the tabernacle of the congregation, which was without the camp. And it came to pass, when Moses went out unto the tabernacle, that all the people rose up, and stood every man at his tent door, and looked after Moses, until he was gone into the tabernacle. And it came to pass, as Moses entered into the tabernacle, the cloudy pillar descended, and stood at the door of the tabernacle, and the Lord talked with

WORSHIP RITUALS

Moses" (Ex. 33:7–10). The tent is described again in Exodus 26. With such a detailed description, it may seem easy to illustrate how the tent looked. But it isn't. It would be just as challenging to picture an automobile engine if we had only a verbal blueprint and had never actually seen one.

Moses spoke with God in this tent. Although Scripture does not say that Moses offered sacrifices in the tent (cf. Ex. 33:7–10), we may assume that he did so, since the altar was there. Moses was seeking the Lord. The people knew God was meeting with Moses because the "cloudy pillar" stood before the tent. This was a familiar sign of God's presence.

Moses and his servant Joshua went into the tent alone while the other people stood by and waited. After Moses first worshiped in the tent, he returned to the mountain to receive new tables of Law. He then came down to relay God's message to His people.

In a sense, Moses was a "go-between" for God and the Israelites. He was not a formal priest, but God did single him out as His leader-messenger. We can see the beginnings of priesthood here; but Moses himself was not actually called a priest until centuries later (cf. Ps. 99:6).

B. The Priesthood. At this point in Israel's history, an ordained priesthood came into being. According to God's command (Ex. 28:1), Moses consecrated his brother Aaron and Aaron's sons as priests. These men came from the tribe of Levi. From this point until intertestamental times, the official priesthood belonged to the Levites.

Moses made a distinction between Aaron and his sons, for he anointed Aaron as the "high priest among his brethren" (Lev. 21:10). He distinguished Aaron's office by giving him special robes (Ex. 28:4, 6–39; Lev. 8:7–9). Upon Aaron's death, the robes and the office were transferred to Eleazar, his eldest son (Num. 20:25–28).

The high priest's most important function was to preside at the annual Day of Atonement. On that day, the high priest could enter the holy of holies of the tabernacle and sprinkle the mercy seat with the blood of sin offerings. By doing this, he atoned for his wrongs, for those of his family, and those of all the people of Israel (Lev. 16:1–25). The high priest also had to sprinkle the blood from the

MODEL OF THE ARK OF THE COVENANT. *The ark was a rectangular box of acacia wood that contained the tables of the Ten Commandments, a pot of manna, and Aaron's rod. The lid, or "mercy seat," was a gold plate surrounded by golden cherubim with outstretched wings. The ark was the symbol of God's presence among His people.*

WORSHIP RITUALS

When Sacrifice Stopped

Judea Capta—"Judea is captured"—read the coins minted by the Romans in commemoration of their victory in A.D. 70. Thousands of Jews died in battle; thousands more were taken into slavery; many others chose to leave the country. Their center of worship, the temple, was burned to the ground and the capital of Judaism had fallen.

The Roman emperors redirected the temple tax, formerly collected from all Jews, to the temple of Jupiter Capitolinus in Rome. Grieving Jews abstained from eating meat and wine, formerly temple staples; they felt it wrong to enjoy what could no longer be offered to God.

With the end of temple worship, the priesthood began to decline. Although the priests could still receive heave offerings and tithes, their revenues were greatly reduced. This loss of income, plus the loss of their temple function, resulted in a loss of influence and authority.

Deuteronomy forbade altars and sacrifices outside the chosen place, Jerusalem. But this was not the first time the Jews had been deprived of their temple and sacrificial worship; during the Exile, the people had assembled regularly to read the Scriptures and to discuss their meaning. These *synagogues* (Greek, "assemblies") again became vital to Judaism after the temple was destroyed.

Jewish people met at the synagogue to pray, sing, and study the Torah. The chief function of the synagogue was to foster understanding and proper observance of the Jewish law. In effect, it became the seat of a spiritual government which ordered and disciplined the lives of the people.

After the destruction of the temple, the sages who interpreted the Law came to be called *tannaim,* and those who were authorized as leaders were given the title *rabbi,* or "doctor of the law." Sages interpreted the laws found in the Pentateuch as well as the traditional, oral laws called the *halakoth.* They were chiefly concerned with how these laws should affect the lives of the people. Followers of the great sage Shammai were noted for their conservative interpretations, while followers of the sage Hillel adhered to more liberal interpretations.

Jabneh (modern Jamnia) on the western Judean plains soon became the center of Jewish learning. During the war with Rome, the sage Johanan ben Zakkai was smuggled out of Jerusalem in a coffin. He made his way to the Roman camp, where he asked Roman authorities to allow him and his disciples to settle the coastal city of Jabneh and to establish an academy there. Johanan rightly perceived that the only important victory to be secured in the war against Rome was the survival of Judaism. If need be, a vitalized tradition could become a "portable homeland" for the Jews. Jabneh became the new center of that tradition.

After the Bar-Kochba revolt in A.D. 135, the center of Jewish studies was moved to Usha in Galilee, near modern Haifa. Here the sages began the assembling and codifying of the halakoth in a document that came to be called *Mishna.*

The sages disagreed as to how the halakoth should be organized. One group thought it should follow the order of the biblical verses to which they referred. Another group, headed by Rabbi Akiba ben Joseph, held out for arranging the sayings by subject matter, the way that was eventually followed.

The task of assembling the Mishna was not completed until the early part of the third century. The Mishna and the *Gemara* (a commentary on the Mishna), comprise the chief parts of the Jewish sacred book called the *Talmud.* This comprehensive compilation of Jewish manners, customs, beliefs, and teachings is still revered and studied by Jewish scholars.

---

sin offerings before the veil of the sanctuary and on the horns of the altar (Lev. 4:3–21).

As the spiritual head of Israel, the high priest had to attain a greater degree of ceremonial purity than did the ordinary priests. Leviticus 21:10–15 outlines requirements for purity of the high priest. Any sin he might commit was a blight upon the entire people of Israel. He had to atone for such a sin with a specially prescribed offering (Lev. 4:3–12).

The high priest also offered the daily meal offering (Lev. 6:19–22) and participated in the general duties of the priesthood (Ex. 27:21). These duties were many. Priests presided over all sacrifices and feasts. They served as med-ical advisors to the community (Lev. 13:15), and they were administrators of justice (Deut. 17:8–9; 21:5; Num. 5:11–13). Only they could give a blessing in the name of God (Num. 6:22–27) and blow the trumpets that summoned the people to war or feast (Num. 10:1–10).

Levites served as priests either from age 30 to 50 (Num. 4:39) or from age 25 to 50 (Num. 3:23–26). After age 50, they were only allowed to assist their fellow priests.

The people's tithe provided food and clothing for the priests (Lev. 32—33); a tenth of the tithe was given to the priests (Num. 18:21, 24–32). Since the tribe of Levi possessed no territory, 48 cities and surrounding pastures were given to them (Num. 35:1–8).

C. The Sacrificial System. The Bible contains many of Moses' regulations for sacrifice, but Leviticus 1—7 is wholly dedicated to the ritual. Many scholars regard this section as a kind of "handbook for sacrifice." It describes five types of sacrifice: burnt offerings, cereal offerings, peace offerings, sin offerings, and trespass offerings.

1. Burnt Offerings. This type of sacrifice was wholly burnt. None of it is eaten by anyone; the fire consumed it all. In fact, the fire was never extinguished: "The fire shall ever be burning upon the altar; it shall never go out" (Lev. 6:13).

The worshiper brought a male animal—a bull, lamb, goat, pigeon, or turtledove (depending largely upon the worshiper's wealth)—to the door of the tent or temple. The animal had to be without blemish. The worshiper then placed his hands upon the animal's head and it was "accepted for him to make atonement for him" (Lev. 1:4). The laying of

hands was a ceremonial act whereby the worshiper blessed or prepared the sacrificial animal. The animal was then killed at the door. Immediately, the priest collected the animal's blood and sprinkled it about the altar. (Priests never drank the blood.) Next, the priest quartered the animal, offered its head and fat on the altar, then washed the legs and entrails in water and offered them. Any remains might be cast aside into the ashes. (For example, this was done with a bird's feathers.)

Besides placing the animal on the altar, the priests were responsible to maintain the fire. They could not permit the ashes to build up in the bottom of the altar, but put them beside the altar at various times. Later, they took the ashes outside the camp or city "unto a clean place." They changed their clothes to do this. (*See* "Clothing and Cosmetics.")

Later in Israel's history, the burnt offering became a continually offered sacrifice: "This is the offering made by fire which ye shall offer unto the Lord; two lambs of the first year without spot day by day, for a continual burnt

MIDIANITE HOLY OF HOLIES. *Shortly after the twelfth century* B.C., *the Midianites set up a sanctuary at a copper-mining site in the Timnah Valley north of Elath. The shrine was roofed with a tent, and its holy of holies contained a copper snake with a gilded head as an object of worship. This sanctuary may resemble early Hebrew shrines, before the tabernacle was built.*

offering" (Num. 28:3). As this passage indicates, two animals were sacrificed each day, one at morning and one at evening. This was done to atone the people's sins against the Lord (Lev. 6:2). The burning symbolized the nation's desire to rid itself of these sinful acts against God.

2. Cereal Offerings. The Israelites sacrificed cereals or vegetable produce in addition to animals. These crops might have been offered independently of the burnt offerings, or along with them. The Hebrew word for "oblation" (*minha*) sometimes refers to these cereal offerings; at other times, *minha* referred to other types of sacrifice.

Leviticus 2 mentions four kinds of cereal offerings and gives cooking instructions for each. A worshiper could offer dough from wheat flour that had been baked in an oven, cooked on a griddle, fried in a pan, or roasted to make bread. (The last method was used for the offering of firstfruits.) All cereal offerings were made with oil and salt; no honey or leaven could be used. Oil and salt would not spoil, while honey and leaven would. In addition to these cooked ingredients, the worshiper was to bring a portion of incense (frankincense). He might also bring portions of the uncooked materials (raw grains, salt, and oil) with the offering.

Worshipers brought cereal offerings to one of two priests, who took it to the altar and threw a "memorial portion" (either of the bread, cake, wafer, or uncooked ingredients) on the fire. He did the same with all the incense. The priest ate the remainder; but if the priest himself was making a cereal offering, he burned the entire sacrifice.

The cereal offering's purpose appears to have been similar to that of the burnt offering—except in case of the "corn" offering, which was linked to the offering of firstfruits (Lev. 2:14). The offering of firstfruits seems to have been intended to sanctify the entire crop. The "corn" offering substituted for the rest of the crop—emphasizing that all of the crop was holy unto the Lord.

3. Peace Offerings. A ritual meal called the "peace offering" was shared with God, the priests, and sometimes other worshipers. It involved male or female oxen, sheep, or goats. The procedure was nearly identical to that of the burnt offering up to the point of the actual burning. In this case, the beast's blood was collected and poured around the edges of the altar. The fat and entrails were burned. Then

the remainder was eaten by the priests and (if the offering was voluntary) by the worshipers themselves. This sacrifice expressed the worshiper's desire to give thanks or praise to God. Sometimes, he was required to do this; at other times he might do so voluntarily.

The required offerings made included unleavened cakes. The priests had to eat all but the memorial portion of the cakes and the remainder of the animal on the same day the sacrifice was made.

When the offering was voluntary, the regulations were not so strict. The worshipers did not need to bring cakes and could eat for two days, not one. The priest's portion was limited to the breast and right thigh of the animal, while anyone who was ceremonially clean could eat of the rest.

Jacob and Laban offered this kind of sacrifice when they made a treaty (Gen. 31:43 ff.). Some scholars call this a "vow offering"; "Thank offerings" and "free-will offerings" followed the same general pattern. Saul's sacrifice (1 Sam. 13:8 ff.) fell into the latter category; although he "forced himself" to do it, he certainly was not required to do it. (In fact, Samuel chastised him, saying that it was illegal.) The vow and thank offerings were required, while free-will offerings were voluntary.

4. Sin Offerings. Sacrifices for sin "paid off" or *expiated* a worshiper's ritual faults against the Lord. These were unintentional faults. "And the Lord spoke unto Moses, saying, Speak unto the children of Israel, saying, if a soul shall sin *through ignorance* against any of the commandments of the Lord concerning things which ought not to be done, and shall do against any of them" (Lev. 4:1–2, italics added). Moses instructed various people to offer different sacrifices in these cases:

Sins of the high priest were atoned with the offering of a bull. The blood was not poured on the altar, but sprinkled from the finger of the high priest seven times on the altar. The fat from the entrails was burned next. The remainder was burned, not eaten, outside the camp or city "unto a clean place, where the ashes are poured out."

Sins of leaders in the community are atoned with the offerings of a male goat. The blood was sprinkled only once, then the remainder was poured around the altar as in the burnt offering.

Sins of private individuals were atoned with

WORSHIP RITUALS

female animals: goats, lambs, turtledoves, or pigeons. If a person could not afford one of those, an offering of grain was acceptable. The procedure for offering the grain was the same as in the cereal offerings.

It would be impossible to name all the ways a person might commit an unintentional sin against God. Some had moral implications. Others, like those of lepers (cf. Luke 5:22 ff.), were purely ceremonial. Another example of sacrifice for a ceremonial fault would be the offering that a woman made after she gave birth, in order to recover her ceremonial cleanliness (Lev. 12). Offerings for the nation and for the high priest covered all these in a collective way. On the Day of Atonement (*Yom Kippur*), the high priest sprinkled blood over the ark of the covenant itself. This was the ultimate ritual of atonement.

5. Trespass Offerings. The trespass offering was similar to the sin offering, and many scholars include it in the former category. It differed only in that the trespass offering was an offering of money. This sacrifice was made for sins of ignorance, connected with fraud. For example, if the worshiper had unwittingly cheated another of money or property, his sacrifice must be equal to the value of the amount taken, plus one-fifth. He offered this amount to the priest, then made a similar restitution to the former property owner. Therefore he repaid twice the amount he had taken plus 40 percent (Lev. 6:5–6).

All of these sacrifices related directly to either *expiation* (guilt removal) or *propitiation* (keeping God's favor). They remind us again of the two strong emotions in all of worship: awe and thankfulness.

D. The Ritual Year. The people of Israel worshiped God at times He chose or whenever they "sought him." But under Moses' leadership, worship became mandatory at certain times of the year. The people began observing the Sabbath and other appointed worship days.

The most important events on the ritual calendar were the three great pilgrim feasts—Passover, the Feast of Weeks (Pentecost), and the Feast of Tabernacles (or Booths). On each of these occasions, the Israelite males journeyed to the central place of worship to offer sacrifices to God.

1. The Sabbath. There seems to have been no observance of a special day of rest among Hebrews before the time of Moses. The first mention of the Sabbath is in Exodus 16:23, when the Hebrews camped in the Wilderness of Sin before they received the Ten Commandments. There God instructed them to observe the Sabbath every seven days, in honor of His work of creation (Ex. 20:8–11; cf. Gen. 2:1–3) and Israel's release from bondage (Deut. 5:12–15; cf. Ex. 32:12). The Sabbath separated the Israelites from work and all other ordinary activity (Ex. 35:2–3); thus it reminded them of Israel's separation from the nations around them, and of their relation to God as a covenant people.

A great deal of legal material in the first five books of the Bible concerns the keeping of the Sabbath. Breaking the Sabbath was like breaking Israel's covenant with God; thus it was punishable by death (Num. 15:32–36). Two lambs were sacrificed on the Sabbath, as opposed to one lamb on other days (Num. 28:9, 19). Twelve cakes of showbread (representing the 12 tribes of Israel) were presented in the tabernacle on the Sabbath (Lev. 24:5–8).

2. Passover and the Feast of Unleavened Bread. During Israel's great pilgrim feasts, all males were required to appear before the sanctuary of the Lord (Deut. 16:16). The first and most important of these was the feast of *Passover.* It combined two observances that originally were separate: *Passover,* the night celebrated in memory of the death angel's passing over the Hebrew households in Egypt, and *the Feast of Unleavened Bread,* which commemorated the first seven days of the Exodus itself. The two celebrations were closely intertwined. For example, leaven had to be removed from the house before the slaying of the Passover lamb (Deut. 16:4). Therefore, the Passover meal itself was one of unleavened bread (Ex. 12:8). Eventually, the people of Israel merged the two celebrations into one.

RITUAL BATH. *Priests washed various cult objects in this basin to achieve ceremonial purity. The early Hebrews considered cleanliness to be both a physical and a moral attribute. Diseased people and the objects they touched were considered unclean (Lev. 15:22).*

This great festival began on the evening of the fourteenth day of Abib (which would have been considered the beginning of the fifteenth day). The lamb or kid was slain just prior to sunset (Ex. 12:6; Deut. 16:6) and was roasted whole and eaten with unleavened bread and bitter herbs. (See "Plants.") The ceremony was full of symbolism: The blood of the animal symbolized the cleansing of sins. Bitter herbs represented the bitterness of bondage in Egypt. And the unleavened bread was a symbol of purity.

Entire families participated in the Passover supper. If the family was small, neighbors joined them until there were enough to eat the entire lamb (Ex. 12:4). The head of the household recited Israel's history during the meal.

The first and seventh days of the celebration were kept as Sabbaths: There was no work and the people came together for a holy gathering (Ex. 12:16; Lev. 23:7; Num. 28:18, 25). On the second day of the festival, a priest waved a sheaf of first-ripe barley before the Lord to consecrate the beginning harvest. In addition to the regular sacrifices in the sanctuary, the priests daily sacrificed two bullocks, one ram, and seven lambs as a burnt offering and a male goat as a sin offering (Lev. 23:8; Num. 28:19–23).

3. The Feast of Weeks (Pentecost). This festival was observed 50 days after the offering of the barley sheaf at the Feast of Unleavened Bread. It marked the end of the harvest and the beginning of the seasonal offering of firstfruits (Ex. 23:16; Lev. 23:15–21; Num. 28:26–31; Deut. 16:9–12). This one-day festival was observed as a Sabbath with a holy gathering at the tabernacle. Two loaves of unleavened bread were offered, along with 10 proper animals for a burnt offering, a male goat for a sin offering, and two yearling male lambs for a peace offering. Priests urged the people to remember the needy at this festival (Deut. 16:11–12), as they were to do at all pilgrim festivals.

Gerizim vs. Jerusalem

"The woman saith unto Him, Sir, I perceive that thou art a prophet. Our fathers worshiped in this mountain; and ye say, that in Jerusalem is the place where men ought to worship" (John 4:20).

These words were spoken by a woman at a well at the foot of Mount Gerizim in Samaria, where Jesus stopped for a drink of water, and reveal a long-standing conflict between the Jews and Samaritans.

Mount Gerizim is the southern member of a pair of mountains, between which lies the site of ancient Shechem. The northern mountain, Ebal, is taller. This is a strategic location since travel routes meet in the pass formed by the mountains. Thus the town of Shechem is frequently mentioned in Genesis. It was on Ebal and Gerizim that the tribes assembled under Joshua to hear the curse and the blessings connected with the violation and observance of the law (Deut. 11:29).

The Samaritans maintained that Shechem, the first capital of Israel, was the place chosen by God for His habitation. Jews claimed that God's chosen spot was Jerusalem. Which was the city of God?

Captured by Assyrians in 722 B.C., the city of Samaria became a military colony. The newcomers intermarried with the Samaritans and accepted their religion.

The Persian Empire fell in 333 B.C., and Macedonians under Alexander the Great proceeded down the coast of Syria toward Egypt. Jerusalem was among the cities that surrendered to the Macedonians. In 332 B.C. Samaria revolted, and in punishment Alexander sent Greek colonists there.

When a Greek colony was established, native villages under Greek control often formed a union around an ancestral sanctuary. This is what happened at Shechem. The "Sidonians (Canaanites) of Shechem" were organized in this Greek style to serve the God of Israel. They would neither accept the Macedonians nor become dependents of Jerusalem. They told the Jews, ". . . We seek your God as you do. . ." (Ezra 4:2), but would not give in to the Jews' demands to worship in Jerusalem.

The people of Shechem founded a new sanctuary. Consecrated to the God of both Jerusalem and Shechem, it stood on the summit of Gerizim, overlooking Shechem.

The chief quarrel between Jew and Samaritan was over which possessed the Holy Temple of God. Later each side invented stories of their own to explain the origins of the Samaritan temple controversy. The Samaritans claimed their temple was founded by Alexander the Great. The Jews said it was founded by the son of a high-priestly family, whom Nehemiah expelled from the temple because he had married a Samaritan girl. Claims such as these obscured the real origin of the schism and confused its dating, which is still not clearly known.

4. The Feast of Tabernacles (Booths). This festival commemorated Israel's wandering in the wilderness. It took its name from the fact that the Israelites lived in tents or arbors during the celebration (Lev. 23:40–42). The festival began on the fifteenth day of the seventh month (Tishri), and lasted for seven days. It fell at the end of the harvest season—thus a third name for the festival, the "Feast of Ingathering" (Ex. 23:16; 34:22; Lev. 23:39; Deut. 16:13–15). The priest offered a special burnt offering of 70 bullocks during the week. Two rams and 14 lambs were the daily burnt offering, and a male goat the daily sin offering (Num. 29:12–34).

Every seventh year, when there was no harvest because of the sabbatical year (*See* "Agriculture."), the Law of Moses was read publicly during the feast. At a later time, another day was added to the Feast of Booths for this purpose. It was known as the *Simhath Torah* ("Joy of the Law"), in honor of the Law.

5. The Day of Atonement. The Law of Moses required only one fast—the Day of Atonement (Ex. 30:10; Lev. 16; 23:36–32; 25:9; Num. 29:7–11). This day fell on the tenth day of Tishri, just before the Feast of Booths.

The day was set aside for the cleansing of sins. It was observed by abstaining from work, fasting, and attending a holy gathering. The high priest replaced his elaborate robes with a simple white linen garment and offered a sin offering for himself, his household, and the entire nation of Israel.

One interesting feature of the day's observance was that the high priest symbolically transferred the sins of the people onto a goat, or *scapegoat*. The high priest laid his hands on the head of the goat and confessed the people's sins. Then the goat was led away into the wilderness, where it was abandoned to die. (In later years, an attendant led the goat out of Jerusalem and pushed it off one of the cliffs surrounding the city.) This act ended the rites of the Day of Atonement. The people, free of sin, danced and rejoiced (cf. Ps. 103:12).

III. From the Monarchy to Exile. Israel's worship patterns changed noticeably from the time of the monarchy (which began when Saul became king in 1043 B.C.) until the time of the Exile (which began when the Babylonians seized Judah in 586 B.C.).

Before this time, the people of Israel worshiped God at many different places; under the kings, their worship would be focused on a central place of sacrifice. Before, a person could make an offering on the spur of the moment; now, he had to follow the procedures established by the Law of Moses.

A. The Temple. Israel's first king, Saul, seemed to be confused about the proper way of worship. Faced with sure defeat at the hands of the Philistines, he reverted to the old ways. He built an altar on the spot of his encampment and asked for God's help. Samuel arrived shortly afterward to remind him of the Lord's commandment not to worship at "every place" (1 Sam. 13:8–14; cf. Deut. 12:13).

Under the leadership of David, Israel became stronger and wealthier as a nation. After

THE SACRED ROCK. *Now in the center of the Mosque of Omar (completed A.D. 691), this rock is located on the site of Solomon's and Herod's temples. Many believe the rock once formed the base of the Jewish altar. The spot is also sacred to the Muslims, who believe that Muhammed ascended into heaven from this point.*

he built a great palace of cedar, it seemed to him wrong that he lived "in a house of cedar, but the ark of God dwelleth within curtains" (2 Sam. 7:2). Therefore, with the prophet Nathan's blessing, David gathered materials and purchased the site for a temple, a house of God (2 Sam. 24:18–25; 1 Chr. 22:3). However, it was not for him to build the temple (1 Chr. 22:6–19), but for his son Solomon.

First Kings 6—7 and 2 Chronicles 3—4 contain descriptions of the temple. There is a remarkable similarity between Solomon's temple and the plans for the tabernacle (Ex. 25—28). For example, each had two chambers or courts. The altars in the temple were bronze with utensils similar to the tabernacle's. Most portrayals of the temple include steps up to a porch with two columns on either side of a doorway. Inside the smaller chamber was the ark of the covenant. A hallway for storing the national treasure surrounded the whole building.

In later days, Solomon's temple was desecrated in various ways by unfaithful Jewish kings (cf. 1 Kin. 14:26; 2 Kin. 12:4–15; 16:8; 18:15–16; 21:4; 23:1–12). It was finally destroyed by Nebuchadnezzar in 586 B.C.

B. The Priests, Prophets, and Kings. A formal priesthood developed among the tribe of Levi in the time of Moses. However, under the monarchy there were examples of non-Levitical priests (2 Sam. 8:17; 20:26; 1 Kin. 4:5). First Kings 12:31 tells us that Jeroboam, the first king of the Northern Kingdom of Israel, set up his own priesthood: "Priests . . . which were not of the sons of Levi."

Priestly assignments were very specialized during the monarchy. For example, one group had charge of the altar, and another of the lamp oil.

But the people recognized that God had spokesmen other than the priests. When the people wanted a king, they went to Samuel, *the prophet*. What role did prophets play in Israel's worship?

We know that prophets gave advice to kings (1 Kings 22), but they also spoke to the people at the sanctuaries. There was actually a formal "prophet-hood," much like there was a distinct priesthood; Amos tells us this by denying that he belongs to it (Amos 7:14). The two groups—priests and prophets—had different purposes and functions. For instance, the Bible does not speak very often about prophets in worship; it speaks more often about their criticism of the worship practices.

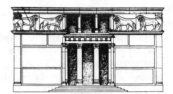

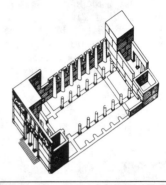

DIAGRAM OF SYNAGOGUE AT ARAQ-EL-EMIR. *This reconstruction of a Jewish synagogue built by the Maccabeans under John Hyrcanus is based on findings from excavations of the site. The facade of the building, erected early in the second century B.C., was decorated with colossal figures of lions in relief. The rectangular interior featured four corner rooms, one of which was a staircase tower.*

The king also played an important role in Israel's worship; some say he had the most important part of all. When he interacted with God, the whole nation felt the impact (2 Sam. 21:1). The high priest anointed the king to signify that God had chosen him for his royal task (cf. 1 Sam. 10:1). As the anointed representative of the people, the king had to make sacrifices (1 Kings 8; 2 Sam. 24:25). He gathered temple materials and ordered the construction. In the end, he had the power to affect everything Israel did concerning worship. Some of the later kings polluted temple activities with foreign rituals and idols. But others forced a return to the proper ways of worship.

The people's understanding of sacrifice was challenged during this period. Notice these words from the prophet Micah: "Wherewith shall I come before the Lord, and bow myself before the high God? shall I come before him with burnt offerings, with calves of a year old? Will the Lord be pleased with thousands of rams, or with ten thousands of rivers of oil? shall I give my firstborn for my transgression, the fruit of my body for the sin of my soul?" (Mic. 6:6–7). The Israelites had to realize that motive is more important than the act of sacrifice itself. They needed to see that the Lord does not require great sacrifices for their own sakes, but justice, love, and kindness (Mic. 6:8). This distinction had far-reaching effects.

Not every animal slaughter was now considered to be sacrificial. The people could kill and eat as much as they desired; but they could not eat the tithe of grain, firstlings, or any other sacrifice. They began to consider some acts of slaughter to be sacred, while some were secular.

C. Feasts. The primary festivals of this period were still the Feast of Weeks, of Unleavened Bread (Passover), and of Booths. Attendance was still required, but they were all held in Jerusalem. (Earlier, they were held wherever the ark of the covenant was located.)

Generally, worship during the monarchy was done in an atmosphere of rejoicing. There was music, shouting, and dancing. But worship was also characterized by prayers, vows, vigils, promises, sacred meals, and ritual washings.

Foreign influences began to creep into Israel's worship and the prophets loudly denounced these. Amos cried out against ritual law breaking (Amos 2:8), ritual prostitution (Amos 2:4), and worship that was not accompanied by repentance (Amos 4:4–6). He said that God detested Israel's feasts (Amos 5:21–24). The prophets also denounced idolatry in Israel's worship (2 Kin. 18:4; Is. 2:8, 20; Hos. 8:4–6; 13:1–2). Even the temple itself— its furnishings, symbolisms, and patterns of worship—showed Canaanite, Phoenician, and Egyptian influences.

The reform under King Josiah (639–608 B.C.) abolished local shrines and did away with local priestly families. All sacrifice was done in Jerusalem once again. Josiah suppressed the local cults and all rites of idolatry (2 Kin. 23:4–25). After his death, however, Judah returned to "that which was evil in the sight of the Lord" (2 Kin. 23:32, 37).

IV. The Exile and the Intertestamental Period. In 586 B.C., Nebuchadnezzar plundered Jerusalem and destroyed the holy temple Solomon had built. Now the Israelites could not worship as they had; they were forced to change. This period of Exile began what we might call the "later years" of Israel's worship.

The Bible says little about what happened at the site of the temple while the Jews were exiled. Ezekiel's "temple" was probably a vision. But Cyrus of Persia ordered the Israelites "to build [God] a house in Jerusalem" (Ezra 1:2). Cyrus also gave them back the holy vessels of gold and silver that Nebuchadnezzar had taken as booty (Ezra 5:14).

In many ways, then, the second temple would be like Solomon's. But the ark of the covenant was permanently lost during the Babylonian invasion. Only a small group of Israelites restored the temple, so capital and labor were minimal. The new building was smaller and less ornate than Solomon's had been. Yet it was styled after Moses' descriptions in Exodus 25—28.

Apparently all Jewish worship was centralized at the new temple. The Mishna tells us that the Psalms were in great use at this time. Psalms of ascents (Ps. 120—134) were used at the Feast of Booths, and the Hallel Psalms (113—118; 136) were used at all the great festivals.

The Jews felt they were under the burden of God's wrath and judgment. To make amends, they began making their offerings and sacrifices once again.

The Levites were among the first to return to Judah: "Then rose up the chief of the fathers of Judah and Benjamin, and the priests, and the Levites, with all them whose spirit God had raised, to go up to build the house for the Lord which is in Jerusalem" (Ezra 1:5). Notice that the Scriptures say "priests and Levites," as if the two were no longer synonymous. Not all Levites were now considered priests—only those who were descendants of Aaron. During the years of the monarchy other branches of the tribe of Levi had been accepted as priests. But following the Exile, all those who claimed to be priests had to prove their descent from Aaron before they were admitted (Ezra 2:61–63; Neh. 7:63–65).

Other temple personnel who returned were the singers, gatekeepers or porters, temple servants (*Nethinim*), and the sons of Solomon's servants (Ezra 2:41–58; cf. 7:24; Neh. 7:44–60). Chronicles refers to the singers and gatekeepers as "Levites," but they were of foreign origin. They were descendants of war captives who had assisted the Levites in Solomon's temple. In Nehemiah's time these people pledged themselves "to walk in God's law" and not to marry foreigners (Neh. 10:28–30).

One very important change took place in this period after the Exile. Leviticus 10:10–11 gave the priests responsibility for both moral

SAMARITAN SACRIFICE. *The Samaritans still make sacrifices in accordance with the Law of Moses, much as their ancestors did. Here lambs are offered on Mount Gerizim in celebration of the Passover.*

instruction and ceremonial matters, but the priest's teaching role seemed to disappear after the Exile. Only one mention of a priestly teaching occurs after the Exile (Hag. 2:10–13). Indeed, the prophet Malachi complained that the priests of his time failed in this important respect (Mal. 2:7–8). Levites other than the priests instructed the people concerning the Law (Neh. 8:7). The high priest became a kinglike entity, combining functions of both religion and state. (*See* "Jews in New Testament Times.")

The joyous atmosphere of the earlier rituals gave way to one of great seriousness and remorse. The ritual feasts had been primarily social meals; now they became awe-inspiring periods of introspection. After the Exile, the Israelites were seeking to learn how they could be more obedient to God's covenant.

One new and more joyous festival—the feast of Purim—was added to the ceremonial observances during this period. This festival was held on Adar 14–15 to commemorate the Jews' deliverance from Haman while they lived under Persian rule. (*See* "The Persians.") Since the time of the Exile, Jews have observed this feast in recognition of God's continued deliverance of His people.

The Purim observance followed a fixed form. Adar 13 was a day of fasting. On the evening of that day (which is the beginning of the fourteenth day), the Jews assembled for a service in their synagogues. Following the service, the book of Esther was read.

When the name of Haman was read, the people cried, "Let his name be blotted out," or "The name of the wicked shall rot." The names of Haman's sons were all read in one breath, to emphasize the fact that they were all hanged at the same time.

The next morning the people again went to the synagogue to finish the formal religious observance. The rest of the day was a time for merrymaking. As in other festival observances, the rich were called on to provide for the poor.

In 333 B.C., Alexander the Great began his conquest of Syria, the Middle East, and Egypt. After his death in 323 B.C., his generals divided the lands among themselves. After many years of political turmoil, a line of Syrian kings known as the Seleucids gained control of Palestine. The Seleucid ruler named Antiochus IV enforced his will upon the Jews by forbidding them to engage in sacrifices, rites, feasts, and worship of any kind.

In 167 B.C., a Syrian officer brought an unnamed Jew to the temple and forced him to make a sacrifice to Zeus. A priest named Mattathias witnessed the event. He slew them both, called for all faithful Jews to follow him, and fled for the hills outside Jerusalem. There he and his sons organized for war against the Seleucids. They swept over Jerusalem, defeated the Syrian army, and secured the city. The Syrian leaders were forced to repeal their ordinances against worship in Israel. Now the temple could be cleansed and true worship could resume. (The biblical account of this period in Israel's history can be found in the deuterocanonical books of 1 and 2 Maccabees. *See also* "Jews in New Testament Times" and "The Greeks and Hellenism" for more detailed account of the history of this period.) Modern Jews remember this great event at the Feast of Dedication or Hanukkah. Jesus Himself was in Jerusalem at the time of a Hanukkah celebration near the end of His earthly ministry (John 10:22). This eight-day feast is celebrated on the twenty-fifth of the month Chislev. Also known as the Feast of Lights, it is marked by the lighting of eight candles— one on each day of the feast. The celebration features the singing of the Hallel Psalms and is somewhat similar to the Feast of Booths.

Under the Maccabees, the Jews worshiped in a nationalistic manner. Their hopes for a God-ruled earth brought new emphasis to their worship, such as the use of apocalyptic literature. (*See* "The Literature of the Bible.") Prophecy gradually diminished as apocalyptic took its place. One apocalyptic writer expressed his hopes for an earthly kingdom of God in this fashion: "And now, O Lord, behold, these heathen, which have ever been reputed as nothing, have begun to be lords over

A spectacular view of the Dead Sea, situated at the lowest point on earth in the hot, desolate wilderness of southern Palestine.

EARLY DOCUMENTS. *Portions of a commentary on the book of Habakkuk—one of the ancient documents included among the Dead Sea Scrolls. (Photo by Howard Vos)*

JERUSALEM MODEL. *A model of Jerusalem as it might have looked in the time of Jesus. The city was protected by massive walls, fortified gates, and defense towers built into the wall system. (Photo by E. B. Trovillion)*

AN ASSYRIAN CLAY TABLET IN ITS ENVELOPE. *Letters and legal documents such as this were sometimes sealed in an outer clay envelope, which protected the document against damage and forgery. The envelope has a description of its contents written on it. The person who received such a letter could break open the envelope to read the message. This particular tablet (from a trading colony in what is now Turkey) dates to about 1800 B.C. (Courtesy Anderson Museum of Bible and Near Eastern Studies)*

A BABYLONIAN CYLINDER SEAL. *The small cylinder at the bottom of this photo was carved from stone and a hole was bored through it. By inserting a wooden dowel through the hole, the owner could roll the seal across a damp clay tablet. Such seals were commonly used to make an impression to validate the decrees of monarchs and other officials, or to legalize contracts. This seal dates back to about 2500 B.C. (Courtesy Anderson Museum of Bible and Near Eastern Studies)*

A REPLICA OF THE MOABITE STONE. *King Mesha of Moab erected this stone in the ninth century B.C. to celebrate his revolt against Israel. The stone was discovered in 1868. Arabs who thought the stone would bless their crops broke it into many fragments; fortunately, most of the slab was recovered. Mesha's revolt is probably the one mentioned in 2 Kings 1:1 and 3:5. (Courtesy Anderson Museum of Bible and Near Eastern Studies)*

BULL'S HEAD FROM UR. *This figure adorned the base of a lyre (a stringed musical instrument) made in about 2500 B.C., recently found in the royal cemetery of Ur. It is constructed of gold and lapis lazuli, a blue semiprecious stone. Four centuries later, Abraham lived among the people of this advanced culture (Gen. 11:31). (Photo by Gustav Jeeninga)*

BILBIL POTTERY. *The people of Cyprus originated this type of ointment juglet, known as bilbil. The juglets were copied and used throughout Palestine. This example of bilbil pottery, dating from the Late Bronze Age, probably held olive oil. (Photo by Gustav Jeeninga)*

RUINS OF THE TEMPLE OF APOLLO, DELPHI. *The oracle of Delphi was renowned throughout the ancient world. If someone wanted to know the future or obtain advice from Apollo, he would ask the attendants of this sanctuary. They would take the request to the high priestess, who would go into a muttering trance. The attendants would interpret this utterance (or oracle) for the person who requested information. (Photo by Gustav Jeeninga)*

DOME OF THE ROCK, JERUSALEM. *The golden dome of a Muslim mosque covers the spot where tradition says Solomon's temple stood. The mosque is called the "Dome of the Rock" because the structure is built around a massive rock. Jewish tradition says the ark of the covenant stood on this rock; Muslim tradition states that Muhammad ascended to the Seven Heavens from this same rock. (Photo by Nancy Arnold)*

RUINS OF HEROD'S TEMPLE, JERUSALEM. *Israeli archaeologists are still uncovering the remains of this temple, which was begun in 19 B.C. by Herod the Great. (It was not completed until A.D. 64.) The building itself was made of white marble, much of which was covered with gold. The temple court was about 176 m. (580 ft.) east to west and about 182 m. (600 ft.) north to south. No wonder the Jews questioned Christ when He said He would destroy and build back this temple in three days (John 2:19–21). (Photo by William White, Jr.)*

ROMAN CAMP AT MASADA. *These are the remains of the encampment from which Roman soldiers laid siege to a band of Jewish Zealots, fortified on the plateau above. For three years after the fall of Jerusalem in A.D. 70, the rebels resisted the Roman legions. After every other Jewish stronghold had fallen to the Romans, the Zealots killed their women and children and then one another. They preferred death to capture. (Photo by William White, Jr.)*

THE JORDAN RIVER. *The Jordan is neither large nor impressive, but it has become the most famous river in the world because of scriptural events associated with it. This is of one of the myriad of bends in the Jordan's path from the Sea of Galilee to the Dead Sea. (Photo by Willem Van Gemeren)*

SHEEP BESIDE THE SEA OF GALILEE. *Shepherds still tend their sheep on the Galilean hillsides as their ancestors did in ancient times. David probably had such a scene in mind when he wrote, "The Lord is my shepherd; I shall not want" (Ps. 23:1). (Photo by Gustav Jeeninga)*

THE WADI ZERED, EDOM. *The Zered flows through part of the rugged desert land of Edom that lies to the south of the Dead Sea. The northern part of the wadi (a dry ravine except during the rainy season) was crossed by the Israelites on their way to the Promised Land (Num. 21:12). The Israelites were refused permission to go through Edom, and they had to go through even more rugged terrain than this (Num. 20:14–21; 21:4–5). (Photo by Gustav Jeeninga)*

PAPYRUS PLANT. *The ancient Egyptians and other peoples crushed papyrus reeds to make a smooth writing material resembling paper. Our English word* paper *is derived from the Greek word for the papyrus plant—papyros. This specimen grows in front of the Cairo Museum. (Photo by Willem van Gemeren)*

ROCK FORMATIONS IN THE NEGEV. *Tradition says that King Solomon operated copper mines in this area south of the Judean hill country. Thus these formations are called "Solomon's Pillars." Many tons of copper would have been required for all the copper (KJV "brass") items used in the temple. (Photo by Gustav Jeeninga)*

MODERN HARBOR OF SIDON. *The ancient Phoenician city of Sidon (or Zidon) was one of the most important seaports of the Mediterranean during the first and second millennia B.C. Because of the city's pride and wickedness, God pronounced judgment on it (Is. 23:2-4, 12). The modern name of the city is Saida. (Photo by Gustav Jeeninga)*

WILDFLOWERS, JORDAN VALLEY. *Palestine supports a beautiful array of wildflowers. Their short life gave the psalmist a striking analogy. "As for man, his days are as grass: as a flower of the field, so he flourisheth. For the wind passeth over it, and it is gone." (Ps. 103:15–16). (Photo by Gustav Jeeninga)*

FIGS. *The fig is still a popular food in Palestine. Notice the small green fruit on this healthy fig tree. Jesus used the fig to illustrate His teachings about the last days. Just as the Jews could observe the sprouting fig leaves and know that summer was approaching, they could observe the signs He described and know that He was about to return (Matt. 24:32–33). (Photo by Gustav Jeeninga)*

THE CANAL AT CORINTH. *This canal connects the Ionian Sea to the Aegean. In* A.D. *67, the emperor Nero made the first attempt to build a canal here; before his time, ships were dragged across the isthmus. The present canal dates from the late nineteenth century. (Photo by Gustav Jeeninga)*

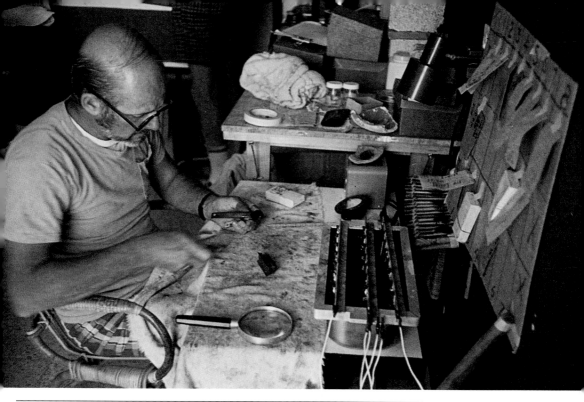

CLEANING COINS. *A numismatist cleans ancient coins at the site of an archaeological dig. He places the coins in the vat before him, where an electrical current dissolves soil and tarnish in a liquid solution. The board identifies where different coins were found at the site. (Photo by Gustav Jeeninga)*

ARCHAEOLOGIST'S RECORDS. *Archaeologists do not just locate and excavate sites; they must keep detailed records of everything they find. This notebook contains the records of a dig at Caesarea Maritima, a city on the coast of the Mediterranean built by Herod the Great (Acts 10:1). Notice the scale drawing of the floor plan of a building that is being excavated. (Photo by Gustav Jeeninga)*

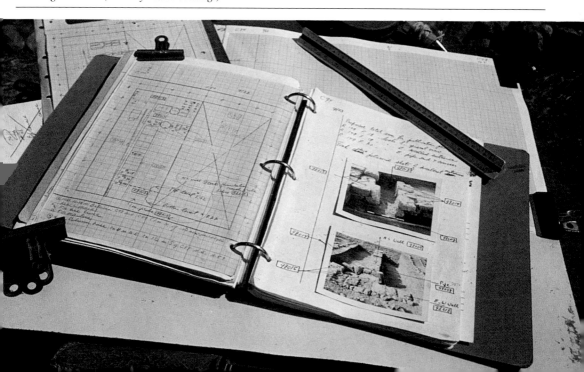

Photo by Gustav Jeeninga

THE COLOSSEUM. *Early Christians may have been forced to fight in gladiatorial contests in the Colosseum, an amphitheater in the city of Rome. (Photo by Gustav Jeeninga)*

Photo by Ben Chapman

THE COLOSSEUM. *Interior view of the massive Colosseum, which covered about six acres and reflected the splendor of ancient Rome. (Photo by Ben Chapman)*

EGYPTIAN SCARABS. *These images of the sacred beetle were carved from stone and wood, with ritual symbols on the flat underside. The Egyptians wore scarabs as charms and used them to print seals on official documents. (Courtesy Anderson Museum of Bible and Near Eastern Studies)*

ABU SIMBEL. *Rameses II of Egypt ordered his craftsmen to carve this enormous temple out of solid rock in the thirteenth century B.C. Some scholars believe that Rameses was the pharaoh of the Exodus, while others place the event much earlier. Lake Nasser formed by the Aswan Dam, would have submerged the temple; so in the early 1960s the entire structure was cut into large blocks and moved piece by piece to higher ground, where it was reconstructed. (Photo by Willem van Gemeren)*

SANCTUARY OF BEL, PALMYRA. *Some people continued to worship the gods of Babylon and Assyria long after these empires fell. The people of Palmyra (an ancient city located in present-day Syria) built this Temple to Bel in the third century* A.D. *Bel or Marduk was the patron god of Babylon (cf. Is. 46:1). (Photo by Gustav Jeeninga)*

GREEK THEATER. *A tour group visits the ruins of a Greek amphitheater on the island of Delos in the Aegean Sea. These theaters were designed so that an actor speaking in a normal voice could be heard by the farthest row of the audience. (Photo by Gustav Jeeninga)*

ROMAN MILEPOST. *This stone marker stood along a major Roman highway in Iconium. The marker told the traveler the distance to various cities along the highway. Notice the title of Caesar in the first line. (Photo by Gustav Jeeninga)*

ROMAN COINAGE. *This coin bears the image of Emperor Diocletian (A.D. 245–313), who launched Rome's last violent persecution of the Christians. Notice the fine detail that Roman craftsmen were able to achieve. (Courtesy Anderson Museum of Bible and Near Eastern Studies)*

ROMAN THEATER. *This Roman amphitheater in Amman, Jordan, is an excellent example of the architecture that dominated Palestine at the time of Jesus. Amman was the chief city of the Ammonites, and in Old Testament times it was known as Rabbah (cf. Amos 1:14). (Photo by Willem van Gemeren)*

WOMAN SELLING GRAPES. *This Arab woman in Jerusalem is selling grapes using a scale similar to those of ancient times. Notice the rocks she uses to weigh the grapes in her scale; these rocks are still commonly employed as weights in the Near East. Their weight is not uniform, but they are popularly accepted. (Photo by Gustav Jeeninga)*

THE TOMB OF BARNABAS, CYPRUS. *Barnabas was born at Cyprus (Acts 4:36) and was converted to Christianity quite early (Acts 4:36–37). He accompanied Paul on many journeys, preaching the gospel to Gentiles. Barnabas is thought to have founded the church at Cyprus (cf. Acts 15:39); his sepulcher was discovered here in A.D. 478. This mausoleum was built in 1953 to cover the sepulcher. (Photo by Gustav Jeeninga)*

SYNAGOGUE ART. *These carvings from the synagogue at Capernaum show how skilled the Jewish artisans had become by the third century* A.D. *One rarely finds Jewish artwork, since the people of Israel were careful to avoid making "graven images" (cf. Ex. 20:4). (Photo by Gustav Jeeninga)*

WALL OF JERUSALEM. *This wall of the "Old City" probably dates to the time of Herod the Great (37—4 B.C.). The city's walls have been rebuilt many different times, usually on top of the ruins of older walls, and so it is difficult to fix a date for any particular section of the fortress. (Photo by William White, Jr.)*

BEDOUIN WOMAN AND CHILD, TRANSJORDAN. *These nomadic Arabs live much like the patriarchs did in Old Testament times. They range across a large area east of the Jordan, primarily in the Arabian and Syrian deserts. They should not be confused with Palestinian Arabs who live in settlements on the west bank of the Jordan. Many Arabs believe they are descendants of Esau, the brother of Jacob (cf. Gen. 25:21–26). (Photo by Gustav Jeeninga)*

us, and to devour us. But we thy people, whom thou hast called thy firstborn, thy only begotten, and thy fervent lover, are given into their hands. If the world now is made for our sakes, why do we not possess an inheritance with the world? how long shall this endure?" (2 Esdras 6:57–59). During this period, however, the seer or apocalyptist spoke for God. He spoke of demons and angels, dark and light, evil and good. He predicted the final triumph of the nation of Israel. This hope flowed as the undercurrent of Jewish worship.

One other feature of worship that became more prominent in this period was the study of the Law. It was primarily a priestly duty, on which the Hasidim (Pharisees) concentrated. They produced many new teachings and doctrines in the process, notably the doctrine of the resurrection of the dead.

V. The New Testament Era. In 47 B.C., Julius Caesar selected Herod Antipater, a Jew of Idumea (the area south of Judea), to be governor of Judea. His son, Herod the Great, inherited the position and called himself "king of the Jews." Realizing the history of unrest among the people, Herod wanted to gain their favor and faith in some way. To do this, he announced the building of a third temple at Jerusalem. Priests specially trained in construction skills did much of the work to make sure the new building followed Moses' floor plan. Most of the construction was completed in about 10 years (*ca.* 20—10 B.C.), but not all was finished until about A.D. 60. (In fact, some scholars feel the new temple had not been completed at the time Jerusalem fell to the Roman general Titus in A.D. 70.) Most worship activities occurred here.

Yet during the persecutions and exiles of Israel, many Jews found themselves too far from Jerusalem to worship there. Did this mean that they were not able to worship at all? By no means! Rather they instituted the custom of local synagogue worship. Although the Old Testament uses the word *synagogue* only once (Ps. 74:8), many of these informal worship places surely existed during the Exile. The New Testament mentions them often (e.g., Matt. 4:23; 23:6; Acts 6:9), but gives us little descriptive information about them. (*See* "Judaism in New Testament Times.") We do know something of the early synagogues from rabbinic sources. We also know that the Law was studied and pronounced there: "For Moses of old time hath in every city them that preach him, being read in the synagogues

WESTERN WALL, JERUSALEM. *The holiest shrine in the Jewish world is the western side of the wall that Herod the Great built to enclose his temple area. The wall is called the "Wailing Wall" for two reasons: First, the Jews gather here to mourn the loss of their temple. Furthermore, legend says that the drops of dew that form on the stones are tears shed by the wall in sympathy with the exiled Jews.*

every sabbath day" (Acts 15:21). Many prayers were recited in synagogue worship (Matt. 6:5). Sources outside the Bible tell us that the synagogue worship services consisted of an invocational prayer, other prayers and benedictions, the reading of the Law of Moses, the reading of the prophets, and a benedictory prayer (Megillah 4:3). Only certain persons were permitted to lead in worship, thus Jesus' right to do so was questioned (Mark 6:2–4). Paul taught at synagogues, but he too had some difficulty (Acts 17:17; 26:11).

Jews considered the followers of Jesus to be a party within Judaism. They were therefore allowed to worship on the Sabbath alongside their fellows at the synagogues and temple.

Jesus loved the temple and respected it. He supported it by encouraging His followers to attend it. He declared it to be sacred (Matt. 23:16 ff.) and believed it to be worthy of cleansing (Matt. 21:12). Yet Jesus said that "in this place is one greater than the temple" (Matt. 12:6), referring to Himself. He charged that the temple had been turned into a "den of thieves" (Matt. 21:13).

At first, the disciples had conflicting emotions about temple and synagogue worship. Eventually, though, the Jews and Christians antagonized each other so much that there was little choice but to worship separately. This conflict did not revolve around the format or the location of worship, but the nature of worship itself. This is reflected in Jesus' conversation with the Samaritan woman at the well. She said, "Our fathers worshiped in this mountain; and ye say, that in Jerusalem is the place where men ought to worship." She clearly thought of worship in terms of external features, such as the location. Jesus replied,

"Woman, believe me, the hour cometh when ye shall neither in this mountain nor yet at Jerusalem, worship the Father. . . . But the hour is cometh, and now is, when the true worshipers will worship the Father in spirit and in truth, for the Father seeketh such to worship him" (John 4:21, 23). Christ and His followers knew that salvation and righteousness came not from offerings and sacrifices, but from obeying God in "spirit and in truth." When God acts and we react in worship, our visible reaction is not so important as our invisible attitude. (Perhaps Abel's offering was acceptable because he had no hatred in his heart, while Cain's offering was unacceptable on account of his hatred for his brother.)

We do not know whether Jesus and the apostles participated in all of the Jewish rituals and feasts. The New Testament gives us no complete account of their activities. But there is some evidence that the early Christians gathered in houses for worship, much as the Jews met in local synagogues. Paul refers to "the church in thy house" (Philem. 2), "the church that is in their house" (Rom. 16:5), and "the church which is in his house" (Col. 4:15). Later, under severe Roman persecution, the places of meeting were even more humble and even secretive. For an extensive account of early Christian worship, *see* "The Early Church."

FAMILY RELATIONSHIPS

Two facts stand out in what the Bible says about the family and its relationships. First, the roles of family members stayed about the same throughout the biblical period. Changing culture and laws did not affect family customs to any great extent. It is true that the folks who lived in the early days of the Old Testament period were semi-nomadic—they often moved from one area to another—so their habits were at some points different from those of settled peoples. The Mosaic Law abolished some of the nomadic practices, such as marrying one's sister. But most of the original family lifestyle persisted, even into the New Testament era.

Second, family life in Bible times reflected a culture quite different from our own. We should recognize this difference when we turn to the Scriptures for guidance in raising our own families. We should search out the principles of Scripture rather than directly copy the specific lifestyles it portrays. These lifestyles were designed for small agricultural communities, and they did not please God in every case.

As an example, the culture of that day allowed a man to have more than one wife, and some men of God did; yet nowhere does Scripture state that God approved this practice. We classify it as a tolerated cultural custom, but not a biblically prescribed one.

Another instance: When Abraham lived in Egypt with Sarah, he told her to say she was his sister, fearing that the Egyptians would kill him because of her great beauty. She was in fact his half sister, a degree of kinship that God later indicated was too close for marriage (cf. Gen. 20:12; Lev. 18:9). As a result, the

RECONSTRUCTED OLD TESTAMENT HOUSE. *The reconstructed interior of a typical house in biblical times shows the cooking stove (to the left of the center) and a water jug with dipper (foreground). A horizontal loom hangs from a pole on the left-hand side in the family's eating area—a circular mat set with bowls. Storage jars, baskets, and bowls sit on shelves, benches, and the floor.*

FAMILY RELATIONSHIPS

pharaoh took Sarah into his house and God afflicted the pharaoh's family with plagues in order to rescue her.

The biblical teaching for family life includes instructions for children, mothers, and fathers. We will see examples of families that followed God's wishes and were greatly blessed; we will also see families that disobeyed God and reaped the consequences. Along the way we will notice how family life changed during the course of Israel's history.

AT THE CITY GATE. *The city gates were centers for conversations and commerce. Gates were often named for the items traded there (e.g., Sheep Gate, Fish Gate). Because the elders often transacted business at the gate, to "sit at the gate" meant to attain a certain social eminence.*

I. The Family Unit. The family was the first social structure that God produced. He formed the first family by joining Adam and Eve together as husband and wife (Gen. 2:18–24). The man and woman became the nucleus of a family unit.

Why did God create the family structure? Genesis 2:18 says that God created the woman as a helper for Adam, which indicates that the man and woman were brought together first for companionship; the wife was to help her husband, and the husband was to care for his wife. Then the two together were to meet the needs of their children, the offspring of their relationship.

A. Husband. The Hebrew word for *husband* partially means "to dominate, to rule." It can also be translated as "master." As head of the family, the husband was responsible for its well-being. For example, when Abraham and Sarah deceived the pharaoh about their marriage, the ruler challenged Abraham rather than Sarah, who had done the actual lying (Gen. 12:10–20). This does not mean that the Hebrew husband was given license to be a tyrant who enjoyed bossing his family around. Rather, he was to assume responsibility for the family and serve the needs of those who were under his authority.

Every Israelite couple married with the idea of having children. They were especially eager to have a male child. A man fortunate enough to father a son was proud indeed. Jeremiah noted, "The man who brought tidings to my father, saying, A man child is born unto thee; [made] him very glad" (Jer. 20:15).

The Israelite father assumed spiritual leadership within the family; he functioned as the family priest (cf. Gen. 12:8; Job 1:5). He was expected to lead his family in observing various religious rites, such as the Passover (Ex. 12:3).

Along with the mother, the father was to "train up a child in the way he should go . . ." (Prov. 22:6). The basis for instruction was the

FAMILY RELATIONSHIPS

GRINDING MEAL, BAKING BREAD. *The Israelites used stones to grind wheat and barley into flour. They kneaded flour, yeast, olive oil, and water or milk into a dough that was stretched thin for baking.*

Law of the Lord. Parents were admonished to "teach them diligently unto thy children, and shalt talk of them when thou sittest in thine house, and when thou walkest by the way, and when thou liest down, and when thou risest up. And thou shalt bind them for a sign upon thine hand, and they shall be as frontlets between thine eyes. And thou shalt write them on the posts of thy house, and on thy gates" (Deut. 6:7–9).

The father could inflict physical punishment when necessary. This was to be done in such a way as not to "provoke your children to wrath: but bring them up in the nurture and admonition of the Lord" (Eph. 6:4).

In biblical times, a man who did not provide adequately for his family was guilty of a serious offense. A man who failed to do this was shunned and mocked by society (cf. Prov. 6:6–11; 19:7). Paul wrote, "If any provide not for his own, . . . he hath denied the faith, and is worse than an infidel" (1 Tim. 5:8).

As husband and father, the man defended his family's rights before the judges when necessary (see Deut. 22:13–19). "The fatherless and the widow" had no man to defend their rights, so they were often denied justice (cf. Deut. 10:18).

Israelites were governed by various traditions. The Talmud says that a father had four responsibilities toward his son, besides teaching him the Law. He was to circumcise his son (cf. Gen. 17:12–13), redeem him from God if he were the firstborn (cf. Num. 18:15–16), find him a wife (cf. Gen. 24:4), and teach him a trade.

A good father thought of his children as full human beings, and took note of their feelings and abilities. A Jewish scholar of the time said that a good father should "push them away with the left hand and draw them near with the right hand." This delicate balance between firmness and affection typified the ideal Israelite father.

B. Wife. In marriage, the woman was expected to take a place of submission to her mate. The wife's responsibility was to be the husband's "helper" (Gen. 2:18, RSV), one who "does him good, and not harm, all the days of her life" (Prov. 31:12). Her main responsibilities were the home and the children, but sometimes it extended to the marketplace and other areas that affected the family's welfare (cf. Prov. 31:16, 24).

A wife's primary goal in life was to bear children for her husband. Rebekah's family spokesman said to her, "Thou art our sister, be thou the mother of thousands of millions and let thy seed possess the gate of those who hate them" (Gen. 24:60). An Israelite family hoped that the wife would become like a fruitful vine, filling the house with many children (Ps. 128:3). So a mother greeted the first child with much happiness and relief.

As children began to arrive, the mother was tied closer to the home. She nursed each child until the age of two or three, besides clothing and feeding the rest of the family. She spent hours each day preparing meals and making clothes. When necessary, the wife helped her husband in the fields, planting or harvesting the crops.

A mother shared the responsibility for training the children. Children spent the early formative years close to their mothers. Eventually, the sons were old enough to go with their fathers into the fields or some other place of employment. The mother then turned her attention more fully to her daughters, teaching them how to become successful wives and mothers.

A woman's performance of her tasks determined the failure or success of the family. The sages said, "A virtuous woman is the crown to her husband, but she that maketh ashamed is as rottenness in his bones" (Prov. 12:4). If the wife worked hard at the task laid before her, it greatly benefited her husband. Israelites believed that a man could rise to a place among the leaders of Israel only if his wife were wise and talented (Prov. 31:23).

C. Sons. In biblical times, sons had to support their parents when they became old and then give them a proper burial. For this reason, a couple usually hoped to have many sons. "As arrows are in the hand of a mighty man; so are children of the youth. Happy is the man that hath his quiver full of them: they shall not be ashamed, but they shall speak with the enemies in the gate" (Ps. 127:4–5).

The firstborn son held a very special place of honor within the family. He was expected to be the next head of the family. All through his life, he was expected to take greater responsibility for his actions and the actions of his brothers. This was why Reuben, as the oldest brother, showed greater concern for the life of Joseph when his brothers agreed to kill him (Gen. 37:21, 29).

When the father died, a firstborn son received a double portion of the family inheritance (Deut. 21:17; 2 Chron. 21:2–3).

The fifth commandment admonished, "Honor thy father and thy mother; that thy days may be long upon the land which the LORD thy God giveth thee" (Ex. 20:12). Both parents were to receive the same amount of respect. However, the rabbis of the Talmud reasoned that if a son ever had to choose, he must give preference to his father. For example, if both parents requested a drink of water simultaneously, the Talmud taught that both the son and the mother should meet the needs of the father.

Jesus was the perfect example of an obedient son. Luke noted that, at the age of 12, Jesus "went down with them and came to Nazareth, and was subject to [his parents]" (Luke 2:51). Even while enduring the agonies of the cross, Jesus thought of His mother and His responsibility toward her as the firstborn son. He asked "the disciple whom he loved" to care for her after His death, thereby fulfilling His duty out of love for her (John 19:26–27).

D. Daughters. In ancient times, daughters were not prized as highly as sons. Some fathers actually looked upon them as nuisances. For example, one father wrote, "The father waketh for the daughter, when no man knoweth; and the care for her taketh away sleep: when she is young, lest she pass away the flower of her age [fail to marry]; and being married, lest she should be hated; in her virginity, lest she should be defiled and gotten with child become pregnant in her father's house; or having an husband, lest she should misbehave herself; and when she is married, lest she should be barren" (Ecclesiasticus 42:9–10).

However, the Hebrews treated their daughters more humanely than some of the surrounding cultures. The Romans actually exposed newborn girls to the elements, in the hope that they would die. The Hebrews believed that all children—male and female—came from God. For this reason, they would never consider killing one of their babies. In fact, when the prophet Nathan sought to describe the intimate relationship of a father to a child, he pictured a daughter in her father's arms with her head on his chest (2 Sam. 12:3).

Firstborn daughters held a special place of honor and duty within the family. For example, Lot's firstborn daughter tried to persuade her younger sister to bear a child for Lot, to preserve the family (Gen. 19:31–38). In the story of Laban and Jacob, the firstborn daugh-

A JEWISH "TABLE." *An Israelite family of Old Testament times would have eaten around a floor mat like this one, where the simple clay dishes were set. This reconstruction is in the Ha-Aretz Museum in Tel Aviv.*

ter Leah was given priority over the younger sister (Gen. 29:26).

If a family was without sons, the daughters could inherit their father's possessions (Num. 27:5–8); but they could keep their inheritance only if they married within their own tribe (Num. 36:5–12).

The daughter was under the legal jurisdiction of her father until her marriage. Her father made all important decisions for her, such as whom she should marry. But the daughter could be asked to give her consent to the choice of a groom, and sometimes she was even allowed to indicate a preference (Gen. 24:58; 1 Sam. 18:20). The father approved all vows the daughter made before they became binding (Num. 30:1–5).

The daughter was expected to help her mother in the home. At a very early age, she began to learn the various domestic skills she needed to become a good wife and mother herself. By the age of 12, the daughter had become a homemaker in her own right and was allowed to marry.

In some Near Eastern cultures, families did not allow their daughters to leave the home. If they did appear in public, they had to wear veils over their faces and were not allowed to speak to males. The Israelites placed no such restrictions on their daughters. Girls were relatively free to come and go, provided their work was done. We see examples of this in Rebekah, who talked to a stranger at the well (Gen. 24:15–21), and the seven daughters of the priests of Midian, who chatted with Moses as they watered their father's flock (Ex. 2:16–22).

The family expected a daughter to remain a virgin until her marriage. Unfortunately, this did not always happen. Some young women were seduced or raped. When this happened, the Mosaic Law made careful distinctions between the punishment for the rape of girls who were engaged and those who were not. (*See* "Marriage and Divorce.")

Often daughters married at an early age. Such early marriages did not create the problems that they do today. Though a bride left the dominion of her father, she entered the new domain of her husband and his family. Her mother-in-law stepped in to continue the guidance and training that her own mother had given her. The bride and her mother-in-law often developed a deep and lasting bond. This is perfectly illustrated in the book of Ruth, when Naomi repeatedly refers to Ruth as "my

daughter." Micah described a strife-filled family as one in which "the daughter riseth up against her mother, the daughter-in-law against her mother-in-law" (Mic. 7:6).

When a young woman went to live with her husband's family, she did not give up all rights in her own family. If her husband died and there were no more brothers-in-law for her to marry, she might return to her father's house. That is exactly what Naomi encouraged her daughters-in-law to do, and Orpah followed her suggestion (Ruth 1:8–18).

E. Brothers and Sisters. Love developed between brothers as they grew up together, sharing responsibilities, problems, and victories. One of the proverbs states, "A man that hath friends must show himself friendly, and there is a friend that sticketh closer than a brother" (Prov. 18:24).

Joseph displayed real love toward his brothers despite the fact that when he was young, his brothers sold him into slavery because of

MORTAR. *This small basalt mortar and pestle found at Jericho was used for grinding cereal grains. It dates from about 1800–1500 B.C.*

FAMILY RELATIONSHIPS

their father's favoritism toward him. Later, when Joseph gained power and position, he could have evened the score with his brothers. Instead, he showed them love and mercy. He said, "Now therefore be not grieved, nor angry with yourselves, that ye sold me hither: for God did send me before you to preserve life" (Gen. 45:5).

The Bible describes many brothers who maintained a deep and abiding love for one another. The Psalmist described the love of brothers by saying, "It is like the precious oil upon the head, running down upon the beard, upon the beard of Aaron, down on the collar of his robes! It is like the dew of Hermon which falls on the mountains of Zion!" (Ps. 133:2–3, RSV).

Brothers and sisters often shared a special bond. When Job's sons entertained they invited their three sisters (Job 1:4). When Dinah was raped, her brothers avenged the crime (Gen. 34).

In earlier times, young men sometimes married their half sisters. Abraham and Sarah had the same father but different mothers (Gen. 20:12). As we have already noted, the Mosaic Law banned this practice (Lev. 18:9; 20:17; Deut. 27:22).

The bond of love between sisters and brothers was so strong that the Mosaic Law allowed even a priest to touch the body of a dead brother, sister, parent, or child (Lev. 21:1–3). This was the only time that a priest could touch a dead person and not become ceremonially unclean.

II. The Extended Family. In the most basic sense, a Hebrew family consisted of a husband, a wife, and their children. When the husband had more than one wife, the "family" included all of the wives and the children in their various relationships (cf. Gen. 30). Normally the family included everyone who shared a common dwelling place under the protection of the head of the family. They might be grandparents, servants, and visitors, as well as widowed daughters and their children. The extended family commonly included sons and their wives and children (Lev. 18:6–18). God counted Abraham's slaves as part of the family group, for He required Abraham to circumcise them (Gen. 17:12–14, 23–27). In Israel's early history, as many as four generations lived together. This was a normal part of the semi-nomadic lifestyle and the later agricultural one.

Even today in the Middle East, semi-

BEDTIME. *During biblical times, most Jewish families slept on pallets on the floor, the children in the middle and a parent at either end. Wealthy people had more elaborate beds (Amos. 6:4).*

nomadic people band together as large families for the sake of survival. Each extended family has its own "father" or *sheik* whose word is law.

In Old Testament days, the extended family was presided over by the oldest male in the household, who was also called the "father." Often this person was a grandfather or a great-grandfather. For example, when Jacob's family moved to Egypt, Jacob was considered to be their "father"—even though his sons had wives and families (cf. Gen. 46:8–27). Jacob continued to preside over his "family" until his death.

The "father" of an extended family seems, in patriarchal times, to have held the power of life and death over its members. We see this when Abraham nearly sacrificed his son, Isaac (Gen. 22:9–12), and when Judah sentenced his daughter-in-law to death because she had committed adultery (Gen. 38:24–26).

Later, the Mosaic Law restricted the father's authority. It assigned the legal right of execution to a court of elders (Deut. 21:18–21). It did not allow a father to sacrifice his child on an altar (Lev. 18:21). It allowed him to sell his daughter, but not to a foreigner and not for prostitution (Ex. 21:7–8; Lev. 19:29). According to the Law, a father could not deny the birthright of his firstborn son, even if he had sons by two different women (Deut. 21:15–17).

Some Hebrew fathers violated these laws. For example, Jephthah vowed to sacrifice whoever came out to greet him upon his victorious return from battle. His daughter was the first. Believing that he had to keep his vow, Jephthah sacrificed her (Judg. 11:31, 34–40). Likewise, King Manasseh burned his son to appease a heathen god (2 Kings 21:6).

We do not know when the extended family of Old Testament times gave way to the family structure we know today. Some scholars feel that it died out during the monarchy of David and Solomon. Others believe that it continued longer than that. But by New Testament times, the meaning of extended family often encompassed parents, children, and slaves (cf. Eph. 5:21—6:9).

The New Testament says that Joseph and Mary traveled as a couple to be registered in Bethlehem (Luke 2:4–5). They went to the temple alone when Mary offered her sacrifices (Luke 2:22). They also traveled alone when they took Jesus into Egypt (Matt. 2:14). These accounts tend to confirm that the "family" of the New Testament consisted only of the husband, wife, and children.

III. The Clan. The extended family was part of a larger group that we call a clan. The clan might be so large that it registered hundreds of males in its ranks (cf. Gen. 46:8–27; Ezra 8:1–14). Members of a clan shared a common ancestry, and thus viewed each other as kinfolk. They felt obligated to help and protect one another.

Often the clan designated one male, called a *goel,* to extend help to clan members in need. In English, this person is referred to as the kinsman-redeemer. His help covered many areas of need.

If a member of the clan had to sell part of his property to pay debts, he gave the kinsman-redeemer the first opportunity to purchase it. The kinsman-redeemer then was supposed to purchase the property, if he could, to keep it in the clan's possession (Lev. 25:25; cf. Ruth 4:1–6). This situation arose when Jeremiah's cousin came to him, saying, "Buy my field . . . that is in Anathoth . . . for the right of inheritance is thine, and the redemption is thine; buy it for thyself" (Jer. 32:6–8). Jeremiah purchased the field and used the event to proclaim that the Jews would eventually return to Judah (Jer. 32:15).

Occasionally, an army would capture hostages and sell them to the highest bidder. Also, a man might sell himself into slavery to repay a debt. In both cases, the slave's next-of-kin was supposed to find the clan's kinsman-redeemer, who would try to purchase his kinsman's freedom (Lev. 25:47–49).

If a married man died without having had a child, the *goel* was supposed to marry the widow (Deut. 25:5–10). This was called a *levirate* ("brother-in-law") marriage. The first son born through this arrangement was considered the offspring of the deceased brother. (*See* "Marriage and Divorce.")

The story of Ruth and Naomi well illustrates the responsibility of the kinsman-redeemer. The widow Naomi had to sell her property near Bethlehem, and she wanted her childless daughter-in-law to remarry. The nearest of kin agreed to purchase the field but was unwilling to marry Ruth. So he gave up both obligations in a ceremony before the elders of the city. Then Boaz, the nearest-of-kin, bought the field and married Ruth (Ruth 4:9–10).

A *goel* was expected to avenge a kinsman's murder. In such a case, he was called the "avenger of blood" (Deut. 19:12). The Law of Moses limited this practice by establishing cities of refuge where killers could flee, but even this did not insure the killer's safety. If the murder was malicious or premeditated, the avenger of blood would follow him to the city of refuge and demand his return. In such a case, the murderer would be turned over to the *goel,* who would kill him (cf. Deut. 19:1–13). Joab killed Abner in this manner (2 Sam. 2:22–23; 3:27).

IV. Erosion of the Family. A family that lives in harmony and exhibits genuine love is a delight to all associated with it. Surely this is what God had in mind when He established the family. Unfortunately, the Bible shows us few families that attained this ideal. Throughout Bible history, families were being eroded by social, economic, and religious pressures. We can identify several of these pressures.

A. Childlessness. Childlessness was a major threat to a marriage in biblical times. If a couple was unable to conceive a child, they looked upon their problem as a chastisement from God. (*See* "Marriage and Divorce.")

Even though he might continue to love his wife, a childless man sometimes married a second woman or used the services of a slave to conceive children (Gen. 16:2–4; 30:3–5;

✦ FAMILY RELATIONSHIPS

ROMAN FAMILY. *The Romans did not value the "extended family" as the Jews did; the immediate family was the basic unit of their society. Roman art often featured family themes—as we see on this grave monument from the Vatican Museum.*

Deut. 21:10–14). Some men divorced their wives in order to do this. While this practice solved the problem of childlessness, it created many other problems.

B. Polygamy. Domestic strife was common when two women shared a husband in Old Testament times. The Hebrew word for the second wife literally meant "rival wife" (1 Sam. 1:6); this suggests that bitterness and hostility usually existed between polygamous wives. Nevertheless, polygamy was not uncommon, especially among the Hebrew patriarchs and Israelite kings. If a man was unable to raise the marriage money for a second wife, he considered buying a slave for that purpose or using one he already had in his household (cf. Gen. 16:1–4; 30:1–8).

In a polygamous marriage, the husband invariably favored one wife over another. This caused complications, such as the need to decide whose child to honor as firstborn son. Sometimes a man wanted to give his inheritance to the son of his favored wife although it was actually owed to the son of the "disliked" wife (Deut. 21:15–17). Moses declared that the firstborn son had to be rightfully honored, and the husband could not shortchange the firstborn's mother to "diminish her food, her clothing, or her marital right" (Ex. 21:10).

Politics was also a motive for polygamy. Often a king sealed a covenant with another king by marrying his ally's daughter. When Scripture speaks of Solomon's large harem, it points out that "he had seven hundred wives, princesses" (1 Kings 11:3). This is likely an indication that most of his marriages were of a political nature. Probably the women came from small city-states and tribes surrounding Israel.

After the Exodus, most Israelite marriages were monogamous (Mark 10:2–9). The book of Proverbs never mentions polygamy, even though it touches on many aspects of Israelite culture. The prophets frequently used the concept of monogamous marriage to describe the Lord's relationship to Israel. Such a marriage was the ideal of family life.

C. Death of Husband. The death of a husband always has far-reaching consequences for his family. For people of biblical times this was true as well. After a period of mourning, the widowed wife might follow one of several courses of action.

If she was childless, she was, according to the levirate law, expected to continue living with her husband's family (Deut. 25:5–10). She was to marry one of her husband's brothers or a near kinsman. If these men were not available, she was free to marry outside the clan (Ruth 1:9).

Widows with children had other options open to them. From the deuterocanonical book of Tobit we learn that some moved back to the family of their father or brother (Tobit 1:8). If the widow were elderly, one of her sons might care for her. If she had become financially secure, she might live alone. For example, Judith neither remarried nor moved into the home of a relative, for "her husband Manasses had left her gold, and silver, and men—servants and maidservants, and cattle, and lands; and she remained upon this estate" (Judith 8:7).

Occasionally a destitute widow had no male relative to depend on. Such women faced great hardships (cf. 1 Kings 17:8–15; 2 Kings 4:1–7).

The childless widow of New Testament times found herself in a much more secure position. If she had no customary means of support, she could turn to the church for help. Paul suggested that young widows should remarry and that elderly widows should be cared for by their children; but if the widow could turn to no one, the church should care for her (1 Tim. 5:16).

D. Rebellious Children. It was a grave sin to dishonor one's father or mother. Moses ordered that a person who struck or cursed his

VILLAGE OF KAFR KENNA. *A village in rural Galilee, Kafr Kenna still looks much like the villages of biblical times. Notice the simple style of the houses.*

parent should be put to death (cf. Ex. 21:15, 17; Lev. 20:9). We have no record of this punishment being carried out, but the Bible describes many instances in which children did dishonor their parents. When Ezekiel enumerated the sins of Jerusalem, he said, "In thee have they set light by father and mother; in the midst of thee have they dealt by oppression with the stranger: in thee have they vexed the fatherless and the widow" (Ezek. 22:7). A similar picture is presented in Proverbs 19:26. Jesus condemned religious leaders of His day for not honoring their parents (Matt. 15:4–9).

Sometimes the parent caused more friction in a family than the child. The prophet Nathan announced to David, "The sword shall never depart from thine house, because thou hast despised me, and hast taken the wife of Uriah the Hittite to be thy wife" (2 Sam. 12:10). From that time on, David had problems with his sons.

Amnon fell passionately in love with Tamar, his half sister, and raped her. Yet David did not punish his son, and Tamar's brother Absalom killed Amnon in revenge. Then Absalom fled to his mother's country, returning later to lead a revolt against his father (2 Sam. 13—15). David urged his men not to kill Absalom, but the young man died in battle. David wept for him (2 Sam. 18).

As David neared his own death, his son Adonijah wanted to succeed him to the throne. David had not tried to restrain his willfulness, in this or anything else. Scripture says that the king "had not displeased [Adonijah] at any time in saying, Why hast thou done so?" (1 Kings 1:6).

E. Sibling Rivalry. Proverbs 18:19 vividly depicts the problem of children who argue with one another: "A brother offended is harder to be won than a strong city: and their contentions are like the bars of a castle." The Bible describes brothers who quarreled for various reasons. Jacob sought to steal Esau's blessing for himself (Gen. 27). Absalom hated Amnon because he raped Absalom's sister (2 Sam. 13). Solomon had his brother Adonijah executed because he suspected that Adonijah wanted his throne (1 Kin. 2:19–25). When Jehoram ascended the throne, he killed all his brothers so that they would never be a threat to him (2 Chr. 21:4).

Sometimes parents provoked sibling rivalry. This was true of Isaac and Rebekah. The Bible says that "Isaac loved Esau . . . but Rebekah loved Jacob" (Gen. 25:28). When Isaac wanted to bless Esau, Rebekah helped Jacob get the blessing for himself. Esau became enraged and threatened to kill Jacob, who fled to a faraway country (Gen. 27:41—28:5). It took an entire generation to reunite their families.

Sadly, Jacob did not learn from his parents' mistakes. He also favored one of his sons, giving Joseph honor before the others. This so enraged the sons that they plotted to kill their father's favorite. Scripture records that "when his brethren saw that their father loved him more than all his brethren, they hated him, and could not speak peaceably unto him" (Gen. 37:4).

F. Adultery. The Israelites considered adultery a serious threat to the family, so they punished adulterers swiftly and harshly. (*See* "Marriage and Divorce.")

V. Summary. The family was a unifying thread in Bible history. When threatened or challenged, the family unit struggled for survival. God used families to convey His message to each new generation.

God has often portrayed Himself as the Father of His redeemed family (Hos. 11:1–3).

FAMILY RELATIONSHIPS

He expects honor from His children (Mal. 1:6). Jesus taught His disciples to pray, "Our Father." Even today, children's prayers prepare them to honor God as the perfect Father who is able to meet all their needs.

God ordained that the family unit be a vital part of human society. Through membership in loving human families, we may begin to understand the awesome privilege we have as members of the "family of God."

WOMEN AND WOMANHOOD

It is fair to say that the people in biblical Israel felt that men were more important than women. The father or oldest male in the family made the decisions that affected the whole family, while the women had very little to say about them. This *patriarchal* (father-centered) form of family life set the tone for the way women were treated in Israel.

For example, a girl was raised to obey her father without question. Then when she married she was to obey her husband in the same way. If she were divorced or widowed, she often returned to her father's house to live.

In fact, Leviticus 27:1–8 suggests that a woman was worth only about half as much as a man. Thus a female child was less welcome than a male. Boys were taught to make decisions and to preside over their families. Girls were raised to get married and have children.

A young woman didn't even think about a career outside the home. Her mother trained her to keep house and to raise children. She was expected to be a helper to her husband and to give him many children. If a woman was childless, she was thought to be cursed (Gen. 30:1–2, 22; 1 Sam. 1:1–8).

Still, a woman was more than an object to be bought and sold. She had a very important role to play. Proverbs 12:4 says, "A virtuous woman is a crown to her husband, but she that maketh ashamed is as rottenness in his bones." In other words, a good wife was good for her husband; she helped him, looked after him, and made him proud. But a bad wife was worse than a cancer; she could painfully destroy him and make him a mockery. A wife could make or break her husband.

Even though most women spent their days as housewives and mothers, there are some exceptions. For example, Miriam, Deborah, Huldah, and Esther were more than good wives—they were political and religious leaders who proved that they could guide the nation as well as any man could.

I. GOD'S VIEW OF WOMEN

II. THE LEGAL POSITION OF WOMEN

III. WOMEN AT WORSHIP

IV. WOMEN IN ISRAEL'S CULTURE
   A. The Ideal Wife
   B. A Woman's Beauty
   C. The Woman as Sexual Partner
   D. The Woman as Mother
   E. A Woman's Work

V. WOMEN LEADERS IN ISRAEL
   A. Military Heroines
   B. Queens
   C. Queen Mothers
   D. Counselors
   E. Religious Leaders

VI. SUMMARY

I. God's View of Women. Toward the end of the first chapter of Genesis, we read: "God created man in his own image, in the image of God created he him; male and female created he them. And God blessed them, and God said to them, Be fruitful, and multiply, and replenish the earth and subdue it: and have dominion over the fish of the sea, and over the fowl of the air, and over every living thing that moveth upon the earth" (Gen. 1:27–28). This passage shows two things about women. First, woman *as well as man* was created in the image of God. God did not create woman to be inferior to man; both are equally important. Second, the woman was also expected to have authority over God's creation. Man and woman are to share this authority—it does not belong only to the man.

God said, "It is not good that the man should be alone; I will make him a helper fit for him" (Gen. 2:18, RSV). So God "caused a deep sleep to fall upon Adam, and he slept: and he took one of his ribs" (Gen. 2:21). God used that rib in the creation of Eve. This account shows how important the woman is to a man: she is part of his very being, and without her man is incomplete.

But Adam and Eve sinned, and God told Eve, "Thy desire shall be to thy husband, and he shall rule over thee" (Gen. 3:16). In New Testament times the Apostle Paul told Christian wives, "Submit yourselves unto your own husbands, as unto the Lord" (Eph. 5:22). But even though a woman was to submit to her husband, she was not inferior to him. It just means that she should be willing to let him

WOMEN AND WOMANHOOD

PORTRAIT HEAD. *The black copper lines set into the eyelids of this ivory sculpture (fourteenth century B.C.) give a lifelike appearance to this representation of an important woman of Ugarit. Along the forehead at the hairline are loops of silver mixed with gold. The high headdress and the hair were once covered with a thin layer of gold.*

could make a religious vow and that it was binding on him; but a vow made by a woman could be cancelled by her father or (if she were married) by her husband (Num. 30:1–15). A woman's father could sell her (Ex. 21:7), and she could not be freed after six years, as a man could (Lev. 25:40). In at least one instance, a man offered his daughter to be used sexually by a mob (Judg. 19:22–25).

But some laws suggested that men and women were to be treated as equals. For example, children were to treat both parents with equal respect and reverence (Ex. 20:12). A son who disobeyed or cursed either parent was to be punished (Deut. 21:18–21). And a man and a woman caught in the act of adultery were both to be executed (Deut. 22:22). (It is interesting to note here that when the Pharisees dragged an adulteress to Jesus and wanted to stone her, they had already broken the law themselves by letting the man get away—John 8:3–11.)

Other biblical laws offered protection for women. If a man took a second wife, he was still bound by law to feed and clothe his first wife, and to continue to have sexual relations with her (Ex. 21:10). Even the foreign woman who was taken captive as a war bride had some rights; if her husband got tired of her, she was to be set free (Deut. 21:14). Any man found guilty of the crime of rape was to be stoned to death (Deut. 22:25–27).

Usually, only men owned property. But when parents had no sons, their daughters could receive the inheritance. They had to marry within the clan to retain the inheritance (Num. 27:8–11; 36:8–9).

Since Israel was a male-dominated society, women's rights were sometimes overlooked. Jesus told of a widow who had to pester a judge who would not take time to listen to her side of the case. Because he didn't want her to keep bothering him, the judge finally agreed to her wishes (Luke 18:1–8). As with many of Jesus' stories, this was something that could really have happened, and perhaps did.

In spite of this, widows were given some special privileges too. For example, they were allowed to glean the fields after the harvest (Deut. 24:19–22) and share a portion of the third-year tithe with the Levite (Deut. 26:12). So in spite of their weaker legal status, women did enjoy some special rights in Jewish society.

lead. In fact, Paul called for submission on the part of both the husband and the wife, "submitting yourselves one to another in the fear of God" (Eph. 5:21). In another letter, Paul clearly stated that there is no difference of status in Christ between a man and a woman. "There is neither Jew nor Greek," he writes, "there is neither bond nor free, there is neither male nor female: for ye are all one in Christ Jesus" (Gal. 3:28).

II. The Legal Position of Women. The legal position of a woman in Israel was weaker than that of a man. For example, a husband could divorce his wife if he "found some uncleanness in her," but the wife was not allowed to divorce her husband for any reason (Deut. 24:1–4). The Law stated that a wife who was suspected of having sexual relations with another man must take a jealousy test (Num. 5:11–31). However, there was no test for a man suspected of being unfaithful with another woman. The Law also said that a man

III. Women at Worship. Women were

WOMEN AND WOMANHOOD

ROMAN MARKET SCENE. *This Roman funerary relief shows the booth of a dealer in poultry and vegetables. A woman vendor stands behind the counter. The lot of Roman women was better than that of most women in the ancient world.*

considered to be members of the "family of faith." As such, they could enter into most of the areas of worship.

The Law directed all men to appear before the Lord three times a year. Apparently the women went with them on some occasions (Deut. 29:10; Neh. 8:2; Joel 2:13, 15–16), but they were not required to go. Perhaps women were not required to go because of their important duties as wives and mothers. For instance, Hannah went to Shiloh with her husband and asked the Lord for a son (1 Sam. 1:3–5). Later, when the child was born, she told her husband, "I will not go up until the child be weaned, and then I will bring him, that he may appear before the Lord, and there abide for ever" (v. 22).

As head of the family, the husband or father presented the sacrifices and offerings on behalf of the entire family (Lev. 1:2). But the wife might also be present. Women attended the Feast of Tabernacles (Deut. 16:13–14), the yearly Feast of the Lord (Judg. 21:19–21), and the Festival of the New Moon (2 Kings 4:23).

One sacrifice that only the women gave to the Lord was offered after the birth of a child: "And when the days of her purifying are fulfilled, for a son, or for a daughter, she shall bring a lamb of the first year for a burnt offering, and a young pigeon, or a turtledove for a sin offering, unto the door of the tabernacle of the congregation, unto the priest" (Lev. 12:6). By New Testament times, Jewish women were perhaps less active in temple or syna-

gogue worship than before. Although there was a special area at the temple known as the "Court of Women," women were not allowed to go into the inner court. Extra-biblical sources indicate that women did not read the Torah or recite prayers in the synagogue; but they could sit and listen in the special women's section.

A different picture unfolds in the early Christian church. Luke 8:1–3 indicates that Jesus welcomed some women as traveling companions. He encouraged Martha and Mary to sit at His feet as disciples (Luke 10:38–42). Jesus' respect for women was something strikingly new.

After Jesus ascended into heaven, several women met with the other disciples in the Upper Room to pray. Even though Scripture does not say so specifically, these women probably prayed audibly in public. Both men and women gathered at the home of John Mark's mother to pray for the release of Peter (Acts 12:1–17), and both men and women prayed regularly in the church at Corinth (1 Cor. 11:2–16). That's why the apostle Paul gave instructions to both men and women about how to pray in public.

This freedom for women was so revolutionary that it caused some problems within the church. Paul therefore gave some early congregations guidelines regarding the role of women. He wrote, "Let your women keep silence in the churches: for it is not permitted unto them to speak, but they are commanded to be under obedience, as also saith the law. And if they will learn any thing, let them ask their husbands at home: for it is a shame for women to speak in the church" (1 Cor. 14:34–35).

In another letter, Paul wrote, "Let the women learn in silence with all subjection. But I suffer not a woman to teach, nor to usurp authority over the man; but to be in silence" (1 Tim. 2:11–12). Opinions differ as to just what prompted Paul to write these things, and how far they constitute a rule for Christians today. Certainly, however, he was correcting behavior that appeared disorderly in his day.

Several Bible women were famous for their faith. Included in the list of faithful people in Hebrews 11 are two women, Sarah and Rahab. Hannah was a godly example of the Israelite mother: she prayed to God; she believed that God heard her prayers; and she kept her promise to God. Her story is found in 1 Samuel 1. Jesus' mother Mary was also a good and godly woman. In fact, Mary must have remembered Hannah's example, for her song of praise to God (Luke 1:46–55) was very similar to Hannah's song (1 Sam. 2:1–10). The apostle Paul reminded Timothy

KNEADING DOUGH. *This crudely modeled human figure from el-Jib in Palestine (ca. sixth century B.C.) bends over a trough to knead dough. Bread was the all-important staple food of the ancient Near East. Bakers mixed flour with water and seasoned it with salt, then kneaded it in the special trough. Then they added a small quantity of fermented dough until all the dough was leavened. The Jews did not use leaven in the offerings made by fire (Lev. 2:11), and its use was forbidden during Passover week.*

of the goodness of his mother and grandmother (2 Tim. 1:5).

Not all Jewish women in Bible times were as loyal to God as the preceding. According to the book of Jewish writings known as the Talmud, some women were "addicted to witchcraft" (Yoma 83b) and paganism. The Talmud also alleged that "the majority of women are inclined to witchcraft" (Sanhedrin 67a). Some rabbis believed this was why God told Moses, "Thou shalt not suffer a witch to live " (Ex. 22:18). (Some translations render the Hebrew word for witch as *sorceress*.)

But to be fair, the Scriptures do not indicate that women were any more interested in the occult than men were. Several scriptural references to women who were involved in the occult (e.g., 2 Kings 23:7; Ezek. 8:14; Hos. 4:13–14) clearly imply that men were also involved. And of the four times that sorcery is mentioned in the Book of Acts, only once was a woman involved (Acts 8:9–23; 13:4–12; 16:16–18; 19:13–16).

IV. Women in Israel's Culture. In Israelite society it was assumed that a woman's place was in the home. She was expected to find fulfillment in life as a wife and mother. Apparently Jewish women accepted that role willingly.

A. The Ideal Wife. Every man wanted to find a suitable wife, one who would do him "good and not evil, all the days of her life" (Prov. 31:12). No man wanted a wife who was bossy or who liked to fight! Proverbs 19:13 compared a wife's quarreling to the continual drip of rain on a person's head. In fact, "it is better to dwell in the wilderness, than with a contentious and an angry woman" (Prov. 21:19).

What qualities went into making the "ideal wife" in ancient Israel? What qualities did parents look for in a bride for their son? What qualities did a mother try to instill in her daughter to prepare her for being a good wife and mother?

Most of these qualities are described in an interesting poem in Proverbs 31. The poem is an *acrostic*—in other words, each verse begins with a different Hebrew letter in alphabetical order. We might call these verses the "ABCs of an Ideal Wife."

According to this poem, the ideal wife has many talents. She knows how to manage a household and provide for her family (vv. 13, 15, 19, 22). She never wastes her time, but spends her time in more important tasks

HAIRDRESSING. *A panel from the sarcophagus of Princess Kawit of Egypt (ca. 2100 B.C.) depicts the elaborate process of hairdressing. A servant braids her mistress's hair, while the princess holds a bowl of milk and a mirror.*

(v. 27). She has a knack for seeing what needs to be done and doing it. She has a good understanding of business, knowing how to buy and sell wisely (vv. 16, 24). However, she is not selfish. She helps the needy and gives advice to those who are less wise (v. 26). She also has a deep reverence for God (v. 30). She tries in every way to be a "helper fit" for her husband. The poem suggests that when she does all these things, her husband will be lifted to an important place in the eyes of the community (v. 23).

A shorter outline of what makes an ideal wife can be found in Ecclesiasticus 26:13–16: "The grace of a wife delighteth her husband, and her discretion will fatten his bones. A silent and loving woman is a gift of the Lord; and there is nothing worth so much as a mind well instructed. A shamefaced [modest] and faithful woman is a double grace, and her continent mind cannot be valued. As the sun when it ariseth in the high heaven, so is the beauty of a good wife in the ordering of her house."

B. A Woman's Beauty. Each society has its own standards of physical beauty. Some cultures associate beauty with plumpness, while others favor thinness. It is difficult to know just what the ancient Hebrews thought in this regard.

Most of the attractive women mentioned in the Bible are not described in detail. The writer usually notes simply that a woman was "beautiful." The biblical concept of beauty is open to different interpretations.

Take, for example, the statement that "Leah's eyes were weak, but Rachel was beautiful and lovely" (Gen. 29:17, RSV). Some scholars think that the Hebrew word for "weak" could be better translated as "tender and charming" (cf. KJV, "tender-eyed"). If so, it might mean that each sister was beautiful in her own way. Leah might have had beautiful eyes, while Rachel had a beautiful body.

The most extensive descriptions of a beautiful woman are found in the Song of Solomon; but even here they are not always all that illuminating. The poet uses a long series of similes and metaphors to portray the woman, and sometimes the poetic technique gets in the way of the description. For example, her teeth are white, like a flock of sheep, with none of them missing. Her lips are like a scarlet thread (Song 4:2–3).

Some of the most important women in the Old Testament were said to be beauties. Sarah (Gen. 12:11), Rebekah (Gen. 26:7), and Rachel (Gen. 29:17) are all described that way. David was tempted to commit adultery with Bathsheba because she was so beautiful (2 Sam. 11:2–3). Tamar, David's daughter, was raped by her half-brother Amnon because of her beauty (13:1). Both Absalom and Job

WOMEN AND WOMANHOOD

WOMAN BATHING. *This crude pottery sculpture depicts a woman seated in a shallow bowl washing her left leg. Hair falls over her shoulders. The figure, dating from about the sixth century B.C. was discovered at the el-Jib cemetery in Palestine. Israelite society required bodily cleanliness, especially of women.*

had beautiful daughters (2 Sam. 14:27; Job 42:15). The struggle between Solomon and Adonijah to succeed David as king was ended when Adonijah asked to marry beautiful Abishag. Not only was his request denied, but it cost him his life (1 Kin. 1:3–4; 2:19–25). The Jews living during the Persian era were saved by a beautiful Jewess named Esther (see the book of Esther).

Of course, not all women were naturally beautiful, but the rich could improve their looks with expensive clothes, perfumes, and cosmetics. (*See* "Clothing and Cosmetics.") The prophet Ezekiel said that the nation of Israel was like a young woman who bathed and anointed herself. She wore fancy clothes and shoes made of leather. God said to the nation, "I decked thee also with ornaments, and I put bracelets upon thy hands, and a chain on thy neck. And I put a jewel on thy forehead, and earrings in thine ears, and a beautiful crown upon thine head. Thus wast thou decked with gold and silver; and thy raiment was of fine linen and silk, and embroidered work" (Ezek. 16:11–13). There is an even more extensive list of jewelry in Isaiah 3:18–23, including anklets, headbands (KJV, "cauls"), amulets (KJV, "tablets"), signet rings, and nose rings. Some of these items have been found by archaeologists.

Jeremiah talked about another practice which was common in his day. Women painted around their eyes to make them more noticeable (Jer. 4:30). Other women put jeweled combs in their hair to make it look nicer. Many of these combs and hundreds of mirrors have also been found, dating all the way back to biblical times.

But there are two kinds of beauty—outer beauty and the inner beauty of a pleasing personality. The Scriptures warned men and women not to place too much importance on physical features and expensive clothes.

One sage said, "As a jewel of gold in a swine's snout, so is a fair woman which is without discretion" (Prov. 11:22). Another sage wrote, "Favor is deceitful, and beauty is vain: but a woman that feareth the Lord, she shall be praised" (Prov. 31:30). Peter and Paul told the women of their day to be more concerned with inner beauty than with good looks (1 Tim. 2:9–10; 1 Pet. 3:3–4).

C. The Woman as Sexual Partner. It was against the Law for an unmarried woman to have sexual relations. She was to remain a virgin until after the marriage ceremony. If anyone could prove that she was *not* a virgin when she married, she was brought to the door of her father's house and the men of the city stoned her to death (Deut. 22:20–21).

Sex was a very important part of married life. God had ordained the sexual relationship to be enjoyed in the proper place and between the right people—marriage partners. The Jews felt so strongly about this that a newly-married man was freed from his military or business duties for a whole year so that he could "cheer up his wife which he hath taken" (Deut. 24:5). The only restriction was that the husband and wife were not supposed to have sexual relations during her menstrual period (Lev. 18:19).

Sex was to be enjoyed by the wife as well as the husband. God told Eve, "Thy desire shall be to thy husband" (Gen. 3:16). In the Song of Solomon, the woman is portrayed as very aggressive, kissing her husband and leading him into the bed chamber. She expresses her love for him over and over, and she urges him to enjoy their physical relationship (Song 1:2; 2:3–6, 8–10; 8:1–4).

In New Testament times, there was a disagreement in the Corinthian church about the role of sex. Some people, it seems, felt that all of life was to be enjoyed, so whatever one wanted to do sexually should be all right—in-

WOMEN AND WOMANHOOD

cluding adultery, prostitution, and homosexual acts. Other people thought that sex was somehow evil and that one should not have any physical relations at all, not even with one's spouse. Paul reminded the Corinthians that adultery and homosexuality were sins and should be avoided (1 Cor. 6:9–11). But he also said that husbands and wives should enjoy God's gift of sex together. Paul's instruction was, "The husband should give to the wife her conjugal rights, and likewise the wife to her husband. . . . Do not refuse one another except perhaps by agreement for a season, that you may devote yourselves to prayer; but then come together again, lest Satan tempt you through lack of self-control" (1 Cor. 7:3, 5, RSV).

D. The Woman as Mother. In ancient times without the benefit of modern medicines and painkillers, childbirth was a very painful experience. In fact, many mothers died while giving birth (e.g., Gen. 35:16–20; 1 Sam. 4:19–20). In spite of these dangers, most women still wanted to bear children.

Being a good wife and mother was extremely important to Hebrew women. The greatest honor a woman could have received would have been to give birth to the Messiah. We can hardly imagine Mary's excitement when the angel Gabriel greeted her with the words, "Hail, thou that art highly favored, the Lord is with thee! Blessed art thou among women!" (Luke 1:28). He then went on to tell her that she would be the Messiah's mother. The greeting that Mary received from Elisabeth was similar (cf. Luke 1:42).

E. A Woman's Work. By today's standards, we would not consider the daily life of the average Israelite mother to have been very stimulating. It was marked by hard work and long hours.

She was up each morning before anyone else, starting a fire in the hearth or oven. The main food in the Jewish diet was bread. In fact, the Hebrew word for bread (*lehem*) was a synonym for food. One of the jobs that the wife and mother had, then, was to grind grain into flour. This involved several steps. (See "Food and Eating Habits.") She obviously had none of the electrical gadgets that are available today, so all of this work had to be done by hand.

She used thorns, stubble, or even animal dung to fuel the oven. The children usually had the job of finding the fuel; but if they were not old enough to leave the house, the woman had to find the fuel herself.

Every household needed water. Sometimes

WOMEN SPINNING WOOL. *This stone relief from Susa depicts a woman holding a spindle in her left hand and a fibrous material, perhaps wool, in her right. Behind her stands a servant with a large fan. Among the Israelites, spinning was mainly the occupation of women (Ex. 35:25–26).*

WOMEN AND WOMANHOOD

WATERSHAFT AND STEPS. *Built in about 1100 B.C., this stairway of 79 steps spirals down to the pool of Gibeon. The stairway and shaft, which required the removal of almost 3,000 tons of limestone, provided access to fresh water from within the city walls. Women of Gibeon made the long descent and climb every day to provide water for their households.*

families built their own private cisterns to store rain water; but most often the water came from a spring or well in the middle of the village. A few cities mentioned in the Old Testament were built above underground springs; Megiddo and Hazor were two of these cities. In Hazor a woman would walk through the streets to a deep shaft. Then she descended 9 m. (30 ft.) on five flights of stairs to the water tunnel, along which she proceeded to the water level to fill her large water jug. She needed considerable strength to climb back out of the watershaft with a heavy water jug. But it wasn't all bad. The trip for water gave her a chance to talk with the other women of the village. The ladies would often gather around the water source in the evening or early morning to exchange news and visit (Gen. 24:11). The woman at the well in Sychar no doubt came at noon because the other women of the town would not have wanted anything to do with her because of her loose living, and so they snubbed her (John 4:5–30). The wife was also expected to make her

family's clothes. (*See* "Clothing and Cosmetics.") Small children had to be nursed, watched, and kept clean. As the children got older, the mother taught them proper manners. She also taught the older daughters how to cook, sew, and do the other things that a good Israelite wife must know about.

In addition, the wife was expected to help bring in the harvest (Ruth 2:23). She prepared some crops like olives and grapes for storage. So her daily routine had to be flexible enough to include these other jobs.

V. Women Leaders in Israel. Most Israelite women never became public leaders, but there were some exceptions. Scripture records the names and deeds of several women who became prominent in political, military, or religious affairs.

A. Military Heroines. The two most famous military heroines mentioned in the Old Testament are Deborah and Jael; both had a part in the same victory. God spoke through Deborah to tell the general named Barak how the Canaanites could be beaten. Barak agreed

WOMEN AND WOMANHOOD

WOMAN'S HEAD OF IVORY. *This ivory head of an Assyrian woman (ca. eighth century B.C.) was carved from a section of a large elephant's tusk. A double-strand fillet or headband holds the hair, which falls in curls down the neck.*

to attack the Canaanites, but he wanted Deborah to go with him into the battle. She did so, and the Canaanites were duly defeated. However, the Canaanite general Sisera escaped on foot. Jael saw him, went out to greet him, and invited him into her tent. There he fell asleep. As he was sleeping, Jael came in and hammered a tent peg through his head, killing him (Judg. 4—5).

Several women helped defend their city of Thebez against attackers. The leader of the attack, Abimelech, moved in close to the tower gate to set it on fire. One of the women saw him at the gate and dropped a millstone on his head. The heavy stone crushed Abimelech's skull. As he lay dying he commanded his armor-bearer, "Draw thy sword and slay me, that men say not of me, A woman killed him" (Judg. 9:54). The attack was called off. Later generations gave the unidentified woman credit for the victory (2 Sam. 11:21).

A popular story told by the Jews in the days of Jesus was about a rich widow named Judith, who was devout and beautiful. The story begins with Israel being invaded by an Assyrian army led by the general Holofernes. He surrounded one of the cities of Israel, cut off its food and supplies, and gave it five days

to surrender. Judith encouraged her fellow townspeople to trust God for a victory. Then she put on beautiful clothes and paid a visit to Holofernes. The general thought she was very lovely and asked her to visit him every day. The last night before the Jews had to surrender, Judith was alone with Holofernes. When he fell into a drunken stupor, Judith took his sword, cut off his head, and put it in a basket. Then she returned to the city. In the morning, after the Assyrians found that their leader was dead, the Jews won an easy victory.

B. Queens. Not all the women in the Bible were known for their good deeds. Queen Jezebel is likely the most notorious woman in the Old Testament. She was a daughter of Ethbaal, king of the Sidonians. She married Ahab, the prince of Israel, and moved to Samaria. When Jezebel became queen, she forced her wishes on the people. She wanted the Israelites to bow down to Baal, so she brought hundreds of Baal's prophets into the country and put them on the government payroll. She also killed as many of the prophets of the Lord as she could find (1 Kin. 18:13). Even godly laymen like Naboth were cut down. The prophet Elijah ran away and hid from Jezebel to save his life. He felt that he was the only true prophet left in the entire country. In fact, it was said that in the entire kingdom there were only 7,000 people who had refused to worship Baal (1 Kings 19:18). Years after Jezebel had been overthrown and killed, the worship of Baal continued.

Herodias was another woman who used her influence to get what she wanted. When John the Baptist spoke out against her marriage to King Herod (Antipas), she influenced the king to arrest John and put him into prison. On Herod's birthday, Herodias' daughter danced for the guests. This pleased Herod very much, so he promised to give her anything she asked for. Herodias told her daughter to ask for the head of John the Baptist. Herod complied, and John was executed.

Of course not all the queens of the Bible were evil. Queen Esther used her position to help the Jews. For a full account of her story, *see* "The Persians."

C. Queen Mothers. The writers of 1 and 2 Kings and 2 Chronicles tell us much about the queen mothers of Judah. In referring to the 20 different kings who ruled in Judah from the time of Solomon to the time of the Exile, only once do these books fail to mention a queen mother. A typical example of what is said

29

WOMEN AND WOMANHOOD

about the queen mother is found in this passage: "In the second year of Joash the son of Jehoahaz king of Israel, Amaziah the son of Joash, king of Judah, began to reign. He was twenty-five years old when he began to reign, and he reigned twenty-nine years in Jerusalem. His mother's name was Jehoaddin of Jerusalem. And he did what was right in the eyes of the Lord" (2 Kin. 14:1–3, RSV).

We assume that the mother of the king must have been an important person in Judah. Unfortunately, very little is known about her role in the government or the society. (*See* "Government.")

One instance of a queen mother's having decisive influence may be noted. Because Adonijah was David's oldest surviving son, he felt that he should be the next king after David. Several high officials agreed with him—including Joab, the general of the army, and Abiathar, the priest. On the other hand, the prophet Nathan and another priest named Zadok believed that Solomon, another of David's sons, would be a better king. Bathsheba, Solomon's mother, persuaded David to designate Solomon as his successor (1 Kings

WOMAN FROM MARI. *A clay statuette from the city of Mari, located along the Euphrates River in Mesopotamia (now Syria), depicts a woman singing. The statuette was made sometime before 2500 B.C.*

1:30). Solomon respected his mother for what she had done (1 Kings 2:19).

However, not all queen mothers were treated so respectfully. When King Asa brought religious reforms to the country, he quite justifiably removed his mother from her position at the court because she had made an image of the goddess Asherah. He also banished the prostitutes and destroyed all the idols, including the one of Asherah (1 Kings 15:9–15).

One queen mother who had tremendous power was Athaliah, the mother of Ahaziah. When her son was killed in battle, Athaliah seized the throne and tried to kill all the rightful heirs. But one of the infant princes was hidden from her. For six years Athaliah ruled Judah with an iron hand; but as soon as the young prince was old enough to become king, Athaliah was overthrown and killed (2 Kin. 11:1–16).

D. Counselors. Most villages had wise persons whom other people often asked for advice. The king's court had many counselors as well. (*See* "Government.") While there are no Scripture references to women counselors in the king's court, there are several examples of village wise women.

When Joab, the commander-in-chief of David's army, wanted to reconcile David and his son Absalom, he got a wise woman from Tekoa to help him. The woman pretended to be a widow with two sons. She said that one of her sons had killed the other in a fit of anger, and that the rest of her family wanted to kill the remaining son. David listened to her story and ruled that she was right to forgive this second son. Then the woman pointed out to the king that he was not practicing what he preached, for he had not forgiven Absalom for a similar crime. David saw that he had been wrong and allowed Absalom to return to Jerusalem (2 Sam. 14:1–23).

Another wise woman saved her town from destruction. A man named Sheba led a revolt against King David. When the revolt failed, Sheba ran away and hid in the city of Abel. David's general Joab surrounded the city and was getting ready to attack it when a wise woman from the city appeared at the wall and asked to speak to Joab. She reminded him how important her town had been to Israel; she said that he was seeking to destroy a city that was "a mother in Israel." So they agreed to a plan. If Sheba were killed, the city would not be attacked. The wise woman returned and told the

WOMEN AND WOMANHOOD

townspeople about the plan. They killed Sheba and watched Joab and his army ride away (2 Sam. 20).

E. Religious Leaders. In Israel, God did not ordain priestesses. A woman could not, in any case, have become a priest because her monthly cycle made her unclean. Priestly ministry was restricted to the male descendants of Aaron. However, women could perform other ritual tasks (Ex. 38:8; 1 Sam. 2:22). They also participated in other forms of public ministry and worship.

Women served as prophetesses—that is, spokeswomen for God. One of the most noteworthy Hebrew prophetesses was Huldah, the wife of Shallum. She was active in ministry during the days of King Josiah. When the book of the Law was found in the temple, the religious leaders came to her and asked what God wanted the nation to do. The whole nation, including King Josiah, tried to carry out her instructions to the last detail, for they were sure God had spoken through her (2 Kings 22:11—23:25).

There are other prophetesses mentioned in the Old Testament, including Miriam (Ex. 15:20), Deborah (Judg. 4:4), and Isaiah's wife (Is. 8:3). The New Testament reports that Anna and the daughters of Philip were prophetesses, but we don't know much else about their lives or their messages (Luke 2:36; Acts 21:9).

Some women used the musical talents that God had given them. Miriam and other women sang a song of praise to God after the Israelites had been delivered from the Egyptians (Ex. 15:20–21). When God helped Deborah and Barak defeat the Canaanites, they sang a victory song as a duet (Judg. 5:1–31). Three daughters of Heman were also musi-

cians; according to 1 Chronicles 25:5, they performed at the temple.

In the church at Cenchreae there was a deaconess named Phoebe, who Paul said was "a helper of many and of [him]self as well" (Rom. 16:1–2, RSV). In a letter to Timothy, Paul wrote that wives of deacons, or women deacons, "must be serious, no slanderers, but temperate, faithful in all things" (1 Tim. 3:11, RSV). But he made it clear that he did not want any woman in the Ephesian church to teach or to have authority over men (2:12).

Other female leaders of the early church included Priscilla, who explained to Apollos "the way of God more perfectly" (Acts 18:24–26). Euodias and Syntyche were two of the spiritual leaders at Philippi. Paul said, "They have labored side by side with me in the gospel together with Clement and the rest of my fellow workers" (Phil. 4:3, RSV). Thus it appears that they were doing a work which was similar to his own.

VI. Summary. An old Jewish story demonstrates how important the woman was in Israel. The story says that a pious man once married a pious woman. They were childless, so they eventually agreed to divorce one another. The husband then married a wicked woman and she made him wicked. The pious woman married a wicked man and made him righteous. The moral of the story is that the woman set the tone for the home.

The Israelite mother held an important place in the life of the family. To a large degree, she could be the key to a successful family or the cause of its failure. She could have incalculable influence on her husband and her children.

Israel's history and its culture owes a great deal to these hard-working women.

MARRIAGE AND DIVORCE

The Bible clearly expresses God's intentions for marriage. In marriage, a man and a woman are meant to find fulfillment that is both spiritual and sexual. This relationship was marred by humankind's fall into sin. The history of Israel tells of changes that affected marriage because the Israelites chose to accept the degrading practices of their ungodly neighbors.

Jesus reaffirmed what marriage means. He rebuked the Jews' attitude toward divorce, and He challenged marriage partners to live in harmony with one another.

I. MARRIAGE
    A. Divinely Established
    B. Marked by Love
    C. Sexually Fulfilling
       1. A Duty to Consummate
       2. Promiscuity and Perversion
       3. Proper Sexual Roles
    D. A Spiritual Symbol

II. BIBLICAL MARRIAGE CUSTOMS

III. LEVIRATE MARRIAGE

IV. VIOLATIONS OF MARRIAGE

V. THE SINGLE PERSON

VI. DIVORCE
    A. Mosaic Law
    B. Jesus' Teachings
    C. Paul's Teachings

I. Marriage. We should notice these Bible passages that describe the purpose of marriage. Scripture gives a full-orbed view of the privileges and duties of the marriage bond.

A. Divinely Established. God first created a pair of human beings, a man and a woman. His first command to them was, "Be fruitful, and multiply, and replenish the earth" (Gen. 1:28). By putting this couple together, God instituted marriage, the most basic of all social relationships. Marriage enabled humankind to fulfill God's command to rule and replenish the earth (Gen. 1:28).

God made both the male and the female in His image, each with a special role and each complemented by the other. Genesis 2 tells us that God created the man first. Then, using a rib from the man, God made a "help meet for him" (Gen. 2:18). When God brought Eve to Adam, He joined them together and said, "Therefore shall a man leave his father and his mother, and shall cleave unto his wife: and they shall be one flesh" (Gen. 2:24).

God intended marriage to be a permanent relationship. It was to be a unique covenantal commitment of two people that excluded all others from its intimacy. God expressly forbade the breaking of that union when He gave the commandment, "Thou shalt not commit adultery" (Ex. 20:14). The New Testament reaffirms the uniqueness of the marriage bond. Jesus said that a man and his wife "are no more twain, but one flesh. What therefore God hath joined together, let not man put asunder" (Matt. 19:6). Paul beautifully compared the love of a man for his wife to the love of Christ for his church (Eph. 5:25). He said that Christ's love was so deep that He died for the church, and in the same way a man's love for his wife should overcome any sense of the imperfections she may have.

Marriage is more than a contract that two people make for their mutual benefit. Because they make their marriage vows in God's presence and in His name, they may draw power from God to fulfill those vows. God becomes a supporting party to the marriage. Proverbs reminds us of this when it says that God gives wisdom, discretion, and understanding so that marriage partners can avoid being lured into unfaithfulness (cf. Prov. 2:6–16). New Testament writers understood that Christian marriage is created and maintained by Christ.

B. Marked by Love. Above all else, love is to mark the union. Note the simplicity with which Scripture describes the marriage of Isaac and Rebekah: "[He] took Rebekah, and she became his wife; and he loved her" (Gen. 24:67). Love, based on true friendship and respect, seals and sustains the marriage bond. Peter calls husbands to "dwell with them [your wives] according to knowledge, giving honor unto the wife, as unto the weaker vessel, and as being heirs together of the grace of life" (1 Pet. 3:7). When this kind of love exists between a man and wife, it purifies their marriage relationship.

MARRIAGE AND DIVORCE

WEDDING PROCESSION. *This artist's conception of a wedding procession in biblical times shows a bridegroom escorting the wedding party back to his house for a feast. Music and dancing were major parts of the celebration, which lasted for one to two weeks.*

The Bible says that husband and wife are equal as persons before God, since both have been made in God's image. Both can be saved from their sins through Jesus (Gen. 1:28; Gal. 3:28; Col. 3:10–11). Together they receive God's gifts and blessings for their marriage (Rom. 4:18–21; Heb. 11:11; 1 Pet. 3:5–7). When they join in marriage, they both have the obligations, though they may have varying degrees of ability to perform the responsibilities they share.

C. Sexually Fulfilling. Another factor in the marriage relationship is the sexual union of the partners. Sexual union consummates marriage on the basis of a mutual matrimonial commitment. The expression, "he knew his wife" (Gen. 4:1, 25, and other places), is the Bible's discreet way of referring to sexual intercourse. But the Bible treats this act with dignity, calling it honorable and undefiled (Heb. 13:4). Scripture calls on God's people to keep their sexual relations pure. They are not

to use sex to fulfill lustful passions, as the ungodly do (1 Thess. 4:3–7). Scripture encourages a married man to delight in the wife of his youth all his life (Eccl. 9:9). He is to be "ravished always with her love" (Prov. 5:15–19).

1. A Duty to Consummate. When a man of Israel became engaged to marry, he was not to let anything keep him from fulfilling his purpose. He was not to go to war, lest he die and another man marry his promised bride (Deut. 20:7). For the first year of marriage, he was not to resume any task that would interfere with his presence at home to "cheer up his wife" (Deut. 24:5). Paul told husbands and wives to be sexually available to each other, without depriving one another, so that Satan would not be able to tempt them to indulge roving affections because they lacked self-control (1 Cor. 7:3–5).

2. Promiscuity and Perversion. Paul says that a man who joins himself "to a harlot is one body [with her], for two [the man and the harlot] . . . shall be one flesh" (1 Cor. 6:16). The body, Paul says, is the temple of Christ. Since a promiscuous sexual union joins the flesh of two individuals, it is a defilement of Christ's holy place.

Here the term *flesh* means more than the sexual organs or even the entire body. It refers to the whole person. Sexual union inescapably involves the whole person, whether within or outside marriage. When God demands that His people live holy lives (1 Pet. 1:15–16), this includes their sexual conduct in relation to their marriage (1 Thess. 4:3–6). He required corresponding holiness of the Israelites (Lev. 18; 20:10–21). The whole person—body no less than soul—is set apart for God.

The cult prostitution of pagan nations eventually found its way into Israel. The very presence of this practice profaned the worship of the Lord (1 Sam. 2:22).

The Bible forbids incest (Lev. 18:6–18; 20:11–12). Also, it denounces homosexual relations as being perverse and despicable in God's eyes. In fact, such relations carried a death penalty in Israel (cf. Lev. 18:22; 20:13; Deut. 23:18; Rom. 1:26–27; 1 Cor. 6:9; 1 Tim. 1:10).

3. Proper Sexual Roles. In biblical times, marriage was thought of as a state in which persons would naturally fulfill their respective sexual roles. Thus the man was head of his family and the wife was to submit to his authority (Ps. 45:11; 1 Pet. 3:4–6); the woman

MARRIAGE AND DIVORCE

was made to be the man's helper, suited to him in that sense. These roles were present at the very beginning. Throughout the time of the Old Testament, the woman found her place in society through her father, then through her husband, and then through her older brother or kinsman-redeemer. (*See* "Family Relationships.") God worked through this role relationship to establish harmony in the family and in the whole of society.

The submission of a Jewish woman to her husband did not depreciate her abilities or demote her to a secondary place in society. The "excellent" wife of the Old Testament (Prov. 31) enjoyed the confidence of her husband and the respect of her children and neighbors. She had a great deal of freedom to use her economic skills to provide for her family. She was recognized as a person of wisdom and a gracious teacher. She was as far as possible from being a chattel slave, which is how a woman was regarded in other Near Eastern cultures.

D. A Spiritual Symbol. Marriage symbolized the union between God and His people. Israel was called the Lord's wife, and the Lord Himself said, "I was a husband unto them" (Jer. 31:32; cf. Is. 54:5). Prophets declared that the nation had committed "fornication" and "adultery" when it turned from God to idols (Num. 25:1; Judg. 2:17; Jer. 3:20; Ezek. 16:17; Hos. 1:2). They said that God had divorced His "unfaithful wife" (Is. 50:1; Jer. 3:8) when He sent the Israelites away into captivity. Yet God had compassion on His "wife," Israel, and called "her" back to be faithful (Is. 54). As a bridegroom delights in his bride (Is. 62:4–5), so the Lord delighted to make Israel the "holy people," His redeemed ones (Is. 62:12).

The New Testament describes the church as the bride of Christ, preparing herself for life in the eternal kingdom (Eph. 5:23). This image underlines the truth that marriage ought to be an exclusive and permanent union of love and fidelity. Husbands should love their wives as Christ loves His ransomed bride, and wives should submit to their husbands, as they submit to Christ.

II. Biblical Marriage Customs. In biblical times, the first step in marriage was taken by the man or his family (Gen. 4:19; 6:2; 12:19; 24:67; Ex. 2:1). Usually the couples' families made the marriage arrangement. Thus Hagar, as head of the family, "took him [Ishmael] a wife out of the land of Egypt" (Gen. 21:21). When Isaac was 40 years old, he was quite ca-

pable of choosing his own wife (Gen. 25:20); yet Abraham sent his servant to Haran to seek a wife for Isaac (Gen. 24).

Abraham gave his servant two strict orders: The bride must not be a Canaanite, and she must leave her home to live with Isaac in the Promised Land. Under no circumstance was Isaac to return to Haran to live according to their former way of life.

Abraham's servant found the Lord's direction in his choice (Gen. 24:12–32). Then, according to Mesopotamian custom, he made arrangements with the girl's brother and mother (Gen. 24:28–29, 33). He sealed the agreement by giving gifts (a dowry) to them and to Rebekah (Gen. 24:53). Finally, they sought Rebekah's own consent (Gen. 24:57). This procedure was very similar to Hurrian marriage practices described in ancient texts from Nuzi.[1]

Under different circumstances, both of Isaac's sons—Jacob and Esau—chose their own wives. Esau's choice caused much distress to his parents (Gen. 26:34–35; 27:46; 28:8–9); but Jacob's choice met with approval.

Jacob was sent to Laban, his uncle in Haran, where he acted on his father's authority to arrange to marry Rachel. Instead of giving Laban a dowry, he worked for seven years. But it was not customary to allow the younger daughter to marry first, so Laban tricked Jacob into marrying Rachel's older sister, Leah. Jacob then accepted Laban's offer to work seven more years for Rachel.

In that region, a man who had no sons often adopted a male heir, giving him his daughter as wife. The adopted son was required to labor in the household. If a natural son were born later, the adopted son lost his inheritance to the natural heir. Laban may have intended to adopt Jacob; but then sons were born to him (Gen. 31:1). Perhaps Laban's sons grew jealous of Jacob because they feared he might claim the inheritance. At any rate, Jacob left Haran secretly to return to his father in Canaan.

Rachel took along the household gods of her father. Since the possession of these gods was a claim to inheritance, Laban followed in hot pursuit; but Rachel concealed the idols so that Laban did not find them. To pacify his uncle, Jacob pledged not to mistreat Laban's daughters or take other wives (Gen. 31:50).

---

[1] *See* E. A. Speiser, *The Anchor Bible: Genesis* (New York: Doubleday and Company, 1964), pp. 182–185.

MARRIAGE AND DIVORCE

Divorce in Babylon

Marriage is an ancient ritual; so is divorce. Perhaps there is nothing so basic to a culture as its rules concerning the relationship of man and woman.

Hammurabi, a Babylonian king who ruled from 1728 to 1686 B.C., constructed intricate laws called the Code of Hammurabi. These laws dealt with all aspects of Babylonian life, including divorce. Hammurabi's divorce laws were almost as complicated as divorce laws today.

A Babylonian husband could simply say to his wife, "Thou art not my wife" (*ul assati atti*), or that he "had left" or "divorced" her. He gave her "leaving money" or "divorce money." It was also sometimes said that he "had cut the fringe of her garment." Since a garment often symbolized the person who wore it, this meant that the husband had cut his marriage tie to his wife. His words were a legal divorce decree.

The Babylonian wife might say that "she has hated" her husband or that she "has left him," which meant that she refused to have sexual relations with him. However, nothing the woman said could dissolve the marriage. She did not have the power to divorce her husband without a court's consent.

Divorce was not an issue unless the marriage had been formalized. "If a man acquire a wife, but did not draw up the contracts for her, that woman is no wife," according to the Hammurabi Code. Once people were legally married, however, the conditions and consequences of divorce were clearly outlined in the Code. There were divorce laws concerning unconsummated marriages, childless marriages, marriage to a priestess, marriage in which the husband was taken captive during a war, marriage in which the wife became seriously ill; and always there were specific provisions about who was to receive what sum of money.

A husband could divorce his wife almost at will. However, if she was not at fault, the man had to give up her dowry, often a large portion of his property. This protected the wife from capricious or casual divorce. If there was misconduct by husband or wife, the courts were expected to assess punishment. A woman could never start divorce proceedings; she had to wait for her husband to apply to the court. If a woman could not prove her own innocence *and* her husband's guilt, she was drowned. Needless to say, only in extreme cases did a woman seek divorce. If the husband was found to be at fault, the wife "incurs no punishment" for her refusal of conjugal rights and could return to her father's house.

A woman could even be divorced if she was "a gadabout, thus neglecting her house and humiliating her husband." If found guilty of this crime, "they shall throw that woman into the water."

Nothing was sacred or perpetual about marriage in Babylonia. It seems to have been a secular agreement rather than a religious or moral commitment.

We should especially note the Old Testament tradition of the "bride price." As we have seen, the husband or his family paid a bride price to the father of the bride to seal the marriage agreement (cf. Ex. 22:16–17; Deut. 22:28–29).

The bride price was not always paid in cash. It might be given in the form of clothing (Judg. 14:8–20) or some other valuable item. A most gruesome one was demanded by Saul, who asked David for physical proof that he had killed 100 Philistines (1 Sam. 18:25).

The giving of a bride price did not indicate that the wife had been sold to the husband and was his property. It was a realization of the economic worth of the daughter. Later the law recognized the practice of buying a female servant to become a man's wife. Such laws protected women from abuse or maltreatment (Ex. 21:7–11).

At times, the groom or his family gave gifts to the bride too (Gen. 24:53). Sometimes the bride's father also gave her a wedding gift, as Caleb did (Josh. 15:15–19). In this connection, it is interesting to note that the Egyptian pharaoh gave the city of Gezer as a wedding gift to his daughter, Solomon's wife (1 Kings 9:16).

The feast was an important part of the marriage ceremony. It was usually given by the bride's family (Gen. 29:22), but the groom's family might give it too (Judg. 14:10).

Both the bride and the groom had attendants to serve them (Judg. 14:11; Ps. 45:14; Mark 2:19). If it were a royal wedding, the bride gave her attendants to her husband to add to the glory of his court (Ps. 45:14).

Even though the bride would adorn herself with jewels and beautiful clothing (Ps. 45:13–15; Is. 49:18), the groom was the center of attention. The Psalmist focuses, not on the bride (as modern Westerners might do), but on the bridegroom as being happy and radiant on the wedding day (Ps. 19:5).

In other Near Eastern nations, the groom customarily went to live with the bride's family. But in Israel, the bride usually went to her husband's home and became part of his family. The right of inheritance followed the male. If an Israelite had only daughters and wanted to preserve his family inheritance, his daughters had to marry within their tribe, because the inheritance could not be transferred to another tribe (Num. 36:5–9).

One of the most important aspects of the marriage celebration was the pronouncement of God's blessing upon the union. This is why Isaac blessed Jacob before sending him to Haran to seek a wife (Gen. 24:60; 28:1–4).

Although Scripture does not describe a marriage ceremony, we assume that it was a very public event. Jesus attended and blessed at least one marriage ceremony. He referred to various aspects of the wedding festivities in His lessons, thus showing that marriage ceremonies were familiar to the common person (Matt. 22:1–10; 25:1–13; Mark 2:19–20; Luke 14:8).

Both families were involved in planning the marriage. The bride's family also assumed responsibility for keeping evidence that she was a virgin on the wedding day, in case her husband later maligned her (Deut. 22:13–19).

III. Levirate Marriage. The Israelites felt that it was very important for a man to have an heir. To preserve the property inheritance that God had given them, they had to convey it through family lines (cf. Ex. 15:17–18; Ps. 127:128).

A woman who was unable to have children often felt the rebuke of her neighbors (Gen. 30:1–2, 23; 1 Sam. 1:6–10; Luke 1:25). She and her family would then retreat into earnest prayer (Gen. 25:21; 1 Sam. 1:10–12, 26–28).

A more serious situation arose if her husband died before she had borne an heir. To solve this problem, the practice of *levirate marriage* was begun. First mentioned in connection with the family of Judah (Gen. 38:8), levirate marriage later became a part of the Law of Moses (Deut. 25:5–10). When a woman was widowed, her dead husband's brother would marry her according to levirate law. The children of this marriage became the heirs of the deceased brother, in order that "his name be not put out of Israel" (Deut. 25:6). If a man refused to marry his widowed sister-

ROYAL COUPLE. *This painted limestone relief from about 1370 B.C. depicts an Egyptian queen offering flowers to the king, who casually leans on his staff. This and other inscriptions show that the queen played a secondary role in the royal family.*

in-law, he was publicly disgraced (Deut. 25:7–10; cf. Ruth 4:1–7).

The most familiar example of this was the marriage of Boaz to Ruth. In this case, the nearest of kin was unwilling to marry Ruth; so Boaz, as the next-nearest of kin, acted as the kinsman-redeemer. Having paid the indebtedness on Elimelech's inheritance, he took Ruth to be his wife "to raise up the name of the dead upon his inheritance, that the name of the dead be not cut off from among his brethren, and from the gate of his place" (Ruth 4:10). David was the third generation from this marriage, and from this line later came Jesus Christ (Ruth 4:17; Rom. 1:3).

IV. Violations of Marriage. Although God ordained marriage as a holy relationship between one man and one woman, it soon was corrupted when some men took two wives (cf. Gen. 4:19). Intermarriage with foreign people and the adoption of pagan ways compounded the problem.

MARRIAGE AND DIVORCE

Scripture records that Abraham followed the heathen custom of begetting a child to be his heir by a slave girl, because his wife was barren. "I pray thee go in unto my maid," Sarah asked her husband. "It may be that I may obtain children by her" (Gen. 16:2). The slave girl, Hagar, soon bore a son for Abraham. Later, Sarah also gave birth to a son. Hagar's arrogance vexed Sarah and caused her to treat Hagar harshly. When Sarah observed Ishmael making fun of her own son, she decided she had endured enough. She demanded that Abraham send Hagar away. Because Hagar had borne him a son, Abraham could not sell her as a slave. He gave Hagar her freedom and sent her away with a gift (Gen. 21:14; 25:6).

Jacob was another Hebrew patriarch who followed pagan marriage customs. Jacob took two wives because his uncle had tricked him into marrying the wrong woman (Gen. 29:21–30). When Rachel realized that she was barren, she gave Jacob her maid "that I may also have children" (Gen. 30:3–6). Leah became jealous and gave Jacob her own servant to bear more children in her name (Gen. 30:9–13). Thus Jacob had two wives and two concubines, but he gave equal status to all his children as heirs of the covenant (Gen. 46:8–27; 49).

Beginning with David, the kings of Israel indulged themselves with the luxury of many wives and concubines, even though God had specifically commanded them not to do this (Deut. 17:17). This practice gave them social status and enabled them to make various political alliances (2 Sam. 3:2–5; 5:13–16; 12:7–10; 1 Kings 3:1; 11:1–4).

David fell into adultery with Bathsheba and eventually committed murder in order to marry her. Death was the customary punishment for this sin (Lev. 20:10; Deut. 22:22). But instead of taking David's life, God decreed that the child of David and Bathsheba should die, and that strife should rise up against David in his own household (2 Sam. 12:1–23).

Solomon also was punished for disobeying God's commands concerning marriage. His many foreign wives led him into idolatry (1 Kings 11:4–5).

The Mosaic Law gave protection to concubines and multiple wives, but not in order to sanction the practice. The Law gave secondary status to concubines and their children to protect these innocent victims of uncontrolled lust (Ex. 21:7–11; Deut. 21:10–17). We should view the Law's allowance of these practices in the light of Jesus' comment on divorce: "Moses, because of the hardness of your hearts, suffered you to put away your wives; but from the beginning it was not so" (Matt. 19:8).

Malachi spoke out against the abuse and neglect that a wife suffered when her husband turned to pagan women and divorced her. The marriage covenant called her to bear "godly seed"; but the man's unfaithfulness led him to ignore his responsibilities to her (Mal. 2:11, 14–16).

Mosaic Law did not allow Israelites to marry foreign women (Deut. 7:3) because they worshiped other gods. When the Israelites returned from captivity, they were reminded that marrying foreign wives was contrary to God's Law. Ezra and Nehemiah spoke on the matter many times (Ezra 10; Neh. 10:30; 13:23–28). Nehemiah rebuked his generation by saying, "Did not Solomon king of Israel sin by these things? . . . even him did outlandish women cause to sin" (Neh. 13:26;

ROMAN COUPLE. *This fresco of a married couple was discovered in a bakery in Pompeii. The scroll and tablet may indicate that the pair were proud of their literacy.*

30

MARRIAGE AND DIVORCE

MARRIAGE AND DIVORCE

WEDDING SCENES. *Scenes from a typical Roman wedding are shown on the sides of this altar. In the scene at left, the couple joins hands at the conclusion of the marriage service. At right, children take part in the procession to the bridegroom's house, carrying an offering for pagan sacrifice.*

cf. 1 Kings 11:4–5). Ezra required every man to end his relationship with his foreign wife. Those who refused were banned from the congregation and their property was seized (Ezra 10:8).

The sexual relationship that God intended was *monogamy*—one man and one woman. But because of degraded human passions, God's Law needed to prohibit specific sexual sins (Lev. 18:1–30; 20:10–24; Deut. 27:20–23).

Even so, some men went to harlots unashamedly (Gen. 38:15–23; Judg. 16:11). The Book of Proverbs warned at length against loose and evil women who solicited young men in the streets (Prov. 2:16–19; 5:1–23; 6:20–35). Canaanite cult prostitution was a grave abuse, which was occasionally practiced in Israel (1 Sam. 2:22–25; 1 Kin. 15:12; 2 Kin. 23:7; Hos. 4:13–14; cf. Deut. 23:17).

Several biblical lists of sins began with sexual immorality (Mark 7:21; Rom. 1:24–27; 1 Cor. 6:9; Gal. 5:19; Eph. 5:5). Any sexual sin mocked the image of God in man. God warned that He would destroy any society that allowed such sin to continue (Lev. 18:24–29).

V. The Single Person. By His words and by His own unmarried life, Jesus showed that marriage was not an end in itself, nor was it essential to the wholeness of a person. As God's servant, a person might not be called to have a mate and children. A Christian disciple might need to forget parents and possessions for the sake of the kingdom of God (Luke 18:29; cf. Matt. 19:29; Mark 10:29–30).

Paul wished that all men could be content to live unmarried like him (1 Cor. 7:7–8). He found full freedom and completeness in attending "upon the Lord without distraction" (1 Cor. 7:35). But he recognized that a person who does not have the gift of self-control in

MARRIAGE AND DIVORCE

this area should marry, so that "he sinneth not" (1 Cor. 7:9, 36).

VI. Divorce. Bible scholars disagree over the way Jesus and Paul interpreted the Mosaic Law concerning divorce. Yet the provisions of the Old Testament are quite clear.

A. Mosaic Law. The Law of Moses allowed a man to divorce his wife when she found "no favor in his eyes, because he hath found some uncleanness in her" (Deut. 24:1). The primary thrust of this piece of legislation was to prevent him from taking her again after she had married another man; this would have been an "abomination before the Lord" (Deut. 24:4).

The Law was supposed to deter divorce rather than encourage it. It required a "writing of divorcement"—a public document granting the woman the right to remarry without civil or religious sanction. Divorce could not be done privately.

The acceptable reason for granting divorce was "some uncleanness." Specific types of "uncleanness" had their own penalties. Adultery carried the death penalty by stoning.

If a man believed his wife was not a virgin when he married her, he could take her to the elders of the city. If they judged her guilty, her punishment was death (Deut. 22:13–21). However, if the man had falsely accused his wife, he would be chastised and required to pay her father twice the usual bride price.

When the husband suspected his wife of adultery, he took her to the priest, who gave her the "jealousy test." This was a "trial by ordeal" typical of ancient Near Eastern cultures. The woman was made to drink bitter water. If she were innocent, then the water did not affect her. If she were guilty, she would become ill. In that case, she was stoned to death as an adulteress (Num. 5:11–31).

Although the Law of Moses allowed a man to divorce his wife, the wife was not allowed to divorce her husband for any reason at all. Many women probably fled from unpleasant circumstances without a bill of divorcement (cf. Judg. 19:2). Legally the wife was bound to her husband as long as they both lived or until he divorced her. If the woman was given a certificate of divorce, she was eligible to remarry any man except a priest (Lev. 21:7, 14; Ezek. 44:22).

However, remarriage defiled her in respect to her first husband—i.e., he could not marry her again, because she had in effect committed adultery against him (cf. Matt. 5:32).

Despite the provisions allowing divorce, God did not approve of it. "He hateth putting away"; He called it "violence" and "dealing treacherously" (Mal. 2:16).

B. Jesus' Teachings. In Jesus' day, there was much confusion about the grounds for divorce. The rabbis could not agree on what constituted the "uncleanness" of Deuteronomy 24:1. There were two opinions. Those following Rabbi Shammai felt adultery was the only grounds for divorce. Those who followed Rabbi Hillel accepted a number of reasons for divorce, including such things as poor cooking.

The Gospels record four statements by Jesus concerning divorce. In two of these, He allowed divorce in the case of adultery.

In Matthew 5:32, Jesus commented on the position of both the woman and her new husband: "Whosoever shall put away his wife, saving for the cause of fornication, causeth her to commit adultery: and whosoever shall marry her that is divorced committeth adultery." In another statement, Jesus spoke of the position of the man who divorced his wife: "Whosoever shall put away his wife, except it be for fornication, and shall marry another committeth adultery" (Matt. 19:9).

These two statements seem to allow divorce on the basis of unfaithfulness. However, in two other contexts, Jesus appears to give no sanction at all to divorce. In Mark 10:11–12 He said, "Whosoever shall put away his wife, and marry another, committeth adultery against her. And if a woman shall put away her husband, and be married to another, she committeth adultery." In Luke 16:18, Jesus makes a similar statement: "Whosoever putteth away his wife, and marrieth another, committeth adultery: and whosoever marrieth her that is put away from her husband committeth adultery."

How do Jesus' statements allowing divorce for infidelity harmonize with the statements that seem to forbid it entirely?

The first clue is found in Jesus' conversations with the Pharisees (Mark 10:5–9; Luke 16:18), in which He is making the point that divorce is contrary to God's plan for marriage. Even though the Law of Moses allowed divorce, it was only a provisional and reluctant allowance. Jesus put "teeth" into the Law by declaring that, even if the divorced couple had not been sexually unfaithful to each other, they would commit adultery in God's sight if they now married other partners.

30

MARRIAGE AND DIVORCE

MARRIAGE AND DIVORCE

Note that Jesus' statements belong in conversations with the Pharisees about the Mosaic Law, which they believed sanctioned divorce on grounds other than adultery (Deut. 24:1–4). Jesus' main point was that divorce should never be considered good, nor should it be taken lightly. So in His statement quoted in Luke 16:18, He did not even broach the subject of adultery. (Apparently, Mark 10:5–9 records only the words of Jesus that bore on the main point of the conversation.)

In the two passages from Matthew (one of them a fuller account of what is recorded in Mark 10), Jesus allows divorce for one reason only—"immorality," or illicit sexual intercourse. His thought is plainly that a person dissolves his marriage by creating a sexual union with someone other than the marriage partner. In that case, the decree of divorce simply reflects the fact that the marriage has already been broken. A man divorcing his wife for this cause does not "make her an adulteress," for she is one already. Divorce for unchastity usually frees the innocent partner to remarry without incurring the guilt of adultery (Matt. 19:9), but sometimes this is questioned.

Although Jesus allowed divorce for adultery, He did not require it. Just the reverse: Insisting that divorce disrupts God's plan for marriage, He opened the door to repentance, forgiveness, and healing in an unfaithful marriage, as He did in the case of other sin-wracked relationships. Reconciliation was Jesus' way of solving marriage troubles.

God had demonstrated this way of reconciliation and forgiveness when He sent Hosea to marry a harlot, then told him to buy her back after she had sold herself to another man. God forgave Israel in just this manner. When the people of Israel continued to worship idols, God sent them into captivity; but He redeemed them and brought them back again to Himself (Jer. 3:1–14; cf. Is. 54).

C. Paul's Teachings. In 1 Corinthians 7:15, Paul says that a Christian whose mate has deserted the marriage should be free to formalize the divorce: ". . . If the unbelieving depart, let him depart. A brother or a sister is not under bondage in such cases."[2] Yet Paul

ARAB WIFE. *Bedouin women of the Near East still perform many of the heavy physical chores that were done by women in biblical times. Here an Arab woman returns from the town market, carrying a basket on her head.*

encourages the believer to keep the marriage together, in hopes that the unbelieving partner might be saved and the children will not suffer. Apparently, Paul is thinking of people who were married before they were converted, because he directs believers never to marry unbelievers (1 Cor. 7:39; 2 Cor. 6:14–18).

Notice that this situation is quite different from the one Jesus addressed in the episode narrated by Matthew 19 and Mark 10. Jesus was speaking to the teachers of the Law—in fact, the misinterpreters of the Law—while Paul was speaking to Christians, many of them Gentiles who had never lived under the Law of Moses. Paul's readers had changed their way of life since they had married, and were trying to influence their spouses to do the same. They were bound to think, not only of their own welfare, but of their spouses' and children's as well. For these reasons, and for the fact that monogamy is God's plan, marriages should be kept together.

Paul sought to discourage divorce, despite its undoubted commonness in the Graeco-Roman culture of pagan Corinth. In so doing, he showed himself to be a true and loyal spokesman of the Law.

---

[2] Some hold that this phrase—"not under bondage"—means that a deserted Christian spouse may lawfully go from divorce to remarriage. But other scholars question this interpretation.

BIRTH AND INFANCY

Today, as in biblical times, the birth of a child is a momentous occasion. But today's parents may well have debated questions that the people living in ancient Israel would have found strange and startling. For example, the following questions would not have entered the minds of the Israelites: "Should we have children?" "If so, should we limit the number to one or two?" Or, "If we do have children, when should we begin?"

The ancient Israelites' attitude could be summed up like this: "We want children. We want them now. We will have as many children as we can because children are very important to us. In fact, we would rather be 'wealthy' with children than with money."

I. THE DESIRE FOR CHILDREN

II. THE CHILDLESS COUPLE

III. MISCARRIAGE

IV. THE "BLESSED EVENT"
    A. Pain in Childbearing
    B. The Delivery

V. NAMING THE CHILD

VI. RITUALS OF CHILDBIRTH
    A. Circumcising the Males
    B. Purifying the Mother
    C. Redeeming the Firstborn

I. The Desire for Children. The very first command of God was, "Be fruitful and multiply, and replenish the earth and subdue it" (Gen. 1:28). The couples in biblical times took this command seriously. As one of the Jewish sages declared, "If anyone does not engage in increase, it is as though he were to shed blood or to diminish God's image."

God's command in Genesis 1:28 was viewed as a great privilege and blessing. The desire to fulfill this command is the subject of many stories in the Bible. Who can forget the son promised to Abraham in his old age (Gen. 15:4; 18:14), or the prophecy that Isaiah delivered to King Ahaz: "Behold, a virgin shall conceive, and bear a son, and shall call his name Immanuel" (Is. 7:14)? And then there was the most miraculous announcement of all, made to the Virgin Mary: "And, behold, thou

shalt conceive in thy womb, and bring forth a son, and shalt call His name Jesus" (Luke 1:31).

Every Jewish couple wanted children. It was considered the main goal of marriage. The couple wanted to be remembered; only through offspring was this assured. To die without descendants might allow an entire family to be wiped out, forgotten forever. In 2 Samuel 14:4–7 we read about a widow with two sons. The sons got into a terrible argument and one killed the other. To make the guilty son pay for his crime, the rest of the relatives insisted that he should be executed. But the mother begged that his life be spared. She pleaded before the king: "And so they shall quench my coal which is left, and shall not leave to my husband neither name nor remainder upon the earth" (2 Sam. 14:7).

Even today many people in the Middle East consider life to be unnatural without children. When a couple's first son is born, the parents often begin to be known by the name of the

MYCENAEAN STATUETTE. *An old woman, a young woman, and a little boy are depicted in this ivory sculpture (thirteenth century B.C.). A close relationship between older and younger women was important in the ancient family structure, especially in the area of rearing children.*

BIRTH AND INFANCY

child. For example, if a son is born named "David," the father is called "Father of David" and the mother becomes "Mother of David."

The hope of having children was in the forefront of a couple's planning. Even before the wedding, their relatives discussed the children that would be born to the marriage. The family of the bride met to pronounce a blessing on the bride, declaring their wish that she might have many children. We need only look at Genesis 24:60 to get a picture of this scene. Here we see Rebekah getting ready for the long journey back to Canaan to become Isaac's wife. Before she leaves, the family gathers around her to pronounce a blessing on her. The spokesman for the family says, "Thou art our sister, be thou the mother of thousands of ten thousands, and let thy seed possess the gate of those which hate them." A similar blessing was given to Ruth before her wedding to Boaz (Ruth 4:11–12, RSV).

A Jewish couple hoped that each new child would be a son, but they gladly accepted either a boy or a girl. This was not the case in some of the surrounding cultures. Newborn girls were often left out in the open to die. Some Gentile parents even sold their baby girls into slavery.

Jewish couples knew that children were God's gift to the couple, "a heritage of the Lord" (Psa. 127:3). As the Psalmist declared, it is God the Lord "who dwelleth on high, who humbleth himself to behold the things that are in heaven, and in the earth: . . . He maketh the barren woman to keep house, and to be a joyful mother of children" (Ps. 113:5–6, 9).

The Bible uses many interesting figures of speech to describe a family. The mother is like a "fruitful vine" (Ps. 128:3). Children are like olive plants surrounding the parent tree (Ps. 128:3). Sons are like arrows in the hand of a warrior (Ps. 127:4).

II. The Childless Couple. The story of Rachel and Leah (Jacob's wives) illustrates how important it was for a woman to give her husband sons (Gen. 30:1–24).

Many Israelite couples were unable to bear children. Today we know that couples may be childless because of the husband's or wife's sterility; but the world of the Bible blamed only the wife for the problem. (For an exception, see Deut. 7:14).

Rachel's cry, "Give me children, or else I die!" (Gen. 30:1), expressed the feelings of every bride. And no doubt many a concerned husband agreed with Jacob's response: "Am I in God's stead, who hath withheld from thee the fruit of the womb?" (Gen. 30:2).

But barrenness was more than a physical or social problem. Deep religious meanings were attached to the problem as well. Moses promised the people that if they obeyed the Lord, blessing would follow: "Thou shalt be blessed above all people: there shall not be male or female barren among you, or among your cattle" (Deut. 7:14). So barrenness was thought to be a result of disobeying God. This idea is seen throughout Israel's history. For example, Abraham openly declared to Abimelech, king of Gerar, that Sarah was his sister. But God revealed to Abimelech in a dream that Sarah was married. When the king returned Sarah to her husband, Abraham asked God to reward him with children. "For the LORD had fast closed up all the wombs of the house of Abimelech, because of Sarah Abraham's wife" (Gen. 20:18). This passage of Scripture describes a barrenness that lasted for only a short period of time. However, the condition could be permanent (cf. Lev. 20:20–21). But whether temporary or permanent, barrenness was thought to be the curse of God.

It is hard for us to imagine how devastating these events would have been for the childless wife. She was spiritually disturbed, socially disgraced, and psychologically depressed. She was married to a husband who wanted a child to assure the continuation of his family line. That husband might continue to love her, but she felt that was small consolation (cf. 1 Sam. 1:6–8). It was in fact a great mercy, for a resentful husband could have made her life unbearable.

A barren couple spent a good deal of time examining their past failures to see if any sin had been unconfessed. Through tears the wife repented of all known sin. Then the husband offered a fitting sacrifice to cover any "unknown" sins (cf. Lev. 4:2). Childlessness became the main theme of the couple's prayers. Note how Isaac begged the Lord to let his wife bear a child (Gen. 25:21). Hannah sobbed before the Lord and promised that if God would give her a son, she would dedicate him to the Lord's service (1 Sam. 1:11).

When sin was ruled out as the cause of the problem, the wife was free to inquire about different kinds of remedies. Her relatives, friends, and neighbors might suggest that she try various love foods or potions that had proved to be helpful to them. One such food is mentioned in Scripture: Rachel requested

BIRTH AND INFANCY

MOTHER AND CHILD. *This crude clay figurine of a mother and her child, dating from about 3000 B.C., comes from Beth-Yerah in northern Israel. The family was a common subject of early Canaanite art.*

"mandrakes" from Leah, her sister (Gen. 30:14–16). Mandrakes were plants believed to produce fertility; they were often used as love charms. Rachel hoped that if she ate this food she would conceive. In rabbinic times women sought to overcome their barrenness by changing their diets. Apples and fish were thought to cause a person to become sexually powerful for procreation.

Modern excavations in Israel have produced many clay fertility figures. They were supposed to help a woman get pregnant by "sympathetic magic." Each figurine was molded to look like a pregnant woman. As the barren woman handled it and kept it near her, she hoped to take on the likeness of the pregnant figure.

Women also wore amulets to insure fertility. Jeremiah the prophet noted another common heathen practice: The women of Judah kneaded cakes, gave drink offerings, and burned incense to the "queen of heaven" to assure fertility (Jer. 44:17–19; cf. Jer. 7:18). The "queen" mentioned in this passage was probably Astarte (Ashtoreth), the Canaanite goddess of sexual love, maternity, and fertility. Of course, all of these superstitious practices were evil in God's sight.

If all the remedies were unsuccessful, the woman was considered to be permanently barren. At this point, the husband might take drastic measures. He might marry another wife or (at least in patriarchal times) use a slave to bear children under his name. This is why Sarah gave her servant Hagar to Abraham (Gen. 16:2) and Rachel asked her husband Jacob to have a child by her handmaid, Bilhah (Gen. 30:3).

Adoption was another way of overcoming the infertility of the wife. The childless couple could adopt an infant or even an adult as their own child. Eliezer of Damascus was a grown man, but Abraham told God that he was to be his heir (Gen. 15:2). The fifteenth-century B.C. tablets discovered at Nuzi show that Abraham was following a common practice for Semitic cultures, although we have few biblical references to it. Adoption solved many problems: The adopted son would care for the couple in their old age, provide them a proper burial, and inherit the family property. However, if the couple had a natural son after one had been adopted, he would become the rightful heir.

Note that after Bilhah's baby was born, it was placed in Rachel's lap. This act was the central part of the adoption ceremony. The baby was then adopted by Rachel as her own (cf. Gen. 30:3). Other references to adoption are in a foreign setting: Pharaoh's daughter adopted Moses (Ex. 2:10—Egypt) and Mordecai adopted Esther (Esth. 2:7, 15—Persia).

If a woman became pregnant after long years of waiting, then she was likely to be the happiest woman in the village. There would be great rejoicing when her baby was born. We dramatically see this in the account of Elisabeth, the mother of John the Baptist. Luke writes, "And her neighbors and her cousins heard how the Lord had showed great mercy upon her; and they rejoiced with her" (Luke 1:58). When Rachel finally conceived and bore a son, she exclaimed, "God has taken away my reproach" (Gen. 30:23). In the hope that this would not be an only child, she called his name *Joseph* meaning "He adds," saying, "The LORD shall add to me another son" (Gen. 30:24).

III. Miscarriage. Just as in our day, not all women in Bible times were able to carry the fetus long enough to give birth. Yet the Bible's references to miscarriage are of a general

BIRTH AND INFANCY

nature. Although the tragedy of miscarriage was probably whispered about in the women's circles, the people's sense of good taste probably kept them from discussing it openly.

Sensing he was about to lose family, health, and possessions, Job wished that he had been "as a hidden untimely birth . . . as infants which never saw light" (Job 3:16). The prophet Jeremiah bitterly professed that it would have been better if he had died in his mother's womb and had never been born (Jer. 20:17–18).

The women in Bible times would not have used modern medical terminology to describe miscarriage. They would have attempted to explain the miscarriage in other terms. They might trace the problem to a food that had been eaten or something that had been drunk. For example, during the days of the prophet Elisha, the women in Jericho were convinced that the water from the nearby spring was causing them to miscarry (2 Kin. 2:19–20).

Sometimes miscarriage was caused by accident. A pregnant woman might be jostled or kicked by an animal. She might get caught between two men who were fighting. According to Mosaic Law, the person who inflicted the blow was fined if the mother miscarried. If the miscarriage caused complications and the woman died as a result, the Law exacted the death penalty (Ex. 21:22–23).

IV. The "Blessed Event." The Hebrews knew something about the growth process, even without current medical data at their fingertips. The Psalmist poetically described God's role in the process when he wrote: "For thou hast possessed my reins: thou hast covered me in my mother's womb. I will praise thee; for I am fearfully and wonderfully made: marvelous are thy works; and that my soul knoweth right well. My substance was not hid from thee when I was made in secret, and curiously wrought in the lowest parts of the earth. Thine eyes did see my substance, yet being unperfect; and in thy book all my members were written, which in continuance were fashioned, when as yet there was none of them" (Ps. 139:13–16).

A. Pain in Childbirth. When Adam and Eve sinned against God in the Garden of Eden, part of God's curse on mankind was that women would experience pain in childbearing (Gen. 3:16). Birth pangs and the cries of a woman in labor were common in a Jewish village.

When the prophets sought to describe God's judgment, they often used the image of a woman in labor. For example, Isaiah said, "Like as a woman with child, that draweth near the time of her delivery, is in pain and crieth out in her pangs; so have we been in thy sight, O Lord. We have been with child, we have been in pain, we have as it were brought forth wind" (Is. 26:17–18). Similarly, Jeremiah said, "For I have heard a voice as of a woman in travail, and the anguish as of her that bringeth forth her first child, the voice of the daughter of Zion, that bewaileth herself, that spreadeth her hands, saying, Woe is me now!" (Jer. 4:31).

Birth pains were sometimes accompanied by complications. The Old Testament records several occasions where the mother's life was endangered. For example, the child born to Tamar was named *Pharez,* meaning "breach." The midwife noticed that the child had made an unusually large breach or tear in the mother (Gen. 38:28). Jacob's beloved wife Rachel

STATUETTE OF PREGNANT WOMAN.
Women who could not conceive often kept fertility figures that looked like pregnant women. These figures were supposed to help produce pregnancy by "sympathetic magic." This ivory statuette depicts a pregnant woman with an exaggerated navel (ca. 3500 B.C.).

BIRTH AND INFANCY

The Hebrew Midwife

A *midwife* is a woman who assists a mother in giving birth. In ancient times, a midwife's duties consisted of cutting the umbilical cord, washing the baby, rubbing it with salt, wrapping it in swaddling cloth, and then presenting it to the father. On one occasion a midwife suggested a name for the infant (Ruth 4:17). The skill and dedication of these women as they assisted at childbirth made theirs an honored profession. The midwife was often a friend and neighbor of the family, and sometimes one of the members of the household.

Midwifery is an ancient practice, first mentioned in the Bible during the time of Jacob (Gen. 35:17). The midwife was experienced in handling the difficulties associated with multiple births, as suggested when Tamar bore Pharez and Zarah (Gen. 38:27–30).

The Bible mentions two women who died during childbirth: Rachel as she bore Benjamin (Gen. 35:17), and Eli's daughter-in-law when Ichabod was born (1 Sam. 4:20–21). In each case the midwife's prompt announcement enabled the mother to name her son.

The two most famous midwives in the Bible are Shiphrah and Puah. They were apparently the chief midwives serving the Hebrew women during the time of slavery in Egypt. Josephus and others believe these were Egyptian women whom pharaoh trusted to carry out his orders to kill male babies of the Hebrews. But the midwives defied the pharaoh with the excuse that Hebrews were more healthy and vigorous during childbirth than Egyptians. (This implied that it would be difficult for the midwives to claim that the babies died in childbirth.)

died while giving birth to Benjamin, her second son (Gen. 35:18–20). Also, Phinehas's wife lost her life in childbirth, though the child was saved (1 Sam. 4:20). The birth of a child was painful and often difficult. The mother suffered without benefit of modern painkillers or sophisticated medical assistance.

B. The Delivery. In some ancient cultures the mother would lie down to deliver a child; in others, the mother would squat in a crouching position. Although Scripture says little about this phase of birth, there is one reference to a birth stool (Ex. 1:16), which implies that the mother did not lie down. Unfortunately, the birth stool is not described. But such stools are well known from other cultures of the Middle East.

The mother was usually assisted by a midwife, a woman specially experienced in helping at the time of childbirth. Sometimes these women were mothers themselves; they had learned by experience what kind of assistance was needed. Some midwives were professional people who performed this service as a full-time occupation.

The midwife served several functions. In addition to delivering the baby, she advised and encouraged the woman in labor. On several occasions, Scripture records the words of midwives as they gave assurance and comfort (cf. Gen. 35:17; 1 Sam. 4:20). If twins were born, the midwife had the responsibility of making the distinction between the first- and second-born. As Tamar gave birth to her twins, the midwife took a scarlet thread and tied it on the hand of the firstborn, telling the mother, "This came out first" (Gen. 38:28).

The mother did not always have the benefit of a midwife. If she had a premature baby or was outside her normal surroundings, she might face this ordeal alone. Scripture suggests that Mary, the mother of Jesus, was alone with her husband when she gave birth to Jesus (Luke 2:7).

In biblical times the infant did not begin life in a sterile hospital setting. It was usually born at home, where the conditions were unsanitary. The floors were probably dirt. Farm animals sometimes shared the same living quarters. The water used to cleanse the child was often polluted; the clothing used to wrap the baby had been washed in the same impure water. Disease-bearing flies and other insects quickly found the infant. The stable where Jesus was born may have been no worse than some of the homes in Bethlehem.

Considering the poor living conditions, infant mortality must have been very high. Demographic studies in Egypt and other ancient cultures show that the infant mortality rate was as high as 90 percent. The many infant burial sites uncovered at various archaeological sites in Israel tend to support this assumption. Also, it is important to remember that the redemption ceremony of the firstborn male was not performed until the child was 30 days old. If he had survived the first month, his chances of growing to adulthood were good.

BIRTH AND INFANCY

Immediately following the delivery, several tasks had to be performed. Until recently, a custom could be seen in Palestine that may reflect the procedure in biblical times. First, the umbilical cord was cut and tied. Then the midwife picked up the baby and rubbed salt, water, and oil over its entire body. The infant was wrapped tightly in clothes or clean rags for seven days, then the process was repeated. This continued until the child was 40 days old. The prophet Ezekiel mentioned salt, cleansing, and swathing bands in reference to the birth of a child (Ezek. 16:4). Luke noted that Mary "brought forth her firstborn son, and wrapped him in swaddling clothes" (Luke 2:7).

The midwife's duties were finished when she handed the baby to the mother to be nursed. It was considered both a privilege and a duty for the Jewish mother to breastfeed her infant. Infants were nursed at the breast for their first year or more. But sometimes a mother was not physically able to nurse her child. When that happened, a wet nurse was secured. This wet nurse was another nursing mother (usually unrelated to the baby) who fed the baby her own breast milk.

Scripture relates something about three of these nurses. Pharaoh's daughter found the infant Moses among the reeds on the River Nile's bank. One of her first orders was to get a woman from among the Hebrew women to nurse the child. Moses' wet nurse was his own natural mother (Ex. 2:7–8). The Bible describes a touching scene that shows the high esteem given these nurses: "But Deborah Rebekah's nurse died, and she was buried beneath Beth-el under an oak: and the name of it was called Allonbachuth [or "Oak of Weeping"]" (Gen. 35:8). Another wet nurse worked with the royal family in Jerusalem. She risked her life by hiding the young prince, who was to inherit the throne when he was old enough to become king (2 Kings 11:1–3).

The midwife announced to the mother that the child had been born and was alive and well. The family's neighbors would ask whether the newborn child was a boy. The birth announcement was simple. It said, "There is a man child conceived" (Job 3:3), or "A man child is born unto thee" (Jer. 20:15). This reminds us of the announcement of the Messiah: "Unto us a child is born, unto us a son is given" (Is. 9:6).

V. Naming the Child. Names were very important in the world of the Old Testament. Hebrew names usually had a meaning that could become an important part of the person's life. Jewish people believed that they must first know a person's name before they could know the person himself. We only have to look at the name *Jacob,* which means "heel grabber," to see the importance of a name. To know Jacob's name was to know his basic character! Therefore, the act of choosing a name for an infant was a serious responsibility.

After the Exile, the meaning of a name was of less importance. A child might be given the name *Daniel* not because of its meaning, but to honor the famous servant of God. But there were exceptions, even during this time. For example, the name *Jesus* is a Greek form of the Hebrew name *Joshua,* which means, "salvation of Yahweh."

The child's name was given by one or both parents. Scripture indicates that the mother usually named the infant. Just as today, other people took it upon themselves to assist in this important task. If Elisabeth's neighbors and kinsfolk had had their way, her son would have been named "Zechariah." But Elisabeth protested, insisting the boy would be called "John" (Luke 1:60–61).

Nowhere does Scripture specifically say when the child was to be named. In some instances, the mother named the child on the day of its birth (1 Sam. 4:21). By New Testament times, a baby boy was usually named on the eighth day, at the time of his circumcision (cf. Luke 1:59; 2:21).

Many of the names in the Bible are *theophoric.* This means that a divine name was joined with a noun or verb, producing a sentence for a name. For example, *Jonathan* means "The Lord has given." The name *Elijah* refers to the prophet's loyalty: "My God [is] the Lord." This was true of many heathen names as well. Many names of the Old Testament contain the word *Baal.* King Saul's grandson was called Meribbaal (1 Chr. 8:34).

Circumstances surrounding the infant's birth sometimes influenced the choice of the child's name. For example, if a woman went to the well for water and had her baby there, she might call the child *Beera,* "[born at the] well." A baby born during a winter rainstorm might be called *Barak,* "lightning." When the Philistines captured the ark of the covenant from Israel, a mother was giving birth to a child. The baby was called *Ichabod,* meaning "No glory." In the words of the mother, "The glory is departed from Israel" (1 Sam. 4:21).

BIRTH AND INFANCY

WOMAN GIVING BIRTH. *This clay statuette from eighth-century Cyprus depicts a woman giving birth. The center figure, in labor, sits upright on the knees of her companion while a midwife attends to her. Some scholars think that Genesis 30:3 refers to this means of giving birth.*

Animal names were commonly used for children. *Rachel* means "sheep." *Deborah* is the Hebrew word for "bee." *Caleb* means "dog," and *Achbor* has reference to a "mouse." We can only guess why these animal names were used. Perhaps they expressed some type of parental wish. A mother might have called her newborn girl *Deborah*, desiring that she would mature into an industrious and busy "bee."

Often the name referred to a personality trait that the parents hoped would describe the child as he reached adulthood. Names like *Shobek* ("Preeminent") and *Azzan* ("Strong") can best be understood in this light. Yet in other cases, the name seems to be the exact opposite of what the parents would want the child to be. *Gareb* suggests a "scabby" condition and *Nabal* means "fool." Some cultures believed that demons want to possess attractive children, so they gave infants names that sounded distasteful. Perhaps names like "Scabby" and "Fool" were given to ward off evil spirits.

Some names were more popular than others. For example, at least a dozen men mentioned in the Old Testament were called *Obadiah* ("servant of Yahweh"). In order to distinguish between many children having the same name, the name of the father might be attached to the son's name. The prophet Micaiah's expanded name was "Micaiah ben Im-

lah," or "Micaiah, the son of Imlah." The apostle Peter's name before Jesus changed it was "Simon Bar-Jona," or "Simon, the son of Jona." This custom also served to remind the son of his ancestors.

Another way to distinguish between people with the same name was to identify each person by the name of his hometown. David's father was called "Jesse the Bethlehemite" (1 Sam. 16:1). The giant that David killed was "Goliath of Gath" (1 Sam. 17:4). One of Jesus' loyal supporters was Mary Magdalene or "Mary of Magdala" (Matt. 28:1).

Sometimes the name of a person was changed after he reached adulthood. The individual himself might ask that his name be changed. Ruth's mother-in-law Naomi asked to be called *Mara* because, she said, "The Almighty has dealt very bitterly [*mara*] with me" (Ruth 1:20). Scripture does not say whether her neighbors took her seriously. The young Pharisee named Saul had been a Christian for years before he changed his name to Paul, after he converted an important official named Sergius Paulus on the island of Cyprus (Acts 13:1–13).

On other occasions, someone else gave a person a new name. An angel of the Lord gave Jacob his new name, *Israel* (Gen. 32:26). Jesus changed Simon's name to *Peter* (Matt. 16:17–18).

VI. Rituals of Childbirth. Ancient Jewish

BIRTH AND INFANCY

culture observed certain rituals in connection with childbirth. The Jewish child was born into a deeply religious community. The following rites had special religious meanings in the development of the child.

A. Circumcising the Males. Many cultures in the world today practice circumcision for hygienic reasons. Some primitive tribes perform the operation on infants and young boys, while others wait until the boys reach the age of puberty or are ready for marriage. These traditions have remained largely unchanged for centuries. Similar practices were common in the Near East in biblical times. Since the Philistines did not practice circumcision, the Jews ridiculed them (cf. 1 Sam. 17:26). In some cases, Israelites were circumcised as adults (Josh. 5:2–5).

Circumcision signified that the infant was being taken into the covenant community. The Lord said to Abraham, "He that is eight days old shall be circumcised among you . . . and my covenant shall be in your flesh for an everlasting covenant" (Gen. 17:12–13). Therefore, this practice was carefully observed. An uncircumcised person was considered to be heathen. When Greek culture came to Palestine two centuries before Christ, many Jews gave up their Jewish customs. Some men submitted to an operation that made them appear "uncircumcised" again. This was tantamount to apostasy.

The Law of Moses does not say who performed the operation on an infant. It is commonly assumed than an adult male cut off the infant's foreskin. On at least one occasion Scripture records that a woman did this; but the circumstances surrounding that particular event were unusual, for the husband seemed to be dying (cf. Ex. 4:25). The Hebrew word for "circumciser" and "father-in-law" is the same. This probably goes back to precovenant days when a young man was prepared for marriage by his future father-in-law.

At first, crude instruments such as flint knives were used for circumcision. Even after metal knives were developed, flint knives were used (Ex. 4:25 and Josh. 5:2). Slowly this tradition was given up, and by New Testament times flint knives had been replaced by metal ones.

The Jewish boy, as we saw, was to be circumcised on the eighth day. God first delivered this commandment to Abraham (Gen. 17:12) and repeated it to Moses in the wilderness (Lev. 12:3). In earlier periods, the Israelites did not always obey this command. But after the Exile, the law was carefully observed. This practice continued through New Testament times (cf. Luke 2:21) and remains a hallmark of Judaism today. When the eighth day fell on the Sabbath, the circumcision rite was still performed—in spite of many rules and regulations about suspending everyday activities that had been developed to keep the Sabbath holy.

Recent studies have confirmed that the safest time to perform a circumcision is on the

INFANT BURIAL. *The remains of an infant were buried in a pottery jar (ca. sixteenth century B.C.) at the site of the Canaanite city of Hazor. The infant mortality rate was extremely high among the early civilizations. Couples had as many children as possible, knowing that not all would survive their first years.*

eighth day of life. Vitamin K, which causes blood to coagulate, is not produced in sufficient amounts until the fifth to seventh day. On the eighth day the body contains 10 percent more prothrombin than normal; prothrombin is also important in the clotting of blood.

B. Purifying the Mother. Childbirth was thought to make a woman ceremonially unclean. That meant she was not allowed to participate in any religious observances or touch any sacred objects. Biblical scholars have long speculated about the reason for this. Did it emphasize that the child was born in sin? Did it demonstrate that sexual acts and the birth of a child were somehow sinful? Or was it designed as a protection for the mother, to keep her from feeling obligated to journey outside her home soon after the birth of a child? Scripture does not give us the reason. However, it is important to remember that anyone—man or woman—was considered ceremonially unclean if they had a discharge of blood, semen, or pus (cf. Lev. 12; 15). Other cultures in biblical times had similar taboos.

According to Leviticus 12, the mother was unclean for 40 days after the birth of a son; she was unclean twice as long if a girl was born. Again, no reason is given.

At the end of this period, after the mother had presented a sin offering and a burnt offering at the central place of worship, she was pronounced ceremonially clean. This tradition is unusual, because sacrifices were normally presented by the males. Also, the Law allowed the woman considerable freedom in choosing the type of animal she would sacrifice, depending upon what she could afford. A wealthy woman was expected to bring a lamb for a burnt offering; but if the family was extremely poor, even two turtledoves were al-

AKHNATON, NEFERTITI, AND CHILDREN. *This painted limestone plaque is a family portrait of Pharaoh Akhnaton (fourteenth century B.C.), his queen, and their three daughters. The queen sits holding two of the daughters, while the king hands an object to the eldest.*

lowed. It is interesting that Mary, the mother of Jesus, could afford only the pair of turtledoves at the time of her purification (Luke 2:22–24).

C. Redeeming the Firstborn. Since all firstborn were God's possession, it was necessary for the family to redeem, or buy back, that firstborn infant from God. The redemption price was five shekels of silver, given to the priests when the child was one month old (Num. 18:15–16).

31

BIRTH AND INFANCY

CHILDHOOD AND SCHOOLING. *A relief from a Roman sarcophagus shows the progress of a child from an infant nursing at his mother's breast (left) to a young boy ready for his first schooling (right).*

BIRTH AND INFANCY

Scripture doesn't tell us about the redemption ceremony itself, but by rabbinic times the following procedure had been established. The joyous occasion was celebrated on the 31st day of the child's life. (If the 31st day happened to fall on the Sabbath, the ceremony was delayed for one day.) The celebration took place in the infant's home, with a priest and other guests present. The rite began as the father presented the infant to the priest. The priest asked the father, "Do you wish to redeem the child or do you want to leave him with me?" The father then answered that he would redeem the child, and he handed the five silver coins to the priest. As the infant was returned, the father gave thanks to God. The priest responded by declaring to the father, "Your son is redeemed! Your son is redeemed! Your son is redeemed!" After the priest pronounced a blessing on the child, he joined the invited guests at a banquet table.

If a child was an orphan at birth, the duty of redeeming him fell to one of the child's male relatives.

The child had survived those first critical weeks. His parents had named him and performed all the essential rites. The mother would continue to nurse the child until he was two or three years old. At that time, he would be weaned and would cross the line that separated infancy from childhood.

CHILDHOOD AND ADOLESCENCE

The people of Bible times respected their elders as a source of wisdom and guidance. They heeded God's command to "rise up before the hoary head, and honor the face of the old man . . ." (Lev. 19:32). Most of the community decisions were made by the village elders, and often these decisions affected the entire clan (cf. Ex. 3:16–18). The title of *elder* indicated a person's age. The Israelites believed that a person gained wisdom as he aged and was therefore a valuable asset to the family (Deut. 32:7; Eccl. 25:6).

We should remember this view of the elderly as we begin to study the children of biblical days. In our society, children are often the center of attention and activity. In ancient times, children were also important—but they could not challenge their parents or elders, nor could they freely express their opinions. Parents were determined to "train up a child in the way he should go" (Prov. 22:6). Part of the "way" was teaching children respect for their parents and elders. Even young adults did not challenge statements made by their elders. For example, Elihu began his speech to Job and his friends in an apologetic tone, saying, "I am young, and ye are very old; wherefore I was afraid, and durst not show you mine opinion" (Job 32:6). Jesus' disciples reflected this attitude when they attempted to shield Jesus from the children. But Jesus told them to "forbid them not, for of such is the kingdom of God" (Luke 18:16).

I. PHYSICAL APPEARANCE AND GROWTH
   A. Growth Stages
   B. Size
   C. Color of Skin and Hair
   D. Children with Physical Problems

II. EDUCATION
   A. The Teaching Model
   B. Parental Responsibility
   C. Synagogue Schools
   D. Vocational Training

III. LEISURE ACTIVITIES
   A. Toys
   B. Games

IV. GOING UP TO JERUSALEM
V. THE EVENING CIRCLE

I. Physical Appearance and Growth. The Gospels give little information about the physical appearance of Jesus, either as an adult or as a child. But the Bible gives sketchy descriptions of some individuals. For example, David is described as being red-haired or ". . . ruddy, and withal of a beautiful countenance, and goodly to look to" (1 Sam. 16:12). However, we do not know what type of person the Israelites considered to be handsome.

Some paintings and sculptures dating back to the time of the Old Testament show how the Israelites might have looked. The problem here is that we cannot determine which features were common and which were used only in the artwork. Still, they add one more piece to the puzzle.

Archaeological excavations give some evidence of the physical characteristics of the Israelites. We'll look at some of these clues below.

A. Growth Stages. The Hebrews used several words to describe stages of a child's growth. A very young child was called a "suckling," which meant that he was still nursing. Then he was referred to as a "weaned one"; this change was an important milestone in a child's life. When the child matured a bit more, the Hebrews said he was a "toddler."

Another plateau was the reaching of puberty. This stage was called *elem* or *almah,* meaning a young person, but sexually mature.

Five stages of human life are outlined in Leviticus 27:1–8; three of these fit into the age of childhood or adolescence. The first stage was from birth until 30 days; the second stage was from one month to five years; and the third from five years until the age of 20. The last two stages were adulthood and old age.

B. Size. The Israelites considered themselves to be smaller than the Canaanites, who inhabited the Promised Land before them. When spies returned from scouting out the

CHILDHOOD AND ADOLESCENCE

GAME BOARD. *Discovered in a grave at Ur, this game board (ca. twenty-fifth century B.C.) was hollowed out to contain the 14 round playing pieces. The board is inlaid with shell, bone, red limestone, and strips of lapis lazuli set in bitumen.*

Promised Land, they reported that the land was filled with giants. They said, "The people is greater and taller than we; the cities are great and walled up to heaven; and moreover we have seen the sons of the Anakim there" (Deut. 1:28). The people referred to as "the Anakim" were legendary descendants of a tribe of giants. But archaeologists have found evidence that the Canaanites were of average size and build. It appears that the spies' report was based on fear rather than fact (Deut. 1:28; Num. 13:28).

By studying the skeletons of adult Israelites, scientists have found that their average size was from 160 to 170 cm. (63 to 67 in.). Their small size was due in part to a poor diet. Drought and locust plagues reduced their crop production drastically. (*See* "Agriculture.") This caused frequent famines among the people (Amos 4:6–10).

In spite of these hardships, there were some overweight people. Eglon, King of Moab, is described as "a very fat man" (Judg. 3:17). But food was often scarce, so that while a rich man could buy more than he needed, a poor man would suffer near-starvation. Scripture condemns the callous selfishness of the rich (cf. Luke 12:13–21), as it does gluttony. For example, God judged Eli and his sons because

they fattened themselves on the choicest parts of the offerings (1 Sam. 2:29).

Though the Israelites may have considered themselves smaller and thinner than their contemporaries, they were not weaker. Everyone worked hard, even the girls. Every day young women filled their water jugs at the local well and carried them home on their heads. When filled with water, each jug weighed as much as 22 kg. (50 lb.). Preparing grain for food was another strenuous and backbreaking task. An ideal wife of that day was one with strong arms (Prov. 31:17).

Life demanded hard work on the part of the men; such work was part of a young boy's growing up too (1 Sam. 16:11). Both men and boys engaged in all sorts of physical labor. For example, they carried sick sheep or goats back to the village from faraway fields. When a house was to be built, they carried the stone with their hands. Most of their traveling was done on foot. All of this contributed to making the Israelites a strong and resilient people.

Sometimes a young man would demonstrate his strength and courage by attacking and killing a wild animal. David told Saul, "Thy servant kept his father's sheep, and there came a lion, and a bear, and took a lamb out of the flock: and I went after him, and smote him,

CHILDHOOD AND ADOLESCENCE

and delivered it out of his mouth; and when he arose against me, I caught him by his beard, and smote him, and slew him. Thy servant slew both the lion and the bear" (1 Sam. 17:34–36). Similar events are recorded in other places in the Bible (e.g., 2 Sam. 23:20).

In every culture there are exceptions to the norm. The Bible says of Saul, "There was not among the children of Israel a godlier person than he: from his shoulders and upward he was higher than any of the people" (1 Sam. 9:2). Goliath was also an exceptionally large man. In 1 Samuel 17:4, we read that his height was six cubits and a span. A *cubit* was the distance from the elbow to the tip of the middle finger, or roughly 45 cm. (18 in.). That would have made Goliath over 270 cm. (9 ft.) tall. At the other end of the scale was Zaccheus, who had to climb a sycamore tree to see over the heads of the crowd (Luke 19:3–4).

C. Color of Skin and Hair. The name *Esau* means "reddish-brown." The descendants of Esau were the reddish-brown people called the Edomites. By contrast, the skin of the Israelites was lighter and more yellowish in color. In our day, Israelis seem to be dark-skinned people because of their constant exposure to the sun.

Young Israelite girls considered light skin to be beautiful, and they avoided the sun's rays as much as possible. We read in the Song of Solomon that the bride-to-be begged her handmaidens to "look not upon me, because I am black, because the sun has looked upon me" (Song 1:6). She was embarrassed that her skin was not as light as the skin of the other girls.

The ancient Israelite youth had dark brown or black hair. Song of Solomon 5:11 describes it as "black as a raven." In the same song, a youth's hair is likened to a flock of goats moving down a hillside (Song 4:1; 6:5); the native goat was black.

Archaeologists have found headbands at various sites in Israel dating from Old Testament times. These relics indicate that men as well as women wore their hair long. Absalom (2 Sam. 14:26) and Samson (Judg. 16:16–19) both had long hair.

Canaanite parents often shaved the heads of their young sons, leaving a lock of hair on top (Lev. 19:27). This was an Egyptian custom that the Israelites were not allowed to follow. The apostle Paul urged women not to shave their heads and men not to wear long hair

CIRCUMCISION. *This relief at Sakkarah depicts the Egyptian rite of circumcision. To the left, an assistant holds the boy's hands while the circumcisor performs the operation with a rounded object, perhaps a flint knife (cf. Exod. 4:25). To the right, the patient braces himself by placing his hand on the head of the circumcisor. Unlike Egyptians, the Hebrews circumcised male infants at the age of eight days, to signify the child's acceptance into the covenant community.*

(1 Cor. 11:14–15); short hair implied that a woman was a prostitute. Hair styles were often a cultural matter; what one generation accepted, another did not. (*See* "Clothing and Cosmetics.")

D. Children with Physical Problems. Birth defects occurred in biblical times just as they do today. A list of some of the more common defects is found in the Pentateuch (Lev. 21:18–21). Apparently, a person with a birth defect was not allowed to perform any priestly duties. Such a person easily became the object of cruel jokes and teasing. This was strictly forbidden by God, who said, "Thou shalt not curse the deaf, nor put a stumblingblock before the blind, but shalt fear thy God: I am the LORD" (Lev. 19:14; cf. Deut. 27:18).

II. Education. The Israelites provided education for their children. It included religious instruction as well as training in practical skills they would need for the workaday world. They were an agricultural people, so

32

CHILDHOOD AND ADOLESCENCE

Greek and Roman Schools

The ancient Romans and Greeks had a sophisticated system of schools. The schools were not compulsory, nor were they run by the government. Still, schooling was widespread.

In the Greek system, boys were sent to school at age six. The school was owned and operated by the teacher. Apparently the Greeks did not have boarding schools.

The Greeks did not teach foreign languages. (They considered their language to be supreme!) Their education had three main divisions: music, gymnastics, writing. All Greek children were taught to play the lyre. Greek girls were taught to read and write by their mothers, who also taught them to weave, dance, and play a musical instrument. Oddly, the few well-educated Greek women were usually prostitutes for the wealthy.

Greek lecturers earned a living by teaching in school halls and even on the streets. Some of these wandering teachers—Socrates, for example—became famous. Greek boys could attend school until they were 16. After that, they were expected to train in sports.

Unlike the Greeks, the Romans used other nationalities to teach their children. Often a Greek nurse started a child's training. Boys and girls entered formal school at age seven. At 13, if they had done well, children went to high school; there were 20 such schools in Rome in A.D. 30. Even Roman secondary education was taught in Greek, and the teachers were generally Greek slaves or freedmen. Like the Greeks, the Romans had more advanced teachers who traveled from school to school.

---

only the religious leaders were taught to read and write.

"Jesus increased in wisdom . . . and in favor with God and man" (Luke 2:52). This verse captures the goal of Jewish education. It strove to impart not only knowledge but wisdom, centered around one's relationship with God.

In ancient Israel, education was an informal process. The parents did most or all of the training. There were no classrooms or structured curricula. By New Testament times, the Jews had adopted a more formal approach to education. They set aside classrooms and qualified teachers to instruct all the children in a village.

A. The Teaching Model. In order to understand the function of the Jewish teacher, we must first consider the divine Teacher after whom he modeled himself. Scripture refers to God as the Teacher who tells His students, "This is the way, walk ye in it" (Isa. 30:20–21). God knows and understands the needs of His students; He is fully versed in His subject; He is the perfect and infallible example for His students. The Jewish teacher had his pattern before him as he went to his work.

We know that God used men to teach the Law to the nation of Israel. These men were not only teachers but examples of godliness—men like Moses, the priests, and prophets such as Elijah. Their students were the adults of the nation of Israel, who were then responsible to pass the knowledge on to their children.

B. Parental Responsibility. The religious education of children was the parents' responsibility (Deut. 11:19; 32:46). No exceptions were made for parents who felt they were too busy to teach.

Even when children came of age and married, the parents' responsibility did not end; they also had an important part in educating the grandchildren (Deut. 4:9). In fact, they often lived in the same house.

The Israelite father was ultimately responsible for the education of the children; but mothers also played a crucial role, especially until a child reached the age of five. During those formative years she was expected to shape the future of her sons and daughters.

When a boy became old enough to work with his father, the father became his principal teacher, even though the mother continued to share in the teaching responsibility (cf. Prov. 1:8–9; 6:20). The mother carried the main responsibility for her daughters, teaching them skills they would need to become in time good wives and mothers.

If someone other than the father had to assume the responsibility of teaching a boy, then that person was considered his "father." In later generations, a person who was specifically assigned to the task of teaching was called "father," and he addressed his pupils as "my sons."

The Jewish parents' major concern was that their children come to know the living God. In Hebrew, the verb "to know" means *to be intimately involved* with a person; Scripture states

CHILDHOOD AND ADOLESCENCE

GIRLS PLAYING. *Young girls dance and play games on this relief (ca. 2200 B.C.) from an Egyptian tomb at Sakkarah. Four of the girls hold mirrors.*

that the reverence or "the fear of the Lord is the beginning of wisdom: and the knowledge of the Holy is understanding" (Prov. 9:10). Godly parents helped their children develop this kind of knowledge about God.

From earliest childhood, a youth learned the history of Israel. In early childhood, he probably memorized a creedal statement and recited it at least once a year, at the offering of the firstfruits. The creed reduced the story of Israel's history to a simple form that was easy to memorize:

A wandering Aramean was my father; and he went down into Egypt and sojourned there, few in number; and there he became a nation, great, mighty, and populous. And the Egyptians treated us harshly, and afflicted us, and laid upon us hard bondage. Then we cried to the Lord the God of our fathers, and the Lord heard our voice, and saw our affliction, our toil, and our oppression; and the Lord brought us out of Egypt with a mighty hand and an outstretched arm, with great terror, with signs and wonders; and he brought us into this place and gave us this land, a land flowing with milk and honey. And behold, now I bring the first of the fruit of the ground, which thou, O Lord, hast given me (Deut. 26:5–10, RSV).

Thus the children learned that the nation of Israel had entered into a covenant with God. This covenant placed certain restrictions on them. They were not free to seek their own desires, but they had a responsibility to God because He had redeemed them. They were diligently taught the guidelines God gave them.

Jesus summarized the essence and intention of these laws when He declared, "Thou shalt love the Lord thy God with all thy heart, and with all thy soul, and with all thy mind. This is the first and great commandment. And the second is like unto it, Thou shalt love thy neighbor as thyself. On these two commandments hang all the law and the prophets" (Matt. 22:37–40).

There were probably no formal schools in Old Testament times. Most learning took place amid everyday life. As opportunities arose throughout the day, parents would instruct their children.

A child might ask, "Father, why are those stones piled there? What do they mean?" (cf. Josh. 4:21). A father would then take time to explain the religious background and significance of the monument.

The education of a child took a lifetime to complete. The Jewish family had the Lord's instructions, "These words, which I command you this day, shall be in thine heart: and thou shalt teach them diligently unto thy children" (Deut. 6:6–7). The phrase "to teach diligently" comes from a Hebrew word that usually refers to sharpening a tool or whetting a knife. What the whetstone is to the knife blade, so training is to the child. Education prepared children to become useful and productive members of society.

C. Synagogue Schools. We are not sure when synagogue schools were first established. Some believe the practice dates back to the Exile in Babylon. (*See* "Jews in New Testament Times.") Whenever it began, by New Testament times the synagogue school was a vital part of Jewish life.

Each Sabbath, Jews faithfully gathered at

32

CHILDHOOD AND ADOLESCENCE

CHILDHOOD AND ADOLESCENCE

the synagogue to hear their rabbi read the Scriptures and explain the Law. The synagogue sponsored special classes apart from the regular times of worship. During the week, boys came to these classes to study the Scriptures under qualified teachers. These classes supplemented the religious education the boys were receiving from their parents.

Jewish fathers were much more concerned with the character of a teacher than with his teaching ability. Naturally, they required him to be competent in his profession; but they were more concerned that he be a proper example to the children. Jewish writings from the New Testament era give us a partial list of the ideal characteristics of a teacher: He must not be lazy. He must have an even temper. He must never show partiality. He must never become impatient. He must never compromise his dignity by jesting. He must never discour-

AMENHOTEP III AND FAMILY. *This colossal family group 7 m. (23 ft.) in height depicts Pharaoh Amenhotep III (ca. 1450 B.C.) in ceremonial beard and headdress. Queen Tiy wears a heavy wig and a crown. Their three daughters are represented by the three small figures along the front of the throne seat. This indicates the insignificant role of children in Egyptian society.*

age the child. He must show sin to be repulsive. He must punish all wrongdoing. He must fulfill all his promises.

Besides the reading of the Scriptures, Jewish boys were also taught manners, music, warfare, and other practical knowledge. We read how young David was said to be "cunning in playing [i.e., a musician], and a mighty valiant man, and a man of valor, a man of war, and prudent in matters, and a comely person" (1 Sam. 16:18). We can tell from this account that David had a well-rounded education, as did most of the Jewish boys.

In New Testament times, the Jewish schools required each student to master several key passages of Scripture. Of primary importance was the *Shema,* the basic creedal statement of the Jews (Deut. 6:4–5). Next in importance was Deuteronomy 11:13–21 and Numbers 15:37–41. The student was also required to learn the *Hallel* ("praise") Psalms (Ps. 113—118), as well as the Creation story (Gen. 1—5) and the sacrificial laws (Lev. 1—8). If a child was unusually bright, he examined more of the book of Leviticus.

Only the boys received formal training outside the home. They began by meeting in the teacher's house, where they read from scrolls containing small portions from the Scriptures, such as the *Shema.* This was the "elementary school" of the day.

When the boys were old enough to learn the sabbatical lessons, they met at the "house of the Book"—the synagogue. Here they entered the room where the Torah scrolls were kept and prepared their lessons under the supervision of the *Hazzan,* the keeper of the scrolls.

Later they were allowed to discuss questions of the Law with the Pharisaic teachers. These discussions constituted the "secondary" level of Jewish education.

In New Testament times, school was in session year-round. During the hot summer months the boys went to school no more than four hours a day. If it was an unusually hot day, school might be dismissed altogether. The class hours were before 10:00 A.M. and after 3:00 P.M. A five-hour break occurred during the hottest part of the day.

The classroom contained a small raised platform where the teacher sat cross-legged. Before him on a low rack were scrolls containing selected Old Testament passages. There were no textbooks. The students sat on the ground at the teacher's feet (Acts 22:3).

Classes were not graded by age; all the stu-

CHILDHOOD AND ADOLESCENCE

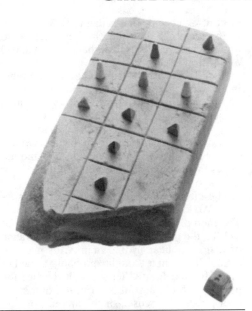

GAME FROM TELL BEIT MIRSIM. *Canaanite children played a game on a board with 10 playing pieces—five in the form of cones and five triangular pyramids, all of blue earthenware. An ivory teetotum, pierced on four sides with holes, completes the set.*

sluggard? When wilt thou arise out of thy sleep? Yet a little sleep, a little slumber, a little folding of the hands to sleep: so shall thy poverty come as one that traveleth, and thy want as an armed man." To survive, a family had to work hard.

The Israelites believed that an undisciplined life would not prepare a youth to cope with what faced him. They taught their children the meaning of responsibility early in life, so when the youngsters reached adulthood they were able to meet its demands with confidence. If a son grew up irresponsibly, he not only embarrassed himself but brought shame to his family. One of the sages noted, "The rod and reproof give wisdom: but a child left to himself bringeth his mother to shame" (Prov. 29:15).

Since Israel was an agricultural society, much of the practical wisdom handed down from father to son was about farming. This included lessons on preparing the soil for planting and cultivating the various crops, as well as harvesting and storing the bounty. Sons learned these skills by working alongside their fathers throughout their youth. Even when the Jewish people began to seek employment other than farming, they were still "people of the land." (*See* "Agriculture.")

It was also the father's responsibility to teach his sons a trade or craft. For example, if the father was a potter, he taught that skill to his sons. One of the Jewish sages affirmed that "he who does not teach his son a useful trade is bringing him up to be a thief."

While the boys were learning these skills, the girls learned baking, spinning, and weaving under the watchful eyes of their mothers (Ex. 35:25–26; 2 Sam. 13:8). If there were no sons in the family, daughters might be required to learn the father's work (Gen. 29:6; Ex. 2:16).

III. Leisure Activities. Young people in biblical times did not have the "time on their hands" that youths have today. But they still had time for recreation and leisure.

A. Toys. Young people had few toys. But terra cotta toys have been found in many excavations. In Egypt, archaeologists have found toys such as carts and wagons in the royal tombs. Israelite girls played with simple clay dolls clothed with rags.

On one occasion, the prophet Isaiah likened God to a person hurling a ball (Is. 22:18). This is the only biblical reference to such a toy. Unfortunately, the prophet described

dents studied together in the same room. For this reason, their instruction had to be individualized. The teacher copied down a verse for the younger students and they recited it aloud until they mastered it. Meanwhile the teacher helped the older boys read a passage from Leviticus. The noise probably would have been very distracting for us, but the Israelite boys soon became accustomed to it. The sages believed that if a verse were not repeated aloud, it would soon be forgotten.

D. Vocational Training. The boys must have been excited to follow their fathers into the fields to work or into the marketplace to buy and sell. They carefully observed their fathers planting, pruning, and harvesting. Sometimes they were allowed to attempt a difficult task, which added to the excitement. A new world had opened to a boy when he was old enough to go with his father.

But the work was monotonous and tiring. As the boy grew older, his responsibilities grew also. Before long, a son was expected to do a full day's work without stopping, other than to rest briefly.

Men encouraged their sons to work hard by admonishing them with Scripture. Proverbs 6:9–11 said, "How long wilt thou sleep, O

32

CHILDHOOD AND ADOLESCENCE

neither the ball nor the game that was played with it.

B. Games. The prophet Zechariah foretold times of peace for Israel by saying, ". . . The streets of the city shall be full of boys and girls playing . . ." (Zech. 8:5). Scripture does not describe the games children might have played, but it does mention their dancing and singing (cf. Job 21:11–12). Jesus said the people of His generation were "like unto children sitting in the market, and calling unto their fellows, And saying, We have piped unto you, and ye have not danced; we have mourned unto you, and ye have not lamented" (Matt. 11:16–17).

Drawings on the walls of ancient Egyptian tombs show children wrestling and playing games such as tug-of-war. No doubt Hebrew boys also played these sports. Footraces and hopscotch were also games children enjoyed.

Children of biblical times loved to explore the caves and crevices that surrounded their world. Shepherd boys often sneaked off to explore or trap wild animals, or practice using a sling or throwing a spear. Even in play, boys were preparing themselves for manhood.

IV. Going up to Jerusalem. The Lord commanded all of the adult Hebrew males to congregate regularly at a central place of worship (Ex. 23:14–17; Deut. 16:16–17). The purpose was primarily religious, but the children considered the trip to be a kind of vacation, full of adventure and excitement. They counted it a privilege to go. Jerusalem was full of new sights and sounds that they were eager to experience. Often the children became so anxious to reach Jerusalem that they ran ahead of the slower adults.

V. The Evening Circle. The evening meal in a Jewish village was eaten about two hours before sundown. Afterward, all of the men gathered in an open-air meeting place, where they sat or lay in a large circle with the older or more respected men in the center. On the outer edges the older boys could stand and listen as the men related the events of that day or long ago.

The circle served as the evening "newspaper." We know what sort of things took place. The men discussed such things as the birth of a child, the illness of a villager, the appearance of a lion or bear in the vicinity, or national events. Then their thoughts probably turned to plans for the future. They might discuss the prospect of a bountiful harvest, the first signs of a plague of locusts, or the amount of rain that had fallen.

We can imagine that as the young men walked home, each reflected on what he had heard. Some stored important information they wanted to remember. Others found their hearts strangely stirred by the tales of daring men of old. Others had simply been entertained by the gossip and proverbs they had heard. But collectively their stock of wisdom and insight had increased, and so their lives had been enriched.

DISEASES AND HEALING

Disease and sickness have plagued man since God cast Adam and Eve out of the Garden of Eden (cf. Gen. 2:19). The Hebrews believed that illness was caused by sin in the individual, which God had to punish (Gen. 12:17; Prov. 23:29–32), the sin of a person's parents (2 Sam. 12:15), or seduction by Satan (Matt. 9:34; Luke 13:16). However, some scriptures show that there is not always such a simple explanation for disease (cf. Job 34:19–20).

Even in Old Testament times, the Hebrews associated healing with God. For example, Malachi spoke of the Sun of Righteousness rising with healing in his wings (Mal. 4:2), and David praised God as the One "that healeth all thy diseases" (Ps. 103:3).

I. TYPES OF DISEASES, AILMENTS, AND MEDICAL PROBLEMS

A. Aphasia
B. Apoplexy
C. Blains
D. Blemishes
E. Blindness and Hearing Loss
F. Boils
G. Cancer
H. Consumption, or Tuberculosis
I. Dysentery
J. Edema ("Dropsy")
K. Endocrine Disturbances
L. Epilepsy
M. Female Disorders
N. Fevers
O. Gangrene
P. Gout
Q. Lameness
R. Leprosy
S. Malaria
T. Mental and Nervous Disorders
U. Palsy
V. Plague
W. Polio
X. Skin Disorders
Y. Smallpox
Z. Sunstroke
AA. Syncope
BB. Venereal Disease
CC. Worms

II. THE USE OF MEDICINE

III. PHYSICIANS AND THEIR WORK

IV. RITUAL CURES AND MIRACULOUS HEALINGS

I. Types of Diseases, Ailments, and Medical Problems. Here we will review some of the diseases and related problems of Bible times. An understanding of these problems is important for every Bible student, because they often affected the course of Israel's history, and Jesus' ministry emphasized the healing of the sick.

A. Aphasia. This is the temporary loss of speech, usually caused by a brain lesion but sometimes attributed to an emotional upset. This happened to the prophet Ezekiel (Ezek. 33:22). When an angel told Zechariah that he was going to be the father of John the Baptist, the old man came out of the temple and could not speak (Luke 1:22).

B. Apoplexy. This term refers to a rupture or obstruction of a brain artery, causing a stroke. When Abigail told Nabal of his insult to David and its dire consequences, Nabal's "heart died within him, and he became like a stone"; 10 days later he died (1 Sam. 25:37–38). These symptoms suggest that he suffered an attack of apoplexy. The same fate may have befallen Uzzah, who touched the ark of the covenant (2 Sam. 6:7), as well as Ananias and Sapphira (Acts 5:5, 9–10).

C. Blains. This term from the KJV probably refers to anthrax, a disease that can be transmitted to humans by cattle, sheep, goats, and horses. The disease is caused by a rod-shaped bacterium that forms spores. These spores, in turn, can infect humans, who develop a boil-like lesion with a *pustule* (blain). In the infective stage, the blain is called a *malignant pustule*. Blains are mentioned only once in the Bible (Ex. 9:9–10). God inflicted them on the Egyptians when the pharaoh refused to let the Hebrews go to the Promised Land.

D. Blemishes. This general term refers to any bodily defect such as blindness, lameness, a broken bone, extra fingers or toes (*polydactylism*), a humped back and so on. A person with blemishes could not offer sacrifices to God (Lev. 21:16–24), nor was he permitted to go beyond the veil of the temple or come near the altar, for this would defile the sanctuary. Imperfect animals could not be used for sacrifices (Ex. 12:5).

DISEASES AND HEALING

CHRIST HEALING A BLIND MAN. *In this detail from the front of a Roman sarcophagus (ca. A.D. 330), Christ touches the eyes of a blind man with a paste of spittle before sending him to the Pool of Siloam (John 9). The Hebrews believed that God would curse those who made the blind wander out of their way (Deut. 27:18).*

E. Blindness and Hearing Loss. Three types of blindness are mentioned in Scripture: sudden blindness caused by flies and aggravated by dirt, dust, and glare; the gradual blindness caused by old age; and chronic blindness. Paul suffered temporary blindness on the road to Damascus (Acts 9:8). Scripture often refers to old persons whose eyes "grew dim" (cf. Gen. 27:1; 48:10; 1 Sam. 4:15). But the Bible more often refers to chronic blindness.

The Israelites had compassion for the blind. In fact, God placed a curse upon those who made the blind wander out of their way (Deut. 27:18). Jesus ministered to many people who were blind. He said, "[God] hath anointed me to preach the gospel to the poor; he has sent me to heal the broken-hearted, to preach deliverance to the captives, and recovering of sight to the blind" (Luke 4:18). Jesus healed a man born blind (John 9:1–41); a blind man whose healing was gradual (Mark 8:24); two blind men sitting by the wayside (Matt. 20:30–34); and a great number of others (Mark 10:46–52; Luke 7:21).

Blindness was often understood to be a punishment for evil-doing. We find examples of this at Sodom (Gen. 19:11); in the Syrian army (2 Kin. 6:18); and in the case of Elymas at Paphos (Acts 13:6–11).

The New Testament occasionally refers to persons who had lost the ability to speak (cf. Matt. 9:32; 15:30; Luke 11:14). This often was the result of hearing loss.

F. Boils. This term refers to any inflamed ulcers on the skin, such as those caused by a staph infection. They may have been confused with "blains" or anthrax. Boils ("shechin" in Hebrew) are first mentioned in Exodus 9:9, when the pharaoh refused to let the Israelites leave Egypt, and boils broke out upon the people. Satan was permitted to afflict Job with boils from the top of his head to the tip of his toes (Job 2:7). King Hezekiah also was afflicted with boils (2 Kin. 20:7), which Isaiah cured by applying a poultice of figs. A fresh fig poultice has a drawing effect. Before the advent of antibiotics, this type of treatment for boils was common.

G. Cancer. Hezekiah was very sick and the Lord told him to prepare to die (2 Kin. 20:1). The Lord inflicted an incurable disease upon Jehoram, and after two years his bowels fell out (2 Chr. 21:18–19). Bible scholars believed these men may have suffered some type of cancer, though chronic dysentery would also have produced Jehoram's symptoms. However, the Bible does not refer to the cancer by name because the disease had not been identified in biblical times.

H. Consumption, or Tuberculosis. Moses warned the rebellious Israelites, "The LORD shall smite thee with a consumption, and with a fever, and with an inflammation and with an extreme burning . . ." (Deut. 28:22). The KJV uses the word *consumption* to refer to tuberculosis, a consumptive infection of the lungs.

I. Dysentery. This is a disease that in its advanced stage, rots the bowels (2 Chr. 21:15–19). The fibrine separates from the inner coating of the intestines and is expelled. The New Testament refers to a severe form of dysentery as the "bloody flux." The father

DISEASES AND HEALING

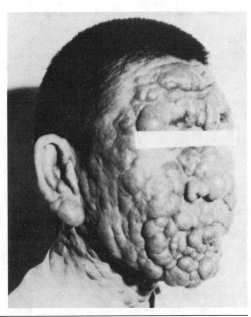

VICTIM OF BOILS. *Certain types of boils (such as the Baghdad boil, produced by a parasite transmitted by the sandfly) are common afflictions among the inhabitants of the Middle East. Job suffered a severe case of boils (Job 2:7–8), possibly similar to the Baghdad boil pictured here.*

of a Christian named Publius lay sick with the bloody flux (Acts 28:8). Paul came in and prayed for him and the man was healed.

J. Edema ("Dropsy"). This describes an abnormal accumulation of serous fluid in the body's connective tissue or in a serous cavity and is a symptom. The accumulation causes swelling. Jesus met at least one victim of edema in a certain Pharisee's house. Asked by Jesus if he thought it lawful to heal on the Sabbath, the Pharisee declined to answer. Jesus thereupon healed the sufferer (Luke 14:1–4).

K. Endocrine Disturbances. The Law of Moses did not permit a dwarfed person to enter the congregation of God's people (Lev. 21:20). Modern science has shown that dwarfism is caused by disturbances in the endocrine glands.

The Bible also mentions a number of giants, such as Goliath (1 Sam. 17:4). True giantism is caused by excessive secretions of the pituitary gland. However, many tall persons inherit their tallness from their forebears.

L. Epilepsy. This is a disorder marked by erratic electrical discharges of the central nervous system and manifested by convulsive attacks. A certain man brought his epileptic son

to Jesus for help (Mark 9:17–29). The KJV says that the boy had a "dumb spirit." Jesus healed him.

An ancient theory held that epilepsy was caused by the moon; people referred to epileptics as being "moonstruck." Psalm 121:6 may reflect this idea when it says, "The sun shall not smite thee by day, nor the moon by night."

M. Female Disorders. According to the Mosaic Law, a woman suffering from menstrual disorders was to be considered unclean (Lev. 15:25). One such woman who had suffered for 12 years (Luke 8:43–48) touched the hem of Jesus' garment and, because of her great faith, was healed immediately.

N. Fevers. The KJV uses the word *ague* to describe a burning fever. Moses warned the rebellious Israelites that "I will ever appoint over you terror, panic, consumption and the burning ague that shall consume the eyes" (Lev. 26:16). Deuteronomy 28:32 also refers to ague.

When Jesus found Simon Peter's mother-in-law ill with this symptom, He rebuked the fever and she was able to rise from her bed and wait on the disciples (Luke 4:38). On another occasion, Jesus healed the feverish son of a government official (John 4:46–54).

Many diseases in ancient Palestine would have been characterized by high fevers, the most common of which were malaria and typhoid. A plague broke out when the Philistines placed the ark of God in an idol's temple (1 Sam. 5:2, 9, 12). The outbreak was associated with mice.

O. Gangrene. This disease is mentioned only once in the Bible: "And their word will eat as doth a canker" (2 Tim. 2:17). Here the KJV translates the Greek *gaggarina* as *canker*. It refers to the circulatory deterioration that we commonly call *gangrene,* which spreads rapidly and eats up tissue.

P. Gout. Excessive uric acid in the blood causes this kidney ailment that manifests itself through painful inflammation of joints. Second Chronicles 16:12–13 says that King Asa had a foot disease, which apparently was gout.

Q. Lameness. Scripture describes many persons who were lame, the most memorable case being recorded in Acts 3:2–11, where we read about a man (born lame) who was carried daily to Jerusalem's Beautiful Gate to beg. One day the beggar saw Peter and John entering the temple and beseeched them for money. Instead, the apostles invoked the name of Jesus to heal the man. Peter lifted up the beggar,

DISEASES AND HEALING

The Leper

Throughout history, leprosy has been one of mankind's most feared diseases. Until this century, men have relied upon various forms of social ostracism in an effort to control the disease. The Hawaiians banished lepers to the island of Molokai. Medieval nobles constructed vast leprosariums. And the ancient Jews cast the leper "without the camp" (Lev. 13:46).

We have little evidence of the actual lives of lepers in biblical times after they had been segregated from the community. Leviticus 13—15 contains the most relevant data on the treatment—or lack thereof—of leprosy in the Old Testament. These chapters mainly detail the symptoms of the disease, the procedures by which a priest determined a case that was cured, and the offerings to be made before the leper could reenter the community.

The leper's condition of life was very simply described in Leviticus: "And the leper in whom the plague is, his clothes shall be rent, and his head bare, and he shall put a covering upon his upper lip, and shall cry, Unclean, unclean. All the days wherein the plague shall be in him he shall be defiled; he is unclean: he shall dwell alone; without

the camp shall his habitation be" (Lev. 13:45–46).

It was a fearsome fate to be condemned to the life of the leper. In medieval times, a priest would often read the burial service over a leper before he was cast out of the city. The miracles of Christ in curing lepers are testimony to His compassion as well as His power (cf. Matt. 8:1–4; Mark 1:40–45; Luke 5:12–14).

Luke is the only Gospel writer to tell of Jesus' cure of 10 lepers during His last journey to Jerusalem. Ten found themselves cured on the way to see the priest, but only one returned to thank Christ. This story is the sole New Testament evidence that lepers congregated together, suggesting that the law of Leviticus had been relaxed. Second Kings 7:3–10 mentions four lepers huddling together outside the gates of a city. But apparently lepers were segregated from the healthy population of towns. In Old Testament times, leprosy was considered a source of physical contamination rather than of moral corruption (which was a popular myth in Jesus' time).

Leprosy was always a disaster, but it took centuries for society to learn how to cope with it.

---

who began to walk. Jesus healed many persons who were lame (cf. Matt. 15:30–31).

R. Leprosy. One of the most dreaded diseases of the world, leprosy is caused by a bacillus and is characterized by formation of nodules that spread, causing loss of sensation and deformity. Now treated with sulfone drugs, leprosy is perhaps the least infectious of all known contagious diseases. Hansen's Disease, as it is more properly known, was often misdiagnosed in biblical times. People believed then that it was highly contagious and hereditary. Leviticus 13:1–17 condemned leprosy as a "plague."

On the basis of a hair in a scab, a pimple, or a spot on the skin that had turned white, the priest would declare a person to be a leper and would quarantine him for seven days. If no change in the spot occurred by then, the quarantine would be extended another week. At that time, if the spot had started to fade, the "leper" would be pronounced cured and returned to his normal life. However, if the spot remained or had spread, he was declared unclean and banished.

Leprosy was very common in the Near East. If a Hebrew was healed of leprosy, he was ex-

pected to offer certain sacrifices and engage in rites of purification (Lev. 14:1–32). Jesus healed lepers on numerous occasions (cf. Luke 5:12–13; 17:12–17).

S. Malaria. This infectious disease was caused by protozoa of the genus *plasmodium*. These one-celled animals can live in the blood of human beings and animals or in the female *Anopheles* mosquito. Once malaria is in the system, it recurs. Paul may have been referring to malaria when he spoke of his "thorn in the flesh" (2 Cor. 12:7).

T. Mental and Nervous Disorders. King Saul seems to have had symptoms of manic depression (cf. 1 Sam. 16:14–23), and the Bible mentions others who may have suffered from mental or nervous disorders. King Nebuchadnezzar is an example (Dan. 4:33).

U. Palsy. The KJV uses this term to refer to total paralysis. The Gospels record a well-known incident in which Jesus healed a paralyzed man at Capernaum (Mark 2:1–12). The book of Acts describes how the apostles healed people with "the palsy" (Acts 8:7; 9:33–34).

V. Plague. Our English versions may use

DISEASES AND HEALING

this word to denote any epidemic disease. It is also used in a general sense in Exodus 7—10, where it refers to the hardships that God inflicted upon the Egyptians.

Epidemics hit the Israelites three times during their wandering in the wilderness. The first time was when they were eating the quail that God sent to satisfy their longing for meat (Num. 11:33). The second time, a "plague" claimed the lives of spies who discouraged the Israelites from entering the Promised Land (Num. 14:37). The third epidemic came as God's punishment upon the Israelites. Aaron stopped this "plague" by offering incense to God (Num. 16:46–47). On one other occasion, Phinehas saved the Israelites from an epidemic by killing a man who brought a Midianite

TREPANNING. *Judean surgeons during the sixth century B.C. practiced trepanning, the surgical removal of bone from the skull to relieve pressure on the brain. The surgeons shaved the patient's head, slit the skin, and pulled it back to expose the bone. Then they used a small saw to remove a section of the skull, which was replaced when the excess fluid had drained off. Archaeologists have found skulls with holes partially cut or with drainage holes left open, which suggest that the operation was frequently unsuccessful.*

LEPROSY. *One of the most dreaded diseases in the world, leprosy is perhaps the least infectious. In biblical times, the deforming disease was incurable and a leper was cast out of society. This modern-day leper suffers from the bacterial form of leprosy, known as true leprosy or Hansen's Disease.*

woman into their midst. Nevertheless, 24,000 people died (Num. 25:8–9).

The Old Testament describes many cases in which God sent "plagues" to chastise His people. One example is found in 2 Samuel, where David says, "Build an altar unto the LORD that the plague may be stayed from the people" (2 Sam. 24:21).

The KJV also uses *plague* to refer to any painful affliction. When the woman with a chronic hemorrhage was healed, she felt that she had been healed of a "plague" (Mark 5:29). We have no evidence that the Bible ever refers to bubonic plague, which would claim millions of lives in medieval Europe.

W. Polio. This is the common name for infantile paralysis, which usually affected children. First Kings 17:17 tells of a woman who brought her son to the prophet Elijah. The boy was so sick that there was no breath in him;

DISEASES AND HEALING

this symptom suggests that he may have had polio, although it also may have been a form of meningitis. Elijah revived the boy through the Lord's intervention in answer to his prayer. However, Scripture does not tell us if the boy was completely cured. The men described in Matthew 12:9–13 and John 5:2 may have had polio.

X. Skin Disorders. The Bible refers to many kinds of skin disorders such as the "itch" (KJV) or ringworm (Lev. 13:30; 21:20). Leviticus 13:39 probably refers to vitiligo, which was confused often with leprosy.

When the KJV uses the word *scurvy,* it is not referring to the vitamin deficiency that causes the problem known by that name today. Instead, the reference is to an itching or scaling condition caused by a fungus (Lev. 21:20, 22).

Y. Smallpox. Some Bible scholars believe that the Hebrew word *maqaq* (literally "waste away") refers to smallpox. The KJV usually translates this word as "pine away," which suggests emotional despair: "And they that were left of you, shall pine away" (Lev. 26:39). "Ye shall not mourn nor weep, but he shall pine away for your iniquities" (Ezek. 24:23). In one instance, the KJV understands *maqaq* to denote a "corruption" of the skin: "My wounds stink and are corrupt because of my foolishness" (Ps. 38:5).

Z. Sunstroke. Isaiah may have referred to sunstroke or heat prostration when he said, "Neither shall heat nor sun smite thee" (Is. 49:10). Second Kings describes a young man who was working among the reapers when he said to his father, "My head, my head." He was carried into the house, where he died (2 Kin. 4:18–20). We would assume that sunstroke was a common malady in the hot summers of the Near East.

AA. Syncope. Arrested heart action or the sudden lowering of blood pressure is normally called *syncope.* When Jacob learned that his son Joseph was still alive, his heart "fainted" (Gen. 45:26)—probably a reference to syncope. When Eli heard that the ark of the covenant had been captured, he fell backwards off his seat, broke his neck, and died (1 Sam. 4:18). This may have been another instance of heart failure or syncope.

BB. Venereal Disease. There is some evidence that venereal diseases were common in Bible times. For example, Zechariah 11:17 warns the shepherd who leaves his flock, saying that his arm will be dried up and his right eye will go blind. These symptoms indicate a disease of the spinal cord, probably a venereal disease. Some believe that Leah had an eye condition that could have been the result of hereditary syphilis (Gen. 29:17).

CC. Worms. Isaiah warned that the rebellious people of Israel would be afflicted with worms (Is. 51:8). He also predicted this fate for Babylon (Is. 14:11). This parasitic disease

ASSYRIAN PRIEST-DOCTORS. *Ancient medical men resorted to exorcism when other remedies failed. This Assyrian tablet depicts priest-doctors dressed as fish, attempting to exorcise an evil spirit from their patient.*

DISEASES AND HEALING

could be fatal because no medical remedies were available.

Scripture says that "an angel of the Lord" smote Herod the Great. Worms ate him up and he died (Acts 12:23).

II. The Use of Medicine. When a person's body began to deteriorate and suffer pain, the victim would naturally look for a remedy. Thus the people of ancient times developed an extensive knowledge of natural medicines.

Probably the first medicines were introduced to the Israelites through the Egyptian people, especially the priests. Egyptians also embalmed their dead with spices and perfume—a custom that the Israelites soon came to accept.

In Bible times, medicines were made from minerals, animal substances, herbs, wines, fruits, and other parts of plants. Scripture often refers to the medicinal use of these substances.

For example, the "balm of Gilead" is mentioned as a healing substance (Jer. 8:22). The "balm" is thought to have been an aromatic excretion from an evergreen tree or a form of frankincense. Wine mixed with myrrh was known to relieve pain by dulling the senses. This remedy was offered to Jesus as He hung on the cross, but He refused to drink it (Mark 15:23). The Israelites anointed their sick with soothing lotions of olive oil and herbs. In the story of the Good Samaritan, oil and wine were poured into the wounds of the beaten man (Luke 10:34). The early Christians continued this practice, anointing the sick as they prayed for them (James 5:14).

Matthew 23:23 mentions certain spices that were often used as antacids. Mandrakes were used to arouse sexual desires (Gen. 30:14). Other plants were used as remedies or stimulants. (*See* "Plants.")

III. Physicians and Their Work. Professional physicians practiced their skills in Bible times, but their work was largely considered to be magical. The Old Testament does not mention the names of any physicians, though it often refers to their work (cf. Gen. 50:2; 2 Chron. 16:12; Jer. 8:22). The deuterocanonical book of Ecclesiasticus (second century B.C.) celebrates the wisdom and skill of

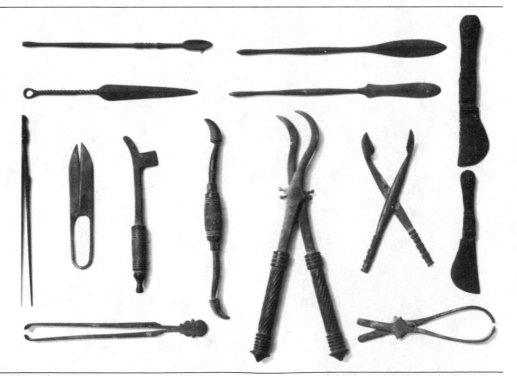

33

DISEASES AND HEALING

SURGEON'S TOOLS. *Knives, scalpels, tweezers, and clamps are among these surgeon's tools found at Pompeii. They indicate that surgical arts were quite sophisticated by the first century A.D.*

DISEASES AND HEALING

physicians (38:1–15). In the New Testament, Luke is mentioned by name as the "beloved physician" (Col. 4:14).

Circumcision is the only type of surgery mentioned in the Bible. This was the ceremonial removal of the foreskin of the male Hebrew child eight days after birth. The practice was begun at God's command by Abraham (Gen. 17:10–14), and God showed anger with Moses for his failure to observe it (Ex. 4:24–26). Even Jesus was circumcised when He was eight days old (Luke 2:21).

IV. Ritual Cures and Miraculous Healings. The Bible refers to some cases in which an ailing person performed a ritual washing in order to receive a cure. When Naaman contracted leprosy, for example, the prophet Elisha instructed him to submerge himself seven times in the Jordan River. Naaman did so and was healed (2 Kings 5:10). Jesus applied mud to the eyes of a blind man and told him to wash it off in the pool of Siloam. The blind man obeyed and received his sight (John 9:7).

On many more occasions, God performed miracles through the ministry of His servants. Elijah and Elisha saw numerous cures of this kind (cf. 1 Kin. 17:17–22; 2 Kin. 4:32–37). When Jesus cured people of all manner of diseases, it confirmed that He was the Messiah (Luke 7:20–22).

The temple priests had several medical functions. Leviticus describes seven forms of ritual purification that had medical significance. They deal with: post-childbirth (Lev. 12), leprosy (Lev. 13), venereal disease (Lev. 15:12–15), the male sexual function (Lev. 15:16–18), sexual intercourse (Lev. 15:18), menstruation (Lev. 15:19–30), and dead bodies (Lev. 21:1–3).

FOOD AND EATING HABITS

From Genesis 1:29 (when God said, "I have given you every herb bearing seed, which is upon the face of the earth . . . ; to you it shall be for meat") to Revelation 22:2 (when John tells about the "tree of life which bare twelve manner of fruits") the Bible is packed with references to food.

Vegetable products formed a major portion of the diet in the warm climate of Palestine. When meat was used, it was often for the purpose of serving strangers or honored guests.

Grains were an important part of the diet. Bread was eaten by itself or with something to increase its flavor, such as salt, vinegar, broth, or honey. Fruits and fish were a favorite part of the diet. Recall the disciples who were called from their fishing nets by Jesus.

The serpent tempted Eve to eat a piece of fruit, and sin entered the world. Esau sold his birthright for a mess of pottage. Jesus was tempted to turn stones into bread, and He used food—bread and wine—as a symbol of our participation in His suffering. Food—an earthy, human necessity—is a fascinating thread woven through the story of God's revelation to humankind.

I. EATING CUSTOMS
A. Breakfast
B. Supper
C. Feasts
D. Hospitality
E. Table
F. Utensils
G. The Sop

II. FASTS

III. WINE

IV. GRAIN
A. Barley
B. Corn
C. Millet
D. Rye
E. Wheat
F. The Mill
G. The Sieve

V. BREAD
A. Showbread
B. Leaven
C. Wafer
D. Cracknels

VI. BAKING
A. The Oven
B. The Hearth

VII. MEAT AND RELATED FOODS
A. Calf
B. Kid
C. Fowl
D. Fish
E. Sheep (Lamb)
F. Fat

VIII. HUNTING

IX. COOKING

X. MILK PRODUCTS
A. Butter
B. Cheese

XI. FRUIT
A. Grapes
B. Raisins
C. Flagon
D. Pomegranate
E. Melon
F. Apple
G. Fig
H. Olive

XII. VEGETABLES
A. Bean
B. Lentil
C. Cucumber
D. Onion and Garlic
E. Leek
F. Pottage
G. Bitter Herbs

XIII. NUTS
A. Almond
B. Pistachio

XIV. HONEY

XV. MANNA

I. Eating Customs. Scripture is filled with references to banquets and feasts; very little is said about day-to-day family meals. All evidence, however, points to the custom of two regular meals a day—breakfast, a light meal in the morning, and supper, a heavier meal in the evening.

Earlier Jews sat on mats on the floor to eat. However, they later adopted the custom of using a table with couches on which they

FOOD AND EATING HABITS

ARABS EATING. *Breaking bread together was the primary expression of hospitality in the ancient Near East, as it is today. Some scholars believe that the Hebrews ate twice a day—a light meal in the morning and a heavier meal in the cool evening. In earlier times, meals were served on floor mats, as shown here. Couches were used in the Roman era.*

reclined (John 21:20). A short prayer or blessing was offered before eating, as when Jesus blessed the bread when He fed the multitude (Matt. 14:19). Washing one's hands was considered essential and was observed as a religious duty, especially by the Pharisees (Mark 7:3).

Breaking bread together, even today, seems to say, We are friends; we share a common bond. Such feelings are apparent throughout the Bible. It is as though eating is more than a matter of ingestion of food; it is participating in all that it means to be human and sharing that mutuality with those around us.

A. Breakfast. The morning meal was usually eaten sometime between nine o'clock and noon. It was a light meal and consisted of bread, fruits, and cheese.

B. Supper. The principal meal of the day was eaten in the evening. The hot temperatures of the daytime hours in Palestine were somewhat cooled by evening and a more relaxed atmosphere prevailed. Meat, vegetables,

butter, and wine were consumed at the evening meal.

C. Feasts. The Jewish people enjoyed celebrations and, according to Scripture, a feast seemed to be a good way to commemorate a joyous event. Music was very much a part of their feasts (Is. 5:12) and dancing was sometimes a part of the entertainment.

The feast was planned and presided over by the "steward" or "governor" of the feast (John 2:8), who directed the servants and tested the food and wine.

Religious festivals, of which feasting was very much a part, may be grouped as follows: (1) The Sabbath, the feast of new moons, the sabbatical year, and the Year of Jubilee; (2) the Passover, Pentecost, and the Feast of Tabernacles; (3) the feasts of Purim and of the dedication. All labor ceased on the principal feast days; the seven-day Passover celebration called for no work on the first and seventh days (Lev. 23).

Feasts were held for marriages (John 2:1–11), on birthdays (Gen. 40:20), at burials

DINING ROOM AT HERCULANEUM.
The dining room of this house at Herculaneum was preserved by volcanic debris in A.D. 79. The Romans used this three-sided arrangement of dining couches to separate three social classes, with special places for the host and guest of honor. The Israelites eventually adopted the Roman practice of dining while stretched out on couches.

FOOD AND EATING HABITS

The Traditional Passover

The Passover ritual is at the center of Jewish worship. Every element of *Pesach* (Hebrew, "Passover") was designed to commemorate the Jews' historic passage from slavery to nationhood under God.

Passover is a seven-day celebration in which the main feast occurs the first night. The *seder* (Hebrew, "service") meal with its accompanying ritual recalls the last meal the Jews ate in Egypt before beginning their journey to the Promised Land. Jews are commanded to remember their history of captivity and liberation on the night of the Seder: "And thou shalt show thy son in that day, saying, This is done because of that which the LORD did unto me when I came forth out of Egypt" (Ex. 13:8).

Of the many traditional ingredients of the Seder table, the most important are those which God specified for that last meal in Egypt: "Your lamb shall be without blemish, a male a year old" (Ex. 12:5). The lambs must be roasted, not boiled. Seder participants are reminded that lamb's blood was smeared on the doorposts of Jewish houses to protect Jews from the plague that struck nonbelievers the first Passover night.

The paschal lamb was to be eaten with bitter herbs, as commanded in Exodus. In Old Testament times bitter lettuce, chicory, or endive were used; today Jewish families are more likely to use grated horseradish or onion. These herbs symbolize the bitterness of captivity under the Egyptians.

Since the first Seder was eaten as Jews prepared for flight, the theme of haste is woven into the feast. Unleavened bread of a cracker-like texture, such as *matzos,* was more suitable for a people in flight than leavened loaves, which require kneading and rising.

Each participant in the Seder has a wine cup. The host of the feast leans on cushions, recalling the ancient mode of eating in a reclining position. In front of the host is placed the Seder plate, with the traditional symbolic foods: three wafers of matzo bread wrapped in a napkin, the bitter herbs, the *haroset* or fruit pulp, the roasted lamb and hard-boiled egg, the sweet vegetables, and a dish of salt water for washing hands.

The best-known part of the Seder ritual is probably the "Four Questions." The youngest male child of the house asks questions about the Seder, beginning with the words, "Why is this night of Passover different from all other nights of the year?" He asks about the use of unleavened bread, bitter herbs, the dipping of vegetables, and the cushions at the host's chair. The host answers the child by reciting the history of Israel's passage from bondage to freedom.

While the preparation for the Seder takes time, none of the traditional foods presents any difficulties. The *haroset* is the only one that requires a special recipe, and there are many versions available. In fact, the important thing about the *haroset* is its texture (which resembles mortar) rather than its ingredients. A simple haroset might include grated apples, chopped nuts, sugar, cinnamon, and sweet red wine. These ingredients are mashed together to the consistency of a dip. Matzo meal can be added, other fruits or nuts substituted, and the sugar and cinnamon added to the individual taste.

(Jer. 16:7–8), at sheep-shearings (1 Sam. 25:2, 36), and on many other occasions. Possibly the one which comes to mind most frequently is the feast prepared by the father of the prodigal son (Luke 15:11–32).

It is interesting to note that women were never present at Jewish meals as guests.

D. Hospitality. Abraham "sat in the tent door in the heat of the day . . . and behold, three men stood in front by him" (Gen. 18:1–2). Abraham gave them water to drink and to wash the dust from their feet. They sat in the shade of his tree and he and Sarah prepared food for them to eat. His guests turned out to be angels!

In Hebrews 13:2 we are entreated, "Be not forgetful to entertain strangers: for thereby some have entertained angels unawares." Hospitality, kindness to strangers, and "especially unto them who are of the household of faith" (Gal. 6:10), had roots in the Old Testament and became an integral part of the teachings of the New Testament.

E. Table. In ancient Palestine the only table was a circular skin or piece of leather placed on the floor mat. Around the edges of this tray-like table were loops through which a cord was drawn. When the meal was finished, the cord was tightened and the "table" was hung out of the way.

In later times a regular table with reclining couches was introduced. Guests leaned on the table with their left elbow and ate with their right hand.

F. Utensils. Various utensils were probably represented by the use of this word. Sacred utensils referred to in Exodus 25:29 include dishes, spoons, and bowls. An ordinary dish

34

FOOD AND EATING HABITS

used in a household comes to mind in 2 Kings 21:13: "I will wipe Jerusalem as a man wipeth a dish, wiping it, and turning it upside down."

G. The Sop. Table utensils were not used among the Hebrews. The *sop* was a piece of bread used to dip in the soup or broth which sat in the center of the table. The master of the feast might dip a sop and give it to a guest. Jesus gave a sop to Judas (John 13:26), indicating that he was the one who was to betray Jesus.

II. Fasts. Feasting was an important part of Jewish life, but fasting (going without food for a period of time) was just as essential. Fasts were prescribed for the Day of Atonement by the Mosaic Code ("afflict your souls," Lev. 16:29), to commemorate the breaking of the tables of the Law, and for other such events in Jewish history.

Fasting was practiced to show humility, sorrow, and dependence upon God. Garments of sackcloth, ashes sprinkled on one's head, unwashed hands, and an unanointed head were signs that a person was observing a fast.

Though fasting became an act of hypocrisy for some (Matt. 6:16–18), we do have record of Jesus' fasting for 40 days and nights when He was in the wilderness (Matt. 4:2). It ap-

WINEPRESS. *Troughs like this one in Jerusalem contained grapes from which wine was made. Holding onto overhead ropes, men stomped on the grapes to extract the juice, which flowed from a hole in the bottom of the trough into a vat (cf. Neh. 13:15).*

pears that it is a matter left mainly to individual choice. (*See* "Worship Rituals.")

III. Wine. The Law of Moses allowed the use of wine; however, drunkenness was forbidden. Wine was used as the drink-offering of the daily sacrifice (Ex. 29:40). Nazirites were forbidden to drink it (Num. 6:3), as were also the priests when they performed the services of the temple (Lev. 10:9). Paul suggests to Timothy that those who are deacons should not be "given to much wine" (1 Tim. 3:8). Excess drinking was a problem then as it continues to be today.

Included in a list of laws and ordinances is the admonition not to "delay to offer the first . . . of thy liquors" (Ex. 22:29). The Hebrew word which the KJV translated as *liquors* seems to have meant the juice of olives and grapes. The "liquor of grapes" mentioned in Numbers 6:3 was a drink made by steeping grapes.

The dregs of wine (lees) were used to improve the flavor, color, and strength of new wine. "Wines on the lees well refined" (Is. 25:6) referred to a rich full-bodied wine—a symbol of the blessings of the feast of the Lord.

Jesus was offered a drink of vinegar on a sponge as He hung on the cross. This was probably the sour wine which the Roman soldiers drank (Matt. 27:48). Though not a desirable drink, vinegar was used for dipping bread (Ruth 2:14). When poured on nitre, vinegar produces an effervescent effect. Thus: "As vinegar upon nitre, so is he that singeth songs to an heavy heart" (Prov. 25:20).

IV. Grain. A generous supply of grain indicates a well-fed people. Think of the importance placed on Joseph's task of storing the extra grain during the seven years of plenty in Egypt (Gen. 41:47–57). "All countries came into Egypt to Joseph for to buy corn" (v. 57). Grain makes bread—and bread sustains nations. (*See also* "Plants.")

A. Barley. Barley was cultivated in Palestine and Egypt and was fed to cattle and horses. Though the Egyptians used barley to feed animals, the Hebrews used it for bread, at least for the poor.

B. Corn. The KJV's references to *corn* (such as Deut. 23:25 and Matt. 12:1) actually mean various kinds of grain, including barley, millet, and wheat. Corn as we know it was not cultivated in the Eastern Hemisphere. Boaz gave Ruth "parched corn" (Ruth 2:14), grain that had been roasted.

FOOD AND EATING HABITS

C. Millet. Mentioned in Ezekiel 4:9 among other grains, millet is a grain with small seeds grown in Palestine and used for bread.

D. Rye. Though rye ("rie") is mentioned in Exodus 9:32, rye was actually never cultivated in Palestine. Authorities believe that the reference signifies another grain such as millet or spelt.

E. Wheat. "A corn of wheat . . . if it die . . . bringeth forth much fruit" (John 12:24). Jesus speaks here of one of the most widely used of all grains among the Hebrews. Referred to throughout the Bible as a staple of the Hebrew diet, wheat is one of the plants which Moses promised could be grown in Canaan, the Promised Land (Deut. 8:8).

F. The Mill. The simplest kind of mill used to grind grain was a hollowed-out stone that held grain to be pounded by another stone. A more efficient mill consisted of two stones, 60 cm. (2 ft.) in diameter and 15 cm. (6 in.) thick. The *nether* (or lower) *stone* was raised in the center. The upper stone was hollowed out and had a hole in the middle. Grain was poured into the hole, and the upper stone was turned by means of a handle. The grain was crushed as it fell between the two stones. To get very fine flour, the grain had to be ground more than once.

The millstone was so important to the Hebrew people that the Law stated that "no man shall take the . . . millstone to pledge," for he would be taking a man's life in pledge (Deut. 24:6).

G. The Sieve. After the meal was sifted in a sieve, what remained would be returned to the millstone to be ground again. Ancient sieves were made of rushes and papyrus. Isaiah speaks of the nations being sifted with the sieve of vanity (Is. 30:28).

V. Bread. "Give us this day our daily bread" (Matt. 6:11). Jesus prayed for bread, meaning food in general. But bread itself was a staple of Hebrew diet. Grain—usually wheat, but also barley—was milled, sifted, made into a dough, kneaded, formed into thin cakes, and then baked.

Expressions like "bread of sorrows" (Ps. 127:2) and "bread of wickedness" (Prov. 4:17) may indicate that these experiences become as much a part of life as daily bread is a part of life.

A. Showbread. Each Sabbath 12 loaves of unleavened bread (for the 12 tribes of Israel) were baked. They were placed in two piles or rows on the golden table in the sanctuary as an

BREAD PAN. *This platter from Lachish (ca. fifteenth century B.C.) may have been used for forming cakes of bread or for baking them (cf. Lev. 2:5).*

offering to the Lord. When the old bread was removed, it could be eaten only by the priests in the court of the sanctuary (Lev. 24:5–9).

B. Leaven. Jesus uses the term *leaven* (a ferment used in bread to make it rise) in a figurative sense, as He does many well-known everyday terms. In Matthew 13:33 He likens the kingdom to leaven, with its power to change the whole.

Perhaps we are most familiar with this term when we use it in connection with unleavened bread. Bread without leavening was used at times in peace offerings and also during the week of the Passover to remind the Israelites of their release from Egyptian bondage.

C. Wafer. This thin unleavened cake made of wheat flour and anointed with oil was used in offerings (Ex. 16:31; Num. 6:15).

D. Cracknels. These hard biscuits or crumbcakes are mentioned in 1 Kings 14:3. They are called *cracknels* in the KJV because they made a cracking noise when they were broken.

VI. Baking. Baking was usually done by women. The hearth was frequently used; but at times a thin dough was formed on a heated stone pitcher and then baked. Typically, dough made of wheat or barley was kneaded in a wooden bowl, made into circular cakes, pricked, and baked around a jar or in a bowl.

FOOD AND EATING HABITS

FLOUR MILL. *Hand mills for grinding grain into flour consisted of two circular stones, the lower having a slightly convex surface to guide the drifting bits of broken grain toward the outer edge, where they dropped off. The millstones had curved furrows that multiplied their cutting and grinding effect as the upper stone was rotated on the lower. Larger grain mills were operated by donkeys or slaves. These Roman flour mills from Pompeii are of the larger type. Notice the bread oven behind them.*

Fresh bread was baked every day. Public bakers are referred to in Hosea 7:4, 6.

A. The Oven. The ovens of the Hebrews were probably of three kinds: (1) The sand oven, in which a fire was built on clean sand and then removed when the sand was hot. Dough was spread on the hot sand in thin layers to bake. (2) The earth oven, the "range for pots" (Lev. 11:35), was a hole in the earth in which stones were heated. Dough was spread in thin layers on the stones after the fire had been removed. (3) Portable ovens, referred to in "baked in the oven" (Lev. 2:4) were probably made of clay. Inside them a fire was built. When they were hot, thin layers of dough were spread on the stones lining the bottom of the oven after the ashes had been removed.

B. The Hearth. Abraham told Sarah to "make cakes upon the hearth" (Gen. 18:6). He was referring to hot stones used for baking bread. The hearth could also mean the fuel that burnt on it (Ps. 102:3) or a portable furnace (Jer. 36:22–23).

VII. Meat and Related Foods. The eating of meat is mentioned in the covenant God made with Noah: "Every moving thing that liveth shall be meat for you" (Gen. 9:3). Though the Hebrews' normal diet consisted of vegetables and fruits, they did eat some meat, particularly for banquets and feasts. The early church had a disagreement concerning eating meat offered to idols, but Paul made it clear that nothing is unclean to those who are pure (Titus 1:15; cf. 1 Tim. 4:4).

A. Calf. When the prodigal son returned home, his father killed a fatted calf for a feast (Luke 15:23). In Hebrew life, the calf was considered the choicest of all meats. It was reserved for the most festive occasions.

B. Kid. The prodigal son's older brother became angry and said to his father, "Thou never gavest me a kid, that I might make merry with my friends" (Luke 15:29). The kid (a young goat) was the more common meat, cheaper, and eaten by the poor. It was used in sacrificial offerings (Num. 7:11–87).

C. Fowl. Some fowl were considered un-

FOOD AND EATING HABITS

clean for food (Deut. 14:20). But partridge, quail, geese, and pigeons might be eaten.

D. Fish. A favorite food in Palestine was fish, caught in large quantities from the Sea of Galilee and the Jordan River. (*See* "Birds and Fish.")

After His resurrection, Jesus prepared a breakfast of fish and bread on a charcoal fire by the seashore for some of the disciples (John 21:9–13). Another time when He appeared to the disciples after the Resurrection He asked for something to eat. Luke tells us, "They gave him a piece of broiled fish, . . . and he took it and did eat before them" (24:42–43).

The Law stated that all fish with fins and scales were clean and therefore could be eaten (Deut. 14:9–10).

E. Sheep (Lamb). Besides its many other uses the sheep was important for its meat, milk, and the fat in its tail, which sometimes weighed as much as fifteen pounds. At the Passover celebration a lamb was killed and eaten to recall the freedom from slavery in Egypt.

F. Fat. The pure fat from an animal was sacrificed to God, since it was considered the richest or best part (Lev. 3:16). It could not be eaten in early times, but this stipulation seemed to be ignored when animals were killed to be used only for food (Deut. 12:15).

VIII. Hunting. Lions, bears, jackals, foxes, hart, roebucks, and fallow-deer are mentioned in the Old Testament. Some of these animals were hunted for food, using a pitfall, a trap, or a net. Isaac instructed Esau to take his bow and quiver and hunt game so that he could have the food he loved (Gen. 27:3–4).

Though not used as utensils for eating as we know them, knives were necessary for killing animals and in preparing them for eating or for sacrifice (Lev. 8:20; Ezra 1:9). (*See* "Tools.")

IX. Cooking. Cooking was woman's work, particularly in the years before the conquest of Canaan. For roasting, a wood fire was built or an oven was used. For boiling, the animal was cut up, put in a kettle (cauldron) with water, and seasoned (Ezek. 24:4–5). The meat and broth were served separately. Vegetables were also boiled.

A cauldron was a large metal vessel used for boiling meat (1 Sam. 2:14). A three-pronged fork was used for removing meat from the cauldron.

SOLDIERS EATING. *David and his followers were wandering soldiers in Judea. They lived off the land and its people, offering protection to those who fed them and taking provisions from the uncooperative. Here several soldiers rest and prepare to eat a meal of lentils, figs, and goat's milk at the house of a Judean peasant.*

X. Milk Products. "A land flowing with milk and honey" was promised to the Israelites (Josh. 5:6), and in that promise they envisioned abundance and prosperity. The Hebrews drank the milk of camels, sheep, and goats. The camel's milk was especially rich and strong, but not very sweet. References to milk are found throughout the Old Testament (cf. Prov. 27:27; Deut. 32:14).

A. Butter. The Hebrew term *chemah* has been variously translated as *cream, curds, cheese,* and *butter.* According to Genesis 18:8, Abraham served butter (*chemah*) to the strangers who visited his tent. Proverbs 30:33 tells us that "the churning of milk bringeth forth butter." Whatever the exact meaning of the Hebrew word, there is agreement that the Hebrews had a kind of butter. It was probably made in the same manner that the Arabs use today. Heated milk, to which a small amount of sour milk is added, is poured into a goatskin bag and shaken until the butter separates. It is drained and after three days is heated again. Butter thus prepared keeps well in the hot climate of Palestine.

B. Cheese. With cheese, we have somewhat the same problem as we have with butter; it is difficult to know for sure what the writers meant. Consider: "Didst thou not . . . curdle me like cheese?" (Job 10:10, RSV); "Take these ten cheeses unto the captain (1 Sam. 17:18); ". . . honey and butter, and sheep, and cheese of kine . . . to eat" (2 Sam. 17:29). In each of these references, the word for *cheese* in the original is a different word. It is likely that cheese in these three instances means a coagulated milk.

XI. Fruit. A favorite food of the Hebrews was the fruit which grew in abundance in the warm climate of that part of the world. (*See also* "Plants.") The spies that Moses sent to Canaan brought back a branch bearing a single cluster of grapes which was so large that they carried it on a pole between them. They also brought back pomegranates and figs (Num. 13:23). These and a variety of other fruits were enjoyed as a part of the regular diet.

A. Grapes. See the section on "Wine," above.

B. Raisins. "Bunches of raisins" were brought to David "for there was joy in Israel" (1 Chron. 12:40). Raisins were grapes that were dried in bunches. They are also mentioned in 1 Samuel 25:18 and 2 Samuel 16:1.

C. Flagon. Though *flagon* in Isaiah 22:24 surely means a kind of vessel, another usage of the word in 2 Samuel 6:19 means "a cake of raisins." It comes from the Hebrew *'ashishah* ("pressed together"). Flagons appear to be dried grapes or raisins that are pressed into a cake. They were used as a sacrifice to idols (Hos. 3:1) and were enjoyed as a delicacy.

D. Pomegranate. This beautiful rose-red fruit with its many seeds was a favorite among the Israelites. The abundance of seeds was symbolic of fertility and it was grown both for its tasty fruit and for its beauty in the garden. The juice of the pomegranate was highly prized (Song 8:2). It was one of the fruits which were grown in the Promised Land (Num. 13:23).

The robe of the high priest was decorated with ornamental "pomegranates of blue, and of purple, and of scarlet, round about the hem thereof" (Ex. 28:33). Two hundred ornamental pomegranates decorated each of the two free-standing pillars (Jachin and Boaz) in Solomon's temple (2 Chr. 3:13).

E. Melon. The Israelites were camped in the hot Arabian Desert with only manna to eat. They complained in the Lord's hearing, "We remember . . . the melons" in Egypt (Num. 11:5). This is the only reference to melons in the Bible. It is impossible to tell whether they meant the muskmelon or the watermelon, or both, since it is possible that both grew in Egypt at that time. Whatever the case, the melon was a refreshing treat when the weather was hot.

F. Apple. The apple or apple tree mentioned in the KJV is probably the citron tree and fruit, although the quince and apricot have also been suggested. From the Bible we learn that the fruit of this "apple tree" is sweet (Song 2:3); its fruit is gold in color (Prov. 25:11); and it is fragrant (Song 7:8).

G. Fig. From the fig leaves used by Adam and Eve as coverings for their nakedness (Gen. 3:7) to the fig tree that Jesus cursed (Mark 11:14), figs are mentioned often in the Bible. They were a common fruit in Palestine. Fig trees grow singly or in small groups and provide a delightful shade with their large leaves (cf. John 1:48). They are eaten fresh from the tree, dried, or pressed into cakes (1 Sam. 25:18).

H. Olive. "And the dove came in to him in the evening; . . . in her mouth was an olive leaf plucked off" (Gen. 8:11). Noah received the symbol of peace and plenty and knew that the waters had gone down. The olive, a common fruit in Palestine, resembles a plum and is first green, then pale in color, and finally black when fully ripe. The tree itself resembles an apple tree and will bear fruit even when very old. The clusters of flowers when the tree is in bloom remind one of lilac.

Olives are beaten or shaken from the tree, and some fruit was to be left for the poor (Deut. 24:20). The fruit was eaten—both green and ripe—but the largest portion of the olive harvest was squeezed for oil.

The best oil comes from the green fruit. It is referred to in Exodus 27:20 as "pure olive oil beaten." The first extraction, shaken in pans or baskets, produces the finest oil; the second and third extractions are inferior. Oil was used for anointing, for food and cooking, and for lamps. A good tree will produce 60 lit. (12 gal.) of oil a year.

Oil was extracted from the olives in heavy stone oil presses called *gath-shemen* (Gethsemane is derived from this word; Matt. 26:36). Micah 6:15 speaks of treading the oil from the olives, as with grapes. Other references suggest that a large millstone was laid on its flat surface and was depressed on the upper surface. Another stone was placed upright on top of this and a beam was passed through its center. A horse or ox or man turned the top stone and the oil was pressed out by the weight.

The "oil-tree" mentioned in Isaiah 41:19 is surely the olive tree. One authority suggests that this refers to the oleaster, a shrub that

ASSYRIAN BANQUET. *Attended by servants and musicians, King Ashurbanipal and his queen feast in their garden in this relief from his palace (ca. sixth century B.C.). Like the Assyrians, the ancient Hebrews frequently celebrated religious and social occasions with feasts, accompanied by music and dancing.*

yields an inferior oil. But general agreement speaks in favor of the olive.

XII. Vegetables. "Let them give us pulse [vegetables] to eat, and water to drink" (Dan. 1:12). Daniel requested the simple food of his people rather than the king's rich diet. "And at the end of 10 days their countenances appeared fairer and fatter in flesh than all the children which did eat the portion of the king's meat" (v. 15).

Vegetables were everyday fare for the Israelites. Vegetable gardens are mentioned in Deuteronomy 11:10 and 1 Kings 21:2.

A. Bean. Beans along with other foods were brought to David as he was fleeing from Absalom (2 Sam. 17:28). Again, in Ezekiel 4:9, a bread made of wheat, barley, lentils, millet, and fitches, with beans, is described. A porridge was made by adding pounded beans to wheat meal or to bruised wheat. Garden beans flavored with oil and garlic were boiled and enjoyed.

B. Lentil. Esau sold his birthright for a bowl of pottage made from red lentils (Gen. 25:29–34). Lentils are similar to garden peas and the red lentils are considered to be the best. As with beans, lentils are sometimes used by the poor to make bread.

C. Cucumber. It is commonly agreed that *cucumber* is a correct translation of the Hebrew words *shakaph* and *miqshah* (Num. 11:5; Is. 1:8). Two types of cucumber were grown in Bible times—the long adder, ready for harvest in July, and the gherkin, which is ready later.

The Hebrews longed for the cucumbers and melons of Egypt when they had nothing but manna to eat in the wilderness (Num. 11:5). An interesting custom among the Hebrews was to build leafy watch places for a guard to sit in

and watch for thieves. When the crop season was over, they were abandoned. In Isaiah 1:8, we are told that Zion was "left as . . . a lodge in a garden of cucumbers"—desolate.

D. Onion and Garlic. These two flavorful bulb-like vegetables grow well in hot countries. Onions and garlic were a part of the memory of the good things of Egypt when the Israelites became fretful in the desert. The reference to these roots in Numbers 11:5 beyond a doubt means the onion and garlic with which we are familiar. Sheep and camels have been known to thrive on them.

E. Leek. The word *leeks* appears only one time in the KJV Bible (Num. 11:5). The same original word appears several times, but in all other cases is translated differently. Various writers identify them as any green vegetable food, such as a vegetable eaten with bread by the poor and made into a meat sauce by the rich, as is today's leek. It is probably a kind of lotus, the root of which was boiled and eaten as a condiment.

F. Pottage. Jacob's pottage is famous (Gen. 25:29–34). Pottage was a soup made of lentils and seasoned with oil and garlic.

Another interesting story about pottage is told in 2 Kings 4:38–41. Other ingredients were used in this type of pottage.

G. Bitter Herbs. This salad-like dish was a part of the Passover feast. It was used to remind the Hebrews of the sorrow they experienced in Egypt before they were free (Ex. 12:8; Num. 9:11). Greens included in the herbs could have been horseradish, lettuce, endive, parsley, and watercress.

XIII. Nuts. Jacob sent nuts as a gift to Joseph in Egypt (Gen. 43:11). Nuts probably did not grow in that country. A nut orchard is spoken of in Song of Solomon 6:11.

FOOD AND EATING HABITS

A. Almond. This early-blooming tree is called *shaked* in the Hebrew language, which means "watch, vigilant." Because of its early flowering, the symbol of the almond is used in Ecclesiastes 12:5 to represent the rapid aging of mankind. Jeremiah also uses the almond to express God's swift performance of His word (Jer. 1:11–12).

Aaron's rod budded, blossomed, and bore almonds in the tabernacle. Through this miracle the people understood that the house of Levi, represented by Aaron, was declared to be the priestly tribe (Num. 17:1–9).

There are two types of almonds. The bitter almond is known for its oil; the sweet almond is used for desserts.

B. Pistachio. The RSV says that Jacob sent pistachio nuts to Joseph in Egypt (Gen. 43:11). This is the only time they are mentioned in the Bible. They were used in confections.

XIV. Honey. The law of the Lord is "sweeter . . . than honey and the honeycomb" (Ps. 19:10). References to this delicacy run throughout the Bible from Genesis to Revelation. The Israelites were led to a "land flowing with milk and honey" (Ex. 3:8); at least 20 references in the Bible are worded similarly. Honey could not be offered on the altar of the Lord (Lev. 2:11), possibly because certain heathen nations practiced such a custom.

Jeroboam, when his child became ill, sent his wife to the prophet Ahijah with "a cruse of honey" (1 Kings 14:3). John the Baptist's "meat was locusts and wild honey" (Matt. 3:4).

The word *honey* in some references may mean the syrup of dates or grapes (Hebrew, *dibs*). The phrase "suck honey out of the rock" (Deut. 32:13) comes from the fact that bees sometimes deposit their honey on the rocks and cover it with a wax.

XV. Manna. The children of Israel, after they left Egypt, came to the Wilderness of Sin, which is between Elim and Sinai. They began to complain to Moses and Aaron: "Would to God we had died . . . in the land of Egypt . . . ; ye have brought us forth . . . to kill [us] with hunger." The Lord heard their complaining and He said, "I will rain bread from heaven for you; and the people shall go out and gather a certain rate every day." On the sixth day, they were to gather an extra day's

FOOD FROM POMPEII. *These serving dishes heaped with food were preserved among the ruins of Pompeii, a Roman city buried by the eruption of Mount Vesuvius in A.D. 79. Excavators also found loaves of bread in the ovens of Pompeii's bakery.*

FOOD AND EATING HABITS

portion for the Sabbath. *Manna* did not fall on the Sabbath. The Lord continued to provide the miraculous bread every morning except the Sabbath for 40 years, until the Israelites entered the land of Canaan (Ex. 16).

Some authorities attempt to give natural explanations for the manna, the most common of which has to do with the tamarisk tree. This tree presently is found in the peninsula of Sinai. A sap drips from this tree during certain seasons of the year and resembles the description of the manna eaten by the Israelites. Exodus 16:14 says it was "a small round thing, as small as the hoar frost on the ground" (v. 14). "It was like coriander seed, white, and the taste of it was like wafers made with honey" (Ex. 16:31).

Some authorities are convinced that tamarisk sap is the same as the original manna. Others contradict this conclusion for the following reasons: (1) The original manna lasted 40 years continuously; the tamarisk manna is unpredictable and seasonal. (2) The quantity produced by the tamarisk manna would not begin to feed three to four million people daily. (3) The original manna fell from heaven; the tamarisk manna fell from twigs on the tree. (4) The original manna could not be kept for more than a day; the tamarisk manna lasts for months. (5) The original manna could be boiled, ground, pounded, and made into cakes; the tamarisk manna could not be so used. (6) The nutrients were different—the original sustained a nation for 40 years; the tamarisk contains little food value.

CLOTHING AND COSMETICS

The Israelites' manner of dress changed gradually over the centuries. Let us note how five basic articles of clothing evolved.

God made garments for Adam and Eve. "Unto Adam also and to his wife did the LORD God make coats of skins, and clothed them" (Gen. 3:21). This garment (Hebrew, *kethon*) was a simple shirt made of animal skin. Later, the Hebrews began making shirts from linen or silk (if the garment was to be worn by an important individual). Thus, we read that Joseph wore the "coat of many colors" (Gen. 37:3), which the RSV renders as a "long robe with sleeves."

While the *kethon* remained the costume of the common people, another form of dress called the *simlah* came into fashion. Shem and Japheth took this garment to cover the

MAKING CLOTHES. *Clothing worn by the Hebrews served as the external symbol of the individual's innermost feelings and desires. Festive and joyful occasions called for bright colors, while the Jew in mourning put on sackcloth, the poorest kind of dress. Israelite families made most of their own clothing. In this family scene, the father is making leather sandals while the mother sews a robe from material she has woven.*

nakedness of their father (Gen. 9:23). At first, the Israelites made the *simlah* of wool, but later camel's hair was used. It was an outer garment resembling a large sheet with a hood, and the Jews used it for additional warmth. The poor used it for their basic dress by day and for cover by night (Ex. 22:26–27).

The Israelites wore the *beged* for special occasions indoors. Isaac and Rebekah dressed their son Jacob in this garment, which they considered their best clothing (Gen. 27:15). The Israelites thought the *beged* a badge of dignity to the wearer, and it was worn by distinguished members of great families. After the temple rituals were instituted, priests wore the *beged*.

The fourth item of clothing, the *lebhosh* (meaning "to clothe"), was a garment used for general wear. However, it eventually became an outer garment for both the rich and the poor. Thus, the Bible says that Mordecai wore a *lebhosh* of sackcloth (Esther 4:2), while a more exquisite *lebhosh* could serve as "royal apparel" (Esth. 8:15). The Psalmist referred to this garment when he wrote, "They part my garments among them, and cast lots upon my vesture" (Ps. 22:18).

Finally, the *addereth* was worn to indicate that the wearer was a person of importance (Josh. 7:21). This garment was also a type of cloak or outer covering. By contrast, such a cloak is worn by various people in Palestine today, regardless of their station in life.

These examples demonstrate how the use of certain garments changed as Jewish society changed. And the manufacture of these garments points to the availability of different textile materials in each era of history.

This article will discuss four different aspects of the clothing of Bible times—fabrics, men's clothing, women's clothing, and priests' clothing. We will also note how Near Eastern people used cosmetics and jewelry.

I. TYPES OF FABRICS
    A. Linen
    B. Wool
    C. Silk
    D. Sackcloth
    E. Cotton

CLOTHING AND COSMETICS

I. Types of Fabrics. Genesis 3:7 tells how Adam and Eve realized they were naked and sewed fig leaves together to make "aprons" (Hebrew, *hagor*). Then the Creator made Adam and Eve shirts of skins, as we saw, before sending them out of the Garden of Eden (Gen. 3:21). Later, various fabrics were used to make clothes.

A. Linen. Linen was one of the most important fabrics for the Israelites. It was made from the flax plant, which was cultivated especially for that purpose. The Canaanites grew flax in Palestine before the Israelites conquered that country (Josh. 2:6).

Linen was a versatile fabric that could be made coarse and thick, or very fine and delicate. The Egyptians had a wide reputation for their fine linen, which was nearly transparent. They also made coarse linen that was so heavy that it could be used for carpets to cover the floors.

The fine linen fabrics were worn by those with positions of status or wealth (cf. Luke 16:19), and the coarser fabrics were worn by the common people. The Egyptians clothed Joseph in fine linen when they made him ruler (Gen. 41:42).

The curtains, veil, and door hangings of the Hebrew tabernacle were made of fine linen (Ex. 26:1, 31, 36), as were the hangings for the gate of the court and for the court itself (Ex. 27:9, 16, 18). The ephod and breastpiece of the high priest contained fine linen (Ex. 28:6, 15). The tunic, girdle, and breeches worn by all priests were also made of fine white linen (Ex. 28:39; 39:27–28).

The Jews made their inner garments, or underclothing, primarily of linen. The graveclothes of Jesus were made from this fabric. Scripture says that Joseph of Arimathea "bought fine linen, and took him down, and wrapped him in the linen" (Mark 15:46). Fine white linen was also a symbol of innocence and moral purity (Rev. 15:6).

B. Wool. The Jews used sheep's wool as the principal material for making clothes. The merchants of Damascus in Syria found a ready market for their fine wool in the port city of Tyre (Ezek. 27:15). Wool is one of the oldest materials used for woven cloth.

God's Law did not allow the Israelites to weave garments from a mixture of wool and linen (Deut. 22:11). This law resembled several other precepts—such as not sowing mingled seed in a field, or not plowing with an ox and an ass together (Lev. 17:19–25). Perhaps these laws symbolically expressed the idea of separateness and simplicity that characterized the ancient people of God. On the other hand, the vestments of the high priest were made of such a mixture. (See the section "Priests'

35

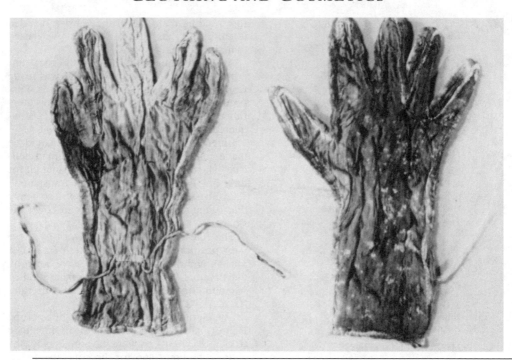

LINEN GLOVES. *Linen was one of the most important fabrics of the ancient world, due to its versatility. Woven coarse and thick, it clothed the poor; finer, more delicately woven linens made up the garments of the wealthy. The photograph shows linen gloves from the tomb of the Egyptian pharaoh Tutankhamen (fourteenth century B.C.).*

Clothing.") Therefore, the mixture may have been considered holy and inappropriate for common apparel.

Wool remained one of the chief materials for dress. Indeed, the economy of Bible lands relied heavily upon wool. (*See* "Trade.")

C. Silk. Ezekiel 16:10, 13 describes silk as a fabric of great value. The Hebrew words for this cloth were *sheshî* and *meshî*. Some scholars think the term found in Proverbs 31:22 (*sheshî*) actually refers to fine linen. We do not know if the Egyptians used silk, but the Chinese and other Asiatics used it in Old Testament times. Silk certainly reached the Bible lands after the conquest of Alexander the Great (*ca.* 325 B.C.). But it may have come to Palestine earlier, since Solomon traded with surrounding countries that might have produced this fabric.

The fineness and vivid color of fabrics increased their value, so silk held an important position in the ancient world. The luxury lovers of New Testament "Babylon" (Rome?) treasured silk (Rev. 18:12). As late as A.D. 275, unmixed silk goods were sold for their weight in gold.

D. Sackcloth. The Israelites used sackcloth as a ritual sign of repentance or a token of mourning. The dark color and coarse texture of this goat's hair material made it ideal for that use. When Joseph's brothers sold him to the Ishmaelites, Jacob put on sackcloth to mourn the loss of his son (Gen. 37:24). In times of extreme sorrow, the Israelites wore this rough material next to their skin, as Job did (Job 16:15).

The New Testament also associated sackcloth with repentance, as we find in Matthew 11:21: "For if the mighty works which were done in you, had been done in Tyre and Sidon, they would have repented long ago in sackcloth and ashes." The sorrowful Israelite would clothe himself in sackcloth, place ashes upon his head, and then sit in the ashes. Our modern Western custom of wearing dark colors to funerals corresponds to the Israelites' gesture of wearing sackcloth.

Sackcloth material was also used to make grain sacks (Gen. 42:25; Josh. 9:4).

E. Cotton. We do not know whether the Israelites used cotton for making clothes. The Hebrew *pishtah* meant a type of material from

CLOTHING AND COSMETICS

Clothing and Climate

Climate is a primary factor in determining a people's style of dress. This can be seen by comparing the dress of ancient Hebrews with the dress of peoples who lived in different climate zones.

Egyptians of the Nile Valley shaved their heads and bodies to keep cool and clean, and developed linen cloth—virtually the lightest of clothing materials—to offset the effects of the sweltering sun in their area. Egyptian workers wore a simple loincloth; in primitive times, this was also accepted garb for men in general. By the time of King Tutankhamen (fourteenth century B.C.), the loincloth had developed into a longer garment, much like an apron. Light cloaks or capes were worn over the shoulder. Women wore a long, loose garment that reached from below the arms to the ankle, and was held in place over the shoulders by one or two straps. The only sleeved garment of the Egyptians was the *kalasiris,* a rectangle of linen cloth with separate sleeves sewn in.

The Egyptians preferred the sheerest of linens. For shoes they wore leather or rush sandals. Headgear consisted of conical hats for men and headbands for women. Many Egyptians carried fans, which served a useful purpose in the hot region, in addition to being decorative.

Contrast the dress of ancient Egyptians with that of the Celts, a barbarian people who lived north of the Alps by at least the sixth century B.C. The Celts were tall, muscular, light-skinned people who lived and worked in a harsh, cold climate. Their basic economy was farming. They raised cattle, cultivated cereal, and engaged in other types of farming—all in climates considerably colder than that of Egypt.

The Celts might wear thick undergarments and a type of stocking or legging, depending on the weather in their region. Men of the Cisalpine tribes wore trousers by the third century B.C. By that time, the Celts also preferred to wear belted tunics or shirts with a cloak. They wrapped cloth about their feet. Celtic women wore a single long garment with a cloak.

The Celts preferred coarse linens and wool for protection against the cold. Their clothing was colored in a wide spectrum, from the darkest shades to sun hues and whites. The Egyptians, on the other hand, preferred white; their only alternate colors were light blues, yellows, and greens.

These extremes in clothing styles—from linen loincloths in Egypt to coarse shirts in northern Europe—points up the role that climate plays in determining the type of garments that different peoples prefer.

---

plants, as opposed to animal material such as wool. The term could refer to the flax plant (as per the RSV) from which linen was made, or possibly to the cotton bush (as per the KJV).

Although the Hebrew word *karpas* was usually translated as if it meant a color (Esth. 1:6; 8:15), it may possibly refer to cotton. Both Syria and Palestine grow cotton today; but we are not sure whether the Hebrews knew of cotton before they came into contact with Persia.

II. Manufacture of Fabrics. Jewish women made clothes out of necessity. The preparation of fabrics and the actual making of clothes were considered to be women's duties. Several processes were involved.

A. Distaff Spinning. Jewish women used distaff spinning to make cloth, since the spinning wheel was unknown at that time. They would attach wool or flax to the *distaff* (a rod or stick), and then use a *spindle* to twist the fibers into threads. The Bible mentions this art in Exodus 35:25–26 and Proverbs 31:19.

B. Weaving. After the women spun the raw materials into thread, they used the thread to weave cloth. We call the lengthwise threads the *warp* and the cross threads the *woof.* The women would attach the woof to a *shuttle,* an instrument that held the thread so that it could be passed over and under the threads of the warp. Scripture does not specifically describe the use of a shuttle, but it is implied in Job 7:6. The warp was attached to a wooden beam at the top or the bottom of the loom, and the weaver stood while working. (The Bible does not mention the loom, only the beam to which the warp was attached—Judg. 16:14.) Various textures of fabric could be produced by this method.

The Israelites were probably acquainted with weaving long before their time of slavery in Egypt. But in Egypt they perfected the art to such a degree that they were able to make the temple hangings mentioned in Exodus 35:35.

The Israelites made various kinds of woven fabrics in their years of wandering in the wilderness. These included woolen garments (Lev. 13:48), twined linen (Ex. 26:1), and the embroidered clothing of the priests (Ex. 28:4, 39).

C. Tanning. Tanning was a process that the

35

CLOTHING AND
COSMETICS

CLOTHING AND COSMETICS

people of Bible times used to dry animal skins, preparing them to wear. They used lime, the juice of certain plants, and the leaves or bark of certain trees to tan the skins.

Jews considered the tanner's trade disreputable. Peter defied this prejudice by stopping with Simon, a tanner, at Joppa (Acts 9:43). Jewish tanners were usually forced to conduct their business outside town.

D. Embroidering. The Hebrews did beautiful needlework. The term *embroider* (Hebrew *shâbâts* and *râqam*) appears in Exodus 28:39; 35:35; 38:23. The "cunning work" (Hebrew, *châshab*) mentioned in Exodus 26:1 may have been more like embroidery than needlework. However, neither would exactly fit our modern idea of embroidery.

The embroiderer wove cloth with a variety of colors and then sewed a pattern onto it. Thus the decorated part of the cloth was on one side of the fabric. In contrast, the "cunning work" was done by weaving gold thread or figures right into the fabric. The Jews did this sophisticated type of embroidery only on the garments worn by the priests.

E. Dyeing. The Israelites were very familiar with the art of dyeing at the time of their Exodus from Egypt (cf. Ex. 26:1, 14; 35:25). The process of dyeing is described in detail on Egyptian monuments; however, Scripture gives us no precise record of how the Hebrews dyed their cloth.

Undyed cotton and linen were used, with some exceptions. Cotton could be dyed indigo blue, but linen was more difficult to dye. Occasionally blue threads decorated the otherwise plain cloth. When the Bible mentions a fabric color other than blue, it indicates that the fabric was wool.

The natural dye colors used by the Jews were white, black, red, yellow, and green. Red was a very popular color for Hebrew clothing.

The purple dye so famous in the ancient Near East came from a species of shellfish in the Mediterranean Sea. The Hebrews valued purple goods very highly, but they loosely used the term to refer to every color that had a reddish tint.

The New Testament tells us that Lydia was a "seller of purple in the city of Thyatira" (Acts 16:14). Thyatira was famous for its cloth dyers, so we assume that Lydia dealt in cloth of purple and possibly in the dye itself.

III. Care of Fabrics. Clothes were laundered by fullers in Bible times. The English term *fuller* means "one who washes" or "one who treads." The professional fuller would clean garments by stamping on them or beating them with a stick in a tub of water. Jeremiah 2:22 and Malachi 3:2 tell us that nitre and soap were used as cleaning agents. Other substances were also used for cleaning, such as alkali and chalk. To whiten garments, fullers would rub "fuller's earth" (cimolite) into them.

The trade of the fuller created an offensive odor, so it was done outside the city. A place called the "fuller's field" on the northern side of the city of Jerusalem was where fullers washed and dried their clothes. Their water supply came from the upper pool of Gihon on the northern side of the city. Scripture tells us how the king of Assyria sent soldiers against Jerusalem from this northern direction (2 Kin. 18:17). It is interesting to note that the fuller's field was so near the city walls that the Assyrian ambassadors standing in the field could be heard on the ramparts.

IV. Men's Clothing. The Israelites were scarcely influenced by the dress of surrounding countries, since their travel was limited. The fashions of Israelite men remained much the same, generation after generation.

A. General Wear. Ordinarily, Jewish men wore an inner garment, an outer garment, a girdle, and sandals. Modern Arabs use the

TUNIC. *The tunic, a kimono-like inner garment reaching to the knees or ankles, was worn next to the skin. Both men and women wore tunics made from cotton, linen, or wool. Held close to the body by a girdle (usually a leather belt), the tunic might be the only garment worn by the poor in warm weather. However, the rich never appeared in public without their outer garments.*

CLOTHING AND COSMETICS

same flowing robes and make the same distinction between "inner" and "outer" garments—the inner garments being of lightweight material and the outer garments being heavy and warm. Modern Arabs also make a visible distinction between the dress of the rich and poor, the rich wearing much finer materials.

1. Inner Garment. The Israelite man's "inner garment" resembled a close-fitting shirt. The most common Hebrew word for this garment (*kethoneth*) is translated variously as *coat, robe, tunic,* and *garment.* It was made of wool, linen, or cotton. The earliest of these garments were made without sleeves and reached only to the knees. Later, the inner garment extended to the wrists and ankles.

A man wearing only this inner garment was said to be naked (1 Sam. 19:24; Is. 20:2–4). The New Testament probably refers to this garment when it says Peter "girt his fisher's coat unto him, (for he was naked,) and did cast himself into the sea" (John 21:7).

2. Girdle. The man's girdle was a belt or band of cloth, cord, or leather 10 cm. or more wide. A fastener attached to the girdle allowed it to be loosened or tightened. The Jews used the girdle in two ways: as a tie around the waist of the inner garment or around the outer garment. When used around the inner garment, it was often called the *loincloth* or *waistcloth.* The use of a girdle increased a person's gracefulness of appearance and prevented the long, flowing robes from interfering with daily work and movements.

The biblical expression "to gird up the loins" meant to put on the girdle; it signified that the person was ready for service (1 Pet. 1:13). On the other hand, "to loose the girdle" meant that the person was either lazy or resting (Is. 5:27).

3. Outer Garment. The Hebrew men wore an "outer garment" consisting of a square or oblong strip of cloth, two to three m. (80 to 120 in.) wide. This garment (*me'yil*) was called the *coat, robe,* or *mantle.* It was wrapped around the body as a protective covering, with two corners of the material being in front. The outer garment was drawn in close to the body by a girdle. Sometimes the Israelites decorated the girdle for this outer garment with rich and beautiful ornaments of metal, precious stones, or embroidery. The poor man used this outer garment as his bed clothing (Ex. 22:26–27). The rich often had a

COAT. *The coat was an outer robe with sleeves. The girdle—sometimes ornamented with precious metals, stones, or embroidery—held this garment close to the body.*

finely woven linen outer garment, and the poor a coarsely woven garment of goat's hair.

Jewish men wore fringes with blue ribbons on the "border" (hemline) of this outer garment (Num. 15:38). The fringes reminded them of the constant presence of the Lord's commandments. Jesus referred to these fringes in Matthew 23:5; apparently, the scribes and Pharisees made these fringes very large so that people could see how faithful they were in doing the Lord's commandments.

The Hebrews often ripped the outer garment in times of distress (Ezra 9:3, 5; Job 1:20; 2:12).

A person's number of robes was a measure of wealth in the Near East (cf. James 5:2). Consequently, a large wardrobe indicated that a person was rich and powerful, and a lack of clothing showed poverty. In this connection, note Isaiah 3:6–7.

4. Purse. The man's purse was actually formed by the girdle, which was sewn double and fastened with a buckle. The other end of the girdle was wrapped around the body and then tucked into the first section, which opened and closed with a leather strap. The contents of the purse were placed beneath the strap. Matthew 10:9 and Mark 6:8 refer to this type of purse. Apparently, the Jews also used a type of purse that was separate from the girdle (Luke 10:4).

Jewish men also used a *scrip,* which may have been similar to our modern purse. Shepherds carried their food or other necessities in this type of bag. It seems that the scrip was worn over the shoulder. In such a bag, David

CLOTHING AND COSMETICS

carried five stones to slay the giant Goliath (1 Sam. 17:40). The scrip mentioned in the New Testament, carried by shepherds and travelers, might have been made of skins (Mark 6:8).

5. Sandals. The term *sandals* is used only twice in the Bible. In its simplest form, the sandal was a sole of wood fastened with straps of leather (thongs). The disciples of Jesus wore these (Mark 6:9). When an angel appeared to Peter in prison, Peter was told to put on his sandals (Acts 12:8). All classes of people in Palestine wore sandals—even the very poor. In Assyria, sandals also covered the heel and the side of the foot. The sandal and the thong (or "shoe latchet") were so common that they symbolized the most insignificant thing, as in Genesis 14:23.

Jews did not wear their sandals indoors (Luke 7:38); they removed them upon entering the house, and the feet were washed. Removing the sandals was also a sign of reverence; Moses was told to do it when God spoke to him from the burning bush (Ex. 3:5).

The Jews considered it a very lowly task to carry or to unloose another person's sandals. When John the Baptist spoke of the coming of Christ, he said, "He it is, who coming after me is preferred before me, whose shoe's latchet I am not worthy to unloose" (John 1:27).

Going without sandals was a mark of poverty (Luke 15:22) or a sign of mourning (2 Sam. 13:30; Is. 20:2–4; Ezek. 24:17, 23).

B. Clothing for Special Occasions. Wealthy Jewish men owned several suits of clothing; each suit consisted of an inner and outer garment. Some of these suits of clothing were made of very thin fabric and were worn over garments of various colors (Is. 3:22).

1. Robes of Honor. Often a man being installed in a position of honor or importance was given a special robe. Joseph was given such a robe when he was put in a position of leadership in Egypt (Gen. 41:42). On the other hand, the removal of a robe signaled a man's dismissal from office. A fine robe was a mark of a man's special honor in a household (Luke 15:22).

2. Wedding Garments. On grand occasions, a host would give special robes to his guests. At Jewish weddings, for instance, the host furnished wedding garments to all the guests (Matt. 22:11). At times, the wedding party wore crowns (Ezek. 16:12).

3. Mourning Garments. See the section on "Sackcloth."

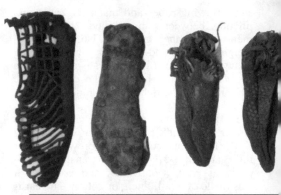

SANDALS. *Most of the people in ancient lands were barefoot or wore sandals. The poor could not afford shoes, since shoes were made of soft leather, which was scarce. Sandals were of tough leather. Some think the Israelites constructed the soles of wood, cane, or palm bark, nailing them to the leather thongs. Archaeologists have found ancient sandals in great variety. These are from Britain during the time of the Roman occupation; notice the hobnails in the sandal second from left.*

4. Winter Clothing. In the winter, people of the Bible lands wore fur dresses or skins. This type of winter clothing may be indicated in 2 Kings 2:8 and Zechariah 13:4. Common cattle skins were worn by the poorest people (Heb. 11:37), but some fur robes were very costly and were a part of the royal wardrobe.

Sheep's clothing (sheepskin) suggested innocence and gentleness; but Matthew 7:15 speaks of it as a symbol of the disguise of false prophets, who lead the people in the wrong way.

C. Ornaments. Jewish men wore bracelets, rings, chains, and necklaces of various kinds. In the Near East, both sexes wore chains of gold for ornament and dignity. Government officials placed such chains on Joseph and Daniel as symbols of sovereignty (Gen. 41:42; Dan. 5:29). Jewish men had a fondness for improving their personal appearance, and they often used jewelry to do this. The craft of jewelry-making probably developed at a very early period (Num. 31:50; Hos. 2:13).

1. Rings. The Jew used the ring as a seal and token of his authority (Gen. 41:42; Dan. 6:17). With his signet ring he would stamp his personal seal on official documents. It could be worn on a cord around the neck or on the finger. Men also wore rings or bands on the upper arms (cf. 2 Sam. 1:10).

As many as nine rings have been found on a single hand of an Egyptian mummy, indicating that the market for jewelry was quite active. In battles, soldiers took bracelets and anklets from their enemy as part of the spoil. When the Amalekite killed Saul, he brought Saul's bracelet to David as proof of Saul's death (2 Sam. 1:10).

2. Amulets. In the superstitious Near Eastern nations many people feared imaginary spirits. To protect themselves, they wore magical charms. The *amulets* referred to in the Bible were earrings worn by women (Gen. 35:4; Judg. 2:13; 8:24), or pendants suspended from chains around the necks of men. The amulet had sacred words or the figure of a god engraved on it. In another form of amulet, the words were written on a papyrus or parchment scroll that was rolled tightly and sewn up in linen.

3. Phylacteries. To counter the idolatrous practice of wearing amulets, Hebrew men began wearing *phylacteries.* There were two kinds of phylacteries: one worn on the forehead between the eyebrows, and one worn on the left arm. The one worn on the forehead was called a *frontlet.* It had four compartments, each of which contained a piece of parchment. On the first was written Exodus 13:1–10, on the second was written Exodus 13:11–16, on the third was written Deuteronomy 6:4–9, and on the fourth, Deuteronomy 11:13–21. These four pieces of paper were wrapped in animal skin, making a square pack. This small bundle was then tied to the forehead with a thong or ribbon. These Scripture passages contained God's commands to remember and obey His Law (e.g., Deut. 6:8).

The phylactery worn on a man's arm was made of two rolls of parchment, on which the laws were written in special ink. The parchment was partially rolled up, enclosed in a case of black calfskin, and tied with a thong to the upper left arm near the elbow. The thong was then wound crisscross around the arm, ending at the top of the middle finger. Some Jewish men wore their phylacteries both evening and morning; others wore them only at morning prayer. Phylacteries were not worn on the Sabbath or on other sacred days; those days were themselves holy signs, so the wearing of phylacteries was unnecessary.

Jesus condemned the practice of "making broad the phylacteries" (Matt. 23:5). The Pharisees made their phylacteries larger than usual, so that casual observers would think they were very holy.

D. Hair Style. Hebrew men considered the hair to be an important personal ornament, so they gave much care and attention to it. Egyptian and Assyrian monuments show examples of elaborate hair arrangements in those cultures. The Egyptians also wore various types of wigs. But we see an important difference between Hebrew and Egyptian hair styles in Genesis 41:14, which says that Joseph "shaved himself" before he was presented to the pharaoh. An Egyptian would have been content to comb his hair and trim his beard; but Hebrew men cut their hair much as modern Western men do, using a primitive kind of scissors (2 Sam. 14:26). The word *polled* in this text means "to cut the hair from the head." The Jews also used razors, as we see in Numbers 6:5.

When a Jewish man made a religious vow, he did not cut his hair (cf. Judg. 13:5). The Israelites were not to shave their hair so closely that they resembled heathen gods who had shaved heads. Nor were they to resemble the Nazirites, who refused to cut their hair at all (Ezek. 44:20). In the New Testament times, long hair on men was considered to be contrary to nature (1 Cor. 11:14).

Men often applied perfumed oil to their hair before festivals or other joyous occasions (Ps. 23:5). Jesus mentions this custom in Luke 7:45, when He says, "My head with oil thou didst not anoint. . . ."

Jewish men also paid much attention to the care of the beard. It was an insult to attempt to touch a man's beard, except when kissing it respectfully and affectionately as a sign of friendship (2 Sam. 20:9). Tearing out the beard, cutting it off entirely, or neglecting to trim it were expressions of deep mourning (cf. Ezra 9:3; Is. 15:2; Jer. 41:5). Egyptian and Roman men preferred clean-shaven faces, although Egyptian rulers did wear artificial beards.

E. Headdress. Apparently, Jewish men wore a headdress for special occasions (Is. 61:3), on holidays, or in times of mourning (2 Sam. 15:30). We first see the headdress mentioned in Exodus 28:40, as a part of the priest's clothing.

Hebrew men probably used a head covering only on rare occasions, though Egyptian and Assyrian men wore them often. Some ancient headdresses were quite elaborate, especially those worn by royalty. The common Egyptian man wore a simple headdress consisting of a square cloth, folded so that three corners hung

35

CLOTHING AND
COSMETICS

CLOTHING AND COSMETICS

MAN IN ROBE. *This statue from Syria (eighth or ninth century B.C.) depicts a man dressed in a long, pleated garment with short sleeves. Over it he wears a shawl with a fringed edge, which is wound about the body at the waist.*

down the back and shoulders. This may have been the type used by the Hebrews.

The Assyrians used a headdress much like a high turban (Ezek. 23:15). Syrian men in Damascus most likely wore the turban.

V. Women's Clothing. Women wore clothing that was very similar to that of men. However, the law strictly forbade a woman to wear anything that was thought to belong particularly to a man, such as the signet ring and other ornaments. According to the Jewish historian Josephus, women were also forbidden to use the weapons of a man. By the same to-

ken, men were forbidden to wear the outer robe of a woman (Deut. 22:5).

A. Inner Garment. This garment was worn by both sexes, and was made of wool, cotton, or linen. (See under "Men's Clothing.")

B. Outer Garment. The Hebrew woman's outer garment differed from that of the man. It was longer, with enough border and fringe to cover the feet (Is. 47:2; Jer. 13:22). It was secured at the waist by a girdle. As with the men, the female's clothing might be made of different materials, according to the social status of the individual.

The front of the woman's outer garment was long enough for her to tuck it up over the girdle to serve as an apron. The word *apron* is first mentioned in Genesis 3:7, when Adam and Eve sewed themselves aprons of fig leaves. This article of clothing may have resembled our modern apron to some degree. The apron might have been used to protect the clothing during work, or to carry some item (cf. Ruth 3:15).

C. Veil. Hebrew women did not wear a veil at all times, as is now the custom in many of the lands of the Near East. Wearing a veil was an act of modesty that usually indicated that a woman was unmarried. When Rebekah first saw Isaac, she was not wearing a veil; but she covered herself with a veil before Isaac saw her (Gen. 24:65). Women of New Testament times covered their heads for worship, but not necessarily their faces (1 Cor. 11:5).

D. Handkerchief. The Hebrew word for *handkerchief* (*mispachoth*) might better be translated as *napkin* or *towel*. These cloths were used to wrap things being carried (Luke 19:20), to wipe perspiration from the face, or to cover the face of the dead.

Some commentators think that the burial napkin was tied under the chin and over the top of the head to keep the dead person's jaw from sagging (John 11:44). John 20:7 says that the napkin that covered the face of the Lord was found rolled and lying separately from the linen grave clothes.

Often the women of modern Near Eastern nations carry handkerchiefs with beautiful needlework. This may also have been the custom in ancient times.

E. Sandals. Jewish women wore sandals, as did the men. There were many variations of the common sandal. The sole might be made of the tough hide of a camel's neck.

CLOTHING AND COSMETICS

Sometimes several thicknesses of hide were sewn together.

One type of woman's sandal had two straps: one strap passed between the big toe and the second toe, and the other went around the heel and over the instep. This shoe could be easily slipped off when coming indoors.

F. Ornaments. The Bible first mentions women's jewelry when Abraham's servant presented earrings and bracelets to Rebekah (Gen. 24:22). Jeremiah well described the Jewish woman's attraction to jewelry when he said, "Can a maid forget her ornaments?" Hebrew women wore bracelets, necklaces, earrings, nose rings, and gold chains. Isaiah 3:16, 18–23 gives a graphic picture of the fashionably ornamented woman of Old Testament times.

1. Bracelets. Both Hebrew women and men wore bracelets (Gen. 24:30). Today, Near Eastern people consider a woman's bracelet to be a badge of high status or royalty, as it probably was in David's time (2 Sam. 1:10). The royal bracelet was probably made of a precious material, such as gold, and was worn above the elbow. The common woman's bracelet might have been worn at the wrist, as it is today (Ezek. 16:11).

Most women's bracelets were made in a full circle to slip over the hand. Some bracelets were made in two pieces that opened on a hinge and closed with a tie or pin. Bracelets varied in size, from several centimeters wide to slender bands.

2. Anklets. Women wore anklets as commonly as bracelets, and these were made of much the same materials (Is. 3:16, 18, 20). Some anklets made a tinkling musical sound as the woman walked. Women of high rank wore hollow anklets filled with pebbles, so that the rattling sound could be heard when they walked.

3. Earrings. Among the Hebrews and Egyptians, only the women wore earrings (cf. Judg. 8:24). Among the Assyrians, both men and women wore earrings.

We are not certain of the form of Hebrew earrings, but Scripture passages suggest that they were round (e.g., Gen. 24:22). Egyptian earrings were generally large single hoops of gold, from 3 to 5 cm. (1 to 2 in.) in diameter. Occasionally, several hoops were fastened together or precious stones were added for effect.

Heathen nations sometimes used earrings as charms. (See the section on "Amulets.") We see this when Jacob's family went to Bethel from Shechem (Gen. 35:4), and they gave up their earrings.

4. Nose Jewels. The woman's nose ring or nose jewel was one of the most ancient ornaments of the East. The ring was made of ivory or precious metals, often with jewels in them. At times, these nose jewels were more than 6 cm. (2.5 in.) in diameter and hung down over the woman's lips. The custom of wearing nose rings still exists in some parts of the Near East, mainly among dancing girls and the lower class of people. However, we have no evidence that Hebrew women wore nose rings.

5. Crisping Pins. The Hebrew word (*charitim*), translated by the KJV as "crisping pins" in Isaiah 3:22 and as "bags" in 2 Kings 5:23, is used only these two times in the Bible. We are not sure what this type of jewelry might have been, or even whether it was a type of jewelry.

6. Cosmetics and Perfumes. Egyptian and Assyrian women used paint as a cosmetic. They colored their eyelashes and the edges of the eyelids with a fine black powder moistened with oil or vinegar, to achieve an effect somewhat like modern mascara.

Hebrew women also painted their eyelashes. But this practice was generally viewed with contempt, as was the case with Jezebel (2 Kin. 9:30). Painting the eyes is disdainfully mentioned in Jeremiah 4:30 and Ezekiel 23:40.

Some women stained their fingers and toes with henna. (*See* "Plants.") This was especially true of the Egyptian women, who also tattooed their hands, feet, and face.

Ancient women used perfume in much the same manner as women do today. Common sources of perfume in Bible times were frankincense and myrrh from Arabia and Africa, aloes and nard from India, cinnamon from Aylon, galbanum from Persia, and stacte and saffron from Palestine. Perfume was a valued item of trade (cf. Gen. 37:25). (*See* "Plants.")

Exodus 30:4–38 tells how the Hebrews made a perfume used in the tabernacle rituals. But the Law forbade the personal use of this perfume.

7. Hair Style. Paul the apostle said that hair was a natural veil, or covering, for the woman; he indicates that in his day it was shameful for a Christian woman to cut her hair (1 Cor. 11:15). The women wore

CLOTHING AND COSMETICS

HOSPITALITY. *God told the Israelites to be hospitable (Lev. 19:34). This meant that they should offer food, shelter, and clothing to travelers passing through their lands. An important Hebrew custom was the washing of the guests' feet, a gesture of welcome in a hot, dusty country where stony roads often made foot travel a painful experience.*

their hair long and braided. The Talmud mentions that Jewish women used combs and hairpins.

Among the Egyptian and Assyrian women, the hair styles were much more elaborate than those worn by the Hebrews, as the monuments of that day show.

8. Headdress. Jewish women used the headdress to some degree, but the apostle Paul urged modest apparel for Christian women (1 Tim. 2:8). The women may have used gold or jewels for hair ornaments (1 Pet. 3:3), as was the practice of women in neighboring countries.

The veil that Jewish women sometimes wore could hardly be considered a headdress, although it did cover the head. In contrast, the headdress for other Near Eastern women was elaborate and costly, depending on the wealth and social position of the wearer.

VI. Priests' Clothing. Priestly dress was much different from that of the common Jew. Furthermore, the high priest's clothing differed from that of the common priest.

A. Breeches. Among the Hebrews, breeches were worn only by the priests. In some neighboring countries, both breeches and trousers were worn by common men.

The Jews used fine linen to make this priestly garment. Apparently, it served as an undergarment so that the priest would not be exposed when he climbed the steps of the temple to minister at the altar (Exod. 28:42–43). This undergarment covered the priest's body from the waist to the knees. Rather than being trousers, "breeches" were probably a double apron. Other references to "breeches" are found in Exodus 39:28; Leviticus 6:10; 16:4; and Ezekiel 44:18.

B. Cassock or Robe. The priests also wore robes of white linen during their temple ministrations. These garments came from the weaver seamless, bound at the waist with a girdle decorated by needlework (Ex. 28:31–34). The garment of Jesus was also a seamless robe, symbolically showing His universal priesthood (John 19:23; Heb. 4:14–15). The priest's robe nearly covered the feet and was woven in a diamond or chessboard pattern.

C. Bonnet. A bonnet was worn by the ordinary priest. This bonnet was made of fine linen (Ex. 39:28). The Hebrew word (*migbaoth*) from which *bonnet* was translated means "to be lofty."

D. Footwear. During all of their ministrations, the priests were to be barefoot. Before they entered the tabernacle, they were to wash their hands and feet. "And he set the laver between the tent of the congregation and the altar, and put water there, to wash withal. And Moses and Aaron and his sons washed their hands and their feet thereat" (Ex. 40:30–31). The area on which the priests were standing was considered holy ground, as was the case with Moses and the burning bush (Ex. 3:5).

E. Hair Care. In Leviticus 21:5, we see that baldness disqualified a man from the priesthood. The priest was not allowed to shave his head or rip his clothes, even to mourn his mother or father's death (Lev. 21:10–11).

VII. High Priest's Clothing. One of the distinctions that separated the high priest from the common priest was the sprinkling of his garments with anointing oil (Ex. 28:41;

CLOTHING AND COSMETICS

29:21). The high priest's clothes were passed on to his successor at his death.

The high priest's garments consisted of seven parts—the ephod, the robe of the ephod, the breastplate, the mitre, the embroidered coat, the girdle, and the breeches (Ex. 28:42).

A. Ephod. The high priest's garments were made of plain linen (1 Sam. 2:18; 2 Sam. 6:14), as were the clothes for all priests. But his ephod was made of "gold, of blue, and of purple, of scarlet, and of fine twined linen" (Ex. 28:6). This indicates that it was a blend of wool and linen, since linen could be dyed only blue. The "cunning work" signifies some type of embroidery.

There were two parts to the ephod: one covering the back and the other covering the breast of the wearer. The garment was fastened at each shoulder by a large onyx stone.

The girdle of the ephod was made of blue, purple, and scarlet fabric interwoven with gold thread (Ex. 28:8).

B. Robe of the Ephod. The robe of the ephod was of inferior material to the ephod, dyed blue (Ex. 39:22). It was worn under the ephod and was longer than the ephod. This robe had no sleeves, only slits in the sides for the arms.

The skirt of this garment had a fringe (trimming) of pomegranates in blue, purple, and scarlet, with a bell of gold hung between each pomegranate. These bells were attached to the bottom of the high priest's robe so that he would be heard as he came or went from the holy place (Ex. 28:32–35).

C. Breastplate. The high priest's breastplate is described in detail in Exodus 28:15–30. It was a piece of embroidered material about 25.4 cm. (10 in.) square and doubled over to make a bag or pouch.

This priestly garment was adorned with twelve precious stones, each bearing the name of one of the twelve tribes of Israel (Ex. 28:9–12). (*See* "Minerals and Gems.") The two upper corners were fastened to the ephod, from which it was not to be loosened (Ex. 28:28). The two lower corners were fastened to the girdle. The rings, chains, and other fastenings were of gold or rich lace.

The breastplate and ephod were called a "memorial" (Ex. 28:12, 29), because they reminded the priest of his relationship to the twelve tribes of Israel. It was also called the "breastplate of judgment" (Exod. 28:15), possibly because it was worn by the priest,

IVORY FIGURE. *The Aramaean figure of ivory dates from about 850 B.C. It shows a man wearing his full, shoulder-length hair parted in the middle. His costume is a long fringed garment, wrapped with a shawl.*

who was God's spokesman of justice and judgment to the Jewish nation. It may also have been called this because it provided a container for the *urim* and *thummim,* the sacred lots, that showed God's judgments upon men (cf. Num. 26:55; Josh. 7:14; 14:2; 1 Sam. 14:42).

D. Mitre. The mitre, or upper turban, was the official headdress of the high priest (Ex. 28:39). It was made of fine linen, had many folds, and had a total length of about 7.3 m. (8 yds.)

This long cloth was wound around the head in turban style. On the front of the mitre was a gold plate bearing the Hebrew words for "HOLINESS TO THE LORD" (Ex. 28:36; 39:28, 30).

E. Embroidered Coat, Girdle, and Breeches. This particular coat was long-

CLOTHING AND COSMETICS

skirted, made of linen, and embroidered with a pattern as if stones were set in it (Ex. 28:4). The common priests also wore this garment. (*See* the section on "Cassock or Robe.")

The girdle of the high priest's garment was wound around the body several times from the breast downwards. The ends of the girdle hung down to the ankles (Ex. 29:5). Beneath the priestly garments, the high priest wore the same type of breeches as did the common priest. (*See* the section on "Breeches.")

ARCHITECTURE AND FURNITURE

Modern people admire the architecture of classical Greece and Rome, with its soaring marble pillars and elaborately decorated arches. But Israel produced very little architecture that we would call innovative or awe-inspiring. The Israelites designed their buildings and furniture to serve their daily needs, giving little thought to esthetic features. Yet their buildings and furniture tell us something of the people's way of life.

The most common dwellings in the ancient world were tents, formed by setting poles in the ground and stretching a covering of cloth or skin over them. The tent dweller would use cords to fasten this covering to stakes driven in the ground (cf. Is. 54:2). Sometimes people used curtains to divide their tents into rooms and covered the ground with mats or carpets. The door was a fold of cloth that could be dropped or raised. The tent dweller kindled his fire in a hole in the middle of the tent floor. His cooking utensils were very few and simple, and were easily moved from place to place.

When people began settling in cities, they built more permanent homes. Apparently they developed skills of architecture at a very early period. But even while the Canaanites and Assyrians built cities, the Hebrews lived in tents; it was not until the conquest of the Promised Land that they abandoned their simple habits. Then they entered the houses that the Canaanites left.

The Bible tells us that the Israelites built large and costly houses in Judea (cf. Jer. 22:14; Amos 3:15; Hag. 1:4). But these houses belonged to wealthy people; many still lived in tents or very crude shelters.

SKETCH OF A HOUSE. *This drawing depicts a large residence in an ancient Israelite village. The house of the average Israelite was small and uncomfortable by modern standards. A favorite spot for relaxation was the roof, reached by a stone staircase or a simple wooden ladder.*

ARCHITECTURE AND FURNITURE

Wealthy people built their houses in the form of a cloister, that is, surrounding an open court. A person entered the house by a door which was ordinarily kept locked, and was tended by someone who acted as a porter (cf. Acts 12:13). This door opened into a porch, furnished with seats or benches. One then walked through the porch to a short flight of stairs leading to the chambers and the open quadrangular court.

I. THE CENTRAL COURT
A. The Master's Quarters
B. Domestic Quarters

II. THE UPPER ROOMS
A. The Alliyah
B. The Roof

III. WINDOWS AND DOORS

IV. FIREPLACES

V. METHODS OF CONSTRUCTION
A. Homes of the Wealthy
B. Homes of the Poor

VI. THE SERVICE OF DEDICATION

VII. FURNITURE

I. The Central Court. The court was the center of a Jewish house. Probably this is where Jesus sat when a group of men lowered a paralytic man "into the midst" to reach Him (Luke 5:19). The court was designed to admit light and air to the rooms around it. Tile or rock paved the floor of the court to shed rain that might come in through the skylight. Sometimes the homeowner built this court around a fountain or well (cf. 2 Sam. 17:18).

The Parthenon

The Parthenon in Athens is one of the finest examples of classic Greek architecture. It physically represents the ancient Greeks' rational, harmonious approach to life. Moreover, it is a marvel of architectural design.

The Greeks erected at least one previous structure on the site of the Parthenon in 488 B.C., when they laid out a massive structure as a thank-offering for their victory over the Persians at Marathon. The limestone foundation for this building extended over 6 m. (20 ft.) into the rock of the Acropolis. Most above-ground work on this site was destroyed, however, when the Persians sacked the Acropolis in 480 B.C.

The Greeks began work on the Parthenon in 447 B.C. and completed it in 438 B.C. They made the structure the main temple on the Acropolis around 432 B.C., when they dedicated it to Athena Parthenos, patron goddess of Athens. Construction on this building was funded by the government of Pericles.

The building was designed to create an optical illusion. The tops of the Parthenon's Doric columns lean toward the center of each colonnade, the steps curve upward at the center, and the columns are more widely spaced at the center of each row than at the end. This makes the columns appear to be evenly spaced. (If they had truly been evenly spaced, the perspective angle would have made them look uneven.)

There are eight columns at each end of the Parthenon and 17 on each side. The Parthenon has a central area, or *cella,* which in turn is divided into chambers. An inner colonnade originally held the great cult statue of Athena, a masterpiece of the sculptor Phidias. This statue has not survived, but we know of its general appearance through smaller copies and through many representations on ancient coins. This statue was seen and described by Greek traveler Pausanias in the second century A.D.

The entire Parthenon is made of marble, including the tiles on the roof. The Greeks used no mortar or cement on the structure; they fitted marble blocks together with the greatest accuracy and secured them with metal clamps and dowels.

An ornamental band of low relief sculpture (*frieze*) decorates the Parthenon. These decorations represent combat among the gods such as Zeus, Athena, and Poseidon. They also picture mounted horsemen, chariot groups, and citizens of Athens.

The Greeks used color to highlight the Parthenon's beauty. The ceiling of the colonnade was colored with red, blue, and gold or yellow. A band running next to the frieze was colored red, and color accented the sculpture and bronze accessories within the Parthenon.

The Parthenon had a varied history. As early as 298 B.C., Lachares stripped the gold plates from the statue of Athena. In A.D. 426 the Parthenon was converted into a Christian church, and the Turks turned it into a mosque in 1460. In 1687 the Venetians, who were battling the Greeks, used the Parthenon as a powder magazine, and accidentally set off an explosion that destroyed the central section of the building. No major repairs were made until 1950, when engineers put fallen columns back in place and repaired the northern colonnade.

ARCHITECTURE AND FURNITURE

WINDOW BALUSTRADE. *Found at Ramat Rahel in southern Israel, this row of limestone pillars (ca. 600 B.C.) appears to have been a window balustrade. It was probably painted red, since traces of red paint were found on the pieces from which these columns were reconstructed. The pillars once graced King Jehoiakim's palace.*

Crowds gathered in a host's court on festive occasions (cf. Esth. 1:5). Usually the host would provide carpets, mats, and chairs for his guests, and might even stretch an awning over the skylight.

The surrounding rooms opened only onto the court, so that a person had to cross the court when entering or leaving the house. In later centuries, builders began erecting balconies or galleries outside the rooms that faced the central court.

A simple stairway of stone or wood led from the court to the rooms above, and to the roof. Larger houses might have more than one set of stairs.

A. The Master's Quarters. On the side of the court that faced the entrance was the reception room of the master of the house. It was furnished handsomely with a raised platform and a couch on three sides, which was a bed by night and a seat by day. The guests who entered took off their sandals before stepping upon the raised portion of the room.

The rooms assigned to the wife and daughters were usually upstairs, but sometimes they were on the level of the central court. No one except the master of the house could enter these apartments. Because the owner bestowed the greatest expense upon these rooms, they were sometimes called "palaces of the house" (1 Kin. 16:18; 2 Kin. 15:25) or "the house of the women" (Esth. 2:3; cf. 1 Kin. 7:8–12).

B. Domestic Quarters. We suppose that in ancient Judea, as in Palestine today, the people used their ground floor for domestic purposes—storing food, housing the servants, and so on. These ground-floor rooms were small and crudely furnished.

II. The Upper Rooms. When a person ascended to the second story by the stairs, he found that the chambers were large and airy, and often furnished with much more elegance than the rooms below. These upper rooms were also higher and larger than the lower rooms, projecting over the lower part of the

36

ARCHITECTURE AND FURNITURE

STABLES. *Archaeologists discovered these ruins of an extensive complex of stables, capable of housing as many as 480 horses, at Megiddo. This is the northern stable compound consisting of five units, each accommodating about 24 horses. Excavators first attributed these stables to Solomon; but subsequent investigation has shown that they date from the time of Ahab, several generations later.*

TABLE FROM JERICHO. *A tomb in Jericho contained this long table with two legs at one end and one at the other.*

building so that their windows hung over the street. They were secluded, spacious, and very comfortable.

Paul preached his farewell sermon in such a room. We can imagine that the crowd had to stand in two circles or ranks, the outer circle being next to the wall and lying on cushions beside the window casement. In that position Eutychus went to sleep and fell into the street (Acts 20:7–12).

A. The Alliyah. The Jews sometimes built another structure called the *alliyah* over the porch or gateway of the house. It consisted of only one or two rooms, and rose one story above the main house. The householder used it to entertain strangers, to store wardrobes, or for rest and meditation. Jesus probably referred to the *alliyah* when He spoke of going into the "closet" to pray (Matt. 6:6). Steps led directly from the street to the *alliyah*, but another flight of stairs connected the *alliyah* with the central court of the house. The *alliyah* afforded a much more private place for worship than the main roof of the house, which might be occupied by the whole family.

The Bible may refer to the *alliyah* when it mentions the "little chamber" of Elisha (2 Kin. 4:10), the "summer chamber" of Eglon (Judg. 3:20–23), the "chamber over the gate" (2 Sam. 18:33), the "upper chamber" of Ahaz (2 Kin. 23:12), and the "inner chamber" where Ben-hadad hid himself (1 Kin. 20:30).

B. The Roof. The roof was an important part of a house in biblical times. A person could climb to the roof by a flight of stairs along the outside wall. In most cases the roof was flat; but sometimes the builders made domes over the more important rooms. Jewish law required each house to have a balustrade or railing around the roof to keep anyone from falling off (Deut. 22:8). Adjoining houses often shared the same roof, and low walls on the roof marked the borders of each house.

The builders covered roofs with a type of cement that hardened under the sun. If this cracked, the householder had to spread a layer of grass on the roof to keep out the rain (cf. 2 Kin. 19:26; Ps. 129:6). Some houses had tiles or flat bricks on the roof.

The Israelites used their roofs as a place of retreat and meditation (Neh. 8:16; 2 Sam. 11:2; Is. 15:3; 22:1; Jer. 48:38). They dried linen, flax, corn, figs, and other fruits on the rooftops (Josh. 2:6). Sometimes they pitched tents on their roofs and slept there at night (2 Sam. 16:22).

The people used their rooftops for private conferences (1 Sam. 9:25). They also went there for private worship (Jer. 19:3; 2 Kin. 23:12; Zeph. 1:5; Acts 10:9) and to shout public announcements or bewail the loss of loved ones (Jer. 48:38; Luke 12:3).

III. Windows and Doors. In ancient houses, the windows were simply rectangular holes in the wall that opened upon the central court or upon the street outside. Sometimes the Israelites built a projecting balcony or porch along the front of the house, carefully enclosed by latticework. They opened the balcony window only for festivals and other special occasions. We suppose that Jezebel was looking out such an outer window when she was seized and put to death by Jehu (2 Kin. 9:30–33). This window was probably called the "casement" (Prov. 7:6; Song 2:9). The Israelites had no glass windows because glass was so expensive.

The doors of ancient houses were not hung on hinges. The jam (or inner side-piece) of the door projected as a circular shaft at the top and bottom. The upper end of this shaft would fit into a socket in the lintel and the lower end fell into a socket in the threshold. The King James Version loosely uses the word *hinges* in referring to the shaft of the door (1 Kin. 26:14; Prov. 26:14).

Often builders equipped the main door of the house with a lock and key. These ancient keys were made of wood or metal, and some

ARCHITECTURE AND FURNITURE

The Herodium

Herod the Great built magnificent structures for his own comfort and protection. Among these projects were his palace-fortress at Masada and the Herodium. In the event of insurrection or military defeat, either would offer strong defense. The Herodium, which was also designed to be Herod's burial place, stands as a tribute to Herod's obsessive fear. It is one of the largest fortresses ever built to guard one man.

The Herodium stands about 11 km. (7 mi.) south of Jerusalem and 5 km. (3 mi.) southeast of Bethlehem, at an altitude of about 700 m. (2300 ft.). It was built on the spot where Herod defeated the forces of the Hasmoneans and their supporters in 40 B.C.—a place of fond memories for Herod. The first-century Jewish historian Josephus tells of the construction of the Herodium in 20 B.C., and of Herod's funeral procession to the site. It was one of the last three strongholds remaining in Jewish hands outside Jerusalem when the Romans destroyed that city in A.D. 70. The Herodium also served as a rebel center during the Bar-Kochba revolt (A.D. 132—135).

V. Corbo led four seasons of excavation at the Herodium (1962–1967). G. Foerster did restoration and exploration at the site of the Herodium in 1967 and 1970, and E. Netzer led a dig at the site in 1972. Together they uncovered an astonishing structure that was surely the greatest engineering feat of intertestamental times.

Viewed from afar, the site looks like a shortened cone. The structure consists of four towers—three semicircular and one round—surrounded by a circular curtain wall, the outer diameter of which is 55 m. (180 ft.). This double wall has a 3-m. (10-ft.) wide passageway between walls. Evidently sand and stone building debris were piled around the outside of the walls soon after construction, leaving only their tops exposed. Thus the hill took on a conical shape.

The eastern half of the Herodium's inner space consisted of an open courtyard surrounded by Corinthian columns, with an *exedra* (outdoor area with seats for informal conversations) on each end. The western half included an elaborately decorated bathhouse complex, with a group of rooms including a dining room occupying the southern side. The dining room was converted into a synagogue, evidently when some of Bar-Kochba's followers held out there in the second century. Above the western rooms rose a second and possibly even a third story, used as living quarters.

A network of huge cisterns honeycombed the interior of the hill. An aqueduct brought water to the site from Solomon's Pools near Bethlehem. One of the inscribed pieces of pottery found by archaeologists at the site mentions Herod.

At the northern base of the hill Netzer uncovered a complex of structures. There was a palace measuring about 53 m. x 122 m. (175 ft. x 400 ft.), from which extended an observation balcony over what appears to have been a hippodrome about 300 m. (1,000 ft.) long, a pool, service building, and other unidentified structures. Obviously, Herod intended to live in style and be buried in splendor.

---

were so large that they were conspicuous when carried in public (Is. 22:22). Treasurers or other civic officers carried these huge keys as a symbol of their high office.

IV. Fireplaces. Ancient houses had no chimneys, even though some versions of the Bible use this word in Hosea 13:3. Smoke from the hearth escaped through holes in the roof and walls. The hearth itself was not a permanent fixture; it was a small metal stove or brazier (cf. Jer. 36:22–23). Since the hearth

was easy to carry from place to place, kings and generals often used it on military campaigns. (For more information about ancient fireplaces, *see* "Food and Eating Habits.")

V. Methods of Construction. We have been describing a typical house of the wealthy people. Individual houses varied from this floor plan; some were more elaborate than this, and others were simpler. But the Israelites used traditional methods of construction in all their homes.

ARCHITECTURE AND FURNITURE

A. Homes of the Wealthy. The materials for building were abundant in Palestine. Well-to-do homeowners could easily obtain stone and brick and the best timber for ornamental work in their houses. They often used hewn stone (Amos 5:11) and highly polished marble (1 Chr. 29:2; Esth. 1:6). They also used large quantities of cedar for their wall paneling and ceilings, often with moldings of gold, silver, and ivory (Jer. 22:14; Hag. 1:4). Perhaps their fondness for ivory accounts for the Bible's

FUNERARY STELE. *Discovered at Nerab in present-day Syria, this funerary tablet (ca. sixth century B.C.) depicts a priest sitting before an offering table, drinking from a cup. The bench and table are constructed in matching style, and the priest's feet rest upon a small footstool—a piece of furniture used in ancient times only by the wealthy.*

references to "houses of ivory" and "ivory palaces" (e.g., 1 Kin. 22:39; Ps. 35:8; Amos 3:15).

Wealthy landowners also built "winter houses" and "summer houses" for their comfort in those seasons (cf. Amos 3:15). They built the summer houses partly underground and paved them with marble. These houses generally had fountains in the central court, and were constructed to bring in currents of fresh air. This made them very refreshing in the torrid heat of summer. We know little about the construction of the winter houses.

We get a glimpse of a typical construction method of Old Testament times when we read how Samson destroyed a temple of the Philistines (Judg. 16:23–30). Samson's enemies brought him into the central court of the temple, which was surrounded by a range of balconies, each supported by one or two pillars. Here the officers of state assembled to transact public business and give public entertainments. If the pillars collapsed, it would upset the building and the people standing on the balconies would tumble to the pavement below.

B. Homes of the Poor. The houses of the common people were hovels of only one room with mud walls. The builders reinforced these walls with reeds and rushes, or with stakes plastered with clay. So the walls were very insecure, and often became breeding places for serpents and vermin (cf. Amos 5:19). The family occupied the same room with their animals, although they sometimes slept on a platform above the animals. Their windows were small holes high in the wall, perhaps barred.

The Bible warns against "leprosy in the house" (Lev. 14:34–53), which was probably a chemical reaction in the mud walls of these poorer homes. The Israelites understood that this "leprosy" would harm their health, so the priests ordered them to remove it.

The peasants made the doors of their homes very low and a person had to stoop to enter them. This kept out wild beasts and enemies. Some say it was a means of preventing the roving bands of Arabs from riding into the houses.

VI. The Service of Dedication. The Israelites dedicated their new homes before they set up housekeeping in them (Deut. 20:5). We suppose they celebrated this event with great joy, and asked God's blessing upon the house and the people who would live in it.

VII. Furniture. To our eyes, the best-furnished houses of Palestine would have appeared empty. On the marble floors of a rich man's house we would have seen beautiful rugs, and on the benches cushions of rich fabric. But the wealthy Israelites did not have the great variety of furniture to which we are accustomed, and the poor people had even less. A well-to-do man might have a mat or a skin to recline on during the day, a mattress to sleep on at night, a stool, a low table, and a brazier—this would be the extent of his furniture. Notice that the rich Shunammite woman furnished the room of Elisha with only a bed (perhaps merely a mattress), a table, a stool, and a candlestick (2 Kin. 4:10–13).

Because the floors of a more fashionable home were of tile or plaster, they often needed sweeping or scrubbing (cf. Matt. 22:11; Luke 15:8). At night the residents threw down thick, coarse mattresses to sleep on. The poorer people used skins for the same purpose. On two or three sides of the rich man's room was a bench, generally 30 cm. (12 in.) high, covered with a stuffed cushion. The master sat upon this bench in the daytime; but at one end of the room it was more elevated, and this was the usual place for sleeping (cf. 2 Kin. 1:4; 4:10). Besides the bench, the very wealthy people had bedsteads made of wood, ivory, or other expensive materials (Amos 6:4; Deut. 3:11). These bedsteads became more common in New Testament times (cf. Mark 4:21).

The Israelites used some of their normal outer garments for bedclothes (Ex. 22:26–27; Deut. 24:12–13). Before lying down for the night, they would simply take off their sandals and their girdle. (*See* "Clothing and Cosmetics.") The pillow of the Hebrews was probably a goat skin stuffed with wool, feathers, or

some other soft material. The poorer people of Palestine use these skins for their pillows today.

Kings and other rulers required a stool for their feet when they sat upon a throne (2 Chr. 9:18), but this piece of furniture was rare in private homes.

On the other hand, lamps were very common. They burned olive oil, pitch, naphtha, or wax, and they had wicks of cotton or flax. (A Jewish tradition says that the priests made wicks for the lamps of the temple from their old linen garments.) The poorer Israelites made their lamps of clay, while the wealthy had lamps of bronze and other metals.

The Israelites let their lamps burn all night, since light made them feel safer. We are told that the family would rather go without food than let their lamps go out, since that indicated they had deserted their house. So when Job predicts the ruin of wicked people, he says, ". . . The light of the wicked is put out . . . The lamp is dark in his tent, and his lamp above him is put out" (Job 18:5–6, RSV). The writer of Proverbs praises the prudent wife, saying, "Her lamp does not go out at night" (Prov. 31:18). Several other Bible passages show that the lamp symbolized the life and dignity of a family (cf. Job 21:17; Jer. 25:10).

Though their furniture was simple, the Israelites lived in much more comfort than their ancestors, who wandered with their flocks. In Jesus' day the typical home was neat and clean, with the functional beauty common to homes in other countries influenced by the Hellenistic culture. Though Palestine was ruled by Rome, few people adopted the ornate tastes of the Romans.

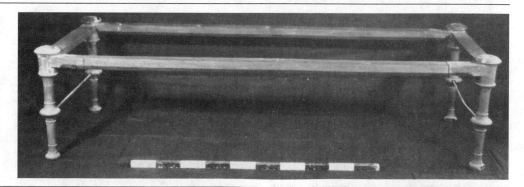

BRONZE FITTINGS FOR BED. *This bed from Tell el-Far'ah in southern Israel has been reconstructed from bronze fittings for the legs and the iron tie-rods that held the legs together. Most Israelites slept on pallets or mats upon the floor. Only the wealthy could afford the luxury of beds, which became more common in New Testament times.*

MUSIC

The Bible gives very little information about Hebrew musical forms and how they developed. For this reason, we must combine Bible study with history and archaeology if we wish to learn about the music of Bible times.

I. DEVELOPMENT OF HEBREW MUSIC
A. Distracting Effect
B. Function in Worship
C. Limits of Our Knowledge

II. TYPES OF INSTRUMENTS
A. Percussion Instruments
  1. Bells
  2. Castanets
  3. Cymbals
  4. Rattler-Sistrum
  5. Tabret
  6. Timbrel
  7. Gong
B. Stringed Instruments
  1. Dulcimer
  2. Harp
  3. Lute
  4. Lyre
  5. Psaltery
  6. Sackbut
  7. Trigon
  8. Viol
C. Wind Instruments
  1. Clarinet
  2. Cornet
  3. Flute
  4. Organ
  5. Pipe
  6. Shophar
  7. Trumpet

I. Development of Hebrew Music. The history of Hebrew music goes back to the first person who beat a stick on a rock, and it extends to the temple orchestra and the "joyous sound" called for in Psalm 150. That first musician heard rhythm as he beat his primitive instrument. As people began to realize they could make music, they created more complex instruments.

For example, David is credited with inventing a number of instruments, although we do not know precisely what they were (cf. Amos 6:5). David called upon a chorus of 4,000 to offer praises to the Lord "with the instruments which I made to praise" (1 Chr. 23:5; cf. 2 Chr. 7:6; Neh. 12:6). David also composed songs, such as his lament over the death of Saul and Jonathan.

Though God directed Israel's social and religious development, the nation absorbed ideas from surrounding cultures. Israel was at a geographical crossroads and was exposed to ideas and customs from other parts of the world (Gen. 37:25), including musical style.

Many men of Israel married foreign wives whose customs gradually crept into Hebrew lifestyle. According to the collection of postbiblical Jewish writings called the *Midrash,* King Solomon married an Egyptian woman whose dowry included 1,000 musical instruments. If this is true, no doubt she brought musicians with her to play those instruments in the traditional Egyptian way.

The purpose the music served and the way in which listeners responded to it also influenced the development of Hebrew music. In times of war, it was often necessary to sound an alarm or send some other kind of urgent signal. Thus the Hebrews developed the *shophar,* an instrument like a trumpet with loud, piercing tones (Ex. 32:17–18; Judg. 7:18–20). Merrymaking and frivolity called for the light, happy tones produced by the pipe or flute (Gen. 31:27; Judg. 11:34–35; Matt. 9:23–24; Luke 15:23–25).

HORN AND DRUM PLAYERS. *This basalt relief from Carchemish in Syria (eighth or ninth century B.C.) depicts four musicians, one blowing a curved horn, one carrying a large drum, and two beating the drum with their open hands. The figure at right appears to wear a neckstrap to help support the drum.*

MUSIC

The World's Oldest Sheet Music?

One scholar recently uncovered controversial evidence suggesting that the ancient Egyptians produced written sheet music during the same centuries as the building of the mighty Sphinx, about 4500 years ago. Maureen M. Barwise claims to have deciphered musical hieroglyphs that date back as far as the fourth dynasty of the old kingdom, roughly 2600 B.C.[1]

According to her translation, the music was written basically in a single melodic line. The earliest sacred pieces featured harps and flutes accompanied by timbrels and percussion sticks, joined later by trumpets, lutes, and lyres.

Ms. Barwise claims the Egyptian musicians used a "gapped" scale, producing music that was beautiful in spite of obvious peculiarities. She notes that it was similar to ancient Gaelic, Welsh, and Scottish folk tunes, with melodies like the droning of the Highland bagpipe.

The researcher undertook the unusual task of reproducing a number of tunes, translating them into the treble-clef keyboard. According to Barwise, the Egyptians understood timing, pitch, rhythm, and harmonic chords in addition to basic melody. The adapted tunes seem to cover a variety of musical moods, from the somewhat playful "Beautiful Moon-Bird of the Nile" to the rather stately grand march, "Honor to the Strong Arm of Pharaoh."

Egyptian music was considered sacred. Therefore, its composition was strictly governed by law and did not develop greatly over the centuries.

Wall paintings, bas-reliefs, and the literature of antiquity clearly show that the Egyptians were skillful musicians. Many experts believe that this early music was preserved in written form, but established archaeological theory holds that the melodies were an oral tradition.

Ms. Barwise's translation of hieroglyphics into music notation challenges the old school of thought and her scholarship has met mixed acceptance. Some critics agree with David Wulston's evaluation, that her work is nothing more than "a whimsical Tolkien-like fantasy [constructed] out of the most unpromising material."[2]

---

[1] Maureen W. Barwise, "Hearing the Music of Ancient Egypt," *The Consort,* Vol. 25 (1968–1969), pp. 345–361.

[2] David Wulston, "The Earliest Music Notation," *Music and Letters,* Vol. 52, No. 4 (Oct. 1971), p. 365.

A. Distracting Effect. Hebrew leaders who ministered in the temple took great care to avoid using music that was associated with sensuous pagan worship. In cultures where fertility rites were common, women singers and musicians incited sexual orgies in honor of their gods. Even instruments not associated with pagan practices were sometimes re-

EGYPTIAN MUSICIANS. *This tomb painting from Thebes (ca. fifteenth century B.C.) portrays Egyptian women playing musical instruments and dancing. From left to right we see a harpist, a lutist, a young dancer, a player of the double pipe, and a lyrist with a seven-stringed instrument. Notice the leopard skin decorating the lower part of the harp frame.*

MUSIC

LUTE. *This terra cotta plaque from Iraq (ca. 2000 B.C.) depicts a musician playing a three-stringed triangular lute. The lute was usually played by women and may have been one of the "instruments of music" mentioned in 1 Samuel 18:6.*

stricted. For example, priests feared that a happy, melodious flute tune in the temple could distract someone's mind from worship. The prophet Amos condemned those "who sing idle songs to the sound of the harp" (Amos 6:5, RSV).

Of course, there were times when the distractions of music could be helpful. The soothing strains of David's lyre refreshed a tormented Saul (1 Sam. 16:23). After Daniel was shut up in the den of lions, King Darius retired to his room and refused to let the "instruments of music" be brought to him (Dan. 6:18).

Music was an important part of everyday life. Merrymaking, weddings, and funerals were not complete without music. Even war relied on music, since special instruments sounded the call to battle. (*See* "Warfare.") Aristocratic diversion and relaxation patronized the musicians and their skills.

B. Function in Worship. Music was also a part of the religious life of Israel. The Israelites' formal worship observed various rituals prescribed by God. (*See* "Worship Rituals.") Music served as an accompaniment to these rituals.

Temple music consisted of singers and an orchestra. The singers and musicians could come only from the males of certain families. Likewise, the types of instruments were restricted. Instruments that were associated with women, with raucous merrymaking (such as the Egyptian *sistrum*), or with pagan worship were banned from the temple orchestra.

The Old Testament lists several kinds of instruments in the temple orchestra (cf. 1 Chr.

15:28; 16:42; 25:1). These instruments include the big harp (*nevel*), the lyre (*kinnor*), the ram's horn (*shophar*), the trumpet (*chatsotserah*), the timbrel (*toph*), and cymbals (*metsiltayim*). After the Israelites returned from the Exile and rebuilt the temple, the orchestra was reestablished (cf. Neh. 12:27). The pipe or flute (*halil*) was probably now included, and vocal music became more prominent.

Beyond formal worship within the temple, music was a part of other religious activities. Instruments not allowed in the temple were played at other religious functions, such as feast days. Often the feast began with a musical proclamation; then music, singing, and even dancing were part of the celebration. Women singers and musicians were allowed to participate (Ezra 2:65; Neh. 7:76; 2 Chr. 35:25).

C. Limits of Our Knowledge. The Old Testament seldom mentions the forms of music, the origins of instruments, and so on. The way to play or make instruments was passed on by oral tradition rather than written record. Most of that oral tradition has been lost, leaving us with only the brief information in the Bible.

Very few ancient musical instruments exist intact, so we must guess at how they looked and sounded. By comparing Scripture references with the artifacts of other cultures, historians and archaeologists have helped fill in many of the gaps in our knowledge of music in Bible times.

This study is a continuing process, as newer translations of the Bible demonstrate. If we compare passages about music from the King James Version with more recent translations, some differences can be noted. The following lists of instruments give the name in the KJV for each instrument mentioned, along with the findings of more recent interpretation.

II. Types of Instruments. Musical instruments fall into three basic classes, according to the way the sound is produced: (1) stringed instruments, which use vibrating strings to produce the sound; (2) percussion instruments, in which the sound is produced by a vibrating membrane or metal shell; and (3) wind instruments, which produce sound by passing air over a vibrating reed.

A. Percussion Instruments. The people of Israel used a variety of percussion instruments to sound out the rhythm of their music.

MUSIC

Rhythm was the vital element of their poetry and songs.

1. Bells. One kind of bell had a name (*metsilloth*) that came from the Hebrew word meaning "to jingle" or "to rattle." This type of bell is mentioned only once in the Bible (Zech. 14:20), where we are told that the Israelites attached these bells to the bridle or breast strap of horses.

Another kind of bell was a tiny, pure gold bell (*paamonim*). It was fastened to the hem of the high priest's robe and alternated with ornamental pomegranates (Ex. 28:33–34). These bells produced a sound only when they touched one another, for they did not have clappers. This jingling sound signified that the high priest was coming before God; others who dared to enter the Holy of Holies would be slain (v. 35).

2. Castanets. *See* "Cymbals" and "Rattler-Sistrum."

3. Cymbals. Cymbals (*metziltayim* or *tziltzal*) were made of copper and were the only percussion instrument in the temple orchestra. They were used when the people were celebrating and praising God. They joined with trumpets and singers to express joy and thanks to the Lord (1 Chr. 15:16; 16:5). Asaph, David's chief musician (1 Chr. 16:5), was a cymbal player. When the people returned from captivity, Asaph's descendants were called to join singers and trumpets in praise to the Lord (Ezra 3:10).

In passages such as 1 Chronicles 16:5, some versions translate the Hebrew as *castanets*. It is now generally believed that this is inaccurate and should be *cymbals*.

4. Rattler-Sistrum. This is the correct translation for 2 Samuel 6:5. (The RSV uses *castanets,* while the KJV uses *cornet.*) The sistrum was a small U-shaped frame with a handle attached at the bottom of the curve. Pieces of metal or other small objects were strung on small bars stretched from one side of the sistrum to the other.

The use of the sistrum goes back to ancient Egypt and has counterparts in other ancient cultures. It was merely a noisemaker, played by women on both joyous and sad occasions.

5. Tabret. *See* "Timbrel."

Story Music

On the surface, the music of the ancient Greeks and Hebrews seemed to have little in common. The Greeks sang of their gods and mythological battles; the Hebrews, on the other hand, devoted their songs to praising the one God. But there is an important link between Greek and Hebrew music, one that involves poetry, song, and religion. That link is the *epic.*

Students of literature know the epic as a long narrative poem that presents the deeds of gods or traditional heroes in a dignified manner. The eighth century B.C. saw the creation of two great Greek epics, the "Iliad" and the "Odyssey," which are attributed to Homer. The "Iliad" describes the clash of arms between Greeks and Trojans "on the ringing plains of windy Troy." The "Odyssey" relates the adventure-filled wanderings of Odysseus in his return to Greece after Troy's fall.

These epics glorify heroic valor and physical prowess. They also provide us with much detail of everyday life in ancient Greece.

The Greeks set many of their epics to music. Music helped narrators recall the wording of the epics, which tended to be extremely long pieces with dozens of verses and many names of people and places. By rhyming the lines, narrators found they could more easily remember the intricate story they had to tell.

The Greeks did not use these "story songs" as part of their worship. (Greek temples were used for sheltering gods, not religious assembly.) The use of the epic song in worship started with the Hebrews, centuries before the Greek epics were written. The earliest Hebrew worship songs arose out of a religious feeling toward God at important moments.

For instance, the first recorded appearance of story music was when Miriam, Moses' sister, sang with joy after the Jews escaped the pharaoh's men (Ex. 15:19–21). Many of the Psalms were epics (e.g., Ps. 114, 136–137) and the prophets sometimes burst forth in epic songs (e.g., Is. 26, Hab. 3).

The Hebrews did not apply intricate melodies to their epics. The tonal range of their songs was probably not great, and they selected rhythm instruments rather than melodic instruments. The melodies of the Psalms and other story songs were well-known in their time, and were probably sung in verses by choirs. It is clear that the Hebrews came to consider the story songs an essential part of their worship. Their music sprang from the soul of a people whose everyday life was religiously ordered.

CAPTIVE LYRISTS. *Three captive lyrists (possibly Jews from Lachish) are conducted through a mountainous area by an Assyrian soldier armed with club and bow. The lyre made a sweet, ringing sound when its strings were plucked with a plectrum (a thin piece of bone or metal). This alabaster relief comes from the ruins of the palace of Sennacherib (704–681 B.C.) at Nineveh.*

6. Timbrel. Modern musicians would classify this instrument as a "membranophone" because the sound is produced by a vibrating membrane. It is correctly translated as either *timbrel* or *tambourine.* (KJV uses the term *tabret.*) It was carried and beaten by the hand. In very early times it may have been made with two membranes, with pieces of bronze inserted in the rim.

7. Gong. The "brass" mentioned in 1 Corinthians 13:1 was actually a metal gong. It was used for weddings and other joyous occasions.

B. Stringed Instruments. Archaeologists have found fragments of harps and other stringed instruments from Egypt and neighboring countries of the Near East. Scripture describes several stringed instruments that were used in Israel.

1. Dulcimer. This term appears in the Bible only in Daniel 3:5, 7, 10, and 15. It is not a precise translation. *See* "Harp."

2. Harp. The harp (KJV also uses *psaltery, viol,* or *dulcimer*) was a favorite instrument of the aristocratic class and was lavishly made (1 Kin. 10:12; 2 Chr. 9:11). It was used in the temple orchestra and was appointed to "raise sounds of joy" (1 Chr. 15:16).

3. Lute. This three-stringed triangular instrument may have been one of the "instruments of music" mentioned in 1 Samuel 18:6. It was usually played by women and was excluded from the temple orchestra.

4. Lyre. Two Hebrew terms are translated as *lyre.* (The KJV uses *harp.*) One is mentioned in only one book of the Bible (Dan. 3:5, 7, 10, 15). This particular lyre (*nevel*) was frequently used for secular music, such as the merrymaking at Nebuchadnezzar's banquet. It was played by plucking the strings with the fingers.

A smaller lyre (*kinnor*) was considered to be the most sophisticated instrument. Its shape and number of strings varied, but all types of lyres produced a most pleasing sound. The lyre was used in secular settings (Is. 23:16), but was welcomed in sacred use too. It was the instrument David used to soothe King Saul. Generally, this "little lyre" was played by stroking the strings with a plectrum, much as a guitar can be played with a pick. However, David seemed to prefer to use his hand instead (1 Sam. 16:16, 23; 18:10; 19:9). Skilled craftsmen made lyres of silver or ivory and decorated them with lavish ornamentation.

5. Psaltery. *See* "Harp."

6. Sackbut. *See* "Trigon."

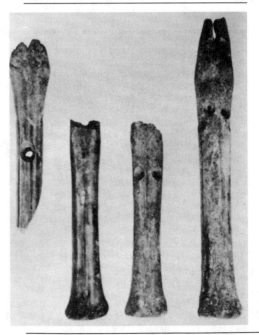

BONE PIPES. *These bone pipes have finger holes that allowed the player to alter the pitch. Chevrons (v-shaped symbols) carved on the flat lower surface may have functioned as thumb rests. Discovered at the site of Tepe Gawra, a city in present-day Iraq, these pipes date from about 3500 B.C.*

STAIRWAY TO HULDA GATES. *Scholars believe that pilgrims may have sung the Songs of Ascent (Ps. 120–134) as they made their journeys to sites hallowed in Israelite tradition. This wide stairway, uncovered south of the temple mount and leading to the Hulda Gates in Jerusalem, is probably the stairway that pilgrims ascended on their way to the inner courts of the temple.*

7. Trigon. The book of Daniel frequently refers to the trigon (Dan. 3:5, 7, 10, 15). The KJV incorrectly calls it the sackbut; the sackbut was not devised until several centuries after biblical times.

We do not know the exact shape and size of the trigon. The instrument appears to have been borrowed from the Babylonians and thus was not common among the instruments of Israel.

8. Viol. *See* "Harp."

C. Wind Instruments. Despite their limited knowledge of metal-working, the Israelites fashioned a variety of horns and other wind instruments.

1. Clarinet. The primitive clarinet was a popular instrument in Bible times. It is mentioned in Isaiah 5:12; 30:29; and Jeremiah 48:36. It is incorrectly translated as *pipe* (KJV) or *flute* (RSV) in these verses. New Testament references include Matthew 9:23; 11:17; Luke 7:32; and 1 Corinthians 14:7. The clarinet probably was not used in the temple but it was a popular instrument for banquets, weddings, or funerals.

2. Cornet. *See* "Trumpet," "Shophar," and "Rattler-Sistrum."

3. Flute. The flute (*mashrokitha*) was actually a big pipe. (The KJV uses *pipe*.) Because it was a big pipe and had a mouthpiece, it produced a sharp, penetrating sound, somewhat like an oboe. The flute was popular for secular and religious use but it was not mentioned as an instrument of the first temple orchestra. It was sometimes allowed in the second temple. Because of its penetrating sound it was used in processions (Is. 30:29).

4. Organ. *See* "Pipe."

5. Pipe. *Pipe* usually refers to a wind instrument that was used to express wild joy or ecstatic lament. It is generally believed to have been a secular instrument, although Psalm 150:4 mentions its use in the temple for a religious celebration.

The King James Version uses the terms *organ* and *flute* instead of *pipe*.

6. Shophar. The *shophar* is best understood as a "ram's horn," as in Josh. 6:4, 6, 8, 13. The KJV often uses *trumpet, cornet,* and *horn* to render this Hebrew word (cf. 1 Chr. 15:28; 2 Chr. 15:14; Hos. 5:8). It was designed to make noise, not music, so it could not play melodies. It was used to give signals and announce special occasions, such as the transfer of the ark (2 Sam. 6). It was also used to frighten away evil spirits and gods of the enemy (Zech. 9:14–15).

7. Trumpet. The trumpet was similar to the *shophar* but was used by the priests. Trumpets were often used in pairs (Num. 10:1–10). Originally two were ordered for the temple; but the number could be increased to 120, depending upon the purpose (2 Chr. 5:12).

Trumpets were made of bones, shell or metals—bronze, copper, silver, gold—all of which produced a high, shrill sound. It is generally believed that these trumpets, like the *shophar,* could not produce sounds in various pitches, so as to make music (melody). However, they could blow legato and staccato notes and trills. Thus, they could convey complicated signals to announce assembly, battle, and ambush.

Gideon used trumpets to terrorize the enemy (Judg. 7:19–20). John heard the sound of a trumpet before he received his vision of the apocalypse (Rev. 1:10). In fact, trumpets are among the prominent symbols of the Judgment (1 Cor. 15:52; 1 Thess. 4:16; Rev. 8:2).

THE JEWS IN NEW TESTAMENT TIMES

I. Introduction. In New Testament times, Jews lived in every part of the Roman Empire. There were more Jews in Egypt than in Jerusalem. Paul's journeys took him through what is today rural Turkey and Greece, and he found communities of Jews everywhere he went. In many places, Jews had built synagogues and were meeting regularly for worship and other activities.

A. Religion of the Jews. What made Jews different from other nations was their religion. Their faith was based on the Scriptures that God had given to them through Moses and the prophets. Moreover, their faith had a geographical center in Jerusalem, which was the traditional capital of the Jewish nation, but, even more important, Jerusalem was the site of the Jewish temple. The temple was designed by Herod to be as magnificent as possible. The platform which supported its courts and buildings was the largest in the known world. The temple compound covered 35 acres, and was more than four times the size of the Acropolis, more than twice the size of the forum in Rome.

Although the Jews could meet for prayer and worship in every city, the sacrifices required by the Law of Moses could only be offered in one place—in the temple in Jerusalem. Jesus' own life took Him from an obscure village to Jerusalem, the capital of His nation and the religious center of his people. As He said, ". . . it cannot be that a prophet should perish away from Jerusalem" (Luke 13:33).

B. The Diaspora. Until recent decades, Judaism in New Testament times was thought of as falling into two separate groups. The first group was made up of Jews living in Palestine. These Jews were thought of as the defenders of orthodoxy and adherents of a unified, conservative faith. Jews living outside Palestine comprised the second group. Technically, this group was referred to as the "Diaspora," or "scattering." Jews in the Diaspora were thought of as being corrupted by the influence of the surrounding cultures in which they lived.

THE JEWS IN NEW TESTAMENT TIMES

STAR OF DAVID. *This six-pointed star is widely used as a symbol of Judaism. The history of its origin is lost, but it decorated Jewish architecture by the third century A.D. Later called the "seal of Solomon," the symbol was apparently first mentioned in Jewish literature of the fourteenth century A.D. It seems that this symbol was not used in biblical times.*

C. Judaism and Greek Culture. The Jews were influenced by the surrounding Greek culture, and this was true for Jews living in Palestine as well as for those living elsewhere. The main culture of the time was Greek culture, or "Hellenism." The process of "hellenization," or the spreading of the influence of Greek culture, really began with Alexander the Great, the general from northern Greece who conquered countries all the way from Greece to the borders of India. Although he died at the age of 33 in 323 B.C., Alexander left behind rulers who were ready to spread the culture of Hellenism in their respective kingdoms.

Jews came under the influence of Hellenism as much any other people. In some matters (such as diet and worship), the Jewish religion made it impossible for its adherents to accept Greek ideas. At the same time, where there was no reason to resist on religious grounds, the Jews were not unwilling to participate in the culture of the day.

In Egypt, the Jews translated all of the Hebrew Bible into Greek. This translation was completed more than 150 years before the time of Christ. Translating the Scriptures was not thought of as compromising the Jewish

MENORAH. Menorah *is the Hebrew word for the seven-branched candlestick which became the primary symbol of Judaism. Although its meaning is lost in antiquity, many scholars believe the menorah is the symbol of the Jewish people as the "light" of God (1 Kings 11:36). Today it is used to symbolize the Jewish state of Israel. This menorah stands before the parliament building in Jerusalem.*

THE JEWS IN NEW TESTAMENT TIMES

SYNAGOGUE SCHOOL. *During the Babylonian Exile, Jews were unable to sacrifice because they lived in an unclean land far from the temple. Their need for a worship community led to the establishment of the synagogue, a place for reading and studying the Old Testament. Jewish boys learned the Law from their rabbi, or teacher, in a synagogue school.*

faith. On the contrary, this translation made it easier for Jews living in areas where Hebrew and Aramaic were not spoken often to follow the commandments. It also made Judaism more attractive to foreigners who might be attracted to the doctrine of one God and to a moral life based on the Law of Moses.

D. Jerusalem, a Crossroad. It is easy to understand why the Jews outside Jerusalem would adapt to the culture around them, but the Jews in Jerusalem also had reason to adapt. Jerusalem itself was a crossroad where more than 100,000 pilgrims would come for Passover, one of the most important holiday seasons of the year. As the book of Acts says, Jews came from "every nation under heaven" (Acts 2:5), and they spoke all kinds of languages. Jerusalem was far from being isolated from the rest of the world, and the Jews from other locales were not out of place in the temple compound.

E. Jewish Art and Architecture. Careful study of ancient Jewish art has changed the notion that there was a strict, orthodox core of Jews residing in Jerusalem and a multitude of less faithful Jews living far from the temple. The synagogues found in Palestine give evidence that Hellenistic culture was accepted to a surprising extent. Popular mythology supplied the subject matter for many of the decorations in the synagogues, but there is no reason to think that there was any compromise in worship. When idolatry seemed to be a possibility, the Jews were quick to defend the purity of their worship. They volunteered to die rather than allow the Romans to bring their military banners and standards into the temple area. These Roman standards were religious icons, and Jews refused to allow them entry into the place where God was worshiped. Yet at the same time, the Jews permitted representations drawn from mythology and the zodiac as adornments in their places of worship.

F. Mysticism. The study of religious experience has also modified our understanding of what Judaism was like in Jesus' day. The mystical speculation of certain Jewish groups was previously thought of as totally excluded from the mainstream of Jewish tradition, commonly referred to as the rabbinic tradition. The scholar Gershom Scholem has shown that even the most prominent figures of the rabbinic tradition did not routinely exclude mystical ideas and other speculations. The truth seems to be that Judaism did not consist of a single tradition surrounded by heretical fringe groups. Rather, different kinds of ideas existed together, and a single person could easily have sympathies with more than one line of thought, and thus be counted in more than one "group" or "movement."

G. Community of the Dead Sea Scrolls. The remarkable discovery of the Dead Sea Scrolls in 1947 has added to the picture of the religious scene in the Judaism of Jesus' time. The Dead Sea community was a kind of fringe group. This group of Jews lived a monastic community in the desert, and they maintained special rules for ritual purity, rules which separated them from other Jewish groups. Nonetheless, the scrolls they left behind included parts from every book in the Hebrew Bible except Esther. A comparison of those texts with today's printed copies of the Hebrew Bible indicates that the wording has been preserved with almost exact precision throughout the centuries. Before the Dead Sea Scrolls were discovered, the earliest available copies of the Hebrew Bible were from the ninth century A.D., almost a thousand years later than the scrolls were hidden (not later

THE JEWS IN NEW TESTAMENT TIMES

than A.D. 68). The Dead Sea community preserved the biblical texts alongside their own traditions.

Formerly, the ideas held by the Dead Sea community were known to us only through what a few other writers had said about them. Now that their own documents have been unearthed, it can be seen that many of their ideas were part of the mix in Israel as a whole. This group in the desert had sympathizers outside their own special community. It may be that John the Baptist had something to do with them, although this cannot be proven. This mix of views suggests that the message of Jesus was proclaimed in an environment of competing and opposing ideas, even within Judaism, and not "in a corner" (Acts 26:26). A closer look at that environment can help us to gain a better understanding of the gospel message.

II. Sources of Knowledge about Judaism. We can turn to several sources to find out what Judaism was like during New Testament times.

A. Old Testament. One of the best sources is the Old Testament, or Hebrew Scriptures, which were written long before the time of Christ. These Scriptures were the foundation of Jewish belief and practice. When Jesus spoke in the synagogue, he read a passage from the Jewish Scriptures (see Luke 4:17). And Peter says that the Jews continued to study the law of Moses on a regular basis (Acts 15:21). The people who relied on the Old Testament were careful to preserve the text in its original language. They also translated their Scriptures into Greek, the most widely spoken language in the Mediterranean area.

B. New Testament. The New Testament gives direct evidence about the Jewish people in the first century. Early Christianity was an offshoot of Judaism. Jesus was a Jew, and almost all of the first Christians were Jews (John 4:22; Rom. 9:5). It goes without saying that the New Testament is an original account of what the earliest Christians believed and how they lived. In addition, the New Testament gives a fair amount of information about other groups. This information is given as needed by the earliest hearers of these writings, but it is not a complete summary or guide, for the writers do not explain whatever they believe their readers and hearers already know. For instance, no general explanation of Roman justice is given, although details about

it are provided when Jesus and Paul are involved.

C. Apocryphal Books. A third source is the books of the Apocrypha. The apocryphal books were written by Jewish authors and were widely read by Jews of the day. Temple worship is described in the Apocrypha, as well as a history of the Maccabean revolt that started in 167 B.C. This war resulted in the establishment of a Jewish political kingdom under the Hasmoneans, a rule that lasted from 142 to 63 B.C. The apocryphal books of the Maccabees are invaluable for an understanding of the vision and courage of many Jews hoping for freedom from the Romans, a vision that lived on in New Testament times. The Jews fought desperately against the Romans from A.D. 67 to 70, only to be defeated terribly. A second uprising took place under the leadership of Bar Kochba (A.D. 132–135), and it was also squelched by the Romans. The forces and longings that led to such sacrifices

SABBATH SERVICE. *Although Jews did not reestablish the temple after the Roman conquest of A.D. 70, they still reverence the site. Jews observing the Sabbath at the Western Wall (site of the temple) in Jerusalem read from the book of the Law.*

were vibrant in New Testament times, and the heroism of the Maccabees was not forgotten.

D. Josephus. The historian who left behind a very important account of the uprising in A.D. 67 to 70 was not a Roman, but a Jew named Flavius Josephus. At first, Josephus fought against the Romans, but after his capture, he gained favor with the emperor of Rome. Part of Josephus's service to the Romans was to write a history of the Jewish War. This book has a detailed description of the siege and collapse of Jerusalem in A.D. 70. Not only was the temple defiled and burned, but the people of Jerusalem suffered horrors that defy the imagination. At one point, the Romans were crucifying more people outside the city walls than could be counted.

To Jewish groups of that period, the war against Rome mingled political and religious commitments that were not easy to separate completely. This makes it easier to understand the sharp interest shown by the Sadducees and the Pharisees in Jesus' ambitions (John 11:47–48). The test question posed to Jesus about whether it was necessary to pay taxes was not simply theoretical in nature (Mark 12:14). In addition, the points of dispute before Pilate about whether Jesus was some kind of king and whether Pilate was really a friend of Caesar were urgent issues (Luke 23:2–3).

E. Philo. Another important Jewish writer, more a philosopher than a historian, was Philo Judaeus (born about 10 B.C. and died about A.D. 45 in Alexandria, Egypt). Philo wrote in Greek and tried to show that the Hebrew Bible really contained the sort of ideas contained in the Greek philosophers. In order to do this, Philo interpreted the Hebrew scriptures as allegories. While Philo had little influence upon the authors of the New Testament, his writings show how Jewish and Greek culture were mingled together. The apostle Paul provides another example of a Jew who was comfortable with and proficient in Greek methods of argumentation and writing. Although Paul's point of view is very different from that of Philo, Paul was not at a loss for something to say when he visited Athens, the center of Greek philosophy (Acts 17:22–34).

F. Rabbinic Traditions. The oral traditions of an important Jewish group of the first century are made known to us through the collections compiled after the fall of Jerusalem (A.D. 70) and also after the failure of the Bar Kochba rebellion (A.D. 135) These traditions, called the "oral Torah" of rabbinic Judaism,

PRAYER TIME. *Beginning about the second century B.C., all male Jews were expected to wear two phylacteries—one on the forehead and one on the left arm—at morning prayers, except on the Sabbath and festival days. The phylacteries were small leather cases containing four passages of Old Testament Scripture: Exodus 13:1–10, 11–16; Deuteronomy 6:4–9; 11:3–21.*

concern in large part questions and responses which focus on legal issues. Basically, these collections of traditions represent the viewpoints of the Pharisees and their descendants. However, the collections themselves were compiled later (about A.D. 200), although sometimes particular sayings or legal rulings are quoted as if they were in force in A.D. 30. There is no reason not to consult these collections for knowledge of first-century Judaism, but caution is necessary because other Jewish groups, such as the Sadducees, are not represented by the traditions and because parts of the tradition could easily have been added at a later date.

G. Other Writers. Several non-Jewish writers provide information that is relevant to our understanding of life in Palestine during New Testament times. Cicero is a good example. In his speeches against Verres, a tax collector, Cicero describes abuses of the tax collection system used by the Romans. Verres had purchased the right to tax Sicily, but he behaved more like a pirate and a robber than an administrator. Cicero also entered into discussions about religion and the gods in which he indicates that he was not prepared to accept any and every strange happening as a miracle. In addition to Cicero, other writers speak about various aspects of ancient societies— their cultures, laws, institutions—in which the Jews lived.

H. Archaeology. Archaeology makes many contributions to our knowledge of Judaism in New Testament times. Besides the study of Jewish art and architecture, which has already been mentioned, archaeologists study and record inscriptions on buildings, monuments, and coins. They also uncover and preserve statues and other objects left behind by ancient peoples. Increasingly, attention is being given to items that add to a more complete picture of the daily life and affairs of ordinary people of that era.

III. Languages in Use. The documents and inscriptions just mentioned are recorded in three languages: Hebrew, Latin, and Greek. These are the three languages found on the sign that Pilate placed on the cross above Jesus' head (John 19:20). In Jerusalem, and even in the villages, many people would have spoken more than one language. Jews spoke Aramaic in their homes, Greek in the marketplace, and Latin in their dealings with the Romans. The Romans used Latin and Greek, but not Hebrew and Aramaic.

A. Hebrew. Hebrew is the language of the Old Testament. Its close relative, Aramaic (written with the same alphabet as Hebrew), was the language commonly spoken in Palestine. Some of Jesus' sayings are recorded in Aramaic, as is the case in Mark 5:41. Psalm 22:1 is quoted in both Hebrew and Aramaic (Matt. 27:46; Mark 15:34), and the two versions differ little.

B. Latin. Latin was the language of Rome. Although Cicero wrote in Latin, other Roman writers employed Greek perhaps because it was considered to be a better language for literature, or perhaps because Greek was more widely spoken in the various regions under Roman rule.

C. Greek. Greek was known throughout the Mediterranean regions. In many places, it was more common than Latin, even in a province like Egypt. There were many Jews

COIN OF ANTIOCHUS IV. *A Seleucid king of Syria, Antiochus IV attempted to prohibit sacrifices in the temple in Jerusalem and erected a Greek altar there. He entered the holy of holies and carried away the sacred vessels. This blasphemous action precipitated the Maccabean revolt (second century B.C.), by which the Jews regained their independence from Syria.*

living outside Jerusalem who did not know Hebrew or could not read it, and for them the Greek translation of the Hebrew Bible (called the Septuagint) was Scripture. The New Testament was written in Greek, and its authors often quote the Septuagint with precision, even in place where the wording of the Septuagint does not agree with the Hebrew text.

IV. Ancient Cities. Several important cities had a large number of Jewish constituents during Jesus' time.

A. Jerusalem. Jerusalem was the capital of Judea and the center of Jewish life and worship. The population of Jerusalem was about 50,000. Since Jerusalem was a crossroad, one filled with pilgrims from other regions during Passover, the city was more cosmopolitan than its size might suggest.

B. Antioch. Antioch, although less well known today, was an important city in ancient times. Located in Syria, north of Israel, Antioch's population was about 100,000 in New Testament times (it may have been several times this size in 150 B.C.). There was a strong Jewish community in Antioch.

C. Ephesus. Ephesus was north and west of Antioch in what is today Turkey. It had as many as 250,000 inhabitants. Little is known about the Jews of Ephesus; however, the largest synagogue discovered yet by archaeologists is in Sardis, only 70 miles away.

D. Rome. Rome was the capital city of the

Roman Empire. Out of Rome's total population of 800,000, perhaps 10,000 were Jews. This population of Jews included many prominent families.

E. Alexandria. Alexandria was the most important city in Egypt. There were probably more than 100,000 Jews living there. Philo said that there were more than a million Jews in Egypt as a whole. Alexandria was known for the scholars and scribes associated with its famous library. The translation of the Hebrew Bible into Greek was accomplished in Alexandria between about 250 to 150 B.C. The Septuagint is the first translation of any lengthy work into another language.

The evidence from these large cities indicates that the Jews of the Diaspora were not at

THE SANHEDRIN. *During most of the Roman period, the internal government of Judea was controlled by the Sanhedrin, the highest tribunal of the Jews. The Sanhedrin, a group of elders, presided over by the high priest, could mete out capital punishment until about 40 years before the destruction of Jerusalem. After that time, it could not execute the sentence of death without the confirmation of the Roman procurator, which is why Jesus had to be tried before Pilate (John 18:31–32).*

all invisible. Many Jews held high positions of status, and many could point to the large public buildings built in their honor or with their funds as proof of their importance. The Jews were not, however, independent. The Romans, not the Jews, ruled the world.

V. Roman Rule in Palestine. From the time of the Maccabean revolt (167–143 B.C.), the Romans were very aware that Palestine was a sensitive area. The Roman general Pompey conquered Judea in 63 B.C., and he set up the different systems of government that are visible in the New Testament. The Romans ruled Jerusalem and Judea through a complicated system that put both Jews and Romans in prominent places. During Jesus' ministry, Pontius Pilate was the Roman governor. His official title was "prefect," as is known from an inscription discovered in Caesarea in 1962. Pilate had the power to impose the death penalty and to pardon, as well as the power to tax.

A. The Herods. The Jewish rulers appointed by the Romans to be in charge of Palestine were from the family of the Herods. Herod the Great, who died in 4 B.C., is mentioned in Luke 1:5. This Herod is responsible for building the magnificent temple in Jerusalem. His son, Herod Antipas, ruled until A.D. 39 (see Matt. 14:1; Mark 6:14; Luke 9:7). Two other Herods mentioned in the New Testament are Herod Agrippa I, who died in A.D. 44 (Acts 12:2); and Herod Agrippa II, who heard Paul's defense (Acts 25:13). After A.D. 6, the Herods were put in charge of the areas surrounding Judea, and thus the region and Jerusalem itself were under direct Roman rule.

B. The Sanhedrin. The Roman government in Jerusalem gave some powers to the Sanhedrin, the ruling council comprised of Jews and headed by the high priest. The Sanhedrin oversaw temple affairs and had some police powers of its own. While the Jews were endowed with some elements of self-rule, there was still tension between the Jews and their Roman rulers. Some of the tension arose from issues clearly political in nature—taxation, for instance—and some of the tension revolved around issues of a religious nature. However, politics and religion were not at all the separate domains in either Rome or Judea that they are in many western nations.

C. Jewish Discontent. Jewish discontent was centered around taxation. In the economy of the time, taxation was heavy. The city of

THE JEWS IN NEW TESTAMENT TIMES

Rome supported itself by imposing and gathering taxes, not by agriculture, industry, or trade. The Roman system allowed for the lease of taxation rights to entrepreneurs, who taxed their region for profit above what was due to Rome. This method of taxation invited trouble. Jews who worked in the tax system were regarded as traitors, even though the situation might have been even worse if foreigners acted as tax agents.

Jewish discontent with Roman rule also had a nationalistic element (John 8:33). The Jews had not forgotten their independence under the Maccabees, and even the Jews who were scattered in many regions throughout the Empire retained their cultural identity. Political discontent was injected with religious fervor because the Jews considered themselves to be a holy nation, and not just a nation among others (Deut. 26:18–19; 27:9).

Some of the Jewish discontent involved the official religious practices of the Roman state.

The flags and standards of the Roman army were regarded as religious items. Roman citizens and subjects were expected to honor these symbols and to participate in public functions when appropriate. When Jews refused to worship the symbols of the Roman state, the Romans looked upon them as traitors. The Romans had made some allowances for the faithfulness and fidelity of the Jews by making Judaism a lawful religion. Nevertheless, the Romans thought that Jews, and Christians also, could practice their own religion while continuing to submit to the religion of the state at the same time. Over time, the Romans introduced the practice of deifying the emperor, that is, making him out to be some kind of god. Julius Caesar (died 44 B.C.) was the first emperor to be deified. In New Testament times, the emperor received worship during his own lifetime. The Jews and the Christians found it impossible to compromise on this issue.

QUMRAN SETTLEMENT. *The Dead Sea Scrolls, one of the greatest archaeological finds of the twentieth century, made Qumran famous. The Roman historian Pliny noted that this area near the Dead Sea was the headquarters of the Essene sect. However, the Dead Sea manuscripts—written between 100 B.C. and A.D. 100—disagree at several points with known Essene writings, causing scholars to speculate on whether this settlement was indeed populated by the Essenes or by some other Hebrew sect.*

THE JEWS IN NEW TESTAMENT TIMES

TETRADRACHMA OF BAR-KOCHBA. *After the fall of Jerusalem in A.D. 70, many groups of Jews continued to fight against the Romans, helping to regain their independence. Simon Bar-Kochba pronounced himself the Messiah and declared the independence of Judea. This Maccabean coin shows the facade of the temple and bears the legend Simeon, i.e., Simon (Bar-Kochba). He seized Jerusalem in A.D. 132, but the Romans retook the city and quashed the rebellion in A.D. 135. The land was desecrated and stripped; Jews were tortured, murdered, and sold as slaves on the open market; and the site of the temple was plowed under. From this time on, Jerusalem increasingly became a Gentile city.*

VI. Jewish Groups and Movements. Various groups of Jews mentioned in the New Testament were sometimes political in orientation, sometimes religious.

A. Zealots. The Zealots. (see Luke 6:15; Acts 1:13) were armed resisters who fought against foreign rule and taxation. They were not a single organization; rather, the name could refer to any group or band that resisted foreign domination. Theirs was the program celebrated in the books of the Maccabees, theirs the struggle that came to an end with the Bar Kochba revolt. Opponents of the Zealots simply called them "bandits." According to Josephus, the Zealots were the leaders in the defense of the temple in Jerusalem who met with defeat in A.D. 70.

B. Sicarii. Sicarii, or "assassins," (Acts 21:38) engaged in a particular kind of armed resistance. Using daggers (*sicarii* in Latin) concealed in their clothing, the Sicarii assassinated their enemies in crowded places, and then ran away before they could be apprehended.

C. Herodians. The Herodians were Jews who sympathized with the Herodian rulers (see Matt. 22:16; Mark 3:6; 12:13).

D. Scribes. "Scribes" is really the name of an occupation, rather than an allegiance (Matt 7:29). Scribes could read and write, and therefore they could work as teachers and secretaries. Since scribes had different employers, or no fixed employer, they had various sympathies. Because the Scriptures were so important to Jews, scribes were often to be found in leadership positions.

E. Priests. Priests were also a professional class (Mark 11:18; 14:10). Priests had official duties in the temple. The high priest was also head of the Sanhedrin in Jerusalem. There were ten other sanhedrins in different locales. Under Roman rule, the high priest was appointed by the Roman governor.

F. Pharisees. The Pharisees (Matt. 5:20) were religious leaders, and both scribes and priests could be found among them. As might be expected, there was some latitude among the Pharisees with regard to how strictly the Law of Moses should be applied. Jesus had dedicated enemies among the Pharisees, who were not only able to appreciate his claims,

DETAIL FROM ARCH OF TITUS. *One of the reliefs from the Arch of Titus in Rome shows Romans triumphantly carrying precious objects from the temple at Jerusalem during the destruction of the city in A.D. 70. Among the artifacts is the golden candlestick with seven branches.*

THE JEWS IN NEW TESTAMENT TIMES

but also to recognize the threat his claims represented to the status quo. Paul was a Pharisee who violently persecuted Christians, but who later became one of most effective defenders of the Christian faith.

The traditions of the Pharisees survived the destruction of the temple and the crushing defeat of the Bar Kochba rebellion. Pharisaic traditions are the source of what is known as rabbinic Judaism. As far as it can be discerned from the Mishnah (a collection of Pharisaic traditions), the teachings of the Pharisees were not fully opposed to Jesus' teachings. That is not surprising, since the basic mission of the Pharisees was to apply the Hebrew Scriptures, especially the five books of Moses, to the living of daily life.

The staunch enemies of Jesus depicted in the Gospel as Pharisees do not necessarily represent all Pharisees. Their interest in particular points of religion, such as fasting and ritual purity, is consistent with their interest in piety. The New Testament is also concerned with those very questions.

G. Sadducees. The Sadducees were aristocratic Jews not sympathetic to the teachings of the Pharisees. The Sadducees maintained that only the five books of Moses had authority and that subsequent traditions handed on by the rabbis did not. According to Mark 12:18, the Sadducees did not believe in the resurrection of the dead. The Sadducees as a group within Judaism did not flourish after the destruction of the temple, which was the locus of their power.

H. Proselytes. "God-fearers" is the conventional translation of the term that appears several times in the New Testament (Acts 10:2, 22; 13:16, 26). These "God-fearers" were proselytes, or converts to Judaism; however, they were not regarded as completely Jewish, perhaps because they were not circumcised. The Jews were willing to receive converts, but it is difficult to tell how many converts there were. It seems unlikely that there was a Jewish "missionary" movement whose aim was gaining converts. When Jesus said that the Pharisees were travelling "sea and land to make a single proselyte," he was referring to their forceful teaching to those inside Judaism, not to a forceful effort to attract those outside Judaism (Matt. 23:15).

I. Essenes. Another movement within Judaism, one which included the community of Qumran, is known as the Essenes. Josephus described the Essenes as strict observers of the Sabbath. They believed in the immortality of the soul. Essenes would not blaspheme God or eat unlawful food, even when threatened with torture. Some Essenes, like those at Qumran, renounced marriage. The New Testament does not explicitly mention the Essenes, but it is clear that many of their ideas could be found in other circles.

J. Common People. Although the "common people" are not a unified group, it is misleading to list only the more readily identifiable groups and movements within Judaism and to omit the Jewish people at large. The participation of the common people in the worship of God and the hearing of God's word was assured by the number of synagogues established in all the regions inhabited by the common people.

VII. The Messiah. The Old Testament records God's promise to David that God's king would always sit on the throne of Israel (2 Sam. 7:16). David and his son, Solomon, were models of what that king would be like, but the Jewish people also drew ideas of what God's king would be like from the books of Moses and the prophets. The Davidic kingdom was overthrown by the Babylonians in 586 B.C. Of course, the Davidic kingdom was later restored, but the interruption of kingly rule was a severe blow. In A.D. 6, Jewish self-government was, for all practical purposes, eradicated by Pompey. The rulers from the family of Herod were not of Davidic descent. Many Jews were hoping that God would send someone to deliver them. That someone would be God's anointed king.

In the Old Testament, when a king was to ascend to his throne, he was first anointed with oil. In a solemn ceremony, olive oil was poured on the head of the king. The English words "Christ" and "Messiah" represent the Greek and Hebrew words for "anointed." Jews who hoped for the Messiah were hoping for an anointed king, a heroic leader like David. As two disciples said about Jesus of Nazareth to the risen Lord himself, ". . . we had hoped that he was the one to redeem Israel" (Luke 24:21). The resurrection of Jesus from the dead removed doubt from the hearts of those who followed Him (John 20:28; Rom. 1:4).

JESUS CHRIST

The New Testament is the only substantial first-century source of information about the life of Jesus. He is hardly mentioned in Jewish or Roman literature of that time.

The first-century Jewish historian Flavius Josephus wrote a book on the history of Judaism, attempting to show the Romans that Judaism was really not so far distant from the Greek and Roman way of life. Josephus said:

"Now there was about this time Jesus, a wise man, if it be lawful to call him a man, for he was a doer of wonderful works, a teacher of such men as receive the truth with pleasure. He drew over to him both many of the Jews and many of the Gentiles, He was [the] Christ. And when Pilate, at the suggestion of the principal men among us, had condemned him to the cross, those that loved him at the first did not forsake him; for he appeared to them alive again the third day; as the divine things concerning him. And the tribe of Christians so named from him are not extinct to this day."[1]

The Roman biographer Suetonius wrote during Nero's reign:

"Punishment [by Nero] was inflicted on the Christians, a class of men given to a new and mischievous superstition."[2]

A distinguished historian of the second century, Tacitus, remarked that Nero attempted to blame the burning of Rome on the Christians. "But the pernicious superstition, repressed for a time, broke out again," he wrote, "not only through Judea, where the mischief originated, but through the city of Rome also. . . ."[3]

The Roman writer Lucian scorned Christians and described Christ as "the man who was crucified in Palestine because he introduced this new cult into the world."[4]

Bear in mind that these remarks about

Christ and Christianity came from men who were hostile to Christianity and not well-informed about it. Yet they show us that Christianity was widespread by the early second century A.D., and that the historical existence of Christ was accepted as a fact, even by His enemies. Apparently they viewed Him as a religious fanatic who had gained more of a following than He really deserved.

The four Gospels are our only primary sources of information about Jesus Christ. They do not present a biography covering His life, but a picture of His person and work. From His birth to His thirtieth year hardly anything is said of Him. Even the account of His ministry is not exhaustive. Much of what John knew and saw, for example, is left unrecorded (John 21:25). What is recorded is sometimes compressed into a few verses. All of the Gospels give considerably more coverage to the events of the last week of Christ's life than they do to anything else.

Because each writer wished to emphasize a somewhat different aspect of Christ's person and work, the accounts vary in detail. It is evident that the original authors selected the facts that best furthered their purposes, and they did not always observe a strictly chronological order. (It is usually assumed that Luke comes nearest to following the actual sequence of events.) The Gospels are more interpretations than chronicles, but there is no reason to doubt that everything they state is completely true.

I. THE ACCOUNT OF JESUS' LIFE
   A. Early Years
   B. Early Judean Ministry
   C. Galilean Ministry
   D. Perean Ministry
   E. The Last Week

II. THE DOCTRINE OF CHRIST
   A. His Person
   B. His Personality
   C. His Position
   D. His Prophetic Office
   E. His Priestly Office
   F. His Kingly Office

I. The Account of Jesus' Life. Though each Gospel was written to stand on its own merits, the four Gospels may be worked

---

[1] Flavius Josephus, *Antiquities of the Jews* (Cambridge, Mass.: Harvard University Press, 1926), Bk. XVII, Chap. iii, Sect. 3. Some scholars think that Christians tampered with Josephus's account to show Jesus in a favorable light.

[2] Suetonius, *Nero* (New York: G.P. Putnam's Sons, 1935), p. 111.

[3] Tacitus, *Annals* (New York: Harper and Brothers, 1858), p. 423.

[4] Lucian, *The Passing of Peregrinus* (London: William Hernemann, Ltd., 1936), pp. 13, 15.

JESUS CHRIST

BETHLEHEM. *This "City of David," earlier named Ephrath (Gen. 35:15), lies a few kilometers south of Jerusalem. It was home to David's ancestors and the prophesied place of the Messiah's birth (Mic. 5:2). When Jesus was born in Bethlehem, He was found and worshiped by shepherds and wise men (Luke 2:1–18; Matt. 2:1–12).*

together into a *harmony,* or single account, of Christ's life. Jesus lived in a Jewish society guided by the Old Testament and basically under the influences of the Pharisaic interpretation of the Law. (*See* "Jews in New Testament Times.")

The Jews of Jesus' day lived in expectation of great events. They were oppressed by the Romans, but strongly convinced that the Messiah would soon come. Various groups pictured the Messiah differently, but hardly a Jew of that day lived without hope in some form. Some in the nation had true faith and looked for the coming of a Messiah who would be their spiritual Savior—e.g., Zechariah and Elizabeth, Simeon, Anna, Joseph and Mary (Luke 1:2; Matt. 1:18 ff.). To such faithful hearts came the first stirrings of the Spirit, preparing them for the birth of God's true Messiah, Jesus Christ (Luke 2:27, 36).

About the year 6 B.C., toward the end of Herod's reign in Israel, the priest Zechariah was officiating in the temple in Jerusalem. He was burning incense at the altar during the evening prayer when an angel appeared to him, announcing the forthcoming birth of his first child, a son. This child would prepare the way for the Messiah; the spirit and power of Elijah would rest upon him (cf. Luke 3:3–6). His parents were to call him John. Zechariah was a truly godly man but it was difficult for him to believe what he heard and conse-

quently he was struck dumb until Elizabeth (his wife) gave birth. The child was born, circumcised and named according to the directions of God. Then Zechariah regained his voice and praised the Lord; this hymn of praise is called the *Benedictus* (Luke 1:5–25, 27–80).

Three months before the birth of John, the same angel (Gabriel) appeared to Mary. This young woman was betrothed to Joseph, a carpenter descended from King David (cf. Is. 11:1). The angel told Mary she would conceive a child by the Holy Spirit, and that she would name the child Jesus. Mary learned to her amazement that although she was a virgin she would have a child who was the very Son of God and the Savior of His people (Luke 1:32–35; cf. Matt. 1:21). Yet she accepted this message with great meekness, glad to be living in God's will (Luke 1:38).

Gabriel also told her that her cousin Elizabeth was pregnant, and Mary hastened to share their mutual joy. When these two godly women met, Elizabeth greeted Mary as the mother of her Lord (Luke 1:39–45). Mary also broke forth in a song of praise (the *Magnificat,* Luke 1:46–56). She stayed three months with Elizabeth before returning home.

Joseph, Mary's betrothed husband, was utterly shocked at what appeared to be the fruit of terrible sin on Mary's part (Matt. 1:19). He decided to put her away quietly. Then an angel in a dream explained the situation to him, and directed him to marry his intended wife as planned.

Jesus was born in Bethlehem to which the newlyweds had been summoned by the command of the emperor, Augustus Caesar (Luke 2:1). Thus the prophecy of Micah 5:2 was fulfilled.

From everywhere in the empire, Jews had to return to their ancestral cities to be registered so that they might be taxed. This census was taken while Cyrenius (Quirinius) was governor of Syria for the first time. Upon their arrival in Bethlehem, Mary and Joseph were unable to find any housing except a stable (perhaps a cave used to house cattle). There the eternal Son of God was born. He was wrapped in baby clothes and laid in a manger. Soon after His birth, shepherds came to see the child; angels had announced His birth to them while they were tending their flocks. Otherwise mankind had not noticed this event.

A. Early Years. We know of five events in the childhood of Jesus. First, in accordance with Jewish Law, He was circumcised and named on the eighth day (Luke 2:21). It is significant that the sinless son of God would undergo this rite binding Him to obedience under the divine covenant and identifying Him with God's people, Israel.

NAZARETH. *The home of Mary and Joseph (Luke 2:39), Nazareth was a Galilean town within the territory of Zebulun. In Bible times, the city lay close to several main trade routes, which afforded it easy contacts with the outside world. At the same time, its position as a frontier town on the border of Zebulun fostered a certain aloofness from the rest of Israel. For this reason, strict Jews scorned the people of Nazareth (John 1:46).*

Second, Jesus was presented at the temple to seal the circumcision. He was also "redeemed" by the payment of the presented five shekels. For her purification, Mary gave the offering of the poor (cf. Lev. 12:8; Luke 2:24). The mission of Jesus was attested at this time by two godly individuals, Simeon and Anna (Luke 2:25–38).

Third, sometime later a group of "wise men" (perhaps Babylonian priests and astrologers) appeared in Jerusalem, inquiring about the birth of a "King of the Jews." They had seen His star in the sky (Matt. 2:2). Ruthless Herod was immediately alarmed. Having learned from the scribes where prophecy said the Messiah was to be born, he sent the wise men to Bethlehem, asking them to return if they found the Messiah there. Herod claimed that he, too, wanted to worship Him. Actually, he wanted to locate the Christ child so he could remove yet another rival. However, an angel told the wise men not to go back to Herod. Before they arrived in Bethlehem the star reappeared and stood over the place Jesus and His parents now lived (Matt. 2:9).

Fourth, after the departure of the wise men, God directed Joseph to flee to Egypt with his family (Matt. 2:13–15). Herod had ordered the execution of all infants aged two and younger who lived in and around Bethlehem. Soon Herod died and God instructed Joseph to return to Nazareth.

The fifth event was Jesus' trip with his parents to the temple when He was 12 years old (Luke 2:41–52). There at the Passover He probably was inducted into the court of the men by being presented to the religious leaders. Unlike His peers, Jesus returned to the temple and continued discussion with the religious teachers (rabbis). He was so engrossed that He did not know His family had departed for home. Amid the confusion of the large group of people with whom they had traveled, His parents were not immediately aware of His absence. When they discovered He was not with them, they returned to Jerusalem and found Him in the temple. When they asked Jesus why He had remained behind, He told them that this was His Father's house and He was about His Father's business.

Scripture says that as a youth Jesus "increased in wisdom and stature, and in favor with God and man" (Luke 2:52).

John the Baptist, Elizabeth's son and Jesus' cousin, was to prepare the way for the ministry of Jesus. He was known as the "Baptist"

JESUS CHRIST

TRADITIONAL SITE OF THE TEMPTATION.
An old Greek Orthodox monastery clings to the cliff on Jebel Qarantal, the traditional Mountain of the Temptation west of Jericho. Qarantal is an Arabic corruption of the Latin word quarantana—*"40 days"—in memory of Christ's 40-day fast during His temptation (Matt. 4:1–11).*

because he preached to his fellow Jews that they should repent and be baptized. Although John cannot easily be identified with any of the Jewish sects, his role as a prophet is clear (Luke 7:24–28). When Jesus was about 30, He went to John to be baptized. However, He repented of no sin, for He had none. He identified with sinners in order to be their sin-bearer. When Jesus came up from the water, the Holy Spirit visibly descended upon Him in the form of a dove. At least Jesus and John (and perhaps the onlookers as well) heard the voice of God stating His approval of Jesus (Matt. 3:13–17); Mark 1:9–11; Luke 3:21–22; John 1:32–33).

The Holy Spirit at once led Jesus into the wilderness to face temptation by the devil (Matt. 4:1–11; Mark 1:12–13; Luke 4:1–13). Jesus was alone with His Father and the Holy Spirit while He fasted. But the devil was also there, tempting Him to (1) satisfy His own hunger, thereby demonstrating distrust of the Father, (2) seize dominion of the world before the Father gave it to Him, and (3) test God to see if He would save Jesus from self-indulged danger, thereby indulging His own self-will.

B. Early Judean Ministry. Only the Gospel of John describes this period of Jesus' life. John first recounts the relationship be-

tween Christ and John the Baptist. John the Baptist told delegates from the highest religious authorities that he was not the Messiah, though indicating that the Messiah was present (John 1:19–27). The next day, seeing Jesus approaching he pointed Him out as the Messiah (John 1:30–34). He said, "Behold the Lamb of God . . . ," implying that his own disciples should follow Jesus (John 1:35–37).

Jesus began to gather disciples to Himself (John 1:38–51). As a result of John the Baptist's testimony, John and Andrew turned to Him. Peter became a follower as a result of his brother's testimony. The fourth follower, Philip, immediately obeyed Jesus' summons to him. Philip brought Nathanael (Bartholomew) to Christ, and when Christ demonstrated that He knew Nathanael's inner thoughts, he also joined the band. (*See* "The Apostles.")

Jesus soon journeyed to Galilee. At a wedding feast in Cana, He turned water into wine (the first recorded miracle). This act revealed to the disciples His authority over nature. After a brief ministry in Capernaum, Jesus and His followers went to Jerusalem for the Passover. There He publicly declared His authority over the worship of men by cleansing the temple.[5] At this time Jesus first hinted at His own death and resurrection: "Destroy this temple and in three days I will raise it up again" (John 2:19).

One of the Jewish leaders, a Pharisee named Nicodemus, came to Jesus by night to talk with Him about spiritual matters. Their well-known conversation focused on the necessity of being "born again" (John 3).

The next six months find Jesus ministering outside Jerusalem, but still in Judea where John the Baptist was also working. Gradually people began to leave John and follow Jesus. This bothered the Baptist's disciples, but not John himself; he no doubt rejoiced to see the Messiah gaining attention (John 3:27–30).

Toward the end of this six months the Baptist was thrown into prison because he denounced Herod Antipas for taking the wife of his brother Philip (Matt. 14:3–5).

Perhaps John's imprisonment prompted Je-

---

[5] At this point John's narrative seems to disagree with the Synoptic Gospels, which say that Jesus cleansed the temple at the *end* of His ministry. Some scholars believe He did this on both occasions. Others think that John relates the event in a different sequence to emphasize Jesus' authority.

sus to go to Galilee to minister. At any rate, He went there. On the way He talked with a Samaritan woman He met at a well. Apparently this woman and some of her countrymen accepted Him as the true Messiah and Savior—a most remarkable thing (John 4:1–42). (For the hatred between Samaritans and Jews, *see* "Jews in New Testament Times.")

C. Galilean Ministry. Jesus' first stop on His return to Galilee was at Cana. There He healed a nobleman's son. The fervency of the nobleman persuaded Jesus to fulfill his request (John 4:45–54). In Nazareth Jesus worshiped in the synagogue on the Sabbath. There He was asked to read (in Hebrew) and explain (perhaps in Aramaic) a portion of Scripture. At first His kinsmen were pleased, but they became angry when they realized He was proclaiming Himself the Messiah. They led Him out of the city to cast Him off a precipice, but Jesus passed "through the midst of them" (Luke 4:30) and escaped.

Then Jesus went to Capernaum, which seems to have become His headquarters (cf. Matt. 9:1). Here He officially called to travel with Him the disciples Peter, Andrew, James, and John, who seem to have returned to their homes and occupations. Jesus taught in the synagogue each Sabbath and healed a demoniac there. He also healed Peter's mother-in-law (Matt. 8:14–15; Mark 1:29–31; Luke 4:38; cf. 1 Cor. 9:5). A crowd of sick folk subsequently gathered, "and he laid his hands on every one of them, and healed them" (Luke 4:40).

In the next stage of Jesus' ministry, He found great popularity among the common people. Now Jesus' primary mission was teaching, so He turned His back on those who would keep him chained to one spot for a ministry of healing only (Luke 4:42–44; cf. Mark 1:35, 37). The people acclaimed His miracles and teaching. Typical of His work on this circuit was the healing of the leper (Luke 5:12–15; cf. Mark 1:40–45). This incident underscored Jesus' submission to the Law, His compassion for men, and His interest in bringing men to salvation. (He commanded the leper to make the long journey to Jerusalem and present himself in the temple for the prescribed purification, submitting himself to God.)

The Date of Christmas

Nearly 2,000 years ago, shepherds in a field near Bethlehem were startled awake by a spectacle never before seen or heard. Wintry clouds were thrust asunder as a heavenly choir burst into majestic song. An angel proclaimed, "We are here to announce the first annual Christmas, which hereafter shall be celebrated throughout the world on December 25."

Fact? Certainly not!

Luke records that angels did announce the birth of "a Savior which is Christ the Lord." And it is true that shepherds received this news. But was the declaration made for December 25?

The fact is that Christmas, as we know it, is a rather modern innovation. Christ's birthday was not celebrated until more than 300 years had gone by, years in which accurate birth records (if there were any) had been lost. The early church remembered and celebrated Christ's Resurrection from the dead, which was more important. But the church was slow in adding Christmas to its list of dates worthy of recognition.

Luke pinpoints the era of Christ's birth by naming Augustus as Rome's imperial ruler. Roman history shows that Caesar Augustus was born 691 years after the founding of the City of Rome. Luke 2 further tells that Cyrenius was Syria's governor; again,

thanks to Rome's exhaustive record of names and events, historians have determined what is believed to be the particular census that Luke described. These dates have minor discrepancies; yet secular history gives us almost the exact year of Christ's birth.

But the month? the day? Winter was wet and chilly in Judea. It is unlikely that shepherds would have spent a December night in an open field, subject to rain and wind. Christ's birth was more likely during the spring lambing season, when nights would have been balmy and shepherds would have needed to be awake, tending the ewes.

So why have we celebrated Christ's birthday on December 25? A pagan festival, *Natalis Invicti,* was a boisterous Roman affair celebrated on December 25, when the sun was in its winter solstice. Worshipers of the Roman sun god enthusiastically pulled their Christian friends into the partying. By A.D. 386, church leaders set up the celebration of "Christ Mass" ("Christ's Coming"), so that Christians could join the festival activities without bending to paganism.

After the Roman Empire dissolved, Christians continued the December 25 birthday custom. By that time, December 25 seemed more fitting than any other date.

TIBERIAS. *This city on the western shore of the Sea of Galilee is mentioned only once in the Gospels (John 6:23). There is no record that Christ ever visited it. Perhaps, since it was a Gentile city, He avoided it in favor of numerous Jewish towns on the lake shore. Of the towns which surrounded the Sea of Galilee during New Testament times, Tiberias is the only one of any size to survive to the present day.*

Back in Capernaum, Jesus demonstrated His authority to forgive sin by curing a paralytic and summoning Matthew, a much-hated tax collector, to become His follower (Luke 5:16–29). Matthew responded immediately. During a feast at Matthew's house, scribes and Pharisees criticized Jesus and His disciples for their self-indulgence. Jesus responded that they were rejoicing at the presence of the Messiah, not revelling in self-indulgence. He alluded to His death and the mourning that would accompany it. But He promised that the mourning would be short-lived, for the spirit of the Gospel could not be confined to the "old wineskins" of Jewish legalism (Luke 5:30–39).

During this period Jesus began to meet increasing hostility from the high Jewish officials. While in Jerusalem for one of the Jews' annual feasts, He was attacked for healing a cripple on the Sabbath (John 5:1–16). He thus asserted His authority over the Sabbath and the Jews at once understood this to be a claim for divine authority. Jesus said that He knew God's mind, that He would judge sin, and that He would raise people from the dead. His critics pointed out that only God can do such things.

Back in Galilee, the Sabbath controversy continued as Jesus defended His disciples for picking grain on the Sabbath. Ultimately He claimed divine Lordship over the day. He healed a man with a withered hand on the Sabbath. The Jewish religious authorities began plotting to destroy Him (Matt. 12:1–14; Mark 2:23—3:6; Luke 6:1–11).

Now Jesus singled out 12 of His disciples who were officially to carry on His ministry. The appointment of the Twelve inaugurated a new period of Christ's ministry, beginning with our version of the great Sermon on the Mount. Jesus delivered this message (also called the Sermon on the Plain) when He descended from the mountain with His newly appointed apostles (Luke 6:20–49; cf. Matt. 5:1–6:29).

Now we read of several interwoven incidents. Perhaps on the very day He delivered the Sermon on the Mount, Jesus healed a centurion's servant. This centurion, a Roman soldier, was sympathetic toward the Jewish religion (Luke 7:5) and apparently embraced Jesus as the true Messiah. The servant was healed "in the selfsame hour" that the centurion made his request (Matt. 8:5–13; cf. Luke 7:1–10).

At Capernaum, perhaps about 11 km. (7 mi.) from the site of the Sermon on the Mount, crowds continued to press upon Jesus. To escape this pressure, He set out for Nain (with many accompanying Him). At the city's entrance He restored a widow's son to life. This incident stirred the excitement of the crowd (Luke 7:11–15).

About this time messengers from John the Baptist came to ask Jesus if He was really the Messiah. Still imprisoned, John had grown perplexed with the course of Jesus' ministry; it was peaceful and merciful, rather than dramatic, conquering, and judgmental. Jesus commended John and denounced the Jewish authorities who had opposed him—indeed, He pointed out that the cities of Galilee that heard John had "repented not." They had not truly come unto Him (Matt. 11:20–24; Luke 7:18–35; cf. 10:12–21).

In one of the cities Jesus visited (perhaps Nain), He was anointed by an outcast woman. He forgave her sins in the presence of His host, Simon the Pharisee. Simon was scandalized, but Jesus was happy to receive her love (Matt. 26:6–13; Mark 14:3–9; Luke 7:36–50).

This brings us to Jesus' second tour of the Galilean cities (Luke 8:1–4). The Twelve and certain devoted women (Mary Magdalene; Joanna, wife of Herod's steward; Susanna; and "many others") accompanied Him. It was on this journey that He cured the demoniac and the Pharisees accused Him of being in league with the devil. For this, Jesus strongly rebuked them (Matt. 8:28–34; Mark 5:1–20; Luke 8:26–39). He emphasized the blessedness of those who "hear the word of God and do it" (Luke 8:21). This same day He spoke many parables from a boat. The parable became Jesus' primary teaching tool, which both revealed and hid the truths He wanted to communicate (Mark 4:10–12; Luke 8:9–10). No doubt He repeated this and other sayings in different contexts, much as present-day ministers repeat their sermons and illustrations.

After preaching from the boat, Jesus crossed over the Sea of Galilee to the western shore. Before He departed, two men approached Him and asked to become His disciples (Matt. 8:18–22). But each made his request in an unrealistic and unworthy way, and Jesus rebuked them.

While crossing the sea, Jesus' life was threatened by a violent storm. He was asleep on a cushion in the stern of the boat, and so His disciples awakened Him. At once He stilled the storm, and the disciples exclaimed, "What manner of man is this! for he commandeth even the winds and water, and they obey him" (Luke 8:25; cf. Mark 4:35–44).

On the other side of Galilee, Jesus met a demoniac and drove the demons from him into a herd of swine, which immediately plunged to their death in the sea. When the townspeople came out to meet Christ, they found the demoniac fully clothed and in his right mind. Surprisingly, they begged Jesus to leave. He did so after He had sent the man to tell his friends of the Messiah (Matt. 8:28; Mark 5:1–20).

We are told of two miracles that Jesus performed when He returned to Capernaum: He raised Jairus' daughter from the dead and cured a woman with an issue of blood when she touched the hem of His garment (Matt. 9:18–26; Mark 5:21–43; Luke 8:40–56).

Jesus made a third tour of Galilee that included a number of miracles and a second rejection at Nazareth. Jesus yearned for more laborers to reap the spiritual harvest. He sent His disciples two-by-two to call the cities of Israel to repentance, granting them power to heal and cast out demons. Thus their ministry extended His own (Matt. 10:5–15; Mark 6:7–13; Luke 9:1–6).

At this point, we read the report of John the Baptist's death. Herod Antipas had long hesitated before killing John because he feared the people; but his wife Herodias plotted John's death using her daughter Salome to achieve her goal. Herod's guilty conscience led him to ask if Jesus was the resurrected John.

Grieving at John's death, beleaguered by crowds, and exhausted from work, Jesus gathered the Twelve and crossed the Sea of Galilee. But the crowds got there before them, and Jesus taught the masses all day. The session was climaxed when Jesus fed the entire multitude (5,000 men) by dividing and multiplying five loaves and two fish. When the leftovers were gathered they filled 12 baskets (Matt. 14:13–21).

Immediately after the miracle Jesus put the Twelve into the boat and sent them back across the Sea of Galilee, even though a storm was brewing. He retreated into the mountains to escape the overly enthusiastic crowd, which wanted to make Him king by force. Three hours after midnight, the disciples were caught in a violent storm in the middle of the lake. They were frightened. But when disaster seemed certain, Jesus came walking toward them on the water (Matt. 14:22–36; Mark 6:45–56). After He calmed their fears, Peter asked Jesus if He would permit him to come and meet Him. On the way, Peter lost heart and began to sink. Jesus took his hand and led

JESUS' BAPTISM. *Jesus came to John the Baptist to be immersed in the Jordan River, to show His obedience to God (Matt. 3:13–15). This photo shows the traditional site of Jesus' baptism, with the Jordan swollen by the melting snows of the northern mountains.*

him back to the boat. The water was calmed immediately.

In Capernaum Jesus began to heal the sick who streamed to Him from everywhere. Soon the crowd who had been fed arrived. Finding Jesus in a synagogue, they heard Him explain that He was the true bread of life from heaven.

They were now faced with accepting the authority of this teaching, spelled out in terms of eating Jesus' flesh and drinking His blood. This offended many of them and they left (John 6:22–66). Jesus asked the Twelve if they too were going to leave. This elicited Peter's well-known confession, "Lord, to whom shall we go? . . . We believe and are sure that thou art that Christ, the Son of the living God" (John 6:69).

After His discourse on the bread of life, Jesus turned from public teaching and devoted Himself to instructing His disciples (Matt. 15:1–20; Mark 7:1–23). The Jewish authorities resented Jesus' rejection of their religious ceremonies and His bold rebuke of their claims to authority. Jesus moved from place to place, seeking to avoid public exposure; but He could not always do this. In the area of Tyre and Sidon He healed a Gentile's daughter (Matt. 15:21–28), and in Decapolis He healed many who were brought to Him by the crowds (Matt. 15:29–31). He fed 4,000 people by multiplying loaves and a few fish (Matt. 15:32–39; Mark 8:1–10).

Back in the area of Capernaum, He was again besieged by the Jewish religious officials. To escape, He took a boat across the Sea of Galilee again. On the way He warned the Twelve of the Pharisees, Sadducees, and Herod (Matt. 16:1–12; Mark 8:11–21). In Bethsaida Jesus healed a blind man (Mark 8:22–26). Then He and His disciples journeyed north to the area of Caesarea Philippi, where Peter confessed Him to be the Messiah, "the Christ, the Son of the living God." Jesus replied that Peter's faith made him a rock, and that He would build His church upon this rock—that is, faith such as Peter had (Matt. 16:13–20; cf. Mark 8:27—9:1). At this point Jesus described His approaching suffering, death, and resurrection.

About a week later, Jesus took Peter, James, and John up a mountain and revealed to them His heavenly glory (the Tranfiguration). He conversed before their eyes with Moses and Elijah (Matt. 17:1–13; Mark 9:2–13; cf. Luke 9:28–36). At the foot of the mountain Jesus healed a demon-possessed boy whom the disciples had been unable to help (Matt. 17:14–23; Mark 9:14–32; Luke 9:37–44).

Jesus again toured Galilee but this time secretly. He again told the Twelve of His coming death and resurrection, and again they were unable to receive what He said.

Jesus paid the temple tax with money that was miraculously provided. On the way to Capernaum, He taught the disciples concerning the true nature of greatness and forgiveness (Matt. 17:22—18:35).

After many months, Jesus went to Jerusalem to celebrate the Feast of Tabernacles. (*See* "Worship Rituals.") He had refused to go with His family but later He made the trip privately. In Jerusalem the people's opinions about Him were divided. Jesus publicly affirmed that He was sent from the Father; He was the Messiah, the Savior of the world. The top religious authorities sent officers to arrest Jesus, but they were so impressed by Him that they were unable to fulfill their task. Then the religious authorities attempted to discredit Him by getting Him to violate the Law. But they were not successful. They brought to Him a woman taken in adultery and He completely turned the incident against them (John 8:1–11).

During this period Nicodemus tried to calm the hatred of the Sanhedrin (the high council of Jewish religious authorities). But while Jesus was in Jerusalem, He healed a blind man on the Sabbath. This provoked a great controversy and the man was cast out of the synagogue (a terrible disgrace). Jesus found the man, who recognized Him as the Messiah (John 9). Here Jesus delivered His famous discourse on the Good Shepherd (John 10:1–21).

D. Perean Ministry. About two months elapsed while Jesus went back to Galilee. Perhaps it was at this time that He sent 70 disciples into the cities of Israel to declare that the Kingdom was near and that Jesus was the Messiah (Luke 10). Jesus attempted to pass through Samaria on His way to Jerusalem, but the people rejected Him. So He crossed the Jordan and traveled through Perea. At one point a lawyer asked Jesus what he needed to do to inherit eternal life. Jesus told him to love God and his neighbor, to which the lawyer replied, "Who is my neighbor?" (Luke 10:28). Then Jesus told him the famous parable of the Good Samaritan. During this journey Jesus performed many miracles, such as healing an infirm woman and a dropsied man on the Sabbath (Luke 13:11–17; 14:1–6). The Sabbath miracles stirred yet more hostility among the Pharisees.

Then the scene shifted to Judea. Perhaps this was the time Jesus visited Bethany and the home of Mary and Martha. Mary sat at Jesus' feet while Martha prepared the meal. Martha complained about her sister's idleness, but Jesus answered that Mary had chosen "that good part"—i.e., listening to His teaching while He was still on earth (Luke 10:42). In Jerusalem at the annual Feast of Dedication, Jesus openly declared Himself to be the Messiah. The Jews regarded this as blasphemy, and they again tried to seize Him. Jesus then retreated across the Jordan to Bethabara. But the opposition of the religious authorities continued to grow.

The outcasts of society rallied to hear His teaching. Again He taught primarily in parables. Jesus privately explained the true meaning of His parables to the Twelve and otherwise continued their special training. One day an urgent message arrived from the home of Mary and Martha: Lazarus, their brother, was

GARDEN OF GETHSEMANE. *A garden east of Jerusalem near the Mount of Olives (Matt. 26:30), Gethsemane was a favorite retreat of Christ and His disciples. The Lord's earnest prayer here (Luke 22:41) gave rise to the Christian custom of kneeling in prayer.*

JESUS CHRIST

mortally ill. By the time Jesus arrived in Bethany, Lazarus had been dead and buried for four days. But Jesus raised him from the tomb. This miracle increased the determination of the religious authorities to get rid of Him (John 11:1–46).

Jesus again retired from the crowds for a time. Then He turned His face toward Jerusalem and death (John 11:54–57). The way to Jerusalem was marked by miracle working, teaching, and confrontation with the Pharisees. While He was on this journey, several parents brought their infants to Jesus for His blessing (Luke 18:15–17). He urged a "rich young ruler" to forsake his wealth and follow Him (Luke 18:18–30). And He again told His disciples of His coming death (Luke 18:31–34). In anticipation of that event, He

ANKLE BONE AND SPIKE. *An iron spike driven through the ankle bone of a 30-year-old man is the result of a first-century crucifixion, a practice that the Greeks and Romans adopted from the Phoenicians. Roman citizens were exempt from the cruel punishment, which was reserved for slaves and rebels. Death came very painfully and very slowly, occasionally taking as long as nine days.*

described the rewards of the Kingdom and instructed His disciples to be servants of their people (Matt. 20:1–16). In the vicinity of Jericho, Jesus healed some blind men, among whom was Bartimaeus, who recognized Jesus as the Messiah (Mark 10:46–52). He ate in the home of Zaccheus the publican, who also received salvation through faith in Him (Luke 19:1–10). From Jericho Jesus went to the home of Lazarus, Mary, and Martha in Bethany.

E. The Last Week. The last week before Jesus' crucifixion occupies a large portion of the Gospel records. Jesus attended a feast in Jericho at the home of Simon the leper, where Mary anointed Him with costly perfumes and wiped His feet with her hair. Some of the disciples protested this act because they felt it was a waste of money, but Jesus commended her. He pointed out that she was anointing Him for His coming burial (Matt. 26:13; Mark 14:3–9).

On the next day (Sunday), Jesus rode into Jerusalem on a colt upon which His followers had spread their garments (John 12). The Passover pilgrims lined the road, waving palm branches and acclaiming Jesus as the Messiah. When the Pharisees told Jesus to rebuke His followers, He replied that if His followers were quiet the stones would cry out. That evening Jesus and the Twelve returned to Bethany (Matt. 21:1–9; Mark 11:1–10; Luke 19:28–38).

The next day they journeyed once again to

PILATE INSCRIPTION. *Discovered in 1961 in the ruins of the Roman theater at Caesarea, this inscription mentions the names of the Emperor Tiberius and Pontius Pilate, who served as governor of Judea from A.D. 26 to 36. The most recent reading of the inscription is: "In honor of Julius Tiberius/Marcus Pontius Pilate/prefect of Judea."*

JESUS CHRIST

Jerusalem. On the way He cursed a fig tree for not having fruit when He required it (Matt. 21:18–19; Mark 11:12–14). By the following morning the fig tree had withered.

On Tuesday the Jewish leaders demanded that Jesus explain the authority by which He acted as He did. Jesus replied by telling several parables. He successfully thwarted the Pharisees' traps to get Him to contradict Moses and be discredited before the crowds. At one point Jesus pointedly denounced the scribes and Pharisees (Matt. 23:1–36). This was followed by an expression of His concern and longing for the people to love Him (Matt. 23:37–39). He also commented on the great sacrifice of the widow's mite (Mark 12:41–44) and talked to some Greeks who had requested an interview (John 12:20). He delivered a discourse on last things (Matt. 24:4—25:15; Mark 13:5–37). Perhaps on Tuesday evening Judas appeared before the council of the Sanhedrin and contracted to betray Jesus for 30 pieces of silver. This bounty was worth less than $20 in today's currency—it was the price of a slave in Jesus' time.

Jesus spent Wednesday resting in Bethany. On Thursday evening He ate the Passover with His disciples (Matt. 26:17–30; Mark 14:12–25). He sent Peter and John to find the place where the meal would be eaten. The feast involved sacrificing a lamb at the temple and eating it while sitting around a table with one's family. Jesus told two of the disciples to meet and follow a man bearing a pitcher who would lead them to the house where the feast would be prepared. They followed Jesus' directions, and the man led them to a house whose owner had already prepared a room for the purpose.

During the meal that evening, the disciples began to argue about which one of them would be most important. Jesus arose and washed their feet, trying to teach them that they should serve one another (John 13:1–17). After the meal Jesus instituted the Lord's Supper, a rite to be observed until He would come again. This symbolic meal consisted of eating bread (representing His body) and drinking wine (representing His blood).

Judas left the meal to finalize his arrangements to betray Jesus. Jesus warned the remaining disciples that they would lose their faith in Him that night. But Peter assured Jesus of his loyalty. Jesus replied that he would deny Him three times before the cock crowed at dawn.

Jesus and His remaining disciples left the Upper Room and went to the Garden of Gethsemane. While Jesus agonized in prayer, the disciples fell asleep. Three times He returned to find them sleeping. Finally He calmed His soul and was ready to face His death and all it would mean (Matt. 26:36–46; Mark 14:32–42). At this point Judas arrived with a company of armed men. He identified Jesus for the soldiers by kissing Him (Matt. 26:47–56; Mark 14:43–52; Luke 22:47–53; John 18:1–14).

Jesus stood trial before both the religious and civil authorities. The religious trial was illegally convened during the night; but it confirmed its decision after daybreak. Even at that, the whole matter was a mockery of justice (Matt. 26:59–68; Mark 14:55–65; Luke 22:65–71).

The civil trial occurred Friday morning before Pilate, who saw no threat or crime in Jesus. He sent Christ to Herod, who mocked Him and returned Him to Pilate (Luke 23:6–16). The Roman official hoped to release Jesus by popular demand but the crowd shouted for him to release Barabbas (a robber and murderer). They insisted that Pilate crucify Christ. Pilate proposed to scourge Christ and release Him to pacify the crowd, and he inflicted on Him other mockeries and punishments. But again the crowd cried, "Crucify Him." Ultimately Pilate gave in and sent Jesus to His death. In the midst of all this tumult, Jesus remained calm and composed (Matt. 27:11–31; Mark 15:2–20; Luke 23:2–25; John 18:28—19:15).

From Pilate's court, Jesus was taken outside the walls of Jerusalem to the hill of Golgotha, where He was crucified at about 9 A.M. on Friday. Accounts of Jesus' execution are found in Matthew 27:32–56 and parallel narratives.

Nicodemus and Joseph of Arimathea took Jesus' body and buried it in Joseph's tomb. Pilate sealed the tomb and set a guard over it to make certain the body was not stolen by Jesus' disciples.

Jesus was buried before dark on Friday ("the first day," since the Jews reckoned days from dusk to dusk). His body remained in the tomb from dusk Friday to dusk Saturday ("the second day") and from dusk Saturday to dawn Sunday ("the third day"). On the morning of the third day the astonished soldiers felt the earth quake and saw an angel roll away the stone sealing the tomb. They fled from the scene. Soon a group of women came to anoint

JESUS CHRIST

He appeared to His apostles, Christ ascended into heaven (Luke 24:49–53; Acts 1:6–11). Jesus promised to return just as He had ascended—visibly and physically. (After the Resurrection Jesus had a real body, although it was not limited by time and space.) He again promised the coming of the Holy Spirit. Although the Holy Spirit has come, the church still awaits the second coming of Christ.

II. The Doctrine of Christ. Christology deals with the person and work of Christ—i.e., the doctrine of Christ.

A. His Person. Understanding Christ's person is no easy task, but there is general agreement on most aspects of the nature of Christ and His personality.

Five titles of Jesus reflect something significant of His person and/or work. The name *Jesus* (which is identical with *Joshua* and means "God is Savior") emphasizes His role as the Savior of His people (Matt. 1:21). *Christ* is the New Testament equivalent of *Messiah*, a Hebrew word meaning "anointed one" (cf. Acts

39

JESUS CHRIST

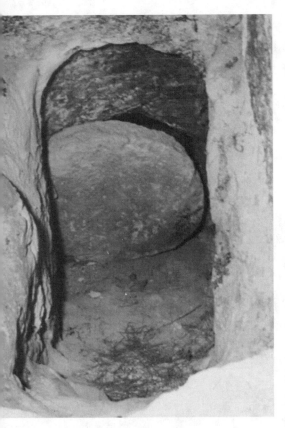

ROCK-HEWN TOMB. *Similar to the one in which the body of Jesus was laid, this tomb was excavated out of the soft limestone rock. The tomb probably contained a first chamber with a ledge around it as a seat and a second chamber with a niche cut into the wall for the body. When the niche was needed for additional bodies, the bones of the first were placed in a hole in the floor. The Gospels state that the tomb of Christ was new (Matt. 27:60; John 19:41), not merely an old tomb that had been emptied.*

Jesus' body with spices. They found the tomb empty. Running back to the city, they reported the news to Jesus' disciples. Peter and John came to the tomb and found it just as they had said (Matt. 27:57—28:10 and parallels). Jesus had risen from the dead.

Jesus appeared to His followers on 10 recorded occasions after His resurrection. At one of these appearances, Jesus commissioned the 11 remaining apostles to go into all the world and make disciples, baptizing and teaching them. This is known as the Great Commission (Matt. 28:19–20). The last time

CRUCIFIXION. *Jesus' atoning death on the cross of Calvary is a central fact of the Gospel. The seventeenth-century Flemish painter Peter Paul Rubens captured the mood of that event in this center panel of a triptych (a three-paneled portrayal of Christ's life) at the Antwerp Cathedral.*

JESUS CHRIST

4:27; 10:38). This title emphasized that Jesus was divinely appointed to His mission, that He had an official relationship to God the Father—that is, He had a job to do and a role to discharge at the Father's appointing.

Son of Man was the title used almost exclusively by Jesus Himself (cf. Matt. 9:6; 10:23; 11:19). Some feel He used it because it most clearly distinguished His Messiahship from the erroneous ideas of His time.

The name *Son of God* was also applied to Jesus in an official or messianic sense (cf. Matt. 4:3, 6; 16:16; Luke 22:70; John 1:49). It emphasized that He was a Person of the triune Godhead, supernaturally born as a human being.

Lord was alternately applied to Jesus as a simple title (somewhat like "Mr."), a title of authority or ownership, or (sometimes) an indication of His equality with God (e.g., Mark 12:36–37; Luke 2:11; Matt. 7:22).

Today Christians believe that Jesus is both God and man—i.e., that He has two distinct natures united "inconfusedly, unchangeably, indivisibly, inseparably" in His one person (Chalcedonian Creed, A.D. 451).

This doctrine is not built on human reason, but on biblical revelation. There is much scriptural proof that Jesus is divine. Scripture states that there is only one God and no lesser gods (cf. Ex. 20:3–5; Is. 42:8; 44:6), yet it clearly affirms that Jesus is God (e.g., John 1:1; Rom. 9:5; Heb. 1:8). The Bible reports that Jesus was worshiped at God's command (Heb. 1:6), while lesser spiritual beings refuse to be worshiped (Rev. 22:8–9) because worship was to be rendered only to God. Only the divine Creator may be worshiped by His creatures. But Jesus Christ, God's Son, is co-creator with His Father (John 1:3; Col. 1:16; Heb. 1:2); therefore both must be worshiped. Again, Scripture declares that Jesus was the Savior of His people (Matt. 1:21), even though Jehovah was the only Savior of His people (Is. 43:11; Hos. 13:4). It states that the Father Himself has clearly called Jesus God (Heb. 1:8).

Scripture also teaches the true humanity of Jesus. The Christ of the New Testament is no illusion or ghost; He is human in every sense. He called Himself man, as did others (e.g., John 8:40; Acts 2:22). He lived in the flesh (John 1:14; 1 Tim. 3:16; 1 John 4:2). He possessed a human body and mind (Luke 23:39; John 11:33; Heb. 2:14). He experienced human wants and sufferings (Luke 2:40, 52;

Heb. 2:10, 18; 5:8). However, the Bible emphasizes that Jesus did not partake of the sin that characterizes all other human beings (cf. Luke 1:35; John 8:46; Heb. 4:15).

B. His Personality. Christ has two distinct natures but is a single person, not two persons under one skin. He is the eternal Logos (divine Word), the second person of the Trinity, yet He assumed human nature in such a way that there was no essential change in the divine nature. We can address Christ in prayer using titles that reflect both His human and divine natures, although His divine nature is the ultimate basis of our worship. The incarnation manifested the *triune* (three-in-One) God by showing us the relationship between Father, Son, and Spirit (cf. Matt. 3:16–17; John 14:15–26; Rom. 1:3–4; Gal. 4:4–5; 1 Pet. 1:1–12). Because Jesus is one Person, and because the unity of His personal life embraces all His character and all His powers, Scripture speaks of Him as being both divine and

EMMAUS. *Described by Luke as about 11 km. (7 mi.) from Jerusalem, the site of Emmaus is uncertain, since the Gospel writer did not say in which direction the village lay. Some scholars identify Emmaus with the modern Amwas, pictured here. Jesus appeared to two of His disciples at Emmaus, following His resurrection (Luke 24:13–35).*

GORDAN'S CALVARY. *The word* Calvary *(Luke 23:33) comes from a Latin translation of an Aramaic word—the* Golgotha *of Matthew 27:33, meaning "skull." Scripture simply says that Calvary was located outside Jerusalem, that it was fairly conspicuous, and that a garden containing the tomb lay nearby. Two sites—the Church of the Holy Sepulcher and Gordan's Calvary—are possible locations of the Crucifixion. The church marks the older spot, which is supported by tradition that goes back at least to the fourth century. Gordan's Calvary, pictured here, contains a rock formation resembling a skull. This site accords with other biblical data, but there is no tradition to support its claim.*

human. It ascribes divine acts and attributes to Christ the eternal Son of God (Acts 20:28).

C. His Position. As we seek to understand Christ, we should examine His position before the Law. He humbled Himself before it; as a result, God exalted Him over it. This is an interesting irony.

The Son laid aside His divine majesty and assumed human nature. He submitted Himself to all the sufferings of His earthly life, including death itself. He did this to accomplish God's plan to redeem mankind from sin.

When the divine Logos became flesh He did not cease to be what He was before. By the same token, the incarnation as such—that is, the Word's bodily existence—continues as He sits at the right hand of God.

Christ was surrounded by sin. The devil repeatedly attacked Him. His own people hated Him and refused to believe He was the Savior. His enemies persecuted Him. Finally, at the end of His earthly life, He endured all the wrath of God against sin. No other person has suffered as intensely as Jesus did.

God the Father exalted Christ by raising Him from the dead, taking Him away to heaven, and seating Him at His own right hand. Christ will return from that place of honor to judge the living and the dead.

D. His Prophetic Office. The Old Testament depicts a prophet as a person who receives God's Word (revelation) and passes it on to his people. In order to function as a prophet, a person had to receive a clear word from God. He stood in God's stead before the people; God used his mouth to communicate what He wished to say.

The Old Testament promised a great prophet who would convey God's Word finally and decisively to His people (Deut. 18:15). Jesus was that prophet (Acts 3:22–24). He acted prophetically even before He came to earth as a man, for He spoke through the writers of the Old Testament (1 Pet. 1:11). During His earthly ministry He taught His followers the things of God, by both word and deed. Now He continues His prophetic work from heaven by operating through the Holy Spirit.

E. His Priestly Office. While the Old Tes-

JESUS CHRIST

tament prophet represented God before the people, the priest represented the people before God. So Christ represents His people before the Father (Heb. 3:1; 4:14).

The Bible tells us that a priest must be appointed by God. He must act on man's behalf in things that pertain to God. For example, He must make sacrifices and offerings for sins, intercede for the people He represents, and bless them (Heb. 5:1; 7:25; cf. Lev. 9:22).

Jesus presented Himself as a priestly sacrifice. The Old Testament sacrifices were *expiatory* (because they "put away" sin, thus restoring the worshiper to the blessings and privileges God intended for him) and *vicarious* (because another life was offered for sin instead of the life of the worshiper). Christ's once-for-all sacrifice was both expiatory and vicarious, and it gained for His people eternal salvation.

Christ reconciles the sinner to God. God expressed His love for mankind by sending Christ to redeem us from our sins (John 3:16). In every event, God has attempted to bring His creatures back to Him. So when Christ came into the world, there was no change in God Himself, only a change in His relation to sinners. Christ's sacrifice covered the guilt that stood between sinners and God.

Christ also intercedes for His people (Heb. 7:25). He entered the Holy Place of heaven by means of the perfect, all-sufficient sacrifice that He offered to the Father. In so doing, He represented those who put their faith in Him and reinstated them before the Father (Heb. 9:24).

In the presence of God, Christ now answers the constant accusations of the devil against believers (Rom. 8:33–34). Our prayers and services are tainted with sin and imperfection; Christ perfects them in the eyes of the Father, speaking constantly to the Father in our behalf. Finally, Christ prays for believers. He pleads for the needs we do not mention in our prayers—things that we ignore, underestimate, or do not see. He does this to protect us from danger and sustain us in faith until we attain victory in the end. He also prays for those who have not yet believed. He constantly does this intercessory work.

F. His Kingly Office. As the second person of the Trinity, co-creator with the Father, Christ is the eternal king over all things. As Savior, He is the king of a spiritual kingdom—that is, He rules in the hearts and lives of His people. By reason of His spiritual kingship, Christ is called the "head" of the church (Eph. 1:22).

Christ rules and governs all things on behalf of His church. He will not allow His purposes to be frustrated in the end. Christ received this universal kingship when God exalted Him to His place of honor in heaven. He will deliver this kingdom to the Father when He accomplishes the final victory over evil (1 Cor. 15:24–28), i.e., when He destroys this world-order once for all and makes it new. Then the universe as we know it will cease to exist. No human kings or diabolical powers will be able to reign. Only Christ and His Kingdom will be preserved.

THE APOSTLES

At the beginning of His ministry, Jesus selected 12 men to travel with Him. These men would have an important responsibility: They would continue to represent Him after He had returned to heaven. Their reputation would continue to influence the church long after they were dead.

So the selection of the Twelve was a great responsibility. "And it came to pass in those days, that he went out into a mountain to pray, and continued all night in prayer to God. And when it was day, he called unto him his disciples: and of them he chose 12, whom he also named apostles" (Luke 6:12–13).

Most of the apostles came from the area of Capernaum, which was despised by polite Jewish society because it was the center of a part of the Jewish state (only recently added) and was known in fact as "Galilee of the Gentiles." Jesus Himself said, "And thou, Capernaum, which art exalted into heaven, shalt be brought down to hell" (Matt. 11:23). Yet Jesus molded these 12 men into strong leaders and articulate spokesmen of the Christian faith. Their success bears witness to the transforming power of Jesus' lordship.

None of the Gospel writers have left us any physical descriptions of the Twelve. Nevertheless, they give us tiny clues that help us to make "educated guesses" about how the apostles looked and acted. One very important fact that has traditionally been overlooked in countless artistic representations of the apostles is their youth. If we realize that most lived into the third and fourth quarter of the century and John into the second century, then they must have been only teenagers when they first took up Christ's call.

Different biblical accounts list the Twelve in pairs. We are not sure whether this indicates family relationships, team functions, or some other kind of association between them.

I. ANDREW

II. BARTHOLOMEW (NATHANAEL?)

III. JAMES, SON OF ALPHEUS

IV. JAMES, SON OF ZEBEDEE

V. JOHN

VI. JUDAS (NOT ISCARIOT)

VII. JUDAS ISCARIOT

VIII. MATTHEW

IX. PHILIP

X. SIMON PETER

XI. SIMON ZELOTES

XII. THOMAS

XIII. JUDAS'S REPLACEMENT

I. Andrew. The day after John the Baptist saw the Holy Spirit descend upon Jesus, he identified Jesus for two of his disciples and said, "Behold the Lamb of God!" (John 1:36). Intrigued by this announcement, the two men left John and began to follow Jesus. Jesus noticed them and asked what they were seeking. Immediately they replied, "Rabbi, where dwellest thou?" Jesus took them to the house where He was staying and they spent the night with Him. One of these men was named Andrew (John 1:38–40).

Andrew soon went to find his brother, Simon Peter. He told Peter, "We have found the Messiah . . ." (John 1:41). Through his testimony, he won Peter to the Lord.

Andrew is our English rendering of the Greek word *Andreas,* which means "manly." Other clues from the Gospels indicate that Andrew was physically strong and a devout, faithful man. He and Peter owned a house together (Mark 1:29). They were sons of a man named Jonah or John, a prosperous fisherman. Both of the young men had followed their father into the fishing business.

Andrew was born at Bethsaida on the northern shores of the Sea of Galilee. Though the Book of John describes Andrew's first encounter with Jesus, it does not mention him as a disciple until much later (John 6:8). The Book of Matthew says that when Jesus was walking along the Sea of Galilee He hailed Andrew and Peter and invited them to become His disciples (Matt. 4:18–19). This does not contradict John's narrative; it simply adds a new feature. A close reading of John 1:35–40 shows that Jesus did not call Andrew and Peter to follow Him the first time they met.

THE APOSTLES

SEA OF GALILEE. *This freshwater lake is also referred to in the New Testament as the "Sea of Tiberias" (John 21:1) and the "lake of Gennesaret" (Luke 5:1). Several of the apostles worked as fishermen along its shores. It measures up to 10 km. (6 mi.) wide and 24 km. (15 mi.) from north to south. Along the shores of the lake were many towns such as Capernaum (in the background), where Christ conducted much of His ministry. In His time, these towns formed an almost continuous belt of settlements around the lake.*

Andrew and another disciple named Philip introduced a group of Greek men to Jesus (John 12:20–22). For this reason, we might say that Andrew and Philip were the first foreign missionaries of the Christian faith.

Tradition says that Andrew spent his last years in Scythia, north of the Black Sea. But a small book entitled the *Acts of Andrew* (probably written about A.D. 260) says that he preached primarily in Macedonia and was martyred at Patras.[1]

Roman Catholic tradition says that Andrew was crucified on an X-shaped cross, a religious symbol that is now known as St. Andrew's Cross. It was believed that he was crucified on November 30, so the Roman Catholic church and Greek Orthodox church observe his festival on that date. Today he is the patron saint of Scotland. The Order of St. Andrew is an association of church ushers who make a special effort to be courteous to strangers.

II. Bartholomew (Nathanael?). We lack information about the identity of the apostle named Bartholomew. He is mentioned only in the lists of apostles. Moreover, while the synoptic Gospels agree that his name was Bartholomew, John gives it as Nathanael (John 1:45). Some scholars believe that Bartholomew was the surname of Nathanael.

The Aramaic word *bar* means "son," so the name *Bartholomew* literally meant "son of Thalmai." The Bible does not identify Thalmai for us, but he may have been named after the King Thalmai of Geshur (2 Sam. 3:3). Some scholars believe that Bartholomew was connected with the Ptolemies, the ruling family of Egypt; this theory is based upon Jerome's statement that Bartholomew was the only apostle of noble birth.

Assuming that Bartholomew is the same person as Nathanael, we learn a bit more about his personality from the Gospel of John. Jesus called Nathanael "an Israelite . . . in whom is no guile" (John 1:47).

Tradition says Nathanael served as a missionary in India. The Venerable Bede said that Nathanael was beheaded by King Astriagis. Other traditions say that Nathanael was crucified head-down.

III. James, Son of Alpheus. The Gospels make only fleeting reference to James, the son of Alpheus (Matt. 10:3; Mark 3:18; Luke 6:15). Many scholars believe that James was a brother of Matthew, since Scripture says that Matthew's father was also named Alphaeus (Mark 2:14). Others believe that this James was identified with "James the Less"; but we have no proof that these two names refer to the same man (cf. Mark 15:40).

If the son of Alphaeus was indeed the same man as James the Less, he may have been a cousin of Jesus (cf. Matt. 27:56; John 19:25). Some Bible commentators theorize that this disciple bore a close physical resemblance to Jesus, which could explain why Judas Iscariot had to identify Jesus on the night of His betrayal (Mark 14:43–45; Luke 22:47–48).

Legends say that this James preached in Persia and was crucified there. But we have no concrete information about his later ministry and death.

IV. James, Son of Zebedee. After Jesus summoned Simon Peter and his brother Andrew, He went a little farther along the shore of Galilee and summoned "James the son of Zebedee and John his brother, who also were in the ship mending their nets" (Mark 1:19). Like Peter and Andrew, James and his brother responded immediately to Christ's invitation.

James was the first of the Twelve to suffer a

[1] Edgar J. Goodspeed, *The Twelve* (Philadelphia: J. C. Winston Company, 1957), p. 99.

THE APOSTLES

martyr's death. King Herod Agrippa I ordered that James be executed with a sword (Acts 12:2). Tradition says this occurred in A.D. 44, when James would have been quite young. (Although the New Testament does not describe the martyrdom of any other apostles, tradition tells us that all except John died for their faith.)

The Gospels never mention James alone; they always speak of "James and John." Even in recording his death, the Book of Acts refers to him as "James the brother of John" (Acts 12:2). James and John began to follow Jesus on the same day, and both of them were present at the transfiguration of Jesus (Mark 9:2–13). Jesus called both men the "sons of thunder" (Mark 3:17).

The persecution that took James's life inspired new fervor among the Christians (cf. Acts 12:5–25). Undoubtedly, Herod Agrippa had hoped to quash the Christian movement by executing leaders such as

James. "But the Word of God grew and multiplied" (v. 24).

Strangely, the Gospel of John does not mention James. John was reluctant to mention his own name, and he may have felt the same kind of modesty about reporting the activities of his brother. Once John refers to himself and James as the "sons of Zebedee" (John 21:2). Otherwise he is silent about the work of James.

Legends say that James was the first Christian missionary to Spain. Roman Catholic authorities believe that his bones are buried in the city of Santiago in northwestern Spain.

V. John. Fortunately, we have a considerable amount of information about the disciple named John. Mark tells us he was the brother of James, son of Zebedee (Mark 1:19). Mark says that James and John worked with the "hired servants" of their father (Mark 1:20).

Some scholars speculate that John's mother was Salome, who observed the crucifixion of

CATACOMB FRESCO. *Dating from A.D. 200–220, this fresco is one of the oldest catacomb paintings yet discovered. It depicts the events of John 21, when seven disciples (i.e., Peter, Thomas, Nathanael, the sons of Zebedee, and two other disciples) feasted on bread and fish.*

THE LAST SUPPER. *Leonardo da Vinci (1452–1519) began work in 1496 on what many art critics consider to be his greatest masterpiece. Christ is shown at the center of the table. He has just revealed that one of them would betray Him. The disciples murmur among themselves, wondering which of them would do this (Luke 22:21–23). Judas, the second figure left of center, sits silently and clutches the disciples' purse (cf. John 12:4–6).*

Jesus (Mark 15:40). If Salome was the sister of Jesus' mother, as the Gospel of John suggests (John 19:25), John may have been a cousin of Jesus.

Jesus found John and his brother James mending their nets beside the Sea of Galilee. He ordered them to launch out into the lake and let down their nets to catch fish. They hauled in a tremendous catch—a miracle that convinced them of Jesus' power. "And when they had brought their ships to land, they forsook all, and followed him" (Luke 5:11). Simon Peter went with them.

John seems to have been an impulsive young man. Soon after he and James entered Jesus' inner circle of disciples, the Master labeled them "sons of thunder" (Mark 3:17). The disciples seemed to relegate John to a secondary place in their company. All of the Gospels mentioned John after his brother James; on most occasions, it seems, James was the spokesman for the two brothers. When Paul mentions John among the apostles at Jerusalem, he places John at the end of the list (Gal. 2:9).

John's emotions often erupted in his conversations with Jesus. On one occasion, John became upset because someone else was ministering in Jesus' name. "We forbade him," he told Jesus, "because he followeth not us" (Mark 9:38). Jesus replied, "Forbid him not . . . For he that is not against us is on our part" (Mark 9:39–40). On another occasion, James and John ambitiously suggested that they should be allowed to sit on Jesus' right

hand in heaven. This idea antagonized the other disciples (Mark 10:35–41).

Yet John's boldness served him well at the time of Jesus' death and resurrection. John 18:15 tells us that John "was known unto the high priest." A Franciscan legend says that John's family supplied fish to the high priest's household.[2] This would have made him especially vulnerable to arrest when the high priest's guards apprehended Jesus. Nevertheless, John was the only apostle who dared to stand at the foot of the cross, and Jesus committed His mother into his care (John 19:26–27). When the disciples heard that Jesus' body was no longer in the tomb, John ran ahead of the others and reached the sepulcher first. However, he allowed Peter to enter the burial chamber ahead of him (John 20:1–4, 8).

If John indeed wrote the fourth Gospel, the letters of John, and the Book of Revelation, he penned more of the New Testament than any of the other apostles. We have no sound reason to doubt John's authorship of these books. (*See* "Outline of the Books of the Bible.")

Tradition says that John cared for Jesus' mother while he was pastor of the congregation in Ephesus, and that she died there. Tertullian says that John was taken to Rome and "plunged into boiling oil, unhurt, and then exiled on an island." This was probably the island of Patmos, where the Book of Revelation was written. It is believed that John lived to an

---

[2] H.V. Morton, *In the Steps of the Master* (New York: Dodd, Mead and Company, 1935).

old age and that his body was returned to Ephesus for burial.

VI. Judas (Not Iscariot). John refers to one of the disciples as "Judas, not Iscariot" (John 14:22). It is not easy to determine the identity of this man. Jerome dubbed him *Trionius*—"the man with three names."

The New Testament refers to several men by the name of Judas—Judas Iscariot (*see below*), Judas the brother of Jesus (Matt. 13:55; Mark 6:3), Judas of Galilee (Acts 5:37), and "Judas, not Iscariot." Clearly, John wanted to avoid confusion when he referred to this man, especially because the other disciple named Judas had such a poor reputation.

Matthew refers to this man as Lebbeus, "whose surname was Thaddeus" (Matt. 10:3). Mark refers to him simply as Thaddeus (Mark 3:18). Luke refers to him as "Judas the son of James" (Luke 6:16; Acts 1:13). The KJV incorrectly translates Luke as saying that this man was the *brother* of James.

We are not sure who Thaddeus's father was. Some think he was James, the brother of Jesus—making Judas a nephew of Jesus. But this is not likely, for early church historians report that this James never married. Others think that his father was the apostle James, son of Zebedee. We cannot be certain.

William Steuart McBirnie suggests that the name Thaddeus was a diminutive form of *Theudas,* which comes from the Aramaic noun *tad,* meaning "breast." Thus, Thaddeus may have been a nickname that literally meant "one close to the breast" or "one beloved." McBirnie believes that the name Lebbeus may be derived from the Hebrew noun *leb,* which means "heart."[3]

The historian Eusebius says that Jesus once sent this disciple to King Abgar of Mesopotamia to pray for his healing. According to this story, Judas went to Abgar after Jesus' ascension to heaven, and he remained to preach in several cities of Mesopotamia.[4] Another tradition says that this disciple was murdered by magicians in the city of Suanir in Persia. It is said that they killed him with clubs and stones.

VII. Judas Iscariot. All of the Gospels place Judas Iscariot at the end of the list of Jesus' disciples. Undoubtedly this reflects Judas's ill repute as the betrayer of Jesus.

The Aramaic word *Iscariot* literally meant "man of Kerioth." Kerioth was a town near Hebron (Josh. 15:25). However, John tells us that Judas was the son of Simon (John 6:71).

If Judas indeed came from the town of Kerioth, he was the only Judean among Jesus' disciples. Judeans despised the people of Galilee as crude frontier settlers. This attitude may have alienated Judas Iscariot from the other disciples.

The Gospels do not tell us exactly when Jesus called Judas Iscariot to join His band of followers. Perhaps it was in the early days when Jesus called so many others (cf. Matt. 4:18–22).

Judas acted as the treasurer of the disciples, and on at least one occasion he manifested a penny-pinching attitude toward their work. When a woman named Mary came to pour rich ointment on the feet of Jesus, Judas complained, "Why was not this ointment sold for 300 pence, and given to the poor?" (John 12:5). John comments that Judas said this "not that he cared for the poor; but because he was a thief" (John 12:6).

As the disciples shared their last meal with Jesus, the Lord revealed that He knew He was about to be betrayed, and He singled out Judas as the culprit. He told Judas, "That thou doest, do quickly" (John 13:27). However, the other disciples did not suspect what Judas was about to do. John reports that "some of them thought, because Judas had the bag, that Jesus had said unto him, 'Buy those things that we have need of against the (Passover) feast . . .'" (John 13:28–29).

Scholars have offered several theories about the reason for Judas' betrayal. Some think that he was reacting to Jesus' rebuke when he criticized the woman with the ointment.[5] Others think that Judas acted out of greed for the money that Jesus' enemies offered him.[6] Luke and John simply say that Satan inspired Judas's actions (Luke 22:3; John 13:27).

Matthew tells us that Judas in remorse attempted to return the money to Jesus' captors:

[3] William Steuart McBirnie, *The Search for the Twelve Apostles* (Chicago: Tyndale House, 1973), p. 196.

[4] Eusebius, *The History of the Church* (Oxford: Penguin Classics, 1965), p. 65.

[5] *The New Westminster Dictionary of the Bible,* ed. by Henry Schneider Gehman (Philadelphia: Westminster Press, 1970), p. 526.

[6] Karl Schmidt, "Judas Iscariot," *The New Schaff-Herzog Encyclopedia of Religious Knowledge,* Vol. 6, ed. by Samuel M. Jackson (Grand Rapids: Baker Books, 1977), p. 244.

"And he cast down the pieces of silver in the temple, and departed, and went and hanged himself" (Matt. 27:5). A folk legend says that Judas hanged himself on a redbud tree, which is sometimes called the "Judas tree." In most modern works, Judas is portrayed as a zealot or extreme patriot who was disappointed at Jesus' failure to lead a mass movement or rebellion against Rome. There is, as yet, little evidence for this viewpoint.

VIII. Matthew. In Jesus' day, the Roman government collected several different taxes from the people of Palestine. Tolls for transporting goods by land or sea were collected by private tax collectors, who paid a fee to the Roman government for the right to assess these levies. The tax collectors made their profits by charging a higher toll than the law required. The licensed collectors often hired minor officials called *publicans* to do the actual work of collecting the tolls. The publicans extracted their own wages by charging a fraction more than their employer required. The disciple Matthew was a publican who collected tolls on the road between Damascus and Accho; his booth was located just outside the city of Capernaum and he may have also collected taxes from the fishermen for their catches.

Normally a publican charged five percent of the purchase price of normal trade items and up to 12.5 percent on luxury items. Matthew also collected taxes from fishermen who worked along the Sea of Galilee and boatmen who brought their goods from cities on the other side of the lake.

The Jews considered a tax collector's money to be unclean so they would never ask for change. If a Jewish man did not have the exact amount that the collector required, he borrowed from a friend. Jewish people despised the publicans as agents of the hated Roman Empire and the puppet Jewish king. Publicans were not allowed to testify in court, and they could not tithe their money to the temple. A good Jew would not even associate with publicans in private life (cf. Matt. 9:10–13).

Yet the Jews divided the tax collectors in two classes. First were the *gabbai,* who levied general agricultural taxes and census taxes from the people. The second group were the *mokhsa,* the officials who collected money from travelers. Most of the *mokhsa* were Jews, so they were despised as traitors to their own people. Matthew belonged to this class of tax collectors.

The Gospel of Matthew tells us that Jesus approached this unlikely disciple as he sat at his tax table one day. Jesus simply commanded Matthew to "follow me," and Matthew left his work to follow the Master (Matt. 9:9).

Apparently Matthew was fairly well-to-do, because he provided a banquet in his own house. "And there was a great company of publicans and of others that sat down with them" (Luke 5:29). The simple fact that Matthew owned his own house indicates that he was wealthier than the typical publican.

Because of the nature of his work, we feel quite certain that Matthew knew how to read

CHALICE OF ANTIOCH. *This large silver cup (19 cm. or 7 1/2 in. high) was discovered in 1916 at Antioch. At first, many scholars thought this was the actual cup used at the Last Supper. However, subsequent study of the artwork on the cup leads authorities to believe it dates no later than the fourth or fifth centuries A.D. The plain metal lining may be a substitute for an original glass vessel. In 1954, Warner Brothers Studios produced a feature-length film about the story of this cup, entitled "The Silver Chalice," starring Paul Newman and Jack Palance.*

and write. Papyrus tax documents dating from about A.D. 100 indicate that the publicans were quite efficient with figures. (Instead of using the clumsy Roman numerals, they preferred the simpler Greek symbols.)

Matthew may have been related to the disciple James, since each of them is said to have been a "son of Alphaeus" (Matt. 10:3; Mark 2:14). Luke sometimes uses the name Levi to refer to Matthew (cf. Luke 5:27–29). Thus some scholars believe that Matthew's name was Levi before he decided to follow Jesus, and that Jesus gave him the new name, which means "gift of God." Others suggest that Matthew was a member of the priestly tribe of Levi.

Even though a former publican had joined His ranks, Jesus did not soften His condemnation of the tax collectors. He ranked them with the harlots (cf. Matt. 21:31), and Matthew himself classes the publicans with sinners (Matt. 9:10).

Of all the Gospels, Matthew's has probably been the most influential. Second-century Christian literature quotes from the Gospel of Matthew more than from any other. The church fathers placed Matthew's Gospel at the beginning of the New Testament canon, probably because of the significance they attributed to it. Matthew's account emphasizes Jesus' fulfillment of Old Testament prophecy. It stresses that Jesus was the promised Messiah, who had come to redeem all mankind.

We do not know what happened to Matthew after the day of Pentecost. In his *Book of Martyrs,* John Foxe stated that Matthew spent his last years preaching in Parthia and Ethiopia. Foxe says that Matthew was martyred in the city of Nadabah in A.D. 60. However, we do not know from what source Foxe got this information (other than from medieval Greek sources) and we cannot judge whether it is trustworthy.

IX. Philip. John's Gospel is the only one to give us any detailed information about the disciple named Philip. (This Philip should not be confused with Philip the evangelist—cf. Acts 21:8.)

Jesus first met Philip at Bethany beyond the Jordan River (John 1:28, RSV). It is interesting to note that Jesus called Philip individually while He called most of the other disciples in pairs. Philip introduced Nathanael to Jesus (John 1:45–51), and Jesus also called Nathanael (or Nathanael Bartholomew) to be His disciple.

When 5,000 people gathered to hear Jesus, Philip asked his Lord how they would feed the crowd. "Two hundred pennyworth of bread is not sufficient for them, that every one of them may take a little," he said (John 6:7).

On another occasion, a group of Greek men came to Philip and asked him to introduce them to Jesus. Philip enlisted the help of Andrew and together they took the men to meet Him (John 12:20–22).

While the disciples ate their last meal with Jesus, Philip said, "Lord, show us the Father, and it sufficeth us" (John 14:8). Jesus responded that they had already seen the Father in Him.

These three brief glimpses are all that we see of Philip in the Gospels. The church has preserved many traditions about his later ministry and death. Some say that he preached in France; others that he preached in southern Russia, Asia Minor, or even India. In A.D. 194, Bishop Polycrates of Antioch wrote that "Philip, one of the twelve apostles, sleeps at Hierapolis." However, we have no firm evidence to support these claims.

X. Simon Peter. The disciple named Simon Peter was a man of contrasts. At Caesarea Philippi, Jesus asked, "But whom say ye that I am?" Peter immediately replied, "Thou art the Christ, the Son of the living God" (Matt. 16:15–16). But seven verses later we read, "Then Peter took him, and began to rebuke him. . . ." Going from one extreme to another was characteristic of Peter.

When Jesus attempted to wash Peter's feet in the Upper Room, the intemperate disciple exclaimed, "Thou shalt never wash my feet." But when Jesus insisted, Peter said, "Lord, not my feet only, but also my hands and my head" (John 13:8–9).

On their last night together, Peter told Jesus, "Although all shall offend thee, yet will not I" (Mark 14:29). Yet within hours, Peter not only denied Jesus but cursed Him (Mark 14:71).

This volatile, unpredictable temperament often got Simon Peter into trouble. Yet the Holy Spirit would mold Peter into a stable, dynamic leader of the early church, a "rockman" (*Peter* means "rock") in every sense.

The New Testament writers used four different names in referring to Peter. One is the Hebrew name *Simeon* (Acts 15:14), which may mean "hearing." A second name was *Simon,* the Greek form of Simeon. A third name was *Cephas,* Aramaic for "rock." The fourth name was *Peter,* Greek for "rock"; the New

THE APOSTLES

Testament writers apply this name to the disciple more often than the other three.

When Jesus first met this man, He said, "Thou art Simon, the son of Jona: thou shalt be called Cephas" (John 1:42). Jonah was a Greek name meaning "dove" (cf. Matt. 16:17; John 21:15–17). Some modern translations render this name as "John."

Peter and his brother Andrew were fishermen on the Sea of Galilee (Matt. 4:18; Mark 1:16). He spoke with the accent of a Galilean, and his mannerisms identified him as an uncouth native of the Galilean frontier (cf. Mark 14:70). His brother Andrew led him to Jesus (John 1:40–42).

While Jesus hung on the cross, Peter was probably among the group from Galilee that "stood afar off, beholding these things" (Luke 23:49). In 1 Peter 5:1 he wrote, "I . . . am also an elder, and a witness of the sufferings of Christ. . . ."

Simon Peter heads the list of apostles in each of the Gospel accounts, which suggests that the New Testament writers considered him to be the most significant of the Twelve. He did not write as much as John or Matthew, but he emerged as the most influential leader of the early church. Though 120 followers of

Jesus received the Holy Spirit on the day of Pentecost, the Scripture records the words of Peter (Acts 2:14–40). Peter suggested that the apostles find a replacement for Judas Iscariot (Acts 1:22). And he and John were the first disciples to perform a miracle after Pentecost, healing a lame man at the Beautiful Gate of Jerusalem (Acts 3:1–11).

The Book of Acts emphasizes the travels of Paul, yet Peter also traveled extensively. He visited Antioch (Gal. 2:21), Corinth (1 Cor. 1:11), and perhaps Rome. Eusebius states that Peter was crucified in Rome, probably during the reign of Nero.

Peter felt free to minister to the Gentiles (cf. Acts 10) but he is best known as the apostle to the Jews (cf. Gal. 2:8). As Paul took a more active role in the work of the church and as the Jews became more hostile to Christianity, Peter faded into the background of the New Testament narrative.

The Roman Catholic church traces the authority of the Pope back to Peter, for it is alleged that Peter was bishop of the church at Rome when he died. Tradition says that the Basilica of St. Peter in Rome is built over the spot where Peter was buried. Modern excavations under the ancient church demonstrate a

Where Is Peter Buried?

Roman Catholic tradition maintains that Peter is buried beneath the magnificent structure in Rome which bears his name—Saint Peter's Basilica. Although the New Testament does not report a visit of Peter to Rome, there is historical evidence that he spent at least part of the latter portion of his life there. There are also extra-biblical references (such as the Acts of Peter) and numerous references in the writings of second- and third-century church scholars which confirm that Peter died in Rome. Eusebius gives A.D. 68 as the approximate date of Peter's death.

The early Christian apologists Tertullian and Origen state that Peter was executed by crucifixion head-downwards in Rome. They say that he was one of thousands of Christians who died under Emperor Nero's persecution. In all probability, Peter was executed at the Neronian Gardens, where the estate of the Vatican is now located. According to Tertullian and Origen, Peter was buried nearby at the foot of Vatican Hill. Gaius of Rome (third century A.D.) mentions this grave.

It is said that Peter's remains were taken to a vault on the Appian Way when Emperor Valerian

began his persecution of the Christians (A.D. 258). There his bones rested with those of Paul, safe from the emperor's threatened desecration of Christian burial grounds. Later, Peter's remains were returned to their original grave, and in about A.D. 325 Constantine erected a magnificent basilica over the location at the foot of Vatican Hill. This basilica was replaced by the present Saint Peter's Basilica in the sixteenth century.

For many centuries, Saint Peter's Basilica has been the most highly revered shrine in the Western world. Thousands of worshipers journey to Rome each year to pray over the spot where Peter is said to be buried. However, in recent years scholars have challenged the claim that Peter is buried beneath the basilica. Vatican archaeologists made several excavations in the early 1960s to investigate the centuries-old claim. They found a first-century Roman cemetery with one hastily dug grave that might have been Peter's. The Vatican researchers felt this was a reasonable conclusion.

Gaius wrote that the tombs of the apostles were close to the Vatican, on the road to Ostia; this suggests another possible site.

THE APOSTLES

very old Roman cemetery and some graves hastily used for Christian burials. A careful reading of the Gospels and the early segment of Acts would tend to support the tradition that Peter was the leading figure of the early church. The tradition that Peter was the leading figure of the apostolic church has strong support.

XI. Simon Zelotes. Matthew and Mark refer to a disciple named "Simon the Canaanite" (modern translations have "Canaanean," which is more correct), while Luke and the Book of Acts refer to one named "Simon Zelotes." These names refer to the same man. *Zelotes* is a Greek word that means "zealous one"; "Canaanite" is an English transliteration of the Aramaic word *kanna'ah,* which also means "zealous one"; thus it appears that this disciple belonged to the Jewish sect known as the Zealots. (*See* "Jews in New Testament Times.")

The Scripture does not indicate when Simon Zelotes was invited to join the apostles. Tradition says that Jesus called him at the same time that He called Andrew and Peter, James and John, Judas Iscariot and Thaddeus (cf. Matt. 4:18–22).

We have several conflicting stories about the later ministry of this man. The Coptic church of Egypt says that he preached in Egypt, Africa, Great Britain, and Persia; other early sources agree that he ministered in the

40

THE APOSTLES

CAESAREA PHILIPPI. *This town was situated at the foot of Mount Hermon, on the main source of the Jordan River. Here Christ asked His disciples who they thought He was. Peter immediately replied, "Thou art the Christ, the Son of the living God" (Matt. 16:16).*

ST. PETER'S BASILICA. *According to tradition, Peter was executed in the circus of Nero, where thousands of Christians suffered martyrdom. In A.D. 319, Emperor Constantine destroyed the circus and built over its northern foundations the first basilica of Saint Peter. The present structure was started in 1450 and took 176 years to build. Michelangelo designed the magnificent dome. St. Peter's is the largest church building in the world.*

British Isles but this is doubtful. Nicephorus of Constantinople wrote: "Simeon born in Cana of Galilee who . . . was surnamed Zelotes, having received the Holy Ghost from above, traveled through Egypt and Africa, then Mauretania and Libya, preaching the Gospel. And the same doctrine he taught to the Occidental Sea and the Isles called Britanniae."[7]

XII. Thomas. The Gospel of John gives us a more complete picture of the disciple named Thomas than we receive from the synoptic Gospels or the Book of Acts. John tells us he was also called Didymus (John 20:4) the Greek word for "twins" just as the Hebrew word *t'hom* means "twin." The Latin Vulgate

used Didymus as a proper name and that style was followed by most English versions until the twentieth century. The RSV and other recent translations refer to him as "Thomas called the Twin."

We do not know who Thomas might have been, nor do we know anything about his family background or how he was invited to join the apostles. However, we know that Thomas joined six other disciples who returned to the fishing boats after Jesus was crucified (John 21:2–3). This suggested that he may have learned the fishing trade as a young man.

On one occasion Jesus told His disciples that He intended to return to Judea. His disciples warned Him not to go because of the hostility toward Him there. But Thomas said, "Let us also go, that we may die with him" (John 11:16).

Yet modern readers often forget Thomas's courage; he is more often remembered for his weakness and doubt. In the Upper Room, Jesus told His disciples, "Whither I go ye know, and the way ye know." But Thomas retorted, "Lord, we know not whither thou goest; and how can we know the way?" (John 14:4–5). After Jesus rose from the dead, Thomas told his friends, "Except I shall see in his hands the print of the nails, and put my finger into the print of the nails, and thrust my hand into his side, I will not believe" (John 20:25). A few days later Jesus appeared to Thomas and the other disciples to give them physical proof that He was alive. Then Thomas exclaimed, "My Lord and my God" (John 20:28).

The early church fathers respected the example of Thomas. Augustine commented, "He doubted that we might not doubt."

Tradition says that Thomas eventually became a missionary in India. It is said that he was martyred there and buried in Mylapore, now a suburb of Madras. His name is carried on by the very title of the Marthoma or "Master Thomas" church.

XIII. Judas's Replacement. Following the death of Judas Iscariot, Simon Peter suggested that the disciples choose someone to replace the betrayer. Peter's speech outlined certain qualifications for the new apostle (cf. Acts 1:15–22). The apostle had to know of Jesus "from the baptism of John, unto that same day that he was taken up from us." He also had to be "a witness with us of his resurrection" (Acts 1:22).

The apostles found two men who met the qualifications: Joseph surnamed Justus and

[7] McBirnie, *The Search for the Twelve Apostles,* p. 213.

THE APOSTLES

Matthias (Acts 1:23). They cast lots to decide the matter and the lot fell to Matthias.

The name Matthias is a variant of the Hebrew name *Mattathias*, which means "gift of God." Unfortunately, Scripture tells us nothing about the ministry of Matthias. Eusebius speculated that Matthias would have been one of the 70 disciples that Jesus sent out on a preaching mission (cf. Luke 10:1–16). Some have identified him with Zaccheus (cf. Luke 19:2–8). One tradition says he preached to cannibals in Mesopotamia; another says he was stoned to death by the Jews. However, we have no evidence to support any of these stories.

Some scholars have suggested that Matthias was disqualified and the apostles chose James the brother of Jesus to take his place (cf. Gal. 1:19; 2:9). But there appear to have been more than 12 men thought of as apostles in the early church and Scripture gives us no indication that Matthias left the group.

40

THE APOSTLES

THE EARLY CHURCH

The Greek word that English versions of the Bible translate as *church* is *ekklesia,* which comes from the Greek word *kaleo* ("I call" or "I summon"). In secular literature, the word *ekklesia* referred to any assembly of people, but in the New Testament the word has a more specialized meaning. Secular literature might use the word *ekklesia* to denote a riot, a political rally, an orgy, or a gathering for any other purpose. But the New Testament uses *ekklesia* to refer only to the gathering of Christian believers to worship Christ. This is why Bible translators render this word as *church* instead of using a more general term like *assembly* or *gathering.*

What is the church? What people comprise this "gathering"? What does Paul mean when he calls the church the "body of Christ"?

To answer these questions fully, we need to understand the social and historical context of the New Testament church. The early church sprang up at the crossroads of Hebrew and Hellenistic cultures. We have already surveyed these cultures in two earlier articles, "Jews in New Testament Times" and "The Greeks and Hellenism."

In this article we turn our attention to the history of the early church itself. We will see what the early Christians understood their mission to be, and how unbelievers viewed them.

I. The Church Is Founded. Forty days after His resurrection, Jesus gave final instructions to His disciples and ascended into heaven (Acts 1:1–11). The disciples returned to Jerusalem and secluded themselves for several days of fasting and prayer, waiting for the Holy Spirit, whom Jesus said would come. About 120 of Jesus' followers waited in the group.

Fifty days after the Passover, on the day of Pentecost, a sound like a mighty rushing wind filled the house where the group was meeting. Tongues of fire rested upon each of them, and they began speaking in languages other than their own as the Holy Spirit enabled them. Foreign visitors were surprised to hear the disciples speaking in their own languages. Some of them mocked the group, saying they must be drunk (Acts 2:13).

But Peter silenced the crowd and explained they were witnessing the outpouring of the Holy Spirit that the Old Testament prophets had predicted (Acts 2:16–21; cf. Joel 2:28–32). Some of the foreign observers asked what they must do to receive the Holy Spirit. Peter said, "Repent, and be baptized every one of you in the name of Jesus Christ for the remission of your sins, and ye shall receive the gift of the Holy Ghost" (Acts 2:38). About 3,000 people accepted Christ as their Savior that day (Acts 2:41).

For several years Jerusalem was the center of the church. Many Jews believed that the followers of Jesus were just another sect of Judaism. They suspected that Christians were trying to start a new "mystery religion" around Jesus of Nazareth.

It is true that many of the early Christians continued to worship at the temple (cf. Acts

THE EARLY CHURCH

AMPHITHEATER, EPHESUS. *Colonized by the Greeks around 1000 B.C., Ephesus enjoyed a long history as an important city of Asia Minor. It occupied a vast area with a population of more than one-third of a million. The city's theater could seat between 25,000 and 50,000 persons. Christianity probably came to Ephesus when Paul visited the city on his second missionary journey (Acts 18:18–19).*

3:1) and some insisted that gentile converts should be circumcised (cf. Acts 15). But Jewish leaders soon realized that the Christians were more than a sect. Jesus had told the Jews that God would make a new covenant with people who were faithful to Him (Matt. 16:18); He had sealed this covenant with His own blood (Luke 22:20). So the early Christians boldly proclaimed that they had inherited the privileges that Israel once knew. They were not simply a part of Israel—they were the new Israel (Rev. 3:12; 21:2; cf. Matt. 26:28; Heb. 8:8; 9:15). "The Jewish leaders had a shuddering fear that this strange new teaching was no narrow Judaism, but merged the privilege of Israel in the high revelation of one Father of all men."[1]

A. The Jerusalem Community. The first Christians formed a close-knit community in Jerusalem after the day of Pentecost. They expected Christ to return very soon.

The Christians in Jerusalem shared all of their material goods (Acts 2:44–45). Many sold their property and gave the proceeds to the church, which distributed these resources among the group (Acts 4:34–35).

The Christians of Jerusalem still went to the

temple to pray (Acts 2:46), but they began sharing the Lord's Supper in their own homes (Acts 2:42–46). This symbolic meal reminded them of their new covenant with God, which Jesus Christ had made by sacrificing His own body and blood.

God worked miracles of healing through these early Christians. Sick people gathered at the temple so that the apostles could touch them on their way to prayer (Acts 5:12–16). These miracles convinced many people that the Christians were truly serving God. Temple officials arrested the apostles in an effort to suppress the people's interest in the new religion. But God sent an angel to deliver the apostles from prison (Acts 5:17–20), which aroused more excitement.

The church grew so rapidly that the apostles had to appoint seven men to distribute goods to the needy widows. The leader of these men was Stephen, "a man full of faith and of the Holy Ghost" (Acts 6:5). Here we see the beginning of church government. The apostles had to delegate some of their duties to other leaders. As time passed, church offices were arranged in a rather complex structure.

B. The Murder of Stephen. One day a group of Jewish men seized Stephen and brought him before the council of the high priest, charging him with blasphemy. Stephen

---

[1] Henry Melvill Gwatkin, *Early Church History,* Vol. I (London: Macmillan and Company, 1927), p. 18.

New Testament Heretics

Since the first century, the church has been plagued by individuals who have tried to twist the truth to suit their own fancy or "refine" it to make it more acceptable or "sensible." Of special concern to the early church were three groups of heretics: Judaizers, Gnostics, and Nicolaitans.

Judaizers. At first the church was composed entirely of converted Jews who recognized that Jesus was the Messiah, God's Anointed One. But as Paul began his ministry among the Gentiles, some of the Jewish Christians warned that a Gentile could not become a Christian *unless* he or she first became a Jew! They said that the Gentile converts should practice physical rituals such as circumcision and adhere to the Law that Jews had kept for hundreds of years (Acts 15:1–31).

As Paul's ministry fanned out, it soon became apparent that Gentiles were flooding into the church with this Jewish indoctrination. Jewish Christian leaders followed in Paul's footsteps, demanding that the gentile believers conform to their beliefs. They used Old Testament Scriptures to support their point. At times these "Judaizers" even preceded Paul on his missionary journeys. In such cases, they caused so much turmoil that little or no evangelistic work could be done.

Gnostics. The Gnostics taught that Jesus wasn't really God's Son. To their minds, matter was evil and spirit was good. Since God was good (and spirit) He could not have personally created a material world (evil). They further argued that since spirit and matter could not intermingle, Christ and God could not have united in the person of Jesus. They took their name from the Greek word *gnosis* ("knowledge"), professing to have special insight into the secret truths of life.

Archaeologists have found several Gnostic papyrus manuscripts in Egypt. Some of them are pseudepigraphical writings, such as the "Wisdom of Jesus Christ" and the "Acts of Peter." Perhaps the best-known Gnostic book is the *Pistis Sophia*

("Faith Knowledge"), which has been translated into English and French.

Many small Gnostic communities were scattered across the Near East. Each developed unique doctrines of its own. Today we must rely on their manuscripts to trace the beliefs of each community, and in many cases it is difficult to tell whether a particular group was Gnostic or a totally different religious sect. A notable example is the community of scribes at Qumran.

Paul mentions three men who deserted the faith for this heresy: Hymenaeus, Alexander, and Philetus (1 Tim. 1:20; 2 Tim. 2:17–18). They claimed the resurrection had already passed, perhaps believing that whatever spirit is "left over" when a man dies is absorbed again into God.

Nicolaitans. John focused on a more extreme form of Gnosticism rampant throughout the first-century church (1 and 2 John; Rev. 2:6, 14, 15). These were the *Nicolaitans.* Supporters of this deadly doctrine claimed that, since their bodies were physical (and therefore evil), only what their spirits did was important. So they felt free to indulge in indiscriminate sexual relationships, to eat food which had been offered to idols, and to do anything they pleased with their bodies.

The early church dealt firmly with those who deviated from Christ's precious truths. They barred heretics from the fellowship and prayed for their salvation. Paul openly rebuked them. (Paul even turned against them at one point, when Peter refused to eat with gentile Christians in the presence of Jewish Christians—Gal. 2:12–15). He felt that heretics had to be cut off from the church before they spread their ruinous ideas.

Irenaeus, Tertullian, and other church fathers denounced the Nicolaitans along with the Gnostics. Irenaeus reported that the sect was named for Nicolaos, a deacon of the first Nicolaitan community, who indulged in adultery.

made an eloquent defense of the Christian faith, explaining how Jesus fulfilled the ancient prophecies of the Messiah who would deliver His people from the bondage of sin. He denounced the Jews as "betrayers and murderers" of God's Son (Acts 7:52). Looking up into heaven, he exclaimed that he saw Jesus standing at the right hand of God (Acts 7:55). This enraged the Jews, who carried him out of the city and stoned him to death (Acts 7:58–60).

This began a wave of persecution that drove many Christians out of Jerusalem (Acts 8:1).

Some of these Christians settled among the Gentiles of Samaria, where they made many converts (Acts 8:5–8). They established congregations in several gentile cities, such as Antioch of Syria. At first the Christians hesitated to welcome Gentiles into the church, because they saw the church as a fulfillment of Jewish prophecy. Yet Christ had instructed His followers to "teach all nations, baptizing them in the name of the Father, and of the Son, and of the Holy Ghost" (Matt. 28:19). So the conversion of Gentiles was "only the fulfillment of the Lord's commission, and the natural

ANTIOCH IN SYRIA. *This city on the Orontes River was one of several cities named Antioch, which were founded by Seleucus I (312–280 B.C.) in honor of his father, Antiochus. Situated on an important trade route between Ephesus and Cilicia, it was a prominent center of Hellenistic culture. Here the disciples were first called Christians (Acts 11:26) and Paul began his missionary journey (Acts 13:1–3).*

result of all that had gone before. . . ."[2] Thus the murder of Stephen began an era of rapid expansion for the church.

II. Missionary Efforts. Christ had established His church at the crossroads of the ancient world. Trade routes brought merchants and ambassadors through Palestine, where they came into contact with the Gospel. Thus in the Book of Acts we see the conversion of officials from Rome (Acts 10:1–48), Ethiopia (Acts 8:26–40), and other lands.

Soon after Stephen's death the church began a systematic effort to carry the Gospel to other nations. Peter visited the major cities of Palestine, preaching to both Jews and Gentiles. Others went to Phoenicia, Cyprus, and Antioch of Syria. Hearing that the Gospel was well received in these areas, the church in Jerusalem sent Barnabas to encourage the new Christians in Antioch (Acts 11:22–23). Barnabas then went to Tarsus to find the young convert named Saul. Barnabas took Saul back to Antioch, where they taught in the church for over a year (Acts 11:26).

---

[2] Gwatkin, *Early Church History,* p. 56.

A prophet named Agabus predicted that the Roman Empire would suffer a great famine under Emperor Claudius. Herod Agrippa was persecuting the church in Jerusalem; he had already executed James the brother of Jesus, and had thrown Peter into prison (Acts 12:1–4). So the Christians in Antioch collected money to send to their friends in Jerusalem, and they dispatched Barnabas and Saul with the relief. Barnabas and Saul returned from Jerusalem with a young man named John Mark (Acts 12:25).

By this time, several evangelists had emerged within the church at Antioch so the congregation sent Barnabas and Saul on a missionary trip to Asia Minor (Acts 13—14). This was the first of three great missionary journeys that Saul (later known as Paul) made to carry the Gospel to the far reaches of the Roman Empire. (*See* "Paul and His Journeys.")

The early Christian missionaries focused their teachings upon the Person and work of Jesus Christ. They declared that He was the sinless servant and Son of God who had given His life to atone for the sins of all people who put their trust in Him (Rom. 5:8–10). He was the One whom God raised from the dead to defeat the powers of sin (Rom. 4:24–25; 1 Cor. 15:17). For a more detailed description of the doctrines of the early church, see "Bible History."

III. Church Government. At first, Jesus' followers saw no need to develop a system of church government. They expected Christ to return soon, so they dealt with internal problems as the need arose—usually in a very informal way.

But by the time Paul wrote his letters to the churches, Christians realized the need to organize their work. The New Testament does not give us a detailed picture of this early church government. Apparently, one or more elders (*presbyters*) presided over the affairs of each congregation (cf. Rom. 12:6–8; 1 Thess. 5:12; Heb. 13:7, 17, 24), just as elders did in Jewish synagogues. These elders were chosen by the Holy Spirit (Acts 20:20), yet apostles appointed them (Acts 14:13). Thus the Holy Spirit worked through the apostles to ordain leaders for the ministry. Some ministers called *evangelists* seem to have traveled from one congregation to another, as the apostles did. Their title means "men who handle the gospel." Some have thought they were all personal deputies of the apostles, as Timothy was

THE EARLY CHURCH

of Paul; others suppose that they gained their name through manifesting a special gift of evangelism. The elders assumed the normal pastoral duties between the visits of these evangelists.

In some congregations, the elders appointed deacons to distribute food to the needy or care for other material needs (cf. 1 Tim. 3:12). The first deacons were the "men of honest report" that the elders of Jerusalem appointed to care for widows in the congregation (Acts 6:1–6).

Some New Testament letters refer to *bishops* in the early church. This is a bit confusing, since these "bishops" did not form an upper tier of church leadership as they do in some churches where the title is used today. Paul reminded the elders of Ephesus that they were bishops (Acts 20:28), and he seems to use the terms *elder* and *bishop* interchangeably (Titus 1:5–9). Both bishops and elders were charged with the oversight of a congregation. Apparently both terms refer to the same ministers in the early church, namely the presbyters.

Paul and the other apostles recognized that the Holy Spirit gave special leadership abilities to certain people (1 Cor. 12:28). So when they conferred an official title upon a Christian brother or sister, they were confirming what the Holy Spirit had already done.

There was no earthly center of power in the early church. The Christians understood that Christ was the center and source of all its powers (Acts 20:28). Ministry meant serving in humility, rather than ruling from a lofty office (cf. Matt. 20:26–28). By the time Paul wrote his pastoral epistles, Christians recognized the importance of preserving Christ's teachings through ministers who devoted themselves to special study, "rightly dividing the word of truth" (2 Tim. 2:15).

The early church did not offer magical powers to individuals through rituals or any other way. The Christians invited unbelievers into their group, the body of Christ (Eph. 1:23), which would be saved as a whole. The apostles and evangelists proclaimed that Christ would return for His people, "the bride of Christ" (cf. Rev. 21:2; 22:17). They denied that individuals could gain special powers from Christ for their own selfish ends (Acts 8:9–24; 13:7–12).

IV. Patterns of Worship. As the early Christians worshiped together, they established patterns of worship that were quite different from the synagogue services. We have no clear picture of early Christian worship un-

til A.D. 150, when Justin Martyr described typical worship services in his writings. We do know that the early Christians held their services on Sunday, the first day of the week. They called this "the Lord's Day" because it was the day that Christ rose from the dead. The first Christians met at the temple in Jerusalem, in synagogues, or in private homes (Acts 2:46; 13:14–16; 20:7–8). Some scholars believe that the reference to Paul's teaching in the school of "one Tyrannus" (Acts 19:9) indicates that the early Christians sometimes rented school buildings or other facilities.[3] We have no evidence that Christians built special facilities for their worship services for more than a century after the time of Christ. Where Christians were persecuted, they had to meet in secret places such as the *catacombs* (underground tombs) in Rome.

Scholars believe that the first Christians worshiped on Sunday evenings, and that their service centered on the Lord's Supper. But at some point the Christians began holding two worship services on Sunday as Justin Martyr describes—one in the early morning and one late in the afternoon. The hours were chosen for secrecy and for the sake of working people who could not attend worship services during the day.

A. Order of Worship. Generally the early morning service was a time for praise, prayer, and preaching. The Christians' impromptu worship service on the day of Pentecost suggests a pattern of worship that might have been generally used. First, Peter read from the Scriptures. Then he preached a sermon that applied the Scriptures to the worshipers' present situation (Acts 2:14–42). People who accepted Christ were baptized, following the example of Christ Himself. The worshipers shared songs, testimonies, or words of exhortation to complete the service (1 Cor. 14:26).

B. The Lord's Supper. The early Christians ate the symbolic meal of the Lord's Supper to commemorate the Last Supper, in which Jesus and His disciples observed the traditional Jewish Passover feast. The themes of the two events were the same. In the Passover, Jews rejoiced that God had delivered them from their enemies and they looked expectantly to their future as God's children. In the Lord's Supper, Christians celebrated how Jesus had delivered them from sin and

---

[3] Lars P. Qualben, *A History of the Christian Church* (New York: Thomas Nelson and Sons, 1964), p. 67.

THE EARLY CHURCH

CLAUDIUS. *Claudius, emperor of Rome from A.D. 41 to 54, had suffered an attack of infantile paralysis that left him with only partial control of his body. His slavering mouth, shaky limbs, and faltering gait gave him a weak appearance; but in reality he was one of the most ingenious and powerful of the Roman emperors. Claudius expelled the Jews from Rome for rioting; this is probably the incident referred to in Acts 18:2.*

verts, some Jewish sects practiced baptism as a symbol of purification, and John the Baptist made baptism an important part of his ministry. The New Testament does not say whether Jesus regularly baptized His converts, but on at least one occasion before John's imprisonment He was found baptizing. (It may, however, have been John's baptism that He was administering.) At any rate, the early Christians were baptized in Jesus' name following Jesus' example (cf. Mark 1:10; Gal. 3:27).

It appears that the early Christians interpreted the meaning of baptism in various ways—as a symbol of a person's death to sin (Rom. 6:4; Gal. 2:12), of the cleansing from sin (Acts 22:16; Eph. 5:26), and of the new life in Christ (Acts 2:41; Rom. 6:3). Occasionally the entire family of a new convert would be baptized (cf. Acts 11:16; 1 Cor. 1:16), which may have signified the person's desire to consecrate all that he had to Christ.

D. Church Calendar. The New Testament gives no evidence that the early church observed any holy days, other than holding its worship on the first day of the week (Acts 20:7; 1 Cor. 16:2; Rev. 1:10). The Christians did not observe Sunday as a day of rest until the fourth century A.D., when Emperor Constantine designated Sunday as a holy day for the entire Roman Empire. The early Christians did not confuse Sunday with the Jewish Sabbath, and they made no attempt to apply Sabbath legislation to Sunday.

The historian Eusebius tells us that Christians celebrated Easter from apostolic times; 1 Corinthians 5:6–8 may refer to such a celebration. Tradition says that the early Christians celebrated Easter at the time of Passover. Around A.D. 120, the Roman Catholic church moved the celebration to the Sunday after the Passover, while the Eastern Orthodox church continued to celebrate it at Passover.

V. New Testament Concepts of the Church. It is interesting to survey the various New Testament concepts of the church. Scripture refers to the early Christians as God's family and temple, as Christ's flock and bride, as salt, as leaven, as fishermen, as a bulwark sustaining God's truth, and in many other ways. The church was thought of as a single worldwide fellowship of believers, of which each local congregation was an outcrop and a sample. Early Christian writers often referred to the church as the "body of Christ" and the "new Israel." These two concepts reveal much

they expressed their hope for the day when Christ would return (1 Cor. 11:26).

At first, the Lord's Supper was an entire meal that Christians shared in their homes. Each guest brought a dish of food to the common table. The meal began with common prayer and the eating of small pieces from a single loaf of bread that represented Christ's broken body. The meal closed with another prayer and the sharing of a cup of wine, which represented Christ's shed blood.

Some people speculated that the Christians were participating in a secret rite when they observed the Lord's Supper, and they fabricated strange stories about these services. The Roman Emperor Trajan outlawed such secret meetings in about A.D. 100. At that time Christians began observing the Lord's Supper during the morning worship service which was open to the public.

C. Baptism. Baptism was a common event of Christian worship in Paul's time (cf. Eph. 4:5). However, Christians were not the first to use baptism. Jews baptized their gentile con-

The Fate of the Seven Churches

Of the seven churches John addressed in the Book of Revelation, four now lie in ruin. The cities of Ephesus, Pergamum (or Pergamos), Sardis, and Laodicea are all desolate; but Smyrna, Thyatira, and Philadelphia still exist as modern cities.

When John wrote to Ephesus (Rev. 2:1–7), he warned the church of pagan influence and urged them to come back to their "first love." Ephesus was a large commercial center, often called "The Market of Asia." The temple of Artemis—one of the seven wonders of the ancient world—was located in Ephesus. In A.D. 262 the Goths destroyed the temple and the entire city of Ephesus. The city never regained its glory or its "first love." A group of Christian bishops held a council in Ephesus as late as A.D. 431, but Ephesus was later attacked by the Arabs, Turks, and finally the Mongols in 1403. Today the city's seaport is a marsh covered with reeds and the city itself is desolate.

In his message to Smyrna (Rev. 2:8–11), John praised the church for being a strong community of believers, but he warned that they would suffer persecution. From the time of John (*ca.* A.D. 90) until about A.D. 312, Christians were continually persecuted. In Smyrna the famous Christian martyr Polycarp was burned to death in A.D. 155. Smyrna was destroyed by an earthquake in A.D. 178, but was quickly rebuilt. Smyrna was one of the few Asian cities to withstand Turkish attacks, and among the last to fall to the Muslims. It was a cultural center, and its survival helped to spur the Renaissance. Smyrna is now the modern city of Izmir—one of Turkey's largest, with a population of half a million.

According to John, the Christians in Pergamum dwelt where "Satan's seat is." He warned that they would be swallowed up in this worldly city (Rev. 2:12–17). The capital city of the Roman province of Asia, Pergamum had magnificent statues of Zeus, Dionysus, and Athena. Christians there suffered, but in A.D. 312 Constantine became the emperor of Rome and ordered an end to Christian persecution. Later he professed Christianity and began molding church and state together. Pergamum became an important center of the state religion of Christianity. Attacked by the Arabs in A.D. 716–717, Pergamum lost its political power. It gradually fell into ruin and is now a scene of desolation.

When John wrote the church in Thyatira (Rev. 2:18–29), he warned about worshiping false idols. There were no great statues of gods in the city, but trade guilds promoted idolatry and excessive drinking. The Arabs and Turks repeatedly attacked Thyatira throughout the years, but each time it was rebuilt. Because the new structures were erected over the ruins, the history of the city is difficult to trace. Now the city is a Turkish town of 50,000 called Akhisar, with little evidence of its character in the apostolic era.

John condemned the church at Sardis for having no life, no spirit (Rev. 3:1–6). After being destroyed by an earthquake in A.D. 117, Sardis was rebuilt by money provided by the Roman Empire. The city slowly lost its affluence, and was attacked and conquered by the Arabs in A.D. 716. There are some reports that Sardis was inhabited again after its destruction by Tamerlane (leader of the Berlas Turks) in 1403. Today a small village renamed Sart stands among the ruins of Sardis.

John praised the church at Philadelphia for its patience (Rev. 3:7–13). Philadelphia was located on a main geological fault line and was subject to frequent earthquakes, so the city was destroyed and rebuilt on several occasions. While the Turks and Muslims flooded across Asia Minor, Philadelphia long remained a Christian city; in fact, Philadelphia was the last Christian outpost in Asia Minor when it fell in 1390. It still stands as a modern Turkish town of 25,000 called Alashehir, meaning "City of God."

Laodicea was located on a trade route that made it a major banking center. By the fourth century, Laodicea had become the episcopal seat of Asia Minor and Christian bishops held a famous council there in A.D. 361. Laodicea's water supply was brought in from nearby cities by a sophisticated aqueduct system. Sunlight heated the water to lukewarm, which was the basis for the striking analogy in Revelation (Rev. 3:14–22). During the wars among the Muslims of the Middle Ages, Laodicea was destroyed and abandoned. By the seventeenth century, travelers noted that the city was inhabited only by wolves and foxes. Its ghostlike ruins remain desolate today.

---

of the early Christians' understanding of their mission in the world.

A. The Body of Christ. Paul describes the church as "one body in Christ" (Rom. 12:5) and "His body" (Eph. 1:23). In other words, the church encompasses in a single communion of divine life all those who are united to Christ by the Holy Spirit through faith. They

share His resurrection (Rom. 6:8), and are both called and enabled to continue His ministry of serving and suffering to bless others (1 Cor. 12:14–26). They are bound together in a community to embody the kingdom of God in the world.

Because they were bound to other Christians, these people understood that what they

THE EARLY CHURCH

did with their own bodies and abilities was very important (Rom. 12:14; 1 Cor. 6:13–19; 2 Cor. 5:10). They understood that the various races and classes become one in Christ (1 Cor. 12:3; Eph. 2:14–22), and must accept and love each other in a way that shows this to be so.

By describing the church as the body of Christ, the early Christians emphasized that Christ was head of the church (Eph. 5:25). He directed its actions and deserved any praise it received. All its power to worship and serve was His gift.

B. The New Israel. The early Christians identified themselves with Israel, God's chosen people. They believed that Jesus' coming and ministry fulfilled God's promise to the patriarchs (cf. Matt. 2:6; Luke 1:68; Acts 5:31), and they held that God had established a new covenant with Jesus' followers (cf. 2 Cor. 3:6; Heb. 7:22; 9:15).

God, they held, had established His new Israel on the basis of personal salvation, rather than family descent. His church was a spiritual nation that transcended all cultural and national heritages. Anyone who placed his faith in God's new covenant by surrendering his life to Christ became Abraham's spiritual descendant and as such a part of the "new Israel" (Matt. 8:11; Luke 13:28–30; Rom. 4:9–25; 11; Gal. 3—4; Heb. 11—12).

C. Common Characteristics. Some common qualities emerge from the many images of the church that we find in the New Testament. They all show that the church exists because God called it into being. Christ has commissioned His followers to carry on His work, and that is the church's reason for existence.

The various New Testament images of the church stress that the Holy Spirit empowers the church and determines its direction. Members of the church share a common task and common destiny under the Spirit's leading.

The church is an active, living entity. It participates in the affairs of this world, it exhibits the way of life that God intends for all people, and it proclaims God's Word for the present age. The spiritual unity and purity of the church stand in bold contrast to the enmity and corruption of the world. It is the church's responsibility in all the particular congregations in which it becomes visible to practice unity, love, and care in a way that shows that Christ truly lives in those who are members of His body, so that their life is His life in them.

VI. New Testament Doctrines. The Bible sets forth the fundamental teachings of the

Christian faith. The early church lived according to these doctrines and preserved them for us today. Let us focus our attention on how the New Testament presents Christianity.

A. Living in Christ. First of all, we are told that God the Father brings Christians into fellowship with Himself, as children in His family, through the death and risen life of Jesus Christ, the eternal Son of God. As Paul wrote, "God was in Christ reconciling the world unto himself" (2 Cor. 5:19). So the eternal Son took on human flesh. Jesus of Nazareth, fully God and fully man, revealed the Father to the world. The early Christians saw themselves as people "who through him are believers in God" (1 Pet. 1:21, NASB). They found new life in Jesus Christ, and came into union with the living God through Him (Rom. 5:1).

Jesus promised that, by being "born again," men and women would find their proper relationship with God and savingly enter the kingdom of God (John 3:5–16; 14:6). The early Christians proclaimed this simple but startling message about Jesus.

Every major religion of the world has claimed that its "founder" had unique insight into the eternal truths of life. But Christians claim far more, for Jesus Himself told us that He is the Truth, not just a teacher of the Truth (John 14:6). First-century Christians rejected the pagan religions and philosophies of their day to accept God's Word in the flesh.

B. Teaching Right Doctrine. The pagan religion of Rome was a rite rather than a doctrine. In effect, the emperor declared: "This you must do, but you can think as you please." Roman worshipers believed they needed only to perform the proper ceremonies of religion, whether they understood them or not. As far as they were concerned, a hypocritical skeptic could be just as "religious" as a true believer, so long as he offered sacrifice in the temple of the gods.

On the other hand, the early Christians insisted that both belief and behavior are vital, that the two go hand in hand. They took seriously Jesus' words that "true worshipers shall worship the Father in spirit and in truth" (John 4:23). What a Christian believed with his mind and felt in his heart, he would do with his hands. So the early Christians obeyed God (1 John 3:22–24), and they contradicted and opposed so-called Christians who tried to spread false teachings (cf. 1 Tim. 6:3–5).

This is essentially what we mean when we

THE EARLY CHURCH

CHURCH OF ST. JOSEPH. *Stairs, cisterns, and a baptismal font are situated in this ancient crypt beneath the church of St. Joseph in Nazareth. Scholars think early Jewish Christians used this underground space for their rites of worship.*

speak of Christianity. It is a new life in Jesus Christ, which brings genuine obedience to His teachings.

The article on "Jesus Christ" describes His teachings in detail. Here we will point out the basic differences between what Jesus and His followers taught, and what their pagan neighbors taught.

1. The Doctrine of God. Nearly every major religion teaches that some Superior Being rules the universe, and that nature demonstrates this all-powerful Being at work. These religions often describe such a Being in terms of natural forces, like the wind and rain. But the early Christians did not look to nature for the truth about God; they looked to Christ. The Christians believed that Jesus fully revealed the heavenly Father (Col. 2:9). So they understood God in terms of Jesus, and they based their doctrine of God upon the life of Christ.

a. The Trinity. Many scholars believe the doctrine of the Trinity is the most crucial element in the Christian understanding of God. The early Christians confessed that they knew God in three Persons—Father, Son, and Holy Spirit—and these three fully share one divine nature.

Many scriptures show that these apostolic Christians understood Jesus Christ in trinitarian terms. For example, Paul said, "Through him [Christ] we both have access by one Spirit

unto the Father" (Eph. 2:18)—describing our relation to the three Persons of the Trinity. The New Testament contains many statements like this.

In no way did the Christian doctrine of the Trinity agree with the pagan teachings of the Egyptians, Greeks, and Babylonians. Nor did it fit in with the abstract philosophies of Greece. None of these ideas—religious or philosophical—could compare with the Christian understanding of God, for the early Christians knew that God was neither the capricious hero of fictional legends nor an impersonal "Force" (1 Cor. 1:9). They knew He was a living personal Creator and Lord; in fact, He came to them as three Persons. Yet He was still one God.

b. God as a Personal Father. Jesus taught His disciples that God is "My Father, and your Father" (John 20:17). In other words, He showed them that God cared for them personally, just as a human father cares for his children. He dared to speak to God the Creator as a child speaks to his parent, and He told His disciples God had given Him "all things" (Matt. 11:27).

Jesus explained that God loves the people who accept Him (Jesus) into their lives (John 17:27). He reminded His followers that their Father-God cared for the smallest details of their everyday needs (Matt. 6:28–32).

Jesus Christ taught that His Father is holy,

THE EARLY CHURCH

BURIAL CHAMBER. *Discovered at Talpioth in south Jerusalem, these ancient chambers contained burial spaces for early Jewish Christians. A stone slab covered the opening to each vault, marked with a cross and the name of the deceased.*

and that He and the Holy Spirit share the same divine holiness and act accordingly (John 15:23–26). Unlike the gods of Greek and Roman myths, who were short-tempered and immoral, the true God is just and righteous (Luke 18:19). He intervenes to save His people from sin. Jesus explained it was to this end that God had sent Him into the world; He brought God's mercy to a sinful and dying humanity, and in Him we see God's holy purpose fulfilled (John 6:38–40). So this holy God does not stand aloof from the affairs of men! He suffers their pain and even submits to the power of death to save His children (John 15:9–14). Again, we see Jesus emphasizing the personal love that God has for every human being.

Jesus demonstrated this love in His own ministry. He went out of His way to find people who were suffering from the effects of sin, so that He could deliver them. C. G. Montefiore says, "The rabbis welcomed a sinner in his repentance. But to *seek out* the sinner . . . was . . . something new in the religious history of Israel."[4] Jesus was willing to pay any price—even the price of death—to save mankind from the clutches of sin. In fact, when one of His disciples advised Him not to do it, He retorted, "Get behind me, Satan!" (Matt. 16:23). Jesus proved that God is the

great Rescuer that the Old Testament prophets had described (cf. Is. 53).

Jesus also broke down the narrow national limits that the Jews had erected around God. Jesus extended the love of God to all people, of all races and nationalities. He sent His disciples "into all the world" to win men back to God (Mark 16:15). The early Christians obeyed His command, carrying the gospel "to the Jew first, and also to the Greek" (Rom. 1:16).

2. The Doctrine of Redemption. Jesus taught that God redeems individuals as well as nations. This was a radically new thought in the Jewish world. Yet the doctrine of personal salvation was the heart of Christian teaching.

a. The Creator God. The Christian doctrine of salvation stood upon the fact that God created the human race. Even this was an unpopular idea in Jesus' day.

Many Greek philosophers and cultists insisted that God could not have made this evil world, and that it "emanated" from God by some natural process, as ripples "emanate" from a pebble dropped in a pond. But the Old Testament showed that God created the world

---

[4] C. G. Montefiore, *Some Elements of the Religious Teaching of Jesus* (Folcroft, Pa.: Folcroft Library Editions, 1910), p. 57.

on His own initiative. He chose to do it. And because God chose to create the world, He could deal with it in any way He wished (Is. 40:28; cf. Rom. 1:20). Cultists taught that evil forces had distorted the "emanations" from God, making the world corrupt. The Bible teaches that God created the world perfectly and made man in His own image, but man chose to rebel against God (Gen. 3). The Greeks believed that the forces of good and evil held the world in a stalemate; they thought evil had corrupted the good, and good kept evil from gaining absolute control of the world. The Christians rejected that idea; they

SARDIS. *All that remains of the temple of Artemis (or Diana) at Sardis are a few magnificent columns. Once the wealthy capital of the Kingdom of Lydia, Sardis lay on an important trade route down the Hermus Valley. By the Roman period, the city had lost the prominence it had in earlier centuries. The letter to the church in Sardis (Rev. 3:1-6) suggests that the Christians there possessed the same spirit as the city, resting on their past without being concerned with present accomplishments.*

taught that the world still belongs to its Creator, and that evil forces cannot finally prevail. Evil has only as much influence as God permits (Rom. 2:3-10; 12:17-21).

b. Fallen Man. Jesus gave the world a new understanding of man. His followers came to realize that each person is a lost child of God that the Father is trying to restore to the family through Christ (John 1:10-13; Eph. 2:19).

Greek myths said that man is a strange mixture of spirit and flesh, swept about by the unpredictable forces of the world. Orphic myths (stories involving the Greek god Orpheus) insisted that man had an inner nature like the gods. Plato had picked up this idea in his philosophy of the World-Soul; he felt that human beings had a spark of divine intelligence, and that a man becomes more god-like as he develops his intellect and his ability to reason.

The Scriptures contradicted this Greek idea of man. They knew that the most important test of a man's character was his moral fiber, not his intellect; and in those terms, man certainly could not claim to be like God! "As it is written," Paul told the Roman Christians, "there is none righteous, no, not one" (Rom. 3:10). The early Christians believed that, even though man is totally unworthy of God's love, God keeps on reaching out to man and trying to bring him back into holy fellowship with Him (Rom. 5:6-8).

The early Christian preachers spoke clearly of man's fall from God's favor in the Garden of Eden. "Death reigned from Adam," Paul wrote, ". . . even over them that had not sinned after the similitude of Adam's transgression . . ." (Rom. 5:14). "For as in Adam all die, even so in Christ shall all be made alive" (1 Cor. 15:22; cf. 15:45). The Christians believed that Adam's sin in Eden was the first key event of human history. It meant that man was a fallen creature who needed to come back to God.

c. The Nature of Sin. Greek and Roman writers criticized the immorality of the ancient world, but they had no definite concept of sin. They feared that reckless living would destroy the harmony of their society, but in no way did they think immorality offended the gods. Why should they? According to their myths, the gods were more lustful and greedy than man would ever imagine.

Jesus taught that sin (defined in 1 John 3:4 as lawlessness) is rebellion against God; it is man's decision to abuse God's love and reject His way, and it brings judgment. ". . . For

THE EARLY CHURCH

if ye believe not that I am he [i.e., the Redeemer], ye shall die in your sins" (John 8:24). Jesus predicted that the Holy Spirit would convict the world of sin "because they believe not on me" (John 16:9). Man chooses to sin, and he is fully responsible for his position in God's sight.

d. Jesus' Sacrificial Death. The Old Testament priests sacrificed animals and sprinkled their blood upon the altar for the people's sins. Jesus told His disciples that He would shed His blood "for the remission of sins" (Matt. 26:28). God Himself, in the person of Jesus Christ, was willing to give Himself to die for man's sins. In this way, He bridged the gap that sin had opened between Him and man. The *incarnation* of the eternal Son of God enabled Him to be the final sacrifice for sin.

Jesus surrendered Himself to Jewish authorities who resented the message He brought to the world. They charged that He was "perverting the nation" by teaching His followers that He was the long-promised Messiah (Luke 23:2). Jesus had not broken any Roman law, but the Roman governor Pontius Pilate allowed his soldiers to execute Jesus to appease the Jewish leaders. So Jesus was not guilty of breaking God's law or man's; even His betrayer Judas Iscariot confessed, "I have sinned in that I have betrayed the innocent blood" (Matt 27:4). Yet Roman centurions nailed Jesus to a cross as if He were a common criminal. In fact, He became God's pure sacrifice for the sin of man, and the early Christians emphasized this in their preaching and teaching (cf. Heb. 10).

e. Jesus' Resurrection. The Christians declared that Jesus' ministry did not end with the cross, because God raised Jesus from the tomb. He ministered among His disciples for several weeks until God took Him up to sit at His right hand in heaven (Acts 7:56).

The early Christians told the world how they had witnessed Jesus' death, resurrection, and ascension. This electrified the Roman Empire, and caused many people to regard the Christians as a group of fanatics (Acts 17:6). But Paul told his Christian friends, "If Christ be not raised, your faith is in vain: ye are yet in your sins. Then they also which are fallen asleep in Christ are perished" (1 Cor. 15:17–18).

3. The Kingdom of God. We have noted that Jesus focused upon God's salvation of the individual; but He also taught that God brings His people into a great community of the redeemed—the realm of God's saving sovereignty, which Jesus called "the Kingdom of God." In this Kingdom (presently expressed in the church), God required His people to live a life of brotherly love. They were to practice the ethics of Christ and work for the redemption of all mankind. Jesus did not limit the Kingdom to the Jews; He explained that everyone who was "bringing forth the fruits thereof" belonged to the Kingdom of God (Matt. 21:43). The Gospel of Matthew in particular records many *parables* (true-to-life illustrations) about the Kingdom; see especially Matthew 20:1–16; 22:2–14; 25:1–30.

Notice that many of these parables point to the end of time, when God will gather all the people of His eternal Kingdom to reign with Him forever. The early Christian evangelists stressed Jesus' message about the end of time, because they believed they lived in the last days. This spurred the Christians to take the gospel to the far corners of the Roman Empire. They had a burning desire to win lost souls for Jesus Christ before the end came.

41

THE EARLY CHURCH

PAUL AND HIS JOURNEYS

"He was a man little of stature," claims an account in the apocryphal second-century Acts of Paul, "partly bald, with crooked legs, of vigorous physique, with eyes set close together and nose somewhat hooked." If this statement is trustworthy, it tells a little more about this man from Tarsus who lived through nearly seven eventful decades after the birth of Jesus. It would fit Paul's own record of a taunt whispered against him in Corinth, "For his letters, say they, are weighty and powerful; but his bodily presence is weak, and his speech contemptible" (2 Cor. 10:10).

What he actually looked like will have to be left to the imagination of the artists—we cannot be sure. But more important matters press for attention—what he felt, what he thought, what he did.

We know what this man from Tarsus came to believe about the person and work of Christ, and other subjects crucial to Christian faith. Letters from his pen, preserved in the New Testament, bear eloquent testimony to the passion of his convictions and the power of his logic.

Here and there in these letters are bits of autobiography. Also, we find a broad outline of Paul's activities in the Acts of the Apostles, recorded by Luke, first-century gentile physician and historian.

So while the theologian has enough material to create endless debate about what Paul believed, the records for the historian are skimpy. A biographer of Paul soon discovers gaps in the apostle's life that cannot be spanned with anything more than a learned guess.

Like a flaming meteor, Paul flashes suddenly into view as an adult in a religious crisis, resolved by conversion. He disappears for many years—years of preparation. He reappears in the role of missionary statesman, and for a time we can trace his movements across the first-century horizon. Before his death, he flames on into the shadows beyond the limits of our straining eyes.

ANCIENT WALL, TARSUS. *The capital city of Cilicia in the eastern part of Asia Minor, Tarsus was the birthplace of the apostle Paul (Acts 21:39), who visited it at least once after his conversion (Acts 11:25). The city was mentioned in historical records as early as the ninth century B.C. and was noted for its schools.*

MILETUS. *The southernmost of the great Greek cities on the west coast of Asia Minor, Miletus flourished as a commercial center before it was destroyed by the Persians in 494 B.C. When Paul arrived here (Acts 20:15; 2 Tim. 4:20), it was part of the Roman province of Asia and declining commercially because its harbor was filling up with silt. Beyond the theater is the former harbor, now a marsh.*

I. Young Saul. But before we can understand Paul, the Christian missionary to the Gentiles, it is necessary to spend some time with Saul of Tarsus, the young Pharisee. We find in Acts Paul's explanation of his identity: "I am a man which am a Jew of Tarsus, a city in Cilicia, a citizen of no mean city" (Acts 21:39). This gives us our first thread for weaving the background of Paul's life.

A. From the City of Tarsus. In the first century, Tarsus was the chief city of the province of Cilicia in the eastern part of Asia Minor. Although about 16 km. (10 mi.) inland, the city was a major port having access to the sea by way of the Cydnus River, which flowed through it.

Just to the north of Tarsus towered the lofty, snow-covered Taurus Mountains, which provided the timber that formed one of the principal objects of trade for Tarsian merchants. An important Roman road ran north out of the city and through a narrow passage in the mountains known as the "Cilician Gates." Many an ancient military struggle was fought at this mountain pass.

Tarsus was a frontier city, a meeting place for East and West, a crossroad for commerce that flowed in both directions by land and sea. Tarsus had a prized heritage. Fact and legend intermingled to make its citizens fiercely proud of its past.

The Roman general Mark Antony granted it the status of *libera civitas* ("free city") in 42 B.C. Thus, though part of a Roman province, it was self-governing, and not required to pay tribute to Rome. The democratic traditions of the Greek city-state had long been established in Paul's day.

In this city, young Saul grew up. In his writings, we find reflections of sights and scenes in Tarsus when he was a lad. In sharp contrast with the rural illustrations of Jesus, the metaphors of Paul spring from city life.

The glint of the Mediterranean sun on Roman helmets and spears would have been a common sight in Tarsus when Paul was a boy. Perhaps this was the background for his illustration concerning Christian warfare, when he insisted that "the weapons of our warfare are not carnal, but mighty through God to the pulling down of strongholds" (2 Cor. 10:4).

Paul writes of "shipwreck" (1 Tim. 1:19), of the "potter" (Rom. 9:21), of being led in "triumph" by Christ (2 Cor. 2:14). He compares the "earthly tent" of this life with "a building of God, a house not made with hands, eternal in the heavens" (2 Cor. 5:1). He takes the Greek word that became *theater* in English and daringly applies it to the apostles, who "are made a spectacle (*theatro*) unto the world" (1 Cor. 4:9).

Such statements reflect the typical life of the city in which Paul spent the formative years of his boyhood. So the sights and sounds of this bustling seaport form a backdrop against which Paul's life and thought become more understandable. Small wonder that he should refer to Tarsus as "no mean city."

The philosophers of Tarsus were mostly Stoics. Stoic ideas, though essentially pagan, produced some of the noblest thinkers of the ancient world. The Tarsian Athenodorus is a splendid example.

When Athenodorus was retiring from public life in Rome to return to his native city, he gave this parting counsel to Augustus Caesar: "When you are angry, Caesar, say nothing and do nothing until you have repeated the letters of the alphabet." He is also credited with saying, "So live with men as if God saw you; so speak with God as if men were listening."

Though Athenodorus died in A.D. 7, when Paul was but a small boy, he long remained a hero in Tarsus. Young Saul could scarcely have escaped hearing something about him.

Just how much contact did young Saul have with this world of philosophy in Tarsus? We do not know; he has not told us. But the marks of wide education and contact with Greek learning are upon him as a grown man. He knew enough about such matters to plead the cause he represented before all sorts of men. He was also aware of the subtle dangers present in the speculative religious philosophies of the Greeks. "See to it that no one makes a prey of you by philosophy and empty deceit, according to human tradition . . . and not according to Christ," he warned the church at Colosse (Col. 2:8, RSV).

B. A Roman Citizen. Paul was not only "a

Paul's Method of Preaching

Paul was a persuasive preacher. His boyhood studies under Gamaliel had strengthened his Hebrew orthodoxy. Redirected by Jesus Christ, Paul exhorted his listeners to believe and be saved.

Paul pointed to his own life and work as proof of his message (2 Cor. 12:12). He heralded good news personally experienced (Phil. 3:12). He wrote, "For to me to live is Christ, and to die is gain" (Phil. 1:21).

Audiences found Paul frank, courageously zealous, poised and sympathetic. Paul reminded his Jewish listeners of their Hebrew history, language, and customs (Acts 13:14–43; 22:2; 23:6–9). Among Gentiles, he appealed to the Greek curiosity about new teachings (Acts 16:37; 17:22 ff.). He compelled their attention with words, gestures, dramatic actions, and warnings (Acts 13:16, 40; 14:14–15).

Paul's one objective was to win men to Christ. His exhortations and warnings were warm and emotional (1 Cor. 15:58). He also used convincing arguments, well-developed summaries (1 Cor. 10:31–33), and personal applications (1 Cor. 11:1; Phil. 3:17).

Paul's preaching corresponded closely to Peter's pattern of preaching at Pentecost. Peter had projected five points: [1] "a man approved of God among you" (Acts 2:22) [2] "ye . . . have crucified and slain" (Acts 2:23) [3] "whom God hath raised up. . . . This Jesus hath God raised up" (Acts 2:24, 32). [4] "God hath made that same Jesus . . . both Lord and Christ" (Acts 2:36). [5] "Ye shall receive the gift of the Holy Ghost" (Acts 2:38).

Paul declared: [1] "God . . . chose our fathers . . . of this man's seed hath God raised unto Israel a Savior" (Acts 13:17, 23). [2] "Desired . . . Pilate that he should be slain" (Acts 13:28). [3] "God raised him from the dead . . . he was seen many days of them" (Acts 13:30–31). [4] "God hath fulfilled . . . unto us their children, in that he hath raised up Jesus" (Acts 13:33). Elsewhere, Paul reveals God's salvation for Gentiles (Acts 14:15–17; 17:22–31).

Paul reflected Jesus' teachings, although he seldom quoted Him. He preached with pastoral love and compassion. His message made many friends and some enemies, but allowed few compromisers. His theology centered in the person and work of Christ. He believed that the ethical demands of Jewish law were to be fulfilled; but he also believed that the new, Spirit-filled man performed from inward motivation what the law's demands had failed to achieve by force.

PAUL AND HIS JOURNEYS

WALL OF DAMASCUS. *Saul of Tarsus, on his way to persecute the Christians of Damascus, was struck to earth and heard the heavenly voice as he neared this city (Acts 9:1–9). This is the traditional site along the wall of Damascus where Paul was lowered in a basket to escape persecution after preaching in the city's synagogues (Acts 9:23–25). Paul had returned to Damascus after a period of solitude in Arabia (Gal. 1:17).*

citizen of no mean city," but a Roman citizen as well. This furnishes still another clue to his boyhood background.

Acts 22:24–29 shows Paul carrying on conversations with a Roman centurion and a Roman tribune. (The *centurion* was a captain over 100 men in the Roman army; the *tribune* in this case would be a military commander.) On orders from the tribune, the centurion was about to have Paul scourged. But the Apostle protested, "Is it lawful for you to scourge a man that is a Roman [citizen], and uncondemned?" (Acts 22:25). The centurion carried the news to the tribune, who queried further. To him Paul not only affirmed his Roman citizenship but explained how he became one: "I was free born" (Acts 22:28). This implies that his father had been a Roman citizen.

Roman citizenship could be obtained in various ways. The tribune in the narrative states that he "bought" his citizenship "for a large sum" (Acts 22:28, RSV). More often, however, citizenship was a reward for some service of unusual distinction to the Roman Empire, or was granted when an individual was freed from slavery.

Roman citizenship was precious, for it carried special rights and privileges, such as exemption from certain forms of punishment. A Roman citizen could not be scourged or crucified.

However, the relationship of the Jews to Rome was not entirely a happy one. Jews rarely became Roman citizens. Most Jews who attained citizenship lived outside of Palestine.

C. Of Jewish Ancestry. We should also consider Paul's Jewish ancestry and the impact of his family's religious faith. He describes himself to the Christians at Philippi as "of the stock of Israel, of the tribe of Benjamin, a Hebrew of the Hebrews; as touching the law, a Pharisee" (Phil. 3:5). On another occasion, he called himself "an Israelite, of the seed of Abraham, of the tribe of Benjamin" (Rom. 11:1).

Thus Paul stood in a proud lineage reaching back to the father of his people, Abraham.

PAUL AND HIS JOURNEYS

From the tribe of Benjamin had come Israel's first king, Saul, after whom the boy of Tarsus was named.

The synagogue school helped Jewish parents pass on the religious heritage of Israel to their children. A boy began reading the Scriptures when he was but five years old. By the time he was ten, he would be studying the Mishna with its involved interpretations of the Law. Thus, he became steeped in the history, customs, Scriptures, and language of his people. Paul's later vocabulary was strongly colored by the language of the Greek Septuagint, which was the Bible of Hellenistic Jews.

Of the major "parties" of the Jews, the Pharisees were the most strict. (*See* "Jews in New Testament Times.") They were determined to resist the efforts of their Roman conquerors to impose new beliefs and ways of life upon them. By the first century, they had become the "spiritual aristocracy" of their people. Paul was a Pharisee, the "son of Pharisees" (Acts 23:6). Thus we can be certain that his religious training found its roots in loyalty to the regulations of the Law, as interpreted by the Jewish rabbis. At 13, he was expected to assume personal responsibility for obedience to that Law.

Saul of Tarsus spent his young manhood in Jerusalem "at the feet of Gamaliel," where he was "taught according to the perfect manner of the law . . ." (Acts 22:3). Gamaliel was the grandson of Hillel, one of the greatest of the Jewish rabbis. The school of Hillel was the more liberal of the two major schools of thought among the Pharisees. Acts 5:33–39, RSV, gives a glimpse of Gamaliel, who is described as "held in honor by all the people."

Rabbinic students were required to learn a trade so that they could eventually teach without becoming a burden to the people. Paul selected a typical Tarsian industry, making tents from goats-hair cloth (Acts 18:3). His skill in this trade later proved a great boon to him in his missionary work.

Upon completion of his studies with Gamaliel, this young Pharisee probably returned to his home in Tarsus for a few years. We have no clear evidence that he met or knew Jesus during the Master's ministry in the flesh.

From Paul's own pen as well as from the book of Acts, we learn that he then returned to Jerusalem and dedicated his energies to the persecution of Jews who accepted the teachings of Jesus the Nazarene. Paul could never quite forgive himself for the hate and violence that characterized his life during these years. "For I am the least of the apostles," he later wrote, ". . . because I persecuted the church of God" (1 Cor. 15:9). In other references, he brands himself as "a persecutor of the church" (Phil. 3:6), one who "persecuted the church of God, and wasted it" (Gal. 1:13).

An autobiographical reference in Paul's first letter to Timothy sheds some light on the question of how a man of such sensitive conscience could become involved in this violence against his own people. "I formerly blasphemed and persecuted and insulted him [Christ, represented by His people]; but I received mercy because I had acted ignorantly in unbelief" (1 Tim. 1:13, RSV). The history of religion is replete with examples of others who made the same mistake. In the same passage, Paul refers to himself as "the foremost of sinners" (1 Tim. 1:15, RSV), undoubtedly because he persecuted Christ Jesus and His followers.

D. The Death of Stephen. Had it not been for the way Stephen died (Acts 7:54–60), young Saul might have turned away unmoved from the stoning, at which he held the executioners' clothing. It would have seemed just another legal execution.

But as Stephen knelt and the martyring stones rained upon his defenseless head, he testified to his vision of Christ in glory, and prayed, "Lord, lay not this sin to their charge" (Acts 7:60). Though this crisis launched Paul on his career as a hunter of heretics, it is natural to suppose that Stephen's words stayed with him so that he became "hunted" as well—hunted by conscience.

E. A Career of Persecution. The events that followed the martyrdom of Stephen do not make pleasant reading. The story is told in a breath: "Saul laid waste the church, and entering house after house, he dragged off men and women and committed them to prison" (Acts 8:3).

II. Conversion on the Damascus Road. The persecution in Jerusalem actually scattered the seed of faith. Believers dispersed, and soon the new faith was being preached far and wide (cf. Acts 8:4). "Yet breathing out threatening and slaughter against the disciples of the Lord" (Acts 9:1), Saul decided it was time to carry the campaign to some of the "foreign cities" in which the scattered disciples had lodged. The long arm of the Sanhedrin could reach to the farthest synagogue in the empire in matters of Jewish religion. At this time, the followers of Christ were still regarded as a heretical Jewish sect.

So Saul set out for Damascus, about 240 km. (150 mi.) away, armed with credentials that would empower him to bring "any of this way, whether they were men or women . . . bound to Jerusalem" (Acts 9:2).

What was in his mind as he tramped on, day after day, in the dust of the road and the burning heat of the sun? The intensely personal self-revelation of Romans 7:7–13 may give us a clue. Here we see a conscientious man's struggle to find peace through observing all the minute ramifications of the Law.

Did it free him? Paul's answer from experience was no. Instead it became an intolerable burden and strain. The influence of Saul's Hellenistic environment in Tarsus must not be overlooked as we try to find the reason for his inner frustration. After his return to Jerusalem, he must have found rigid Pharisaism galling, even though he professed to accept it wholeheartedly. He had breathed freer air most of his life, and he could not renounce the freedom to which he had become accustomed.

However, the deeper reason for his distress was spiritual. He had tried to keep the Law, but learned that he could not do so, by reason of his sinful fallen nature. How then could he ever be right with God?

With Damascus in sight, a momentous thing happened. In one blinding flash, Saul saw himself stripped of all pride and pretension, as the persecutor of God's Messiah and His people. Stephen had been right, and he was wrong. In the face of the living Christ, Saul capitulated. He heard a voice that said, "I am Jesus, whom thou persecutest. . . . Arise, and go into the city, and it shall be told thee what thou must do" (Acts 9:5–6). And Saul obeyed.

During his stay in the city, "He was three days without sight, and neither did eat nor drink" (Acts 9:9). A disciple at Damascus by the name of Ananias became a friend and counselor, a man not afraid to believe that Paul's[1] conversion had been genuine. Through his prayers, God restored Paul's sight.

III. Early Ministry. Paul began witnessing to his newfound faith in the synagogue at Damascus. The burden of his message concerning Jesus was, "He is the Son of God" (Acts 9:20). But Paul had bitter lessons to learn before he could emerge as a trusted and effective Christian leader. He discovered that people do not forget easily; a man's mistakes can haunt him for a long time, even after he has forsaken them. Paul was suspected by many of the disciples and hated by his former companions in persecution. He preached briefly in Damascus, went away to Arabia, and then returned to Damascus.

Paul's second attempt to preach in Damascus did not work out well, either. A year or two had elapsed since his conversion, but the Jews remembered how he had deserted his original mission to Damascus. Hatred against him flamed anew, and "the Jews took counsel to kill him" (Acts 9:23). The story of Paul's dramatic escape over the wall in a basket has captured the imagination of many readers.

Paul's days of preparation were not over. The Galatian account continues by saying, "After three years I went up to Jerusalem . . . ." (Gal. 1:18). There he met the same hostile reception as at Damascus. Once more he had to flee.

Paul dropped from view for several years. These hidden years brought the ripened convictions and spiritual stature he would need for his ministry.

In Antioch, Gentiles were being converted to Christ. The church in Jerusalem had to decide how to care for these new converts. It was then that Barnabas remembered Paul and went to Tarsus to look for him (Acts 11:25). Barnabas had already been instrumental in introducing Paul in Jerusalem, in an effort to allay suspicions against him.

These two men were entrusted with the task of carrying relief funds back to Judea, where the followers of Jesus were suffering from a famine. When Barnabas and Paul returned to Antioch, mission accomplished, they brought young John Mark, Barnabas' nephew, with them (Acts 12:25).

IV. Missionary Journeys. The thriving young church at Antioch now sent out Barnabas and Paul as missionaries. The first port of call on the first missionary journey was Salamis on the island of Cyprus, the home country of Barnabas. This fact, together with the Bible's frequent listing of these

---

[1] Tradition says that God gave Saul the Hellenistic name Paul at the time of his conversion. Scripture does not say whether Saul adopted the name or whether it was given to him; nor does the Bible say when this change of name occurred. He is still called "Saul" during the time of his first missionary journey (Acts 13:19). But for the sake of convenience, we shall refer to him as "Paul" from this point.

PAUL AND HIS JOURNEYS

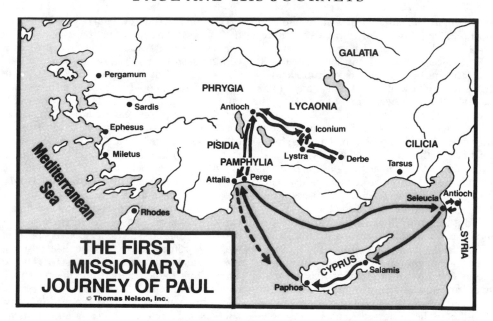

missionaries as "Barnabas and Saul," indicates that Paul was playing the lesser role. This was Bar-nabas' journey, Paul was second in command, and the two of them "had John [Mark] to assist them" (Acts 13:5, RSV).

The success of their missionary endeavors on that island fired Paul and his partners to press on into more difficult territory. They made a longer sea voyage, this time across to Perga on the mainland of Asia Minor. From there Paul meant to travel inland on a dangerous mission to Antioch in Pisidia.

But just at this point, something happened that was to cause much heartache for all three. The helper, John Mark, "departing from them returned to Jerusalem" (Acts 13:13), his home. We are not told why, though it is natural to guess that his courage and confidence had failed. Mark's sudden change of plans would later cause friction between Paul and Barnabas.

In Antioch, Paul became the spokesman and a familiar pattern developed. Some believed his message and rejoiced; others rejected his message and stirred up opposition. It happened first at Antioch, then at Iconium. At Lystra he was stoned and left for dead (Acts 14;19), but he survived to press on to one more city, Derbe.

The visit of Paul and Barnabas to Derbe completed their first journey. Soon Paul decided to retrace the difficult route over which he had come, in order to strengthen, encour-

age, and organize the Christian groups he and Barnabas had established.

In this we discern Paul's plan of planting congregations in the principal cities of the Roman Empire. He did not leave his converts unorganized and without suitable leadership; but by the same token, he did not remain long in one place.

The Jews often made converts among the Gentiles, but these gentile converts were kept in a "second-class" position. Unless they were ready to undergo circumcision and accept the Pharisaic interpretation of the Law, they remained on the fringes of the Jewish congregation. Even if they went that far, the fact that they were not born Jewish still barred them from complete fellowship.

So what would be the relationship of gentile converts to the Christian community? Paul and Barnabas journeyed to Jerusalem to confer with the leaders there regarding this fundamental issue.

At Jerusalem, Paul set forth his convictions and won the day. Paul's own description of the controversy in Galatians[2] states that he was given "the right hands of fellowship," along with Barnabas. The elders at Jerusalem agreed that these men "should go unto the heathen" (Gal. 2:9).

Following the conference in Jerusalem,

---

[2] If indeed this is what the passage refers to; it may be describing an earlier visit to Jerusalem.

PAUL AND HIS JOURNEYS

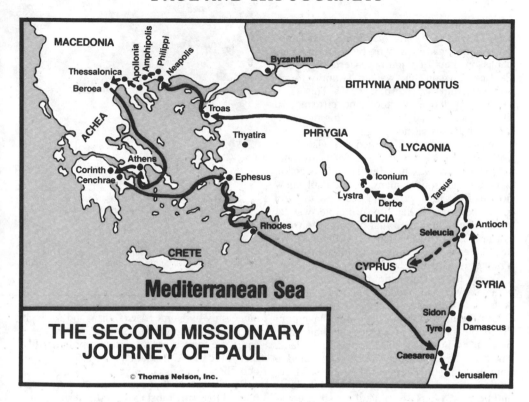

MACEDONIA
Amphipolis
Apollonia
Philippi
Neapolis
Byzantium
Thessalonica
Beroea
BITHYNIA AND PONTUS
Troas
ACHEA
Thyatira
PHRYGIA
LYCAONIA
Athens
Corinth
Cenchrae
Ephesus
Iconium
Lystra
Derbe
Tarsus
CILICIA
Rhodes
Antioch
Seleucia
CRETE
CYPRUS
SYRIA
Mediterranean Sea
Sidon
Tyre
Damascus
Caesarea
Jerusalem

THE SECOND MISSIONARY JOURNEY OF PAUL

© Thomas Nelson, Inc.

42

PAUL AND HIS JOURNEYS

Paul and Barnabas "continued in Antioch, teaching and preaching the word of the Lord" (Acts 15:35). Here, two incidents put severe strains upon Paul's working relationships with Peter and Barnabas.

The first of these incidents arose out of the same problems that brought on the Jerusalem conference. The conference had freed Gentiles from the Jewish regulation of circumcision. However, it had not decided whether Christians of Jewish background could eat with gentile converts. Peter took his stand with Paul in favor of this practice, which involved relaxing the Jewish food regulations. In fact, Peter set the example by eating with the Gentiles. But later he "withdrew and separated himself" (Gal. 2:12), and "Barnabas also was carried away with their dissimulation" (v. 13).

Paul, regarding these acts as a new threat to his mission to the Gentiles, resorted to drastic action. "I opposed [Peter] to his face, because he stood condemned" (Gal. 2:11, RSV). He did this "before them all" (v. 14). In other words, he resorted to public rebuke.

This incident helps us to understand the second one, which Luke records in Acts 15:36–40. Barnabas wanted young Mark to

accompany them on a second missionary journey; Paul opposed the idea. And the narrative says "there arose a sharp contention" (v. 39, RSV).

We do not know whether Paul and Barnabas ever met again. They "agreed to disagree" and embarked on separate journeys. No doubt the gospel was thereby furthered more than it would have been had they stayed together.

Then "Paul chose Silas, and departed, . . . and he went through Syria and Cilicia, confirming the churches" (Acts 15:40–41). After revisiting Derbe, which had been the last point visited on the first journey, Paul and his company pressed on to Lystra to see their converts in that place. Here Paul found a young Christian named Timothy (Acts 16:1), and perhaps saw in him a potential replacement for Mark.

What happened here redeemed Paul from any charge of not being willing to place confidence in men younger than himself. In 1 Timothy 1:2, Paul addressed Timothy as "my own son," and in the second epistle he speaks of him as "my dearly beloved son" (2 Tim. 1:2). In the second epistle we also read, "I am reminded of your sincere faith, a faith that dwelt first in your grandmother Lois and your mother Eunice and now, I am sure, dwells in you" (1:15, RSV). This may imply that Timothy's family had been won by Paul and Barnabas on their first journey. Certainly, when Paul came again, he "wanted Timothy to accompany him" (Acts 16:3, RSV). This same verse adds that Paul "took and circumcised him because of the Jews." Was this inconsistent with Paul's earlier judgment upon Peter? Or was it that he had learned the wisdom of not forcing unnecessary issues? At any rate, since Timothy was half-Jewish, this decision would avoid trouble many times. Paul knew how to fight for a principle and how to yield for expediency when no principle was at stake. Paul maintained that circumcision was not necessary to salvation (cf. Galatians), yet he was ready to circumcise a Christian Jew as a matter of expediency.

When the evangelistic party (directed in some unspecified way by the Holy Spirit— Acts 16:6–8) reached Troas and stood gazing across the narrow strait, they must have pondered the prospect of advancing their campaign to what is now the European mainland. The decision came when "a vision appeared to Paul in the night; There stood a man of Macedonia . . . saying, Come over into Macedonia and help us" (Acts 16:9). Paul's response was immediate. The party set sail for Europe. Many writers have suggested that this "man of Macedonia" may have been Luke the physician. At any rate, he seems to enter the travel drama at this point, for now he begins referring to the missionaries as "we."

The journey continued along the great Roman road running westward through the principal cities of Macedonia—from Philippi to Thessalonica, and from Thessalonica to Berea. For three weeks, Paul spoke in the synagogue at Thessalonica; then he moved on to Athens, center of Greek learning and a "city wholly given to idolatry" (Acts 17:16). Restlessly, he journeyed on to Corinth.

His first major mission to the gentile world extended to almost three years. Then he turned back to Antioch.

After a short stay in Antioch, Paul set out on his third missionary journey in A.D. 52. This time his first stops were in Galatia and Phrygia. After visiting the churches in Derbe, Lystra, Iconium, and Antioch, he decided to do some intensive missionary work in Ephesus. Ephesus was the capital of the Roman province of Asia. Strategically located for commerce, it was surpassed in size and impor-

STREET IN EPHESUS. *Paul's words incited a mob of angry Ephesians to riot in the theater at the end of this marble street (Acts 19:21-41). Demetrius, who made small silver models of the great temple of Diana, stirred up the trouble when he found that Paul's preaching endangered his craft. Paul left the city, choosing Timothy to remain behind and prevent the church from being corrupted by false doctrine (1 Tim. 1:3).*

tance only by Rome, Alexandria, and Antioch. As the outcome of Paul's labors there, it became the third most important city in the history of early Christianity—Jerusalem, Antioch, then Ephesus.

Paul came to Ephesus to undertake what proved to be the most extended and successful of his missionary efforts in any one locality. But these were strenuous years for him. Since he supported himself by working at his trade, his days were long. Following the custom of laborers in such a hot climate, he would be up and working at his trade before dawn. His afternoon hours were given to teaching and preaching, and likely his evening hours as well. He did this "daily" for "two years." In his own description of these labors, Paul adds that he not only taught in public, but "from house to house" (Acts 20:20). He succeeded—too well. We are told of "special miracles" (Acts 19:11) that took place during these stirring days in Ephesus. The new faith made such an impact on the city that "a number of those who practiced magic arts brought their books together and burned them" (Acts 19:19, RSV). This aroused the hatred of pagan worshipers, who feared that the Christians would undermine the influence of their religion.

After three winters in Ephesus, Paul spent the next one in Corinth, in line with the promise and hope expressed in 1 Corinthians 16:5–7. There Paul made further preparation for a visit to Rome. He penned a letter, telling

PAUL AND HIS JOURNEYS

the Christians in Rome, "I long to see you, . . . Oftentimes I purposed to come unto you" (Rom. 1:11, 13), and "I hope to see you in passing as I go to Spain" (Rom. 15:24, RSV).

Paul ignored warnings of the dangers that threatened him if he should appear in Jerusalem again. He felt that it was crucial that he return in person, bearing the gift of the gentile congregations. He was "ready not to be bound only, but also to die at Jerusalem for the name of the Lord Jesus" (Acts 21:13). So Paul came again to Jerusalem, and Luke writes that "the brethren received us gladly" (21:17). But lurking in the shadows was a reception committee with different intentions.

V. Imprisonment and Trial. The Christians in Jerusalem were happy to hear Paul's report of the spread of the Christian faith. However, some of the Jewish Christians doubted Paul's sincerity. To show his respect for the Jewish Christians, Paul helped four men who were keeping a Nazarite vow at the temple. Some Jews from Asia seized Paul and falsely accused him of bringing Gentiles into the temple (Acts 21:27–29). The tribune of the Roman garrison took Paul into custody to prevent a riot. Upon learning that Paul was a Roman citizen, the tribune removed his chains and asked the Jews to convene the Sanhedrin to interrogate him.

Paul realized that the heated mob might send him to death. So he told the Sanhedrin that he had been arrested because he was a Pharisee and believed in the resurrection of the dead. This divided the Sanhedrin into its Pharisaic and Sadducean factions, and the Roman tribune had to rescue Paul again.

Hearing that the Jews were plotting an ambush for Paul, the tribune sent him by night to Caesarea, where he was guarded in Herod's palace. Paul spent two years under arrest there.

When Paul's Jewish accusers arrived, they charged that the apostle had tried to profane

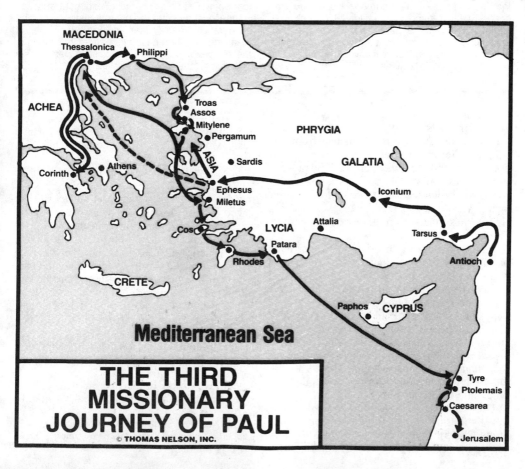

THE THIRD MISSIONARY JOURNEY OF PAUL

© THOMAS NELSON, INC.

Gamaliel

Gamaliel is only mentioned twice in the New Testament (Acts 5:34; 22:3), but he may have exerted a more profound influence on the course of Christianity than these brief references indicate. He was one of the few Jewish leaders who earned the title of *Rabban* ("our master, our great one") rather than the ordinary title *Rabbi* ("my master"). Gamaliel held a respected place on the Sanhedrin, the governing body of the Jewish religion. The Jews' high esteem for Gamaliel is demonstrated by one rabbi's comment made upon his death: "When Rabban Gamaliel the Elder died, the glory of the Law ceased and purity and abstinence died."

We find clues to Gamaliel's influence upon Christianity in the two Scripture references to him. In the first instance (Acts 5:34), the Sanhedrin met in a specially called session to deal with the Christians, who insisted that the Sanhedrin was responsible for the Messiah's death. In this emotionally heated session, Gamaliel rose and asked that Peter and the other Christians be excused for a moment so that he could speak. When this was done, he proceeded with a surprisingly insightful speech that obviously swayed the Sanhedrin: "And now I say unto you, Refrain from these men, and let them alone: for if this counsel or this work be of men, it will come to nought: But if it be of God, you cannot overthrow it; lest haply ye be found even to fight against God!" (Acts 5:38–39). Rather than the flogging they anticipated, Peter and the apostles were given a severe warning and were released.

The second reference (Acts 22:3) was made by Paul, Gamaliel's former pupil. Paul was appealing to a Jewish mob, and he was not hesitant to link himself to this great teacher.

Gamaliel's greatness lay in his devotion to God and the Law. These incidents paint at least a partial portrait of his personality and Jewish tradition tells us that this elder statesman stressed the importance of repentance rather than of "works." Perhaps Paul's emphasis on this great Christian doctrine had its roots in Gamaliel's teaching.

Gamaliel's further influence on Paul can only be surmised. Surely Paul's great zeal—first for the Law, then for Christ—was captured from Gamaliel. Paul's love for the truth and his exhaustive understanding of the Scriptures might also be attributed to his teacher. With this training, anointed by the Holy Spirit, Paul built his New Testament treatises on the Christian faith, the church, justification, and regeneration. Paul's clear and logical manner of explaining the great doctrines of the Christian faith was no doubt the result, at least in part, of his schooling "at the feet of Gamaliel."

---

the temple and had created a civil riot in Jerusalem (Acts 24:1–9). The Roman procurator Felix demanded more evidence from the tribune in Jerusalem. But before new evidence could arrive, Felix was replaced by a new procurator, Porcius Festus. This new official asked for Paul's accusers to come to Caesarea again. When they arrived, Paul exercised his right as a Roman citizen to present his case to Caesar.

While waiting for the ship to Rome, Paul had an opportunity to plead his cause before King Agrippa II, who visited Festus. Acts 26 records Paul's speech, in which he recounted the events of his life up to that point.

Festus committed Paul to the charge of a centurion named Julius, who was taking a shipload of prisoners to the imperial city. After a very rough voyage, the ship was wrecked on the island of Melita (Malta). Three months later, Paul and the other prisoners boarded another ship for Rome.

The Christians of Rome traveled about thirty miles from the city to welcome Paul (Acts 28:15). Julius delivered Paul to "the captain of the guard" (Acts 28:16), who placed the apostle under house arrest. Acts 28:30 tells us that Paul rented a house for two years while waiting for Caesar to hear his case.

The New Testament gives us no account of Paul's death. Many modern scholars believe that Caesar freed Paul, and that the apostle engaged in more missionary work before being arrested a second time and executed.[3]

Two books written before A.D. 200—the First Epistle of Clement and the Acts of Paul—assert that this happened. They indicate that Paul was beheaded in Rome near the end of the reign of Emperor Nero (*ca.* A.D. 67).

VI. Paul's Personality in His Letters. Paul's epistles are the mirror of his soul. They reveal his inner motives, his deepest passions, his basic convictions. Without the surviving letters of Paul, he would be only a dim figure for us.

Paul was more interested in persons and what was happening to them than in literary

---

[3] *The New Westminster Dictionary of the Bible*, ed. by Henry S. Gehman (Philadelphia: Westminster Press, 1970), p. 721.

PAUL AND HIS JOURNEYS

OLD APPIAN WAY. *Paul traveled to Rome on this, the oldest and most famous highway in Italy (Acts 28:14–16). Appius Claudius began its construction in 312 B.C. Roman tombs, catacombs, and towering cypress trees line the way for many kilometers.*

formalities. As we read Paul's writings we note that his words may come tumbling out in hot haste, as in the first chapter of Galatians. Sometimes he breaks off abruptly to plunge into a new line of thought. At points he draws a long breath and dictates a sentence almost without end.

Second Corinthians 10:10 gives a clue as to how Paul's letters were received and regarded. Even his enemies and critics acknowledged the impact of what he had to say, for they were known to comment, "His letters are weighty and powerful . . ." (2 Cor. 10:10).

Strong leaders, such as Paul, tend to attract or repel those they seek to influence. Paul had both devoted followers and bitter enemies. Consequently, his contemporaries held widely differing opinions about him.

Paul's earliest writings antedate most of the four Gospels. They mirror him as a man of courage (2 Cor. 2:3), of integrity and high motive (vv. 4–5), of humility (v. 6), and of gentleness (v. 7).

Paul knew how to differentiate between his own opinion and a "commandment of the Lord" (1 Cor. 7:25). He was humble enough to say "I think" on some matters (v. 40). He was very aware of the urgency of his commission

(9:16–17), and of the fact that he was not beyond the danger of being "disqualified" through succumbing to temptation (1 Cor. 9:27, RSV). He recalls with sorrow that once he "persecuted the church of God" (15:9).

Read Romans 16 with special attention to Paul's generous attitude toward his co-laborers. He was a man who loved and appreciated people and prized the fellowship of the believers. In the letter to the Colossians, we see how warm and friendly Paul could be, even with Christians whom he had not met. "I want you to know how greatly I strive for you . . . and for all who have not seen my face," he writes (Col. 2:1, RSV).

In the Colossian letter, we also read about a man named Onesimus, a runaway slave (Col. 4:9) who had evidently added theft to the crime of forsaking his owner, Philemon. Now Paul had won him to the Christian faith and had persuaded him that he should return to his master. But knowing the severity of punishment meted out to runaway slaves, the apostle wanted to persuade Philemon to treat Onesimus as a brother. Here we see Paul the reconciler. He maneuvered to ensure a Christian welcome for Onesimus as he returned to Philemon. As we would say it today, he put

PAUL AND HIS JOURNEYS

Philemon "on the spot" in the eyes of the church and in terms of his personal relationship to Paul. And he did all this in behalf of a man on the bottom rung of the ladder in Roman society. Contrast this with the behavior of young Saul, guarding the garments of those who stoned Stephen. Observe how profoundly Paul had changed in his attitude toward persons.

In these writings we see Paul as a generous, warmhearted friend, a man of great faith and courage—even in the face of extreme circumstances. He was utterly committed to Christ, whether in life or death. His testimony is one deep anchorage in spiritual realities: "I know both how to be abased, and I know how to abound: every where and in all things I am instructed both to be full and to be hungry, both to abound and to suffer need. I can do all things through Christ which strengtheneth me" (Phil. 4:12–13).

OUTLINE OF THE BOOKS OF THE BIBLE

Our English word *Bible* comes from the Greek word *biblia,* which means "the books." Christians have regarded their collection of Scriptures as being "the Book" since the Council of Carthage drew up the final list of New Testament books in A.D. 397.

The Bible contains many different kinds of writings. (*See* "Literature.") Here we will give outlines of the Bible books in each major section of the biblical literature. The Jews organized the Old Testament into three major sections: the five Books of Moses (*Torah*), the Prophets (*Nebi'im*), and the Writings (*Kethubim*). But here we will follow the major divisions that we find in the Greek Septuagint version.

I. Pentateuch. We must consider the books of Genesis, Exodus, Leviticus, Numbers, and Deuteronomy together, because they were all written by Moses. Jewish rabbis recognize the close connection of these five, and call them "the five-fifths of the Law." The Greek translators called them the *Pentateuch* (*pente,* "five," and *teuchos,* "a volume"—i.e., "the fivefold book"). Indeed, it is probable that all five books were originally one continuous narrative, and the 70 translators who made the Septuagint version divided it into the present five books. In the Jewish Hebrew manuscripts, the Pentateuch still forms one single unbroken document, marked only with the divisions for reading. Ezra, Nehemiah, and Chronicles variously refer to the Pentateuch as "the Law of Moses," "the Books of Moses," "the Book of the Covenant," and "the Book of the Law." Deuteronomy was rediscovered in the reign of Josiah, after having been long unknown to the nation of Israel (2 Chr. 34:14).

The Pentateuch was written or compiled by Moses at different times during his life. At what times, we cannot say; but (with the exception of Genesis) the Pentateuch must have been written between the time of the Exodus from Egypt and the author's death. (*See* "Chronology.")

The first eleven chapters of Genesis constitute a history of the Creation and of the early generations of the world. Then it focuses on the story of Abraham and his descendants. The remainder of Genesis brings us to the death of Joseph. The rest of the Pentateuch gives the history of the Israelites from the death of Joseph to the entrance into Canaan, together with the elaborate code of moral laws and civil government that God revealed to Moses.

A. Genesis. The word *genesis* is a Greek word meaning "origin" or "generation." It occurs frequently in the Septuagint version of this book. The Hebrew title of the book is *Bereshith,* which we translate as, "In the beginning."

1. Authorship. The Old Testament names Moses as the author of the Pentateuch (Josh. 8:31; 23:6; 2 Kin. 14:6; 2 Chr. 25:4; 35:12; Ezra 6:18; Neh. 8:1; 13:1). There is nothing improbable in this. Moses' education in the court of Pharaoh brought him in contact with the literature of the ancient world (Acts 7:22). Moses may well have used these documents of great antiquity in writing his account of Creation. The book is a literary masterpiece as well as a tremendous presentation of God and the origins of things; it could only have been written by a man of Moses' stature.

2. Contents. Genesis sets the stage for all of the rest of the Bible. It gives us a survey of God's work of Creation and His establishment of a covenant with Abraham's family. The early chapters describe the position of man in the universe and his relationship with the Creator. They also declare God's first laws for man, which define human sin and divine righteousness. Genesis establishes the major themes of Scripture—Creation, Fall, and Redemption. The writer organized this book into eleven sections (*see below*).

OUTLINE OF GENESIS

OUTLINE OF THE BOOKS OF THE BIBLE

---

*Genesis has 50 chapters, 1,533 verses,
and ca. 38,267 words.*

B. Exodus. Our title for this book comes from the Greek word that means "departure" or "going out." The Hebrew name for the book is the first phrase, "These are the names," or *We'alleh Shemoth*.

1. Authorship. Moses is the personality of this book, as well as being its author. However, scholars debate his dating of some events. (*See* "Chronology.")

2. Contents. Exodus takes up where Genesis leaves off. The period between Joseph and Moses is covered by two verses, 1:6–7. The favored guests of Pharaoh had become a nation of slaves, as the new Pharaoh sought to control the Hebrews. God prepared Moses, then used him to deliver the Hebrews. God led the Israelites out of Egypt so that He might bring them into the Promised Land. The theme of Exodus is not simply God's deliverance of Israel, but His adoption of them as the people of God.

The Exodus influenced the religion and life of Israel more than we can imagine. When God called this slave people out of Egypt and made them a great nation, He revealed Himself as the Lord of history and the Redeemer of those who call upon Him. The Exodus is the central event in the Old Testament, just as the cross is in the New Testament.

OUTLINE OF EXODUS

---

*Exodus has 40 chapters, 1,213 verses, and
ca. 32,692 words.*

C. Leviticus. The name *Leviticus* comes from the Greek word *Levitikon* ("of the Levites"), which is part of the book's title in the Septuagint version. The Hebrew title is *Wayyiqra* ("And he called").

1. Authorship. "And they set the priests in their divisions, and the Levites in their courses, for the service of God, which is at Jerusalem; as it is written in the book of Moses" (Ezra 6:18).

Ezra the scribe refers to Leviticus in describing the proper procedure for dedicating the rebuilt temple. Leviticus stresses that Moses recorded the regulations God gave for proper worship in the tabernacle. Moses was the central leader in the establishment of tabernacle worship.

2. Contents. Leviticus continues the narrative of Exodus without a break. It describes the priestly practices and the rituals of worship in ancient Israel. Chapter 16 explains God's law for the Day of Atonement, which was a forerunner of the atoning death of Jesus Christ in New Testament times.

OUTLINE OF LEVITICUS

Leviticus has 27 chapters, 859 verses, and ca. 24,546 words.

D. Numbers. The title *Numbers* is our English translation of *Arithmoi,* the title of this book in the Greek Septuagint. Various Hebrew manuscripts entitle this book *Wayed habber* ("And he spoke") or *Bemidhbar* ("In the wilderness")—both come from the first words of this book.

1. Authorship. Like the rest of the Pentateuch, this book was written by Moses. In fact, the book of Numbers names Moses as its author more than eighty times. Only the account of Balaam and Balak (Num. 22—24) does not specifically mention Moses; but we have no reason to doubt that Moses wrote that section also.

2. Contents. In Numbers, God teaches His people how to function as a camp. He sets their religious, civil, and military economies in order, in preparation for their journeying as a nation.

Laws and instructions are interspersed throughout the book. Numbers 1:1–2 tells us that Israel took a census and received additional instructions, largely ceremonial (chaps. 5—10). The Israelites left Sinai on the twentieth day of the second month, in the second year after the Exodus (10:11). Numbers records Israel's movements from that time until they arrived in the Plains of Moab, east of the Jordan River (Num. 22:1; 26:3, 33–50).

From Sinai, Israel journeyed north to the Paran Wilderness. There spies brought back an "evil report" about Canaan and the people refused to enter the land. They were turned back to wander in the wilderness 38 more years (chaps. 13—14). After this, they traveled to the Plains of Moab and occupied all of Transjordan north of the Arnon River. Here they fell into sin with the Moabite and Midianite women and worshiped their gods. Another census numbered the new generation of Israel (chap. 26), and at the command of God they destroyed the Midianites (chap. 31). Gad, Reuben, and the half-tribe of Manasseh were given land east of the Jordan (chap. 32).

Moses appointed Joshua his successor (27:18–23). Chapters 20—36 deal with events of the fortieth year (36:13).

OUTLINE OF NUMBERS

Numbers has 36 chapters, 1,288 verses, and ca. 32,902 words.

E. Deuteronomy. Our English title for this last book of the Pentateuch comes from the Greek words *deuteronomion touto,* which mean "this second law giving." The Hebrew manuscripts call it *'Elleh Haddevarim* ("These are the words") or *Mishmeh Hattorah* ("Repetition of the law"). This comes from a phrase in Deuteronomy 17:18.

1. Authorship. Scholars have argued that some later author or authors wrote the book of Deuteronomy. But Christians and Jews have traditionally held that Moses wrote this book, apart from the few verses describing his death (34:5–12). The book of Deuteronomy itself says that Moses wrote it (31:9, 24).

2. Contents. Jesus quoted the book of Deuteronomy more often than any other Old Testament book. In fact, the New Testament refers to it more than eighty times. Deuteronomy tells how God renewed His covenant with Israel on the Plains of Moab, just before they entered the Promised Land. The generation that accepted God's covenant at Sinai had died out, so God wanted to seal a new covenant with the people who could actually take the land of Canaan.

OUTLINE OF DEUTERONOMY

OUTLINE OF THE BOOKS OF THE BIBLE

Deuteronomy has 34 chapters, 959 verses, and ca. 28,461 words.

■

II. Other Works of the Mosaic Period. A number of ancient Hebrew books besides the Pentateuch existed during the time of Moses. Among them were the books Moses used in compiling the Pentateuch—such as "the Book of the Wars of the Lord" (cf. Num. 21:14). Bible scholars have their theories about what these books contained, but we have no copies of them, so we cannot be sure.

Note that Ezra or some other scribe must have added the account of Moses' death and burial, and perhaps a few other passages in the Pentateuch. But the bulk of it is Mosaic.

III. The Historical Books. We call the next section the historical books; it includes the 12 books from Joshua to Esther. Jews call the first six (Joshua, Judges, 1 and 2 Samuel, 1 and 2 Kings) the "former Prophets," because prophetic people wrote them. Altogether, the historical books give us the history of Israel from the death of Moses to the reconstruction of the temple under Nehemiah.

It is remarkable that the history of so small a nation has been preserved so fully. There are particular reasons for this.

The Jews were extremely industrious and careful in tracing and preserving their genealogies, which they could frequently link to Abraham. Many of these genealogical documents survived the Babylonian Captivity and even the first Roman conquest; but in the final dispersion of the Jews under the Emperor Hadrian in A.D. 135, the genealogies were mostly destroyed. Some special uses for the Jewish genealogies helped to preserve them in Old Testament times. No one was permitted to become a priest unless he could present a perfect and authentic genealogical record of his priestly descent. Accordingly, the priests were doubly diligent in preserving the documents that gave the required qualifications for their dignified office. With these records they pre-served the Book of the Law (the Pentateuch), which contained all the early part of the Jewish history. Furthermore, families divided up the land of Canaan, and their inheritance in each generation depended upon their being able to trace their descent. Lastly, God had promised that the Messiah would appear to the house of David; and as time passed, thousands of Jews zealously preserved the proof of their Davidic descent, hoping that they might bear the child who would make theirs the most illustrious household of all earthly history.

The tabernacle (and later the temple) became the treasure house for the genealogies of the nation. Scribes who researched and wrote genealogies used this place for keeping their records. And as other narratives of the past were compiled, the writers naturally laid them up in the literary storehouse of their people.

A. Joshua. This book bears the name of its principal character, Joshua. It continues the historical narrative of the Pentateuch, describing the conquest of Canaan in detail.

1. Authorship. We have no clear proof of who wrote the Book of Joshua. Many Jews and Christians believe it was written by Joshua himself. As in the case of Moses, it is believed that the account of Joshua's death was added by a later writer. Others have ascribed it to various writers—Phinehas, Eleazar, Samuel, Jeremiah, one of Joshua's elders, someone in the time of Jonah, someone in the time of Saul, or someone after the Babylonian Captivity. But none of these views is any more reasonable than the traditional view that the great Jewish general wrote it himself, with a few subsequent additions.

2. Contents. The book of Joshua stresses the uniqueness and holiness of Israel, which entitled God's people to conquer Canaan. By the time of Joshua, Canaanite religious observances had degenerated to licentiousness and brutality, as we learn from the Ugaritic tablets and the relics unearthed at Beth-shean and Megiddo. The immoral devotees of the Canaanite deities practiced the most demoralizing rites of the ancient Near East. (*See* "Pagan Religions and Cultures.")

OUTLINE OF JOSHUA

Joshua has 24 chapters, 685 verses, and ca. 18,858 words.

B. Judges. The title *Judges* is a direct English translation of the Hebrew title, *shoffim.* The Septuagint and the Latin Vulgate picked up this title and carried it into our modern English versions.

1. Authorship. Different scholars have attributed this book to Phinehas, Hezekiah, Jeremiah, Ezekiel, Ezra, or to some unknown prophet who is supposed to have drawn the materials from the public records. Jews believe it was written by the prophet Samuel. But we have no proof for any of these ideas. It was probably written during the first years of David's reign, because it came after the fall of Shiloh (18:31). But it must have been written before David's capture of Jebus, because Jebusites were still living in Jerusalem (1:21).

2. Contents. Judges continues the narrative of Joshua. However, it reflects the general social and political chaos at the end of the Amarna Age (*ca.* 1200 B.C.), when Egypt had lost her empire in Asia Minor. The book shows God's deliverance in the face of Israel's many foes. The writer stresses that the people needed to repent and return to the Lord.

OUTLINE OF JUDGES

B. The crime at Gibeah and the war against Benjamin . . . . 19:1—21:25

Judges has 21 chapters, 618 verses, and ca. 18,976 words.

C. Ruth. The book of Ruth is named after its heroine, a Moabite woman who journeyed to Bethlehem with her mother-in-law after the death of her husband. We remember Ruth because she was a foreign ancestor of King David and Jesus Christ.

1. Authorship. This sweet and graceful pastoral narrative is written by some wholly unknown author, though it has been credited to Samuel, Hezekiah, and Ezra. We cannot determine who wrote it. But it is reasonable to suppose that it was written about the time of David, since it mentions him (4:18–22) and doesn't mention Solomon, his son.

2. Contents. In telling about the experiences of Ruth, this book gives us a very detailed account of Israelite village life in the time of the judges. The book also demonstrates the ancient law of levirate marriage, by which a male relative would marry a dead man's widow to provide offspring to carry the family name.

OUTLINE OF RUTH

I. THE FAMILY OF ELIMELECH MIGRATES TO MOAB *1:1–5*

II. ELIMELECH'S WIDOW AND DAUGHTER-IN-LAW RETURN FROM MOAB *1:6–8*

III. NAOMI AND RUTH ARRIVE AT BETHLEHEM *1:19–22*

IV. RUTH GLEANS IN THE FIELDS OF BOAZ *2:1–23*

V. RUTH FINDS A REDEEMER *3:1–18*

VI. BOAZ MARRIES RUTH *4:1–17*

VII. RUTH BECOMES AN ANCESTRESS OF DAVID *4:18–22*

Ruth has 4 chapters, 85 verses, and ca. 2,578 words.

D. First Samuel. This book is named after the key person in its narrative. At first, the Hebrew Bible did not divide this narrative into two books (1 and 2 Samuel). The Septuagint and Vulgate versions made this division, and Hebrew Bibles printed after A.D. 1488 have followed suit.

1. Authorship. It is likely that Samuel wrote only the sections that deal with the history of Israel prior to his retirement from public office. Some scholars suggest that Abiathar wrote much of 1 and 2 Samuel, especially the parts that describe the court life of David. Abiathar was intimately associated with David during his civil war with Saul. Also, he came from a priestly family and undoubtedly had learned the art of writing. Another suggestion is that one of Samuel's students finished the history of Israel begun by his master.

2. Contents. First Samuel continues the history of Israel from the period of the judges down to the establishment of the monarchy under Saul. The chief character and probable author of the first section of the book is Samuel, the last judge of Israel and the first major prophet.

The books of Samuel emphasize that God rules in the lives of men and nations. In judgment and in blessing, God works to prepare His people for the coming of the Messiah. Many sub-themes play around this major one. For example, God's call of the boy Samuel and His revelation of the coming judgment continue the theme of God's effort to redeem a rebellious nation. The rise and fall of King Saul illustrates how the nation had turned away from God. God's final rejection of Saul was a warning of the pitiful plight of Israel if it continued to rebel.

OUTLINE OF 1 SAMUEL

I. THE LIFE AND MINISTRY OF SAMUEL *1:1—7:17*
   A. The birth and childhood of Samuel . . . . 1:1—4:1a
   B. The capture and return of the ark . . . . 4:1b—7:1
   C. The victory over the Philistines 7:2–17

First Samuel has 31 chapters, 810 verses, and ca. 25,061 words.

E. Second Samuel. Early English Bibles called this book 2 Kings, because it is the second book about the kings of Israel. (Those early versions called 1 and 2 Kings by the names 3 Kings and 4 Kings, respectively.) But later Bible publishers attached Samuel's name to this book, because Samuel played such an important role in setting up the monarchy in Israel.

1. Authorship. This book does not mention its author. It may have been written by a scribe in the court of King Solomon, or even later. The writing contains many archaic Hebrew words and quotations from earlier documents.

2. Contents. Second Samuel begins by telling how David's men wiped out Saul's family, opening the way for David to rule Israel. It describes David's reign very objectively, showing both his strengths and weaknesses.

OUTLINE OF 2 SAMUEL

Second Samuel has 24 chapters, 695 verses, and ca. 20,612 words.

F. First Kings. The two books of Kings were originally one in the Hebrew Bible. The translators of the Septuagint divided them; the Vulgate and English versions later did the same. As we noted under the section on "Second Samuel," the earliest English Bibles called these books 3 and 4 Kings.

1. Authorship. The book does not identify its author. But the Jewish Talmud claims that Jeremiah wrote it, because Jeremiah 52 and 2 Kings 24—25 are nearly identical. Modern scholars agree that 1 Kings was written during the time of Jeremiah, but the style of 1 Kings doesn't seem to match that of Jeremiah. The writer of 1 Kings tells us that he referred to several other documents in compiling his narrative, including "the Book of the Acts of Solomon" (11:41), "the Book of the Chronicles of the Kings of Judah" (14:29), and "the Book of the Chronicles of the Kings of Israel" (14:19).

2. Contents. The books of Kings do not give a detailed history of all the kings of Judah and Israel. They give only passing reference to powerful kings like Omri and Jeroboam II, but they emphasize the prophets Elijah and Elisha, and some of the less politically influential kings who reigned in the days of the prophets, such as Josiah.

The author was not concerned simply with giving an account of the kings of the divided nation. He dwelt upon the men and events that taught a prophetic message.

The writer has certain religious standards by which he evaluates each king. For example, he believed that the king's role included the giving of support to the temple and its worship. This was impossible for the kings of the Northern Kingdom; but the writer believed that was part of God's judgment upon them because they had separated themselves from the temple. He saw the fall of the Northern Kingdom as punishment for its idolatry. It was his belief that God's people must always separate themselves from the religious practices of the pagan nations surrounding them.

The theme of these books is that God blesses the king and the nation when they keep the covenant. God's judgment falls with inevitable certainty upon those who disobey His law.

Outline of 1 Kings

First Kings has 22 chapters, 816 verses, and ca. 24,524 words.

G. Second Kings. This book continues the history of Israel and Judah as begun by 1 Kings, and carries it up to the Babylonian Captivity.

1. Authorship. Like 1 Kings, this book does not name its author. But it probably was written by the same person who compiled the narrative of 1 Kings.

2. Contents. Second Kings describes the fall of Israel and the last throes of Judah. Like 1 Kings, it shows that God tried to warn these nations through His prophets, but the corrupt kings ignored Him. Here we see the climax of the prophetic ministry of Elijah and Elisha.

Outline of 2 Kings

*Second Kings has 25 chapters, 719 verses,
and ca. 23,532 words.*

OUTLINE OF 1 CHRONICLES

*First Chronicles has 29 chapters, 942
verses, and ca. 20,369 words.*

H. First Chronicles. First and 2 Chronicles comprised one book in the Hebrew Bible, called *Divere Hayyanim* ("The words of the days"). The Septuagint translators divided this material into the two books we have today; they called them the *Paraleipomena* ("Things omitted"). Jerome's Latin Vulgate gave them the title that we now use: "Chronicles." They form a religious history of the monarchy from David on, complementing the more political narrative of the books of Samuel and Kings, which they often summarize.

1. Authorship. Hebrew tradition says that Ezra wrote Chronicles as well as Ezra. The books do have the same style of language and type of contents. We see it in their frequent genealogies, their similar stress upon ritual, and their common devotion to the Law of Moses. The closing verses of 2 Chronicles (36:22–23) are repeated as opening verses of Ezra (1:1–3a). This seems to indicate that Ezra and Chronicles were originally one consecutive history. The fact that 2 Chronicles breaks off in the middle of Cyrus' decree suggests that Ezra was deliberately guiding his readers to the Book of Ezra.

2. Contents. First Chronicles starts by setting forth the genealogies of Jewish priests and laymen. These records were the only proof of a person's right to priestly office and an individual's claim to the property of his ancestors. So when the Jews returned from Exile, they had to rely on these accounts for reestablishing temple worship and resettling the land. The rest of the book tells the story of David's reign, with special emphasis on the details of Israelite worship during that period.

I. Second Chronicles. This book describes the reign of Solomon, the division of the kingdom, and the subsequent history of the Southern Kingdom of Judah. The account seems to end with 36:21, and the last two verses of the book take up the subject of the Book of Ezra.

1. Authorship. Jewish tradition says that Ezra wrote this book, along with the narrative of 1 Chronicles. If that is so, it was written after the Jews returned from their Exile in Babylon.

2. Contents. This book describes the history of some of the kings in more detail than the books of Kings. For example, it devotes about thirty verses to the religious reforms and military exploits of King Asa, while *Kings* gives us less than half of that material (1 Kings 15:9–24).

OUTLINE OF 2 CHRONICLES

I. THE REIGN OF SOLOMON 1:1— 9:31
A. Solomon's inaugurations... 1:1–17
B. Solomon's temple......... 2:1—7:22
1. Preparations 2:1–18
2. Construction.......... 3:1—4:22
3. Dedication............ 5:1—7:22
C. Solomon's kingdom ...... 8:1—9:31
1. Its achievements....... 8:1–18
2. Its splendor........... 9:1–31

II. THE KINGDOM OF JUDAH 10:1—36:23
A. The division of the kingdom 10:1—11:23
B. The rulers of Judah .... 12:1—36:16
1. Rehoboam............ 12:1—16
2. Abijah 13:1–22
3. Asa.................. 14:1—16:14
4. Jehoshaphat .... 17:1—20:37
5. Jehoram 21:1–20
6. Ahaziah............. 22:1–9
7. Athaliah.............. 22:10—23:21
8. Joash 24:1–27
9. Amaziah 25:1–28
10. Uzziah 26:1–23
11. Jotham............... 27:1–9
12. Ahaz................. 28:1–27
13. Hezekiah .... 29:1—32:33
14. Manasseh 33:1–20
15. Amon 33:21–25
16. Josiah................ 34:1—35:27
17. Jehoahaz, Jehoiakim, Jehoiachin, and Zedekiah 36:1–16
C. The Exile............... 36:17–23

Second Chronicles has 36 chapters, 822 verses, and ca. 26,074 words.

us a very reliable account of the Jewish restoration.

OUTLINE OF EZRA

I. THE EXILES' RETURN FROM BABYLON 1:1—2:70
A. The decree of Cyrus....... 1:1–4
B. Preparations for the journey 1:5–11
C. Those who returned...... 2:1–70

II. TEMPLE BUILDING BEGUN 3:1—4:24
A. The altar and the foundation 3:1–13
B. Opposition to the work 4:1–24

III. THE BUILDING COMPLETED 5:1—6:22
A. Work resumed 5:1–5
B. Tatnai's letter to Darius.... 5:6–17
C. Decrees of Cyrus and Darius 6:1–12
D. The temple finished 6:13–22

IV. EZRA'S JOURNEY TO JERUSALEM 7:1—8:36
A. Ezra introduced 7:1–10
B. Letter of Artaxerxes to Ezra 7:11–28
C. The journey to Jerusalem .. 8:1–36

V. THE GREAT REFORMATION 9:1—10:44
A. The tragic report and Ezra's prayer 9:1–15
B. The abandonment of mixed marriages 10:1–17
C. List of those with foreign wives 10:18–44

Ezra has 10 chapters, 280 verses, and ca. 7,441 words.

43

OUTLINE OF THE BOOKS OF THE BIBLE

J. Ezra. This book is a continuation of Chronicles. Ezra, a priest and a scribe, was well fitted for writing this historical narrative. It begins with Cyrus' decree, permitting Zerubbabel to lead the Jews back to Jerusalem and rebuild the temple. It ends with Ezra's moral reform among the Jewish people.
1. Authorship. Scholars think the priest Ezra wrote part of this book and compiled the rest. They believe Ezra wrote chapters 7—10 from his own experiences and gathered the rest of the material from earlier histories.
2. Contents. The book of Ezra describes how the Jews returned from Exile and restored their worship rituals in Jerusalem. Since it was an eyewitness who prepared this book, it gives

K. Nehemiah. This book tells the story of the third great leader of the Jews' return from Exile. King Artaxerxes sent Nehemiah, a Jew, to serve as governor of the restored city of Jerusalem. The Book of Nehemiah recounts this man's struggle to reestablish Israel as a nation.
1. Authorship. Scholars believe Nehemiah wrote much of the book himself, though later scribes added more material to detail the history of this period. The Hebrew Bible included this book with the book of Ezra; the Septuagint and Vulgate versions called it "Second Ezra."
2. Contents. Though Nehemiah was not a priest, he proved to be as pious as Ezra, the great religious leader of the period—and he

was a more practical statesman than Ezra. He came to Jerusalem 13 years after Ezra arrived, and spent the rest of his life there, except for a brief return to Persia.

OUTLINE OF NEHEMIAH

Nehemiah has 13 chapters, 406 verses, and ca. 10,483 words.

L. Esther. The Hebrew name of this book is *Megillah Esther,* or "The Volume of Esther." *Esther* is a Persian name that the Persian royal court gave to Hadassah, the daughter of Abihail; it comes from the Persian word *stara,* meaning "star."

1. Authorship. We do not know who wrote the book of Esther, though the Jewish historian Josephus says it was Mordecai. The text suggests it was written by someone who lived at the time of Esther.

2. Contents. Jews have valued this book very highly as a patriotic rallying point. They like its story of Esther's revenge against the wicked court official Haman, who tried to exterminate the Jews. But the book of Esther does not even mention the name of God. This

troubled Jewish scholars for centuries, but the book has earned its place in the canon by tradition, and is in fact a telling portrayal of God's hidden hand in providence. The Deuterocanon adds six chapters to Esther that most Protestant Bibles do not contain.

OUTLINE OF ESTHER

Esther has 10 chapters, 167 verses, and ca. 5,637 words.

IV. The Poetic Books. These are six in number: Job, Psalms, Proverbs, Ecclesiastes, Song of Solomon, and Lamentations. We give the name of *poetry* to compositions that possess imaginative thought, figurative language, and an arrangement in lines of regulated lengths and accents. Hebrew poetry has all of this, yet it uses techniques that are quite different from what we find in English-language poems. (*See* "Poetry.")

A. Job. Some scholars believe this book was written before any other book of the Old Testament—even before the Pentateuch. But most conservative Bible experts think it was written during the reign of King Solomon. Job lived in the land of Uz, somewhere east of Palestine; perhaps in the area of Idumaea.

1. Authorship. Tradition says that Job himself wrote the book; but as we've already noted, more recent scholars dispute that claim. Across the years, Bible students have supposed that it was written by Moses, Elihu, Solomon, Isaiah, or someone else. We have no proof for any of these theories, and the book does not name its author.

2. Contents. This book describes Job's questioning of God in the aftermath of several tragedies that befell the "upright man" of Uz. It addresses the age-old question, "Why do the righteous suffer?"

OUTLINE OF JOB

Job has 42 chapters, 1,070 verses, and ca. 10,102 words.

B. Psalms. The Hebrew name for this book means "Praises." The present name is Greek, and was first given in the Septuagint translation; it means "poems with musical accompaniment."

We may add here the meanings of several Hebrew words found in the titles of some of the Psalms, such as *Maschil*, "instruction" or "homily"; *Michtam*, "private memorial"; *Eduth*, "testimony"; *Shoshannim*, "lilies"; *Shiggaion*, "irregular ode." The three words *Neginoth, Nehiloth,* and *Sheminith* probably are names of musical instruments. *Mahalath* means a kind of dance, and *Mahalath-Leannoth,* a responsive psalm for such a dance.

The meaning of the word *Selah* is unknown, and a great many useless opinions have been given about it. For instance, some think it is a musical term meaning "pause" or "repeat." Others believe it marks a change of meter or the coming in of the accompaniment. Still others think it was supposed to call attention to a peculiarly important thought, or that it designated the end of a prayer. Any of these theories is as good as the others. The Hebrew scholar W.A. Wright ends a long list of these opinions by quietly calling it a "hopeless subject."

1. Authorship. Besides 73 Psalms that are ascribed to David, we have about 30 that are attributed to other authors and about 50 that are anonymous. Solomon is supposed to have written Psalms 72 and 127, and he may also have written some of the anonymous Psalms. Many Psalms are ascribed to Asaph (the head of the temple musicians in David's time) and "the sons of Korah" (probably Levite writers who descended from Korah).

43

2. Contents. The book of Psalms is the songbook of the ancient Hebrews. It contains hymns that the priests sang during temple worship and ballads that express the feelings of the Hebrew people at different stages in their history.

3. Outline. We have already noted that the Psalms seem to fall into five sections, according to their authorship or date of compilation. (*See* "Poetry.") Beyond this, we cannot outline the subject matter of the book, because very few of the Psalms are grouped in a topical sequence.

C. Proverbs. In this case, the Hebrew and English names of the book mean the same, since the first words of the book in both languages name its contents—"The Proverbs of Solomon." No doubt this collection of pithy religious and moral sayings was mainly composed by the wise king whose name it bears.

1. Authorship. Even though Solomon wrote most of the Proverbs, the book was not compiled until the time of King Hezekiah, whose scribes "copied out" the sayings of Solomon (Prov. 25:1). We do not know the identity of "Agur the son of Jakeh" and the mother of "King Lemuel," who wrote latter portions of the book (Prov. 30—31).

2. Contents. Proverbs is a collection of sharp ethical precepts about practical living. Like the Psalms, it arranges its material in balanced pairs of thoughts by the method of contrasting parallelism. (*See* "Poetry.")

OUTLINE OF PROVERBS

Proverbs has 31 chapters, 915 verses, and ca. 15,043 words.

D. Ecclesiastes. The Hebrew name of this book is *Qoheleth,* which means "Preacher" or "One Who Assembles." The Septuagint translators gave it its current Greek name, which means "Member of the Assembly." It scorns the sinful ways of man and condemns the futility of most human endeavors. It is very different from Proverbs in style and content. Hebrew scholars at the end of the first century A.D. debated whether it should be included in the Bible, and it remains one of the most difficult Bible books to understand.

1. Authorship. Tradition says that King Solomon wrote this book in his later years, after he had repented of his sinful ways. But modern scholars reject this view, saying it was probably written after the Exile. They believe the writer wrote the book in the character of Solomon for literary effect.

2. Contents. Ecclesiastes blasts the emptiness of greed and materialism and exhorts the reader to "remember now thy Creator . . ." (Eccl. 12:1). Overall the book has a disillusioned tone, save in its repeated celebration of ordinary everyday pleasures, and the message of abiding hope for God's faithful people emerges only at the end of the last chapter.

OUTLINE OF ECCLESIASTES

II. THE THEME DEMONSTRATED
(I)   *1:4—2:26*
A. **By this life** 1:4–11
B. **By knowledge** 1:12–18
C. **By pleasure** 2:1–11
D. **By the fate of all men** 2:12–17
E. **By toil** 2:18–23
F. **Sum: Enjoy life now** 2:24–26

III. THE THEME DEMONSTRATED
(II)   *3:1—4:16*
A. **By the laws of God** 3:1–15
B. **By mortality** 3:16–22
C. **By oppression** 4:1–3
D. **By work** 4:4–6
E. **By miserliness** 4:7–12
F. **By fleeting acclaim** 4:13–16

IV. WORDS OF ADVICE (A)   5:1–7

V. THE THEME DEMONSTRATED
(III)   *5:8–6:12*
A. **By enjoying wealth** 5:8–20
B. **By unenjoyable wealth** 6:1–9
C. **By the fixity of fate** 6:10–12

VI. MORE WORDS OF ADVICE
(B)   *7:1—8:9*
A. **Honor over luxury** 7:1
B. **Sobriety superior to fun.** . . . 7:2–7
C. **Caution over rashness** 7:8–10
D. **Wisdom and money beat wisdom only** 7:11–12
E. **Patience superior to fury** . . . 7:13–14
F. **Reserve superior to excess.** . 7:15–22
G. **Men are better than women!** 7:23–29
H. **Compromise incidentals usually** 8:1–9

VII. THE THEME DEMONSTRATED
(IV)   *8:10—9:16*
A. **By the incongruity of life** . . . 8:10–14
B. **Sum: enjoy life now** . . . . 8:15—9:16

VIII. WORDS OF ADVICE (C)   9:17—12:8
A. **Some lessons on wisdom and folly** . . . . 9:17—10:15
B. **Some lessons about rulers** . . 10:16–20
C. **Some lessons on overcautiousness.** 11:1–8
D. **Some lessons on pleasure** . . . 11:9—12:8

IX. CONCLUSION   *12:9–14*
A. **The preacher's intent** 12:9–10
B. **His teaching endorsed** 12:11–12
C. **The end can be good** 12:13–14

Ecclesiastes has 12 chapters, 222 verses, and ca. 5,584 words.

███████

E. Song of Solomon. The Hebrew Bible calls this book "The Song of Songs"—that is, the most beautiful of all songs. It expresses a young man's love for a maiden, and many Bible scholars have found symbolic or allegorical meanings within it.

1. Authorship. Tradition says that Solomon wrote this book, probably while he was a young man. However, it seems more to be about him than by him, and it does not portray him in a favorable light at all.

2. Contents. Probably no book of the Bible has been interpreted in as many different ways as the Song of Solomon. Basically, these interpretations fall into two categories—literal or allegorical. The Jewish Talmud teaches that the book is an allegory of God's love for Israel. Many Christian writers feel that it is an allegory of God's love for the church. Some Roman Catholic commentators conclude that it is an allegory of God's love for the Virgin Mary. On the literal side, Theodore of Mopsuestia (fourth century A.D.) believed it was a straightforward poem that Solomon wrote in honor of his marriage. Johann David Michaelis believed the book simply expressed God's approval of marriage, while Johann F. W. Bousset supposed that it was a poetic marriage drama used in ancient times. The modern scholar Calvin Seerveld sees it as an ancient love story with a strong religious and spiritual message. Despite these differing opinions, the book is one of the most beautiful examples of Hebrew poetry found in the Old Testament.

43

OUTLINE OF THE BOOKS OF THE BIBLE

OUTLINE OF SONG OF SOLOMON

I. THE MUTUAL AFFECTION OF BRIDE AND BRIDEGROOM   *1:1—2:7*

II. THE BRIDE SPEAKING OF HER BRIDEGROOM. HER FIRST DREAM ABOUT HIM   *2:8—3:5*

III. THE BRIDAL PROCESSION; THE BRIDE'S SECOND DREAM; HER CONVERSATION WITH THE DAUGHTERS OF JERUSALEM   *3:6—6:3*

IV. THE BRIDEGROOM'S FURTHER PRAISE OF HIS BRIDE'S BEAUTY. HER DESIRE FOR HIM   6:4—8:4

V. FINAL EXPRESSIONS OF MUTUAL LOVE 8:5–14

Song of Solomon has 8 chapters, 117 verses, and ca. 2,661 words.

F. Lamentations. The Jewish name of this book literally means "Ah, how!"—from the first words of the text. Our present name of the book is the English translation of *Thrēnoi,* the title the Septuagint translators gave it.

1. Authorship. Jewish tradition says that Jeremiah wrote this book, and the Septuagint even added a verse of introduction that named Jeremiah as the author. Second Chronicles 35:25 affirms that Jeremiah wrote this type of literature.

2. Contents. The book consists of five separate elegies or lamentations, corresponding to the five chapters of the English version. It is poetical throughout—more elaborately poetical than any other portion of the Bible. Each of the five elegies or chapters is arranged in 22 portions, corresponding with the 22 letters of the Hebrew alphabet.

OUTLINE OF LAMENTATIONS

Lamentations has 5 chapters, 154 verses, and ca. 3,415 words.

V. The Prophetic Books. Strictly speaking, a *prophet* is not simply a person who foretells the future; he is one who "speaks for" God, interpreting God's will to His people. The divine spokesman would often predict future events, but that was not his primary duty. The prophetic books of the Bible contain many predictions of the future, but they also contain many inspired sermons about conditions in Israel at the time the prophets were writing.

A. Isaiah. The name of this prophet literally means "Salvation of Yahweh." Though Isaiah lived and wrote later than some of the other prophets, our modern Bibles place his book before the rest because his predictions were so important for the future of Israel and all mankind.

1. Authorship. Isaiah undoubtedly compiled this book, though he may have been assisted by a scribe or secretary. Bible critics have claimed that Isaiah did not write the latter chapters, 40—66, but they build their argument on the supposition that God does not reveal the future to His prophets. If we accept that God could show Isaiah in advance how Judah would be destroyed, taken captive, and then restored, there is no good reason to doubt that the prophet wrote the whole book.

2. Contents. Isaiah proclaimed God's Word under a succession of kings, warning them that God would destroy Judah because of their evil ways. They did not heed him, and an old Jewish tradition says that King Manasseh executed Isaiah by having him sawn in two.

OUTLINE OF THE BOOKS OF THE BIBLE

OUTLINE OF ISAIAH

Isaiah has 66 chapters, 1,292 verses, and ca. 37,044 words.

B. Jeremiah. This name literally means "the appointed one of the Lord." Jeremiah lived and prophesied about two centuries after Isaiah. He was a priest from the city of Anathoth, and he ministered in Judah for more than forty years. Jewish tradition says that the Jewish refugees stoned him to death in Egypt, because he criticized their life in the Exile.

1. Authorship. This book contains the prophecies of Jeremiah as they were recorded by his scribe, Baruch. Jeremiah spoke some of these prophecies under Kings Josiah, Jehoiakim, and Zedekiah; some under Governor Gedaliah; and some in Egypt, where some people of Judah had fled from the Babylonian armies.

2. Contents. The book of Jeremiah describes the prophet's attempt to call his people back to God just before the Babylonians seized the nation of Judah. Occasionally, the writer uses a secret script called *Atbash* to conceal the names of nations or cities God has doomed, in case the scroll fell into the hands of enemies.

OUTLINE OF JEREMIAH

I. *ORACLES AGAINST JUDAH* 1:1—25:38
   A. The call of Jeremiah....... 1:1–19
   B. Reproofs and admonitions . 2:1—20:18
      1. Israel's neglect of God . . . 2:1—3:5
      2. Judah warned by the doom of the northern kingdom .... 3:6—6:30
      3. Judah's wrong religion . . 7:1—10:25
      4. Israel rejected for breaking God's covenant .... 11:1—13:27
      5. Jeremiah prays......... 14:1—17:27
      6. Lesson from imprisonment .... 18:1—20:18
   C. Later prophecies.......... 21:1—25:38
      1. The siege 21:1–14
      2. An exhortation to king and people 22:1–9
      3. The fate of Shallum 22:10–12
      4. An oracle against Jehoiakim 22:13–23
      5. An oracle against Jehoiakim............. 22:24–30
      6. The messianic King 23:1–8
      7. Against the false prophets 23:9–40
      8. The vision of figs. 24:1–10
      9. The judgment on Judah . 25:1–38

II. *THE LIFE OF JEREMIAH* 26:1—45:5
   A. The temple sermon and Jeremiah's arrest 26:1–24
   B. The yoke of Babylon ...... 27:1—29:32
   C. The Book of Consolation . . . 30:1—33:26
      1. The Day of the Lord..... 30:1–24
      2. The restoration of the nation 31:1–40
      3. Jeremiah buys land 32:1–44
      4. Promises of restoration . . 33:1–26
   D. Some experiences .... 34:1—36:32
      1. Truth to Zedekiah 34:1–7
      2. The Covenant and slaves. 34:8–22
      3. The Rechabites 35:1–19
      4. Jeremiah's secretary 36:1–32
   E. Jeremiah under pressure... 37:1—39:18
      1. Jeremiah jailed......... 37:1–21
      2. In a miry dungeon 38:1–28
      3. Jerusalem falls 39:1–18
   F. Jeremiah's last years ...... 40:1—45:5
      1. Gedaliah murdered ..... 40:1—41:18
      2. Refugees to Egypt....... 42:1—43:7
      3. Jeremiah in Egypt ...... 43:8—44:30
      4. Baruch advised......... 45:1–5

III. *AGAINST FOREIGN NATIONS* 46:1—51:64
   A. Oracle against Egypt 46:1–28
   B. Against the Philistines 47:1–7

OUTLINE OF THE BOOKS OF THE BIBLE

Jeremiah has 52 chapters, 1,364 verses, and ca. 42,659 words.

▬▬▬

C. Ezekiel. This prophet's name means "God strengthens." He came from a family of priests and served as a priest in the temple until he was carried away into captivity by Nebuchadnezzar. He delivered his prophecies during this captivity, somewhere along the Chebar River (a tributary of the Euphrates).

1. Authorship. There is no doubt that the prophet Ezekiel wrote this book. It reflects the times in which Ezekiel lived, and it carries the burden of his message to the Jews in captivity.

2. Contents. When Nebuchadnezzar captured the temple in Jerusalem, he stunned the Israelites. They believed God would never allow their enemies to violate the holy sanctuary. But Jeremiah had predicted this would happen, and Ezekiel reminds his fellow exiles that God had brought it to pass, and justly so. His later chapters look forward to restoration from exile and spiritual renewal.

OUTLINE OF EZEKIEL

Ezekiel has 48 chapters, 1,273 verses, and ca. 39,407 words.

D. Daniel. The Book of Daniel comes from the Babylonian Captivity, and recounts several miraculous divine interventions in the lives of certain of the exiles. It also predicts how God would destroy the nations that held the Israelites in bondage, and bring in the Messiah.
1. Authorship. Daniel spent his adult life in the royal court of the Babylonian and Persian empires. Though he lived after the Jews returned to Palestine, we doubt that he went with them. Some scholars deny that Daniel wrote this book because they doubt the reality of predictive prophecy. But the book names him as the author and the New Testament confirms it, even in the words of Jesus, who speaks of "Daniel the prophet" (Matt. 24:15). Archaeological evidence supports the book's record of history.
2. Contents. The book of Daniel consists of two parts. The first, including the first six chapters, contains an account of the life of Daniel at the Babylonian court and of various occurrences of the reigns of Nebuchadnezzar, Belshazzar, and Darius. The second part is prophetic. A wide variety of interpretations have been put forth by Bible-believing scholars. The traditional view states that it predicts

various political changes, the coming of the Messiah, the rebuilding of Jerusalem and the temple, their subsequent second destruction, and the Messiah's return to judgment.

OUTLINE OF DANIEL

Title: Prophecies of the Nations of the World and of Israel's Future in Relation to Them in the Plan of God.

Daniel has 12 chapters, 357 verses, and ca. 11,606 words.

E. Hosea. This prophet was a native of Israel, and he addressed his prophecies to the people of the Northern Kingdom. Like the other prophets of this period (such as Isaiah), Hosea seems to have exhorted his people in vain.
1. Authorship. It seems certain that the prophet Hosea actually wrote this book. God

instructed him to marry a prostitute as an object lesson of God's persistent love for Israel. This makes Hosea's prophetic message intensely personal.

2. Contents. The book consists of threats and denunciations against the wickedness of the Israelites, mingled with predictions of the final restoration of God's people. Hosea's prophecies are obscure and difficult because of their brief and condensed style, their sudden transitions from one subject to another, and the indistinct nature of their allusions. Hosea is remarkable for his intensity of passion, both in wrath and in tenderness.

OUTLINE OF HOSEA

Hosea has 14 chapters, 197 verses, and ca. 5,175 words.

■

F. Joel. In Hebrew, this prophet's name means "Yahweh is God." Scholars disagree about the time of this prophet's ministry; but most believe that he lived around 400 B.C., while the Jews were still under the power of the Persian Empire.

1. Authorship. Some Bible critics of the nineteenth century supposed that several authors wrote this book. More recent researchers believe it was all penned by Joel, though some later scribes may have changed a few verses.

2. Contents. The book of Joel takes occasion from a plague of locusts to appeal to the Jews to repent, threatens them with destruction otherwise, and predicts the final glory of the Jewish nation. However, Joel does not refer to known historical events specifically enough to fix the date of his book.

OUTLINE OF JOEL

C. Judgment upon the nations. 3:1–17
1. The avenging of wrongs committed
against the Jews 3:1–3
2. Judgment upon
Phoenicia 3:4–8
3. World judgment 3:9–17
D. The blessings following the
judgment 3:18–21

*Joel has 3 chapters, 73 verses, and ca.
2,034 words.*

■

G. Amos. The prophet Amos must have written this book soon after the events he describes in it. He prophesied under King Uzziah of Judah and Jeroboam II of Israel. (*See* "Chronology.") Although Amos was a native of Judah, he prophesied in Israel.

1. Authorship. This book tells us that Amos lived in Tekoa, about 19 km. (12 mi.) south of Jerusalem. He earned his living as a shepherd and a tender of "sycamore" trees (a fruit tree quite different from the sycamores of North America). Yet he had learned a great deal about the history of Israel, as we see from the many civic and religious symbols that crop up in his book.

2. Contents. Israel neglected the worship of God and indulged in extravagant luxury. Rich merchants oppressed the poor and worshiped the pagan idols that Jeroboam I had introduced to the nation. God brought Amos into this situation to warn the Israelites of God's anger, and judgment to come.

OUTLINE OF AMOS

**I. PROPHECIES AGAINST THE
NATIONS**   **1:1—2:16**
A. Superscription and
proclamation 1:1–2
B. Indictment of neighboring
nations . . . . 1:3—2:3
C. Indictment of Judah 2:4–5
D. Indictment of Israel 2:6–16

**II. THREE SERMONS AGAINST
ISRAEL**   **3:1—6:14**
A. A declaration of judgment . . 3:1–15
B. The depravity of Israel 4:1–13
C. A lamentation for Israel's sin and
doom . . . . 5:1—6:14

**III. FIVE VISIONS OF ISRAEL'S
CONDITION**   **7:1—9:10**
A. The devouring locusts 7:1–3

B. The flaming fire 7:4–6
C. The plumb line 7:7–9
D. Ecclesiastical opposition . . . 7:10–17
E. The basket of ripe fruit 8:1–14
F. The judgment of the Lord . . 9:1–10

**IV. THE PROMISE OF ISRAEL'S
RESTORATION**   **9:11–15**

*Amos has 9 chapters, 146 verses, and ca.
4,217 words.*

■

H. Obadiah. This short book of prophecy tells us nothing specific about Obadiah's native land or the time in which he lived. It denounces the Edomites for taking advantage of the Jews when Judah was under attack, and it predicts that God will restore the glory of His people.

1. Authorship. The first nine verses of this book resemble Jeremiah 49, and so both prophets may have used some statements from earlier prophetic documents. But it's clear that Obadiah wrote and organized this book on his own.

2. Contents. As we've already noted, Obadiah directs his attention to the Edomites. He condemns them for joining the other enemies of Judah to plunder and burn the city of Jerusalem. He warns that God will judge the Edomites for their actions.

OUTLINE OF OBADIAH

I. SUPERSCRIPTION   **V. 1A**

**II. NATIONS ARRAYED AGAINST
EDOM**   **V. 1B**

**III. PUBLIC ENEMY NUMBER ONE
ARRAIGNED**   **VV. 2–7**

IV. EDOM INDICTED   **VV. 8–14**
A. The Judge's intention . . . . . . vv. 8–9
B. The case against Edom . . . . vv. 10–14

V. EDOM SENTENCED   **VV. 15–20**
A. Judgment . . . . vv. 15–16
B. Vindication . . . . vv. 17–20

VI. THE LORD TO BE KING V. 21

*Obadiah has 1 chapter, 21 verses, and ca.
670 words.*

■

43

**OUTLINE OF THE BOOKS
OF THE BIBLE**

I. Jonah. This is the story of an eighth-century prophet who ignored God's call to preach against Nineveh. It narrates how God prepared a great fish to swallow Jonah, and how Jonah had a change of heart. It also describes the prophet's bitterness toward God after the city repented of its evil and found forgiveness.

1. Authorship. Tradition says that Jonah himself wrote this book, but the book does not name him as its author. Some scholars think it is a book *about* Jonah, but not written *by* Jonah.

2. Contents. This book teaches impressively that God will forgive the wicked if they repent. Perhaps God intended the mission of Jonah to have a reforming effect upon the Israelites themselves after his return. They assuredly needed a reform, for in the time of Jonah they generally worshiped the golden calves at Bethel and Dan. But we have no proof that Jonah's teachings produced any effect upon his countrymen, or that he made any effort to sway them.

J. Micah. The name of this prophet is a shortened form of *Mîckayahû,* which means "Who is like Yahweh?" He declared God's Word under the reigns of Kings Jotham, Ahaz, and Hezekiah in Israel and Kings Pekah and Hoshea of Judah. (*See* "Chronology.")

1. Authorship. Some Bible critics doubt that Micah wrote the entire book, because the prophecies seem too sketchy and disjointed. But this argument is weak. It is more reasonable to accept the book's own witness that Micah wrote it (1:1).

2. Contents. Micah declares God's anger against both Israel and Judah. He delivered his prophecies at different times, and we find it rather difficult to follow the historical sequence of the book.

OUTLINE OF JONAH

I. FLEEING   1:1–17
A. The Lord's command...... 1:1–2
B. A ship to Tarshish......... 1:3
C. A storm at sea............ 1:4–14
1. Asleep during a storm ... 1:4–6
2. The culprit found 1:7–10
3. Sailors in distress 1:11–14
D. Cast overboard........... 1:15–17

II. PRAYING   2:1–10
A. Cast out................. 2:1–4
B. Brought up 2:5–6
C. Paying vows 2:7–9
D. Delivered............... 2:10

III. PREACHING   3:1–10
A. The Lord's second command................. 3:1–2
B. Declaring the message 3:3–4
C. Nineveh's repentance...... 3:5–9
1. In sackcloth and ashes... 3:5–6
2. The king's decree 3:7–9
D. Judgment withheld........ 3:10

IV. LEARNING   4:1–11
A. Complaint............... 4:1–3
B. The gourd and the worm... 4:4–7
C. The wind and the sun...... 4:8
D. The lesson 4:9–11

Jonah has 4 chapters, 48 verses, and ca. 1,321 words.

OUTLINE OF MICAH

Superscription 1:1

I. APPROACHING JUDGMENT OF ISRAEL AND JUDAH   1:2–16
A. The call to attention....... 1:2
B. Jehovah's coming announced and described.................. 1:3–4
C. The sins of Jerusalem representative of Judah.................... 1:5
D. Fearful consequences..... 1:6–7
E. Micah's vision of judgment. 1:8–16

II. DOOM OF THE UNGODLY 2:1—3:12
A. Woe to land thieves 2:1–5
B. Preaching thieves 2:6–13
1. Efforts to stop the preaching of the true prophet 2:6
2. False preaching that the Spirit of Jehovah is straitened 2:7
3. The insecurity problem .. 2:8–13
C. False leaders denounced ... 3:1–7
1. Micah's answer......... 3:1
2. Wicked oppressors...... 3:2–3
3. Jehovah would not hear.. 3:4
4. More false prophets 3:5–7
D. Micah's consciousness of power from the Spirit 3:8
E. "Sin is a reproach"........ 3:9–12

III. VISION OF HOPE THROUGH THE COMING ONE   4:1—5:15
A. Final triumph of Jerusalem. 4:1—5:1
1. Revival of true religion and return to Jehovah................. 4:1–2
2. Peace and prosperity 4:3–5
3. Return of those in captivity promised 4:6–7
4. Jerusalem to be restored to greater splendor and power 4:8
5. Redemption preceded by suffering for sin................... 4:9–10

6. Enemies to see Jehovah's vindication of his people. 4:11–12
7. Victory after siege . . . . . . 4:13—5:1
B. Coming mighty leader to be born in Bethlehem and to restore the remnant of Jacob 5:2–15
1. The Messiah to be born in Bethlehem 5:2–3
2. The Messiah's beneficent reign. 5:4–7
3. Spiritual Israel to become a great conqueror 5:8–9
4. Spiritual Israel to be deprived of supposed strength and help. . 5:10–15

IV. LAWSUIT OF JEHOVAH 6:1—7:20
A. First complaint of Jehovah . 6:1–5
B. Israel's first reply 6:6–8
C. Second complaint of Jehovah 6:9–16
D. Israel's second reply. 7:1–10
E. Israel's promised blessing . . 7:11–13
F. Final plea for Israel 7:14–17
G. The triumph of grace. 7:18–20
1. The forgiving LORD 7:18
2. The redeeming LORD 7:19
3. The faithful LORD. 7:20

Micah has 7 chapters, 105 verses, and ca. 3,153 words.

K. Nahum. The name of this prophet literally means "Consoler." He brought God's message of comfort to Judah just before the Babylonians invaded it.

1. Authorship. Nahum was born at Elkosh, a village of Galilee. He tells the people of Judah that God will destroy the city of Nineveh because its people had opposed the Jews for so long. Archaeologists tell us that Nineveh fell in 612 B.C., so Nahum must have delivered his prophecy shortly before that time.

2. Contents. The prophecy of Nahum is a single poem of great eloquence, sublimity, and ardor. Its theme is "The burden of Nineveh"— that is, the coming punishment of that city and empire in retribution for the Assyrians' cruel treatment of the Jews.

OUTLINE OF NAHUM

I. GOD'S MAJESTY 1:1–14

II. THE COMING DESTRUCTION OF NINEVEH 1:15—2:13

III. THE REASON FOR NINEVEH'S FALL 3:1–19

Nahum has 3 chapters, 47 verses, and ca. 1,285 words.

L. Habakkuk. This prophet lived just before Nebuchadnezzar took the city of Jerusalem. His book denounces the sins of the Jews and predicts that the Babylonians will conquer them as a result.

1. Authorship. We know virtually nothing about the prophet himself. His name seems to come from a Hebrew word that means "to embrace," and Jerome believed *Habakkuk* literally meant "the embracer."

2. Contents. As we have already mentioned, most of this book is a stern warning for the people of Judah. However, it closes with a beautiful hymn of petition and praise that the Jews might have sung in their temple services.

OUTLINE OF HABAKKUK

I. INTRODUCTION 1:1

II. THE PROPHET'S COMPLAINT OF UNCHECKED VIOLENCE IN JUDAH 1:2–4

III. THE LORD'S ANSWER: THE CHALDEAN IS HIS INSTRUMENT OF PUNISHMENT 1:5–11

IV. A SECOND PROBLEM: THE CHALDEANS ARE MORE WICKED THAN THE JUDEANS 1:12—2:1

V. THE LORD'S SECOND ANSWER: THE PURPOSE IS CERTAIN AND FAITH WILL BE REWARDED 2:2–4

VI. FIVE WOES UPON INIQUITY, WHETHER JEWISH OR CHALDEAN 2:5–20

VII. A VISION OF DIVINE JUDGMENT 3:1–16

VIII. THE TRIUMPH OF FAITH 3:17–19

Habakkuk has 3 chapters, 56 verses, and ca. 1,476 words.

M. Zephaniah. The name of this prophet means "the Lord hides." He foretold the downfall of Judah, as well as God's wrath for the Philistines and the other pagan neighbors of Judah.

1. Authorship. Some Bible students suppose that Zephaniah's father, "Hizkiah" (1:1), was actually King Hezekiah of Judah. But we have no positive proof of this. Zephaniah prophesied during King Josiah's reign. (*See* "Chronology.")

2. Contents. Zephaniah lashes his people's hypocrisy and idolatrous worship. Even though King Josiah tried to reform them, they continued to wallow in their sins. Zephaniah foretold that this would lead them to destruction, though there would be a restoration afterwards.

He was the first prophet to address the Jews who returned from the Exile in Babylon, beginning his work in the second year of King Darius (1:1). He urged the Jews to finish rebuilding the temple so that they could restore their traditional ways of worship.

1. Authorship. We have no reason to doubt that the prophet Haggai actually wrote this brief book. It expresses a very natural concern of the time—to renew Israel's cultic covenant with God.

2. Contents. The Jews had begun rebuilding the temple when they first returned to Jerusalem. But their neighbors harassed and discouraged them, and they had suspended work on the project. So God sent Haggai to bolster the people's spirits and prod them to finish the task. Under Haggai's preaching the Jews completed the temple in four years.

OUTLINE OF ZEPHANIAH

Zephaniah has 3 chapters, 53 verses, and ca. 1,617 words.

N. Haggai. We know very little about the life of Haggai, whose name means "festive."

OUTLINE OF HAGGAI

Haggai has 2 chapters, 38 verses, and ca. 1,131 words.

O. Zechariah. This prophet lived during the time of Haggai and began work in the second year of Darius' reign (1:1). Like Haggai,

OUTLINE OF THE BOOKS OF THE BIBLE

Zechariah encouraged his people to rebuild the temple and restore their nation under God.

1. Authorship. Zechariah delivered all of his prophecies at Jerusalem after the Jews returned from captivity in 539 B.C. (*See* "Chronology.") Besides that, we know very little about him. He was a visionary prophet to whom was given vivid insight into God's plans for the future.

2. Contents. Zechariah not only exhorted the people to rebuild God's temple; he gave them hope for the restored nation of Israel. He devotes over a chapter of his book to instructing his people in the ways of holy fasting to prepare them for God's commission.

OUTLINE OF ZECHARIAH

Zechariah has 14 chapters, 211 verses, and ca. 6,444 words.

P. Malachi. This name is probably a short form of the Hebrew name *Malachiah,* which means "the messenger of the Lord." Malachi was the last prophet to preach to the Jews after they returned from the Exile and indeed the last prophet of the Old Testament era.

1. Authorship. The book of Malachi indicates that the Jews had rebuilt the temple, restored their worship, and then had fallen away from God again. This means that Malachi probably wrote late in the fifth century B.C.

2. Contents. If, as seems to be the case, Malachi prophesied in the time of Nehemiah, the immediate purpose of his prophecy would have been to uphold and perfect the reforms introduced by Nehemiah when he returned from his visit to the Persian court.

OUTLINE OF MALACHI

Malachi has 4 chapters, 55 verses, and ca. 1,782 words.

VI. The Deuterocanon, or "Apocrypha." This is the proper place to discuss the deutero-canonical books, since they were written between the time of the Exile and the birth of Christ. Collectively, these books are also called the *Apocrypha,* a Greek term that properly means "hidden" or "secret things." Many spurious sacred books were put forth in early times, often claiming a mystical or secret quality. Many Jewish and Christian writings came over the years to be called "apocryphal."

OUTLINE OF THE BOOKS OF THE BIBLE

The deuterocanon—which Protestants call "the Apocrypha"—consists of books written at various times from about 300 B.C. to 30 B.C. They include several valuable accounts of intertestamental history, along with didactic and devotional compositions. In 1546 A.D., the Council of Trent declared these books to be authoritative Scripture. However, Protestant churches have never accepted these books as part of the canon.

Judith, Tobit, 1 Maccabees, and Ecclesiasticus appear to have been first written in Hebrew, but were translated into Greek. The rest of the deuterocanon was written in Greek by Alexandrian Jews. The Jews never admitted these books into their canon, but Alexandrian Jews wrote them in the same rolls with the Septuagint, and hence they found a degree of respect with some of the early Christian fathers.

Luther's whole German Bible (1534) printed the deuterocanonical books separately from the canon, asserting that they were not inspired, but profitable. The Anglican 39 Articles spoke of them the same way. The Council of Trent formally received them all except the two books of Esdras and the Prayer of Manasses.

We may very briefly describe the deuterocanonical books as follows:

A. First Esdras. This is mainly an historical account of the return from the Babylonian Captivity and the reestablishment of the temple and its worship. It was compiled mostly from Nehemiah, Ezra, and Chronicles.

B. Second Esdras. This book contains some visions and revelations of the early Jewish rabbis. It is a helpful specimen of Jewish thought and literature a little before the time of Christ.

C. Tobit. This pious fiction about good and evil spirits teaches several lessons in morals.

D. Judith. This is a pious tale of a woman who murdered the Assyrian(?) general Holofernes. It aims to show God's ability to deliver His people from dire circumstances.

E. The Rest of the book of Esther. This section was probably written by an Alexandrian Jew who wanted to embellish the book of Esther itself. These additional chapters are unreliable as history, but they do show us more of the Jews' high regard for Esther.

F. The Wisdom of Solomon. This is a collection of teachings in a system of moral philosophy, supposedly written in the style of Solomon. It reflects the morality of the book of Proverbs, but scholars do not believe that Solomon wrote it. It seems to have been composed in Greek about the first century B.C.

G. Ecclesiasticus. This collection of proverbs and moral sayings also imitates the style of Solomon. However, it contains more acute thought and elegance of expression than the Wisdom of Solomon.

H. Baruch. This book was supposed to have been written by Jeremiah's scribe, Baruch. It offers encouragement to the Jews in exile.

I. The Song of the Three Children; the History of Susanna; Bel and the Dragon. These are collections of stories about the prophet Daniel and his friends. They all extol the virtues of righteous living.

J. The Prayer of Manasses. This is a pious composition, but wholly spurious.

K. The books of Maccabees. These two narratives contain much valuable historical matter about the valiant priests, soldiers, and rulers of the Maccabean family. (This surname is probably derived from the Hebrew, *macaba*—"a hammer.") The first book of Maccabees is a history of the Jews from the beginning of the reign of Antiochus Epiphanes to the death of Simon Maccabeus. The second book begins its account just before the time of the first book, and goes over much of the same ground. It contradicts the first book and has less historical authority.

There are three other so-called books of Maccabees; but they have never been reckoned canonical, except the third (by the Greek Orthodox Church).

VII. New Testament Historical Books. The historical books of the New Testament comprise the four Gospels and the book of Acts. The name *gospel* is Anglo-Saxon, from *god* ("good") and *spel* ("word" or "tidings"). It is a literal translation of the Greek name *Euangelion,* which was evidently the title which the authors gave to these books. Bible students often refer to the first three Gospels together as the "Synoptics" [Greek, *synoptikos*—"yielding a single view"] because they give a consecutive account of Christ's life and actions, whereas John concentrates on His character and office. The four Gospels thus give an authentic account of what Christ said and did, and of what He felt and meant.

The book of Acts advances the story about thirty years beyond the Crucifixion. Except for what Acts tells us, and incidental statements in the Epistles, we have to depend upon

OUTLINE OF THE BOOKS OF THE BIBLE

later church and secular history for knowledge of the progress of Christianity.

A. Matthew. Part, at least, of the Gospel of Matthew was probably first written in the Syriac, Syro-Chaldaic, Aramaic, or popular Hebrew language. A second-century writer named Papias affirms this, and the Gospel reads as if it were written for Jews rather than Gentiles. Jerome asserts that he found an Aramaic copy of this Gospel in the library of Pamphilus at Caesarea and translated it into Greek and Latin. Scholars have in the past supposed that Matthew wrote his Gospel over again in Greek some years later, with a view to making his narrative more widely useful. It was most likely written in Palestine, and the whole texture of the book confirms that its primary purpose was to convince the Jews that Jesus was the Messiah.

1. Authorship. Christian tradition says that the apostle Matthew wrote this book, and we have no reason to doubt it. His apparent use of Mark's Gospel as a source is no problem; though himself an eyewitness of Jesus, he would naturally have welcomed Mark's pioneer work of putting the story of Jesus' ministry into shape, and availed himself of it. As a tax collector, Matthew would have mastered the art of writing and would have given careful attention to details.

2. Contents. As we have already said, Matthew wrote this account of Jesus' life to convince the Jews that Jesus was their Messiah. However, we also see a strong appeal to new Christians in the book, as Matthew stresses Jesus' exhortations to His followers.

OUTLINE OF MATTHEW

43

OUTLINE OF THE BOOKS OF THE BIBLE

Matthew has 28 chapters, 1,071 verses, and ca. 23,684 words.

B. Mark. This Gospel was recorded sometime before Matthew was written. An ancient tradition says that Mark was only the scribe for this book, and the apostle Peter dictated it to him while they were both at Rome. It evidently embodies eyewitness testimony, and was probably composed in Greek (although some Roman Catholic theologians have held that it was first written in Latin).

1. Authorship. The ancient church fathers agreed that John Mark, Peter's assistant, wrote down this account of Jesus' life. Mark came from Jerusalem (Acts 12:12), and must have spoken the Aramaic language, which the Greek style of the Gospel often seems to echo. The outline of this Gospel resembles Peter's sermon at Caesarea (Acts 10:34–43), which supports the theory that Peter dictated it. Or, as some traditions say, Mark may have written it after Peter's death. The book itself does not say who wrote it.

2. Contents. This Gospel was written for gentile Christians; we can tell by the careful way Mark explains religious terms that would have been familiar to the Jews. Clement of Alexandria says that the Christians of Rome asked Mark to write this Gospel to preserve what they had been hearing from Peter. This may well be so.

OUTLINE OF MARK

Mark has 16 chapters, 678 verses, and ca. 15,171 words.

C. Luke. This Gospel gives the fullest account of Jesus' birth, youth, and ministry that we have. It was the first of two volumes, the second being the book of Acts. Both books were addressed to Theophilus, who probably was a community leader or government official.

1. Authorship. The ancient church fathers tell us that Luke, a companion of Paul, wrote this Gospel. Paul called Luke "the beloved physician" (Col. 4:14). Undoubtedly the early Christians respected him highly.

2. Contents. The Gospel of Luke focuses on Jesus' ministry as the Savior. Luke shows how Jesus lifted lost men and women out of their sins and brought them back to God. He describes some events that the other Gospels do not; no doubt he distilled this information

OUTLINE OF THE BOOKS OF THE BIBLE

from the apostles' preaching or from his conversations with other eyewitnesses.

OUTLINE OF LUKE

Luke has 24 chapters, 1,151 verses, and ca. 25,944 words.

IV. John. We find a remarkable contrast between the Gospel of John and the Synoptics. The fourth-century writer Theodore of Mopsuestia said that the apostle John wrote this book in Ephesus. Theodore writes: "It now occurred to the Christians of Asia that St. John was a more credible witness than all others, forasmuch as from the beginning, even before Matthew, he was with the Lord, and enjoyed more abundant grace through the love which the Lord bore to him. And they brought him the books [i.e., the Gospels of Matthew, Mark, and Luke], and sought to know his opinion of them. Then he praised the writers for their veracity, and said that a few things had been omitted by them, and that all but a little of the teaching of the most important miracles was recorded. And he added that they who discourse on the coming of Christ in the flesh ought not to omit to speak of His divinity, lest in course of time men who are used to such discourses might suppose that Christ was only what He appeared to be. Thereupon the brethren exhorted him to write at once the things which he judged the most important for instruction, and which he saw omitted by the others. And he did so. And therefore at the beginning he discoursed about the doctrine of the divinity of Christ, judging this to be the necessary beginning of the Gospel and from it he went on to the incarnation."

1. Authorship. Some modern scholars doubt that the apostle John wrote this book, because he was an unlearned fisherman. But we should not think it impossible that God could inspire John to write a book of such depth and beauty; though he was a fisherman, he was not necessarily lacking in insight or power to think and express himself. Irenaeus and other early writers affirm that John was the author.

2. Contents. The material in the Gospel suggests that, while preparing a history of Jesus' life that would supplement the three previous ones, John wanted to present the teachings of Christ in a way that would refute certain heretical doctrines that were then

43

OUTLINE OF THE BOOKS OF THE BIBLE

prevailing among the Christians. These were the doctrines of the Gnostics, and especially of Cerinthus, who believed that Jesus was only a man inhabited by the spirit of Christ. John presented the story of Jesus' life in a very compelling way, which must have reclaimed the attention of the Christians who had fallen under the Gnostics' exotic teachings.

OUTLINE OF JOHN

John has 21 chapters, 878 verses, and ca. 19,099 words.

V. Acts of the Apostles. This book takes up the history of Christianity and continues it for a period of about thirty years, to the arrival of Paul at Rome. Like the Gospel of John, it was written later than some of the Epistles. Luke wrote the second half of it from his own observation of the facts narrated.

1. Authorship. This book does not identify its author, but church tradition says it was Luke. The opening verses link it with Luke's Gospel.

2. Contents. The book of Acts does two crucial things: It describes the Holy Spirit's work in the lives of the apostles, and it shows how God brought the Gentiles into the early church. Thus it proved that Jesus fulfilled His promise to send the Holy Spirit to His followers, and it silenced the arguments of Jewish Christians who opposed the easy admission of Gentiles to the church.

OUTLINE OF ACTS

Acts has 28 chapters, 1,007 verses, and ca. 24,250 words.

VIII. The Epistles. A collection of letters on theology and practical religion forms the second great division of the New Testament. These 21 letters were written by five of the apostles—Paul, James, Peter, John, and Jude. Fourteen of them were written by Paul. The apostles wrote these epistles to congregations of Christian converts or to individuals upon different occasions. But they agree as to facts and doctrines, and they thus constitute an authentic and invaluable commentary on the meaning of the life and teachings of Christ.

The epistles do not stand in the order in which they were written, but in the order of the importance of the audiences addressed. Thus, Romans comes first because Rome was the capital of the empire. Corinthians comes next, because Corinth was the next most important city, and so on. Paul's epistles to individuals follow those to collective audiences, and our Bibles also place them in an order of dignity: first the letter to Timothy, the favorite disciple; then the letter to Titus, the evangelist; and then the letter to Philemon, a private Christian. Hebrews appears last, because there is good reason to doubt whether it is by Paul.

After Paul's epistles come the seven "catholic," or general, epistles—so called because they were addressed to Christians generally. They appear roughly in the order of their length.

Christians adopted this order of the epistles as early as the time of Eusebius in the beginning of the third century. Our modern editions of the Bible retain this order because of the uncertainty that exists about the precise dates of some of the epistles, and the difficulty of introducing any change in an order of such long standing and universal acceptance.

A. Romans. Paul wanted to contact the church at Rome for various reasons. Relatives and friends of his were connected with it. It was an important church, because Rome was the capital of the empire. This majestic epistle is a spontaneous outpouring of the great apostle to Christians he had never seen.

1. Authorship. Paul wrote this letter on his third missionary journey, probably while he was staying in Corinth. Paul hoped he would visit Rome someday; but first he had to return to Jerusalem with an offering to help the persecuted Christians in that city. Little did he know that his Jewish enemies would arrest him there and send him to Rome in chains.

2. Contents. In this letter, Paul addresses himself to Jewish converts and Gentile converts alike. He sets forth a body of Christian doctrine so broadly conceived, so fully stated that it would accomplish all that Paul could do if he were able to preach in Rome.

OUTLINE OF ROMANS

Romans has 16 chapters, 433 verses, and ca. 9,447 words.

B. First Corinthians. Paul established the church at Corinth on his second missionary journey, when he stayed a year and a half in that city. While this church was zealous and prosperous, it was also prone to great troubles. Corinth was a wealthy commercial city; it was famous even among the heathen for its sensual worship of Venus. The church itself consisted of Jews, Greeks, and other Gentiles. It felt the temptations of heathen vice from without and tendencies to bigotry and idle philosophizing within.

OUTLINE OF THE BOOKS OF THE BIBLE

While Paul was still at Ephesus during his third missionary journey, he received unpleasant news from Corinth. Members of Chloe's household told him of the spread of immorality and dissension in that church. Nearly at the same time, three members of the church came to obtain advice on some of the very points Paul's messages had mentioned: marriage, things sacrificed to idols, spiritual gifts, and charitable collections. To deal with all these matters, Paul wrote the First Epistle to the Corinthians.

1. Authorship. The book identifies the Apostle Paul as its author, and the early church fathers such as Clement of Rome confirm this. The content of the letter also proves Paul's authorship of First Corinthians.

2. Contents. When most people reflect on this letter, they think of Paul's great rhapsody on Christian love in the thirteenth chapter. But the entire book contains a wealth of practical advice on Christian conduct, designed to help the Corinthians deal with the problems in their congregation.

OUTLINE OF 1 CORINTHIANS

First Corinthians has 16 chapters, 437 verses, and ca. 9,489 words.

C. Second Corinthians. Paul wrote his second letter to the Corinthian church within a year after the first one. Having dispatched the first epistle, Paul went to Troas, where he expected to meet Titus and to learn the effect of his admonitions upon the church at Corinth. Titus was not there, so Paul went on into Macedonia. There he found Titus and received the information desired. The news was partly good and partly bad. Many of the Corinthian Christians had corrected their beliefs and conduct according to Paul's instructions in the first epistle. But some of them still opposed the Apostle's authority and teaching. So this second letter defends Paul's motives, authority, and labors. It also gives directions about taking collections for the poor of the church at Jerusalem. This epistle was written in Macedonia (probably at Philippi).

1. Authorship. Some modern biblical scholars have debated whether Paul wrote this entire letter at one time. They think that 2 Corinthians 6:14—7:1 might have been inserted later, since it seems to break the letter's train of thought. In spite of this, they agree that Paul wrote the letter, and the book itself says so.

Outline of 2 Corinthians

I. THE CONCILIATION   **1:1—7:16**
- A. **Paul's distress mutual** 1:1–7
  - 1. **Salutation** 1:1–2
  - 2. **Adoration** 1:3
  - 3. **Agonizing tribulation**.... 1:4–7
- B. **Paul's desperation relieved** . 1:8–14
- C. **Paul's diversion justified** ... 1:15—2:17
  - 1. **The plan contemplated** .. 1:15–16
  - 2. **The plan criticized** 1:17
  - 3. **The plan comprehended** . 1:18–22
  - 4. **The plan changed** .... 1:23—2:4
  - 5. **The plan chastened** 2:5–11
  - 6. **The plan consummated** .. 2:12–17
- D. **Paul's dispensation superior** 3:1–18
  - 1. **In documentation** 3:1–3
  - 2. **In dynamism** 3:4–6
  - 3. **In degree** 3:7–9
  - 4. **In destination** 3:10–11
  - 5. **In diagnosis** 3:12–17
  - 6. **In solution** 3:18
- E. **Paul's dualism explained** ... 4:1–18
  - 1. **The hidden and the open**. 4:1–2
  - 2. **The blinded and the enlightened** 4:3–4
  - 3. **Slaves and the Master** ... 4:5
  - 4. **Darkness and light** 4:6
  - 5. **The frail and the Mighty** . 4:7
  - 6. **Trials and triumphs** 4:8–10
  - 7. **Death and life** 4:11–12
  - 8. **The written and the spoken** 4:13
  - 9. **The past and the future** .. 4:14
  - 10. **Grace and thanksgiving**. . 4:15
  - 11. **The outer and the inner man** 4:16
  - 12. **Affliction and glory** 4:17
  - 13. **The seen and the unseen** . 4:18a
  - 14. **The temporal and the eternal** 4:18b
- F. **Paul's dedication motivated** 5:1—6:10
  - 1. **Motivated by knowledge** . 5:1–9
  - 2. **Motivated by judgment**. . 5:10
  - 3. **Motivated by fear** 5:11
  - 4. **Motivated by unselfishness** 5:12–13
  - 5. **Motivated by love** 5:14–15
  - 6. **Motivated by regeneration** 5:16–17
  - 7. **Motivated by reconciliation** 5:18–21
  - 8. **Motivated by time** 6:1–2
  - 9. **Motivated by suffering** .. 6:3–10
- G. **Paul's dissuasion urged** .... 6:11—7:1
  - 1. **The thesis: Change your attitude toward me** 6:11–13
  - 2. **The antithesis: Change your attitude toward the world** 6:14–16
  - 3. **The synthesis: Obey and live** .... 6:17—7:1
- H. **Paul's delight exemplified** .. 7:2–16
  - 1. **Paul's high regard** 7:2–4
  - 2. **Why such regard** 7:5–16

II. THE COLLECTION   **8:1—9:15**
- A. **The first reason for its completion**............... 8:1–8
- B. **The second reason for its completion: the example of Christ**........ 8:9
- C. **The third reason for its completion: the requirements of honor**....... 8:10—9:5
- D. **The fourth reason for its completion: the requirements of stewardship**.............. 9:6–15

III. THE CREDENTIALS   **10:1—13:14**

Second Corinthians has 13 chapters, 257 verses, and ca. 6,092 words.

D. Galatians. On this third missionary journey, Paul went into Galatia and Phrygia, where he made an inspection tour of the churches, exhorting and advising as he found needful. He then proceeded to Ephesus. While there, he heard from the Galatian churches that they were being troubled by persons who were teaching doctrines of a Jewish sort, insisting on circumcision for salvation. These persons were also attacking the authority of Paul.

1. Authorship. This letter identifies Paul as the author, and its contents support that. It agrees with Paul's teachings in other epistles.

2. Contents. This letter refutes the teachings of the Judaizers, who wanted the new Christians to be circumcised and to adopt other Jewish rituals.

Outline of Galatians

I. INTRODUCTION   **1:1–9**
- A. **Salvation** 1:1–5
- B. **Theme of the epistle** 1:6–9

II. PAUL'S APOSTLESHIP DEFENDED   **1:10—2:21**
- A. **A special apostleship affirmed**................ 1:10–17

Galatians has 6 chapters, 149 verses, and ca. 3,098 words.

E. Ephesians. After Paul arrived in Rome, he wrote the Epistle to the Ephesians in about A.D. 61. So it is one of the last items of his life's work. This epistle has the same general character of the Epistle to the Romans, and for somewhat similar reasons. It was written to fortify the Christian faith and practice of the church at Ephesus.

1. Authorship. Few scholars would deny that Paul wrote this letter. There are reasons for thinking it was a circular to several churches, of which that at Ephesus was one. The letter clearly identifies Paul as the author, and its content fits the general pattern of Paul's work.

2. Contents. In this letter, Paul emphasizes that Christ is the head of the church. He exhorts his fellow Christians to live worthy of their high calling as Jesus' disciples.

OUTLINE OF EPHESIANS

OUTLINE OF THE BOOKS OF THE BIBLE

D. The wise walk .... 5:15—6:9
E. The Christian walk as a
   warfare 6:10–20
   1. Being strong in the Lord . 6:10–17
   2. A prayer for all 6:18–20
F. Closing greetings 6:21–24

*Ephesians has 6 chapters, 155 verses, and
ca. 3,039 words.*

F. Philippians. Paul established the first
European congregation of the church in the
Greek city of Philippi. He wrote this letter
from prison to encourage his friends in the
Philippian church.

1. Authorship. This letter names Paul as
its author, and the early church fathers testify
that this is true. The letter certainly reflects
Paul's love for the Philippian church.

2. Contents. Paul expresses his thanks to
the Philippians for a gift they had sent him in
prison. In the process, he warns them to correct some problems arising in the church.

OUTLINE OF PHILIPPIANS

I. *PAUL'S GRATITUDE AND
   PRAYER*   *1:1–11*

II. *WARNINGS AGAINST FALSE
    DOCTRINE*   *1:12–18*

III. *PAUL'S PLAN TO RETURN 1:19–30*
   A. Hope for good results from his imprison-
      ment 1:19–26
   B. Words of encouragement ... 1:27–30

IV. *THE LORDSHIP OF
    CHRIST*   *2:1–18*
   A. "He humbled Himself" 2:1–11
   B. Therefore "be blameless and
      harmless" 2:12–18

V. *A RECOMMENDATION OF
   TIMOTHY AND
   EPAPHRODITUS*   *2:19–30*

VI. *A HOPEFUL FUTURE   3:1—4:23*
   A. Paul's zeal to "press on" ... 3:1–21
   B. "Rejoice . . . and think on these
      things" 4:1–9
   C. Words of gratitude 4:10–20
   D. Final greetings 4:21–23

*Philippians has 4 chapters, 104 verses,
and ca. 2,002 words.*

G. Colossians. Paul wrote this epistle at
about the same time as Ephesians and probably sent it to the church at Colossae by the
same messengers, Tychicus and Onesimus.
Epaphras, the teacher of the church at Colossae, was at Rome with Paul at the time and
had told him about the church. Besides, some
of Paul's personal friends lived at Colossae, so
he was eager to advise and encourage the
church there. Paul requested that the Colossians share this letter with the church at
Laodicea, which presumably wanted to consult him on the points he discusses in it.

1. Authorship. A few scholars doubt that
Paul wrote this letter, but their arguments are
not very convincing. The letter is true to
Paul's teachings, and its description of the
church of Colossae fits what Paul would have
known about the congregation.

2. Contents. Some leaders of the Colossian
church said that Gentiles had to adopt Jewish
rituals and learn to worship angels when they
became Christians. At the same time, these
leaders were dabbling in Gnostic philosophy—*theosophy,* we should call it—and skirt-
ing very close to heresy. Paul attempted to
correct these trends with the letter.

OUTLINE OF COLOSSIANS

I. *INTRODUCTION*   *1:1–2*

II. *THE NATURE OF CHRIST'S
    LORDSHIP*   *1:3—2:7*
   A. Thanksgiving for the Colossians' faith in
      Christ. 1:3–8
   B. Prayer for their growth in
      Christ. 1:9–14
   C. Christ as Lord 1:15–19
      1. Lord of creation 1:15–17
      2. Lord of the new creation . 1:18–19
   D. Christ as God's reconciler .. 1:20–23
      1. Reconciler of all things .. 1:20
      2. Reconciler of the Colossians
         Christians 1:21–23
   E. Paul: Christ's minister of
      reconciliation 1:24–29
      1. Sharer of Christ's sufferings 1:24
      2. Proclaimer of the Christian
         mystery 1:25–27
      3. Instructor of the saints ... 1:28–29
   F. Paul's concern for the Lycus Valley
      Christians 2:1–7

III. *CHRIST'S LORDSHIP AND THE
     FALSE TEACHING AT
     COLOSSAE*   *2:8—3:4*

OUTLINE OF THE BOOKS OF THE BIBLE

*Colossians has 4 chapters, 95 verses, and
ca. 1,998 words.*

H. First Thessalonians. Of Paul's many epistles that we now have, this one was written first. The church at Thessalonica was the second congregation Paul and his friends founded in Europe, and he wrote this letter from Athens in A.D. 51 or 52.

1. Authorship. We have no doubt that Paul wrote both First and Second Thessalonians. In the book of Acts, Luke tells us about the events surrounding the time Paul wrote them (chap. 18).

2. Contents. In this first letter, Paul reminisces about his earlier work in Thessalonica and encourages the Thessalonians to live holy lives. He also explains the destiny of the dead, giving us one of the most detailed discussions of the Christian hope in the New Testament.

OUTLINE OF 1 THESSALONIANS

*First Thessalonians has 5 chapters, 89
verses, and ca. 1,857 words.*

I. Second Thessalonians. Paul wrote his second epistle to the Thessalonians not long after the first. It is an addition or supplement to the first epistle because the Thessalonians had misunderstood the first one. They had gathered from it that Christ was just about to return in their own lifetime.

1. Authorship. (See the section on First Thessalonians above.)

2. Contents. Paul explains that very troublesome times will come before Christ returns to save His people. He urges his Christian friends to guard against laziness or vain confidence and instructs them in ways they can make the best use of the time that remains.

OUTLINE OF 2 THESSALONIANS

I. INTRODUCTION — 1:1–2

II. ENCOURAGEMENT IN PERSECUTION — 1:3–12
  A. Commendation for steadfastness ... 1:3–4
  B. Explanation of the purpose of persecution ... 1:5–10
  C. Intercession for continued spiritual growth ... 1:11–12

III. INSTRUCTION CONCERNING THE DAY OF THE LORD — 2:1–12
  A. To come in the future ... 2:1–2
  B. To be preceded by definite signs ... 2:3–12

IV. THANKSGIVING AND EXHORTATION — 2:13–17
  A. Praise for their calling ... 2:13–15
  B. Prayer for their comfort and stability ... 2:16–17

V. CONFESSION OF CONFIDENCE — 3:1–5
  A. Request for prayer ... 3:1–2
  B. Reminder of God's faithfulness ... 3:3–5

VI. COMMANDMENTS TO WORK — 3:6–15
  A. Shun the idle ... 3:6
  B. Imitate us ... 3:7–9
  C. Work or do not eat ... 3:10
  D. Exhort the idle ... 3:11–13
  E. Warn and discipline the disobedient ... 3:14–15

VII. CONCLUSION — 3:16–18
  A. Blessing ... 3:16
  B. Paul's signature ... 3:17
  C. Benediction ... 3:18

Second Thessalonians has 3 chapters, 47 verses, and ca. 1042 words.

J. First Timothy. We call the two letters to Timothy and the letter to Titus the "Pastoral Epistles," because they are letters of advice for exercising the pastoral office. While the dates of all three letters are somewhat uncertain, they were probably written toward the close of Paul's life. Paul wrote the first epistle to Timothy while that young Christian missionary was in charge of the church at Ephesus. It consists principally of instructions for exercising his office as Paul's deputy.

1. Authorship. The letter identifies Paul as its author, and despite the doubts of scholars we feel quite certain this is so. Paul took Timothy under his charge very early in the young man's ministry, and here he reviews again for Timothy the proper conduct of pastoral work.

2. Contents. Paul emphasizes the importance of the trust that God has placed in Timothy's hands. He advises the young pastor about the proper function of various classes of people in the Christian congregation.

OUTLINE OF 1 TIMOTHY

I. SALUTATION AND INTRODUCTION — 1:1–20
  A. Salutation, with special notes of authority and hope ... 1:1–2
  B. Charge to Timothy ... 1:3–16
    1. Sound versus false teaching ... 1:3–4
    2. The purpose of sound teaching ... 1:5–7
    3. The true doctrine of the Law ... 1:8–11
    4. Paul's testimony and gospel ... 1:12–16
  C. Doxology ... 1:17
  D. Charge and encouragement 1:18–20

II. EXHORTATIONS AND INSTRUCTIONS TO THE CHURCH OF THE LIVING GOD — 2:1–6:2
  A. To the witnessing church ... 2:1–3:13
    1. Public prayer as related to the missionary purpose of the church ... 2:1–8
    2. Conduct of women as related to the testimony of the church ... 2:9–15
    3. Qualifications of church officers ... 3:1–13
  B. To the church as pillar and ground of the truth ... 3:14–4:5
    1. Its exalted position as organ of the gospel doctrine ... 3:14–15
    2. Hymn of praise: Poetic statement of true doctrine ... 3:16
    3. Prophetic warning of false doctrine ... 4:1–5

OUTLINE OF THE BOOKS OF THE BIBLE

C. To the witnessing individual 4:6—6:2
1. To Timothy, as a good minister 4:6–16
2. To men 5:1
3. To women, especially widows 5:2–16
4. To elders 5:17–25
5. To servants 6:1–2a–c

III. CONCLUSION   6:2D–21
A. A solemn charge 6:2d–15a
1. Warnings against false teachers 6:3–5
2. Right attitudes of true teachers 6:6–10
3. The motives of the man of God 6:11–15a
B. The exalted Christ 6:15b–16
C. Personal admonitions 6:17–21

First Timothy has 6 chapters, 113 verses, and ca. 2,269 words.

K. Second Timothy. Paul wrote this letter primarily to call Timothy back to Rome. But it also contains a kind of spiritual bequest, in case Paul died before Timothy arrived. This consists of general instructions for ministerial duty.

1. Authorship. (See the section on "First Timothy.")

2. Contents. This letter follows much the same pattern as the first. But here Paul emphasizes the need to pass the gospel on to faithful men who would proclaim the Good News to succeeding generations.

OUTLINE OF 2 TIMOTHY

I. SALUTATION AND
INTRODUCTION   1:1–18
A. Salutation of special authority and affection 1:1–2
B. Thanksgiving for Timothy's faith 1:3–5
C. Reminder of responsibility for the gospel 1:6–18
1. The gift of God 1:6–7
2. Challenge to endure afflictions incident to the ministry 1:8–12
3. Challenge to hold fast the form of sound words 1:13–14
4. Personal illustrations of loyalty and opposition 1:15–18

II. THE GOSPEL: A TRUST
REQUIRING
FAITHFULNESS   2:1—3:17
A. To be diligently committed to others 2:1–7
1. As a soldier 2:1–4
2. As an athlete 2:5
3. As a farmer 2:6–7
B. To be firmly guarded and cherished 2:8–26
1. The central truth of the gospel 2:8
2. Paul's example of faithfulness 2:9–10
3. The truth embodied in a "faithful saying" 2:11–13
4. The truth rightly handled 2:14–19
5. The truth applied to the life 2:20–26
C. To be recognized as a bulwark 3:1–17
1. Against apostasy 3:1–9
2. In defense of the faithful 3:10–12
3. The inspired Scriptures: Our confidence 3:13–17

III. CHARGE TO TIMOTHY, AND
CONCLUSION   4:1–22
A. The solemn charge 4:1–5
B. Paul's final testimony 4:6–8
C. His love and concern 4:9–22

Second Timothy has 4 chapters, 83 verses, and ca. 1,703 words.

L. Titus. Paul wrote this letter to Titus, another young minister whom he had left as his deputy in Crete, and to whom he wanted to give a refresher course in pastoral work. Paul offers a great deal of practical advice on the personal ethics of a minister.

1. Authorship. Some scholars doubt that Paul wrote this book because its language and style differ a bit from his other letters. Also, the letter indicates that the churches had developed a rather complex system of administration, and it is supposed that Paul died before that. But these arguments don't change the fact that the letter identifies Paul as its author. It's possible that church administration developed more rapidly than we would have expected. It's also possible that Paul lived longer than we usually suppose, and may have been imprisoned twice. (*See* "Paul and His Journeys.")

2. Contents. Paul explains that sound doctrine should produce a godly life. So a minister like Titus needs to do more than teach the gospel; he must make sure that he and his congregation are putting it into practice.

OUTLINE OF TITUS

I. SALUTATION 1:1–4

II. TITUS' MISSION: TO SET MATTERS IN ORDER 1:5—3:11
A. The appointment and need of the teaching elder.................... 1:5–16
1. Qualifications of elders .. 1:5–9
2. Need for elders to combat error 1:10–16
B. The pastoral work of the teaching elder.................... 2:1—3:11
1. Application of sound doctrine to particular cases............... 2:1–10
2. Proclamation of sound doctrine: The grace of God 2:11–15
3. Demonstration of sound doctrine: The root and the fruit 3:1–11

III. ZEALOUS OF GOOD WORKS 3:12–15

Titus has 3 chapters, 46 verses, and ca. 921 words.

▬▬▬

M. Philemon. Paul wrote this brief epistle at the same time as he wrote to the Colossians and Ephesians. He sent it by Tychicus and Onesimus, along with the other letters. In it he recommends Onesimus to his Christian brother, Philemon. Onesimus had been Philemon's slave and had become a Christian through Paul since running away.

1. Authorship. Paul wrote this letter to an individual, yet the early church valued it for its pertinent words on Christian brotherhood. Congregations shared the letter from an early date, receiving it as an inspired letter from Paul.

2. Contents. As we have already mentioned, the Letter to Philemon was supposed to be a personal communication on behalf of Onesimus. But Paul's counsel on Christian brotherhood makes it useful for all Christian readers.

OUTLINE OF PHILEMON

I. INTRODUCTION VV. 1–3
II. THANKSGIVING VV. 4–7

III. PAUL'S APPEAL FOR ONESIMUS VV. 8–21
IV. CONCLUSION VV. 22–25

Philemon has 1 chapter, 25 verses, and ca. 445 words.

▬▬▬

N. Hebrews. Tradition says that Paul wrote this letter to the converted Jewish congregations in Jerusalem. It makes a profound argument to converts from Judaism, to convince them of the truth and finality of Christianity as compared with Judaism.

1. Authorship. This letter does not name its author, but its dissimilarity to Paul's letters in style, language and method of arguing rules out the idea that Paul composed it. It may have been written by one of Paul's pupils or a Christian leader in Alexandria.

2. Contents. This letter displays Jesus as God, man, and high priestly mediator, the fulfillment of all Jewish hopes. Beyond that, it shows how Jesus by His once-for-all self-offering opened the door for all people to approach God and find forgiveness of their sins.

OUTLINE OF HEBREWS

I. INTRODUCTION 1:1–4
A. God's self-revelation 1:1–2
B. Christ superior to the prophets 1:3–4

II. THE MAIN ARGUMENTS INTRODUCED AND EXPLAINED 1:5—10:18
A. Christ "greater than"; the argument for superiority .... 1:5—7:28
1. Superior to angels 1:5–14
2. The greater salvation, and a warning against neglect 2:1–4
3. Christ as the perfect man 2:5–18
4. Christ superior to Moses . 3:1–6
5. The superiority of the rest of Christ over the rest of Israel under Moses and Joshua .... 3:7—4:13
6. Christ as high priest in the order of Melchizedek, superior to Aaron................. 4:14—5:10
7. A rebuke for lack of understanding and for immaturity .... 5:11—6:20
8. The priesthood of Melchizedek 7:1–28

Hebrews has 13 chapters, 303 verses, and ca. 6,913 words.

O. James. This letter is addressed to Hebrew converts. It is intended to strengthen them in the Christian life by correcting various tendencies to sin and by instructing them in the truth that faith must show itself alive by the way it works.

1. Authorship. The man who wrote this epistle was probably the brother of Christ. Tradition says he was the leader of the Christian church at Jerusalem for many years and was martyred there by a mob. The date of its composition has been variously set between A.D. 45 and 62.

2. Contents. This letter challenges Christians to exercise their faith in their daily lives. It calls for clean, vibrant living that glorifies Christ.

OUTLINE OF JAMES

James has 5 chapters, 108 verses, and ca. 2,309 words.

P. First Peter. Peter probably wrote this letter at "the mystical Babylon"—i.e., Rome—in A.D. 64. He addresses it to "the strangers" in Asia Minor—people he had converted from Judaism on several visits to that area.

1. Authorship. At several points, the letter identifies the apostle Peter as its author. Most scholars accept this as a fact. The different Greek styles of Peter's two letters (they are different; and neither suggests an ex-Galilean fisherman) are to be explained as belonging to two different penmen whose skills Peter used. (1 Pet. 5:12 gives us the name of the first, Silvanus.)

2. Contents. The epistle contains miscellaneous exhortations and instructions to help these new Christians to persevere in the faith. Also, it shows how they must apply the doctrines of Christianity in the duties of daily life.

OUTLINE OF 1 PETER

OUTLINE OF THE BOOKS OF THE BIBLE

First Peter has 5 chapters, 105 verses, and ca. 2,482 words.

Q. Second Peter. We suppose that Peter wrote this letter also from Rome to the Christians of Asia Minor. He probably penned it a couple of years after the first letter, since we now see him addressing a new problem on the scene—false teachers.

1. Authorship. (See the section on "First Peter.")

2. Contents. This letter is Peter's last testament of faith. It contains his final instructions and exhortations to his beloved Christian friends.He calls on them to press on in faith, holiness, and hope, and to grow in grace.

OUTLINE OF 2 PETER

Second Peter has 3 chapters, 61 verses, and ca. 1,559 words.

R. First John. The apostle John probably wrote the three letters that bear his name in the city of Ephesus, where he spent the later years of his life. They are general letters of counsel to the Christians scattered throughout the Roman Empire.

1. Authorship. Scholars have long debated whether the apostle John or another Christian leader named John wrote these letters. The arguments pro and con are very complicated. But many scholars support the traditional belief that the apostle wrote the Gospel of John and these letters as well.

2. Contents. This letter dwells on the nature of Christ, His mission, and His principal doctrines (concerning the Christian life). It also shows the distinction between true and false believers.

OUTLINE OF 1 JOHN

OUTLINE OF THE BOOKS OF THE BIBLE

First John has 5 chapters, 105 verses, and ca. 2,523 words.

S. Second John. Scholars disagree about the identity of the "elect lady" to whom John addressed this book. Some think he refers to the whole church, the "bride of Christ." Others think this was an individual whose name we do not know. Still others think she was an individual with the name of *Kyria* (the Greek word that our Bibles translate as "elect lady"). At any rate, John encourages this "lady" in the raising of her "children," and he advises her in several doctrinal matters that troubled the early Christians.

1. Authorship. (See the section on "First John.")

2. Contents. In this brief epistle, John warns against the heresy of denying the Incarnation and reminds his Christian friends to obey God's commandment of love.

OUTLINE OF 2 JOHN

Second John has 1 chapter, 13 verses, and ca. 303 words.

T. Third John. The apostle John wrote this epistle to a man named Gaius, who was well-known for his hospitality. The epistle simply commends Gaius for his Christian virtues, cautions him against Diotrephes (a schemer and false teacher) and recommends a man named Demetrius.

1. Authorship. (See the section on "First John.")

2. Contents. It seems obvious that John wrote this letter to a real individual, rather than using the name *Gaius* for a group of people. The letter gives Gaius personal praise and advice.

OUTLINE OF 3 JOHN

Third John has 1 chapter, 14 verses, and ca. 299 words.

U. Jude. We do not know where this epistle was written, and we have no knowledge of the life or labors of Jude. This epistle is addressed to all Christians, and it is principally a strong denunciation of false teachers.

1. Authorship. Matthew 13:55 and Mark 6:3 state that a man named Jude was a brother of Jesus. The writer identifies himself as "a brother of James." This is all we know of him. Whether he was Jesus' brother or another Jude, we cannot say.

2. Contents. Jude warns his Christian friends to avoid the heresy of Gnosticism. The

OUTLINE OF THE BOOKS OF THE BIBLE

Gnostics taught that matter is evil and only spirit is good, so that the physical side of life is spiritually irrelevant, and sensual indulgence is in no way harmful. Jude reminded his readers of the apostles' prediction that false teachers would try to make them doubt the truth.

OUTLINE OF JUDE

I. IDENTIFICATION, SALUTATION, AND PURPOSE   *VV. 1–4*

II. ADMONITIONS AGAINST FALSE TEACHERS   *VV. 5–16*

III. EXHORTATIONS TO CHRISTIANS   *VV. 17–23*

IV. BENEDICTION   *VV. 24–25*

Jude has 1 chapter, 25 verses, and ca. 613 words.

V. Revelation. This last book of the New Testament is a prophetic vision of the future. Bible scholars have interpreted it in many different ways, and it remains one of the most controversial books of the Bible.

1. Authorship. The early church fathers reported that the apostle John wrote this book, and we have no sufficient reason to doubt their word. The book of Revelation resembles the Gospel of John in many ways—for example, both of them refer to Jesus as the divine Word (*Logos*) and the "Lamb of God."

2. Contents. We cannot be sure precisely what is meant by all the gorgeous, impressive, and mysterious pictures of this book. Because much of it is still unfulfilled, we have to be cautious in our guesses as to what events John's symbols have in view. However, the book's powerful prophecy of the final happiness of the good and the final misery of the wicked makes it an unfailing source of warning and encouragement to Christians.

OUTLINE OF REVELATION

I. MESSAGES TO THE SEVEN CHURCHES OF ASIA   *1:1—3:22*
  A. John's vision of Christ 1:1–20
  B. The message to Ephesus . . . 2:1–7
  C. The message to Smyrna 2:8–11
  D. The message to Pergamos . . 2:12–17
  E. The message to Thyatira . . . 2:18–29
  F. The message to Sardis 3:1–6
  G. The message to Philadelphia 3:7–13
  H. The message to Laodicea . . . 3:14–22

II. OPENING THE BOOK WITH SEVEN SEALS   *4:1—9:21*
  A. God upon His throne 4:1–11
  B. The sealed book is brought out 5:1–14
  C. The first six seals are opened 6:1–17
  D. The throng of the redeemed 7:1–17
  E. The seventh seal is opened. . 8:1—9:21

III. THE HOUR OF RECKONING   *10:1—13:18*
  A. The "little book". 10:1–11
  B. Symbols of the end . . . . 11:1—12:17
  C. The two beasts 13:1–18

IV. GOD POURS OUT HIS WRATH   *14:1—16:21*
  A. The Lamb of God. 14:1–13
  B. The harvest of souls 14:14–20
  C. Seven vials of judgment. . . . 15:1—16:21

V. THE DEFEAT OF EVIL   *17:1—20:15*
  A. "Babylon" falls . . . . 17:1—18:24
  B. The marriage supper of the Lamb 19:1–10
  C. A rider from heaven. . . . . . . 19:11—20:10
  D. The judgment 20:11–15

VI. GOD'S NEW CREATION   *21:1—22:21*
  A. A new heaven and a new earth . . . . 21:1—22:5
  B. Christ to return soon 22:6–16
  C. Invitation and benediction . 22:17–21

Revelation has 22 chapters, 404 verses, and ca. 12,000 words.

Outline of the Books of the Bible

The Order of the Books

"We believe in all 39 books of the Old Testament," a Christian tells his Hebrew friend. He replies, "But we only have 24 in our Bibles." It's true! An English text of Jewish Scriptures has only 24 books, but these 24 books contain the same material as the Christian 39!

The distinction is caused by two different traditions, Jewish and Latin. The Jewish people arranged their books according to the official position or status of the writers—Moses, the prophets, and the other writers—though this sequence did not indicate degrees of inspiration. Most modern Jews believe that all the books of their Bible are equally inspired and equally authoritative. So the order of the books in the Hebrew (Masoretic Text) Bible is as follows:

1. *The Law of Moses* (5 books):
   Genesis, Exodus, Leviticus, Numbers, Deuteronomy
2. *The Prophets* (8 books):
   a. *The Former Prophets* (4 books):
      Joshua, Judges, Samuel, Kings
   b. *The Latter Prophets* (4 books):
      Isaiah, Jeremiah, Ezekiel, "The Twelve" (Minor Prophets)
3. *The Writings* (11 books):
   a. *Poetical Books* (3):
      Psalms, Proverbs, Job
   b. *The Five Rolls* (5):
      Song of Solomon, Ruth, Lamentations, Ecclesiastes, Esther
   c. *The Historical Books* (4):
      Daniel, Ezra, Nehemiah, Chronicles

This division is mentioned in the prologue to the deuterocanonical book of Ecclesiasticus and again in the Gospels (cf. Luke 24:44).

Josephus, the great Jewish historian of the first century A.D., divided the Hebrew Scriptures into the same three parts but in a different order, having 22 books—one for each letter of the Hebrew alphabet. The Law of Moses remained the same, but he had 13 prophetical books and four books in the writings (Psalms, Proverbs, Ecclesiastes, and Job or Song of Solomon). He grouped the rest with others among the prophets (for example, Ruth with Judges and Lamentations with Jeremiah).

Protestants and Catholics follow the order given in the Septuagint, which Jerome changed slightly when he issued the Latin Vulgate in the fourth century A.D. The Septuagint had the Minor Prophets first among the Latter Prophets, while the Vulgate placed Isaiah, Jeremiah, and Ezekiel first. The Vulgate's order—based on topics rather than the importance of the original writers—is the one we know. Most Protestants exclude the books of the Deuterocanon from Scripture, though they are found in the Septuagint and modern Catholic Bibles.

The order of the books in the New Testament is based on subject categories. First come the historical books—the Gospels and Acts. Then come the epistles—first the Pauline collection, then those of the other writers. The Apocalypse, or Revelation, comes at the end.

Early church tradition has the Gospels in the order they are today, with the synoptic Gospels coming first, then the Gospel of John. The early church fathers also arranged the Pauline epistles in two categories—the epistles to the churches and personal letters. They generally arranged the epistles to the churches according to size or length, and the personal letters seemed to follow the same structure, as did the general epistles (non-Pauline writings)—Hebrews was placed first, followed by the writings of James, Peter, John, and Jude.

This order has been constant since about the fourth century A.D., but many lists circulating during the first three centuries did not include all of the books. Athanasius (A.D. 297?–373), one of the great early church fathers, gave the following list in his writings: Matthew; Mark; Luke; John; Acts; James; 1 and 2 Peter; 1, 2, 3 John; Jude; Romans; 1 and 2 Corinthians; Galatians; Ephesians; Philippians; Colossians; 1 and 2 Thessalonians; Hebrews; 1 and 2 Timothy; Titus; Philemon; and Revelation.

43

OUTLINE OF THE BOOKS OF THE BIBLE

OUTLINE OF THE BOOKS OF THE BIBLE

When the Books Were Written (or Compiled)

The books of the Bible are not arranged in the order in which they were written. The Scriptures are generally organized by subject.

Scholars have been able to use information from secular writers to determine the dates when some books were written. The Scriptures occasionally refer to historical events that help to date the writing. An example of this is Luke's mention of government officials by name: "Now in the fifteenth year of the reign of Tiberius Caesar . . ." (Luke 3:1).

The following list is arranged chronologically according to the most probable dates for the books of the Bible. Deuterocanonical books appear in italics:

Genesis—*ca.* 1400 B.C.
Exodus—*ca.* 1400 B.C.
Leviticus—*ca.* 1400 B.C.
Numbers—*ca.* 1400 B.C.
Deuteronomy—*ca.* 1400 B.C.
Psalms—970–500 B.C.
Joshua—1235 B.C.
Judges—1025 B.C.
1 Samuel—1000–850 B.C.
2 Samuel—1000–850 B.C.
Ruth—990 B.C.
1 Kings—970–850 B.C.
Ecclesiastes—962–922 B.C.
Song of Solomon—962–922 B.C.
Job—*ca.* 900 B.C.
Proverbs—*ca.* 900 B.C.
2 Kings—850–586 B.C.
Obadiah—848–841 B.C.
Joel—835–796 B.C.
Jonah—780–750 B.C.
Amos—765–750 B.C.
Hosea—755–715 B.C.
Isaiah—700–680 B.C.
Micah—700–690 B.C.
Nahum—630–612 B.C.
Habakkuk—625 B.C.
Baruch—608–539 B.C.
Song of the Three Children—605–539 B.C.
Story of Susanna—605–539 B.C.
Bel and the Dragon—605–539 B.C.
Ezekiel—593–571 B.C.
Zephaniah—*ca.* 621 B.C.
Jeremiah—585 B.C.
Lamentations—585 B.C.

Haggai—520 B.C.
Zechariah—520–515 B.C.
Zechariah (chaps. 9–14)—after 500 B.C.
Esther—486–465 B.C.
Malachi—450 B.C.
Nehemiah—445 B.C.
Ezra—445 B.C.
1 Chronicles—350 B.C.
2 Chronicles—350 B.C.
The Rest of the Book of Esther—250 B.C.
Prayer of Manasses—199–100 B.C.
Judith—*ca.* 199–100 B.C.
Ecclesiasticus—175 B.C.
2 Maccabees—175–160 B.C.
1 Maccabees—167–134 B.C.
Tobit—*ca.* 150 B.C.
1 Esdras—*ca.* 100 B.C.
Mark—A.D. 60's
Wisdom of Solomon—50 B.C.
James—A.D. 45
1 Thessalonians—A.D. 51–52
2 Thessalonians—A.D. 51–52
1 Corinthians—A.D. 54–55
2 Corinthians—A.D. 55–56
Galatians—A.D. 55–56
Romans—A.D. 56–58
Luke—A.D. 58–63
Ephesians—A.D. 61–62
Philippians—A.D. 61–62
Philemon—A.D. 62
Colossians—A.D. 62–63
Acts—A.D. 63
1 Peter—A.D. 64
1 Timothy—A.D. 64
2 Timothy—A.D. 64
2 Peter—A.D. 66
Titus—A.D. 64
Hebrews—A.D. 68
Matthew—A.D. 75
1 John—A.D. 85–90
John—A.D. 90–100
Jude—A.D. 90
Revelation—A.D. 96
2 John—A.D. 96
3 John—A.D. 97
2 Esdras (chaps. 1–14)—*ca.* A.D. 100
2 Esdras (chaps. 15–16)—A.D. 270

PEOPLE OF THE BIBLE

This article identifies people whose proper names occur in the Bible, excluding the deuterocanonical books.

The names are set out alphabetically as they are spelled in the King James Version, with variant spellings enclosed in brackets [ ]. The meaning of the name is then given in parentheses (). Under each entry, various individuals bearing this name are differentiated by boldface brackets, like this: **[1]**; **[2]**; and so on. Then follows a description of the character, with several Bible verses listed where the name occurs. (Not all verses could be given; so if the reader is considering a passage that is not cited in the section, he must choose the character that would most likely be identical with the person in his passage.)

We have made no attempt to designate each person as a Palite, Harodite, Gileadite, and so on. Many of these designations refer to the ancestor of an individual; in other cases, they refer to the person's city, district, or distinctive clan. It is often a guess as to which meaning is intended.

The meanings of the names are not infallibly accurate; they are simply interesting possibilities. These names are ancient and their history is obscure and uncertain.

Many people in Scripture bear the same name. In dozens of cases, we cannot determine whether an individual in one book is identical with someone having the same name in another book. In the ancient world, a person was often called by more than one name.

In the transmission of Scripture, copyists occasionally made errors. Surely Reuel was not also called Deuel, nor Jemuel called Nemuel, and so on. Yet which is original? Only in a few cases do we have any clues.

We find variant forms and contractions of names through the Bible. They probably presented little difficulty to an ancient reader. But this further complicates the identification problem for us.

The Hebrew genealogies are abbreviated at many points. At times it is difficult to distinguish a man from his ancestor. Consider also the problem of trying to match an abbreviated list with a fuller list. Either the names in the abbreviated list are independent of the longer list or they are already included in it. In other words, we may find the same person included in two lists or two different people in two lists.

In a few cases, our English versions use the same word to transliterate several similar Hebrew names. In these instances, we have recorded a separate entry for each Hebrew name (e.g., Iddo).

MOUNT HOR. *The burial place of Aaron (Deut. 32:50), Mount Hor is traditionally identified with the modern-day peak of Jebel Nebi Harun. Over 1,500 m. (4,800 ft.) high, the mountain stands to the west of Edom.*

A

Aaron ("enlightened, rich, mountaineer"), the brother of Moses. He became the first high priest of Israel (Exod. 4:14, 30; 7:2, 19; 17:9–12; 29; Num. 12; 17).

Abagtha ("happy, prosperous"), one of the seven chamberlains of King Ahasuerus (Esth. 1:10).

Abda ("servant; worshiper"). **[1]** Father of Solomon's tribute officer, Adoniram (1 Kings 4:6). **[2]** A chief Levite after the Exile (Neh. 11:17). He is called Obadiah in First Chronicles 9:16.

Abdeel ("servant of God"), the father of

PEOPLE OF THE BIBLE

Shelemiah, who was commanded to arrest Baruch and Jeremiah (Jer. 36:26).

Abdi ("servant of Jehovah"). **[1]** One whom David set over the song service (1 Chron. 6:44). **[2]** One who took a foreign wife during the Exile (Ezra 10:26). **[3]** A Levite contemporary with Hezekiah (2 Chron. 29:12).

Abdiel ("servant of Jehovah"), ancestor of a clan of Gad (1 Chron. 5:15).

Abdon ("service, servile"). **[1]** A judge of Israel for eight years (Judg. 12:13, 15). *See* Bedan. **[2]** A descendant of Benjamin who dwelt in Jerusalem (1 Chron. 8:23). **[3]** First-born son of Jehiel, mentioned in Chronicles (1 Chron. 8:30; 9:36). **[4]** One sent to Huldah to inquire of the meaning of the Law (2 Chron. 34:20). He is called Achbor in Second Kings 22:12. Possibly he is identical with [2]. See also "Places of the Bible."

Abed-nego ("servant of Nebo; servant of Ishtar"), name given to Azariah, one of the three friends of Daniel who were carried captive to Babylon. He was thrown into a fiery furnace (Dan. 1:7; 2:49; 3:12–30).

Abel ("a breath, vapor; shepherd"), second son of Adam and Eve, slain by his brother Cain (Gen. 4:1–10; Heb. 11:4; 12:24).

Abi, the mother of King Hezekiah (2 Kings 18:2). *Abi* is a contraction of *Abijah* ("Jehovah is father"), which she is called in Second Chronicles 29:1. *See* Abi-albon; Abi-ezer.

Abia [**Abiah, Abijah**] ("Jehovah is father"). **[1]** A son of Samuel and wicked judge of Israel (1 Sam. 8:2; 1 Chron. 6:28). **[2]** The wife of Hezron (1 Chron. 2:24). **[3]** Son of Rehoboam and successor to the throne of Judah, an ancestor of Christ (1 Chron. 3:10; 2 Chron. 11:20—14:1; Matt. 1:7). He was also known as Abijam. **[4]** The seventh son of Becher the son of Benjamin (1 Chron. 7:8). **[5]** A descendant of Aaron appointed by David in connection with the priestly courses (1 Chron. 24:10; cf. Luke 1:5). **[6]** A son of Jeroboam I of Israel (1 Kings 14:1–8). **[7]** A priest of Nehemiah's time who sealed the covenant (Neh. 10:7). Possibly the same as the priest mentioned in Nehemiah 12:1, 4, 17. **[8]** *See* Abi.

Abi-Albon ("father of strength"), one of David's "valiant men" (2 Sam. 23:31). Also called Abiel (1 Chron. 11:32).

Abiasaph [**Ebiasaph**] ("my father has gathered"), a Levite whose descendants were doorkeepers of the Tabernacle (Exod. 6:24; 1 Chron. 6:23; 9:19).

Abiathar ("father of super-excellence or pre-eminence"), the only priest to escape Saul's massacre at Nob, he was a high priest in David's time. He was deposed by Solomon (1 Sam. 22:20–23; 1 Kings 2:27; 1 Chron. 15:11–12). First Samuel 21 says that Ahimelech **[1]** was the high priest when David ate the showbread, yet Mark 2:26 states this occurred in the days of Abiathar the high priest. There are several possible ways to resolve this problem (a) An old rabbinic tradition says that the son of a high priest could also be designated a high priest; however, we cannot be sure how old this tradition is. (b) Abiathar may have been assisting his father as high priest and thus could be so designated. (c) Abiathar was more prominent in history than was his father Ahimelech, so he is mentioned here instead of Ahimelech. If this is so (and it seems to be), then Abiathar is called the "high priest" before he actually assumed that office. Notice that Mark does *not* say that Abiathar was present when David ate the showbread; there is no need to suppose an error in this passage.

Abida [**Abidah**] ("father of knowledge"), a son of Midian listed in Genesis and Chronicles (Gen. 25:4; 1 Chron. 1:33).

Abidan ("father is judge"; "my father"), a prince of Benjamin (Num. 1:11; 2:22; 7:60, 65; 10:24).

Abiel ("God is father"). *See* Abi-albon, Ner.

Abi-ezer [**Abiezer**] ("father of help"). **[1]** A descendant of Manasseh (Josh. 17:2; 1 Chron. 7:18). *See* Jeezer. **[2]** One of David's mighty men (2 Sam. 23:27; 1 Chron. 11:28; 27:12).

Abigail ("father [i.e., cause] of delight"). **[1]** A wife of Nabal and afterwards of David (1 Sam. 25:3, 14–44). **[2]** Mother of Amasa, whom Absalom made captain (2 Sam. 17:25; 1 Chron. 2:16–17).

Abihail ("father of might"). **[1]** A chief man of the descendants of Merari (Num. 3:35). **[2]** The wife of Abishur (1 Chron. 2:29). **[3]** Head of a family of Gad (1 Chron. 5:14). **[4]** A wife of Rehoboam (2 Chron. 11:18). **[5]** Father of Esther (Esther 2:15; 9:29).

Abihu ("he is my father"), a son of Aaron, destroyed with his brother for offering strange fire to God (Exod. 6:23; Lev. 10:1).

Abihud ("father of honor"), a son of Bela listed in Chronicles (1 Chron. 8:3).

Abijah ("the Lord is my father"). *See* Abia.

Abijam ("father of the sea [or west]"). *See* Abia [3].

Abimael ("my father is God"), a son of Joktan listed in Genesis and Chronicles (Gen. 10:26–28; 1 Chron. 1:20–22). The name may

PEOPLE OF THE BIBLE

denote an Arabian tribe. Some scholars suggest a locality in Arabia is intended.

Abimelech ("father of the king"). **[1]** Many scholars believe the King(s) Abimelech(s) of Gerar in Genesis 20, 21, and 26 are not proper names but a royal title borne by the Philistine kings. The Psalm 34 title mentions Abimelech where Achish should occur. Since the story of Achish was well known, it seems improbable to regard this as a mistake, but rather a royal title of Achish, king of Gath. *See* Phichol. **[2]** A son of Gideon who tried to become king of Israel, and did reign for three years (Judg. 8:30—10:1). **[3]** *See* Ahimelech [2].

Abinadab ("father or source of liberality or willingness"). **[1]** A man of Judah in whose house the ark was placed (1 Sam. 7:1; 2 Sam. 6:3–4; 1 Chron. 13:7). **[2]** A brother of David (1 Sam. 16:8; 17:13; 1 Chron. 2:13). **[3]** Son of Saul slain by the Philistines (1 Sam. 31:2; 1 Chron. 8:33; 9:39; 10:2). **[4]** Father of one of Solomon's officers (1 Kings 4:11).

Abiner. *See* Abner.

Abinoam ("father of pleasantness"), father of Barak the general (Judg. 4:6, 12; 5:1, 12).

Abiram ("father of elevation"). **[1]** One who conspired against Moses and was destroyed (Num. 16:27; Psa. 106:17). **[2]** First-born son of Hiel who died when his father began to rebuild Jericho (1 Kings 16:34; cf. Josh. 6:26).

Abishag ("my father was a wanderer"), a beautiful woman chosen to nurse the aged David (1 Kings 1:3, 15; 2:17, 21–22). This woman may also be the heroine of the Song of Solomon, where she is simply called "the Shulamite."

Abishai ("my father is Jesse; source of wealth"), a son of David's sister, Zeruiah. He was one of David's mighty men (1 Sam. 26:6–9; 2 Sam. 2:18; 10:10; 23:18).

Abishalom [Absalom] ("father of peace"), father of Maachah, the wife of Rehoboam (1 Kings 15:2, 10). He is called Absalom, another form of the name, in Second Chronicles 11:20, 21, and Uriel in Second Chronicles 13:2. *See* Absalom.

Abishua ("father of safety"). **[1]** A son of Phinehas, descendant of Aaron mentioned in Chronicles and Ezra (1 Chron. 6:4, 5, 50; Ezra 7:5). **[2]** A descendant of Benjamin listed in Chronicles (1 Chron. 8:4).

Abishur ("father of oxen"), a son of Shammai listed in Chronicles (1 Chron. 2:28–29).

Abital ("source of dew"), a wife of David (2 Sam. 3:4; 1 Chron. 3:3).

Abitub ("source of good"), a descendant of Benjamin listed in Chronicles (1 Chron. 8:11).

Abiud ("my father is majesty; father of honor"), a son of Zerubbabel and ancestor of Christ (Matt. 1:13).

Abner [Abiner] ("my father of light"), a shortened form of *Abiner;* the captain of the host under Saul and Ishbosheth (1 Sam. 14:50–51; 26:5, 7; 2 Sam. 2; 3).

Abraham [Abram], the founder of the Jewish nation and an ancestor of Christ. His name was changed from Abram ("the father is exalted") to Abraham ("father of multitudes") (Gen. 11—26; Matt. 1:1–2).

Absalom ("father of peace"), a son of David who tried to usurp the throne from his father (2 Sam. 3:3; 13—19). *See* Abishalom.

Achaicus ("belonging to Achaia"), a Corinthian Christian who visited Paul at Philippi (1 Cor. 16:17).

Achan [Achar] ("trouble"), one who stole part of the spoil of Jericho and brought "trouble" on his people. He was killed for this

TOMB OF ABSALOM. *According to Jewish tradition, David's son Absalom was buried under this stone monument in a cemetery along the Kidron Valley near Jerusalem. It has been called "Absalom's Pillar" because of the account in 2 Samuel 18:18, which says that Absalom set up a pillar in his own honor. But this monument was erected at least 500 years after Absalom's death.*

PEOPLE OF THE BIBLE

(Josh. 7:1–24). In First Chronicles 2:7, he is called *Achar.*

Achaz, Greek form of Ahaz (q.v.).

Achbor ("a mouse"). **[1]** Father of a king of Edom (Gen. 36:38–39; 1 Chron. 1:49). **[2]** The father of the one sent to bring Urijah from Egypt (Jer. 26:22; 36:12). **[3]** *See* Abdon [4].

Achim ("woes"), ancestor of Christ (Matt. 1:14).

Achish ("serpent-charmer"). **[1]** A king of Gath to whom David fled for safety (1 Sam. 21:27–29). **[2]** Another king of Gath who bore the same name but reigned during Solomon's time (1 Kings 2:39–40). However, many believe the kings to be identical.

Achsa [Achsah] ("serpent-charmer"), a daughter of Caleb who married her uncle Othniel (Josh. 15:16–17; Judg. 1:12–13; 1 Chron. 2:49).

Adah ("pleasure; beauty"). **[1]** One of the two wives of Lamech (Gen. 4:19–20, 23). **[2]** One of the wives of Esau (Gen. 36:2, 4, 10, 12, 16). *See* Esau's Wives.

Adaiah ("pleasing to Jehovah; Jehovah has adorned"). **[1]** A son of Shimhi found in First Chronicles 8:12–21. **[2]** A Levite ancestor of Asaph (1 Chron. 6:41). Also called Iddo (1 Chron. 6:21). **[3]** Father of a captain who aided Jehoiada (2 Chron. 23:1). **[4]** Father of Jedidah, the mother of King Josiah (2 Kings 22:1). **[5]** One whose descendants resided in Jerusalem (Neh. 11:5). **[6]** One who married a foreign wife (Ezra 10:29). **[7]** Another who did the same (Ezra 10:39). **[8]** A Levite descendant from Aaron (1 Chron. 9:12; Neh. 11:12).

Adalia ("honor of Ized"), one of the sons of Haman slain by the Jews (Esther 9:8).

Adam ("of the ground; firm"), the first man. His sin caused a curse to fall upon all the race (Gen. 2—3; 1 Cor. 15:22, 45). He is listed in the genealogy of Christ (Luke 3:38). *See also* "Places of the Bible."

Adbeel ("languishing for God"), a son of Ishmael listed in Genesis and Chronicles (Gen. 25:13; 1 Chron. 1:29).

Addan. *See* Addon.

Addar ("height; honor"), a son of Bela listed in Chronicles (1 Chron. 8:3). *See* Ard [2].

Addi ("my witness"), an ancestor of Christ (Luke 3:28).

Addon [Addan] ("strong"), a man who was unable to prove his Jewish ancestry when he returned from Exile (Neh. 7:61; Ezra 2:59).

Ader ("a flock"), a son of Beriah listed in Chronicles (1 Chron. 8:15).

Adiel ("ornament of God"). **[1]** A descendant of Simeon listed in Chronicles (1 Chron. 4:36). **[2]** A descendant of Aaron (1 Chron. 9:12). **[3]** Father of David's treasurer, Asmaveth (1 Chron. 27:25).

Adin ("ornament"). **[1]** Ancestor of returned captives (Ezra 2:15; Neh. 7:20). **[2]** One whose descendant returned with Ezra (Ezra 8:6). **[3]** A family who sealed the covenant (Neh. 10:14–16).

Adina ("ornament"), a captain of David's (1 Chron. 11:42).

Adino ("ornament"), a chief of David's mighty men (2 Sam. 23:8). Some identify him with Jashobeam [2]; others deny this.

Adlai ("lax; weary"), father of an overseer of David's herds (1 Chron. 27:29).

Admatha ("God-given"), one of the seven princes of Persia (Esther 1:14).

Adna ("pleasure"). **[1]** One who took a foreign wife (Ezra 10:30). **[2]** A priest listed in Nehemiah (Neh. 12:12–15). *See also* Adnah.

Adnah ("pleasure"). **[1]** A captain who joined David at Ziklag (1 Chron. 12:20). **[2]** A chief captain of Jehoshaphat (2 Chron. 17:14). *See also* Adna.

Adoni-bezek ("lord of lightning [Bezek]"), a king of Bezek who was captured by Israel (Judg. 1:5–7).

Adonijah ("Jehovah is my lord"). **[1]** A son of David, executed by Solomon for trying to usurp the throne (2 Sam. 3:4; 1 Kings 1:2). **[2]** One sent by Jehoshaphat to teach the law (2 Chron. 17:8). **[3]** One who sealed the new covenant with God after the Exile (Neh. 10:14–16). **[4]** *See* Tob-adonijah.

Adonikam ("my lord has risen"), ancestor of returned captives (Ezra 2:13; 8:13; Neh. 7:18).

Adoniram. *See* Hadoram [3].

Adoni-zedek ("lord of justice or righteousness"), a king of Jerusalem defeated by Joshua (Josh. 10:1–27).

Adoram. *See* Adoniram; Hadoram [3].

Adrammelech ("honor of the king; Adar is a king"), a son of the Assyrian king Sennacherib who, with his brother, killed his father (2 Kings 19:37; Isa. 37:38).

Adriel ("honor of God; my help is God"), the man whom Merab married although she had been promised to David (1 Sam. 18:19; 2 Sam. 21:8).

Aeneas ("praise"), the paralytic of Lydda who was healed by Peter (Acts 9:33–34).

PEOPLE OF THE BIBLE

Agabus ("locust"), a prophet of Jerusalem who foretold suffering for Paul if he went to Jerusalem (Acts 11:28; 21:10).

Agag ("high; warlike"), a name or title of the kings of Amalek; it is probably not a proper name. However, if it is a proper name, it is used to refer to two persons: **[1]** A king mentioned by Balaam (Num. 24:7). **[2]** A king that Saul spared, but who was later executed by Samuel (1 Sam. 15).

Agar ("wandering"), the Greek form of Hagar (q.v.).

Agee ("fugitive"), father of one of David's mighty men (2 Sam. 23:11).

Agrippa. *See* Herod.

Agur ("gathered"), a sage who wrote Proverbs 30.

Ahab ("father's brother [uncle]"). **[1]** The seventh king of Israel. He was wicked and idolatrous and married a woman of the same character—Jezebel (1 Kings 16:28—22:40). **[2]** A false prophet killed by Nebuchadnezzar (Jer. 29:21–22).

Aharah ("brother's follower"). *See* Ahiram.

Aharhel ("after might; brother of Rachel"), a descendant of Judah (1 Chron. 4:8).

Ahasai ("my holder; protector"), a priest of the family of Immer (Neh. 11:13). *See* Jahzerah.

Ahasbai ("blooming; shining"), father of one of David's mighty men (2 Sam. 23:34).

Ahasuerus ("prince"). **[1]** The king of Persia whom Esther married. He is known as Xerxes to historians (Esther 1:1; 2:16; 10:3) **[2]** The father of Darius the Mede (Dan. 9:1). **[3]** Another name for Cambyses, king of Persia (Ezra 4:6).

Ahaz [Achaz] ("he holds"). **[1]** The eleventh king of Judah and an ancestor of Christ (1 Kings 15:38—16:20; Matt. 1:9). **[2]** A descendant of Benjamin (1 Chron. 8:35–36; 9:41–42).

Ahaziah [Azariah] ("Jehovah holds or sustains"). **[1]** The eighth king of Israel. He was weak and idolatrous (1 Kings 22:51; 2 Kings 1:18). **[2]** The sixth king of Judah; he reigned only one year (2 Kings 8:24–29; 9:16f). He was also known as Jehoahaz (2 Chron. 21:17; 25:23). His being called Azariah in Second Chronicles 22:6 is an error; over fifteen Hebrew manuscripts and all recent versions read Ahaziah. *See* Jehoahaz.

Ahban ("brother of intelligence"), the son of Abishur of Judah (1 Chron. 2:29).

PLAIN OF JEZREEL. *King Ahab and his wife Jezebel conspired to murder a man named Naboth and seize his vineyard, which grew in this fertile region (1 Kings 21:1–15). The mountains of Gilboa rise in the background; their streams water the rich soil of the plain.*

Aher ("one that is behind"), a descendant of Benjamin (1 Chron. 7:12). *See also* Ahiram.

Ahi ("my brother"). **[1]** Head of a family of Gad (1 Chron. 5:15). **[2]** A man of the tribe of Asher (1 Chron. 7:34).

Ahiah ("Jehovah is brother"). **[1]** A grandson of Phinehas (1 Sam. 14:3, 18). Some identify him with Ahimelech [2]. **[2]** One of Solomon's scribes (1 Kings 4:3). **[3]** A descendant of Benjamin (1 Chron. 8:7). *See also* Ahijah.

Ahiam ("a mother's brother"), one of David's mighty men (2 Sam. 23:33; 1 Chron. 11:35).

Ahian ("brother of day"), a descendant of Manasseh (1 Chron. 7:19).

Ahiezer ("helping brother"). **[1]** A prince of Dan who helped Moses take a census (Num. 1:12; 2:25; 7:66). **[2]** One who joined David at Ziklag (1 Chron. 12:3).

Ahihud ("brother of honor"). **[1]** A prince of Asher (Num. 34:27). **[2]** A member of the family of Ehud, descended from Benjamin (1 Chron. 8:7).

Ahijah ("Jehovah is brother; my brother is Jehovah"). **[1]** A prophet who prophesied the splitting away of the ten tribes (1 Kings 11:29–30; 14:2, 4–5). **[2]** Father of Baasha who conspired against Nadab (1 Kings 15:27, 33; 21:22). **[3]** A son of Jerahmeel (1 Chron. 2:25). **[4]** One of David's mighty men (1 Chron. 11:36). **[5]** One who sealed the new covenant with God after the Exile (Neh. 10:26). **[6]** One set over the temple treasures (1 Chron. 26:20). *See also* Ahiah; Ahimelech.

PEOPLE OF THE BIBLE

Ahikam ("my brother has risen"), a member of the group sent to consult Huldah the prophetess (2 Kings 22:12, 14; 25:22; Jer. 26:24; 39:14).

Ahilud ("a brother born; child's brother"), father of a recorder appointed by David (2 Sam. 8:16; 20:24; 1 Kings 4:3, 12).

Ahimaaz ("powerful brother"). [1] Father of Ahinoam, wife of Saul (1 Sam. 14:50). [2] One of Solomon's officers (1 Kings 4:15). [3] Son of Zadok who remained loyal to David (2 Sam. 15:27, 36; 17:17, 20; 18:19–29).

Ahiman ("brother of man or fortune"). [1] A son of Anak who dwelt in Hebron (Num. 13:22; Josh. 15:14; Judg. 1:10). [2] A porter in the temple (1 Chron. 9:17).

Ahimelech ("brother of the king; my brother is king"). [1] A Hittite friend of David (1 Sam. 26:6). [2] A priest, son of Abiathar and grandson of [3] (2 Sam. 8:17; 1 Chron. 24:6). Some think the readings in these passages have been transposed (i.e., they speak of Ahimelech the son of Abiathar instead of Abiathar the son of Ahimelech). But this seems unlikely, especially in First Chronicles 24. He is called Abimelech in First Chronicles 18:16. The Septuagint has Ahimelech here also. [3] One of the priests of Nob slain for helping David (1 Sam. 21:1–8; 22:9–20). *See also* Abimelech; Ahiah.

Ahimoth ("brother of death"), a descendant of Kohath (1 Chron. 6:25).

Ahinadab ("brother of liberality or willingness"), one of Solomon's royal merchants (1 Kings 4:14).

Ahinoam ("pleasant brother"). [1] Wife of King Saul (1 Sam. 14:50). [2] A woman of Jezreel who married David (1 Sam. 25:43; 27:3; 1 Chron. 3:1).

Ahio ("his brother"). [1] Son of Abinadab, in whose house the ark stayed for 20 years (2 Sam. 6:3–4; 1 Chron. 13:7). [2] A descendant of Benjamin (1 Chron. 8:14). [3] A descendant of Saul (1 Chron. 8:31; 9:37).

Ahira ("brother of evil"), a chief of the tribe of Naphtali (Num. 1:15; 2:29; 7:78).

Ahiram ("exalted brother; my brother is exalted"), a descendant of Benjamin (Num. 26:38). He is called Ehi, possibly a contraction of Ahiram, in Genesis 46:21 and Aharah in First Chronicles 8:1. He is possibly the same as Aher (q.v.).

Ahisamach ("supporting brother"), one who helped build the tent of meeting (Exod. 31:6; 35:34; 38:23).

Ahishahar ("brother of the dawn"), one of the sons of Bilhan (1 Chron. 7:10).

Ahishar ("brother of song; my brother has sung"), an officer of Solomon (1 Kings 4:6).

Ahithophel ("brother of foolishness"), the real leader of Absalom's rebellion against David. When he saw that victory was impossible, he committed suicide (2 Sam. 15—17).

Ahitub ("a good brother; my brother is goodness"). [1] A son of Phinehas (1 Sam. 14:3; 22:9, 11–12, 20). [2] Father of Zadok the high priest (2 Sam. 8:17; 15:27; 1 Chron. 6:7–8). [3] A high priest of the same family who served during Nehemiah's time (1 Chron. 6:11; 9:11; Neh. 11:11).

Ahlai ("Jehovah is staying"). [1] A daughter of Sheshan listed in First Chronicles 2:31. [2] Father of one of David's mighty men (1 Chron. 11:41).

Ahoah ("a brother's reed; brotherly"), a son of Bela (1 Chron. 8:4).

Aholiab ("a father's tent"), one of the workers who erected the tabernacle (Exod. 31:6; 35:34; 36:1–2).

Aholibamah ("tent of the high place"). [1] A wife of Esau (Gen. 36:2, 5, 14, 18). [2] A duke of Edom (Gen. 36:41). *See also* Esau's Wives.

Ahumai ("heated by Jehovah"), a descendant of Judah (1 Chron. 4:2).

Ahuzam ("possession"), a son of Ashur, a descendant of Judah through Caleb (1 Chron. 4:16).

Ahuzzath ("holding fast"), a friend of Abimelech, king of Philistia (Gen. 26:26).

Aiah [Ajah] ("a vulture"). [1] A son of Zibeon (Gen. 36:24; 1 Chron. 1:40). [2] Father of Saul's concubine, Rizpah (2 Sam. 3:7; 21:8, 10–11).

Akan. *See* Jaakan.

Akkub ("lain in wait; pursuer"). [1] One descendant from David mentioned in Chronicles (1 Chron. 3:24). [2] A porter in the temple (1 Chron. 9:17; Neh. 11:19; 12:25). [3] Ancestor of a family of porters (Ezra 2:42; Neh. 7:45). [4] Ancestor of Nethinim who returned from the Exile (Ezra 2:45). [5] A priest who helped the people understand the Law (Neh. 8:7).

Alameth ("hidden"), a son of Becher (1 Chron. 7:8).

Alemeth ("hiding place"), a descendant of Jonathan (1 Chron. 8:36; 9:42). *See also* "Places of the Bible."

Alexander ("helper of man"). [1] A son of the Simon who bore Christ's cross (Mark

PEOPLE OF THE BIBLE

PETRA. *Selah, the towering rock fortress of the Edomites, was the foundation of the city of Petra. The defeat of this stronghold prompted Amaziah of Judah to challenge Jehoash of Israel to war (2 Kings 14:7–12).*

15:21). **[2]** A kinsman of Annas and a leading man in Jerusalem (Acts 4:6). **[3]** A Christian with Paul when the Ephesians had a riot (Acts 19:33). Perhaps the same as [1]. **[4]** A convert who apostatized (1 Tim. 1:20). **[5]** A person who did much harm to Paul (2 Tim. 4:14). Perhaps the same as [4].

Aliah [Alvah] ("sublimity"), a duke of Edom (1 Chron. 1:51). He is called Alvah in Genesis (Gen. 36:40).

Alian [Alvan] ("sublime"), a descendant of Seir (1 Chron. 1:40). He is called Alvan in Genesis 36:23.

Allon ("an oak"), a chief of Simeon (1 Chron. 4:37). *See also* "Places of the Bible."

Almodad ("the agitator"), a son of Joktan (Gen. 10:26; 1 Chron. 1:20). Perhaps the name refers to an Arabian people that settled in South Arabia.

Alpheus ("leader; chief"). **[1]** The father of Levi (Matthew) (Mark 2:14). **[2]** The father of the apostle James (Matt. 10:3; Mark 3:18; Acts 1:13). Some identify him with Cleophas. *See* Cleophas.

Alvah. *See* Aliah.

Alvan. *See* Alian.

Amal ("laboring"), a descendant of Asher (1 Chron. 7:35).

Amalek ("warlike; dweller in the vale"), a son of Eliphaz and progenitor of the Amalekites (Gen. 36:12, 16; 1 Chron. 1:36; cf. Exod. 17:8–9).

Amariah ("Jehovah has said"). **[1]** Grandfather of Zadok the high priest (1 Chron. 6:7, 52; Ezra 7:3). **[2]** Son of Azariah, a high priest in Solomon's time (1 Chron. 6:11). **[3]** A descendant of Kohath (1 Chron. 23:19; 24:23). **[4]** A chief priest in the reign of Jehoshaphat (2 Chron. 19:11). **[5]** The one appointed to distribute the tithes (2 Chron. 31:15). **[6]** One who took a foreign wife during the Exile (Ezra 10:42). **[7]** One who sealed the new covenant with God after the Exile (Neh. 10:3; 12:2, 13). **[8]** One whose descendants dwelled in Jerusalem after the Exile (Neh. 11:4). **[9]** Ancestor of Zephaniah the prophet (Zeph. 1:1).

Amasa ("burden-bearer; people of Jesse"). **[1]** A nephew of David who became the commander of Absalom's army (2 Sam. 17:25; 19:13; 20:4–12). **[2]** One who opposed making slaves of captured Jews (2 Chron. 28:12).

Amasai ("burden-bearer"). **[1]** A man in the genealogy of Kohath (1 Chron. 6:25, 35; 2 Chron. 29:12). **[2]** A captain who joined David at Ziklag (1 Chron. 12:18). **[3]** A priest who assisted in bringing up the ark of the covenant to Obed-edom (1 Chron. 15:24).

Amashai ("carrying spoil"), a priest of the family of Immer (Neh. 11:13).

Amasiah ("Jehovah bears; Jehovah has strength"), a chief captain of Jehoshaphat (2 Chron. 17:16).

Amaziah ("Jehovah has strength"). **[1]** Son and successor of Joash to the throne of Judah.

He was murdered at Lachish (2 Kings 12:21—14:20). **[2]** A man of the tribe of Simeon (1 Chron. 4:34). **[3]** A Levite descendant from Merari (1 Chron. 6:45). **[4]** An idolatrous priest of Bethel (Amos 7:10, 12, 14).

Ami [Amon] ("master workman"), a servant of Solomon whose descendants returned from captivity (Ezra 2:57). In Nehemiah 7:59, he is called Amon.

Aminadeb ("people of liberality"), Greek form of Amminadab (q.v.).

Amittai ("truthful"), father of the prophet Jonah (2 Kings 14:25; Jon. 1:1).

Ammiel ("my people are strong; my kinsman is God"). **[1]** One of those who spied out the Promised Land (Num. 13:12). **[2]** father of Machir, David's friend (2 Sam. 9:4–5; 17:27). **[3]** *See* Eliam [1]. **[4]** A porter of the tabernacle in the time of David (1 Chron. 26:5).

Ammihud ("my people are honorable or glorious"). **[1]** Father of Elishama, the chief of Ephraim (Num. 1:10; 2:18; 7:48). **[2]** A Simeonite whose son helped to divide the Promised Land (Num. 34:20). **[3]** A Naphthalite whose son helped divide the Promised Land (Num. 34:28). **[4]** Father of Talmai, king of Geshur (2 Sam. 13:37). **[5]** A descendant of Pharez (1 Chron. 9:4).

Amminadab [Aminadab] ("my people are willing or noble"). **[1]** Aaron's father-in-law (Exod. 6:23). **[2]** A prince of Judah and ancestor of Christ (Num. 1:7; 2:3; Ruth 4:19–20; Matt. 1:4). **[3]** A son of Kohath (1 Chron. 6:22). **[4]** One who helped to bring the ark of the covenant from the house of Obed-edom (1 Chron. 15:10–11).

Ammi-shaddai ("the Almighty is my kinsman; my people are mighty"), father of Ahiezer, a captain of Dan during the wilderness journey (Num. 1:12; 2:25).

Ammizabad ("my people are endowed; my kinsman has a present"), one of David's captains (1 Chron. 27:6).

Ammon. *See* Ben-ammi.

Amnon ("upbringing; faithful"). **[1]** Eldest son of David, by Ahinoam, slain by Absalom (2 Sam. 3:2; 13:1–39). **[2]** A son of Shimon of the family of Caleb (1 Chron. 4:20).

Amok ("deep"), a priest who returned to Jerusalem with Zerubbabel (Neh. 12:7, 20).

Amon ("workman" or "trustworthy"). **[1]** Governor of Samaria in Ahab's time (1 Kings 22:26; 2 Chron. 18:25). **[2]** Son and successor of Manasseh to the throne of Judah; an ancestor of Christ (2 Kings 21:19–25; Jer. 1:2; Zeph. 1:1; Matt. 1:10). **[3]** *See* Ami.

Amos ("burden-bearer; burdensome"). **[1]** A prophet during the reigns of Uzziah and Jeroboam (Amos 1:1; 7:10–12, 14). **[2]** An ancestor of Christ (Luke 3:25).

Amoz ("strong"), father of the prophet Isaiah (2 Kings 19:2, 20; Isa. 1:1; 2:1; 13:1).

Amplias ("large"), a Roman Christian to whom Paul sent greetings (Rom. 16:8).

Amram ("people exalted; red"). **[1]** A descendant of Levi and father or ancestor of Aaron, Moses, and Miriam (Exod. 6:18, 20; Num. 3:19; 26:58–59). **[2]** One who had taken a foreign wife (Ezra 10:34). **[3]** *See* Hemdan.

Amraphel ("powerful people"), a king of Shinar who warred against Sodom (Gen. 14:1, 9).

Amzi ("my strength"). **[1]** A Levite of the family of Merari (1 Chron. 6:46). **[2]** An ancestor of returned exiles (Neh. 11:12).

Anah ("answering"). **[1]** The mother (father?) of one of Esau's wives (Gen. 36:2, 14, 18, 25). If the father, he is the same as Beeri the Hittite (Gen. 26:34). *See* Esau's Wives. **[2]** A son of Seir and a chief of Edom (Gen. 36:20, 29; 1 Chron. 1:38). **[3]** A son of Zibeon (Gen. 36:24; 1 Chron. 1:40–41).

Anaiah ("Jehovah has covered; Jehovah answers"). **[1]** One who stood with Ezra at the reading of the Law (Neh. 8:4). **[2]** One who sealed the new covenant with God after the Exile (Neh. 10:22).

Anak ("giant; long necked"), ancestor of the giant Anakim (Num. 13:22, 28, 33; Josh. 15:14).

Anamim ("rockmen"), a descendant of Mizraim (Gen. 10:13; 1 Chron. 1:11). Possibly an unknown Egyptian tribe.

Anan ("he beclouds; cloud"), one who sealed the new covenant with God after the Exile (Neh. 10:26).

Anani ("my cloud"), a descendant of David who lived after the Babylonian Captivity (1 Chron. 3:24).

Ananiah ("Jehovah is a cloud [i.e., protector]"), ancestor of a returned exile (Neh. 3:23). *See also* "Places of the Bible."

Ananias ("Jehovah is gracious"). **[1]** A disciple struck dead for trying to deceive the apostles (Acts 5:1, 3, 5). **[2]** A disciple of Damascus who helped Paul after receiving a vision (Acts 9:10–17; 22:12). **[3]** A high priest in Jerusalem who opposed Paul (Acts 23:2; 24:1).

Anath ("answer"), father of the judge Shamgar (Judg. 3:31; 5:6).

Anathoth ("answers"). **[1]** A son of Becher

(1 Chron. 7:8). **[2]** One who sealed the new covenant with God after the Exile (Neh. 10:19). *See also* "Places of the Bible."

Andrew ("manly; conqueror"), the brother of Peter and one of the twelve apostles (Matt. 4:18; 10:2; John 1:40, 44; 6:8).

Andronicus ("conqueror"), a kinsman of Paul at Rome, to whom Paul sent greetings (Rom. 16:7).

Aner ("sprout; waterfall"), an Amorite chief (Gen. 14:13, 24). *See also* "Places of the Bible."

Aniam ("lamentation of the people"), a descendant of Manasseh (1 Chron. 7:19).

Anna ("grace"), a prophetess of the tribe of Asher in Christ's time (Luke 2:36).

Annas ("grace of Jehovah"), high priest of the Jews who first tried Christ (Luke 3:2; John 18:13, 24; Acts 4:6).

Antipas, a Christian martyr of Pergamos (Rev. 2:13).

Anto-thijah ("answers of Jehovah; belonging to Anathoth"), a son of Shashak (1 Chron. 8:24).

Anub ("strong; high"), descendant of Judah through Caleb (1 Chron. 4:8).

Apelles, a Roman Christian to whom Paul sent greetings (Rom. 16:10).

Aphiah ("striving"), an ancestor of Saul (1 Sam. 9:1).

Aphses ("the dispersed"), chief of the eighteenth temple chorus (1 Chron. 24:15).

Apollos ("a destroyer"), a Jewish Christian, mighty in the Scripture, who came to Ephesus and was instructed by Aquila and Priscilla (Acts 18:24; 19:1; 1 Cor. 1:12; 3:4–6; Titus 3:13).

Appaim ("face; presence; nostrils"), a son of Nadab (1 Chron. 2:30).

Apphia, a female Christian Paul mentioned when writing Philemon (Philem. 2).

Aquila ("eagle"), a pious Jewish Christian, husband of Priscilla and friend of Paul (Acts 18:2, 18, 26; Rom. 16:3; 1 Cor. 16:19).

Ara ("strong"), a son of Jether (1 Chron. 7:38).

Arad ("fugitive"). One of the chief men of Aijalon (1 Chron. 8:15). *See also* "Places of the Bible."

Arah ("wayfarer"). **[1]** A son of Ulla; member of the tribe of Asher (1 Chron. 7:39). **[2]** Ancestor of a family returned from the Exile (Ezra 2:5; Neh. 7:10). **[3]** Grandfather of the wife of Tobiah, who opposed Nehemiah in rebuilding the temple (Neh. 6:18).

Aram ("high; exalted"). **[1]** A son of Shem (Gen. 10:22–23; 1 Chron. 1:17). The Aramean people possibly are referred to. **[2]** A son of Abraham's nephew, Kemuel (Gen. 22:21). **[3]** a descendant from Asher (1 Chron. 7:34). **[4]** The Greek form of Ram (q.v.). *See also* "Places of the Bible."

Aran ("firmness"), a son of Seir (Gen. 36:28; 1 Chron. 1:42).

Araunah ("Jehovah is firm"). *See also* Ornan.

Arba ("four; strength of Baal"), an ancestor of the Anakim (Josh. 14:15; 15:13; 21:11).

Archelaus ("people's chief"), the son of Herod the Great who succeeded his father as the ruler of Idumea, Judea, and Samaria (Matt. 2:22).

Archippus ("chief groom"), a "fellow-soldier" whom Paul addresses (Col. 4:17; Philem. 2).

Ard ("sprout; descent"). **[1]** A son of Benjamin (Gen. 46:21). **[2]** A son of Bela listed in Numbers 26:40. Possibly identical with the Adar of First Chronicles 18:3.

Ardon ("descendant"), a son of Caleb of Judah mentioned in Chronicles (1 Chron. 2:18).

Areli ("valiant; heroic; God's hearth"), one of the sons of Gad (Gen. 46:16; Num. 26:17).

Aretas ("pleasing; virtuous"), Aretas IV, Philopatris. King of the Nabataeans whose deputy tried to seize Paul (2 Cor. 11:32).

Argob ("mound"), an officer of Pekahiah slain by Pekah (2 Kings 15:25).

Aridai ("delight of Hari"), a son of Haman slain by the Jews (Esther 9:9).

Aridatha ("given by Hari"), a son of Haman, hanged with his father (Esther 9:8).

Arieh ("lion of Jehovah"), a man of Israel killed by Pekah (2 Kings 15:25).

Ariel ("lion of God"), one sent by Ezra to secure the temple ministers (Ezra 8:16).

Arioch ("lion-like"). **[1]** A king of Ellasar in Assyria who took part in the expedition against Sodom and Gomorrah (Gen. 14:1, 9). **[2]** A captain of Nebuchadnezzar's guard commanded to slay the "wise men" (Dan. 2:14–15, 24–25).

Arisai, a son of Haman slain by the Jews (Esther 9:9).

Aristarchus ("the best ruler"), a faithful companion who accompanied Paul on his third missionary journey (Acts 19:29; 20:4; Col. 4:10).

Aristobulus ("best counselor"), a person in Rome whose household Paul saluted (Rom. 16:10).

Armoni ("of the palace"), a son of Saul by Rizpah (2 Sam. 21:8).

Arnan ("joyous; strong"), a descendant of David and founder of a family (1 Chron. 3:21).

Arod ("descent; posterity"), a son of Gad, progenitor of the tribe of Arodi (Num. 26:17; cf. Gen. 46:16).

Arphaxad, a son of Shem and an ancestor of Christ (Gen. 10:22, 24; 1 Chron. 1:17–18; Luke 3:36). Possibly the reference is to a tribe or people. Formerly identified with the mountainous land north of Nineveh.

Artaxerxes ("fervent to spoil"). [1] A king of Persia, Artaxerxes I Longimanus, at whose court Ezra and Nehemiah were officials (Ezra 7:1, 7, 11–12; Neh. 2:1; 5:14). [2] Some suppose that Ezra 4:7 uses "Artaxerxes" to refer to the pseudo-Smerdis king of Persia, but the reference is probably to [1].

Artemas ("whole; sound"), a friend of Paul's at Nicopolis (Titus 3:12).

Arza ("firm"), a steward of King Elah of Israel (1 Kings 16:9).

Asa ("physician; healer"). [1] The third king of Judah and an ancestor of Christ (1 Kings 15:8—16:29; Matt. 1:7–8). [2] Head of a Levite family (1 Chron. 9:16).

Asahel ("God is doer; God has made"). [1] A son of David's sister, Zeruiah. He was slain by Abner (2 Sam. 2:18–32; 3:27, 30). [2] A Levite sent to teach the Law (2 Chron. 17:8). [3] A Levite employed as an officer of the offerings and tithes (2 Chron. 31:13). [4] Father of Jonathan, appointed to take a census of foreign wives (Ezra 10:15).

Asahiah [Asaiah] ("Jehovah is doer; Jehovah has made"), one sent to inquire of the Lord concerning the Book of the Law (2 Kings 22:12, 14; 2 Chron. 34:20).

Asaiah ("Jehovah is doer; Jehovah has made"). [1] A prince of Simeon who helped defeat the people of Gedor (1 Chron. 4:36). [2] A descendant of Merari who helped bring up the ark (1 Chron. 6:30; 15:6, 11). [3] A resident of Jerusalem (1 Chron. 9:5). [4] *See also* Asahiah.

Asaph ("collector; gatherer"). [1] One of David's three chief musicians (1 Chron. 6:39; 15:17, 19). Author of Psalms 50, 73—83. [2] Father of Joah the recorder to Hezekiah (2 Kings 18:18, 37; 2 Chron. 29:13). [3] A Levite whose descendants lived in Jerusalem (1 Chron. 9:15). [4] One whose descendants were porters in David's time (1 Chron. 26:1). The text should possibly read Abiasaph (q.v.).

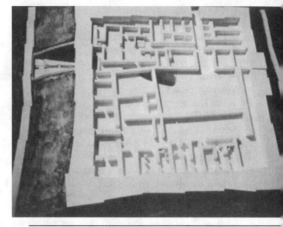

FORTRESS AT ARAD. *King Azariah (Uzziah) built several large fortresses to protect the highways of his expanded territories in the Negev Desert. This model of a fort at Arad shows the type of construction that Azariah's builders used.*

[5] A keeper of the royal forests in Judah (Neh. 2:8).

Asareel ("God is joined or ruler"), a descendant of Judah through Caleb (1 Chron. 4:16).

Asarelah ("Jehovah is joined; whom God has bound"), one appointed to the temple service by David (1 Chron. 25:2). He is called Jesharelah ("of Jesharel") in verse 14. This may be another name for Azarael [2].

Asenath ("dedicated to [the deity] Neit"), the Egyptian wife of Joseph (Gen. 41:45, 50; 46:20).

Aser, Greek form of Asher (q.v.).

Ashbea ("man of Baal"), a family of linen-workers that sprang from Shelah, son of Judah (1 Chron. 4:21).

Ashbel ("man of Baal"), son of Benjamin (Gen. 46:21; Num. 26:38; 1 Chron. 8:1).

Ashchenaz [Ashkenaz] ("a fire that spreads"), a son of Gomer (Gen. 10:3; 1 Chron. 1:6). Possibly a race or tribe who dwelt near Ararat and Minni in eastern Armenia.

Asher [Aser] ("happy"), the eighth son of Jacob and an ancestor of one of the twelve tribes of Israel (Gen. 30:13; 35:26; 46:17; 49:20; 1 Chron. 2:2). *See also* "Places of the Bible."

Ashkenaz. *See* Ashchenaz.

Ashpenaz, prince of Nebuchadnezzar's eunuchs who had charge of the captives from Judah (Dan. 1:3).

Ashriel. *See* Asriel.

PEOPLE OF THE BIBLE

Ashur ("free man; man of Horus"), a son of Hezron and head of the inhabitants of Tekoa (1 Chron. 2:24; 4:5).

Ashvath ("made; wrought"), a son of Japhlet; a descendant of Asher (1 Chron. 7:33).

Asiel ("God is doer or maker"), a descendant of Simeon and grandfather of Jehu (1 Chron. 4:35).

Asnah ("thornbush"), one whose descendants returned from Exile (Ezra 2:50).

Asnapper (alternative form of Osnapper), one who brought men from Susa and Elam to Samaria (Ezra 4:9). Formerly believed to have been Esarhaddon, he is now believed to have been Ashurbanipal, king of Assyria and Esarhaddon's son.

Aspatha ("horse-given"), son of Haman, slain by the Jews (Esther 9:7).

Asriel [Ashriel] ("God is joined; vow of God"), a son of Manasseh (Num. 26:31; 1 Chron. 7:14).

Asshur [Assur] ("level plain"). [1] A son of Shem (Gen. 10:22; 1 Chron. 1:17). Possibly the people of Assyria are intended. [2] Genesis 10:11, if denoting a person, refers to a son of Ham or to [1]. However, many scholars translate: "From that land he (Nimrod) went into Assyria (Asshur)." *See also* "Places of the Bible."

Assir ("prisoner"). [1] A son of Korah (Exod. 6:24; 1 Chron. 6:22). [2] A son of Ebiasaph (1 Chron. 6:23, 37). [3] A son of Jeconiah (Jehoiachin), king of Judah (1 Chron. 3:17).

Assur. *See* Asshur.

Asuppim, a word which should be translated "storehouse" as in Nehemiah 12:25. First Chronicles 26:15 should read: "The lot for the South Gate (southward) fell to Obededom, and the lot for the storehouse fell to his sons."

Asyncritus ("incomparable"), one at Rome whom Paul salutes (Rom. 16:14).

Atarah ("crown; ornament"), a wife of Jerahmeel (1 Chron. 2:26).

Ater ("bound; lame"). [1] One who sealed the new covenant with God after the Exile (Neh. 10:17). [2] Ancestor of a family of gatekeepers (Ezra 2:42; Neh. 7:45). [3] Ancestor of a family that returned from the Exile (Ezra 2:16; Neh. 7:21).

Athaiah ("Jehovah is helper"), a descendant of Judah dwelling in Jerusalem (Neh. 11:4).

Athaliah ("whom Jehovah has afflicted; Jehovah is strong"). [1] The daughter of Jezebel, wife of King Jehoram, and afterwards ruler of Judah for six years (2 Kings 8:26; 11:1–20; 2 Chron. 22:2—23:21). [2] A son of Jeroham (1 Chron. 8:26). [3] Father of a returned exile (Ezra 8:7).

Athlai ("Jehovah is strong"), one who married a foreign wife (Ezra 10:28).

Attai ("seasonable; timely"). [1] One who joined David at Ziklag (1 Chron. 12:11). [2] A son of King Rehoboam (2 Chron. 11:20). [3] Descendant of Pharez (1 Chron. 2:35–36).

Augustus (i.e., "consecrated" or "holy"). Acts 25:21, 25; 27:1 use the Greek rendering of the title "reverend" in this fashion, since Augustus had been dead many years.

Augustus Caesar. The imperial name of Octavian, a nephew of Julius Caesar who became emperor of Rome. During his reign, Christ was born (Luke 2:1).

Azaliah ("Jehovah is noble"), father of Shaphan the scribe (2 Kings 22:3; 2 Chron. 34:8).

Azaniah ("Jehovah is hearer"), father of one who signed the new covenant with God after the Exile (Neh. 10:9).

Azarael [Azareel] ("God is helper"). [1] One who joined David at Ziklag (1 Chron. 12:6). [2] One who ministered in the song service of the temple (1 Chron. 25:18). [3] A prince of Dan (1 Chron. 27:22). [4] One who took a foreign wife (Ezra 10:41). [5] A priest of the family of Immer (Neh. 11:13). [6] One who played the trumpet at the dedication of the new temple (Neh. 12:36).

Azariah ("Jehovah has helped"). [1] *See* Uzziah. [2] A ruler of Solomon's officers (1 Kings 4:5). [3] A descendant of David's high priest (1 Kings 4:2). [4] A descendant of Judah (1 Chron. 2:8). [5] A descendant of Je-rahmeel (1 Chron. 2:38–39). [6] A son of Ah-imaaz (1 Chron. 6:9). [7] A high priest and grandson of [6] (1 Chron. 6:10–11). [8] A son of Hilkiah the high priest under Josiah (1 Chron. 6:13–14; 9:11; Ezra 7:1). [9] An ancestor of Samuel the prophet (1 Chron. 6:36). [10] A prophet who went to Asa (2 Chron. 15:1). [11], [12] Two sons of King Jehoshaphat (2 Chron. 21:2). [13] *See* Ahaziah [2]. [14] A captain who helped to place Joash on the throne (2 Chron. 23:1). [15] Another man who helped Joash (2 Chron. 23:1). [16] A high priest who opposed Uzziah (2 Chron. 26:17, 20). [17] A chief of Ephraim (2 Chron. 28:12). [18] A descendant of Kohath and father of Joel (2 Chron. 29:12). [19] One who helped cleanse the temple (2 Chron. 29:12). **[20]** A chief of the family of Zadok, priest in Hezekiah's time (2 Chron. 31:10, 13). **[21]** Ancestor of Zadok and Ezra (Ezra 7:3). **[22]** One who repaired the wall of Jerusalem (Neh. 3:23–24). **[23]** One who came up to Jerusalem with Zerubbabel (Neh. 7:7). Perhaps this is another name of Seraiah (Ezra 2:2); if not, his name is omitted in this passage. **[24]** A priest who explained the Law (Neh. 8:7). **[25]** *See* Ezra [1]. **[26]** A prince of Judah (Neh. 12:33). **[27]** One who charged Jeremiah with false prophecy (Jer. 43:2). **[28]** A captive carried to Babylon with Daniel (Dan. 1:6–7, 11, 19; 2:17). *See* Abed-nego.

Azaz ("strong; powerful"), a descendant of Reuben (1 Chron. 5:8).

Azaziah ("Jehovah is strong"). **[1]** A Levite who took part in the musical service when the ark was brought to the temple (1 Chron. 15:21). **[2]** Father of a prince of Ephraim in David's time (1 Chron. 27:20). **[3]** A Levite who had the oversight of the dedicated things of the temple under Hezekiah (2 Chron. 31:13).

Azbuk ("pardon"), the father of a man named Nehemiah (Neh. 3:16).

Azel ("noble"), a descendant of King Saul (1 Chron. 8:37–38; 9:43–44). *See also* "Places of the Bible."

Azgad ("worship; supplication; Gad is strong"). **[1]** One whose descendants returned from the Exile with Zerubbabel (Ezra 2:12; Neh. 7:17). **[2]** One who came back to Jerusalem with Ezra (Ezra 8:12). **[3]** One who sealed the new covenant with God after the Exile (Neh. 10:15).

Aziel ("God is might"). *See* Jaaziel.

Aziza ("strong"), one who married a foreign wife (Ezra 10:27).

Azmaveth ("counsel or strength of death"). **[1]** One of David's mighty men (2 Sam. 23:31; 1 Chron. 11:33). **[2]** A descendant of Saul (1 Chron. 8:36; 9:42). **[3]** Father of two men who joined David at Ziklag (1 Chron. 12:3). **[4]** A treasury officer of David's (1 Chron. 27:25). *See also* "Places of the Bible."

Azor ("helper"), an ancestor of Christ (Matt. 1:13–14).

Azriel ("God is helper"). **[1]** A chief of the tribe of Manasseh (1 Chron. 5:24). **[2]** Father of a ruler of Naphtali in David's time (1 Chron. 27:19). **[3]** Father of an officer sent to capture Baruch (Jer. 36:26).

Azrikam ("my help has risen"). **[1]** One of the family of David (1 Chron. 3:23). **[2]** A son

of Azel of the family of Saul (1 Chron. 8:38; 9:44). **[3]** A descendant of Merari (1 Chron. 9:14; Neh. 11:15). **[4]** The governor of Ahaz's house (2 Chron. 28:7).

Azubah ("forsaken"). **[1]** The mother of King Jehoshaphat (1 Kings 22:42; 2 Chron. 20:31). **[2]** Wife of Caleb, the son of Hezron (1 Chron. 2:18–19).

Azur ("helper; helpful"). **[1]** Father of a prince that Ezekiel saw in a vision (Ezek. 11:1). **[2]** Father of the false prophet Hananiah (Jer. 28:1). *See also* Azzur.

Azzan ("sharp; thorn"), father of a chief of Issachar (Num. 34:26).

Azzur ("helper; helpful"), one who sealed the covenant (Neh. 10:17). *See also* Azur.

B

Baal ("master; lord"). **[1]** A descendant of Reuben (1 Chron. 5:5). **[2]** The fourth of ten sons of Jehiel (1 Chron. 8:29, 30; 9:36). *See also* "Places of the Bible."

Baal-hanan ("the lord is gracious"). **[1]** The seventh of the kings of Edom (Gen. 36:38–39; 1 Chron. 1:49–50). **[2]** A tender of olive and sycamore trees in David's time (1 Chron. 27:28).

Baalis ("lord of joy"), the king of the Ammonites after Jerusalem was taken (Jer. 40:14).

Baana [Baanah] ("son of grief; patient"). **[1]** One of Solomon's royal merchants (1 Kings 4:12). **[2]** Another merchant of Solomon, responsible for Asher (1 Kings 4:16). **[3]** Father of Zadok, the builder of the temple (Neh. 3:4). **[4]** Father of one of David's mighty men (2 Sam. 23:29; 1 Chron. 11:30). **[5]** A captain in Ish-bosheth's army (2 Sam. 4:2, 5–6, 9). **[6]** One who returned from the Exile with Zerubbabel (Ezra 2:2; Neh. 7:7; 10:27).

Baara ("a wood; the burning one"), a wife of Shaharaim (1 Chron. 8:8).

Baaseiah ("Jehovah is bold"), an ancestor of Asaph (1 Chron. 6:40).

Baasha ("boldness"), the third king of Israel; war and wickedness characterized his reign (1 Kings 15:16—16:13).

Bakbakkar ("diligent; searcher"), a Levite who returned from the Babylonian Captivity (1 Chron. 9:15). *See* Bakbukiah [1].

Bakbuk ("waste; hollow"), one whose descendant returned from the Exile (Ezra 2:51; Neh. 7:53).

PEOPLE OF THE BIBLE

Bakbukiah ("wasted by Jehovah"). **[1]** A Levite who lived in Jerusalem (Neh. 11:17). Perhaps identical with Bakbakkar (q.v.). **[2]** A Levite who returned with Zerubbabel (Neh. 12:9). **[3]** A Levite and guard of the temple storehouse (Neh. 12:25).

Balaam ("a pilgrim; lord [Baal] of the people"), a prophet that the king of Moab induced to curse Israel. Instead, God put words of blessing in his mouth (Num. 22—24; 31:8).

Balac, Greek form of Balak (q.v.).

Baladan ("having power"), father of the king of Babylon in Hezekiah's time (2 Kings 20:12; Isa. 39:1).

Balak [Balac] ("void; empty"), the king of Moab that hired Balaam to curse Israel (Num. 22—24; Josh. 24:9).

Bani ("posterity"). **[1]** One of David's mighty men (2 Sam. 23:36). **[2]** A descendant of Merari (1 Chron. 6:46). **[3]** A descendant of Pharez (1 Chron. 9:4). **[4]** Father of a family that returned from the Babylonian Captivity (Ezra 2:10; 10:29). In Nehemiah 7:15, he is called Binnui. **[5]** One whose descendants had taken foreign wives during the Exile (Ezra 10:34). **[6]** A descendant of [5] who took a foreign wife during the Exile (Ezra 10:38). **[7]** A Levite who helped to repair the wall of Jerusalem (Neh. 3:17; 8:7). **[8]** A Levite who assisted in the devotions of the people (Neh. 9:4; 10:13). **[9]** One who sealed the new covenant with God after the Exile (Neh. 10:14). **[10]** A Levite whose son was an overseer of the Levites after the Exile. Perhaps the same as [7] or [8] (Neh. 11:22). **[11]**, **[12]**, **[13]** Three Levites who participated in the temple worship (Neh. 9:4–5).

Bar (Aramaic for the Hebrew "bēn," "son.") "Bar" and "ben" are frequently prefixed to names to indicate direct relationship. Thus Peter is called Bar-jonah (son of Jonah) because his father was named Jonah (Matt. 16:17) and perhaps Nathanael was called Bartholomew (son of Tolmai) because his father was named Tolmai. It can also designate characteristics or conditions. For example, Joses was called Barnabas ("son of consolation") because of the aid he rendered the apostles (Acts 4:36).

Barabbas ("father's son"), a murderer whom the people demanded that Pontius Pilate should release instead of Christ (Matt. 27:17, 20–21, 26; Mark 15:7). *See* Bar.

Barachel ("blessed of God"), father of Elihu, a figure in Job (Job 32:2, 6).

Barachias (Greek form of Barachiah), the father of a prophet whom the Jews killed (Matt. 23:35). It is quite possible the reference is to the author of the Book of Zechariah, Zechariah [11], or else an unknown prophet. *See* Berechiah.

Barak ("lightning"), the general of the judge Deborah; he helped to defeat Sisera (Judg. 4:6—5:15).

Bariah ("fugitive"), a descendant of David (1 Chron. 3:22).

Bar-jesus. *See* Elymas; Bar.

Bar-jonah. *See* Peter; Bar.

Barkos ("partly colored"), an ancestor of captives returning from the Exile (Ezra 2:53; Neh. 7:55).

Barnabas ("son of consolation"), a Jewish Christian who traveled widely with Paul (Acts 4:36; 9:27; 11:22–30; Gal. 2:1). His original name was Joses, but he was named Barnabas by the apostles (Acts 4:36); obviously they considered him to be *their* consoler. *See* Bar.

Barsabas ("son of Saba"). *See* Bar; Joseph [11]; Juda [12].

Bartholomew ("son of Tolmai"), one of Jesus' twelve apostles (Matt. 10:3; Mark 3:18; Acts 1:13). He is probably the same as Nathanael (q.v.). *See* Bar.

Bartimaeus (Aramaic *bar*, "son" and Greek *timaios,* "honorable"), a blind beggar healed by Christ (Mark 10:46–52). *See* Bar.

Baruch ("blessed"). **[1]** Jeremiah's friend and scribe (Jer. 32:12–13, 16; 36). **[2]** One who helped to rebuild the wall of Jerusalem (Neh. 3:20; 10:6). **[3]** A descendant of Perez who returned from the Exile (Neh. 11:5).

Barzillai ("strong"). **[1]** One who befriended David when he fled from Absalom (2 Sam. 17:27; 19:31–39). **[2]** Husband of Merab, Saul's eldest daughter, and father of Adriel (2 Sam. 21:8). **[3]** A priest whose genealogy was lost during the Exile (Ezra 2:61; Neh. 7:63).

Bashemath [Basmath] ("fragrant"). **[1]** A daughter of Solomon (1 Kings 4:15). **[2]** A wife of Esau (Gen. 26:34). *See also* Esau. **[3]** Another wife of Esau, whom he married to appease his father (Gen. 36:3–4, 10, 13). *See also* Esau's Wives.

Basmath. *See* Bashemath.

Bath-sheba ("the seventh daughter; daughter of the oath"), the beautiful wife of Uriah the Hittite, and afterward the wife of David (2 Sam. 11:3; 12:24; 1 Kings 1:11—2:19). She was the mother of Solomon and an ancestor of Christ (Matt. 1:6). She is called Bath-shua in First Chronicles 3:5.

Bath-shua ("daughter of prosperity"). [1] Another name of Bath-sheba (q.v.). [2] The wife of Judah. In Genesis 38:2 and First Chronicles 2:3, the KJV incorrectly renders her name as "daughter of Shua"; Bath-shua is really a proper name.

Bavai ("wisher"), one who helped to rebuild the wall of Jerusalem (Neh. 3:18).

Bazlith [Bazluth] ("asking"), one whose descendants returned from the Exile (Ezra 2:52; Neh. 7:54).

Bealiah ("Jehovah is lord"), a man who joined David at Ziklag (1 Chron. 12:5).

Bebai ("fatherly"). [1] An ancestor of captives returning from the Exile (Ezra 2:11; Neh. 7:16). [2] An ancestor of some returning from the Exile with Ezra (Ezra 8:11; 10:28); perhaps the same as [1]. [3] One who sealed the new covenant with God after the Exile (Neh. 10:15).

Becher ("youth; firstborn"). [1] A son of Benjamin (Gen. 46:21). [2] A son of Ephraim (Num. 26:35); perhaps the same as Bered in First Chronicles 7:20.

Bechorath ("first birth"), an ancestor of Saul (1 Sam. 9:1).

Bedad ("alone"), father of Hadad, fourth king of Edom (Gen. 36:35; 1 Chron. 1:46).

Bedan ("son of judgment"). [1] A leader of Israel mentioned as a deliverer of the nation (1 Sam. 12:11). The Septuagint, Syriac, and Arabic read *Barak* instead; however, many think this is a reference to Abdon. [2] A descendant of Manasseh (1 Chron. 7:17).

Bedeiah ("servant of Jehovah"), one who had married a foreign wife during the Exile (Ezra 10:35).

Beeliada ("the lord knows"), a son of David (1 Chron. 14:7) also known as Eliada (2 Sam. 5:16; 1 Chron. 3:8).

Beera [Beerah] ("expounder"). [1] A descendant of Asher (1 Chron. 7:37). [2] A prince of Reuben who was carried captive to Assyria (1 Chron. 5:6).

Beeri ("man of the springs" or "expounder"). [1] Father of Judith, a wife of Esau (Gen. 26:34). *See also* Esau's Wives. [2] Father of the prophet Hosea (Hos. 1:1).

Bela [Belah] ("consumption"). [1] A king of Edom, the first mentioned in Scripture (Gen. 36:32–33; 1 Chron. 1:43–44). [2] A son of Benjamin and one of the left-handed heroes (Gen. 46:21; 1 Chron. 7:6–7). [3] Descendant of Reuben (1 Chron. 5:8). *See also* "Places of the Bible."

Belshazzar (Hebrew form of the Babylonian name Bel-shar-usur—"[the god] Bel has protected the king [ship]"), the son of Nabonidus and co-regent in Babylon. He witnessed strange handwriting on the wall of his palace before his kingdom was overthrown by Persia (Dan. 5; 7:1; 8:1).

Belteshazzar (Hebrew form of the Babylonian name, Balat-usu-usur—"Protect his life!"), the name given to Daniel in Babylon (Dan. 1:7). *See* Daniel.

Ben ("son"), an assistant in the temple musical service at the time of David (1 Chron. 15:18).

Benaiah ("Jehovah has built"). [1] The third leader of David's army, counselor to the kings, and loyal friend of both David and Solomon (2 Sam. 8:18; 20:23; 1 Kings 1:8—2:46). [2] One of David's mighty men (2 Sam. 23:30; 1 Chron. 11:31). [3] Head of a family of the tribe of Simeon (1 Chron. 4:36). [4] One of David's priests (1 Chron. 15:18, 20, 24; 16:5–6). [5] Father of one of David's counselors (1 Chron. 27:34). [6] The grandfather of Jahaziel (2 Chron. 20:14). [7] An overseer of the temple during Hezekiah's reign

BEN-HADAD'S CAPITAL. *When Ben-hadad II united the Arameans (who lived in the territory northwest of Israel) he strengthened Damascus as the capital of his domain. Ben-hadad's armies defeated the combined forces of Israel and Judah in a battle at Ramoth-gilead, in which King Ahab was killed (1 Kings 22:1–35). Modern Damascus shows the strong influence of Muslim culture.*

(2 Chron. 31:13). **[8]**, **[9]**, **[10]**, **[11]** Four men who married foreign wives during the Exile (Ezra 10:25, 30, 35, 43). **[12]** Father of Pelatiah, a prince of Judah (Ezek. 11:1, 13).

Ben-ammi ("son of my people"), the ancestor of the Ammonites (Gen. 19:38), born to Lot and his daughter.

Ben-hadad ("son of [the god] Hadad"). **[1]** Ben-hadad I, the king of Syria who made a league with Asa of Judah and invaded Israel (1 Kings 15:18, 20; 2 Chron. 10:2, 4). **[2]** Ben-hadad II, another king of Syria defeated by Ahab; he eventually laid siege to Samaria itself (1 Kings 20; 2 Kings 6:24; 8:7, 9. **[3]** The son of Hazael who reigned over Syria as the empire disintegrated (2 Kings 13:3, 24–25; Amos 1:4). **[4]** Possibly a general title of the Syrian kings (Jer. 49:27).

Ben-hail ("strong; son of strength"), a prince of Judah under Jehoshaphat (2 Chron. 17:7).

Ben-hanan ("son of grace"), a son of Shimon of the tribe of Judah (1 Chron. 4:20).

Beninu ("our son"), one who sealed the new covenant with God after the Exile (Neh. 10:13).

Benjamin ("son of the right hand"). **[1]** The youngest son of Jacob; his descendants became one of the twelve tribes of Israel (Gen. 35:18, 24; 42:4, 36; 43—45. **[2]** A descendant of Benjamin (1 Chron. 7:10). **[3]** A descendant of Harim (Ezra 10:32). **[4]** One who helped to repair the wall of Jerusalem (Neh. 3:23). **[5]** One who helped to dedicate the wall of Jerusalem (Neh. 12:34).

Beno ("his son"), a descendant of Merari (1 Chron. 24:26–27).

Benoni ("son of my sorrow"), name given to Rachel's child as she died bearing him; Jacob changed his name to Benjamin (q.v.).

Ben-zoheth ("son of Zoheth; corpulent; strong"), a descendant of Judah through Caleb (1 Chron. 4:20).

Beor [Bosor] ("shepherd"). **[1]** Father of Bela, the king of Edom (Gen. 36:32; 1 Chron. 1:43). **[2]** Father of the prophet Balaam (Num. 22:5; 24:3, 15; 31:8).

Bera ("gift"), a king of Sodom in the time of Abram (Gen. 14:2).

Berachah ("blessing"), one who joined David at Ziklag (1 Chron. 12:3). *See also* "Places of the Bible."

Berachiah. *See* Berechiah [2].

Beraiah ("unfortunate"), a chief of Benjamin (1 Chron. 8:21).

Berechiah [Berachiah] ("Jehovah is bless-ing"). **[1]** A descendant of Jehoiakim (1 Chron. 3:20). **[2]** Father of Asaph, the chief singer (1 Chron. 6:39; 15:17). **[3]** A Levite who lived near Jerusalem (1 Chron. 9:16). **[4]** One of the tabernacle doorkeepers (1 Chron. 15:23). **[5]** A descendant of Ephraim in the time of Pekah (2 Chron. 28:12). **[6]** Father of one who repaired the wall of Jerusalem (Neh. 3:4, 30; 6:18). **[7]** The father of the prophet Zechariah (Zech. 1:1, 7). *See* Barachias.

Bered ("seed place"), a descendant of Ephraim (1 Chron. 7:20); perhaps the same as Becher (Num. 26:35). *See also* "Places of the Bible."

Beri ("expounder"), a descendant of Asher (1 Chron. 7:36).

Beriah ("unfortunate"). **[1]** A descendant of Asher (Gen. 46:17; Num. 26:44–45; 1 Chron. 7:30–31). **[2]** A descendant of Ephraim (1 Chron. 7:23). **[3]** A descendant of Benjamin (1 Chron. 8:13, 16). **[4]** A descendant of Levi (1 Chron. 23:10–11).

Bernice ("victorious"), the immoral daughter of Herod Agrippa I. She and her brother Agrippa (with whom she was living in incest) sat in judgment on Paul (Acts 25:13, 23; 26:30).

Berodach-baladan, a copyist's mistake or another form of Merodach-baladan (q.v.).

Besai ("treading down"), one who returned to Jerusalem with Zerubbabel (Ezra 2:49; Neh. 7:52).

Besodeiah ("given to trust in Jehovah"), one of the repairers of the old gate of Jerusalem (Neh. 3:6).

Beth-rapha ("place of fear"), a descendant of Judah or a city Eshton built (1 Chron. 4:12).

Bethuel ("dweller in God"), a son of Nahor, Abraham's brother (Gen. 22:22–23; 28:5). *See also* "Places of the Bible."

Bezai ("shining; high"). **[1]** An ancestor of 323 captives returning from the Exile (Ezra 2:17; Neh. 7:23). **[2]** One who sealed the new covenant with God after the Exile (Neh. 10:18).

Bezaleel ("God is protection"). **[1]** A chief worker and designer of the tabernacle (Exod. 31:2; 35:30; 36:1–2). **[2]** One who had married a foreign wife (Ezra 10:30).

Bezer ("strong"), one of the heads of Asher (1 Chron. 7:37). *See also* "Places of the Bible."

Bichri ("youth; firstborn"), an ancestor of Sheba, who rebelled against David (2 Sam. 20:1).

Bidkar ("servant of Ker [Kar]"), a captain

in the service of Jehu who executed the sentence on Ahab's son (2 Kings 9:25).

Bigtha ("given by fortune"), a chamberlain of Ahasuerus (Esther 1:10).

Bigthan [Bigthana] ("given by fortune"), a chamberlain who conspired against Ahasuerus (Esther 2:21; 6:2).

Bigvai ("happy; of the people"). **[1]** Head of one of the families who returned with Zerubbabel (Ezra 2:2, 14; 8:14; Neh. 7:7, 19). **[2]** One who sealed the covenant with Nehemiah (Neh. 10:16).

Bildad ("lord Adad; son of contention"), one of Job's three "friends" (Job 2:11; 8:1; 18:1; 25:1; 42:9).

Bilgah ("bursting forth; firstborn"). **[1]** A priest in the tabernacle service (1 Chron. 24:14). **[2]** A priest who came up to Jerusalem with Zerubbabel (Neh. 12:5, 18).

Bilgai ("bursting forth"), one who sealed the new covenant with God after the Exile (Neh. 10:8); perhaps the same as Bilgah [2].

Bilhah ("tender"), the handmaid of Rachel and mother of Dan and Naphtali (Gen. 29:29; 30:3–5, 7). *See also* "Places of the Bible."

Bilhan ("tender"). **[1]** A descendant of Seir (Gen. 36:27; 1 Chron. 1:42). **[2]** A descendant of Benjamin (1 Chron. 7:10).

Bilshan ("searcher"), a prince who returned from the Exile (Ezra 2:2; Neh. 7:7).

Bimhal ("circumcised"), a descendant of Asher (1 Chron. 7:33).

Binea ("wanderer"), a descendant of Saul (1 Chron. 8:37; 9:43).

Binnui ("being a family"). **[1]** A Levite appointed by Ezra to weigh gold and silver (Ezra 8:33). **[2],[3]** Two men who married foreign wives during the Exile (Ezra 10:30, 38). **[4]** One who repaired the wall of Jerusalem (Neh. 3:24; 10:9). **[5]** A Levite who came up with Zerubbabel (Neh. 12:8). **[6]** *See* Bani [4].

Birsha ("thick; strong"), a king of Gomorrah in the days of Abraham (Gen. 14:2).

Birzavith ("olive well"), descendant of Asher (1 Chron. 7:31).

Bishlam ("peaceful"), a foreign colonist who wrote a letter of complaint against the Jews (Ezra 4:7).

Bithiah ("daughter of Jehovah"), a daughter of the pharaoh and wife of Mered (1 Chron. 4:18); her name implies her conversion.

Biztha ("eunuch"), one of Ahasuerus' eunuchs (Esther 1:10).

Blastus ("a bud"), the chamberlain of Herod Agrippa I (Acts 12:20).

HOUSE OF CAIAPHAS. *A monastery built in 1931 stands on the traditional site of the house of high priest Caiaphas, on the eastern slope of Mount Zion in Jerusalem. Caiaphas (high priest A.D. 18–36) was the son-in-law of the former high priest, Annas, and worked in close cooperation with him (cf. John 18:13). He presided at the trial of Jesus (Matt. 26:57).*

Boanerges, the surname bestowed upon James and John, the sons of Zebedee. It means "sons of thunder" (Mark 3:17).

Boaz [Booz] ("fleetness; strength"), a Bethlehemite of Judah who became the husband of Ruth and an ancestor of Christ (Ruth 2—4; Matt. 1:5; Luke 3:32).

Bocheru ("youth"), a descendant of King Saul (1 Chron. 8:38; 9:44).

Bohan ("stumpy"), a descendant of Reuben for whom a boundary stone between Judah and Benjamin was named (Josh. 15:6; 18:17). *See also* "Places of the Bible."

Booz, Greek form of Boaz (q.v.).

Bosor, Greek form of Beor (q.v.).

Bukki ("proved of Jehovah; mouth of Jeho-

PEOPLE OF THE BIBLE

vah"). **[1]** An ancestor of Ezra and descendant of Aaron (1 Chron. 6:5, 51; Ezra 7:4). **[2]** A prince of the tribe of Dan (Num. 34:22).

Bukkiah ("proved of Jehovah; mouth of Jehovah"), a son of Heman and musician in the temple (1 Chron. 25:4, 13).

Bunah ("understanding"), a son of Jerahmeel (1 Chron. 2:25).

Bunni ("my understanding"). **[1]** An ancestor of Shemaiah the Levite (Neh. 11:15). **[2]** A Levite who helped Ezra in teaching the Law (Neh. 9:4). **[3]** One who sealed the new covenant with God after the Exile (Neh. 10:15).

Buz ("contempt"). **[1]** The second son of Nahor, the brother of Abraham (Gen. 22:21). **[2]** A descendant of Gad (1 Chron. 5:14).

Buzi ("despised by Jehovah"), a descendant of Aaron and father of Ezekiel (Ezek. 1:3).

C

Caesar, the name of a branch of the aristocratic family of the Julii, which gained control of the Roman government; afterward it became a formal title of the Roman emperors. *See* Augustus Caesar; Tiberius Caesar; Claudius Caesar.

Caiaphas ("depression"), the high priest who took a leading role in the trial of Jesus (Matt. 26:3, 57–68; John 11:49).

Cain ("acquired; spear"), the eldest son of Adam who killed his brother Abel (Gen. 4:1–25). *See also* Tubal-cain; "Places of the Bible."

Cainan [Kenan] ("acquired"). **[1]** A son of Enosh and ancestor of Christ (Gen. 5:9; Luke 3:37). The KJV inconsistently spells the same name *Kenan* in First Chronicles 1:2. **[2]** A son of Arphaxad and an ancestor of Christ (Luke 3:36). It should be noted that this name occurs in the Septuagint text and not in the Hebrew of Genesis 10:24; 11:12. The presence of this name shows that the early lists in Genesis were not meant to be complete.

Calcol ("sustaining" or "nourishment"), a descendant of Judah (1 Chron. 2:6). *See also* Chalcol.

Caleb [Chelubai] ("impetuous; raging with madness"). **[1]** One of the spies sent out by Moses to see the Promised Land (Num. 13:6; Josh. 14—15). **[2]** A son of Hezron and grandfather of [1] (1 Chron. 2:18–19, 42).

Canaan ("low"), a son of Ham and grandson of Noah (Gen. 10:6–19; 1 Chron. 1:8, 13).

Possibly a reference to the inhabitants of Canaan.

Candace ("contrite one"), a dynastic title of Ethiopian queens (Acts 8:27).

Caphtorim [Caphthorim], a son of Mizraim (Gen. 10:14; 1 Chron. 1:12). Possibly a reference to the people from Caphtor.

Carcas ("severe"), a chamberlain of Ahasuerus (Esther 1:10).

Careah. *See* Kareah.

Carmi ("fruitful; noble"). **[1]** A son of Reuben who went to Egypt with him (Gen. 46:9; Exod. 6:14; 1 Chron. 5:3). **[2]** A descendant of Judah (Josh. 7:1; 1 Chron. 2:7). **[3]** Another son of Judah (1 Chron. 4:1); some identify him with [2].

Carpus ("fruit; wrist"), a friend with whom Paul left his cloak (2 Tim. 4:13).

Carshena ("distinguished; lean"), one of the seven princes of Persia and Media during Ahasuerus' reign (Esther 1:14).

Casluhim ("fortified"), a son of Mizraim (Gen. 10:14; 1 Chron. 1:12). Possibly a people related to the Egyptians. They were the ancestors of the Philistines.

Cephas. *See* Peter.

Chalcol ("sustaining"), a wise man with whom Solomon was compared (1 Kings 4:31).

Chedorlaomer (Elamite, Kutir-Lakamar—"servant of [the goddess] Lakamar"), a king of Elam who came up against Sodom and Gomorrah (Gen. 14:1–24).

Chelal ("completeness"), a man who took a foreign wife during the Exile (Ezra 10:30).

Chelluh ("robust"), a man who married a foreign wife during the Exile (Ezra 10:35).

Chelub ("boldness"). **[1]** A descendant of Judah (1 Chron. 4:11). **[2]** Father of Ezri (1 Chron. 27:26).

Chelubai. *See* Caleb [2].

Chenaanah ("flat; low"). **[1]** A son of Bilhan (1 Chron. 7:10). **[2]** Father of the false prophet Zedekiah (1 Kings 22:11, 24).

Chenani ("Jehovah, creator"), a Levite in the time of Ezra (Neh. 9:4).

Chenaniah ("established by Jehovah"). **[1]** A head Levite when David brought the ark of the covenant to the temple (1 Chron. 15:22, 27). **[2]** An officer of David (1 Chron. 26:29). *See also* Conaniah.

Cheran ("lyre; lamb; union"), a son of Dishon (Gen. 36:26).

Chesed ("gain"), son of Nahor and Milcah and nephew of Abraham (Gen. 22:22).

Chidon. *See* Nachon.

Chileab ("restraint of father"), a son of David (2 Sam. 3:3); probably also called Daniel (1 Chron. 3:1).

Chilion ("pining"), son of Naomi and husband of Orpah (Ruth 1:2, 5).

Chimham ("pining"), a friend and political supporter of David (2 Sam. 19:37–38, 40; Jer. 41:17).

Chislon ("strength"), a prince of the tribe of Benjamin (Num. 34:21).

Chloe ("a tender sprout"), a Corinthian woman or an Ephesian woman who knew of the problems at Corinth (1 Cor. 1:11).

Christ. *See* Jesus.

CYRUS CYLINDER. *King Cyrus of Persia allowed the Jews to return home and rebuild their temple. Inscribed on this clay cylinder are the king's words: "As to the region from . . . as far as Ashur and Susa, Akkad . . . , as well as the towns of the Gutians, ... I also gathered all their former inhabitants and returned to them their habitations."*

Chushan-rishathaim ("man of Cush; he of the twofold crime"), a king of Mesopotamia that God chose to punish Israel (Judg. 3:8, 10).

Chuza ("seer"), steward of Herod Antipas whose wife ministered to Christ and the apostles (Luke 8:3).

Cis, Greek form of Kish (q.v.).

Claudia ("lame"), a Roman Christian who sent greetings to Timothy (2 Tim. 4:21).

Claudius Caesar ("lame ruler"), Roman emperor who banished the Jews from Rome (Acts 18:2).

Claudius Lysias ("lame dissolution"), a Roman officer, chief captain in Jerusalem (Acts 23:26).

Clement ("mild"), a co-worker with Paul at Philippi (Phil. 4:3).

Cleopas ("renowned father"), one of the disciples whom Jesus met on the way to Emmaus (Luke 24:18). *See also* Cleophas.

Cleophas ("renowned"), the husband of one of the Marys who followed Jesus (John 19:25); possibly the same as Alphaeus (q.v.). *See also* Alphaeus; Cleopas.

Col-hozeh ("wholly a seer"). **[1]** Father of Shallum, who helped to rebuild the wall of Jerusalem (Neh. 3:15). **[2]** A man of Judah (Neh. 11:5); possibly the same as [1].

Conaniah [Cononiah] ("Jehovah has founded"). **[1]** A Levite appointed to be overseer of the tithes and offerings at the temple (2 Chron. 31:12–13). **[2]** A chief of the Levites (2 Chron. 35:9). *See also* Chenaniah.

Coniah. *See* Jehoiachin.

Cononiah. *See* Conaniah.

Core, Greek form of Korah (q.v.).

Cornelius ("of a horn"), a Roman centurion who was converted to Christianity (Acts 10:1–31).

Cosam ("diviner"), an ancestor of Christ (Luke 3:28).

Coz ("thorn; nimble"), a descendant of Judah through Caleb (1 Chron. 4:8).

Cozbi ("deceitful"), a Midianite woman slain by Phinehas at Shittim (Num. 25:6–18).

Crescens ("increasing"), an assistant with Paul at Rome (2 Tim. 4:10).

Crispus ("curled"), a ruler of the Jewish synagogue at Corinth who was converted to Christ (Acts 18:7–8; 1 Cor. 1:14).

Cush ("black"). **[1]** Eldest son of Ham (Gen. 10:6–8; 1 Chron. 1:8–10). **[2]** A descendant of Benjamin and enemy of David (Psa. 7, title). *See also* "Places of the Bible."

Cushi ("black"). **[1]** Father of Zephaniah (Zeph. 1:1). **[2]** Great-grandfather of Jehudi

PEOPLE OF THE BIBLE

EN-GEDI. *This spring of fresh water is En-gedi, where David hid from Saul (1 Sam. 23:29). Located in the northeast corner of the Negev Desert, the fountain creates an oasis rich with semitropical vegetation and celebrated for its palms, vineyards, and balsam (Song of Sol. 1:14).*

(Jer. 36:14). **[3]** The messenger that told David of the defeat of Absalom (2 Sam. 18:21–32).

Cyrenius [Quirinius] ("of Cyrene"), the governor of Syria (Luke 2:2).

Cyrus, founder of the Persian Empire; he returned the Jews to their land (Ezra 1:1–4, 7; 3:7; Isa. 44:28; 45:1–4; Dan. 6:28).

D

Dalaiah ("Jehovah is deliverer" or "Jehovah has raised"), a descendant of Judah (1 Chron. 3:24). *See also* Delaiah.

Dalphon ("swift"), a son of Haman slain by the Jews (Esther 9:6–7, 10).

Damaris ("heifer"), an Athenian woman converted by Paul (Acts 17:34).

Dan ("judge"), the fifth son of Jacob and ancestor of one of the twelve tribes of Israel (Gen. 30:6; 49:16–17). *See also* "Places of the Bible."

Daniel ("God is my judge"). **[1]** A prophet at the time of Nebuchadnezzar and Cyrus. His wisdom and faith earned him a position of esteem under Nebuchadnezzar and Darius (Dan. 1:1–6; 2; 6:1–2). **[2]** One of the sons of David (1 Chron. 3:1). *See* Chileab. **[3]** A Levite of the line of Ithamar (Ezra 8:2; Neh. 10:6).

Dara ("bearer [pearl] of wisdom"), a son of Zerah (1 Chron. 2:6). Possibly the same as Darda (q.v.).

Darda ("bearer [pearl] of wisdom"), a wise man with whom Solomon was compared (1 Kings 4:31). *See also* Dara.

Darius ("he that informs himself"). **[1]** The sub-king of Cyrus who received the kingdom of Belshazzar (Dan. 5:30—6:28); also known as Darius the Mede. **[2]** The fourth king of Persia (Ezra 4:5; Hag. 1:1; Zech. 1:1); also called Hystaspis. **[3]** Darius II (Nothus) who ruled Persia and Babylon (Neh. 12:22).

Darkon ("carrier"), a servant of Solomon whose descendants returned to Palestine after the Exile (Ezra 2:56; Neh. 7:58).

Dathan ("fount"), a chief of the tribe of Reuben who tried to overthrow Moses and Aaron (Num. 16; 26:9; Deut. 11:6).

David ("beloved"), the great statesman, general, and king of Israel. He united the divided tribes of Israel and made many preparations for the temple, which his son Solomon would complete (1 Sam. 16—1 Kings 2:11). He was an ancestor of Christ (Matt. 1:6).

Debir ("oracle"), a king of Eglon defeated by Joshua (Josh. 10:3).

Deborah ("bee"). **[1]** The nurse of Rebekah (Gen. 24:59; 35:8). **[2]** Prophetess and judge of Israel who helped to deliver her people from Jabin and Sisera (Judg. 4:4–14; 5).

Dedan. [1] A descendant of Cush (Gen. 10:7). Possibly a people of Arabia in the neighborhood of Edom. **[2]** A son of Jokshan and grandson of Abraham (Gen. 25:3). *See also* Dedan in "Places of the Bible."

Dekar ("lancer"), father of one of Solomon's commissaries (1 Kings 4:9).

Delaiah ("Jehovah has raised; Jehovah is deliverer"). **[1]** One of David's priests (1 Chron. 24:18). **[2]** A prince who urged Jehoiakim not to destroy the roll containing Jeremiah's prophecies (Jer. 36:12, 25). **[3]** Ancestor of a postexilic family that had lost its genealogy (Ezra 2:60; Neh. 7:62). **[4]** The father of Shemaiah (Neh. 6:10). *See also* Dalaiah.

Delilah ("longing; dainty one"), a woman

whom the Philistines paid to find Samson's source of strength (Judg. 16).

Demas ("popular"), a friend of Paul at Rome who later forsook him (Col. 4:14; 2 Tim. 4:10; Philem. 24).

Demetrius ("belonging to Demeter"). **[1]** A Christian praised by John (3 John 12). **[2]** A silversmith who led the opposition against Paul at Ephesus (Acts 19:24–41).

Deuel ("knowledge of God"), father of Eliasaph (Num. 1:14). He is called Reuel in Numbers 2:14; we do not know which name is original.

Diblaim ("two cakes; double embrace"), father-in-law of Hosea (Hos. 1:3).

Dibri ("eloquent" or "on the pasture born"), a descendant of Dan whose daughter married an Egyptian; her son was stoned for blasphemy (Lev. 24:11).

Didymus. *See* Thomas.

Diklah ("place of palms"), a son of Joktan (Gen. 10:27; 1 Chron. 1:21). Possibly a people who dwelt in Arabia is intended.

Dinah ("justice"), the daughter of Jacob and Leah who was violated by Hamor; this resulted in a tribal war (Gen. 34).

Dionysius ("Bacchus"), a member of the supreme court at Athens converted by Paul (Acts 17:34).

Diotrephes ("nourished by Jupiter"), a person who opposed John's authority (3 John 9–10).

Diphath. *See* Riphath.

Dishan ("antelope" or "leaping"), a son of Seir (Gen. 36:21, 28, 30; 1 Chron. 1:38, 42). *See also* Dishon.

Dishon ("antelope" or "leaping"). **[1]** A son of Seir (Gen. 36:21, 30; 1 Chron. 1:38). **[2]** A grandson of Seir (Gen. 36:25; 1 Chron. 1:41). *See also* Dishan.

Dodai. *See* Dodo.

Dodanim [Rodanim], the son of Javan (Gen. 10:4). First Chronicles 1:7 states his name as Rodanim; many scholars consider Rodanim to be original. Possibly a reference to the inhabitants of Rhodes and the neighboring islands.

Dodavah ("loved of Jehovah"), father of Eliezer (2 Chron. 20:37).

Dodo [Dodai] ("beloved"). **[1]** The grandfather of Tola, a judge (Judg. 10:1). **[2]** A commander of one of the divisions of David's army and father of Eleazar **[3]** (2 Sam. 23:9; 1 Chron. 11:12; 27:4). **[3]** Father of Elhanan **[2]** (2 Sam. 23:24; 1 Chron. 11:26).

Doeg ("anxious; cared for"), a servant of King Saul who executed the priests of Nob on Saul's orders (1 Sam. 21:7; 22:9–19).

Dorcas. *See* Tabitha.

Drusilla ("watered by dew"), a Jewess, the daughter of Herod Agrippa I and wife of Felix; she and Felix heard a powerful message of Paul's (Acts 24:24–25).

Dumah ("silence"), a descendant of Ishmael (Gen. 25:14; 1 Chron. 1:30). *See* "Places of the Bible."

E

Ebal [Obal] ("bare" or "naked"). **[1]** A son of Shobal the Horite (Gen. 36:23; 1 Chron. 1:40). **[2]** A son of Joktan, descendant of Shem (1 Chron. 1:22). He is called Obal in Genesis 10:28. Possibly an Arabian people is meant. *See also* "Places of the Bible."

Ebed ("servant"). **[1]** A companion of Ezra on his return to Jerusalem (Ezra 8:6). **[2]** Father of Gaal who rebelled against Abimelech (Judg. 9:26–35).

Ebed-Melech ("the king's servant"), an Ethiopian eunuch who rescued Jeremiah (Jer. 38:7–12; 39:16).

Eber ("the other side; across"). **[1]** A descendant of Shem and an ancestor of Christ (Gen. 10:21, 24–25; 11:14–17; Luke 3:35). His name occurs as Heber in Luke 3:35. Possibly the Hebrews and certain Aramean people are intended. **[2]** A descendant of Benjamin (1 Chron. 8:12). **[3]** Head of a priestly family (Neh. 12:20). *See* Heber.

Ebiasaph. *See* Abiasaph.

Eden ("delight"). **[1]** A descendant of Gershom (2 Chron. 29:12). **[2]** A Levite in the time of Hezekiah (2 Chron. 31:15). *See also* "Places of the Bible."

Eder ("flock"), a grandson of Merari, son of Levi (1 Chron. 23:23; 24:30). *See also* "Places of the Bible."

Edom ("red"), name given to Esau, the elder son of Isaac, because of his red skin (Gen. 25:30). *See* Esau; Obed-edom. *See also* "Places of the Bible."

Eglah ("calf"), one of David's wives (2 Sam. 3:5; 1 Chron. 3:3).

Eglon ("circle"), a king of Moab who oppressed Israel in the days of the judges (Judg. 3:12–17).

Ehi. *See* Ahiram.

Ehud ("strong"). **[1]** A judge who delivered Israel from the oppression of Eglon of Moab (Judg. 3:15–30). **[2]** Great-grandson of Ben-

PEOPLE OF THE BIBLE

TRAVELLER'S REST, KADESH. *An Arab traveller dozes beneath a broom bush in the wilderness along the Negev Desert. In this same area Elijah stopped to rest beneath a juniper tree and received encouragement from an angel of the Lord (1 Kings 19:4–7).*

jamin (1 Chron. 7:10; 8:6); perhaps the same as [1].

Eker ("root"), a descendant of Judah (1 Chron. 2:27).

Eladah ("God is ornament"), a descendant of Ephraim (1 Chron. 7:20).

Elah ("oak"). **[1]** A chieftain of Edom (Gen. 36:41; 1 Chron. 1:52). **[2]** Father of a commissary officer under Solomon (1 Kings 4:18). **[3]** The son and successor of Baasha, king of Israel. He was murdered by Zimri (1 Kings 16:6–14). **[4]** The father of Hoshea, last king of Israel (2 Kings 15:30; 17:1). **[5]** A son of Caleb, son of Jephunneh (1 Chron. 4:15). **[6]** A descendant of Benjamin (1 Chron. 9:8). *See also* "Places of the Bible."

Elam ("highland"). **[1]** A son of Shem (Gen. 10:22; 1 Chron. 1:17). Some consider the people of Elam, a region beyond the Tigris east of Babylonia, to be intended. It was bounded on the north by Assyria and Media, on the south by the Persian Gulf, and on the east and southeast by Persia. **[2]** A descendant of Benjamin (1 Chron. 8:24). **[3]** A descendant of Korah (1 Chron. 26:3). **[4]** A leader of the people who sealed the new covenant with God after the Exile (Neh. 10:14). **[5]** A priest of Nehemiah's time who helped to cleanse Jerusalem (Neh. 12:42). **[6]** One whose descendants returned from the Exile (Ezra 2:7). **[7]** Another whose descendants returned from the Exile (Ezra 2:31). **[8]** Yet another whose descendants returned from the Exile (Ezra 8:7). **[9]** Ancestor of some who married foreign wives during the Exile (Ezra 10:2).

Elasah ("God is doer"). **[1]** One who married a foreign wife (Ezra 10:22). **[2]** Ambassador of Zedekiah (Jer. 29:3). **[3]** *See* Eleasah.

Eldaah ("whom God calls"), a son of Midian (Gen. 25:4; 1 Chron. 1:33).

Eldad ("God is a friend"), one of two elders who received the prophetic powers of Moses (Num. 11:26–27).

Elead ("God is witness"), a descendant of Ephraim slain by invaders (1 Chron. 7:21).

Eleasah ("God is doer"). **[1]** A descendant of Judah (1 Chron. 2:39–40). **[2]** A descendant of King Saul (1 Chron. 8:37; 9:43). *See* Elasah.

Eleazar ("God is helper"). **[1]** Third son of Aaron and successor to the high priest's office (Exod. 6:23; Num. 3:32; 20:28). **[2]** One sanctified to keep the ark of the covenant (1 Sam. 7:1). **[3]** One of David's mighty men (2 Sam. 23:9; 1 Chron. 11:12). **[4]** A descendant of Merari who had no sons (1 Chron. 23:21–22; 24:28). **[5]** A priest who accompanied Ezra when he returned to Jerusalem (Ezra 8:33). **[6]** A priest who assisted at the dedication of the walls of Jerusalem (Neh. 12:42); possibly the same as [5]. **[7]** An ancestor of Jesus (Matt. 1:15).

Elhanan ("whom God gave; God is gracious"). **[1]** The warrior who killed Lahmi, the brother of Goliath (1 Chron. 20:5; 2 Sam. 21:19). **[2]** One of David's mighty men (2 Sam. 23:24; 1 Chron. 11:26).

Eli ("Jehovah is high"), high priest at Shiloh and judge of Israel. He is remembered for his lack of firmness (1 Sam. 1—4). *See also* Heli.

Eliab ("God is father"). **[1]** A prince of Zebulun (Num. 1:9; 2:7; 7:24, 29; 10:16). **[2]** Father of the wicked pair, Dathan and Abiram (Num. 16:1, 12; 26:8). **[3]** Son of Jesse and brother of David (1 Sam. 16:6); he is called Elihu in First Chronicles 27:18. **[4]** Ancestor of Samuel (1 Chron. 6:27); he is called Eliel in First Chronicles 6:34 and Elihu in First Samuel 1:1. **[5]** A warrior of David (1 Chron. 12:8–9, 14). **[6]** A Levite musician in the time of David (1 Chron. 15:18, 20; 16:5). **[7]** *See* Eliel.

Eliada [Eliadah] ("God is knowing"). **[1]** A mighty man of Jehoshaphat (2 Chron. 17:17). **[2]** Father of Rezon (1 Kings 11:23). **[3]** *See* Beeliada.

Eliah. *See* Elijah.

Eliahba ("God hides"), one of David's 30-man guard (2 Sam. 23:32; 1 Chron. 11:33).

Eliakim ("God is setting up"). **[1]** Successor of Shebna as master of Hezekiah's household (2 Kings 18:18, 26; Isa. 22:20). **[2]** Original name of King Jehoiakim (q.v.). **[3]** A priest in Nehemiah's time (Neh. 12:41). **[4]** An ancestor of Christ (Matt. 1:13).

Eliam ("my God is a kinsman; God is founder of the people"). **[1]** Father of Bathsheba (2 Sam. 11:3). By transposition of the two parts of the name he is called Ammiel (1 Chron. 3:5). **[2]** One of David's mighty men (2 Sam. 23:34).

Elias, Greek form of Elijah (q.v.).

Eliasaph ("God is gatherer"). **[1]** Head of the tribe of Gad (Num. 1:14; 2:14; 7:42, 47). **[2]** A prince of Gershon (Num. 3:24).

Eliashib ("God is requiter"). **[1]** A priest in the time of David (1 Chron. 24:12). **[2]** A descendant of David (1 Chron. 3:24). **[3]** The high priest in Nehemiah's time (Neh. 3:1, 20–21). **[4]**, **[5]**, **[6]** Three men who married foreign wives during the Exile (Ezra 10:24, 27, 36). **[7]** One who assisted Ezra in resolving the matter of the foreign wives (Ezra 10:6; Neh. 12:10); possibly the same as [3].

Eliathah ("God is come"), one appointed for the song service in the temple (1 Chron. 25:4, 27).

Elidad ("God is a friend"), a chief of the tribe of Benjamin (Num. 34:21).

Eliel ("God, my God"). **[1]** Head of a family of the tribe of Manasseh (1 Chron. 5:24). **[2]** A descendant of Benjamin (1 Chron. 8:20). **[3]** Another descendant of Benjamin in Chronicles (1 Chron. 8:22). **[4]** A captain of David's

army (1 Chron. 11:46). **[5]** One of David's mighty men (1 Chron. 11:47). **[6]** One who joined David at Ziklag (1 Chron. 12:11); perhaps the same as [4] or [5]. **[7]** A chief of Judah (1 Chron. 15:9); perhaps [4]. **[8]** A chief Levite whom David commissioned to bring the ark of the covenant to the temple (1 Chron. 15:11). **[9]** The Levite overseer of the dedicated things of the temple under Hezekiah (2 Chron. 31:13). **[10]** *See* Eliab [4].

Elienai ("unto God are my eyes"), a chief of Benjamin (1 Chron. 8:20).

Eliezer ("God is help"). **[1]** Abraham's chief servant (Gen. 15:2). **[2]** The second son of Moses and Zipporah (Exod. 18:4; 1 Chron. 23:15, 17). **[3]** A descendant of Benjamin (1 Chron. 7:8). **[4]** A priest who assisted with bringing the ark of the covenant to the temple (1 Chron. 15:24). **[5]** A prince of Reuben in the time of David (1 Chron. 27:16). **[6]** A prophet who rebuked Jehoshaphat (2 Chron. 20:37). **[7]** A leader who induced others to return to Jerusalem (Ezra 8:16). **[8]**, **[9]**, **[10]** Three men who took foreign wives during the Exile (Ezra 10:18, 23, 31). **[11]** An ancestor of Christ (Luke 3:29).

Elihoenai ("to Jehovah are my eyes"), ancestor of some returned exiles (Ezra 8:4). *See also* Elioenai.

Elihoreph ("God of harvest grain"), a scribe of Solomon (1 Kings 4:3).

Elihu ("God himself"). **[1]** One who joined David at Ziklag (1 Chron. 12:20). **[2]** A porter at the tabernacle at the time of David (1 Chron. 26:7). **[3]** The youngest "friend" of Job (Job 32:2, 4–6). **[4]** *See* Eliab [3]. **[5]** *See* Eliab [4].

Elijah [Eliah; Elias] ("Jehovah is my God"). **[1]** A great prophet of God; he strenuously opposed idolatry and was caught up in a chariot of fire at death (1 Kings 17:1— 2 Kings 2:11; Matt. 17:3). **[2]** A chief of the tribe of Benjamin (1 Chron. 8:27). **[3]** One who married a foreign wife during the Exile (Ezra 10:26). **[4]** Another who took a foreign wife during the Exile (Ezra 10:21).

Elika ("God is rejector"), one of David's warriors (2 Sam. 23:25).

Elimelech ("my God is King"), the husband of Naomi and father-in-law of Ruth. He died in Moab (Ruth 1:2–3; 2:1, 3; 4:3, 9).

Elioenai ("to Jehovah are my eyes"). **[1]** A descendant of David (1 Chron. 3:23–24). **[2]** A chief of the tribe of Simeon (1 Chron. 4:36). **[3]** A chief of Benjamin (1 Chron. 7:8). **[4]**, **[5]** Two men who had married foreign wives dur-

PEOPLE OF THE BIBLE

ing the Exile (Ezra 10:22, 27). **[6]** A priest in the days of Nehemiah (Neh. 12:41); possibly the same as [4]. **[7]** A doorkeeper of the temple (1 Chron. 26:3). **[8]** *See* Elihoenai.

Eliphal ("God is judge"), one of David's mighty men (1 Chron. 11:35).

Eliphalet [Eliphelet; Elpalet] ("God is escape"). **[1]** The last of David's thirteen sons (2 Sam. 5:16; 1 Chron. 3:8; 14:7). **[2]** Another of David's sons (1 Chron. 3:6); called Elpalet in First Chronicles 14:5. **[3]** One of David's mighty men (2 Sam. 23:34). **[4]** A descendant of Benjamin and Saul (1 Chron. 8:39). **[5]** One who came back to Jerusalem with Ezra (Ezra 8:13). **[6]** One who took a foreign wife during the Exile (Ezra 10:33).

Eliphaz ("God is dispenser"). **[1]** The leader of Job's three "friends" who confronted

him (Job 2:11; 4:1; 15:1). **[2]** A son of Esau (Gen. 36:4, 10–12; 1 Chron. 1:35–36).

Elipheleh ("Jehovah is distinction"), a Levite set over the choral service of the temple when the ark of the covenant was returned (1 Chron. 15:18, 21).

Eliphelet. *See* Eliphalet.

Elisabeth ("God is swearer; oath of God"), the wife of Zacharias and mother of John the Baptist (Luke 1:5–57).

Eliseus, Greek form of Elisha (q.v.).

Elisha [Elishah; Eliseus] ("God is Savior"). **[1]** The disciple and successor of Elijah; he held the prophetic office for 55 years (1 Kings 19:16–17, 19; 2 Kings 2—6; Luke 4:27). **[2]** Eldest son of Javan and grandson of Noah (Gen. 10:4). Possibly the people of Cyprus or the inhabitants of Alasiya, a country

---

The Herods

The family of the Herods exerted Rome's control over Palestine during the time of Christ and the founding of the Christian church. This family ruled tyrannically—and often violently—for about 100 years.

The family that became known as the Herods were Idumean by birth. (Idumea was an area south of Bethlehem and Jerusalem, populated by the Edomites—former Jews who had refused to "inhabit the land" of Canaan.) The Maccabean leader John Hyrcanus I had conquered the Idumeans in about 126 B.C. and compelled them to accept orthodox Judaism. The Herod family ruled Idumea when the Maccabean dynasty began to lose control of Palestine.

The Maccabean family had led the Jews in a heroic struggle to free themselves from foreign rule. However, political intrigue and family jealousy among the Maccabeans left the Jewish state in a weakened condition, making it a prey to Rome. The last strong ruler of the Maccabean (later called the Hasmonean) line was Alexander Jannaeus. When he died (*ca.* 78 B.C.), he left the kingdom to his widow, Alexandra Salome. She made her older son, John Hyrcanus II, high priest and hoped to groom him for the throne. But Alexandra suddenly became ill and died, and her younger son Aristobulus proclaimed himself king. The Herods took advantage of this confused situation.

Antipater I of Idumea, father of Herod the Great, was cunning, wealthy, and ambitious. He allied himself with John Hyrcanus II in a bid to overthrow Aristobulus. They drew the Romans into the struggle and won. Antipater reinstated Hyrcanus II as

high priest, and Julius Caesar later appointed Antipater as governor of Judea.

Antipater gave two of his sons positions in the government—Phasael was made prefect of Jerusalem and Herod was governor of Galilee. Herod ("the Great") was intelligent, charming in manners, and quite capable in statecraft. Like his father he was highly ambitious. But the Sanhedrin (Jewish legal council) turned against the young ruler when he executed some Jews without official consent; in fact, they demanded his death. He appealed to the Roman governor of Syria, who dismissed the Jews' charges and extended Herod's governorship to Coele-Syria and Samaria.

When Cassius, one of Julius Caesar's murderers, became ruler of the eastern sector of the Roman Empire, Herod and his father Antipater gave him their full cooperation. Many Jewish groups opposed their rule, and Antipater died of poisoning in 43 B.C. just after he paid a large tax to Cassius.

Then Mark Antony assumed control of the eastern provinces, and Jewish leaders clamored to denounce Herod as a tyrant. But Antony confirmed Herod and Phasael *tetrarchs* (i.e., each was ruler of one-fourth of the region) of Judea.

In 40 B.C., the Hasmonean leader Antigonus (a nephew of John Hyrcanus I) ousted Herod from power and was proclaimed king of Judea. He ordered his men to cut off the ears of Hyrcanus II, so that he could no longer be high priest. (It was unlawful for a mutilated person to serve as priest.) Herod appealed to Antony for aid. Octavian and Antony advised the Roman senate to appoint Herod king of the Jews, but it took him three years of hard fighting to regain his kingdom. From that

near Cilicia. Others suggest it includes the Italians and Peloponnesians.

Elishama ("God is hearer"). **[1]** Grandfather of Joshua (Num. 1:10; 2:18; 1 Chron. 7:26). **[2]** A son of King David (2 Sam. 5:16; 1 Chron. 3:8). **[3]** Another son of David (1 Chron. 3:6); also called Elishua in Second Samuel 5:15 and First Chronicles 14:5. **[4]** A descendant of Judah (1 Chron. 2:41). **[5]** One of the "royal seed" and grandfather of Gedaliah (2 Kings 25:25; Jer. 41:1). **[6]** A scribe or secretary of Jehoiakim (Jer. 36:12, 20, 21). **[7]** A priest sent by Jehoshaphat to teach the Law (2 Chron. 17:8).

Elishaphat ("God is judge"), one of the captains of hundreds commissioned by Jehoiada (2 Chron. 23:1).

Elisheba ("God is swearer; God is an oath"), the wife of Aaron and mother of Nadab, Abihu, Eleazar, and Ithamar (Exod. 6:23).

Elishua ("God is rich"). *See* Elishama [3].

Eliud ("God my praise"), an ancestor of Jesus (Matt. 1:14–15).

Elizaphan [Elzaphan] ("God is protector"). **[1]** A chief of the family of Kohath (Num. 3:30; 1 Chron. 15:8); he is also called Elzaphan (Exod. 6:22; Lev. 10:4). **[2]** A prince of the tribe of Zebulun (Num. 34:25).

Elizur ("God is a rock"), a chief of the tribe of Reuben who assisted Moses in taking the census (Num. 1:5; 2:10; 7:30, 35).

Elkanah [Elkonah] ("God is possessing"). **[1]** Grandson of Korah (Exod. 6:24; 1 Chron. 6:23). **[2]** Father of the prophet Samuel and a descendant of [1] (1 Sam. 1:1–23; 2:11, 20).

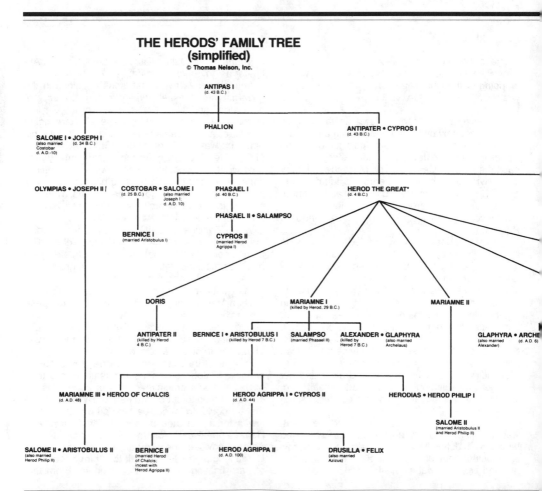

THE HERODS' FAMILY TREE
(simplified)
© Thomas Nelson, Inc.

PEOPLE OF THE BIBLE

[3] A descendant of Levi (1 Chron. 6:25, 36). [4] A descendant of Levi (1 Chron. 6:26, 35); perhaps the same as [3]. [5] A Levite ancestor of Berechiah (1 Chron. 9:16). [6] One who joined David at Ziklag (1 Chron. 12:6). [7] A doorkeeper of the ark of the covenant (1 Chron. 15:23); perhaps the same as [6]. [8] An officer of King Ahaz (2 Chron. 28:7).

Elmodam ("measure"), an ancestor of Christ (Luke 3:28).

Elnaam ("God is pleasant"), the father of two of David's warriors (1 Chron. 11:46).

Elnathan ("God is giving"). [1] Father of Nehushta, Jehoiakim's queen (2 Kings 24:8; Jer. 26:22). [2], [3], [4] Three Levites in the time of Ezra (Ezra 8:16).

Elon ("oak; strong"). [1] Father of a wife of Esau (Gen. 26:34; 36:2). [2] A son of Zebulun

(Gen. 46:14; Num. 26:26). [3] A judge of Israel for ten years (Judg. 12:11–12). *See also* "Places of the Bible."

Elpaal ("God is working"), a descendant of Benjamin (1 Chron. 8:11–12).

Elpalet. *See* Eliphalet [2].

Eluzai ("God is strong"), one who joined David at Ziklag (1 Chron. 12:5).

Elymas ("a sorcerer"), a false prophet who opposed Saul and Barnabas at Paphos (Acts 13:8); he was also called Bar-jesus (v. 6).

Elzabad ("God is endowing"). [1] One who joined David at Ziklag (1 Chron. 12:12). [2] A descendant of Levi (1 Chron. 26:7).

Elzaphan. *See* Elizaphan.

Emmor, Greek form of Hamor (q.v.).

Enan ("eyes; fountain"), father of a prince of Naphtali (Num. 1:15; 2:29).

---

time until his death 33 years later, Herod governed his realm as a loyal ally of Rome.

When Octavian defeated Antony and Cleopatra at Actium in 31 B.C., Herod wisely surrendered his kingdom to his new master. Octavian confirmed Herod as king of Judea and added still more territory to his domain.

Herod the Great married a total of ten women—Doris, Mariamne I, Mariamne II, Malthace, Cleopatra, Pallas, Phaedra, Elpis, and two whose names are unknown (in that order). In all, they bore him at least 15 children.

Herod divorced Doris in order to marry Mariamne (known historically as Mariamne I). She was a member of the Hasmonean family, and Herod hoped to gain political status through this marriage. Eventually, Herod ordered his men to execute Mariamne I and her grandfather John Hyrcanus II. By doing this, Herod exterminated the Hasmonean family.

Herod the Great tried to win the Jews' favor by rebuilding their temple on a magnificent scale. Yet he also built temples dedicated to pagan gods. The Jewish people resented Herod's Idumean ancestry and his marriage to Malthace, a Samaritan.

The last years of Herod's life were dismal and full of grief; he deteriorated mentally and physically. His mad jealousy caused him to order many executions. Three of his sons—Antipater II, Alexander, and Aristobulus I—were among the victims.

Herod's death in 4 B.C. brought a new era to Judea. Just before his death, Herod formally gave the Roman emperor power to supervise his kingdom. (Rome had been the real ruler of Palestine since the overthrow of Aristobulus in 63 B.C., but it now exerted its control more directly.) In his will,

JOSEPH III
(d. 38 B.C.)

PHRERORAS
(d. 5 B.C.)

ACE

CLEOPATRA**
**

AS II • HERODIAS
(also married
Herod Philip I)

OLYMPIAS
(married
Joeseph II)

HEROD

SALOME II • HEROD PHILIP II
(also married
Aristobulus)
(d. A.D. 34)

*Also married five other wives of lesser importance: Pallas, Phaedra, Elpis, and two who are anonymous. This chart traces Herod's descendants through the first five wives.
**Not the Cleopatra of Egypt.
• Denotes marriage

Enoch [Henoch] ("teacher"). **[1]** The eldest son of Cain (Gen. 4:17–18). **[2]** A son of Jared and an ancestor of Christ (Gen. 5:18–19, 21; 1 Chron. 1:3; Luke 3:37; Heb. 11:5). *See also* "Places of the Bible."

Enos [Enosh] ("mortal"), son of Seth and ancestor of Christ (Gen. 4:26; 5:6–11; 1 Chron. 1:1; Luke 3:38).

Enosh. *See* Enos.

Epaenetus ("praised"), a Christian at Rome to whom Paul sent greetings (Rom. 16:5).

Epaphras (shortened form of *Epaphroditus—"lovely"*), a Christian worker with Paul who served as missionary to Colossae (Col. 1:7; 4:12; Philem. 23).

Epaphroditus ("lovely"), a Philippian Christian who worked so strenuously that he lost his health (Phil. 2:25; 4:18).

Ephah ("obscurity"). **[1]** A concubine of Caleb (1 Chron. 2:46). **[2]** A descendant of Judah (1 Chron. 2:47). **[3]** A grandson of Abraham (Gen. 25:4; 1 Chron. 1:33).

Ephai ("obscuring"), one whose children were left in Judah after the Exile (Jer. 40:8).

Epher ("calf; young deer"). **[1]** A grandson of Abraham and son of Midian (Gen. 25:4; 1 Chron. 1:33). **[2]** One of the descendants of Judah (1 Chron. 4:17). **[3]** A chief of the tribe of Manasseh east of the Jordan River (1 Chron. 5:24).

Ephlal ("judging"), a descendant of Pharez through Jerahmeel (1 Chron. 2:37).

Ephod ("oracular"), father of a prince of the tribe of Manasseh (Num. 34:23).

Ephraim ("doubly fruitful"), the second son of Joseph by Asenath. Although Ephraim

---

Herod the Great divided his kingdom among three of his sons. Archelaus received Judea, Samaria, and Idumea; Antipas II received Galilee and Perea; and Herod Philip II received the northeastern territories.

Herod Archelaus ruled "in the room of his father Herod" (Matt. 2:22), although without the title of king. He was Herod's oldest son by Malthace and had the worst reputation of all Herod's children. He angered the Jews by marrying Glaphyra, the widow of his half-brother Alexander. Rival Jews and Samaritans sent a united delegation to Rome, threatening to revolt if Archelaus were not removed. Accordingly, in A.D. 6, he was deposed and banished. Judea then became a Roman province, administered by governors appointed by the emperor.

Herod Antipas II was Herod's younger son by Malthace. The Gospels depict him as wholly immoral. He divorced his first wife to marry Herodias, the wife of his half-brother Herod Philip I; since Herodias was also his niece, their union was doubly sinful. He imprisoned John the Baptist for denouncing this marriage (Mark 6:17–18). Herodias made full use of her husband's pledge to give her daughter (possibly Salome II) anything that she wished (Mark 6:19–28). She demanded John's head on a platter, and so Antipas had him executed. However, Herod Antipas II was the ablest of Herod's sons; in A.D. 22 he built the city of Tiberias on the Sea of Galilee. Emperor Caligula exiled him in A.D. 39 after Herod Agrippa I accused him of plotting against Rome.

Herod Philip II was unlike the rest of the Herodian clan, for he was dignified, moderate, and just. He ruled for 37 years as the "tetrarch of Iturea, and of the region of Trachonitis" (Luke 3:1). He married Salome II, the daughter of Herod Philip I, his half-brother.

Herod Agrippa I was the son of Aristobulus I and a grandson of Herod the Great. In A.D. 37, Emperor Caligula gave Agrippa the title of king, with territories northeast of Palestine. When Antipas II was banished in A.D. 39, Galilee and Perea were added to Agrippa's kingdom. Emperor Claudius further extended Agrippa's territory by giving him Judea and Samaria in A.D. 41. Agrippa I killed the apostle James and persecuted the early church. Because of his arrogance, God took his life (Acts 12). Among his children were Bernice II, Herod Agrippa II, and Drusilla (who married Felix, the Roman governor of Judea—cf. Acts 24:24).

Emperor Claudius gave Herod Agrippa II the title of king, with territories north and northeast of Palestine; these territories were increased by Emperor Nero in A.D. 56. His incestuous relationship with his sister Bernice II was a scandal among the Jews; the New Testament mentions that he and Bernice heard Paul (Acts 25:13—26:32). He urged his countrymen to remain loyal to Rome during the Jewish revolts; when the nation fell he moved to Rome, where he died in about A.D. 100.

Herod Philip I was the Herod the Great's son by Mariamne II. For a time, he was included in Herod's will; but the king later revoked this grant. Philip remained a private citizen and his life story is unclear. His wife, Herodias, left him to live with his half-brother Antipas II (cf. Mark 6:17–18).

Christ, the apostles, and the early Christians lived during the turbulent days of the Herods. While the Herods built many splendid edifices and strengthened Judea militarily, the verdict of their subjects was that they were guilty—of oppression, tyranny, and burden in the highest degree.

PEOPLE OF THE BIBLE

CITY OF EXILE. *An ancient clay tablet shows a map of Nippur, a city located along the Chebar River in Babylonia. Ezekiel and the other exiles of Judah were taken to cities like Nippur (Ezek. 1:1–3). However, the exact city where Ezekiel stayed is not known.*

Esaias, Greek form of Isaiah (q.v.).

Esarhaddon ("Ashur has given a brother"), the son of Sennacherib and a powerful king of Assyria (2 Kings 19:37; Ezra 4:2; Isa. 37:38).

Esau ("hairy"), eldest son of Isaac and twin brother of Jacob. He is the progenitor of the tribe of Edom (Gen. 25:25). He sold his birthright to Jacob (Gen. 25:26–34; 27; 36).

Esau's Wives: There are two lists of Esau's wives—Genesis 26:34; 28:9 list them in this fashion: **[1]** Judith, the daughter of Beeri the Hittite. **[2]** Bashemath, daughter of Elon the Hittite and **[3]** Mahalath, the daughter of Ishmael, Abraham's son. The other list in Genesis 36:2–3 runs thus: **[1]** Aholibamah, the daughter of Anah the daughter of Zibeon. **[2]** Adah, the daughter of Elon the Hittite and **[3]** Bashemath, the daughter of Ishmael. Some scholars suppose we are dealing with six women, but this seems unlikely. In the ancient world, many women received new names at marriage and this fact would account for the different names. Thus, **[1]** Judith is Aholibamah, **[2]** Bashemath is Adah, and **[3]** Mahalath is Bashemath. As far as Judith is concerned, Beeri might be her father and Anah her mother; or perhaps Anah is another name of Beeri. Some even think Beeri ("man of the

44

PEOPLE OF THE BIBLE

was the younger of the two sons of Joseph, he received the firstborn's blessing. He was an ancestor of one of the twelve tribes of Israel (Gen. 41:52; 46:20; 48; 50:23). *See also* "Places of the Bible."

Ephratah [Ephrath] ("fertility"), the second wife of Caleb (1 Chron. 2:19, 50; 4:4). *See also* "Places of the Bible."

Ephron ("strong"), a Hittite from whom Abraham bought a field with a cave, which became Sarah's burial place (Gen. 23:8, 10, 13–14; 49:30). *See also* "Places of the Bible."

Er ("watcher"). **[1]** Eldest son of Judah, slain by God (Gen. 38:3, 6–7; 1 Chron. 2:3). **[2]** A son of Shelah (1 Chron. 4:21). **[3]** An ancestor of Jesus (Luke 3:28).

Eran ("watcher; watchful"), the son of Ephraim's oldest son (Num. 26:36).

Erastus ("beloved"). **[1]** Christian sent with Timothy into Macedonia while Paul stayed in Asia (Acts 19:22). **[2]** An important person in Corinth sending greetings to Rome (Rom. 16:23). **[3]** One who remained at Corinth (2 Tim. 4:20). Perhaps some or all of the above are identical.

Eri ("watcher"), a son of Gad (Gen. 46:16; Num. 26:16).

WHERE FELIX AND FESTUS HELD COURT. *Scattered columns, broken walls, and a large open well are the only remains of Caesarea Maritima, the lavish Roman port where Felix and Festus heard Paul's testimony (Acts 24–26). Paul remained imprisoned in this city for about two years before facing the emperor in Rome.*

springs") is a nickname rather than a proper name.

Esh-baal ("man or servant of Baal"), altered to a curse. *See* Ishbosheth.

Eshban ("man of understanding"), son of Dishon (Gen. 36:26; 1 Chron. 1:41).

Eshcol ("a cluster of grapes"), the brother of Mamre and Aner who helped Abraham defeat Chedorlaomer (Gen. 14:13–24). *See also* "Places of the Bible."

Eshek ("oppressor"), a descendant of King Saul (1 Chron. 8:39).

Eshtemoa ("bosom of women"), a Maacathite, a son of Ishbah (1 Chron. 4:17, 19).

Eshton ("rest"), a descendant of Judah through Caleb (1 Chron. 4:11–12).

Esli ("reserved"), an ancestor of Christ (Luke 3:25).

Esrom, Greek form of Hezron (q.v.).

Esther ("star; [the goddess] Ishtar"), the Persian name of Hadassah, who was chosen by Ahasuerus to be his queen. The book of Esther tells her story.

Etam ("wild beast's lair"), a name occurring in Judah's genealogy list (1 Chron. 4:3). It may be a place name.

Ethan ("ancient"). **[1]** A wise man in the days of Solomon (1 Kings 4:31; Psa. 89 title). **[2]** A descendant of Judah (1 Chron. 2:6, 8). He is possibly identical with [1]. **[3]** *See* Jeduthun. **[4]** A descendant of Levi (1 Chron. 6:42).

Ethbaal ("Baal's man; with Baal"), king of Sidon and father of Ahab's wife Jezebel (1 Kings 16:31).

Ethnan ("gift"), grandson of Ashur through Caleb, son of Hur (1 Chron. 4:7).

Ethni ("my gift"), one whom David set over the song service of the temple (1 Chron. 6:41).

Eubulus ("of good counsel"), one of the

HOME OF GIDEON'S ENEMIES. *A simple village stands at the site of Midian, the center for a tribe that threatened to take the Promised Land from the newly arrived Israelites. Gideon and an army of 300 men repelled the Midianites in a surprise attack near Mount Moreh (Judg. 7).*

PEOPLE OF THE BIBLE

Roman Christians that remained loyal to Paul (2 Tim. 4:21).

Eunice ("conquering well"), the pious mother of Timothy (2 Tim. 1:5; cf. Acts 16:1).

Euodias ("fragrant"), a Christian woman at Philippi (Phil. 4:2). The KJV is mistaken at this point, giving a man's name for a woman's. The name should read *Euodia.*

Eutychus ("fortunate"), a young man at Troas whom Paul restored to life (Acts 20:6–12).

Eve ("life; life-giving"), the first woman, Adam's wife (Gen. 3:20; 4:1; 2 Chron. 11:3).

Evi ("desire"), one of the five kings of Midian slain by Israel (Num. 31:8; Josh. 13:21).

Evil-merodach (Babylonian, Arvil-Marduk—"the man of [the god] Marduk"), the king of Babylon who released Jehoiachin from imprisonment. He succeeded his father, Nebuchadnezzar (2 Kings 25:27–30; Jer. 52:31).

Ezar. *See* Ezer [6].

Ezbai ("shining; beautiful"), the father of one of David's mighty men (1 Chron. 11:37).

Ezbon ("bright"). **[1]** A son of Gad (Gen. 46:16), called Ozni ("Jehovah hears") in Numbers 26:16. **[2]** A descendant of Benjamin (1 Chron. 7:7).

Ezekias, Greek form of Hezekiah (q.v.).

Ezekiel ("God strengthens"), a prophet of a priestly family carried captive to Babylon. He prophesied to the exiles in Mesopotamia by the river Chevar, and is the author of the book bearing his name (Ezek. 1:3; 24:24).

Ezer ("help"). **[1]** A son of Ephraim slain by the inhabitants of Gath (1 Chron. 7:21). **[2]** A priest in Nehemiah's time (Neh. 12:42). **[3]** A descendant of Judah through Caleb (1 Chron. 4:4); perhaps the same as Ezra [2]. **[4]** A valiant man who joined David at Ziklag (1 Chron. 12:9). **[5]** A Levite who assisted in repairing the wall of Jerusalem (Neh. 3:19). **[6]** ("union"), a son of Seir (Gen. 36:21, 27, 30; 1 Chron. 1:42); he is also called Ezar (1 Chron. 1:38). *See* Abi-ezer; Romamti-ezer.

Ezra ("help"). **[1]** Head of one of the courses of priests that returned from the Exile (Neh. 12:1). The full form of his name, *Azariah,* occurs in Nehemiah 10:2. **[2]** A descendant of Judah through Caleb (1 Chron. 4:17). *See* Ezer [3]. **[3]** A prominent scribe and priest descended from Hilkiah the high priest (Ezra 7:1–12; 10:1; Neh. 8:1–13). *See* Azariah.

Ezri ("my help"), one of David's superintendents of farm workers (1 Chron. 27:26).

F

Felix ("happy"), Roman governor of Judea that presided over the trial of Paul at Caesarea (Acts 23:23–27; 24:22–27).

Festus ("swine-like"), successor of Felix to the governorship of Judea. He continued the trial of Paul begun under Felix (Acts 25; 26).

Fortunatus ("fortunate"), a Corinthian Christian who cheered and comforted Paul at Ephesus (1 Cor. 16:17–18).

G

Gaal ("rejection"), a son of Ebed. He tried to lead a rebellion against Abimelech (Judg. 9:26–41).

Gabbai ("collector"), a chief of the tribe of Benjamin after the return from the Exile (Neh. 11:8).

Gad ("fortune"). **[1]** The seventh son of Jacob and an ancestor of one of the twelve tribes (Gen. 30:11; 49:19). **[2]** David's seer who frequently advised him (1 Sam. 22:5; 1 Chron. 21:9–19).

Gaddi ("my fortune"), one of those sent to spy out Canaan (Num. 13:11).

Gaddiel ("fortune of God"), one of the spies (Num. 13:10).

Gadi ("fortunate"), father of King Menahem of Israel (2 Kings 15:14, 17).

Gaham ("blackness"), a son of Nahor (Gen. 22:24).

Gahar ("prostration; concealment"), one whose family returned from captivity (Ezra 2:47; Neh. 7:49).

Gaius ("lord"). **[1]** One to whom John's third epistle is addressed (3 John 1). **[2]** A native of Macedonia and a companion of Paul (Acts 19:29). **[3]** A man of Derbe who accompanied Paul as far as Asia (Acts 20:4). **[4]** The host to Paul when he wrote to the Romans (Rom. 16:23). **[5]** A convert whom Paul baptized at Corinth (1 Cor. 1:14); some think he is identical with [4].

Galal ("great; rolling"). **[1]** A returned exile (1 Chron. 9:15). **[2]** A Levite who returned from the Exile (1 Chron. 9:16; Neh. 11:17).

Gallio (meaning unknown), Roman proconsul of Achaia before whom Paul was tried in Corinth (Acts 18:12–17).

Gamaliel ("reward or recompense of God"). **[1]** A prince of the tribe of Manasseh (Num. 1:10; 2:20). **[2]** A great Jewish teacher of the Law. He persuaded his fellow Jews to let the apostles go free (Acts 5:33–40; 22:3).

Gamul ("weaned"), a chief priest (1 Chron. 24:17).

Gareb ("reviler; despiser"), one of David's mighty men (2 Sam. 23:38; 1 Chron. 11:40). *See also* "Places of the Bible."

Gashmu. *See* Geshem.

Gatam ("burnt valley"), an Edomite chief, grandson of Esau (Gen. 36:11, 16; 1 Chron. 1:36).

Gazez ("shearer"). **[1]** A son of Caleb (1 Chron. 2:46). **[2]** A grandson of Caleb (1 Chron. 2:46).

Gazzam ("devourer; swaggerer"), one whose descendants returned (Ezra 2:48; Neh. 7:51).

Geber ("man; strong one"). **[1]** The father of one of Solomon's officers (1 Kings 4:13). **[2]** One of Solomon's commissaries (1 Kings 4:19).

Gedaliah ("Jehovah is great"). **[1]** Governor of Jerusalem after the Exile (2 Kings 25:22; Jer. 40:5–6). **[2]** A Levite musician (1 Chron. 25:3, 9). **[3]** A priest who had married a foreign wife during the Exile (Ezra 10:18). **[4]** A chief of Jerusalem that imprisoned Jeremiah (Jer. 20:1–6). **[5]** Grandfather of the prophet Zephaniah (Zeph. 1:1).

Gedeon, Greek form of Gideon (q.v.).

Gedor ("wall"). **[1]** An ancestor of Saul (1 Chron. 8:31). **[2]** A descendant of Judah (1 Chron. 4:4). **[3]** A descendant of Judah (1 Chron. 4:18). *See also* "Places of the Bible."

Gehazi ("valley of vision; diminisher"), the dishonest servant of Elisha (2 Kings 4:12–37; 5:20–27; 8:4).

Gemalli ("camel owner"), father of Ammiel (Num. 13:12).

Gemariah ("Jehovah has accomplished"). **[1]** One who sought to stop Jehoiakim from burning Jeremiah's prophecies (Jer. 36:10–11, 12, 25). **[2]** One of Zedekiah's ambassadors to Babylon (Jer. 29:3).

Genubath ("theft"), a son of Hadad the Edomite (1 Kings 11:20).

Gera ("enmity" or "grain"). **[1]** A son of Benjamin (Gen. 46:21). **[2]** A son of Bela (1 Chron. 8:3, 5, 7). **[3]** Father of Ehud (Judg. 3:15). **[4]** Father or ancestor of Shimei (2 Sam. 16:5; 19:16, 18; 1 Kings 2:8). [Note: All of these may be identical.]

Gershom ("exile"). **[1]** Firstborn son of Moses and Zipporah (Exod. 2:22; 18:3). **[2]** *See* Gershon. **[3]** A descendant of Phinehas

(Ezra 8:2). **[4]** Father of Jonathan, a Levite during the time of the judges (Judg. 18:30).

Gershon [Gershom] ("exile"), an important priest, the eldest son of Levi (Gen. 46:11; Exod. 6:16; 1 Chron. 6:1). He is also called Gershom (1 Chron. 6:16–17, 20; 15:7).

Gesham ("firm"), a descendant of Caleb (1 Chron. 2:47).

Geshem [Gashmu] ("rainstorm" or "corporealness"), an Arabian opponent of Nehemiah (Neh. 2:19; 6:1–2).

Gether. **[1]** A descendant of Shem (1 Chron. 1:17). Possibly an unknown family of Arameans is meant. **[2]** The third of Aram's sons (Gen. 10:23).

Geuel ("salvation of God"), the spy sent out from Gad to bring back word about Canaan (Num. 13:15).

Gibbar ("high; mighty"), one who returned to Jerusalem with Zerubbabel (Ezra 2:20).

Gibea ("highlander"), a descendant of Caleb (1 Chron. 2:49). *See also* "Places of the Bible."

Giddalti ("I have magnified"), a son of Heman in charge of one of the courses at the temple (1 Chron. 25:4).

Giddel ("very great"). **[1]** One whose descendants returned to Jerusalem with Zerubbabel (Ezra 2:47; Neh. 7:49). **[2]** Head of a family of Solomon's servants (Ezra 2:56; Neh. 7:58).

Gideon [Gedeon] ("feller [i.e., great warrior]"), the great judge of Israel who delivered his people from Midian (Judg. 6—8); he was given the name Jerubbaal (q.v.).

Gideoni ("feller"), a descendant of Benjamin (Num. 1:11; 2:22).

Gilalai ("rolling; weighty"), one of a party of priests who played on David's instruments at the consecration of the Jerusalem walls under Ezra (Neh. 12:36).

Gilead ("strong; rocky"). **[1]** A son of Machir (Num. 26:29–30). **[2]** Father of Jephthah the judge (Judg. 11:1–2). **[3]** A descendant of Gad (1 Chron. 5:14). *See also* "Places of the Bible."

Ginath ("protection"), father of Tibni (1 Kings 16:21–22).

Ginnetho [Ginnethon] ("great protection"), a prince or priest who sealed the new covenant with God after the Exile (Neh. 10:6; 12:4, 16).

Ginnethon. *See* Ginnetho.

Gispa ("listening; attentive"), an overseer of the Nethinim (Neh. 11:21).

Gog ("high; mountain"). **[1]** A descendant

PEOPLE OF THE BIBLE

of Reuben (1 Chron. 5:4). **[2]** A prince of Rosh, Meshech, and Tubal (Ezek. 38:2; 39:1, 11). In Revelation 20:8 Gog appears to have become a nation as is Magog, thus indicating the name is to be understood symbolically. *See also* Magog.

Goliath ("an exile or soothsayer"). **[1]** The Philistine giant who was slain by David (1 Sam. 17:4–54). **[2]** Another giant, possibly the son of [1] (2 Sam. 21:19).

Gomer. [1] Eldest son of Japheth (Gen. 10:2–3; 1 Chron. 1:5–6). Possibly a people inhabiting the north, probably including or identical with the Cimmerians of classical history. **[2]** The immoral wife of Hosea (Hos. 1:3; 3:1–4).

Guni ("protected"). **[1]** Son of Naphtali found in three lists (Gen. 46:24; Num. 26:48; 1 Chron. 7:13). **[2]** Father of Abdiel (1 Chron. 5:15).

H

Haahashtari ("the courier"), a son of Ashur listed in the descendants of Judah (1 Chron. 4:6).

Habaiah ("Jehovah is protection"), ancestor of a priestly family (Ezra 2:61; Neh. 7:63).

Habakkuk ("love's embrace"), a prophet during the reigns of Jehoiakim and Josiah (Hab. 1:1; 3:1).

Habaziniah ("Jehovah's light"), the grandfather of Jaazaniah, the founder of a Jewish sect (Jer. 35:3).

Hachaliah ("Jehovah is hidden"), the father of Nehemiah the governor of Israel (Neh. 1:1).

Hachmoni ("the wise"), father of Jehiel, the royal tutor (1 Chron. 27:32).

Hadad ("thunderer"). **[1]** One of the twelve sons of Ishmael and grandson of Abraham (1 Chron. 1:30). He is called Hadar, due to a copyist's mistake or a dialectal variant in Genesis 25:15. **[2]** A king of Edom who fought Midian (Gen. 36:35–36; 1 Chron. 1:46). **[3]** The last of Edom's early kings (1 Chron. 1:50–51). Due to a copyist's mistake or dialectal variant he is called Hadar in Genesis 36:39. **[4]** A member of the royal family of Edom who opposed Israel's rule of Edom (1 Kings 11:14–22, 25).

Hadadezer [Hadarezer] ("[the god] Hadad is my help"), the king of Zobah in Syria that warred against David and Joab (2 Sam. 8:3–12). His name is also written Hadarezer;

perhaps this is a dialectal variant (2 Sam. 10:16; 1 Chron. 18:3–10).

Hadar. *See* Hadad [1], [3].

Hadarezer. *See* Hadadezer.

Hadassah ("myrtle"), the Hebrew name of Esther (q.v.).

Hadlai ("resting"), the father of Amasa, a chief man of the tribe of Ephraim (2 Chron. 28:12).

Hadoram ("Hadad is high"). **[1]** The son of Joktan, a descendant of Noah (Gen. 10:27; 1 Chron. 1:21). Possibly the name denotes an Arabian tribe. **[2]** The son of the king of Hamath; he bore presents to David (1 Chron. 18:10). He is called Joram in 2 Samuel 8:9–10, perhaps as a token to honor David's God (i.e., Joram means "Jehovah is high"). **[3]** The superintendent of forced labor under David, Solomon, and Rehoboam. He is variously called Adoniram ("my lord is exalted"), and Adoram, a contraction of the former (2 Sam. 20:24; 1 Kings 4:6; 12:18; 2 Chron. 10:18). *See also* Jehoram.

Hagab ("locust"), an ancestor of captives returning with Zerubbabel (Ezra 2:46). *See* Hagaba.

Hagaba [Hagabah] ("locust"), an ancestor of some of the captives returning with Zerubbabel (Ezra 2:45; Neh. 7:48). *See* Hagab.

Hagabah. *See* Hagaba.

Hagar [Agar] ("wandering"), an Egyptian servant of Sarah; she became the mother of Ishmael by Abraham (Gen. 16:1–16; 21:14–17).

Haggai ("festive"), the first of the prophets who prophesied after the Babylonian Captivity (Ezra 5:1; Hag. 1:1, 3, 12).

Haggeri ("wanderer"), the father of one of David's mighty men (1 Chron. 11:38).

Haggi ("festive"), the second son of Gad (Gen. 46:16; Num. 26:15).

Haggiah ("feast of Jehovah"), a descendant of Levi (1 Chron. 6:30).

Haggith ("festal"), the fifth wife of David and mother of Adonijah (2 Sam. 3:4; 1 Kings 1:5, 11).

Hakkatan ("the little one"), the father of Johanan, who returned with Ezra (Ezra 8:12).

Hakkoz ("the nimble"), a priest and chief of the seventh course of service in the sanctuary (1 Chron. 24:10). *See* Koz [1].

Hakupha ("incitement"), ancestor of a family returning from captivity (Ezra 2:51; Neh. 7:53).

Hallohesh [Halohesh] ("the whisperer; the slanderer"). **[1]** The father of one who repaired the wall (Neh. 3:12). [2] A man or family that sealed the new covenant with God after the Exile (Neh. 10:24); some identify him with [1].

Halohesh. *See* Hallohesh.

Ham ("hot"), the youngest son of Noah. Because of his wickedness, his son Canaan was cursed (Gen. 5:32; 9:22–27). *See also* "Places of the Bible."

Haman ("celebrated Human [Humban]"), the prime minister of Ahasuerus who plotted against the Jews (Esther 3—9).

Hamath. *See* Hemath.

Hammedatha ("given by the moon"), the father of Haman (Esther 3:1).

Hammelech. This is not a proper name. It is a general title that means "the king" (Jer. 36:26; 38:6).

Hammoleketh ("the queen"), an ancestor of Gideon. It may be a proper name or title (1 Chron. 7:18).

Hamor [Emmor] ("ass"), the prince of Shechem whose son Shechem brought destruction on himself and his family (Gen. 33:19; 34:2–26).

Hamran. *See* Hemdan.

Hamuel ("wrath of God"), a descendant of Simeon (1 Chron. 4:26).

Hamul ("pity"), the younger son of Pharez (Gen. 46:12; 1 Chron. 2:5).

Hamutal ("kinsman of the dew"), one of King Josiah's wives (2 Kings 23:31; 24:18; Jer. 52:1).

Hanameel ("gift or grace of God"), a cousin of Jeremiah's who sold him a field (Jer. 32:6–9).

Hanan ("merciful"). [1] A descendant of Benjamin (1 Chron. 8:23). [2] A descendant of Benjamin through Saul (1 Chron. 8:38; 9:44). [3] One of David's heroes (1 Chron. 11:43). [4] A returned captive (Ezra 2:46; Neh. 7:49). [5] A Levite who assisted Ezra when reading the Law (Neh. 8:7). [6] A Levite who sealed the covenant with Nehemiah (Neh. 10:10; 13:13). Perhaps identical with [5]. [7] A chief or family who sealed the covenant with Nehemiah (Neh. 10:22). [8] A chief or family who also sealed the covenant (Neh. 10:26). [9] A temple officer whose sons had a chamber in the temple (Jer. 35:4). [Note: This name should not be confused with Baal-hanan.]

Hanani ("gracious"). [1] A musician and head of one of the courses of the temple services (1 Chron. 25:4, 25). [2] The father of the prophet Jehu; cast into prison by Asa (1 Kings 16:1, 7; 2 Chron. 16:7–10). [3] A priest who

married a foreign wife (Ezra 10:20). [4] A brother of Nehemiah and a governor of Jerusalem under him (Neh. 1:2; 7:2). [5] A priest and musician who helped to purify the walls of Jerusalem (Neh. 12:36).

Hananiah ("Jehovah is gracious"). [1] A descendant of Benjamin (1 Chron. 8:24). [2] An officer of Uzziah (2 Chron. 26:11). [3] The father of a prince under Jehoiakim (Jer. 36:12). [4] The leader of the sixteenth division of David's musicians (1 Chron. 25:4, 23). [5] The grandfather of Irijah (Jer. 37:13). [6] A false prophet who opposed Jeremiah (Jer. 28). [7] One of Daniel's friends at Babylon (Dan. 1:7, 11, 19). *See also* Shadrach. [8] A son of Zerubbabel (1 Chron. 3:19, 21). [9] A Levite who married a foreign wife during the Exile (Ezra 10:28). [10] A druggist and priest who helped to rebuild the wall of Jerusalem (Neh. 3:8). [11] One who helped to rebuild the gate of Jerusalem (Neh. 3:30); perhaps the same as [10]. [12] A faithful Israelite placed in charge of Jerusalem (Neh. 7:2). [13] One who sealed the new covenant with God after the Exile (Neh. 10:23). [14] A priest present at the dedication of the walls of Jerusalem (Neh. 12:12, 41).

Haniel [Hanniel] ("God is gracious"). [1] A prince of the tribe of Manasseh (Num. 34:23). [2] A hero of Asher (1 Chron. 7:39).

Hannah ("grace"), a prophetess, the mother of Samuel (1 Sam. 1).

Hanniel. *See* Haniel.

Hanoch [Henoch] ("dedicated"). [1] A grandson of Abraham (Gen. 25:4), called Henoch in First Chronicles 1:33. [2] The eldest son of Reuben, and founder of the Hanochite clan (Gen. 46:9; 1 Chron. 5:3). [3] Enoch, the son of Jared (1 Chron. 1:3).

Hanun ("gracious"). [1] A king of Ammon who involved the Ammonites in a disastrous war with David (2 Sam. 10:1–6). [2] One who repaired the wall (Neh. 3:30). [3] One who repaired the valley gate of Jerusalem (Neh. 3:13).

Haran ("strong; enlightened"). [1] A brother of Abraham who died before his father (Gen. 11:26–31). [2] A descendant of Levi (1 Chron. 23:9). [3] A son of Caleb (1 Chron. 2:46). *See also* "Places of the Bible."

Harbona [Harbonah] ("ass-driver"), a chamberlain under Ahasuerus (Esther 1:10; 7:9).

Hareph ("early born"), a son of Caleb (1 Chron. 2:51), not to be confused with Hariph (q.v.).

PEOPLE OF THE BIBLE

Harhaiah ("Jehovah is protecting"), father of Uzziel, a builder of the wall of Jerusalem (Neh. 3:8).

Harhas [Hasrah] ("glitter"), grandfather of Shallum, the husband of the prophetess Huldah (2 Kings 22:14). Another form of the name is Hasrah (2 Chron. 34:22).

Harhur ("nobility; distinction"), ancestor of returned captives (Neh. 7:53; Ezra 2:51).

Harim ("snub-nosed"). **[1]** A priest in charge of the third division of temple duties (1 Chron. 24:8; Ezra 2:39; 10:21; Neh. 3:11). **[2]** An ancestor of some returning from captivity (Ezra 2:32; Neh. 7:35). **[3]** One whose descendants took foreign wives during the Exile (Ezra 10:31). **[4]** One who sealed the new covenant with God after the Exile (Neh. 10:5). **[5]** A family that sealed the new covenant with God after the Exile (Neh. 10:27). **[6]** An ancestor of a family, perhaps [4] (Neh. 12:15). [Note: Many of those named Harim may be identical; there are many uncertainties.]

Hariph ("early born"). **[1]** An ancestor of returning captives (Neh. 7:24). **[2]** Head of a family who sealed the new covenant with God after the Exile (Neh. 10:19). He is called Jorah in Ezra 2:18.

Harnepher ("panting"), a descendant of Asher (1 Chron. 7:36).

Haroeh ("the seer"), a descendant of Judah (1 Chron. 2:52); perhaps Reaiah (1 Chron. 4:2).

Harsha ("artificer"), an ancestor of returning captives (Ezra 2:52; Neh. 7:54).

Harum ("elevated"), a descendant of Judah (1 Chron. 4:8).

Harumaph ("slit-nosed"), father of Jedaiah the wall-builder (Neh. 3:10).

Haruz ("industrious"), mother of King Amon (2 Kings 21:19).

Hasadiah ("Jehovah is kind"), a descendant of Jehoiakim (1 Chron. 3:20).

Hasenuah ("the violated"), a descendant of Benjamin (1 Chron. 9:7). The original name was probably Senuah, to which the Hebrew definite article (Ha-) is prefixed. *See also* Senuah.

Hashabiah ("Jehovah is associated"). **[1]** A descendant of Levi (1 Chron. 6:45). **[2]** Another descendant of Levi (1 Chron. 9:14). **[3]** A son of Jeduthun (1 Chron. 25:3). **[4]** A descendant of Kohath (1 Chron. 26:30). **[5]** A son of Kemuel who was a prince of the Levites (1 Chron. 27:17). **[6]** A chief of a Levite clan (2 Chron. 35:9). **[7]** A Levite who returned with Ezra from Babylon (Ezra 8:19).

ANTONIA FORTRESS (MODEL). *Named for Mark Antony, this fortress was built by Herod the Great at the northwest corner of his temple. The structure is called "the castle" in Acts 21:34. It also served as a palace, and many scholars believe it was the place where Christ was tried before Pilate.*

44

PEOPLE OF THE BIBLE

[8] A chief of the family of Kohath (Ezra 8:24). **[9]** One who repaired the wall of Jerusalem (Neh. 3:17). **[10]** One who sealed the covenant with Nehemiah (Neh. 10:11). **[11]** A Levite in charge of certain temple functions (Neh. 11:15). **[12]** An attendant of the temple (Neh. 11:22). **[13]** A priest in the days of Jeshua (Neh. 12:21). **[14]** A chief Levite (Neh. 12:24). [Note: It is quite possible that [9], [12], and [14] refer to the same person.]

Hashabnah ("Jehovah is a friend"), one who sealed the new covenant with God after the Exile (Neh. 10:25).

Hashabniah ("Jehovah is a friend"). **[1]** Father of Hattush who helped to rebuild the wall of Jerusalem (Neh. 3:10). **[2]** A Levite who officiated at the fast under Ezra and Nehemiah when the covenant was sealed (Neh. 9:5).

Hashbadana ("judge"), an assistant to Ezra at the reading of the Law (Neh. 8:4).

Hashem ("shining"), father of several of David's guards (1 Chron. 11:34).

Hashub [Hasshub] ("associate"). **[1]** A Levite chief (1 Chron. 9:14; Neh. 11:15). **[2]** A builder of the wall of Jerusalem (Neh. 3:11). **[3]** One of the signers of the new covenant with God after the Exile (Neh. 10:23). **[4]** One who repaired the wall of Jerusalem (Neh. 3:23).

Hashubah ("association"), a descendant of Jehoiakim (1 Chron. 3:20).

Hashum ("shining"). **[1]** One whose descendants returned from the Babylonian Captivity (Ezra 2:19; 10:33; Neh. 7:22). **[2]** One who sealed the covenant (Neh. 8:4; 10:18).

Hashupha [Hasupha] ("stripped"), an ancestor of returning captives (Ezra 2:43; Neh. 7:46).

Hasrah. *See* Harhas.

Hassenaah ("the thorn hedge"), an ancestor of those who rebuilt the Fish Gate at Jerusalem (Neh. 3:3). The name is probably identical with the Senaah of Ezra 2:35 and Nehemiah 7:38, which most English translators have understood to have the Hebrew definite article (Ha-) prefixed.

Hasshub. *See* Hashub.

Hasupha. *See* Hashupha.

Hatach, a chamberlain of Ahasuerus (Esther 4:5–10).

Hathath ("terror"), son of Othniel (1 Chron. 4:13).

Hatipha ("taken; captive"), an ancestor of returning captives (Ezra 2:54; Neh. 7:56).

Hatita ("exploration"), a temple gatekeeper or porter whose descendants returned from the Babylonian Captivity (Ezra 2:42; Neh. 7:45).

POOL OF SILOAM. *The pool is located in the Kidron Valley and was connected to the spring of Gihon by the Siloam Tunnel. King Hezekiah of Judah knew that the Assyrians would lay seige to Jerusalem. In order to assure a free flow of water into the city, he ordered that the waters of Gihon be diverted underground into a tunnel hewn out of stone (2 Chron. 32:1–5, 30). These waters flowed into the pool of Siloam, located within the city walls.*

Hattil ("decaying"), an ancestor of some who returned from the Babylonian Captivity (Ezra 2:57; Neh. 7:59).

Hattush ("contender"). **[1]** Descendant of the kings of Judah, perhaps of Shechaniah (1 Chron. 3:22). **[2]** A descendant of David who returned from the Exile with Ezra (Ezra 8:2). **[3]** A priest who returned from the Exile with Zerubbabel (Neh. 12:2). **[4]** One who helped to rebuild the wall of Jerusalem (Neh. 3:10). **[5]** A priest who signed the covenant (Neh. 10:1, 4). [Note: entries [1], [2], [3], and [5] may refer to the same person.]

Havilah (perhaps "sandy"). **[1]** Son of Cush (Gen. 10:7; 1 Chron. 1:9). Possibly an unknown tribe is intended. **[2]** A descendant of Shem in two genealogies (Gen. 10:29; 1 Chron. 1:23). Possibly a tribe of Arabians who inhabited central or south Arabia is meant. *See also* "Places of the Bible."

Hazael ("God sees"), the murderer of Benhadad II who usurped the throne of Syria (1 Kings 19:15, 17; 2 Kings 8:8–29).

Hazaiah ("Jehovah is seeing"), a descendant of Judah (Neh. 11:5).

Hazar-maveth ("court of death"), the third son of Joktan (Gen. 10:26; 1 Chron. 1:20). Possibly the name refers to a people who dwelt in the peninsula of Arabia.

Hazelelponi ("protection of the face of"), a daughter of Etam in the genealogy of Judah (1 Chron. 4:3).

Haziel ("God is seeing"), a descendant of Levi in the time of David (1 Chron. 23:9).

Hazo ("vision; seer"), a son of Nahor and nephew of Abraham (Gen. 22:22).

Heber (properly Eber—"the other side; across"). **[1]** Head of a family of Gad (1 Chron. 5:13). **[2]** A descendant of Benjamin (1 Chron. 8:22). *See* Eber.

Heber ("companion"). **[1]** A descendant of Asher (Gen. 46:17; 1 Chron. 7:31–32). **[2]** The husband of Jael, who killed Sisera (Judg. 4:11, 17, 21; 5:24). **[3]** Head of a clan of Judah (1 Chron. 4:18). **[4]** A descendant of Benjamin (1 Chron. 8:17). **[5]** Used in Luke 3:35 to refer to Eber [1].

Hebron ("ford; company"). **[1]** A son of Kohath (Exod. 6:18; Num. 3:19; 1 Chron. 6:2, 18). **[2]** A descendant of Caleb (1 Chron. 2:42–43).

Hegai [Hege], a chamberlain of Ahasuerus (Esther 2:3, 8, 15).

Helah ("tenderness"), a wife of Asher (1 Chron. 4:5, 7).

Heldai ("enduring"). **[1]** A captain of

PEOPLE OF THE BIBLE

LAND OF EPHRAIM. *The prophet Hosea predicted that God would punish the tribe of Ephraim, which lived in these fertile hills north of Jerusalem (cf. Hosea 12–13). Hosea said, "Now they sin more and more, and have made them . . . idols according to their own understanding. . ." (Hosea 13:2).*

the temple service (1 Chron. 27:15). **[2]** An Israelite who returned from the Babylonian Captivity and was given special honors (Zech. 6:10); he is called Helem in verse 14.

Heleb [Heled] ("fat"), one of David's mighty men (2 Sam. 23:29; 1 Chron. 11:30).

Heled. *See* Heleb.

Helek ("portion"), a descendant of Manasseh (Num. 26:30; Josh. 17:2).

Helem ("strength"). **[1]** A descendant of Asher (1 Chron. 7:35). **[2]** Another name for Heldai [2] (q.v.).

Helez ("vigor"). **[1]** One of David's mighty men (2 Sam. 23:26; 1 Chron. 11:27; 27:10). **[2]** A descendant of Judah (1 Chron. 2:39).

Heli ("high," perhaps a contracted form of "God is high." Heli is the Greek form of Eli.), the father of Joseph in Luke's genealogy (Luke 3:23).

Helkai ("Jehovah is my portion"), the head of a priestly family (Neh. 12:15).

Helon ("valorous"), the father of Eliab, the prince of Zebulun (Num. 1:9; 2:7; 7:24; 10:16).

Hemam. *See* Homam.

Heman ("faithful"). **[1]** A musician and seer appointed by David as a leader in the temple's vocal and instrumental music (1 Chron.

6:33; 15:17; 2 Chron. 5:12; 35:15). **[2]** A wise man with whom Solomon was compared (1 Kings 4:31; 1 Chron. 2:6). He composed a meditative Psalm (Psa. 88, title).

Hemath ("warmth"), father of the house of Rechab (1 Chron. 2:55); also called Hamath (Amos 6:14).

Hemdan ("pleasant"), a descendant of Seir (Gen. 36:26). The KJV wrongly rendered his name *Amram* in First Chronicles 1:41—the reading there is Hamran, possibly a copyist's mistake.

Hen ("favor"), a son of Zephaniah (Zech. 6:14); he is probably the same as *Josiah* in verse 10.

Henadad ("Hadad is gracious"), a head of a Levite family that helped to rebuild the temple (Ezra 3:9; Neh. 3:18, 24; 10:9).

Henoch. *See* Hanoch [1] and Enoch [2].

Hepher ("a digging; a well"). **[1]** The youngest son of Gilead and founder of the Hepherites (Num. 26:32; Josh. 17:2). **[2]** A man of Judah (1 Chron. 4:6). **[3]** One of David's heroes (1 Chron. 11:36). *See also* "Places of the Bible."

Hephzi-bah ("my delight is in her"), the mother of King Manasseh (2 Kings 21:1).

Heresh ("work; silence"), head of a Levite family (1 Chron. 9:15).

Hermas ("Mercury; interpreter"), a Christian to whom Paul sent greetings (Rom. 16:14).

Hermes ("Mercury [the god]; interpreter"), a Greek Christian in Rome to whom Paul sent greetings (Rom. 16:14).

Hermogenes ("born of Hermes"), a Christian who deserted Paul at Rome or Ephesus (2 Tim. 1:15).

Herod ("heroic"). **[1]** Herod the Great, the sly king of Judea when Christ was born. In order to maintain power, he murdered the children of Bethlehem, thinking that he would be killing the Messiah (Matt. 2:1–22; Luke 1:5). **[2]** Herod Antipas, son of the former, was tetrarch of Galilee and Perea. He was the murderer of John the Baptist (Matt. 14:1–10; Luke 13:31–32; Luke 23:7–12). **[3]** Herod Philip, son of Herod the Great, was tetrarch of Iturea and Trachonitis (Luke 3:1). **[4]** Herod Philip, another son of Herod the Great, is the Philip whose wife Herod Antipas lured away (Matt. 14:3). **[5]** Herod Agrippa I, tetrarch of Galilee and eventual ruler of his grandfather's (i.e., Herod the Great's) old realm. He bitterly persecuted Christians (Acts 12:1–23). **[6]** Herod Agrippa II, son of Agrippa I and king of various domains, witnessed the preaching of Paul (Acts 25:13–26; 26:1–32). (*See* "The Herods' Family Tree," pp. 634–635.)

Herodias ("heroic"), granddaughter of Herod the Great, wife of Antipas, and ultimate cause of John the Baptist's death (Matt. 14:3–9; Luke 3:19).

Herodion ("heroic"), a Jewish Christian to whom Paul sent greetings (Rom. 16:11).

Hesed ("kindness"; [God has kept] "faithfulness"), father of one of Solomon's officers (1 Kings 4:10); not to be confused with Jushab-hesed (q.v.).

Heth, a son of Canaan (Gen. 10:15; 1 Chron. 1:13). Possibly a reference to the Hittite people.

Hezeki ("Jehovah is strength"), a descendant of Benjamin (1 Chron. 8:17).

Hezekiah [Ezekias; Hizkijah] ("Jehovah is strength"). **[1]** One who returned from Babylon (Ezra 2:16; Neh. 7:21). He, or his representative, is called Hizkijah (a form of Hezekiah) in Nehemiah 10:17. **[2]** The twelfth king of Judah; an ancestor of Christ. He instituted religious reform and improved the overall safety and prosperity of the nation (2 Kings 18—20; 2 Chron. 29—32; Matt. 1:9–10). **[3]** A son of Neariah, a descendant of the royal family of Judah (1 Chron. 3:23).

Hezion ("vision"), the grandfather of Ben-hadad, king of Syria (1 Kings 15:18). Many scholars identify him with Rezon (q.v.).

Hezir ("returning home"). **[1]** A Levite in the time of David (1 Chron. 24:15). **[2]** A chief of the people that sealed the new covenant with God after the Exile (Neh. 10:20).

Hezrai [Hezro] ("blooming; beautiful"), one of David's warriors (2 Sam. 23:35). He is also called Hezro (1 Chron. 11:37).

Hezro. *See* Hezrai.

Hezron [Esrom] ("blooming"). **[1]** A son of Perez and an ancestor of Christ (Gen. 46:12; 1 Chron. 2:5, 9, 18, 21, 24–25; Matt. 1:3; Luke 3:33). **[2]** A son of Reuben (Gen. 46:9; Exod. 6:14). *See also* "Places of the Bible."

Hiddai [Hurai] ("mighty; chief"), one of David's mighty men (2 Sam. 23:30). He is called Hurai ("free; noble") in First Chronicles 11:32.

Hiel ("God is living"), a man who rebuilt Jericho (1 Kings 16:34) and sacrificed his sons, in fulfillment of Joshua's curse (Josh. 6:26).

Hilkiah ("Jehovah is protection" or "my portion"). **[1]** One who stood with Ezra at the reading of the Law (Neh. 8:4). **[2]** A Levite who kept the children of the temple officials (1 Chron. 6:45). **[3]** A gatekeeper of the tabernacle (1 Chron. 26:11). **[4]** Master of the household of King Hezekiah (2 Kings 18:18, 26; Isa. 22:20; 36:3). **[5]** A priest of Anathoth and father of Jeremiah (Jer. 1:1). **[6]** High priest and the discoverer of the Book of the Law in the days of Josiah (2 Kings 22:4, 8; 23:4). **[7]** The father of Gemariah (Jer. 29:3). **[8]** A chief of priests who returned from captivity (Neh. 12:7) and his later descendants (Neh. 12:12, 21).

Hillel ("praised greatly"), the father of Abdon, one of the judges (Judg. 12:13, 15).

Hinnom, an unknown person who had a son(s) after whom a valley near Jerusalem was named. Human sacrifices took place there in Jeremiah's day, and garbage was later incinerated in this defiled place (Josh. 15:8; 18:16; Neh. 11:30; Jer. 7:31–32).

Hirah ("distinction"), a friend of Judah (Gen. 38:1, 12).

Hiram [Huram] (abbreviated form of Ahiram, "My brother is the exalted"). **[1]** A king of Tyre who befriended David and Solomon (2 Sam. 5:11; 1 Kings 5; 9:11; 10:11). **[2]** The skillful worker in brass whom Solomon secured from King Hiram (1 Kings 7:13, 40, 45;

PEOPLE OF THE BIBLE

ISAIAH INSCRIPTION. *Archaeologists excavating the Western Wall of the temple in Jerusalem found this stone, bearing a portion of Isaiah 66:14. Carved during the fourth century A.D., the inscription encouraged the Jews with Isaiah's prophetic words: "And when ye see this, your heart shall rejoice, and your bones shall flourish like an herb . . ." Less than 32 km. (20 mi.) to the southeast is the barren territory of the Dead Sea.*

2 Chron. 4:11, 16). **[3]** A descendant of Benjamin (1 Chron. 8:5).

Hizkiah [Hizkijah] ("Jehovah is strength"). **[1]** An ancestor of the prophet Zephaniah (Zeph. 1:1). *See* Hezekiah [1].

Hobab ("beloved"), the father-in-law or brother-in-law of Moses (Num. 10:29; Judg. 4:11). The phrase "father-in-law" in Judges 4:11 may possibly mean nothing more than "in-law," or perhaps Jethro was also named Hobab; but the identity is uncertain. *See also* Jethro.

Hod ("majesty"), one of the sons of Zophah (1 Chron. 7:37).

Hodaiah ("honorer of Jehovah"), a descendant of the royal line of Judah (1 Chron. 3:24); possibly an alternate spelling of Hodaviah (q.v.).

Hodaviah ("honorer of Jehovah"). **[1]** A chief of the tribe of Manasseh (1 Chron. 5:24). **[2]** A descendant of Benjamin (1 Chron. 9:7). **[3]** An ancestor of returning captives (Ezra 2:40). He is also called Hodevah ("Jehovah is honor") in Nehemiah 7:43. *See also* Hodaiah.

Hodesh ("new moon"), a wife of Shaharaim (1 Chron. 8:9).

Hodevah. *See* Hodaviah.

Hodiah [Hodijah] ("splendor [or honor] of Jehovah"). **[1]** A brother-in-law of Naham (1 Chron. 4:19). The KJV incorrectly identifies him as the "wife" of Naham. **[2]** One of the Levites who explained the Law (Neh. 8:7; 10:10, 13). **[3]** One who sealed the new covenant with God after the Exile (Neh. 10:18).

Hodijah. *See* Hodiah.

Hoglah ("partridge"), a daughter of Zelophehad (Num. 26:33; 27:1; Josh. 17:3).

Hoham ("whom Jehovah impels; Jehovah protects the multitude"), an Amorite king slain by Joshua (Josh. 10:1–27).

Homam [Hemam] ("raging"), a Horite descendant of Esau (1 Chron. 1:39). He is called Hemam in Genesis 36:22 (probably a copyist's error).

Hophni ("strong"), the unholy son of Eli slain at the battle of Aphek (1 Sam. 1:3; 2:22–24, 34).

Horam ("height"), a king of Gezer defeated by Joshua (Josh. 10:33).

Hori ("free; noble"). **[1]** A descendant of Esau (Gen. 36:22; 1 Chron. 1:39). **[2]** The father of one of the men sent to spy out the Promised Land (Num. 13:5).

Hosah ("refuge"), one of the first doorkeepers of the ark of the covenant (1 Chron. 16:38; 26:10–11, 16). *See also* "Places of the Bible."

Hosea [Osee] ("help; i.e., Jehovah is help"), a prophet of Israel; he denounced the idolatries of Israel and Samaria (Hos. 1:1–2).

Hoshaiah ("whom Jehovah helps"). **[1]** The father of Jezaniah or Azariah (Jer. 42:1; 43:2). **[2]** A man who led half of the princes of Judah in procession at the dedication of the walls (Neh. 12:32).

Hoshama ("whom Jehovah heareth"), a son or descendant of Jeconiah or Jehoiakim (1 Chron. 3:18).

Hoshea [Hosea] ("Jehovah is help or salvation"). **[1]** A chief of the tribe of Ephraim in the days of David (1 Chron. 27:20). **[2]** The last king of Israel; he was imprisoned by Sargon of Assyria (2 Kings 15:30; 17:1, 4, 6; 18:1). **[3]** One who sealed the covenant with Nehemiah (Neh. 10:23). **[3]** The original name of Joshua (q.v.).

Hotham [Hothan] ("determination"). **[1]** A descendant of Asher (1 Chron. 7:32). **[2]** Father of two of David's best men (1 Chron. 11:44).

Hothan. *See* Hotham.

Hothir ("abundance"), son of Heman in charge of the twenty-first course of the tabernacle service (1 Chron. 25:4, 28).

Hul ("circle"), grandson of Shem (Gen. 10:23; 1 Chron. 1:17). Possibly an Aramean tribe is referred to; some have suggested the people of Hūlīa near Mt. Masius.

Huldah ("weasel"), a prophetess in the days of King Josiah (2 Kings 22:14; 2 Chron. 34:22).

Hupham ("coast-inhabitant; protected"), the head of a family descendant from Benjamin (Num. 26:39). In Genesis 46:21 and First Chronicles 7:12, his name is listed as Huppim ("coast-people" or "protection").

Huppah ("protection"), a priest in the time of David who had charge of one of the courses of service in the sanctuary (1 Chron. 24:13).

Huppim. *See* Hupham.

Hur ("free; noble"). **[1]** One of the men who held up Moses' arms during the battle with Amalek (Exod. 17:10, 12; 24:14). **[2]** A son of Caleb (Exod. 31:2; 35:30; 38:22; 1 Chron. 2:19, 50; 4:1, 4). **[3]** A Midianite king slain by Israel (Num. 31:8; Josh. 13:21). **[4]** An officer of Solomon on Mount Ephraim (1 Kings 4:8). **[5]** The ruler of half of Jerusalem under Nehemiah (Neh. 3:9).

Hurai ("free; noble"). *See* Hiddai.

Huram. *See* Hiram.

Huri ("linen weaver"), a descendant of Gad (1 Chron. 5:14).

Hushah ("haste"), a descendant of Judah (1 Chron. 4:4).

Hushai ("quick"), a friend and counselor of David (2 Sam. 15:32, 37; 16:16–18; 17:5–15).

Husham ("hasting; alert"), a descendant of Esau who became king of Edom (Gen. 36:34–35; 1 Chron. 1:45–46).

Hushim ("hasting; hasters"). **[1]** A son of Dan (Gen. 46:23); in Numbers 26:42, his name is Shuham. **[2]** A descendant of Benjamin (1 Chron. 7:12). **[3]** One of the two wives of Shaharaim (1 Chron. 8:8, 11).

Huz. *See* Uz.

Hymenaeus ("nuptial"), an early Christian who fell into apostasy and error (1 Tim. 1:20; 2 Tim. 2:17).

I

Ibhar ("chooser; Jehovah chooses"), one of David's sons born at Jerusalem (2 Sam. 5:15; 1 Chron. 3:6).

Ibneiah [Ibnijah] ("Jehovah builds up"). **[1]** A descendant of Benjamin (1 Chron. 9:8). **[2]** A man of Benjamin whose descendants lived in Jerusalem (1 Chron. 9:8).

Ibnijah. *See* Ibneiah.

Ibri ("one who passes over; a Hebrew"), a descendant of Merari in the time of David (1 Chron. 24:27).

Ibzan ("famous; splendid"), a Bethlehemite who judged Israel for seven years (Judg. 12:8–10).

Ichabod ("inglorious"), son of Phinehas, born after his father's death and after the ark was taken (1 Sam. 4:19–22).

Idbash ("honey-sweet"), one of the sons of Abi-etam (1 Chron. 4:3).

Iddo ("honorable; happy"), the official of Casiphia who provided Levites for Ezra (Ezra 8:17).

Iddo ("beloved"). **[1]** Captain of the tribe of Manasseh in Gilead (1 Chron. 27:21). **[2]** A descendant of Gershon (1 Chron. 6:21); called Adaiah in First Chronicles 6:41.

Iddo ("timely"). **[1]** Father of Abinadab (1 Kings 4:14). **[2]** Grandfather of the prophet Zechariah (Ezra 5:1; Zech 1:7).

Iddo ("adorned"). **[1]** A prophet who wrote about the kings of Israel (2 Chron. 9:29; 2 Chron. 12:15). **[2]** A priest who returned to

JACOB'S WELL. *This well near Sychar is traditionally identified as Jacob's well, located near the land the patriarch gave to his son Joseph. It was here that Jesus talked with the woman of Samaria (John 4).*

Jerusalem with Zerubbabel (Neh. 12:4); perhaps the same as [1].

Igal [Igeal] ("Jehovah redeems"). **[1]** One of the twelve spies sent to search out Canaan (Num. 13:7). **[2]** One of David's heroes (2 Sam. 23:36). **[3]** A descendant of the royal house of Judah (1 Chron. 3:22).

Igdaliah ("Jehovah is great"), ancestor of persons who had a "chamber" in the temple (Jer. 35:4).

Igeal. *See* Igal.

Ikkesh ("subtle" or "crooked"), father of Ira, one of David's mighty men (2 Sam. 23:26; 1 Chron. 11:28; 27:9).

Ilai ("exalted"). *See* Zalmon.

Imla [Imlah] ("fullness"), father of Micaiah (2 Chron. 18:7–8).

Imlah. *See* Imla.

Immer ("loquacious; prominent"). **[1]** A priest in the time of David (1 Chron. 24:14). **[2]** A priest of Jeremiah's time (Jer. 20:1). **[3]** The father of Zadok (Neh. 3:29). **[4]** A family of priests who gave their name to the sixteenth course of the temple service (1 Chron. 9:12; Ezra 2:37; Neh. 7:40). *See also* "Places of the Bible."

Imna [Jimna; Jimnah; Imnah] ("lugging"). **[1]** A descendant of Asher (Gen. 46:17; 1 Chron. 7:35). **[2]** A son of Asher (Num. 26:44; 1 Chron. 7:30). **[3]** Father of Kore in Hezekiah's reign (2 Chron. 31:14).

Imnah. *See* Imna.

Imrah ("height of Jehovah" or "stubborn"), a descendant of Asher (1 Chron. 7:36).

Imri ("talkative; projecting"). **[1]** A descendant of Judah (1 Chron. 9:4). **[2]** Father of Zaccur, one of Nehemiah's assistants (Neh. 3:2).

Iphedeiah ("Jehovah redeems"), a descendant of Benjamin (1 Chron. 8:25).

Ir ("watcher" or "city"), a descendant of Benjamin (1 Chron. 7:12); possibly the same as Iri (v. 7). Not to be confused with Ir-nahash.

Ira ("watchful"). **[1]** A priest to David (2 Sam. 20:26). **[2]** One of David's thirty mighty men (1 Chron. 11:28; 2 Sam. 23:38) and a captain of the temple guard (1 Chron. 27:9). **[3]** Another of David's thirty (1 Chron. 11:40; 2 Sam. 23:26).

Irad ("fleet"), a descendant of Enoch (Gen. 4:18).

Iram ("citizen"), a duke of Edom (Gen. 36:43).

Iri ("watchful"), a descendant of Benjamin (1 Chron. 7:7); possibly the same as Ir (v. 12).

Irijah ("seen of Jehovah"), a captain of the gate who arrested Jeremiah (Jer. 37:13–14).

Ir-nahash ("serpent city"), a descendant of Judah (1 Chron. 4:12).

Iru ("watch"), a son of Caleb (1 Chron. 4:15).

Isaac ("laughter"), the son of Abraham and Sarah, born to them in their old age. He was the father of Jacob and Esau and an ancestor of Christ (Gen. 21—25; Matt. 1:2).

Isaiah [Esaias] ("salvation of Jehovah"), called the "prince of prophets"; his career lasted over sixty years. He foretold the coming of Christ (Isa. 1:1; 7:14; 9:6; 52:12–53).

Iscah ("Jehovah is looking" or "who looks"), daughter of Haran, sister of Milcah, and niece of Abraham (Gen. 11:29).

Iscariot. *See* Juda(s) [8].

Ishbah ("praising; appeaser"), a descendant of Judah (1 Chron. 4:17).

Ishbak ("leaning; free"), son of Abraham and father of a northern Arabian tribe (Gen. 25:2; 1 Chron. 1:32).

Ishbi-benob ("dweller at Nob"), one of the sons of Rapha the Philistine; he attacked David but was killed by Abishai (2 Sam. 21:15–22).

Ishbosheth ("man of shame"), son and successor of King Saul. He reigned two years before being defeated by David (2 Sam. 2:8–15; 3:8, 14–15; 4:5–12). He also was known as Esh-baal (1 Chron. 8:33; 9:39).

Ishi ("my husband" or "salutary"). **[1]** A descendant of Pharez, son of Judah (1 Chron. 2:31). **[2]** A descendant of Judah (1 Chron. 4:20). **[3]** A descendant of Simeon

(1 Chron. 4:42). [4] A chief of the tribe of Manasseh (1 Chron. 5:24).

Ishiah. *See* Isshiah.

Ishijah. *See* Isshiah.

Ishma ("high" or "desolate"), a brother of Jezreel and Idbash, all descendants of Caleb (1 Chron. 4:3).

Ishmael ("God hears"). [1] Son of Abraham and Hagar; his descendants are the Arabian nomads (Gen. 16:11–16; 17:18–26; 25:9–17; 28:9; 36:3). [2] The cunning son of Nethaniah and traitor of Israel (Jer. 40:8—41:18). [3] A descendant of Benjamin (1 Chron. 8:38). [4] Father of Zebadiah (2 Chron. 19:11). [5] A captain in the time of Jehoiada and Joash (2 Chron. 23:1). [6] A Levite who married a foreign wife during the Exile (Ezra 10:22).

Ishmaiah [Ismaiah] ("Jehovah hears"). [1] A chief of Zebulun in David's time (1 Chron. 27:19). [2] A chief of Gibeon who joined David at Ziklag (1 Chron. 12:4).

Ishmerai ("Jehovah is keeper" or "to guard"), a descendant of Benjamin (1 Chron. 8:18).

Ishod ("man of majesty"), a man of Manasseh (1 Chron. 7:18).

Ish-pan ("he will hide"), a chief man of Benjamin (1 Chron. 8:22).

Ishuah [Isuah] ("he will level" or "even"), second son of Asher (Gen. 46:17; 1 Chron. 7:30).

Ishui [Ishuai; Isui; Jesui] ("equal"). [1] Third son of Asher (Gen. 46:17; Num. 26:44; 1 Chron. 7:30). [2] A son of King Saul by Ahinoam (1 Sam. 14:49). Some believe he is identical with Ishbosheth.

Ismachiah ("Jehovah will sustain"), an overseer under King Hezekiah (2 Chron. 31:13).

Ismaiah. *See* Ishmaiah.

Ispah ("firm"), a descendant of Benjamin (1 Chron. 8:16).

Israel. *See* Jacob.

Issachar ("reward"). [1] Ninth son of Jacob and ancestor of one of the twelve tribes of Israel (Gen. 30:17–18; 49:14–15). [2] A tabernacle porter (1 Chron. 26:5).

Isshiah [Ishiah; Ishijah] ("Jehovah exists"). [1] One of David's chiefs (1 Chron. 7:3). [2] *See* Jesiah [2]. [3] A man who took a foreign wife during the Exile (Ezra 10:31). [4] A descendant of Moses (1 Chron. 24:21). *See* Isaiah.

Isuah. *See* Ishuah.

Isui. *See* Ishui.

Ithai ("being"), one of David's thirty mighty men (1 Chron. 11:31). He is called Ittai in 2 Samuel 23:29.

Ithamar ("land; island of palms"), a son of Aaron (Exod. 6:23; 28:1); Eli was high priest of his line (1 Chron. 24:6).

Ithiel ("God is"), a man of the tribe of Benjamin (Neh. 11:7).

Ithiel and **Ucal** ("signs of God"; or verb meaning "to be weary"), the names of two wise men to whom Agur spoke his words. Some scholars believe these are not proper names, but two verbs. If so, the last part of verse 1 would read: "The man said, I have wearied myself, O God, I have wearied myself, O God, and am consumed" (Prov. 30:1).

Ithmah ("purity"), a Moabite, one of David's guards (1 Chron. 11:46).

Ithra ("abundance"), the father of Amasa, Absalom's captain (2 Sam. 17:25). He was also known as Jether (1 Kings 2:5, 32).

Ithran ("excellent"). [1] A descendant of Seir (Gen. 36:26). [2] A son of Zophah of Asher (1 Chron. 7:37).

Ithream ("residue of the people"), a son of David probably by Eglah (2 Sam. 3:5).

Ittai ("timely"). [1] A Philistine friend and general of David (2 Sam. 15:11–22; 18:2, 4, 12). [2] *See* Ithai.

Izehar [Izhar] ("shining"), a Levite, the father of Korah (Exod. 6:18–21; Num. 3:19).

Izrahiah ("Jehovah shines"), a descendant of Issachar (1 Chron. 7:3).

Izri ("creator"), leader of the fourth musical course (1 Chron. 25:11); perhaps the same as Zeri (v. 3).

J

Jaakan [Jakan] ("intelligent"), a son of Ezer, son of Seir (Deut. 10:6; 1 Chron. 1:42). In Genesis 36:27, he is called Akan. Many scholars believe the reference in the Deuteronomy passage is to a city. *See* Beeroth [1] in "Places of the Bible."

Jaakobah ("to Jacob"), a descendant of Simeon (1 Chron. 4:36).

Jaalah [Jaala] ("elevation"), a servant of Solomon whose descendants returned from the Exile (Ezra 2:56; Neh. 7:58).

Jaalam ("hidden"), a duke of Edom (Gen. 36:5, 14, 18; 1 Chron. 1:35).

Jaanai ("answerer"), a descendant of Gad (1 Chron. 5:12).

Jaare-oregim ("foresters"), father of Elhanan, slayer of Goliath the Gittite (2 Sam.

JEROBOAM'S CAPITAL. *King Jeroboam of Israel fortified the city of Shechem and made it his capital for a time. Jeroboam incurred God's wrath by building shrines in Dan and Bethel to rival the Jerusalem temple.*

21:19). Some suggest this is a copyist's error for Jair (cf. 1 Chron. 20:5), the "oregim" ("weavers") being a mistaken repetition of the last word in the verse.

Jaasau ("maker"), one who married a foreign wife (Ezra 10:37).

Jaasiel [Jasiel] ("God is maker"). **[1]** One of David's mighty men (1 Chron. 11:47). **[2]** A cousin of Saul's (1 Chron. 27:21).

Jaazaniah ("Jehovah is hearing"). **[1]** A captain of the forces who joined Gedaliah (2 Kings 25:23). He is the Jezaniah ("Jehovah determines; Jehovah hears") of Jeremiah 40:8; 42:1, and possibly the Azariah of Jeremiah 43:2. **[2]** A chief of the tribe of Reuben, a son of a certain man named Jeremiah but not the prophet (Jer. 35:3). **[3]** One enticing the people to idolatry (Ezek. 8:11). **[4]** A wicked prince of Judah seen in Ezekiel's vision (Ezek. 11:1).

Jaaziah ("Jehovah is determining"), a descendant of Merari living in Solomon's day (1 Chron. 24:26–27).

Jaaziel ("God is determining"), a temple musician in David's time (1 Chron. 15:18). He is called Aziel in verse 20.

Jabal ("moving"), son of Lamech, a nomad (Gen. 4:20).

Jabesh ("dry place"), father of Shallum, who killed Zechariah and reigned in his place (2 Kings 15:10–14). *See also* Jabesh-gilead of "Places of the Bible."

Jabez ("height"), head of a family of Judah

(1 Chron. 4:9–10). *See also* "Places of the Bible."

Jabin ("intelligent; observed"). **[1]** A king of Hazor defeated by Joshua (Josh. 11:1). **[2]** Another king of Hazor who oppressed Israel and was defeated by Deborah (Judg. 4).

Jachan ("afflicting"), a descendant of Gad (1 Chron. 5:13).

Jachin ("founding" or "he will establish"). **[1]** A son of Simeon (Gen. 46:10; Exod. 6:15; Num. 26:12). He is called Jarib in First Chronicles 4:24. **[2]** A priest in Jerusalem after the Babylonian Captivity (1 Chron. 9:10; Neh. 11:10). **[3]** Head of a family of Aaron (1 Chron. 24:17). *See* Jarib.

Jacob ("supplanter; following after"). **[1]** Son of Isaac, twin of Esau, and an ancestor of Christ. He bought Esau's birthright and became the father of the Jewish nation (Gen. 25—50; Matt. 1:2). God changed his name from Jacob to Israel ("God strives"; Gen. 32:28; 35:10). **[2]** The father of Joseph, the husband of Mary (Matt. 1:15–16). *See also* Heli.

Jada ("knowing"), a descendant of Judah (1 Chron. 2:28, 32).

Jadau ("friend"), one who married a foreign wife (Ezra 10:43).

Jaddua ("very knowing; known"). **[1]** One who sealed the covenant (Neh. 10:21). **[2]** The last high priest mentioned in the Old Testament (Neh. 12:11, 22).

Jadon ("judging"), one who helped repair the wall (Neh. 3:7).

Jael ("a wild goat"), wife of Heber who killed Sisera (Judg. 4:17–22; 5:6, 24).

Jahath ("comfort; revival"). **[1]** A descendant of Judah (1 Chron. 4:2). **[2], [3], [4], [5]** Four descendants of Levi (1 Chron. 6:30, 43; 23:10–11; 24:22). **[5]** An overseer of temple repair (2 Chron. 34:12).

Jahaziah ("Jehovah reveals"), one who assisted in recording those who had foreign wives (Ezra 10:15).

Jahaziel ("God reveals"). **[1]** One who joined David at Ziklag (1 Chron. 12:4). **[2]** A priest who helped bring the ark of the covenant into the temple (1 Chron. 16:6). **[3]** Son of Hebron (1 Chron. 23:19; 24:23). **[4]** A Levite who encouraged Jehoshaphat's army against the Moabites (2 Chron. 20:14). **[5]** A chief man whose son returned from Babylon (Ezra 8:5).

Jahdai ("Jehovah leads" or "leader; guide"), one of the family of Caleb the spy (1 Chron. 2:47).

Jahdiel ("union of God; God gives joy"), head of a family of Manasseh east of the Jordan (1 Chron. 5:24).

Jahdo ("union"), descendant of Gad (1 Chron. 5:14).

Jahleel ("God waits; wait for God"), a son of Zebulun (Gen. 46:14; Num. 26:26).

Jahmai ("Jehovah protects"), head of a clan of Issachar (1 Chron. 7:2).

Jahzeel [Jahziel] ("God apportions"), a son of Naphtali listed three times (Gen. 46:24; Num. 26:48; 1 Chron. 7:13).

Jahzerah ("Jehovah protects"), a priest of the family of Immer whose descendants dwelt in Jerusalem (1 Chron. 9:12). Perhaps another name for Ahasai (q.v.).

Jahziel. *See* Jahzeel.

Jair ("Jehovah enlightens"). **[1]** A descendant of Judah through his father and of Manasseh through his mother (Num. 32:41; Deut. 3:14; 1 Kings 4:13; 1 Chron. 2:22). **[2]** Judge of Israel for twenty-three years (Judg. 10:3–5). **[3]** The father of Mordecai, Esther's cousin (Esther 2:5). **[4]** *See* Jaareoregim.

Jairus ("enlightened"), a ruler of a synagogue near Capernaum whose daughter Jesus raised from the dead (Luke 8:41).

Jakan. *See* Jaakan.

Jakeh ("hearkening"), the father of Agur, the wise man (Prov. 30:1).

Jakim ("a setter up"). **[1]** Descendant of Benjamin (1 Chron. 8:19). **[2]** Head of a family descended from Aaron (1 Chron. 24:12).

Jalon ("Jehovah abides"), a descendant of Caleb the spy (1 Chron. 4:17).

Jambres, one of the Egyptian magicians who opposed Moses (Exod. 7:9–13; 2 Tim. 3:8; cf. Exod. 7:9–13).

James (Greek form of Jacob). **[1]** The son of Zebedee and brother of John called to be one of the Twelve. He was slain by Herod Agrippa I (Matt. 4:21; Mark 5:37; Luke 9:54; Acts 12:2). **[2]** The son of Alpheus, another of the twelve apostles. He is probably the same as James "the less," the son of Mary. By "the less" is his age or height in relation to James the son of Zebedee (Matt. 10:3; Mark 15:40; Acts 1:13). **[3]** The brother of Jesus (Matt. 13:55). After Christ's resurrection, he became a believer (1 Cor. 15:7) and a leader of the church at Jerusalem (Acts 12:17; Gal. 1:19; 2:9). He wrote the Epistle of James (James 1:1). **[4]** Unknown person mentioned as "the brother of Judas." Most view this as an incorrect translation and would render

JEREMIAH'S HOME. *The mound of Ras el-Harrubeh 5 km. (3 mi.) northeast of Jerusalem is thought to be the site of biblical Anathoth, the home of Jeremiah. This well-fortified city stood on a ridge overlooking the Jordan River Valley. Destroyed by Babylonian armies in the late seventh century B.C., Anathoth was repopulated by Jews returning from the Exile (Neh. 11:32).*

". . . Judas, the son of James" (Luke 6:16; Acts 1:13).

Jamin ("right hand; favor"). **[1]** A son of Simeon (Gen. 46:10; Exod. 6:15; Num. 26:12; 1 Chron. 4:24). **[2]** A descendant of Ram (1 Chron. 2:27). **[3]** A priest who explained the Law (Neh. 8:7).

Jamlech ("Jehovah rules"), a prince of Simeon (1 Chron. 4:34).

Janna, an ancestor of Christ (Luke 3:24).

Jannes ("he who seduces"), an Egyptian magician who opposed Moses (2 Tim. 3:8–9; cf. Exod. 7:9–13).

Japheth ("the extender; fair; enlarged"), second son of Noah, considered the father of the Indo-European races (Gen. 5:32; 6:10; 7:13; 9:18, 23, 27; 1 Chron. 1:4–5).

Japhia ("high"). **[1]** Amorite king of Lachish defeated by Joshua (Josh. 10:3). **[2]** A son of David (2 Sam. 5:15; 1 Chron. 3:7; 14:6). *See also* "Places of the Bible."

Japhlet ("Jehovah causes to escape"), a descendant of Asher (1 Chron. 7:32–33).

Jarah ("unveiler; honey"), a son of Ahaz of the family of Saul (1 Chron. 9:42). He is called Jehoadah in First Chronicles 8:36.

Jareb ("contender; avenger"), a king of Assyria (Hos. 5:13; 10:6); surely a nickname.

Jared [Jered] ("descending"), a descendant of Seth and ancestor of Christ (Gen. 5:15–20; 1 Chron. 1:2; Luke 3:37).

Jaresiah ("Jehovah gives a couch"), a descendant of Benjamin (1 Chron. 8:27).

Jarha, an Egyptian servant who married his master's daughter (1 Chron. 2:34–35).

Jarib ("striving"). **[1]** A chief man under Ezra (Ezra 8:16). **[2]** A priest who took a foreign wife during the Exile (Ezra 10:18). **[3]** *See* Jachin [1].

Jaroah ("new moon"), a descendant of Gad (1 Chron. 5:14).

Jashen ("shining"), the father of some, or one, of David's mighty men (2 Sam. 23:32). But the text probably should read thus: ". . . Jashen, Jonathan the son of Shammah the Hararite." Thus, Jashen would be one of the mighty men, and Shage (1 Chron. 11:34) is the same as Shammah (2 Sam. 23:33). *See also* Hashem.

Jasher ("upright"), one who wrote a now lost book (Josh. 10:13; 2 Sam. 1:18).

Jashobeam ("the people return"). **[1]** One of David's mighty men (1 Chron. 11:11; 27:2). **[2]** One who joined David at Ziklag (1 Chron. 12:6). *See* Adino.

Jashub ("turning back"). **[1]** One who took a foreign wife (Ezra 10:29). *See* Jashubi-lehem. **[2]** *See* Job [2].

Jashubi-lehem ("turning back to Bethlehem"), a descendant of Judah (1 Chron. 4:22).

Jasiel. *See* Jaasiel.

Jason ("healing"). **[1]** Paul's host during his stay at Thessalonica (Acts 17:5–9). **[2]** A Jewish Christian kinsman of Paul who sent salutations to Rome (Rom. 16:21). Both are possibly identical.

Jathniel ("God is giving"), a gatekeeper of the tabernacle (1 Chron. 26:2).

Javan, fourth son of Japheth (Gen. 10:2, 4; 1 Chron. 1:5, 7). The name corresponds etymologically with Ionia and may denote the Greeks (cf. Is. 66:19).

Jaziz ("shining"), David's chief shepherd (1 Chron. 27:31).

Jeaterai ("steadfast"), a descendant of Gershon (1 Chron. 6:21).

Jeberechiah ("Jehovah is blessing"), the father of the Zechariah whom Isaiah took as a witness (Isa. 8:2).

Jecamiah [Jekamiah] ("may Jehovah establish"). **[1]** A descendant of Judah (1 Chron. 2:41). **[2]** A son of King Jeconiah (Jehoiachin; 1 Chron. 3:18).

Jecholiah [Jecoliah] ("Jehovah is able"), mother of Uzziah (or Azariah), king of Judah (2 Kings 15:2; 2 Chron. 26:3).

Jechonias, Greek form of Jeconiah. *See* Jehoiachin.

Jecoliah. *See* Jecholiah.

Jeconiah. *See* Jehoiachin.

Jedaiah ("Jehovah is praise"). **[1]** A descendant of Simeon (1 Chron. 4:37). **[2]** One who helped repair the wall (Neh. 3:10).

Jedaiah ("Jehovah is knowing"). **[1]** A priest of Jerusalem (1 Chron. 9:10; 24:7; Ezra 2:36; Neh. 7:39). **[2]** A priest who returned with Zerubbabel (Neh. 11:10; 12:6, 19). **[3]** Another priest who came up with Zerubbabel (Neh. 12:7, 21). **[4]** One who brought gifts to the temple (Zech. 6:10, 14).

Jediael ("God knows"). **[1]** A son of Benjamin (1 Chron. 7:6, 10–11). Possibly the same as Ashbel (1 Chron. 8:1). **[2]** One of David's mighty men (1 Chron. 11:45). **[3]** One who joined David at Ziklag (1 Chron. 12:20). **[4]** A descendant of Korah, son of Meshelemiah (1 Chron. 26:2).

Jedidah ("beloved"), mother of King Josiah (2 Kings 22:1).

Jedidiah ("beloved of Jehovah"), the name God gave Solomon through Nathan (2 Sam. 12:25).

Jeduthun ("a choir of praise"). **[1]** One of the three chief musicians of the service of song (1 Chron. 9:16; 25:1–6; Neh. 11:17). He was also named Ethan (1 Chron. 6:44; 15:17, 19). **[2]** The father of Obed-edom (1 Chron. 16:38). Some believe him identical with [1].

Jeezer (contracted form of Abiezer, "father of help"), a descendant of Manasseh (Num. 26:30). Probably the same as the Abiezer of Joshua's time (Josh. 17:2; 1 Chron. 7:18).

Jehaleleel [Jehalelel] ("God is praised").

PEOPLE OF THE BIBLE

JESUS' HOMETOWN. *This town in Galilee was the home of Mary and Joseph (Luke 2:39). Jesus lived here for about 30 years, and He was therefore called "Jesus of Nazareth." Nazareth sits in a high valley about 360 m. (1,200 ft.) above sea level, among the southernmost limestone hills of the Lebanon range.*

[1] A descendant of Judah through Caleb the spy (1 Chron. 4:16). **[2]** A descendant of Merari in the time of Hezekiah (2 Chron. 29:12).

Jehdeiah ("union of Jehovah"). **[1]** A descendant of Levi in David's time (1 Chron. 24:20). **[2]** An overseer of David (1 Chron. 27:30).

Jehezekel ("God is strong"), a priest with sanctuary duty (1 Chron. 24:16).

Jehiah ("Jehovah is living"), a Levite gatekeeper of the ark (1 Chron. 15:24). He was also called Jeiel (1 Chron. 15:18; 2 Chron. 20:14).

Jehiel ("God is living"). **[1]** A singer in the tabernacle in David's time (1 Chron. 15:18; 16:5). **[2]** A descendant of Gershon (1 Chron. 23:8; 29:8). **[3]** A companion of the sons of David (1 Chron. 27:32). **[4]** A son of Jehoshaphat (2 Chron. 21:2). **[5]** A son of Heman the singer (2 Chron. 29:14). **[6]** A Levite in charge of the dedicated things in the temple (2 Chron. 31:13). **[7]** A chief priest in Josiah's day (2 Chron. 35:8). **[8]** Father of one who returned from the Exile (Ezra 8:9). **[9]** Father of the one who first admitted taking a foreign wife during the Exile (Ezra 10:2). **[10], [11]** Two who had taken foreign wives (Ezra 10:21, 26).

Jehieli, a Levite set over the treasures of the sanctuary in David's time (1 Chron. 26:21–22). *See* Jehiel.

Jehizkiah ("Jehovah is strong" or "Jehovah strengthens"), an opponent of those who would have made fellow Jews slaves (2 Chron. 28:12). *See* Hezekiah.

Jehoadah ("Jehovah unveils; Jehovah has numbered"). *See* Jarah.

Jehoaddan ("Jehovah gives delight"), mother of King Amaziah and wife of King Joash (2 Kings 14:2; 2 Chron. 25:1).

Jehoahaz ("Jehovah upholds"). **[1]** Son and successor of Jehu on the throne of Israel. His reign was one of disaster (2 Kings 10:35; 13:2–25). **[2]** The son of Josiah and ruler of Judah for three months before he was deposed by Pharaoh Necho (2 Kings 23:30–34; 2 Chron. 36:1–4). He was also called Shallum before becoming king (1 Chron. 3:15; Jer. 22:11). **[3]** *See* Ahaziah [2].

Jehoash [Joash] ("Jehovah has given; Jehovah supports"). **[1]** The ninth king of Judah. Until the time of Jehoiada the priest's death Jehoash followed God; afterwards, he brought idolatry and disaster to his country (2 Kings 11:21—12:21). He is more frequently called by the shortened form of his name, Joash. **[2]** The twelfth king of Israel; he was successful in many military campaigns (2 Kings 13:9—14:16). He is most frequently called Joash, an abbreviated form of his name.

Jehohanan ("Jehovah is gracious"). **[1]** A gatekeeper of the tabernacle in David's time (1 Chron. 26:3). **[2]** A chief captain of Judah (2 Chron. 17:15). **[3]** Father of one who aided

PEOPLE OF THE BIBLE

Jehoiada (2 Chron. 23:1). **[4]** One who married a foreign wife during the Exile (Ezra 10:28). **[5]** A priest who returned to Jerusalem with Zerubbabel (Neh. 12:13). **[6]** A singer at the purification of the wall of Jerusalem (Neh. 12:42). **[7]** Son of Tobiah the Ammonite (Neh. 6:17–18).

Jehoiachin ("Jehovah establishes"), ruler of Judah when it was captured by Nebuchadnezzar. He was an ancestor of Christ (2 Kings 24:8–16; 2 Chron. 36:9–10; Matt. 1:11–12). Jeconiah [Jechonias] ("Jehovah is able") is an altered form of his name (1 Chron. 3:16–17; Jer. 24:1) as is Coniah ("Jehovah is creating"; Jer. 22:24, 28; 37:1).

Jehoiada ("Jehovah knows"). **[1]** The father of one of David's officers (2 Sam. 8:18; 1 Kings 1:8, 26). **[2]** The chief priest of the temple for many years of the monarchy. He hid Joash from Athaliah for 6 years (2 Kings 11—12:9). **[3]** One who joined David at Ziklag (1 Chron. 12:27). **[4]** A counselor of David (1 Chron. 27:34). **[5]** One who helped to repair a gate of Jerusalem (Neh. 3:6). **[6]** A priest replaced by Zephaniah (Jer. 29:26). See Joiada.

Jehoiakim ("Jehovah sets up" or "Jehovah has established"), the name given to Eliakim by Pharaoh Necho when he made him king of Judah. The name probably means that Necho claimed Jehovah had authorized him to put Eliakim on the throne (2 Kings 23:34—24:6). Not to be confused with Joiakim.

Jehoiarib ("Jehovah contends"). **[1]** Head of a family of Aaron (1 Chron. 24:7). **[2]** See Joiarib [3].

Jehonadab [Jonadab] ("Jehovah is liberal"). **[1]** Descendant of Rechab, who forbade his followers and descendants to drink wine and live in houses (Jer. 35:6–19; 2 Kings 10:15, 23). **[2]** The sly son of David's brother, Shimeah (2 Sam. 13:3, 5, 32, 35).

Jehonathan ("Jehovah gives"). **[1]** An overseer of David's storehouses (1 Chron. 27:25). **[2]** One sent by Jehoshaphat to teach the Law (2 Chron. 17:8). **[3]** A priest (Neh. 12:18). He is called Jonathan in Nehemiah 12:35.

Jehoram [Joram] ("Jehovah is high"). Joram is a shortened form of the name. **[1]** Son and successor of Jehoshaphat to the throne of Judah and an ancestor of Christ (2 Kings 8:16–24; Matt. 1:8). **[2]** The ninth king of Israel, slain by Jehu (2 Kings 1:17; 3:1–6; 9:24). **[3]** A priest commissioned to teach the people (2 Chron. 17:8).

Jehoshabeath [Jehosheba] ("Jehovah makes oath"), a daughter of Jehoram, king of Judah, who helped conceal Joash (2 Chron. 22:11). In Second Kings 1:2, she is called Jehosheba.

Jehoshaphat [Josaphat] ("Jehovah is judge"). **[1]** The recorder of David (2 Sam. 8:16; 20:24; 1 Kings 4:3). **[2]** An officer of Solomon (1 Kings 4:17). **[3]** Father of Jehu,

44

PEOPLE OF THE BIBLE

Jezebel's Idolatry

Jezebel, daughter of King Ethbaal of Sidon, was raised in Sidon, a commercial city on the coast of the Mediterranean Sea. Sidon was considered to be a center of vice and ungodliness. When Jezebel married King Ahab of Israel, she moved to Jezreel, a city that served Jehovah. Jezebel soon decided to turn Jezreel into a city similar to her native town.

Jezebel tried to convince her husband to begin serving the golden calf, under the pretense that such worship would really be a service to Jehovah. Actually, the calf was a central idol in the worship of Baal, a sun-god who was important to ancient Phoenicians. Because Baal was believed to have power over crops, flocks, and the fertility of farm families, the golden calf was often linked with him. As the worship of Baal spread to countries bordering Phoenicia, more peoples adopted the religion's lascivious rites, which included human sacrifice, self-torture, and kissing the image. The practices of the Baal cult offended pious Jews, but because

King Ahab was easily manipulated by Jezebel, beautiful temples honoring Baal were soon erected throughout Israel.

The priests of Jehovah opposed Jezebel; many of them were murdered. Even the great prophet Elijah fled from her wrath (1 Kings 18:4–19).

In her effort to erase the mark of Jehovah throughout Israel, Jezebel became the first female religious persecutor in Bible history. She so effectively injected the poison of idolatry into the veins of Israel that the nation suffered.

Elijah said, "The dogs shall eat Jezebel by the wall of Jezreel" (1 Kings 21:23). This prophesy came true; only Jezebel's skull, feet, and the palms of her hands were left to bury (2 Kings 9:36–37).

The hearts of the Israelites must have been ripe for idolatry, or Jezebel would not have been able to so pervert their religion. King Ahab committed a grave sin against God by marrying her, because Jezebel worshiped Baal (1 Kings 21:25–26).

who conspired against Joram (2 Kings 9:2, 14). **[4]** A priest who helped to bring the ark of the covenant from Obed-edom (1 Chron. 15:24). **[5]** Faithful king of Judah and an ancestor of Christ (1 Kings 22:41–50; Matt. 1:8).

Jehosheba. *See* Jehoshabeath.

Jehoshua. *See* Joshua.

Jehozabad ("Jehovah endows"). **[1]** A servant who killed Jehoash (2 Kings 12:21; 2 Chron. 24:26). **[2]** A gatekeeper descended from Korah (1 Chron. 26:4). **[3]** A chief captain of Jehoshaphat (2 Chron. 17:18). Not to be confused with Jozabad.

Jehozadak. *See* Josedech.

Jehu ("Jehovah is he"). **[1]** The prophet who brought tidings of disaster to Baasha of Israel (1 Kings 16:1–12; 2 Chron. 19:2). **[2]** The tenth king of Israel (1 Kings 19:16–17; 2 Kings 9—10). His corrupt leadership weakened the nation. **[3]** A descendant of Hezron (1 Chron. 2:38). **[4]** A descendant of Simeon (1 Chron. 4:35). **[5]** One who joined David at Ziklag (1 Chron. 12:3).

Jehubbah ("hidden"), a descendant of Asher (1 Chron. 7:34).

Jehucal [Jucal] ("Jehovah is able"), a messenger of Zedekiah (Jer. 37:3; 38:1).

Jehudi ("a Jew"), a man who brought Baruch to the princes and read the king Jeremiah's prophecies (Jer. 36:14, 21, 23).

Jehudijah ("the Jewess"), the wife of Ezra and descendant of Caleb (1 Chron. 4:18).

Jehush ("collector"), a man of the family of Saul (1 Chron. 8:39).

Jeiel [Jehiel] ("God snatches away"). **[1]** A chief of the tribe of Reuben (1 Chron. 5:7). **[2]** An ancestor of Saul (1 Chron. 9:35). **[3]** One of David's mighty men (1 Chron. 11:44). **[4]** A singer and gatekeeper of the tabernacle (1 Chron. 15:18, 21; 16:5). **[5]** A descendant of Asaph (2 Chron. 20:14). **[6]** A scribe or recorder of Uzziah (2 Chron. 26:11). **[7]** A Levite in Hezekiah's time (2 Chron. 29:13). **[8]** A chief Levite in the days of Josiah (2 Chron. 35:9). **[9]** One who returned to Jerusalem with Ezra (Ezra 8:13). **[10]** One who married a foreign wife during the Exile (Ezra 10:43).

Jekameam ("standing of the people"), a descendant of Levi (1 Chron. 23:19; 24:23).

Jekamiah. *See* Jecamiah.

Jekuthiel ("God is mighty"), a descendant of the spy Caleb (1 Chron. 4:18).

Jemima ("little dove"), first daughter of Job to be born after his restoration from affliction (Job 42:14).

Jemuel ("God is light"). *See* Nemuel.

Jephthae, Greek form of Jephthah (q.v.).

Jephthah [Jephthae] ("an opposer"), a judge of Israel who delivered his people from Ammon (Judg. 11—12:7).

Jephunneh ("appearing"). **[1]** A man of Judah and father of Caleb the spy (Num. 13:6; 14:6; Deut. 1:36). **[2]** Head of a family of the tribe of Asher (1 Chron. 7:38).

Jerah ("moon"), a son of Joktan (Gen. 10:26; 1 Chron. 1:20). Possibly an Arabian tribe is intended.

Jerahmeel ("God is merciful"). **[1]** A son of Hezron, grandson of Judah (1 Chron. 2:9, 25–27, 33, 42). **[2]** A son of Kish (1 Chron. 24:29). **[3]** An officer of Jehoiakim (Jer. 36:26).

Jered ("low; flowing"). **[1]** A son of Ezra, a descendant of Caleb (1 Chron. 4:18). **[2]** *See* Jared.

Jeremai ("Jehovah is high"), one who took a foreign wife during the Exile (Ezra 10:33).

Jeremiah [Jeremias; Jeremy] ("Jehovah is high"). **[1]** A dweller of Libnah whose daughter married King Josiah (2 Kings 23:31; Jer. 52:1). **[2]** Head of a family of the tribe of Manasseh (1 Chron. 5:24). **[3]** One who joined David at Ziklag (1 Chron. 12:4). **[4]** A man of Gad who joined David at Ziklag (1 Chron. 12:10). **[5]** Another who joined David at Ziklag (1 Chron. 12:13). **[6]** A priest who sealed the new covenant with God after the Exile (Neh. 10:2; 12:1, 12). **[7]** A descendant of Jonadab (Jer. 35:3). **[8]** A prophet whose activity covered the reigns of the last five kings of Judah. He denounced the policies and idolatries of his nation (Jer. 1; 20; 26; 36).

Jeremias, Greek form of Jeremiah (q.v.).

Jeremoth ("elevation"). **[1]** A son of Beriah (1 Chron. 8:14). **[2], [3]** Two who married foreign wives (Ezra 10:26–27). **[4]** A son of Mushi, descendant of Levi (1 Chron. 23:23). He is called Jerimoth in First Chronicles 24:30. **[5]** One appointed by David to the song service of the temple (1 Chron. 25:22). He is called Jerimoth in First Chronicles 25:4.

Jeriah [Jerijah] ("Jehovah is foundation"), a descendant of Hebron in the days of David (1 Chron. 23:19; 24:23; 26:31).

Jeribai ("Jehovah contends"), one of David's mighty men (1 Chron. 11:46).

Jeriel ("foundation of God"), a descendant of Issachar (1 Chron. 7:2).

Jerijah. *See* Jeriah.

Jerimoth ("elevation"). **[1]** A son of Bela (1 Chron. 7:7). **[2]** A son of Becher, son of

PEOPLE OF THE BIBLE

A BOOTH. *Jonah made a booth to shelter him from the hot sun while he waited to see what would happen to Nineveh (Jonah 3:4—4:5). The people of biblical times often made such crude shelters by weaving together the boughs of saplings; soldiers and farmers used them for watch duty. The Israelites lived in booths during the Feast of Tabernacles, which commemorated their bondage in Egypt (Lev. 23:34, 40–43).*

Benjamin (1 Chron. 7:8). **[3]** One who joined David at Ziklag (1 Chron. 12:5). **[4]** A ruler of the tribe of Naphtali (1 Chron. 27:19). **[5]** A son of David (2 Chron. 11:18). **[6]** *See* Jeremoth [4], [5].

Jerioth ("tremulousness"), a wife or concubine of Caleb (1 Chron. 2:18).

Jeroboam ("enlarger; he pleads the people's cause"). **[1]** The first king of Israel after the division of the kingdom. He reigned for 22 years (1 Kings 11:26–40; 12:1—14:20). **[2]** The thirteenth king of Israel; his Israel was strong but overtly idolatrous (2 Kings 14:23–29).

Jeroham ("loved"). **[1]** A Levite, the grandfather of Samuel (1 Sam. 1:1; 1 Chron. 6:27). **[2]** A descendant of Benjamin (1 Chron. 9:8). **[3]** Head of a family of Benjamin (1 Chron. 8:27). **[4]** A priest whose son lived in Jerusalem after the Exile (1 Chron. 9:12; Neh. 11:12). **[5]** Father of two who joined David at Ziklag (1 Chron. 12:7). **[6]** Father of Azareel, prince of Dan (1 Chron. 27:22). **[7]** Father of one who helped Jehoiada to set Joash on the throne of Judah (2 Chron. 23:1).

Jerubbaal ("let Baal contend" or possibly "let Baal show himself great"), the name given to Gideon by his father (Judg. 6:32; 7:1; 8:29).

Jerubbesheth ("contender with the idol"), name given to Jerubbaal (Gideon) by those who wanted to avoid pronouncing Baal (2 Sam. 11:21).

Jerusha [Jerushah] ("possession"), the wife of King Uzziah (2 Kings 15:33; 2 Chron. 27:1).

Jesaiah [Jeshaiah] ("Jehovah is helper"). **[1]** A grandson of Zerubbabel (1 Chron. 3:21). **[2]** One appointed to the song service (1 Chron. 25:3, 15). **[3]** A grandson of Moses (1 Chron. 26:25). **[4]** One who returned from the Babylonian Captivity (Ezra 8:7). **[3]** A descendant of Merari who returned from Exile (Ezra 8:19). **[6]** One whose descendants dwelled in Jerusalem (Neh. 11:17).

Jesharelah. *See* Asarelah.

Jeshebeab ("seat of the father"), head of the fourteenth course of priests (1 Chron. 24:13).

Jesher ("rightness"), a son of Caleb (1 Chron. 2:18).

Jeshishai ("Jehovah is ancient" or "aged"), a descendant of Gad (1 Chron. 5:14).

Jeshohaiah ("humbled by Jehovah"), a descendant of Simeon (1 Chron. 4:36).

Jeshua [Jeshuah] ("Jehovah is deliverance"). **[1]** A priest of the sanctuary (1 Chron. 24:11; Ezra 2:36; Neh. 7:39). **[2]** A Levite in charge of various offerings to the temple (2 Chron. 31:15). **[3]** A priest who returned to Jerusalem with Zerubbabel (Ezra 2:2; 3:2–9; 4:3; Neh. 7:7; 12:1–26). **[4]** Father of Jozabad the Levite (Ezra 8:33). **[5]** One whose descendants returned from the Exile (Ezra 2:6; Neh. 7:11). **[6]** Father of one who repaired the wall of Jerusalem (Neh. 3:19). **[7]** A Levite who explained the Law to the people (Neh. 8:7; 9:4–5). **[8]** One who sealed the new covenant with God after the Exile (Ezra 2:40; Neh. 7:43; 10:9). Some believe he is identical with [6]. **[9]** *See* Joshua. *See also* "Places of the Bible."

Jesiah ("Jehovah exists"). **[1]** One who joined David at Ziklag (1 Chron. 12:6). **[2]** A descendant of Uzziel and a Levite (1 Chron. 23:20). He is called Isshiah in First Chronicles 24:25.

Jesimiel ("God sets"), a descendant of Simeon (1 Chron. 4:36).

Jesse ("Jehovah exists; wealthy"), father of David and an ancestor of Christ (Ruth 4:17, 22; 1 Sam. 17:17; Matt. 1:5–6).

Jesui. *See* Ishui.

Jesus (Greek form of Joshua). **[1]** A Christian who, with Paul, sent greetings to the

TERRAIN NEAR JERICHO. *This rugged mountain valley is typical of the area near Jericho, the city overwhelmed by Joshua. In this view, the monastery of St. George of Koziba overlooks the Wadi Qilt.*

Colossians (Col. 4:11); he was also called Justus. [2] *See* Joshua.

Jesus Christ (*Jesus*—"Jehovah is salvation," *Christ*—"the anointed one"), the son of the Virgin Mary who came to earth to fulfill the prophecies of the King who would die for the sins of His people. The account of His ministry is found in the Gospels of Matthew, Mark, Luke, and John.

Jether ("pre-eminent"). [1] The firstborn son of Gideon (Judg. 8:20). [2] A son of Jerahmeel (1 Chron. 2:32). [3] A descendant of Caleb the spy (1 Chron. 4:17). [4] A descendant of Asher (1 Chron. 7:38). [5] *See* Ithra.

Jetheth ("subjection"), a duke of Edom (Gen. 36:40; 1 Chron. 1:51).

Jethro ("pre-eminence"), the father-in-law of Moses. He advised Moses to delegate the administration of justice (Exod. 3:1; 4:18; 18:1–12). He is called Reuel in Exodus 2:18. In Numbers 10:29, the KJV calls him Raguel; but the Hebrew text reads Reuel.

Jetur, a son of Ishmael (Gen. 25:15; 1 Chron. 1:31).

Jeuel ("snatching away"), a descendant of Judah (1 Chron. 9:6).

Jeush ("collector"). [1] A son of Esau (Gen. 36:5, 14, 18; 1 Chron. 1:35). [2] A descendant of Benjamin (1 Chron. 7:10). [3] A descendant of Gershon and the head of a clan (1 Chron. 23:10–11). [4] A son of Rehoboam (2 Chron. 11:19).

Jeuz ("counselor"), son of Shaharaim, a descendant of Benjamin (1 Chron. 8:10).

Jezaniah. *See* Jaazaniah [1].

Jezebel ("unexalted; unhusbanded"). [1] The wicked, idolatrous queen of Israel (1 Kings 16:31; 18:4—21:25; 2 Kings 9:7–37). [2] A false prophetess at Thyatira (Rev. 2:20). Possibly the name is symbolic and not the prophetess's real name.

Jezer ("formation"), the third son of Naphtali (Gen. 46:24; Num. 26:49; 1 Chron. 7:13).

Jeziah ("Jehovah unites"), one who took a foreign wife (Ezra 10:25).

Jeziel ("God unites"), man of valor who joined David at Ziklag (1 Chron. 12:3).

Jezliah ("Jehovah delivers"), a descendant of Benjamin (1 Chron. 8:18).

Jezoar, a descendant of Caleb, the son of Hur (1 Chron. 4:7).

Jezrahiah ("Jehovah is shining"), an overseer of the singers at the purification of the people (Neh. 12:42). *See* Izrahiah.

Jezreel ("God sows"). [1] A descendant of Etam (1 Chron. 4:3). [2] The symbolic name of a son of Hosea (Hos. 1:4). *See also* "Places of the Bible."

Jibsam ("lovely scent"), a son of Tola (1 Chron. 7:2).

Jidlaph ("melting away"), son of Nahor and nephew of Abraham (Gen. 22:22).

Jimna. *See* Imna.

Joab ("Jehovah is father"). [1] A son of Zeruiah, David's sister. He was captain of David's army (2 Sam. 2:13–32; 3:23–31; 18; 1 Kings 2:22–23). [2] A descendant of Judah (1 Chron. 2:54). Some scholars believe a city of Judah is referred to here. The name would include the four words that follow in the KJV and be written: Atroth-beth-joab. [3] One of the tribe of Judah (1 Chron. 4:14). [4] An ancestor of returned captives (Ezra 2:6; 8:9; Neh. 7:11).

Joah ("Jehovah is brother"). [1] A son of Asaph, the recorder in the time of Hezekiah (2 Kings 18:18, 26; Isa. 36:3, 11, 22). [2] A descendant of Gershom (1 Chron. 6:21; 2 Chron. 29:12). [3] A porter in the tabernacle (1 Chron. 26:4). [4] A Levite commissioned to repair the Lord's house (2 Chron. 34:8).

Joahaz ("Jehovah helps"), father of Joah, Josiah's recorder (2 Chron. 34:8).

Joanna ("God-given"). [1] An ancestor of Christ (Luke 3:27). [2] The wife of Chuza,

PEOPLE OF THE BIBLE

Herod's steward, who ministered to Christ and the apostles (Luke 8:3; 24:10).

Joash (abbreviated form of Jehoash). **[1]** A man of Judah (1 Chron. 4:22). **[2]** Father of Gideon the judge (Judg. 6:11–32). **[3]** A son of Ahab (1 Kings 22:26; 2 Chron. 18:25). **[4]** One who joined David at Ziklag (1 Chron. 12:3). **[5]** *See* Jehoash [1]. **[6]** *See* Jehoash [2].

Joash ("Jehovah has aided"). **[1]** A son of Becher, a descendant of Benjamin (1 Chron. 7:8). **[2]** The keeper of David's stores of oil (1 Chron. 27:28).

Joatham, Greek form of Jotham (q.v.).

Job ("hated; persecuted"). **[1]** A pious man of Uz. His endurance in fierce trial resulted in marvelous blessing (Job 1—3; 42; Ezek. 14:14, 20). **[2]** The third son of Issachar (Gen. 46:13); he is also called Jashub (Num. 26:24; 1 Chron. 7:1).

Jobab. [1] A son of Joktan (Gen. 10:29; 1 Chron. 1:23). The name may possibly refer to an unknown Arabian tribe. **[2]** A king of Edom (Gen. 36:33–34; 1 Chron. 1:44–45). **[3]** A king of Canaan conquered by Joshua (Josh. 11:1). **[4]** A descendant of Benjamin (1 Chron. 8:9). **[5]** Another descendant of Benjamin (1 Chron. 8:18).

Jochebed ("Jehovah is honor or glory"), a descendant of Levi and mother of Moses (Exod. 6:20; Num. 26:59).

Joed ("Jehovah is witness"), a son of Pedaiah, a descendant of Benjamin (Neh. 11:7).

Joel ("Jehovah is God"). **[1]** The firstborn son of Samuel the prophet (1 Sam. 8:2; 1 Chron. 6:33; 15:17). *See also* Vashni. **[2]** A descendant of Simeon (1 Chron. 4:35). **[3]** The father of Shemaiah, a descendant of Reuben (1 Chron. 5:4, 8). **[4]** A chief of the tribe of Gad (1 Chron. 5:12). **[5]** An ancestor of the prophet Samuel (1 Chron. 6:36). **[6]** A descendant of Tola (1 Chron. 7:3). **[7]** One of David's mighty men (1 Chron. 11:38). **[8]** A Levite in David's time (1 Chron. 15:7, 11; 23:8). **[9]** A keeper of the treasures of the Lord's house (1 Chron. 26:22). **[10]** A prince of Manasseh west of the Jordan (1 Chron. 27:20). **[11]** A Levite who aided in cleansing the temple (2 Chron. 29:12). **[12]** One who married a foreign wife during the Exile (Ezra 10:43). **[13]** An overseer of the descendants of Benjamin in Jerusalem (Neh. 11:9). **[14]** A prophet in the days of Uzziah (Joel 1:1; Acts 2:16).

Joelah ("God is snatching; may it avail!"), one who joined David at Ziklag (1 Chron. 12:7).

Joezer ("Jehovah is help"), a warrior who joined David at Ziklag (1 Chron. 12:6).

Jogli ("exiled"), a prince of Dan (Num. 34:22).

Joha ("Jehovah is living"). **[1]** A descendant of Benjamin (1 Chron. 8:16). **[2]** One of David's valiant men (1 Chron. 11:45).

Johanan ("Jehovah is gracious"). **[1]** A captain who allied with Gedaliah after the fall of Jerusalem (2 Kings 25:23; Jer. 40:8, 13). **[2]** Eldest son of Josiah, king of Judah (1 Chron. 3:15). **[3]** A son of Elionai (1 Chron. 3:24). **[4]** Father of a priest in Solomon's time (1 Chron. 6:9–10). **[5], [6]** Two valiant men who joined David at Ziklag (1 Chron. 12:4, 12). **[7]** One who opposed making slaves of Judean captives in Ahaz's time (2 Chron. 28:12). **[8]** A returned exile (Ezra 8:12). **[9]** A priest who beckoned the exiles to Jerusalem (Ezra 10:6). **[10]** A son of Tobiah the Ammonite (Neh. 6:18). **[11]** A priest in the days of Joiakim (Neh. 12:22–23).

John (a contraction of Jehohanan, "gift of God"). [1] The son of Zacharias and Elisabeth who came to prepare the way for the Messiah. He was called John the Baptist and was beheaded by Herod (Matt. 3; 11:7–18; 14:1–10; Luke 1:13–17). **[2]** A son of Zebedee and one of the twelve apostles. He is traditionally accorded the authorship of the Revelation, the fourth Gospel, and the three epistles bearing his name (Matt. 4:21; 10:2; Acts 1:13; Gal. 2:9; Rev. 1:1). **[3]** A relative of the high priest Annas, who sat in judgment on Peter (Acts 4:6). **[4]** A missionary better known by his surname, Mark (q.v.). *See also* Jehohanan; Johanan.

Joiada ("Jehovah knows"), an ancestor of the priest Jeshua (Neh. 12:10–11, 22; 13:28). *See* Jehoiada.

Joiakim ("Jehovah sets up"), the son of Jeshua who returned from the Babylonian Captivity (Neh. 12:10, 12, 26). Not to be confused with Jehoiakim.

Joiarib ("Jehovah knows"). **[1]** One whom Ezra sent to persuade ministers to return to the land of Israel (Ezra 8:16). **[2]** An ancestor of a family living in Jerusalem (Neh. 11:5). **[3]** A priest who returned from captivity (Neh. 11:10; 12:6, 19). He is called Jehoiarib in First Chronicles 9:10.

Jokim ("Jehovah sets up"), a descendant of Judah (1 Chron. 4:22).

Jokshan ("fowler"), a son of Abraham by Keturah (Gen. 25:2–3; 1 Chron. 1:32).

Joktan, a son of Eber of Shem's line (Gen.

GIBEON (?) *Archaeologists believe that this site, known as el-Jib, is the biblical Gibeon. God instructed Joshua to destroy all of the people of Canaan when the Israelites took the land, but the people of Gibeon tricked him into making a treaty with them. Neighboring Amorite kings attacked Gibeon for defecting to the Israelites, and Joshua came to their aid. God granted a hailstorm and an extension of the daylight hours to help Joshua defeat the Amorites (Josh. 9—10; 11:19). The treaty remained in force during the time of Saul and David. When the Gibeonites demanded justice for murders that Saul had committed there, David gave them seven of Saul's sons to be executed (2 Sam. 21:1–11).*

10:25–26; 1 Chron. 1:19–20, 23). Perhaps the reference is to an Arabian tribe from whom many other Arabian groups sprang.

Jona [Jonah; Jonas] ("a dove"). **[1]** The father of Simon Peter (John 1:42; 21:15–17). **[2]** A Hebrew prophet sent to preach to Nineveh in the days of Jeroboam II. He was the first Hebrew prophet sent to a heathen nation (2 Kings 14:25; Jon. 1:1, 3, 5, 17; 2:10; Matt. 12:39–41).

Jonadab. *See* Jehonadab.

Jonah. *See* Jona.

Jonan ("grace"), an ancestor of Christ (Luke 3:30).

Jonathan ("Jehovah is given"). **[1]** A priest of an idol shrine in the territory of Ephraim (Judg. 18:30). **[2]** A son of Abiathar the high priest (2 Sam. 15:27, 36; 17:17; 1 Kings 1:42). **[3]** A son of Shimea, David's brother (2 Sam. 21:21; 1 Chron. 20:7). **[4]** One of David's mighty men (2 Sam. 23:32; 1 Chron. 11:34). **[5]** A grandson of Onam (1 Chron. 2:32–33). **[6]** An uncle of David (1 Chron. 27:32). **[7]** Father of one who returned with Ezra (Ezra 8:6). **[8]** One involved with the foreign wife

controversy (Ezra 10:15). **[9]** A descendant of Jeshua the high priest (Neh 12:11). **[10]** A priest (Neh. 12:14). **[11]** A scribe in whose house Jeremiah was kept prisoner (Jer. 37:15, 20; 38:26). **[12]** One who joined Gedaliah after the fall of Jerusalem (Jer. 40:8). **[13]** A son of Saul and close friend of David (1 Sam. 14; 18:1–4; 31:2). **[14]** *See* Jehonathan [3].

Jorah ("harvest-born"). *See* Hariph [2].

Jorai ("taught of God"), a chief of the tribe of Gad (1 Chron. 5:13).

Joram (shortened form of Jehoram). **[1]** A descendant of Moses (1 Chron. 26:25). **[2]** *See* Hadoram [2]. **[3]** *See* Jehoram [1], [2].

Jorim (a shortened form of Jehoram), an ancestor of Christ (Luke 3:29).

Jorkoam ("spreading the people"), a son of Raham, or a city he founded (1 Chron. 2:44).

Josabad. *See* Jozabad.

Josaphat, Greek form of Jehoshaphat (q.v.).

Jose, an ancestor of Christ (Luke 3:29). Not to be confused with Joses.

Josedech ("Jehovah is righteous"), a priest and father of Jeshua the high priest (Hag. 1:1, 12, 14; Zech. 6:11). He is also called Jozadak (Ezra 3:2, 8; 5:2; 10:18; Neh. 12:26) and Jehozadak (1 Chron. 6:14–15).

Joseph ("increaser"). **[1]** The son of Jacob and Rachel. He was sold into slavery but became the prime minister of Egypt (Gen. 37; 39—50). **[2]** Father of one of the spies sent into Canaan (Num. 13:7). **[3]** A son of Asaph (1 Chron. 25:2, 9). **[4]** One who married a foreign wife during the Exile (Ezra 10:42). **[5]** A priest of the family of Shebaniah (Neh. 12:14). **[6]** The husband of Mary, mother of Jesus (Matt. 1:16–24; 2:13; Luke 1:27; 2:4). **[7]** A converted Jew of Arimathea in whose tomb Jesus was laid (Matt. 27:57, 59; Luke 15:43). **[8]** An ancestor of Christ (Luke 3:24). **[9]** Another ancestor of Christ (Luke 3:26). **[10]** Yet another ancestor of Christ (Luke 3:30). **[11]** A disciple considered to take the place of Judas Iscariot (Acts 1:23). He was also known as Barsabas and Justus.

Joses ("helped"). **[1]** One of the brothers of Christ (Matt. 13:55; Mark 6:3). **[2]** The son of Mary, the wife of Cleophas (Matt. 27:56; Mark 15:40, 47). Not to be confused with Jose.

Joshah ("Jehovah is a gift"), a descendant of Simeon (1 Chron. 4:34).

Joshaphat ("Jehovah judges"), one of David's valiant men (1 Chron. 11:43). Not to be confused with Jehoshaphat.

PEOPLE OF THE BIBLE

Joshaviah ("Jehovah is equality"), one of David's valiant men (1 Chron. 11:46).

Joshbekashah ("seated in hardness"), a son of Heman, David's song leader (1 Chron. 25:4, 24).

Joshua [Jehoshua; Jeshua] ("Jehovah is salvation"). [1] The successor of Moses; the general who led the conquest of the Promised Land (Exod. 17:9–14; 24:13; Deut. 31:1–23; 34:9). Moses changed his name from Hoshea ("Jehovah is help") to Joshua. Oshea is another form of Hoshea (Num. 13:8, 16; Deut. 32:44). Joshua and Jehoshua are forms of the same name. He is also called Jeshua (Neh. 8:17). [2] A native of Beth-shem in the days of Eli (1 Sam. 6:14, 18). [3] The governor of Jerusalem under Josiah (2 Kings 23:8). [4] High priest at the rebuilding of the temple (Hag. 1:1, 12, 14; 2:2, 4; Zech. 3:1, 3, 6).

Josiah [Josias] ("Jehovah supports"). [1] Godly king of Judah during whose reign the Book of the Law was found (1 Kings 13:2; 2 Kings 22:1—23:30). He was an ancestor of Christ (Matt. 1:10–11). [2] A son of Zephaniah living in Jerusalem (Zech. 6:10). *See also* Hen.

Josias, Greek form of Josiah (q.v.).

Josibiah ("Jehovah causes to dwell"), a descendant of Simeon (1 Chron. 4:35).

Josiphiah ("Jehovah abides"), father of one who returned from the Exile (Ezra 8:10).

Jotham [Joatham] ("Jehovah is perfect"). [1] The son of Gideon who managed to escape from Abimelech (Judg. 9:5, 7, 21, 57). [2] A son of Jahdai (1 Chron. 2:47). [3] The twelfth king of Judah and an ancestor of Christ (2 Kings 15:5–38; Isa. 1:1; 7:1; Matt. 1:9).

Jozabad [Josabad] ("Jehovah endows"). [1] One who joined David at Ziklag (1 Chron. 12:4). [2], [3] Two descendants of Manasseh who joined David at Ziklag (1 Chron. 12:20). [4] An overseer of the dedicated things of the temple under Hezekiah (2 Chron. 31:13). [5] A chief of the Levites in Josiah's time (2 Chron. 35:9). [6] One who helped weigh the sanctuary vessels (Ezra 8:33). [7], [8] Two who had married foreign wives (Ezra 10:22–23). [9] One who interpreted the Law (Neh. 8:7). [10] A chief Levite after the Exile (Neh. 11:16). Not to be confused with Jehozabad.

Jozachar ("Jehovah remembers"), the servant and murderer of King Joash of Judah (2 Kings 12:21). He is called Zabad in Second Chronicles 24:26.

Jozadak. *See* Josedech.

Jubal ("playing; nomad"), son of Lamech; he was skilled with musical instruments (Gen. 4:21).

Jucal. *See* Jehucal.

Juda [Judah; Judas; Jude] ("praise"). [1] A son of Jacob by Leah and an ancestor of Christ. He acquired the birthright Reuben lost. His descendants became one of the twelve tribes of Israel (Gen. 29:35; 37:26–28; 43:3–10; Matt. 1:2–3; Luke 3:33). [2] An ancestor of one who helped to rebuild the temple (Ezra 3:9). [3] One who married a foreign wife during the Exile (Ezra 10:23). [4] Second in authority over Jerusalem after the Exile (Neh. 11:9). [5] One who came up to Jerusalem with Zerubbabel (Neh. 12:8). [6] A prince of Judah (Neh. 12:34). [7] A priest and musician (Neh. 12:36). [8] One of the twelve apostles. He betrayed his Lord and hanged himself (Matt. 10:4; 26:14, 25, 47; 27:3; Luke 6:16; 22:3, 47–48). He was called Iscariot, apparently meaning "a man of Kerioth," a town 19 km. (12 mi.) from Hebron. [9] One of the brothers of Jesus (Matt. 13:55; Mark 6:3). He wrote the epistle bearing his name (Jude 1). [10] A Galilean who caused a rebellion against Rome (Acts 5:37). [11] One with whom Paul stayed at Damascus (Acts 9:11). [12] A prophet sent to Antioch with Silas (Acts 15:22, 27); he was surnamed Barsabas. [13] *See* Thaddeus. [14], [15] Two ancestors of Christ (Luke 3:26, 30). *See also* "Places of the Bible."

Judith ("Jewess"), a wife of Esau (Gen. 26:34). *See* Esau's Wives.

Julia ("soft-haired"), a Christian woman to whom Paul sent greetings (Rom. 16:15).

Julius ("soft-haired"), a centurion who delivered Paul to Rome (Acts 27:1, 3).

Junia ("youth"), a man or woman (probably a man) to whom Paul sent greetings (Rom. 16:7).

Jushab-hesed ("kindness is returned"), a son of Zerubbabel (1 Chron. 3:20).

Justus ("just"). [1] A believer in Corinth with whom Paul lodged (Acts 18:7). [2] *See* Jesus [2]. [3] *See* Joseph [11].

44

PEOPLE OF THE BIBLE

K

Kadmiel ("God the primeval" or "before God"). [1] One whose descendants returned from the Exile (Ezra 2:40; Neh. 7:43). [2] One who helped rebuild the temple (Ezra 3:9). [3]

Levite who led the devotions of the people (Neh. 9:4, 5; 10:9).

Kallai ("Jehovah is light" or "swift"), a priest who returned with Zerubbabel (Neh. 12:20).

Kareah [Careah] ("bald head"), the father of Johanan and Jonathan (Jer. 40:8). The KJV spells the name Careah in Second Kings 25:23.

Kedar ("powerful" or "dark"), second son of Ishmael (Gen. 25:13; 1 Chron. 1:29).

Kedemah ("eastward"), a son of Ishmael, head of a clan (Gen. 25:13; 1 Chron. 1:31).

Keilah ("fortress"), a descendant of Caleb (1 Chron. 4:19).

Kelaiah ("Jehovah is light; swift for Jehovah"), one of the priests who married a foreign wife during the Exile (Ezra 10:23). Possibly the same as Kelita (q.v.).

Kelita ("littleness"). [1] A priest who explained the Law when it was read by Ezra (Neh. 8:7). [2] One of those who sealed the covenant (Neh. 10:10); possibly the same as [1]. One or both of these may be identical with each other and/or Kelaiah (q.v.).

Kemuel ("God stands" or "God's mound"). [1] A son of Nahor and a nephew of Abraham (Gen. 22:21). [2] A prince of Ephraim (Num. 34:24). [3] A Levite (1 Chron. 27:17).

Kenan. *See* Cainan.

Kenaz [Kenez] ("side" or "hunting"). [1] A duke of Edom (Gen. 36:42; 1 Chron. 1:53). [2] The fourth son of Eliphaz (Gen. 36:11, 15; 1 Chron. 1:36); perhaps the same as [1]. [3] Father of Othniel the judge (Josh. 15:17; Judg. 1:13). [4] A grandson of Caleb (1 Chron. 4:15).

Keren-Happuch ("horn of antimony"), the third daughter of Job to be born after his restoration to health (Job 42:14).

Keros ("fortress; crooked"), ancestor of a clan who returned from the Exile to the land of Israel (Ezra 2:44; Neh. 7:47).

Keturah ("incense"), a wife of Abraham (Gen. 25:1, 4; 1 Chron. 1:32).

Keziah ("cassia"), the second daughter of Job to be born after his restoration from affliction (Job 42:14).

Kish [Cis] ("bow; power"). [1] A son of Gibeon (1 Chron. 8:30; 9:36). [2] A Levite in David's time (1 Chron. 23:21; 24:29). [3] A descendant of Levi who assisted in the cleansing of the temple under Hezekiah (2 Chron. 29:12). [4] Great-grandfather of Mordecai (Esther 2:5). [5] The father of King Saul (1 Sam. 9:1, 3; 14:51; Acts 13:21).

Kishi ("snarer; fowler"), father of Ethan, also known as Kushaiah (1 Chron. 6:44; 15:17).

Kittim ("knotty"), a son of Javan (Gen. 10:4; 1 Chron. 1:7). Possibly the name refers to the inhabitants of Cyprus and the islands nearby.

Koa ("male camel"), a prince or people dwelling between Egypt and Syria; named as enemy of Jerusalem (Ezek. 23:23).

Kohath ("assembly"), the second son of Levi and beginning of a priestly clan (Gen. 46:11; Exod. 6:16, 18).

Kolaiah ("voice of Jehovah"). [1] A descendant of Benjamin (Neh. 11:7). [2] Father of the false prophet Ahab (Jer. 29:21).

Korah [Core] ("baldness"). [1] A son of Esau by Aholibamah (Gen. 36:5, 14, 18; 1 Chron. 1:35). [2] A son of Eliphaz (Gen. 36:16). [3] A son of Hebron (1 Chron. 2:43). [4] Grandson of Kohath and ancestor of some sacred musicians (1 Chron. 6:22; Psa. 42; 45—46 titles). He was one of the leaders of the rebellion against Moses and Aaron; the earth swallowed them up (Num. 16:1–35).

Kore ("one who proclaims; quail"). [1] A Levite in charge of the freewill offerings in Hezekiah's time (2 Chron. 31:14). [2] A son of Asaph whose descendants were gatekeepers at the tabernacle (1 Chron. 9:19; 26:1, 19).

Koz ("thorn"). [1] The ancestor of a priestly family returning from captivity (Ezra 2:61; Neh. 7:63). In the Hebrew text, the name appears as *Hakkoz;* the KJV considers the *Ha-* of the name to be the prefixed Hebrew definite article—here denoting a *certain* family. Others take all the word as a name (i.e., *Hakkoz*). If this be the case, the Hakkoz of First Chronicles 24:10 probably also refers to this person. [2] An ancestor of one who helped to repair the walls of Jerusalem (Neh. 3:4, 21).

Kushaiah ("bow of Jehovah"). *See* Kishi.

L

Laadah ("order; festival"), a descendant of Judah (1 Chron. 4:21).

Laadan ("festive-born; ordered"). [1] A descendant of Ephraim (1 Chron. 7:26). [2] A Levite from the family of Gershon (1 Chron. 23:7–9; 26:21). Also known as Libni (Exod. 6:17; Num. 3:18).

Laban ("white; glorious"), the brother of Rebekah and father of Rachel and Leah. Jacob served him for seven years in order to marry

PEOPLE OF THE BIBLE

Rachel, but Laban tricked him by substituting Leah at the wedding festivals (Gen. 24—31). *See also* "Places of the Bible."

Lael ("belonging to God"), a descendant of Gershon (Num. 3:24).

Lahad ("oppression; dark colored"), a descendant of Judah (1 Chron. 4:2).

Lahmi ("warrior"), brother of Goliath, the giant (1 Chron. 20:5).

Laish ("lion"), father of Phalti, who became the husband of Michal (1 Sam. 25:44; 2 Sam. 3:15). *See also* "Places of the Bible."

Lamech ("strong youth; overthrower"). **[1]** Father of Noah and ancestor of Christ (Gen. 5:25–31; Luke 3:36). **[2]** Father of Jabal and Jubal; he is the first recorded polygamist (Gen. 4:18–26).

Lapidoth ("flames; torches"), the husband of Deborah, the prophetess (Judg. 4:4).

Lazarus (abridged form of Eleazar, "God has helped"). **[1]** The brother of Mary and Martha whom Jesus raised from the dead (John 11:1—12:17). **[2]** A believing beggar who was carried to Abraham's bosom (Luke 16:19–31).

Leah ("weary"), Jacob's wife through the deception of her father, Laban (Gen. 29—31).

Lebana [Lebanah] ("white"), chief of a family of returning exiles (Ezra 2:45; Neh. 7:48).

Lebanah. *See* Lebana.

Lebbaeus. *See* Thaddeus.

Lecah ("walking; addition"), a descendant of Judah (1 Chron. 4:21).

Lehabim ("flame, red"), a descendant of Mizraim (Gen. 10:13; 1 Chron. 1:11). Possibly a reference to a tribe of Egyptians.

Lemuel ("Godward; dedicated"), an unknown king often supposed to be Solomon or Hezekiah, whose words are recorded in Proverbs 31:1–9.

Letushim ("hammered"), a son of Dedan (Gen. 25:3).

Leummim ("nations"), a son of Dedan (Gen. 25:3).

Levi ("joined"). **[1]** The third son of Jacob who avenged Dinah's wrong (Gen. 34:25–31), and went to Egypt with his father (Gen. 39:34; Exod. 6:16). His descendants became the priests of Israel. **[2]** An ancestor of Christ (Luke 3:24). **[3]** An ancestor of Christ (Luke 3:29). **[4]** Another name of Matthew (q.v.).

Libni ("whiteness; distinguished"). **[1]** A son of Merari (1 Chron. 6:29). **[2]** *See* Laadan.

Likhi ("learned"), a descendant of Benjamin (1 Chron. 7:19).

Linus ("net"), a Roman friend of Paul (2 Tim. 4:21).

Lo-ammi ("not my people"), symbolic name of Hosea's son (Hos. 1:9).

Lois ("pleasing; better"), the pious grandmother of Timothy (2 Tim. 1:5).

Lo-ruhamah ("receiving no compassion"), a figurative name of Hosea's daughter, indicating God's rejection of Israel (Hos. 1:6).

Lot ("veiled"), Abraham's nephew that escaped from wicked Sodom (Gen. 13:1–14; Gen. 19).

Lotan ("hidden"), an Edomite duke (Gen. 36:20–29).

Lucas. *See* Luke.

Lucifer (Latin, "light-bearer"), an epithet for the king of Babylon (Isa. 14:12). Lucifer translates a Hebrew word meaning "light-bearer." The title came to be applied to Satan.

Lucius ("morning born; of light"). **[1]** A prophet or teacher from Cyrene ministering at Antioch (Acts 13:1). **[2]** A Jewish Christian who saluted the community at Rome (Rom. 16:21). Perhaps the same as [1].

Lud, a son of Shem (Gen. 10:22). Possibly the Lydians are intended.

Ludim, a son of Mizraim (Gen. 10:13). Possibly a reference to the inhabitants of an unknown country connected with the Egyptians.

Luke [Lucas] ("light-giving"), evangelist, physician, and author of the third Gospel and Acts (Col. 4:14; 2 Tim. 4:11; Philem. 24).

Lydia ("native of Lydia"), a woman convert of Thyatira (Acts 16:14–15). *See also* "Places of the Bible."

Lysanias ("that drives away sorrow"), the tetrarch of Abilene (Luke 3:1).

Lysias. *See* Claudius Lysias.

M

Maachah [Maacah] ("oppression"). **[1]** The son of Nahor, Abraham's brother (Gen. 22:24). **[2]** One of David's wives and mother of Absalom (2 Sam. 3:3; 1 Chron. 3:2). **[3]** A king of Maachah (2 Sam. 10:6). Some translate "the king of Maacah." **[4]** Father of Achish, king of Gath (1 Kings 2:39). He is called Maoch in First Samuel 27:2. **[5]** The mother of Asa, king of Judah (1 Kings 15:10, 13; 2 Chron. 15:16). She is called Michaiah (2 Chron. 13:2). **[6]** Concubine of Caleb (1 Chron. 2:48). **[7]** Wife of Machir, son of

Manasseh (1 Chron. 7:15–16). **[8]** Wife of Jehiel (1 Chron. 8:29; 9:35). **[9]** Father of one of David's warriors (1 Chron. 11:43). **[10]** Father of Shephatiah, ruler of Simeon (1 Chron. 27:16).

Maadai ("Jehovah is ornament"), one who married a foreign wife (Ezra 10:34; Neh. 12:5).

Maadiah ("Jehovah is ornament"), a priest who returned from the Babylonian Captivity (Neh. 12:5). He is called Moadiah in Nehemiah 12:17.

Maai ("Jehovah is compassionate"), a priest who helped to purify the people who returned from the Exile (Neh. 12:36).

Maaseiah ("Jehovah is a refuge"). **[1]** A Levite of the praise service (1 Chron. 15:18, 20). **[2]** A captain who helped to make Joash king (2 Chron. 23:1). **[3]** Officer of King Uzziah (2 Chron. 26:11). **[4]** A son of Ahaz, king of Judah (2 Chron. 28:7). **[5]** Governor of Jerusalem under Josiah's reign (2 Chron. 34:8). **[6], [7], [8], [9]** Four men who took foreign wives during the Exile (Ezra 10:18, 21–22, 30). **[10]** Father of Azariah, who repaired part of the wall of Jerusalem (Neh. 3:23). **[11]** A priest who stood with Ezra while he read the Law (Neh. 8:4). **[12]** A priest who explained the Law (Neh. 8:7); possibly the same as [11]. **[13]** One who sealed the new covenant with God after the Exile (Neh. 10:25). **[14]** A descendant of Pharez living in Jerusalem (Neh. 11:5). **[15]** One whose descendants lived in Jerusalem (Neh. 11:7). **[16], [17]** Two priests who took part in the purification of the wall of Jerusalem (Neh. 12:41–42). **[18]** A priest whose son was sent by King Zedekiah to inquire of the Lord (Jer. 21:1; 29:25). **[19]** Father of a false prophet (Jer. 29:21). **[20]** An officer of the temple (Jer. 35:4). **[21]** Grandfather of Baruch, Jeremiah's scribe (Jer. 32:12).

Maasiai ("work of Jehovah"), a descendant of Aaron (1 Chron. 9:12).

Maath ("small"), an ancestor of Christ (Luke 3:26).

Maaz ("counselor"), a son of Ram (1 Chron. 2:27).

Maaziah ("strength of Jehovah"). **[1]** Priest to whom certain sanctuary duties were charged (1 Chron. 24:18). **[2]** A priest who sealed the new covenant with God after the Exile (Neh. 10:8).

Machbanai ("thick"), warrior who joined David at Ziklag (1 Chron. 12:13).

Machbenah ("knob, lump"). **[1]** A descen-

HOUSE OF MARY AND MARTHA. *Christ visited the home of Mary and Martha at Bethany, where He ate a meal. This is the traditional site of their home. Martha complained that Mary was not helping in preparation of the food; Christ replied that Mary had chosen a better task by remaining to converse with Him (Luke 10:38). Six days before Passover, Christ again ate a supper at Bethany. On this occasion, Mary anointed the Lord's feet with precious ointment, wiping them with her hair (John 12:1–8).*

dant of Caleb (1 Chron. 2:49). **[2]** Possibly a place identical with Cabbon (q.v.).

Machi ("decrease"), father of one of the spies sent into Canaan (Num. 13:15).

Machir ("salesman; sold"). **[1]** A son of Manasseh (Gen. 50:23; Num. 26:29; Josh. 13:31). **[2]** A descendant of Manasseh living near Mahanaim (2 Sam. 9:4–5; 17:27).

Machnadebai ("liberal; gift of the noble one"), one who had married a foreign wife (Ezra 10:40).

Madai, son of Japheth (Gen. 10:2; 1 Chron. 1:5). The name possibly refers to the inhabitants of Media.

Magdiel ("God is renowned"), a duke of Edom (Gen. 36:43; 1 Chron. 1:54).

Magog ("covering; roof"), the second son of Japheth (Gen. 10:2; 1 Chron. 1:5). Possibly

PEOPLE OF THE BIBLE

a people inhabiting the north land. The name may denote the Scythians or be a comprehensive term for northern barbarians.

Magor-missabib ("terror is about"), symbolic name given to Pashur by Jeremiah (Jer. 20:1–3).

Magpiash ("collector of a cluster of stars; moth-killer"), one who sealed the new covenant with God after the Exile (Neh. 10:20).

Mahalah ("tenderness"), descendant of Manasseh (1 Chron. 7:18). *See* Mahlah.

Mahalaleel [Maleleel] ("God is splendor"). **[1]** Son of Cainan and an ancestor of Christ (Gen. 5:12–13, 15; Luke 3:37). **[2]** One whose descendants lived at Jerusalem (Neh. 11:4).

A TAX COLLECTOR. *While the Romans controlled Palestine, they contracted local businessmen to collect taxes. These businessmen appointed scribes known as* publicans *to do the actual work of collecting the tax. The publicans levied more than the legal tax, keeping the excess for themselves and their employers. Roman law did not limit the amount that they could charge, so most publicans overtaxed the people to a painful degree. For this reason, Jewish observers were scandalized when Jesus called a publican named Matthew to become one of His disciples (Luke 5:27–31).*

Mahalath ("mild"). **[1]** One of Esau's wives (Gen. 28:9). *See* Esau's Wives. **[2]** Wife of Rehoboam (2 Chron. 11:18).

Mahali. *See* Mahli.

Maharai ("hasty"), one of David's warriors (2 Sam. 23:28; 1 Chron. 11:30; 27:13).

Mahath ("dissolution; snatching"). **[1]** A descendant of Kohath who helped to purify the sanctuary (1 Chron. 6:35; 2 Chron. 29:12). **[2]** A Levite overseer of dedicated things during Hezekiah's reign (2 Chron. 31:13).

Mahazioth ("visions"), one set over the song service of the temple (1 Chron. 25:4, 30).

Maher-shalal-hash-baz ("the spoil hastens, the prey speeds"), symbolic name of Isaiah's son (Isa. 8:1–4).

Mahlah ("mildness; sick"), eldest daughter of Zelophehad allowed a share of the land because her father had no sons (Num. 26:33; 27:1; Josh. 17:3). *See* Mahalah.

Mahli [Mahali] ("mild; sickly"). **[1]** A son of Merari (Exod. 6:19; Num. 3:20; 1 Chron. 6:19, 29; Ezra 8:18). **[2]** A descendant of Levi (1 Chron. 6:47; 23:23; 24:30).

Mahlon ("mild; sickly"), the first husband of Ruth who died in Moab (Ruth 1:2–5).

Mahol ("dancer"), father of renowned wise men (1 Kings 4:31).

Malachi ("messenger of Jehovah" or "my messenger"), the last of the prophets recorded in the Old Testament; he was contemporary with Nehemiah (Mal. 1:1).

Malcham ("their king"), a descendant of Benjamin (1 Chron. 8:9).

Malchiah [Malchijah; Melchiah] ("Jehovah is king"). **[1]** A leader of singing under David's reign (1 Chron. 6:40). **[2]** An Aaronite whose descendants dwelled in Jerusalem after the Captivity (1 Chron. 9:12; Neh. 11:12). **[3]** Head of a priestly family (1 Chron. 24:9). **[4], [5], [6]** Three who married foreign wives during the Exile (Ezra 10:25, 31). **[7], [8],** Three who helped to rebuild the wall of Jerusalem (Neh. 3:11, 14, 31). **[10]** A prince or Levite who stood beside Ezra as he read the Law (Neh. 8:4). **[11]** A priest who helped to purify the wall of Jerusalem (Neh. 10:3; 12:42). **[12]** Father of Pashur (Jer. 21:1; 38:1).

Malchiel ("God is a King"), a descendant of Asher (Gen. 46:17; Num. 26:45; 1 Chron. 7:31).

Malchijah. *See* Malchiah.

Malchiram ("my king is exalted"), a descendant of King Jehoiakim (1 Chron. 3:18).

Malchi-shua. *See* Melchi-shua.

Malchus ("counselor; ruler"), a servant of

the high priest whose ear Peter cut off (John 18:10).

Maleleel, Greek form of Mahalaleel (q.v.).

Mallothi ("Jehovah is speaking"), one who was set over the song service of the temple (1 Chron. 25:4, 26).

Malluch ("counselor; ruling"). **[1]** A descendant of Levi (1 Chron. 6:44). **[2], [3]** Two who took foreign wives during the Exile (Ezra 10:29, 32). **[4]** A priest who sealed the covenant (Neh. 10:4). **[5]** A leader who sealed the new covenant with God after the Exile (Neh. 10:27). **[6]** One of the priests who returned with Zerubbabel (Neh. 12:2); he is called Melicu in verse 14.

Mamre ("firmness; vigor"), an Amorite chief who allied with Abraham (Gen. 14:13, 24). *See also* "Places of the Bible."

Manaen ("comforter"), a teacher or prophet at Antioch (Acts 13:1).

Manahath ("resting place; rest"), a descendant of Seir (Gen. 36:23; 1 Chron. 1:40). *See also* "Places of the Bible."

Manasseh [Manasses] ("causing forgetfulness"). **[1]** The first son of Joseph (Gen. 41:51). His descendants became one of the twelve tribes of Israel and occupied both sides of the Jordan (Josh. 16:4–9; 17). **[2]** The idolatrous successor of Hezekiah to the throne of Judah. He was an ancestor of Christ (2 Kings 21:1–18; Matt. 1:10). **[3]** One whose descendants set up graven images at Laish (Judg. 18:30). Most scholars suggest that we should read Moses here instead. Perhaps a scribe felt an idolatrous descendant would cast reproach on the great lawgiver. A few manuscripts of the Septuagint, Old Latin, and the Vulgate read Moses here. **[4], [5]** Two who had taken foreign wives (Ezra 10:30, 33).

Manasses, Greek form of Manasseh (q.v.).

Manoah ("rest"), the father of Samson the judge (Judg. 13:1–23).

Maoch ("poor"). *See* Maachah [4].

Maon ("abode"), a son of Shammai or a city he founded (1 Chron. 2:45).

Mara ("bitter"), name assumed by Naomi after the death of her husband (Ruth 1:20).

Marcus. *See* Mark.

Mareshah ("possession"). **[1]** Father of Hebron (1 Chron. 2:42). **[2]** Son of Laadah (1 Chron. 4:21). *See also* "Places of the Bible."

Mark [Marcus] ("polite; shining"), a Christian convert and missionary companion of Paul (Acts 12:12, 25; 15:37, 39; Col. 4:10). Mark is his Latin name, John his Hebrew name. He wrote the Gospel bearing his name.

Marsena ("worthy"), a prince of Persia (Esther 1:14).

Martha ("lady"), sister of Mary and Lazarus in Bethany (Luke 10:38, 40–41; John 11:1–39).

Mary (Greek form of Miriam, "strong"). **[1]** The mother of Jesus Christ; her song of faith (Luke 1:46–55) reveals her deep faith (Matt. 1:16–20; cf. John 2:1–11). **[2]** Mary the sister of Martha. She anointed the Lord with ointment and received His approval (Luke 10:39, 42; John 11:1–45). **[3]** A woman of Magdala in Galilee. She had been converted after having "seven devils" cast out of her (Matt. 27:56, 61; 28:1; Luke 8:2; John 19:25). **[4]** The mother of John Mark (Acts 12:12). **[5]** A Roman Christian to whom Paul sent greetings (Rom. 16:6). **[6]** Mary, the mother of Joses (Mark 15:47) and James (Luke 24:10), the "other Mary" (Matt. 28:1), and the Mary, wife of Cleophas (John 19:25), are possibly to be identified as the same person (Mark 15:40).

Mash ("drawn out"), son or grandson of Shem (Gen. 10:23). In First Chronicles 1:18 he is called Meshech. Possibly an Aramean people dwelling near Mt. Masius in northern Mesopotamia is meant.

Massa ("burden; oracle"), a son of Ishmael (Gen. 25:14; 1 Chron. 1:30).

Mathusala, Greek form of Methuselah (q.v.).

Matred ("God is pursuer" or "expulsion"), mother of Mehetabel, wife of Hadar (Gen. 36:39; 1 Chron. 1:50).

Matri ("Jehovah is watching" or "rainy"), ancestor of a tribe of Benjamin to which Saul belonged (1 Sam. 10:21).

Mattan ("gift"). **[1]** A priest of Baal slain by the Jews (2 Kings 11:18; 2 Chron. 23:17). **[2]** Father of a prince of Judah (Jer. 38:1).

Mattaniah ("gift of Jehovah"). **[1]** The original name of King Zedekiah (2 Kings 24:17). **[2]** A descendant of Asaph whose family dwelt at Jerusalem (1 Chron. 9:15; 2 Chron. 20:14; Neh. 11:17, 22; 13:13). **[3]** A son of Heman the singer (1 Chron. 25:4, 16). **[4]** One who helped to cleanse the temple (2 Chron. 29:13). **[5] [6], [7], [8]** Four who married foreign wives during the Exile (Ezra 10:26–27, 30, 37). **[9]** One of the gatekeepers (Neh. 12:25).

Mattatha ("gift"), ancestor of Jesus (Luke 3:31). Not to be confused with Mattathah.

Mattathah ("gift"), one who married a foreign wife (Ezra 10:33). Not to be confused with Mattatha.

PEOPLE OF THE BIBLE

Mattathias ("God's gift"). **[1]** An ancestor of Jesus (Luke 3:25). **[2]** Another ancestor of Christ (Luke 3:26).

Mattenai ("gift of Jehovah"). **[1], [2]** Two who married foreign wives during the Exile (Ezra 10:33, 37). **[3]** A priest who returned from the Exile (Neh. 12:19).

Matthan ("gift"), an ancestor of Jesus (Matt. 1:15).

Matthat ("gift"). **[1]** Grandfather of Joseph and ancestor of Jesus (Luke 3:24). **[2]** Another ancestor of Jesus (Luke 3:29).

Matthew ("gift of God"), one of the twelve apostles; he was a tax collector before his call. He was also known as Levi (Matt. 9:9; 10:3; Mark 2:14). He wrote the third Gospel.

Matthias ("God's gift"), a Christian chosen to become an apostle to fill the place of Judas (Acts 1:23, 26). He was surnamed Justus.

Mattithiah ("gift of Jehovah"). **[1]** A Levite in charge of "things made in pans" (1 Chron. 9:31). **[2]** A Levite singer and gatekeeper (1 Chron. 15:18, 21; 16:5). **[3]** A son of Jeduthun (1 Chron. 25:3, 21). **[4]** One who took a foreign wife during the Exile (Ezra 10:43). **[5]** One who stood with Ezra when he read the Law (Neh. 8:4).

Mebunnai ("built up"). *See* Sibbecai.

Medad ("love"), one of the elders of the Hebrews on whom the spirit fell (Num. 11:26–27).

Medan ("judgment"), a son of Abraham by Keturah (Gen. 25:2; 1 Chron. 1:32).

Mehetabel [Mehetabeel] ("God is doing good"). **[1]** Wife of King Hadar of Edom (Gen. 36:39; 1 Chron. 1:50). **[2]** Father of Delaiah who defied Nehemiah (Neh. 6:10).

Mehida ("famous"), an ancestor of returned captives (Ezra 2:52; Neh. 7:54).

Mehir ("dexterity"), a descendant of Caleb of Hur (1 Chron. 4:11).

Mehujael ("God is combating"), a descendant of Cain (Gen. 4:18).

Mehuman ("true"), one of the chamberlains of Ahasuerus (Esther 1:10).

Melatiah ("Jehovah delivers"), an assistant wall-builder (Neh. 3:7).

Melchi ("my King"). **[1]** An ancestor of Jesus (Luke 3:24). **[2]** Another ancestor of Jesus (Luke 3:28).

Melchiah. *See* Malchiah.

Melchisedec, Greek form of Melchizedek (q.v.).

Melchi-shua [Malchi-shua] ("the king, i.e., [God] is salvation"), the third son of King Saul (1 Sam. 14:49; 31:2; 1 Chron. 8:33).

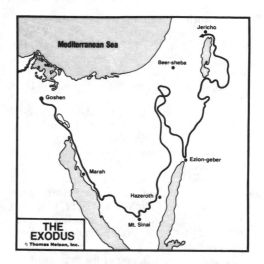

THE EXODUS
© Thomas Nelson, Inc.

Melchizedek [Melchisedec] ("king of righteousness"), king and high priest of Salem. He was a prophetic symbol or "type" of Christ (Gen. 14:18–20; Psa. 110:4; Heb. 5–7).

Melea ("full"), ancestor of Christ (Luke 3:31).

Melech ("King"), great-grandson of Saul (1 Chron. 8:35; 9:41).

Melicu. *See* Malluch [4].

Melzar ("the overseer"), one to whom Daniel and his companions were entrusted (Dan. 1:11, 16); this is possibly a title, rather than a proper name.

Memucan, a Persian prince (Esther 1:14–21).

Menahem ("comforter"), the idolatrous and cruel usurper of the throne of Israel who killed Shallum (2 Kings 15:14–23).

Menan, an ancestor of Christ (Luke 3:31).

Meonothai ("Jehovah is dwelling" or "my dwelling"), a descendant of Judah (1 Chron. 4:14).

Mephibosheth ("idol breaker"). **[1]** Son of Saul by his concubine Rizpah (2 Sam. 21:8). **[2]** A grandson of Saul. He was loyal to David, even though Ziba told David he was a traitor (2 Sam. 4:4; 9:6–13). He was also called Merib-baal ("Baal contends") (1 Chron. 8:34; 9:40).

Merab ("increase"), daughter of Saul promised to David but given to Adriel (1 Sam. 14:49; 18:17, 19). Apparently she was a sister of Michal.

Meraiah ("revelation of Jehovah"), a priest of Jerusalem in the days of Joiakim (Neh. 12:12).

PEOPLE OF THE BIBLE

Meraioth ("revelations"). **[1]** A descendant of Aaron and ancestor of Azariah (1 Chron. 6:6–7, 52; Ezra 7:3). **[2]** Another priest of the same line (1 Chron. 9:11; Neh. 11:11). **[3]** Another priest at the end of the Exile (Neh. 12:15); possibly the same as Meremoth [1] or [3].

Merari ("bitter; excited"), the third son of Levi and founder of a priestly clan (Gen. 46:11; Exod. 6:16, 19; Num. 3; 4:29–45).

Mered ("rebellious"), son of Ezra, descendant of Judah (1 Chron. 4:17–18).

Meremoth ("strong; firm"). **[1]** A priest who weighed the gold and silver vessels of the temple (Ezra 8:33; Neh. 3:4, 21). **[2]** One who took a foreign wife during the Exile (Ezra 10:36). **[3]** One who sealed the new covenant with God after the Exile (Neh. 10:5; 12:3).

Meres ("worthy"), one of the seven princes of Persia (Esther 1:14).

Merib-baal. *See* Mephibosheth.

Merodach-baladan (Babylonian, *Marduk-baladan*—"[the god] Marduk has given a son"), a king of Babylon in the days of Hezekiah (Jer. 50:2). Also called Berodach-baladan (2 Kings 20:12).

Mesha ("freedom"). **[1]** A king of Moab who rebelled against Ahaziah (2 Kings 3:4). **[2]** Eldest son of Caleb (1 Chron. 2:42). **[3]** A descendant of Benjamin (1 Chron. 8:9). *See also* "Places of the Bible."

Meshach ("the shadow of the prince; who is this?"), the name given to Mishael after he went into Babylonian captivity. He was delivered from the fiery furnace (Dan. 1:7; 3:12–30).

Meshech [Mesech] ("long; tall"). **[1]** A son of Japheth (Gen. 10:2; 1 Chron. 1:5). Possibly a people inhabiting the land in the mountains north of Assyria; it was called Musku. **[2]** *See* Mash.

Meshelemiah ("Jehovah recompenses"), a descendant of Levi (1 Chron. 9:21; 26:1–2, 9). He is also called Shelemiah (1 Chron. 26:14).

Meshezabeel ("God is deliverer"). **[1]** A priest who helped rebuild the wall (Neh. 3:4). **[2]** One who signed the covenant (Neh. 10:21). **[3]** A descendant of Judah (Neh. 11:24).

Meshillemith ("retribution"), a priest whose descendants lived in Jerusalem (1 Chron. 9:12). He is called Meshillemoth in Nehemiah 11:13.

Meshillemoth ("recompense"). **[1]** A descendant of Ephraim (2 Chron. 28:12). **[2]** *See* Meshillemith.

Meshobab, a prince of Simeon (1 Chron. 4:34).

Meshullam ("associate; friend"). **[1]** Grandfather of Shaphan, a scribe (2 Kings 22:3). **[2]** A descendant of King Jehoiakim (1 Chron. 3:19). **[3]** Head of a family of Gad (1 Chron. 5:13). **[4]** A descendant of Benjamin (1 Chron. 8:17). **[5]** One whose son lived in Jerusalem (1 Chron. 9:7). **[6]** One who lived in Jerusalem (1 Chron. 9:8). **[7]** A descendant of Aaron and an ancestor of Ezra (Neh. 11:11; 1 Chron. 9:11). He is also called Shallum (Ezra 7:2; 1 Chron. 6:12–13). **[8]** A priest (1 Chron. 9:12). **[9]** An overseer of the temple work (2 Chron. 34:12). **[10]** A chief man who returned with Ezra to Jerusalem (Ezra 8:16). **[11]** One who had assisted in taking account of those who had foreign wives after the Exile (Ezra 10:15). **[12]** One who took a foreign wife during the Exile (Ezra 10:29). **[13], [14]** Two who rebuilt part of the wall of Jerusalem (Neh. 3:4, 6, 30; 6:18). **[15]** A prince or priest who stood with Ezra while he read the Law (Neh. 8:4). **[16]** A priest who sealed the new covenant with God after the Exile (Neh. 10:7). **[17]** One who sealed the new covenant with God after the Exile (Neh. 10:20). **[18]** One whose descendants lived in Jerusalem (Neh. 11:7). **[19]** A priest who assisted in the dedication of the wall of Jerusalem (Neh. 12:13, 33). **[20]** A descendant of Ginnethon (Neh. 12:16). **[21]** A Levite and gatekeeper after the Exile (Neh. 12:25).

Meshullemeth ("friend"), wife of Manasseh and mother of Amon (2 Kings 21:19).

Methusael ("man of God"), the father of Lamech (Gen. 4:18).

Methuselah [Mathusala] ("man of the dart"), the longest-living human recorded in the Bible, the grandfather of Noah and an ancestor of Christ (Gen. 5:21–27; Luke 3:37).

Mezahab ("offspring of the shining one"), grandfather of Mehetabel, wife of Hadar, the eighth king of Edom (Gen. 36:39; 1 Chron. 1:50).

Miamin ("fortunate"). **[1]** One who took a foreign wife during the Exile (Ezra 10:25). **[2]** A priest who returned from the Exile (Neh. 12:5).

Mibhar ("choice; youth"), one of David's mighty men (1 Chron. 11:38).

Mibsam ("sweet odor"). **[1]** A son of Ishmael (Gen. 25:13; 1 Chron. 1:29). **[2]** A son of Simeon (1 Chron. 4:25).

Mibzar ("fortified"), chief of Edom (Gen. 36:42; 1 Chron. 1:53).

NEHEMIAH'S WALL. *Nebuchadnezzar of Babylon razed the walls of Jerusalem in 586 B.C. and captured the city. When Cyrus allowed the Jews to return to Jerusalem, Nehemiah (the governor of Judea) ordered his men to rebuild the wall of the old material (Neh. 2:13–15; 4:1–2, 7). This section of Nehemiah's wall is found on the hill of Ophel.*

Mica [Micah, Micha, Michah—all probably contractions of Micaiah]. **[1]** Owner of a small private sanctuary (Judg. 17:1–5). **[2]** A descendant of Reuben (1 Chron. 5:5). **[3]** A son of Merib-baal, Mephibosheth in Second Samuel 4:4 (1 Chron. 8:34). **[4]** A descendant of Kohath, son of Levi (1 Chron. 23:20; 24:24). **[5]** The father of Abdon (2 Chron. 34:20). He is called Michaiah in Second Kings 22:12. **[6]** A prophet (Jer. 26:18; Mic. 1:1). **[7]** The son of Zichri (1 Chron. 9:15; Neh. 11:17). **[8]** One who signed the covenant (Neh. 10:11).

Michael ("who is like God?") **[1]** One sent to spy out the land of Canaan (Num. 13:13). **[2]** A descendant of Gad (1 Chron. 5:13). **[3]** Another descendant of Gad (1 Chron. 5:14). **[4]** An ancestor of Asaph (1 Chron. 6:40). **[5]** A chief of the tribe of Issachar (1 Chron. 7:3). **[6]** One residing in Jerusalem (1 Chron. 8:16). **[7]** A warrior who joined David at Ziklag (1 Chron. 12:20). **[8]** Father of Omri, a prince of Issachar (1 Chron. 27:18). **[9]** A son of Jehoshaphat (2 Chron. 21:2). **[10]** An ancestor of one who returned from the Exile (Ezra 8:8).

Michah. *See* Mica.

Michaiah [Micaiah] ("who is like Jehovah?"). **[1]** Wife of Rehoboam (2 Chron. 13:2). She is also called Maachah (1 Kings 15:2; 2 Chron. 11:20). *See* Maachah [5]. **[2]** *See* Mica [5]. **[3]** A prince of Judah (2 Chron. 17:7). **[4]** The son of Zaccur (Neh. 12:35). **[5]** One present at the dedication of the wall (Neh. 12:41). **[6]** A prophet who predicted Ahab's downfall (1 Kings 22:8—28; 2 Chron. 18:7–27).

Michal ("who is like God?"), a daughter of Saul whom David married (1 Sam. 14:49). Michal "had no child unto the day of her death" (2 Sam. 6:23). Yet Second Samuel 21:8 states she had five sons. The KJV rendering, "whom she brought up for Adriel," is not a permissible translation—the Hebrew text states she bore them. A few Hebrew, Greek, and Syriac manuscripts read: "the five sons of Merab" instead of Michal, which seems a plausible solution to the problem. See First Samuel 18:19.

Michri ("Jehovah possesses"), an ancestor of a clan of Benjamin in Jerusalem (1 Chron. 9:8).

Midian ("contention"), a son of Abraham by Keturah and founder of the Midianites (Gen. 25:2, 4; 36:35; 1 Chron. 1:32). *See also* "Places of the Bible."

Mijamin ("fortunate"). **[1]** A priest in the time of David (1 Chron. 24:9). *See also* Miniamin [2]. **[2]** One who sealed the new covenant (Neh. 10:7). **[3]** One who married a foreign wife (Ezra 10:25).

Mikloth ("twigs; sticks"). **[1]** A descendant of Benjamin living in Jerusalem (1 Chron. 8:32; 9:37–38). **[2]** A chief military officer under David (1 Chron. 27:4).

Mikneiah ("Jehovah is zealous"), a Levite musician (1 Chron. 15:18, 21).

Milalai ("Jehovah is elevated"), a priest who aided in the purification of the wall (Neh. 12:36).

Milcah ("counsel"). **[1]** A daughter of Haran, Abraham's brother, and wife of Nahor (Gen. 11:29; 22:20, 23). **[2]** A daughter of Zelophehad (Num. 26:33; 27:1).

Miniamin ("fortunate"). **[1]** A Levite who

apportioned the tithes (2 Chron. 31:15). **[2]** A priest in the days of Joiakim (Neh. 12:17). He is possibly the same as Mijamin in First Chronicles 24:9. *See* Mijamin [1]. **[3]** A priest who helped dedicate the wall (Neh. 12:41).

Miriam ("fat; thick; strong"). **[1]** The sister of Moses and Aaron. She rebelled against Moses with Aaron at Hazeroth (Exod. 2:4–10; Num. 12:1–15; 20:1). **[2]** A woman descendant of Judah (1 Chron. 4:17).

Mirma ("height"), descendant of Benjamin (1 Chron. 8:10).

Mishael ("who is what God is?"). **[1]** One who carried away the dead Nadab and Abihu (Exod. 6:22; Lev. 10:4). **[2]** One who stood with Ezra at the reading of the Law (Neh. 8:4). **[3]** One of the companions of Daniel in Babylon (Dan. 1:6–7, 11, 19). *See* Meshach.

Misham ("impetuous; fame"), a descendant of Benjamin (1 Chron. 8:12).

Mishma ("fame"). **[1]** A son of Ishmael (Gen. 25:14; 1 Chron. 1:30). **[2]** A descendant of Simeon (1 Chron. 4:25).

Mishmannah ("strength; vigor"), one who joined David at Ziklag (1 Chron. 12:10).

Mispar. *See* Mispereth.

Mispereth ("writing"), one who returned from captivity (Neh. 7:7). He is called Mispar in Ezra 2:2.

Mithredath ("given by [the god] Mithra"). **[1]** The treasurer of Cyrus through whom he restored the temple vessels (Ezra 1:8). **[2]** One who wrote to the king of Persia protesting the restoration of Jerusalem (Ezra 4:7).

Mizraim, the second son of Ham (Gen. 10:6, 13; 1 Chron. 1:8, 11). Possibly the Egyptian people are intended.

Mizzah ("terror; joy"), a duke of Edom (Gen. 36:13, 17; 1 Chron. 1:37).

Mnason ("remembering"), a Cyprian convert who accompanied Paul from Caesarea on Paul's last visit to Jerusalem (Acts 21:16).

Moab ("from my father"), the son of Lot by his daughter and an ancestor of the Moabites (Gen. 19:34–37). *See also* "Places of the Bible."

Moadiah. *See* Maadiah.

Molid ("begetter"), a descendant of Judah (1 Chron. 2:29).

Mordecai ("dedicated to Mars"). **[1]** A Jewish exile who became a vizier of Persia. He helped save the Jews from destruction (Esther 2—10). **[2]** A leader who returned from the Babylonian Captivity (Ezra 2:2; Neh. 7:7).

Moses ("drawer-out; child; one-born"), the great prophet and lawgiver of Israel. He led his people from Egyptian bondage. The book of Exodus tells his story. He wrote the first five books of the Bible.

Moza ("origin; offspring"). **[1]** A son of Caleb (1 Chron. 2:46). **[2]** A descendant of Saul (1 Chron. 8:36–37; 9:42–43).

Muppim ("obscurities"), a son of Benjamin (Gen. 46:21). He is also called Shuppim (1 Chron. 7:12, 15; 26:16), Shupham (Num. 26:39), Shephuphan (1 Chron. 8:5). These last three names mean "serpent." While this individual may have borne many names, probably copyists' errors account for some of the diversity.

Mushi ("drawn out; deserted"), a son of Merari, son of Levi (Exod. 6:19; Num. 3:20; 1 Chron. 6:19, 47).

N

Naam ("pleasantness"), a son of Caleb (1 Chron. 4:15).

Naamah ("pleasant"). **[1]** Daughter of Lamech and Zillah (Gen. 4:22). **[2]** A wife of Solomon and mother of Rehoboam (1 Kings 14:21; 2 Chron. 12:13). *See also* "Places of the Bible."

Naaman ("pleasantness"). **[1]** A Syrian general who was healed of leprosy by bathing in the Jordan (2 Kings 5; Luke 4:27). **[2]** Grandson of Benjamin (Gen. 26:38, 40). **[3]** A son of Benjamin and founder of a tribal family (Gen. 46:21).

Naarah ("a girl" or "posterity"), a wife of Ashur (1 Chron. 4:5–6). *See also* "Places of the Bible."

Naarai ("youthful"), one of David's valiant men (1 Chron. 11:37). Probably the same as Paarai (2 Sam. 23:35).

Naashon. *See* Nahshon.

Naasson, Greek form of Nahshon (q.v.).

Nabal ("foolish; wicked"), a wealthy Carmelite who refused David and his men food (1 Sam. 25).

Naboth ("a sprout"), the owner whom Jezebel had killed in order to obtain his vineyard (1 Kings 21:1–18).

Nachon ("stroke"). Scripture refers to the threshing floor of Nachon/Chidon (1 Sam. 6:6; 1 Chron. 13:9). This is either the combined name of two individuals, of two place names, or a combination of both. *Chidon* possibly means "destruction or a javelin."

Nachor, Greek form of Nahor (q.v.).

Nadab ("liberal"). **[1]** Firstborn son of

PEOPLE OF THE BIBLE

Aaron, struck dead for offering "strange fire" to God (Exod. 6:23; Lev. 10:1–3). **[2]** A descendant of Jerahmeel (1 Chron. 2:28, 30). **[3]** A brother of Gibeon (1 Chron. 8:30). **[4]** Son of Jeroboam I; he ruled Israel for two years (1 Kings 15:25–31).

Nagge ("splendor"), ancestor of Jesus (Luke 3:25). *See also* Neariah.

Naham ("comfort"), a descendant of Judah, a chieftain (1 Chron. 4:19).

Nahamani ("compassionate"), one who returned with Zerubbabel (Neh. 7:7).

Naharai [Nahari] ("snorting one"), Joab's armor-bearer (1 Chron. 11:39; 2 Sam. 23:37).

Nahari. *See* Naharai.

Nahash ("oracle" or "serpent"). **[1]** The father of Abigail and Zeruiah (2 Sam. 17:25). **[2]** An Ammonite king that was defeated by Saul (1 Sam. 11:1–2; 12:12). **[3]** Another king of Ammon (2 Sam. 10:2; 17:27; 1 Chron. 19:1–2). Not to be confused with Ir-nahash.

Nahath ("lowness"). **[1]** A descendant of Esau (Gen. 36:13; 1 Chron. 1:37). **[2]** An overseer of the offerings at the temple (2 Chron. 31:13). **[3]** *See* Toah.

Nahbi ("Jehovah is protection"), the spy of Naphtali whom Moses sent out to explore Canaan (Num. 13:14).

Nahor [Nachor] ("piercer"). **[1]** Grandfather of Abraham and ancestor of Christ (Gen. 11:22–25; Luke 3:34). **[2]** A brother of Abraham (Gen. 11:26–27, 29; 22:20, 23; Josh. 24:2).

Nahshon [Naashon; Naasson] ("oracle"), a descendant of Judah and ancestor of Christ. Perhaps Aaron's brother-in-law (Exod. 6:23; Num. 1:7; Matt. 1:4).

Nahum ("comforter"), one of the later prophets; he prophesied against Nineveh (Nah. 1:1). Not to be confused with Naum.

Naomi ("pleasantness; my joy"), mother-in-law to Ruth (Ruth 1:2—4:17).

Naphish ("numerous"), son of Ishmael (Gen. 25:15; 1 Chron. 1:31).

Naphtali ("wrestling"), the sixth son of Jacob (Gen. 30:7–8). His descendants became one of the twelve tribes.

Naphtuhim, a son of Mizraim (Gen. 10:13; 1 Chron. 1:11). Many think this refers to a district in Egypt, possibly a designation for the people of the Egyptian Delta.

Narcissus (meaning unknown), a Roman Christian (Rom. 16:11).

Nathan ("gift"). **[1]** Prophet and royal advisor to David (2 Sam. 7:2–17; 12:1–25). **[2]** A son of King David and ancestor of Christ (2 Sam. 5:14; 1 Chron. 3:5; Luke 3:31). **[3]** Father of Igal (2 Sam. 23:36). **[4]** A descendant of Jerahmeel (1 Chron. 2:36). **[5]** A companion of Ezra (Ezra 8:16). **[6]** One of those who had married a foreign wife (Ezra 10:39). **[7]** Brother of Joel, one of David's valiant men (1 Chron. 11:38). **[8]** Father of Solomon's chief officer (1 Kings 4:5). **[9]** A chief man of Israel (Zech. 10:10). *See* Nathan-melech.

Nathanael ("God has given"), a Galilean called by Christ to be a disciple. He is probably to be identified with Bartholomew (John 1:45–49; 21:2; Acts 1:13). *See also* Bartholomew.

Nathan-Melech ("King's gift"), an official under Josiah (2 Kings 23:11).

Naum ("comforter"), an ancestor of Christ (Luke 3:25). Not to be confused with Nahum.

Neariah ("Jehovah drives away"). **[1]** A descendant of David (1 Chron. 3:22). **[2]** A descendant of Simeon who smote the Amalekites in Mount Seir (1 Chron. 4:42).

Nebai ("projecting"), a co-covenanter with Ezra (Neh. 10:19).

Nebaioth [Nebajoth] ("husbandry"), oldest son of Ishmael (Gen. 25:13; 28:9; 36:3; 1 Chron. 1:29).

Nebajoth. *See* Nebaioth.

Nebat ("cultivation"), father of Jeroboam I (1 Kings 11:26).

Nebo ("height"), an ancestor of Jews who had taken foreign wives during the Exile (Ezra 10:43). This reference quite possibly refers to a city.

Nebuchadnezzar **[Nebuchadrezzar]** (Babylonian, *Nabur-kudurri-utsur*—"may [the god] Nabu guard my boundary stones"), great king of the Babylonian Empire; he captured Jerusalem three times and carried Judah into captivity (2 Kings 24:1, 10–11; 25:1, 8, 22; Dan. 1—4).

Nebushasban ("Nabu delivers me"), a Babylonian prince (Jer. 39:13).

Nebuzaradan (Babylonian, "[the god] Nabu has given seed"), a Babylonian captain of the guard at the siege of Jerusalem (2 Kings 25:8, 11, 20).

Necho, pharaoh of Egypt who fought Josiah at Megiddo (2 Chron. 35:20).

Nedabiah ("Jehovah is willing"), a descendant of Jehoiakim king of Judah (1 Chron. 3:18).

Nehemiah ("Jehovah is consolation"). **[1]** Governor of Jerusalem; he helped rebuild the fallen city (Neh. 1:1; 8:9; 12:47). **[2]** A chief man who returned from the Exile (Ezra 2:2;

44

PEOPLE OF THE BIBLE

Neh. 7:7). **[3]** One who repaired the wall of Jerusalem (Neh. 3:16).

Nehum. *See* Rehum.

Nehushta ("basis; ground"), wife of Jehoiakim; mother of Jehoiachin (2 Kings 24:8).

Nekoda ("herdsman"). **[1]** Head of a family of Nethinim (Ezra 2:48; Neh. 7:50). **[2]** The head of a family without genealogy after the Exile (Ezra 2:60; Neh. 7:62).

Nemuel ("God is speaking"). **[1]** A descendant of Reuben (Num. 26:9). **[2]** A son of Simeon (Num. 26:12; 1 Chron. 4:24). In Genesis 46:10; Exodus 6:15, he is called Jemuel.

Nepheg ("sprout; shoot"). **[1]** A brother of Korah (Exod. 6:21). **[2]** A son of David (2 Sam. 5:15; 1 Chron. 3:7; 14:6).

Nephishesim [Nephusim] ("expansions"), ancestor of returned captives (Neh. 7:52). He is called Nephusim in Ezra 2:50. This man is possibly identical with Naphish.

Nephusim. *See* Nephishesim.

Ner ("light"). **[1]** An uncle (?) of Saul, father of Abner (1 Sam. 14:50). **[2]** Grandfather of Saul (1 Chron. 8:33; 9:39). These relationships are unclear. Abner may have been Saul's uncle. If so, Ner [1] and [2] are the same. He is also called Abiel (1 Sam. 9:1). It is also possible that Ner [2] (Abiel) had sons named Ner [1] and Kish, the father of Saul.

Nereus ("lamp"), a Roman Christian (Rom. 16:15).

Nergal-sharezer ("May the god Nergal defend the prince"), a Babylonian officer who released Jeremiah (Jer. 39:3, 13–14).

Neri ("whose lamp is Jehovah"), ancestor of Christ (Luke 3:27).

Neriah ("whose lamp is Jehovah"), father of Baruch (Jer. 32:12, 16; 36:4, 8, 32).

Nethaneel ("God gives"). **[1]** Chief of Issachar whom Moses sent to spy out the land of Canaan (Num. 1:8; 2:5; 7:18, 23; 10:15). **[2]** Fourth son of Jesse (1 Chron. 2:14). **[3]** One of the trumpet blowers when the ark of the covenant was brought up (1 Chron. 15:24). **[4]** A Levite (1 Chron. 24:6). **[5]** A son of Obededom and gatekeeper of the tabernacle (1 Chron. 26:4). **[6]** A prince commissioned by Jehoshaphat to teach the people (2 Chron. 17:7). **[7]** A Levite in the days of Josiah (2 Chron. 35:9). **[8]** A priest who married a foreign wife (Ezra 10:22). **[9]** A priest in the days of Joiakim (Neh. 12:21). **[10]** Levite musician at the purification ceremony (Neh. 12:36).

Nethaniah ("Jehovah gives"). **[1]** A musician in David's worship services (1 Chron. 25:2, 12). **[2]** A Levite whom Jehoshaphat sent

to teach in Judah's cities (2 Chron. 17:8). **[3]** Father of Jehudi (Jer. 36:14). **[4]** Father of Ishmael, the murderer of Gedaliah (Jer. 40:8, 14–15; 41:11).

Neziah ("preeminent"), head of a Nethinim family that returned to Jerusalem with Zerubbabel (Ezra 2:54; Neh. 7:56).

Nicanor ("conqueror"), one of the seven chosen in the ministry to the poor (Acts 6:5).

Nicodemus ("innocent blood"), a Pharisee and ruler of the Jews who assisted in Christ's burial (John 3:1–15; 7:50–52; 19:39–42).

Nicolaus ("conqueror of the people"), one of the seven chosen to aid in the ministration to the poor (Acts 6:5).

Niger, surname of Simeon (q.v.).

Nimrod ("valiant; strong"), a son of Cush (Gen. 10:8–9; 1 Chron. 1:10). His kingdom included Babel, Erech, Accad, and Calneh, cities in Shinar, but also included Assyria.

Nimshi ("Jehovah reveals"), an ancestor of Jehu (1 Kings 19:16; 2 Kings 9:2, 14).

Noadiah ("Jehovah assembles"). **[1]** Son of Binnui to whom Ezra entrusted the sacred vessels of the temple (Ezra 8:33). **[2]** A prophetess opposed to Nehemiah (Neh. 6:14).

Noah [Noe] ("rest"), son of Lamech; the patriarch chosen to build the ark. Only his family survived the flood (Gen. 5:28–32; 6:8–22; 7—10). He was an ancestor of Christ (Luke 3:36).

Noah ("flattery; movement"), a daughter of Zelophehad (Num. 26:33; Josh. 17:3).

Nobah ("prominent"), a descendant of Manasseh who conquered Kenath (Num. 32:42). *See also* "Places of the Bible."

Noe, Greek form of Noah (q.v.).

Nogah ("splendor"), a son of David (1 Chron. 3:7; 14:6).

Nohah ("rest"), a son of Benjamin (1 Chron. 8:2).

Non. *See* Nun.

Nun [Non] ("continuation; fish"). **[1]** A descendant of Ephraim (1 Chron. 7:27); possibly the same as [2]. **[2]** The father of Joshua (Exod. 33:11; 1 Kings 16:34).

Nymphas ("bridegroom"), a Christian of Laodicea to whom Paul sends greetings (Col. 4:15). Some manuscripts read Nympha, which would make this individual a woman.

O

Obadiah ("servant of Jehovah"). **[1]** The governor or prime minister of Ahab who tried to protect the prophets against Jezebel (1 Kings 18:3–16). **[2]** A descendant of David (1 Chron. 3:21). **[3]** A chief of the tribe of Issachar (1 Chron. 7:3). **[4]** A descendant of King Saul (1 Chron. 8:38; 9:44). **[5]** A man of the tribe of Zebulun (1 Chron. 27:19). **[6]** A chief of the Gadites who joined David at Ziklag (1 Chron. 12:9). **[7]** One of the princes whom Jehoshaphat commissioned to teach the Law (2 Chron. 17:7–9). **[8]** A Levite overseer in work done on the temple (2 Chron. 34:12). **[9]** The chief of a family that returned to Jerusalem (Ezra 8:9). **[10]** One who sealed the covenant with Nehemiah (Neh. 10:5). **[11]** A gatekeeper for the sanctuary of the temple (Neh. 12:25). **[12]** The fourth of the "minor prophets." His message was directed against Edom (Obad. 1). **[13]** *See* Abda [2].

Obal. *See* Ebal.

Obed ("servant"). **[1]** A son of Boaz and Ruth, father of Jesse, and ancestor of Christ (Ruth 4:17; Matt. 1:5; Luke 3:32). **[2]** A descendant of Judah (1 Chron. 2:37–38). **[3]** One of David's warriors (1 Chron. 11:47). **[4]** A Levite gatekeeper in David's time (1 Chron. 26:7). **[5]** Father of Azariah, who helped make Joash king of Judah (2 Chron. 23:1).

Obed-edom ("servant of [the god] Edom"). **[1]** A man who housed the ark for three months (2 Sam. 6:10–12; 1 Chron. 13:13–14). **[2]** One of the chief Levitical singers and doorkeepers (1 Chron. 15:18, 21, 24; 16:5, 38; 26:4, 8, 15). **[3]** A temple treasurer or official, or perhaps the tribe that sprang from [2] (2 Chron. 25:24).

Obil ("camel-keeper" or "leader"), a descendant of Ishmael who attended to David's camels (1 Chron. 27:30).

Ocran ("troubler"), a descendant of Asher (Num. 1:13; 2:27).

Oded ("aiding" or "restorer"). **[1]** Father of Azariah the prophet (2 Chron. 15:1). **[2]** A prophet of Samaria who persuaded the northern army to free their Judean slaves (2 Chron. 28:9–15).

Og ("giant"), the giant king of Bashan, defeated at Edrei (Num. 21:33–35; Deut. 3:1–13).

Ohad ("strength"), a son of Simeon (Gen. 46:10; Exod. 6:15).

Ohel ("tent"), a son of Zerubbabel (1 Chron. 3:20).

Olympas (meaning unknown), a Roman Christian (Rom. 16:15).

Omar ("speaker; mountaineer"), a grandson of Esau and a duke of Edom (Gen. 36:15).

Omri ("Jehovah apportions; pupil"). **[1]** The sixth king of Israel and founder of the third dynasty. He founded Samaria and made it Israel's capital (1 Kings 16:15–28). **[2]** A descendant of Benjamin, the son of Becher (1 Chron. 7:8). **[3]** A descendant of Perez living at Jerusalem (1 Chron. 9:4). **[4]** A prince of Issachar in the days of David (1 Chron. 27:18).

On ("sun" or "strength"), a Reubenite who rebelled against Moses and Aaron (Num. 16:1). *See also* "Places of the Bible."

Onam ("vigorous"). **[1]** A grandson of Seir (Gen. 36:23; 1 Chron. 1:40). **[2]** A son of Jerahmeel of Judah (1 Chron. 2:26, 28).

Onan ("vigorous"), the second son of Judah. He was slain by God for disobedience (Gen. 38:4–10; Num. 26:19).

Onesimus ("useful"), a slave on whose behalf Paul wrote an epistle to his master, Philemon (Col. 4:9; Philem. 10, 15).

Onesiphorus ("profit-bringer"), a loyal friend of Paul's who often refreshed him in prison (2 Tim. 1:16; 4:19).

Ophir ("fruitful; rich"), a son of Joktan (Gen. 10:29; 1 Chron. 1:23). The name may possibly refer to a tribe who inhabited modern Somaliland. *See also* "Places of the Bible."

Ophrah ("fawn; hamlet"), a descendant of Judah (1 Chron. 4:14). *See also* "Places of the Bible."

Oreb ("raven"), a Midianite chieftain defeated by Gibeon and beheaded by the Ephraimites (Judg. 7:25). *See also* "Places of the Bible."

Oren ("pine; strength"), a son of Jerahmeel of Judah (1 Chron. 2:25).

Ornan ("active"), a Jebusite from whom David bought a piece of land, on which Solomon's temple was erected (1 Chron. 21:15–25). He is called Araunah in Second Samuel 24:16.

Orpah ("fawn; youthful freshness"), daughter-in-law of Naomi (Ruth 1:4–14).

Osee, Greek form of Hosea (q.v.).

Oshea. *See* Joshua.

Othni ("Jehovah is power"), a Levite, son of Shemaiah and tabernacle gatekeeper in David's time (1 Chron. 26:7).

Othniel ("God is power"), Caleb's younger brother who liberated Israel from foreign rule (Judg. 1:13; 3:8–11; 1 Chron. 27:15).

Ozem ("strength"). **[1]** A brother of David (1 Chron. 2:15). **[2]** A son of Jerahmeel of Judah (1 Chron. 2:25).

Ozias, Greek form of Uzziah (q.v.).

Ozni. *See* Ezbon [1].

44

PEOPLE OF THE BIBLE

P

Paarai ("revelation of Jehovah" or "devotee of Peor"), one of David's mighty men (2 Sam. 23:35); probably the same as Naarai (1 Chron. 11:37).

Padon ("redemption"), one who returned with Zerubbabel (Ezra 2:44; Neh. 7:47).

Pagiel ("God's intervention"), a chief of Asher (Num. 1:13; 2:27).

Pahath-Moab ("ruler of Moab"), a Jewish family named after an ancestor of the above name or title (Ezra 2:6; Neh. 3:11). The one who sealed the covenant bearing this name is either another Jew or else the above family is intended (Neh. 10:1, 14).

Palal ("judge"), one who helped rebuild the wall (Neh. 3:25).

Pallu [Phallu] ("distinguished"), a son of Reuben (Gen. 46:9; Exod. 6:14; 1 Chron. 5:3).

Palti ("Jehovah delivers"). **[1]** The man selected from Benjamin to spy out the land (Num. 13:9). **[2]** *See* Paltiel [2].

Paltiel [Phaltiel] ("God delivers"). **[1]** A prince of the tribe of Issachar (Num. 34:26). **[2]** The man who married David's wife (2 Sam. 3:15). He is called Phalti in First Samuel 25:44.

Parmashta ("stronger"), a son of Haman (Esther 9:9).

Parmenas ("steadfast"), one of the seven deacons (Acts 6:5).

Parnach ("gifted"), a descendant of Zebulun (Num. 34:25).

Parosh [Pharosh] ("fleeing; fugitive"). **[1]** One whose descendants returned from the Exile (Ezra 2:3; Neh. 7:8). **[2]** Another whose family returned from the Exile (Ezra 8:3). **[3]** One whose descendants had taken foreign wives during the Exile (Ezra 10:25). **[4]** One who sealed the covenant (Neh. 10:14). **[5]** The father of one who helped repair the wall of Jerusalem (Neh. 3:25). All of these are possibly the same.

Parshandatha ("given by prayer"), a son of Haman slain by the Jews (Esther 9:7).

Paruah ("blooming"), father of Jehoshaphat (1 Kings 4:17).

Pasach ("limping"), a descendant of Asher (1 Chron. 7:33).

Paseah [Phaseah] ("limping"). **[1]** A descendant of Judah through Caleb (1 Chron. 4:12). **[2]** One whose family returned (Ezra 2:49; Neh. 7:51). **[3]** Father of Jehoiada, who helped repair the wall (Neh. 3:6).

Pashur ("splitter; cleaver"). **[1]** Head of a priestly family (Ezra 2:38; 10:22; Neh. 7:41). **[2]** A priest who sealed the covenant with God after the Exile (Neh. 10:1, 3). Possibly identical with [1]. **[3]** A priest, the "chief governor in the house of the Lord," who persecuted Jeremiah (Jer. 20:1–6). **[4]** Son of Melchiah, whose family returned to Jerusalem (1 Chron. 9:12; Neh. 11:12; Jer. 21:1; 38:1).

Pathrusim a descendant of Mizraim (Gen. 10:14; 1 Chron. 1:12). Possibly the inhabitants of Pathros.

Patrobas ("paternal"), a Roman Christian (Rom. 16:14).

Paul (Latin, *Paulus*—"little"), a Pharisee who studied Jewish law under Gamaliel (Acts 21:39). He was converted and made an Apostle to the Gentiles (Acts 26:12–20). Perhaps he used his Roman name in humility. The Book of Acts tells of his missionary journeys.

Pedahel ("whom God redeems"), a prince of Naphtali (Num. 34:28).

Pedahzur ("the rock delivers"), father of Gamaliel (Num. 1:10; 2:20).

Pedaiah ("Jehovah delivers"). **[1]** Father of Joel (1 Chron. 27:20). **[2]** Grandfather of King Josiah (2 Kings 23:36). **[3]** Son or grandson of Jeconiah (1 Chron. 3:18–19). **[4]** One who helped to rebuild the wall of Jerusalem (Neh. 3:25). **[5]** One who stood with Ezra when he read the Law (Neh. 8:4; 13:13). **[6]** A descendant of Benjamin (Neh. 11:7).

Pekah ("opening"), a usurper of the throne of Israel; he ruled for twenty years (2 Kings 15:25–31).

Pekahiah ("Jehovah watches"), son and successor of Menahem on the throne of Israel. He was murdered by Pekah (2 Kings 15:22–26).

Pelaiah ("Jehovah is distinguished"). **[1]** A son of Elioenai (1 Chron. 3:24). **[2]** A Levite who explained the Law when Ezra read it (Neh. 8:7). **[3]** A Levite who sealed the covenant (Neh. 10:10); he may be the same as [2].

Pelaliah ("Jehovah judges"), a priest whose grandson dwelled in Jerusalem after the Exile (Neh. 11:12).

Pelatiah ("Jehovah delivers"). **[1]** One who sealed the new covenant with God after the Exile (Neh. 10:22). **[2]** A descendant of David (1 Chron. 3:21). **[3]** A captain of Simeon (1 Chron. 4:42–43). **[4]** A wicked prince seen in Ezekiel's vision (Ezek. 11:1, 13).

Peleg [Phalec] ("division"), son of Eber and ancestor of Christ (Gen. 10:25; 11:16; Luke 3:35).

PEOPLE OF THE BIBLE

Pelet ("deliverance"). **[1]** A son of Jahdai of the family of Caleb (1 Chron. 2:47). **[2]** One who joined David at Ziklag (1 Chron. 12:3).

Peleth ("flight; haste"). **[1]** Father of On (Num. 16:1). **[2]** A son of Jonathan and a descendant of Pharez (1 Chron. 2:33).

Peninnah ("coral; pearl"), second wife of Elkanah, father of Samuel (1 Sam. 1:2, 4).

Penuel ("face of God"). **[1]** A descendant of Benjamin (1 Chron. 8:25). **[2]** A chief or father of Gedar (1 Chron. 4:4).

Peresh ("separate"), son of Machir, son of Manasseh (1 Chron. 7:16).

Perez **[Phares; Pharez]** ("bursting through"), eldest son of Judah and an ancestor of Christ (1 Chron. 27:3; Neh. 11:4). He is also called Pharez (Gen. 38:29; 46:12; Luke 3:33).

Perida [Peruda] ("separation"), one whose descendants returned from the Exile (Neh. 7:57; Ezra 2:55).

Persis ("Persian"), a Christian woman at Rome (Rom. 16:12).

Peruda. *See* Perida.

Peter ("stone; rock"), a fisherman called to be an apostle of Christ. He became one of the leaders of the early church (Matt. 4:18–20; 16:15–19; Acts 2). Christ changed this man's name from Simon to a name meaning "rock" (*Cephas* in Aramaic, *Peter* in Greek).

Pethahiah ("Jehovah opens up"). **[1]** A chief Levite in the time of David (1 Chron. 24:16). **[2]** A Levite having a foreign wife (Ezra 10:23). **[3]** A descendant of Judah (Neh. 11:24). **[4]** A Levite who regulated the devotions of the people after Ezra had finished reading the Law (Neh. 9:5).

Pethuel ("God's opening"), father of Joel the prophet (Joel 1:1).

Peullethai ("Jehovah's seed"), a son of Obed-edom and gatekeeper in the time of David (1 Chron. 26:5).

Phalec, Greek form of Peleg (q.v.).

Phallu. *See* Pallu.

Phalti. *See* Paltiel [2].

Phaltiel. *See* Paltiel.

Phanuel ("vision of God"), father of Anna (Luke 2:36).

Pharaoh ("inhabitant of the palace"), royal title of Egyptian kings, equivalent to our word *king* (Gen. 12:15; 37:36; Exod. 2:15; 1 Kings 3:1; Isa. 19:11).

Phares, Greek form of Perez (q.v.).

Pharez. *See* Perez.

Pharosh. *See* Parosh.

Phaseah. *See* Paseah.

TOMB OF RACHEL. *This is the traditional spot where Jacob erected a pillar to mark the tomb of his wife Rachel, who died near Bethlehem (Gen. 35:19–20). Today, this small building commemorates the site.*

Phebe ("shining"), a servant of the church at Corinth or Cenchrea who helped Paul (Rom. 16:1).

Phichol ("dark water"), a captain or captains of the army of Abimelech, king of the Philistines (Gen. 21:22; 26:26). Some scholars think this is not a proper name (nor Abimelech), but a Philistine military title. Abraham and Isaac journeyed to Gerar many years apart yet both encountered an Abimelech and Phichol residing there. If these names are titles, that would help explain this puzzling situation; *See* Abimelech.

Philemon ("friendship"), a convert at Colossae to whom Paul wrote an epistle on behalf of his runaway servant, Onesimus (Philem. 1, 5—7).

Philetus ("amiable"), a convert who was condemned by Paul because of his stand on the Resurrection (2 Tim. 2:17).

Philip ("lover of horses"). **[1]** One of the twelve apostles of Christ (Matt. 10:3; John 1:44–48; 6:5–9). **[2]** An evangelist mentioned several times in Acts (Acts 6:5; 8:5–13). **[3]** *See* Herod [3], [4].

Philistim. The reference to Philistim in Genesis 10:14 is to the Philistines.

Philologus ("a lover of learning"), a Roman Christian to whom Paul sent greetings (Rom. 16:15).

Phinehas ("mouth of brass"). **[1]** Grandson

of Aaron and high priest (Exod. 6:25; Num. 25:6–18; 1 Chron. 6:4; 9:20). **[2]** Younger son of Eli; he was a priest who abused his office (1 Sam. 1:3; 2:22–24, 34). **[3]** Father of Eleazar (Ezra 8:33).

Phlegon ("burning"), a Roman Christian (Rom. 16:14).

Phurah ("beauty"), a servant of Gideon (Judg. 7:10–11).

Phut [Put] ("bow"), the third son of Ham (Gen. 10:6; 1 Chron. 1:8). Possibly a reference to a people related to the Egyptians. Many consider the reference to be to a people related to the Libyans. *See also* "Places of the Bible."

Phuvah [Pua; Puah] ("utterance"). **[1]** Second son of Issachar (Gen. 46:13; Num. 26:23; 1 Chron. 7:1). **[2]** Father of Tola the judge (Judg. 10:1).

Phygellus ("fugitive"), one who deserted Paul in Asia (2 Tim. 1:15).

Pilate. *See* Pontius Pilate.

Pildash ("flame of fire"), a son of Nahor, Abraham's brother (Gen. 22:22).

Pileha ("worship"), one who sealed the covenant (Neh. 10:24).

Piltai ("Jehovah causes to escape"), a priest in Jerusalem in the days of Joiakim (Neh. 12:17).

Pinon ("darkness"), a chief of Edom (Gen. 36:41; 1 Chron. 1:52).

Piram ("indomitable" or "wild"), an Amorite king slain by Joshua (Josh. 10:3).

Pispah ("expansion"), a descendant of Asher (1 Chron. 7:38).

Pithon ("harmless"), a son of Micah and great-grandson of Saul (1 Chron. 8:35).

Pochereth ("binding"), one whose children returned (Ezra 2:57; Neh. 7:59).

Pontius Pilate (Latin, *Pontius Pilatus*— "marine dart-carrier"), a Roman procurator of Judea. When Christ was brought before him for judgment, Pilate, fearing the Jews, turned Him over to the people even though he found Him not guilty (Matt. 27:2–24; John 18:28–40).

Poratha ("favored"), a son of Haman slain by the Jews (Esther 9:8).

Porcius Festus. *See* Festus.

Potiphar ("belonging to the sun-god"), Egyptian captain of the guard who became the master of Joseph (Gen. 37:36; 39).

Poti-pherah ("given of the sun-god"), a priest of On; father-in-law of Joseph (Gen. 41:45, 50).

Prisca, shortened form of Priscilla (q.v.).

Priscilla [Prisca] ("ancient one"), the wife of Aquila; a Jewish Christian deeply loyal to her faith (Acts 18:2, 18, 26; Rom. 16:3).

Prochorus ("choir leader"), one of the seven deacons (Acts 6:5).

Pua. *See* Phuvah.

Puah. *See* Phuvah.

Publius ("common; first"), governor of Malta who courteously received Paul and his company when they were shipwrecked (Acts 28:1–10).

Pudens ("shame faced"), a Roman Christian (2 Tim. 4:21).

Pul. *See* Tiglath-pileser. *See also* "Places of the Bible."

Put. *See* Phut.

Putiel ("God enlightens"), father-in-law of Eleazer, son of Aaron (Exod. 6:25).

Q

Quartus ("fourth"), a Corinthian Christian who sent greetings to the church in Rome (Rom. 16:23).

R

Raamah ("trembling"), a son of Cush (Gen. 10:7; 1 Chron. 1:9). Possibly a reference to the inhabitants of a place in southwest Arabia.

Raamiah ("Jehovah causes trembling"), a chief who returned to the land (Neh. 7:7). In Ezra 2:2, he is called Reelaiah ("Jehovah causes trembling").

Rabmag ("chief magician" or "priest"), not a proper name, but an official position of some sort. It is unclear whether it is a high religious or governmental position (Jer. 39:3, 13). Nergal-sharezer of Babylonia bore this title.

Rabsaris. Not a proper name, but an official position in the Babylonian and Assyrian governments. Its precise nature is unknown (Jer. 39:3, 13; 1 Kings 18:17).

Rabshakeh, the title of an office in the Assyrian government. Its precise function is unknown, but suggestions include that of a field marshal or governor of the Assyrian provinces east of Haran (2 Kings 18:17–28; 19:4, 8).

Rachab, Greek form of Rahab (q.v.).

Rachel [Rahel] ("ewe"), daughter of Laban, wife of Jacob, and mother of Joseph and Benjamin (Gen. 29—35).

PEOPLE OF THE BIBLE

Raddai ("Jehovah subdues" or "beating down"), brother of David (1 Chron. 2:14).

Ragau, Greek form of Reu (q.v.).

Raguel. *See* Jethro.

Rahab [Rachab] ("broad"), the harlot of Jericho who helped the Hebrew spies and who became an ancestor of Christ (Josh. 2:1–21; 6:17–25; Matt. 1:5).

Raham ("pity; love"), a descendant of Caleb (1 Chron. 2:44).

Rahel. *See* Rachel.

Rakem ("friendship"), a descendant of Manasseh (1 Chron. 7:16).

Ram [Aram] ("exalted"). **[1]** An ancestor of David and of Christ (Ruth 4:19; Matt. 1:3–4; Luke 3:33). **[2]** Son of Jerahmeel of Judah (1 Chron. 2:27). **[3]** Head of the family of Elihu (Job 32:2).

Ramiah ("Jehovah is high"), one who married a foreign wife during the Exile (Ezra 10:25).

Ramoth ("heights"), one who had taken a foreign wife (Ezra 10:29).

Rapha ("fearful"). **[1]** The fifth son of Benjamin (1 Chron. 8:2). He is called Rephaiah in First Chronicles 9:43. **[2]** A descendant of King Saul (1 Chron. 8:37).

Raphu ("feared; one healed"), father of a spy sent into Canaan (Num. 13:9).

Reaia [Reaiah] ("Jehovah sees"). **[1]** A descendant of Reuben (1 Chron. 5:5). **[2]** One whose descendants returned from the Exile (Ezra 2:47; Neh. 7:50). **[3]** A descendant of Judah (1 Chron. 4:2); perhaps the same as Haroeh (1 Chron. 2:52).

Reba ("fourth part"; "sprout"; or "offspring"), one of the Midianite chieftains slain by the Israelites under Moses (Num. 31:8; Josh. 13:21).

Rebecca, Greek form of Rebekah (q.v.).

Rebekah [Rebecca] ("flattering"), wife of Isaac and mother of Jacob and Esau (Gen. 22:23; 24—28).

Rechab ("companionship"). **[1]** A descendant of Benjamin who murdered Ishbosheth (2 Sam. 4:2, 5–9). **[2]** Founder of a tribe called Rechabites (2 Kings 10:15; Jer. 35). **[3]** A descendant of Hemath (1 Chron. 2:55). **[4]** One who helped to build the wall of Jerusalem (Neh. 3:14).

Reelaiah. *See* Raamiah.

Regem ("friendship"), a descendant of Caleb (2 Chron. 2:47). *See* Regem-melech.

Regem-melech ("royal friend"), a messenger sent out by some Jews. Some authorities do not take this as a proper name but read: ". . . Sherezer, the friend of the king" (Zech. 7:2).

Rehabiah ("Jehovah is a widener"), eldest son of Eliezer, son of Moses (1 Chron. 23:17; 24:21).

Rehob ("width; breadth"). **[1]** Father of Hadadezer, king of Zobah (2 Sam. 8:3, 12). **[2]** A Levite who sealed the covenant (Neh. 10:11). *See also* "Places of the Bible."

Rehoboam [Roboam] ("freer of the people"), the son of Solomon; when he was king, ten tribes revolted from him and he set up the southern kingdom of Judah (1 Kings 11:43; 12; 14). He was an ancestor of Christ (Matt. 1:7).

Rehum ("pity"). **[1]** A chief man that returned from the Exile with Zerubbabel (Ezra 2:2). He is called Nehum ("comfort") in Nehemiah 7:7. **[2]** A chancellor of Artaxerxes (Ezra 4:8, 17). **[3]** A Levite who helped to repair the wall of Jerusalem (Neh. 3:17). **[4]** One who sealed the covenant (Neh. 10:25). **[5]** One who went up with Zerubbabel (Neh. 12:3).

Rei ("friendly"), a friend of David (1 Kings 1:8).

Rekem ("friendship"). **[1]** A Midianite king slain by the Israelites (Num. 31:8; Josh. 13:21). **[2]** A son of Hebron (1 Chron. 2:43–44). *See also* "Places of the Bible."

Remaliah ("Jehovah increases" or "whom Jehovah has adorned"), father of Pekah (2 Kings 15:25–37). This is perhaps not a proper name, but a slur on Pekah's impoverished background.

Rephael ("God has healed"), firstborn son of Obed-edom and tabernacle gatekeeper (1 Chron. 26:7).

Rephah ("healing; support"), a descendant of Ephraim (1 Chron. 7:25).

Rephaiah ("Jehovah is healing"). **[1]** Head of a family of the house of David (1 Chron. 3:21). **[2]** A captain of Simeon (1 Chron. 4:42). **[3]** A son of Tola (1 Chron. 7:2). **[4]** One who helped to rebuild the wall of Jerusalem (Neh. 3:9). **[5]** *See* Rapha [1].

Resheph (the name of a Canaanite deity; meaning unknown), a descendant of Ephraim (1 Chron. 7:25).

Reu [Ragau] ("friendship"), son of Peleg and ancestor of Christ (Gen. 11:18–21; Luke 3:35).

Reuben ("behold, a son"), eldest son of Jacob and Leah; he lost his birthright through sin against his father (Gen. 29:32; 35:22;

37:29). His descendants became one of the twelve tribes of Israel.

Reuel ("God is his friend"). **[1]** A son of Esau by Bashemath (Gen. 36:4; 1 Chron. 1:35, 37). **[2]** Descendant of Benjamin (1 Chron. 9:8). **[3]** See Jethro. **[4]** See Deuel.

Reumah ("pearl; coral"), Nahor's concubine (Gen. 22:24).

Rezia ("Jehovah is pleasing"), a descendant of Asher (1 Chron. 7:39).

Rezin ("dominion"). **[1]** The last king of Syria who, along with Pekah, fought Judah (2 Kings 15:37; 16:5–10). **[2]** One whose descendants returned from the Babylonian Captivity (Ezra 2:48; Neh. 7:50).

Rezon ("prince; noble"), a Syrian rebel who set up his own government in Damascus (1 Kings 11:23). Many scholars think Rezon simply is a title denoting a prince and identify him with Hezion (q.v.).

Rhesa ("head"), an ancestor of Christ (Luke 3:27).

Rhoda ("rose"), a maid in the house of Mary (Acts 12:12–15).

Ribai ("Jehovah contends"), father of Ittai, one of David's valiant men (2 Sam. 23:29; 1 Chron. 11:31).

Rimmon ("pomegranate"), father of Ishbosheth's murderers (2 Sam. 4:2–9). See also "Places of the Bible."

Rinnah ("praise to God; strength"), a descendant of Judah (1 Chron. 4:20).

Riphath ("spoken"), a son of Gomer (Gen. 10:3). A copyist's mistake makes him Diphath in First Chronicles 1:6. Possibly a reference to the Paphlagonians on the Black Sea.

Rizpah ("variegated" or "hot stone"), a concubine of Saul (2 Sam. 3:7; 21:8–11).

Roboam, Greek form of Rehoboam.

Rodanim. See Dodanim.

Rohgah ("outcry; alarm"), a chief of Asher (1 Chron. 7:34).

Romamti-ezer ("highest help"), son of Heman appointed over the service of song (1 Chron. 25:4, 31).

Rosh ("head"), a descendant of Benjamin (Gen. 46:21).

Rufus ("red"). **[1]** A son of Simon of Cyrene (Mark 15:21). He was probably well-known to those to whom Mark wrote his Gospel. **[2]** A Roman Christian (Rom. 16:13); some identify him with [1].

Ruth ("friendship; companion"), Moabite wife of Mahlon and Boaz; she was the great-grandmother of David and an ancestor of Christ (Ruth 1:4–5, 14–16; 4:10; Matt. 1:5).

S

Sabta [Sabtah] ("striking"), the third son of Cush (Gen. 10:7; 1 Chron. 1:9). Possibly a people of southern Arabia is intended.

Sabtecha [Sabtechah] ("striking"), the fifth son of Cush (Gen. 10:7; 1 Chron. 1:9). Possibly a reference to a people of south Arabia.

Sacar ("hired"). **[1]** The father of one of David's mighty men (1 Chron. 11:35). He is called Sharar ("strong") in Second Samuel 23:33. **[2]** A Levite tabernacle gatekeeper in the days of David (1 Chron. 26:4).

Sadoc (Greek form of Zadok—"righteous"), an ancestor of Christ (Matt. 1:14).

Sala [Salah] ("petition; sprout"), a son of Arphaxad and ancestor of Christ (Gen. 10:24; 11:12; Luke 3:35). He is called Shelah in First Chronicles 1:18, 24.

Salathiel, Greek form of Shealtiel (q.v.).

Sallai ("rejecter"). **[1]** A chief man of the tribe of Benjamin (Neh. 11:8). **[2]** A priest who returned with Zerubbabel from the Exile (Neh. 12:20). He is called Sallu in Nehemiah 12:7.

Sallu ("weighed; dear"). **[1]** A descendant of Benjamin dwelling in Jerusalem (1 Chron. 9:7; Neh. 11:7). **[2]** See Sallai [2].

Salma [Salmon] ("strength; clothing"). **[1]** A son of Caleb, son of Hur (1 Chron. 2:51, 54). **[2]** Father of Boaz and ancestor of Christ (Ruth 4:20–21; Matt. 1:4–5; Luke 3:32). Not to be confused with Zalmon.

Salome ("clothing; strength"). **[1]** One of the women who saw the Crucifixion (Mark 15:40; 16:1). Matthew 27:56 mentions that the mother of the sons of Zebedee was present; she is probably to be identified with Salome. John 19:25 lists the sister of Jesus' mother among those near the cross; some scholars identify her with Salome, but others deny this. **[2]** The daughter of Herodias who danced before Herod (Matt. 14:6; Mark 6:22).

Salu ("miserable; unfortunate"), father of Zimri, who was slain (Num. 25:14).

Samgar-nebo, a Babylonian officer who sat with other officials in the middle gate of Jerusalem (Jer. 39:3). Some take this as a proper name (perhaps meaning "be gracious, Nebo"). Others view it as a title of Nergal-sharezer.

Samlah ("garment"), king of Edom (Gen. 36:36; 1 Chron. 1:47–48).

Samson ("distinguished; strong"), judge of Israel for 20 years. His great strength and moral weakness have made him famous (Judg. 13:24; 14—16).

Samuel [Shemuel] ("asked of God; heard of God"), prophet and last judge of Israel. He anointed Saul and later David as king (1 Sam. 1:20; 3—13; 15—16; 19; 25:1; Heb. 11:32).

Sanballat ("strong"), a leading opponent of the Jews at the time they were rebuilding the walls of Jerusalem (Neh. 2:10; 4:1, 7; 6:1–14).

Saph ("preserver"), a descendant of Rapha the giant (2 Sam. 21:18). He is called Sippai ("Jehovah is preserver") in First Chronicles 20:4.

Sapphira ("beautiful; sapphire"), the dishonest wife of Ananias, who was struck dead by God (Acts 5:1–10).

Sara, Greek form of Sarah (q.v.).

Sarah [Sara; Sarai] ("princess"), the wife of Abraham and mother of Isaac (Gen. 17—18; 20—21; Heb. 11:11; 1 Pet. 3:6). Her name was changed from Sarai ("Jehovah is prince") to Sarah ("princess") because she would be the progenitor of a great nation (Gen. 17:15). *See* Serah.

Sarai. *See* Sarah.

Saraph ("burning"), a descendant of Judah (1 Chron. 4:22).

Sargon ("[the god] has established the king [ship]"), an important king of Assyria who finished the siege of Samaria and carried away Israel. He is called by name only once in Scripture (Isa. 20:1).

Sarsechim ("chief of the eunuchs"), a prince of Babylon who sat at the gate (Jer. 39:3).

Saruch, Greek form of Serug (q.v.).

Saul [Shaul] ("asked"). **[1]** The first king of Israel; God eventually gave him up. He tried several times to slay David, but was killed himself at Gilboa (1 Sam. 9—31). **[2]** The original name of Paul (q.v.). **[3]** *See* Shaul [1].

Sceva ("fitted"), a Jewish priest at Ephesus whose sons attempted to cast out a demon, but were wounded by it instead (Acts 19:14–16).

Seba ("drunkard"), eldest son of Cush (Gen. 10:7; 1 Chron. 1:9). Not to be confused with Sheba. Possibly the name refers to a people of southern Arabia. *See also* "Places of the Bible."

Secundus ("second"), a Thessalonian Christian and friend of Paul (Acts 20:4).

Segub ("might; protection"). **[1]** Younger son of Hiel who rebuilt Jericho in the days of Ahab (1 Kings 16:34). **[2]** A grandson of Judah (1 Chron. 2:21–22).

Seled ("exultation"), a descendant of Judah (1 Chron. 2:30).

Sem, Greek form of Shem (q.v.).

Semachiah ("Jehovah supports"), a gatekeeper of the tabernacle in David's day (1 Chron. 26:7).

Semei (Greek form of Shimei), an ancestor of Christ (Luke 3:26).

Senaah. *See* Hassenaah.

Sennacherib (Babylonian, *Sin-ahi-eriba*—"[the god] Sin has substituted for my brother"), an Assyrian king who killed his brother to usurp the throne. He unsuccessfully invaded Judah. The amazing story of the destruction of his army is told in Second Kings 19 (2 Kings 18:13; Isa. 36:1; 37:17, 21, 37).

Senuah ("the violated"), a descendant of Benjamin (Neh. 11:9). Possibly the same as Hasenuah (q.v.).

Seorim ("fear; distress"), a priest in the days of David (1 Chron. 24:8).

Serah ("extension"), a daughter of Asher (Gen. 46:17; 1 Chron. 7:30). Numbers 26:46 should read Serah, not Sarah.

Seraiah ("Jehovah is prince; Jehovah has prevailed"). **[1]** A scribe of David (2 Sam. 8:17). In 2 Samuel 20:25, he is called Sheva and Shavsha in First Chronicles 18:16. He is also called Shisha in First Kings 4:3. **[2]** Chief priest of Jerusalem (2 Kings 25:18; 1 Chron. 6:14; Ezra 7:1). **[3]** One whom Gedaliah advised to submit to Chaldea (2 Kings 25:23; Jer. 40:8). **[4]** The brother of Othniel (1 Chron. 4:13–14). **[5]** A descendant of Simeon (1 Chron. 4:35). **[6]** A priest that returned to Jerusalem with Zerubbabel (Ezra 2:2). **[7]** A leader sent to capture Jeremiah (Jer. 36:26). **[8]** A prince of Judah who went to Babylon (Jer. 51:59, 61). **[9]** A son of Hilkiah dwelling in Jerusalem after the Exile (Neh. 11:11). **[10]** A chief of the priests who returned from Babylon (Neh. 12:1, 7).

Sered ("escape; deliverance"), eldest son of Zebulun (Gen. 46:14; Num. 26:26).

Sergius Paulus, the Roman deputy of Cyprus who was converted because Elymas was struck blind (Acts 13:7).

Serug [Saruch] ("strength; firmness"), father of Nahor and ancestor of Christ (Gen. 11:20, 21; Luke 3:35).

Seth [Sheth] ("compensation; sprout"), son of Adam and Eve, and an ancestor of Christ (Gen. 4:25–26; 1 Chron. 1:1; Luke 3:38).

Sethur ("secreted; hidden"), one sent to spy out the land (Num. 13:13).

Shaaph ("union; friendship"). **[1]** A descendant of Judah (1 Chron. 2:47). **[2]** A son of Caleb (1 Chron. 2:49).

Shaashgaz ("lover of beauty; one anxious to learn"), a chamberlain of Ahasuerus (Esther 2:14).

Shabbethai ("sabbath-born"). **[1]** An assistant to Ezra (Ezra 10:15). **[2]** One who explained the Law to the people (Neh. 8:7). **[3]** A chief Levite in Jerusalem (Neh. 11:16). All three may be identical.

Shachia ("fame of Jehovah"), a descendant of Benjamin (1 Chron. 8:10).

Shadrach ("servant of [the god] Sin"), the name given to Hananiah at Babylon. He was cast into a fiery furnace and rescued (Dan. 1:7; 3).

Shage ("erring; wandering"), father of one of David's mighty men (1 Chron. 11:34). Possibly another name of Shammah (q.v.).

Shaharaim ("double dawn"), a descendant of Benjamin who went to Moab (1 Chron. 8:8).

Shallum [Shallun] ("recompenser"). **[1]** The youngest son of Naphtali (1 Chron. 7:13). He is also called Shillem (Gen. 46:24; Num. 26:49). **[2]** A descendant of Simeon (1 Chron. 4:25). **[3]** A descendant of Judah (1 Chron. 2:40–41). **[4]** One who usurped the throne of Israel and reigned for one month (2 Kings 15:10–15). **[5]** Husband of Huldah the prophetess (2 Kings 22:14; 2 Chron. 34:22). **[6]** See Jehoahaz [2]. **[7]** See Meshullam [7]. **[8]** A gatekeeper of the tabernacle (1 Chron. 9:17–19, 31; Ezra 2:42; Neh. 7:45). **[9]** Father of Jehizkiah (2 Chron. 28:12). **[10], [11]** Two who married foreign wives during the Exile (Ezra 10:24, 42). **[12]** One who helped to repair the wall of Jerusalem (Neh. 3:12). **[13]** One who helped to repair the gate of Jerusalem (Neh. 3:15). **[14]** An uncle of Jeremiah (Jer. 32:7). **[15]** Father of one who was a temple officer in the days of Jehoiakim (Jer. 35:4).

Shalmai ("Jehovah is recompenser"), ancestor of returned exiles (Ezra 2:46; Neh. 7:48).

Shalman, the king who sacked Beth-arbel (Hos. 10:14). Perhaps he was either Shalmaneser V of Assyria or Shalman king of Moab.

Shalmaneser (Babylonian, *Shulmaner-asharidu*—"[the god] Shulman is chief"), the king of Assyria to whom Hoshea became subject was Shalmaneser V (2 Kings 17:3). Either Shalmaneser or Sargon, his successor, was the king to whom Samaria fell after a long siege (2 Kings 17:6; 18:9).

Shama ("hearer"), one of David's heroes (1 Chron. 11:44).

Shamariah. *See* Shemariah.

Shamed ("destroyer"), a son of Elpaal (1 Chron. 8:12).

Shamer ("preserver"). **[1]** A descendant of Merari (1 Chron. 6:46). **[2]** A descendant of Asher (1 Chron. 7:34). He is called Shomer in First Chronicles 7:32.

Shamgar ("cupbearer; fleer"), judge of Israel who rescued his people from the Philistines (Judg. 3:31; 5:6).

Shamhuth ("fame; renown"), a captain of David's army (1 Chron. 27:8).

Shamir ("thorn hedge; approved"), a son of Micah, a Levite (1 Chron. 24:24). *See also* "Places of the Bible."

Shamma ("fame; renown"), a descendant of Asher (1 Chron. 7:37). *See* Shammah.

Shammah ("fame; renown"). **[1]** A grandson of Esau (Gen. 36:13, 17; 1 Chron. 1:37). **[2]** A son of Jesse (1 Sam. 16:9; 17:13). He is also called Shimeah or Shimea (2 Sam. 13:3; 21:21; 1 Chron. 20:7), and Shimma (1 Chron. 2:13). **[3]** One of David's mighty men or the father of one of David's mighty men (2 Sam. 23:11). **[4]** Another of David's mighty men (2 Sam. 23:33), called Shammoth in First Chronicles 11:27. **[5]** Yet another of David's mighty men (2 Sam. 23:25).

Shammai ("celebrated"). **[1]** A descendant of Judah (1 Chron. 2:28, 32). **[2]** A descendant of Caleb, son of Hezron (1 Chron. 2:44–45). **[3]** A son or grandson of Ezra (1 Chron. 4:17).

Shammoth. *See* Shammah [4].

Shammua [Shammuah] ("famous"). **[1]** One sent to spy out the land of Canaan (Num. 13:4). **[2]** One of David's sons (2 Sam. 5:14; 1 Chron. 14:4). In First Chronicles 3:5, he is called Shimea. **[3]** A Levite who led the temple worship after the Exile (Neh. 11:17). He is also called Shemaiah (1 Chron. 9:16). **[4]** The head of a priestly family in Nehemiah's day (Neh. 12:18).

Shamsherai ("heroic"), a descendant of Benjamin (1 Chron. 8:26).

Shapham ("youthful; vigorous"), a chief of Gad (1 Chron. 5:12).

Shaphan ("prudent; sly"). **[1]** A scribe of Josiah who read him the Law (2 Kings 22:3; 2 Chron. 34:8–21). **[2]** Father of a chief officer under Josiah (2 Kings 22:12; 2 Chron. 34:20). **[3]** Father of Elasah (Jer. 29:3). **[4]** Father of Jaazaniah whom Ezekiel saw in a vision

PEOPLE OF THE BIBLE

(Ezek. 8:11). Many scholars consider all of the above to be identical.

Shaphat ("judge"). [1] One sent to spy out the land of Canaan (Num. 13:5). [2] Father of Elisha the prophet (1 Kings 19:16, 19; 2 Kings 3:11; 6:31). [3] One of the family of David (1 Chron. 3:22). [4] A chief of Gad (1 Chron. 5:12). [5] One over David's herds in the valley (1 Chron. 27:29).

Sharai ("Jehovah is deliverer"), one who took a foreign wife (Ezra 10:40).

Sharar. *See* Sacar [1].

Sharezer [Sherezer] (Babylonian, *Sharutsur*—"he has protected the king"). [1] A son of the Assyrian king Sennacherib who, with his brother, killed their father (2 Kings 19:37; Isa. 37:38). [2] One sent to consult the priests and prophets (Zech. 7:2).

Shashai ("noble; free"), one who married a foreign wife during the Exile (Ezra 10:40).

Shashak ("assaulter; runner"), a descendant of Benjamin (1 Chron. 8:14, 25).

Shaul [Saul] (variant form of Saul). [1] The sixth king of Edom (Gen. 36:37–38; 1 Chron. 1:48–49). [2] A descendant of Levi (1 Chron. 6:24). [3] A son of Simeon found in several lists (Gen. 46:10; Exod. 6:15; 1 Chron. 4:24).

Shavsha. *See* Seraiah [1].

Sheal ("request"), one who took a foreign wife (Ezra 10:29).

Shealtiel [Salathiel] ("lent by God"), father of Zerubbabel and an ancestor of Christ (Ezra 3:2, 8; 5:2; Hag. 1:1, 12; Matt. 1:12).

Sheariah ("Jehovah is decider"), a descendant of Saul (1 Chron. 8:38; 9:44).

Shear-jashub ("a remnant returns"), symbolic name given a son of Isaiah (Isa. 7:3).

Sheba ("oath; covenant"). [1] A chief of Gad (1 Chron. 5:13). [2] One who rebelled against David and was beheaded for it (2 Sam. 20). [3] A grandson of Abraham (Gen. 25:3; 1 Chron. 1:32). [4] A descendant of Shem (Gen. 10:28; 1 Chron. 1:22). Some scholars identify [5] with [4]. They believe Sheba is a tribe or people and stress that close genealogical ties account for the occurrence of the name in both Ham's and Shem's genealogy. [5] A descendant of Ham (Gen. 10:7; 1 Chron. 1:9). *See also* "Places of the Bible."

Shebaniah ("Jehovah is powerful"). [1] A priest who aided in bringing the ark of the covenant to the temple (1 Chron. 15:24). [2] A Levite who guided the devotions of the people (Neh. 9:4–5; 10:10). [3], [4] Two priests who sealed the covenant (Neh. 10:4, 12, 14).

Sheber ("breach"), a descendant of Jephunneh (1 Chron. 2:48).

Shebna ("youthfulness"), the scribe or secretary of Hezekiah replaced by Eliakim (2 Kings 18:18; Isa. 22:15–25; 36:3–22).

Shebuel ("God is renown"). [1] A son of Gershom (1 Chron. 23:16; 26:24). [2] A son of Haman, chief singer in the sanctuary (1 Chron. 24:4). He is called Shubael in verse 20.

Shechaniah [Shecaniah] ("Jehovah is a neighbor"). [1] Head of a family of the house of David (1 Chron. 3:21–22). [2], [3] Two whose descendants returned from the Babylonian Captivity (Ezra 8:3, 5). [4] One who took a foreign wife during the Exile (Ezra 10:2). [5] Father of one who repaired the wall of Jerusalem (Neh. 3:29). [6] Father-in-law to one who opposed Nehemiah (Neh. 6:18). [7] A priest who returned from the Exile (Neh. 12:3). [8] A priest in the time of David (1 Chron. 24:11). [9] A priest in Hezekiah's day (2 Chron. 31:15).

Shechem [Sychem] ("shoulder"). [1] Son of Hamor who defiled Dinah; he and his family were soon destroyed for that act (Gen. 33:19; 34). [2] A descendant of Manasseh (Num. 26:31; Josh. 17:2). [3] Another descendant of Manasseh (1 Chron. 7:19). *See also* "Places of the Bible."

Shedeur ("shedder of light"), one who helped number the people (Num. 1:5; 2:10; 7:30, 35).

Shehariah ("Jehovah is the dawn"), a descendant of Benjamin (1 Chron. 8:26).

Shelah ("peace"). [1] The youngest son of Judah (Gen. 38:5–26; 1 Chron. 2:3; 4:21). [2] *See* Sala.

Shelemiah ("Jehovah is recompense"). [1] *See* Meshelemiah. [2], [3] Two who married foreign wives during the Exile (Ezra 10:39, 41). [4] Father of Hananiah (Neh. 3:30). [5] A priest over the treasury (Neh. 13:13). [6] An ancestor of one who was sent by the princes to get Baruch (Jer. 36:14). [7] One ordered to capture Baruch and Jeremiah (Jer. 36:26). [8] Father of one sent to Jeremiah to ask for prayers (Jer. 37:3; 38:1). [9] Father of the guard who apprehended Jeremiah (Jer. 37:13).

Sheleph ("drawn out"), a son of Joktan (Gen. 10:26; 1 Chron. 1:20). A Semitic people dwelling in Arabia is possibly intended.

Shelesh ("might"), a descendant of Asher (1 Chron. 7:35).

Shelomi ("Jehovah is peace"), father of a prince of Asher (Num. 34:27).

Shelomith ("peacefulness"). [1] Mother of

44

PEOPLE OF THE BIBLE

one stoned for blasphemy in the wilderness (Lev. 24:11). **[2]** Daughter of Zerubbabel (1 Chron. 3:19). **[3]** A descendant of Gershon (1 Chron. 23:9). **[4]** A descendant of Levi and Kohath (1 Chron. 23:18). **[5]** One over the treasures in the days of David (1 Chron. 26:25–28). **[6]** Child of Rehoboam (2 Chron. 11:20). **[7]** An ancestor of a family that returned from the Exile (Ezra 8:10). Not to be confused with Shelomoth.

Shelomoth ("peacefulness"), a descendant of Izhar (1 Chron. 24:22). Many identify him with Shelomith [4].

Shelumiel ("God is peace"), a chief of Simeon appointed to assist Moses (Num. 1:6; 2:12; 7:36).

Shem [Sem] ("name; renown"), son of Noah and ancestor of Christ (Gen. 5:32; 6:10; 10:1; Luke 3:36).

Shema ("fame; repute"). **[1]** A son of Hebron (1 Chron. 2:43–44). **[2]** A descendant of Reuben (1 Chron. 5:8). **[3]** A chief of the tribe of Benjamin (1 Chron. 8:13). **[4]** One who stood with Ezra when he read the Law (Neh. 8:4). *See also* "Places of the Bible."

Shemaah ("the fame"), father of two valiant men who joined David (1 Chron. 12:3).

Shemaiah ("Jehovah is fame" or "Jehovah hears"). **[1]** A prophet who warned Rehoboam against war (1 Kings 12:22; 2 Chron. 11:2). **[2]** A descendant of David (1 Chron. 3:22). **[3]** Head of a family of Simeon (1 Chron. 4:37). **[4]** Son of Joel (1 Chron. 5:4). **[5]** A descendant of Merari (1 Chron. 9:14; Neh. 11:15). **[6]** One who helped to bring the ark of the covenant to the temple (1 Chron. 15:8, 11). **[7]** A Levite who recorded the allotment in David's day (1 Chron. 24:6). **[8]** A gatekeeper for the tabernacle (1 Chron. 26:4, 6–7). **[9]** A Levite whom Jehoshaphat sent to teach the people (2 Chron. 17:8). **[10]** One who helped to cleanse the temple (2 Chron. 29:14). **[11]** A Levite in Hezekiah's day (2 Chron. 31:15). **[12]** A chief Levite in Josiah's day (2 Chron. 35:9). **[13]** One who returned with Ezra (Ezra 8:13). **[14]** A person sent to Iddo to enlist ministers (Ezra 8:16). **[15], [16]** Two who married foreign wives during the Exile (Ezra 10:21, 31). **[17]** One who helped to repair the wall of Jerusalem (Neh. 3:29). **[18]** One who tried to intimidate Nehemiah (Neh. 6:10). **[19]** One who sealed the new covenant with God after the Exile (Neh. 10:8). **[20]** One who helped to purify the wall of Jerusalem (Neh. 12:36). **[21]** One at the dedication of the wall of Jerusalem (Neh. 12:42). **[22]** Father of the prophet Urijah (Jer. 26:20). **[23]** One who wanted the priests to reprimand Jeremiah (Jer. 29:24, 31). **[24]** Father of a prince of the Jews (Jer. 36:12). **[25]** *See* Shammua [3]. **[26]** A prince of Judah who took part in the dedication of the wall (Neh. 12:34). **[27]** A Levite of the line of Asaph (Neh. 12:35). **[28]** A chief of the priests who returned with Zerubbabel (Neh. 12:6–7).

Shemariah [Shamariah] ("whom Jehovah guards"). **[1]** One who joined David at Ziklag (1 Chron. 12:5). **[2]** A son of King Rehoboam (2 Chron. 11:19). **[3], [4]** Two who married foreign wives during the Exile (Ezra 10:32, 41).

Shemeber ("splendor of heroism"), the king of Zeboim in the days of Abraham (Gen. 14:2).

Shemer ("watch"), owner of the hill which Omri bought and on which he built Samaria (1 Kings 16:24).

Shemida [Shemidah] ("fame of knowing"), a grandson of Manasseh (Num. 26:32; Josh. 17:2; 1 Chron. 7:19).

Shemidah. *See* Shemida.

Shemiramoth ("fame of the highest"). **[1]** A Levite in the choral service (1 Chron. 15:18, 20; 16:5). **[2]** One sent by Jehoshaphat to teach the Law (2 Chron. 17:8).

Shemuel (variant form of Samuel—"asked of God"). **[1]** One appointed to divide the land of Canaan (Num. 34:20). **[2]** Head of a family of Issachar (1 Chron. 7:2). **[3]** *See* Samuel.

Shenazar ("ivory keeper; Sin [the god] protect"), son or grandson of Jeconiah (1 Chron. 3:18).

Shephathiah [Shephatiah] ("Jehovah is judge"). **[1]** A son of David by Abital (2 Sam. 3:4; 1 Chron. 3:3). **[2]** Father of Meshullam who dwelled in Jerusalem (1 Chron. 9:8). **[3]** A valiant man who joined David at Ziklag (1 Chron. 12:5). **[4]** A prince of Simeon (1 Chron. 27:16). **[5]** A son of Jehoshaphat (2 Chron. 21:2). **[6]** An ancestor of returned captives (Ezra 2:4; Neh. 7:9). **[7]** One of Solomon's servants whose descendants returned from the Babylonian Captivity (Ezra 2:57; Neh. 7:59). **[8]** An ancestor of returned captives (Ezra 8:8). He is possibly identical with **[6]**. **[9]** A descendant of Pharez whose descendants dwelled in Jerusalem (Neh. 11:4). **[10]** A prince of Judah in Zedekiah's time (Jer. 38:1).

Shephi [Shepho] ("unconcern"), a descen-

PEOPLE OF THE BIBLE

TIGLATH-PILESER'S CAPTURE OF ASHTAROTH. *A bas relief from the palace of tiglath-pileser III at Calah shows the Assyrian army carrying off the spoils of Ashtaroth, a city just east of the Sea of Galilee. Tiglath-pileser's soldiers ravaged much of Israel and the surrounding territory between 738 and 726 B.C.*

44

PEOPLE OF THE BIBLE

dant of Seir the Horite (1 Chron. 1:40). He is called Shepho in Genesis 36:23.

Shepho. *See* Shephi.

Shephuphan. *See* Muppim.

Sherah ("blood-relationship"), a woman descendant of Ephraim (1 Chron. 7:24). She was either his daughter or granddaughter; the text is unclear.

Sherebiah ("Jehovah is originator"). **[1]** A priest who returned from the Exile (Ezra 8:18, 24; Neh. 8:7; 9:4–5). **[2]** A Levite who sealed the new covenant with God after the Exile (Neh. 10:12; 12:8, 24).

Sheresh ("union"), a descendant of Manasseh (1 Chron. 7:16).

Sherezer. *See* Sharezer.

Sheshai ("free; noble"), a son of Anak slain by Caleb (Num. 13:22; Josh. 15:14).

Sheshan ("free; noble"), a descendant of Judah through Jerahmeel (1 Chron. 2:31, 34, 35).

Sheshbazzar ("O Shamash [the god], protect the father"), the prince of Judah into whose hands Cyrus placed the temple vessels. Many believe he is the same as Zerubbabel, but others deny this. They claim Sheshbazzar was governor under Cyrus and Zerubbabel under Darius (Ezra 1:8, 11; 5:14–16).

Sheth ("compassion"), a chief of the Moabites (Num. 24:17). Not to be confused with Seth.

Sheth ("tumult"), a descriptive name given

to Moabites (Num. 24:17). Possibly an ancient tribal name of the Moabites.

Shethar ("star; commander"), one of the seven princes of Persia and Media (Esther 1:14). Not to be confused with Shethar-boznai.

Shethar-boznai ("starry splendor"), an official of the king of Persia (Ezra 5:3, 6; 6:6, 13).

Sheva ("self-satisfying"). **[1]** A son of Caleb (1 Chron. 2:49). **[2]** *See* Seraiah [1].

Shilhi ("a warrior; one with darts"), grandfather of King Jehoshaphat (1 Kings 22:42; 2 Chron. 20:31).

Shillem ("retribution"). *See* Shallum [1].

Shiloni ("weapon; armor"), father of Zechariah (Neh. 11:5).

Shilshah ("might; heroism"), a son of Zophath (1 Chron. 7:37).

Shimea [Shimeah] ("[God] has heard [a prayer]"). **[1]** A descendant of Merari (1 Chron. 6:30). **[2]** Father of Berachiah (1 Chron. 6:39). **[3]** *See* Shammah [2]. **[4]** *See* Shammua [2]. **[5]** One of the family of King Saul whose descendants dwelled in Jerusalem (1 Chron. 8:32; 9:38). In the latter passage he is called Shimeam.

Shimeam ("fame; rumor"). *See* Shimeah [2].

Shimeath ("fame"), mother of one who aided in killing King Jehoash (2 Kings 12:21; 2 Chron. 24:26).

Shimei [Shimhi; Shimi] ("Jehovah is fame; Jehovah hear me"). **[1]** A son of Gershon and a grandson of Gershon (Exod. 6:17; Num. 3:18, 21; Zech. 12:13). **[2]** A descendant of Benjamin who cursed David when he was fleeing from Absalom (2 Sam. 16:5–13; 19:16–23). **[3]** A loyal officer of David (1 Kings 1:8). **[4]** An officer of Solomon (1 Kings 4:18). **[5]** Grandson of King Jeconiah (1 Chron. 3:19). **[6]** A man who had sixteen sons and six daughters (1 Chron. 4:26–27). **[7]** A descendant of Reuben (1 Chron. 5:4). **[8]** A son of Libni (1 Chron. 6:29). **[9]** Father of a chief of Judah (1 Chron. 8:21). **[10]** A Levite (1 Chron. 23:9). **[11]** A Levite in the temple song service in the days of David (1 Chron. 25:17). **[12]** One in charge of many vineyards (1 Chron. 27:27). **[13]** One who helped to cleanse the temple (2 Chron. 29:14). **[14]** A Levite in charge of the temple offerings under Hezekiah (2 Chron. 31:12–13). **[15], [16], [15], [16], [17]** Three men who took foreign wives during the Exile (Ezra 10:23, 33, 38). **[18]** Grandfather of Mordecai (Esther 2:5).

Shimeon ("hearing"), one who married a foreign wife (Ezra 10:31). Not to be confused with Simeon.

Shimhi. See Shimei.

Shimi. See Shimei.

Shimma. See Shammah [2].

Shimon ("trier; valuer"), a descendant of Caleb (1 Chron. 4:20).

Shimrath ("watch"), a descendant of Benjamin (1 Chron. 8:21).

Shimri [Simri] ("Jehovah is watching"). **[1]** Head of a family of Simeon (1 Chron. 4:37). **[2]** Father of one of David's mighty men (1 Chron. 11:45). **[3]** Gatekeeper of the tabernacle in David's day (1 Chron. 26:10). **[4]** One who helped to cleanse the temple (2 Chron. 29:13).

Shimrith ("watch"), a woman of Moab, mother of Jehozabad who killed Joash (2 Chron. 24:26). She is called Shomer in Second Kings 12:21.

Shimrom [Shimron] ("watch"), the fourth son of Issachar (Gen. 46:13; Num. 26:24; 1 Chron. 7:1). See also Shimron in "Places of the Bible."

Shimshai ("Jehovah is splendor"), a scribe who, with Rehum, wrote to the king of Persia opposing the rebuilding of the wall of Jerusalem (Ezra 4:8–9, 17, 23).

Shinab, the king of Admah attacked by Chedorlaomer and his allies (Gen. 14:2).

Shiphi ("Jehovah is fulness"), father of a chief of Simeon (1 Chron. 4:37).

Shiphrah ("beauty"), one of the Hebrew midwives at the time of the birth of Moses (Exod. 1:15).

Shiphtan ("judge"), father of Kemuel, a chief of Ephraim (Num. 34:24).

Shisha ("distinction; nobility"), father of two of Solomon's scribes (1 Kings 4:3). Possibly the same as Seraiah [1].

Shishak, another name for Shishak I, king of Egypt. He sheltered Jeroboam against Solomon and in later years invaded Judah (1 Kings 11:40; 14:25; 2 Chron. 12).

Shitrai ("Jehovah is deciding"), a man in charge of David's herds in Sharon (1 Chron. 27:29).

Shiza ("splendor"), father of one of David's valiant men (1 Chron. 11:42).

Shobab ("returning"). **[1]** A son of David (2 Sam. 5:14; 1 Chron. 3:5). **[2]** A son of Caleb (1 Chron. 2:18).

Shobach ("expansion"), captain of the army of Hadarezer of Zobah (2 Sam. 10:16, 18); he is also called Shophach (1 Chron. 19:16).

Shobai ("Jehovah is glorious"), a tabernacle gatekeeper whose descendants returned from the Babylonian Captivity (Ezra 2:42; Neh. 7:45).

Shobal ("wandering"). **[1]** A son of Seir (Gen. 36:20, 23; 1 Chron. 1:38, 40). **[2]** A son of Caleb, son of Hur (1 Chron. 2:50, 52). **[3]** A son of Judah (1 Chron. 4:1–2).

Shobek ("free"), one who sealed the covenant with Nehemiah (Neh. 10:24).

Shobi ("Jehovah is glorious"), a man who helped David when he fled from Absalom (2 Sam. 17:27).

Shoham ("leek-green beryl"), a descendant of Merari (1 Chron. 24:27).

Shomer ("keeper"). **[1]** See Shamer [2]. **[2]** See Shimrith.

Shophach. See Shobach.

Shua [Shuah] ("prosperity"). **[1]** A daughter of Heber (1 Chron. 7:32). **[2]** A Canaanite whose daughter Judah married (Gen. 38:2, 12; 1 Chron. 2:3).

Shuah ("depression"). **[1]** A son of Abraham by Keturah (Gen. 25:2; 1 Chron. 1:32). **[2]** A brother of Chelub; descendant of Caleb (1 Chron. 4:11).

Shual ("jackal"), the third son of Zophah (1 Chron. 7:36).

Shubael ("God's captive"). **[1]** A son or descendant of Amram, a descendant of Levi (1 Chron. 24:20). **[2]** *See* Shebuel [2].

Shuham ("depression"). *See* Hushim [1].

Shuni ("fortunate"), a son of Gad (Gen. 46:16; Num. 26:15).

Shupham. *See* Muppim.

Shuppim ("serpent"). **[1]** A gatekeeper in the days of David (1 Chron. 26:16). **[2]** *See* Muppim.

Shuthelah ("setting of Telah"). **[1]** A son of Ephraim (Num. 26:35–36; 1 Chron. 7:20). **[2]** Another descendant of Ephraim (1 Chron. 7:21).

Siaha [Sia] ("congregation"), ancestor of returned captives (Ezra 2:44; Neh. 7:47).

Sibbechai ("Jehovah is intervening"), a mighty man who killed a Philistine giant (2 Sam. 21:18; 1 Chron. 11:29; 20:4). He is called Mebunnai in Second Samuel 23:27.

Sidon [Zidon] ("fortress"), eldest son of Canaan, son of Ham (Gen. 10:15). He is called Zidon in First Chronicles 1:13. Possibly a reference to the inhabitants of the ancient city of Sidon.

Sihon ("great; bold"), an Amorite king that was defeated by Israel (Num. 21:21–31; Deut. 1:4; 2:24–32; Josh. 13:15–28).

Silas [Silvanus] ("forest; woody; third; asked"), an eminent member of the early church who traveled with Paul through Asia Minor and Greece and was imprisoned with him at Philippi (Acts 15:22, 32–34; 2 Cor. 1:19; 1 Thess. 1:1).

Silvanus. *See* Silas.

Simeon [Simon] ("hearing"). **[1]** The second son of Jacob by Leah (Gen. 29:33; 34:25; 48:5; 49:5). His descendants became one of the twelve tribes of Israel. **[2]** A devout Jew who blessed the Christ child in the temple (Luke 2:25–34). **[3]** An ancestor of Jesus (Luke 3:30). **[4]** A disciple and prophet at Antioch (Acts 13:1); he was surnamed Niger ("black"). **[5]** Original name of Peter (q.v.). Simon is but another form of Simeon. Not to be confused with Shimeon.

Simon ("hearing"). **[1]** Original name of the apostle Peter (Matt. 4:18; 16:16–17; Luke 4:38; Acts 10:18). **[2]** Another of the twelve apostles, called Simon the Canaanite, indicating his fierce loyalty either to Israel or to his faith (Matt. 10:4; Mark 3:18; Luke 6:15; Acts 1:13). **[3]** One of Christ's brothers (Matt. 13:55; Mark 6:3). **[4]** A leper of Bethany in whose house Christ was anointed (Matt. 26:6; Mark 14:3). **[5]** A Cyrenian who was forced to bear the cross of Christ (Matt. 27:32; Mark

15:21). **[6]** A Pharisee in whose house the feet of Christ were anointed (Luke 7:40, 43, 44). **[7]** The father of Judas Iscariot (John 6:71; 12:4; 13:2). **[8]** A sorcerer who tried to buy the gifts of the Holy Spirit (Acts 8:9, 13, 18, 24). **[9]** A tanner of Joppa with whom Peter lodged (Acts 9:43; 10:6, 17, 32).

Simri. *See* Shimri.

Sippai. *See* Saph.

Sisamai ("Jehovah is distinguished"), a descendant of Jerahmeel, son of Pharez (1 Chron. 2:40).

Sisera ("mediation; array"). **[1]** Captain of the army of Jabin who was murdered by Jael (Judg. 4:1–22; 5:26, 28). **[2]** One whose descendants returned (Ezra 2:53; Neh. 7:55).

So ("vizier"), a king of Egypt, either Osorkon IV or Tefnakht. Others believe this name is a reference to a city (2 Kings 17:3–7).

Socho ("brambly"), a son of Heber (1 Chron. 4:18).

Sodi ("Jehovah determines"), father of one of the spies sent into Canaan (Num. 13:10).

Solomon ("peace"), son of David by Bathsheba and king of a united, strong Israel for forty years. His wisdom and carnal sin stand out in his multi-faceted character (1 Kings 1:11; 2:11). He was an ancestor of Christ (Matt. 1:6–7).

Sopater ("one who defends the father"), a man of Berea who accompanied Paul to Asia (Acts 20:4). Perhaps the same as Sosipater (q.v.).

Sophereth ("learning"), servant of Solomon whose ancestors returned from exile (Ezra 2:55; Neh. 7:57).

Sosipater ("one who defends the father"), one who sent greetings to the Roman Christians (Rom. 16:21). He was Jewish (a "kinsman" of Paul) and is possibly the same as Sopater (q.v.).

Sosthenes ("strong; powerful"). **[1]** Chief ruler of the synagogue at Corinth, beaten by the Greeks (Acts 18:17). **[2]** A believer who united with Paul in addressing the Corinthian church (1 Cor. 1:1). Some believe he was [1] after conversion.

Sotai, head of a family of servants (Ezra 2:55; Neh. 7:57).

Stachys ("ear of corn"), a believer of Rome to whom Paul sent greetings (Rom. 16:9).

Stephanas ("crown"), one of the first believers of Achaia (1 Cor. 1:16; 16:15–17).

Stephen ("crown"), one of the seven deacons. He became the first martyr of the church after Christ (Acts 6:5–9; 7:59; 8:2).

PEOPLE OF THE BIBLE

Suah ("riches; distinction"), a son of Zophah, a descendant of Asher (1 Chron. 7:36).

Susanna ("lily"), one of the women who ministered to Christ and was His follower (Luke 8:3).

Susi ("Jehovah is swift or rejoicing"), father of one of the spies (Num. 13:11).

Syntyche ("fortunate"), a woman of the church at Philippi (Phil. 4:2).

T

Tabbaoth ("spots; rings"), one whose descendants returned with Zerubbabel (Ezra 2:43; Neh. 7:46).

Tabeal [Tabeel] ("God is good"). [1] Father of a man the kings of Israel and Damascus planned to make king of Judah (Isa. 7:6). [2] A Persian official who tried to hinder the rebuilding of the wall of Jerusalem (Ezra 4:7).

Tabeel. See Tabeal.

Tabitha ("gazelle"), the Christian woman of Joppa whom Peter raised from the dead (Acts 9:36–42). Dorcas is the Greek form of the name.

Tabrimon ("[the god] Rimmon is good"), father of Ben-hadad I, king of Syria (1 Kings 15:18).

Tahan ("graciousness"). [1] A descendant of Ephraim (Num. 26:35). [2] Another descendant of Ephraim (1 Chron. 7:25).

Tahath ("depression; humility"). [1] A descendant of Kohath (1 Chron. 6:24, 37). [2] A descendant of Ephraim (1 Chron. 7:20). [3] A grandson of the above (1 Chron. 7:20). See also "Places of the Bible."

Tahpenes, an Egyptian queen, wife of the Pharaoh, who received the fleeing Hadad, an enemy of Solomon (1 Kings 11:18–20).

Tahrea [Tarea] ("flight"), son of Micah, descendant of Saul (1 Chron. 8:35; 9:41).

Talmai ("bold; spirited"). [1] A man or clan defeated by Caleb (Num. 13:22; Josh. 15:14; Judg. 1:10). [2] King of Geshur and father-in-law of David (2 Sam. 3:3; 13:27).

Talmon ("oppressor; violent"), a Levite in Ezra's day; a temple porter (1 Chron. 9:17; Ezra 2:42; Neh. 7:45).

Tamah [Thamah] ("combat"), one whose descendants returned from the Babylonian Captivity (Ezra 2:53; Neh. 7:55).

Tamar [Thamar] ("palm"). [1] The wife of Er, mother of Perez, and an ancestor of Christ (Gen. 38:6, 11, 13; Ruth 4:12; Matt. 1:3). [2]

The daughter of David violated by Amnon (2 Sam. 13:1–32). [3] A daughter of Absalom (2 Sam. 14:27). See also "Places of the Bible."

Tanhumeth ("comfort"), father of one of Gedaliah's captains (2 Kings 25:23; Jer. 40:8).

Taphath ("ornament"), a daughter of Solomon (1 Kings 4:11).

Tappuah ("apple; hill place"), a descendant of Judah (1 Chron. 2:43). See also "Places of the Bible."

Tarea [Tharshish]. See Tahrea.

Tarshish ("hard"). [1] A son of Javan and grandson of Noah (Gen. 10:4; 1 Chron. 1:7). Possibly a people who inhabited a region in Spain (Tartessus), near Gibraltar. [2] One of the seven princes of Persia (Esther 1:14). [3] A descendant of Benjamin (1 Chron. 7:10). See also "Places of the Bible."

Tartan (meaning unknown), the title of a high Assyrian officer. There is evidence that the office was second only to the king. There are two tartans mentioned in Scripture (2 Kings 18:17; Isa. 20:1).

Tatnai ("gift"), a Persian governor of Samaria in the days of Zerubbabel (Ezra 5:3; 6:6, 13).

Tebah ("thick; strong"), a son of Nahor, the brother of Abraham (Gen. 22:24).

Tebaliah ("Jehovah is protector; Jehovah has purified"), a Levite gatekeeper in the days of David (1 Chron. 26:11).

Tehinnah ("entreaty; supplication"), a descendant of Judah (1 Chron. 4:12).

Telah ("vigor"), a descendant of Ephraim (1 Chron. 7:25).

Telem ("a lamb"), one who married a foreign wife during the Exile (Ezra 10:24). See also "Places of the Bible."

Tema ("south" or "sun burnt"), a son of Ishmael (Gen. 25:15; 1 Chron. 1:30).

Teman ("south" or "sun burnt"). [1] A grandson of Esau (Gen. 36:11, 15; 1 Chron. 1:36). [2] A duke of Edom (Gen. 36:42; Chron. 1:53).

Temeni ("fortunate"), a son of Ashur (1 Chron. 4:5–6).

Terah [Thara] ("turning; duration"), the father of Abraham and ancestor of Christ (Gen. 11:27–32; Luke 3:34).

Teresh ("strictness; reverence"), a chamberlain of the Persian court that plotted against the crown (Esther 2:21; 6:2).

Tertius ("third"), the scribe to whom the epistle to the Romans was dictated (Rom. 16:22). Some conjecture that he is Silas (q.v.).

Tertullus ("third"), an orator hired by the

PEOPLE OF THE BIBLE

Jews to state skillfully their case against Paul before Felix (Acts 24:1–8).

Thaddeus (a name derived from an Aramaic word for the female breast), one of the twelve apostles (Matt. 10:3; Mark 3:18). He is the same as Judas, the brother of James (Luke 6:16; John 14:22; Acts 1:13). He was also named Lebbeus ("heart").

Thahash ("reddish"), a son of Nahor, Abraham's brother (Gen. 22:24).

Thamah. *See* Tamah.

Thamar, Greek form of Tamar (q.v.).

Thara, Greek form of Terah (q.v.).

Theophilus ("loved by God"), an unknown person, possibly a Roman official, to whom Luke addressed his Gospel and Acts (Luke 1:3; Acts 1:1).

Theudas ("the gift of God"), instigator of a rebellion against the Romans, which was crushed by them (Acts 5:36).

Thomas ("twin"), one of the twelve apostles of Jesus. When Christ rose from the dead, he was most skeptical (Matt. 10:3; Mark 3:18; John 20:24–29). His Aramaic name is Didymus in Greek.

Tiberius ("son of [the river] Tiber"), third emperor of the Roman Empire (Luke 3:1).

Tibni ("intelligent"), one who rivaled Omri for the throne of Israel (1 Kings 16:21–22).

Tidal ("splendor; renown"), king of Goyim who, with his allies, invaded the Cities of the Plain (Gen. 14:1, 9).

Tiglath-pileser (Babylonian, *Tukulti-apil-Esharra*—"my trust is in the son of Asharra"), a king of Assyria who invaded Naphtali during the time of Pekah of Israel. He conquered northern Palestine and deported many from Naphtali (2 Kings 15:29; 16:7, 10; 1 Chron. 5:6, 26). His native name was Pul (2 Kings 15:19). Realizing he bore two names, we should translate First Chronicles 5:26, ". . . God . . . stirred . . . Pul king of Assyria *even* [not *and*] Tilgath-pilneser king of Assyria."

Tikvah [Tikvath] ("hope"). **[1]** The father-in-law of Huldah the prophetess (2 Kings 22:14; 2 Chron. 34:22). **[2]** The father of Jahaziah (Ezra 10:15).

Tilon ("mockery; scorn"), a descendant of Judah (1 Chron. 4:20).

Timaeus ("honorable"), father of the blind Bartimaeus (Mark 10:46).

Timna [Timnah] ("allotted portion; restraining"). **[1]** A concubine of a son of Esau (Gen. 36:12). **[2]** A daughter of Seir the Horite (Gen. 36:22; 1 Chron. 1:39). **[3]** A chief of Edom (Gen. 36:40; 1 Chron. 1:51). **[4]** A son

of Eliphaz (1 Chron. 1:36). *See also* "Places of the Bible."

Timon ("honorable"), one of the seven deacons (Acts 6:1–6).

Timotheus [Timothy] ("honored of God"), a young friend and convert of Paul; he traveled extensively with the apostle. He was from Lystra and was the son of Eunice, a Jewess, and a Greek father (Acts 16:1; 17:14, 15; 1 Tim. 1:2, 18; 6:20).

Timothy. *See* Timotheus.

Tiras ("longing"), youngest son of Japheth (Gen. 10:2; 1 Chron. 1:5). Possibly the inhabitants of Thrace. Other scholars consider reference to be to the Tyrsenoi, a people who inhabited the islands and coastlands of the Aegean.

Tirhakah, a king of Ethiopia and Egypt who aided Hezekiah in his fight against Sennacherib (2 Kings 19:9; Isa. 37:9).

Tirhanah ("kindness"), a descendant of Hezron (1 Chron. 2:48).

Tiria ("foundation"), a descendant of Judah (1 Chron. 4:16).

Tirshatha ("reverend—i.e., his excellency"), a title of the governor of Judea under Persian rule (Ezra 2:63; Neh. 7:65, 70; 8:9; 10:1).

Tirzah ("delight"), youngest daughter of Zelophehad (Num. 26:33; 27:1; Josh. 17:3). *See also* "Places of the Bible."

Titus ("pleasant"), a converted Greek entrusted with a mission to Crete (2 Cor. 2:13; Gal. 2:1; Titus 1:4).

Toah ("depression; humility"), an ancestor of Samuel the prophet (1 Chron. 6:34). He is called Nahath in verse 26 and Tohu in First Samuel 1:1.

Tob-adonijah ("the Lord Jehovah is good"), one sent by Jehoshaphat to teach the Law (1 Chron. 17:8).

Tobiah [Tobijah] ("Jehovah is good"). **[1]** A Levite sent by Jehoshaphat to teach the Law (2 Chron. 17:8). **[2]** An ancestor of returning captives who had lost their genealogy (Ezra 2:60; Neh. 7:62). **[3]** An Ammonite servant of Sanballat who opposed Nehemiah (Neh. 2:10–20). **[4]** A leader who returned from the Babylonian Captivity (Zech. 6:10, 14).

Tobijah. *See* Tobiah.

Togarmah, a son of Gomer (Gen. 10:3; 1 Chron. 1:6). Possibly a people of the far north who inhabited the mountains northwest of Mesopotamia, between the Anti-Taurus and the Euphrates, or possibly the area on the upper Euphrates between Samosata and Melita.

PEOPLE OF THE BIBLE

Tohu. *See* Toah.

Toi [Tou] ("error; wandering"), a king of Hamath who sent his son to congratulate David on his victory over Hadadezer (2 Sam. 8:9–10; 1 Chron. 18:9–10).

Tola ("warm; crimson"). **[1]** A son of Issachar (Gen. 46:13; 1 Chron. 7:1–2). **[2]** A judge of Israel (Judg. 10:1).

Tou. *See* Toi.

Trophimus ("a foster child"), a Christian convert and afterward a companion-in-travel with Paul (Acts 20:4; 21:29; 2 Tim. 4:20).

Tryphena ("dainty; shining"), a Christian woman of Rome to whom Paul sent greetings (Rom. 16:12).

Tryphosa ("delicate; shining"), a Christian woman at Rome sent greetings by Paul (Rom. 16:12).

Tubal, a son of Japheth (Gen. 10:2; 1 Chron. 1:5). Possibly a reference to a people in eastern Asia Minor; they are called Tabal in Assyrian inscriptions.

Tubal-cain, one of the sons of Lamech and expert metalsmith (Gen. 4:22).

Tychicus ("fortunate"), a disciple and messenger of Paul (Acts 20:4; Eph. 6:21; 2 Tim. 4:12).

Tyrannus ("tyrant"), a Greek rhetorician or Jewish rabbi in whose school Paul taught at Ephesus (Acts 19:9).

U

Ucal ("I can"; or a verb meaning "to be consumed"). *See* Ithiel.

Uel ("will of God"), a son of Bani who had taken a foreign wife (Ezra 10:34).

Ulam ("solitary" or "preceding"). **[1]** A descendant of Manasseh, the son of Peresh (1 Chron. 7:16–17). **[2]** A descendant of Benjamin whose sons were "mighty men of valor" (1 Chron. 8:39–40).

Ulla ("elevation; burden"), a descendant of Asher (1 Chron. 7:39).

Unni ("answering is with Jehovah"). **[1]** One of the Levites chosen as singers (1 Chron. 15:10, 18, 20). **[2]** A Levite that returned to the land with Zerubbabel (Neh. 12:9).

Ur ("flame; light"), father of one of David's mighty men (1 Chron. 11:35).

Urbane [Urbanus] ("pleasant; witty"), a faithful Roman Christian whom Paul greeted (Rom. 16:9).

Uri ("enlightened; my light"; a contracted form of Uriah). **[1]** The son of Hur, and father

of Bezaleel (Exod. 31:1–2; 1 Chron. 2:20). **[2]** The father of Geber (1 Kings 4:19). **[3]** A porter of Levi who had married a foreign wife (Ezra 10:24).

Uriah [Urias; Urijah] ("Jehovah is my light"). **[1]** A Hittite soldier in David's army. He was killed in a fierce battle, for David, desiring to marry his wife, Bath-sheba, had placed him on the front battle line (2 Sam. 11). **[2]** A priest under Ahaz who built a pagan altar on the king's command; then placed it in the temple (2 Kings 16:10–16). **[3]** A prophet whose message of judgment so offended Jehoiakim that he murdered him (Jer. 26:20–23). **[4]** A priest, the father of Meremoth (Ezra 8:33; Neh. 3:4, 21). **[5]** A man who stood by Ezra when he read the Law (Neh. 8:4). Possibly the same as [4]. **[6]** A priest whom Isaiah took as a witness (Isa. 8:2).

Urias, Greek form of Uriah (q.v.).

Uriel ("God is my light"). **[1]** A chief of the sons of Kohath (1 Chron. 6:24; 15:5, 11). Possibly the same as Zephaniah [2]. **[2]** Father of Michaiah, one of Rehoboam's sons (2 Chron. 13:2).

Urijah. *See* Uriah.

Uthai ("my iniquity; Jehovah is help"). **[1]** A son of Bigvai who returned to the land of Israel with Ezra (Ezra 8:14). **[2]** A descendant of Judah (1 Chron. 9:4).

Uz [Hur] ("counsel; firmness"). **[1]** Eldest son of Aram (Gen. 10:23). Possibly the name refers to an Aramean tribe or people. **[2]** A son of Shem (1 Chron. 1:17). The Septuagint makes this Uz identical with [1] naming Aram as his father. It is also possible the Hebrew text was abbreviated here. **[3]** A son of Dishan, son of Seir (Gen. 36:28). **[4]** The son of Nahor by Milcah (Gen. 22:21).

Uzai ("hoped for"), the father of Palal (Neh. 3:25).

Uzal ("wandering"), a son of Joktan (Gen. 10:27; 1 Chron. 1:21). Possibly the name refers to an Arabian tribe.

Uzza [Uzzah] ("strength"). **[1]** A man who was struck dead by God when he touched the ark of the covenant (2 Sam. 6:2–7; 1 Chron. 13:6–10). **[2]** A descendant of Merari (1 Chron. 6:29). **[3]** A descendant of Ehud (1 Chron. 8:7). **[4]** An ancestor of a Nethinim family that returned from Babylon (Ezra 2:49; Neh. 7:51). *See also* "Places of the Bible."

Uzzah. *See* Uzza.

Uzzi ("Jehovah is strong" or "my strength"). **[1]** A descendant of Issachar (1 Chron. 7:1–3). **[2]** Chief of a priestly family of

Jedaiah (Neh. 12:19, 42). **[3]** Descendant of Benjamin (1 Chron. 7:7). **[4]** The overseer of the Levites at Jerusalem (Neh. 11:22). **[5]** The father of Elah, a descendant of Benjamin (1 Chron. 9:8). **[6]** A son of Bukki; even though in the line of high priests, he does not seem to have held this office (1 Chron. 6:5–6, 51; Ezra 7:4).

Uzzia ("Yahweh is strong"), one of David's valiant men (1 Chron. 11:44).

Uzziah [Ozias] ("Jehovah is strong" or "my strength is Jehovah"). **[1]** The eleventh king of Judah. When he attempted to offer incense unlawfully, God struck him with leprosy. He was also called Azariah (2 Kings 15:1–8; 2 Chron. 26). He was an ancestor of Christ (Matt. 1:8–9). **[2]** A Levite descended from Kohath and ancestor of Samuel (1 Chron. 6:24). **[3]** Father of Jehonathan (1 Chron. 27:25). **[4]** A priest who had married a foreign wife (Ezra 10:21). **[5]** A descendant of Judah (Neh. 11:4).

Uzziel ("God is my strength" or "God is strong"). **[1]** The ancestor of the Uzzielites; the son of Kohath (Exod. 6:18). **[2]** Captain of the sons of Simeon (1 Chron. 4:42). **[3]** A son of Bela and grandson to Benjamin (1 Chron. 7:7). **[4]** An assistant wall-builder (Neh. 3:8). **[5]** A Levite, son of Jeduthun, who helped to cleanse the temple (2 Chron. 29:14). **[6]** A musician set by David over the service of song in the temple (1 Chron. 25:4). Uzziel is the same as Azareel in verse 18.

V

Vajezatha ("born of Ized" or "given-of-the-Best-One"), one of the sons of Haman slain by the Jews (Esther 9:9).

Vaniah ("praise, or nourishment, of Jehovah"), a son of Bani who had sinned by marrying a foreign wife (Ezra 10:36).

Vashni ("the second"), according to First Chronicles 6:28, the firstborn son of Samuel, but First Samuel 8:2 states Joel was his firstborn. Because of this, some scholars follow the Septuagint and Syriac versions, where verse 28 reads thus: "And the sons of Samuel: the firstborn, Joel, and *the second* Abiah."

Vashti ("beautiful woman; best"), the queen of Persia who was divorced by King Ahasuerus because she refused to come to his great feast (Esther 1:10–22).

Vophsi ("fragrant; rich"), a descendant of Naphtali, the father of Nahbi the spy (Num. 13:14).

Z

Zaavan [Zavan] ("causing fear"), a descendant of Seir (Gen. 36:27). Also called Zavan (1 Chron. 1:42).

Zabad ("endower"). **[1]** A descendant of Jerahmeel of Judah (1 Chron. 2:36–37). **[2]** A man of Ephraim and son of Tahath (1 Chron. 7:21). **[3]** Son of Alai and one of David's mighty men (1 Chron. 11:41). **[4], [5], [6]** Three who married foreign wives during the Exile (Ezra 10:27, 33, 43). **[7]** *See* Jozachar.

Zabbai ("roving about; pure"). **[1]** One who took a foreign wife during the Exile (Ezra 10:28). **[2]** Father of Baruch (Neh. 3:20).

Zabbud ("endowed"), one who returned from the Exile with Ezra (Ezra 8:14).

Zabdi ("Jehovah is endower"). **[1]** Father of Carmi (Josh. 7:1, 17–18); called Zimri in First Chronicles 2:6. **[2]** A descendant of Benjamin (1 Chron. 8:19). **[3]** One of David's storekeepers (1 Chron. 27:27). **[4]** An ancestor of Mattaniah (Neh. 11:17); also called Zichri (1 Chron. 9:15) and Zaccur (1 Chron. 25:2, 10; Neh. 12:35).

Zabdiel ("my gift is God"). **[1]** Father of Jashobeam, David's captain (1 Chron. 27:2). **[2]** An overseer of the priests (Neh. 11:14).

Zabud ("bestowed"), officer and friend of Solomon (1 Kings 4:5).

Zabulon. Greek form of Zebulun (q.v.).

Zaccai ("pure"), one whose descendants returned (Ezra 2:9; Neh. 7:14). Possibly the same as Zabbai [2].

Zaccheus ("pure"), a publican with whom Jesus lodged during His stay at Jericho (Luke 19:1–10).

Zaccur [Zacchur] ("well remembered"). **[1]** A descendant of Simeon (1 Chron. 4:26). **[2]** Father of Shammua, one of the spies (Num. 13:4). **[3]** Descendant of Merari (1 Chron. 24:27). **[4]** *See* Zabdi [4]. **[5]** A Levite who sealed the covenant (Neh. 10:12). **[6]** Father of Hanan (Neh. 13:13); possibly the same as [5]. **[7]** One who rebuilt part of the wall of Jerusalem (Neh. 3:2).

Zachariah [Zechariah] ("memory of the Lord"). **[1]** Son and successor of Jeroboam II. He reigned only six months (2 Kings 14:29; 15:8–11). **[2]** Father of Abi or Abijah, mother of Hezekiah (2 Kings 18:2); written *Zechariah* in Second Chronicles 29:1.

Zacharias (Greek form of Zechariah—"memory of the Lord"). **[1]** The prophet whom the Jews stoned (Matt. 23:35; Luke

11:51). Some believe this prophet to be identical with Zechariah [11] or [16], though it is possible the reference is to an unknown prophet. [2] A priest, father of John the Baptist (Luke 1).

Zacher ("fame"), son of Jeiel (1 Chron. 8:31); called Zechariah in First Chronicles 9:37.

Zadok ("righteous"). [1] A high priest in the time of David (2 Sam. 8:17; 15:24–36; 1 Kings 1:8–45). [2] Father of Jerusha, wife of Uzziah and mother of Jotham, both kings of Israel (2 Kings 15:33; 2 Chron. 27:1). [3] Son of Ahitub and father of Shallum or Meshullam (1 Chron. 6:12, 13; Ezra 7:2). [4] A young man of valor (1 Chron. 12:28). [5], [6] Two who repaired the wall of Jerusalem (Neh. 3:4, 29). [7] One who sealed the covenant with Nehemiah (Neh. 10:21). [8] A scribe under Nehemiah (Neh. 13:13).

Zaham ("fatness"), a son of Rehoboam (2 Chron. 11:19).

Zalaph ("purification"), the father of one who repaired the wall of Jerusalem (Neh. 3:30).

Zalmon ("terrace; accent"), the Ahohite who was one of David's guards (2 Sam. 23:28). He is called Ilai ("exalted") in First Chronicles 11:29. Not to be confused with Salmon. *See also* "Places of the Bible."

Zalmunna ("withdrawn from protection"), a Midianite king slain by Gideon (Judg. 8:5–21).

Zanoah ("broken district"), one of the family of Caleb (1 Chron. 4:18).

Zaphnath-paaneah ("savior of the world; revealer of secrets"), name given to Joseph by Pharaoh (Gen. 41:45).

Zara, Greek form of Zara or Zerah (q.v.).

Zarah. *See* Zerah.

Zattu [Zatthu] ("lovely; pleasant"). [1] One whose descendants returned from the Exile (Ezra 2:8; 10:27; Neh. 7:13). [2] A co-sealer of the new covenant (Neh. 10:14).

Zavan. *See* Zaavan.

Zaza ("projection"), a son of Jonathan (1 Chron. 2:33).

Zealotes. *See* Simon [2].

Zebadiah ("Jehovah is endower"). [1] A descendant of Benjamin (1 Chron. 8:15). [2] A son of Elpaal (1 Chron. 8:17). [3] One who joined David (1 Chron. 12:7). [4] A descendant of Levi through Kohath (1 Chron. 26:2). [5] A son of Asahel (1 Chron. 27:7). [6] A Levite sent by Jehoshaphat to teach the Law (2 Chron. 17:8). [7] A son of Ishmael

(2 Chron. 19:11). [8] Head of a family who returned from exile (Ezra 8:8). [9] A priest who had taken a foreign wife (Ezra 10:20).

Zebah ("victim"), Midianite king slain by Gideon (Judg. 8:5–21).

Zebedee ("the gift of Jehovah"), a fisherman of Galilee, husband of Salome, and father of the apostles James and John (Matt. 4:21; 27:56; Mark 1:19–20).

Zebina ("bought"), one who married a foreign wife during the Exile (Ezra 10:43).

Zebudah ("endowed"), wife of Josiah, king of Judah (2 Kings 23:36).

Zebul ("dwelling"), ruler of Shechem (Judg. 9:28–41).

Zebulun [Zabulon] ("dwelling"), tenth son of Jacob and ancestor of one of the twelve tribes (Gen. 30:20; 49:13; 1 Chron. 2:1).

Zechariah ("Jehovah my righteousness"). [1] A chief of the tribe of Reuben (1 Chron. 5:7). [2] A Levite gatekeeper in the days of David (1 Chron. 9:21; 26:2, 14). [3] A Levite set over the service of song in the days of David (1 Chron. 15:18, 20; 16:5). [4] A priest in the days of David (1 Chron. 15:24). [5] A descendant of Levi through Kohath (1 Chron. 24:25). [6] A descendant of Levi through Merari (1 Chron. 26:11). [7] Father of Iddo (1 Chron. 27:21). [8] A prince of Jehoshaphat sent to teach the people (2 Chron. 17:7). [9] A Levite who encouraged Jehoshaphat against Moab (2 Chron. 20:14). [10] A son of Jehoshaphat (2 Chron. 21:2). [11] A son of Jehoiada who was stoned (2 Chron. 24:20). *See* Zacharias [1]. [12] Prophet in the days of Uzziah (2 Chron. 26:5). [13] A Levite who helped to cleanse the temple (2 Chron. 29:13). [14] A descendant of Levi (2 Chron. 34:12). [15] A prince of Judah in the days of Josiah (2 Chron. 35:8). [16] A prophet in the days of Ezra. His book still exists (Ezra 5:1; 6:14; Zech. 1:1, 7; 7:1, 8). [17] A chief man of Israel (Ezra 8:3). [18] One who returned from the Exile (Ezra 8:11). The chief man in Ezra 8:16 was probably [17] or [18]. [19] One who took a foreign wife during the Exile (Ezra 10:26). [20] A prince with Ezra (Neh. 8:4). [21] A descendant of Perez (Neh. 11:4). [22] One whose descendants dwelled in Jerusalem (Neh. 11:5). [23] A priest (Neh. 11:12). [24] A Levite trumpeter (Neh. 12:35–36). [25] A priest who took part in the dedication ceremony (Neh. 12:41). [26] One whom Isaiah took as a witness (Isa. 8:2). [27] *See* Zachariah [2]. [28] *See* Zacher.

Zedekiah ("Jehovah my righteousness; Je-

PEOPLE OF THE BIBLE

hovah is might"). **[1]** A false prophet who encouraged Ahab to attack the Syrians at Ramoth-gilead (1 Kings 22:11, 24; 2 Chron. 18: 10, 23). **[2]** A false prophet (Jer. 29:21–23). **[3]** A prince of Judah in the days of Jehoiakim (Jer. 36:12). **[4]** The last king of Judah; his rebellion spelled the doom of Judah (2 Kings 24:18—25:7; 2 Chron. 36:11–21). He is probably referred to in First Chronicles 3:16 as a "son" or successor of Jeconiah. *See* Mattaniah [1].

Zeeb ("wolf"), a prince of Midian slain by Gideon (Judg. 7:25; 8:3).

Zelek ("split"), an Ammonite, a valiant man of David (2 Sam. 23:37; 1 Chron. 11:39).

Zelophehad ("firstborn"), grandson of Gilead (Num. 26:33; 27:1, 7; Josh. 17:3).

Zemira ("song"), a son of Becher, a descendant of Benjamin (1 Chron. 7:8).

Zenas ("living"), a Christian who had been a teacher of the Law (Titus 3:13).

Zephaniah ("Jehovah is darkness; Jehovah has treasured"). **[1]** A prophet in the days of Josiah (Zeph. 1:1). **[2]** A Levite or priest, ancestor of Samuel (1 Chron. 6:36). Possibly the same as Uriel [1]. **[3]** Son of Josiah the priest (Zech. 6:10, 14). **[4]** A priest who opposed Babylonian rule (2 Kings 25:18; Jer. 21:1; 37:3).

Zephi [Zepho] ("watch"), a son of Eliphaz (Gen. 36:11, 15; 1 Chron. 1:36).

Zepho. *See* Zephi.

Zephon ("dark; wintry"), a son of Gad (Num. 26:15). Also called Ziphion in Genesis 46:16.

Zerah [Zara; Zarah] ("sprout"). **[1]** A son of Reuel (Gen. 36:13, 17; 1 Chron. 1:37). **[2]** Father of Jobab (Gen. 36:33; 1 Chron. 1:44). **[3]** A son of Judah (Gen. 38:30; 1 Chron. 2:4, 6). **[4]** A descendant of Gershon (1 Chron. 6:21). **[5]** A Levite (1 Chron. 6:41). **[6]** A king of Ethiopia who warred with Asa (2 Chron. 14:9). **[7]** *See* Zohar [2].

Zerahiah ("Jehovah has come forth"). **[1]** A priest of the line of Eleazar (1 Chron. 6:6, 51; Ezra 7:4). **[2]** Head of a family who returned from the Exile with Ezra (Ezra 8:4).

Zeresh ("gold"), wife of Haman (Esther 5:10, 14; 6:13).

Zereth ("brightness"), a descendant of Judah (1 Chron. 4:7).

Zeri ("balm"), a musician in the days of David (1 Chron. 25:3); perhaps the same as Izri (v. 11).

Zeror ("bundle"), an ancestor of Kish (1 Sam. 9:1).

Zeruah ("full-breasted"), the mother of Jeroboam I (1 Kings 11:26).

Zerubbabel [Zorobabel] ("seed of Babylon"). **[1]** The leader of a group who returned from exile; he began the rebuilding of the temple (Ezra 3—5; Neh. 7:7; 12:1, 47). He was an ancestor of Christ (Matt. 1:12–13). **[2]** An ancestor of Christ (Luke 3:27); perhaps the same as [1].

Zeruiah ("balm"), a daughter of Jesse and David's sister (1 Sam. 26:6; 2 Sam. 2:13, 18).

Zetham ("shining"), son or grandson of Laadan (1 Chron. 23:8; 26:22).

Zethan ("olive tree"), a descendant of Benjamin (1 Chron. 7:10).

Zethar ("conqueror"), a eunuch of Ahasuerus (Esther 1:10).

Zia ("terrified"), a descendant of Gad (1 Chron. 5:13).

Ziba ("plantation"), a steward of Saul (2 Sam. 9:2–13; 16:1–4; 19:17–29).

Zibeon ("wild robber"). **[1]** A Hivite man (Gen. 36:2, 14). **[2]** A son of Seir (Gen. 36:20, 24; 1 Chron. 38, 40).

Zibia ("gazelle"), a descendant of Benjamin (1 Chron. 8:9).

Zibiah ("gazelle"), mother of King Joash of Judah (2 Kings 12:1; 2 Chron. 24:1).

Zichri ("renowned"). **[1]** A son of Izhar (Exod. 6:21). **[2]** A descendant of Benjamin (1 Chron. 8:19). **[3]** A descendant of Benjamin of Shishak (1 Chron. 8:23). **[4]** A descendant of Benjamin of Jeroham (1 Chron. 8:27). **[5]** A descendant of Eliezer in the days of Moses (1 Chron. 26:25). **[6]** Father of Eliezer, a descendant of Reuben (1 Chron. 27:16). **[7]** Father of Amaziah (1 Chron. 27:16). **[8]** Father of Elishaphat (2 Chron. 23:1). **[9]** A man of valor who slew the son of King Ahaz (2 Chron. 28:7). **[10]** Father of Joel (Neh. 11:9). **[11]** A priest of the sons of Abijah (Neh. 12:17). **[12]** *See* Zabdi [4].

Zidkijah ("Jehovah my righteousness"), a chief prince of the Jews (Neh. 10:1).

Zidon. *See* Sidon.

Ziha ("dried"). **[1]** One whose children returned from the Babylonian Captivity (Ezra 2:43; Neh. 7:46). **[2]** A ruler of the Nethinim (Ezra 2:43; Neh. 11:21).

Zillah ("protection; screen"), one of the wives of Lamech (Gen. 4:19, 22–23).

Zilpah ("myrrh dropping"), mother of Gad and Asher (Gen. 29:24; 30:9–13; 35:26).

Zilthai ("shadow"). **[1]** A descendant of Benjamin (1 Chron. 8:20). **[2]** A captain who joined David at Ziklag (1 Chron. 12:20).

44

PEOPLE OF THE BIBLE

PEOPLE OF THE BIBLE

Zimmah ("counsel"). **[1]** A Levite of the family of Gershon (1 Chron. 6:20). **[2]** A Levite in the fourth or fifth degree of temple service (1 Chron. 6:42). **[3]** A Levite who assisted in cleansing the temple (2 Chron. 29:12).

Zimran ("celebrated"), a son of Abraham by Keturah (Gen. 25:2; 1 Chron. 1:32).

Zimri ("celebrated"). **[1]** A disobedient Israelite slain by Phinehas (Num. 25:14). **[2]** A captain who slew Elah (1 Kings 16:9–20). **[3]** A son of Zerah of Judah (1 Chron. 2:6). **[4]** A descendant of Benjamin (1 Chron. 8:36; 9:42).

Zina ("fruitful"), second son of Shimei (1 Chron. 23:10). He is called Zizah in verse 11.

Ziph ("refining place"). **[1]** Grandson of Caleb (1 Chron. 2:42). **[2]** A son of Jehaleleel (1 Chron. 4:16). *See also* "Places of the Bible."

Ziphah ("lent"), a son of Jehaleleel (1 Chron. 4:16).

Ziphion ("looking out; serpent; dark"). *See* Zephon.

Zippor ("bird"), father of Balak, king of Moab (Num. 22:2, 4, 10, 16).

Zipporah ("little bird"), the wife of Moses and daughter of Reuel (Exod. 2:21; 4:25; 18:2).

Zithri ("Jehovah is protection"), a descendant of Levi through Kohath (Exod. 6:22).

Ziza [Zizah] ("shining; brightness"). **[1]** A chief of Simeon (1 Chron. 4:37). **[2]** A son of King Rehoboam (2 Chron. 11:20). **[3]** *See* Zina.

Zobebah ("the affable"), a descendant of Judah (1 Chron. 4:8).

Zohar ("nobility; distinction"). **[1]** Father of Ephron, from whom Abraham bought a field (Gen. 23:8; 25:9). **[2]** A son of Simeon of Judah (Gen. 46:10; Exod. 6:15). He is also called Zerah (1 Chron. 4:24).

Zoheth ("strong"), a descendant of Judah (1 Chron. 4:20).

Zophah ("watch"), a descendant of Asher (1 Chron. 7:35–36).

Zophai ("watcher"), a brother of Samuel (1 Chron. 6:26). He is called Zuph in verse 35.

Zophar ("hairy; rough"), a Naamathite and "friend" of Job (Job 2:11; 11:1; 20:1).

Zorobabel, Greek form of Zerubbabel (q.v.).

Zuar ("little"), father of Nethaneel and a chief of Issachar (Num. 1:8; 2:5).

Zuph. *See* Zophai. *See also* "Places of the Bible."

Zur ("rock"). **[1]** A prince of Midian slain by Phinehas (Num. 25:15; 31:8). **[2]** A son of Jehiel (1 Chron. 8:30; 9:36).

Zuriel ("God is my rock"), a chief of the Levites, descendant from Merari (Num. 3:35).

Zurishaddai ("the Almighty is a rock"), father of Shelumiel (Num. 1:6; 2:12).

PLACES OF THE BIBLE

This article identifies places named in the Bible, excluding the deuterocanonical books. The place names are arranged alphabetically as they appear in the King James Version, with variant spellings enclosed in brackets [ ]. The suggested meaning of the names is then given in parentheses ( ). Under each entry, various places bearing this name are differentiated by boldface brackets, like this **[1]**; **[2]**; and so on. Then follows a description of each place, with several Bible references to it.

The meanings of the names are not infallibly accurate; they are simply interesting possibilities. These place names are ancient, many are pre-Israelite, and their history is obscure and uncertain.

Often a Hebrew name refers to both a place and a person. In such cases, you will find the same name in "People of the Bible."

Different names were used to refer to certain sites in different periods of history (e.g., Accho and Ptolemais). We have grouped these names under the most familiar biblical name, cross-referencing the other names to it. Modern place names are given under most of the biblical names.

A

Abana ("stony"), a river that runs through Damascus, purported to have healing qualities (2 Kin. 5:12). A more accurate rendering of the name would be Amana.

Abarim ("mountain beyond"), a large mountain range in Moab near Heshbon, which includes Mount Nebo (Num. 27:12; 33:47–48; Deut. 32:49).

Abdon ("servile"), a city belonging to the tribe of Asher, located at the present site of Khirbet Abdeh (Josh. 21:30; 1 Chr. 6:74). It was once called Hebron; *see* Hebron [2]. *See also* "People of the Bible."

Abel ("meadow," "brook," "stream"), a prefix attached to several towns. **[1]** In Second Samuel 20:14–18, a city specifically related to Abel-beth-maacah is mentioned. Some suppose that Abel and Beth-maacah were towns so close together that they were thought of as being one. However, others believe only one town is referred to in this passage. **[2]** The KJV reading in First Samuel 6:18, "the great stone of Abel," is not very likely. It is a combination of the Hebrew, "the great meadow [*abel*]," and the Septuagint, "the great stone." A city is not referred to here. *See* Abel-beth-maacah. *See also* "People of the Bible."

Abel-beth-maacah ("meadow [brook] of the house of Maacah"), a town of the tribe of Naphtali, located in northern Palestine (2 Sam. 20:14–15). Verse 14 probably refers to one city, not two. In verse 18 the city is simply called Abel. *See also* Abel [1], Abel-maim.

Abel-maim ("meadow [brook] of waters"), probably another name for Abel-beth-maacah (2 Chr. 16:4).

Abel-meholah ("meadow [brook] of dancing"), the birthplace of Elisha, located on the western side of the Jordan Valley (Judg. 7:22; 1 Kin. 4:12).

Abel-mizraim. *See* Atad.

Abel-shittim ("meadow [brook] of Acacias"), largest campsite of the wandering Israelites, located on the plains of Moab (Num. 33:49).

Abez ("lofty"), a town in northern Palestine apportioned to the tribe of Issachar (Josh. 19:20).

Abilene ("stream," "brook"), a Syrian tetrarchy located 29 to 32 km. (18 to 20 mi.) northwest of Damascus (Luke 3:1).

Accad [Akkad] ("fortress"), a city built by Nimrod on the Plain of Shinar (Sumer), north of Babylonia (Gen. 10:10).

Accho ("compressed"), a town on the coast of Palestine about 40 km. (25 mi.) south of Tyre, apportioned to the tribe of Asher (Judg. 1:31); also called Ptolemais in Acts 21:7.

Aceldama [Potter's Field] ("field of blood"), a field purchased by the priests of Jerusalem with the 30 pieces of silver that bought the betrayal of Jesus (Acts 1:19); also called Potter's Field (Matt. 27:7).

Achaia ("trouble"), an ancient district of the Peloponnesus in Greece ruled by the Romans (Acts 18:12; Rom. 15:26).

Achmetha [Ecbatana] ("a place of horses"), a provincial city of the Medes that was the summer residence of Persian kings

PLACES OF THE BIBLE

VALLEY OF AIJALON. *Bordering the Plain of Sharon between the city of Jericho and the Mediterranean Sea, the valley of Aijalon (or Ajalon) was the site of Joshua's famous battle with the Amorites (Josh. 10:12–14). The biblical town of Aijalon, located nearby, should not be confused with a city by the same name in modern Jordan.*

(Ezra 6:2); also called Ecbatana. The city stood near present-day Hamadan.

Achor ("trouble"), a valley south of Jericho, in which Achan was stoned (Josh. 7:24); and which formed the northern boundary of Judah (Josh. 15:7).

Achshaph ("sorcery"), a city of Canaan captured by Joshua (Josh. 12:20), and a landmark on the boundary of the land apportioned to the tribe of Asher (Josh. 19:25).

Achzib [Chezib] ("false"). **[1]** A Canaanite city in the lowlands of Judah, captured by Joshua (Gen. 38:5; Josh. 15:44). **[2]** A seashore town on the northern side of Galilee near the Lebanon border (Josh. 19:29; Judg. 1:31).

Adadah ("holiday"), a town in the southern district of Judah (Josh. 15:22).

Adam ("red; of the earth"), a city on the east bank of the Jordan River that was given to

the tribe of Reuben (Josh. 3:16). *See also* "People of the Bible."

Adamah ("earth"), a fortified city in northern Palestine apportioned to the tribe of Naphtali (Josh. 19:36); its exact location is not known.

Adami [Adami-Nekeb] ("fortified"), a border town assigned to the tribe of Naphtali (Josh. 19:33); perhaps located on the site of modern Khirbet ed-Damiyeh, 8 km. (5 mi.) southwest of Tiberias.

Some consider this to be the same as Nekeb and hence join the words to form one: Adami-Nekeb. Others deny this—either view is possible. Adami also might be identical with Adamah (q.v.).

Adar [Hazar-Addar] ("height"), a fortress town located on the southwestern border of Judah between Kadesh-barnea and Karka (Josh. 15:3). This place is called Hazar-Addar in Numbers 34:4.

Addan [Addon] ("stony"), a place in Babylon that served as a staging area for exiles returning to Israel (Ezra 2:59; Neh. 7:61).

Adithaim ("double crossing"), a town in the lowlands of Judah (Josh. 15:36).

Admah ("redness"), one of the Cities of the Plain that God destroyed with Sodom and Gomorrah (Gen. 19:25–29); its location may now be submerged by the southern end of the Dead Sea.

Adoraim ("two mounds"), a city in Judah built by Rehoboam (2 Chr. 11:9).

Adramyttium ("from Adramys, brother of Craesus"), a port city of Mysia in the northwestern part of the Roman province of Asia (Acts 27:2; cf. 16:7).

Adria ("from [the city] Adria of Italy"), originally a name referring to the sea east of Italy. In later times, the term included the Mediterranean between Greece and Sicily (Acts 27:27).

Adullam ("refuge"), a town of Judah near Succoth. David made the headquarters of his rebellion against Saul in a cave near this town (Josh. 12:7–15; 1 Sam. 22; 2 Sam. 23:13).

Adummim ("bloody things"), a pass from the Jordan Valley to the hill country of Judah. It is the shortest route from Jericho to Jerusalem, and may have been the setting for Jesus' parable of the good Samaritan (Josh. 15:7; cf. Luke 10:30–37).

Aenon ("fountains"), a place noted for its abundant supply of water, where John baptized his converts. Most likely this site was at

PLACES OF THE BIBLE

the head of the Valley of Shechem (John 3:23).

Ahava ("water"), a site about 14 km. (9 mi.) north of Babylon; a staging area for Jews preparing to return to Palestine (Ezra 8:15, 31).

Ahlab ("fertile"), a town assigned to Asher, but never captured from the Canaanites (Judg. 1:31); its probable location is about 6 km. (4 mi.) northeast of Tyre.

Ai [Aiath; Aija] ("heap of ruins"). **[1]** One of the strongest Canaanite cities, located east of Bethel (Josh. 7:2; Neh. 11:31). In Isaiah 10:28 the Hebrew feminine form of the name (Aiath) occurs. **[2]** A city of the Ammonites, probably located near Heshbon (Jer. 49:3).

Aijalon [Ajalon] ("place of harts"). **[1]** A town located 22.5 km. (14 mi.) northwest of Jerusalem, designated as a Levitical city (Josh. 19:42; 21:24; 2 Chr. 28:18). **[2]** A site belonging to the tribe of Zebulun west of the Sea of Galilee, where the judge Elon was buried (Judg. 12:12). Its exact location is unknown.

Ain ("eye"). **[1]** A town of Judah near Rimmon, assigned to the Levites serving the tribe of Simeon (Josh. 15:32; 19:7; 21:16; 1 Chr. 4:32). **[2]** A site on the boundary line of the Promised Land, west of Riblah (Num. 34:11). Its exact location is unknown.

Ajalon. *See* Aijalon.

Akrabbim. *See* Maaleh-acrabbim.

Alammelech ("king's oak"), a village assigned to the tribe of Asher (Josh. 19:26).

Alemeth [Almon] ("hidden"), a city given to the priests of the tribe of Benjamin (1 Chr. 6:60; Josh. 21:18). *See also* "People of the Bible."

Alexandria ("city of Alexander the Great"), a city on the Mediterranean coast of Egypt, which served as Egypt's capital city for many years (Acts 27:6; 28:11–13).

Allon ("an oak"), a town in south Naphtali (Josh. 19:33). *See also* "People of the Bible."

Almon. *See* Alemeth.

Almon-diblathaim ("hiding place of two fig sacks"), a site between the Arnon River and Shittim where the Israelites camped during their wandering in the wilderness (Num. 33:46).

Aloth ("ascents; steeps"), a district from which King Solomon drew provisions (1 Kin. 4:16).

Alush ("crowd"), a site where the Israelites camped on their journey from Egypt to Mount Sinai (Num. 33:14).

Amad ("enduring"), a frontier town of the tribe of Asher (Josh. 19:26).

Amam ("gathering place"), a village located on the Wadi-es-Sini in southern Judah (Josh. 15:26).

Amana ("forth"), a range of mountains in Lebanon, probably south of the Amana [Abana] River (Song 4:8).

Ammah ("head"), a hill in the wilderness of the Jordan Valley near Gibeon; Joab and Abner fought here (2 Sam. 2:24).

Amphipolis ("surrounded city"), the chief city of Macedonia, located in the region of Thrace (Acts 17:1).

Anab ("grape"), a town in the mountains of Judah (Josh. 11:21; 15:50).

Anaharath ("gorge"), a frontier town of the tribe of Issachar (Josh. 19:19).

Ananiah ("Jehovah has covered"), a town inhabited by the tribe of Benjamin after the Exile (Neh. 11:32). *See also* "People of the Bible."

Anathoth ("answer"), a town of the tribe of Benjamin, located about 4 km. (2.5 mi.) northeast of Jerusalem (Josh. 21:18; Ezra 2:23); the birthplace of the prophet Jeremiah (Jer. 1:1; 11:21). *See also* "People of the Bible."

Anem ("two fountains"), a city of the tribe of Issachar, assigned to the Levites (1 Chr. 6:73). It is identical with En-gannim [2].

Aner ("spout; waterfall"), a city of the tribe of Manasseh located west of the Jordan; it was assigned to the Levites (1 Chr. 6:70). *See also* "People of the Bible."

Anim ("fountains"), a town in the hills of Judah (Josh. 15:50).

Antioch ("speedy as a chariot"). **[1]** A Syrian city on the south side of the Orontes River, where the followers of Jesus were first called Christians (Acts 11:19–26). **[2]** A city of Phrygia near the border of Pisidia, visited by Paul and Barnabas on their missionary journey (Acts 13:14).

Antipatris ("for his father"), a city built on the Plain of Sharon by Herod the Great (Acts 23:31).

Aphek [Aphik] ("strength"). **[1]** A city north of Sidon (Josh. 13:4). **[2]** A town assigned to the tribe of Asher but never captured from the Canaanites; located just southeast of Accho (Josh. 19:30; Judg. 1:31). **[3]** A town on the Plain of Sharon northeast of Joppa, whose king was killed by Joshua (Josh. 12:18). **[4]** A town between Shunem and Jezreel, whose soldiers fought in the war between Saul and the Philistines (1 Sam. 28:4;

45

PLACES OF THE BIBLE

29:1, 11; 31:1). This may have been the town where Ben-hadad fought Ahab (1 Kin. 20:26–30), and where "Jehoash" of Israel would defeat the Syrians (2 Kin. 13:14–19). However, these two passages may refer to Aphek in Golan, about 5 km. (3 mi.) east of the Sea of Galilee.

Aphekah ("fortress"), a city of Judah (Josh. 15:53).

Aphrah ("house of dust"), a city of Philistia (Mic. 1:10).

Apollonia ("city of Apollo"), a Macedonian town visited by Paul on his way to Thessalonica (Acts 17:1).

Appii Forum ("marketplace of Appius"), a town in Italy about 64 km. (40 mi.) from Rome. Roman Christians met Paul here when he was brought to plead his case before Caesar (Acts 28:15).

Ar ("city"), the chief city of Moab, located on the northern boundary of Moabite territory (Num. 21:15; Is. 15:1).

Arab ("ambush"), a town in the hills of Judah east of Dumah (Josh. 15:52).

Arabah ("steppe"), the depression of land holding the Sea of Galilee and the Dead Sea (Josh. 18:18). The "valley" of Joshua 11:2 probably refers to Arabah.

ARNON RIVER. *Sometimes described as the "brook" Arnon, the mighty Arnon River carves a deep gorge that bisects the highlands east of the Dead Sea. For this reason, the Arnon is nearly always mentioned in the Bible as a frontier—first as the southern frontier of the Amorites, and later as a border of Reuben (Num. 21:13).*

ANATHOTH. *From the mound that covers the site of ancient Anathoth, one can see the modern village of Anata. Anathoth was a city of the tribe of Benjamin that was assigned to the Levites (Josh. 21:18). It was the home of the high priest Abiathar (1 Kin. 2:26), the prophet Jeremiah (Jer. 1:1), and David's famed warrior, Jehu (1 Chr. 12:3). Today the site is known as Ras el-Harrubeh; it is located about 5 km. (3 mi.) north of Jerusalem.*

Arabia ("desert"), a large peninsula bounded on the east by the Persian Gulf and the Gulf of Oman, on the west by the Red Sea, and on the south by the Indian Ocean. It was the home of many nomadic tribes, and was sometimes called the "East Country" (2 Chr. 21:16; Is. 13:20).

Arad ("wild ass"), a Canaanite city in the wilderness of Judea (Josh. 12:14). *See also* "People of the Bible."

Aram ("high"), the plain extending eastward from the Lebanon Mountains beyond the Euphrates River, occupied by the Aramaeans, mistakenly termed "Syrians" by the KJV (Num. 23:7; 1 Kin. 20:1). *See also* "People of the Bible."

Ararat ("high land"), a mountainous, hilly land in western Asia (Jer. 51:27) later known as Armenia (Is. 37:38; 2 Kin. 19:37). Noah's ark rested on mountains in this area (Gen. 8:4).

Areopagus ("hill of Ares [Mars]"), a hill west of the acropolis in Athens, where Paul addressed several Greek philosophers; also known as Mars Hill (Acts 17:19–34).

Argob ("region of clods"), a district of Bashan that was taken by King Solomon (Deut. 3:4; Josh. 13:30; 1 Kin. 4:13). *See also* "People of the Bible."

Arimathea ("heights"), the home of a businessman named Joseph, who gained permission to bury the body of Jesus (Matt. 27:57;

PLACES OF THE BIBLE

Luke 23:51). Its exact location is not known, but is generally believed to have been about 16 km. (10 mi.) northeast of Lydda on the western edge of the hill country of Ephraim. *See also* Ramah.

Armageddon (Hebrew, *Har Megiddo*—"hill of Megiddo"), the site of the final battle between Christ and Satan (Rev. 16:16). *See also* Megiddo.

Armenia. *See* Ararat.

Arnon ("rushing water"), a river that pours into the Dead Sea (Num. 21:13; Josh. 13:16).

Aroer ("naked"). **[1]** A town on the northern bank of the Arnon River (Deut. 2:36; Josh. 12:2). **[2]** A city of Gilead east of Rabbath-Ammon (Josh. 13:25). **[3]** A village of Judah about 19 km. (12 mi.) southeast of Beer-sheba (1 Sam. 30:28).

Arpad [Arphad] ("strong"), a Syrian city 20 km. (13 mi.) north of Aleppo (Is. 36:19; Jer. 49:23).

Aruboth ("windows"), a district belonging to King Solomon (1 Kin. 4:10).

Arumah ("heights"), a town near Shechem once occupied by Abimelech (Judg. 9:41).

Arvad ("wandering"), the northernmost Phoenician city, noted for its mariners (Ezek. 27:8). The modern city of Ruwad is located on this site.

Arzob. *See* Bashan.

Ashan ("smoke"), a lowland town assigned to the tribe of Judah, then to Simeon (Josh. 15:42; 19:7; 1 Chr. 4:32); probably located just northwest of Beer-sheba. It is possibly identical with Chor-ashan (q.v.).

Ashbea ("idolatry"), a place where linen workers lived (1 Chr. 4:21); its exact location is unknown.

Ashdod ("stronghold"), one of the five chief Canaanite cities; the seat of the worship of the fish god Dagon; located halfway between present-day Jaffa and Gaza (Josh. 11:22; 1 Sam. 5:1). In the N.T. the city is called Azotus (Acts 8:40).

Asher ("happy"), a town on the southern border of Manasseh (Josh. 17:7). *See also* "People of the Bible."

Ashkelon [Askelon] ("wandering"), one of the five chief Canaanite cities, the seat of the worship of the goddess Derceto; located about 19 km. (12 mi.) north of the present-day city of Gaza (Josh. 13:3; Jer. 47:5).

Ashnah ("hard; firm"). **[1]** A village in the

45

PLACES OF THE BIBLE

TELL EZ-ZAKARIYEH. *Scholars believe this mound located in the low agricultural plains along Judah's west coast is the site of the biblical Azekah. Joshua pursued the Amorites as far as Azekah (Josh. 10:10–11), and in the days of Rehoboam the city was a fortified border town (2 Chr. 11:5). Azekah was one of the last cities to fall to Nebuchadnezzar during the Babylonian invasion (Jer. 24:7).*

lowlands of Judah near Zorah (Josh. 15:33). **[2]** Another village of Judah, farther south (Josh. 15:43).

Ashtaroth. *See* Ashteroth-karnaim.

Ashteroth-karnaim ("[the goddess] Ashtaroth of the two horns"), a town of Bashan, the seat of the worship of the goddess Ashtaroth (Gen. 14:5). The city is possibly to be identified with Astaroth (Ashtaroth) (Deut. 1:4; Josh. 9:10), though this is not certain.

Asia ("eastern"), the term used by the Bible to refer to Asia Minor (1 Cor. 16:19; Acts 2:9).

Askelon. *See* Ashkelon.

Asshur [Assur] ("level plain"), a city in Assyria which was sometimes the capital, or the nation itself may be referred to (Num. 24:22, 24). *See also* "People of the Bible."

Assos ("approaching"), a seaport of Mysia, near Troas (Acts 20:13).

Assyria ("country of Assur"), a Semitic nation on the Tigris River, whose capital was Nineveh (Gen. 2:14; 2 Kin. 15:10, 20).

Atad ("a thorn"), the campsite near Hebron used by Joseph and his brothers as they prepared to take Jacob's body back to Canaan (Gen. 50:11). The new name given the site was a pun: The Canaanites saw the mourning [Hebrew, *ēbhel*] of the Egyptians and called the place *Abel* [Hebrew, *ābhel*]—"meadow"; *mizraim*—"of the Egyptians."

Ataroth ("crowns"). **[1]** A town east of the Jordan River rebuilt by the tribe of Gad (Num. 32:3, 34). **[2]** A town on the edge of the Jordan Valley at the border of Ephraim (Josh. 16:7). **[3]** The house of Joab mentioned in the genealogy of Judah (1 Chr. 2:54). The site is unknown. Some take the "House of Joab" to be part of the town's title; in Hebrew this would be Atroth-bethjoab. **[4]** *See also* Atarothaddar.

Ataroth-addar [Ataroth-adar] ("crown of Addar"), a village on the southern frontier of Ephraim (Josh. 16:5; 18:13). The town is probably to be identified with Ataroth (Josh. 16:2).

Athach ("stopping place"), a town in southern Judah, to which David sent some of the spoil of Ziklag (1 Sam. 30:30).

Athens ("city of Athena"), the greatest city of classical Greece, capital of the Greek city-state of Attica, where Paul founded a Christian church (Acts 17:15–18).

Atroth ("crowns"), a city of the tribe of Gad (Num. 32:35). Some believe Atroth and Shophan are one city and render the name Atroth-shophan. *See also* Shophan.

Attalia, a seaport of Pamphylia near Perga through which Paul and Barnabas passed after their first missionary journey (Acts 14:25).

Ava ("region"), an Assyrian city that sent settlers to colonize Samaria (2 Kin. 17:24).

Aven ("nothingness"). **[1]** Another name for the Egyptian city of On, called Heliopolis by the Greeks (Ezek. 30:17). **[2]** A valley town in the kingdom of Damascus; probably Awaniyek (Amos 1:5).

Avim, a city of the tribe of Benjamin, probably near Bethel (Josh. 18:23). Some translate "Bethel and (the village of) the Arvim," thus indicating a group of people.

Avith ("ruins"), a city of Edom, home of King Hadad (Gen. 36:35; 1 Chr. 1:46).

Azal ("noble; slope"), a place near Jerusalem (Zech. 14:5). *See also* "People of the Bible."

Azekah ("dug up place"), a city in the lowlands of Socoh, less than 32 km. (20 mi.) southwest of Jerusalem; the kings besieging Gibeon were driven here (Josh. 10:10; 1 Sam. 17:1).

Azem. *See* Ezem.

Azmaveth. *See* Beth-Azmaveth. *See also* "People of the Bible."

Azmon ("strong"), a place on the western boundary of Canaan (Num. 34:4).

Aznoth-Tabor ("peaks [ears] of Tabor"), an incline near Mount Tabor, west of Kadesh-Barnea (Josh. 19:34).

Azotus. *See* Ashdod.

Azzah. *See* Gaza.

B

Baal ("master"), a city of Simeon, identical with Baalath-beer (1 Chr. 4:33). *See also* "People of the Bible."

Baalah ("mistress"). **[1]** A Simeonite town in southern Judah (Josh. 15:29). The city is also called Bilhah (1 Chr. 4:29) and Balah in Joshua 19:3. **[2]** A hill in Judah between Ekron and Jabneel (Josh. 15:11). **[3]** *See* Kirjath-jearim.

Baalath ("mistress"), a town of the tribe of Dan, located near Gezer (Josh. 19:44; 1 Kin. 9:18; 2 Chr. 8:6).

Baalath-beer ("mistress of a well"), a border town of the tribe of Simeon, sometimes called "Ramoth (or Ramath) of the south" (Josh. 19:8). It is identical with Baal (q.v.).

Baale-judah. *See* Kirjath-jearim.

Baal-gad ("the lord of fortune; Gad is

lord"), a town at the foot of Mount Hermon that marked the northern limit of Joshua's conquest (Josh. 11:17; 12:7).

Baal-hamon ("lord of a multitude"), a place where King Solomon had a vineyard (Song 8:11); its exact location is unknown.

Baal-hazor ("lord of Hazor [enclosure]"), the place near Ephraim where Absalom had Amnon killed (2 Sam. 13:23); the probable site is about 7 km. (4.5 mi.) northeast of Bethel.

Baal-hermon ("lord of Hermon"), the site of Canaanite rituals on the eastern slope of Mount Hermon, which marked the northwest boundary of the half-tribe of Manasseh (Judg. 3:3; 1 Chr. 5:23).

Baal-meon ("lord of the house"), an Amorite city on the north border of Moab (Num. 32:38; Ezek. 25:9). The city is called Beon in Numbers 32:3, Beth-baal-meon in Joshua 13:17 and Beth-meon in Jeremiah 48:23.

Baal-perazim ("lord of breaches"), a place near the Valley of Rephaim, where King David won a battle with the Philistines (2 Sam. 5:20). It is called simply Perazim in Isaiah 28:21.

Baal-shalisha ("lord of a third part"), a village that presented food to the prophet Elisha; probably located about 22 km. (13.5 mi.) northwest of Gilgal (2 Kin. 4:42).

Baal-tamar ("lord of palms"), a place near Gibeah and Bethel in the territory of Benjamin, where the Israelites repelled the army of Gibeah (Judg. 20:33).

Baal-zephon ("lord of the North"), the site that the Israelites faced when they encamped between Migdol and the Red Sea on their Exodus from Egypt (Ex. 14:2; Num. 33:7).

Babel ("gate of God"), a city built by Nimrod on the Plain of Shinar (Gen. 10:10).

Babylon (meaning unknown). **[1]** The capital city of the Babylonian Empire, famous for its hanging gardens; a focal point of the Jewish captivity beginning in 586 B.C. (2 Kin. 17:24–25; Is. 39:3, 6–7). **[2]** Most scholars believe the references in First Peter 5:13 and Revelation 14:8; 18:2, 10–21 are to Rome. However, some believe Peter refers to [1].

Babylonia (meaning unknown). The eastern portion of the Fertile Crescent having Babylon (2 Kin. 17:24–25) for its capital. It is also called Shinar (Gen. 10:10) and the land of the Chaldeans (Jer. 24:5; Ezek. 12:13) in the Old Testament.

Baca ("weeping; balsam tree"), a valley of Palestine; possibly the Valley of Rephaim, where many balsam trees are found (Ps. 84:6).

Bahurim ("low ground"), a village near the Mount of Olives on the road from Jerusalem to the Jordan River (2 Sam. 3:16; 16:5; 17:18; 19:16).

Bajith ("house"), a Moabite city or temple (Is. 15:2).

Balah. *See* Baalah [1].

Bamah ("high place"), the reference in Ezekiel 20:29 is possibly to a prominent high place of idolatrous worship like the one at Gibeon (1 Kin. 3:4).

Bamoth ("high places"), an Israelite encampment north of the Arnon River (Num. 21:19). The city is probably the Baal of Numbers 22:41.

Bamoth-baal ("high places of Baal"). *See* Bamoth.

Bashan ("fertile plain"), a district stretching from the Upper Jordan Valley to the Arabian Desert, containing "the whole region of Arzob" (Deut. 3:4–5, 10, 13; 1 Kin. 4:13; Ps. 22:12; Ezek. 27:6; 39:18).

Bashan-havoth-jair. *See also* Havoth-jair.

Bath-rabbim ("daughter of multitudes"), a gate of Heshbon (Song 7:4).

Bealoth ("mistresses; possessors"), a village in southern Judah (Josh. 15:24).

BETH-ABARA. *John the Baptist was preaching and baptizing converts at Beth-abara when the Pharisees sent messengers to ask whether he was the Messiah. John denied that he was, but he said, ". . . There standeth one among you, whom ye know not; He it is who coming after me is preferred before me, whose shoe's latchet I am not worthy to unloose" (John 1:26–27). Today this town is known as Qasr el-Yehud.*

PLACES OF THE BIBLE

POOL OF BETHESDA. *Said to possess healing virtues, the Pool of Bethesda was located in Jerusalem near the Sheep Gate (John 5:2–4). Excavations near the Church of St. Anne in 1888 revealed this pool with five porches and a faded wall fresco depicting an angel and water. Apparently, this pool was regarded as Bethesda in the early Christian era.*

Beautiful Gate, a portion of the east gate of Jerusalem where Peter and John healed a lame man (Acts 3:2).

Beer ("a well"). **[1]** A temporary encampment of the Israelites in the wilderness (Num. 21:16–18); possibly the same as Beer-elim. **[2]** A place where Jotham sought refuge from his brother Abimelech (Judg. 9:21); possibly the same as Beeroth.

Beer-elim ("well of Elim"), a village in southern Moab (Is. 15:8).

Beer-lahai-roi [Lahai-roi] ("well of the living one who sees me"), the well of Hagar, located between Kadesh and Bered on the road to Shur, about 80 km. (50 mi.) southwest of Beer-sheba (Gen. 16:14). It is shortened to Lahai-roi in Genesis 24:62.

Beeroth ("wells"). **[1]** A place on the border of Edom where the wandering Israelites camped; also called Beeroth, Bene-Jaakan, or Bene-jaakan (Deut. 10:6; Num. 33:31). **[2]** A city of Gibeon assigned to the tribe of Benjamin (Josh. 9:17; 18:25).

Beer-sheba ("well of oaths"), a city in southern Judah, site of Abraham's covenant with Abimelech; it is located about 45 km. (28 mi.) southwest of Hebron (Gen. 21:14, 22–31; Josh. 15:28).

Beeshterah ("temple of Ashterah"). *See* Ashtaroth-Karnaim.

Bela [Belah] ("destroying"), one of the Cities of the Plain, probably Zoar (Gen. 14:2). *See also* "People of the Bible."

Bene-berak ("sons of lightning"), a town of the tribe of Dan, about 6 km. (4 mi.) east of modern Jaffa (Josh. 19:45).

Bene-jaakan ("sons of Jaakan"). *See* Beeroth [1].

Beon ("house of On"). *See* Baal-meon.

Berachah ("blessing"), a valley in Judah near Tekoa, named by Jehoshaphat (2 Chr. 20:26). *See also* "People of the Bible."

Berea ("watered"), a city in Macedonia about 80 km. (50 mi.) west of Thessalonica (Acts 17:10); now called Verria, or Salonica.

Bered ("hail"), a place in the wilderness of Shur in southern Palestine, not far from Kadesh (Gen. 16:14). *See also* "People of the Bible."

Berothah [Berothai; Chun] ("of a well"), a town in northern Palestine between Hamath and Damascus, captured by David; also called Chun (2 Sam. 8:8; 1 Chr. 18:8; Ezek. 47:16).

Besor ("cold"), a brook south of Ziklag (1 Sam. 30:9–10, 21).

PLACES OF THE BIBLE

Betah ("confidence"), a city of Amam-Zobah (2 Sam. 8:8). It is identical with Tibhath (q.v.).

Beten ("valley"), a village of the tribe of Asher (Josh. 19:25); Eusebius noted that it was about 12 km. (7.5 mi.) east of Accho.

Beth-abara ("house at the ford"), a place on the eastern side of the Jordan River where John the Baptist baptized his converts (John 1:28). The majority of Greek manuscripts read Bethany here instead; however, this city was not identical with Bethany proper.

Beth-anath [Beth-anoth] ("house of reply"). [1] A fortress town of the tribe of Naphtali (Josh. 19:38; Judg. 1:33). [2] A town in the mountains of Judah, about 6 km. (4 mi.) from Hebron (Josh. 15:59).

Bethany ("house of affliction; place of unripe figs"), a settlement on the hill leading to the Mount of Olives, about 2.6 km. (1.6 mi.) from Jerusalem (Mark 11:1; Luke 19:29).

Beth-arabah ("house of the desert"), a village in the Judean wilderness on the boundary between the territories of Judah and Benjamin (Josh. 15:6, 61; 18:22).

Beth-aram [Beth-haran] ("house of the heights"), a town of the tribe of Gad, located in the Jordan Valley and noted for its hot springs (Num. 32:36; Josh. 13:27).

Beth-arbel ("house of ambush"), a town destroyed by Shalman (Hos. 10:14). Now known as Irbid, it is located about 6 km. (4 mi.) west-northwest of Tiberias.

Beth-aven ("house of idols"), a town of the tribe of Benjamin, located in the wilderness near Ai (Josh. 7:2; 18:12; 1 Sam. 13:5).

Beth-azmaveth ("house of Azmaveth"), a town near Jerusalem, halfway between Geba and Anathoth; perhaps the same as Hizmeh (Neh. 7:28). It is also called simply Azmaveth (Ezra 2:24; Neh. 12:29).

Beth-baal-meon ("Baal's dwelling place"). *See also* Baal-meon.

Beth-barah, a place in the vicinity of the Jordan Valley, possibly a ford or crossing near the confluence of the Jordan and the Wadi Farah (Judg. 7:24).

Beth-birei [Beth-biri] ("house of my creation"), a town of the tribe of Simeon (1 Chr. 4:31); perhaps the same as Bethlebaoth (q.v.).

Beth-car ("house of the lamb"), a Philistine stronghold in Judah, site of a battle between the Israelites and the Philistines (1 Sam. 7:11).

Beth-dagon ("house of Dagon"). [1] A town located on the border between Asher and Zebulun (Josh. 19:27); probably modern Jelamet el-Atika at the foot of Mount Carmel. [2] A town in the Judean lowlands (Josh. 15:33, 41); possibly modern Khirbet Dajun.

Beth-diblathaim ("house of fig cakes"), a town in Moab (Jer. 48:21–22); possibly the same as Almon-diblathaim (q.v.).

Beth-el [Bethel] ("house of God"). [1] A town located about 18 km. (11 mi.) north of Jerusalem; an important site throughout the history of Israel (cf. Gen. 13:3; 28:18–19; Josh. 16:2; Judg. 21:19). It was formerly called Luz. The modern town of Bertin is located near the ruins. [2] *See also* Bethuel.

Beth-emek ("house of the valley"), a town near the border of Asher; it is bounded on the north side by the ravine of Jiphtah-el (Josh. 19:27). The modern name of this site is Amkah.

Bether. Many scholars believe the text of The Song of Solomon 2:17 should read "rugged mountains" instead of Bether. Others suggest the reference is to "the hills where the spice [cinnamon?] grows."

Bethesda ("house of outpouring or overflowing water"), a pool near the Sheep Gate of Jerusalem reputed to have healing qualities (John 5:2–3).

Beth-ezel ("a place near"), a town of southern Judah (Micah 1:11); present-day Deil el-'Asal.

Beth-gader ("house of walls"), a town of Judah founded by Hareph (1 Chr. 2:51).

Beth-gamul ("camel house"), a city of Moab about 10 km. (6 mi.) east of Dibon (Jer. 48:23).

Beth-haccerem ("house of vines"), a town of Judah that maintained a beacon station (Neh. 3:14; Jer. 6:1); probably present-day 'Ain Karim, 7 km. (4 mi.) west of Jerusalem.

Beth-haran. *See* Beth-aram.

Beth-hogla [Beth-hoglah] ("partridge house"), a Benjamite village about 6 km. (4 mi.) southeast of Jericho (Josh. 15:6; 18:19, 21).

Beth-horon ("cave house"), twin towns located on the boundary between the territories of Ephraim and Benjamin. Upper Beth-horon was situated on a mountain pass between Jerusalem and the plain to the west. Lower Beth-horon was about 2 km. (1.5 mi.) farther northwest (Josh. 16:3; 18:13; 2 Chr. 8:5; 1 Kin. 9:17). The modern names for these towns are Beit 'Ur et Tahta (Lower) and Beit 'Ur el Foka (Upper).

Beth-jeshimoth [Beth-jesimoth] ("house

45

PLACES OF THE
BIBLE

RUINS OF CAESAREA. *Built by Herod the Great, this magnificent city stood on the Mediterranean shore of Palestine. Named in honor of Augustus Caesar, it was a celebrated trading center and seaport. Paul departed from Caesarea on his way to Tarsus, having escaped his Jewish enemies in Damascus (Acts 9:30).*

of deserts"), a town in Moab near the Dead Sea (Num. 33:49; Josh. 12:3).

Beth-lebaoth ("house of lionesses"), a town of southern Judah assigned to the tribe of Simeon (Josh. 19:6). The city is also known as Lebaoth (Josh. 15:32). It is perhaps identical with Beth-birei (q.v.).

Bethlehem ("house of bread"). **[1]** A town about 10 km. (6 mi.) south of Jerusalem; birthplace of Jesus Christ (Matt. 2:5) and Ephrath (Gen. 35:16, 19; Ruth 4:11; cf. Mic. 5:2). Only in later times was it known as Bethlehem. It was originally called Ephratah (Ephrath) (Gen. 35:16; Ruth 4:11). **[2]** A city of the tribe of Zebulun located about 11 km. (7 mi.) northwest of Nazareth (Josh. 19:15). *See also* "People of the Bible."

Beth-maachah. *See also* Abel-beth-maachah.

Beth-marcaboth ("house of chariots"), a city in the Negeb near Ziklag (Josh. 19:5).

Beth-meon ("dwelling place"). *See also* Baal-meon.

Beth-nimrah ("house of the leopardess"), a fortified city built by the tribe of Gad east of the Jordan River (Num. 32:36); also called Nimrah (Num. 32:3).

Beth-palet [Beth-phelet] ("house of escape"), a town in the southernmost part of Judah (Josh. 15:27; Neh. 11:26); probably modern el-Meshash.

Beth-pazzez ("house of dispersion"), a town of the tribe of Issachar (Josh. 19:21); its modern name is Kerm el-Haddatheh.

Beth-peor ("house of Peor"), a site near Pisgah where the Israelites placed their main camp while warring against Og (Deut. 3:29; 4:46).

Bethphage ("house of unripe figs"), a settlement near Bethany on the road from Jerusalem to Jericho, probably at the descent from the Mount of Olives (Matt. 21:1; Mark 11:1).

Beth-rapha. *See also* "People of the Bible."

Beth-rehob ("place of a street" [or market]), a town of the Upper Jordan Valley (Judg. 18:28; 2 Sam. 10:6). The city is called Rehob (Num. 13:21).

Bethsaida ("fish house"), a fishing town on the Sea of Galilee; birthplace of Philip, Andrew, and Simon (Matt. 11:21; Luke 9:10; Mark 6:45).

Beth-shean [Beth-shan] ("house of rest"), the southern border town of the region of Galilee; largest of the ten cities of the Decapolis (Josh. 17:11; 1 Chr. 7:29).

Beth-shemesh ("house of the sun"). **[1]** A town on the road from Ashkelon and Ashdod to Jerusalem; it is located about 38 km. (24 mi.) west of Jerusalem (Josh. 15:10). **[2]** A Canaanite city in the territory of Naphtali (Josh. 19:38; Judg. 1:33). **[3]** A city of the tribe of Issachar, probably on the Jordan River near the Sea of Galilee (Josh. 19:22). **[4]** Another name for the Egyptian city of Heliopolis (Jer. 43:13).

Beth-shittah ("house of acacia"), a town of the Jordan Valley between Jezreel and Zererah, noted for its acacia trees (Judg. 7:22).

Beth-tappuah ("house of apricots"), a settlement in the hills of Judah about 8 km. (5 mi.) west of Hebron (Josh. 15:53).

Bethuel [Bethul] ("dweller of God"), a town apportioned to the tribe of Simeon (Josh. 19:4; 1 Chr. 4:30). The town was also called Bethel (1 Sam. 30:27). *See also* "People of the Bible."

Beth-zur ("house of rock"), a city in the hill country of Judah, fortified during the era of Rehoboam (Josh. 15:58; 2 Chr. 11:7). *See also* "People of the Bible."

Betonim ("bellies"), a town assigned to the tribe of Gad (Josh. 13:26).

Beulah ("married"), Isaiah's name for the Promised Land after the Babylonian Captivity (Is. 62:4).

Bezek ("lightning"). **[1]** A town near Jerusalem (Judg. 1:4–5). **[2]** The place where Saul assembled his army (1 Sam. 11:8).

Bezer ("fortress"), a fortified city within the territory of Reuben (Deut. 4:43; Josh. 20:8); probably present-day Umm el-'Amad, about 9 km. (5.5 mi.) east of Heshbon. *See also* "People of the Bible."

Bileam ("foreigners"), a settlement on the western side of the Jordan River assigned to the tribe of Manasseh (1 Chr. 6:70).

Bilhah. *See* Baalah [1]. *See also* "People of the Bible."

Bithron ("ravine"), a gorge in the Aravah east of the Jordan River (2 Sam. 2:29).

Bithynia ("violent rainfall"), a country of northwestern Asia Minor, bounded on the north by the Black Sea (Acts 16:7; 1 Pet. 1:1).

Bizjothjah (meaning uncertain), a town in the southernmost portion of Judah (Josh. 15:28).

Bochim ("weepers"), a site near Gilgal where the Israelites repented of their sins (Judg. 2:1–5).

Bohan ("thumb; stumpy"). The "stone of Bohan" was a boundary mark separating the NE frontier of Judah from Benjamin. The site is uncertain (Josh. 18:17). *See also* "People of the Bible."

Boscath. *See* Bozkath.

Bozez ("shining"), the name of two crags near Geba; the northernmost crag faces Michmash (1 Sam. 14:4).

Bozkath [Boscath] ("craggy"), a town near Lachish in southern Judah (Josh. 15:39; 2 Kin. 22:1).

Bozrah ("stronghold"). [1] The capital of Edom (Gen. 36:33; 1 Chr. 1:44). [2] A city of Moab; probably Bezer (Jer. 48:24).

Brook of the Willows. *See* Willows, Brook of the.

C

Cabbon ("understanding"), a town of lowland Judah (Josh. 15:40). *See also* Machbenah in "People of the Bible."

Cabul ("displeasing; obscurity"). [1] A town of the tribe of Asher noted for its dry climate (Josh. 19:27). [2] A district of Galilee; the northern part of the territory of Naphtali (1 Kin. 19:13).

Caesarea [Caesarea Maritima] ("city of Caesar"), coastal city of Palestine that served as capital of the Roman province (Acts 8:40). Built by Herod the Great, it is located 37 km. (23 mi.) from the foot of Mount Carmel; also called Caesarea Maritima.

CILICIAN GATES. *This deep cleft in the Taurus Mountains leads from Asia Minor to the fertile plain of Cilicia, in what is now Turkey. Paul probably passed through the Cilician Gates on his second and third missionary journeys.*

Caesarea Philippi ("Caesar's city of Philippi"), a town located at the foot of Mount Hermon; the northernmost extent of Jesus' ministry (Matt. 16:13–20).

Cain, a town in the hill country of Judah (Josh. 15:57). *See also* "People of the Bible."

Calah ("old age"), a city built by Nimrod that later became the capital of the Assyrian Empire; located about 29 km. (18 mi.) south of Nineveh (Gen. 10:11).

Caleb-ephratah, the place where Hezron died (1 Chr. 2:24). Many scholars translate the verse: "after the death of Hezron, Caleb went in to Ephrathah, the wife of Hezron his father, and she bore him Ashhur, the father of Tekoa" (RSV) following the LXX. *See also* Ephratah in "People of the Bible."

Calneh ("fortress"). [1] A Babylonian city belonging to Nimrod (Gen. 10:10). [2] A city located about 10 km. (6 mi.) from Arpad (Amos 6:2); probably the present-day Kullani.

Calno ("futility"), a city conquered by the Assyrians (Is. 10:9); probably the same as Calneh [2].

Calvary. *See* Golgotha.

Camon ("standing place"), the place Jair was buried (Judg. 10:5).

Cana ("reeds"), a village of Galilee where Jesus performed the miracle of changing water into wine. It is located 16 km. (10 mi.) northeast of Nazareth (John 2:1, 11; 4:46).

Canaan ("purple"), the native name of Palestine, the land given to Abraham and his descendants (Gen. 11:31; Ex. 6:4). *See also* "People of the Bible."

Canneh ("distinguished"), a town on the southern coast of Arabia (Ezek. 27:23); present-day Canne.

Capernaum ("village of Nahum"), a town

Corinth at the Crossroads

Corinth rose from ashes to occupy a position of prominence at the trading crossroads of the ancient world. The original city was destroyed in 146 B.C. in a Greek revolt against the Roman Empire. Rebuilt in the time of Julius Caesar (*ca.* 46 B.C.), Corinth soon regained its former position as a center of commerce. Within 21 years, this rapidly growing metropolis became the capital of the province of Achaia in Greece.

Corinth was one of the wealthiest and most influential cities of its time. Located on a narrow strip of land between mainland Greece and the Peloponnesus (the peninsula of southern Greece), Corinth had two main harbors, which gave the city access to the Aegean and Ionian seas. This strategic location allowed Corinth to control the traffic of the eastern and western seas, along a principal trade route of the Roman Empire. Corinth was the fourth largest city of the empire (after Rome, Alexandria, and Antioch), and had a population of nearly half a million.

Corinth was also situated at a cultural crossroads. Residents migrated to this rapidly developing area from every corner of the Mediterranean world. Egyptians, Syrians, Orientals, and Jews who settled there brought a wide variety of cultural influences.

One might well call ancient Corinth a "sin city." While rather low moral values were held by the general Roman public, Corinth had a reputation for embracing the lowest of the low. Even prior to the time of the apostle Paul, "to live like a Corinthian" was a slang phrase denoting loose, immoral conduct.

Oddly, religion contributed to this atmosphere of moral corruption. Many of the fertility cults that existed in the city included acts of magic and sexual perversion as part of their "worship." Corinth's temple of Aphrodite, the goddess of love, at one time had one thousand priestess-prostitutes within its confines.

To this complex city came the Apostle Paul. Arriving around A.D. 52, Paul remained there for about a year and a half, ministering to one of the greatest churches of Jesus Christ. A city at the crossroads, both physically and spiritually, Corinth heard the gospel of Christ through Paul's ministry.

Corinth was rebuilt after earthquakes in 1858 and 1928. The Doric columns of one old temple of Apollo are one of the few reminders of Corinth's early days left above the ground. Corinth today has a population of about 20,000. It is still an important sea town, with exports of olive oil, silk, and currants, which take their name from the city.

on the northwest shore of the Sea of Galilee; an important center of Jesus' ministry (Matt. 4:13; Luke 4:31).

Caphtor ("isle"), the island or seacoast region from which the Philistines originally

came (Jer. 47:4; Amos 9:7); probably Crete and other nearby islands.

Cappadocia ("five horses"), a Roman district in eastern Asia Minor (Acts 2:9; 1 Pet. 1:1).

CARAVAN OF DEDANITES. *These Arabs are descendants of Dedan, the grandson of Abraham mentioned in Genesis 25:3. The Dedanites figured prominently in the trade and commerce of the Ancient Near East.*

PLACES OF THE BIBLE

Carchemish [Charchemish] ("city [fortress] of Chemosh"), a city west of the Euphrates River; the eastern capital of the Hittites (2 Chr. 35:20; Is. 10:9; Jer. 46:2).

Carmel ("orchard"). [1] A string of mountains that run about 24 km. (15 mi.) through central Palestine and jut into the Mediterranean Sea (Jer. 46:18). [2] A town in the mountains of Judah about 14 km. (9 mi.) south-southeast of Hebron (Josh. 15:55; 1 Sam. 25:5); modern Kermel. [3] *See* Rachal.

Casiphia, an unidentified place in Babylon to which Ezra sent for ministers of the house of God (Ezra 8:17).

Cedron. *See* Kidron.

Cenchrea ("millet"), a harbor about 11 km. (7 mi.) east of Corinth, visited by Paul (Acts 18:18).

Chaldea ("demons"), the southern region of the Babylonian Empire (Jer. 50:10; Ezek. 11:24).

Champaign, a word derived from the Latin campus, a field. The Hebrew text reads Arabah (Deut. 11:30).

Charashim [Charran] ("ravine of craftsmen"), a valley that ran along the back of the Plain of Sharon, east of modern Jaffa (1 Chr. 4:14). Compare Nehemiah 11:35, where the valley is called Charran.

Charran. Greek form of Haran (q.v.). *See* Charashim.

Chebar ("strength"), a river of Chaldea; the Jewish exiles, including Ezekiel, lived along its banks (Ezek. 1:3).

Chephar-haammonai ("village of the Ammonites"), a town assigned to the tribe of Benjamin (Josh. 18:24); probably modern Khirbet Kafr 'Ana, east of Jifna.

Chephirah ("town"), a city of Gibeon given to the tribe of Benjamin (Josh. 9:17); modern Kefireh, located 13 km. (8 mi.) west-northwest of Jerusalem.

Cherith ("gorge"), a small stream east of the Jordan River, where birds fed the prophet Elijah (1 Kin. 17:3–5).

Cherub, a place in Babylonia (Ezra 2:59; Neh. 7:61).

Chesalon ("hopes"), a town on Mount Jearim of Judah, about 16 km. (10 mi.) west of Jerusalem (Josh. 15:10).

Chesil ("fool"), a village in the southernmost portion of Judah (Josh. 15:3); perhaps the same as Bethuel (q.v.).

Chesulloth ("loins"), a town 6 km. (4 mi.) southeast of Nazareth in the territory of Issachar (Josh. 19:18).

MOUNT GERIZIM AND MOUNT EBAL. *As the Israelites prepared to enter the Promised Land, Joshua gathered them in front of Gerizim (1) and Ebal (2) to hear him read the Law of Moses (Josh. 8:30–35). The two mountains form a natural amphitheater, where thousands of people could have listened to Joshua's voice.*

Chezib. *See* Achzib.

Chidon [Nachon] ("javelin"), the place where Uzzah was struck dead for touching the ark of the covenant (1 Chr. 13:9); in Second Samuel 6:6 the place is called Nachon. Its exact location is unknown.

Chilmad ("closed"), a nation on the Euphrates River that traded with Tyre (Ezek. 27:23).

Chinnereth [Chinneroth; Cinneroth] ("harps"). [1] Another name for the Sea of Galilee (Num. 34:11; Josh. 12:3). [2] A city on the north shore of the Sea of Galilee (Deut. 3:17). [3] The region surrounding the city of Chinnereth (1 Kin. 15:20).

Chios ("open"), an island of the Greek chain at the entrance to the Gulf of Smyrna (Acts 20:15).

Chisloth-tabor ("loins of tabor"), a city of Zebulun at the foot of Mount Tabor (Josh. 19:12). It is perhaps identical with Tabor [2].

Chittim, the island of Cyprus (Is. 23:1, 12). The term referred in a more general way to the coastlands of the Mediterranean (Jer. 2:10). The ships of Chittim in Daniel 11:30 probably refer to Rome. *See also* Kittim in "People of the Bible."

Chor-ashan ("smoking furnace"), a town in Judah given to Simeon (1 Sam. 30:30). It is possibly identical with Ashan (q.v.).

Chorazin ("secret"), a coastal city of the Sea of Galilee where Jesus Christ performed many miracles (Matt. 11:21; Luke 10:13).

PLACES OF THE BIBLE

Chozeba ("untruthful"), a village of Judah inhabited by the descendants of Shelah (1 Chr. 4:22); probably the same as Achzib [1].

Chub. Many scholars believe this is a textual error and should be read as in the LXX, "Lub," i.e., Libya (q.v.) (Ezek. 30:5).

Chun ("founding"). *See* Berothah.

Cilicia ("rolling"), a district of southeast Asia Minor. Paul was born in Tarsus, the principal city of this district (Acts 21:39).

Cities of Refuge, six Levitical cities set aside as sanctuaries for certain criminals: Bezer, Ramoth-gilead, Golan, Kedesh, Shechem, and Kirjath-arbu (Deut. 4:41–43; Josh. 20:7–9).

Cities of the Plain, five cities located on the Plain of Jordan: Sodom, Gomorrah, Admah, Zeboim, and Zoar (Gen. 10:19; 13:10).

City of David. [1] Jebusite city of Zion captured by David's men. David made it his royal city and renamed it Jerusalem (2 Sam. 5:6–9; 1 Chr. 11:5, 7). [2] *See* Bethlehem.

Jerusalem and History

The most famous city in Bible lands is Jerusalem. From early times it was an important center. For example, Abram gave gifts to Melchizedek, who was the "king of Salem" (Gen. 14:18). This "Salem" was most likely the city of Jerusalem.

When the Israelites conquered the Promised Land, Benjamin's tribe was assigned the territory that included Jerusalem. But the invading armies were not strong enough to capture the city, and it was not until King David's time that Jerusalem finally became Hebrew territory (2 Sam. 5:6–7). David made the city his capital. He brought the ark of the covenant there, pitched a suitable tent for it, and began planning a temple to house the ark. His son Solomon completed the job (2 Sam. 7:12–16 and 1 Kin. 5—6).

Later kings neglected both the temple and the city of Jerusalem. But at the height of its glory, Jerusalem was a showplace of the nation and the temple was world-famous. The greatest era in the history of the city and temple was under Solomon.

The city was protected by God when the national leaders worshiped Him and trusted Him. When Sennacherib attempted to destroy it, the Assyrian army was destroyed by a miracle from God (2 Kin. 19:35–37).

In 587 B.C., Nebuchadnezzar of Babylon invaded Palestine, overran the city, and took the people away as slaves. The expensive treasures that were housed in the city and the many skilled craftsmen who maintained the valuable works of art and architectural design, are described in 2 Kin. 24:10–17.

For 50 years the city of Jerusalem lay in waste, but in 537 B.C. Zerubbabel and 50,000 followers were allowed to return and start rebuilding (Ezra 2:64–65; 3:8). Nehemiah rebuilt the walls of Jerusalem in about 444 B.C. (Neh. 6:15). Slowly, the Hebrews returned from their captivity and worked at rebuilding other sections of their city. Other strong nations arose—the Greeks under Alexander the Great, the Egyptians, and the Persians. In 198 B.C., Jerusalem became a part of the Seleucid empire. Judas Maccabee, one of Israel's greatest heros, retook the city in 165 B.C. and purified the temple.

In 63 B.C., Roman armies swept through Palestine and captured Jerusalem, ruining what was left of Zerubbabel's attempts to rebuild the temple. However, in 37 B.C., Herod the Great began rebuilding the temple on a grand scale; his work was so complex that the temple wasn't complete when Jesus was taken there as a baby (Luke 2:21–39). The end of Jerusalem's history in biblical times came when Titus, the Roman emperor, leveled the city and temple in A.D. 70.

Despite the troubled history of the "holy city," it still stands as a symbol of the Jewish people. "Zion" is one name given to it (although this really refers to one of the several hills around Jerusalem). The Bible calls the city by various names of honor: "city of David" (2 Sam. 5:7); "city of God" (Ps. 46:4); "city of truth" (Zec. 8:3); "holy city" (Neh. 11:1); "throne of the Lord" (Jer. 3:17) and many more.

The Egyptian pharaoh's daughter visited Solomon there (1 Kin. 3:1); the Queen of Sheba also visited (1 Kin. 10:1–2). Many events of Jesus' earthly ministry occurred there: Palm Sunday, the meal in an upper room, the trials and death of Christ, and His appearance after the Resurrection (Luke 24:33ff).

In both Hebrews and Revelation, Jerusalem symbolizes the future hope of Christians who are faithful. The fact that heaven is called the "New Jerusalem" (Rev. 21:2) shows that eternal life will be beautiful and wonderful, even as a perfect Jerusalem would be (Heb. 12:22; Rev. 21:10; 22:19).

Even today, Jerusalem is a center for historical study and international struggle. Three world religions claim it as a holy city—Islam, Judaism, and Christianity.

City of Salt, a city in the wilderness of Judah near En-gedi (Josh. 15:62).

Clauda ("lamentable"), an island southwest of Crete passed by Paul during his journey to Rome (Acts 27:16).

Cnidus ("age"), a city on the southwestern coast of Asia Minor near the Isle of Cos passed by Paul on his journey to Rome (Acts 27:7).

Colosse [Colossae] ("punishment"), a city in the district of Phrygia in Asia Minor (Col. 1:2).

Coos, an island between Rhodes and Miletus (Acts 21:1).

Corinth ("ornament"), a Greek city located on the isthmus between the Pelopennesus and mainland Greece, about 64 km. (40 mi.) west of Athens (Acts 18:1; 1 Cor. 1:2).

Corner Gate, a gate near the northwest corner of the wall of Jerusalem (2 Kin. 14:13).

Crete ("carnal"), a large island southeast of Greece (Titus 1:5).

Cush ("black"), the area of the Upper Nile south of Egypt; traditional homeland of the descendants of Ham (Gen. 10:6–8). *See also* "People of the Bible."

Cushan, the name of a place or people, possibly Midian (Hab. 3:7).

Cuth ("burning"), a Babylonian city (2 Kin. 17:30); present-day Tell Ibrahim, northeast of Babylon.

Cyprus ("fairness"), an island in the northeastern Mediterranean Sea about 96 km. (60 mi.) east of Syria (Acts 13:4; 15:39).

Cyrene ("wall"), a city of Libya in northern Africa (Matt. 27:32); probably modern Shahhat.

D

Dabbasheth ("camel hump"), a border town of the tribe of Zebulun (Josh. 19:11).

Daberath [Dabareh] ("pasture"), a city of the tribe of Issachar, assigned to the Levites (Josh. 19:12; 1 Chr. 6:72); probably modern Daburiyeh at the western base of Mount Tabor. The KJV renders the same Hebrew word as Dabareh in Joshua 21:28.

Dale, the King's. *See* Shaveh.

Dalmanutha ("bucket"), a fishing village on the western coast of the Sea of Galilee (Mark 8:10).

Dalmatia ("deceitful"), a province of Illyricum on the eastern shore of the Adriatic Sea; noted for its wild inhabitants (Rom. 15:19; 2 Tim. 4:10). Dalmatia later became the official name of the province.

Damascus ("sackful of blood"), an important Syrian trade center; Paul was converted on the road from Jerusalem to this city (Gen. 14:15; Acts 9:2).

Dan ("judge"), a town of the tribe of Dan in the northwest portion of Palestine (Josh. 19:47; Judg. 20:1). *See also* "People of the Bible."

Dan-jaan ("judgment"), a place or city between Gilead and Sidon; possibly Dan (2 Sam. 24:6).

Dannah ("judging"), a small village in the hill country of Judah (Josh. 15:49); modern Deir esh-Shemsh or Simya.

Dead Sea. *See* Salt Sea.

Debir ("oracle"). **[1]** A town in the hill country of Judah assigned to the Levites (Josh. 15:15). The city is also called Kirjath-sannah (Josh. 15:49) and Kirjath-sepher (Judg. 1:11–13). **[2]** A town near the Valley of Achor, probably on the road between Jerusalem and Jericho (Josh. 15:7). **[3]** A border town of the tribe of Gad, located east of the Jordan River near Mahanaim (Josh. 13:26).

Decapolis ("ten cities"), a league of ten cities forming a Roman district on the Plain of Esdraelon and the Upper Jordan Valley (Matt. 4:25).

Dedan ("low"), a district near Edom between Sela and the Dead Sea (Jer. 25:23; Ezek. 25:13). Isaiah 21:13 mentions the "caravans of the Dedanim" in the wilds of Arabia. *See also* "People of the Bible."

Derbe ("sting"), a city of southeastern Asia Minor, where Paul sought refuge after being stoned at Lystra (Acts 14:6–20).

Diblath ("round cake"), a place or city in Palestine (Ezek. 6:14); its exact location is unknown, but it was probably Riblah [1].

Dibon [Dimon; Dimonah] ("wasting"). **[1]** A city of the tribe of Gad located north of the Arnon River (Num. 21:30; 32:3; Is. 15:2, 9); the famous Moabite Stone was found here in 1868. **[2]** A village of Judah, also known as Dimonah (Neh. 11:25; Josh. 15:22).

Dibon Gad ("wasting of Gad"), a halting place of the Israelites leaving Egypt (Num. 33:45–46). It is probably the same as Dibon [1].

Dilean ("cucumber"), a city in the lowlands of Judah (Josh. 15:38).

Dimnah ("dung"). *See* Rimmon [3].

Dimon. *See* Dibon.

Dimonah. *See* Dibon [2].

Dinhabah ("give judgment"), a city belonging to the king of Edom (Gen. 36:32); its exact location is unknown.

Dizahab ("have gold"), a place near where Moses gave his farewell speech to the nation of Israel (Deut. 1:1); its exact location is unknown, but it may be Edh-Dheilbeh, east of Heshbon.

Dophkah ("drover"), a place in the wilderness of Sinai between the Red Sea and Rephidim (Num. 33:12–13).

Dor ("dwelling"), a Canaanite town on the Mediterranean coast about 13 km. (8 mi.) north of Caesarea (Josh. 11:2; 12:23).

Dothan ("two wells"), a city of the tribe of Manasseh west of the Jordan River and northeast of Samaria, near Mount Gilboa; here Joseph was sold into slavery (Gen. 37:17; 2 Kin. 6:13).

Dragon Well [Jackal's Well], a well located between the Dung Gate and the Valley Gate of Jerusalem (Neh. 2:13).

Dumah ("silence"). **[1]** A town in Judah (Josh. 15:52). **[2]** A symbolic name of Edom or a place in Arabia (Is. 21:11). *See also* "People of the Bible."

Dung Gate, a gate in the southwest wall of Jerusalem (Neh. 2:13; 12:31).

Dura ("fortress"), the Babylonian plain where King Nebuchadnezzar set up a golden idol (Dan. 3:1).

E

East Land [East Country; Dawn Land], a general reference to all of the lands east of Palestine; sometimes used to refer specifically to the Arabian and Syrian Deserts (Zech. 8:7).

East Sea. *See* Salt Sea.

Ebal ("stone"), a mountain beside Mount Gerizim (Deut. 27:12–13); modern Jebel Es-lamiyeh. *See also* "People of the Bible."

Eben-ezer ("stone of help"). **[1]** The site of the defeat of Israel by the Philistines (1 Sam. 4:1–22). It was in the north of Sharon near Aphek. **[2]** Name of a stone Samuel erected to commemorate his victory over the Philistines (1 Sam. 7:12). The stone was possibly named after [1] to give the idea that Israel's defeat there had been reversed.

Ebez. *See* Abez.

Ebronah ("passage; opposite"), a stopping place for the Israelites in the wilderness just north of Ezion-geber on the Gulf of Aqabah (Num. 33:34–35).

Eden ("pleasure"). **[1]** The garden that God created as the first residence of man (Gen. 2:15); its exact location is unknown. It may have been between the Tigris and Euphrates Rivers near the head of the Persian Gulf. **[2]** A region in Mesopotamia (2 Kin. 19:12; Is. 37:12). *See also* "People of the Bible."

Eder [Edar] ("flock"). **[1]** A tower or possibly a town between Bethlehem and Hebron; Jacob once camped near here (Gen. 35:21). **[2]** A town of southern Judah about 7 km. (4.5 mi.) south of Gaza (Josh. 15:21); modern el-Adar. *See also* "People of the Bible."

Edom ("red"), a mountainous region south of Moab, which stretches from the Dead Sea to the Gulf of Aqabah. It was settled by the Edomites (Gen. 32:3; Ex. 15:15). *See also* "People of the Bible."

Edrei ("fortress"). **[1]** The capital of Bashan; site of Israel's battle with Og (Deut. 3:10; Josh. 12:4). **[2]** A city of Naphtali between Kedesh and En-hazor (Josh. 19:37).

Eglaim ("pond"), a town of Moab (Is. 15:8).

Eglon ("of a calf"), a town in the lowlands of Judah (Josh. 15:39); its exact location is unknown. *See also* "People of the Bible."

Egypt ("land of the soul of Ptah"), northeast corner of Africa where the Israelites were held in bondage until Moses led them to the Promised Land (Gen. 45:9; 47:6).

Ekron ("migration"), the northernmost of the five chief cities of Philistia, apportioned to the tribe of Judah (Josh. 13:3); present-day 'Akir, located 10 km. (6 mi.) west of Gezer.

Elah ("oak" or "terebinth"), a valley mentioned in First Samuel 17:2. Possibly the Wadi es-Sunt ("valley of the terebinth") or part of its intended. Es-Sunt is 11 mi. southwest of Jerusalem. *See also* "People of the Bible."

Elath [Eloth] ("terebinth tree"), a major port city of the Gulf of Elath or Aqaba on the Red Sea (Deut. 2:8).

El-beth-el ("God of Bethel"), name Jacob gave the scene of his vision at Luz (Bethel) (Gen. 35:7).

Elealeh ("ascent of God"), a town of the tribe of Reuben about 3 km. (2 mi.) north-northeast of Heshbon (Num. 32:3); modern el-Al.

Eleph ("ox"), a city of the tribe of Benjamin, near Jerusalem (Josh. 18:28).

Elim ("oaks"), the second resting place of the Israelites after they crossed the Red Sea (Ex. 15:27; 16:1); probably the modern oasis of Wadi Gharandel, located 101 km. (63 mi.) from Suez.

Elkosh (meaning unknown), the birthplace of Nahum the prophet (Nah. 1:1).

Ellasar ("oak"), a city of lower Babylonia, formerly known as Larsa (Gen. 14:1, 9); present-day Senkereh.

Elon ("oak; terebinth tree"), a city assigned to the tribe of Dan (Josh. 19:43); its exact location is unknown. *See also* "People of the Bible."

Elon-Beth-Hanan ("oak of the house of grace"), one of three towns of the tribe of Dan that formed a district of King Solomon (1 Kin. 4:9).

Eloth. *See* Elath.

El-Paran. ("oak of Paran"). *See* Paran.

Eltekeh ("grace"), a town of the tribe of Dan assigned to the Levites (Josh. 19:40, 44; 21:20, 23); probably modern Khirbet el-Mukanna, located about 10 km. (6 mi.) south-southeast of Akir (Ekron).

Eltekon (meaning uncertain), a village in the hill country of Judah (Josh. 15:59); probably modern Khirbet ed-Deir, located about 6 km. (4 mi.) west of Bethlehem.

Eltolad ("kindred of God"), a town about 21 km. (13 mi.) southeast of Beer-sheba in southern Judah; apportioned to the tribe of Simeon (Josh. 19:4) in First Chronicles 4:29 the city is simply called Tolad.

Emmaus ("despised people"), a settlement about 16 km. (10 mi.) west of Jerusalem (Luke 24:13); its exact location is unknown.

Enam ("double fountains"), a village of lowland Judah near Jarmuth (Josh. 15:20, 34).

En-dor ("fountain of habitation"), a town of the tribe of Manasseh where Saul consulted a witch about his future (Josh. 17:11); probably modern Indur on the northeastern shoulder of the Little Hermon Mountain, 10 km. (6 mi.) southeast of Nazareth.

En-eglaim ("fountain of two calves"), a place on the northwestern coast of the Dead Sea (Ezek. 47:10).

En-gannim ("fountain of gardens"). **[1]** A town of lowland Judah (Josh. 15:20, 34). **[2]** A border town of the tribe of Issachar, about 11 km. (7 mi.) southwest of Mount Gilboa (Josh. 19:21); sometimes called Anem (1 Chr. 6:73). Its modern name is Jenin.

En-gedi ("fountain of the goat"), a town on the western shore of the Dead Sea assigned to the tribe of Judah; originally called Hazazon-tamar (Josh. 15:62; 2 Chr. 20:2).

En-haddah ("flowing strongly"), a village

SEA OF GALILEE. *This freshwater lake, fed by the Jordan River, is enclosed by hills except where the Jordan enters and leaves. Called a "sea" because of its considerable size, the lake is below sea level and has a semitropical climate. Violent storms can suddenly sweep down onto the lake from nearby Mount Hermon.*

RUINS OF GEBAL. *King Solomon hired stone masons from the Phoenician coastal city of Gebal (later called Byblos) to help build the temple in Jerusalem (1 Kin. 5:18, RSV). Their skill is evidenced by these stone monuments at Gebal, 40 km. (25 mi.) north of Beirut. The craftsmen of Gebal also had a reputation for shipbuilding (Ezek. 27:9).*

of the tribe of Issachar, located about 10 km. (6 mi.) east of Mount Tabor (Josh. 19:21).

En-hakkore ("well of the one who called"), a spring at Lehi, which God brought forth as an answer to Samson's prayer (Judg. 15:18–19).

En-hazor ("fountain of the village"), a fortified city of the tribe of Naphtali (Josh. 19:37). It has been identified with modern Khirbet Hasireh, near the ruins of Hazzûtr.

En-mishpat ("fountain of judgment"). *See also* Kadesh-barnea.

Enoch ("initiated"), a city built by Cain (Gen. 4:17). *See also* "People of the Bible."

En-rimmon. *See* Rimmon [1].

En-rogel ("fuller's fountain"), a spring outside the city of Jerusalem near the Hinnom Valley (2 Sam. 17:17).

En-shemesh ("eye of the sun"), a well and town east of Bethany on the road between Jerusalem and Jericho (Josh. 15:1, 7).

En-tappuah ("apple spring"), a town on the border of Ephraim (Josh. 17:7–8).

Ephes-dammim [Pas-dammim] ("boundary of blood"), a Philistine settlement near Socoh, apportioned to the tribe of Judah (1 Sam. 17:1). It is called Pas-dammim ("portion of blood") in First Chronicles 11:13.

Ephesus ("desirable"), a town on the western coast of Asia Minor between Miletus and Smyrna; an important trading center (Acts 19:1).

Ephraim ("fruitful"). [1] The territory allotted to the tribe of Ephraim in the Promised Land (Num. 1:33). [2] A city near Baal-hazor, probably the same as "Ephraim near the Wilderness" (2 Sam. 13:23; John 11:54). It is identified with modern et-Taiyibeh, about 6 km. (4 mi.) northeast of Bethel. [3] A gate on the north wall of old Jerusalem (2 Kin. 14:13; 2 Chr. 25:23). [4] A rough area (not forest) where Absalom was slain (2 Sam. 18:6). [5] A mountain allotted to the tribe of Ephraim (1 Sam. 1:1). *See also* "People of the Bible."

Ephrain ("fruitful"), a city that Abijah took from Jeroboam (2 Chr. 13:19); probably another name for Ephraim [2].

Ephratah. *See* Bethlehem [1].

Ephrath. *See* Bethlehem [1].

Ephron ("dust"), a ridge of mountains between Nephtoah and Kirjath-jearim on the boundary between Judah and Benjamin (Josh. 15:1, 9). *See also* "People of the Bible."

Erech ("length"), a city built by Nimrod on the Plain of Shinar, south of Babylon (Gen. 10:10).

Esek ("strife"), a well dug by Isaac in the Valley of Gerar; claimed by the Philistines (Gen. 26:20).

Eshan ("support"), a mountain village near Dumah, about 16 km. (10 mi.) from Hebron; apportioned to the tribe of Judah (Josh. 15:52).

Eshcol ("cluster of grapes"), a valley north of Hebron, famous for its grapes (Num. 13:24). *See also* "People of the Bible."

Eshean. *See* Eshan.

Eshtaol ("way"), a settlement in the hills of Judah about 21 km. (13 mi.) west of Jerusalem; burial place of Samson (Josh. 15:33; Judg. 13:25).

Eshtemoa [Eshtemoh] ("bosom of women"), a village in the hill country of Judah about 14 km. (9 mi.) south of Hebron, famed for its prophetic oracle (Josh. 15:20, 50). *See also* "People of the Bible."

Etam ("lair"). [1] A town of the tribe of Simeon (1 Chr. 4:32); identified with modern 'Aitun, about 18 km. (11 mi.) west-southwest of Hebron. [2] A cleft of rock near Zorah (Judg. 15:8, 11). [3] A resort town near Jerusalem, used by King Solomon (2 Chr. 11:6); Josephus wrote that it was located about 11 km. (7 mi.) from Jerusalem. *See also* "People of the Bible."

Etham ("sea-bound"), a place where the Israelites camped before they entered the wilderness of Sinai (Ex. 13:20; Num. 33:6); apparently it was located north of Timsah Lake.

Ether ("plenty"). [1] A village of the tribe of Judah located within 3 km. (2 mi.) of modern Beit-Jibrin (Josh. 15:42). [2] A village of the tribe of Simeon (Josh. 19:7), sometimes called Tochen (1 Chr. 4:32). This is probably modern Khirbet 'Attic, 25 km. (15.5 mi.) northeast of Beer-sheba.

Ethiopia [Cush?] ("burnt face"), a nation located in the upper region of the Nile River (Ps. 68:31; Is. 18:1). It is not the same as modern Ethiopia. *See also* Cush.

Euphrates (meaning unknown), a major river of western Asia, which begins in Armenia and joins the Tigris River before flowing into the Persian Gulf. It formed the western boundary of Mesopotamia (Gen. 2:14; 15:18).

Ezel ("division; separation"), a craggy hiding place of David during his rebellion against Saul (1 Sam. 20:19).

Ezem [Azem] ("bone"), a village about

PLACES OF THE BIBLE

MOUNT GERIZIM. *Now called Jebel et-Tor, Gerizim remains the sacred mountain of the Samaritans, who have worshiped here for countless generations. According to Samaritan tradition, Gerizim is Mount Moriah, on which Abraham was instructed to sacrifice his son Isaac (Gen. 22:2) and where God chose to reveal His name (Deut. 12:5). However, Jewish tradition identifies Mount Moriah with the Temple Mount in Jerusalem.*

5 km. (3 mi.) south of Beer-sheba, near the border of Edom (Josh. 15:29).

Ezion-geber [Ezion-gaber] ("giant's backbone"), a village west of the port of Elath on the Gulf of Aqaba (Num. 33:35).

F

Fair Havens, an anchorage on the southern coast of the island of Crete, near Lasea (Acts 27:8).

G

Gaash ("earthquake"), a hill in the territory of Ephraim, just south of Timnath-serah; the burial place of Joshua (Josh. 24:30).

Gaba. *See* Geba.

Gabbatha ("pavement"), an open space at the front of Herod's temple in Jerusalem, where Pontius Pilate sat to judge Jesus Christ (John 19:13).

Gad ("lot; fortune"), the territory settled by the tribe of Gad, east of the Jordan River (1 Sam. 13:7; Josh. 13:24). *See also* "People of the Bible."

Gadara ("walls"), a town located east of the Jordan River, 11 km. (7 mi.) south of the Sea of Galilee (Mark 5:1; Luke 8:26). It was one of the Decapolis cities (q.v.). *See also* Gergesa.

Gai. *See* Gath.

Galatia ("land of Galli"), a district of central Asia Minor (Acts 16:6).

Galeed. *See* Jegar-sahadutha.

Galilee ("circle"), one of the largest Roman districts of Palestine; the primary region of Jesus' ministry (Luke 3:1; 23:6).

Galilee, Sea of, a large lake in northern Palestine, fed by the Jordan River; several of Jesus' disciples worked as fishermen on this lake (John 6:1). The lake was also known as the Sea of Chinnereth (q.v.), the Sea of Tiberias, and the Sea of Gennesaret (q.v.). *See also* Chinnereth [1] and Gennesaret [2].

Gallim ("heaps"), a village near Gibeah of

PLACES OF THE BIBLE

Saul (Is. 10:29–30; 1 Sam. 25:44); probably modern Khirbet Ka'Kūl.

Gareb ("scab"), a hill in the vicinity of Jerusalem (Jer. 31:39). *See also* "People of the Bible."

Gath ("wine press"), one of the five chief Philistine cities; home of the giant Goliath (1 Sam. 17:4; 2 Kin. 12:17; 2 Chr. 26:6). Its exact location is not known.

Gath-hepher [**Gittah-hepher**] ("wine press of digging"), a city of the tribe of Zebulun, located about 5 km. (3 mi.) northeast of Nazareth; home of the prophet Jonah (Josh. 19:13; 2 Kin. 14:25).

Gath-rimmon ("pomegranate press"). [1] A city of the tribe of Dan assigned to the Levites; it probably was located on the Plain of Joppa (Josh. 19:45; 1 Chr. 6:69). [2] A town of the tribe of Manasseh, assigned to the Levites (Josh. 21:25); probably the same as Bileam.

Gaza [**Azzah**] ("strong"). [1] The southernmost of the five chief Philistine cities, located 72 km. (44.5 mi.) south of modern Jaffa and 4 km. (2.4 mi.) from the Mediterranean Sea. It was the scene of Samson's exploits (Josh. 11:22; Judg. 16:1–3; 2 Kin. 18:8; Jer. 25:20). [2] A town of the tribe of Ephraim located on a small plain near Shiloh (1 Chr. 7:28).

Gazer. *See* Gezer.

Geba [**Gaba**] ("hill"), a Benjamite city in the extreme northern portion of Judah, about 10 km. (6 mi.) north-northeast of Jerusalem (Josh. 18:24); modern Jeba'.

Gebal ("mountain"). [1] A Phoenician seaport 68 km. (42 mi.) north of Sidon; also called Byblos (Ezek. 27:9). [2] The northern portion of the mountains of Edom (Ps. 83:7).

Gebim ("ditches"), a settlement just north of Jerusalem near Michmash (Is. 10:31).

Geder ("wall"), a town in the extreme southern portion of Judah, captured by Joshua (Josh. 12:13); perhaps the same as modern Beth-gador or Gedor.

Gederah ("sheepfold"), a town in the lowlands of Judah, 6 km. (4 mi.) northwest of Zorah (Josh. 15:36); modern Jedireh.

Gederoth ("sheepfolds"), a town in the lowlands of Judah, about 6 km. (4 mi.) southwest of Ekron (Josh. 15:41); modern Katrah.

Gederothaim ("two sheepfolds"), a town of Judah (Josh. 15:36), perhaps the same as Gederoth.

Gedor ("wall"). [1] A town in the hills of Judah about 11 km. (7 mi.) northwest of Hebron (Josh. 15:58). [2] A town of the tribe of

Simeon, near the southwestern limits of Palestine (1 Chr. 4:39). [3] A village in the territory of Benjamin (1 Chr. 12:7); modern Khirbet el-Judeira. *See also* "People of the Bible."

Geharashim. *See* Charashim.

Geliloth ("circles"), a landmark on the southern boundary of Benjamin (Josh. 18:17). *See also* Gilgal [4].

Gennesaret ("garden of the prince"). [1] The region on the northwest shore of the Sea of Galilee (Matt. 14:34). [2] Another name for the Sea of Galilee (Luke 5:1).

Gerar ("halting place"), a Philistine city on the southern edge of Palestine, near Gaza (Gen. 26:1; 2 Chr. 14:13); its exact location is unknown.

Gergesa ("pilgrims"), a town or district which would have been located on the eastern side of the Lake of Galilee. Its location is not certain, but some have suggested modern-day Kersa (Matt. 8:28). Some scholars have questioned the reliability of the Gospel accounts of the healing of the demoniac, for Matthew says that it occurred in Gergesa while Mark 5:1 and Luke 8:26 say that it occurred in Gadara. However, this really is no problem for Gadara was a strong city and probably had economic and political influence over the entire area.

Gerizim ("cutters; wasteland"), a steep mountain in central Palestine facing Mount Ebal (Deut. 11:29); its peak is 872 m. (2,840 ft.) above sea level.

Geshur ("bridge"), an Aramean kingdom just east of Maacah, between Mount Hermon and the district of Bashan. Absalom sought refuge here after he killed his half-brother Amnon (2 Sam. 3:3; 13:37).

Gethsemane ("oil press"), a garden east of Jerusalem, beyond the brook Kidron at the foot of Mount Olivet; the site of Christ's betrayal (Matt. 26:36–56).

Gezer [**Gazer**] ("dividing"), a Canaanite town beside the Mediterranean Sea near Lachish and Lower Beth-horon; a battleground in King David's wars (2 Sam. 5:25; 1 Chr. 14:16).

Giah ("waterfall"), a settlement between Gibeon and a ford across the Jordan River (2 Sam. 2:24).

Gibbethon ("high house"), a village of the tribe of Dan where Nadab was assassinated (Josh. 19:44; 1 Kin. 15:27); probably modern Tell el-Melat, directly east of Ekron.

Gibeah ("hill"). [1] A Judean town about

PLACES OF THE BIBLE

HAMATH. *The modern Syrian city of Hama stands on the site of biblical Hamath. The city marked the northern boundary that God assigned to the people of Israel (Num. 34:8; Josh. 13:5). In King David's time, the Aramean people of Hamath were friendly toward Israel (2 Sam. 8:9–10). The Orontes River flows through the city.*

16 km. (10 mi.) northwest of Hebron (Josh. 15:57). **[2]** A town midway between Jerusalem and Ramah; home and capital of King Saul (1 Sam. 10:26; 15:34). The town is called Gibeath in Joshua 18:28. **[3]** A town or hill in the territory of Ephraim (Josh. 24:33); probably near Timnah [1]. **[4]** A hill in Kiriath-jearim on which was located the house of Abinadad (2 Sam. 6:3–4).

Gibeon ("hill height"), the chief city of the Hivites, assigned to the tribe of Benjamin; located 9 km. (5.5 mi.) north-northwest of Jerusalem (Josh. 11:19; 2 Sam. 20:1–9). Its modern name is El-Jib.

Gidom ("desolation"), a village of the tribe of Benjamin, located between Gibeah [1] and Rimmon [2] (Judg. 20:45).

Gihon ("stream; bursting forth"). **[1]** One of the four rivers of Eden [1] (Gen. 2:13). **[2]** An intermittent spring outside the walls of Jerusalem, south of the temple area (1 Kin. 1:38–45; 2 Chr. 32:30).

Gilboa ("hill country"), a mountain overlooking the Plain of Jezreel; site of King Saul's death (1 Sam. 28:4; 31:1); modern Jebel Fuku'a.

Gilead ("strong; rocky; rough"). **[1]** A region east of the Jordan River, stretching from Moab to the Yarmuk River (Deut. 3:16–17). **[2]** A mountain jutting onto the Plain of Jezreel (Judg. 7:3). **[3]** A city in the region of Gilead (Hos. 6:8). *See also* "People of the Bible."

Gilgal ("rolling"). **[1]** The first campsite of the Israelites after they crossed the Jordan River into Canaan, probably near Jericho (Josh. 4:19–24). **[2]** A village 11 km. (7 mi.) northeast of Bethel, from which Elijah and Elisha began their journey (2 Kin. 2:1–4; 4:38); present-day Jiljilia. **[3]** A town on the edge of the Plain of Sharon, about 8 km. (5 mi.) north-northeast of Antipatris (Josh. 10:6–9, 15). **[4]** A place on the northern boundary of Judah, near Debir (Josh. 15:7); perhaps the same as Geliloth.

Giloh ("he that overturns"), a town in the hill country of Judah, 8 km. (5 mi.) north-northwest of Hebron (Josh. 15:51).

Gimzo ("sycamore"), a town of northern Judah, about 5 km. (3 mi.) southeast of Lydda (2 Chr. 28:18); modern Jimzu.

Gittah-hepher. *See* Gath-hepher.

Gittaim ("two winepresses"), a Benjamite town of refuge near Beeroth (Neh. 11:33); probably the site of modern el-Ramleh.

Goath ("constancy"), a site near Jerusalem (Jer. 31:39); its exact location is unknown.

Gob ("cistern"), a site of several battles during Israel's wars with the Philistines (2 Sam. 21:18); its exact location is unknown, but may be the same as Gezer or Gath.

Golan ("passage"), a city of Bashan east of

the Jordan River, assigned to the Levites as a city of refuge (Deut. 4:43; Josh. 21:27). It is probably the site of modern Sahem el-Jaulan, 27 km. (17 mi.) east of the Sea of Galilee.

Golgotha [Calvary] ("skull"), a hill just outside the walls of ancient Jerusalem; the site of Jesus' crucifixion (Matt. 27:33; John 19:17). Its exact location is unknown, but it was probably inside the walls of what is now called the "old city."

Gomorrah ("submersion"), one of the five Cities of the Plain destroyed along with Sodom (Gen. 18:20; 19:24, 28). Many scholars believe it was submerged by the southeastern tip of the Dead Sea.

Goshen ("drawing near"). **[1]** A cattle-raising district of the Nile delta assigned to the Israelites before they were placed in bondage (Gen. 46:28). **[2]** A town in the hill country of Judah (Josh. 15:51); probably modern Dahariyeh, about 21 km. (13 mi.) southwest of Hebron. **[3]** A region of Judah that probably derived its name from the town of Goshen (Josh. 10:41; 11:16).

Gozan ("food"), a district and town of Mesopotamia, located on the Habor River (2 Kin. 17:6; 18:11). The KJV refers to it as a river, but this does not seem likely.

Greece [Grecia] (meaning uncertain), a country of Southern Europe between Italy and Asia Minor; one of the most powerful nations of the ancient world (Dan. 8:21; Zech. 9:13; Acts 20:2).

Gudgodah ("incision"), a place where the Israelites camped in the wilderness, near Ezion Geber (Deut. 10:7); perhaps the same as Hor-hagidgad (q.v.).

Gur ("whelp"), a hill near Ibleam where Jehu killed Ahaziah (2 Kin. 9:27).

Gur-baal ("dwelling place of Baal"), a desert district south of Beer-sheba between Canaan and the Arabian peninsula (2 Chr. 26:7).

H

Habor ("fertile"), a tributary of the Euphrates River (2 Kin. 17:6; 18:11); probably the Khabur River.

Hachilah ("gloomy"), a hill in the wilderness southeast of Hebron, near Maon (1 Sam. 26:1–3).

Hadadrimmon (compound of two divine names: Hadad and Rimmon). The KJV takes this as a reference to a place in the Valley of

HAZOR. *Joshua defeated King Jabin of Hazor during the conquest of Canaan (Josh. 11:1–13; 12:19). King Solomon later fortified the city, but the Assyrians destroyed it in the eighth century B.C. and carried away its people (1 Kin. 9:15; 2 Kin. 15:29). From 1955 to 1958, Israeli archaeologists led by Yigael Yadin excavated the ruins of Hazor, just northwest of the Sea of Galilee.*

Jezreel, near Megiddo (Zech. 12:11). Many believe, however, the reference is to the lamentation for a divinity analogous to the weeping for Tammuz (Ezek. 8:14).

Hadashah ("new"), a village in the lowlands of Judah about 5 km. (3 mi.) from Beth-horon (Josh. 15:37); perhaps modern Khirbet el-Judeideh.

Hadattah ("new"), a town in southern Judah (Josh. 15:25), probably near Hazor [2].

Hades. *See* Hell.

Hadid ("point"), a Benjamite town located 5 km. (3 mi.) east-northeast of Lydda (Ezra 2:33; Neh. 11:34).

Hadrach ("dwelling"), a Syrian country associated with Hamath and Damascus, encompassing an area along the Orontes River south of Hamath (Zech. 9:1).

Halah ("moist table"), a portion of the Assyrian kingdom, encompassing the basin of the Habor and Saorkoras Rivers (2 Kin. 17:6; 1 Chr. 5:26).

Halak ("smooth"), a mountain in southern Palestine (Josh. 11:17; 12:7); possibly present-day Jebel Halaq, just north-northeast of Abdeh.

Halhul ("tremble"), a Judean village located about 6 km. (4 mi.) north of Hebron (Josh. 15:58); said to be the burial place of Jonah.

Hali ("sickness"), a town of Judah, located near the border of Asher (Josh. 19:25).

Ham. [1] A name for Egypt used only in poetry (Ps. 78:51). **[2]** A place between

PLACES OF THE BIBLE

Ashteroth-Karnaim in Bashan and the Moabite country (Gen. 14:5). Possibly modern Ham about 5 mi. south of Irbid in the 'Ajlūn district. *See also* "People of the Bible."

Hamath [Hemath] ("anger"). **[1]** A Hittite city on the Orontes River about 200 km. (125 mi.) north of Damascus; a supply base for Solomon's armies (2 Chr. 8:4). **[2]** The ideal northern boundary of Israel (Num. 13:21; 34:8).

Hamath-zobah, a city captured by Solomon (2 Chr. 8:3).

Hammath [Hemath] ("hot springs"), a city of Naphtali allotted to the Levites (Josh. 19:35). It is probably identical with Hammon (1 Chr. 6:76) and Hammoth-dor (Josh. 21:32).

Hammon ("hot waters"). **[1]** A frontier village of the tribe of Asher, assigned to the Levites, located about 16 km. (10 mi.) south of Tyre (Josh. 19:28). **[2]** *See* Hammath.

Hammoth-dor. *See* Hammath.

Hamonah ("multitude"), symbolic name of the city where Gog is to be defeated (Ezek. 39:16).

Hamon-gog ("multitude of Gog"), the valley where Gog and his armies will be defeated in their final struggle against God's people (Ezek. 39:11–15).

Hananeel ("given of God"), a tower of Jerusalem, located near the Sheep Gate (Jer. 31:38; Zech. 14:10).

Hanes ("Mercury"), an Egyptian town

Hebron and History

The city of Hebron is first mentioned in the Bible when Abram separated his camp from Lot's and settled at Hebron (Gen. 13:18). Years later, Abraham bought the cave at Machpelah in Hebron to bury Sarah. The burial place later served for Abraham, Isaac and Rebecca, and Jacob and Leah (Gen. 49:29–33).

When the Hebrews returned from Egyptian bondage to inhabit the Promised Land, they feared the size of the inhabitants; so they only gradually captured Canaan from the clans of Anak, or made alliances with them (Num. 13:14). After Hebron's king joined with other kings to attack a Hebrew ally, Gibeon, the Hebrews attacked and captured Hebron and other cities (Josh. 10). The Bible gives credit for the capture of Hebron to three people or groups of people: Caleb (Josh. 15:13–15), the tribes of Judah (Judg. 1:8–10), and Joshua (Josh. 10:36–37). After the capture, Hebron was turned over to Caleb, as God had promised earlier (Num. 14).

Generations later, the inhabitants of Hebron assisted David and his army as he pursued the Philistines. Victorious, David shared "the spoil of the enemies of the Lord" (1 Sam. 30—31) with the people of Hebron and other cities. As David grew in power, the men of Judah gathered at Hebron and anointed him their king. David ruled the southern kingdom from Hebron for seven and a half years.

After David united the two kingdoms (with the seat of government at Jerusalem), Hebron is mentioned only briefly in the Bible. David's son Absalom launched an unsuccessful revolt against him from Hebron (2 Sam. 15:7–10). Later Rehoboam strengthened the city's fortifications so that Hebron could protect Jerusalem, which lay about nineteen miles to the north (2 Chr. 11:5, 10).

Hebron was designated a city of the Levites. The descendants of Levi (i.e., the priests) were given these cities and surrounding pastures as places to live (cf. Josh. 21:1–12). Hebron was also named a city of refuge. If a person unintentionally killed someone, he could flee to one of the six cities of refuge, where he would be protected until he stood trial (Num. 35:9–15).

Modern Hebron has a population of about 40,000 and is located on an important road junction in the highland area of western Jordan. The stone-built town has small, winding streets, and active marketplaces, which sell the wares of local craftsmen, such as glassblowers. Dr. Philip C. Hammond of the University of Utah, who has excavated many artifacts at Hebron, considers the city the oldest continuously occupied unwalled city in the world.

PLACES OF THE BIBLE

VALLEY OF HINNOM. *In the sixth century* B.C., *the people of Judah began worshiping idols of the pagan god Molech in this valley south of Jerusalem; King Josiah ended this practice (Jer. 7:30–31; 2 Kin. 23:25). Later the people of Jerusalem made this valley a dumping ground for garbage and burned the bodies of criminals upon the heaps.*

about 80 km. (50 mi.) south of Memphis (Is. 30:4).

Hannathon ("dedicated to grace"), a town of the tribe of Zebulun located on a road between Megiddo and Accho (Josh. 19:14).

Haphraim ("two pits"), a frontier town assigned to the tribe of Issachar (Josh. 19:19). It may be modern Khirbet el-Farriyeh, about 10 km. (6 mi.) northwest of Megiddo; or it may be modern et Taiyibeh, northwest of Bethshean.

Hara ("hill"), a place in Assyria to which the Israelite captives were taken (1 Chr. 5:26); it may be the proper name of a settlement or the Hebrew term for "mountains of the Medes."

Haradah ("fear"), a place where the Israelites camped during their wilderness wanderings (Num. 33:24); its exact location is unknown.

Haran [**Charran**] ("mountains"), a Mesopotamian city located 386 km. (240 mi.) northwest of Nineveh and 450 km. (280 mi.) north-northeast of Damascus (Gen. 11:31; 12:4–5). *See also* "People of the Bible."

Hareth ("thicket"), a forest of Judah in which David hid (1 Sam. 22:5).

Harmon (KJV reads "the palace"), a place to which the people of Samaria were exiled, perhaps in the area of Rimmon (Amos 4:3).

Harod ("trembling"), a spring (Judg. 7:1); commonly thought to be modern 'Ain Jalud on the northwest side of Mount Gilboa, about 1.5 km. (1 mi.) southeast of Jezreel.

Harosheth ("carving"), a small village on the northern bank of the Kishon River 26 km. (16 mi.) north-northwest of Megiddo (Judg. 4:2, 13).

Hashmonah ("fruitfulness"), a place where the Israelites camped in the wilderness (Num. 33:29–30); possibly modern Wadi el-Hashim.

Hauran ("black land"), a district bordering the region of Gilead south of Damascus, noted for the fertility of its soil (Ezek. 47:16, 18).

Havilah ("circle"), a region of central Arabia populated by the descendants of Cush (Gen. 10:7; 1 Sam. 15:7; cf. Gen. 25:18). This term may have referred to the territory of the Arabian Desert for several hundred miles north of modern Al-Yamanah. *See also* "People of the Bible."

PLACES OF THE BIBLE

Havoth-jair ("tent villages of Jair"), an area in the northwest part of Bashan, containing several unwalled cities (Num. 32:41). The area is called Bashan-havoth-jair in Deuteronomy 3:14.

Hazar-Addar. *See* Adar.

Hazar-enan ("village of fountains"), a small village on the northern border of Palestine (Num. 34:9; Ezek. 48:1); probably modern Kiryatein.

Hazar-gaddah ("town of Gadah"), a village on the southern border of Judah southwest of Ras Zuiveira (Josh. 15:27); possibly modern Khirbet Ghazza.

Hazar-hatticon ("enclosure"), a village on the border of Havran (Ezek. 47:16).

Hazar-maveth ("enclosure"), a very small district of Arabia in the southern portion of the Arabian Peninsula (Gen. 10:26).

Hazar-shual ("fox village"), a town in southern Judah apportioned to the tribe of Simeon (Josh. 15:28; 19:3). Perhaps it is modern el-Watan, located between Beer-sheba and Tell es-Saba.

Hazar-susah [Hazar-susim] ("captive mare[s]"), a small village in the extreme south of the territory of Simeon (Josh. 19:5; 1 Chr. 4:31); it may be modern Susiyeh, located 3 km. (2 mi.) east of Eshtemoa.

Hazazon-tamar [Hazezon-tamar] ("sandy surface of the palm tree"), said to be another name for En-gedi (Gen. 14:7; 2 Chr. 20:2); this name may in fact refer to modern Tamar, about 32 km. (20 mi.) south-southeast of the Dead Sea on the road to Elath.

Hazeroth ("enclosures"), a place where the Israelites camped in the wilderness (Num. 11:35); possibly modern Ain Hudra, about 58 km. (36 mi.) north-northeast of Mount Sinai.

Hazor ("enclosure"). [1] The capital of the Canaanite kingdom, later included in the territory of Naphtali in northern Palestine (Josh. 11:1, 10, 13); site of a major archaeological excavation. [2] A place in extreme southern Judah (Josh. 15:23); possibly modern el-Jebariyeh. [3] Another city in southern Judah (Josh. 15:25). Hezron was a district or region of the city or another name for the city itself (verse 25). [4] A village of the tribe of Benjamin, to which the Jewish exiles returned (Neh. 11:33); modern Khirbet Hazzur, 6 km. (4 mi.) north-northwest of Jerusalem. [5] A region of the Arabian Desert east of Palestine (Jer. 49:28, 30, 33).

Hebron ("friendship"). [1] A city in the hills of Judah, 32 km. (20 mi.) south of Jerusalem (Gen. 13:18; Num. 13:22). [2] A town of the tribe of Asher, more frequently called Abdon (Josh. 19:28). *See also* "People of the Bible."

Helam, a place east of the Jordan, where David defeated the king of Syria (2 Sam. 10:16–19). Possibly 'Almā or 'Ilmā, 10 mi. southwest of Busr el-Harīrī.

Helbah ("fertile"), a town of the tribe of Asher on the Phoenician plain northeast of Tyre (Judg. 1:31); probably the same as Ahlah.

Helbon ("fat"), a village of Syria near Damascus, known for its wines (Ezek. 27:18); probably modern Khalbun, 21 km. (13 mi.) north-northwest of Damascus.

Heleph ("passing over"), a town marking the boundary of the tribe of Naphtali, just northeast of Mount Tabor (Josh. 19:33).

Helkath ("part"), a town marking the boundary of the tribe of Asher (Josh. 19:25); probably modern Tell el-Harboj.

Helkath-hazzurim ("field of rock"), an area of smooth ground near the pool of Gibeon (2 Sam. 2:16).

Hell ("conceal"), the place of woe for the departed. "Hades" is the New Testament name for "Sheol," which was conceived as a place where the souls of all dead resided (Ps. 16:10; Matt. 11:23; Acts 2:27). The KJV also has *hell* as its translation of *Gehenna,* a valley outside Jerusalem that Jesus used as a symbol of woe for lost souls. For believers, He said that Hades would be a paradise (Luke 23:43); for the godless, it would be "Gehenna" (cf. Luke 16:22–23).

Hemath. *See* Hammath.

Hena ("troubling"), a city about 32 km. (20 mi.) from Babylon (2 Kin. 19:13; Is. 37:13); probably the same as modern Anah on the Euphrates River.

Hepher ("pit"), a town west of the Jordan River (Josh. 12:17); probably modern Tell Ibshar on the Plain of Sharon. *See also* "People of the Bible."

Heres ("sun"). [1] A mountain in the district of Aijalon (Judg. 1:35). [2] An Egyptian city that the KJV calls "the city of destruction" (Is. 19:18).

Hermon ("devoted to destruction"), the highest mountain of the Anti-Lebanon range, marking the northeast boundary of Palestine (Deut. 3:8; Josh. 11:17; 1 Chr. 5:23).

Heshbon ("stronghold"), the Amorite capital on the boundary between Reuben and Gad,

JERUSALEM. *The name of this sacred city and capital of Israel comes from Hebrew words that mean "foundation of peace" or "secure habitation." Jerusalem is located at one of the highest points on the central ridge of Palestine. This aerial view shows the site where Solomon's temple stood. The site is now covered by the Dome of the Rock, an Islamic mosque.*

standing between the Arnon and Jabbok Rivers (Num. 21:26; Josh. 13:17).

Heshmon ("rich soil"), a place in the far southern region of Judah (Josh. 15:27); possibly same as Azmon.

Hethlon ("fearful dwelling"), a mountain pass at the northern border of Palestine, connecting the Mediterranean coast with the Plain of Hamath (Ezek. 47:15; 48:1).

Hezron ("blooming"). [1] *See* Hazor [5]. [2] A place on the southern border of Judah, not far from Kadesh-barnea (Josh. 15:3). *See also* "People of the Bible."

Hiddekel ("sound"), an archaic name for the Tigris River (Gen. 2:14; Dan. 10:4). It is narrower than the Euphrates, but carries more water. It joins the Euphrates 100 miles from the Persian Gulf at Al Qurna.

Hierapolis ("holy city"), a city of the province of Phrygia in Asia Minor, at the confluence of the Lycas and Meander Rivers (Col. 4:13).

Hilen [Holon] ("grief"), a city of the tribe of Judah, allotted to the Levites (Josh. 15:51; 1 Chr. 6:58).

Hinnom ("their riches"), a narrow valley

southwest of Jerusalem (Josh. 15:8; 18:16; 2 Chr. 28:3).

Hobah ("love"), the town north of Damascus that was the farthest point to which Abraham pursued the defeated eastern kings (Gen. 14:15).

Holon ("grief"). [1] A Moabite town (Jer. 48:21); possibly modern Horon. [2] *See* Hilen.

Hor ("hill"). [1] A mountain on the boundary of Edom (Num. 20:22; 33:37); tradition identifies it as modern Jebel Harun, but Jebel Madeirch is more likely the location. [2] A mountain between the Mediterranean Sea and the entrance of Hamath [2], possibly in the Lebanon range (Num. 34:7–8).

Horeb ("desert"), a range of mountains on the Sinai Peninsula, of which Mount Sinai is the highest (Ex. 17:6); now called the Serbal range.

Horem ("dedicated to God"), a fortress of the tribe of Naphtali (Josh. 19:38); modern Hurah at the southern end of the Wadi el-Ain.

Hor-hagidgad ("cleft mountain"), a place where the wandering Israelites camped (Num. 33:32); probably located on what is now called the Wadi Ghadaghed. It is perhaps identical with Gudgodah (q.v.).

Hormah ("dedicated to God"), a Canaanite city located near Ziklag; originally called Zephath (1 Sam. 30:30); perhaps the same as modern Tell el-Milk, east-southeast of Beersheba.

Horonaim ("double caves"), a sanctuary town of Moab, near Zoar (Is. 15:5; Jer. 48:3).

Hosah ("refuge"), a landmark city of the tribe of Asher on the boundary near Tyre (Josh. 19:29). *See also* "People of the Bible."

Hukkok ("hewn"), a place on the border of Naphtali (Josh. 19:34); probably modern Yakuk.

Hukok ("ditch"), a city marking the boundary of Asher (1 Chr. 6:75). It is identical with Helkath (q.v.).

Humtah ("place of lizards"), a city in the mountains of Judah near Hebron (Josh. 15:54).

I

Ibleam ("ancient people"), a city of the tribe of Manasseh (Josh. 17:11; Judg. 1:27); generally believed to be another name for Bileam (q.v.).

Iconium ("coming"), capital of the province of Lycaonia in Asia Minor (Acts 13:51; 14:1).

Idalah ("land of slander"), a city of the tribe of Zebulun (Josh. 19:15); modern Khirbet el-Huvara.

Idumea ("red"), an area in southwestern Palestine. After the fall of Jerusalem in 586 B.C. many Edomites migrated into this area thus giving it the name Idumea (the Greek form of the Hebrew Edom) (Mark 3:8).

Iim ("heaps"). **[1]** A town in extreme southern Judah (Josh. 15:29); modern Deir el-Ghawi. **[2]** A town east of the Jordan River,

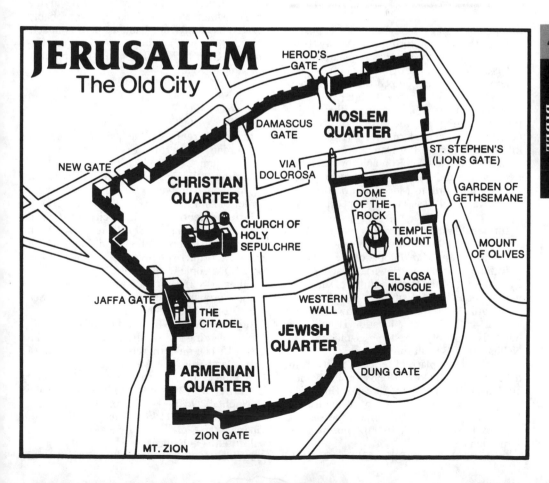

PLACES OF THE BIBLE

KINGDOM OF ISRAEL
Mediterranean Sea
Mt. Carmel
Samaria
Shechem
Mt. Gerizim
Ashdod
Jerusalem
Hebron
KINGDOM OF JUDAH

ISRAEL AND JUDAH
© Thomas Nelson, Inc.

perhaps the Moabite fortress of Mahaiy (Num. 33:45); probably the same as Ije-abarim.

Ije-abarim ("ruins of Abraham"), a place where the Israelites camped in the territory of Moab (Num. 33:45). *See also* Iim [2].

Ijon ("heap; ruin"), a city of northern Palestine belonging to the tribe of Naphtali (1 Kin. 15:20); modern Merj 'Ayun, a few kilometers northwest of Dan.

Illyricum ("joy"), a Roman province on the east coast of the Adriatic Sea, stretching from Italy on the north to Macedonia on the south (Rom. 15:19). It was later renamed Dalmatia (q.v.).

Immer ("lamb"), a person or place in Babylonia (Ezra 2:59; Neh. 7:61); its exact location is unknown. *See also* "People of the Bible."

India (meaning unknown), a land on the eastern limit of the Persian Empire, surrounding the Indus River (Esth. 1:1; 8:9).

Ir-nahash ("serpent city"), a town of Judah (1 Chr. 4:12); its exact location is unknown, but it is probably the same as modern Deir Nahhas, near Beit Jibrin.

Iron ("pious; place of terror"), a city of the tribe of Naphtali (Josh. 19:38); probably modern Yarun, 16 km. (10 mi.) west of Hula Lake.

Irpeel ("God heals"), a city of the tribe of Benjamin (Josh. 18:27); perhaps the same as modern Rafat, 10 km. (6 mi.) northwest of Jerusalem.

Ir-shemesh ("city of the sun"), a city of the

tribe of Dan (Josh. 19:41); probably another name for Beth-shemesh (q.v.).

Ish-tob ("good man"), a small state of Aram (2 Sam. 10:6, 8).

Israel ("who prevails with God"), the northern kingdom of the Hebrews in Palestine, inhabited by the ten tribes that followed Ishbosheth and Jeroboam. The cities of Jericho and Gezer marked its southern boundary (2 Chr. 35:18; cf. Gen. 32:32). *See also* Jacob in "People of the Bible."

Italy ("abounding with calves"), the peninsula jutting from the Alps into the Mediterranean Sea, bounded on the south by the straits of Messina (Acts 18:2; 27:1).

Ithnan ("given"), a town in extreme southern Judah (Josh. 15:23).

Ittah-kazin ("gather"), a landmark on the boundary of Zebulun near modern Sepphoris (Josh. 19:13).

Ituraea ("mountains"), a small province on the northwest boundary of Palestine at the base of Mount Hermon (Luke 3:1). It probably derived its name from Jetur, a son of Ishmael.

Ivah ("hamlet"), a city located on the Euphrates River (2 Kin. 18:34; 19:13); perhaps the same as Ava.

J

Jaazer [Jazer] ("God helps"), a city east of the Jordan River, in or near the region of Gilead (Num. 21:32; 32:1).

Jabbok ("flowing"), an eastern tributary of the Jordan River, which served as the western border of Ammon (Gen. 32:22; Deut. 2:37).

Jabesh-gilead ("dry"), a city of Gilead (Judg. 21:8; 1 Sam. 11:1). It may have been located at a site now called Wadi Yabis, about 23 km. (20 mi.) south of the Sea of Galilee. *See also* "People of the Bible."

Jabez ("sorrow"), a dwelling place of scribes, probably in Judah (1 Chr. 2:55). *See also* "People of the Bible."

Jabneel [Jabneh] ("building of God"). **[1]** A city marking the northern border of Judah (Josh. 15:11); modern Yebnah, about 6 km. (4 mi.) inland from the Mediterranean Sea and 14.5 km. (9 mi.) north-northeast of Ashdod (2 Chr. 26:6). **[2]** A border town of the tribe of Naphtali (Josh. 19:33); probably modern Khirbet Yemman, 11 km. (7 mi.) southwest of Tiberias.

Jabneh. *See* Jabneel.

Jachin ("God establishes"), the right hand

PLACES OF THE BIBLE

pillar of Solomon's porch on the temple of Jerusalem (1 Kin. 7:21). *See also* "People of the Bible."

Jagur ("husbandman"), a town in extreme southern Judah (Josh. 15:21); probably modern Tell Ghurr.

Jahaz [Jahaza, Jahazah] ("a place trodden under foot"), a battlefield on the wastelands of Moab (Num. 21:23); its exact location is unknown.

Janoah [Janohah] ("resting"). **[1]** A city of the tribe of Naphtali, north of Galilee (2 Kin. 15:29); possibly modern Yanuh, 10.5 km. (6.5 mi.) southeast of Tyre. **[2]** A town on Ephraim's border (Josh. 16:6); possibly modern Yanun, 11 km. (7 mi.) southeast of Shechem.

Janum ("sleeping"), a town in the mountains of Judah, west-southwest of Hebron (Josh. 15:53).

Japhia ("enlarging"), a boundary town of Zebulun, 3 km. (2 mi.) southwest of Nazareth (Josh. 19:12). *See also* "People of the Bible."

Japhleti ("to shine"), a landmark on the southern boundary of Ephraim, near Beth-horon (Josh. 16:3).

Japho ("beauty"), a Palestinian city on the Mediterranean coast 56 km. (34 mi.) west of Jerusalem (Josh. 19:46). It was later called Joppa (q.v.).

Jarmuth ("height"). **[1]** A city in the lowlands of Judah (Josh. 10:3); modern Khirbet Yarmuk. **[2]** A city of the tribe of Issachar assigned to the Levites (Josh. 21:29); the same as Ramoth [3].

Jattir ("preeminence"), a town in the mountains of Judah, assigned to the Levites (Josh. 15:48; 21:14); possibly modern Khirbet 'Atti, 21 km. (13 mi.) south-southwest of Hebron.

Javan ("Ionians"), a trading post in southern Arabia (Ezek. 27:13). *See also* "People of the Bible."

Jearim ("woods"), mountains marking the boundary of Judah about 13 km. (8 mi.) northeast of Beth-shemesh (Josh. 15:10).

Jebus ("manager"), another name for Jerusalem (Judg. 19:10–11).

Jegar-sahadutha [Galeed] ("heap of witness"), a pile of stones erected by Laban to memorialize his pact with Jacob; near Mount Gilead north of the Jabbok River (Gen. 31:47). Galeed is Hebrew and Jegar-sahadutha is Aramaic; both mean the same thing.

Jehoshaphat ("judged of God"), the valley where the Last Judgment will take place (Joel 3:2); tradition identifies it as the Kidron Valley (q.v.). *See also* "People of the Bible."

Jehovah-jireh ("the Lord will provide"), the place where Abraham attempted to offer Isaac as a sacrifice (Gen. 22:14); its exact location is unknown.

Jehovah-nissi ("the Lord my banner"), the altar that Moses built at Rephidim in honor of Israel's victory over Amalek (Ex. 17:15).

Jehovah-shalom ("the Lord send peace"), an altar that Gideon built at Ophrah [2] (Judg. 6:24).

Jehud ("praising"), a town of the tribe of Dan located between Baalath and Bene-berak (Josh. 19:45); probably modern el-Yehudiyeh.

Jekabzeel ("congregation of God"). *See* Kabzeel.

Jericho ("his sweet smell"), a fortified city of Canaan located about 8 km. (5 mi.) from the north end of the Dead Sea and 16 km. (10 mi.) northwest of the Jordan River (Num. 22:1; Deut. 32:49). Today it is the oldest continually inhabited city in the world.

Jeruel ("vision of God"), a wilderness area in Judah near the cliff of Ziz and En-gedi (2 Chr. 20:16).

Jerusalem ("possession of peace"), capital of the southern kingdom of Judah, located 48 km. (30 mi.) from the Mediterranean Sea and 27 km. (18 mi.) west of the Jordan River (Josh. 10:1; 2 Sam. 5:5).

Jeshanah ("old"), a city in the hill country of Ephraim (2 Chr. 13:19); variously

LACHISH LETTER. *This is one of 21 ostraca (broken pottery pieces) discovered at Tell ed-Duweir, located on the site of ancient Lachish. Messages dating from the beginning of Nebuchadnezzar's conquest of Judah (ca. 586–87 B.C.) are scribbled on the potsherds. In this letter, a subordinate officer at an outpost near Azekah states: ". . . we are watching for the fire-signals of Lachish . . . for we cannot see Azekah." The message implies that Azekah had already fallen to the Babylonians.*

PLACES OF THE BIBLE

identified as modern 'Ain Sinya, 6 km. (4 mi.) north of Bethel, or Burj el-Isanah, about 10 km. (6 mi.) north of Bethel.

Jeshimon ("solitude"). **[1]** A wilderness area lying west of the Dead Sea a few kilometers south of Hebron (1 Sam. 23:19; 26:1, 3). **[2]** A wilderness on the northeast end of the Dead Sea, near Pisgah and Peor (Num. 21:20).

Jeshua ("a savior"), a town in southern Judah that was repopulated by Jews returning from the Babylonian Captivity (Neh. 11:26); probably modern Tell es-Sa'roeh, about 18 km. (11 mi.) east-northeast of Beer-sheba. *See also* "People of the Bible."

Jeshurun [Jesurun] ("blessed"), a symbolic name for Israel (Deut. 32:15; Is. 44:2).

Jesurun. *See* Jeshurun.

Jethlah a town of Dan (Josh. 19:42).

Jezreel ("seed of God"). **[1]** A city on the Plain of Jezreel between Mount Gilboa and Mount Carmel (Josh. 19:18; 1 Kin. 21:1). **[2]** A town in Judah's hill country (Josh. 15:56); probably modern Khirbet Terrama on the Plain of Dibleh. *See also* "People of the Bible."

Jiphtah ("breaking through"), a city in Judah near Ashnah and Nezib (Josh. 15:43).

Jiphthah-el ("God opens"), a valley that served as the boundary between the territories of Zebulun and Asher (Josh. 19:14, 27).

Jogbehah ("high"), a city east of the Jordan River, inhabited by the tribe of Gad (Num. 32:35); present-day Jubeihat, located 10 km. (6 mi.) northwest of Rabbath-ammon.

Jokdeam ("anger of the people"), a city in the mountains of Judah south of Hebron (Josh. 15:56).

Jokmeam ("revenge of the people"), a city of the tribe of Ephraim, given to the Levites. It stood nearly opposite the mouth of the Jabbok River (1 Chr. 6:68); probably the same as Kibzaim (q.v.).

Jokneam ("building up of the people"). **[1]** A city in Zebulun allotted to the Levites (Josh. 21:34). It stood on or near Mount Carmel, probably Tell Kaimun, about 11.3 km. (7 mi.) northwest of Megiddo. **[2]** A city in Ephraim

LEBANON MOUNTAINS. *The snow-capped Lebanon Mountains parallel the Palestinian coast for a distance of about 161 km. (100 mi.) from Kadesh to Sidon. At its highest point, the range reaches more than 3,300 m. (10,000 ft.) above sea level. These mountains formed the northwestern boundary of the Promised Land (Deut. 1:7).*

PLACES OF THE BIBLE

(1 Kin. 4:12). We should probably read Jokmeam (q.v.).

Joktheel ("subdued by God"). **[1]** A city located in the lowlands of Judah (Josh. 15:38). **[2]** The name given to Sela [now Petra], capital of the Edomites (2 Kin. 14:7).

Joppa ("beauty"), a town on the coast of Palestine (2 Chr. 2:16; Acts 9:36). *See* Japho.

Jordan (meaning uncertain), the major river of Palestine. It rises in a valley between Mount Lebanon and Hermon. It follows a twisting route to enter the north end of the Dead Sea (Gen. 13:10; Josh. 2:7).

Jorkoam ("paleness"), a place belonging to the tribe of Judah (1 Chr. 2:44). It may be identical with Jokdeam (q.v.).

Jotbah ("pleasantness"), the city of Haruz, the father of Meshullemeth (2 Kin. 21:19).

Jotbath [Jotbathah] ("goodness"), an encampment of the Israelites in the wilderness. Apparently it was near Ezion-geber (Num. 33:33; Deut. 10:7); it is possibly modern el-Taba.

Judah [Joda] ("the praise of the Lord"), the territory of one of the original twelve tribes. Judah, along with Benjamin, formed the southern kingdom after Solomon's death. The uncertain border between Israel and Judah ran between Bethel in Israel and Ramah in Judah. Jerusalem was its capital (2 Chr. 13:18; 15:8). *See also* "People of the Bible."

Judea [Jewry] ("the praise of the Lord"), first mentioned as a Persian province (Ezra 3:8). Later it became a Roman province (Matt. 2:1). Its northern boundary was Joppa on the west to a point 16.1 km. (10 mi.) north of the Dead Sea on the east. Its southern boundary was about seven miles southwest of Gaza, through Beer-sheba, to the southern end of the Dead Sea.

Juttah ("turning away"), a city in the mountains of Judah. It is near Maon, Carmel, and Ziph (now Yatta), 8.8 km. (5.5 mi.) southwest of Hebron (Josh. 15:55; 21:16).

K

Kabzeel ("the congregation of God"), a city in Judah (Josh. 15:21; 2 Sam. 23:20); probably modern Khirbet Hora. The city was also known as Jekabzeel (q.v., Neh. 11:25).

Kadesh. *See* Kadesh-barnea; also Meribah [2].

Kadesh-barnea ("holy"), a wilderness on Palestine's southern frontier. It was on the border between the wilderness of Paran on the south and the wilderness of Zin on the north of the Sinai Peninsula (Num. 32:8; 34:4). It is also called simply Kadesh (Num. 13:26; 20:1). In Genesis 14:7 the region is called En-mishpat.

Kadesh-barnea. *See* Kadesh.

Kanah ("of reeds"). **[1]** A stream that divided the territories of Ephraim and Manasseh; perhaps Wadi Kanah which enters the Mediterranean 6.4 km. (4 mi.) north of Joppa (Josh. 16:8; 17:9). **[2]** A city in Asher not far from Sidon, presently known as Ain Kanah (Josh. 19:28).

Karkaa ("floor; deep ground"), an unknown site on the southern boundary of the tribe of Judah (Josh. 15:3).

Karkor ("they rested; even or deep ground"), a city in Gad, east of the Jordan. The site of Gideon's victory over Zebah and Zalmunna (Judg. 8:10). It is present-day Karkar.

Kartah ("city"), a city in Zebulun given to the Merarite Levites (Josh. 21:34). The site has been identified with 'Ailit on the seacoast 14.5 km. (9 mi.) south of the point where Carmel reaches the sea.

Kartan ("town; city"), city of Naphtali given to the Gershonite Levites (Josh. 21:32); it is the same as Kirjathaim in First Chronicles 6:76 and is modern Khirbet el-Kureiyeh.

Kattath ("small"), a town in Zebulun (Josh. 19:15). It is probably identical with the Kitron in Judges 1:30.

Kedemoth ("antiquity; old age"), a Levitical town east of the Dead Sea (Josh. 13:18; 21:37; 1 Chr. 6:79).

Kedesh ("holy"). **[1]** A city of the Canaanites near the northern border, defeated by Joshua (Josh. 12:22; 19:37). **[2]** Levitical city of refuge in Naphtali. It was sometimes called Kedesh Naphtali (Josh. 20:7; Judg. 4:6, 9). It is probably modern Kades, about 7.2 km. (4.5 mi.) northwest of Lake Huleh. **[3]** A Levitical city in Issachar (1 Chr. 6:72). **[4]** A city of Judah near Hazor and Ithan (Josh. 15:23).

Kehelathah ("a whole; a congregation"), a desert encampment of the Israelites (Num. 33:22, 23). It is probably Krintilet Krayeh, also called Ajrud.

Keilah ("fortress"), a town in the lowlands of Judah (1 Sam. 23:1, 13; Josh. 15:44). It is 8.5 mi. north of Hebron at Khirbet Kila. *See also* "People of the Bible."

Kenath ("possession"), a town on the

extreme northeastern border of Israelite territory, the easternmost of the ten cities of the Decapolis (Num. 32:42). It is identified with Kanawat.

Kerioth [Kirioth] ("the cities"). **[1]** A town in extreme southern Judah (Josh. 15:25). **[2]** A city of Moab (Jer. 48:24, 41; Amos 2:2); possibly the same as Ar.

Keziz ("the angle; border; cassia tree"), a valley and town of Benjamin (Josh. 18:21).

Kibroth-hattavah ("the graves of lust"), a campsite on the Sinai Peninsula where the Israelites grew tired of manna (Num. 11:34–35). This may be Rueis el-Ebeirig, northeast of Jebel Mesa.

Kibzaim ("double gathering"), a city of Ephraim given to the Levites (Josh. 21:22). It may be the same as Jokmeam.

Kidron [Cedron] ("obscure; making black or sad"), a valley in Jerusalem between the Mount of Ophel and the Mount of Olives (2 Sam. 15:23; John 18:1). Today it is called Wadi Sitti Maryan.

Kinah ("buying; dirge; lamentation"), a city on the extreme southern boundary of Judah (Josh. 15:22).

Kir ("a city; wall; meeting"). **[1]** An eastern country whose location has not been determined (2 Kin. 16:9; Amos 9:7). The Arameans migrated from this place to Syria. It may have been the area between the Caspian and Black Seas, the modern Georgia. **[2]** *See* Kir-haraseth.

Kir-haraseth [Kir-hareseth, Kir-haresh, Kir-heres] ("city of the sun; wall of burnt brick"), a fortified city, probably the same as Kir (2 Kin. 3:25; 16:9; Is. 16:7, 11; Jer. 48:31). Its modern name is Kerak and it is located about 17.7 km. (11 mi.) east of the south bay of the Dead Sea.

Kir-heres. *See* Kir-haraseth.

Kirioth. *See* Kerioth.

Kirjath ("city; vocation; meeting"), a city belonging to the tribe of Benjamin (Josh. 18:28). It is probably Kirjath-jearim (q.v.).

Kirjathaim [Kiriathaim] ("double city"). **[1]** A Moabite city on the east of the Jordan (Num. 32:37); probably Khirbet-el-Kureiyat, north of the Arnon. **[2]** *See* Kartan.

Kirjath-arba ("fourth city"), an early name for the city of Hebron (Gen. 23:2; Josh. 14:15). *See* Hebron.

Kirjath-arim. *See* Kirjath-jearim.

Kirjath-baal. *See* Kirjath-jearim.

Kirjath-huzoth ("city of streets"), a town of Moab (Num. 22:39). Its location is un-

known, but Kirjathaim and Kerioth are possibilities.

Kirjath-jearim ("city of woods"), originally one of the cities of the Gibeonites located at the northwestern boundary of Judah (Josh. 9:17; Judg. 18:14). It is identical with Baalah (Josh. 15:9), Kirjath-arim (Ezra 2:25), Kirjath-baal (Josh. 18:14), and Baale-judah (2 Sam. 6:2). It is thought to be modern Deir el-Azhar, about 13.4 km. (8.3 mi.) northwest of Jerusalem. *See also* "People of the Bible."

Kirjath-sannah ("city of instruction"). *See* Debir [1].

Kirjath-sepher ("city of books"). *See* Debir [1].

Kishion [Kishon] ("hardness"), a city on the boundary of the tribe of Issachar (Josh. 19:20; 21:28). It is probably modern Tell el-Ajjul, 20.1 km. (12.5 mi.) northeast of Megiddo.

Kishon [Kison] ("bending; crooked"), a river in central Palestine which rises in Mount Tabor and, flowing westward, drains the valley of Esdraelon [Jezreel] (Judg. 4:7, 13; 1 Kin. 18:40; Ps. 83:9). Next to the Jordan, it is the most important river in Palestine. *See* Kishion.

Kithlish ("it is a wall"), a city located in the lowlands of Judah, perhaps the same as Dilean (Josh. 15:40); identified with Khirbet el-Makhaz.

Kitron ("making sweet"), one of the towns of Zebulun (Judg. 1:30); perhaps the same as Kattath. It is identified with modern Tell el-Far, about 9.7 km. (6 mi.) southeast of Haifa.

L

Laban ("whiteness"), an obscure place in the Sinai Peninsula (Deut. 1:1); perhaps the same as Libnah [1]. *See also* "People of the Bible."

Lachish ("who exists of himself"), a southern city of Judah midway between Jerusalem and Gaza (Josh. 10:3, 5; 2 Kin. 18:17). The modern site of this Amorite city is Tell-ed-Duweir.

Lahai-roi. *See* Beer-lahai-roi.

Lahmam ("their bread"), a city located in the lowlands of Judah (Josh. 15:40); probably Khirbet el-Lahm.

Laish [Leshem] ("a lion"). **[1]** The northern limit of the tribe of Dan (Judg. 18:7–29; Is. 10:30; Josh. 19:47). The Danites changed its name to Dan (q.v.). **[2]** A place named in

PLACES OF THE BIBLE

Isaiah 10:30 with Gallim and Anathoth. *See also* "People of the Bible."

Lakum ("fortress"), one of the landmarks on the boundary of Naphtali (Josh. 19:33); probably modern Mansura near the head of Wadi Fejjas.

Laodicea ("just people"), a chief city of Phrygia in Asia Minor (Col. 2:1; 4:15; Rev. 1:11). It is located on the Lycous River, a tributary of the Meander.

Lasea ("wise"), a seaport of Crete (Acts 27:8). It is about 8 km. (5 mi.) east of Fair Havens.

Lasha ("to anoint"), a Canaanite boundary somewhere in the southeast of Palestine (Gen. 10:19). It has been identified with Callirhoe, a ravine east of the Dead Sea known for its hot springs. Now called Wadi Zerka Ma'in, it enters the Dead Sea about 17.7 km. (11 mi.) east of the mouth of the Jordan.

Lasharon ("of or to Sharon"), a town belonging to the Canaanites (Josh. 12:18). It may be the same as Aphek [3].

Lebanon ("white"), one of two ranges of mountains in northern Palestine (Deut. 1:7; Josh. 1:4). The second is called the Anti-Lebanons; Mount Hermon is its highest peak. Running for about 161 km. (100 mi.), the

ROAD TO MEDEBA. *A Roman milestone stands beside the ancient road from Dibon to Medeba (visible in the distance). The Moabite town of Medeba was given to the tribe of Reuben (Josh. 13:9, 16); but the city later defected to the Moabites once again (cf. Is. 15:2). During the intertestamental period, the Jewish military leader John Maccabeus was killed in this town.*

MEGIDDO. *Joshua conquered the city which stood at this site in the Carmel Mountains during his conquest of Canaan (Josh. 12:21); it was then given to the tribe of Manasseh (Josh. 17:11). King Solomon fortified the city and established accommodations for his chariots and horses here (1 Kin. 9:15–19). Many people believe that the end-time battle of Armageddon (Hebrew, "hill of Meggido") will take place in this area.*

chain begins about 24.1 km. (15 mi.) southeast of Sidon and runs north to about 19.3 km. (12 mi.) north-northeast of Tripolis in Syria.

Lebaoth ("lioness"), one of the towns of southern Judah in Simeon (Josh. 15:32). It is the same as Beth-lebaoth and perhaps identical with Beth-birei (q.v.).

Lebonah ("incense"), a place 12.9 km. (8 mi.) north of Bethel (Judg. 21:19).

Lehi ("elevation of the jawbone"), the location in Judah where Samson slew many Philistines (Judg. 15:9, 14, 19). The site is unknown. In v. 17 it is called Ramath-lehi ("elevation of the jawbone").

Leshem. *See* Laish.

Libnah ("white"). **[1]** An encampment of the Israelites during their journey in the wilderness (Num. 33:20–21). It may be identical with Laban. **[2]** A Levitical city of Jerusalem (Josh. 10:29–31; 2 Kin. 19:8). It is now called Tel-el-safieh.

Libya ("heart of the sea"), the Greek name for the continent of Africa, west of Egypt (Acts 2:10). The Hebrews called this region Phut [Put]. Even though the Hebrew text of Ezekiel 30:5 and 38:5 read Phut, the KJV rendered the word *Libya. See also* Lubim.

Lod ("nativity"), a city of Benjamin in the Plain of Sharon (1 Chr. 8:12; Ezra 2:33). Today it is Ludd, about 17.7 km. (11 mi.) southeast of Joppa. In New Testament times it was called Lydda.

Lo-debar ("barren"), a place east of the Jordan River (2 Sam. 9:4); probably the same as Debir [3].

Lubim ("dwellers in a thirsty land"), the North African continent west of Egypt (Neh. 3:9). *See also* Libya.

Luhith ("made of boards"), a town in Moab, between Areopolis and Zoar (Is. 15:5; Jer. 48:5).

Luz ("separation"). **[1]** A city 17.7 km. (11 mi.) north of Jerusalem. In later times it was called Beth-el (Gen. 28:19; Josh. 16:2). **[2]** A town of the Hittites (Judg. 1:22–26). The ruin Luweiziyeh, about 4.5 miles northwest of Baniyas, has been proposed as the site.

Lycaonia ("she-wolf"), an inland district of Asia Minor. Paul twice visited in the cities of Derbe and Lystra here (Acts 14:6–11). It was bordered on the north by Galatia and on the south by Cilicia.

Lycia ("land of Lycus"), a region in southwestern Asia Minor (Acts 27:5); the place juts into the Mediterranean Sea.

Lydda ("a standing pool"), a town located

on the Plain of Sharon (Acts 9:32). It is identical with Lod (q.v.).

Lydia ("Lydus land"), a country and people in Northern Africa, west of Egypt (Ezek. 30:5). *See also* "People of the Bible."

Lystra ("that dissolves"), a city of Lycaonia in central Asia Minor. Paul was stoned here (Acts 14:6–21).

M

Maachathi [properly Maacah], a small kingdom that adjoined Geshur on the western border of Bashan (Deut. 3:14), the inhabitants of which were called Maachathites (Josh. 12:5; 13:13).

Maaleh-acrabbim [Akrabbim] ("ascent of scorpions"), a high place which marks part of the boundary of Judah between Kedish and the Dead Sea (Josh. 15:3; Num. 34:4). Akrabbim is a shortened form of the name.

Maarath ("den"), a town located in the mountains of Judah (Josh. 15:59). It is near Beth-aron and is now called Umman.

Macedonia (meaning unknown), a nation lying to the north of Greece proper (Acts 16:9; 18:5).

Machpelah ("double"), the place where the burial cave of Abraham is located, near Hebron (Gen. 23:17; 25:9).

Madian. *See* Midian.

Madmannah ("measure of a gift"), a town near Gaza in southern Judah (Josh. 15:31). It is perhaps the same as Beth-marcaboth, which is Umm pemneh, about 19.3 km. (12 mi.) northeast of Beer-sheba. *See also* "People of the Bible."

Madmen ("dunghill"), a location in Moab (Jer. 48:2). It may be modern Khirbet Dimneh, 4 km. (2.5 mi.) northwest of Rabba.

Madmenah ("dung heap"), a village north of Jerusalem in the territory belonging to Benjamin (Is. 10:31).

Madon ("strife"), a city of northern Canaan (Josh. 11:1; 12:19). The name still exists in Khirbet Madin, 5 km. (3 mi.) south of Hattin.

Magbish (probably "sturdy; strong"), an unidentified town in Benjamin (Ezra 2:30).

Magdala ("tower"), a village located on the western edge of the Sea of Galilee (Matt. 15:39). It is present-day el-Mejdel, 4.8 km. (3 mi.) north-northwest of Tiberias.

Magog ("region of Gog"), a country of undetermined location, generally described as being in a northerly direction from Palestine

(Ezek. 38:2; 39:6). The first-century Jewish historian Josephus identified the land with the Scythians.

Mahanaim ("tents"), a place on the boundary between Reuben and Gad (Gen. 32:2; Josh. 21:38). It is east of the Jordan and south of the Jabbok. The exact site is undetermined.

Mahaneh-dan ("tents of judgment"), a campsite between Zorah and Eshtaol (Judg. 18:12). It is west of Kirjath-jearim.

Makaz ("an end"), a place mentioned in First Kin. 4:9; it is thought to be Khirbet el-Mukheigin, south of Ekron.

Makheloth ("congregations"), a desert encampment of the Israelites (Num. 33:25); probably modern Kuntilet Krayeh or Ajurd.

Makkedah ("worshipping"), a city of the Canaanites located on the plain of Judah (Josh. 10:10; 12:16). It is 19.3 km. (12 mi.) southwest of Jerusalem in the plain country of Judah, and is now called Mughar.

Maktesh ("mortar"), a section of Jerusalem where merchants gathered (Zeph. 1:11); probably the northern portion of the city.

Mamre ("firmness; vigor"), a place in the Hebron district, west of Machpelah (Gen. 23:17, 19; 49:30). The site has been identified at Râmet el-Khálil, 2 mi. north of Hebron. *See also* "People of the Bible."

Manahath ("resting place; rest"), a city of Benjamin (1 Chr. 8:6). *See also* "People of the Bible."

Maon ("place of sin"), a mountain city of Judah (Josh. 15:55; 1 Sam. 23:24). It is modern Tell Ma'in, about 13.8 km. (8.5 mi.) south of Hebron. *See also* "People of the Bible."

Marah ("bitter"), the fountain of bitter water in the wilderness of Shur where the Israelites first halted after crossing the Red Sea (Ex. 15:23; Num. 33:8). The traditional site is 'Ain Hawarah, about 75.6 km. (47 mi.) from Suez.

Maralah ("sleep"), a boundary village of Zebulun (Josh. 19:11). It is probably Tell Ghalta in the Plain of Kishon.

Mareshah ("from the beginning"), a city in the lowlands of Judah (Josh. 15:44; 2 Chr. 11:8). Its ruins are placed at 1.6 km. (1 mi.) southeast of Beit Jibrin. *See also* "People of the Bible."

Maroth ("bitterness"), a town in the lowlands of Judah (Mic. 1:12); possibly the same as Maarath (q.v.).

Mars Hill. *See* Areopagus.

Mashal ("parable"), a city in Asher given to the Levites (1 Chr. 6:74). It is probably located on the plain south of Accho. It is identical with Mishal (q.v.).

Masrekah ("whistling"), an ancient city in Edom (Gen. 36:36; 1 Chr. 1:47). It is Jebel el-Mushrat, about 35.4 km. (22 mi.) south-south-west of Ma'an.

Massah ("temptation"), the name of a spot in the vicinity of Horeb where the Israelites tempted God (Ex. 17:7; Deut. 6:16). *See also* Meribah [1].

Mattanah ("gift of Jehovah"), an encampment during the latter part of Israel's wandering (Num. 21:18–19). It was north of the Arnon River and west of the wilderness of Kedemoth.

Meah ("hundred"), a tower at Jerusalem not far from the Sheep Gate (Neh. 3:1; 12:39).

Mearah ("den"), a place, possibly a cavern, in Sidon in northern Canaan (Josh. 13:4).

Medeba ("waters of grief"), a Moabite town on the Jordan River in the territory of Reuben east of the Arnon (Num. 21:30; Josh. 13:9). It is now Madaba, 9.7 km. (6 mi.) south of Heshbon.

Media ("middle land"), a country of Asia located south of the Caspian Sea, west of Parthia, north of Elam, and east of the Yagros Mountains. During the 400's B.C. the Persians and Medes had a powerful empire here (Esth. 1:3, 14, 18; Dan. 8:20).

Megiddo [Megiddon] ("declaring a message"), a city on the southern edge of the Plain of Esdraelon (Jezreel) at the northeast of Mount Carmel (Josh. 12:21; 17:11; Zech 12:11).

Megiddon. *See* Megiddo.

Me-jarkon ("the waters of Jordan"), a city in the territory of Dan near Joppa (Josh. 19:46).

Mekonah ("provision"), a town of Judah named in connection with Ziklag and other towns of the far south (Neh. 11:28).

Melita ("affording honey"), the island of Malta, located in the Mediterranean Sea (Acts 28:1). It is 96.5 km. (60 mi.) south of Sicily.

Memphis ("abode of the good"), an ancient Egyptian city located on the western bank of the Nile in the central portion of the country (Hos. 9:6). It was also called Noph (Jer. 2:16).

Meonenim ("regardless of time"), a place near Shechem in Ephraim (Judg. 9:37).

Mephaath ("force of waters"), a city allotted to Reuben and assigned to the Levites (Josh. 13:18). It was near Kedemoth or Kirjath-aim.

PLACES OF THE BIBLE

STREET SCENE, NAZARETH. *Nazareth was a small city of low repute, yet Jesus' parents lived here and it became the boyhood home of the Savior (Luke 2:39–51). This narrow, winding alley of Nazareth looks much as the streets of Jesus' times would have appeared.*

Merathaim ("double rebellion"), the country of the Chaldeans, also known as Babylon (Jer. 50:21).

Meribah ("quarrel"). **[1]** The desert location where Moses smote the rock (Ex. 17:7). **[2]** Another name for Kadesh-barnea in the wilderness of Zin, where the Hebrew people rebelled against Moses (Num. 20:13). In Deuteronomy 32:51 the place is called Meribah-Kadesh.

Meribah-Kadesh. *See* Meribah [2].

Merom ("elevations"), a lake 16.1 km. (10 mi.) north of the Sea of Galilee (Josh. 11:5, 7).

Meroz ("secret"), a place near Kishon (Judg. 5:23). Its exact location is unknown, but may be modern Khirbet Marus, about 12.1 km. (7.5 mi.) south of Kedesh of Naphtali.

Mesha ("salvation"), a boundary marker of the descendants of Joktan (Gen. 10:30). It

seems to be west of Sephar. *See also* "People of the Bible."

Mesopotamia ("between two rivers"), a region located between the Tigris and Euphrates Rivers (Gen. 24:10; Deut. 23:4), excluding the mountain regions where the rivers take their rise and the low-lying plains of Babylon.

Metheg-ammah ("bridle of bondage"), a stronghold of the Philistines captured by David (2 Sam. 8:1). Many scholars believe that the name refers to Gath.

Michmash [Michmas] ("he that strikes"), a town of Benjamin (1 Sam. 13:5; Is. 10:28; Ezra 2:27). The pass of Mukkmas retains the name. The town is 12.1 km. (7.5 mi.) northeast of Jerusalem and east of Bethaven.

Michmethah ("the gift of a striker"), a landmark boundary of Manasseh on the western side of the Jordan, east of Shechem (Josh. 17:7).

Middin ("judgment"), a village in the wilderness of Judah (Josh. 15:61). It is probably modern Khirbet Abu Tabak in the Valley of Achor.

Midian [Madian] ("contention"), the land of the descendants of Midian beyond the Jordan. It included Edom, the Sinai Peninsula, and Arabian Petra (Ex. 2:15–16; Judg. 6:1; Acts 7:29). *See also* "People of the Bible."

Migdalel ("tower of God"), a fortified city of Naphtali (Josh. 19:38). It may be modern Mujeidil 20.1 km. (12.5 mi.) northwest of Kedesh [Kades].

Migdalgad ("tower compassed about"), a lowland city of Judah (Josh. 15:37); probably modern Khirbet el-Mejdeleh 8 km. (5 mi.) south of Beit Jibrin.

Migdol ("tower"). **[1]** A location in the extreme north of Egypt (Jer. 44:1; 46:14). **[2]** An encampment of the Israelites west of the Red Sea (Ex. 14:2; Num. 33:7).

Migron ("fear"). **[1]** A Benjamite village north of Michmash (Is. 10:28). It may be modern Makrum. **[2]** If there were two Migrons, the second was located at the outermost part of Gibeah and considerably south of Michmash (1 Sam. 14:2). Tell Miryam has been suggested as the site.

Miletus [Miletum] ("scarlet"), a coastal city of Ionia (Acts 20:15; 2 Tim. 4:20). It was 57.9 km. (36 mi.) south of Ephesus.

Millo ("fulness"). **[1]** A bastion in Jerusalem built in anticipation of an Assyrian siege (2 Sam. 5:9; 1 Kin. 9:15). **[2]** An acropolis of Shechem, a high platform of artificial fill (Judg. 9:6, 20).

PLACES OF THE BIBLE

AMPHITHEATER IN PERGAMUM. *The citizens of Pergamum (KJV, Pergamos) were the first to establish the worship of the Roman emperor, Augustus Caesar; John referred to the city as the "seat of Satan" (Rev. 2:13). It is located 80 km. (50 mi.) north of Smyrna in present-day Turkey. In the heart of the city the Greeks built this magnificent amphitheater with 78 rows of seats. Behind the row of columns was the Asclepieum, where the people of Pergamum worshiped the god of healing, Asclepias.*

Minni ("prepared"), a portion of the land of Armenia (Jer. 51:27). It was directly south of Lake Urmia and next to the Kingdom of Ararah of the Araxes River.

Minnith ("prepared"), a location east of the Jordan where Jephthah slaughtered the Ammonites (Judg. 11:33; Ezek. 27:17). It may be modern Khirbet Hamzeh 6.4 km. (4 mi.) northeast of Hebron.

Miphkad ("appointment; census"), a gate in or near the northern end of the east wall of Jerusalem (Neh. 3:31).

Misgab ("light"), an unidentified location in Moab (Jer. 48:1).

Mishal [Misheal] ("requiring"), a territorial town of Asher (Josh. 19:26; 21:30); not to be confused with Mashal.

Misrephoth-maim ("hot waters"), a location in northern Palestine (Josh. 11:8; 13:6). It was on the frontier of the country of the Sidonians. It is identified with modern Khirbet el-Musheir-efeh 17.7 km. (11 mi.) north of Ac-

cho and 8 km. (5 mi.) from the Mediterranean.

Mithcah ("sweetness"), an unidentified encampment of the Israelites in the wilderness (Num. 33:28).

Mitylene ("purity"), the principal city of the Island of Lesbos off the western coast of Asia Minor (Acts 20:14).

Mizar ("little"), a hill east of the Jordan, probably within sight of Mount Hermon, on Lebanon's eastern slope (Ps. 42:6).

Mizpah [Mizpeh] ("a watchtower"). **[1]** A mound of stones on Mount Gilead (Gen. 31:49). **[2]** A Hivite settlement in northern Palestine at the foot of Mount Hermon (Josh. 11:3). **[3]** A city in the lowlands of Judah (Josh. 15:38). It was just north of Eleutheropolis [Beit Jibrin]. **[4]** A town in Gilead east of the Jordan (Judg. 11:34). It is possibly identical with Ramath-Mizpeh. **[5]** A town of Benjamin just north of Jerusalem (Josh. 18:26; 1 Kin. 15:22). The exact site is uncertain. **[6]** A place in Moab (1 Sam. 22:3); perhaps modern Rujm el-Meshrefeh west-southwest of Madaba.

Moab, a land that consisted of the plateau east of the Dead Sea between the wadis Arnon and Zered, though at certain periods extending to the north of the Arnon (Deut. 1:5; Num. 22—25). *See also* "People of the Bible."

Moladah ("generation"), a southern city of Judah (Josh. 15:26; Neh. 11:26).

Moreh ("stretching"). **[1]** The first stopping place of Abraham after he entered Canaan (Gen. 12:6). It was near Shechem. **[2]** A hill lying at the foot of the valley of Jezreel (Judg. 7:1). It is probably modern Jebel Dahy or Little Hermon about 12.9 km. (8 mi.) northwest of Mount Gilboa.

Moresheth-gath ("possession of Gath"), the hometown of Micah (Mic. 1:14). It may be modern Tell ej-Judeiyeh about 32 km. (2 mi.) north of Eleutheropolis.

Moriah ("bitterness of the Lord"). **[1]** An elevation in Jerusalem on which Solomon built the temple (2 Chr. 3:1). Probably the same hilltop was used as the threshing floor of Araunah. The name Moriah was possibly ascribed by the Chronicler because of its traditional meaning (2 Sam. 24:18; 2 Chr. 3:1). **[2]** The hill on which Abraham was prepared to sacrifice Isaac (Gen. 22:2). The site is uncertain, but Samaritans identify Moriah with Moreh [1]. This seems unlikely.

Mosera ("bonds"), the location of an Israelite wilderness encampment near Mount Hor on the border of Edom (Deut. 10:6).

Moseroth ("discipline"), a desert encampment of the Hebrews (Num. 33:30). Some identify it with Mosera (q.v.).

Mozah ("unleavened"), a city allotted to Benjamin (Josh. 18:26); probably Kalunya 7.6 km. (4.7 mi.) northwest of Jerusalem on the road to Jaffa.

Myra ("weep"), a town of Lycia where Paul changed ships on his way to Rome (Acts 27:5). It is now called Dembre.

Mysia ("abominable"), a province in northwestern Asia Minor (Acts 16:7). Lydia is to the south and the Aegean Sea to the west of this province.

N

Naamah ("beautiful"), a town in the southwestern lowlands of Judah (Josh. 15:41). It is probably modern Khirbet Fered near Arak Ma'aman. *See also* "People of the Bible."

Naaran [Naarath] ("youthful"), a border town of Ephraim (1 Chr. 7:28). It was east of Bethel and near Jericho, and was also called Naarath (Josh. 16:7).

Naarath. *See* Naaran. *See also* "People of the Bible."

Nachon. *See* Chidon.

Nahalal [Nahallal; Nahalol] ("pasture"), a city of Zebulun assigned to the Levites (Josh. 19:15; 21:35; Judg. 1:30). It is probably modern Khirbet el-Teim, south of Accho.

Nahaliel ("valley of God"), an Israelite encampment north of the Arnon River and east of Moab (Num. 21:19). It may be modern Wadi el-Waleh or Wadi Zerka Ma'in.

Nahallal. *See* Nahalal.

Nahalol. *See* Nahalal.

Nahor, a city mentioned in Genesis 24:10. This is possibly Haran so-called after Abraham's brother, Nahor. *See also* "People of the Bible."

Nain ("beauty"), a village in Galilee where Christ resurrected a widow's son (Luke 7:11). It is located 3.2 km. (2 mi.) south of Mount Tabor and a little southwest of the Sea of Galilee.

Naioth ("habitation"), the place in Ramah where a community of prophets gathered around Samuel (1 Sam. 19:18–23; 20:1). Its location is not clearly identified. *See also* Ramah [2].

Naphtali [Nephthalim] ("that struggles"), a territory assigned to the tribe of Naphtali, located in mountainous northern Palestine (Josh. 19:32–39; Matt. 4:13). It was bounded on the east by the Upper Jordan River and the Sea of Galilee and on the west by the territories of Zebulun and Asher. *See also* "People of the Bible."

Nazareth ("sanctified"), the hometown of Jesus in lower Galilee, north of the Plain of Esdraelon [Jezreel] (Matt. 4:13; Mark 1:9). It is 8 km. (5 mi.) west-southwest of Tiberias, 32.2 km. (20 mi.) southwest of modern Tell Hum [Capernaum] and 141.6 km. (88 mi.) north of Jerusalem.

Neah ("moved"), a landmark boundary of Zebulun (Josh. 19:13). It is probably modern Tell el-wawiyat.

Neapolis ("the new city"), a seaport of Philippi in Macedonia (Acts 16:11; cf. 20:6). It is on the Strymonian Gulf 16.1 km. (10 mi.) east-southeast of Philippi.

Neballat ("prophecy"), a town of Benjamin repopulated after the Babylonian Captivity (Neh. 11:34). It is now Beit Nabala 6.4 km. (4 mi.) northeast of Lydda.

PHILIPPI. *Alexander the Great named this city after his father, Philip II. It was located near rich gold and silver mines, and was a staging point for the Battle of Actium in 31 B.C. During the apostle Paul's visit to Philippi in about A.D. 52, the Philippian jailer and a woman named Lydia were converted to the gospel of Christ (Acts 16:12–14).*

Nebo ("that prophesies"). **[1]** The mountain from which Moses saw the Promised Land (Deut. 32:49; 34:1). It is a peak in the Abarim Mountains east of the Jordan, opposite Jericho; probably modern Jebel en Neba, 12.9 km. (8 mi.) east of the mouth of the Jordan. On a clear day, all of Palestine can be seen from this peak. **[2]** A city of Reuben that fell again to the Moabites (Num. 32:3, 38; 33:47). It is probably modern Khirbet el-Mekhayyet, south of Mount Nebo. **[3]** A city in Judah (Ezra 2:29; Neh. 7:33), probably modern Beth-Nube, near Lydda.

Neiel ("commotion of God"), a landmark boundary of Asher (Josh. 19:27). It is probably modern Khirbet ya'nin on the edge of the Plain of Acre [Accho].

Nekeb ("cave"), a town on the boundary of the territory of Naphtali (Josh. 19:33); perhaps the same as Adami (q.v.).

Nephthalim. *See* Naphtali.

Nephtoah ("open"), a spring that marks the boundary between Judah and Benjamin (Josh. 15:9). It is identified with modern Lifta, 3.2 km. (2 mi.) northwest of Jerusalem.

Netophah, a city in Judah (Ezra 2:22). A Netophathite is one from this city (1 Chr. 2:54).

Nezib ("standing-place"), a city in the lowlands of Judah (Josh. 15:43). It is now Beit Nasib, near Ashna.

Nibshan ("prophecy"), a wilderness town of Judah (Josh. 15:62); possibly modern Khirbet el-Makari south of Jericho between Betharaban and En-gev.

Nicopolis ("the city of victory"). **[1]** A town in Epirus in western Greece about 6.4 km. (4 mi.) north of Actium. **[2]** A city on both sides of the Nestus River, the boundary between Thrace and Macedonia. Paul referred to one of the above in Titus 3:12; the first is preferred.

Nile ("dark blue"), the greatest river of Egypt and the world's longest. It is simply referred to in Scripture as "the river" (Gen. 13:1; Ex. 2:3; 7:21). The Nile is about 6,669.3 km. (4,145 mi.) long.

Nimrah. *See* Beth-Nimrah.

Nimrim ("bitterness"), a brook in Moab (Is. 15:6; Jer. 48:34). The name still exists in Wadi en-Nemeirah near the southeast end of the Dead Sea.

Nineveh [Nineve] (meaning unknown), the capital of the Kingdom of Assyria (Nah. 1:1; cf. 3:1; Zeph. 2:13; Luke 11:32). It was located east of the Tigris River in the area north of the point the Tigris joins the Upper Zab. The ruins are now called Tell Kuyunjik and Tell Nebi Yunus.

No ("stirring up"), an Egyptian city better known as Thebes (Ezek. 30:14–16; Jer. 46:25). It was the capital of Upper Egypt.

Nob ("prophecy"), a city of the tribe of Benjamin located northeast of Jerusalem, within sight of the city (1 Sam. 21:1; 22:19).

Nobah ("prominent"), a town of Gad east of the Jordan (Judg. 8:11). Its site is a tell near Safut. *See also* "People of the Bible."

Nod ("vagabond"), an unidentified land east of Eden to which Cain fled after the murder of Abel (Gen. 4:16). Some suppose it to be China, but this is speculation.

Noph. *See* Memphis.

Nophah ("fearful"), a city in Moab (Num. 21:30). It is not referred to elsewhere and may not be a place name. However, it may be another name for Nobah (q.v.).

O

Oboth ("desires"), an encampment of the Israelites east of Moab (Num. 21:10; 33:43). It is probably modern 'Ain el-Weiba.

Olives, Mount of [Mount of Corruption; Olivet], a ridge east of Jerusalem and separated from Jerusalem by the Kidron Valley (2 Sam. 15:30; Mark 11:1; Acts 1:12). It is

PLACES OF THE BIBLE

called the Mount of Corruption in Second Kin. 23:13.

On ("strength"), an ancient city of Lower Egypt situated on the Nile Delta (Gen. 41:45, 50). It is identical with Beth-Shemesh [4], 30.6 km. (19 mi.) north of Memphis. *See also* "People of the Bible."

Ono ("grief of him"), a city of Benjamin (1 Chr. 8:12; Ezra 2:33). It is probably modern Kafr 'Ana 11.3 km. (7 mi.) southeast of Joppa.

Ophel ("small white cloud"), a hill in southeastern Jerusalem (2 Chr. 27:3; Neh. 3:26; 11:21). It was near the Water Gate, Horse Gate, Pool of Siloam, the east court of the temple, and the Kidron Valley.

Ophir ("fruitful region"), a region where Solomon mined gold (1 Kin. 9:28; 1 Chr. 29:4). The location is highly uncertain. Josephus thought it was India, but the African coast in modern Somaliland is more probable. *See also* "People of the Bible."

Ophni ("wearisomeness"), a city of Benjamin (Josh. 18:24). It was 4.8 km. (3 mi.) north-northwest of Bethel.

Ophrah ("a fawn"). **[1]** A city of Benjamin (Josh. 18:23; 1 Sam. 13:17). It is probably modern el Taiyibeh, about 6.4 km. (4 mi.) east-northeast of Bethel. **[2]** A city in Manasseh (Judg. 6:11, 24; 9:5). It is now called Arrabeh. *See also* "People of the Bible."

Oreb ("a raven"), the rock east of Jordan near Beth-bareh where the Midianite chieftain Oreb died (Judg. 7:25; Is. 10:26). It is now called Ash-el-Ghorab. *See also* "People of the Bible."

P

Padan-aram [Padan] ("plain [tableland] of Aram"), the plain region of Mesopotamia from the Lebanon Mountains to beyond the Euphrates, and from the Taurus Mountains on the north to beyond Damascus on the south (Gen. 25:20; 28:2; 31:18). It is called simply Padan in Genesis 48:7.

Pai [Pau] ("howling"), the capital of Hadar, King of Edom (Gen. 36:39; 1 Chr. 1:50). Its location is unknown.

Palestine [Palestina] ("which is covered"), an ill-defined region between the Jordan River and the Dead Sea on the east and the Mediterranean on the west (Gen. 15:18; Ex. 15:14; Joel 3:4). Its northern border is roughly the Lebanon Mountain range. It stretches in a southwesterly triangle to the Gulf of Aqaba on the Red Sea.

Pamphylia ("a nation made up of every tribe"), a southern coastal area in Asia Minor; its main city is Perga (Acts 13:13; 14:24; 27:5).

Paphos ("that which boils"), a town on the southwest extremity of Cyprus; it was visited by Paul and Barnabas (Acts 13:6–13). It is modern Baffa.

Paradise ("pleasure ground; park"), figurative name for the place where God dwells (2 Cor. 12:3) and the abode of the righteous (Luke 23:43; Rev. 2:7).

Parah ("increasing"), a town of Benjamin (Josh. 18:23). It is probably modern Wadi el-Farah 5.5 miles northeast of Jerusalem.

Paran ("beauty"), a wilderness seven days' march from Mount Sinai (Gen. 21:21; Num. 10:12; 1 Sam. 25:1). It is located east of the wilderness of Beer-sheba and Shurj, and it merges with the Wilderness of Sin with no clearly marked boundary. The area borders on Edom and Midian; it is sometimes called Mount Paran (Hab. 3:3) and El-Paran (Gen. 14:6).

Parbar ("a suburb"), an area on the west side of the temple containing officials' chambers and cattle stalls (1 Chr. 26:18).

Parvaim ("eastern"), a place where gold was obtained for the decoration of Solomon's temple (2 Chr. 3:6). It may be modern Sak el-Farwain in southern Arabia.

Pas-dammim. *See* Ephes-dammim.

Patara ("trodden under foot"), a seacoast city of southwest Lycia in Asia Minor (Acts 21:1).

Pathros ("persuasion of ruin"), the country of Upper Egypt inhabited by the Pathrusim (Is. 11:11; Jer. 44:1–12), one of the seven peoples coming out of Egypt.

Patmos ("mortal"), a barren island to which John was banished (Rev. 1:9). It is in the Greek archipelagos and is now called Patino.

Pau. *See* Pai.

Peniel. *See* Penvel.

Penvel [Peniel] ("face of God"), an encampment of the Hebrews east of Jordan (Gen. 32:30–31; Judg. 8:8, 17). It derived its name from the fact that Jacob had seen God face-to-face there.

Peor ("opening"), a mountain peak near Pisgah in Moab (Num. 23:28). It stood across the Jordan River from Jericho.

Perazim. *See* Baal-perazim.

Perez-Uzzah ("breech of Uzzah"), the name David gave to the place Uzzah was struck by God (2 Sam. 6:8).

PLACES OF THE BIBLE

Perga ("very earthy"), the capital of Pamphylia in Asia Minor during the Roman period (Acts 13:13).

Pergamos ("elevation"), a city of Mysia in northwest Asia Minor and the site of one of the seven churches of Asia (Rev. 2:12–17).

Persia ("cuts or divides"), a great empire including all of western Asia and parts of Europe and Africa (Ezra 1:8; Ezek. 38:5). Persia proper corresponded to what is now the province of Fars in Iran.

Pethor ("soothsayer"), the residence of Balaam (Num. 22:5; Deut. 23:4). The town was near the Euphrates River and the mountains of Aram. It was a few kilometers south of Carchemish.

Pharpar ("that produces fruit"), one of the two rivers of Damascus (2 Kin. 5:12). It is probably the modern Nahr el-'A'waj.

Phenice ("land of palm trees"). **[1]** A harbor in southern Crete (Acts 27:12). **[2]** *See* Phoenicia.

Philadelphia ("love of a brother"), a town of Lydia in Asia Minor. It was the site of one of the seven churches of Asia (Rev. 1:11; 3:7–13). It was 45.5 km. (28.3 mi.) southeast of Sardis.

Philippi ("the same"), a city of Macedonia founded by Philip the Great and named for him (Acts 16:12; 20:3–6). It lies inland about 16.1 km. (10 mi.) northwest of its seaport, Neapolis.

Philistia ("land of sojourners"), an area on the southwest coast of Palestine (Ps. 60:8; 87:4; 108:9). This land, which was the home of traditional enemies of Israel, was 80 km. (50 mi.) long and only 24 km. (15 mi.) wide.

Phoenicia [Phenice] ("land of palm trees"), a thin strip of territory between the Mediterranean Sea on the west and on the east the mountains of Lebanon (Acts 21:2; 11:19;

ROMAN FORUM. *The forum was the ancient meeting place, marketplace, and political center of Rome. It was established about 500 B.C. in the valley between the Capitoline and Palatine hills. The city's legendary founder, Romulus, is said to be buried in the forum. Here Cicero spoke to the Senate and Julius Caesar was murdered. The forum's monumental architecture remained intact until the sixth century A.D., but has since been destroyed by war, vandals, and the ravages of nature.*

PLACES OF THE BIBLE

RUINS OF SAMARIA. *A city with a long history, Samaria was capital of the northern kingdom of Israel from the reign of Omri in the ninth century* B.C. *This basilica near the forum at Samaria was built by Herod the Great, who named the town Sebaste in honor of his Roman patron, Augustus (Sebaste is the Greek equivalent of the Latin Augustus). The evangelist Philip preached here, as did Peter and John (Acts 8:5–25).*

15:3). It included the hills running south from those mountains.

Phrygia ("barren"), a large and important inland province of Asia Minor (Acts 2:10; 16:6).

Phut. *See* Libya. *See also* "People of the Bible."

Pibeseth ("house of Bast"), an Egyptian town located on the west bank of the Pelusiac branch of the Nile (Ezek. 30:17). It is now called Tell Basta, about 72.4 km. (45 mi.) east-northeast of Cairo.

Pi-hahiroth ("the mouth"), the location of the final Israelite encampment prior to crossing the Red Sea (Ex. 14:2, 9; Num. 33:7–8). The site is uncertain, but it may be the swamps of Jeneffel at the edge of the pass between Baal-zephon and the Great Bitter Lake.

Pirathon ("princely"), the town where Abdon the judge was buried (Judg. 12:15). It is now called Ferata and is 12 km. (7.5 mi.) southwest of Shechem.

Pisgah ("fortress"), the mountain ranges from which Moses viewed the Promised Land (Num. 21:20; Deut. 3:27). This part of the Abarim Range is near the northeast end of the Dead Sea.

Pisidia ("pitch"), an island district of Asia Minor with Antioch as its capital (Acts 13:14).

Pison ("changing"), a river of Eden (Gen. 2:11). It has traditionally been identified with the Phasis (modern Rion) or the Kur, a tributary of the Araxes. The Palla Copas canal has been suggested also.

Pithom ("their mouthful"), an Egyptian store-city built by the Israelites (Ex. 1:11). It was located in the valley connecting the Nile and Lake Timsah. The ruins are at Tell el-Maskhutah.

Pontus ("the sea"), a district in northeastern Asia Minor on the Pontus Euxinus (Acts 2:9; 1 Pet. 1:1).

Potter's Field. *See* Aceldama.

Praetorium. The Praetorium was originally the headquarters of a Roman camp, but in the provinces the name was used to designate the official residence. Jesus was brought to Pilate's Praetorium in Jerusalem (Mark 15:16).

Ptolemais. *See* Accho.

Pul ("Lord"), a country of undetermined location (Is. 66:19), sometimes considered to be Libya. *See also* "People of the Bible."

Punon ("precious stone"), an Israelite encampment during the last portion of the wilderness wandering (Num. 33:42). It is probably modern Feeinan on the east side of the Aravah.

Put. *See* Libya. *See also* "People of the Bible."

Puteoli ("sulphurous wells"), a seaport on the northern shore of the Bay of Naples (Acts 28:13). The modern city of Pozzuoli stands there.

Q

Quicksands, the. *See* Syrtis.

R

Raamah ("to constrain, humiliate"), a place near Ma'in in southwest Arabia (Ezek. 27:22). It is called Regma in inscriptions from that area. *See also* "People of the Bible."

Raamses ("child of the sun"), one of the cities the Israelites built for the Egyptians (Ex. 1:11). It is thought to be San el-Hazar or modern Kantir.

PLACES OF THE BIBLE

Rabbah [Rabbath] ("great"). **[1]** The chief city of the Ammonites (Deut. 3:11; Josh. 13:25). It was located 37 km. (23 mi.) east of the Jordan River at the headwaters of the Jabbok. **[2]** A city in Judah near Kirjath-jearim (Josh. 15:60).

Rabbith ("great"), a boundary town of Issachar (Josh. 19:20). It is perhaps the present village of Raba 12.9 km. (8 mi.) south of Mount Gilboa.

Rachal ("to whisper"), a town in Judah (1 Sam. 30:29). Some believe the text should read Carmel and would be identical with Carmel [2].

Rakkath ("empty"), a fortress city in Naphtali on the western shore of the Sea of Galilee (Josh. 19:35); probably Tell el-latiyeh.

Rakkon ("void"), a place near Joppa in the territory of Dan (Josh. 19:46).

Ramah [Rama] ("elevated"). **[1]** A town in Benjamin near Gibeah, Geba, and Bethel (Josh. 18:25; Judg. 4:5; Is. 10:29; Matt. 2:18). It has been identified as modern Er-Ram 8 km. (5 mi.) north of Jerusalem. **[2]** The town where Samuel was born (1 Sam. 1:1). It is also called Ramathaim-zophim (1 Sam. 1:11). Its location is uncertain but has been identified with Ramah [1] and modern-day Rentis, about 14.5 km. (9 mi.) northeast of Lydda. It may be Arimathea. **[3]** A frontier town of Asher (Josh. 19:29). If not the same as Ramah [4] it may be Rameh, about 20.9 km. (13 mi.) south-southeast of Tyre. **[4]** A fortified city of Naphtali (Josh. 19:36). The site may be modern Rameh, 27.4 km. (17 mi.) east-northeast of Accho. **[5]** See Ramoth-gilead. **[6]** See Ramath.

Ramath [Ramoth] ("height, elevation"), a city of Simeon called "Ramath of the South" (Josh. 19:8). It is now Kurnab. It is also called "Ramoth" in First Samuel 30:27.

Ramathaim-Zophim. See Ramah [2].

Ramath-lehi ("elevation of the jawbone"). See Lehi.

Ramath-mizpeh ("place of the watchtower"), a city of Gad in Gilead (Josh. 13:26). It was 24 km. (15 mi.) northwest of Rabbath of Ammon, at the Jabbok. It may be identical with Mizpeh [4].

Rameses ("child of the sun"), a fertile district of Egypt where the Israelites settled (Gen. 47:11; Ex. 12:37). It was possibly the Land of Goshen.

Ramoth ("high places" or "heights"). **[1]** A Levitical city of Gilead in Gad (Deut. 4:43; Josh. 20:8). It is identical with Ramoth-gilead.

SHECHEM. *Situated in the hill country of Ephraim (Josh. 20:7) near Mount Gerizim, Shechem is today known as Tell Balata. The first Palestinian site mentioned in Genesis, Shechem was the place where Abraham built an altar to the Lord (Gen. 12:6–7). Here also the Israelites buried the bones of Joseph, which they had brought from Egypt (Josh. 24:32).*

45

PLACES OF THE BIBLE

[2] A city of Levi in Issachar (1 Chr. 6:37). It is identical with Jarmuth [2] and Remeth (q.v.). **[3]** See Ramath.

Ramoth-gilead [Ramoth] ("heights of Gilead"), the chief city of Gad. It was a city of refuge ascribed to the Levites (1 Kin. 4:13; 22:4). Sometimes it is called simply Ramoth (Deut. 4:43; Josh. 20:8). It has been identified with both Tell Ramith and Tell el-Hush.

Rechah ("uttermost part"), a village in Judah (1 Chr. 4:12). Its location is not known.

Red Sea, a sea that divides Egypt and Arabia. It was across this body of water that the Israelites escaped from Egypt (Ex. 10:19). The Hebrews called it the Sea of Deliverance; others called it the "Sea of Reeds."

Refuge, Cities of. See Cities of Refuge.

Rehob ("breadth; width"). **[1]** See Beth-rehob. **[2], [3]** Two towns of Asher (Josh. 19:28, 30). One of them was given to the Levites and one remained in the hands of the Canaanites (Josh. 21:31; Judg. 1:31). See also "People of the Bible."

Rehoboth ("spaces"). **[1]** A well dug by Isaac in the Valley of Gerar (Gen. 26:22). It is probably modern Wadi Ruheibeh, 30.6 km. (19 mi.) southwest of Beer-sheba. **[2]** A suburb of Nineveh (Gen. 10:11). **[3]** A city somewhere in northern Edom (Gen. 36:37; 1 Chr. 1:48). Its location is unidentified.

PLACES OF THE BIBLE

MOUNT SINAI. *Viewed from a trail leading to its summit, Jebel Musa (right) is traditionally considered to be the biblical Mount Horeb, or Sinai. The Lord revealed himself to Moses on this mountain, giving him the Ten Commandments and other laws (Ex. 20:1–17). Jebel Musa is located on the southern portion of the Sinai Peninsula between the Red Sea and the Gulf of Aqaba.*

Rèkem ("mercy"), a city of Benjamin (Josh. 18:27). It is probably modern Ar Kalandujeh. *See also* "People of the Bible."

Remeth ("height"), a city of the tribe of Issachar (Josh. 19:21); not to be confused with Ramath.

Remmon. *See* Rimmon.

Remmon-methoar. *See* Rimmon [3].

Rephaim, Valley of ("valley of giants"), the site in Judah where David defeated the Philistines (Is. 17:5; 2 Sam. 5:18). It lies between Jerusalem and Bethlehem, southwest of Jerusalem and the Valley of Hinnom. It is probably the present-day Valley el-Bukaa.

Rephidim ("beds"), an Israelite encampment between the Wilderness of Sin and Mount Sinai (Ex. 17:1, 8). It may be the Wadi Refayid, northwest of Jebel Musa.

Resen ("bride"), a city between Nineveh and Calah in Assyria (Gen. 10:12).

Rezeph ("pavement"), a city of Syria taken by Sennacherib (2 Kin. 19:12; Is. 37:12). It is perhaps the modern Rusafah several kilometers west of the Euphrates toward Palmyra.

Rhegium ("fracture"), a town located in southern Italy (Acts 28:13). It was opposite Messina in Sicily and is now called Reggio.

Rhodes ("rose"), an island located off the coast of Caria in southwest Asia Minor (Acts 21:1).

Riblah ("quarrel"). **[1]** A city on the Orontes where the sons of Zedekiah were slain (Jer. 39:5–7; 2 Kin. 23:33). It was 80 km. (50 mi.) south of Hamath. It may be modern Ribleh in the Plain of Coelesyria. **[2]** A border city of the Promised Land (Num. 34:11). It is perhaps modern Harmel northeast of the source of the Orontes.

Rimmon [Remmon] ("pomegranate"). **[1]** A town in southern Judah (Josh. 15:32; 1 Chr. 4:32; Zech. 14:10) near Khirbet Umm er-Ramāmīn about 9 mi. from Beer-sheba. **[2]** A rock near Gibeah (Judg. 20:45–47; 21:13). It is possibly a limestone projection 3 1/2 mi. east of Bethel. **[3]** A border town of Zebulun (1 Chr. 6:77). The town is called Dimnah in Joshua 21:35, a reading many scholars consider a corruption of Rimmon. The site is referred to in Joshua 19:13 as Remmon-methoar. Many translate verse 13: . . . [the border] goes out to Ittah-Kazin and goes to Kemmon and bends [methoar] to Neah.

Rimmon-parez ("pomegranates of the wrath"), the fifteenth encampment of the Israelites (Num. 33:19). It is somewhere between Rithmah and Libnah and is possibly Nakt el-Biyar.

PLACES OF THE BIBLE

Rissah ("dew"), an encampment in the wilderness (Num. 33:21–22). It is probably modern Kuntilet el-Jerafi.

Rithmah ("noise"), the fourteenth encampment of Israel in the wilderness (Num. 33:18). It is perhaps the same as Kadesh.

Rogelim ("footmen"), the dwelling place of Barzillai (2 Sam. 17:27). It was located in Gilead and is probably Bersiniya 8.8 km. (5.5 mi.) southwest of Irbid.

Rome ("city of Romulus"), the capital of the great Roman Empire (Acts 23:11). It is located in Italy on the Tiber River.

Rumah ("exalted"), a town whose locality is uncertain (2 Kin. 23:36). Perhaps it is Arumah near Shechem or Rumah [Khirbet Rumeh] in Galilee, 9.7 km. (6 mi.) north of Nazareth.

S

Salamis ("shaken"), a town located on the east end of Cyprus (Acts 13:5). It is 4.8 km. (3 mi.) northwest of modern Famagusta.

Salcah [Salchah] ("thy lifting up"), a city located at the extreme limits of Bashan (Deut. 3:10; Josh. 12:5). It is now Salkhad 106.2 km. (66 mi.) east of the Jordan, opposite Bethshean in Samaria.

Salem ("perfect peace"), the city of Melchizedek (Gen. 14:18; Ps. 76:2). It is possibly modern Salim; however, many believe it to be Jerusalem.

Salim ("path"), the place where John baptized (John 3:23). It is near the waters of Aenon which were probably north of Shechem, although the site is uncertain.

Salmon. *See* Zalmon.

Salmone ("peace"), the easternmost point of the island of Crete (Acts 27:7). It is now known as Cape Sidero. *See also* "People of the Bible."

Salt, City of. *See* City of Salt.

Salt Sea [Dead Sea; East Sea], the body of water at the southern end of the Jordan Valley, which contains no marine life because of its heavy mineral contents (Gen. 14:3; Num. 34:12). Its modern name is the Dead Sea.

Salt, Valley of, a plain traditionally located at the lower end of the Dead Sea (2 Sam. 8:13). Another such valley, the Wadi el-Milh (salt), is east of Beer-sheba, and may be the site of the defeat of the Edomites.

Samaria ("watch mountain"). **[1]** The capital of the northern kingdom of Israel (1 Kin.

SUCCOTH. *In this area, Jacob built a house for himself and booths for his cattle (Gen. 33:17); hence the city that grew up at this spot was called Succoth (Hebrew, "tents" or "booths"). The city was given to the tribe of Gad (Josh. 13:27). The mound that now marks the site is known as Tell Deir 'Alla.*

20:1; 2 Chr. 18:2; Jer. 41:5). It was 67.6 km. (42 mi.) north of Jerusalem. **[2]** Another name for the kingdom of Israel (1 Kin. 13:32; 2 Kin. 17:24). **[3]** A district of Palestine in Christ's time (Luke 17:11–19). Galilee was on its north and Judea on the south.

Samos ("full of gravel"), an island of Greece (Acts 20:15). It is off the eastern coast of Asia Minor southwest of Ephesus.

Samothracia ("of the Samians and Thracians"), a small island in the Aegean Sea off the southern coast of Thrace (Acts 16:11).

Sansannah ("branch"), a village in extreme southern Judah (Josh. 15:31). It is probably modern Khirbet esh-Shamsaniyat about 16.1 km. (10 mi.) north-northeast of Beer-sheba.

Saphir ("delightful"), a town in Judah (Mic. 1:11). It was west of Hebron and may be Khirbet el-Kom.

Sardis ("prince of joy"), the capital city of Lydia where a church was located (Rev. 1:11; 3:1, 4). It was on the east bank of the Pactolus River about 80.5 km. (50 mi.) east of Smyrna.

Sarid ("survivor"), a landmark in the territory of Zebulun (Josh. 19:10, 12). It is modern Tell Shadud in the northern portion of the Plain of Esdraelon [Jezreel] about 8 km. (5 mi.) southwest of Nazareth.

Saron, the Greek form of Sharon (q.v.).

Seba (meaning unknown), an African nation bordering the land of Cush (Ps. 72:10; Is. 43:3). There is some confusion between Sheba and Seba, but they are probably two

PLACES OF THE BIBLE

distinct locations. *See also* "People of the Bible."

Secacah ("thicket"), a city of Judah near the Dead Sea (Josh. 15:61). It was situated in the Valley of Achor.

Sechu ("defense"), a location with a well on the route from Gibeah to Ramah (1 Sam. 19:22).

Seir ("tempest"). **[1]** The valley and mountains of Aravah from the Dead Sea south to the Elanitic Gulf (Gen. 14:6; 32:3). Seir was the name of the mountain range in Edom and the name came to include the entire territory. **[2]** A ridge on Judah's border west of Kirjath-jearim (Josh. 15:10). *See also* "People of the Bible."

Seirath ("tempest"), a place in Mt. Ephraim to which Ehud fled after he murdered Eglon (Judg. 3:26).

Sela [Selah] ("a rock"). **[1]** The capital of Edom, located between the Dead Sea and the Gulf of Aqaba (2 Kin. 14:7; Is. 16:1). It is also called Petra. **[2]** A rock formation about 1,160 m. (3,800 ft.) above sea level, which dominates the city of Petra (cf. Judg. 1:36). It is now called Ummel-Bizarah.

Sela-hammahlekoth ("rock of divisions"), a cliff in the wilderness near Maon where David escaped from Saul (1 Sam. 23:28).

Seleucia ("beaten by the waves"), a Syrian seaport from which Paul and Barnabas began their first missionary journey (Acts 13:4). It is located 8 km. (5 mi.) north of the mouth of the Orontes River.

Seneh ("enemy"), the more southerly of two rocks in the passage between Michmash and Geba (1 Sam. 14:4–5). It is 10.5 km. (6.5 mi.) northeast of Jerusalem.

Senir. *See* Shenir.

Sephar ("scribe"), an area in the southeastern portion of Arabia (Gen. 10:30).

Sepharad ("a book descending"), a place where the Jerusalem exiles lived (Obad. 20). It is probably Sardis in Asia Minor (q.v.).

Sepharvaim ("the two scribes"), a city formerly identified with Sippar on the east bank of the Euphrates; it is now believed to be the Syrian city Shabara' (Is. 37:13).

Shaalabbin [Shaalbim], a city of Dan (Josh. 19:42; Judg. 1:35). It may be modern Silbit 4.8 km. (3 mi.) northwest of Aijalon.

Shaaraim [Sharaim] ("gates"). **[1]** A town in lowland Judah west of Socoh (Josh. 15:36; 1 Sam. 17:52). **[2]** A town of Simeon (1 Chr. 4:31). It is identified with Tell el-Far'ah about 24.9 km. (15.5 mi.) south-southeast of Gaza.

Shahazimah ("heights"), a city of Issachar

MONASTERY ON MOUNT TABOR. *Looking west from the summit of Mount Tabor, one sees the Greek monastery that commemorates Jesus' transfiguration (Matt. 17:1–13). Christians have identified this as the site of the transfiguration since at least the fourth century* A.D.

PLACES OF THE BIBLE

TIRZAH(?) *Archaeologists believe that Tell el-Far'ah is the site of ancient Tirzah, a Canaanite city that served as the capital of the northern kingdom of Israel from the time of Jeroboam I to Omri (cf. 1 Kings 15:21, 33). Omri moved the capital to the nearby city of Samaria. Tell el-Far'ah is one of the largest tells (mounds) near Samaria, but excavators have not found conclusive proof that the site is indeed that of ancient Tirzah.*

(Josh. 19:22). It is between Mount Tabor and the Jordan, and is probably modern Tell el-Mekarkash [Mukarkash].

Shalem ("peaceful; secure"), a town near Shechem (Gen. 33:18). Most scholars translate: "And Jacob came in peace [Shalem] to the city of Shechem."

Shalim ("foxes"), a district in Ephraim through which Saul passed when searching for his father's livestock (1 Sam. 9:4).

Shalisha ("the third"), an area near Mount Ephraim through which Saul passed when searching for his father's livestock (1 Sam. 9:4). It was probably northeast of Lydda.

Shamir ("thorn"). **[1]** A city in the mountainous district of Judah (Josh. 15:48). It is probably modern el-Bireh. **[2]** A town in Mount Ephraim (Judg. 10:1–2). Sanur be-

tween Samaria and En-gannim have been suggested as sites. *See also* "People of the Bible."

Shapher ("bright"), a mountain encampment during the Hebrews' wanderings in the wilderness (Num. 33:23). Jebel 'Araif en-Nakah, south of Kadesh, has been suggested as the site.

Sharaim. *See* Shaaraim [1].

Sharon [Saron] ("his song"). **[1]** A region that lies between the Mediterranean Sea from Joppa to Carmel and the central portion of Palestine (1 Chr. 27:29; Acts 9:35). **[2]** A district east of the Jordan occupied by the tribe of Gad (1 Chr. 5:16).

Sharuhen ("gracious house"), a city in Simeon near Beth-lebaoth (Josh. 19:6). It is perhaps identical with Shaaraim [2].

Shaveh ("the plain"), a place near Salem

PLACES OF THE BIBLE

mentioned as the King's Valley (Gen. 14:17; 2 Sam. 18:18). It may be the same as the Kidron Valley.

Shaveh Kiriathaim ("plains of Kiriathaim"), a plain near Kirjathaim [1], the dwelling place of the Emim (Gen. 14:5).

Shearing house, the location where the royal family of King Ahaziah of Judah were slaughtered (2 Kin. 10:12–14). The Hebrew name is *Beth 'eked;* the site is probably Beit Kad, about 25.7 km. (16 mi.) north-northeast of Samaria.

Sheba ("oath"). **[1]** A country in southwest Arabia (1 Kin. 10:1–13; 2 Chr. 9:1–12). Its capital was Ma'rib, which was about 60 miles east-northeast of San'a, the present capital of Yemen. **[2]** A town of Simeon mentioned after Beer-sheba (Josh. 19:2). Its location is uncertain. *See also* "People of the Bible."

Shebah ("seven"), the well at Beer-sheba where Isaac made a covenant with Abimelech (Gen. 26:33).

Shebam ("fragrance"), a city east of the Jordan given to the tribes of Reuben and Gad (Num. 32:3). It is located 8 km. (5 mi.) from Heshbon. It is identical with Sibmah (q.v.).

Shebarim ("hopes"), a place to which the Israelites ran on their flight from Ai (Josh. 7:5). The location of the site is unknown.

Shechem [Sichem; Sychem] ("portion"), an ancient city in central Palestine (Gen. 12:6; 33:18; Josh. 24:32; Acts 7:16) in the hill country of Ephraim. It is present-day Nablus, located about 66 km. (41 mi.) north of Jerusalem between Mount Ebal and Mount Gerizim. *See also* "People of the Bible."

Shen ("tooth"), a place near which Samuel erected a stone memorial to the victory over the Philistines (1 Sam. 7:12).

Shenir [Senir] ("light that sleeps"), the Amorite name for Hermon (Deut. 3:9; Ezek. 27:5).

Shepham ("wild"), a location on the northeastern boundary of the Promised Land near Riblah (Num. 34:10).

Sheshach ("humiliation"), possibly a cipher form of Babel (Babylon) (Jer. 25:26). Other scholars view this as a part of Babylon or a Babylonian district.

Shibmah. *See* Sibmah.

Shicron ("his wages"), a town on the northern boundary of Judah (Josh. 15:11).

Shihon ("wall of strength"), a town near Mount Tabor (Josh. 19:19). It is perhaps at modern Ayun esh-Sha'in.

Shihor [Sihor] ("blackness"), the east branch of the Nile River (1 Chr. 13:5; Jer. 2:18). Ideally, this was to be Israel's southern boundary.

Shihor-libnath ("black of whiteness"), a boundary stream of Asher (Josh. 19:26). It is probably the Nahr ez-Zirka 9.7 km. (6 mi.) south of Dor.

Shilhim ("armed"), a city in southern Judah near Lebaoth (Josh. 15:32). It is identified with Shaaraim [2].

Shiloah [Siloah] ("sent"), a waterway of Jerusalem (Is. 8:6; Neh. 3:15). It carried water from the spring of Gihon to the Pool of Shelah to irrigate the Kidron Valley outside the city. It is identical with Siloam [1].

Shiloh ("peace"), a town in Ephraim (Josh. 18:1–10; Judg. 21:19). It is halfway between Shechem and Bethel.

Shimron ("watch-height"), an ancient city belonging to Zebulun (Josh. 11:1; 19:15). It is possibly Semuniyeh 10.1 km. (6.3 mi.) west of Nazareth. *See also* "People of the Bible."

Shimron-meron, a royal city of the Canaanites, whose king was slain by Joshua (Josh. 12:20). Probably the full name of Shimron (q.v.).

Shinar ("watch of him that sleeps"), the plains later known as Babylonia or Chaldea, through which the Tigris and Euphrates Rivers flow (Gen. 10:10; Is. 11:11).

Shittim ("thorns"). **[1]** The final Israelite encampment before crossing the Jordan. Here Moses bade farewell and the Law was completed (Num. 25:1; Josh. 2:1). It was in Moab, east of Jordan, opposite Jericho. **[2]** A dry and unfruitful valley (Joel 3:18). The name may not denote any particular valley, but it may refer to the Kidron Wadi which starts northwest of Jerusalem, moves toward the east and runs toward the Dead Sea. It may also be a portion of the Arabah around the Dead Sea.

Shoa ("kings"), a location mentioned along with Babylon, Chaldea, and Assyria (Ezek. 23:23); it probably refers to a settlement of the Sutu nomads of the Syrian Desert.

Shocho [Shochoh; Shoco; Socoh; Socho; Sochoh] ("defense"). **[1]** A town in lowland Judah or the hilly border of the Valley of Elah (Josh. 15:35; 2 Chr. 11:7; 28:18; 1 Sam. 17:1). **[2]** A town in Judah's hill country (Josh. 15:48). It is modern Khirbet Shuweikeh 16.1 km. (10 mi.) south-southwest of Hebron. **[3]** A place in one of Solomon's administrative districts (1 Kin. 4:10). It is modern Tell-er-Ras about 16.1 km. (10 mi.) northwest of Samaria.

PLACES OF THE BIBLE

Shochoh. *See* Shocho.

Shoco. *See* Shocho.

Shophan ("burrow"), a fortress city east of the Jordan River that was captured and rebuilt by the tribe of Gad (Num. 32:35).

Shual ("fox"), a district north of Michmash (1 Sam. 13:17). *See also* "People of the Bible."

Shunem ("their sleep"), a town near Jezreel that was allotted to the tribe of Issachar (Josh. 19:18; 1 Sam. 28:4). It was opposite Mount Gilboa. The site is present-day Solem or Sulam.

Shur ("wall"), a desert in the northwest part of the Sinai Peninsula (Gen. 16:7; 25:18). It was outside the eastern border of Egypt and was probably a caravan route between Egypt and Beer-sheba.

Shushan [Susa] ("a lily"), the capital of Elam inhabited by the Babylonians; later a royal residence and capital of the Persian Empire (Neh. 1:1; Dan. 8:2). The city was also known as Susa. The site is modern Shush on the Ulai River.

Sibmah [Shibmah] ("to be cold"), a town of Reuben and Gad (Num. 32:38; Josh. 13:19). It is identical with Shebam (q.v.).

Sibraim ("twofold hope"), a northern boundary marker of Canaan (Ezek. 47:16). It is probably Sepharvaim.

Sichem. *See* Shechem.

Siddim ("the tilled field"), a valley near the Dead Sea (Gen. 14:3, 8, 10), full of bitumen pits.

Sidon [Zidon] ("hunting"), an ancient city of Canaan (Gen. 10:15, 19; Josh. 11:8; Luke 4:26). *See also* "People of the Bible."

Sihor. *See* Shihor.

Silla ("exalting"), a place near Millo where King Joash was murdered (2 Kin. 12:20).

Siloah. *See* Shiloah.

Siloam ("sent"). **[1]** A famous pool of Jerusalem at the south end of Hezekiah's tunnel (John 9:7). It is identical with Shiloah (q.v.). **[2]** A tower on the Ophel ridge near Siloam (Luke 13:4).

Sin ("bush"). **[1]** A city on the eastern side of the Nile (Ezek. 30:15–16). It is possibly Pelusium; but is also identified with Syene, which is present-day Aswan at the first cataract of the Nile. **[2]** A wilderness area located between the Gulf of Suez and Sinai (Ex. 16:1; Num. 33:11–12).

Sinai [Sina] ("a bush"). **[1]** An area in the center of the peninsula that lies between the horns of the Red Sea, the Gulf of Suez, and the Gulf of Aqaba (Ex. 16:1; Acts 7:30–38). **[2]** A mountain, called also Horeb, where the Israelites received the Ten Commandments (Ex. 19:18). The location of the site is uncertain, although it is generally agreed to be in central Sinai. The traditional site is Jebel Musa, but other possibilities are Mount Serbal and Ras es-Safsafeh.

Sinim ("south country"), a land from which the scattered Israelites were again to be gathered (Is. 49:12). It probably refers to Syene on the southern Egyptian frontier where there was a Jewish garrison. Earlier scholars believed that China was indicated, but that view has been abandoned.

Sion ("breastplate"). **[1]** Another name for Mount Hermon (Deut. 4:48). **[2]** *See* Zion.

Siphmoth ("fruitful"), a place in southern Judah frequented by David (1 Sam. 30:28).

Sirah ("turning"), a well near Hebron where Abner was recalled by Joab (2 Sam. 3:26). It is probably modern 'Ain Sarah.

Sirion ("breastplate"), the name given to Mount Hermon by the Sidonians (Deut. 3:9; Ps. 29:6).

Sitnah ("hatred"), the second well dug by Isaac, located in the Valley of Gerar (Gen. 26:21).

Smyrna ("myrrh"), a city on the western coast of Asia Minor (Rev. 2:8–11). It is 64.4 km. (40 mi.) north of Ephesus.

Socho. *See* Shocho.

Sochoh. *See* Shocho.

Socoh. *See* Shocho.

Sodom [Sodoma] ("their secret"), one of the five Cities of the Plain (Gen. 10:19; Rom. 9:29), destroyed because of its wickedness. The exact location of the site is unknown, but it is in the Dead Sea area.

Solomon's Pools, a repository of water built by Solomon near Bethlehem (Eccl. 2:6).

Solomon's Porch, a colonnade built by Solomon on the east side of the temple (John 10:23; Acts 3:11).

Sorek ("vine"), a valley in Gaza where Delilah lived (Judg. 16:4). It is modern Wadi es-Saran, which begins 20.9 km. (13 mi.) southwest of Jerusalem and twists northwest toward the Mediterranean.

South Ramoth. *See* Ramath.

Spain ("rain"), a peninsula in southwestern Europe (Rom. 15:24). The nation was known as Hispania to the Romans.

Succoth ("tents"). **[1]** A town where Jacob built himself a house (Gen. 33:17; Josh.

13:27). It was east of the Jordan between Peniel and Shechem. Its probable location is Deir 'Alla, about 1.6 km. (1 mi.) west of where the Jabbok bulges and turns south. **[2]** The first camping ground of the Israelites after leaving Egypt (Ex. 12:37; 13:20).

Sukkiims ("booth-dwellers"), a nation that assisted Shishak of Egypt when he invaded Judah (2 Chr. 12:3). Its population was probably of Libyan origin.

Sur ("rebellion"), a gate in Jerusalem, possibly leading from the king's palace to the temple (2 Kin. 11:6). The parallel passage calls it the Gate of the Foundation (2 Chr. 23:5).

Susa. *See* Shushan.

Sychar ("end"), a town of Samaria near Jacob's well (John 4:5).

Sychem. *See* Shechem.

Syene ("a bush"), a town on the southern frontier of Egypt (Ezek. 29:10; 30:6).

Syracuse ("that draws violently"), a city on the east coast of Sicily (Acts 28:12).

Syria (a form of the word *Assyria*), the country lying north and east of Palestine (Judg. 10:6; 1 Kin. 10:29; Acts 15:23). It stretched far inland from the Mediterranean and was bounded by the Taurus Mountains to the north.

Syrtis Quicksands ("shallows"), two shoals off the coast of Africa between Carthage and Cyrene (Acts 27:17). The greater Syrtis is now called the Gulf of Sidra, the lesser Syrtis the Gulf of Gabes.

T

Taanach [Tanach] ("who humbles thee"), an ancient city in Canaan whose king was conquered by Joshua (Josh. 12:21; 21:25; Judg. 1:27). Its ruins, Tell Ta'annak, are on the southern edge of the Valley of Jezreel about 8 km. (5 mi.) southeast of Megiddo.

Taanath-shiloh ("breaking down a fig tree"), a border town between Manasseh and Ephraim (Josh. 16:6). It is now Khirbet Ta'na 11.3 km. (7 mi.) east-southeast of Shechem.

Tabbath ("celebrated"), a place where the Midianites stayed after Gideon's attack (Judg. 7:22). It is located in the Jordan Valley at Ras Abu Tabat.

Taberah ("burning"), a place three days north of Mount Sinai where Israel was punished for murmuring against God (Num. 11:3; Deut. 9:22).

Tabor ("purity"). **[1]** A mountain located in the northern part of the Valley of Jezreel (Judg. 4:6, 12, 14; Ps. 89:12). It is now called Jebel el-Tur and is 8.8 km. (5.5 mi.) southeast of Nazareth. **[2]** A town of Zebulun given to the Levites (1 Chr. 6:77). Its location is uncertain. It may be the Chisloth-tabor of Joshua 19:12 or Khirbet Dabural, which is on a hill between Tabor and Nazareth. **[3]** An oak (not a plain as in KJV) in Benjamin (1 Sam. 10:3).

Tadmor ("bitterness"), a city known to the Greeks and Romans as Palmyra; it facilitated trade with the East (1 Kin. 9:18; 2 Chr. 8:4). Its ruin is Tadmor in an oasis east-northeast of Damascus about midway between the city and the Euphrates. Some believe the reading in First Kin. should be *Tamar;* the Masoretic Hebrew scholars read *Tadmor* in the margin but *Tamar* in the text. If we read Tamar then the reference is to a city probably in southern Judah.

Tahath ("fear"), a desert encampment of the Israelites (Num. 33:26–27). *See also* "People of the Bible."

Tahapanes [Tahpanhes; Tehaphnehes] ("secret temptation"), an Egyptian city on the Pelusiac channel of the Nile (Jer. 2:16; 43:7–9; 44:1; Ezek. 30:18). It is identified with modern Tell Defneh.

Tahtim-hodshi ("lowlands of Hodshi"), a location between Gilead and Dan-jaan visited by Joab during the census of Israel (2 Sam. 24:6). The location of the site is unknown.

Tamar ("palm tree"), a place somewhere to the southwest of the Dead Sea; some identify the site with the village of Thamara, near Kurnub and Ain el-Arūs. Others deny this (Ezek. 47:18–19; 48:28). *See also* "People of the Bible."

Tanach. *See* Taanach.

Tappuah ("swelling"). **[1]** A city in the lowlands of Judah (Josh. 15:34). It is probably modern Beit Nettif 6.4 km. (4 mi.) north of Hebron. **[2]** A border town of Ephraim west of Shechem (Josh. 16:8; 17:7–8). It is probably Sheikh Abu Zarad, about 12.9 km. (8 mi.) south of Shechem. *See also* "People of the Bible."

Tarah ("wretch"), the twelfth Israelite encampment in the wilderness (Num. 33:27). It was between Tahath and Mithcah.

Taralah ("strength"), a city allotted to the tribe of Benjamin (Josh. 18:27). It was near Irpeel.

Tarshish [Tharshish] ("contemplation"), a

PLACES OF THE BIBLE

city in southern Spain with which the Phoenicians traded (1 Kin. 10:22; Jer. 10:9; Ezek. 27:12). It is believed to be modern Tartessus near Gibraltar. *See also* "People of the Bible."

Tarsus ("winged"), the most prominent city of Cilicia located on the river Cydnus in Asia Minor; it was the birthplace of Paul (Acts 9:11).

Tehaphnehes. *See* Tahapanes.

Tekoa [Tekoah] ("that is confirmed"), a town of Judah on the hills near Hebron (2 Sam. 14:2; Jer. 6:1). It is modern Taku 'ais, a ruined village 9.7 km. (6 mi.) south of Bethlehem.

Tel-abib ("heap of new grain"), a town of Babylonia near the river Chebar where Jewish exiles were placed (Ezek. 3:15).

Telaim ("lambs"), the place where Saul gathered and numbered his forces before the attack on Amalek (1 Sam. 15:4). It was probably in extreme southern Judah.

Telassar [Thelasar] ("taking away"), a city near Harran and Orfa in western Mesopotamia (2 Kin. 19:12; Is. 37:12).

Telem ("their shadow"), a town in extreme southern Judah (Josh. 15:24). *See also* "People of the Bible."

Tel-harsa [Tel-haresha] ("suspension of the plow"), a Babylonian village used as a grouping point for Jews returning to Palestine (Ezra 2:59; Neh. 7:61).

Tel-melah ("hill of salt"), a Babylonian town mentioned in Ezra 2:59; Nehemiah 7:61. It possibly was situated on the low salt tract near the Persian Gulf.

Tema ("south; south country; sun burnt"), a son of Ishmael (Gen. 25:15). The place his descendants dwelt was also called Tema (Job 6:19). It was located in Arabia midway between Damascus and Mecca.

Temple, the structure in which the Israelites worshiped and offered sacrifices to God. There were three temples: Solomon's, Zerubbabel's, and Herod's.

Tharshish. *See* Tarshish.

Thebez ("muddy"), a place in the district of Neapolis (Judg. 9:50). It was 20.9 km. (13 mi.) southwest of Scythopolis [Beth-shean].

Thelasar. *See* Telassar.

Thessalonica ("victory at sea"), a city situated on the Macedonian coast at the head of the Thermaic Gulf (Acts 17:1, 11, 13; 27:2). It is known as Salonika today.

Thimnathah ("a portion"), a city in the allotment of Dan (Josh. 19:43). It was located between Elon and Ekron. Many identify it with Timnath [2]. *See also* Timnah.

Three Taverns, a station on the Appian Way near the modern city of Cisterna (Acts 28:15).

Thyatira ("sacrifice of labor"), a city between Pergamos and Sardis (Acts 16:14; Rev. 2:18–29). It was in Lydia in Asia Minor.

Tiberias ("good vision"), a city on the west coast of the Sea of Galilee (Josh. 6:1; 21:1).

Tibhath ("extension"), a city of Amam-Zobah (1 Chr. 18:8). It is identical with Betah (q.v.).

Timnah ("allotted portion"). **[1]** A town on the northern border of Judah (Josh. 15:10). It was allotted to Dan and is called Thimnathah in Joshua 19:43. It was also known as Timnath (Gen. 38:12–14). Its site is Khirbet Tibnah, 15 mi. from Jerusalem. **[2]** A town in the hill country of Judah (Josh. 15:57). Possibly identical with [1]. *See also* Timna of "People of the Bible."

Timnath ("image"). **[1]** A border town in Judah (Gen. 38:12–14). It is probably identical with Timnah. **[2]** A city in the territory of Dan near Philistia (Judg. 14:1–2, 5). *See also* Timnah.

Timnath-heres ("extra portion"), a village in Ephraim (Judg. 2:9). It is identical with Timnath-serah.

Timnath-serah ("image of the sun"), the home and burial place of Joshua (Josh. 19:50; 24:30). It is probably modern Tibnah, 19.3 km. (12 mi.) northeast of Lydda. It is identical with Timnath-heres.

Tiphsah ("passage"). **[1]** A crossing located on the Euphrates River (1 Kin. 4:24). It is probably modern Thapsacus. **[2]** A place mentioned in connection with Tirzah (2 Kin. 15:16). It may be the ruined village of Tafsah 10.5 km. (6.5 mi.) southwest of Shechem. Others identify it with Tappuah (q.v.).

Tirzah ("benevolent"), a Canaanite city located north of Jerusalem (Josh. 12:24; 1 Kin. 14:17). It was 48.3 km. (30 mi.) from Jerusalem. *See also* "People of the Bible."

Tob ("good"), an area east of the Jordan between Gilead and the eastern deserts (Judg. 11:3, 5).

Tochen ("middle"), a town of Simeon (1 Chr. 4:32), near Rimmon. It is identical with Ether [2].

Togarmah ("all bone"), a country that supplied horses and mules to the Tyrians and soldiers to the army of Gog (Ezek. 27:14; 38:6). Many identify this land with Armenia.

Tolad. *See* Eltolad.

Tophel ("ruin"), an area north of Bozra, toward the southeast corner of the Dead Sea (Deut. 1:1). It is perhaps Tafileh.

Tophet [Topheth] ("a drum"), once a part of a king's garden in Hinnom; it became a place where people in Jerusalem sacrificed their children (2 Kin. 23:10; Is. 30:33; Jer. 19:6, 11–14).

Trachonitis ("strong"), a Roman province south of Damascus and north of Jordan (Luke 3:1). It is now called al-Seja.

Treasure Cities [Treasure House; Store Cities], designated cities at which the kings of the ancient world kept their treasures and tithes (Ex. 1:11; Ezra 5:17).

Troas ("penetrated"), an important city on the coast of Mysia (Acts 16:8; 2 Tim. 4:13). It was in northern Asia Minor and is also called Alexandria.

Trogyllium ("fruit port"), a rocky projection of the ridge of Mycale and a town (Acts 20:5). They were both located on the western coast of Asia Minor opposite the island of Samos.

Tyre [Tyrus] ("rock"), a city on the central coast of Phoenicia noted for its commercial activity (Josh. 19:29; 2 Sam. 5:11; Jer. 25:22). It is located halfway between Accho and Sidon.

Tyrus. *See* Tyre.

U

Ulai ("pure water"), a river surrounding Shushan in Persia (Dan. 8:2, 16). It is now called Kerah or Kerkhah.

Ummah ("darkened"), a city of Asher on the Mediterranean coast (Josh. 19:30). It was near Aphek or Rehob; now it is called Alma.

Uphaz ("pure gold"), a city generally regarded as being identical with Ophir (Jer. 10:9; Dan. 10:5).

Ur ("light"), the city which Abram left to go to Haran (Gen. 11:28, 31). Ur is generally identified as ancient Ur (Uri), modern Tell el-Muqayyar located on the Euphrates in south Iraq.

Uz ("counsel; firmness"). **[1]** The country where Job lived (Job 1:1). The two most likely locations are Hauran, south of Damascus, and the area between Edom and north Arabia. **[2]** A kingdom not far from Edom (Jer. 25:20; Lam. 4:21). Perhaps identical with [1].

Uzza, Garden of ("strength"), the place where Manasseh, king of Judah, and Amon, his son, were buried (2 Kin. 21:18, 26). *See also* "People of the Bible."

Uzzen-sherah ("ear of the flesh"), a town established by Sherah, a daughter of Ephraim (1 Chr. 7:24). It was near the two Beth-horons and is now called Beit Sira.

V

Valley Gate, a gate in the southwest wall of Jerusalem leading to the Hinnom Valley (Neh. 2:13).

Vineyards, Plain of the, a place east of the Jordan River, site of the battle in which Jephthah defeated the forces led by Ammon (Judg. 11:33). Many translations take this as a proper name and render it *Abel-cheramin.*

W

Water Gate, a gate on the east side of Jerusalem, above the spring of Gihon (Neh. 8:1, 3).

Wilderness, the area in which the Israelites wandered for 40 years before entering Canaan (Deut. 1:1; Josh. 5:6). Several places are encompassed in the designation Wilderness; these are listed under their individual names (e.g., Paran, Zin, etc.).

Willows, Brook of the, a small stream that marks the boundary between Moab and Edom (Is. 15:7). It is possibly the lower course of Wadi el-Hesa where it meets the upper course of Seil el-Kerahi.

Z

Zaanaim. *See* Zaanannim.

Zaanan ("pointed"), a town in Judah (Mic. 1:11). It is probably identical with Zenan (q.v.). The site is probably modern Arak el-Kharba.

Zaanannim [Zaanaim], a place on the southern border of Naphtali (Josh. 19:33; Judg. 4:11).

Zair ("small"), the place in or near Edom where Joram defeated the Edomites (2 Kin. 8:21). It is possibly Sa'ir, about 8 km. (5 mi.) north-northeast of Hebron. Some identify the city with Zior (q.v.).

Zalmon [Salmon] ("shady"), a wooded

area in Shechem (Judg. 9:48–49; Ps. 68:14). *See also* "People of the Bible."

Zalmonah ("shade"), an Israelite encampment in the desert (Num. 33:41–42). It was probably east of Jebel Harien.

Zanoah ("marsh"). **[1]** A town in lowland Judah (Josh. 15:34; Neh. 3:13). It is Khirbet Zanu' or Zanuh about 4.8 km. (3 mi.) southsoutheast of Beth-shemesh. **[2]** A town in Judah's hill country about 2.1 km. (1.3 mi.) northwest of Yatta (Josh. 15:56; 1 Chr. 4:18). *See also* "People of the Bible."

Zaphon ("north"), a place allotted to the tribe of Gad in the Jordan Valley east of the river (Josh. 13:27).

Zareah ("wasp; hornet"). *See also* Zorah.

Zared [Zered] ("brook"), a brook and valley that marks the greatest limit of the Hebrews' wandering in the wilderness (Num. 21:12; Deut. 2:13–14). It was south of the Arnon, probably Wadi el-Hesa.

Zarephath ("smelting place"), a town located near Zidon (Sidon) that was the residence of Elijah (2 Kin. 17:9). It is probably modern Sarafand, 12.9 km. (8 mi.) south of Zidon.

Zaretan [Zartanah; Zarthan] ("cooling"), a village near Beth-shean in the territory of Manasseh (Josh. 3:16; 1 Kin. 4:12). It is probably Tell es-Sa'idiyeh. The city is probably identical with Zereda (q.v.).

Zareth-shahar ("beauty of the dawn"), a town allotted to the tribe of Reuben (Josh. 13:19). It is probably at Zarat on the eastern shore of the Dead Sea.

Zartanah. *See* Zaretan.

Zarthan. *See* Zaretan.

Zebaim ("gazelles"), the home of one whose descendants returned from the Babylonian Captivity (Ezra 2:57; Neh. 7:59). It is perhaps identical with Zeboim (q.v.).

Zeboim [Zeboiim] ("gazelles"). **[1]** One of the five Cities of the Plain (Gen. 10:19; 14:2, 9). **[2]** A valley between Michmash and the wilderness to the east (1 Sam. 13:16–18). **[3]** A Benjamite town (Neh. 11:34). It is probably north of Lydda, perhaps at Khirbet Sabeyah.

Zebulun ("dwelling"), the territory given to the tribe of Zebulun (Josh. 19:27, 34). It was north of Issachar, east of Asher, and southwest of Naphtali. *See also* "People of the Bible."

Zedad ("mountainside"), a northern boundary mark of Canaan (Num. 34:8; Ezek. 47:15). It is probably a tower and has been identified with Sadad, southwest of Homs.

Zelah ("rib"), a town of Benjamin contain-

ing Kish's tomb (2 Sam. 21:14). It is probably Khirbet Salah northwest of Jerusalem.

Zelzah ("noontide"), a town near Rachel's tomb (1 Sam. 10:2). It was 8 km. (5 mi.) southeast of Jerusalem.

Zemaraim ("wool"). **[1]** A city north of Jericho (Josh. 18:22); we now know that it was 6.4 km. (4 mi.) away from Jericho. **[2]** A mountain in Ephraim's hill country (2 Chr. 13:4). Possible locations are Burkah and Kafr Nata.

Zenan ("coldness"), a village in the allotment of Judah (Josh. 15:37). It is probably identical with Zaanan (q.v.).

Zephath ("which beholds"), a city of Canaan in the mountains of Kadesh near the Edomite border (Judg. 1:17). It was later called Hormah (q.v.).

Zephathah ("watchtower"), the valley in Judah's territory near Mareshah in which Asa and Zerah battled (2 Chr. 14:9–10). It is possibly modern Wadi Safiyeh.

Zer ("perplexity"), a fortress city of Naphtali (Josh. 19:35). It was located near the southwest bank of the Sea of Galilee. It may be Madon (q.v.).

Zered. *See* Zared.

Zereda ("ambush"), a village in Manasseh (1 Kin. 11:26). It was located to the north of Mount Ephraim about 24.1 km. (15 mi.) southwest of Shechem. It is identical with Zaretan (q.v.).

Zeredathah ("cool"), a village near Bethshean (2 Chr. 4:17). Many suppose this place is identical with Zaretan (q.v.).

Ziddim ("huntings"), a fortress city of Naphtali (Josh. 19:35). It is possibly Hattim, 8.8 km. (5.5 mi.) northwest of Tiberias.

Zidon. *See* Sidon.

Ziklag ("measure pressed down"), a city in the south of Judah (1 Sam. 30:1; 2 Sam. 1:1; 4:10). It is probably Tell el-Khutweilfel about 16.1 km. (10 mi.) north of Beer-sheba.

Zin ("swelling"), a wilderness on the southern border of Canaan, not to be confused with the Wilderness of Sin. It was either a part of the Wilderness of Paran or bordered on the wilderness which contained Kadesh-barnea (Num. 20:1; 27:14; Josh. 15:1–3).

Zion [Sion] ("monument; fortress; set up"), one of the hills on which Jerusalem stood. It came to be applied to the temple and the whole of Jerusalem and its people as a community whose destiny depends on God (2 Sam. 5:7; Ps. 48:11; Is. 8:18; Joel 2:23). Zion also was a symbol of heaven (Rev. 14:1).

PLACES OF THE BIBLE

Zior ("smallness"), a city in Judah near Hebron (Josh. 15:54). Some identify the city with Zair (q.v.).

Ziph ("falsehood"). **[1]** A city in southern Judah (Josh. 15:24). It was located between Ithnan and Telem and is probably modern ez-Teifah. **[2]** A town in Judah's hill country (Josh. 15:55; 2 Chr. 11:8). It is Tell Zif, 4 mi. southeast of Hebron. *See also* "People of the Bible."

Ziphron ("rejoicing"), a place specified by Moses as the northern boundary of the Promised Land (Num. 34:9). It is probably Za'feranh southeast of Restan.

Ziz ("flower"), the pass that runs from the western shore of the Dead Sea north of En-gedi to the wilderness of Judah (2 Chr. 20:16). It is probably Wadi Hasasah.

Zoan ("motion"), a city on the eastern bank of the Nile Delta on the Tanitic branch of the river (Ezek. 30:14). It was known to the Greeks as Tanis and is now San el-Hagar.

Zoar ("small"), one of the five Cities of the Plain of the Jordan (Gen. 14:2; 19:22). It probably was located at the southeast end of the Dead Sea near es-Safi. The original site is believed to be under the Dead Sea's waters.

Zobah [Zoba] ("station"), a portion of Syria east of Coelesyria that was a separate empire during the days of Saul, David, and Solomon (1 Sam. 14:47; 2 Sam. 8:3; 10:6).

Zoheleth ("that creeps; serpent"), a stone beside En-rogel near the Well of the Virgin. It was here that Adonijah sacrificed animals (1 Kin. 1:9).

Zophim ("place for a watchman"), a place on top of Pisgah where Balaam viewed the Israelite camp (Num. 23:14). It is possibly Tal'al es-Safa.

Zorah ("leprosy"), a city in the lowlands of Judah allotted to the tribe of Dan (Josh. 19:41; 2 Chr. 11:10). The site is Sar'ah about 22.5 km. (14 mi.) west of Jerusalem. It is identical with Zorean (q.v.). It is called Zoreah [Zareah] in Joshua 15:33 and Nehemiah 11:29.

Zoreah ("wasp; hornet"). *See also* Zorah.

Zuph ("covering"), a district of unknown location (1 Sam. 9:5). The usual location given is about 40.2 km. (25 mi.) southwest of Shechem. *See also* "People of the Bible."

ACKNOWLEDGMENTS

The publisher gratefully acknowledges the cooperation of these sources, whose illustrations appear in the present work:

American Baptist Association, 209; American Bible Society, 56; Antwerp Cathedral, 525 (bottom); Archives Photographique (Paris), 299; Armed Forces Institute of Pathology, 461; Ashmolean Museum (Oxford), 32; Augsburg Publishing House, 482, 483; Baker Book House, 243, 244, 250, 251, 341, 366, 644, 654; Denis Baly, 184, 199, 201, 242, 249, 617, 704; P. Benoit, 553; LaMar Berrett, 2 (bottom), 216, 262, 294 (bottom), 409, 505 (top), 515, 538, 541, 629, 653, 708 (top), 729; Bildarchiv Foto Marburg, 149, 436, 449 (top); Bildarchiv Preussicher Kulturbesitz, 27 (top), 101 (bottom); W. Braun, 494; British Library, 44; British Museum, 1, 22 (right), 36 (top), 89, 94, 96, 109 (top), 117, 134, 140, 144, 148, 179, 224, 260, 266, 274 (bottom), 273, 292, 303, 327 (top and bottom), 350, 364, 391 (top), 452, 475, 484, 498, 502 (top), 628; British School of Archaeology, 495; Brooklyn Museum, 45, 67, 227; G. G. Cameron, 339; Capitoline Museum, 152 (top); J. Cools, 72; Gaalyah Cornfeld, 18, 313, 332, 352, 367, 373, 464, 493 (top), 503, 512 (top), 549, 647, 718; Judith Dekel, 308; Department of Antiquities (Amman, Jordan), 4 (top); Department of Museums (Cyprus), 447; Dover Publications, 90; J. Dupont, 40, 652; Ecce Homo Orphanage, 643; Editorial Photocolor Archives, 468 (bottom); William B. Eerdmans, 47, 52; Egyptian National Museum, 91, 102 (bottom), 103, 107, 316, 425, 453, 456; Lee Ellenberger, 71; Elsevier Publishing Projects, 383, 645, 683; Foreign Missions Board, 191, 192, 200 (bottom), 202, 527, 552, 560, 734; Fototeca Unione, 165, 171 (top), 334, 423; Fratelli Alinari, 418, 437, 476; Richard Frye, 146; Ewing Galloway, 98, 102, 150, 163 (bottom), 164 (top), 167, 229, 519, 521, 532, 735; German Archaeological Institute, 438; Giegel (Zurich), 419; Giraudon (Paris), 11, 113 (bottom), 449 (bottom); L. H. Grollenberg, 67 (top), 188, 246, 289, 357, 362, 694, 697, 709 (bottom), 712, 722, 725 (top and bottom), 728, 737, 738, 739; Ha-Aretz Museum, 411, 414; The Hague, Kon. Kab. van Munten en Pennigen, 545; Harvard Semitic Museum, 380; Historical Picture Service, 51, 509; Institute for Creation Research, 2 (top); Iraq Museum, 120, 206, 301, 305, 429; Israel Department of Antiquities and Museums, 99, 195, 208, 214, 217, 266 (top); 268, 277, 278, 282, 309, 310, 316, 345, 348, 403, 415, 424, 426, 443, 457, 471, 497, 620, 721; Israel Government Office of Tourism, 171 (bottom), 505 (bottom), 507; Israel Government Press Office, 8, 12 (bottom), 66, 186, 197 (top), 370, 388, 406, 408; Israel Information Service, 258; Israel Museum (Jerusalem), 73 (bottom); Istanbul Museum, 275; Istituto di archeologia Cristiana, 531; Gustav Jeeninga, 76, 80, 131 (bottom), 530; Jeep Express, 193 (top); Jewish Theological Seminary of America, 385; Jordan Archaeological Museum, 486; H. D. Laxague, 631; Levant Photo Service, 14, 18, 158, 168, 173 (top), 200 (top), 238, 252, 329 (bottom), 440, 472, 512 (bottom), 525, 611, 638, 669, 700, 703, 731, 733; Thomas de Liagre Böhl, 16; Seton Lloyd (Ankara), 3; The Louvre, 87, 135, 162, 222, 338 (bottom), 340, 381 (top), 427, 489, 496; Charles Ludwig, 329 (top); Matson Photo Service (Episcopal Home), 5, 10, 12 (top), 30, 38, 176, 180, 185, 186, 194, 233, 289, 398, 405, 468 (top); 516, 522, 526, 537, 543, 555, 626, 649, 651, 664, 675, 694, 696 (top), 699, 702, 711, 714, 716; B. Mazar, 281; Metropolitan Museum of Art, 257, 258, 314, 336, 499, 534; R. H. Mount, Jr., 399; Museum of Fine Arts (Boston), 376; Naples Museum, 88, 157, 172, 323; National Gallery (London), 360; Oriental Institute, 27, 34 (bottom), 36 (bottom), 79, 97, 105 (bottom), 114, 119, 134 (bottom), 136, 137, 138, 139, 141, 145, 218, 270, 274, 296, 318 (bottom), 320, 335, 379, 455, 493 (bottom), 500; Palestine Archaeological Museum, 295; Palestine Exploration Fund, 73 (top), 217, 276; Photopress, 26 (right); Pontificium Institutum Biblicum (Jerusalem), 75; J. B. Pritchard, 338 (top); Readers Digest Association, 463 (top), 473; Religious News Service, 7, 23, 50 (left); H. Armstrong Roberts, 55; Beno Rothenberg, 401; John Rylands Museum, 50 (right); Claude Schaeffer-Forrer, 122, 123, 124, 125, 127, 129 (top and bottom), 131 (top), 381 (bottom), 422; S. J. Schweig, 21; Charles Scribner's Sons and B. T. Batsford Ltd., 491; Amikam Shoob, 224, 232; Standard Publishing Company, 231, 412, 413, 416, 433, 478, 488, 506, 508, 510, 665; Lawrence M. Stone, 347; Studium Biblicum Franciscanum, 548; The Times (London), 176 (bottom); Trans World Airlines, 104; University Museum, 112, 113 (top), 264, 322, 326, 391 (bottom), 394, 428, 502 (bottom), 637 (top); University of Michigan, 342; University of Tel-Aviv, 397; Willem Van de Poll, 13, 195, 615, 624, 705, 734; A.A.M. Van der Heyden, 155, 353, 460; M. J. Van der Ploeg, 613, 657, 658, 660; Bastian Van Elderen, 550; Vatican Museum, 306; Howard Vos, 205, 470; Wellcome Trust, 463 (top); William White, Jr., 67 (top), 68, 70, 84, 85, 100, 160 (bottom), 170 (top), 193 (bottom), 197 (bottom), 220, 230, 239, 247, 253, 256, 337 (bottom), 511, 517, 523 (top and bottom), 637 (bottom); Wolfe Worldwide Films, 463 (bottom); Bryant G. Wood, 289; Yale University Art Gallery, 82; Yigael Yadin, 300, 448.

PUBLISHED SOURCES

Budge, E. A. Wallis. *The Gods of the Egyptians,* Volume II. (New York: Dover Publications, Inc., 1969)—109. Gilbertson, Merrill T. *The Way It Was In Bible Times.* (Minneapolis: Augsburg Publishing House, 1959)—479, 480. *Great People of the Bible and How They Lived.* (New York: The Reader's Digest Association, Inc., 1974)—462 (bottom), 471. Greenlee, J. Harold. *Introduction to New Testament Textual Criticism.* (Grand Rapids, Michigan: William B. Eerdman's Publishing Co., 1964)—69, 74. Heaton, E. W. *Everyday Life in Old Testament Times.* (London: B. T. Batsford Limited, 1956)—487. Kenyon, Kathleen, *Archaeology in the Holy Land.* (London: Ernest Benn, Ltd., rev. ed. 1979)—490. LaHaye, Tim F. and John D. Morris. *The Ark on Ararat.* (Nashville and San Diego: Thomas Nelson Inc., Publishers and Creation-Life Publishers, 1976)—27 (top).

The Publisher has attempted to observe the legal requirements with respect to the rights of the suppliers of photographic materials. Nevertheless, persons who have claims are invited to apply to the Publisher.

INDEX

This index is designed as a guide to proper names and other significant topics. Page numbers in italics indicate pages where a related illustration or sidebar appears. Headings in italics indicate the title of a book or some other important work of literature. Use the index to find related information in various articles. For example, the index shows that "law" is discussed in the section entitled "Laws and Statutes," but also in several other sections of the book.

INDEX

INDEX

INDEX

INDEX

INDEX

INDEX

INDEX

INDEX

INDEX

INDEX

INDEX

INDEX

INDEX

INDEX

INDEX

INDEX

INDEX

INDEX

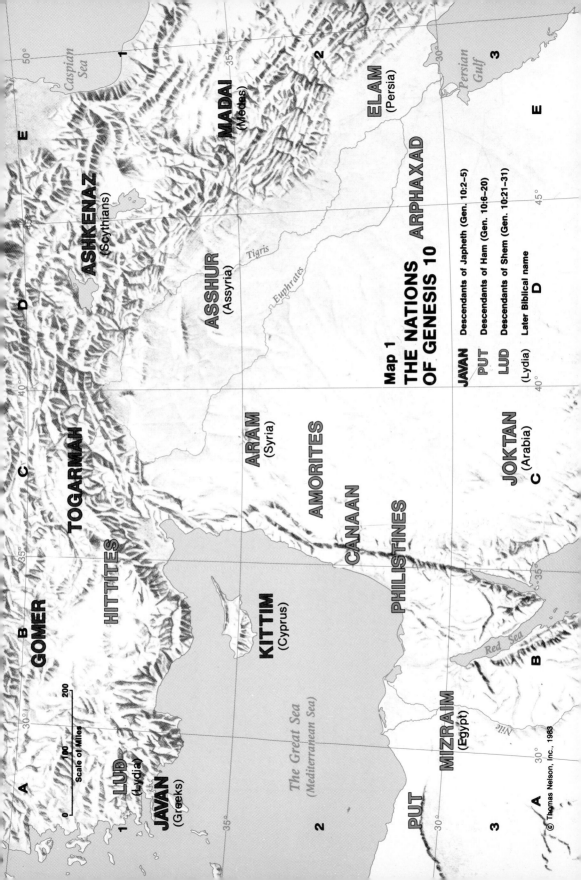

Map 1

THE NATIONS OF GENESIS 10

JAVAN — Descendants of Japheth (Gen. 10:2–5)
PUT — Descendants of Ham (Gen. 10:6–20)
LUD — Descendants of Shem (Gen. 10:21–31)
(Lydia) — Later Biblical name

GOMER

TOGARMAH

HITTITES

ASHKENAZ
(Scythians)

MADAI
(Medes)

ASSHUR
(Assyria)

ELAM
(Persia)

ARPHAXAD

ARAM
(Syria)

AMORITES

CANAAN

PHILISTINES

KITTIM
(Cyprus)

JOKTAN
(Arabia)

LUD
(Lydia)

JAVAN
(Greeks)

MIZRAIM
(Egypt)

PUT

The Great Sea
(Mediterranean Sea)

Caspian Sea

Persian Gulf

Tigris

Euphrates

Nile

Red Sea

Scale of Miles

0   100   200

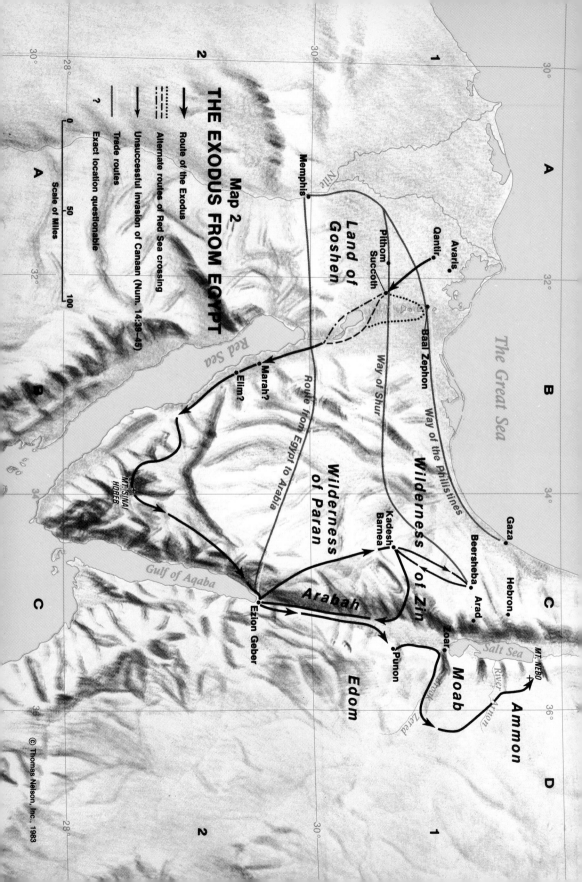

Map 2
THE EXODUS FROM EGYPT

Route of the Exodus
Alternate routes of Red Sea crossing
Unsuccessful invasion of Canaan (Num. 14:39–45)
Trade routes
? Exact location questionable

Scale of Miles
0   50   100

© Thomas Nelson, Inc., 1983

Memphis

Nile

Land of Goshen

Pithom
Succoth

Qantir

Avaris

Baal Zephon

Way of Shur

Way of the Philistines

The Great Sea

Gaza
Hebron
Beersheba
Arad

Red Sea

Marah?
Elim?

Route from Egypt to Arabia

Wilderness of Shur

Wilderness of Paran

Wilderness of Zin

MT. SINAI
HOREB

Gulf of Aqaba

Kadesh Barnea

Arabah

Ezion Geber

Punon

Edom

Zoar

Salt Sea

MT. NEBO

Moab

River Arnon

Zered

Ammon

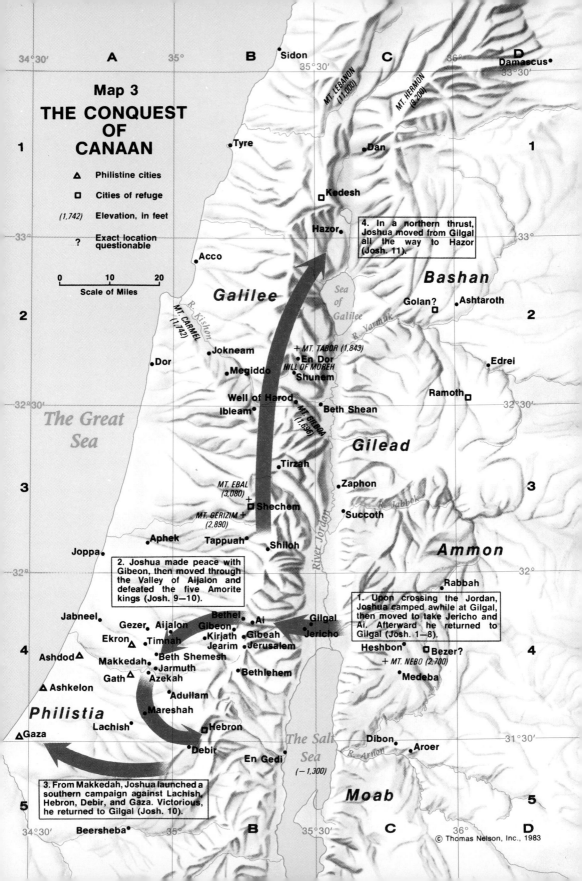

Map 3
THE CONQUEST OF CANAAN

△ Philistine cities

◻ Cities of refuge

(1,742) Elevation, in feet

? Exact location questionable

Scale of Miles
0   10   20

4. In a northern thrust, Joshua moved from Gilgal all the way to Hazor (Josh. 11).

2. Joshua made peace with Gibeon, then moved through the Valley of Aijalon and defeated the five Amorite kings (Josh. 9—10).

1. Upon crossing the Jordan, Joshua camped awhile at Gilgal, then moved to take Jericho and Ai. Afterward he returned to Gilgal (Josh. 1—8).

3. From Makkedah, Joshua launched a southern campaign against Lachish, Hebron, Debir, and Gaza. Victorious, he returned to Gilgal (Josh. 10).

Sidon
Damascus•
MT. LEBANON (11,000)
MT. HERMON (9,200)
Tyre•
Dan•
◻ Kedesh
Hazor•
Bashan
Acco•
Golan? ◻   •Ashtaroth
Galilee
Sea of Galilee
R. Yarmuk
MT. CARMEL (1,742)
Jokneam•
+ MT. TABOR (1,843)
•En Dor
HILL OF MOREH
Edrei•
Megiddo•
Shunem•
•Dor
Ramoth ◻
Well of Harod•
MT. GILBOA (1,696)
Ibleam•
•Beth Shean
The Great Sea
Gilead
Tirzah•
Zaphon•
MT. EBAL (3,080) +
Succoth•
R. Jabbok
+ Shechem ◻
MT. GERIZIM + (2,890)
Aphek•
Tappuah•
•Shiloh
Ammon
Joppa•
River Jordan
Rabbah•
Jabneel•
Bethel• •Ai
•Gilgal
Gezer• Aijalon• Gibeon•
Jericho•
Heshbon• ◻ Bezer?
Ekron △ •Timnah
Kirjath Jearim• •Gibeah
Jerusalem•
+ MT. NEBO (2,700)
Ashdod △ Makkedah• •Beth Shemesh
•Medeba
Gath△ •Jarmuth
•Azekah
•Bethlehem
△ Ashkelon
•Adullam
•Mareshah
Philistia
Lachish•
◻ Hebron
The Salt Sea (−1,300)
Dibon•
△Gaza
•Debir
•Aroer
En Gedi•
R. Arnon
Moab
Beersheba•

© Thomas Nelson, Inc., 1983

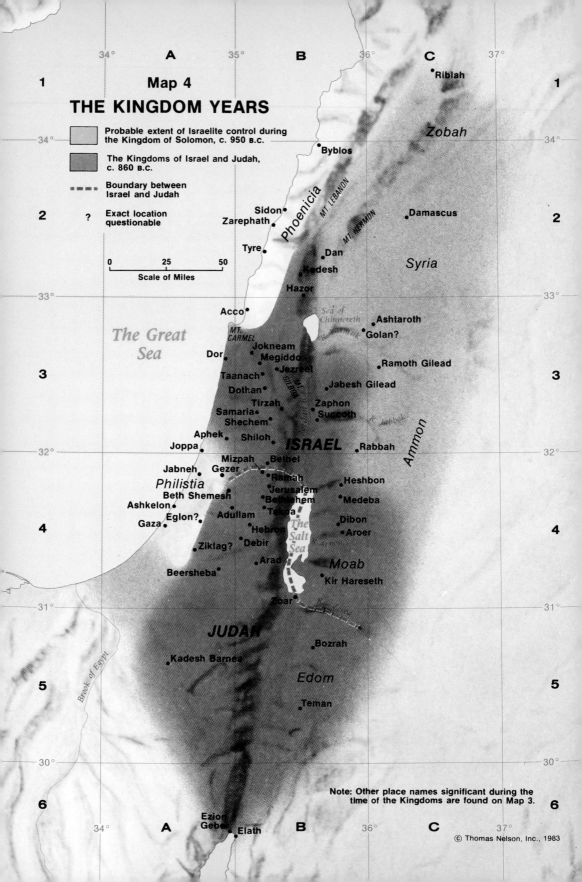

Map 4
THE KINGDOM YEARS

Probable extent of Israelite control during the Kingdom of Solomon, c. 950 B.C.

The Kingdoms of Israel and Judah, c. 860 B.C.

Boundary between Israel and Judah

? Exact location questionable

0 25 50
Scale of Miles

The Great Sea

Riblah

Zobah

Byblos

Phoenicia

MT. LEBANON

Sidon
Zarephath

Damascus

Tyre

MT. HERMON

Dan
Kedesh

Syria

Hazor

Sea of Chinnereth

Ashtaroth
Golan?

Acco

MT. CARMEL

Jokneam
Dor   Megiddo
Jezreel

Ramoth Gilead

Taanach
Dothan

Jabesh Gilead

Tirzah
Samaria   Zaphon
Shechem   Succoth

Aphek   Shiloh
Joppa

ISRAEL

Rabbah

Ammon

Mizpah   Bethel
Jabneh   Gezer
Philistia   Ramah
Beth Shemesh   Jerusalem
Ashkelon   Bethlehem   Heshbon
Eglon?   Tekoa   Medeba
Gaza   Adullam
Hebron   Dibon
Ziklag?   Debir   Aroer
Arad   *The Salt Sea*
Beersheba   *Moab*
Kir Hareseth

Zoar

JUDAH

Bozrah

Kadesh Barnea

Edom

Teman

Brook of Egypt

Ezion Geber
Elath

Note: Other place names significant during the time of the Kingdoms are found on Map 3.

© Thomas Nelson, Inc., 1983

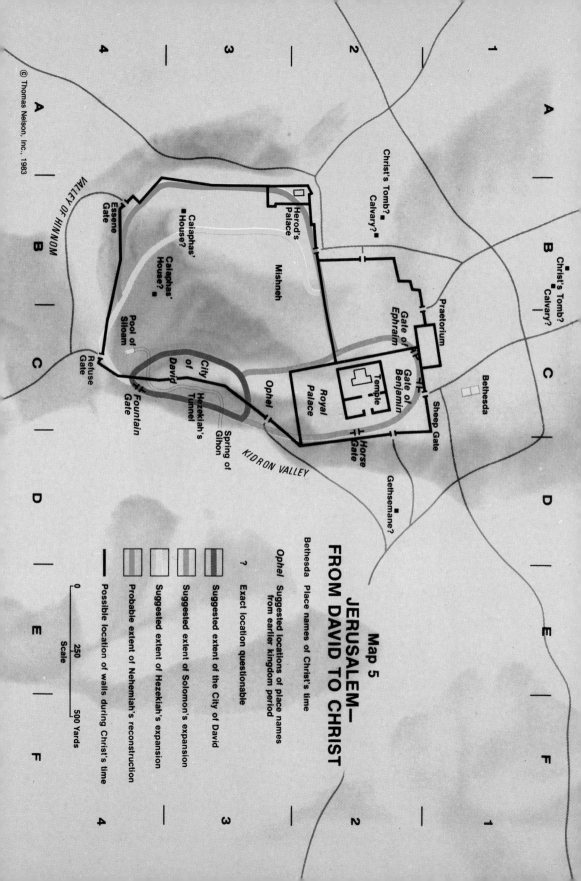

Map 5
JERUSALEM—
FROM DAVID TO CHRIST

© Thomas Nelson, Inc., 1983

VALLEY OF HINNOM

KIDRON VALLEY

Christ's Tomb?
Calvary?

Christ's Tomb?
Calvary?

Herod's Palace

Mishneh

Caiaphas' House?

Caiaphas' House?

Essene Gate

Pool of Siloam

Refuse Gate

City of David

Hezekiah's Tunnel

Fountain Gate

Spring of Gihon

Ophel

Gate of Ephraim

Praetorium

Gate of Benjamin

Sheep Gate

Temple

Royal Palace

Horse Gate

Bethesda

Gethsemane?

Bethesda Place names of Christ's time

Ophel Suggested locations of place names from earlier kingdom period

? Exact location questionable

Suggested extent of the City of David

Suggested extent of Solomon's expansion

Suggested extent of Hezekiah's expansion

Probable extent of Nehemiah's reconstruction

Possible location of walls during Christ's time

Scale

0   250   500 Yards

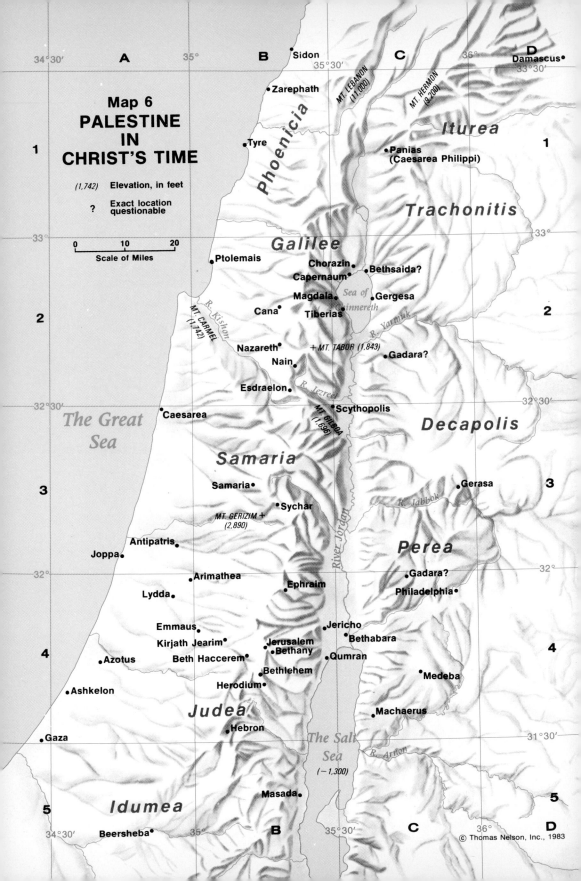

Map 6
PALESTINE
IN
CHRIST'S TIME

(1,742) Elevation, in feet

? Exact location
questionable

0   10   20
Scale of Miles

A · 34°30' · 35° · **B** · Sidon · 35°30' · **C** · 36° · 33°30' · **D** · Damascus

Zarephath

Phoenicia

MT. LEBANON
(11,000)

MT. HERMON
(9,200)

Iturea

Tyre **1**

Panias
(Caesarea Philippi) **1**

Trachonitis

33° 33°

Galilee

Ptolemais

Chorazin
Capernaum Bethsaida?

Magdala Gergesa

Sea of
Cinnereth

Cana Tiberias

R. Kishon

MT. CARMEL
(1,742)

R. Yarmuk

2 Nazareth + MT. TABOR (1,843) Gadara? **2**

Nain

Esdraelon R. Jezreel

MT. GILBOA
(1,696)

32°30' Scythopolis 32°30'

The Great
Sea

Caesarea

Decapolis

Samaria

Samaria

Gerasa **3**

3 Sychar

R. Jabbok

MT. GERIZIM +
(2,890)

Antipatris Perea

Joppa 32° Gadara? 32°

Arimathea Ephraim Philadelphia

Lydda

Emmaus Jericho

Kirjath Jearim Jerusalem Bethabara
Bethany

4 Beth Haccerem Qumran Medeba **4**

Azotus Bethlehem

Ashkelon Herodium

Judea Machaerus

Gaza Hebron

The Salt
Sea
(−1,300)

R. Arnon

5 Masada **5**

Idumea

Beersheba **A** 34°30' 35° **B** 35°30' **C** 36° **D**

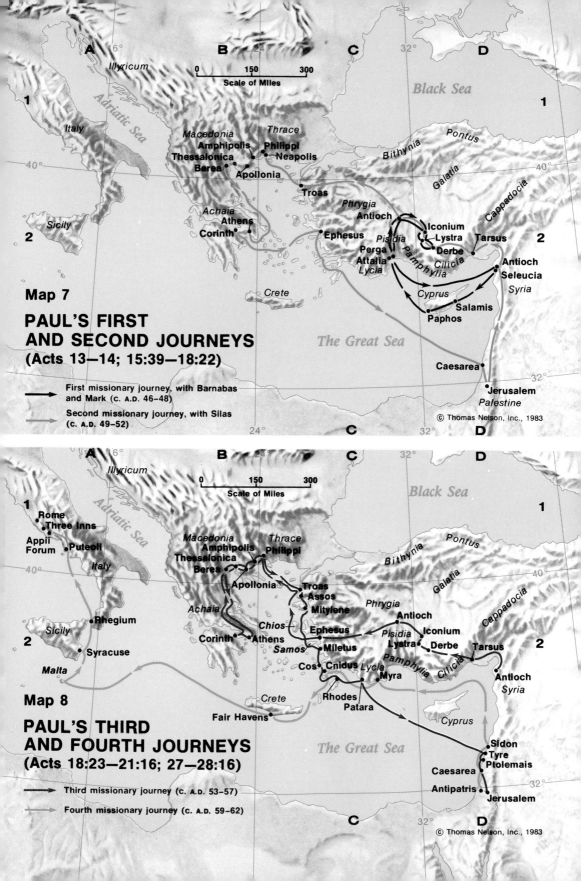

Map 7

PAUL'S FIRST AND SECOND JOURNEYS
(Acts 13—14; 15:39—18:22)

First missionary journey, with Barnabas and Mark (c. A.D. 46–48)

Second missionary journey, with Silas (c. A.D. 49–52)

Illyricum

Italy

Adriatic Sea

Sicily

Macedonia
Amphipolis
Thessalonica
Berea
Apollonia

Thrace
Philippi
Neapolis

Troas

Achaia
Athens
Corinth

Ephesus

Crete

Black Sea

Bithynia

Pontus

Galatia

Cappadocia

Phrygia
Antioch

Pisidia
Perga
Attalia
Lycia

Iconium
Lystra
Derbe
Pamphylia
Cilicia

Tarsus

Antioch
Seleucia
Syria

Cyprus

Salamis
Paphos

The Great Sea

Caesarea

Jerusalem
Palestine

© Thomas Nelson, Inc., 1983

Map 8

PAUL'S THIRD AND FOURTH JOURNEYS
(Acts 18:23—21:16; 27—28:16)

Third missionary journey (c. A.D. 53–57)

Fourth missionary journey (c. A.D. 59–62)

Illyricum

Adriatic Sea

Rome
Three Inns
Appii
Forum
Puteoli
Italy

Sicily
Rhegium
Syracuse
Malta

Black Sea

Macedonia
Amphipolis
Thessalonica
Berea

Thrace
Philippi

Apollonia

Achaia
Corinth
Athens
Samos

Troas
Assos
Mitylene

Chios

Ephesus
Miletus
Cos
Cnidus

Crete
Fair Havens
Rhodes
Patara

Phrygia
Antioch

Pisidia
Lystra

Iconium
Derbe
Pamphylia
Cilicia

Tarsus

Antioch
Syria

Lycia
Myra

Cyprus

The Great Sea

Caesarea
Antipatris

Sidon
Tyre
Ptolemais

Jerusalem

© Thomas Nelson, Inc., 1983

Map 9

THE HOLY LAND
IN MODERN TIMES

Area occupied by Israel
since June, 1967

Scale of Miles
0   25   50

LEBANON

Tripoli

Beirut

BEKAA VALLEY

LEBANON MTS.

ANTI-LEBANON MTS.

Sidon

Damascus

SYRIA

Tyre

Dan

U.N. Buffer Zone
1973 Line

Qiryat
Shemona

Quneitra
1967 Cease-Fire Line

Nahariyya

Safad

Golan
Heights

Akko

Sea of
Galilee

Haifa

Tiberias

Dera

Nazareth

Ramtha

Afula

Mediterranean Sea

Beth Shean

Hadera

Jarash

Netanya

Tulkarm

Herzliyya

Nablus

Tel Aviv

West
Bank

Yafo

Petah
Tiqwa

Rishon le Zion

Amman

Ramla

Lod

Ashdod

Ramalah

Jericho

Ashqelon

Jerusalem

Jordan River

Bethlehem

Madaba

Gaza

Qiryat
Gat

Hebron

Dead
Sea

En Gedi

Dhiban

Al-Arish

Beersheba

Karak

JORDAN

ISRAEL

EGYPT

Negev

Arabah

Sinai

Elat

Aqaba

© Thomas Nelson, Inc., 1983